Western Pacific Operations

HISTORY OF U. S. MARINE CORPS
OPERATIONS IN WORLD WAR II

VOLUME IV

By

GEORGE W. GARAND

TRUMAN R. STROBRIDGE

Historical Division, Headquarters, U. S. Marine Corps

1971

Originally published 1971

Reprinted by
The Battery Press, Inc.
P.O. Box 198885
Nashville, Tennessee 37219
Seventh in The Battery Press Official History Series

1994
ISBN: 0-89839-198-9
Printed in the United States of America

Foreword

This book is the fourth in the five-volume history of Marine Corps operations in World War II. The story of Peleliu, Iwo Jima, and Marine artillery and aviation in the Philippines, as previously narrated in separate detail in preliminary monographs, has been reevaluated and rewritten to depict events in proper proportion to each other and in correct perspective to the war as a whole. New material, particularly from Japanese and other sources that has become available since the earlier monograph series was published, has been included to provide fresh insight into the Marine Corps' contribution to the final victory in the Pacific.

The period covered by this history, essentially from mid-September 1944 to late March 1945, covers the continuation of the United States drive from the Central Pacific to the Western Carolines and the Volcano-Bonin Islands at the very doorstep of Japan. Once again it became the task of the Marine Corps to put into practice the amphibious doctrine that had been developed during the prewar years, modified and perfected during earlier operations in the Solomons, Gilberts, Marshalls, and Marianas. The course of events on Peleliu and Iwo Jima demonstrated the basic soundness of Marine Corps tactics and techniques in the face of skillful and tenacious resistance offered by a highly motivated and well trained foe who was determined to defend his possessions to the last.

While the American amphibious assault team fought its way through the Japanese defenses towards the Home Islands, Marine aviation wrote a glorious chapter of its own. Frequently denied the opportunity of flying direct support in amphibious operations, Marine aviators developed and put into practice a doctrine of close air support that more than proved its worth during the recapture of the Philippines. The continuous neutralization of bypassed enemy-held islands in the Central Pacific by Marine air isolated sizable Japanese garrisons from their bases of supply and rendered them powerless to support the enemy war effort until their surrender at the end of the war.

The numbers of men and quantities of materiel employed during the operations narrated in this volume defy the imagination. In this connection it is worth recalling that the successful execution of these operations depended on joint Army-Navy-Marine cooperation, which became ever more pronounced as the war approached its final phase. Combined with improved tactics and weapons on the field of battle was the highly flexible and efficient Marine command organization designed to meet the requirements of modern warfare.

As on other battlefields before World War II and since, the Marines who fought and died in the Philippines, on Peleliu, and on Iwo Jima wrote with their blood an indelible account of courage and sacrifice that will live on in their country's history, to serve as a guide and inspiration to future generations.

L. F. CHAPMAN, JR
GENERAL, U.S. MARINE CORPS
COMMANDANT OF THE MARINE CORPS

Reviewed and approved
26 May 1970

Preface

In a series of boldly conceived and executed operations, American forces in the Pacific Theater captured and developed a number of strategically placed islands that were to serve as springboards for the inexorable advance towards the Japanese home islands. The Guadalcanal campaign, first offensive step after a year of reverses in this theater, marked the beginning of the American counteroffensive that gathered momentum until a steamroller of unprecedented force smashed its way across the vast expanses of the Central and Western Pacific.

Hand in hand with the accelerating tempo of operations went improvements in the techniques employed in the amphibious assault and the sometimes protracted operations inland. By the time the Peleliu operation was launched in mid-September 1944, the Japanese had changed their tactics of defending the beaches and launching a final *banzai* once the inevitable end was in sight to a far more sophisticated defense that amounted to an extended delaying action conducted from well dug tunnels and cave positions which had to be taken at great cost to the attacking force. The battle for Iwo Jima, which got under way on 19 February 1945, represented a battle of attrition in the truest sense, with losses in men and materiel far out of proportion to the size of the objective. Aside from its tactical value, Iwo Jima assumed strategic importance in signalling the Japanese government and people that the United States was determined to bring the war in the Pacific to a victorious conclusion and that even the heaviest losses would not deter Americans from this purpose.

New tactics employed by the Marine Corps in the course of the war were not limited to fighting on the ground. The speedy expansion of Marine strength following the Pearl Harbor debacle was accompanied by a proportionate growth of the air arm that had existed in miniature size up to that time. Denied the use of carriers during the early years of the war, Marine aviators discovered through trial and error that they could make an important contribution to the ground troops in furnishing a type of close air support that could be rendered quickly and with devastating results to the enemy. Together with this support came the creation and perfection of the air liaison team which provided a direct and vital link between troops on the ground, whether Marine or Army, and the supporting aircraft. The bombing of bypassed islands in the Central Pacific, as carried out by Marine aviation over a prolonged period of time, underscored the fact that enemy bastions of considerable strength could be effectively neutralized from the air without having to be subjected to costly ground assault.

A section of this volume has been devoted to the evolution of the organization that had to be created to coordinate the training, flow of replacements and supplies, and overall employment of Marine field components. This was the Fleet Marine Force, which was conceived long before World War II. Its growth and development clearly mirror the organizational demands made on the Corps during the war years. The chapters provide the reader with a better understanding of the command organization that made possible many of the famous amphibious assaults of World War II.

Our purpose in publishing this operational history in durable form is to make the Marine Corps record permanently available for study by military personnel and the general public as well as by serious students of military history. We have made a conscientious effort to be objective in our treatment of the actions of Marines and of the men of other services who fought at their side. We have tried to write with understanding about our former enemies and in this effort have received invaluable help from the Japanese themselves. Few people so militant and unyielding in war have been as dispassionate and analytical about their actions in peace. We owe a special debt of gratitude to Mr. Susumu Nishiura, Chief of the War History Office, Defense Agency of Japan and to the many researchers and historians of his office that reviewed our draft manuscripts.

This five-volume series was planned and outlined by Mr. Henry I. Shaw, Jr., Chief Historian, while Mr. George W. Garand was responsible for Volume IV itself. Mr. Truman R. Strobridge, originally assigned as the author of this volume, wrote the first four chapters of the Peleliu campaign before he left the Marine Corps to become a historian with the Department of the Army. Mr. Garand wrote the rest of this book, revising and editing it for publication. In his research on the Peleliu operation, Mr. Garand frequently consulted the material assembled for the monograph *The Assault on Peleliu* by Major Frank O. Hough; material dealing with the Philippines was obtained from the monograph *Marine Aviation in the Philippines* by Major Charles W. Boggs, Jr. In preparing the narrative for Iwo Jima, the monograph *Iwo Jima: Amphibious Epic*, prepared by Lieutenant Colonel Whitman S. Bartley, served as a valuable guide. Mr. Garand also prepared all the appendices. The Director of Marine Corps History made the final critical review of portions of the manuscript.

A number of leading participants in the actions described have commented on the preliminary drafts of pertinent portions of the book. Their valuable assistance is gratefully acknowledged. Several senior officers, in particular General Oliver P. Smith, Admiral George H. Fort, Admiral

Jesse B. Oldendorf, Lieutenant General Julian C. Smith, Lieutenant General Merwin H. Silverthorn, Lieutenant General Thomas A. Wornham, Lieutenant General Louis E. Woods, Major General Ford O. Rogers, Major General Dudley S. Brown, and Brigadier General John S. Letcher made valuable contributions through their written comments, as did Lieutenant General Lewis B. Puller and Brigadier General John R. Lanigan during personal interviews.

Special thanks are due to the historical agencies of the other services for their critical readings of draft chapters of this book. Outstanding among the many official historians who measurably assisted the authors were: Dr. Stetson Conn, Chief Historian and Mr. Robert R. Smith, Head, General History Branch, Office of the Chief of Military History, Department of the Army; Dr. Dean C. Allard, Head, Operational Archives Branch, Naval History Division, Department of the Navy; and Dr. Robert F. Futrell, Historian, Historical Research Division, Air University, Maxwell Air Force Base, Alabama.

Captain Charles B. Collins and his predecessors as Historical Division/Branch Administrative Officers, Chief Warrant Officer Jo E. Kennedy, Second Lieutenant Gerald S. Duncan, and First Lieutenants John J. Hainsworth and D'Arcy E. Grisier ably handled the many exacting duties involved in processing the volume from first drafts through final printed form. The bulk of the early preliminary typescripts was prepared by Miss Kay P. Sue, who, with the assistance of Sergeant Michael L. Gardner, also expertly handled the painstaking task of typing the final manuscript for the printer. Miss Sue, assisted by Miss Charlotte L. Webb, also performed the meticulous work demanded in preparing the index.

The maps were drafted by Sergeant Earl L. Wilson and his successor, Sergeant Kenneth W. White.

F. C. CALDWELL
COLONEL, U.S. MARINE CORPS (RETIRED)
DIRECTOR OF MARINE CORPS HISTORY

Contents

PART I BACKGROUND

CHAPTER	PAGE
1. Introduction	3

PART II FLEET MARINE FORCE, PACIFIC

1. The Development of FMFPac	13
2. Administration and Aviation	33

PART III THE PALAUS: GATEWAY TO THE PHILIPPINES

1. Strategic Situation	51
2. Pre-Assault Preparations	77
3. D-Day on Peleliu	106
4. The Drive Inland: 16–22 September	132
5. Angaur and Ulithi	162
6. Securing the North: 23–30 September	185
7. The Umurbrogol Pocket: 29 September–15 October	219
8. To the Bitter End	254

PART IV MARINES IN THE PHILIPPINES

1. Background and Planning	291
2. The Leyte Landings	309
3. The Luzon Campaign	334
4. Southern Philippines Operations	358

PART V MARINE AVIATION IN THE WESTERN PACIFIC

1. Mounting The Offensive	393
2. Marine Aviation in the Marianas, Carolines, and at Iwo Jima	422

PART VI IWO JIMA

CHAPTER	PAGE
1. Background to DETACHMENT	443
2. Offensive Plans and Preparations	462
3. The Preliminaries	482
4. D-Day on Iwo Jima	502
5. The Struggle for Suribachi	528
6. Drive to the North	547
7. 3d Marine Division Operations on Iwo Jima	571
8. Airfield Development and Activities Behind the Lines	594
9. The 5th Marine Division Drive on the Left	616
10. The 4th Marine Division Drive on the Right	645
11. Final Operations on Iwo Jima	684
12. Summary	713
13. Conclusions	729

APPENDICES

A.	Bibliographical Notes	739
B.	Guide to Abbreviations	752
C.	Military Map Symbols	758
D.	Chronology	759
E.	Fleet Marine Force Status—31 August 1944	765
F.	Table of Organization F-100 Marine Division	780
G.	Marine Task Organization and Command List	782
H.	Marine Casualties	797
I.	Unit Commendations	798

Index 813

ILLUSTRATIONS

Amphibious Exercises, Puerto Rico	18
Testing Higgins Boat	18
Landing Exercise, New River, N. C.	37
Change of Command, FMFPac, 1945	37
Assault Troops Off Peleliu	107
Peleliu Beach on D-Day	107
Abortive Enemy Tank Attack, Peleliu	125
Machine Gun In Action, Peleliu	125
Artillery in Firing Position	140

ILLUSTRATIONS—Continued

	PAGE
Marine Tanks at Peleliu Airfield	140
Close Fighting Near Airfield	149
Casualty Evacuation	149
U. S. Army Troops Assault Angaur	167
Closing in on the Enemy, Angaur	167
Men and Supplies Crossing Peleliu Reef	188
U. S. Army Troops Arrive at Peleliu	188
Marine Aircraft Preparing for Napalm Attack	194
Bombing of Japanese Ridge Positions, Peleliu	194
Assault on Ngesebus	213
Advance Inland, Ngesebus	213
Battle of the Ridges, Peleliu	243
Final Operations on Peleliu	243
Navy Planes at Dulag Airfield, Leyte	313
Marine Night Fighters, Leyte	313
Close Air Support for U. S. Army Troops, Luzon	355
Marine Dive Bombers on Luzon Returning from Mission	355
New Dive Bombers for Marine Aviation in the Philippines	360
Filipino Guerrillas On Mindanao	360
LSTs Unloading at Zamboanga	369
U. S. Army Ceremony Honors Marine Aviation	369
Marine Dive Bombers En Route to Bypassed Islands	419
U. S. Personnel Touring Mille Island, Marshalls	419
Bombs Away at Iwo Jima	488
Amphibious Assault, Iwo Jima	488
4th Marine Division Troops on Iwo Beach	507
Landing of 2/27, Iwo Jima	507
Japanese Painting of Iwo Invasion	511
War Dog and Handler Approach Enemy Cave	511
37mm Gun in Action	529
Debris of Battle, D plus 2	529
Flamethrowers in Action	532
Marine on Mt. Suribachi and View of Landing Beaches	532
First Flag Raising on Iwo Jima	541
Second Flag Goes Up on Suribachi	544
Marines at Mass	596
First "Grasshopper" Lands on Iwo	596
B-29 Superfortress After Emergency Landing	599
4th Marine Division Observation Post	599

ILLUSTRATIONS—Continued

	PAGE
155mm Gun in Action	606
Rocket Fire Support	606
Birdseye View of Iwo Beachhead	609
Shore Parties Hauling Supplies	609
Captured Japanese Tank	619
Combat Patrol in Northern Iwo	619
Enemy Positions near Nishi Village	696
Japanese Prisoner and Escort	696
Air Force Bivouac Area on Iwo After Banzai	709
Motoyama Airfield No. 1 After Restoration	709

MAPS

1.	Strategic Situation, Central and Western Pacific	53
2.	Palau Islands	56
3.	Japanese Defense Plan, Peleliu	74
4.	D-Day, Peleliu	111
5.	Peleliu, Second Operational Phase	133
6.	Angaur Island	164
7.	Ulithi Atoll	182
8.	Commitment of the U.S. Army 321st Infantry Regiment, Peleliu	191
9.	Isolation of Umurbrogol	196
10.	North Peleliu and Ngesebus	203
11.	Securing the North	215
12.	Umurbrogol Pocket	220
13.	Drive from the North	239
14.	Final Marine Action, Peleliu	247
15.	Final 81st Infantry Division Operations, Peleliu	255
16.	Philippine Islands	295
17.	Sixth Army Area of Operations	311
18.	Lingayen Gulf Landing	338
19.	Luzon	341
20.	Route to Manila and XI Corps Landings	345
21.	Main U. S. Drives in the Victor V Operation	364
22.	Area of Responsibility, Commander Aircraft, Northern Solomons	394
23.	Marshall Islands—MAG-22 Operations, 1944	406
24.	Iwo Jima—Sulphur Island	446
25.	Japanese Defense Sectors	460

MAPS—Continued PAGE

26. Landing Plan, Iwo Jima 470
27. Naval Gunfire Areas of Responsibility, D-3 and D-2 . 494
28. VAC Front Lines D-Day, 19 February 1945 524

 I. Scene of Battle, 1944-1945 . . . . Map Section
 II. Progress of the Attack, VAC Front Lines, D-Day—
     D Plus 5 . . . . Map Section
III. 3d Marine Division Zone of Action, Iwo Jima,
     25 February–1 March 1945 . . . . Map Section
 IV. 3d Marine Division Zone of Action, Iwo Jima,
     1–10 March 1945 . . . . Map Section
  V. 5th Marine Division Zone of Action, Iwo Jima,
     24 February–2 March 1945 . . . . Map Section
 VI. 5th Marine Division Zone of Action, Iwo Jima,
     2–10 March 1945 . . . . Map Section
VII. 4th Marine Division Zone of Action, Iwo Jima,
     24–28 February 1945 . . . . Map Section
VIII. 4th Marine Division Zone of Action, Iwo Jima,
     5–7 March 1945 . . . . Map Section
 IX. 3d Marine Division, Final Operations . . . . . Map Section
  X. 4th Marine Division, Final Operations . . . . . Map Section
 XI. 5th Marine Division, Final Operations . . . . . Map Section

CHARTS

1. Genealogy of Fleet Marine Force, Pacific 22
2. Japanese Command Organization—Defense of the Philippines 299
3. Organization of Air Command, Southwest Pacific Area . . . 302

MAPS—Continued   PAGE

26. Landing Plan, Iwo Jima   470
27. Naval Gunfire Areas of Responsibility, D-3 and D-2 .   494
28. VAC Front Lines D-Day, 19 February 1945   524

  I. Scene of Battle, 1944-1945 . . . . Map Section
 II. Progress of the Attack, VAC Front Lines, D-Day—
     D Plus 5 . . . . Map Section
III. 3d Marine Division Zone of Action, Iwo Jima,
     25 February–1 March 1945 . . . . Map Section
 IV. 3d Marine Division Zone of Action, Iwo Jima,
     1–10 March 1945 . . . . Map Section
  V. 5th Marine Division Zone of Action, Iwo Jima,
     24 February–2 March 1945 . . . . Map Section
 VI. 5th Marine Division Zone of Action, Iwo Jima,
     2–10 March 1945 . . . . Map Section
VII. 4th Marine Division Zone of Action, Iwo Jima,
     24–28 February 1945 . . . . Map Section
VIII. 4th Marine Division Zone of Action, Iwo Jima,
     5–7 March 1945 . . . . Map Section
 IX. 3d Marine Division, Final Operations . . . . . Map Section
  X. 4th Marine Division, Final Operations . . . . . Map Section
 XI. 5th Marine Division, Final Operations . . . . . Map Section

CHARTS

1. Genealogy of Fleet Marine Force, Pacific   22
2. Japanese Command Organization—Defense of the Philippines 299
3. Organization of Air Command, Southwest Pacific Area . . . 302

PART I

Background

CHAPTER 1

Introduction

The military operations narrated in this volume cover neither the beginning of the greatest global conflict in history nor its end. They do, however, describe in detail two of the major amphibious campaigns in the Western Pacific, Peleliu and Iwo Jima, and the prolonged fighting that followed until all enemy resistance was quelled. In addition, the little-known exploits of Marine artillery and air in the Philippines and the accomplishments of Marine flying squadrons in the reduction of enemy positions in the Central and Western Pacific are covered.

In themselves, the day-by-day accounts of terrain seized, sorties flown, rounds fired, numbers of enemy killed, and casualties sustained tend to have a numbing effect. The mere recitation of the thousands of tons of artillery ammunition expended in the preliminary bombardment and small arms ammunition fired in weeks of close combat tend to overwhelm the imagination. Nor does the spectacle of 90,000 men battling for weeks at close quarters appear realistic unless it is remembered that such combat actually took place on Iwo Jima. Even though this volume tells of the exploits of Marines, both ground and air, in the Western Pacific, it should be recalled that their heroism was but a small part in the mosaic of global war, and that their sacrifice was directly linked with that of the remaining military services of the United States and its Allies.

World War II had its roots in the political, economic, and social conditions that arose or prevailed in the years following the end of the greatest conflagration the world had experienced up to that time. In a carefully prepared address to the Senate on 22 January 1917, President Woodrow Wilson had voiced the view that any lasting peace had to be a peace without victory, since "victory would mean peace forced upon a loser, a victor's peace imposed upon the vanquished. Only a peace between equals can last."[1]

Almost prophetically, the President continued that "peace must be followed by some concert of powers which will make it virtually impossible that any such catastrophe should ever overwhelm us again."[2]

As part of the peace settlement following the end of World War I, the German island possessions in the Central Pacific, notably the Marianas, Carolines, and Marshalls, were mandated to the Japanese, who also gained control of former German concessions in China.

---

[1] President Woodrow Wilson's address to the U.S. Senate, 22Jan17, as cited in Oscar Theodore Barck, Jr., and Nelson Manfred Blake, *Since 1900—A History of the United States* (New York: The Macmillan Company, 1965), pp. 210-211.

[2] *Ibid.*

While Germany was being stripped of her outlying possessions and the groundwork for future trouble was being laid in Central Europe, where strips of territory inhabited by ethnic Germans were being incorporated into adjacent countries, Japan emerged as the strongest power in the western Pacific. While the Japanese, under the terms of the mandate given to them by the League of Nations, were permitted to govern and develop the islands placed under their charge, they were forbidden to construct fortifications on them, a point further underscored by the Washington Naval Treaty of 1922.

Quite possibly, given a few decades of global peace, the major nations of the world might well have succeeded in restoring their shattered economies, rebuilding their political structures, and learning to live with their neighbors across the multitude of newly created borders. Unfortunately, this was not to be the case. The severe bloodletting that the big powers had undergone in World War I bred distrust, dissatisfaction, and an increasing trend towards national and international violence among the victors and vanquished alike.

Even before the end of World War I, two major upheavals occurred in Russia, with inherent loss of life and destruction of property unheard of since the Mongol invasion. While the Red and White factions were locked in a struggle to the death, the peasants, workers, and remnants of the erstwhile aristocracy suffered drastic privations. In the end little changed, and one oppressive regime was succeeded by another. Lack of faith in their respective leaders and/or national destinies was to cause overwhelming changes in Italy and Germany where fascist dictatorships were established without recourse to civil war, once the people had lost faith in the parliamentary forms of government they had enjoyed since the end of the war.

In the United States, following the conclusion of the armistice, there was a considerable amount of confusion as to the shape in which the postwar world was to be rebuilt. President Wilson was an ardent advocate of a League of Nations in which every member, regardless of size, would have one vote. The five big powers, Great Britain, France, Italy, Japan, and the United States, were to sit on an executive council permanently, while non-permanent seats were to be allotted to four of the smaller nations. A permanent Court of International Justice was to arbitrate disputes between the member nations. Among the foremost functions of the League of Nations was the preservation of peace, as expressed in Article 10, which President Wilson regarded as the heart of its constitution. This article provided that:

> The Members of the League undertake to respect and preserve as against external aggression the territorial integrity and existing political independence of all members of the League. In case of any threat of danger of such aggression the Council shall advise upon the means by which this obligation shall be fulfilled.[3]

Enforcement of a global peace was predicated on the assumption that no aggressor could withstand the combined strength of outraged humanity, and that all member nations would take con-

---

[3] Article 10 of the Constitution, League of Nations, as cited in *ibid.*, p. 251.

certed action without delay against any form of aggression. The United States had joined the Allies "in order to make the world safe for democracy," and President Wilson clearly perceived that the future of world peace could be safeguarded only if all the major powers combined their strength, manpower, and resources in stabilizing a shaky world. Many influential Americans felt now that the war had been won, in no small measure by virtue of their efforts, that the time had come to withdraw from the arena of international politics. In this they were guided by the parting words of the first President of the United States who had clearly stated:

> The great rule of conduct for us in regard to foreign nations is, in extending our commercial relations to have with them as little political connections as possible . . . It is our true policy to steer clear of permanent alliances . . . Taking care always to keep ourselves by suitable establishments on a respectable defensive posture, we may safely trust to temporary alliances for extraordinary emergencies.[4]

Continued upheavals in Europe, economic considerations, and disillusionment with prolonged bickering at the conference table soon led the United States to revert to its hallowed tradition of isolationism, thus deserting Wilson's leadership that, had it been carried out to its fullest extent, might have assured the world a period of peace and stability. Instead, the American nation rejected not only Wilson's vision of a just peace, but along with it his political party and the League of Nations. On the positive side, the Republican administration of President Warren G. Harding convened a disarmament conference in July 1921, initially limited to Great Britain, France, Italy, and Japan. The number of participants was subsequently expanded to include several of the smaller countries. Soviet Russia, socially still unacceptable and far removed from obtaining official United States recognition, was excluded.

On 12 November 1921, three years after the World War I armistice, the conference was held in Washington. Considering the differences that existed between the attending powers, substantial agreement was quickly reached by the three major nations, the United States, Great Britain, and Japan, as well as by France and Italy, with reference to the ratio to be employed as to the ships to be retained by each country's navy and the number to be scrapped. At the same time, the participants agreed to halt the construction of warships, but not aircraft carriers, in excess of 10,000 tons or equipped with guns larger than 8 inches in caliber for a period of 10 years. The participants agreed to the terms of the agreement largely because it resulted in a sizable cut in military spending at a time when the various treasuries were badly depleted by the drain of World War I. Japan received an additional incentive as her reward for agreeing to the ratio, which was to become a major factor in shaping the policies that the major powers were to adopt in dealing with various areas of the Pacific.

By way of a compromise, the United States agreed that she would not fortify any of the islands under her control in

---

[4] Victor Platsits, ed., *Washington's Farewell Address* (New York: New York Public Library, 1935), pp. 155-56.

the Pacific, except for Hawaii. The United States specifically agreed not to fortify the Philippines, Guam, Wake, or the Aleutian Islands; Great Britain likewise agreed not to fortify Hong Kong, Borneo, the Solomons, and the Gilberts. In turn, the Japanese agreed not to fortify Formosa or any of the former German possessions in the Pacific north of the equator, including specifically the Marianas less Guam, which was under American control, and the Carolines.

A Four-Power Pact, to which England, France, Japan, and the United States were signatories called for a mutual recognition of insular rights in the Pacific. This pact, which was to be in force for a 10-year period, called for the adjustment of any difficulties that might arise by way of the conference table. In order to eliminate a further source of irritation in the Far East, a Nine-Power Treaty, subscribed to by the United States, Great Britain, Japan, Portugal, Belgium, Italy, The Netherlands, France, and China attempted to regulate the often precarious and complicated relations of China with various outside powers. At least on the surface, the Washington Conference seemed to assure a period of international cooperation that, coupled with a reduction in armaments, could lead to a lengthy span of global peace.

Under the terms of the Naval Treaty of 1922, the United States destroyed 19 capital ships of pre-World War I vintage and 13 that were still under construction. Expressed in tonnage, the United States destroyed 842,380 tons; Great Britain 447,750 tons; and Japan 354,709 tons. On the part of American naval experts the scrapping of major ships as well as the agreement to leave the western Pacific area unfortified evoked sharp criticism, since "the strict observance of these treaties left the United States crippled."[5] It was to become apparent soon enough that the Washington Conference had left a major loophole in that the quota system did not apply to submarines, cruisers, and destroyers. As a result, it was not long before those nations interested in evading the provisions of the disarmament treaty concentrated their efforts on the construction of these "permitted" vessels.

By 1927, the euphoria that had followed in the wake of the Washington Conference had largely given way to a spirit of sober contemplation. In an attempt to revive the hopeful spirit of 1922, and in order to put an end to the smaller vessel naval armaments race that had been developing, President Calvin Coolidge deemed it advisable to hold a second disarmament conference, which convened in late June 1927 at Geneva. Even though once again the United States offered her good offices in reviving the feeling of trust and conviviality that had marked the Washington Conference, the climate abroad had undergone a distinct change in the five years that had passed since the earlier conference. Both Italy and France refused to participate at all; the United States, Japan, and Great Britain failed

---

[5] Maj C. Joseph Bernardo and Dr. Eugene H. Bacon, *American Military Policy—Its Development Since 1775* (Harrisburg: The Military Service Publishing Company, 1957), p. 391.

INTRODUCTION

to reach any substantial agreement in limiting the construction of the smaller naval vessels and, in consequence, the Geneva Conference ended in failure.

Nearly three more years were to pass before the London Naval Treaty of April 1930 once more brought some semblance of order into the international naval armament situation, though once again France and Italy refused to comply with the terms of the agreement. A World Disarmament Conference, convened at Geneva in 1932 under the auspices of the League of Nations, failed to yield concrete results, even though the United States, this time under the leadership of President Herbert Hoover, attempted to have all offensive weapons outlawed, and, failing this, made an effort to at least obtain a sizable reduction in such weapons. Once again, the American proposals fell on deaf ears in a world increasingly beset by social, political, and economic problems. One history was to sum up the overall situation in these words:

> America had entered the postwar period with hopeful visions of a new world order in which reason, logic, and disarmament would pave the way toward world peace. But the unsettled problems and bitterness of the Versailles Peace Conference provided anything but the proper milieu for the entertainment of such thoughts. The world was in ferment, but America slept, trusting in diplomacy and disarmament to protect her from a cruel and implacable fate.¹

It was the fate of the United States to emerge on the international scene as a dominant power at the very time that the problems of the major nations cried for a solution that even an older and more experienced country might have been able to mediate only with great difficulty. World War I had brought forth only bitter fruit for victors and vanquished alike and the balance of power that had existed prior to 1914 had largely vanished. It was succeeded by new forms of government and tenuous alliances more often engaged in as fleeting expediences rather than solutions of a more permanent nature. Seemingly abounding in material wealth, possessed by a sharp sense of business, and dwarfing the Old World powers with her sheer physical size and enormous resources, the appearance of the young giant on the world scene, and particularly in the sphere of diplomacy, was greeted by her elders with a mixture of amusement, admiration, envy, and scorn. Few could deny President Wilson's sincerity in putting forward his Fourteen Points aimed at restoring stability to a troubled postwar world. Even fewer could question the honesty of the attempts made by Presidents Harding, Coolidge, and Hoover in forestalling a general world armaments race that sooner or later was bound to result in a shooting war that once again might engulf one nation after another. Yet, in assessing its own political aspirations on the international scene, a nation embarked on pursuit of its national destiny, real or imagined, could not help but feel a sense of frustration and irritation at the continuous American efforts that could well be considered as direct or indirect interference in the affairs of others. No matter how well meant or inspired the American quest for world

---
¹ *Ibid.*, p. 392.

peace, the very honesty and often lack of complexity within these proposals could hardly fail to act as an irritant to those nations that by virtue of age, culture, and social fabric considered themselves somewhat superior to the sometimes clumsy diplomacy of the New World.

On the international scene, fluctuations in American foreign policy occasioned by succeeding administrations that were in themselves reflections of internal developments within the country frequently were misinterpreted by foreign observers. Central and South America were generally regarded as the preserve of the United States, and several small-scale military incursions by U.S. forces into these areas whenever American interests were threatened underscored this point. In other parts of the world, the United States attempted to make available its good offices in mediating disputes, but isolationism within the country failed to furnish the outside world with an image of firmness and resolution, backed by military power.

The isolationism that gripped the United States in the early 1930s in itself was the outgrowth of several factors, all of which combined to imbue Americans with a spirit of withdrawal from the troubles of other nations. The prolonged economic depression with its side effects of widespread discontent further contributed to a public apathy towards external developments underscored by growing public disillusionment with the state of the world in general. As one history dealing with this particular subject matter was to comment:

> To many Americans, World War I had been fought in vain; the world had not been made safe for democracy. There was a growing feeling that wars were engineered by munitions makers so that they might make money.... Another factor in the isolationist trend was the failure of the debtors to repay what they had borrowed during World War I. And what made it worse, Americans felt that this money was being used to build up national armaments which would lead to future wars.[7]

The rising number of dictatorships across the globe could also serve as a barometer warning of future trouble in international affairs. By the end of the 1920s a growing number of nations had entrusted their destinies to the hands of "strong men," notably the Soviet Union, Hungary, Italy, Spain, Portugal, and Poland. The trend toward authoritarian forms of government was still gaining ground and the concept of a single-party state that, at the cost of individual freedom, could operate more efficiently in a state of crisis than the parliamentary system, made great inroads. Thus, the six million unemployed in Germany resulting from the Great Depression, played an important part in the rise to power of the National Socialist Party. In Japan, the militarists were also moving into the saddle by degrees, though the Emperor continued to rule supreme. As the evil of totalitarianism spread, the differences between opposing systems became diffused:

> Communism and fascism became more clearly movements international in character, each thriving in the fertile soil of popular frustration and social distress, and on fears aroused by the other. After 1933, when the National Socialists took absolute control of Germany, the accumulating crises merged into one supreme crisis: The direct challenge of unbridled

---

[7] Barck and Blake, *op. cit.*, p. 551.

INTRODUCTION

organized violence to all that men had tried to achieve in 1919 and had still hoped to achieve in 1925.[8]

Trouble in Europe and Asia was not to be long delayed. In Central Europe, within three years after Adolf Hitler's rise to power, there occurred the German remilitarization of the Rhineland, followed by the annexation of Austria in early 1938 and occupation of the Sudetenland in September of that year under a policy of appeasement by the Western European powers. Within six months of the Munich settlement, the Germans occupied the remainder of Bohemia. In September 1939, Hitler launched his fateful attack against Poland, thus ushering in a global conflict of then unheard of dimensions. On the other side of the globe, Japan had launched an attack on Manchuria in September 1931 and by May 1933 had withdrawn from the League of Nations. Italy, under the leadership of Benito Mussolini, launched a war of aggression of its own against Ethiopia and in late 1935 thwarted League action condemning the attack. In 1936 Germany, Italy, and Japan aligned themselves, ostensibly against the threat of Communism, but each with her own separate interests. Both China and Spain represented additional trouble spots, each country engaged in civil war that was fuelled from outside sources. The League of Nations, lacking an effective police force to check the spiralling aggression of the totalitarian powers, proved unable to assert its authority; its role eventually was reduced to that of a debating society whose members, when chastized, walked out at will.

During the 1930s, some Americans were watching the increasing trend towards international violence with rising concern, though the country was still in the throes of the Great Depression. Considering the state of the United States' defenses, this concern was only too well justified. In 1933, the then Chief of Staff of the Army, General Douglas MacArthur, estimated "that the United States stood seventeenth in rank among the world's armies."[9] In order to counter the general apathy towards military preparedness then engulfing the country, several veterans' organizations spoke up in behalf of increased allocations for the armed forces, but theirs was a voice crying in the wilderness in a country still beset by major economic troubles. As to the outlook for bolstering America's armed forces during this period, the situation was bleak:

> A new administration would take office in 1933, faced not only with the grim specter of hunger stalking the streets, but also the sound of marching boots in Europe and Asia. The Roosevelt Administration was to fall heir to a depleted military establishment, acute economic distress, and intensified international difficulties.[10]

Within the budget-starved military establishment of the United States there existed a force that was lean in numbers but strong in history, tradition, and reputation: the United States Marine Corps. In 1933, the entire Corps consisted of 1,192 officers and 15,343 men. As war clouds gathered over Europe in

---

[8] David Thomson, ed. *The Era of Violence, 1898–1945—The New Cambridge Modern History*, vol. xii (Cambridge: Cambridge University Press, 1960), p. 558, used with permission.

[9] Bernardo and Bacon, *op. cit.*, p. 401.
[10] *Ibid.*, p. 400.

the summer of 1939, this number saw only a nominal increase, though a substantial enlargement was authorized by executive order of 8 September 1939. Specializing in the amphibious assault, the U.S. Marine Corps was to occupy a unique position in World War II. One of the official histories in this series, which discusses the role of Marines prior to and following America's entry into the war in detail, makes this observation:

> While his country battled a coalition of enemies, and most of his countrymen in arms were fighting halfway across the globe from him, the Marine trained to meet only one enemy—Japan. As the war moved inexorably onward, the men who flocked to join the Corps in unprecedented numbers were literally and consciously signing up to fight the Japanese. This orientation toward a single enemy and towards one theater, the Pacific, colored every Marine's life in and out of battle and had an incalculable but undeniably beneficial effect on the combat efficiency of the Fleet Marine Force.[11]

The development of the Fleet Marine Force in conjunction with the evolution of amphibious doctrine will be discussed in greater detail in the following chapters as a prelude to the account of two of the major amphibious operations undertaken by the U.S. Marine Corps in the Western Pacific. To this end, an understanding of the principles of the amphibious assault and knowledge of the Marine command organization that evolved in the Pacific during World War II, should prove helpful.

---

[11] Henry I. Shaw, Jr. and Major Douglas T. Kane, *Isolation of Rabaul—History of U.S. Marine Corps Operations in World War II*, v. II (Washington: Hist Br, G-3 Div, HQMC, 1963), p. 4, hereafter Shaw and Kane, *Isolation of Rabaul.*

PART II

Fleet Marine Force, Pacific

CHAPTER 1

The Development of FMFPac[1]

BACKGROUND[2]

During World War II, the primary tactic employed by the United States in the Pacific Theater was the amphibious assault. In photographs, newsreels, and books dealing with the progress of American operations against Japan, there appears the familiar sight of United States Marines wading through the surf to assault a hostile beach or of waves of amphibian tractors approaching enemy-held shores. So closely has the U.S. Marine Corps been identified in the public mind with amphibious warfare that such terms as "The Marines have landed" have long since become a commonly-used phrase in the American vocabulary. Amphibious warfare and amphibious assault, over a period of many years, have assumed a very definite meaning: that of landing a force to wrest islands or other terrain from the enemy, as opposed to uncontested amphibious landings. Generally, the preparedness of the United States to conduct amphibious operations during the early phase of World War II has been conceded to be the result of foresight and planning on the part of the U.S. Navy and Marine Corps.[3]

In order to obtain a balanced picture of the U.S. Marine Corps, its organization and its tactics in World War II, it

---

[1] Unless otherwise noted, the material in this chapter is derived from: Administrative History of Fleet Marine Force, Pacific, 10Apr44–31Aug45, dtd 15May46, hereafter *FMFPac Administrative History*; Historical Outline of the Development of Fleet Marine Force, Pacific, 1941–1950 (Preliminary), HQMC, n.d., hereafter *The Development of FMFPac*; LtCol Frank O. Hough, Maj Verle E. Ludwig, and Henry I. Shaw, Jr., *Pearl Harbor to Guadalcanal—History of U. S. Marine Corps Operations in World War II*, v. I (Washington: HistBr, G-3, HQMC, 1958), hereafter Hough, Ludwig, and Shaw, *Pearl Harbor to Guadalcanal*; Henry I. Shaw, Jr., Bernard C. Nalty, and Edwin T. Turnbladh, *Central Pacific Drive—History of U. S. Marine Corps Operations in World War II*, v. III (Washington: HistBr, G-3, HQMC, 1966), hereafter Shaw, Nalty, and Turnbladh, *Central Pacific Drive*; Maj Edwin N. McClellan, *The United States in the World War* (Washington: HistBr, G-3, HQMC, 1968 Reprint of 1920 Edition); General Holland M. Smith and Percy Finch, *Coral and Brass* (New York: Charles Scribner's Sons, 1949), hereafter Smith and Finch, *Coral and Brass*, used with permission; Jeter A. Isely and Philip Crowl, *The U. S. Marines and Amphibious War, Its Theory, and Its Practice in the Pacific* (Princeton: Princeton University Press, 1951), hereafter Isely and Crowl, *U. S. Marines and Amphibious War*; Clyde H. Metcalf, *A History of the United States Marine Corps* (New York: G. P. Putnam's Sons, 1939), hereafter Metcalf, *A History of the U. S. Marine Corps*; Robert D. Heinl, Jr., *Soldiers of the Sea—The United States Marine Corps, 1775–1962* (Annapolis: United States Naval Institute, 1962), hereafter Heinl, *Soldiers of the Sea*.

[2] Additional information in this section is derived from: William H. Russell, "The Genesis of FMF Doctrine: 1879–1899," *Marine Corps Gazette*, v. 35, nos. 4–7 (Apr–July 1951); LtGen Holland M. Smith, "The Development of Amphibious Tactics in the U. S. Navy," in *Marine Corps Gazette*, v. 30, nos. 6–10 (Jun–Oct 1946).

[3] Isely and Crowl, *U. S. Marines and Amphibious War*, chaps. 1–2.

13

becomes necessary to follow the evolution of that service since its inception. The tradition of Marines serving on board ships and landing on foreign shores dates back to the Revolutionary War. Throughout the Nineteenth Century, as occasion demanded and as dictated by the expanding interests of the United States, Marines distinguished themselves in operations on the seas or on foreign soil. Their exploits became legend at home and abroad; their existence and immediate availability in time of need became a factor in the foreign policy of the United States. To those viewing this country with unfriendly eyes, they became a force to be reckoned with.

Even though, from the very inception of the Corps, ship-based Marines had made landings on enemy soil, real interest in amphibious warfare, as the term has since become widely known, did not develop until the Spanish-American War. At that time, both in Cuba and in the Philippines, a military force was needed to accompany the fleet to seize and hold advanced bases.[4] Once this requirement had been established, The General Board of the Navy recommended the activation of a permanent base force. In November 1901, the Secretary of the Navy ordered the Commandant of the Marine Corps to organize a battalion for such advance base work. Instruction of Marines in this special activity began in 1902 at Newport, Rhode Island and Annapolis, Maryland. The training covered field fortifications, transportation of guns, construction of telegraph and telephone lines, and the planting of land mines. Of necessity, it was limited in scope, since the Marine Corps was fully occupied with other commitments abroad. Amphibious landing exercises were not held until 1914. Advance base training was shifted to New London, Connecticut in 1910 and to Philadelphia a year later. There it remained until 1920, when the activity moved to Quantico, Virginia.

During World War I, the Marine Corps gained little combat experience in advance base warfare despite the existence of an Advance Base Force of more than 6,000 officers and men. The big battles of that war were fought on *terra firma* by large land armies locked for weeks or months in trench warfare that featured little movement. As in the past, Marines distinguished themselves on the battlefield, but the war they waged was that of the foot soldier. Since armies tend to refight battles of a previous war in peacetime in anticipation of the next conflict, instruction in the years following World War I emphasized the Army-type of fighting that had become the trademark of that war. As a result, emphasis in those years was on land warfare at the expense of amphibious training.

Another reason for a lack of interest in amphibious warfare in the immediate post-World War I years was the dismal experience of the British in launching their ill-fated Dardanelles-Gallipoli operation in 1915. The general conclusion among military strategists at the time was that large scale amphibious opera-

[4] For a detailed account of Marine involvement in shaping the concept of amphibious warfare, see Hough, Ludwig, and Shaw, *Pearl Harbor to Guadalcanal*, Pt. I.

tions against a defended shore were comparable to a "Charge of the Light Brigade," particularly if such an assault were attempted in the daytime. Still, there were others who did not share this pessimism. The subject of amphibious landings was discussed in the Annual Report of the Commandant of the Marine Corps in 1921. At the same time, a then unknown student at the Naval War College at Newport, Rhode Island, Major Holland M. Smith, began to expound his views on behalf of the role he envisioned for the Marine Corps of the future in the realm of amphibious warfare.[5]

During the immediate postwar period, the voices raised in support of the feasibility of amphibious warfare were crying in the wilderness. By mid-1921, at a time of isolationism and retrenchment, the strength of the U.S. Marine Corps diminished to 1,087 officers and 21,903 enlisted men,[6] a figure that was to drop even lower during the late 1920s and early 1930s. In the wake of demobilization the entire Corps was suffering from a letdown that invariably follows the return of a military organization to peacetime conditions. Most of the men who had signed up for the emergency had returned to their civilian pursuits. Many wartime officers had left the service and wholesale demotions in rank had become necessary, while recruiting was slow. The status of the officers who remained was uncertain and, as with the other Services, retrenchment and budgetary restrictions obscured the peacetime mission and status of the Corps.

Postwar economy and public apathy subjected the Marine Corps and the other Services to severe limitations in men and resources, notwithstanding the fact that Marines were deployed in the Caribbean and later in Central America on peace-keeping missions that occasionally extended to fighting brushfire wars. The lean years, which were to extend to the very eve of World War II, placed severe restrictions on the scope of Corps operations, yet the maxim that "necessity is the mother of invention" once again proved its validity during this period. Lack of manpower and equipment forced Marines to concentrate on intellectual pursuits, primarily that of defining their mission and planning ahead for the future. At times, bigness tends to stifle initiative; lacking all but the most elementary resources, Marines relied on improvisation that, despite some manifest disadvantages, was to serve them well in the years to come.[7]

Two factors combined to bring about a gradual reversal of the negative thinking regarding amphibious operations. One resulted from the Five-Power Washington Conference of 1921-1922, which put an end to the further fortifi-

---

[5] Smith and Finch, *Coral and Brass*, pp. 47–54.

[6] *Historical Statistics of the United States—Colonial Times to 1957* (Washington: Department of Commerce, Bureau of the Census, GPO, 1961), hereafter *U. S. Historical Statistics*.

[7] Recalling this period many years later, one Marine was to comment: "Prior to World War II, the Marine Corps was a great "make do" outfit despite extremely limited means. Where else could you find men who, after four years, shipped over for PFC?" Col R. M. Baker ltr to Head, Hist Br, G-3 Div, HQMC, dtd 21Jul69, in FMFPac History Comment File.

cation of naval bases in the Pacific west of the Hawaiian Islands; the other was the emergence of the Japanese presence in the Pacific, one of the consequences of the Treaty of Versailles, the bitter fruits of which were not to be confined to Europe alone. Having jumped on the Allied bandwagon just in time in World War I, Japan was free to consolidate and expand her foothold in the Central and Western Pacific.

Among the first to recognize that expansion-minded Japan might well become a major adversary in any future war was Major Earl H. Ellis, a Marine Corps officer who by 1921 foresaw the possibility that the United States some day would have to seize bases from Japan in the Marshall, Caroline, and Palau Islands.[8] Though high-ranking Marines, including the Commandant, Major General John A. Lejeune, shared his views, little concrete planning could be accomplished at the time. Major Ellis went on to write an ingenious plan for "Advanced Base Operations in Micronesia," which was to become a partial blueprint for American operations in the Central Pacific 20 years later during World War II. But Major Ellis was far ahead of his time and was destined to perish obscurely in the Palaus—either on a personal or semi-official reconnaissance—before his seeds could fall on fertile soil.

CREATION OF THE FLEET MARINE FORCE [9]

During the early 1920s, the Marine Corps involvement with amphibious warfare very gradually gained ground, though a number of years were to elapse before it became the Corps' primary mission. In 1921, the Advance Base Force at Quantico was superseded by the Marine Corps Expeditionary Force. Emphasis was on support of the fleet and in 1924 and 1925 this force took part in extensive maneuvers in the Caribbean and in Hawaii. By 1927, a Joint Army-Navy Board recommended that the Marine Corps, in keeping with its close association with the Navy, be given special preparation for the conduct of amphibious warfare.

Thus was laid the groundwork for what was to become the main occupation of the Corps. But the road from recommendation to concrete planning to actual implementation was a rocky and tortuous one, and in the late 1920s a clear definition of the primary Corps mission was still lacking. By this time, large Leatherneck contingents were stationed abroad, notably in Nicaragua and China. Neither funds nor personnel were available for the creation of an amphibious force as envisioned by some of the farsighted Marine commanders. Once again, internal and external developments lent a helping hand to the budding amphibious force. The year 1929

---

[8] As a captain prior to World War I, Ellis had already written on "The Security of Advanced Bases and Advanced Base Operations" (IntelSec, DivOps and Trng Files, HistDiv, HQMC).

[9] Additional material in this section is derived from: MajGen John H. Russell, "The Birth of the FMF," *U. S. Naval Institute Proceedings*, v. 2, no. 515 (Jan 1946).

saw a significant reduction in the number of Marines on foreign service; by early 1933 the last contingent had left Nicaragua.

Major General John H. Russell, who commanded the Marine Corps at the time, took the initiative in approaching the Chief of Naval Operations with a plan that would supplant the Expeditionary Force Staff at Quantico with a "Fleet Base Defense Force" or "Fleet Marine Force." Under the new concept espoused by the Commandant, this force would not be subject to continuous interruption in training through detachment or diversion to other tasks. It was visualized that the new force would become an integral unit within the Fleet under operational control of the Commander in Chief, U. S. Fleet. General Russell's recommendations were approved and thus was created on 7 December 1933 the Fleet Marine Force[10] with headquarters at Quantico, Virginia, an event that was to be described as perhaps "the most significant development within the Marine Corps."[11]

Immediately following the establishment of the 3,000-man Fleet Marine Force, the Marine Corps Schools at Quantico prepared an amphibious operations manual which set forth a philosophy of command relations, modern concepts, and techniques for a controlled ship-to-shore movement; possible means of ship-to-shore communications; doctrines for air support and naval gunfire; combat loading of troops and supplies; and basics of shore party organization. The finished guide was introduced as the *Tentative Landing Operations Manual.* Within four years, the manual was to be adopted by the Navy as official doctrine for all landing operations. Subsequently, with additional modifications, it also emerged as an Army Field Manual.

In September 1935, Headquarters, Fleet Marine Force moved from Quantico to San Diego. At the same time, the Fleet Marine Force was organized into two brigades. The 1st Brigade was stationed at Quantico, while the 2d moved to the Marine Corps Base, San Diego. In order to have available an organization that could cope with the testing of equipment that was to be used for amphibious warfare, a Marine Corps Equipment Board was established at Quantico, which subsequently was instrumental in the development of the amphibian tractor.

Beginning in February 1934, units of the Fleet Marine Force took part in the annual maneuvers of the U. S. Fleet. In the Pacific, such maneuvers were held off the coast of California, in Hawaii, and at Midway, while similar landing exercises in the Atlantic were conducted in the Caribbean. In 1936 and again in 1938, elements of the U. S. Army participated in some of the exercises, but in 1939 the Army declined to take part, thus for all practical purposes leaving the field of amphibious warfare entirely in the hands of the Marine Corps. Along with the refinement in landing techniques during the late 1930s came the introduction of suitable vessels that

---

[10] Navy Dept GO No. 241, as cited in *The Development of FMFPac*, pp. 6-7.

[11] Metcalf, *A History of the U. S. Marine Corps*, p. 550.

AMPHIBIOUS EXERCISES *at Culebra, Puerto Rico, 1936. (USMC 529463)*

MARINES *in steel Higgins boat, 1939. (USMC 526331)*

would move an assault force from the troop transports to its objective. Following extensive experimentation and controversy, Higgins-designed landing craft were found to be best suited to this purpose, and their manufacture in large numbers was initiated.

When World War II broke out in Europe in September 1939, the Marine Corps, with a strength of less than 20,000 men, already had laid a sound basis for its subsequent expansion. This got under way when President Roosevelt proclaimed a state of limited national emergency and, in keeping with a general expansion of the armed forces, increased Marine Corps strength to 25,000. While the war in Europe ran its course and a victorious German Army overran Poland, Denmark, Norway, the Low Countries, and finally France—in the end placing Great Britain under threat of imminent invasion—the Marine Corps continued to train for a war in which the United States might eventually become involved.

In the autumn of 1940, the 1st Marine Brigade departed from Quantico for Cuba and subsequently underwent extensive amphibious training in the West Indies. On 1 February 1941, the newly organized 7th Marines joined the 1st Brigade at Culebra, where the two combined units were designated as the 1st Marine Division, commanded by Holland M. Smith, who up to this time had headed the 1st Marine Brigade.

In the course of the landing exercises conducted by the division, various types of landing craft and new tank and artillery lighters were tested. The boats employed to bring the Marines ashore were totally unsuitable in high surf, such as existed off Culebra, as were the Navy tank lighters tested. On the other hand, the Higgins boat, which made its first appearance during 1940, had much to recommend it and, according to General Smith, "this craft, in my opinion, did more to help win the war in the Pacific than any other single piece of equipment. . . . Without it our landings on Japanese-held beaches in large numbers would have been unthinkable."[12]

Also on 1 February 1941, the 2d Brigade was designated the 2d Marine Division. It is interesting to note that at the very threshold of the greatest expansion the Marine Corps had even seen, the Fleet Marine Force was temporarily disbanded. This development resulted from war plans that called for the establishment of a two-divisional expeditionary force with each fleet for the specific purpose of carrying out amphibious assaults as required. These amphibious forces were to be further supplemented by an additional division per fleet obtained from the Army and to be trained by the Marines. Upon the recommendation of the Commandant of the Marine Corps, Major General Thomas Holcomb, the 1st and 2d Marine Divisions were assigned to the Atlantic and Pacific Fleets respectively, while the defense battalions of the Fleet Marine Force, which had been created in 1939 for advance base service, were distributed to other commands.

For all practical purposes, the Fleet Marine Force was converted into a training command that would pass on its knowledge and experience to the other Services. In June of 1941, barely

---

[12] Smith and Finch, *Coral and Brass*, p. 72.

six months before the attack on Pearl Harbor, certain organizational changes occurred. Major General Holland M. Smith on 13 June relinquished command of the 1st Marine Division and became Commanding General of I Corps (Provisional), U. S. Atlantic Fleet, composed of the 1st Marine Division and the Army's 1st Infantry Division. Two weeks later, the organization was redesignated as Task Force 18, U.S. Atlantic Fleet, followed within two days, on 28 July 1941, by a redesignation to the 1st Joint Training Force, U. S. Atlantic Fleet. By mid-August 1941, the title had been changed again to Atlantic Amphibious Force, and in late October of the same year, the organization became the Amphibious Force, Atlantic Fleet. This designation was retained until 3 March 1942, at which time the command received yet another title, that of Amphibious Corps, Atlantic Fleet.[13] Significantly, regardless of this multitude of titles bestowed upon the organization, there was a continuity of command if not in name, and General Holland Smith continued to preside at each consecutive baptism.

By mid-1941, with war clouds now looming ominously over the Pacific, Marine Corps strength had doubled over that of the preceding year totalling over 54,000.[14] The rapid expansion continued throughout 1941 and skyrocketed after the Japanese attack on Pearl Harbor. By 30 June 1942 the Marine Corps numbered 142,613 officers and men.[15] Even during the period of rapid expansion in the summer of 1941, no one could surmise the scope of global warfare in which the United States would shortly become involved. Thus, in May of that year the Navy General Board, in dealing with the expansion of the Marine Corps, concluded that:

> The composition, organization and strength of the Marine Division as submitted to the General Board by the U. S. Marine Corps appear to be satisfactory for the overseas landing operations to be required of Marine Corps ground troops. The question as to the number of Marine Divisions necessary has been fully discussed and while it appears that a major war conducted in both the Atlantic and Pacific might require three Marine Divisions, most of the probable operations incident to the seizure of any one outlying overseas base probably can be carried through successfully with one Marine Division fully supported as it would be by a Naval Attack Force.[16]

The global commitment of the Marine Corps was to go far beyond the strength contemplated in early 1941, but at the time a steady increase in strength over a protracted period of time was envisioned. Hand in hand with the augmentation of the Corps went the enlargement of existing bases and acquisition of new ones. One of these on the East Coast was the New River base in North Carolina, later to become Camp Lejeune; another was the Marine air station at Cherry Point, North Carolina. On the West Coast, Camp Holcomb, subsequently renamed Camp Elliott, came into being. Early in the year, the first planes of the 2d Marine Aircraft Group were sta-

---

[13] *Ibid.*, pp. 82–83.
[14] *U. S. Historical Statistics*, p. 736.
[15] *Ibid.*

[16] Report of General Board on Expansion of U. S. Marine Corps, G. B. No. 432, Serial No. 139, dtd 7 May 1941, in Organization and Expansion of the USMC, 1940s (OAB, NHD).

tioned on Oahu at Ewa.[17] Marine defense battalions at the outbreak of the war were stationed on Midway, Palmyra, and Johnston Islands, and on Wake. Other detachments held forward outposts in the Pacific in American Samoa, at Subic Bay, Luzon, and in the Aleutians.

As the expansion of the armed forces of the United States continued and was further accelerated during 1942, a concept was adopted which charged the Army with primary responsibility in the Atlantic, while the Navy was to reign in the Pacific. As a result of this concept, amphibious training activities on the East Coast of the United States generally became the responsibility of the Army, while similar activities on the West Coast were assigned to the Marine Corps. In line with this thinking, the 2d Joint Training Force had been created on 1 November 1941 at Camp Elliott near San Diego. This force had been planned as a joint Marine-Army training organization, paralleling General Holland Smith's setup on the East Coast. There were similar gyrations in name and title to those the Marine establishment on the East Coast had experienced. On 10 February 1942, Major General Clayton B. Vogel's command became the Amphibious Force, U. S. Pacific Fleet, to be rechristened as Amphibious Corps, Pacific Fleet, less than two months later. (See Chart 1.) Effective 3 August 1942, General Vogel, who up to this time had also acted as the senior Fleet Marine Force commander at San Diego, was placed in command of all Fleet Marine Force units, both ground and air, in the 11th Naval District.

WORLD WAR II EXPANSION [18]

By mid-1942 it had become apparent that predominance of the Army on the East Coast had deprived the Amphibious Training Staff, Fleet Marine Force, of the lion's share of its training mission in the Atlantic or the Caribbean. At the same time, developments in the Pacific Theater left very little doubt that the offensive in the South Pacific would be based on large-scale amphibious warfare, all or most of which would be carried out by the Marine Corps. As a consequence of this shift in strategic emphasis, General Smith and his Amphibious Training Staff, Fleet Marine Force, departed from Quantico in September of 1942 and proceeded to San Diego. There, the Amphibious Training Staff was disbanded and its personnel assigned to Headquarters, Amphibious Corps, Pacific Fleet. At the same time, General Smith took over as Commander of the Amphibious Corps and as Commanding General, Fleet Marine Force, San Diego Area. General Vogel, who had been displaced by the arrival of General Smith, took charge of the I Marine Amphibious Corps (IMAC) at San Diego, a unit whose staff was composed largely of personnel who had previously served with General Vogel on the staff of the Amphibious Corps, Pacific Fleet. Shortly thereafter, General Vogel left

---

[17] The growth of Marine Corps aviation and the evolution of its command organization will be dealt with in a separate chapter.

[18] Additional material in this section is derived from: BGen D.A.D. Ogden (AUS), "Amphibious Operations," Reprint of Lecture at the U. S. Army Engineer School, Ft. Belvoir, Va., 15Mar49.

GENEALOGY OF FLEET MARINE FORCE, PACIFIC

```
Headquarters,
2d Joint Training Force
1 Nov 41 - 9 Feb 42
        │
Headquarters,
Amphibious Force, Pacific Fleet
10 Feb 42 - 31 Mar 42
        │
Headquarters,
Amphibious Corps, Pacific Fleet
1 Apr 42 - 24 Aug 43
        │
Headquarters,
V Amphibious Corps
25 Aug 43 - 11 Jul 44
       ├──────────────────────────┐
Headquarters, Marine          Headquarters
Administrative Command        V Amphibious Corps
V Amphibious Corps
10 Apr 44 - 11 Jun 44

Headquarters,
Fleet Marine Forces, Pacific
12 Jul 44 - 23 Aug 44

Headquarters
Administrative Command
Fleet Marine Forces, Pacific
12 Jun 44 - 23 Aug 44

Provisional Headquarters,
Fleet Marine Force, Pacific
24 Aug 44 - 16 Sep 44

Headquarters,
Fleet Marine Force, Pacific
17 September 1944
```

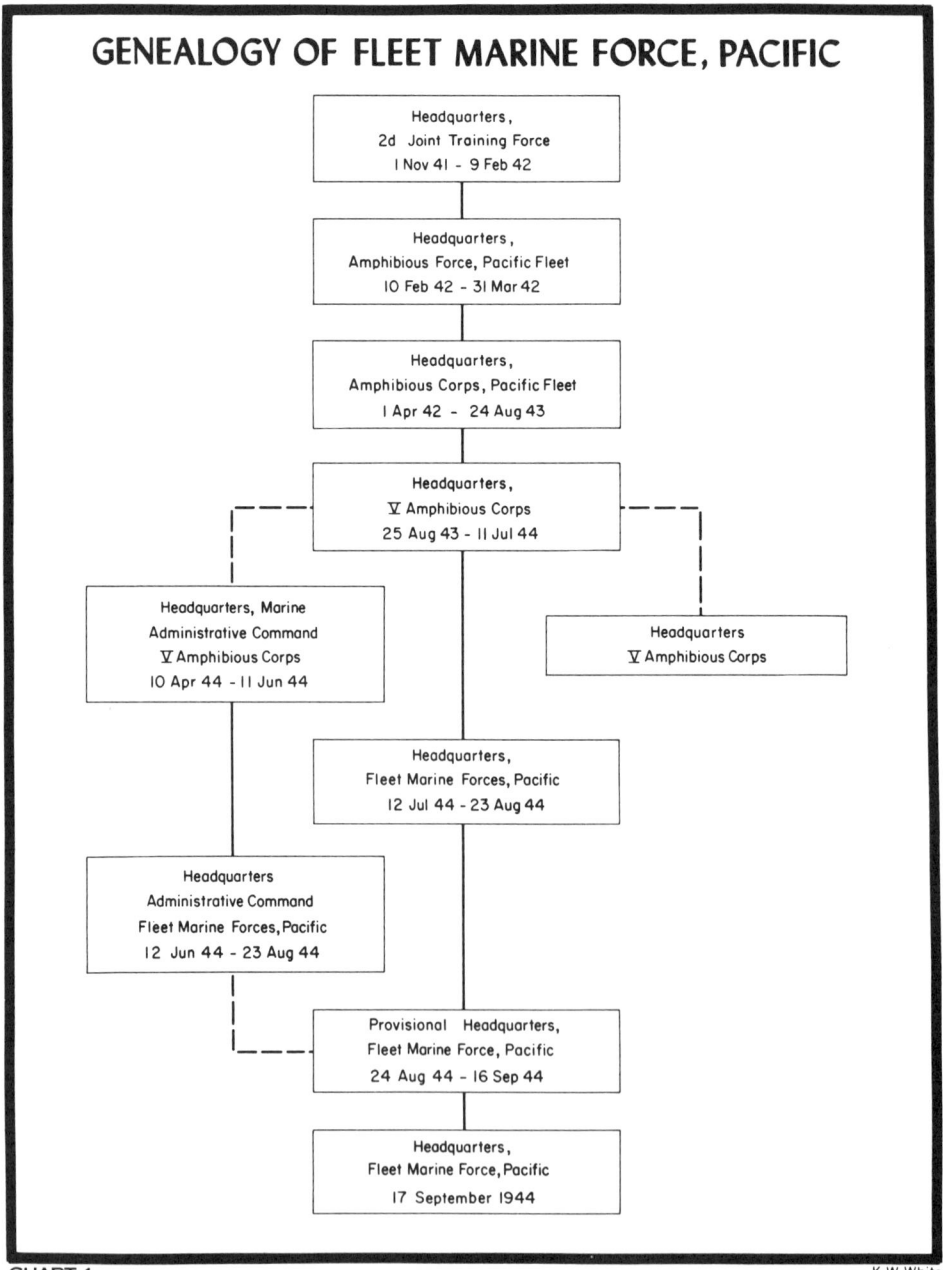

CHART 1 K.W. White

the West Coast to assume command of the IMAC in the South Pacific.

Despite the tortuous and somewhat confusing road that the Marine Corps command organization had travelled, an effective command organization was beginning to emerge by the middle of 1942, though many difficulties remained to be overcome. In his capacity as Commanding General, Amphibious Corps, Pacific Fleet, General Smith was responsible for the organization and training of Fleet Marine Force units as they became available for employment with the Amphibious Force, Pacific Fleet. At the same time, in his dual capacity as Commanding General, Fleet Marine Force, San Diego Area, General Smith was charged with the administration of training activities at San Diego, Camp Pendleton, and Camp Dunlap, as well as command of Fleet Marine Force units that were not specifically assigned to the Corps. Since the Amphibious Corps was a joint command and consisted of U. S. Army as well as Marine units, its primary mission for a number of months was to train Army units, specifically for operations in the Aleutians.

Meanwhile, American troops were pouring into the Pacific Area in ever increasing numbers, making it necessary for the I Marine Amphibious Corps, originally planned only as an administrative command for Marine units, to assume tactical functions. By late 1943, augmentation of the Pacific Fleet and availability of manpower made possible the initiation of the Central Pacific offensive, whose purpose was to strike out westward across the Pacific along the most direct route to Japan. Pursuant to this mission, Vice Admiral Raymond A. Spruance became commander of the Central Pacific Force and the Fifth Fleet. In August 1943, the Fifth Amphibious Force was organized under Rear Admiral Richmond K. Turner, and later that month the Amphibious Corps, Pacific Fleet, was redesignated as the V Amphibious Corps (VAC), with General Holland Smith in command.

Even though the newly-created VAC directly succeeded the Amphibious Corps, Pacific Fleet, there was a major difference in its mission, which became a dual one. First, the organization was to constitute an administrative command with control of Marine units in the Central Pacific. Secondly, it had the tactical mission of directing amphibious assaults of both Marine and U. S. Army troops. At the time of these administrative changes, the new organization turned over its responsibility for amphibious training on the West Coast of the United States to a newly established Troop Training Unit, Amphibious Training Command, Pacific Fleet. In September 1943, VAC moved to Hawaii, where preparations were then in full swing for the invasion of the Gilbert Islands.

It soon became apparent that the organizational expedient that had been sought in establishing such a multitude of organizations whose missions were bound to overlap would not be a happy one. In the words of one history dealing with this organizational maze:

> Assumption of tactical functions by Amphibious Corps headquarters gave rise once again to the problem of conduct of administrative matters of Fleet Marine Force units in the Pacific. Now two parallel echelons functioned directly with Headquarters, Marine Corps while performing duplicate administrative activities

with respect to subordinate units. It became necessary to divorce tactical elements from administrative elements during operations, hence the formation of rear echelons of substantial size for each amphibious corps headquarters.[19]

The Joint Chiefs of Staff had decided as early as 1942 to split command in the Pacific Theater between the Southwest Pacific Area under General MacArthur and the Pacific Ocean Areas under Admiral Nimitz. Until 1944, most FMF units had served in the Southwest Pacific under MacArthur, but the new Central Pacific drive demanded trained amphibious troops and the Navy wanted Marines for the assault role. Effective 25 March 1944, the I Marine Amphibious Corps passed to the command of Admiral Nimitz, who now controlled it in addition to the V Amphibious Corps.

General Holland Smith, who had just received his promotion to lieutenant general, recognized that the time was ripe for a reorganization of the Marine command structure under the new setup in the Central Pacific. He recommended the creation of Headquarters, Amphibious Troops, Pacific, to include I Marine Amphibious Corps, II Marine Amphibious Corps, an Army Corps, along with Defense Troops, Expeditionary Troops Artillery, and the Service of Supply, Amphibious Troops Pacific. The new organization, which for all practical purposes constituted a field army, would be divided into two echelons: an administrative rear headquarters in Hawaii to take care of administrative and logistical matters, and a forward headquarters to command and direct amphibious assaults.[20]

On 29 March 1944 the Commander in Chief, United States Fleet, authorized the Commanding General, VAC, to exercise, as an additional duty, complete administrative control and logistical responsibility for all Fleet Marine Force units committed for operations in the Central Pacific.[21] General Alexander A. Vandegrift, who had been appointed as Commandant of the Marine Corps on 1 January, was on an inspection tour in Hawaii when the above authorization arrived and on this occasion proposed the establishment of an Administrative Command, VAC. The latter was to function just below VAC with responsibility for the administrative work of all Pacific Fleet Marine Force units concerning supply, evacuation, sanitation, construction, salvage, personnel management, quartering and general supervision of censorship. Further, it was to handle the command and administration of all Fleet Marine Force units in the Pacific which remained at bases during combat operations or which were assigned by the Commanding General, VAC. Finally, the Administrative Command was to supervise the routine administrative activity of units that would normally be handled by the rear echelon of the Corps headquarters.

Admiral Nimitz expressed his belief that the efficiency of both the administration of Marine units in the Pacific Ocean Areas and the logistic support of

---

[19] *FMFPac Administrative History*, p. 11.

[20] Smith and Finch, *Coral and Brass*, p. 154.
[21] CominCh ltr ser 001015, dtd 29Mar44 as cited in *FMFPac Administrative History*, p. 11.

their combat operations would be greatly improved by the measures proposed by General Vandegrift, except that he desired the new organization to be designated as the V Amphibious Corps Marine Administrative Command in order to avoid any misconception that the functions assigned to the new organization would affect such Army units as were assigned or attached to VAC. The Commandant's recommendations were put into effect without further delay and on 10 April 1944, the Marine Administrative Command, VAC, was activated.[22]

Under the reorganization, the newly created unit consisted of Headquarters, Marine Administrative Command, VAC, and Marine Supply Service, VAC. At the same time that the organizational changes became effective, the Commanding General, I Marine Amphibious Corps, was relieved of his administrative functions, retaining only those of a tactical nature, unless otherwise directed by the Commanding General, VAC. Under the new setup, the functions of the Supply Service, IMAC and those of the Marine Supply Service, VAC, were consolidated.

While the above reorganization and consolidation no doubt were steps in the right direction, it soon became evident that additional changes were necessary as a consequence of the constantly changing tactical situation in the Pacific Theater. By April 1944 the Fleet Marine Force units in the theater consisted of four divisions, a brigade which lacked only a regimental combat team in order to constitute a full division, corps troops and a steadily expanding Supply Service. The 5th Marine Division was still being trained and equipped in the Continental United States, but its arrival in the theater was also expected around the turn of 1944–1945.

During 1944, imminent operations in the Marianas made the establishment of an overall Marine Command in the Pacific highly desirable, if not imperative. Since operations in the Marianas were to be carried out in two major phases—an attack against Saipan and Tinian in the north, followed by the assault against Guam farther south, two task forces would be necessary. One of these was the Northern Attack Force under Vice Admiral Richmond Kelly Turner, who also led the Joint Expeditionary Force. The Southern Attack Force came under Rear Admiral Richard L. Connolly. General Holland Smith was to wear two hats during the operations, for he was to serve as Commanding General, Expeditionary Troops and at the same time as Commanding General, Northern Troops and Landing Force. Major General Roy S. Geiger, commanding the III Amphibious Corps (IIIAC), a new title for IMAC, was to command the Southern Troops and Landing Force in the assault on Guam.[23] In order for General Smith to exercise tactical command in both IIIAC and VAC, a higher headquarters had to be organized. Prior to the landings, VAC thus had to set up

---

[22] VAC GO No. 53–44, dtd 6Apr44, as cited in *FMFPac Administrative History*, p. 14.

[23] The redesignation which became effective on 15 April 1944, reflected the fact that the corps, like VAC, was a command including troops of all Services, not just Marines.

two tactical staffs. Organization of the staff took place at Pearl Harbor on 12 April 1944, on the same date that the Marine Administrative Command was formed. For all practical purposes, a Headquarters, Fleet Marine Force, Pacific was now in existence in all respects except for the name.

Events occurring during the spring of 1944 were designed to correct this deficiency. On 27 May 1944, the Commander in Chief, U. S. Fleet queried the Commander in Chief, U. S. Pacific Fleet with respect to the desirability of creating a Headquarters, Fleet Marine Force, Pacific Ocean Areas, under General Holland Smith. In reply, Admiral Nimitz expressed his concurrence and recommended that the change become effective upon completion of the assault phase of the campaign in the Marianas. As far as the organizational structure was concerned, Admiral Nimitz recommended that the Fleet Marine Force, Pacific Ocean Areas, consist of a headquarters with the IIIAC, the VAC, and the Administrative Command, Fleet Marine Force, Pacific Ocean Areas, as subordinate units.

Following the above discussions, on 5 June 1944 Admiral King designated the Commanding General, VAC, as the type commander for all Fleet Marine Force ground units in the Pacific Ocean Areas effective that date. He further specified that, as ordered by the Commander in Chief, U. S. Pacific Fleet, a Headquarters, Fleet Marine Force, Pacific, be established under the command of General Holland Smith. The Marine Administrative Command, VAC, was to be redesignated as Administrative Command, Fleet Marine Force, Pacific.[24]

Since at the time General Holland Smith was participating in the Saipan-Tinian campaign as Commanding General, VAC, the Commander in Chief, Pacific Ocean Areas directed that in his absence the Commanding General, Marine Administrative Command, Fleet Marine Force, Pacific, assume additional duty as Deputy Commander, Fleet Marine Force, Pacific. Upon his return from the Marianas, General Smith assumed command of Fleet Marine Force, Pacific. On 24 August 1944 Headquarters, Administrative Command, Fleet Marine Force, Pacific, was redesignated Provisional Headquarters, Fleet Marine Force, Pacific.[25] Subordinate units of the Administrative Command, Fleet Marine Force, Pacific were redesignated units of Fleet Marine Force, Pacific. Headquarters and Service Battalion, Administrative Command, Fleet Marine Force, Pacific, also underwent a change in that it became Provisional Headquarters and Service Battalion, Fleet Marine Force, Pacific.

Presumably, the term "provisional" was inserted in the titles of Force Headquarters and Force Headquarters and Service Battalion because it had previously been stipulated that the Administrative Command would continue to function as a separate entity under Headquarters, Fleet Marine Force, Pacific. Instead, the Provisional Headquarters, Fleet Marine Force, Pacific

---

[24] *FMFPac Administrative History*, p. 15.
[25] FMFPac SpecO No. 2-44, dtd 23Aug44.

THE DEVELOPMENT OF FMFPAC   27

now assumed those functions previously assigned to the Administrative Command.

Within a week, there was to be a further change in the round of redesignations and reorganizations. On 31 August 1944, the Commandant ordered the abolition of the Administrative Command and organization of the Fleet Marine Force, Pacific. At the same time an organizational chart was drawn up listing as components of the Fleet Marine Force, Pacific, the FMFPac Headquarters Troops, III Amphibious Corps, V Amphibious Corps, FMF Air Pacific, Force Artillery, Force Antiaircraft Artillery, Force Amphibian Tractor Group, Force Reserve, FMF Supply Service, Force Service Troops, FMF Transient Center, and Marine units under island commands for administration only.[26] In line with this authority from CMC, Headquarters, Fleet Marine Force, Pacific, and Headquarters and Service Battalion, Fleet Marine Force, Pacific were formally activated effective 17 September 1944.[27]

As of this date, the following major elements comprised Fleet Marine Force, Pacific:

    Headquarters, Fleet Marine Force, Pacific
    Headquarters, III Amphibious Corps, and Corps Troops
    Headquarters, V Amphibious Corps, and Corps Troops
    1st Marine Division
    2d Marine Division
    3d Marine Division
    4th Marine Division
    5th Marine Division
    6th Marine Division
    Aircraft, Fleet Marine Force, Pacific, with
        1st Marine Aircraft Wing
        2d Marine Aircraft Wing
        3d Marine Aircraft Wing
        4th Marine Aircraft Wing
    Marine Fleet Aircraft, West Coast
    1st 155mm Howitzer Battalion
    2d 155mm Howitzer Battalion
    3d 155mm Howitzer Battalion
    4th 155mm Howitzer Battalion
    5th 155mm Howitzer Battalion
    7th 155m Gun Battalion
    8th 155mm Gun Battalion
    9th 155mm Gun Battalion
    10th 155mm Gun Battalion
    11th 155mm Gun Battalion
    12th 155mm Gun Battalion
    1st Antiaircraft Artillery Battalion
    2d Antiaircraft Artillery Battalion
    3d Antiaircraft Artillery Battalion
    4th Antiaircraft Artillery Battalion
    5th Antiaircraft Artillery Battalion
    7th Antiaircraft Artillery Battalion
    8th Antiaircraft Artillery Battalion
    9th Antiaircraft Artillery Battalion, Reinforced
    10th Antiaircraft Artillery Battalion
    11th Antiaircraft Artillery Battalion
    12th Antiaircraft Artillery Battalion
    14th Antiaircraft Artillery Battalion, Reinforced

---

[26] CMC ltr to CG, FMFPac, Serial 003E23944, dtd 31Aug44.
[27] FMFPac GO No. 12-44, dtd 18Sep44.

15th Antiaircraft Artillery Battalion
16th Antiaircraft Artillery Battalion
17th Antiaircraft Artillery Battalion
18th Antiaircraft Artillery Battalion
52d Defense Battalion, with two detachments

1st Seacoast Artillery Battalion
1st Amphibian Tractor Battalion
2d Amphibian Tractor Battalion
3d Amphibian Tractor Battalion
4th Amphibian Tractor Battalion
5th Amphibian Tractor Battalion
6th Amphibian Tractor Battalion
8th Amphibian Tractor Battalion
10th Amphibian Tractor Battalion
11th Amphibian Tractor Battalion
1st Armored Amphibian Battalion
2d Armored Amphibian Battalion
3d Armored Amphibian Battalion (Provisional)
1st Base Headquarters Battalion
3d Base Headquarters Battalion
1st Separate Engineer Battalion
2d Separate Engineer Battalion

Supply Service, Fleet Marine Force, Pacific, with
1st Field Depot
3d Field Depot
4th Base Depot
5th Field Depot
6th Base Depot
7th Field Depot
8th Field Depot
16th Field Depot
1st Service and Supply Battalion
2d Service and Supply Battalion
3d Service and Supply Battalion
4th Service and Supply Battalion[28]

The far-reaching changes in the organizational structure of the Marine Corps found their echo in the status of the Fleet Marine Force aviation units in the Pacific, which also was subject to modification. On 7 September 1944, General Vandegrift acted on instructions received from Admiral King and ordered deletion of FMF Air Pacific from the initial organizational chart of 31 August, leaving the command status of aviation units to be clarified at a later date. On 16 September, Marine Aircraft Wings, Pacific, was redesignated as Aircraft, Fleet Marine Force, Pacific.

A final decision on the status of the aviation units of the Fleet Marine Force, Pacific, was reached on 11 October 1944 in Pacific Fleet Letter 53L-44, which also regulated the status of FMFPac. Accordingly, the Commanding General, FMFPac, was a type commander for all units comprising his command and in this capacity came under the direct command of the Commander in Chief, Pacific Fleet. He had responsibility for the overall administration and supply of all subordinate units, except for aviation supplies. He was charged with coordinating the activities of the Fleet Marine Force; establishing policies relating to its organization, maintenance, and support; issuing directives for its training, operations, administration, and supply, except for the operation of aircraft. Further, he was to keep the Commander

---

[28] *FMFPac Administrative History*, pp.113-114.

in Chief, Pacific Fleet, informed of matters affecting the readiness or operating capabilities of subordinate units; allocate and distribute personnel; and exercise operational control of all FMF units (except aviation) unless they were otherwise assigned. In addition to the above, the Commanding General, FMFPac was to act as advisor to the Commander in Chief, Pacific Fleet and Pacific Ocean Areas on matters pertaining to the Marine Corps in general and on amphibious operations. He was to study and keep abreast of the strategic situation and make recommendations for the employment of the Fleet Marine Force. Finally, he was to command a task force in combat operations when directed to do so.[29]

With reference to the aviation units, the same letter spelled out the status of Aircraft, FMFPac. The latter organization was defined as a major unit of FMFPac. Its Commanding General was charged with performing type-command functions under the Commanding General, FMFPac within the latter's field of responsibility. In aviation matters, the Commanding General, Aircraft, FMFPac, was to perform type-command functions under the Commander, Air Force, Pacific Fleet. Operational control of Aircraft, FMFPac tactical units was to remain with the Commander, Air Force, Pacific Fleet, unless such units were otherwise assigned.

Even though the letter more clearly spelled out the mission and responsibilities of FMFPac, and as such signified a large step forward for the Marine Corps command structure, it still fell short of one objective. There now existed an amphibious organization in the Pacific which had come a very long way from the basic structure that had existed at the time of the Pearl Harbor attack. Nevertheless, the new establishment still had not attained the status of a tactical field army type of headquarters that General Smith had envisioned and proposed in March 1944 and which the Commandant had previously endorsed. A gap in the doorway had been opened through the provision that the Commanding General, FMFPac, could at times act as a task force commander in combat operations, but at this stage the door was still far from ajar.

In November 1944, General Smith submitted proposed tables of organization for his headquarters staff. These proposals rested on the premise that FMFPac would represent a tactical headquarters for a Marine field army of two corps, as well as an administrative headquarters in the rear. In the course of January 1945 these proposals formed the subject of discussion between representatives of General Vandegrift, Admiral Nimitz, and General Smith. When it became apparent that no operations were scheduled calling for the commitment of a Marine field army, and in the light of personnel shortages, it was decided that the staff of Headquarters, FMFPac would be large enough only to take care of the administrative duties, with sufficient additional personnel for inspection parties, observers, and small task force staffs.[30]

---

[29] Pacific Fleet Letter 53L-44, dtd 11Oct44.

[30] *FMFPac Administrative History*, pp. 19-22, 33-34.

Assurances were provided that General Holland Smith in his capacity as Commanding General, FMFPac, would retain responsibility for conducting combat operations as a task force commander when directed to do so. In practice, he was able to exercise such command only during the Iwo Jima operation in February–March 1945. Prior to the end of World War II, the status and organizational structure of Headquarters, FMFPac remained essentially unchanged. The only other major change was the redesignation of the Supply Service, FMFPac, as Service Command, FMFPac, which became effective on 1 June 1945.

At the time of the Japanese surrender, FMFPac consisted of the Service Command, FMFPac, the III and V Amphibious Corps, composed of six Marine divisions, and Aircraft, FMFPac consisting of four Marine Aircraft Wings and Marine Fleet Air, West Coast.

The American drive across the Pacific to the doorstep of Japan rendered acute the question of the forward displacement of Headquarters, FMFPac. It was proposed initially to move elements of Headquarters, FMFPac, from Hawaii to Guam in the Marianas. A study of the question brought out the fact that there was a continuing necessity for certain sections of General Smith's headquarters to maintain liaison with Headquarters, Commander in Chief, Pacific. There was an additional requirement for other headquarters sections to advise the Commanding General, FMFPac, in the forward area. Basically, the latter would comprise the personnel who would act as the operating staff of the Fleet Marine Force in the field.

As of December 1944, it was envisioned that major portions of the G-2 and G-4 Sections, Headquarters, FMFPac, would remain in Hawaii, since the Joint Intelligence Center, POA, and most of the logistical operating sections would also remain there. The Deputy Commander, FMFPac, was to remain at Pearl Harbor, and all staff sections were to be represented on his staff, so that normal administrative functions as an area command could be retained. Since a Field Service Command was already present on Guam, no further displacement of Headquarters, Supply Service, FMFPac, was anticipated.

After a considerable delay resulting from General Holland Smith's participation in the Iwo Jima operation, he recommended to Admiral Nimitz that Headquarters, FMFPac, and Headquarters, Supply Service, FMFPac, displace forward either to Guam or Okinawa once VAC embarked upon its next amphibious operation. General Smith felt that since FMFPac constituted a major element within the Pacific Fleet, the eventual location of his headquarters should depend on that of the Pacific Fleet. In any case, he felt that all of the Fleet Marine Force should in time be located either in the Marianas or further west, in any case at least as far west as Guam.[31]

On 26 April 1945, the Commander in Chief, Pacific Ocean Areas authorized the forward displacement of Administrative Headquarters, FMFPac, to Guam

---

[31] *Ibid.*, pp. 73–74.

subsequent to 1 July. However, inasmuch as the primary function of the Commanding General, FMFPac, was that of an administrative commander, General Smith felt that it would not be feasible for the main body of the administrative staff to remain in Hawaii while he himself relocated to Guam. Since he was divorced from operational duties, the bulk of the daily decisions dealt with questions of personnel and logistics whose solution required immediate access to all of the records retained in Headquarters, FMFPac. The physical separation of the major portion of his staff from these records would, for all practical purposes, strip him of his primary function as administrative commander of FMFPac while delegating the command of that headquarters to the Deputy Commander, FMFPac.

An additional factor mitigating against the forward displacement of FMFPac was the lack of headquarters facilities on Guam. There was a critical shortage of engineers and it was felt while some construction could be completed for subordinate elements of FMFPac with limited space requirements, adequate housing for the Headquarters would not be available on Guam for an indefinite period. In view of this problem, the Commanding General, Fleet Marine Force, Pacific reversed his thinking as to the forward displacement of his headquarters and requested that his earlier recommendation to this effect be held in abeyance, pending a major change in the overall situation.

In July 1945, following the assumption of the command of FMFPac by Lieutenant General Roy S. Geiger on 3 July, action on the forward move of the headquarters was again initiated. It was tentatively planned that the forward headquarters would consist of the commanding general and a small operating staff and that initially the bulk of the administrative work would be handled in Hawaii under the Deputy Commander, FMFPac. As before, Guam was to serve as the forward location. Initial housekeeping support at the forward headquarters was to be provided by small advance echelons of the Headquarters and Service Battalion, the Signal Battalion, the Marine Detachment (Provisional), Marianas Area, and the Transient Center, Marianas Area. Subsequent echelons were to displace forward over an extended period of time. In order to provide for an uninterrupted handling of the workload, it was anticipated that certain Headquarters files and records would have to be duplicated and that certain special staff sections would have to be combined with appropriate general staff sections at either location.

In response to General Geiger's request, the Commander in Chief, U. S. Pacific Fleet and Pacific Ocean Areas on 19 July 1945 authorized FMFPac to establish an advance headquarters on Guam, to consist of approximately 72 officers and 350 enlisted men. However, it was specified that the Island Commander, Guam, was not in a position to furnish engineering assistance for the construction of the necessary facilities. Despite difficulties that could be expected with reference to office space and quarters, final preparations for the forward displacement were all but completed by early August 1945. The initial echelon which was to include General Geiger, the Chief of Staff, G-3 Section, and appropriate general and special staff representatives, was slated to be established on Guam on or about 3 September 1945.[32] The main body of Headquarters, FMFPac was to remain in Hawaii under the Deputy Commander, FMFPac, as stipulated in the earlier plan.

During the absence of General Geiger, the Deputy Commander was to exercise the former's administrative functions, in addition to controlling and supervising units and the staff groups remaining in Hawaii. The division of staff functions between the forward and rear echelon was to be handled in such a way that operational planning, allocation of troop units, training directives, organization, and troop movements would all be taken care of on Guam while personnel administration, allocation of replacement drafts, intelligence functions, procurement of maps and aerial photographs, supply and evacuation, transportation, and other administrative matters both special and routine would be the responsibility of the Deputy Commander.

The end of the war forestalled the forward displacement of FMFPac, and the headquarters remained at Pearl Harbor.[33] The immediate problems inherent in the invasion of Japan, for which planning was well under way by the time of the Japanese surrender, could now be shelved as the uncontested occupation of the Home Islands became a reality. In nearly four years of global warfare, the Marine Corps had succeeded in putting an untried concept of amphibious warfare to the acid test. The evolution of the administrative structure of the FMFPac represented a small but vital link in the chain of events that led from prewar experimentation with the ways and means of amphibious assault on the peaceful shores of islands in the Caribbean to such places as Tarawa, Saipan, Tinian, Guam, Iwo Jima, and Okinawa. To make these assaults feasible required not only vast quantities of materiel and men trained in their use, but also an efficient organization that could assure that both were available when and where needed.

The twists and turns taken during the evolution of the Fleet Marine Force are but a reflection of the ever-changing war situation that called for a highly flexible command organization. Thus, the development of the Fleet Marine Force saw its beginnings before war came to the United States; it was destined to continue long after the last shot had been fired. The lessons of that war, many of them learned by trial and error, were to become an invaluable asset in the overall offensive and defensive capability of the United States, to be available as needed for the use of future generations.

---

[32] FMFPac GO No. 75–45, dtd 30Aug45.

[33] The Japanese surrender voided the imminent move of Headquarters, FMFPac to Guam. Detailed notes pertaining to this move for the period 12–27Aug45 are contained in LtGen Merwin H. Silverthorn ltr to HistBr, G-3 Div, HQMC, dtd 20Jun69, in *FMFPac History Comment File*.

CHAPTER 2

Administration and Aviation[1]

ADMINISTRATIVE FUNCTIONS AND CONTACTS

When the guns fell silent in 1945, the time had arrived to take stock and determine where the organizational structure of the Marine Corps had gone during the war years and what direction it would take in the future. The expanded Fleet Marine Force in the summer of 1945 bore little resemblance to the embryo organization that had existed during the early days of World War II, when a few defense units had been scattered among widely separated islands in the Pacific. Within the overall structure of the Marine Corps and the remaining armed forces of the United States, the Fleet Marine Force was not an isolated entity. All of its titles and functions resulted from tactical considerations; in fact, the numerous changes in both were inherently the result of a flexible response to widely varying demands made on the Corps in the course of the evolution of amphibious warfare.

One name that recurs unfailingly during all of World War II in connection with this evolution is that of General Holland M. Smith. This officer, among others, made it his life purpose to perfect amphibious doctrine and organization to a point where both won general acceptance, despite numerous skeptics and critics who still remembered the unsuccessful Allied expedition to the Dardanelles in World War I. The experience of the U.S. Marine Corps in all aspects of amphibious landings during World War II removed that type of warfare once and for all from the sphere of experimentation that had occupied much thought and time of planners during the 1920s and 1930s. It was fortunate that "this tough, egocentric, cantankerous, exacting little Marine general, who became one of the most controversial figures in World War II, provided the main power drive to all amphibious training on the east coast in the crucial year of 1941."[2] Nor did this drive diminish during the war years, for throughout the war General Smith kept in mind the fundamental reason for the existence of the Fleet Marine Force: the Navy's need for an efficient, highly mobile striking force

---

[1] Unless otherwise noted, the material in this chapter is derived from: *FMFPac Administrative History; The Development of FMFPac*; Shaw, Nalty, and Turnbladh, *Central Pacific Drive*; Reports of Organization and Expansion of the U. S. Marine Corps during the 1940s (OAB, NHD); Smith and Finch, *Coral and Brass*; Isely and Crowl, *U. S. Marines and Amphibious War*; Heinl, *Soldiers of the Sea*; Robert Sherrod, *History of Marine Corps Aviation in World War II* (Washington: Combat Forces Press, 1952), hereafter, Sherrod, *Marine Corps Aviation in World War II*; *U. S. Historical Statistics*.

[2] Isely and Crowl, *U. S. Marines and Amphibious War*, p. 62.

that was the master of amphibious assault. In assessing the role played by Holland Smith in the evolution of his command and in enumerating some of his personal qualities, one historical account concluded:

> Whatever may be the judgment of his contemporaries or of history concerning his role in the Pacific War, there can be little doubt that he played the leading part in forging a fighting amphibious team that made possible the eventual successful landings in both the Atlantic and the Pacific. General Smith's primary qualifications for the particular job at hand were that he was a driver and a perfectionist. Never did he allow himself the comfortable satisfaction of believing that the training exercises under his direction came off as well as might have been expected under the circumstances and therefore could pass muster. Never did he allow his subordinates in the Navy and Marine Corps or his equals and superiors in the Navy to relax in the drive for perfect planning and execution of all phases of landing operations.[3]

The very nature of the successively redesignated commands he headed dictated that General Smith should work in close coordination with elements of the other Services. Thus, during the early phase of World War II, he not only supervised the amphibious training of the 1st Marine Division but at the same time initiated the U.S. Army's 1st and 9th Infantry Divisions into the intricacies of amphibious warfare. While this activity was in progress on the East Coast of the United States, the 2d Marine Division and the Army's 3d Infantry Division were similarly trained in California. Once his activities had shifted to the West Coast, General Smith took over the amphibious training of the 2d Marine Division and the Army's 7th Infantry Division. Almost from the very outset, both the embarkation and debarkation of troops from the vessels then available posed serious problems as did accommodations on the transports themselves. At the time, the Higgins craft with bow ramp remained to be perfected. Once a landing force made it ashore, endless confusion ensued until an effective shore party organization could be established.

Within the scope of any amphibious landing, overall coordination and the quantity and quality of naval gunfire support loomed as ominous factors. The controversy regarding the effectiveness of such support was to flare up here and there across the Pacific throughout the war. In 1941 there were no concrete answers to this question since during the landing exercises held at the time all naval gunfire support was simulated. One problem arising in the course of these exercises was the difficulty of coordinating the efforts of the three Services; the naval shore observation parties were without adequate communications equipment and lacked experience, while Army officers were generally unfamiliar with standard naval signal procedure.[4]

Similar exercises conducted in 1942 resulted in answers to some of these problems only to have new ones crop up, notably in connection with the shore party. In the end, the elements of amphibious training were decentralized so that various centers could devote their full resources to a specified activity. In consequence, special schools to conduct

---
[3] Ibid.

[4] Ibid., p. 65.

the training of shore fire control parties were set up at Quantico and Parris Island. Transport-loading training was given at Quantico and Norfolk, while both Quantico and Fort Bragg, N. C., provided much needed theoretical and practical instruction in radio code, the operation of message centers, and the fundamentals of joint Army-Navy communications procedure. The effects of this training were to be felt across the globe as the Marine and Army divisions who had absorbed it headed for different theaters of operations.

Along with improvements in training came significant technological developments in the machinery of war that would move amphibious assault troops to their objectives. First came the Higgins boats, which had already been tested and improved during the late 1930s, followed in 1941 by the adoption of the Higgins tank lighters which were to become the standard medium landing craft (LCM) used in amphibious landings throughout World War II. The development of the tracked landing vehicle, subsequently to become known as the LVT, followed a tortuous path similar to that of the Higgins boat. Initially invented for rescue work in the Everglades of Florida, the amphibian tractor first came to the attention of the Marine Corps in the 1930s. In late 1940 the first of the Roebling "Alligators" was demonstrated at Quantico, after which time funds were set aside by the Navy for the large-scale production of this vehicle.

While these developments were in progress, the Marine Corps Equipment Board was working on plans for an armored amphibian vehicle based on the design of the "Alligator." As this project got under way:

> Plans called for a vehicle of over twenty feet in length, twelve feet wide, and six and one half feet high. The hull was to be composed of structural steel, turrets were to be of ⅜-inch steel castings and would be operable by hand. Each such vehicle was to be armed with a 37-millimeter gun and one .30 caliber machine gun in the center turret, one .50-caliber machine gun in each side turret, and two fixed .50 caliber machine guns fired by the driver by means of buttons at the top of the two steering levers. Propulsion would be obtained from 4-inch T-shaped curved cleats bolted to roller chains. Roebling accepted the idea with modifications. By November 1940, Marine Corps Headquarters had given approval, and production of the first model armored amphibian (LVTA) was begun.[5]

Also during the early phase of the war, rapid improvements were made in naval gunnery that would assure an assault force effective fire support as it approached and seized an enemy shore. Once again, General Smith, on this occasion with the active support of Admiral Ernest J. King, initiated a general reorganization of the shore fire control party. One of the basic changes adopted was the substitution of a Marine or U. S. Army officer for naval personnel who had previously acted as naval gunfire spotters. Henceforth, specially trained naval officers were to act as liaison officers of the shore fire control party. Signal personnel of the assault units, either Marine or Army, were to be made available to the gunfire spotter. In order to familiarize naval personnel with the problems that an amphibious assault force could expect to

---
[5] *Ibid.*, p. 69.

face during actual landings, a number of naval gunfire liaison officers were sent to Quantico and Parris Island where they received joint training with Marine artillery officers between September 1941 and March 1942. Artillery officers of the 1st Marine Division received similar training with those of the Army's 9th Infantry Division at Fort Bragg, N. C. around the same period. Eventually the graduates of these courses, though their number remained small, found their way into the various theaters of operations, where their special training benefited those headquarters to which they were assigned.

In a parallel development, naval observation pilots received special instruction in spotting shore targets during early 1942, both at Quantico and at Fort Bragg. In order to train these officers in practical gunnery without having to resort to extensive travel in the Caribbean, an island was purchased off the eastern shore of Maryland in Chesapeake Bay to serve as a firing range for naval bombardment. It was the first amphibious gunnery range ever established for this specific purpose, and a new chapter in the history of naval gunfire training got under way.

As combat operations expanded and the size, mission, and capabilities of the Marine Corps increased, the administrative contacts between the various components of the Corps became more complex. The directive establishing the Fleet Marine Force, Pacific, had defined the role of the commander of that organization as that of a type commander for all units comprising FMFPac. As such General Smith came under the direct command of the Commander in Chief, U. S. Pacific Fleet.[6] At the same time, however, the Commander, FMFPac also was a direct administrative subordinate of the Commandant of the Marine Corps. In line with this organizational structure, overall tactical control of the Fleet Marine Force was vested in the Commander in Chief, U. S. Pacific Fleet, while CMC handled routine administrative matters. Since no distinct line existed between matters of tactical and administrative concern, there evolved a no-man's-land in which the Commander in Chief, U. S. Pacific Fleet, exercised a certain influence. Any change in the organization of the Fleet Marine Force, for example, could have a direct and profound effect on the tactical employment of Marine units despite the administrative nature of such changes.

During the Central Pacific Campaign successive islands were seized, which made it incumbent upon General Smith's headquarters to establish and maintain contact with the commanders of the more recently seized islands, notably those on Tinian, Guam, and Peleliu. In their capacity as island commanders these Marines were indirectly subordinate to the Commander in Chief, Pacific Ocean Areas, the channel of command leading to them from the latter by way of the area commander.

There was no chain of command between Headquarters, FMFPac and the Commander, Marianas Area, or the Commander, Marshall-Gilberts Area. Each of the latter was directly under the Commander in Chief, Pacific Ocean

---

[6] Pac Flt ltr 53L-44 dtd 11Oct44.

MARINE INFANTRY AND ARTILLERY *landing exercise, New River, N.C. 1942.*
(USMC 5125)

LIEUTENANT GENERAL ROY S. GEIGER *takes command of the Fleet Marine Force, Pacific, from Lieutenant General Holland M. Smith at Oahu, Hawaii, 7 March 1945.*
(USMC 127386)

Areas. The area commanders exercised operational control over certain units of the Fleet Marine Force, either through the island or the atoll commanders. In relation to the business of these commands, the normal flow of communications passed through the Commander in Chief, Pacific Ocean Areas, though shortcuts were frequently taken to simplify procedures and conserve time.

The Commander, Amphibious Forces, U. S. Pacific Fleet and the Commander, Air Force, U. S. Pacific Fleet were type commanders under the direct control of the Commander in Chief, U. S. Pacific Fleet. Their status thus paralleled that of the Commanding General, FMFPac. In the case of these commands, the Commander in Chief, Pacific Ocean Areas acted as the hub of the wheel, though liaison officers were often directly employed between the commands.

Even though no administrative command relationship existed between units of the U. S. Army and the Fleet Marine Force in the Pacific Ocean Areas, it was inevitable that interservice cooperation and coordination would be required on an ever increasing scale as joint operations became more commonplace. During the early phase of the war in 1942, the Joint Chiefs of Staff had already authorized the creation of the amphibious corps, under a Marine officer whose staff included such Army and Navy personnel as were required. Of necessity, such officers provided the necessary liaison with their respective Services. In line with this concept, most of the U. S. Army personnel attached to Headquarters, VAC, were transferred to Headquarters, FMFPac when that organization was activated.[7] There, they remained in their respective capacities and continued to serve on the general and special staffs until the cessation of hostilities.

By early 1945, it had become common practice to exchange staff representatives monthly between Headquarters, Marine Corps and FMFPac. Such an exchange provided a better liaison between the two headquarters in addition to routine communication that already existed. At the same time, a liaison officer of the Fleet Marine Force attached to the staff of Admiral Nimitz looked after the interests of his organization. The principal contacts between Headquarters, FMFPac, and Headquarters, Department of the Pacific pertained to the exchange of administrative information on personnel matters and business mutual to Marine garrison units of the Navy's shore establishment and the Fleet Marine Force. A similar exchange of information took place with the Commanding General, Marine Garrison Forces, Fourteenth Naval District, since no chain of command existed between that command and Headquarters, FMFPac.

During the early part of 1945, the trend towards representation of the Fleet Marine Force, Pacific, on Army staffs continued in the Pacific Theater. Towards this end, based on purely tactical considerations, the Marine Detachment, Tenth Army was activated on the first day of the year and assigned to Headquarters, U. S. Tenth Army, where it carried out a vital liaison func-

---

[7] FMFPac SO No. 3-44, dtd 26Aug44.

tion during the planning and execution of the Okinawa campaign. The Marine Detachment, U. S. Sixth Army, was slated for a similar role during the impending assault on Kyushu in the Home Islands, in which VAC was to participate.

Pursuant to an agreement reached between the Commander in Chief, Army Forces, Pacific, and the Commander in Chief, Pacific Ocean Areas on 16 May 1945, provision was made for Headquarters, FMFPac to be represented on the staff of the Commanding General, United States Army Forces, Western Pacific. The liaison officers thus assigned were to provide the Army headquarters with information on the capabilities of FMFPac, obtain logistic support for Fleet Marine Force units under U. S. Army operational control, and make certain that directives of Army commanders corresponded to the capabilities of FMFPac. It was intended that representatives of the Fleet Marine Force would become an integral part of the Army staffs to which they were assigned; their primary duty would be to assist in planning for future operations. In their capacity as representatives of FMFPac, they could contact that headquarters directly in all matters pertaining to Fleet Marine Force policy. Activation of the Marine Detachment (Provisional), U. S. Army Forces, Western Pacific, took place on 19 June 1945. This detachment remained attached to the Army headquarters until the end of the war.

The expansion of Marine Corps staffs and headquarters in the course of World War II can be understood only when viewed in an overall relationship with the expanded responsibilities and size of the Corps. From a total strength of 54,359 officers and men in the summer of 1941, the Marine Corps expanded eight-fold within the span of four years; on 30 June 1945, within six weeks of the war's end, the Corps numbered 37,067 officers and 437,613 men, a total of 474,680.[8]

By the time the war entered its final phase, the Marine Corps in the Continental United States had become a huge replacement training organization. The last Fleet Marine Force unit to be organized was the 29th Marines. When that unit left Camp Lejeune in 1944, training shifted for the most part to individual replacements who, upon completion of boot camp, either went on to technical schools or moved in a steady flow towards the combat areas of the Pacific Theater, according to the dictum that "there are only two kinds of Marines: those who have been overseas and those who are going."[9] Thus, in a few short years, the Fleet Marine Force truly had come a long way, eventually comprising some 185,000 trained men in ground organizations, organized into six divisions and other supporting units.[10]

Beyond training members of the U. S. Marine Corps, an additional temporary function emerged for the Fleet Marine Force in 1943, when Dutch Marines were trained at Quantico and Camp Lejeune in line with the reorganization of the Royal Netherlands Marine Corps,

---

[8] *U. S. Historical Statistics*, p. 736.

[9] Statement attributed to General Vandegrift in Heinl, *Soldiers of the Sea*, p. 508.

[10] Furer, *Administration of the Navy Department in World War II*, p. 595.

which was then being reconstituted in exile. Before the end of World War II, several thousands of these Netherlands Marines were to absorb some of the doctrine and experiences of their American counterparts.

THE DEVELOPMENT OF AIRCRAFT, FMFPAC[11]

The development of the aviation arm of FMFPac during World War II paralleled that of the ground units. It portrayed the gradual ascendancy of an instrument of war which, long neglected in peacetime appropriations like most of the military establishment, was to be forged into a potent striking force. The history of Marine aviation passed through several stages of growth. Following the establishment of the Fleet Marine Force in the 1930s, the fledgling force grasped for a clearcut mission. The years prior to World War II saw the training of pilots and ground crews and the acquisition of newer type aircraft. After the Pearl Harbor attack, Marine aviation initially maintained a defensive posture during the early months of the war in the face of overwhelming enemy superiority. Eventually, there followed the establishment and consolidation of bases along the outer perimeter of the Japanese advance; and finally, a gradual movement got under way to the northwest, across the Pacific, towards the Japanese Home Islands, slow at first, but steadily accelerating as the offensive across the Pacific gained momentum.

The mission of Marine aviation, as set forth by the Navy General Board in 1939, was primarily to support the Fleet Marine Force in landing operations and in the field. As a secondary mission, Marine air was to furnish replacement squadrons for carrier-based naval aircraft. To carry out their mission, Marine pilots had to utilize airfields within a relatively short range of the objective; the only alternative to nearby airfields was to station Marine squadrons on carriers. During the early 1930s, Marine aviators gained considerable experience in that type of operation when stationed on board the *Saratoga* and *Lexington*. A lack of carriers, on the other hand, precluded such combat employment of Marine squadrons until the final phase of World War II.

Attempts to obtain carriers for the exclusive use of Marine aviation invariably resulted in a rebuff similar to that administered by the Chief of Naval Operations, Admiral H. R. Stark, who on 15 March 1941 made this comment:

> In fleet landing exercises recently completed, naval squadrons were landed from and marine squadrons embarked in both carriers available, and so doing is considered to be in accordance with correct principles. Assignment of a few particular carriers to the Fleet Marine Force would inevitably fail to meet possible requirements in carrier operation of marine squadrons. At the same time it would permanently reduce the number available for purely naval operations. Thus there would be imposed definite disadvantages

---

[11] Unless otherwise noted, the material in this section is derived from: Division of Aviation, Marine Corps Aviation Status Sheet (Pers& Loc, May42–Dec46); Aircraft, Fleet Marine Force, Pacific Administrative History, 7Aug 42–16Sep44, hereafter *AirFMFPac Administrative History*; Marine Aircraft Wings, Pacific, War Diary, Aug1942–Sep1944, hereafter MAWPac WarD; Aircraft, Fleet Marine Force, Pacific, War Diary, Sep1945–Dec1946, hereafter AirFMFPac WarD; Sherrod, *Marine Corps Aviation in World War II*.

without adequate compensating advantages.

The assignment of a carrier to operate marine squadrons only could not be permitted to involve any replacement of the ship's own personnel by marines. It could not, without definite reduction of efficiency and definite violation of principles of unquestionable standing, be permitted to involve command of important units, such as carriers and their necessary supporting ships, by marine officers.[12]

The U. S. Navy's attitude with respect to the exclusive assignment of carriers to Marine aviation is understandable enough when it is recalled that during the 1930s the *Saratoga* and the *Lexington* were the only carriers the Navy had. As more of these types of ships became available, they had to be assigned to other uses. As a result, for most of World War II, Marine air support of amphibious ooperations was limited to landings carried out within range of land-based airfields.

Organizationally, Marine Corps aviation had humble beginnings. There were 129 Marine pilots in 1931, a figure that had increased by 9 four years later. By mid-1940, there were 245 Marine pilots; expansion of the Corps then under way resulted in an increase to 425 by the end of that year.[13] In 1935, Marine aviation was transferred from the Division of Operations and Training at Headquarters, Marine Corps and established as an independent section under the Commandant. Less than a year later, on 1 April 1936, the Officer in Charge,

Colonel Ross E. Rowell, was appointed Director of Marine Corps Aviation. In this capacity, he continued the functions his predecessors had carried out since the days of Major Alfred A. Cunningham in 1919, by advising the Commandant on all matters pertaining to Marine aviation and acting as liaison between the Marine Corps and the Navy Bureau of Aeronautics.

When Congress established a 10,000-plane program for the U. S. Navy in June 1940, Marine Corps aviation was allotted slightly more than 10 percent of this number, a total of 1,167 planes. In line with this expansion, the 1st and 2d Marine Aircraft Wings were activated at Quantico, Virginia and San Diego, California, respectively. On paper, a wing was authorized 4 air groups with 16 squadrons, though at the time there were not even enough aircraft on hand to equip a single group. When the Japanese struck at Pearl Harbor, the total Marine aviation organization consisted of 13 squadrons with a total of 204 aircraft of all types, as follows:[14]

---

[12] CNO ltr to Chairman, General Board, Op-12A-4-drc (SC) A21-2/CV, Ser 020512, dtd 15 Mar41, in Organization and Expansion of the U. S. Marine Corps, 1940s (OAB, NHD).

[13] Sherrod, *Marine Corps Aviation in World War II*, p. 30.

[14] In this table, adapted from Sherrod, *Marine Corps Aviation in World War II*, p. 33, V equals aircraft (heavier-than-air); M stands for Marine; F equals fighter; SB stands for scout bomber; J designates utility; R equals transport; O stands for observation. (*) On maneuvers at New Bern, N. C. Returned to Quantico 9 December. (**) No record has been found which indicates how many planes were at San Diego in wing headquarters, if any. The same is true of group headquarters at Ewa. (***) Commissioned 1 December at Naval Air Station, San Diego. No record of any planes received by 6 December. (****) Available records show only 204 planes in the Marine organization as of 6 December 1941, as compared to a figure of 251 compiled in Historical Division, HQMC in 1944.

MARINE CORPS AVIATION, 6 DECEMBER 1941

Director: COL RALPH J. MITCHELL

1st Marine Aircraft Wing, BGen Roy S. Geiger, Quantico
Wing Hq, 1 JRB-2, 1 SBC-4

MAG-11, LtCol Harold D. Campbell, Group Hq, 2 SBD-1

VMF-111*	15 F4F-3A	2 SNJ-3	Maj Thomas J. Walker, Jr.
VMF-121*	20 F4F-3	2 SNJ-3	Maj Samuel S. Jack
VMO-151*	12 SBC-4		Maj Thomas C. Green
VMSB-131	18 SB2U-3	5 spares	Capt Paul Moret
VMSB-132	19 SBD		Maj Albert D. Cooley
VMJ-152	1 JO-2	3 J2F-4	Maj Thomas J. McQuade
	2 R3D	1 J2F-1	

2d Marine Aircraft Wing, BGen Ross E. Rowell, San Diego
Wing Hq**

MAG-21, LtCol Claude A. Larkin, Ewa, T.H.

VMF-211	12 F4F-3	at Wake	Maj Paul A. Putnam
	10 F4F-3	1 SNJ at Ewa	
VMF-221	12 F2A-3	in *Saratoga*	Maj Verne J. McCaul
VMO-251***			Capt Elliott E. Bard
VMSB-231	18 SB2U-3	in *Lexington*	Maj C. J. Chappell, Jr.
	7 SB2U-3	at Ewa	
VMSB-232	19 SBD-1	3 SBD-2	Maj Ira L. Kimes
VMJ-252	2 R3D-2	1 JO-2	Maj Perry K. Smith
	2 J2F-4	1 SB2U-3	
	1 JRS-1	1 SBD-1	

Virgin Islands, Base Air Detachment 3

VMS-3	7 J2F-4	1 JRF	Maj Roger T. Carleson

Total planes, 204****

Just one week prior to the Pearl Harbor attack, the Chief of Naval Operations, Admiral Stark, once more commented on the size of the Marine Corps contemplated under the then existing state of limited emergency. In outlining the overall mission of the Corps in the immediate future, the Admiral foresaw three types of operations calling for the employment of Marines. These were broken down into:

a. small expeditions for the seizure of

small islands, such as a small atoll; or a compact group of islands, well separated from other islands or land masses, such as the Azores;

b. large expeditions requiring the simultaneous or successive capture of several islands spread over a considerable area, with a view to developing a secure advanced base area for future operations of the fleet, and

c. large expeditions to overseas continental areas for the seizure of bases to be used subsequently as bridgeheads for extensive land campaigns.[15]

In cautioning against too large an expansion of the Marine Corps, Admiral Stark stated:

It seems apparent that were the Navy to insist on building up amphibious assault troops in numbers sufficient for all three of the categories of operations mentioned in paragraph 3, the effect would be that the Navy would be attempting to create a separate army of its own, entirely independent of the United States Army, and of a size greater than has heretofore been contemplated. Unfavorable reactions would ensue, which might even result in the absorption by the Army of all Marine Corps units at shore stations. Were this to occur, the Navy would be deprived of troops especially trained to work with the fleet, and to take the lead in amphibious operations. Assembling all the equipment for a third Marine division would be of little use, because it takes a long time to enlist and train the personnel of a division, and during the training period the two existing divisions would be more or less broken up to provide for the new division a nucleus of trained men. The net result would be that, for a considerable period, the Navy would be without the services of even one trained division.[16]

At the same time the Chief of Naval Operations also outlined his objections to provisions that the General Board had made in the summer of 1941 with respect to the 15,000-plane program then recommended. This plan called for two air wings, each to be attached to a Marine division, and the establishment of four base defense air groups for the defense of advance bases in cooperation with Marine defense battalions. According to the program that the General Board had approved, medium bombers were to be eliminated from the aircraft wing and dive bombers substituted in their place. In view of the mission of the Marine Corps which was to capture positions and defend them once they had been seized, Admiral Stark felt that medium range bombers would be far more valuable than dive bombers. In outlining his objections to the proposed course of action, the Chief of Naval Operations added:

Once the wing is established ashore after capture of the position, medium range bombers are needed for reaching into back areas for attack on enemy reinforcements which may be coming up, or, if established on an island, to reach out at considerable distances to attack enemy bases or naval vessels. Providing only dive bombers for Marine aircraft organizations is considered unsound, since dive bombers are not effective against well armed ships or shore bases except at considerable sacrifice. War experience has demonstrated the need not only for dive bombers, but also for long range bombers and torpedo planes.[17]

---

[15] CNO ltr to SecNav, dtd 1Dec41 Op.12-VDS (SC) P-16-1KK Serial 0120712, in Organization and Expansion of the U. S. Marine Corps, 1940s (OAB, NHD).

[16] *Ibid.*, p. 2.
[17] *Ibid.*, p. 4.

This high-altitude bomber versus dive bomber controversy remained unsolved, for the Japanese attack on Pearl Harbor, immense enemy victories during the initial phase of the war in the Pacific, and requirements in men and material that now became global in nature put an end to the gradual increase of Marine Corps strength. In the words of one historical account:

> The amphibious character of the war in the Pacific imposed on the Marine Corps greater tasks than any it had ever been called on to perform. Expanding the Corps and equipping it with the weapons and support facilities demanded by modern amphibious undertakings was an administrative achievement of the first magnitude but was overshadowed by the readiness of the Fleet Marine Force to undertake the Guadalcanal Operation at a critical time early in the war when other ground forces were still undergoing training.[18]

The development of the command organization of Marine aviation was to follow a course that was somewhat similar to that of the ground units. In August 1942, at a time when Marine aviation was undergoing a rapid expansion in line with the demands of the war in the Pacific, the need for a command echelon above that of the Marine air wing became apparent. In order to meet this requirement the Commandant, General Holcomb, on 10 August 1942 ordered the establishment of a new command to be known as Marine Aircraft Wings, Pacific, under Major General Ross E. Rowell, who up to this time had commanded the 2d Marine Aircraft Wing.

The new command was to consist of the Headquarters, a Service Group, the 1st Marine Aircraft Wing, the 2d Marine Aircraft Wing, and the 4th Marine Base Defense Aircraft Wing.[19] While Headquarters was to be located at Pearl Harbor, the Service Group was to be situated at a place where it could best carry out its function of dealing with personnel and supplies. The 1st and 2d Marine Aircraft Wings were to retain all units assigned to them at this time, except for squadrons and groups stationed at outlying bases for defense purposes. These latter units were to be incorporated into the 4th Marine Base Defense Aircraft Wing.

Operating under Admiral Nimitz, the new headquarters was responsible for the organization, administration, and distribution of personnel and supplies within the command. Its area of responsibility extended to all Marine aviation units in the Pacific except for those assigned to a specific task organization. General Rowell was to make recommendations to Admiral Nimitz as to the employment of Marine aviation units in the Pacific Theater.

Headquarters Squadron, Marine Aircraft Wings, Pacific, was activated at the Naval Air Station, San Diego on 15 August 1942. Initially, the organization consisted of 10 officers and 24 enlisted men.[20] Five days later, the Service Group was activated, in accordance with the original authority which had stated that the group was to be established "for the distribution of personnel and material with operating

---

[18] Furer, *Administration of the Navy Department in World War II*, p. 595.

[19] CMC ltr to MajGen Ross E. Rowell, dtd 10Aug52, App 1 to MAWPac WarD, p. 1.

[20] *MAWPac Hist*, p. 2.

agencies at such localities as may be appropriate."[21] The first officer to command the Service Group was Colonel Lewie G. Merritt.

One of the first measures initiated by General Rowell was to field the 1st Marine Aircraft Wing, commanded by Brigadier General Roy Geiger. Orders to this effect were issued on 21 August, directing Headquarters and Service Squadron, 1st MAW and MAG-12 to head for the South Pacific. There, the battle for Guadalcanal was just getting under way, and General Geiger's pilots would soon make a name for themselves in the defense of Henderson Field. By 24 August, the 4th Marine Base Defense Aircraft Wing was organized under Colonel Claude A. Larkin. Initially, this wing was to consist of units of the 1st and 2d Marine Aircraft Wings which were assigned to the defense of outlying bases.

Once the 4th Wing had been organized, the time had come for Marine Aircraft Wings, Pacific, to leave the Continental United States. Accordingly, Admiral Nimitz on 5 September requested General Rowell to move his headquarters to Hawaii, where it was to be based at Ewa, which had been commissioned as a Marine Air Station only five days earlier. The move to Hawaii was designed to bring about closer liaison between Marine Aircraft Wings, Pacific, its subordinate units in the Pacific Theater, and the headquarters of Admiral Nimitz. Pursuant to these orders[22] General Rowell left San Diego for Hawaii on 16 September, followed less than two weeks later by Headquarters Squadron, Marine Air Wings, Pacific, which made the voyage by ship and reached Pearl Harbor on 4 October. On 19 November, MAG-23 returned from Guadalcanal en route to the Continental United States, where personnel of this group were broken up and split into cadres that were to become Marine Aircraft Groups 41, 42, 43, and 44. Some of these cadres became the nuclei for new Marine air stations to be established at El Centro, Santa Barbara, and Mojave.[23]

Meanwhile, the expanding needs of Marine aviation in the Pacific Theater placed a heavy workload on the Service Group, both with respect to personnel replacement and the procurement of materiel. In order to furnish additional support for the Service Group, which had remained in the Continental United States, General Rowell on 3 December 1942 ordered it to be expanded into a larger unit designated as Marine Fleet Air, West Coast. This organization was activated on 22 January 1943 under the command of Colonel Merritt, who had previously been in charge of the now defunct Service Group.

One of the immediate problems facing General Rowell's recently constituted headquarters was that of channeling replacements into the combat area. The 1st Wing estimated at the time that 5 percent enlisted ground personnel, 25 percent pilots, and 20 percent radioman-gunner replacements would be required for each month of combat in the South Pacific.[24] In re-

---
[21] CMC ltr to MajGen Rowell, dtd 10Aug42, *Ibid.*

[22] CinCPac Dispatch #050113, as cited in *MAWPac Hist*, p. 1.

[23] *MAWPac Hist*, p. 4.

[24] *Ibid.*, p. 5.

sponse to this problem, the 2d Marine Aircraft Wing, commanded by Colonel Francis P. Mulcahy, was ordered into the South Pacific area to relieve General Geiger's wing in late February 1943.

Major General Ralph J. Mitchell, who had served as Director of Aviation until late March 1943 assumed command of Marine Aircraft, South Pacific on 21 April, thus heading the principal subordinate echelon of Marine Aircraft Wings, Pacific. Both the 1st and the 2d Marine Aircraft Wings came under his headquarters. In a reflection of the stepped up operations in the South Pacific during the summer of 1943, several changes were made in the organization of Marine aviation. In August, Admiral Nimitz ordered Headquarters of the 4th Marine Base Defense Aircraft Wing to be established in Samoa, where it was to function under the operational control of the Commanding General, Samoan Force. On the 21st of the month, Brigadier General Harold D. Campbell assumed command of the Aircraft Defense Force, Samoan Area. Embarkation of the first echelon of the 4th Wing for Samoa got under way on 28 August.

The continued expansion of Marine aviation in the field necessitated additional changes in the areas farther to the rear. Accordingly, on 1 September 1943, Marine Aircraft, Hawaiian Area was activated. In another development highlighting the increasingly important part played by Marine aviation in the South Pacific, General Mitchell, in November 1943, became Commander of Aircraft in the Solomons Area (ComAir Sols) in addition to his other duties, relieving Army Air Forces Major General Nathan Twining.

As of the beginning of 1944, Marine Air Wings, Pacific, still commanded by General Rowell, functioned under Air Force, Pacific Fleet, alternately designated as Task Force 59.11. The units subordinated to General Rowell's headquarters at this time were Marine Aircraft, South Pacific; the 4th Marine Base Defense Aircraft Wing; Marine Aircraft, Hawaiian Area, and Marine Fleet Air, West Coast. By this time the staff at Headquarters, Marine Air Wings, Pacific, numbered 27 officers and 118 enlisted men.[25]

On 8 May 1944 the 3d Marine Aircraft Wing, which had previously been a training command on the East Coast, and was on this date commanded by Brigadier General Walter G. Farrell, who had just taken over from Brigadier General Larkin, reached Ewa. There, it assumed the functions which had previously been assigned to Marine Aircraft, Hawaiian Area. The latter headquarters was deactivated.[26] All elements of the former command were incorporated into the new wing.

The establishment of Headquarters, Fleet Marine Force, Pacific, in the summer of 1944 brought with it the question as to who was to control the Fleet Marine Force aviation units. In August of that year, the Commandant had directed

---

[25] *Ibid.*, p. 7.
[26] *MAWPac Chronology* in MAWPac WarD, p. 4.

that Marine aviation in the Pacific was to be under the newly organized Fleet Marine Force, Pacific. This order had been revoked at the direction of Admiral Nimitz, and for a month the status of these aviation units remained unclarified. This uncertainty ended on 11 October 1944, when Marine Aircraft Wings, Pacific was redesignated as Aircraft, Fleet Marine Force, Pacific.[27] The implementation order issued by General Mulcahy, who had assumed command of Marine Aircraft Wings, Pacific on 16 September, spelled out in detail:

> Aircraft Fleet Marine Force, Pacific, is a major unit of the Fleet Marine Force, Pacific. The Commanding General, Aircraft, Fleet Marine Force performs type command functions under the Commanding General, Fleet Marine Force with respect to matters for which the latter is responsible. He also performs type command functions under Commander Air Force, Pacific Fleet, with respect to aviation matters. The operational control of the tactical units of Aircraft, Fleet Marine Force, rests with Commander Air Force, Pacific Fleet, unless they are otherwise assigned.[28]

Two additional subordinate commands were established on 21 October 1944. One was the Provisional Air Support Command at Ewa under Colonel Vernon E. Megee. The overall purpose of this command was to act as a liaison group in amphibious operations between ground forces and supporting aircraft. The other was Marine Carrier Groups, Aircraft, FMFPac, which was organized at Santa Barbara, California, under the command of Colonel Albert D. Cooley. Creation of the latter organization marked the end of years of Marine efforts to have men and aircraft assigned to carriers. Colonel Cooley's command consisted of MBDAG-48 at Santa Barbara and MAG-51 at Mojave, shortly thereafter redesignated as Marine Air Support Groups. Each Air Support Group was to consist of four carrier air groups, each with an 18-plane fighter squadron and a 12-plane torpedo-bomber squadron.

At the beginning of 1945, the units subordinate to Aircraft, Fleet Marine Force, Pacific, were the 1st, 2d, 3d, and 4th Marine Air Wings; Marine Fleet Air, West Coast, and the newly established Provisional Air Support Command. This organization remained in effect during the early months of 1945, though changes in command were frequent. Thus, on 23 February, Major General James T. Moore, who had led the 2d Marine Aircraft Wing during the campaign in the Palaus, traded commands with Major General Mulcahy. General Moore became Commanding General, Aircraft, FMFPac, while General Mulcahy assumed command of the 2d Wing, which subsequently was to take part in the invasion of Okinawa.

One final change was to mark the Marine aviation organization in the Pacific Theater prior to the end of the war. On 21 April 1945, the Provisional Air Support Command was disbanded and

---

[27] Pacific Flt Ltr 53L-44, dtd 11Oct44, in Organization and Expansion of the U. S. Marine Corps, 1940s (OAB, NHD).

[28] FMFPac GO No. 3-44, dtd 24Oct 44, App 2 to MAWPac WarD.

the personnel and equipment of that unit were taken over by the newly established Marine Air Support Control Units, Amphibious Forces, Pacific. This command, under Colonel Megee, consisted of a headquarters and four teams designed to furnish close air support control for ground forces in amphibious operations. The command, functioning under the Commander, Amphibious Forces, Pacific, continued to carry out its administrative function at Ewa until the end of the war.

The evolution of Marine Corps aviation administrative headquarters must be viewed from the organizational requirements levied on that arm. Thus, by the end of World War II, Marine aviation had expanded to a total of 103 tactical squadrons, numbering 10,049 pilots and a total of 116,628 personnel.[29] Not included in these figures are those nontactical squadrons used for transport and observation. In a span of four years, Marine aviation had mushroomed from 2 aircraft groups with 9 aircraft squadrons to 5 aircraft wings, 32 aircraft groups, and 131 aircraft squadrons.[30]

In retrospect, the organization of Marine Aviation met the demands made upon it, oftentimes by trial and error, within the limitations imposed by time and recurrent shortages in manpower and materiel. The flexibility of the administrative support available to the tactical squadrons in the field contributed much in helping these units to carry out their tactical missions. Thus, when compared to the development of the Fleet Marine Force organization as outlined in the previous chapter, it becomes readily apparent that the growth of Marine aviation was directly proportionate to overall Marine strength. The effect of this administrative expansion on the units in the field will be demonstrated in subsequent parts of this volume which describe in detail the performance of Marine aviators and their equipment in a tactical environment.

---

[29] Sherrod, *Marine Corps Aviation in World War II*, p. 422.

[30] *Ibid.*, p. 434. An additional monthly breakdown of Marine aviation units, location, and personnel is contained in Division of Aviation Monthly Status Sheets, Mar43–Dec46, Division of Aviation, HQMC.

PART III

The Palaus: Gateway To The Philippines

CHAPTER 1

Strategic Situation [1]

Most American planners agreed by early 1944 that the next important goal in the increasingly successful war against Japan was to secure a base in the strategic triangle formed by the Philippines, Formosa, and the coast of China. Such a move would sever the lines of communication between Japan's home islands and her rich conquered lands in the Netherlands Indies and Southeast Asia. Moreover, the plan envisaged sites for long range bomber airfields, as well as a valuable base from which future invasions, including the ultimate assault of Japan itself, could be mounted. After much debate over the proper avenues of advance, the Joint Chiefs of Staff agreed to a compromise which would set in motion a two-pronged attack along the two most practicable routes of approach: one through the Central Pacific, and the other along the New Guinea-Mindanao axis originating from the Southwest Pacific.

Both of these offensives were well advanced by the summer months of 1944. By a series of amphibious landings, General Douglas MacArthur's Southwest Pacific Area forces had reached the western extremity of New Guinea. As a result, the island was neutralized as a base for enemy operations, and the way was cleared for a move against Mindanao (See Map 1). In the Central Pacific, meanwhile, troops controlled by Admiral Chester W. Nimitz, Commander in Chief, Pacific Ocean Areas (CinCPOA) had seized Saipan and consolidated their hold on the Marianas. When these two avenues of attack converged in a pincer movement on the Philippines, the

---

[1] Unless otherwise noted, the material in this section is derived from: Maj Frank O. Hough, *The Assault on Peleliu* (Washington: HistDiv, HQMC, 1950), hereafter Hough, *Assault on Peleliu*; Isely and Crowl, *U. S. Marines and Amphibious War*; *The War Reports of General of the Army George C. Marshall—General of the Army H. H. Arnold—Fleet Admiral Ernest J. King* (Philadelphia and New York: J. B. Lippincott Company, 1947), hereafter *War Reports* with appropriate originator; Robert Ross Smith, *The Approach to the Philippines—The War in the Pacific—U. S. Army in World War II* (Washington: OCMH, DA, 1953), hereafter Smith, *Approach to the Philippines*; USSBS(Pac), NavAnalysis Div, *The Campaigns of the Pacific War* (Washington, 1946), hereafter USSBS(Pac), *Pacific Campaigns*; Samuel Eliot Morison, *Leyte June 1944–January 1945—History of United States Naval Operations in World War II*, v. XII (Boston: Little, Brown and Company, 1958), hereafter Morison, *Leyte*; Wesley Frank Craven and James Lea Cate, eds., *The Pacific: Matterhorn to Nagasaki—The Army Air Forces in World War II*, v. V (Chicago: The University of Chicago Press, 1953), hereafter Craven and Cate, *The Pacific*. Where location citations for documentary sources for this part are missing, the material is in the following files of the Archives, Historical Division, Headquarters Marine Corps: Palaus Area Operations; Peleliu Monograph and Comment File; Unit Historical Report.

51

planned encirclement of bypassed Japanese bases would be complete, and the Central Pacific for all practical purposes would be turned into an American lake. First, however, thought had to be given to the safeguarding of MacArthur's invasion route north from New Guinea.

Some 530 miles directly east of Mindanao lay Japan's main bastion in the Western Carolines, the Palau Islands. General MacArthur believed that he could not mount an amphibious campaign against the Philippines unless this potential threat to his lines of communications was eliminated. It appeared that land-based aircraft could not neutralize this danger, for the enemy stronghold was too far distant from newly-acquired bases for sustained and effective air attacks. Permanent neutralization of the Palaus, Pacific planners decided, could be gained only by amphibious assault.

Although three excellent targets stood out in the Western Carolines—the Palaus' airfields and anchorages, Yap's air base, and Ulithi's exceptionally spacious and deep anchorage—the high level planners envisioned, at first, only the seizure of the Palaus. This undertaking was given the rather prophetic code name of Operation STALEMATE, for revisions, postponements, and drastic changes characterized it right up to the moment of actual consummation. Before the campaign initiated by STALEMATE was ended, all three of the targets were to be included in its operation plans, although only the islands of Peleliu and Angaur in the southern Palaus and the Ulithi Atoll actually would be invaded.

As Admiral Nimitz later explained, the reasons for STALEMATE were twofold: "first, to remove from MacArthur's right flank, in his progress to the Southern Philippines, a definite threat of attack; second, to secure for our forces a base from which to support MacArthur's operations into the Southern Philippines."[2] On the same day proposed for the landing on Peleliu, infantry units of the Southwest Pacific command would assault the island of Morotai in the Moluccas, thus securing MacArthur's left flank and providing him with a suitable airfield site for land-based aircraft to support his invasion armada mounting from New Guinea.

Whether or not the Palau Operation was a necessary prerequisite for MacArthur's return to the Philippines remains a matter of unproductive speculation. Except for those who participated in it, Peleliu largely remains a forgotten battle, its location unknown, its name calling forth no patriotic remembrance of self-sacrifice or gallant deeds as do the battles of Guadalcanal, Tarawa, and Iwo Jima. For the Marines who stormed ashore on Peleliu, however, the strategic value of the island may not have been clear, but duty was. They had been given a job to do, and they went ahead and did it. As Major Frank O. Hough, a veteran of the fighting on "Bloody" Peleliu, commented:

> Whatever might have been, the Marines hit the Peleliu beaches on 15 September 1944, and history records that nine days after the assault phase was declared at an

---

[2] FAdm Chester W. Nimitz ltr to Philip A. Crowl, dtd 5Oct49, cited in Isely and Crowl, *U. S. Marines and Amphibious War*, p. 392.

STRATEGIC SITUATION

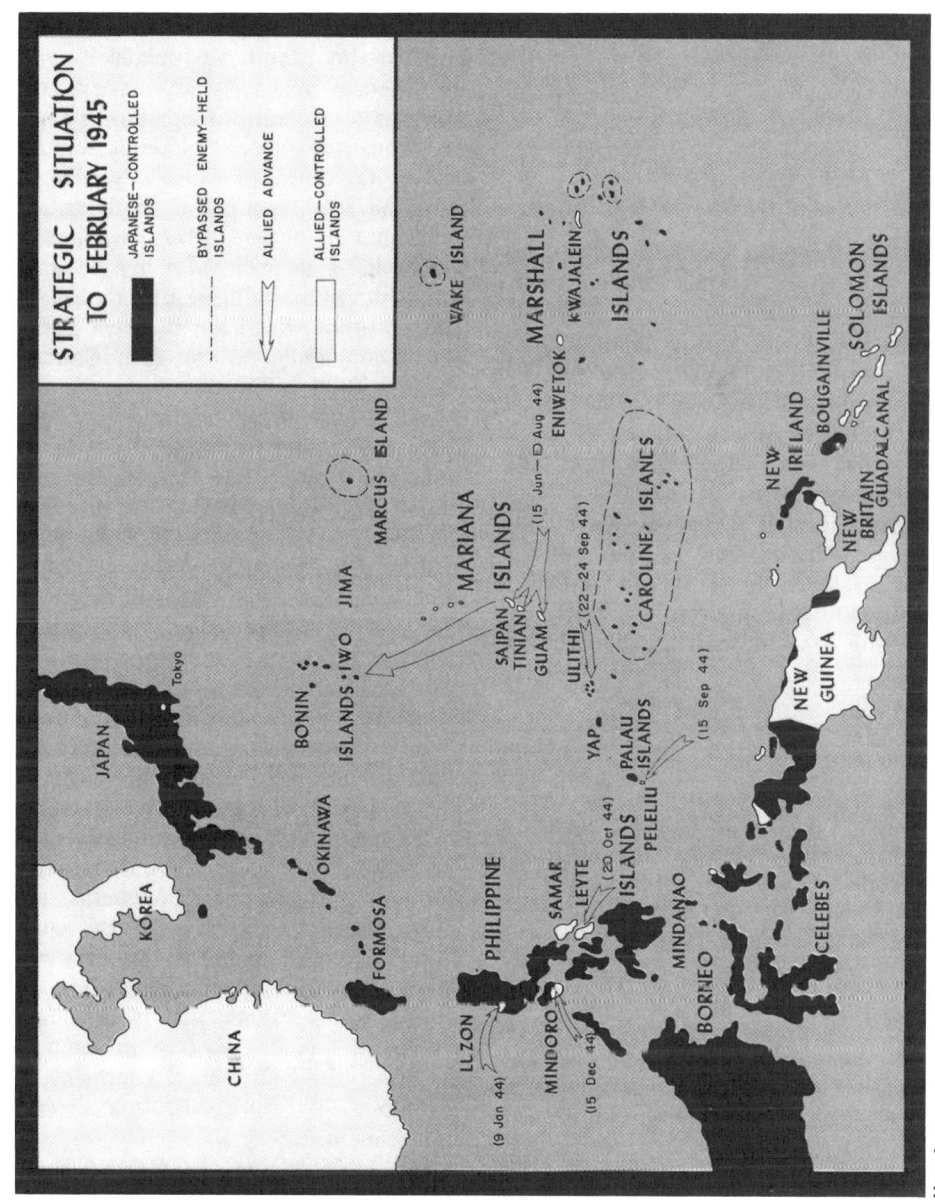

Map 1

end, MacArthur invaded Leyte. For better or for worse, his flank had been secured, and with the action which followed the Pacific War entered a new and decisive phase.[3]

GEOGRAPHICAL AND HISTORICAL BACKGROUND[4]

As the westernmost extremity of the vast Carolines Islands chain, which spans some 33 degrees of longitude across the Pacific Ocean just north of the equator, the Palaus lie roughly 500 miles from both the Philippines to the west and New Guinea to the south, and 240 miles from Yap to the east. This remoteness, especially from the rest of Micronesia, long retarded the islands' development and delayed knowledge of their existence to the outside world.

Although Ruy Lopez de Villalobos is generally credited with the discovery of the Palaus in 1543, the first recorded visit to the island was made in 1712 by Spanish missionaries. Afterwards, Spain was to maintain a shadowy claim of ownership over the Palaus and the rest of the Western Carolines; yet she made no real attempts at the economic development or social improvement of them. Except for visits by English ships in 1738 and 1791, the Palaus remained unknown to the Western World until the middle of the 18th Century when trading ships plying the Chinese market rediscovered them.

By 1885, Spain's long failure to develop the Western Carolines encouraged Imperial Germany, anxious at this time for overseas colonies to supplement her rapidly growing industrial factories, to land naval forces at Yap and take possession. This challenge to Spanish sovereignty proved fruitless, for a neutral arbitrator soon disallowed the Germans' claim to the disputed islands. In 1899, however, Spain suddenly decided to withdraw completely from the Pacific area; she wanted no more territorial losses such as she had suffered in the Spanish-American War. As a result, she sold the Carolines, Marshalls, and Marianas to the Germans, who immediately began to exploit the islands with vigor. By 1914, this exploitation had provided the Palaus with a telegraph station and modernized transportation facilities. In addition, the mining of phosphates and the production of copra had been initiated.

At this point, the outbreak of World War I gave Japan a golden opportunity for expanding into the Central Pacific. Quickly joining the Allies, she organized naval expeditions and set about

---

[3] Hough, *Assault on Peleliu*, p. 1.

[4] Unless otherwise noted, the material in this section is derived from: Joint Intelligence Study Publishing Board, Joint Army-Navy Intelligence Study of Palau Islands (JANIS No. 103), 2 vols, dtd Apr44, hereafter *JANIS No. 103*; CinCPac-CinCPOA Bulletin No. 124-44, Southern Palau, dtd 15Aug44; JICPOA, Information Bulletin: Palau, dtd 15Feb44, hereafter *JICPOA Bulletin No. 17-44*; JICPOA, Information Bulletin: Palau Islands, dtd 1Jun44, hereafter *JICPOA Bulletin No. 87-44*; Hough, *Assault on Peleliu*; Herbert W. Krieger, *Island Peoples of the Western Pacific Micronesia and Melanesia: Smithsonian Institution War Background Studies Number 16* (Washington: The Smithsonian Institution, 1943); R. W. Robson, *The Pacific Islands Handbook 1944: North American Edition* (New York: The Macmillan Company, 1945); LCdr Dorothy E. Richard, *United States Naval Administration of the Trust Territory of the Pacific Islands*, 3 vols (Washington: CNO, 1957).

seizing Germany's Pacific possessions. This energetic land-grab was more or less legitimized after the war, when the new League of Nations granted Japan a mandate over the former German colonies north of the equator. After their abrupt withdrawal from the League in 1935, the Japanese continued exercising a *de facto* sovereignty over the Palau Islands, as well as the rest of the mandated islands.

Geographically, the Palaus consist of several large islands and well over a hundred smaller ones, extending generally in a northeast-southwest direction for nearly 100 miles (See Map 2). Except for Angaur in the south and two small atolls in the north, the whole group lies within a great encircling coral reef which is largely a barrier reef on the west and a fringing reef on the east. The maximum width between the outer reefs is about 20 miles, and the whole island group covers approximately 175 square miles. All of the islands are irregularly shaped and most are hilly, but they vary greatly in physical character, ranging from flat atolls in the north to volcanic central islands and, finally, to coral-limestone islands in the south.

Lying only a few degrees above the equator, the Palaus have a humid and hot climate typically equatorial, and the seasons are monotonously uniform and unchanging. In any month, the rainfall is rarely less than 4 inches, and the mean monthly temperature is seldom less than 80 or more than 82 degrees Fahrenheit. While temperatures are not excessively hot, the relative humidity (82%) remains high at all times and is most discomforting and debilitating. Also typical of equatorial conditions are the threats to health caused by dengue and dysentery; strangely enough, however, malarial mosquitoes are not present in the Palaus.

During the fall season (September-November), westerly winds predominate, and there are usually three heavy thunderstorms a month, while typhoons are an ever-present threat. In addition, these fall months normally have 18 to 20 rainy days, the average rainfall for any one month being just over 10 inches. Visibility is usually good, however, with mean monthly amounts of cloud cover varying from four-tenths to six-tenths. Fogs are rare and mists infrequent.

The natives inhabiting these equatorial islands are basically Micronesians, a racial blend of the lighter Polynesian and the darker Melanesian stocks. Physically, however, Palauans most nearly resemble the Malay people of the Netherlands Indies, probably because of interracial mixing that occurred as the result of an eastward seaborne immigration of the Malays. The Palau language shows obvious Malayan influences also. In fact, Americans found great language and cultural differences between the people of the Western Carolines and those whom they encountered in Micronesia.

Like other native ethnic groups in the Pacific islands, the Palauans suffered a population decline following the coming of the white man, usually as a result of his diseases. From an estimated 40,000 in 1800, the number of Palauans had shrunk to a pre-World War II total of 6,500. An estimated 20,000 Japanese civilians, who had emigrated from the

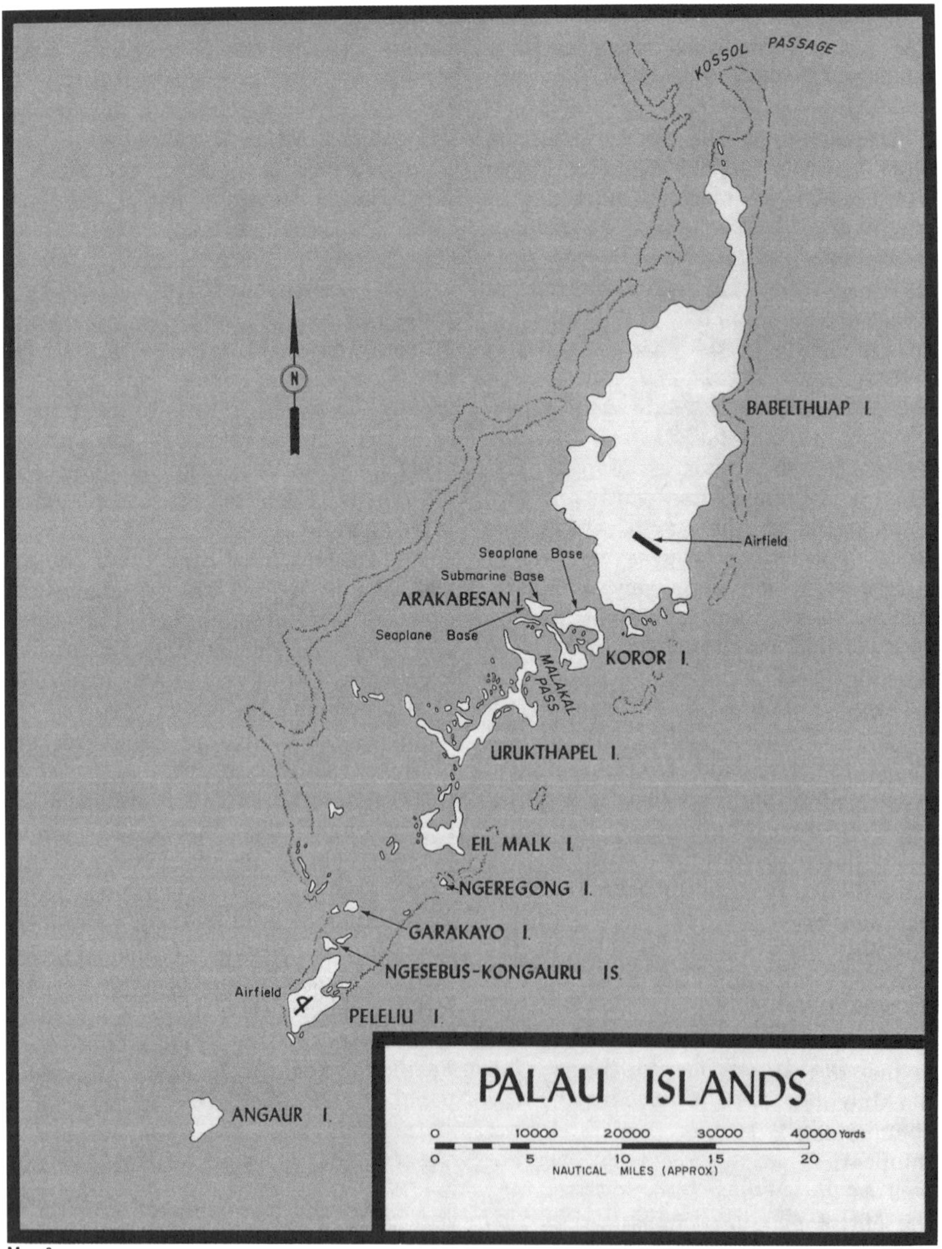

Map 2

E.L.Wilson

Home Islands prior to the war, lived in the Palaus. As a result, a certain intermingling of Japanese and Palauan blood lines occurred.

While the natives enjoyed an adequate food supply due to the islands' staple taro crop, large quantities of rice had to be imported from the Home Islands each year to feed the numerous Japanese living there. Fish from the surrounding waters, of course, provided an important dietary supplement. The only agricultural export produced by the natives was copra, but the extensive phosphate deposits on Angaur and Peleliu supplied the Palaus' most valuable export. Trade between the various islands and the outside world was restricted by the Japanese almost solely to the Home Islands.

The principal islands in the Palau chain from north to south are Babelthuap, Koror, Arakabesan, Malakal, Urukthapel, Eil Malk, Peleliu, and Angaur. Larger than all others combined, Babelthuap has a rugged interior with heights up to 800 feet, and is covered with a typical rainforest growth. Just north of the large island lies Kossol Passage, a valuable naval anchorage because of its spacious reef-enclosed area with a coral and sand bottom. Centrally located and near the best anchorages and harbors, the town of Koror on the island of the same name is just to the south of Babelthuap. Under Japanese rule, it functioned as the commercial, administrative, and communication hub for the island group, as well as governmental headquarters for the entire mandated territory. It was, however, the southernmost islands, Peleliu and Angaur, upon which the attention of the American planners came to focus.

Located just inside the southwest tip of the huge Palau reef, Peleliu is an oddly shaped island with two elongated arms of land. Often described as resembling the claw of a lobster, this coral-limestone island is approximately six miles long, is aligned in a north-south direction, and has a maximum width of slightly more than two miles. The relatively flat and wide southern section contrasts sharply with the northern elongated arm which is dominated by an irregular series of broken coral ridges, narrow valleys, and rugged peaks. The key terrain from a military viewpoint, this ridge system derived its name from the 550-foot Umurbrogol Mountain. Literally honeycombed with natural caves, a nightmare of crags, pinnacles, and coral rubble, this type of terrain lends itself well to defensive tactics (See Map 3).

To the east, Peleliu's other peninsula soon tapers off into a series of smaller islets, separated from each other and the longer northern arm by a complex of swamps and shoal coral. This eastern arm of land extending out from the southern portion of Peleliu is virtually separated from it by a tidal coral flat choked with mangroves. The southernmost part of the island, on the other hand, terminates into two promontories with a cove between. The southwestern promontory, sometimes called Ngarmoked Island, is larger and more rugged than the southeastern one, which is connected to the mainland only by a narrow spit of sand.

The island is heavily wooded with a thick scrub jungle growth, and on the thin topsoil of the Umurbrogol ridges grew a sparse, scraggly vegetation that cloaked the contours beneath and defied all attempts of pre-invasion aerial reconnaissance. A dense tropical growth thrives along most of the island's shores, with mangrove swamps bordering the northeastern beaches. The island has no rivers or lakes, and except for a few swamps, its soils drain within a few hours after a heavy rainfall. For their water supply, Peleliu's inhabitants depended chiefly upon rain water stored in cisterns.

Amphibious planners found no dearth of suitable beaches on Peleliu, for landings were feasible at almost any point, providing the reef was passable. Along the east coast is a narrow reef which borders the shoreline, except to the south where small bays occur, and to the north where the reef lies 1,200 to 5,000 yards offshore. On the western side of Peleliu, there is a broad, shallow reef shelf, varying in width from over a mile in the north to 400 yards in the south. The outer part, somewhat higher than the inner portion, was strewn with boulders. At a few points, there are breaks in the reef, where restricted channels permit passage of small boats at high tide. The northern part of the reef is from 1,400 to 1,600 yards offshore, while in the south it averages 500 yards. During the fall months, the west shores of Peleliu receive only a light to moderate surf, and the mean range of its tides is from 3.3 to 3.9 feet.

The beaches on the western side, the best in terms of amphibious assaults, are extensive. Composed of coarse textured coral sands, they are trafficable at all times, particularly when wet. Their surface is generally rough and rubbly, with much coral debris lying about. The slope of the beaches is usually moderate to steep, and passage inland encounters, in general, only moderately rising wooded areas.

The main military value of Peleliu, and of the Palaus, lay in its southern lowlands, where the Japanese had already built two unusually good runways in an X pattern. Surfaced with hard-packed coral, this airfield was suitable for bombers and fighters, and was served by ample taxiways, dispersal areas, and turning circles. A scrub jungle, interspersed with wild coconut trees and an occasional grassy clearing, flanked the field on both the west and south, while a dense mangrove swamp bordered it on the east. To the north was an extensive area of buildings, and right behind them began the sharp ridges of the Umurbrogol system, which were to prove such an ideal position for the defenders. Also of military interest was the auxiliary fighter strip in the process of being constructed on Ngesebus Island, which lay off the northern tip of Peleliu, connected by a wooden causeway across a shallow reef to the mainland.

The Japanese airfield, near the village of Asias, was the central focus of Peleliu's road system. From the airfield, the West and East Roads ran up the northern peninsula, flanking the Umurbrogol highlands. In the north where the ridges flatten out briefly, these two roads converged into one that continued to the northernmost tip of Peleliu and the village of Akalokul, site of a phosphate crushing plant and a hand-operated, narrow-gauge railroad.

About half way up the West Road, near the village of Garekoru, a trail angled across the ridges to link up with the East Road. From Asias, a road ran northeast across the narrow causeway and up the eastern peninsula to Ngardololok, where the Japanese had set up a radio-direction finder, a power plant, and a few other military installations. A southern extension of the East Road served the promontories to the south.

The other island attracting the attention of American planners was smaller and more compact than Peleliu. Angaur is the southernmost of the Palau Islands and lies outside of the complex of reefs surrounding them. The island is composed of raised coral and is shaped somewhat like a half-moon, with its concave side facing to the west. Approximately 5,000 yards north to south and nearly 4,000 yards at its maximum width, Angaur has an estimated area of 2,000 acres. Its highest elevation, about 200 feet, is in the more rugged northwest corner, and there are steep 20- to 40-foot cliffs along much of the shoreline. The remainder of the densely wooded island, however, is almost flat, and its capability of being readily transformed into a heavy bomber site made it a military objective worthy of seizure. Barriers to overland movement were the dense jungle growth, swampy areas inland, steep cliffs, two small lakes formed by water collecting in abandoned phosphate diggings, and the broken ridges of the northwest corner.

Several excellent beaches for landing operations occur on Angaur, with movement immediately inland hampered only by the rainforest and thick undergrowth. Where reefs fringe the coast, they are generally narrow and drop off sharply into deep water. A sheltered water area exists on the west side near the village of Saipan. The port and trade center of the island, this village was connected with the other coasts by roads, trails, and narrow-gauge railway lines.

Two other potential targets, besides the Palaus, also played an important role in the evolution of STALEMATE: Yap Island and Ulithi Atoll. Yap, actually a cluster of islands grouped together on a triangular reef, possessed a well-developed and strongly garrisoned Japanese airbase. None of Ulithi's some 30 islands, on the other hand, was considered suitable by Japanese engineers for the construction of an airstrip, and the atoll was only lightly held. Ulithi, however, possessed an excellent sheltered anchorage, and occupied a central position in respect to other Pacific islands the Americans had seized or intended to seize. After its capture, it was destined to become the vital hub of naval operations in the Western Pacific during the last days of the war.

OPERATION STALEMATE II[5]

Initial Allied planning for the capture of the Palaus started during the First

---

[5] Unless otherwise noted, the material in this section is derived from: ComThirdFlt, Rpt on Seizure of Southern Palau Islands and Ulithi, Concurrent Ops in Support of the Seizure of Morotai, dtd 14Nov44, hereafter *ThirdFlt AR*; ComWesPacTFs OPlan No. 14-44, dtd 1Aug44; III PhibFor, Rpt on STALEMATE II Op, dtd 11Nov44, hereafter *III PhibFor STALEMATE II Rpt*; TF 31 OPlan A302-44, dtd 4Aug44;

Quebec Conference (QUADRANT) in August 1943. During this top level meeting, a tentative date of 31 December 1944 was fixed for the assault on the Palaus; the campaign would follow the seizure of the Marshalls and Truk, but precede the attack on the Marianas. Subsequent strategic revisions, however, provided for the bypassing of Truk and the capture of the Palaus in September following the occupation of Saipan, Tinian, and Guam. This new schedule was formulated by the Joint Chiefs of Staff directive of 12 March 1944.

Preliminary steps, meanwhile, had already been initiated by top Pacific commands. A Marine general, passing through Pearl Harbor on his way to the front in January 1944, found the Planning Section of CinCPOA Staff, headed by Colonel Ralph R. Robinson, USMC, far advanced in its preparation for a future assault of Babelthuap. In fact, the general noted that the planners were utilizing the same landing area as used by a Marine Corps Schools problem in the thirties.[6] A month later, Joint Intelligence Center, Pacific Ocean Areas distributed a bulletin setting forth what was then known about the Palaus. This was little enough, for such convenient intelligence sources as coast-watchers and trading ships' captains, often available in earlier campaigns, were totally lacking. Until the Americans actually landed in the Palaus, any terrain studies of the islands would have to be made solely from aerial or submarine reconnaissance.

Operation STALEMATE was formally launched on 10 May, when Admiral Nimitz issued the Joint Staff Study for the Palau Operation. This study contained the general organization of the forces to be employed, the allocation of ground, air, and naval units, the scheme of maneuver, and the logistic support plan. The date for the landing was tentatively set for 15 September 1944. As copies came into the hands of the assault and support echelons concerned, detailed planning began immediately. The planning for the Marianas campaign was minutely scrutinized, with a view of profiting from previous errors and of eliminating all unnecessary detail from the plans of each subordinate command.

This flurry of activity among the staffs of the various Pacific commanders accelerated appreciably on 29 May, when CinCPOA promulgated a warning order envisioning the capture of the entire Palau Group with a target date of 8 September. This ambitious undertaking, larger in scale than any previous Pacific operation, would employ four assault divisions, organized into two corps.

ExTrps, ThirdFlt, SAR, Palau Op, dated 12Oct44, hereafter *ExTrps SAR;* IIIAC, Op-Rpt-PalausOps, dtd 24Oct44, hereafter *IIIAC Palaus Rpt*; *Peleliu Comment File*; Hough, *Assault on Peleliu*; Smith, *Approach to the Philippines*; Morison, *Leyte*; RAdm Worrall Reed Carter, *Beans, Bullets, and Black Oil: The Story of Fleet Logistics Afloat in the Pacific during World War II* (Washington: GPO, 1952), hereafter, Carter, *Beans, Bullets, and Black Oil*; Craven and Cate, *The Pacific*.

[6] MajGen Oliver P. Smith, "Personal Narrative," p. 62, being a typed copy of Smith's personal journal with the inclusive dates, 28Jan44-1Nov44, hereafter cited as Smith, *Narrative*.

STRATEGIC SITUATION

Earlier, on 7 April, while in Pearl Harbor in connection with the planning for the Marianas Operation (FORAGER), Major General Roy S. Geiger, Commanding General, III Amphibious Corps (IIIAC), had been forewarned by Nimitz that his corps would participate in the coming Palau campaign. Immediately upon his return to Guadalcanal and in spite of the scarcity of available information, General Geiger had his staff institute a study of the Palaus, concurrent with its planning for the close-at-hand Guam assault.

Just prior to embarking for the Marianas, Geiger detached a provisional planning staff from IIIAC and sent it to Pearl Harbor, where it became operative on 12 June. Initially headed by Colonel Dudley S. Brown and charged with the planning for the seizure of the Palaus, this group was later redesignated X-Ray Provisional Amphibious Corps, and Major General Julian C. Smith, who possessed sufficient rank and seniority to sustain Marine Corps views in subsequent planning conferences, was placed in command. At this time, General Smith was stationed in Pearl Harbor as Deputy Commander, V Amphibious Corps, and he was to fill both positions for some time.

Because so many echelons had staffs located in the Pearl Harbor area, planning for the Palau campaign benefited from a closer coordination between the various assault and support commands than was customary in similar operations. Right from the start, however, complications arose to plague the planners and high echelon commanders. Unbeknown to them, STALEMATE plans were to wend an involved and tortuous path and undergo numerous revisions before actual consummation.

The troop basis for the Palau Operation had been predicated upon the use of units already slated for the Marianas, a campaign that proved more difficult and time-consuming than originally estimated. As a result, units earmarked for STALEMATE had become deeply involved in the Marianas fighting. Unless the landing was delayed, it would be impossible to re-equip and ready these forces in sufficient time to meet the deadline of 8 September. Accordingly, CinCPOA directed, on 29 June, that such substitutions or improvisations be made as necessary for the execution of the Palau campaign.

Such last minute shifts of troop assignments, however, did not resolve the problem of insufficient forces. By early July, planners were becoming disturbed by reports that alarming increases in the enemy forces garrisoning Babelthuap and the other islands were occurring. Doubts were voiced about the adequacy of a two-division landing force for the large island. After all, it had taken three divisions 25 days to secure the smaller and less rugged Saipan.

Questions were raised also about the suitability of Babelthuap's terrain for airfield construction, hitherto a contributory reason for its being a target. Peleliu, on the other hand, already had a fine airfield and an auxiliary fighter strip under construction on offshore Ngesebus. Their seizure and rapid development as a base for American planes would permit neutralization of the remaining Japanese-held Palau Islands without the need of actually invading them. In addition, the small island of Yap, Palaus' nearest neighbor, already possessed a good airbase and was a much easier target than Babelthuap.

Although its anchorage facilities was another reason for Babelthuap's capture, the excellent and spacious fleet anchorage at Ulithi Atoll was available at little cost, as the Japanese had only a handful of soldiers outposting it. The substitution of Yap and Ulithi for Babelthuap, with its unfinished airfields and fair anchorage, would provide instead a good operative airbase and a superb fleet anchorage.

Other factors added complications to the STALEMATE planners. Shipping allocated to the Palau Operation was heavily committed to the slow-moving Marianas campaign, as were the available fire support ships. Then in mid-June, the Joint Chiefs of Staff queried the top Pacific commanders as to the possibility of bypassing the Western Carolines completely in exchange for a speedup of the Pacific timetable and an earlier strike at Formosa, or even Japan itself. Only one answer was in the affirmative, that of Admiral William F. Halsey, but the changed strategic picture in the Central Pacific at this time did bring about a radical revision of the proposed Palau Operation.

After a re-examination of the situation, Nimitz cancelled the original Palau concept in favor of a much less ambitious venture. The southern islands of Peleliu and Angaur would still be seized, but the atolls of Ulithi and Yap, known to be easier targets, would be substituted for Babelthuap.

On 7 July, a new warning order was forwarded to all subordinate commands, replacing the earlier one of 29 May. The overall operation, under the new designation of STALEMATE II, was to be a two-phase assault carried out by two separate landing forces. Phase I would consist of the capture of the Southern Palaus and the neutralization of the Babelthuap and Koror areas, while Phase II would involve the seizure of Yap and the Ulithi Atoll. The target date for Phase I was postponed to 15 September 1944, thus coinciding with the assault on Morotai, and the date for the initiation of Phase II was established tentatively as 5 October.

Overall command for the operation resided in Admiral Halsey as Commander, Western Pacific Task Forces. The combat ships of his Third Fleet were to cover the approach of the Joint Expeditionary Forces to their objectives. In addition, he was expected to furnish naval support for the Southwest Pacific Forces simultaneously assaulting Morotai while, in return, General MacArthur's air would aid in the pre-invasion softening up of the Palaus and other air support missions.

Incidentally, out of this planning by Central and Southwest Pacific air liaison officers for STALEMATE II came a most closely coordinated, integrated, and far-reaching series of strategic air support missions. The major objective of the combined operation–gaining control over the eastern approaches of the Luzon - Formosa - China coast area—caused the air planners to widen the scope of the proposed air activities to a degree not encountered in any previous Pacific amphibious undertakings.

STRATEGIC SITUATION

The magnitude of Halsey's task is still difficult to imagine. Upon his Third Fleet fell the duty of transporting and protecting the landing forces en route to the target, furnishing the necessary naval gunfire and air support, plus such related support missions as supplying the troops ashore after a beachhead was secured. Before STALEMATE II was over, every major command in the Pacific participated in it, and it eventually involved 800 vessels, 1,600 aircraft, and an estimated 250,000 Navy, Army, and Marine personnel. As the largest naval amphibious venture thus far in the Pacific, the attacking force alone included 14 battleships, 16 carriers, 20 escort carriers, 22 cruisers, 136 destroyers, and 31 destroyer escorts, not counting the numerous types of landing craft or service ships, nor the support ships for the Morotai landing. Supplying such a vast and complicated assortment of men and ships taxed the logistic support of all available Allied commands.

In order to handle adequately the job of shepherding the troop transports and attached vessels to their destination, plus fulfilling related support missions, Admiral Halsey was forced to divide his powerful Third Fleet into two parts. He retained direct control of the Covering Forces and Special Groups (TF 30), and Vice Admiral Theodore S. Wilkinson commanded the Third Amphibious Force (TF 31). For direct support of the landings, TF 31 was further divided into the Eastern Attack Force (TF 33), scheduled for the Yap-Ulithi assaults, and the Western Attack Force (TF 32), which would cover the Peleliu and Angaur operations. Admiral Wilkinson retained direct control of TF 33, but delegated control of TF 32 to Rear Admiral George H. Fort. This latter force was again divided into the Peleliu Attack Group (TG 32.1, under Fort's tactical control), the Angaur Attack Group (TG 32.2, Rear Admiral William H. P. Blandy), and the Kossol Passage Detachment (TG 32.9, Commander Wayne R. Loud), which had the mission of sweeping the area free of mines and organizing it as a temporary fleet anchorage and seaplane base.

Although the U. S. Navy had the task of transporting, protecting, and landing the assault troops, the man designated to control all ground action for Operation STALEMATE was Major General Julian C. Smith in his role as Commanding General, Expeditionary Troops. Immediate control would be exercised by his subordinate Western and Eastern Landing Forces. The Western Landing Force and Troops, Major General Geiger's IIIAC, would seize Peleliu using the 1st Marine Division (Major General William H. Rupertus) and complete Phase I by capturing Angaur with the 81st Infantry Division (Major General Paul J. Mueller, USA). Phase II, the seizure of Yap and Ulithi, was assigned to the Eastern Landing Force and Troops, commanded by Major General John R. Hodge, USA. He had the XXIV Corps, consisting of two infantry divisions and, upon release by the Western Landing Force and Troops, units of the 81st.

For backup, General Smith had as floating reserve the 77th Infantry Division, which would be embarked at Guam. He also could call upon the newly-formed 5th Marine Division in area reserve, should the need arise.

With the successful securing of the objectives, General Smith's duties as overall ground commander for STALEMATE II would cease. At this time, the defense and subsequent development of the newly-acquired bases as major airfields and fleet anchorages would become the sole responsibility of Admiral John H. Hoover, Commander, Forward Area, Central Pacific Command.

Except for a few minor redesignations in units and commanders, Phase I plans remained unchanged until D-Day. Upon his return from Guam on 15 August, General Geiger assumed command of X-Ray Provisional Amphibious Corps which was then redesignated IIIAC, and took over command of Western Landing Forces and Troops from General Smith, who then reverted to his higher role as Commanding General, Expeditionary Troops, Third Fleet. Phase II, on the other hand, was destined to undergo still another radical revision due to startling developments arising out of the far-sweeping support actions of the U. S. Navy.

One portion of the Third Fleet's mission was to "Seek out and destroy hostile air and naval forces which threaten interference with the STALEMATE II operations, in order to inflict maximum damage on the enemy and to protect our own forces."[7] This provision for blunting the enemy's potential to counteract a landing was by this time standard operating procedure in any amphibious undertaking. This time, however, Halsey had ordered his naval officers to seek out every opportunity for engaging the Japanese major naval forces in a decisive sea battle.

In his eagerness to close with the enemy's surface fleet, Halsey made this mission the primary one, overriding the customary one of protecting the landing force. His operation order clearly directed this radical departure from accepted amphibious doctrine by stating, "In case opportunity for the destruction of a major portion of the enemy fleet offers itself or can be created, such destruction will become the primary task."[8] Subordinate naval echelons, of course, reflected this viewpoint. Admiral Wilkinson directed his heavier warships in the Fire Support Group to "Concentrate and engage enemy task forces encountered. Supoort the Covering Force or provide striking groups if so directed."[9] As in the recent Marianas campaign, the covering naval forces for STALEMATE II were on the lookout for a decisive sea battle with the Imperial Fleet rather than being primarily concerned with the protection of the amphibious landing forces.

In hopes of being in on just such a decisive naval engagement, Admiral Halsey personally led the strongest combat component of the Covering Forces and Special Groups, Vice Admiral Marc A. Mitscher's Fast Carrier Task Force (TF 38), out of Eniwetok Atoll on 28 August 1944 for strikes against the Bonins, Palaus, Yap, and Mindanao. Chichi Jima and Iwo Jima were struck by carrier-launched aircraft on 31 Au-

---

[7] ComWesPac TFs OPlan No. 14-44, dtd 1Aug44, p. 3.

[8] *Ibid.*

[9] TF 31 OPlan A302-44, dtd 4Aug44, p. 3.

gust-2 September, the Palaus on 6-8 September, and Mindanao on 9-10 September. Everywhere the enemy's air resistance proved surprisingly weak, and the great success of the last strike persuaded Halsey to shift his intended follow-up attack on Mindanao instead to the Central Philippines.

Exploiting the enemy's weakness by pressing in close to the coast, the carriers of TF 38 actually stationed themselves within sight of the Samar Mountains from 12-14 September, during which time 2,400 sorties were launched against the Visayas bases of the Japanese. The phenomenal success of this air attack, which had achieved tactical surprise, proved dazzling. American pilots claimed the destruction of some 200 enemy planes, the sinking or damaging of many ships, and the infliction of tremendous damage upon Japanese installations. American losses in comparison were minute: 8 planes in combat, 1 operationally, and 10 men.

Halsey could report to his superior that the "Enemy's non-aggressive attitude [was] unbelievable and fantastic."[10] Later he would recall that "We had found the central Philippines a hollow shell with weak defenses and skimpy facilities. In my opinion, this was the vulnerable belly of the Imperial dragon."[11]

This astonishing victory, coupled with the lack of serious Japanese reaction, prompted Halsey to send a dispatch to Nimitz stating his belief that "the Palau and Yap-Ulithi operations were unnecessary to support the seizure of the Philippines"[12] and that an invasion of the Leyte-Samar area be undertaken at the earliest possible date using the troops slated for STALEMATE II. Admiral Nimitz passed on the recommendation concerning Phase II to the Joint Chiefs of Staff, but due to commitments already made, he decided Phase I would have to go through as planned.

From then on, events on the strategic stage moved rapidly. In answer to a Joint Chiefs of Staff inquiry about General MacArthur's willingness to advance Leyte's target date if given the troops of XXIV Corps, his staff officers, took it upon themselves—MacArthur was maintaining radio silence on board a cruiser off Morotai—to radio an affirmative reply on 15 September.[13]

Word to this effect was immediately relayed to the Joint Chiefs of Staff, then in Quebec with President Roosevelt for the OCTAGON conference. So impressed were they by this dramatic agreement between the top Pacific Theater commanders that 90 minutes after the dispatch was received they were able to flash their approval. Thus the XXIV Corps departed the Central Pacific to play its important part in the dramatic 'Liberation' campaign.[14]

To further compound the difficulties, Halsey on the following day, the second

---

[10] CinCPac WarD, dtd 14Sep44, p. 1, hereafter *CinCPac WarD*, with appropriate date.

[11] FAdm William F. Halsey and LCdr Julian Bryan, III, *Admiral Halsey's Story* (New York: McGraw-Hill Book Company, Inc., 1947), p. 199, hereafter Halsey and Bryan, *Admiral Halsey's Story*.

[12] *ThirdFlt AR*, p. 4.

[13] George C. Kenney, *General Kenney Reports: A Personal History of the Pacific War* (New York: Duell, Sloan and Pearce, 1949), p. 432, hereafter Kenney, *Reports*, used with permission.

[14] Hough, *Assault on Peleliu*, p. 191.

day of the Peleliu fighting, directed the seizure of Ulithi "as early as practical . . . with resources at hand."[15] The only uncommitted force was the corps reserve, a single regimental combat team (RCT), and its removal from the immediate area would leave the Marines still battling desperately ashore to secure Peleliu without any reinforcements should they be needed.[16] What resulted, however, when this happened, will be narrated later in its proper sequence.

THE JAPANESE BOLSTER DEFENSES[17]

The thick veil of secrecy with which the Japanese cloaked their prewar activities in the mandated Palaus revealed an early awareness of the military potentialities of the islands. Under the League of Nations' terms, none could be fortified, but Japan's extreme sensitivity concerning them aroused suspicions. As one American visitor stated, "Officials and officers swarm here in such numbers that the visitor does not draw a breath without an appropriate note being made in the archives."[18] Here, it was, also, that a Marine colonel died under very mysterious circumstances in 1923, while traveling in the disguise of a commercial trader.[19]

On the other hand, there was no concrete evidence of any extensive fortification of the Palaus prior to World War II. Harbors had been dredged, some naval facilities erected, and an airfield built, but the Peleliu airfield, while pos-

---

[15] *III PhibFor, STALEMATE II Rpt*, p. 8.

[16] "In explanation of Halsey's decision, 3dPhibFor's serial 00314 of 11 Nov 1944 (p. 8) notes that Halsey acted after receiving a report of the local situation. Further, the RCT was not expected to depart until 21 September and Halsey provided for the use of the RCT in Peleliu prior to that date if the situation required." RAdm E. M. Eller ltr to Hd, HistBr, G-3 Div, HQMC, dtd 18Jul66, in *Peleliu Comment File*, hereafter *Eller ltr*.

[17] Unless otherwise noted, the material in this section is derived from: *ExTrps SAR*; *IIIAC Palaus Rpt*; *1stMarDiv, SAR, PalauOp*, dtd 16Nov44, hereafter *1st MarDiv SAR*; *Peleliu Comment File*; CinCPac-CinCPOA Bulletin No. 173-45, Japanese Military Caves on Peleliu: 'Know Your Enemy!', dtd 23Jul45; *JICPOA Bulletin No. 17-44*; JICPOA Bulletin No. 87T-44, Target Analysis: Palau Islands, dtd 20Jun44, hereafter *JICPOA Bulletin No. 87T-44*; USSBS(Pac), *Interrogations*, II, VAdm Shigeru Fukudome, Cdr Chikataka Nakajima; HistSec, G-2, GHQ, FEC, Japanese Studies in World War II, Japanese Monograph No. 48, *Operations in the Central Pacific*, hereafter *Japanese Ops in the CenPac*; Japanese Research Div, MilHistSec, GHQ, FEC, Japanese Monograph No. 49, *Central Pacific Operations Record*, Volume II, April-November 1944, hereafter *Japanese CenPac Ops*; Gen MacArthur's Staff, Historical Report of Operations in the Southwest Pacific Area, 2 vols. (Tokyo, 1951), hereafter *MacArthur's History*, with appropriate volume; Saburo Hayashi, in collaboration with Alvin D. Coox, *Kōgun: The Japanese Army in the Pacific War* (Quantico, Va.: The Marine Corps Association, 1959) hereafter Hayashi and Coox, *Kōgun*; Hough, *Assault on Peleliu*; Smith, *Approach to the Philippines*; Morison, *Leyte*.

[18] Willard Price, "Hidden Key to the Pacific," *The National Geographic Magazine*, v. LXXXI, No. 6 (Jun42), p. 784.

[19] For those interested in the mysterious disappearance of Lieutenant Colonel Earl H. Ellis, see: LtCol Philip N. Pierce, USMC, "The Unsolved Mystery of Pete Ellis," *Marine Corps Gazette*, v. 46, No. 2 (Feb62), pp. 34-40, which incorporated the findings of LtCol Waite W. Worden, USMC, who visited Koror in 1950 and interviewed its residents concerning Ellis' death. Copies of Worden's findings are also in the possession of RefBr, HistDiv, HQMC.

sessing great military value, was equally useful for peaceful civilian pursuits.

Immediately following Pearl Harbor, however, the islands served as a jumping-off point for Japan's attack against the Philippines. Out of its naval base had sortied the small carrier task force which launched the first air raids against American forces in the Philippines, while troops staged at the Palaus for the later Philippines land campaign. Afterwards, the islands came to be used primarily as an intermediate staging base and supply point for offensives along the outer perimeter of the Japanese advance. During the struggle for the Solomons, thousands of Imperial soldiers staged through the Palaus, utilizing them as training and practice areas, on their way to the front.

The Japanese high command, during the early stages of the Pacific War, paid slight attention to the ability of the Palaus to defend themselves. The full vigor of Japan's war effort was then concentrated upon the outer fringes of newly conquered territories, where mounting Allied counterattacks absorbed available Japanese troops and war material in ever increasing amounts. Any development of a strategic inner defense line was deferred until dramatic reversals in New Guinea, the Solomons, and other points forced the Imperial war planners to reassess the hopeless battle on the outer perimeter.

Finding herself unable to match the superior Allied air and naval strength, Japan began concentrating her energies upon the creation of a powerful defensive bastion which would halt the Allied advance and hurl it back. Accordingly, in September 1943, the *Imperial General Headquarters (IGHQ)* at Tokyo created a second line of defense which embraced the areas west of the Marianas-Carolines-Western New Guinea line. It was then decreed that this was the zone of absolute defense where each Japanese soldier would fight to the death.

Initial steps in girding this decisive battle area for the eventual assault called for bolstering the garrisons with first-string combat troops. For the first time in the Pacific War, *IGHQ* planners were forced to draw upon the battle-ready divisions of the *Kwantung Army* in Manchuria. Maintained at peak combat readiness, this unit served the purpose of immobilizing the large number of Russian troops in nearby Siberia, thereby preventing their redeployment to the European front for use against Japan's ally, Germany. The needs of the crucial Pacific sector, however, sent the *35th Division*, among others of the *Kwantung* units, hurrying southward. The *35th* arrived during March 1944 in the Palaus, until then garrisoned only by rear-echelon troops, but it was almost immediately dispatched farther westward to a more critical front, leaving only one understrength regiment to defend the island group.

Earlier in 1944, the American seizure of the Admiralties and Marshalls had brought all of the Carolines within effective striking range of Allied land-based bombers. In the face of this new threat, the *Combined Fleet* transferred its headquarters from the now highly vulnerable Truk to the Palaus, which would be used as a temporary forward naval base until a permanent one could be constructed in the Philippines. No sooner had the Japanese settled down in their new location, than a successful carrier raid by the U. S. Fifth Fleet in late March denied them the use of the Palaus even temporarily.

This large scale air strike also spurred the defensive efforts of the Japanese Army and caused some drastic reshuffling of troop assignments. Since an American attack was believed imminent, the *14th Division,* already en route from Manchuria, was dispatched with all possible speed to the Palaus. Landing there on 24 April, the *14th* took over the responsibility for the islands' defenses, releasing the regiment of the *35th* to rejoin its parent organization already committed to the fighting farther westward.

To handle the overall task of defending the Central Pacific area, *IGHQ* had established the *Thirty-first Army* with headquarters in the Marianas. Its zone of responsibility stretched along the Bonins-Marianas-Carolines line of the strategic area of absolute defense. The commanding general was to have control over all army units in the theater and be directly responsible to the *Central Pacific Fleet,* but his displeasure in being subordinated to a naval officer precipitated a furious interservice squabble which was smoothed over only when the Navy and Army commanders orally pledged each other not to assume complete responsibility.

With the arrival of the hardened veterans of the *14th Division* on Babelthuap, after a delay while their transports evaded would-be American attackers, an effective defense of the islands approached reality. The *14th* was one of the oldest and best military units in the Japanese Army, and its infantry regiments, the *2d, 15th,* and *59th,* all had excellent reputations. Its commanding officer, Lieutenant General Sadae Inoue, was made Commander, *Palau Sector Group,* the organization responsible to the *Thirty-first Army* for the defense of all the Palaus, Yap, and nearby islands. Military units already based in the Palaus, such as the Sea Transport Units (landing craft and crews) of the *1st Amphibious Brigade,* and the service and support troops for the Japanese forces in New Guinea, passed to the control of General Inoue as group commander, who later reorganized them into the *53d Independent Mixed Brigade (IMB).* Inoue's orders from the superior headquarters were concise:

> The Palau Sector Group Commander will secure the Palau Islands (including Angaur) and the Yap Island area. . . . The islands must be held to the very last as the final position barring the enemy from penetrating into the Pacific. Peleliu and Angaur must be fortified as an important air base.[20]

Within a matter of weeks after his arrival, General Inoue successfully deployed his units in scattered defensive positions. Headquarters of both the division and group, naturally, were located on Koror, the administrative center of the islands, and the major part of the troops were deployed on nearby Babelthuap where Inoue planned to make his final fight.

As the main infantry force on Peleliu, Inoue allocated the *2d Infantry.* Its commander, Colonel Kunio Nakagawa, was designated Commander, *Peleliu*

---

[20] *Japanese Ops in the CenPac,* p. 24.

STRATEGIC SITUATION

Sector Unit, which also had artillery, mortar, signal, and light tank units attached to it. The *346th Independent Infantry Battalion* of the *53d IMB* and the *3d Battalion, 15th Infantry,* were also assigned to Nakagawa's command to bolster his combat strength. In addition, the Navy had the *144th* and *126th Antiaircraft* units, and the *45th Guard Force Detachment,* plus construction units and the airbase personnel. In all, Nakagawa had approximately 6,500 combat troops available for the defense of Peleliu, and the service troops and non-combatants brought his garrison total up to about 10,500.

The *Peleliu Sector Unit* commander confidently expected his troops to man their assigned positions until death, for the Imperial Japanese infantryman, schooled in the strict *Bushido* code of the warrior, prided himself on his tenacious fighting ability without regard for personal safety. The *esprit de corps* of the *15th Infantry,* whose *2d* and *3d Battalions* were destined to be wiped out during the fighting on Peleliu, was typical of the Japanese fighting units. First organized in 1884, the regiment was presented its colors the following year and covered them with great honor in several hard-fought battles. More recently, it had received a citation for a battle in North China. As the regimental commander reported:

> All the officers and men carried in mind the meaning of our sacred war, and the leaders, burning with the will to be 'Breakwater of the Pacific,' and feeling the obligation of this important duty, and being a picked Manchukuoan regiment that does not expect to return alive and will follow to the death an imperial order, devoted themselves to the endeavor of being the type of soldier who can fight hundreds of men....
>
> Using all wisdom especially while acquiring our antilanding training we will overcome the hardships of warfare and under the battle flag which displays our battle glory we vow with our unbreakable solidarity we will complete our glorious duty and establish the 'Breakwater of the Pacific.'[21]

Such was the caliber of the men slated to fight to the last in a hopeless struggle on Peleliu. About the only Japanese lacking this fanatical viewpoint were those portions of the naval garrison consisting of the labor troops and the Korean labor force. Most of these noncombatants, however, were forced by the combat troops to resist aggressively the American attacks; only a few ever succeeded in surrendering.

On Angaur, Inoue stationed the *59th Infantry,* less one battalion. Late in July, however, most of these infantrymen were withdrawn to strengthen Babelthuap where the main attack was expected, leaving only the *1st Battalion* as garrison. Its commander, Major Ushio Goto, was then assigned as Commander, *Angaur Sector Unit.* His remaining garrison forces totaled some 1,400 men, including supporting artillery, antiaircraft, mortar, engineer, and service units.

Within easy reinforcing distance of both Peleliu and Angaur were some 25,000 troops on the other Palau Islands, many specially trained in amphibious operations. Among the other places under General Inoue's command, only Yap was heavily garrisoned. As

---

[21] CinCPac-CinCPOA Item No. 9764, "Report on the 15th Infantry Regiment," dtd 16May44.

late as 27 August 1944, American intelligence officers reported its defending forces as 8,000 to 10,000 men.[22]

Immediately upon assuming responsibility for the defense of the *Palau Sector Group,* General Inoue became bogged down in that long-standing rivalry between the Japanese Army and Navy. The naval officers had regarded the Palaus as their own private domain for so long that the sudden arrival of a lieutenant general, senior to their own commander, aroused their excessive sensitivity and displeasure.

The Army commander, right from the start, was made to feel the Navy's resentment over the new state of affairs. Inoue found it practically impossible to obtain civilian help in erecting fortifications, for the Navy had already monopolized all available labor and organized the workers into pools to be used for naval projects only. Nor would the naval officers allow any Army personnel to utilize their caves or installations. As a result, Inoue had to drive his men night and day in a frantic effort to prepare adequate defensive positions quickly. The situation became unusually severe on Peleliu, where the Navy garrison was commanded by a flag officer—who was, of course, senior to Colonel Nakagawa. Finally, in desperation, Inoue assigned his next senior officer, Major General Kenjiro Murai, in nominal command of the Peleliu garrison in order to make any progress at all in fortifying the island.

There was also another reason for General Murai's presence on Peleliu.

Since the group commander considered the island's airfields of prime importance, he had selected his most able officer, Colonel Nakagawa, to direct its defense. As Inoue explained in a postwar interview, he had assigned Murai to Peleliu while leaving Nakagawa in actual command for two reasons. First, Inoue wanted to remove the pressure of naval animosity from Nakagawa's shoulders and second, as a form of insurance, "to see that Colonel Nakagawa didn't make any mistakes."[23] This unusual arrangement proved unnecessary, as later events indicated that all orders right up to the bitter end of the fighting were issued in Nakagawa's name.

Actually, the Palaus' defenses actively entered into the strategic defense plans of *IGHQ* only for the relatively brief period from April to July 1944. During this time, men and supplies were rushed to the islands to hasten their preparations for an expected imminent assault. With the successful American attack upon the Marianas, however, the greater strategic value of the Philippines necessitated the writing off of the Palaus and their garrisons and the concentration of all available strength in the Philippines area.

The overshadowing importance of the Philippines also caused a lack of Japanese air support for the Palaus, a serious flaw in their defense preparations. Most, if not all, of the planes already in the Palaus were destroyed in the Fifth Fleet's carrier raid of late March, when jubilant American fliers claimed a total of 168 aircraft destroyed. At any

---

[22] 96th InfDiv, STALEMATE II FO No. 14, dtd 27Aug44, Anx B, p. 1.

[23] LtCol Waite W. Worden ltr to CMC, dtd 4Apr50, in *Peleliu Comment File,* hereafter *Worden ltr.*

rate, none of the Peleliu-based Japanese airplanes survived the pre-invasion bombardment; only a few float planes at Koror escaped intact. Nor could replacements be spared. By this time, Japan's aircraft reserves were becoming limited. Besides, all available planes were being hoarded for the planned decisive battle to be forced with the Americans in the Philippines.

Even though written off by *IGHQ* strategists, the doomed Palaus garrisons were expected to conduct a tenacious defense in the event of American attack, thereby delaying utilization of the coveted airfields by the invaders. Besides, combat losses to the assaulting units would delay their reemployment in future campaigns. Time, a most precious commodity in war, would be gained by the Japanese for perfecting defenses in more strategic areas.

By July 1944, also, the point had finally been driven home to the Japanese high command that a blind adherence to the usual doctrine of attempting to annihilate the invaders on the beach was futile. Recent battles involving American amphibious assaults against well-fortified beaches revealed that the Americans' ability to unleash a devastating preparatory bombardment made total reliance upon beach defense useless.

Only one limited success stood out. Instead of uselessly expending his forces in suicidal *Banzai* counterattacks, the Japanese commander at Biak had prolonged the fighting substantially by having his men dig in, thus forcing the Americans to rout out each defender in a long, bloody, mopping-up campaign. This successful innovation, the protracted resistance on Saipan, and the long list of failures of Japanese commanders in attempting to hold the beachline, undoubtedly spurred the *IGHQ* planners to undertake a detailed study of the problem.

As a result, *IGHQ* decided in July 1944 on a new approach, and orders to employ new tactics in protracted ground battles were circulated to all Japanese commands in the Pacific. Briefly, these tactics involved the preparation of a main line of resistance far enough inland from the beach to minimize the effects of the pre-invasion bombardment, the organization of a defense in depth designed to wear down the attacking forces, and the hoarding of sufficient reserves to mount successful counterattacks at the appropriate times.

On 11 July 1944, General Inoue issued "Palau Sector Group Training for Victory," a document incorporating the new defensive concepts of *IGHQ*. His instructions revealed a departure from Japanese tactics employed earlier in the Pacific war and a unique attempt by the Japanese to profit from past errors. Inoue's instructions emphasized that victory would depend upon "our thorough application of recent battle lessons, especially those of Saipan,"[24] and that the "ultimate goal of this training is to minimize our losses in the severe enemy pre-landing naval and aerial bombardment." Among other things, Inoue urged the holding back of sufficient reserves in prepared defensive positions inland to permit a massive

---

[24] All quotes from this document were taken from CinCPac-CinCPOA Item No. 11,190, "Palau Sector Group Headquarters: Palau Sector Group Training for Victory," dtd 11Jul44.

counterattack and the destruction of the invaders in one fell swoop before their beachhead became secure. In deploying these reserve troops for the attack, careful attention was to be given so that there "will be no rapid exhaustion of battle strength," and the soldiers were to advance "at a crawl, utilizing terrain, natural objects and shell holes." As a last resort, he instructed the "construction of strong points from which we can cover our airfields up to the last moment, regardless of the situation," and it was Inoue's contention that "if we repay the Americans (who rely solely upon material power) with material power it will shock them beyond imagination."

As it turned out, Peleliu was where the battle was joined and the wisdom of Inoue's defensive tactics tested. Basically, the Japanese planned their troop and weapon dispositions on the island for a defense in depth. The resulting defense system was well organized and carefully integrated, and it possessed great inherent strength and flexibility. The enemy utilized the rugged terrain to construct mutually supporting defensive positions, and Peleliu was divided into four sectors, each manned by a reinforced battalion, with another one in reserve.

Regardless of which beaches the Americans chose to land on, they would be resisted by the major portion of Colonel Nakagawa's available forces. Swift redeployment of his troops would be possible, since the Japanese commander had the advantage of interior lines to operate over. Nor would naval or air attempts at interdiction prevent this concentration, for the earlier American air raids had been utilized by the Japanese to provide actual troop training in advancing under fire. Detailed plans dealing with proposed counterattacks were prepared and rehearsed. A few infantry companies were even reorganized into special counterattack units, rather than in the conventional platoons. Most companies also had several teams of two to three men prepared to infiltrate and to knock out attacking tanks.

To forestall an invasion of Peleliu, all potential landing beaches were heavily mined with mine belts often extending 100 yards or so inland. Offshore obstacles were erected, anti-tank barriers constructed, and barbed wire strung. Everywhere, the dominating terrain was utilized for the placement of artillery, previously zeroed-in on the beaches, to wreak havoc among the assaulting troops. All defensive positions took full advantage of man-made and natural cover and concealment, while yet dominating all invasion approaches (See Map 3).

Peleliu's southwestern beaches, where the American assault actually came, were typical of the Japanese beach defense preparations. The natural offshore obstacles there were augmented by the effective positioning of tetrahedron-shaped tank obstacles, strung barbed wire, and over 300 single and double-horned anti-invasion mines. The beaches themselves and all routes leading inland were strewn with tangled barbed wire and land mines, as well as with huge aerial bombs adapted to serve as mines. To prevent advancing infantrymen from working their way through the obstacles on the beaches under the covering fire of their tanks, long antitank trenches running roughly parallel to the beaches were dug.

These antitank ditches, as well as the beaches, were covered by fields of fire from pillboxes and gun casemates, located in dominating positions and all linked together in a system of mutual cover and support. The casemates mounted 37mm or 47mm antiboat and antitank guns, and were made of reinforced concrete with coral packed against the sides and over the top.

Just to the north of the beaches, a natural fortress formed by a prominent coral hill was riddled with covered rifle pits and pillboxes, each large enough for two or three infantrymen armed with rifles or automatic weapons. Near the base of the cliff was a reinforced concrete casemate housing a 47mm gun which could provide enfilade fire on approaching amphibious waves or interdictory fire on the beaches. Peleliu's southwestern promontory and a small island, a few hundred yards offshore, were used for the location of anti-boat guns and machine guns to furnish enfilade fire.

On the flat terrain farther inland from the beaches, the defense consisted of direct fire against advancing troops from well-camouflaged pillboxes and other defensive positions, while observed artillery and mortar fire could be laid down from the dominating ridges to the north of the airfield. Dug into these ridges were pillboxes and a casemate for a 75mm mountain gun, which commanded the entire southern portion of the island. At least one steel-reinforced concrete blockhouse had as many as 16 mutually supporting automatic weapons.

If the invaders survived the landing and were able to consolidate the beachhead, the Japanese planned to fall back to previously prepared defensive positions that commanded the ground between them and the attacking forces. If all else failed and the secondary line of defense was overrun and the commanding ground seized, last ditch resistance would center around the extensive cave fortifications that literally honeycombed the rugged terrain of northern Peleliu. Below is a description of the area by a former Marine, who was wounded in the fighting:

> It was this high ground which made Peleliu so perfectly adaptable to defense-in-depth, for it was neither ridge nor mountain but an undersea coral reef thrown above the surface by a subterranean volcano. Sparse vegetation growing in the thin topsoil atop the bedrock had concealed the Umurbrogol's crazy contours from the aerial camera's eye. It was a place that might have been designed by a maniacal artist given to painting mathematical abstractions—all slants, jaggeds, straights, steeps, and sheers with no curve to soften or relieve. Its highest elevation was 300 feet in the extreme north overlooking the airfield-islet of Ngesebus 1,000 yards offcoast there. But no height rose more than 50 feet before splitting apart in a maze of peaks and defiles cluttered with boulders and machicolated with caves. For the Umurbrogol was also a monster Swiss cheese of hard coral limestone pocked beyond imagining with caves and crevices. They were to be found at every level, in every size—crevices small enough for a lonely sniper, eerie caverns big enough to station a battalion among its stalactites and stalagmites."[25]

[25] Robert Leckie, *Strong Men Armed: The United States Marines Against Japan* (New York: Random House, 1962), p. 391, used with permission.

Map 3

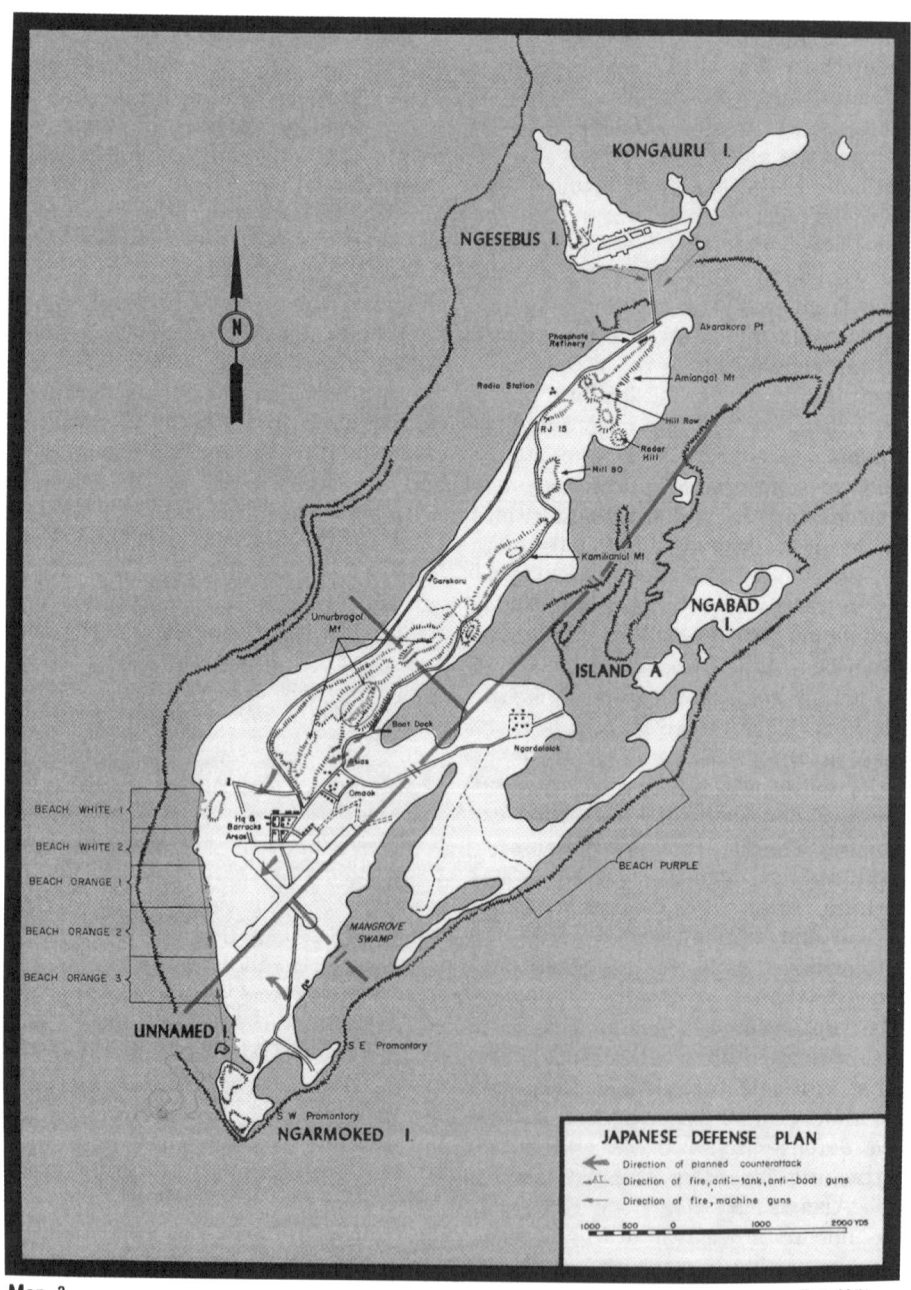

STRATEGIC SITUATION

The Umurbrogol ridges were, of course, the key to a successful defense of Peleliu, and the Japanese made the utmost use of its rugged terrain. They developed the natural caves that existed practically everywhere or blasted others into the almost perpendicular cliffs in order to deploy their troops and locate their weapons for a last-ditch stand. If driven from prepared positions, enemy soldiers could take refuge in the abundant natural cavities in the ridges, and by sniping from and defending every cave, crack, or crevice large enough for a man to squeeze into, could tenaciously prolong the resistance.

Due to bitter inter-service rivalry, both the Army and the Navy independently developed their own caves. The Navy, with the help of the *214th Naval Construction Battalion* and a tunnel construction unit, was able to build some rather elaborate underground installations. These were located mainly in the north of Peleliu and consisted for the most part of tunnels, ranging from single ones up to networks of 10 or more. The hollowed-out chambers usually measured 10 feet across and 6 feet high, often with separate rooms for food and ammunition storage, living quarters, and medical facilities. Some even had the benefits of electric lights, ventilation systems, and wooden floors. Designed primarily as shelters against air and naval bombardment, these underground positions had no prepared defenses against the onslaughts of attacking infantry/tank teams.

The Army's caves, on the other hand, while not so large, elaborate, nor ingeniously constructed as those of the Navy, were built and prepared for prolonged land combat. Whenever practicable, two or more staggered levels were constructed, and the multiple entrances led to tortuous passageways within a single huge tunnel system, where any number of safe refuges would protect the occupants from the concussive effect of bombing and shelling and provide cover from direct fire. Every effort, of course, was taken to camouflage skillfully all cave openings, while still preserving protection and clear fields of fire. Siege defense preparations consisted of jamming every nook and crevice with food and ammunition and building troughs to collect the water dripping from overhead stalactites.

Tactical reasons alone determined the location of the Army's caves. Fortifications were built, weapons sited, and soldiers deployed in order to provide a mutually interlocking system of concrete pillboxes, entrenchments, gun emplacements, and riflemen's positions dominating the strategic areas. Near every important artillery or mortar emplacement were other underground dwellings housing automatic weapons to provide protective fire. Communication trenches or tunnels connected these mutually supporting locations, while observation posts often were placed on top of the ridge in a natural limestone cavity or crevice. The approaches to vital installations, such as command posts, were covered from all angles by fire from cleverly located caves half way up the surrounding ridges. At most strategic points and in the final defensive area were numerous smaller underground positions designed to provide interlocking support fire from small arms. These were intended to be held to the death, and no escape routes had been provided for their occupants.

With their final defensive positions prepared, the Japanese garrison on Peleliu could view the future only gloomily. After July, when the Palaus were written off by the Imperial high command, whose attention was centered on the approaching decisive battle in the Philippines, even the receipt of the more essential supplies dwindled to a mere trickle due to shipping losses by attacks from American submarines and aircraft. The future prospects seemed dim indeed.

The Americans had the choice of either assaulting the islands or bypassing them, thereby allowing the Japanese garrison to degenerate into a state of combat ineffectiveness through lack of supplies and food. If the invasion came, then the enemy soldier faced the dilemma of either surrendering or waging a bitter fight to the death. No hope of relief or reinforcements could be expected.

After communications with the *Thirty-first Army's* headquarters on Saipan ceased in August, the *Palau Sector Group* was reassigned by *IGHQ*, for administrative purposes, to the *Southern Army* which controlled operations in the Philippines, and operationally to *Headquarters, Combined Fleet*. When advance intelligence indicated an imminent American assault, it was the *Southern Army* that notified General Inoue on 3 September as to the probable time and place of the landing. A few days later, Japanese intelligence officers estimated the size of the attacking force to be probably a division. Just before the actual invasion, the Japanese learned that the assault force commander was Major General Julian C. Smith.

General Inoue immediately notified all of the forces under his command that the long awaited opportunity to annihilate the Americans was near at hand. But as late as 8 September, *Palau Sector Group Headquarters* thought the carrier strikes might be just feinting actions, with the main assault coming elsewhere. When the heavy calibered shells of the American battleships began falling on 12 September, however, Inoue knew, without doubt, that the decisive moment had arrived. With great eloquence, he informed his command of the approaching battle:

> This battle may have a part in the decisive turn of tide in breaking the deadlock of the 'Great Asiatic War.' The entire Army and people of Japan are expecting us to win this battle. There will never be another chance as these few existing days for the people living in the empire to repay the emperor's benevolence again. Rouse yourselves for the sake of your country! Officers and men, you will devote your life to the winning of this battle, and attaining your long cherished desire of annihilating the enemy.[26]

---

[26] *Japanese Ops in the CenPac*, p. 75.

CHAPTER 2

Pre-Assault Preparations[1]

THE BEACH AND THE PLAN[2]

Detailed planning by the assault unit scheduled for the Peleliu landing began on 2 June 1944, when CinCPOA's warning order of 29 May was received by the 1st Marine Division. It was now resting and reorganizing on Pavuvu in the Russells, a small island group about 65 miles northwest of Guadalcanal, having arrived there in April following the strenuous New Britain campaign.

Although Major General Rupertus was absent in Washington arranging for replacements, Brigadier General Oliver P. Smith, the Assistant Division Commander, immediately initiated a staff study of the proposed assault. As soon as the G-2 officer assembled all available maps and aerial photographs of Peleliu and adjacent islands, the staff members began a careful examination of the beaches. In spite of the fact that higher echelons provided very little guidance during this early phase of the planning or that little intelligence of the island was available, the division managed to have a workable plan by the time of the commanding general's return.

Knowledge of Peleliu's beaches and terrain came almost solely from photographs, for it was nearly impossible to land a reconnaissance patrol and expect it to scout successfully the interior of the small, strongly-held island. The Fifth Fleet's carrier strike in March had made the first systematic aerial surveillance of the Palaus, and subsequent flights by carrier planes and the

[1] Unless otherwise noted, the information for this chapter has been derived from: ComWesPac TF OPlan No. 14-44, dtd 1Aug44; *Third-Flt AR; III PhibFor STALEMATE II Rpt*; TF 31 OPlan A302-44, dtd 4Aug44; *ExTrps SAR*; ExTrps OPlan No. 1-44, dtd 9Jul44; TF 32 Rpt of Amph Op to Capture Peleliu and Angaur, dtd 16Oct44, hereafter *TF 32 Peleliu and Angaur Rpt*; TF 32 OPlan A501-44, dtd 15Aug44; *IIIAC Palaus Rpt; 1st MarDiv SAR*; 1st MarDiv WarDs, Jun-Sep44, hereafter *1st MarDiv WarD*, with appropriate date; 1st MarDiv OPlan 1-44, dtd 15Aug44; *Peleliu Comment File*; Smith, *Narrative*; Hough, *Assault on Peleliu*; George McMillan, *The Old Breed: A History of the First Marine Division in World War II* (Washington: Infantry Journal Press, 1949), hereafter McMillan, *The Old Breed;* Sherrod, *Marine Corps Aviation in World War II;* Isely and Crowl, *U.S. Marines and Amphibious War;* Morison, *Leyte;* Smith, *Approach to the Philippines;* Craven and Cate, *The Pacific;* The 81st Wildcat Division Historical Committee, *The 81st Infantry Wildcat Division in World War II* (Washington: Infantry Journal Press, 1948), hereafter Historical Committee, *81st Infantry Division.*

[2] Additional sources used for this section are: WesLandFor, STALEMATE II, OPlan No. 1-44, dtd 23Jul44; 7th Mar OPlan No. 1-44, dtd 1Aug44; Theodore Roscoe, *United States Submarine Operations in World War II* (Annapolis, Maryland: United States Naval Institute, 1949), hereafter Roscoe, *Submarine;* Cdr Francis Douglas Fane, USNR, and Don Moore, *The Naked Warriors* (New York: Appleton-Century-Crofts, Inc., 1956), hereafter Fane and Moore, *The Naked Warriors.*

77

land-based aircraft of the Fifth Air Force obtained up-to-date vertical and oblique shots of the island chain. In addition, photographic profiles of all potential beaches were taken by the submarine, USS *Seawolf,* during the period 23-28 June.

A month later, another submarine surfaced off Peleliu with the intention of landing small underwater demolition teams (UDTs) by rubber boats. Bright moonlit nights, coupled with active Japanese radar and constant air and sea patrols, however, kept the USS *Burrfish* submerged for two weeks, during which time it could only take periscope photographs of the island's shore lines. Finally, on a dark night, a five-man landing party succeeded in paddling ashore on a beach later used in the assault. Much valuable data was obtained, but vital beach information, such as depth of water, nature of shoals, and type of bottom, had to wait upon the explorations of the UDTs working under the protective cover of naval gunfire just prior to the landing.

The intelligence officers of X-Ray Provisional Amphibious Corps regularly passed on to the 1st Marine Division and other assault units the latest maps and photographs as well as the current estimate of the enemy's strength. The standard map of Peleliu for the operation was compiled by CinCPOA cartographers and drawn on a scale of 1:20,000. Although the map contained some errors, it was workable and accurate for most of the island. Front line units received blown-up sections on the larger scale of 1:10,000 and 1:5,000. Following the fortuitous capture on Saipan of certain *31st Army* Headquarters files, Americans knew almost to a man the size of the Japanese garrisons in the Palaus. Although modified by later findings, this estimate served as the basis for tactical planning by the assault forces.

Right from the start, the Marine planners noted that the Peleliu landing would be different from any of the 1st Marine Division's earlier operations. To cross the 600-700-yard reef all along the prospective beachhead—similar to the situation encountered at Tarawa— would necessitate transporting the troops, equipment, and supplies across the coral obstacles solely by amphibian tractors. In addition, while the southern part of the island was flat and low, like an atoll, the parallel ridges just to the north of the airfield possessed some of the most rugged and easily defended terrain yet encountered by American forces in the Pacific. Peleliu, therefore, would repeat many of the difficulties encountered at Tarawa, as well as some which were met on Saipan.[3]

Although Peleliu abounded with beaches suitable in size for a division landing, the Marine staff quickly selected the western ones as being most preferable. The eastern beaches, backed by sprawling swamps that would hinder movement inland, had been discarded early, as were the extreme northern ones which were too far from the

---

[3] "The 1st Marine Division, while experienced in other amphibious operations, had not previously landed over a coral reef. They were short of amtracs and very deficient in mine detection and disposal." Vice Admiral George H. Fort, USN (Ret) ltr to Head, HistBr, G-3 Div, HQMC dtd 18May66 in *Peleliu Comment File,* hereafter *Fort ltr.*

prime objective of the assault, the airfield.

The division planners finally narrowed the choice down to three courses of action: (1) to land on the beaches overlapping the airfield; (2) to land on the beaches overlapping the airfield, while at the same time landing on the two promontories at the southern end of the island; or (3) to land on the beaches north of the airfield.

At first, the Marine officers had leaned toward the idea of making a two-pronged assault, with one regiment landing on the southern promontories while another one attacked across the beaches overlapping the airfield. Later, however, a more complete photographic coverage revealed that the promontories were strongly fortified and that the reef between them was covered with concrete tetrahedrons and was heavily sown with mines. An expert in UDT techniques warned, also, that the pillboxes ringing the coves could prohibit demolition work on the reef. The third possibility, landing in the north, was discarded because the ground rose abruptly into jungle-covered cliffs which would deprive the division of maneuver space.

By the time General Rupertus returned on 21 June, his staff members felt that an attack over the western beaches overlapping the airfield best favored success; after making his own estimate, the division commander agreed. The code name of White and Orange were given to the selected beaches.

Although the 1st Marine Division's staff inaugurated the detailed planning for the Peleliu landing, the amphibious corps slated for the assault (X-Ray—redesignated IIIAC on 15 August 1944) passed on the proposed plan before giving it a stamp of approval. For instance, when Rupertus wanted to assault the objective with two regiments, holding the other afloat as reserve, General Julian C. Smith recommended a simultaneous landing by three infantry regiments, with a RCT of the 81st Infantry Division as division reserve. After returning from Guam and assuming charge of X-Ray, General Geiger ruled that the Marine division would land with three regiments abreast, less one battalion landing team as the division's sole reserve.

The reserve's small size was not considered risky, for the embarked troops of the 81st Infantry Division were not to be committed to the Angaur landing until the situation on Peleliu had passed the critical assault phase. In addition, one RCT of the 81st was to be held afloat as corps reserve. Disturbing for the future, however, was Rupertus' apparent unwillingness to make use of available Army troops. This early reluctance foreshadowed the division commander's marked refusal, later, to employ Army units as reinforcements during the critical first week ashore on Peleliu.

General Smith, as the Marine Corps spokesman during the inter-service planning, took exception to the Navy's proposal for Angaur's seizure before the Peleliu landing. This course of action, the general explained, would permit the Japanese to rush reinforcements from Babelthuap down the island chain onto Angaur, thus prolonging the fighting there. To seize Peleliu first, he argued, would make it impossible for additional enemy troops to reach Angaur. Eventually, the naval planning staff was brought around to Smith's way of thinking "but, desiring Angaur for construction of a second airfield, continued throughout to press for the earliest possible landing on that island."[4]

As finally approved, the scheme of maneuver for the Peleliu assault called for the landing of three RCTs abreast on a 2,200-yard-wide beachhead, followed by a drive straight across the island to seize the airfield and to divide the enemy forces. On order, a reinforced battalion would make a shore-to-shore assault against Ngesebus Island and capture its fighter strip.

On the left (north) flank of the beachhead, over the White Beaches, the 1st Marines would land two of its battalions abreast, with the remaining one in regimental reserve. After driving inland and helping to secure the airfield, the regiment was to pivot left and attack toward the high ground north of the airfield.

Landing in the center over Beaches Orange 1 and 2, the 5th Marines would use two battalions in assault and one in support. While the left battalion tied in with elements of the 1st Marines, the other assaulting battalion would push straight across the island to the eastern shore. The support battalion, to be landed at H plus 1, would attack across the airfield and then participate in a wheeling movement northward. Once the airfield was captured, the mission of the 5th Marines would be to seize the northeastern peninsula and its nearby islets.

Only one beach, Orange 3, was assigned to the 7th Marines, for it was to land in a column of battalions, with its 2d Battalion remaining afloat as division reserve. The first battalion ashore was to attack eastward in conjunction with the 5th Marines, while the following battalion was to swing right and attack southward. After the opposite shore had been reached, all of the might of the 7th would be thrown into a push to the southern promontories, wiping out any Japanese holdouts in that area.

The 11th Marines, reinforced by the 8th 155mm Gun Battalion and the 3d 155mm Howitzer Battalion, both from corps artillery, was to land on order after H plus 1 over the Orange Beaches. Once ashore, the regiment would set up so that its 1st and 2d Battalions would be in direct support of the 1st and 5th Marines, respectively, while its 3d and 4th Battalions, together with the corps artillery, would be in support of the division. Four hours after the 11th Marines was ashore, all battalions were to be prepared to mass their fires on the ridges north of the airfield. In addition, the 8th 155mm Gun Battalion had the assignment of locating its artillery pieces so as to provide supporting fire for the Army division's later assault on Angaur.

---

[4] LtGen Julian C. Smith intvw by Maj Frank O. Hough, dtd 23Nov49, as cited in Hough, *Assault on Peleliu*, p. 11. In rebuttal of the above, the Naval Histories Division has commented: "We are unable to locate documentation in our records supporting General Smith's statement that the Navy proposed to seize Angaur prior to Peleliu." *Eller ltr.*

PRE-ASSAULT PREPARATIONS

The scheme of maneuver selected by the division commander contained the best features of the two discarded courses of action. The approach to the White and Orange beaches avoided the enemy-emplaced hazards on the reef off the southern beach. Once ashore, the massed division could attack inland swiftly over the low flat ground that was well-suited for the employment of tanks. Such a rapid advance would quickly gain the island's airfield, uncover maneuver room for the division, and strike the main enemy beach defenses on the east coast from the rear. With the early seizure of the opposite shore, the division could operate multiple unloading points in order to speed up the disgorging of the thousands of tons of cargo needed to sustain the offensive.

The scheme did have one real danger, however. The Marines would be forced to attack across the low flat ground while the dominating ridges remained in enemy hands. The Japanese were sure to have guns of large caliber emplaced on those commanding heights. Nevertheless, the division officers willingly accepted this risk, because of the scheme's other obvious advantages. They also figured that the 7th Marines would easily mop up the southern portion of Peleliu on the first day, after which it could help the 1st Marines take the key ridges north of the airfield. Until such time as the combined striking power of the two RCTs could be massed against the defenders on the ridges, the 1st Marines would be supported by the concentrated fire of planes, gunfire ships, artillery, and tanks.

Even with the benefit of hindsight, it still is difficult to challenge the Marine officers' reasoning. After the war, however, some criticism was raised as to whether there would have been fewer Marine dead, if the landing had taken place on the north beaches at the foot of the commanding ridges.[5] Granted that a successful assault at this point could have given the division control of the key terrain early in the campaign, anything less than 100 percent execution would have been fatal. If the momentum of the initial assault failed to seize the ridgeline, then the Marines would have been stranded on a narrow low beachhead, without room to maneuver or emplace supporting artillery, while the enemy would be literally looking down their throats.

The unanimity of opinion among Marines who participated in the operation and later had a chance to examine the island's terrain and Japanese defenses in great detail is that the correct course of action was taken. Typical of their attitude is the following comment:

> None of the remaining beaches which might permit a landing in force would allow the rapid development of an adequate beachhead which is so essential in a landing operation. The Division Command was confronted with the problem of select-

---

[5] See McMillan, *The Old Breed*, p. 262, and Fletcher Pratt, *The Marines' War: An Account of the Struggle for the Pacific from Both American and Japanese Sources* (New York: William Sloane Associates, Inc., 1948), p. 345, hereafter Pratt, *The Marines' War*.

ing the least undesirable of several beaches. In the light of those factors as well as the later developments, the correctness of the decision to land on the White and Orange beaches is hardly open to question.[6]

LOGISTIC CONSIDERATIONS[7]

While the assault Marines received more newspaper coverage than did the logistic commands, the latter are, of course, just as essential to victory on the battlefield. The service units, performing the unquoted tasks of tending the wounded, furnishing tactical and logistical transport, providing all combat equipment and supplies, and repairing troop weapons, vehicles and other equipment, were a decisive factor behind every successful amphibious landing in the Pacific War. STALEMATE II was no exception.

To supply the vast and complex assortment of ships, equipment, and troops required for the Palau Operation, all the major Pacific commands had to be called upon for support. Only the closest liaison among these various echelons made it possible for logisitic preparations to proceed smoothly. "Overall requirements for supplies, materials, and service personnel needed for the Palau operations were ascertained by joint study. Policies affecting the Army, Navy, and Marines were implemented by interservice and intra-staff planning."[8] Available shipping, always a limiting factor in amphibious undertakings, had to be tightly scheduled, while the estimated arrival dates of the cargo vessels bringing the heavier base development equipment directly from the United States had to be carefully calculated.

The basic guidelines for STALEMATE II's logistic planning were set forth on 1 August 1944 by Admiral Halsey's Operation Plan 14-44, which also instructed all combatant and auxiliary ships to make a special effort to ensure they sailed from the mounting points for the target with the maximum authorized loads of ammunition, fuel, and fresh provisions. Now began an intense period of activity as all the major bases of the Pacific commands pitched in to provide the necessary logistic support, and a 24-hour workday with 12-hour shifts became the norm.

While the various warships and cargo ships took on dry provisions, the fleet tankers loaded to half capacity with Diesel oil and aviation gasoline and topped to maximum draft with fuel oil. Fresh and frozen foods, however, were available only in limited quantities, and battleships, cruisers, and carriers were provisioned to serve at least one completely dry ration every sixth day. By the last part of August, the stocks had been exhausted, and a Marine unit re-

---

[6] BGen Walter A. Wachtler ltr to CMC, dtd 1Mar50, in *Peleliu Comment File,* hereafter *Wachtler ltr.*

[7] Additional sources used for this section are: ExTrps AdminO No. 1-44, dtd 22Jul44; 1st MarDiv AdminO No. 1-44, dtd 7Aug44; USAFor-MidPac and Predecessor Commands during World War II, 7Dec41-2Sep45, History of G-4 Section, n.d., hereafter *USAFor MidPac G-4 Hist;* Carter, *Beans, Bullets, and Black Oil;* Kenneth W. Condit, Gerald Diamond, and Edwin T. Turnbladh, *Marine Corps Ground Training in World War II* (Washington: HistBr, G-3, HQMC, 1956), hereafter Condit, Diamond, and Turnbladh, *Marine Corps Ground Training.*

[8] *USAFor MidPac G-4 Hist,* p. 408.

PRE-ASSAULT PREPARATIONS

questing fresh meat and vegetables for its troops was forced to sail for Peleliu with only a supply of emergency rations instead.

All types of vessels, from the 90,000-ton floating dry-dock to the hospital ships, steamed toward the designated staging areas. In the Tulagi-Purvis Bay region of the Solomons alone, there were gathered at one time 255 vessels, with ship movements averaging 122 daily during the last week of August. From the far reaches of the Pacific, the various vessels began to rendezvous at the mounting areas of Manus, in the Admiralty Islands, about 1,000 miles in a southwesterly direction from the objective, and Eniwetok Atoll, some 1,500 miles northeast of Peleliu.

The IIIAC assault elements and accompanying garrison forces were directed by Headquarters, Expeditionary Troops, to carry with them sufficient rations for 32 days, water enough for 5 days when pro-rated at 2 gallons per man per day, medical supplies to last 30 days, and a 20-day supply of clothing, fuel, lubricants, and miscellaneous equipment. For the assault phase, all weapons would be allowed five units of fire—a unit of fire being that amount of ammunition which CinCPOA had determined from previous campaigns would last for one day of heavy fighting.[9] In addition, the 105mm howitzers would be issued another two units, and the 57mm antitank guns supplied with five more. The 1st Marine Division, moreover, arranged to carry an additional 10 units of flamethrower fillers and explosives, since it expected to encounter numerous fortified positions on Peleliu.

Detailed planning for Marine and naval cooperation during the Peleliu assault began 8 August, when a joint conference at Pavuvu was attended by the staffs of General Rupertus and Admiral Fort, commander of the Western Attack Force. At this time, the division's proposed scheme of maneuver was presented, thus permitting Admiral Fort to determine what support would be required of his force. Naval gunfire and air support plans were worked on jointly by the respective staff members concerned with these matters, and the use of UDTs for clearing away underwater obstacles and the selection of potential landing beaches for the various amphibious craft were discussed in detail.

Two days later, the Commander of Transport Group 3, the division's assigned lift, arrived with members of his staff. This time, the regimental commanders and their staffs joined the conferences planning the combat loading of the assault forces for the Peleliu operation.[10] During this phase of joint planning, the details of boat allocation,

---

[9] *1st MarDiv SAR*, Part III to Anx C, lists the number of rounds in the CinCPOA unit of fire for the various weapons in the Marine division. The unit of fire for the M-1 rifle, for example was 100 rounds; .30 caliber carbine, 45; .45 caliber pistol, 14; .30 caliber machine gun, 1,500; .50 caliber machine gun, 600; 60mm and 81 mm mortars, 100; 105mm howitzers, 200; 155mm howitzers, 145; and 155mm gun, 100.

[10] By combat loading is meant the method of embarking troops and loading their equipment and supplies in such a manner that they can be rapidly unloaded at the objective in the desired priority for sustaining the attack.

landing plans, and control of the landing waves were ironed out. Lieutenant Colonel Robert G. Ballance, commanding the 1st Pioneer Battalion, was involved frequently in these conferences, for he was to be the division shore party commander.

By the time of STALEMATE II, the Marine Corps' amphibious techniques for an assault landing over a fringing reef had been battle-tested, modified where necessary, and molded into a smooth working ship-to-shore operation. Since previous Pacific campaigns had revealed that the LVT (Landing Vehicle, Tracked) was indispensable to the uninterrupted flow of assault troops past the coral barriers guarding the enemy's shores, every man in the assault forces at Peleliu was transported to the beach in an amphibian tractor.

These vehicles and their infantry passengers, as well as the LVT(A)s (armored amphibian tractors), were carried to the target by LSTs (Landing Ships, Tank). At a distance safe from enemy shore batteries, the LSTs opened their massive doors and disgorged the amphibians loaded with the assault Marines. The LVTs then proceeded to within roughly 4,000 yards of the beach. Here, along the line of departure, the vehicles were reformed into waves and headed in succession toward the beaches. Patrol craft and submarine chasers were stationed at this and other control lines to regulate movement. These vessels served also to facilitate communications between the various elements of this complex amphibious operation.

Upon reaching the reef, the amphibian tractors would crawl over and continue landward. At a point several hundred yards offshore, the LVT(A)s, which made up the initial assault wave, would begin firing their cannon for the last minute support of the assault troops in the following waves of LVTs. Once ashore, the Marines could get prompt artillery support from 75mm pack howitzers landed, ready for action, from the rear ramps on the most recent version of the LVT. Additional support was to be furnished by 105mm howitzers, brought onto the beach by DUKWs (2½-ton amphibious cargo trucks) which had been specially equipped with an A-frame unloading device to land the completely-assembled 105.

The division's tanks would be preloaded in LCTs (Landing Craft, Tank) which, in turn, were loaded unto the well decks of LSDs (Landing Ships, Dock). Once in the unloading zone, the decks of these floating drydocks were flooded with water. After the huge stern gates of the LSDs had swung open, the LCTs emerged for a run to the reef, where the tanks, specially waterproofed beforehand, debarked and continued ashore under their own power.

An innovation first tested at Peleliu was the use of LVTs to guide these tanks onto the beaches. Evolved to prevent delays and casualties such as those experienced during the Marianas campaign, this successful technique was described by a Marine tank officer in the following account:

> An LVT was placed on each LCT to lead the tanks ashore. These LVTs were used to test the depth of the water, and as long as they propelled themselves along the bottom the tanks would follow, but if the

LVTs became waterborne the tanks would stop until the LVTs could reconnoiter a safe passage. . . . Fuel, ammunition and maintenance supplies were loaded on these LVTs which enabled the tank units to have a mobile supply dump available to them upon reaching the beach.[11]

For the rest of the troops, equipment, and supplies, the passage to the target area was made in assault cargo and personnel transports. The Marines were moved from their transports to the line of departure by LCVPs (Landing Craft, Vehicle, Personnel), where they were formed into waves and dispatched to a transfer line just seaward of the coral. For the remainder of the trip to the beachhead, the troops and their equipment were transferred into empty LVTs and DUKWs which had returned from the beach to shuttle the rest of the Marines and their gear to shore.

Since the LVTs had a waterborne speed of about 4.5 miles per hour, the trip from the line of departure to the beach was estimated as 30 minutes and from the transfer line, 15 minutes. Preceding the first wave of troops and scheduled to hit the beaches at H-Hour were the armored amphibians. A minute later, the initial assault troops would land, with the following waves scheduled to land at five-minute intervals. Within the first 20 minutes, five assault battalions, comprising some 4,500 men, were to be on their assigned beaches, and tanks would begin landing over the edge of the reef. Four minutes later, the regimental weapons companies were to begin landing and, by H plus 85 minutes, with the coming ashore of three more infantry battalions, there would be 8,000 combat Marines on the beachhead.

To follow, of course, would be the remaining 17,000 men of the reinforced division, their equipment, and the some 34,500 tons of initial supply support. The division logisticians planned to leave practically all the bulk cargo either in the cargo nets or on the pallets loaded on board the ships at the embarkation points in order to expedite unloading at the target.[12] When these pre-packaged loads made the trip from ship to the supply dump on land, they would be moved intact at each necessary transfer point by crane instead of being unloaded and reloaded, piece by piece, by manpower. If necessary, the pallets could be dumped on the edge of the reef and hauled to the beach by bulldozer. In all, the division utilized some 2,200 pallets, attempting to palletize a representative portion of the bulk cargo. As it turned out, however, the items found most suitable for palletizing were ammunition, barbed wire, and pickets.

In charge of all unloading activities to the seaward of the beaches was the transport group beachmaster. Under him were three transport division beachmasters, each responsible for the unloading in front of a regimental beach. Each of these beaches was assigned a reef beach party and a shore

---

[11] Capt George E. Jerue ltr to CMC, dtd 2Mar50, in *Peleliu Comment File*.

[12] The pallet, an Army innovation first used in the Marshalls, was simply a sled, four by six feet, with wooden runners, which could be loaded to a height of about three feet and with a weight of approximately 3,000 pounds, the load being fastened securely on the pallet by means of flat metal strappings.

beach party. The reef beach party was responsible for the amphibian vehicles and boats when afloat and had the task of marking approaches over the reef and points on it where craft unable to negotiate the coral barrier could be beached. The shore beach party became the naval platoon of the regimental shore party and, as such, performed its normal functions in connection with marking of the beaches, salvage, and evacuation.

As the division shore party commander at Peleliu, Lieutenant Colonel Ballance supervised the handling of supplies on and in the rear of the beaches, as well as the casualties arriving from the battalion aid stations. He had the further responsibility of providing for the close-in defenses of the beach areas.

Initially, the division shore party was to be decentralized with a detachment of the subordinate regimental shore party going in with each assault battalion. Each regiment had been furnished a company of pioneers from Lieutenant Colonel Ballance's 1st Pioneer Battalion as the framework for its shore party.

As soon as possible, the regimental shore party commander was to take over and consolidate the unloading operations on his beach. In turn, Lieutenant Colonel Ballance, upon landing, was to assume control of all shore party activities and to select the best beaches over which supplies would continue to be unloaded. To insure that the vital stream of supplies continued to flow into the supply dumps on the beaches, the colonel planned to maintain the closest of coordination with the various beach parties.

Later, when all assault shipping was ashore, the beach dumps were to be taken over by the 16th Field Depot, a Marine supply agency designated as part of the Island Command but attached to the 1st Marine Division for the assault phase. This innovation worked extremely well from the Marines' standpoint, for it made the field depot subject to the direct orders of the division's commanding general. According to the commanding officer of the 1st Service Battalion, this arrangement made all "the difference between ordering and asking."[13]

Another technique, first improvised during the Marianas campaign, was included in the original plans for the Peleliu assault. Two provisional companies of infantry replacements were attached to the shore party, until such time as they would be needed to fill depleted ranks in the rifle regiments. The shore party could make good use of these extra men during the critical unloading phase, and they would be readily available for deployment as riflemen on the front lines when needed. The heavy losses of the 1st Marines during the first week of the Peleliu campaign accentuated the wisdom of planning for combat replacements and, in the later Iwo Jima operation, each Marine division had two replacement drafts attached to its shore party.

Logistic support on D-Day was expected to be hectic and difficult. The assault battalions would be able to take in with them only limited quantities of

---

[13] Col John Kaluf ltr to CMC, dtd 7Mar50, in *Peleliu Comment File*, hereafter *Kaluf ltr*.

rations, water, and ammunition, and the anticipated heavy fighting would make it particularly important to assure an adequate resupply of ammunition and water. To safeguard this vital flow of supplies reaching the embattled Marines ashore, certain improvisations were made and precautions taken by the logistic planners.

Until such time as a pontoon causeway could be constructed over the reef to the Peleliu beaches, the creation of an artificial, waterborne supply beach seaward of the reef was imperative. For this purpose, 24 pontoon barges were lashed to the sides of LST's for the journey from the Solomons to the target. These barges had been formed by fastening pontoon cells, seven cells long and three wide, into a single unit. When an outboard motor was attached, they became self-propelled. Once in the unloading area, only the lines holding the barges to the sides of the LSTs had to be loosened and the barges would be launched into the water, ready to proceed under their own power.

Nine of these barges, which had been modified to allow the mounting of cranes on them, would be dropped into the sea early on D-Day. After having swing cranes lowered onto them and secured, the barges would proceed to a point approximately 1,000 yards seaward of the reef. Their job was to facilitate the transfer of bulk supplies from the boats bringing them from the cargo ships to the amphibians for transportation across the reef and onto the beach. If shore-based enemy fire proved too dangerous, the barges could move under their own power to a safer spot farther out.

Three other barges were to provide fuel and lubricating oil for the LVTs. After being launched from the LSTs, these self-propelled barges were to be loaded with 80-octane gasoline and lubricating oil and dispatched to a point just off the reef. One was assigned to each regimental beach, and they all were ordered to erect a large banner, marked "Gas," so that the LVTs could easily recognize them.

The remaining 12 barges would be used to establish floating dumps. Since the transports and cargo ships were expected to retire to safer waters out to sea at nightfall, provision had to be made for an accessible supply of critical items which would be needed by the assault battalions during the hours of darkness. Upon being launched, these barges would proceed to designated cargo ships, where they would take on predetermined loads of infantry and tank ammunition, flamethrower fuel, motor fuel, lubricants, emergency rations, and water in drums, before continuing on to report to their assigned transport division beachmasters for mooring off the reef. Large painted numbers on the sides of the barges would aid the drivers of the LVTs and DUKWs in identifying the type of load contained in each. The amphibians could come alongside the barge and load by hand, or the barge might be placed next to a crane for speedier loading.

The problem of how to insure an immediately accessible supply of high expenditure rate items, such as mortar and machine gun ammunition and flamethrower fuel, for the assaulting troops during the afternoon of D-Day was also resolved. At Peleliu, the amphibian cargo trailer would be utilized in quantity for the first time. This Marine-designed vehicle had an axle and two pneumatic tires on the bottom while its top could be bolted into place, making it waterproof. Pre-loaded in the Russells, the trailers could be lowered into the sea by cranes at the transport area and towed by LCVPs to the reef, where amphibians would hook onto them, drag them across the jagged coral barrier, and finish towing them the rest of the way to the beach. Each rifle regiment was allotted 13 of these trailers and the artillery regiment 20.

Another method of handling priority cargo was by means of specially loaded LCVPs. Certain of the assault ships would set aside eight LCVPs, preloaded with infantry ammunition, flamethrower fuel, and water. On D-Day, these LCVPs would be dispatched to the reef off their assigned regimental beaches. The respective regimental shore parties would be briefed on the contents of the different type loads and could send out LVTs or DUKWs to locate the correct LCVP and take on a load. In a similar manner, LCMs (Landing Craft, Mechanized) were to be loaded with artillery ammunition in order to meet urgent requests for resupply of the Marine batteries ashore.

Since Peleliu lacked surface water and its enervating climate would accelerate consumption, preparations were made to insure an adequate supply for the attacking infantrymen. Every available 5-gallon can was pre-filled to the brim and scheduled for an early trip to shore, while scoured-out 55-gallon oil drums would hold a reserve supply. After the engineers managed to set up distillation apparatus and drill new wells, the water problem was expected to vanish.

Throughout the logistic planning for STALEMATE II, the short supply of shipping in the Pacific was always a limiting factor. An unfortunate example of this situation was the fact that only four LSDs were available and these were equally divided by IIIAC planners between the Peleliu and Angaur assault units. The division found itself able to lift only 30 tanks and had to leave 16 behind. This decision aroused criticism, for Peleliu was more heavily defended and more suitable for tank operations than Angaur, where, as it turned out, only one company of tanks was ever employed at one time. As the commanding officer of the 1st Tank Battalion later stated:

> ... it is my belief that a serious error, indefensible from the tank viewpoint, was made in splitting the available tank shipping ... as events proved it was extremely unsound in view of the desperate need for additional tanks throughout the first five (5) days of the operation ... our Corps staff at that time did not include a tank section, greatly handicapping tank planning at Corps level.[14]

The lack of shipping space, coupled with the planners' belief that Peleliu's limited land area would not cause a serious transportation problem, resulted in the breaking up of the 1st Motor Transport Battalion as an integral unit. Only Company A was allowed to lift its organic equipment, including repair facilities, and, even

---

[14] LtCol Arthur J. Stuart ltr to CMC, dtd 25Apr50, in *Peleliu Comment File*, hereafter *Stuart ltr*.

PRE-ASSAULT PREPARATIONS

then, its platoons were distributed among the infantry regiments to expedite the movement of supplies from the beach to the forward areas during the initial advance inland. Company C was detached during the operation and its men utilized as amphibian tractor drivers, and Headquarters and Service Company was assigned the responsibility for the division's maintenance and fuel supply, while Marines of Company B were to serve as stretcher bearers, relief drivers, and reserve troops throughout the campaign. Since each individual unit of the division down to company level was allowed to lift up to five vehicles, depending upon its mission, the total number of trucks carried to the target approximated the number that would have been organic to the 1st Motor Transport Battalion, but the lack of centralized control proved far from satisfactory. In the battalion commander's view:

> This proved to be a serious handicap in the direct supply of troops. With few exceptions, there were no trucks available for the movement of troops even though the tactical situation of then [during the Peleliu campaign] called for the expeditious movement of troops by vehicular transportation.[15]

PAVUVU, TROOP TRAINING, AND SHORTAGES[16]

Following the Cape Gloucester campaign in the debilitating rain forests of New Britain, the Marines of the 1st Division were badly in need of rest and rehabilitation. A suitable camp was already available on Guadalcanal but, instead, General Geiger chose the small island of Pavuvu, in hopes of sparing his exhausted men the distasteful task of furnishing large working parties each day to the Island Command as was customary on the larger island. He had made the selection following a reconnaissance of Pavuvu by air and with the expectation that a battalion of Seabees would be there preparing facilities.

Upon the Marines' arrival in April 1944, they discovered to their dismay that the 10-mile long piece of coral was virtually a jungle, with the abandoned plantation long overgrown and rats and rotting coconuts practically everywhere. The 15th Naval Construction Battalion, having completed a 1,300 bed hospital on nearby Banika Island on 26 March, had little time to work on the camp on Pavuvu before the Marines arrived. Typical of the Marines' bitterness was that of the officer who barged into General Smith's tent and shouted, "Great God! Who picked this dump? More like a hog lot than a rest camp."[17]

Instead of getting a chance to relax, the battle weary Marines found them-

---

[15] Maj Robert B. McBroom ltr to CMC, dtd 13Mar50, in *Peleliu Comment File*.

[16] Additional sources used for this section are: History of the 1st Marine Regiment, 26Aug-10Oct44, n.d., hereafter *1st Mar Hist;* LtCol Kimber H. Boyer, USMC, "Formation and Employment of an Armored Amphibian Battalion, Palau Operation, 15 September 1944-20 October 1944: A Study of the Use of Special Equipment," (Quantico, Va.: Marine Corps Schools, Amphibious Warfare School, Senior Course 1946-1947), hereafter Boyer, *Armd AmphibianBn;* Condit, Diamond, and Turnbladh, *Marine Corps Ground Training*.

[17] Burke Davis, *Marine! The Life of LtGen Lewis B. (Chesty) Puller, USMC (Ret)*, (Boston: Little, Brown and Company, 1962), p. 202, hereafter Davis, *Marine!*, used with permission

selves turned to constructing a livable camp area. Disposing of the rotting coconuts alone took over a month; wells for drinking water had to be dug;[18] and for weeks, the men were forced to live, work, and sleep in mud until they had laboriously bucket-hauled enough coral to surface the access roads and living area.

Not surprisingly, the morale of the division hit an all-time low. The majority of the veterans had been in the Pacific for over two years, and their exertions in two strenuous jungle campaigns had sapped their reserves of energy. Alternately racked by malarial chills or burning up with its fever—which the tropical climate of Pavuvu did nothing to alleviate—weakened by poor rations, and rotten with a variety of fungus growths in various parts of their bodies, these Marines were both physically and mentally exhausted.

The number answering sick call increased alarmingly, averaging "200 to 250 cases daily. . . . Hospitalization would not have been required in many of these cases had water, clean surroundings and clean clothing and of course good food been available to all units on the Island."[19] Because of the Marines' weakened condition, their letdown following the recent tensions and stresses of combat, and the countless frustrations encountered on Pavuvu, they tended to behave in a manner that people back home might consider eccentric and to give credulity to wild rumors that ordinarily would have been laughed down.[20]

Adding to their woes, the food on Pavuvu, while adequate, was monotonous, unappetizing, and limited—for example, fresh meat appeared on the mess tables only once a week—the movies were usually second-run features or worse, and beer was limited to only a few cans a week.[21] Contributing to the men's dissatisfaction with their lot was the widespread belief that service troops on Banika and Guadalcanal were eating and drinking much better than the combat-returned Marines.

Welding these dispirited, malady-ridden, and exhausted men once again into a keenly-edged fighting team was the first task faced by the division's officers, who set about immediately preparing the Marines physically and

---

[18] ". . . and when that water was reached, it was the most god-awful stuff you can imagine. Its unique flavor was not enhanced by the rotting coconuts which had seeped through the coral-streaked mud to the water supply and one was forced to spike it with the lemonade component of K-rations which, in itself, was more like battery acid and more suitable for burnishing canteen cups and mess gear than for drinking." Mr. Benis M. Frank comments on draft MS, dtd 29Mar63.

[19] Cdr Emil E. Napp ltr to CMC, dtd 9Mar50, in *Peleliu Comment File*.

[20] "Less eccentric by Pavuvu standards was the man who ran out of his tent at dusk and began to pound his fists against a coconut tree, sobbing angrily: " 'I hate you, goddammit, I hate you!' 'Hit it once for me,' came a cry from a nearby tent, the only comment that was made then or later by the man's buddies." McMillan, *The Old Breed*, p. 231.

[21] "The only USO show to reach this miserable hole was not scheduled to come at all; it arrived only by dint of the personal efforts of Bob Hope and at considerable inconvenience to his troupe, who managed to sandwich in a morning performance between rear echelon engagements shortly before the division shoved off for Peleliu." Hough, *Assault on Peleliu*, p. 27.

psychologically for their role in the forthcoming assault. Training, however, had to be conducted under the severe limitations of space, equipment shortages, and the detailing of men and equipment for the construction of camp facilities. In addition, the division experienced an influx of some 260 officers and 4,600 enlisted men replacing those Marines being rotated home. All of the newcomers had to be broken in on their new jobs for the imminent battle.

The amount of terrain on Pavuvu suitable for training purposes proved to be small even for a platoon to maneuver about, let alone a whole division. As a result, Marines on field problems found themselves slipping between the tents and messhalls of their bivouac area.[22] With large-scale maneuvers out of the question, the only recourse was to place a much greater emphasis upon small unit exercises, practicing with rifles, automatic weapons, grenades, bazookas, and portable flamethrowers. Meticulous attention was paid to the details of each unit's proposed scheme of maneuver ashore at the target. Over and over again, the movements of the scheme were rehearsed until each rifleman, specialist, and leader knew exactly where he was to be and what he was to do throughout the different phases of the assault.

---

[22] One story, perhaps apocryphal, has it that "one Saturday morning a battalion of the Fifth Marines was holding inspection while a battalion of the First Marines was conducting a field problem. The result was that during the inspection, fire groups of the latter were infiltrating through the statue-like ranks of the former." Maj Robert W. Burnette ltr to CMC, dtd 9Mar49, in *Peleliu Comment File*.

Stressed also was instruction in close-in fighting with the bayonet, knife, club, hip-level snap shooting, and judo. The use of hikes, excellent in hardening men for the rigors of combat, was handicapped by the lack of space; the marching units kept bumping into each other.

Unfortunately, practical experience in tank/infantry coordination, destined to be of inestimable value in the coming battle, was limited to one day for each rifle regiment. Each squad, however, did actually coach the movements and firing of a tank by visual signals and the external telephone in the rear of the tank.

Wherever suitable terrain could be found, firing ranges and combat areas were set up, and their use was rigidly controlled by a tight scheduling. In the combat areas, platoon-sized groups employed flamethrowers, bazookas, demolitions, antitank guns, machine guns, and rifles while practicing simulated assaults against log bunkers. On the infiltration course, Marines negotiated barbed wire and other obstacles, while live ammunition forced them to keep down. Other subjects covered were the techniques of night defense, chemical warfare, patrolling with war dogs, and coordination of fire teams using all organic weapons. The ground phase of the training closed in the middle of August with combat firing by all units.

Even more difficult and nightmarish than the infantry's efforts were the attempts of the division's supporting arms to train with their bulkier equipment on Pavuvu. The 11th Marines rehearsed massing fires with time, impact, and ricochet bursts, but due to lack of space, the artillery "was reduced to the pitiful expedient of firing into the water with the observers out in a boat or DUKW."[23] Without room to maneuver, tank training had to stress gunnery, flamethrower operations, fording, night security, all-around defense, and textbook study of tactics. On the whole, organic support units spent the majority of their training period breaking in replacements, repairing battered equipment, and shaking down new vehicles.

During the division's training period, two newly developed weapons were received. The Navy Mark I flamethrower was capable of throwing a flame of blazing napalm[24] to a distance of 150 yards and sustaining it for 80 seconds. Three of the flamethrowers were mounted on LVTs, while another LVT was equipped to serve as a supply carrier for the napalm mixture. Although slated for employment primarily against beach pillboxes during the assault landings, the new weapon was to prove its great value in reducing dug-in fortifications farther inland.

The other new weapon was the 60mm shoulder mortar, adapted to fire from a light machine gun mount and designed for flat trajectory fire against pillbox and cave openings. Some of its parts, however, proved too weak to stand the rough wear and tear of combat, and Marines who had to lug the weapon around complained of its heaviness. Even more serious was the recoil, which was so severe that the gunner had to be relieved after firing only two to four rounds. Since this new weapon's function duplicated that of the bazooka, which gave a good performance on coral-surfaced Peleliu, Marines were inclined to hold the shoulder mortar in less regard than the older and more familiar weapon.

Hindering the whole training schedule of the division, but especially the amphibious phases, were critical shortages of equipment. These embraced such a wide array of items that about the only things in adequate supply were the basic arms of the individual infantrymen. Shortages in armored amphibians, amphibian tractors, flamethrowers, demolitions, automatic weapons, bazookas, engineering equipment, and waterproofing material existed right up to the last stages of training, while final allotments in some categories arrived barely in time to be combat-loaded with the troops. In addition, some of the supplies furnished with the division were not of A-1 quality:

> Belts of machine gun ammunition had rotted . . . powder rings on mortar ammunition were disintegrating and bourrelets rusted, shotgun shells swollen or, if brass, corroded. All ammunition had to be unstowed, inspected and in large part replaced and restowed at the last minute.[25]

To complicate matters further, the division had been ordered early in July to form two provisional amphibian tractor battalions, "utilizing personnel of the 1st Amphibian Tractor Battalion, augmented by personnel from units of the

---

[23] LtCol Leonard F. Chapman, Jr., ltr to CMC, dtd 9Mar50, in *Peleliu Comment File*.

[24] The gelled fuel resulting from combining napalm powder with gasoline for use in incendiary bombs and flamethrowers.

[25] LtCol Spencer S. Berger ltr to CMC, dtd 19Mar50, in *Peleliu Comment File*, hereafter *Berger ltr*.

division."[26] These Marine elements preparing for imminent combat, however, objected strenuously to parting with any of their skilled men, and often did not without a fight. In addition, those Marines reassigned to the amphibian tractor battalions had to be retrained in the operation of the unfamiliar equipment. Often, due to lack of time to practice, these inexperienced drivers would be performing on-the-job training with tractors filled with Marines practicing assault landings.

Further complications arose for the newly formed 3d Armored Amphibian Battalion (Provisional), because it was scheduled to receive the recently developed LVT(A), or armored amphibian tractor, which would form the initial assault wave at Peleliu and furnish fire support for the following troop waves. Lacking any of the new vehicles for demonstration purposes, the battalion's Marines, completely unfamiliar with the LVT(A) or its armament, were forced to rely solely upon blueprints for acquaintance with the tractor they would be handling in combat. Although the first delivery of the armored amphibians arrived early in August, difficulties still persisted. After feverishly practicing with the new vehicles, the crews were dumbfounded to find that the next shipments were of a later model, mounting 75mm howitzers instead of the 37mm's with which the crews had previously familiarized themselves. Approximately two-thirds of the battalion had to be retrained as a result.

"That the battalion should turn in an outstanding performance after such unpropitious beginnings might well rank as one of the minor miracles of the campaign."[27] The man responsible for the battalion's good showing on the Peleliu beaches was Lieutenant Colonel Kimber H. Boyer. He "did one of the greatest training jobs I ever saw or heard of,"[28] said a fellow officer. Although beset by overwhelming problems and forced to obtain his men in driblets from whatever source he could find, Lieutenant Colonel Boyer managed to train and shape his crews into a finely tuned combat team by the time of the assault. The commanding officer of the newly formed 6th Amphibian Tractor Battalion, Captain John I. Fitzgerald, Jr., "faced with almost the same problems and circumstances [as Boyer], performed as admirably."[29]

The amphibious training, not only of the amphibian battalions but also of the entire division, was retarded seriously by the insufficiency of amphibious vehicles and the lack of repair parts for them. Upon its arrival at Pavuvu, the division had only 48 of the 248 LVTs authorized for the Peleliu campaign. Of these 48, more than half were inoperative, awaiting vital parts. When the first shipment did arrive, there remained less than a month in which to prepare the vehicles, train the crews, and familiarize the several thousand assault troops in LVT ship-to-shore techniques.

As a result, the division was forced to substitute the DUKWs as personnel carriers and to use them in the amphib-

---

[26] 1st MarDiv SAR, Phase 1, p. 5.

[27] Hough, Assault on Peleliu, p. 31.
[28] LtCol Joseph E. Buckley ltr to CMC, dtd 10Mar50, in Peleliu Comment File.
[29] Maj Robert F. Reutlinger ltr to CMC, dtd 10Mar50, in Peleliu Comment File, hereafter Reutlinger ltr.

ious exercises with the infantry regiments. It was during such a landing drill that General Rupertus fell from an amphibian tractor and severely fractured his ankle, an injury that might have caused a less determined man to miss the Peleliu campaign. The amphibious trucks used by the infantry, however, had to be taken away from the artillery units, which had been practicing their own assault techniques of loading and unloading howitzers and radio jeeps in the LVTs and DUKWs. Consequently, the training time available to the 11th Marines was drastically reduced.

Training for the 1st Marine Division culminated in large-scale landing rehearsals at the Cape Esperance area on Guadalcanal. By this time, 27 and 29 August, the assault units were already embarked on board the vessels which would carry them to the target, and the warships scheduled to provide naval gunfire support for the operation were also on hand.

The first rehearsal was designed solely to test communications. After the new radio equipment, which had been rushed by air from Pearl Harbor to supply the division's minimum requirements, was accurately calibrated, the rehearsal went off smoothly. On the 29th, the naval guns and planes blasted at the beaches prior to the landing and continued deep supporting fires after the Marines debarked and moved inland. Spreading out, the assault units went through the motions of their assigned missions, and everything went off smoothly.

At a critique held the next day, and attended by all of the ranking commanders of both naval and ground forces, not a single serious criticism was raised; in fact, nothing in the way of constructive revisions was even discussed. The two practice landings, however, had served their purpose of familiarizing the troops with their debarkation and transfer stations, snapping in the new crews of the amphibian vehicles, coordinating the preliminary gunfire and bombardment plans, and ironing out any possible kinks in the complicated ship-to-shore maneuver, which depended upon split-second timing and scheduling for success.

On 3 September, a shore party exercise was held at Tetere Beach on Guadalcanal, but no supplies were unloaded. The next landing performed by Marines of the division would be over Peleliu's coral reef and onto the enemy-held beaches.

Despite its frustrations with Pavuvu's shortcomings, the equipment shortages, and the training difficulties, the 1st Marine Division had done an admirable job of fusing the new replacements with the older veterans of Guadalcanal and Cape Gloucester into a recharged, combat-ready fighting unit. When the 1st Division's Marines stormed ashore at Peleliu, they were once again a topnotch assault outfit.

MOUNTING THE ATTACK[30]

The logistical problem confronting the 1st Marine Division in mounting out from Pavuvu for the Peleliu campaign and the many heartbreaking diffi-

---

[30] Additional sources used for this section are: TF 32 MovO No. A503-44, dtd 20Aug44; ComLSTFlot 13 Trng MovO No. 3-44, dtd 24Aug44; 1st MarDiv AdminO No. 1-44, dtd 7Aug44.

culties encountered in solving it cannot be overemphasized. What the situation would have been if the division had not been lifted by an experienced transport group is hard to imagine, because the loading of the naval vessels had to be closely coordinated with the final plans for the beach assault.

Fortunately, the transport group commander, his staff, and the vessels' crews were veterans in complicated ship-to-shore movements and experts in working with Marines to solve related problems. The group staff, according to one Marine officer:

> . . . worked in the closest liaison, not only with the Division's Operations and Planning Officers, but with the commanders and staff officers of subordinate units, together with the Navy Control Officers designated for each beach. The consolidated scheme was a product of close and effective joint planning.[31]

The embarkation warning order reached the Marine division on 5 August, only 10 days before the actual assault loading was to begin. Planning by staff officers started immediately but, without any idea of the number, type, or characteristics of the allotted ships, only the most general plans could be made. Although the transport group commander and his staff arrived at Pavuvu on 10 August, the necessary, detailed information was not obtained until two days later. Even after the ships finally appeared, it was discovered that several had reserved holds for ship's stores or carried extra equipment which was not shown on the ship's characteristics. As a result, confusion and misunderstanding marked the loading arrangements of the division, causing numerous changes, compromises, and improvisations right up until the last.

To complicate the Marines' logistic problem even further, loading operations would have to be conducted at the widely separated staging areas of Pavuvu, Banika, Guadalcanal, and Tulagi, as well as in the New Hebrides, where the transports would pick up the ground echelons and equipment of the Marine air units slated to be based on the Peleliu airfield as soon as it was seized and operative. If the principle of combat loading was to be adhered to, a prodigious amount of load planning and close coordination of ships' routes would be necessary to prevent wasted effort or back-tracking. Compounding the difficulties were the limits to dockage and lighterage at certain of these staging areas, which necessitated a tight scheduling of the ships' movements to forestall any needless delays.

The first units of the LST flotilla assembled from scattered Pacific bases, arrived off Pavuvu on 11 August, and the Marine division began loading the next day. Since the flotilla commander, Captain Armand Robertson, had been too busy readying his ships for sea to come to Pavuvu during the planning phase, the Marines had requested him to delegate a liaison officer with the authority to make decisions in his name, but none was ever furnished. Admiral Fort, who was Captain Robertson's superior, held daily conferences with the Marines on Pavuvu after 8 August, thus to some extent offsetting the gap created by the absence of a liaison officer.

---
[31] Col Harold O. Deakin ltr to CMC, dtd 10Mar50, in *Peleliu Comment File*.

Nevertheless, shortly after his arrival, Captain Robertson ordered the loading plans for eight LSTs to be changed. The Marines knew from past experience that understowing[23] was indispensable in keeping within allotted load limits and yet lifting all the required tonnage. It was only with the greatest reluctance, however, that the flotilla commander permitted his LSTs to be so loaded.

Even after the Marines were finally embarked, they discovered to their amazement that certain vessels transporting two regiments would be in launching areas different from those planned by the division. If not rectified, this drastic change would force the amphibians and craft, carrying the 5th and 7th Marines ashore, to crisscross in order to get these regiments to the proper beaches. Such a maneuver, difficult to execute and contrary to the accepted doctrine for ship-to-shore procedures, could not be tolerated and, as a result, troops already embarked on board nine vessels had to be shifted.

Actually, the last of the LST flotilla did not put in an appearance at Pavuvu until 25 August, at which time the troops were already embarked on board the transports in preparation for their final training rehearsals. In spite of all these last-minute complications, however, the 30 LSTs, 17 transports, and 2 LSDs allotted to the division for the Peleliu operation were fully combat-loaded by 31 August.

After their final landing exercises at Guadalcanal, the Marines had a chance to go ashore before departing for the Peleliu assault. These last few days were spent in conditioning hikes, small-unit maneuvers, and recreation. The other assault unit of the IIIAC, the 81st Infantry Division, meanwhile, had mounted out in Hawaii and rendezvoused off Guadalcanal for its final rehearsals and movement to the target.

Unlike the Marine division with its two major campaigns under its belt, the newly activated Army division was still untested in battle. Neither during their training nor mounting out had the soldiers endured any of the difficulties experienced by the Marines on Pavuvu. According to the 81st's history, "the loading worked out well," and after "its long stateside training, its intensive refresher courses, the rehearsal, and the relaxation in the [Hawaiian] Islands, the Division was a bronzed, tough crew, ready for action."[33]

On 4 September, LSTs carrying the initial assault elements of both the 1st Division and the 81st lifted anchor and departed with their naval escort ships for the Palaus. Four days later, the faster-moving transports and LSDs followed with their screening forces. The two convoys were expected to rendezvous in the target area early on D-Day. Prior to the departure of the transport echelon, the Peleliu Fire Support Unit and Escort Carrier Group had left in order to arrive at the target on 12 September to begin the bombardment and bombing of the objective, as well as to

---

[32] Understowing consisted simply of the loading of the tank deck of an LST with flat or well-packaged cargo, such as rations, barbed wire, or ammunition, next covering the whole with a layer of dunnage, and then storing LVTs on top of the dunnage.

[33] Historical Committee, *81st Infantry Division*, pp. 45, 59.

PRE-ASSAULT PREPARATIONS   97

start the underwater demolition of artificial obstacles.

The approach route lay northwestward through the Solomons and then along a course generally parallel to the northern coast of New Guinea. For the embarked troops, the 2,100-mile trip over smooth seas was uneventful, the monotony being broken only by the periodic antiaircraft exercises which used the naval planes flying from the escort carriers as tracking targets. On 14 September, D minus 1, the transports made contact with the slower-moving LSTs, and they proceeded together to their respective stations off the Palaus.

On the same day, the Marine troop commanders and the civilian news correspondents opened General Rupertus' sealed letter, which had been given to each of them just prior to the departure from Guadalcanal with instructions not to open it until D minus 1. Apparently, the division's commanding general had not consulted with anyone, "with the possible exception of"[34] his chief of staff, before issuing the letter. In it, Rupertus expressed his opinion that the fighting on Peleliu would be extremely tough but short, lasting not more than four days. This viewpoint, according to the official Marine Corps monograph on the campaign was:

> ... perhaps the most striking manifestation of that preoccupation with speedy conquest at the highest division level which was to color tactical thinking ashore for a month to follow.[35]

---

[34] LtCol William E. Benedict ltr to CMC, dtd 27Feb50, in *Peleliu Comment File*.

[35] Hough, *Assault on Peleliu*, p. 35. "Most officers believed this unusual document [was] intended in the nature of a pep talk. This was

MARINE AIR PREPARES[36]

Since the Western Carolines lay too far distant from any Allied base for land-based aircraft to provide cover during STALEMATE II, naval planes operating off carriers would furnish the needed air support until such time as the airfield on Peleliu had been captured and readied for use by American aviation units. Destined to be the major component of this garrison air force was the 2d Marine Aircraft Wing (2d MAW) which, in mid-1944, was located in the Solomons and functioned primar-

---

not its effect on news correspondents, however: many of the 36 accredited to the division did not come ashore at all, and only six (one of whom was killed) chose to stay through the critical early phases. Hence, news coverage of the operation was sketchy, often misleading, and, when quick conquest failed to materialize, tinged with biting criticism." *Ibid.*

[36] Additional sources used for this section are: Garrison AF Western Carolines WarDs, 30May-Sep44, n.d., hereafter *Garrison AF WarD*, with appropriate date; Island Comd, Peleliu WarDs, Jul-Sep44, hereafter *Peleliu Island Comd WarD*, with appropriate date; 2d MAW WarDs, June-Sep44, hereafter *2d MAW WarD*, with appropriate date; 2d MAW UHist, 7Dec41-20Feb46, dtd 12Mar46, hereafter *2d MAW UHist*; HqSq-2, 2d MAW WarD, Jul-Sep44, hereafter *HqSq-2, 2d MAW WarD*, with appropriate date; MAG-11 WarD, Jun-Sep44, hereafter *MAG-11 WarD*, with appropriate date; MAG-11 UHist, 1Aug41-1Jul44, dtd 19Jun45, hereafter *MAG-11 UHist*; MAG-11 Rpt on Palau Ops with 4th MAW comments, dtd 22Dec44, hereafter *MAG-11 Palau Rpt*; VMF-114 WarD, Jun-Sep44, hereafter *VMF-114 WarD*, with appropriate date; VMF-114 UHist, 1Jul43-1Jan45, dtd 10May45, hereafter *VMF-114 UHist*; VMF(N)-541 WarD, Jun-Sep44, hereafter *VMF(N)-541 WarD*, with appropriate date; VMF(N)-541 UHist, 15Feb44-30Apr46, dtd 30Apr46, hereafter *VMF(N)-541 UHist*.

ily as a training command for squadrons flying combat missions in more active zones. Assignment to the wing, whose headquarters was on Efate Island in the New Hebrides, meant that a squadron's pilots could receive additional training as well as enjoy a welcome break from the rigors of daily flights over enemy-held territory, before returning to combat.

The 2d Wing first suspected it was slated for a more active war role when it received a dispatch on 14 June ordering it to become an "independent and self sustaining unit"[37] as rapidly as possible. Eleven days later, the wing was directed to move to Espiritu Santo Island, a staging area farther north in the same island chain, for possible deployment to an active combat zone.

A forward echelon moved to the new base to pave the way for the rest of the command, and the 2d MAW officially began operating from there on 3 July. During the remainder of the month, the wing busied itself with completing the move, bringing itself up to authorized strength, gathering and readying its own lower echelons, and streamlining its staff organization for efficient functioning under any possible combat contingency.

This tailoring of the air unit to fit the requirement of its assigned mission resulted in the 2d MAW reverting back to a one-group wing. Only the month previously, it had been brought up to a two-group wing in anticipation of an active combat role. Since Marine Aircraft Group 11 (MAG-11) was expected to furnish sufficient tactical air support for STALEMATE II once it was based on the captured and repaired Peleliu airfield, the unneeded MAG-25 was detached from the 2d MAW on 25 July.[38]

In preparation for basing on Peleliu, MAG-11 was authorized a new provisional table of organization on 26 July. All elements, except group and squadron headquarters, and operations and intelligence sections, were to be transferred to the service squadron, which would then be placed under the operational control of the Air Base Commander, a subordinate of the Island Commander. Although these changes made the service squadron large and unwieldy, besides complicating the command structure, this arrangement was to remain in effect throughout the Palau campaign.

Earlier, on 6 July, the 2d MAW had lost its commander, when CinCPOA summoned Brigadier General Harold D. Campbell to Pearl Harbor to organize a headquarters for his forthcoming role as Island Commander, Peleliu. This joint Army-Navy-Marine Corps command, known as the Third Island Base Headquarters until 16 November 1944, was to have the mission of defending the captured base from all possible enemy attacks and improving the island's facilities in accordance with the base development plan.

No sooner had the new wing commander, Major General James T. Moore, assumed command, than a dispatch from Admiral Nimitz on 9 July desig-

---

[37] *2d MAW WarD*, Jun44, p. 1.

[38] The 2d MAW became a two-group wing again on 8 October 1944, the date that Marine Base Defense Air Group 45 (redesignated MAG-45 on 15 November) arrived at Ulithi Atoll.

nated the Marine officer as Commander Garrison Air Force, Western Carolines. As was common in the intricate amphibious air-sea-land operations of the Pacific War, General Moore was to head a staff composed of Army, Navy, and Marine Corps officers whose mission was to "defend the Western Carolines area by employing in mutual support against hostile air threats all air defense units based in that area."[39] Once his squadrons began operating from the captured Peleliu airfield, the Marine general would have three major tasks: defending all ground troops and convoys in the Western Carolines from enemy air attacks, providing close air support for the infantry units still fighting on Peleliu, and neutralizing the remaining enemy bases in the Western Carolines.

Although still the 2d Wing's commander, General Moore found it necessary to locate at Pearl Harbor near the headquarters of Marine Aircraft Wings, Pacific, because the planning and organizing of his new command necessitated frequent conferences with the staffs of higher and subordinate echelons. Finally, on 22 August, the Marine general flew to Espiritu Santo and assumed personal command of the wing during final preparations for the Peleliu campaign.

Scheduled to land with the assault units at Peleliu were the ground echelons of Marine Fighter Squadron 114 (VMF-114), VMF-121, VMF-122, and Marine Night Fighter Squadron 541 (VMF(N)-541) of MAG-11. Their flight echelons were to remain at Es-

piritu until such time as they could be flown by stages to the repaired and operative airfield. As soon as possible, other units of MAG-11 would be flown in, to be followed later by wing headquarters.

With combat imminent, the group's squadrons underwent intensified training.[40] The typical day's flight schedule was designed to improve the skills and abilities of the pilots, as well as to determine the condition of the aircraft and equipment. The final weeks prior to mounting out found the fighter squadrons stressing dive and glide bombing exercises, for which their assigned aircraft, the F4U (Corsair), was admirably suited. In addition to this increased emphasis upon tactics which could be used in close support of ground troops, the basics of squadron air work were practiced in instruments, intercepts, and division tactics.

The Marine air units, not unlike the ground troops, were experiencing their own difficulties with shortages, as MAG-11 reported:

> The first major difficulty encountered was in obtaining the proper quantities and types of aviation ordnance. Allowances were specifically laid down by ComAirPac [Commander Air Forces, Pacific Fleet] who then made ComSoPac [Commander, South Pacific] responsible for their delivery. ComSoPac passed this task to the 16th Field Depot, a Marine unit, at Guadalcanal. Due to shortages, lack of knowledge of aviation ordnance and lack of belting equipment, the specified allowances were never obtained. The Group went on the operation short of certain bombs, fuses,

---

[39] *Garrison AF WarD*, 30May-30Sep44, p. 3.

[40] During July and August, training accidents resulted in 2 pilots killed, 1 missing, 1 wounded, and 4 aircraft lost.

etc., and had to take all unbelted ammunition. Belting and handling a million and a quarter rounds of .50 caliber ammunition was done after landing and proved to be a major problem.[41]

Since the Peleliu landing would be the first time that ground echelons of Marine squadrons would accompany the assault troops ashore, the aviators preparing for their role in STALEMATE II found themselves confronted by some unique problems. The question of the composition of the parties to accompany the general assault units and the amount and type of gear the parties should take with them was a difficult one to resolve, according to MAG-11, which noted:

> At present, there is no table of allowances which prescribes the kind and amount of aviation materiel, Marine Corps equipment, transportation and personnel that should be taken in with the assault echelons. As a result of this, every Group and Squadron Commander had to make his own decision in the matter, with the result that the amount and kind of material and number of personnel taken in during the early stages of an operation varies greatly.[42]

Adding to the Marine aviators' woes was the fact that, because shipping space was at a premium, equipment had to be reduced to the barest necessities. Liaison officers had been sent to Pavuvu for coordination of loading plans with the 1st Marine Division, but the limitation of pace on the ships transporting the assault elements and the staging of STALEMATE II at five widely separated points complicated the situation. The S. S. *Mormacport*, for example, after loading the ground echelons and equipment of MAG-11 and Marine Torpedo Bombing Squadron 134 (VMTB-134) in the New Hebrides, would stop at the Russells and embark another task force unit "on top of the Group and squadron gear."[43] As a result, VMTB-134 would be flying antisubmarine patrols long before its equipment or spare parts were ashore at Peleliu.

The newly organized VMF(N)-541, which arrived at the Espiritu Santo staging area from the United States just in time for its ground echelons to be loaded on board the assault ships, had its own unique problem. Commissioned 15 February 1944 at Cherry Point, North Carolina, this night fighter squadron had been equipped and trained for its mission of providing protection against enemy air attacks during the hours of darkness. Its assigned aircraft, a modified version of the Navy's standard fighter, the F6F (Hellcat) contained very complicated precision radar to aid in the night interception of enemy bombers. Although excellent in operating aspects and accurate at times for distances up to 60 miles, this radar required a great deal of maintenance to keep it in acceptable working condition.

The misfortunes of VMF(N)-541 began when it travelled some 10,000 miles from its staging area at Cherry Point and continued until its planes touched down on the repaired Peleliu airfield. At no time in this two-month period was there ever any testing or maintenance of the delicate radar equipment installed in the Hellcats, even though the flight echelon had flown over 5,000 miles. The

---

[41] *MAG-11 Palau Rpt*, p. 1.
[42] *MAG-11 Palau Rpt*, 1st End, p. 1.

[43] *MAG-11 Palau Rpt*, p. 2.

not unexpected result was that "every one required almost a major overhaul at a time when top performance was required."[44]

Loading out at Espiritu Santo began 25 August, when the ground echelons of VMF-114, VMF-121, VMF-122, and VMF(N)-541 went on board the USS *Tryon* and *Centaurus*. These vessels sailed on the 25th and 27th, respectively, to rendezvous with the main naval task force at Guadalcanal. On 30 August, the ground echelons of VMTB-134 and the Headquarters and Service Squadrons of MAG-11 embarked in the S. S. *Mormacport* for their journey to Peleliu. Remaining behind at Espiritu Santo were the flight echelons and the rear echelon which would service the aircraft prior to departure for the Palaus and supervise the loading of the remaining gear.

SOFTENING THE ENEMY'S DEFENSES[45]

Owing to the detailed planning by SWPA and CinCPOA air liaison officers, STALEMATE II's plans called for a wide-sweeping series of closely-meshed air support missions by both carrier- and land-based aircraft embracing the period prior to, during, and after the amphibious landing. As early as March 1944, the Palaus had been struck by fast carrier forces of the Fifth Fleet, and further carrier-based attacks were again launched during July and August. SWPA's long-range planes, meanwhile, had flown reconnaissance and bombing runs over the target area and, in August, the Fifth Air Force's B-24s (Liberators) began a concentrated effort to knock out enemy defenses throughout the island chain.

A series of night flights from 8 August through 14 September dumped 91.2 tons of fragmentation, demolition, and incendiary bombs over the Palaus and, beginning 25 August, the heavy bombers braved Japanese fighters and heavy antiaircraft fire to make daylight bombing runs over the objective. In a total of 394 sorties, the Liberators dropped 793.6 tons of high explosives on the enemy defenses. In Koror Town alone, some 507 buildings were completely demolished, and major Japanese installations throughout the island chain were destroyed. By 5 September, photo reconnaissance revealed only 12 Japanese fighters, 12 floatplanes, and 3 observation aircraft still based in the Palaus. The enemy's airstrips, moreover, were badly cratered, and only the most extensive repairs would ever make them fully operative again.

Although the Palaus were beyond the range of CinCPOA's shore-based planes, other Japanese-held islands in the Carolines were not. Yap, Woleai, and Truk, for example, were hit repeatedly by naval bombers operating from recently captured Allied bases, while the Libera-

---

[44] VMF(N)-541 Rpt (Night Fighter Squadron, plane, personnel, and material requirements), dtd 25Nov44, hereafter *VMF(N)-541 Rpt*.

[45] Additional sources used for this section are: TG 38.3 OpO No. 1-44, dtd 25Aug44; TF 32 MovO No. A503-44, dtd 20Aug44; TG 32.1 AtkO No. A502-44, dtd 20Aug 44; TG 32.15 AtkO No. 8-44, dtd 30Aug44; TU 32.7.1 OpO No. 1-44, dtd 5Sep44; VMF-314 Rpt of Observers aboard Aircraft Carriers during STALEMATE, dtd 17Nov44, hereafter *VMF-314 Rpt of Observers*; Fane and Moore, *The Naked Warriors*; Roscoe, *Submarine*.

tors of SWPA flew coordinated, reinforcing strikes against the same objectives. In addition, the B-24s struck at enemy airdromes on Celebes and in the southern Philippines in preparation for the later-scheduled carrier strikes by the Third Fleet.

To prevent confusion and to coordinate strategic air support missions, the heavy bombers of SWPA were to shift to night bombing runs as soon as American carriers began operations in the vicinity of the Palaus. In late August, one group of Admiral Mitscher's fast carriers made a diversionary raid against the enemy-held Volcano-Bonin Islands, while the other three proceeded to the Palaus and initiated a three-day aerial bombardment with a fighter sweep on the afternoon of 6 September. During the next two days, as the warplanes ranged over the islands, bombing and strafing, the cruisers and destroyers of the covering screen blasted away at the Japanese defenses ashore. These fast carrier groups then continued on to their additional mission of interdictory strikes against the enemy airbases in the southern Philippines.

After completing its diversionary raid in the Volcano-Bonins, the remaining fast carrier group struck at Yap and, on 10 September, its planes hit the Palaus. Notwithstanding the target's previous bombardment by both aircraft and warships, the naval pilots could lament that so many Japanese antiaircraft batteries were still active that "Much time and many bombs were expended before return fire was sufficiently reduced to let us get down low for close observation and detection of small but important enemy positions, bivouac areas, etc."[46] This carrier group remained near the Palaus, for it was scheduled to augment the striking power of the escort carriers during the prelanding bombardment and to provide additional firepower on D-Day, if needed.

Land-based planes of both the Southwest and Central Pacific commands, meanwhile, flew search and reconnaissance missions screening the approach to the target by transports and support ships of the Western Attack Force. The pilots, flying daylight patrols some 50 to 100 miles in advance of the main naval forces, had orders to attack and destroy any enemy planes encountered.

A unique addition to the screening forces was the Submarine Offensive Reconnaissance Group, which was utilized by Halsey during the Palau operation only. Composed of three wolf packs of three submarines each, the group was strung out in attack formation over a 300-mile front. The submarines, upon sighting any enemy forces, were to radio a warning of danger to the Western Attack Force and then attack to inflict the maximum damage. In addition, they were to provide rescue service for downed aviators and furnish on-the-spot weather information.

Before dawn on 12 September, the first echelon of the Escort Carrier Group and the warships of the Fire Support Group were off Peleliu ready to begin preliminary bombardment operations. The four escort carriers, soon to be

---

[46] Air IntelGru, CNO, "Comments on 'softening up' strikes in preparation for landing operations, taken from the report of R. L. Kibbe, Cdr, USN, Commander of Air Group Thirteen for the period 6-16 September 1944," dtd 25Nov44.

joined by another six, had the task of safeguarding the approach of the Western Attack Force to the target, assisting in the softening up of the island's defenses prior to the landing, and providing close air support once the Marines were ashore on Peleliu. In addition, four seaplane tenders were to arrive in Kossol Passage one day before the landing and, after their squadrons had joined them, were to provide air-sea rescue and lifeguard, weather, and reconnaissance missions.

The activity of all planes in the target area was closely coordinated with the naval gunfire and minesweeping operations by Admiral Wilkinson's Commander Support Aircraft. Control of the close fire support furnished to the infantry would be handled by the Joint Assault Signal Company (JASCO) teams. Each Marine battalion was assigned such a team, consisting of a naval gunfire officer, an aviation liaison officer, and a shore party officer, with the required communications personnel and equipment. Once ashore, the battalion commander had only to turn to an officer at his side and heavy guns firing shells up to 16-inch or planes capable of bombing, strafing, or launching rockets were at his disposal. The Commander, Support Aircraft, could, at his discretion, relinquish control of all planes in the area to the ground commander once the expeditionary troops were firmly established on the beachhead.

First to venture in close to the target were the vessels of the Kossol Passage Detachment, which began minesweeping operations along the approaches to the designated transport and fire support areas. Later, these minesweepers would clear the Kossol Passage, which would be utilized as a roadstead where ships might await call to Peleliu for unloading and in which replenishment of fuel, stores, and ammunition could be accomplished.

At 0530 on the 12th, the large caliber guns of Rear Admiral Jesse B. Oldendorf's Fire Support Group, consisting of 5 old battleships, 4 heavy cruisers, 4 light cruisers, and 14 destroyers, began blasting away at Peleliu's defenses. For two hours, the warships steamed in a zigzag pattern off the island and fired at preselected targets. When this naval barrage ceased temporarily, carrier planes appeared over Peleliu's interior and began flying strikes against the defenses there. Following this two-hour aerial bombardment, the heavy naval guns resumed their deliberate fire. This alternating of naval gunfire and aerial bombardment was the procedure followed during the three days prior to the assault. During this time, the warships expended some 519 rounds of 16-inch shells, 1,845 rounds of 14-inch, 1,427 rounds of 8-inch, 1,020 rounds of 6-inch, and 12,937 rounds of 5-inch, for a total of 2,255 tons of ammunition.

Special UDTs, meanwhile, had been landed on the reef, where they began their important tasks of removing underwater obstacles, blasting ramps for LSTs and pathways for DUKWs in the coral, clearing boulders from roadways, and placing buoys and markers. Clad only in swimming trunks, these underwater experts were constantly fired at by Japanese with rifles and machine guns during the dangerous process of destroying the underwater obstructions, which an American admiral described as "the most formidable which we encountered in the entire Pacific."[47]

Originally, the gunfire support plan called for only two days of preparatory bombardment prior to D-Day, but the strong protests of General Geiger had persuaded Admiral Wilkinson to add another day. This extra time, however, did not mean that a larger number of shells were fired; instead, the extra day merely allowed the same amount of ammunition to be expended with greater deliberation over a longer period of time. Since the Japanese had skillfully camouflaged their artillery positions and refused to be goaded into returning fire, Admiral Oldendorf was of the opinion that the "best that can be done is to blast away at suspected positions and hope for the best."[48] As a result, he ended the bombardment early, explaining that all targets on Peleliu worthy of naval gunfire had been destroyed.

Although the awesome weight, explosive power, and armor-piercing quality of the shells expended had transformed Peleliu's exterior "into a barren wasteland,"[49] neither the enemy nor his prepared defenses had been obliterated. Artillery had been hidden carefully in underground caves, some of which had steel doors to protect their interiors, while the troops had been placed in sheltered areas, from which they could emerge, unscathed and combat-ready, after the American barrage lifted. Frustrating as it was for one Japanese soldier in a machine cannon company to remain huddled in his shelter while the warships shelled Peleliu with impunity —the sight so infuriated him that he "could feel the blood pounding in my veins throughout my body"[50]—the fact remains that only one man in his outfit was injured by the prelanding bombardment, and then only slightly. As Oldendorf later admitted, "My surprise and chagrin when concealed batteries opened up on the LVTs can be imagined."[51] In addition, one huge Japanese blockhouse, which the assaulting Marines confidently believed would be demolished since it was pinpointed on their maps, was later found to have escaped damage completely from any of the naval shells.[52]

Oldendorf's decision to break off fire has been described as being "entirely correct," by Admiral Fort, who was present at the bombardment of Peleliu. The "idea which some people seem to have of just firing at an island is," said the admiral, "an inexcusable waste of ammunition."[53] Colonel William H. Har-

---

[47] Adm Jesse B. Oldendorf ltr to DirMCHist, dtd 25Mar50, in *Peleliu Comment File*, hereafter *Oldendorf ltr.*

[48] *Oldendorf ltr.*

[49] CinCPac-CinCPOA Translations Item No. 12,190, "Extracts taken from the diary of an unidentified man," 15May-15Sep44.

[50] *Ibid.*

[51] *Oldendorf ltr.*

[52] Admiral Oldendorf commented that this blockhouse was not shown on the maps furnished him and that during "the preliminary bombardment and until several days after the landing, my entire staff was on the sick list, only my flag lieutenant remaining on his feet. This threw a heavy load on me, as I not only had to supervise the details of the daytime operations but also operate tactically at night during withdrawals." *Ibid.*

[53] RAdm George H. Fort ltr to DirMCHist, dtd 20Mar50, in *Peleliu Comment File*, hereafter *Fort ltr.*

rison, commanding the 11th Marines at Peleliu, held somewhat similar views, for he doubted "whether 10 times the gunfire would have helped."[54]

Among the Marines actually storming the shelled and bombed beaches at Peleliu and assaulting the still intact Japanese defenses and fortifications, however, there grew a belief, verging later on a feeling of bitterness, that the preparatory naval gunfire left something to be desired. After the war, this belief was shared by two historians of amphibious warfare, Isely and Crowl, who wrote that:

> ... the conclusion cannot be avoided that preliminary naval gunfire on Peleliu was inadequate, and that the lessons learned at Guam were overlooked. ... Peleliu, like Tarawa and to a lesser extent Saipan, demonstrated that the only substitute for such prolonged bombardment was costly expenditure of the lives of the assault troops.[55]

---

[54] Comments on the Palau (Peleliu) Monograph by Col William H Harrison, n.d., hereafter *Harrison cmts.*

[55] Isely and Crowl, *U.S. Marines and Amphibious War*, p. 403.

CHAPTER 3

D-Day on Peleliu [1]

FIRST WAVES ASHORE [2]

Dawn on 15 September 1944 broke calm and clear at 0552. Sharply silhouetted against the first rays of sunlight were the American warships which filled the waters off White and Orange Beaches at Peleliu as far as the eye could see. Fortunately for the Marine division scheduled to assault the strongly held enemy island, the weather was ideal for amphibious operations. Only a slight surf was running, and visibility was unlimited in practically every direction.[3]

With his fire support ships already in position, Admiral Oldendorf in the U. S. heavy cruiser *Louisville* gave the command and, about 0530, shells began slamming into the target areas. By this time, the green-clad Marines slated to comprise the assault waves already were loaded in their assigned LVTs and were being dispatched toward the line of departure. As the amphibian tractors formed into waves behind the LVT(A)s and began their approach to the beaches, the steady stream of naval shells overhead increased in fury.

On board their amphibious command ships, USS *Mount Olympus* and *Mount McKinley*, the ranking Navy and Marine commanders observed the complicated landing operation, while the staff of the 1st Marine Division functioned from the

---

[1] Unless otherwise noted, the material in this chapter is derived from: *III PhibFor STALEMATE II Rpt*; *ExTrps SAR*; *IIIAC Palaus Rpt*; *1st MarDiv SAR*; 1st MarDiv WarD, 15Sep44; 1st MarDiv D-2 Jnl, dtd 15Sep44, hereafter *1st MarDiv D-2 Jnl*, with appropriate date; 1st MarDiv D-3 Jnl, dtd 15Sep44, hereafter *1st MarDiv D-3 Jnl*, with appropriate date; 1st MarDiv D-3 Periodic Rpt, dtd 15Sep44, hereafter *1st MarDiv D-3 Periodic Rpt*, with appropriate date; 4th War Dog Platoon, IIIAC, Peleliu OpRpt, 15–30 Sep44, dtd 20Nov44, hereafter *4th War Dog Plat Peleliu OpRpt*; *Peleliu Comment File*; *Japanese CenPac Ops*; Smith, *Narrative*; Hough, *Assault on Peleliu*; Morison, *Leyte*; Smith, *Approach to the Philippines*; Isely and Crowl, *U.S. Marines and Amphibious War*; McMillan, *The Old Breed*; Historical Committee, *81st Infantry Division*.

[2] Additional sources used for this section are: *TF 32 Peleliu and Angaur Rpt*; TF 32 OPlan A501–44, dtd 15Aug44; *"1st Mar Hist"*; 5th Mar OpRpt, 17Aug–16Oct44, n.d., hereafter *5th Mar OpRpt*, with appropriate date; 3/1 Rec of Events, 26Aug–10Oct44, n.d., hereafter *3/1 Rec of Events*, with appropriate date; 3/7 WarD, 24Aug–30Oct44, dtd 18Nov44, hereafter *3/7 WarD*, with appropriate date; Boyer, *ArmdAmphibianBn*; Cdr. C. M. Blackford, USCG, "They were all Giants at Peleliu," *USNI Proceedings*, v. 76, no. 10 (Oct50), pp. 1114–1117, hereafter Blackford, "Giants at Peleliu."

[3] Flying conditions, in fact, were so phenomenally good, not only on D-Day but throughout the period of carrier air support, that on "no occasion was it necessary to deny a mission request from an air liaison party because of adverse weather, and on only a few occasions was it necessary to postpone temporarily the granting of a mission because of local weather conditions." *TF 32 Peleliu and Angaur Rpt*, Encl F, p. 4.

D-DAY ON PELELIU

MARINES *boarding landing craft off Peleliu. (USMC A94889)*

ASSAULT FORCE *under enemy fire at Orange Beach 3. Note burning amtracs in background. (USMC 94937)*

U. S. assault transport *DuPage*. Although this vessel had been equipped as a command ship, the Marines still had to furnish much of their own equipment for communication purposes while afloat.

Beginning at 0750, 50 carrier planes bombed enemy gun positions and installations on the beaches. Not once during this 15-minute aerial strike did the roar of the ships' guns cease, since the plan called for the pilots to remain above the flat trajectory of the naval shells. While the Commander, Support Aircraft, was busy coordinating air operations with naval gunfire, the Advance Commander, Support Aircraft, who had handled this task during the preliminary bombardment, prepared to go ashore, where he would be able to assume control in the event the *Mount Olympus* became disabled. Destroyers, meanwhile, had placed white phosphorus shells on the ridges of the Umurbrogol to blanket observation by the Japanese artillerymen there, while the heavier warships had shifted to close fire support and begun firing high explosives on the beaches to pulverize their defenses.

The initial assault wave of LVT(A)s crossed the line of departure at 0800 and churned toward White and Orange Beaches, closely followed by the LVTs filled with infantry. Preceding were the 18 LCIs (Landing Craft, Infantry), which had been equipped with 4.5-inch rocket launchers. After approaching within 1,000 yards of the shore, these vessels took up positions and began unleashing salvos of 22 rockets each. When the third assault wave passed the LCIs, they moved to the flanks of the landing beaches, ready to deliver "on call" fire. Four other LCIs, mounting 4.2-inch mortars, were stationed on the left (north) flank just off the reef to keep up a continuous fire on the rugged terrain in back of White Beach 1.

No sooner had the sound of the rocket salvos ceased, than 48 fighter-bombers flown by naval fliers appeared in the skies overhead. Peeling off, these planes struck at the landing beaches in a finely coordinated maneuver which kept at least eight of them in attack at any one time. Employing bombs, rockets, and machine guns, they poured down an effective neutralizing fire after the support ships had shifted their targets inland and to the flanks of the beaches and during the amphibian tractors' final run to the shore. As the foremost wave approached the water's edge, the fire of the planes gradually moved inland, at no time coming closer to the LVT(A)s than 200 yards.

At 0832, the armored amphibians clambered out of the water onto land, their 37mm and 75mm cannon placing fire upon the beach defenses. A minute later, the first troop wave touched the shoreline, whereupon the assault Marines hurriedly departed their LVTs and fanned out over the coral sands. Succeeding waves continued to land at one-minute intervals. The sight greeting these early arrivals on the beachhead has been aptly described by one of the participants:

> Our amtrac [LVT] was among the first assault waves, yet the beach was already a litter of burning, blackened amphibian tractors, of dead and wounded, a mortal garden of exploding mortar shells. Holes

had been scooped in the white sand or had been blasted out by the shells, the beach was pocked with holes—all filled with green-clad helmeted Marines.[4]

Only the few scattered Japanese that somehow had survived the bombardment opposed the landing, but as the LVT(A)s led the attack inland off the beach, a steadily increasing volume of enemy artillery, mortar, machine gun, and rifle fire hampered the advance. Strewn over the beaches and reaching about 100 yards inland were numerous land mines, many of them naval types whose "horns (lead covered bottles of acid) had not been maintained properly and practically all of these mines failed to detonate. Had these mines been effective the results would have been disastrous."[5] For reasons unknown, many of the mines had been set on "safe," a possible indication that the Japanese may have expected the landing on the eastern shore, where the mines were fully armed and fused.[6]

The Marines advanced inland beyond the beaches, maintaining their initial momentum despite increasing resistance and heavy losses. As a chaplain with the assault waves marvelled later, "how we got through the murderous mortar fire which the Japs were laying down on the reef we'll never know. The bursts were everywhere and our men were being hit, left and right."[7] Carefully sited Japanese high velocity weapons also wreaked havoc on the advancing tractors. A 47mm cannon hidden in a coral point jutting into the sea just north of White Beach 1 and antiboat guns located on the southwestern promontory and on a nearby small island kept up a devastating enfilading fire upon the approaches to the beaches, as well as upon the beach flanks themselves.

As more and more LVTs were destroyed, and their burning hulls cluttered up the beaches, a shortage of these all-important vehicles was soon felt. The division's action report gave the official number of LVTs destroyed that day as 26, but "unofficial estimates by assault unit commanders bring the total knocked out at least temporarily in excess of 60."[8] This discrepancy in figures probably arose because of the observers' inability to differentiate between the blazing LVTs and DUKWs, as well as the Marines' great skill and ingenuity in repairing crippled LVTs and thus restoring them to usefulness.

Despite the heavy losses in amphibian tractors, subsequent waves continued to

---

[4] Robert Leckie, *Helmet for My Pillow* (New York: Random House, 1957), p. 286, hereafter Leckie, *Helmet*, used with permission.

[5] LtCol William E. Benedict ltr to CMC, dtd 27Feb50, in *Peleliu Comment File*, hereafter *Benedict ltr*. "The two types most frequently encountered were 50 kg. aerial bombs buried with the tail assembly down and a pressure detonating fuse extending some three inches above the ground, and the two-horn naval anti-invasion mine. Regarding the latter, it is of interest to note that a great majority were not armed." *1st MarDiv SAR*, Phase II, Part I to Anx C, p. 6.

[6] *Fort ltr*.

[7] Chaplain Edgar E. Siskin ltr, reproduced in *Hebrew Union College Bulletin* (Apr45), pp. 7–8.

[8] Hough, *Assault on Peleliu*, p. 37. Oddly enough, this was the same number that the Japanese claimed to have destroyed on D-Day. *Japanese CenPac Ops*, p. 84.

move shoreward. Landing simultaneously with the fourth wave were the division's tanks (M-4 Shermans). Because of their excellent waterproofing for the operation, they successfully negotiated the reef, where the worst of the underwater obstacles had been removed by UDTs, and continued toward land in six parallel columns led by their respective LVT guides. The enemy fire, however, proved so intense that over half of 30 tanks organic to the division suffered from one to four hits during the 10 minutes necessary to cross the reef. In the 1st Marines' zone, for example, only one of the assigned tanks escaped being hit during the trip ashore. Only three, however, were completely knocked out of action. "Thus within a half hour after the initial landing the infantry had full tank support—a record unsurpassed in any previous Marine landing in the Central Pacific, except for the Marshalls."[9]

TROUBLE ON THE LEFT[10]

Colonel Lewis B. Puller's 1st Marines came in over the White Beaches on schedule. Its 3d Battalion (3/1)[11] landed

---

[9] Isely and Crowl, *U.S. Marines and Amphibious War*, p. 404.

[10] Additional sources consulted for this section are: *1stMarHist*; 1/1 UHist, dtd 23Nov44, hereafter *1/1 UHist*; *3/1 Rec of Events*, 15Sep44; George P. Hunt, *Coral Comes High* (New York: Harper & Brothers, 1946), hereafter Hunt, *Coral Comes High*.

[11] For ease of reference, this numerical abbreviation will be used throughout the volume. For example, the 2d Battalion, 5th Marines will be referred to sometimes simply as 2/5. This designation should be understood to include the reinforcing troops that make a battalion a BLT.

on White Beach 1, the 2d on White Beach 2, with the 1st landing over White Beach 1 at 0945 as regimental reserve. Colonel Puller rode in with the first troop wave and, as his LVT grounded:

> .... went up and over that side as fast as I could scramble and ran like hell at least twenty-five yards before I hit the beach, flat down.... Every platoon leader was trying to form a line of his own, just as I was.... That big promontory on my left hadn't been touched by the ship's guns and planes, and we got a whirlwind of machine gun and anti-tank fire.[12]

Landing with Companies K and I in assault, 3/1 (Lieutenant Colonel Stephen V. Sabol) ran into the most determined resistance, which, coupled with the severe enemy shelling and unexpected obstacles, hindered its progress toward phase line 0-1 (See Map 4). As the left assault unit, Company K was to act as the pivot when the regiment turned north. Its immediate objective was the Point—a jagged coral outcropping jutting into the sea and rising some 30 feet above the water's edge—from which Japanese gunners were placing a dangerous enfilading fire upon the division's flank. Company K, led by Captain George P. Hunt, was destined to execute a classic example of a small-unit attack on a fortified position.

The assault rifle platoons climbed out of their LVTs onto the white coral sand only to find themselves about 100 yards to the right of their assigned area. Company K immediately attacked inland, nevertheless, and initiated its turning movement northward with two platoons in assault. The 3d Platoon on the left

---

[12] Quoted in Davis, *Marine!*, pp. 217–218.

D-DAY ON PELELIU

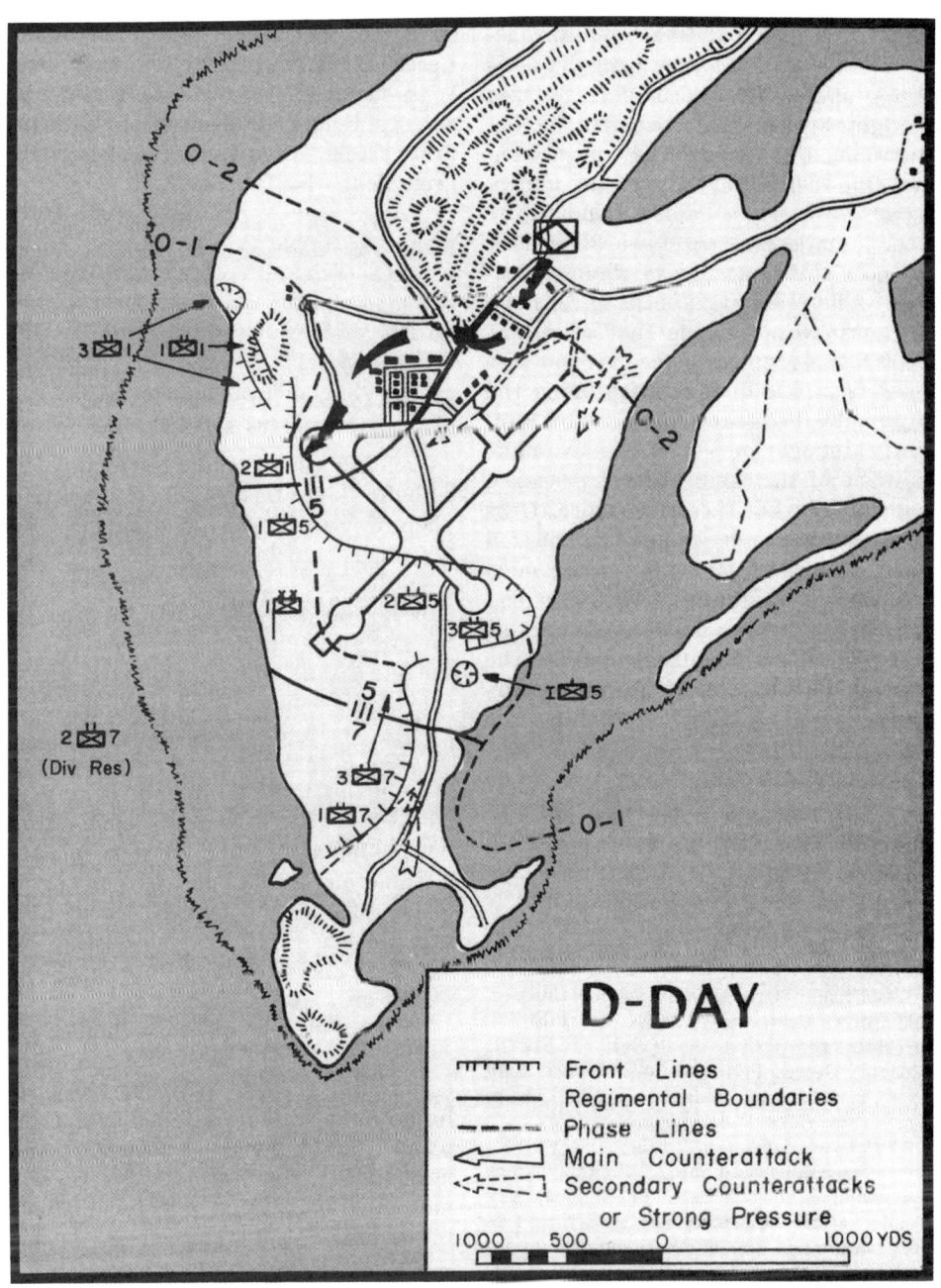

D-DAY

- Front Lines
- Regimental Boundaries
- Phase Lines
- Main Counterattack
- Secondary Counterattacks or Strong Pressure

Map 4

E. L. Wilson

close to the shore fought its way to within 50 yards of The Point before its attack stalled. The 2d Platoon pushed straight ahead some 75 yards before stumbling into a tank trap and becoming pinned down by heavy fire coming from the northern end of a long coral ridge that loomed up some 30-40 feet to the right front of the startled Marines. The precipitous face of this obstacle, shown on none of the photographs or maps supplied to the 1st Marines, was honeycombed with caves and dug-in positions swarming with Japanese soldiers. By this time, the heavy fighting against stiff enemy resistance had reduced the effective strength of each of the assault platoons to approximately a squad, and contact between the two units had been severed.

Ignoring the gap between his assault units, Captain Hunt sent his reserve platoon forward to press the attack against the assigned objective, The Point.[13] Before this formidable stronghold could be seized, Company K would have to overcome five reinforced-concrete pillboxes, one of which housed a 47mm cannon, and the others, heavy machine guns. Each pillbox had from 6 to 12 occupants, while other Japanese infantrymen, some with light machine guns, had been placed in nearby dug-in positions and coral depressions to provide protective fire. All of these carefully prepared defenses were still intact at the time of the Marine assault, despite Colonel Puller's having insisted upon, and received, assurances from naval officers that this strategic area enfilading his flank would be properly blanketed with fire during the preliminary bombardment.[14]

Since The Point's fires were oriented primarily towards the landing beach area, the Marines decided to assault the bastion from the rear (east). Gathering up the remnants of the 3d Platoon, Second Lieutenant William A. Willis and his 1st Platoon began slugging their way toward the top of the objective in the face of concentrated enemy fire. After killing off its protecting infantrymen, the Marines approached each pillbox from its blind spot to blast the occupants with grenades. Finally, the attackers broke through the maze of infantry positions and pillboxes to storm the crest of The Point, but beneath them at the water's edge could be heard the roar of the 47mm cannon that had wreaked havoc among the Marines all morning.

Stealthily easing down toward the reinforced-concrete casemate from above, Lieutenant Willis managed to lob a smoke grenade right in front of the embrasure, temporarily blinding the gunners inside. Mere seconds later, another Marine fired a rifle grenade through the

---

[13] "If any portion of my plan was to break down, the seizure of the Point must not. Should we fail to capture and hold the Point the entire regimental beach would be exposed to heavy fire from the flank." Hunt, *Coral Comes High*, p. 17.

[14] Davis, *Marine!*, p. 214. "At a conference on the flagship sometime prior to D-Day Col Puller requested that naval gunfire be put down on this point even though no enemy gun emplacements could be detected from photographs." Col Richard P. Ross, Jr., memo to DirMCHist, dtd 7Nov49. *3/1 Rec of Events*, 15Sep44, states that "The entire point and its defenses were untouched by naval gunfire; in fact, the entire length of Beach White One was only moderately damaged by our preparatory firings and bombings."

gun port. This bursting grenade probably ignited some stacked ammunition, for the whole interior almost immediately became seared with white-hot flames. When the fleeing Japanese, their clothes aflame and their cartridge belts exploding from the intense heat, dashed out, pre-positioned Marine riflemen cut them down.

By 1015, Company K had fulfilled its mission, killing a counted 110 enemy soldiers in the process. As a result, the enfilading fire from the left flank had been silenced, but the cost to the Marines had been high. Out of the two-platoon assault force, Captain Hunt could find only 32 survivors with whom to set up a hasty perimeter defense, for his other platoon was still pinned down in the antitank trap near the coral ridge. Hurriedly a captured Japanese machine gun was rushed into use, for this handful of men soon found themselves isolated on the extreme left flank of the division and the object of determined counterattacks by small enemy groups.

By this time, the 3d Battalion's 81mm mortar platoon, which had suffered 11 casualties and lost a base plate soon after landing, was working its way southward on the crowded beach, seeking room to set up firing positions. The early confusion of the landing was severely intensified by heavy enemy fire, for mortars and artillery continued to shell the shallow beachhead, while Japanese on the coral ridge some 70 yards inland swept the area with light and heavy machine gun and rifle fire. From time to time, the ammunition in a shattered, blazing tractor would explode, scattering burning debris over the beach and its scurrying occupants. To avoid

certain destruction, succeeding waves of amphibian vehicles merely dumped their contents in the midst of support platoons engaged in clearing out small pockets of enemy resistance and hurried back to the reef for another load.

Efforts of 3/1 to expand the beachhead area proved disappointing. Not only had a gap been opened between elements of Company K, but its contact with Company I, attacking on the right through swampy terrain near the 2d Battalion, had been severed. Within 15 minutes of The Point's seizure, Lieutenant Colonel Sabol ordered two platoons from his reserve (the recently landed Company L) to fill the gap between the two assault companies. Before these riflemen could complete the mission, they too were stopped by heavy fires from the southern portion of the same ridge that had kept the right assault platoon of Company K pinned down. Despite repeated attempts at both flanking and frontal assaults, the reserve group failed to dislodge the entrenched foe. Thus there was no resumption of the advance to establish contact. The battalion commander, meanwhile, had thrown in his last reserve platoon to plug the undesirable gap in Company K's lines between The Point and the long coral ridge.

While 3/1 attempted to remedy its frontline problems, the Japanese had become aware of this opening between Company K's assault platoon and had thrust massed troops into the area. When the reserve platoon arrived on the scene, these enemy soldiers aggressively resisted all attempts by the small Marine force to expel them. Since he had exhausted all the battalion's reserves,

Lieutenant Colonel Sabol requested regimental assistance to deal with this dangerous enemy-held salient in the Marine line.

The Marines of 1/1's Company A hurled themselves into the breach between The Point and the ridge, but superior and concentrated Japanese fire from the coral ridge to their right front caused the attack to bog down by inflicting severe casualties. For several hours, the Marines pressed determined attacks, including tank/infantry assaults, against both the enemy salient and the dug-in foe on the ridge. Finally, elements of Company A succeeded in storming the southern slopes of the ridge where some Marines secured a foothold and made contact with Company I on their right. Late in the afternoon, Company B of 1/1 passed through the depleted ranks of Company A to press the attack, but enemy fire from the ridge halted the advance for the day.

After commitment, the regiment's reserve battalion established contact between the assaulting rifle companies and narrowed the gap between The Point and the ridge, but the opening still was there and the danger to the division's left flank remained. Had the Japanese launched a major counterattack down the corridor between the ridge and the sea, they might have succeeded in penetrating to the beaches, which were cluttered with the men, gear, and supplies brought in by later waves. The effect upon the beachhead could have been disastrous; in fact, the possibility existed that the Marines might have been driven into the sea.

To counter this threat, Colonel Puller used the remainder of the regimental reserve, as well as headquarters personnel and 100 men of the 1st Engineer Battalion, to form a secondary line of defense blocking the route down the corridor. The feared counterattack in force did not come, either because the Japanese failed to capitalize upon this tactical opportunity or because the Marines' fire support overwhelmed enemy attempts at massing the troops necessary to exploit the gap.

In contrast to the opposition encountered by 3/1, the 2d Battalion (Lieutenant Colonel Russell E. Honsowetz) found relatively less resistance. Upon hitting White Beach 2, the assault companies of 2/1 spread out and drove inland, as a corporal later recorded in his diary:

> I rushed forward with the others—dashing, dodging and jumping over logs and bushes. We must have moved in a hundred yards or so when we came to a swamp. . . . I fell flat on my face and pushed my nose deep into the moist jungle floor, waiting for more fire from the Japs; maybe I could spot them . . . started to wade into the swamp, the Nips again opened fire—burst after burst, and some did find the mark. . . .[15]

Advancing inland against resistance described as moderate, the Marines, making use of all their organic weapons and paced by surviving LVT(A)s, pushed on through the heavy woods and swamps, bypassing well-organized enemy strongholds or eliminating them with flamethrowers and demolitions, until they reached the 0-1 phase line—about 350 yards inland—by 0945. Here, in the wooded area facing the airfield, the battalion made a firm contact with

---

[15] Quoted in McMillan, *The Old Breed*, p. 283.

elements of the 5th Marines, thus securing the right flank of the regiment, and held up, awaiting orders to proceed to the next phase line. The 2d Battalion remained here, however, until the following morning because of the precarious situation on the left.

CENTRAL DRIVE
TO THE AIRFIELD[16]

The 5th Marines, commanded by Colonel Harold D. Harris, landed in the center with two battalions abreast, the other as reserve following closely. As the left flank unit, the 1st Battalion came in over Orange Beach 1 with two rifle companies in assault, while the 3d Battalion landed in the same formation over Orange 2. The enemy had made extensive use of double-horned mines on both beaches. Altogether, there were three rows of them, laid in a checkerboard pattern and emplaced at about one-meter intervals. Rough weather prior to D-Day had deposited almost a foot of sand on these mines and substantially decreased their effectiveness. A number of LVTs and DUKWs were disabled by them, however, and became easy targets for the enemy artillery.

[16] Additional sources used for this section are: *5th Mar OpRpt*, 15Sep44; B-3 Jnl, 15Sep–16Oct44, hereafter *1/5 B-3 Jnl*, with appropriate date; 2/5 OpRpt, 17Aug44–1Jan45, n.d., hereafter *2/5 OpRpt*, with appropriate date; 3/5 Rpt of Opns, 26Aug–7Nov44, n.d., hereafter *3/5 Rpt of Ops*, with appropriate date; *3/7 WarD*, 15Sep44; 2/11 SAR, 24Aug–29Sep44, n.d., hereafter *2/11 SAR*; LtCol Robert W. Boyd, "1st Battalion, Fifth Marines, 1st Marine Division in the Palau Operation: A Summary of Offensive Action," (Quantico, Va.: Marine Corps Schools, Amphibious Warfare School, Senior Course 1948–1949), hereafter Boyd, *1/5 PalauOp*.

Another period of rough weather soon after D-Day washed the sand from atop these mines and made their location and removal easier.[17]

The assault troops of 1/5 (Lieutenant Colonel Robert W. Boyd) disembarked from their LVTs about 25 yards inland and began a rapid advance eastward through the coconut palms. Encountering only scattered Japanese riflemen and an occasional machine gun, the infantrymen pushed on until they reached the open area on the west edge of the airfield at 0900. Shortly after reaching the phase line 0-1, they tied in with Marine elements on both flanks.

Across the airfield lay phase line 0-2, but when orders did not come for the advance to continue, the battalion readied its riflemen and automatic weapons along a defensive line. Other Marines with grenade launchers and bazookas took up positions to provide cover both along the front and in depth; four 37mm antitank guns were placed in defilade in shell craters across the front; and machine guns were set up to serve as breakthrough guns in the event the Japanese counterattacked. When three tanks of Company B, 1st Tank Battalion, arrived, they were spaced out and placed in hull defilade among the bomb craters.

The caution exercised by the battalion during this phase of the operation derived from the preparatory phase. Shortly before the division left the Russell Islands, a careful study of aerial photographs had unearthed something

[17] BGen Harold D. Harris ltr to HistBr, dtd 12Jun66, in *Peleliu Comment File*, hereafter *Harris ltr*.

that bore a very marked resemblance to tank tracks. A tank-supported counterattack debouching from the area north of the airfield seemed highly probable, since this area offered both cover and concealment. Based on this conclusion, the bulk of the anti-tank weapons and the limited number of tanks available to the 5th Marines were assigned to back up 1/5.[18]

By early afternoon, a battery of 2/11's 75mm pack howitzers was ashore and digging firing positions just to the right rear of 1/5. All of the artillery batteries' guns, ammunition, and equipment had to be manhandled to this position from the beach, since antitank obstacles prevented the use of LVTs. The mission of 2/11 was to support the attack of the 5th Marines, as well as to supply reinforcing fires in the zone of the 1st Marines. By 1510, the battalion's Fire Direction Center (FDC) was functioning and, 55 minutes later, the first artillery mission was fired at a Japanese gun emplacement. As these howitzers went into action, they replaced the LVT(A)s in providing supporting fire for infantry units.

Although 1/5 was to remain poised on phase line 0-1 because of the 1st Marines' failure to advance, the 5th Marines' 3d Battalion (Lieutenant Colonel Austin C. Shofner) was to surge deep into the interior of Peleliu. It came in over Beach Orange 2 with Company I on the left, K on the right, and L in reserve. After the assault troops oriented themselves, they immediately cleared the beach and attacked directly east. Company I soon tied in with elements of 1/5 and gained the first objective, phase line 0-1, within an hour of landing.

Company K, meanwhile, had run into trouble. In fact, for at least 15 minutes after H-Hour, it was the right flank unit of the entire division landing. The LVTs carrying 3/7, scheduled to land on Beach Orange 3, encountered some serious underwater obstacles, which, coupled with the heavy enfilading fire from the right, caused the drivers to veer to the left. Accordingly, about half of 3/7's assault units actually landed on Beach Orange 2, where they became intermingled with 3/5's elements.[19]

No sooner had 3/5's Company K extricated itself from the predicament on the beach and begun its advance, than a heavy enemy mortar barrage on the southern part of Beach Orange 2 and just inland halted its forward progress. When the barrage lifted a half hour later, and after elements of 3/7 took up their positions on the right flank of Company K, the delayed movement toward phase line 0-1 began. Upon reaching the edge of the airfield, the attacking company ran into several mutually-supporting concrete and log pillboxes, which had to be reduced before the first objective could be reached. About 1000, however, the company tied in with Company I on the first phase line.

When the push to the east was resumed some 30 minutes later, Company K retained contact with the advancing

---

[18] *Harris ltr.*

[19] "It was noted in this connection that having the third battalions of two regiments as adjacent units added to the difficulty of reorganization on the beach since there were two 'I' Companies, two 'K' Companies, and two 'L' Companies involved." *3/7 WarD*, 15Sep44.

elements of 3/7 on the right flank, but quickly lost touch with Company I on the left, for this unit had the responsibility of remaining tied in with 1/5. As Company K continued to push through the scrub forest, the commanding officer had trouble maintaining contact between his platoons. Not only did the thick undergrowth limit visibility to a few feet, but enemy snipers kept up a heavy harassing fire. Company L, which had been sent up to plug the gap between Companies I and K, found the going much easier through the light underbrush in its zone. Shortly after noon, the two assaulting companies were stalled by a series of mutually supporting pillboxes and trenches manned by Japanese with automatic weapons. Only after a platoon of tanks could be brought up was this obstruction reduced, but by this time, contact between Company K and elements of 3/7 on the right had been severed.

The 2d Battalion (regimental reserve), meanwhile, had finished landing over Beach Orange 2 by 1015. Quickly clearing the beach, 2/5 pushed on to the front, where it relieved Company I. This unit then passed around the rear of Company L and assumed a position between the other assaulting companies of 3/5, thereby reducing Company K's frontage. Following its relief of Company I, the 2d Battalion launched a vigorous drive eastward. Later that afternoon, 2/5 shifted the direction of its attack northward. Upon the completion of this turning movement, during which time the battalion's left flank was kept anchored to 1/5's static defensive positions, the assault elements of the 2d Battalion were deployed around the entire southern edge of the airfield. On the battalion's right and still retaining contact was Company L of 3/5, which was attacking straight across the island in coordination with the other rifle companies of 3/5.

After the reduction of the nest of pillboxes that had pinned 3/5 down, the battalion's advance resumed. Control of that afternoon's attack, however, proved extremely difficult and, even today, what actually happened is not completely known. In advancing through the thick scrub jungle that was devoid of any easily recognizable landmark, the riflemen were guided by maps that only sketchily portrayed the terrain. Difficulties in maintaining direction, control, and contact were compounded by steady enemy resistance. Flank elements had to take but a few extra steps to the side and contact became lost with neighboring units. The battalion's control problem was further complicated because of the earlier loss of the LVT carrying practically all of the wire and equipment of 3/5's communication platoon. Although most of these Marines managed to wade ashore and join the battalion early in the afternoon, they had been able to salvage for future use little of the vital equipment.

During the delay caused by the Japanese pillboxes, 3/5 had lost contact on its right flank with elements of 3/7. Shortly after resuming the advance, Lieutenant Colonel Shofner received a radio message from 3/7's command post (CP) stating that its left flank unit was on a north-south trail about 200 yards ahead of 3/5's right flank element. Shofner ordered Companies I and K to push rapidly forward. The left flank unit of 3/7, meanwhile, was to hold up waiting for Company K to come abreast. The two 5th Marines companies pressed on across the island, almost reaching the eastern beaches, but never did contact any of 3/7's elements. About 1500, another radio message from 3/7's CP informed Shofner that the position of 3/7's left flank unit had been given incorrectly. Actually, at the time Company K began its push inland, 3/7's left flank was some 200 yards in the rear of that 5th Marines company. The attack of Company K, while 3/7's left flank elements held up, served to widen the existing gap.

When the true location of 3/7's left flank became known, Shofner ordered Company K to bend its right flank back in an effort to tie in with the adjoining regiment. Because its rifle platoons were already committed, the company had to press headquarters personnel into service in order to extend the line far enough, but even then the flanking 3/7's elements were not sighted by dark. During this late afternoon attack, moreover, Shofner's unit was experiencing trouble in retaining contact between its rifle companies. Only 3/5's left flank unit, Company L, managed to press its advance eastward, all the while remaining tied in with elements of 2/5 on the left. Company L was to have the distinction of being the only Marine unit to cut completely across the island and reach the opposite beach on D-Day.

All cohesion as a battalion ceased about 1700 when 3/5's CP was struck by a well-placed enemy mortar barrage which wounded the battalion commander. Following Shofner's evacuation, Lieutenant Colonel Lewis W. Walt, executive officer of the 5th Marines, assumed command, only to be faced with the problem of regaining control over the scattered units. Setting out on a personal reconnaissance, Walt first located Company L, one platoon of which was still tied in with 2/5 on the airfield while the other two were preparing a perimeter defense for the night some 100 yards farther south in the jungle. After ordering the two isolated platoons back to the airfield to set up a linear defense in conjunction with 2/5, the battalion commander next discovered the long-lost left flank of 3/7, which was already digging in for the night on the edge of the airfield some 400 yards in from the beach.

Not until 2100, however, did Walt and his runner find Company I, and then only after a difficult passage through the jungle in the dark. The Marines, isolated from all other friendly troops and in a perimeter defense, were some 200 yards south of the airfield and about 300 yards short of the eastern shore. Walt dispatched the company toward the airfield with orders to tie in on the right flank of Company L. Some 100 yards farther southwest from Company I, the battalion commander located the last of his units, Company K. It was sent back to the airfield to tie in between Company I and the left flank company of 3/7, thereby finishing the forming of a defensive line along the edge of the airfield.

The new line was never fully completed, however, for Company I failed to locate its assigned position on the edge of the airfield due to the darkness. The unit finally deployed in the woods in front of the gap in the 5th Marines' lines, thereby minimizing the danger. That night, as the commanding officer admitted. "No Japanese counterattack as such hit our lines, which was, of course, fortunate."[20]

PROGRESS TO THE SOUTH[21]

The 7th Marines, commanded by Colonel Herman H. Hanneken, landed over Beach Orange 3 in column of battalions. The 3d Battalion (Major E. Hunter Hurst) landed at H-Hour, with the 1st following immediately, while the 2d was to remain afloat as division reserve. To carry out their mission more efficiently, the two assaulting battalions made use of an unusual command structure:

> During the landing and initial operations ashore, Company A was attached to 3/7; to revert to control of CO 1/7 upon his landing. Company A had the mission of advancing south in the left half of 1/7 zone of action. This maneuver was to provide initial flank protection for 3/7 as it was advancing eastward. The support company of 3/7 was attached to CO 1/7 for the landing and reverted to CO 3/7 upon landing.[22]

[20] Maj John A. Crown ltr to CMC, dtd 13 Feb50, in *Peleliu Comment File*, hereafter *Crown ltr*.
[21] Additional sources consulted for this section are: 7th Mar R-2 Jnl, 15Sep-17Oct44, n.d., hereafter *7th Mar R-2 Jnl*, with appropriate date; 1/7 Combined Bn 2-3 Jnls, 15 Sep-17Oct44, n.d., hereafter *1/7 Bn 2-3 Jnls*, with appropriate date; 1/7 HistRpt, 15Sep-30Oct44, n.d., hereafter *1/7 HistRpt*, with appropriate date; 2/7 WarD, 25Aug-26Oct44, n.d., hereafter *2/7 WarD*, with appropriate date; 3/7 WarD, 24Aug-30Oct44, dtd 18Nov 44, hereafter *3/7 WarD*, with appropriate date; *3/5 Rpt of Ops*, 15Sep44.
[22] LtCol John J. Gormley ltr to CMC, dtd 3Nov49, in *Peleliu Comment File*, hereafter *Gormley ltr I*. "It is believed that the decision

Exposed as it was on the extreme right flank, the 7th Marines was subjected to heavy antiboat, mortar, and machine gun fire from Japanese weapons sited on the southwest promontory and the small unnamed islet nearby,[23] as well as to the artillery and mortar fire that was falling along the entire landing front. Both "natural and man-made obstacles on the reef necessitated [an] approach to the beach in column rather than normal wave formation"[24] and, as explained earlier, approximately half of the lead battalion landed to the left of its assigned beach in 3/5's landing area.

Despite the resultant confusion and dispersion, 3/7 quickly reunited and attacked inland with Company I on the left and K on the right. Fortunately, the battalion had encountered fewer than 30 live Japanese still on the beach, and these were so dazed from the preparatory fires that they were disposed of quickly by the assault troops as they pushed inland. Although mines, barbed

made during the planning phase to have LT [Landing Team] 1/7 and LT 3/7 swap a company was a wise one and that much time was saved during the early part of the attack since LT 1/7, landing in column behind LT 3/7, did not have to pass through the beachhead line of another unit." *3/7 WarD*, 15Sep44.
[23] "While the Naval Gunfire Support plan was under discussion, I strongly urged heavy caliber fire on the unnamed island just south of Orange 3, both in the prelanding and assault phases. This island was a 'natural' for enfilading the reef and Orange Beaches. During the ship-to-shore move I did not see a single indication of friendly fire on this target." *Harris ltr*.
[24] LtCol John J. Gormley ltr to CMC, dtd 27Feb50, in *Peleliu Comment File*, hereafter cited as *Gormley ltr II*.

wire entanglements, and spotty resistance from enemy soldiers in mutually supporting pillboxes and trenches hindered the advance, the Marines obtained unexpected help from one enemy obstacle, a large antitank trench just inland of Beach Orange 3. Spotted early that morning by an air observer, its existence was radioed to the staff of 3/7 just prior to landing. According to Major Hurst, the trench simplified the reorganization problem:

> Once officers were able to orient themselves, it (the antitank ditch) proved an excellent artery for moving troops into the proper position for deployment and advance inland since it crossed the entire width of our zone of action approximately parallel to the beach. With respect to the battalion CP, I am convinced that it enabled us to join the two principal echelons of CP personnel and commence functioning as a complete unit at least an hour earlier than would otherwise have been possible.[25]

By 0925, 3/7 had seized its beachhead at a cost of 40 Marine casualties and, with two companies in assault, the battalion was moving rapidly inland against resistance described as moderate. In little over an hour, the front had advanced some 500 yards farther east into the island's interior, and Company K reported the capture of an enemy radio direction tower. Early in the afternoon, however, Company I came up against a well organized defense "built around a large blockhouse, the concrete ruins of a barracks area, several pillboxes, concrete gun emplacements and mutually supporting gun positions."[26]

To prevent needless casualties, the Marines were halted pending the arrival of the landing team's tanks which had been briefed for this particular mission.

As the Shermans moved up, making a wide sweep around the antitank trench, they chanced upon some Marines working their way along the southern fringe of the airfield. When the troops identified themselves as being of Company I, the tank commander attached his Shermans to this group of Marines and operated with them for some time before discovering that they were from 3/5's Company I instead of 3/7's Company I. All this time, of course, Hurst's battalion had been held up, awaiting the arrival of the tanks. Accordingly, 3/7's "time schedule, which had worked perfectly up to that point," explained the commanding officer, "was thrown completely off by the delay entailed, and I believe that to be principally responsible for our not reaching the east beach on the first day."[27]

While waiting for the Shermans to arrive and reduce the obstructions to its advance, Company I of 3/7 lost all contact with 3/5's Company K on the left flank. Accordingly, Major Hurst placed Company L, which had landed with 1/7, in a reserve position behind Company I and echeloned it toward the left rear to safeguard that flank and to allow the attack to continue. Patrols from Company L were dispatched to

---

[25] LtCol E. Hunter Hurst ltr to DirMCHist, dtd 23Nov49, in *Peleliu Comment File*, hereafter *Hurst ltr. I*.

[26] *3/7 WarD*, 15Sep44.

[27] *Hurst ltr I*. "Incidentally, this incident is one of many which reflect on the lack of training prior to Peleliu. With adequate tank-infantry training behind us, the tank personnel would have known to which I Co they had attached themselves." *Ibid.*

the north in search of the adjoining regiment's right flank unit, but the foremost patrol emerged upon the airfields hundreds of yards in the rear of the unit it was attempting to locate.

The 1st Battalion (Lieutenant Colonel John J. Gormley), meanwhile, had landed but suffered from the same antiboat fire and underwater obstacles that had scattered the lead battalion. As a result, some of 1/7's men ended up on Orange 2. Once ashore, the 1st quickly regrouped and began clearing the beach. Its zone of action was on the extreme right of the division landing, that portion of the beach which Company A of 1/7 had seized earlier when landing attached to 3/7. This company, after rejoining its parent unit, attacked directly east on the left, while Company C advanced southward on the right, and Company B remained in reserve. Until about noon, the resistance to the battalion's advance was described as light, although heavy mortar fire was received.

Immediately after moving off the beach, the Marines ran into a thick mangrove swamp which extended across a large portion of 1/7's front. When Marines of Company C tried to make their way along the only path skirting the western (right) edge of the watery obstacle, they received heavy machine gun and rifle fire from Japanese entrenched in pillboxes constructed out of large pieces of coral. As a result, their progress was seriously hindered. Company A, on the other hand, had worked its way around the eastern fringe of the swamp only to find itself some 250 yards within 3/7's zone of action. Lieutenant Colonel Gormley ordered the reserve company up to tie in between the assaulting companies, as the heavy fighting which had begun about noon continued.

Since the 7th Marines had failed to keep on schedule, all of its elements pushed on as rapidly as possible in the gathering dusk. Not until 1715 did the frontline units receive orders to dig in for the night. No sooner did the Marines attempt to tie in their lines, than the enemy began executing a forward movement by means of light machine gun teams operating in mutual support. Lateral movement along the front became difficult and the Marines were forced to organize only hasty defensive positions.

Although several localized counterattacks were launched against the 7th Marines' lines during the hours of darkness, only one posed any real danger. Company C was hit at approximately 0200, when a strong Japanese force swarmed out of the swamp and attacked the Marines' night defenses. Some enemy troops even succeeded in penetrating the forward positions, whereupon a number of beach party personnel were pressed into service as a mobile reserve. During the four hours of fighting, the Marines inflicted some 50 casualties upon the attackers before the Japanese broke off the action.[28]

---

[28] *Gormley ltr I.* "It is my recollection that the Reconnaissance Co. was deployed just behind 1/7 on the night of D Day. . . . During the night a runner supposedly from 1/7 CP contacted men with orders to move forward and plug up the lines which were being breached by the enemy. . . . The Second Platoon then moved forward under fire and took its place in a gap about 40 yards . . . [and]

JAPANESE COUNTERATTACKS[29]

It was not until late afternoon of D-Day that the Japanese, whose failure to seize tactical advantage from the fluid situation was puzzling, made their major bid to drive the invaders into the sea, but by then it was too late. The Marines had already established a beachhead and had made preparations to frustrate any bold attempt by the enemy to smash through to the vital supply dumps and unloading areas.

First warning of the Japanese intentions came about 1625, when particularly heavy enemy artillery and mortar fire began falling on Marine positions. Then, at 1650, Japanese infantry in estimated company-strength appeared on the northern edge of the airfield and began advancing across it. To Marines hoping for a massive *banzai* charge to facilitate their task of wiping out enemy resistance, the cool professional way in which these enemy soldiers negotiated the open area, taking maximum advantage of every dip and shell hole in the terrain over which they passed, was disappointing.

A large number of Japanese tanks, meanwhile, was forming up behind the protective shield of the ridges to the north of the airfield. They debouched in two columns upon the open terrain about 600 yards to the left front of 1/5 in full view of the Marines. After skirting the northern fringe where the jungle growth gave some scant cover, the enemy tanks swung out "in what can best be described as two echelon formation [and] headed for the center of the 1st Battalion. About half of the enemy tanks had from eight to a dozen Japanese soldiers riding (tied) on the outside of the tanks."[30]

These light tanks, really tankettes by American standards,[31] soon came abreast the infantry advancing in dispersed formation across the open airfield and quickly left them far behind. The Japanese tank commander employed his only sound tactic, which was racing straight ahead at full throttle for the Marine lines. If the tank officers had attempted to coordinate their attack with the slower moving infantry, not one of the enemy tanks would have gained the Marine lines, for many of the organic weapons of a rifle batttalion could have knocked them out.

Fortunately for the Marines, the place where this tank/infantry attack was aimed, the junction between the 1st and 5th Marines in the woods southwest of the airfield, was held by the units best organized to withstand a determined thrust of this type. Colonel Harris, knowing that the forward elements of his 5th Marines would end up facing the level terrain where conditions were ideal for tank maneuvers, had ordered

---

accounted for at least 30 of the enemy killed during the night." 1stLt Robert L. Powell, Jr., ltr to CMC, n.d., in *Peleliu Comment File*, hereafter *Powell ltr*.

[29] Additional sources used for this section are: *5th Mar OpRpt*, 15Sep44; *1/5 B-3 Jnl*, 15Sep44; *2/5 OpRpt; 3/5 Rpt of Ops*, 15Sep 44; *2/11 SAR;* Boyd, *1/5 PalauOp*.

[30] Boyd, *1/5 PalauOp*, p. 16.

[31] The Marine tank commander on Peleliu described the Japanese light tanks as merely "light reconnaissance vehicles" possessing "only ¼" to ⅜" armor," and stated that these "tankettes were not worthy of the name tank and were doomed to certain destruction in any heavy action." *Stuart ltr*.

that heavy machine guns and 37mm antitank guns be unloaded with the assault troops and set up on phase line 0-1 as soon as this initial objective was seized. It was for this reason that Lieutenant Colonel Boyd had placed the three Shermans attached to his 1st Battalion in hull defilade when further advance did not seem likely. Although the Americans had exact intelligence as to the number of enemy tanks and expected some form of violent reaction from the Japanese during the day, the sudden appearance of the tanks on the airfield and the speed of their charge towards the Marine lines caused some surprise.

The course of the enemy tank attack ran diagonally across the front of 2/1, whose men opened up with every weapon they had. Two of the tanks suddenly veered right and crashed into the battalion's lines. Some 50 yards inside, the tanks hurled over an embankment and landed in a bog. When the Japanese attempted to escape their mired vehicles, nearby infantrymen quickly dispatched them.

Although all except one of 2/1's attached Shermans had returned to the beach to rearm, they only had to move some 50 yards to gain a clear field of fire and to engage the enemy tanks.[32] Once the Marines opened fire, the dust became so dense that sighting by the Shermans was possible only between the dust clouds, which slowed down their rate of fire. The first few rounds had been armor-piercing, but these shells,

to the Marines' dismay, passed completely through the thin hulls of the Japanese light tanks to detonate harmlessly on the ground. After the gunners switched to high explosive ammunition, however, the effect of the Shermans' fire was devastating.

Other Marine tanks working through the woods on the southern side of the airfield with advance elements of 2/5, meanwhile, spotted the enemy armor early and "moved out on the airstrip and were shooting as soon as the first Jap tank touched the other side of the airport."[33] The part that these Shermans played in the following action was witnessed by Lieutenant Colonel Walt from an advantageous position just right of the 1/5 lines:

> . . . four Sherman tanks came onto the field in the 2/5 zone of action on the south end of the airfield and opened fire immediately on the enemy tanks. These four tanks played an important role in stopping the enemy tanks and also stopping the supporting infantry, the majority of which started beating a hasty retreat when these Shermans came charging down from the south. They fought a running battle and ended up in the midst of the enemy tanks.[34]

Men of 1/5, meanwhile, opened up with their 37mm's and heavy machine guns, while their immobile Shermans added cannon fire. Just inside the battalion's front lines were set up the only artillery pieces ready to function at this time. Battery E of 2/11 began firing

---

[32] Capt Robert E. Brant ltr to CMC, dtd 9Feb50, in *Peleliu Comment File*, hereafter *Brant ltr*. ". . . the tank commanders were adjusting fires from their turrets just as if they were on a gunnery range." *Ibid.*

[33] Maj Jack R. Munday ltr to CMC, dtd 13Mar50, in *Peleliu Comment File*, hereafter *Munday ltr*.

[34] LtCol Lewis W. Walt ltr to CMC, dtd 25Mar50, in *Peleliu Comment File*, hereafter *Walt ltr*.

at maximum rate as soon as the Japanese tanks appeared on the airfield. Once the enemy vehicles came within range, Marines employing bazookas and grenade launchers took them under fire. Overhead, a Navy dive bomber swooped down to plant a 500-pound bomb right in the midst of the onrushing enemy tanks, adding air power's destructive capability to the holocaust already engulfing the counterattack from every available Marine weapon in range.

Under the weight of this combined fire, the tank-infantry charge quickly began melting away. Some of the tanks exploded, spreading flaming fragments far and wide, while the hitchhiking soldiers just seemed to disintegrate. Not all of the Japanese tanks were knocked out, however, and these survivors smashed into the front lines of 1/5. Penetrating far to the rear past startled Marines, these tanks created confusion and dismay among the beachhead defenders.

As the commanding officer of 1/5 described the scene, these tanks "were running around wildly, apparently without coordination, within our lines firing their 37mm guns with the riders on those tanks carrying external passengers yelling and firing rifles."[35] One Japanese vehicle headed straight for the firing howitzers in an attempt to overrun them. A Battery E gunner hit the tank with the first round of direct fire, stopping it in its tracks, and a bazooka team finished the job. Another tank nearly reached the beach before firepower from rear area troops knocked it out. Marines in frontline positions, however, did not panic. Once the enemy vehicles passed them, they remained in place, ready to engage the following Japanese infantrymen.

When the smoke of battle cleared, no enemy riflemen were in sight. They had either been destroyed by the overwhelming firepower brought to bear upon them or preferred to retreat in the face of it. Two Marines were found crushed to death by enemy tanks and a few other men had been wounded by flying fragments of exploding tanks. One Sherman had even suffered three hits by bazookas, indicative of the confusion caused by the counterattack. The commanding officer of the 1st Tank Battalion, however, thought that the swift collapse of the tank-infantry counterattack was "no grounds for smugness in regard to our antitank prowess. Had the Japanese possessed modern tanks instead of tankettes and had they attacked in greater numbers the situation would have been critical."[36]

What actually happened during those few brief minutes of furious combat has remained cloudy and unclarified down to the present. For example, if all the claims of individual Marines were accepted, the total of Japanese tanks destroyed that day would be several times higher than what the enemy garrison had on Peleliu. Even the number of tanks engaged in the charge is in doubt, and those destroyed were so fragmentized and riddled by marks of various Marine weapons that no accurate count could be made or credit definitely granted to the weapon responsible for

---

[35] Boyd, *1/5 PalauOp*, p. 16.

[36] *Stuart ltr.*

AFTERMATH *of enemy tank attack on Peleliu airfield. (USMC 95921)*

.30 CALIBER MACHINE GUN *in action on Peleliu. (USMC 95248)*

the vehicle's demise. Apparently, two of the Japanese light tanks escaped, leaving 11 as the number destroyed.[37]

Although foiled in their major attempt to annihilate the invaders, the Japanese did not lose heart. During the rest of the day and night, they pressed against the Marine lines, attempted to infiltrate these positions, and launched numerous localized counterattacks. The next major threat came about 1750, when two Japanese light tanks, this time coordinating their movement with supporting infantry, started across the northern runway, aimed as before at the junction between the 1st and 5th Marines. The heavier weapons of the Marine division quickly dispatched the two tanks, while the approaching soldiers were cut down or scattered well forward of the front lines by the hurricane of automatic fire unleashed by nearby units. About a half hour later, the enemy engaged the Marines at the junction of 1/5 and 2/5 in a fire fight which soon faded out. The next morning in a pre-dawn attack, two more Japanese light tanks accompanied by a group of soldiers attempted an attack upon 1/5's lines, but without any success.

Throughout the hours of darkness, the use of star shells and 60mm mortar illuminating ammunition precluded any surprise movements by the Japanese, while those artillery pieces already ashore kept up harassing fires to prevent regrouping of the enemy's forces. Probably because of this, no major counterattack developed on the extreme left flank of the division to exploit the precarious situation there. The small band of Marines isolated on the Point, however, was reduced through attrition by numerous small, but determined, enemy thrusts until only 18 men, relying on a single captured machine gun, remained to resist a counterattack.

Farther south, Marine units were subjected to infiltration tactics and minor counterattacks by a determined foe throughout the night, but 2/1 and 1/5 were tied in on phase line 0-1. Except for the difficulties of 3/5 and the two assault battalions of the 7th Marines in locating each other and establishing contact, the situation appeared to be in good shape. Before halting for the night, 2/5 had surged half way across the open airfield to make the biggest gain of any Marine battalion for the day. The advance in the southern portion of the island, although nowhere near the optimistic goals set by the division commander, had opened up much-needed space for the emplacing of artillery and the locating of inland supply dumps to relieve some of the beach congestion.

SUPPORT OPERATIONS[38]

While assault Marines aggressively expanded the shallow beachhead, other

---

[37] *5th Mar OpRpt*, 15Sep44; *1/5 B-3 Jnl*, 15Sep44; *Walt ltr*.

[38] Additional sources consulted for this section are: *2d MAW UHist; MAG-11 UHist; MAG-11 Palau Rpt;* 11th Mar OpRpt, dtd 10Nov44, hereafter *11th Mar OpRpt; 5th Mar OpRpt;* 5th Mar Rpt on Sup and Evac, n.d., hereafter *5th Mar Sup-Evac-Rpt;* QM, 5th Mar Rpt on Sup, PeleliuOp, dtd 4/Oct44, hereafter *5th Mar SupRpt; 3/5 Rpt of Ops;* 8th Amphibian TractorBn, IIIAC, OpRpt, dtd 30Oct 44, hereafter *8th Amphibian TractorBn OpRpt;* LtCol W. A. Bean, Canadian Army, Observer's Report—Palau, dtd 31Oct44, hereafter Bean, *Observer's Rpt—Palau*.

members of the task force labored strenuously to organize the beach area and to maintain a steady stream of vital supplies moving shoreward and inland. On the whole, this essential job was performed well, despite the enemy's heavy artillery, mortar, and machine gun fire upon the beaches. Although the shore party suffered twice the number of casualties on Peleliu than had been the case in any previous 1st Marine Division operation, such losses "did not affect the constant unloading of supplies."[39]

The decision to create a waterborne supply dump by means of floating barges proved to be "an excellent solution to an extremely important problem . . . and enabled the force ashore to get along on a minimum margin of supply and also avoided congesting the beach with large quantities of supplies before it was prepared for their reception."[40] Another example of good foresight was the use of large numbers of amphibian trailers, which succeeded in staving "off a threatened shortage of artillery and machine gun ammunition until unloading could be resumed at dawn on Dog plus One."[41]

The unloading of mechanized equipment proceeded on schedule so that by late afternoon, most of the cranes and bulldozers were in operation. Some of the shore party's labor forces, however, did not arrive at their assigned locations until the morning after D-Day owing to the lack of LVTs and DUKWs to transport them. The intense enemy fire took its toll of the advancing amphibian waves and "resulted in a continuous shortage of amphibious vehicles into which to transfer boat waves, and these waves hit the beach further and further behind schedule."[42]

This unfortunate situation was intensified by the fact that damaged LVTs were being dispatched to a repair ship which was already loaded to capacity with other amphibians in need of repair, thereby forcing these LVTs to mill about until they could be taken aboard. "Unnecessary wear and tear on damaged tractors resulted. In addition, as many as four (4) LVTs were towing other LVTs, thereby taking out of service from the beach badly needed tractors."[43] When it was discovered that it was possible to bring LCVPs over the reef to the beach at high tide, the situation was alleviated somewhat.

Participating actively in the logistic effort were the forward ground echelons of MAG-11's squadrons. Previously organized working parties operated small boat platoons for the unloading of equipment and evacuating of the wounded, while other Marines served as stretcher bearers, ammunition carriers, and even riflemen and grenade throwers on the front lines. Moreover, some 50 men from VMF(N)-541 landed in a group and manned a second line of defense against Japanese infiltration of the 7th Marines' mortar positions.

---

[39] *1st MarDiv SAR*, Phase II, Part I to Anx C, p. 2.

[40] Bean, *Observer's Rpt—Palau*, p. 13.

[41] *1st MarDiv SAR*, Phase II, Part I to Anx C, p. 3.

[42] Bean, *Observer's Rpt—Palau*, p. 11.

[43] *8th Amphibian TractorBn, OpRpt*. "In one case, an LVT with a damaged hull came alongside the repair ship, and not being able to get aboard, sank alongside." *Ibid.*

Ashore, the assault forces were encountering and solving their own logistic headaches. The trials of the 5th Marines, in particular, revealed that complications arise even in the best laid plans. By afternoon, the heavy fighting experienced by 3/5 during its advance across the island had resulted in a critical supply shortage, for almost all the assault companies' rifle and machine gun ammunition had been expended. Replacement of these essential items to the assaulting battalion, however, was hampered seriously by the LVT shortage and the heavy enemy shelling. Japanese observers kept the entire regimental beach under strict surveillance and continually called down artillery and mortar fire whenever amphibian vehicles reached the shore. Even the 5th Marines' assigned amphibian trailers, which were being employed at Peleliu specifically to provide timely replacement of high expenditure-rate ammunition, did not help to alleviate the shortage. These trailers were not received by the regiment until after the initial supply problem had been solved, and even then, all except two were delivered in damaged condition.

Complicating the whole supply situation for the 5th Marines was the early loss of its assigned beach party commander. This naval officer had been wounded almost immediately upon arrival ashore, and his successor fell to a sniper bullet soon after. As a result, the regimental quartermaster was forced to step in and assume this additional responsibility, an unwanted command of which he was not relieved until late in the afternoon. Just one of the many problems connected with this new task was the mounting number of casualties. Because of the shortage of amphibian vehicles, a speedy evacuation of the wounded was impossible, and the first aid stations on the beaches soon reached the overflowing stage. Too late, the Marine commander learned that the beach party had not marked the regimental beach properly, and when the evacuation LVTs finally arrived, they encountered difficulties in locating their assigned landing points.

The need on the front lines for water, rations, and ammunition, meanwhile, was so great that every available vehicle of the 5th Marines was kept busy hauling these critical items up to the embattled infantrymen. Accordingly, the work of clearing the rest of the regiment's equipment off the beach was hindered, and the unloading areas steadily became further congested. Despite these handicaps, however, the Marines of the 5th managed to surmount these logistic stumbling blocks by one means or another, and the regiment's drive across the enemy-infested island pressed on.

Like the other assault units of the division, the 5th Marines quickly discovered that the water supply contained in the 55-gallon drums, while drinkable, was extremly unpalatable. The oil drums had been improperly steam-scoured and, as a result, the water in them became fouled. Marines also found that those drums which had not been filled flush with the top had rusted in the tropical heat, polluting the water.

At any rate, the lack of a readily available water supply on the coral island was "one of the most critical items in this operation."[44] One tank officer jotted down in his notebook that the infantrymen in the front lines on D-Day were begging for water "like dying men."[45] The enervating heat of Peleliu, when coupled with the island's lack of surface water, caused numerous cases of heat prostration among the attacking troops. Although these men bounced back to full combat effectiveness after a few days aboard ship where water was plentiful, their much-needed presence during the critical assault phase was lost.[46]

By nightfall, most of the 11th Marines' artillery was ashore and its batteries had completed registration firing,[47] but not before encountering various complications. Some artillery units, finding their assigned firing positions still in enemy hands, had to search for new sites on the crowded beachhead; others, discovering their designated landing beaches too congested and the enemy fire too intense, had to divert their Marines and equipment to areas more appropriate for getting ashore and setting up to engage the Japanese. Two 105mm howitzer batteries of 3/11 were actually ashore, but still aboard their DUKWs, when ordered back to the LSTs for the night. During the return trip to the ships across the jagged coral reef, the already damaged hulls of three of the DUKWs were further holed, causing them to sink with the loss of all howitzers and equipment aboard. The surviving 105mm's were landed again early the following morning, as was the corps artillery, which had been prevented from landing on D-Day because of the shallow width of the beachhead.

TWENTY-FOUR HOUR TOE HOLD[48]

Although General Rupertus remained on board ship during D-Day, his assistant, Brigadier General Oliver P. Smith, went ashore with a skeleton staff as soon as confirmation came that the assault battalions of the 5th Marines held a firm foothold on the beach. Smith arrived on Peleliu about 1130 and set up an advance command post in an antitank ditch a short distance inland from Beach Orange 2. Almost immediately, he made contact with the CPs of the 5th and 7th Marines, as well as with the command ship, but even attempts by radio failed to bring a response from Puller's regiment.[49]

---

[44] *Worden ltr.* "Lack of water during the first three days ashore caused scores of men in my battalion (1/7) to become real casualties—unfit to fight, unable to continue ... as many casualties as enemy fire." *Ibid.*

[45] *Munday ltr*

[46] Fortunately, this water situation was alleviated somewhat when potable water was discovered by digging shallow holes in the sand near the shore, and the problem vanished completely once the engineers got their distillation units operating on the island.

[47] "By 1800 the artillery had one and a half Bns [Battalions] of 75mm pack howitzers and one and a third Bns of 105mm howitzers in position, registered and ready to furnish supporting fires." *1st MarDiv D-3 Periodic Rpt,* 15Sep44.

[48] Additional sources used for this section are: *1stMarHist; 11th Mar OpRpt; 7th Mar R-2 Jnl,* 15Sep44; *2/7 WarD,* 15Sep44.

[49] To facilitate communications ashore, the division had been allotted an experimental LVT(A) that had been extensively modified as a mobile radio station. "This vehicle, while not

Earlier, the 1st Marines had suffered the loss of many skilled radio operators and much communications equipment when enemy fire had scored direct hits upon the five LVTs carrying the regimental headquarters ashore. To make matters worse, the CP was no sooner set up ashore when it was hit by a mortar shell that caused further damage and disorganization. Accordingly, neither Puller nor the division had a clear picture of the tactical situation confronting the 1st's assault platoons or of the units' casualties. It was not until late afternoon that Smith was able to talk to Puller by radio, and even then no inkling of the true precariousness of the situation on the division's left flank was gained.

When reports began trickling out to the command ship about the heavy fighting developing ashore, Rupertus' natural concern was over the loss of the initial momentum of the assault. His attention was drawn early to the plight of the 7th Marines, for just after midmorning the division commander learned of the loss by that regiment of 18 LVTs, and shortly before noon he received the 7th Marines' report of "Heavy casualties. Need ammo, reinforcements."[50] It was, therefore, the failure of the 7th to achieve the speedy conquest of the south rather than the bitter dug-in enemy resistance to the north, which worried the division commander. He knew, moreover, that the 7th Marines had suffered heavy losses.

By noon, Rupertus had ordered that the Division Reconnaissance Company, part of the floating reserve, go ashore for commitment with the 7th Marines.[51] That afternoon, when the situation in the south still had not remedied itself, and after requesting General Smith's and Colonel Hanneken's opinions, Rupertus committed 2/7, the remaining division reserve. Before the BLT could be landed, however, the approach of darkness and the shortage of amphibian vehicles resulted in its being ordered back to the ships. Some of the returning boats failed to locate the Marines' ship in the darkness and spent the entire night searching, while the troops in them remained in cramped quarters. The Marines in two other boats, because of the "confusion caused by conflicting orders,"[52] were landed by LVTs later in the night. Since neither Smith nor Hanneken really desired the additional combat troops because their arrival would only further congest the already overcrowded beaches, 2/7's inability to land had no decisive effect upon the first day's fighting.

As the day wore on the situation ashore worsened—"it was a pretty grim

---

completely successful, performed a highly useful service for General Smith's Advance CP on D-Day." LtCol Frederick A. Ramsey, Jr., ltr to CMC, dtd 28Feb50, in *Peleliu Comment File*, hereafter *Ramsey ltr*.

[50] *7th Mar R–2 Jnl*, 15Sep44.

[51] "When he committed the Reconnaissance Company it was not, in the CG's [Commanding General] mind, (in my opinion) that it was a unit but that it was a group of individual infantry replacements." *Fields ltr*. "This was an improper use of the Reconnaissance Company, as there later developed several opportunities for employment of this company in the manner for which it had been trained." Smith, *Narrative*, p. 30.

[52] *2/7 WarD*, 15Sep44.

outlook at that time,"[53] recalled Rupertus' chief of staff, Colonel John T. Selden—the Marine commander began to express anxiety to be on the scene himself, a desire which was intensified when he learned that General Geiger, corps commander, was already ashore. Colonel Selden and other staff members, fearful that a single enemy round might wipe out the entire top echelon during the perilous journey to the beach, finally prevailed upon Rupertus to remain afloat. Selden insisted, however, that the bulk of the command echelon go ashore.

Upon reaching the transfer line, the command group discovered 2/7's Marines still waiting for amphibian vehicles to transport them across the reef. Because he "decided that superimposing a second staff on General Smith was useless and ridiculous,"[54] and that what was needed ashore was more combat troops and artillery, Colonel Selden arranged for his party to lie off the transfer line until elements of 2/7 cleared it. When LVTs or DUKWs still had not arrived by darkness, Selden sent off a message to Rupertus stating his intention of returning to the command ship, and then brought his party back.[55]

On D-Day, Rupertus had expected that his assault troops would seize Objective O-1, which included a 300-yard penetration behind the northern beaches and all of Peleliu south of the airfield. Then he had hoped to attack across the open runways to capture Objective O-2, which embraced all of the island south of the ridges behind the airfield. Actually, at day's end the Marines had penetrated approximately 300 yards behind the northern beaches, but held only a narrow wedge of terrain across the island behind Beach Orange 3. This shallow beachhead "had cost the division 210 dead (killed in action, died of wounds, missing presumed dead), and 901 wounded in action; total casualties of 1,111, not including combat fatigue and heat prostration cases."[56]

In contrast to the Marine commander's concern over the progress of his assault troops ashore on Peleliu, the Japanese commander's report on the day's fighting glowed with optimism:

> . . . by 1000 hours, our forces successfully put the enemy to rout. . . . At 1420 hours, the enemy again attempted to make the perilous landing on the southwestern part of our coastline. The unit in that sector repulsed the daring counter-attack, and put the enemy to rout once more. However in another sector of the coastline near AYAME [Beach Orange 3] the enemy with the aid of several tanks were successful in landing, although they were encountering heavy losses inflicted by our forces. . . . Our tank unit attacked the enemy with such a cat-like spring at dusk, that they were able to inflict heavy damages on the enemy. . . .[57]

---

[53] BGen John T. Selden ltr to HistDiv, HQMC, dtd 26Oct49, in *Peleliu Comment File*, hereafter *Selden ltr*.

[54] *Ibid.*

[55] "During this period, we had to shift position on more than one occasion due to high velocity guns that were beginning to register too close for comfort." *Selden ltr.*

[56] Hough, *Assault on Peleliu*, p. 75. "These were very heavy losses and could not have been sustained for very many days in succession without destroying the combat efficiency of the division." Smith, *Narrative*, p. 34.

[57] *Japanese CenPacOps*, p. 85.

CHAPTER 4

The Drive Inland: 16-22 September [1]

THE MORNING AFTER [2]

The "whiskery, red-eyed, dirty Marines," observed a civilian combat artist on the morning of 16 September, "had spent the night fighting in foxholes filled with stinking swamp water; they were slimy, wet and mean now."[3] The intervening hours of darkness had been filled with the roar of artillery and the rattle of automatic weapons as the infantrymen beat back localized counterattacks. From time to time, star shells and flares from the U.S. cruiser *Honolulu*, the six destroyers, and four LCI gunboats remaining in support cast a greenish pallor over the embattled island. Small groups of Japanese, some wearing helmets of dead Marines, infiltrated behind the frontline positions, and furious hand-to-hand struggles occurred in the rear. Three enemy soldiers even made a brief appearance near the division CP before a burst of fire from an alert sentry cut them down.

Under the cover of darkness, shore party and support troops made use of available LVTs and DUKWs to rush ammunition and water up to the front and to evacuate the wounded. In some cases, vital supplies had to be laboriously hand-carried forward so that the morning attack could start on schedule. No new orders were needed. All regiments were to resume the assault and bend every effort to seize the objectives previously assigned (See Map 5).

Following a half-hour air and naval gunfire bombardment, the division jumped off along the entire line at 0800. Two hours later, General Rupertus came ashore to assume direct control of the advance. The day turned extremely hot —105 degrees in the shade—and the men, already enervated by their previous day's exertions and their night-long vigil, suffered greatly as they fought exposed to the merciless sun. Canteens quickly emptied, and a rapid resupply proved impossible. As panting men slumped to the ground, often with "tongues so swollen as to make it impossible for them to talk or to swallow,"[4] the strength of the attacking units deteriorated rapidly.

---

[1] Unless otherwise noted, the material in this chapter is derived from *IIIAC Palaus Rpt*; *1st MarDiv SAR*; 1st MarDiv WarD, 15–23 Sep44; *1st MarDiv D–2 Jnl*, 15–23Sep44; *1st MarDiv D–3 Periodic Rpt*, 15–23Sep44; *Peleliu Comment File*; *Japanese CenPac Ops*; Smith, *Narrative*; Boyer, *Armd Amphibian Bn*; Hough, *Assault on Peleliu*; Morison, *Leyte*; Smith, *Approach to the Philippines*; Isely and Crowl, *U.S. Marines and Amphibious War*; McMillan, *The Old Breed*.

[2] Additional sources consulted for this section are: 1st MarDiv POW Interrogation Rpts Peleliu, 16Sep–16Oct44, hereafter *1st MarDiv POW Interrogation Rpts Peleliu*; Richard, *U.S. Naval Administration*.

[3] Tom Lea, *Peleliu Landing* (El Paso: Carl Hertzog, 1945), p. 22.

[4] *Worden ltr*.

THE DRIVE INLAND

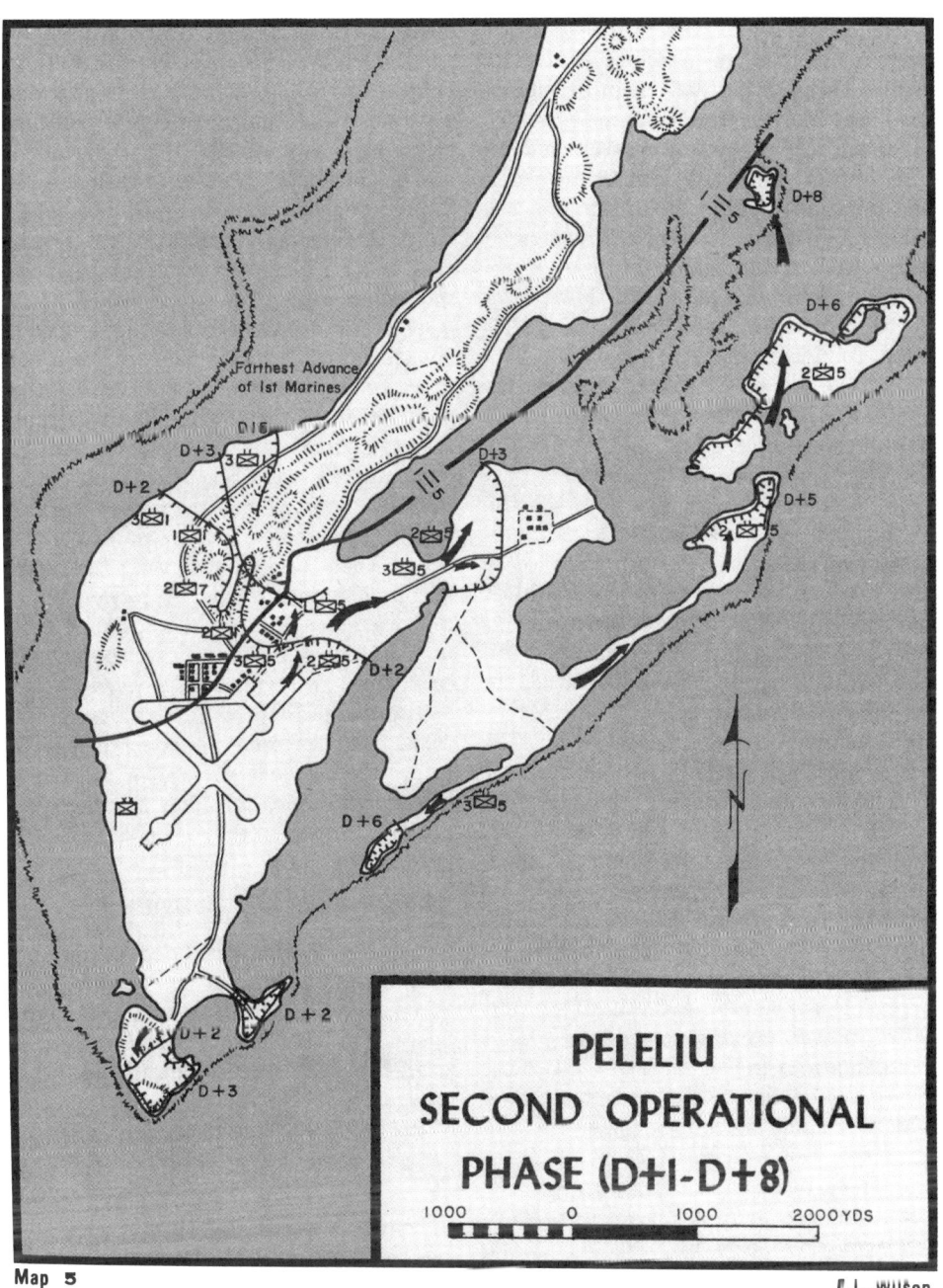

Map 5

PELELIU
SECOND OPERATIONAL
PHASE (D+1-D+8)

The majority of the riflemen, however, continued to advance in swift rushes through a steady rain of enemy artillery, mortar, and machine gun fire to reach the Japanese entrenched in blockhouses, pillboxes, and other fortified positions. Paced by Shermans, the Marines employed flamethrower and demolition charges to eliminate these enemy strongholds or called down supporting arms fire upon particularly difficult fortifications.

On the coral ridges to the north, Puller's 1st Marines ran into bitter dug-in resistance that held down the day's gains. In the center, the 5th Marines cooperated with 2/1 to seize the airfield and to expand east and northeast, while the 7th Marines drove east and south to overrun all of the southern portion of Peleliu except the promontories. Within a few days, both the 5th and 7th Marines accomplished their initial missions and turned their attention northward to aid the hard-pressed 1st, which was finding the going slow over the central ridges.

The second day of the assault, in addition, witnessed two events of some significance: the capture of the first prisoner of war and the official establishment of military government on Peleliu. Members of the naval unit responsible for handling the native population posted the first of ten scheduled proclamations in the name of CinCPOA. To their chagrin, however, not a single Palauan made an appearance, for the Japanese had evacuated them all from the island prior to the landing. Accordingly, the ten men of the military government unit were utilized in various capacities by the Marine division until their transfer to the Island Command on 7 October. Eventually, 15 natives turned up, but they were promptly dispatched to Angaur where a refugee camp already existed.

The prisoner of war taken on 16 September responded freely to questions. A former fisherman from Koror, this second class private had been inducted in July 1944 and trained along with 500 other men as part of a special counterlanding force; 200 of these soldiers were assigned to Peleliu after completion of the course. Their mission was to swim out and destroy the American landing vehicles and tanks with grenades and mines. The men of this specially-trained force remained holed up in their caves, however—to escape the bombs and shells of naval planes and warships—until the arrival of riflemen of the 1st Marines. Although the prisoner's information proved to be vague and of little military value, he did make one extremely accurate prediction. When asked about the morale of the Peleliu garrison, the Japanese replied, "Though they die, they will defend."[5]

SWEEP TO THE SOUTH[6]

As soon as the scheduled D plus one preparatory fires to its front were lifted, the 7th Marines attacked vigorously. On the left, the 3d Battalion pushed rapidly across the island, while

---

[5] Preliminary Interrogation Rpt No. 1, dtd 16Sep44, G-2 Sec, 1st MarDiv, in *1st MarDiv POW Interrogation Rpts Peleliu.*

[6] Additional sources used for this section are: *7th Mar R-2 Jnl*, 16-18Sep44; *1/7 Bn 2-3 Jnls*, 16-18Sep44; *1/4 HistRpt*, 16-18Sep44; *3/7 WarD*, 16-18Sep44.

the 1st drove south toward the promontories. Bitterly resisting this two-pronged assault was the *3d Battalion, 15th Infantry*, whose veteran troops tenaciously defended their fortified positions till death in true *Bushido* spirit.

Companies K and I advanced directly east, with L following in reserve. First task of the left flank unit, Company K, was to reduce the fortifications that had held up the unit on the previous day. Aided by point-blank fire from the tanks that paced their advance, the infantrymen quickly seized the barracks area and the three gun positions, but the blockhouse proved to be a more difficult problem. Its five-foot thick reinforced concrete walls withstood direct hits from naval gunfire, 75mm tank cannon, and bazookas; even flamethrowers failed, for one-inch armor plates shielded the blockhouse's gun ports and its two underground entrances. Only after demolition teams worked their way forward under the cover of smoke to lay their charges directly against its massive walls and breached this fortification was forward movement resumed.

The 3d Battalion gained the eastern shore by 0925; then, while Company I organized beach positions to defend against any possible enemy reaction and to support the advance by fire, the battalion shifted its assault south toward the promontories. Company K led the way, followed closely by L in reserve. Free use of flamethrowers and bazookas was made, for numerous pillboxes and concrete gun emplacements were encountered. By noon, however, the foremost elements had eliminated the last two pillboxes barring the way to the sandpit leading out to the southeast promontory. The rifle company, unfortunately, was "unable to continue its advance until a resupply of water could be effected."[7] The battalion waited in vain until 1500 before the necessary water arrived. By this time, only a few hours of daylight remained, so the battalion was ordered to dig in, postponing the final assault until the following morning.

What daylight remained was used to bring up tanks that destroyed with pointblank fire one blockhouse, two pillboxes, and several machine gun positions guarding the approach to the promontory. Under the cover of this protective fire, a detail of combat engineers ventured forth onto the sandspit to remove or disarm the numerous enemy mines there, paving the way for the scheduled attack the next morning. The Marines manned positions facing their objective during the hours of darkness, but the only enemy opposition consisted of sniper fire in the rear areas.

The 1st Battalion, meanwhile, had been supported in its southward drive by artillery, naval gunfire, and air strikes, as well as by rocket concentrations from the LCIs that paced the Marines' advance along the western shore. The riflemen succeeded in overrunning numerous enemy-held pillboxes and bunkers, in addition to four 5-inch guns and three lighter dual-purpose antiaircraft guns. By noon, the Marines had reached the shore opposite Ngarmoked Island, but their strenuous ex-

---

[7] *3/7 WarD*, 16Sep44. Colonel Hanneken received the following message at 1324: "3/7 out of water. Troops having dry heaves." *7th Mar R-2 Jnl*, 16Sep44.

ertions in the blazing sun had so dehydrated them that a halt was called until water could be brought up to restore the troops' strength. Sufficient water did not arrive until late afternoon, however, and the order was given to dig in for the night.

During the lull, the battalion regrouped and prepared to resume the attack. Additional engineers were rushed up to clear away Japanese mines on the beaches to the Marines' front, and a 75mm self-propelled half-track and four 37mm antitank guns had been brought up to the battalion by 1530. Later, under the cover of darkness, demolition experts searched the narrow strip of land linking Ngarmoked Island to Peleliu and dug up the enemy mines that could bar the employment of tanks in the morning attack.[8]

At 0730 on 17 September, the 3d Battalion's objective, the southeast promontory, was hit by an air strike, but a scheduled mortar preparation was called off when combat engineers, ranging far in advance of the infantrymen, discovered another extensive minefield in their path. For an hour and a half, Shermans and riflemen provided covering fire while the engineers performed their dangerous task of disarming or removing the deadly Japanese mines. Then, at 1000, a platoon from Company L, the reserve of the previous day, began working its way across the sandspit in coordination with two tanks. Twenty-six minutes later, a foothold had been seized on the objective, whereupon the remainder of the company was transported over the open stretch of ground in LVTs that provided protection from small arms fire.

After regrouping, Company L immediately attacked. Opposing the advance were Japanese soldiers manning automatic weapon and rifle positions among the coral crevices or entrenched in pillboxes with mutually supporting lanes of fire. The Marines, slowly battling their way forward, recognized that blazing napalm was the most effective method of rooting out the diehard defenders, and a hurried call went throughout the battalion for additional flamethrowers. Once they reached the front and began burning the enemy out, the advance quickened. By 1215, the rifle company had seized enough ground for the siting of weapons to provide supporting fires for 1/7's assault of Ngarmoked Island; an hour later, the 3d Battalion reported the capture of the entire southeastern promontory.

The two-day struggle southward cost the Marine battalion 7 dead and 20 wounded. In contrast, the last-ditch stand by the isolated Japanese resulted in 441 enemy killed. The startling discrepancy between these two casualty figures clearly demonstrated the outstanding success and superb skill with which the highly-trained Marines employed small unit assault tactics against stubbornly-defended fortified positions.

---

[8] "During the night of D plus 1 many Japs were annihilated while attempting to cross from the southwestern promontory to the unnamed island during low tide. Mortar illuminating shells provided excellent observation of this movement by our troops and the Japs were easy targets for our machine gun and rifle fire." *Gormley ltr I.*

Success, however, did not come so quickly for the 1st Battalion in its final assault on Ngarmoked Island, the southwestern promontory. Early on the 17th, a platoon from Company B, the battalion reserve of the previous day that now held assault positions opposite the objective, moved out in the wake of naval gunfire and mortar fire to gain the far end of the causeway. Here, the onrushing riflemen and their supporting tanks ran head-on into heavily-fortified positions, and the attack ground to an abrupt halt. After an hour of stubborn fighting failed to expand the bridgehead, Colonel Hanneken approved a withdrawal to give the supporting arms a chance to pulverize the enemy fortifications holding up the advance.

While naval gunfire, artillery, and mortars hammered the objective, preparations to resume the attack were made. All available tanks, LVT(A)s, halftracks, and 37mm guns were dispatched forward. By early afternoon, the successful completion of 3/7's mission permitted Major E. Hunter Hurst to release his tank and weapons support for use by Lieutenant Colonel John J. Gormley's 1st Battalion. Company B, which had been badly mauled by enemy fire that raked the causeway, was replaced in the frontlines by Company A, which jumped off at 1430 following a 10-minute air strike.

In short order, the Marines, now supported by three tanks, broke through the battered Japanese positions and began fighting their way southward. An hour later, Company I moved into reserve behind 1/7, releasing Company C, which crossed over to the promontory and joined the attack on A's right. Shortly thereafter, Company B also moved to Ngarmoked Island and took up reserve positions immediately behind the two assault units that were pressing the attack with vigor. A measure of revenge was granted the fast moving Marines, for they finally succeeded in knocking out the high velocity guns that had enfiladed the Orange beaches for so long. When darkness halted the day's advance, the two rifle companies had a firm hold on both the eastern and western shores and a defensive line running almost halfway across the promontory.

The next day, 18 September, the resumption of the attack was delayed until 1000 to permit a more thorough preparation. Marine artillery blanketed the enemy-held part of Ngarmoked Island, while riflemen, with their armor and supporting weapons, carefully deployed into the most advantageous jump-off positions. Just to the front loomed a sizeable swamp, approximately in the center of the promontory. Company A attacked to the left of this impassable terrain, Company C to the right, with both units reestablishing contact on the opposite side. Company B had the task of seizing a piece of land that protruded from the eastern shore just in front of the line of departure.

Attacking units were instructed to leave bypassed Japanese for later destruction by demolition teams, but Company C was early treated to an example of the enemy's tactics of passive infiltration, *i.e.*, allowing positions to be overrun in order to be in the rear of the

American attacking force. During the advance south around the swamp, 15 riflemen were detailed to remain behind to guard suspected cave openings and pillboxes where Japanese might still be lurking. No sooner had the front lines surged forward than a large number of enemy soldiers suddenly emerged from their concealed holes and took the small Marine detachment under fire. The situation became so critical that both the Division Reconnaissance Company, attached to the regiment since D-Day, and most of Company I had to be committed to maintain control of the bypassed areas.

By 1344, the two attacking rifle companies of the 1st Battalion had seized the southern shore of Ngarmoked Island. Company B, on the other hand, had experienced tougher going; its assault squads, attacking towards the eastern shore, ran squarely into the extensive fortifications that the Japanese had prepared to prevent any penetration into the cove between the two promontories. The advancing Marines continued a yard by yard conquest of the dug-in positions, which seemed to be crowded literally on top of each other. At 1354 the attack stalled, after the Shermans had withdrawn to rearm and the half-tracks had become bogged down in the miry ground. By this time, the company had killed an estimated 350 enemy soldiers and had restricted the pocket of resistance to an area of some 50 square yards.

While waiting for a bulldozer to arrive, Marines in the frontlines could hear the sound of shots, as some of their opponents, faced with the inevitable choice of death or surrender, chose to commit suicide. Other Japanese leaped into the sea and attempted to escape across the tetrahedrons to the southeastern promontory, only to run into 3/7's riflemen, who promptly slew some 60 of them. After the bulldozer extricated the half-tracks, Company B resumed the assault and quickly overran the last remaining defenders, bringing the unit's estimated total of enemy killed that day to 425.

The 7th Marines informed division at 1525 on 18 September that its initial mission on Peleliu was completed. In seizing the southern part of the island, the regiment uncovered much-needed maneuver area and destroyed to the last man an excellently trained and well-equipped Japanese infantry battalion. During its first four days of fighting, the 7th Marines, less its 2d Battalion, accounted for an estimated 2,609 enemy dead. The fierce determination of the Japanese was reflected by the fact that not a single one was taken prisoner. In accomplishing its mission, the regiment suffered 47 killed, 414 wounded, and 36 missing in action. The disproportionate number of Marine casualties to enemy dead was surprising, for the four-day long assault had constantly pitted exposed Marines against entrenched Japanese in strongly fortified positions. Using proven small-unit assault tactics and making full utilization of all supporting arms, especially demolitions and flamethrowers, the Marines succeeded in annihilating the enemy garrison. Only a unit like the 1st Division, containing a sizable number of veteran troops who had been tested in battle, could have executed such a mission with a minimum of casualties.

ACROSS THE AIRFIELD AND UP THE PENINSULA[9]

The first task confronting the 5th Marines as 16 September dawned was seizure of the airfield, the primary objective on Peleliu. Fortunately for the battalions, their night positions placed them in an advantageous location for that day's advance which was to be a turning movement northward, using the extreme left flank of the division as a pivot point. On the left was the 1st Battalion strung out along the woods' edge. The 2d was deployed in the middle about halfway across the open terrain, and the 3d was on the right at the southern fringe of the airfield.

With the coming of daylight, the enemy laid down an intense shelling upon these frontlines. One Japanese shell landed directly on the regimental CP, and another one destroyed vital communications equipment. Several staff officers became casualties, and Colonel Harris' knee was severely injured, making it extremely difficult for him to move about. Division rushed replacements to staff the 5th's CP adequately, which allowed the regiment to jump off on schedule.

At 0800, the 1st Battalion moved out of the woods onto the open runways with two companies in assault, the other in reserve and echeloned to the left rear. Although a few riflemen benefited somewhat from the cover provided by the scrub growth and rubble along the northern fringe of the airfield, most had to brave the open runways in an open order formation with intervals of about 20 yards. "The advance of the assault companies across the fireswept airfield," reminisced the battalion commander, "was an inspiring and never to be forgotten sight."[10] Despite heavy casualties, the Marines surged across the exposed runways to reach the main hangar area on the northeast side of the airfield in little more than an hour.

Here, the leading troops encountered stiff resistance from enemy soldiers entrenched among the ruins of the buildings, a large V-shaped antitank ditch, and two stone revetments that housed 20mm guns. As large numbers of the attackers became casualties, the advance faltered, for the Marines' strength had been severely weakened by numerous heat exhaustion cases. When LVTs attempted to evacuate the wounded, they attracted such a deadly rain of fire from Japanese guns emplaced in the commanding ground north of the airfield that Shermans had to run interference for the thin-skinned amphibian vehicles.

A platoon moving in defilade of a Marine tank finally managed to outflank the enemy positions holding up the attack, and, once the reserve company was committed, a vigorous assault overran the Japanese defenders in the hangar area after some furious hand-to-hand fighting. Pushing on, the 1st Battalion gained phase line 0–2 before dark, but Japanese gunners on nearby ridges unleashed such an intense and

---

[9] Additional sources used for this section are: *5th Mar OpRpt*, 16–23Sep44; *1/5 B 3 Jnl*, 16–23Sep44; *2/5 OpRpt*, 16–23Sep44; *3/5 Rpt of Ops*, 16–23Sep44; 5th War Dog Plat IIIAC, Peleliu OpRpt, 16Sep–18Oct44, dtd 17Nov44, hereafter *5th War Dog Plat Peleliu OpRpt*; Boyd, *1/5 PalauOp*.

[10] Boyd, *1/3 PalauOp*, p. 19.

75MM GUN *in firing position on Peleliu. (USMC 95050)*

1st MARINE DIVISION *tanks at Peleliu airfield. (USMC 94876)*

accurate fire upon the exposed infantrymen that the decision was made to withdraw to the antitank ditch to set up night defenses.

The 2d Battalion spent the day fighting its way up the east side of the airfield through an almost impassable scrub jungle that degenerated into a thick mangrove swamp along the eastern shore. Supporting Shermans could operate only along the fringe of the woods, and the riflemen had to plunge alone into the thicket infested by enemy soldiers, who often had to be ousted in close combat. When darkness began closing in, the Marines tied in with 1/5 on the left flank and fell back a short distance on the open airfield in order to have clear fields of fire to their front.

On the extreme right, the 3d Battalion soon found itself in an unusual predicament as the attack progressed. Company I started the day in reserve, but was shifted northward about noon and used to cover a threatening gap that developed between assault units of the 1st Marines. Company L, meanwhile, remained tied in with 2/5's drive northeastward, while Company K renewed its eastern advance on the left flank of 3/7. As a result, the 3d Battalion's two rifle companies had to overextend themselves to retain contact as they assaulted in different directions. About 1500, Major John H. Gustafson, formerly executive officer of 2/5, replaced Lieutenant Colonel Walt as battalion commander. Walt promptly returned to the 5th's CP and resumed his duties as regimental executive officer, thereby taking some of the load off the injured Colonel Harris. Shortly after this change in command, the 3d Battalion was ordered to displace forward in preparation for relieving the 1st Battalion the following morning.

Before passing into reserve on 17 September, however, the 1st drove forward against light resistance to regain the previous day's positions on phase line 0-2. During this advance, one of the rifle platoons was subjected to a rocket strike from a carrier plane. This unfortunate incident occurred when the man responsible for removing the panels signalling an earlier air strike "had been evacuated as a casualty and provisions had not been made for someone else to take over his responsibilities."[11] After taking over 1/5's zone, the 3d Battalion moved out in coordination with elements of 2/5 on its right, but the heavy flanking fire from the Japanese on the central ridges with their clear fields of fire and excellent observation effectively prevented any real gains that day.

On the right, the 2d Battalion resumed its slow advance through the dense jungle between the airfield and the mangrove swamp. When a Sherman attempted to assist infantrymen working their way through the undergrowth at the edge of the airfield, Japanese observers on the ridges called down such a concentration of artillery and mortar fire upon the tank that it departed to spare the nearby Marines. As the men attempted to maintain a skirmish line while moving through the jungle against the sporadic fire of scattered snipers, the enervating heat caused greater casualties than did the Japanese. Pla-

---

[11] Boyd, *1/5 PalauOp.* p. 25

toon leaders halted their men frequently for rest periods, but the number dropping from heat prostration continued to mount. Day's end, nevertheless, found the battalion some 600 yards beyond phase line 0–2, with one flank anchored on the swamp and the other firmly tied in with 3/5's right flank.

On this day, the Japanese fired a few rockets, possibly of the spin stabilized type, although they had a very erratic corkscrew type of trajectory. These rockets appeared to be about the size of 5-inch shells and were loaded with picric acid. The bright, yellow burst caused brief excitement when a few cries of "Mustard Gas" were raised. Prompt reassurance by radio that it was only explosion of picric acid quelled the excitement.[12]

The next day, 18 September, the 5th Marines' attack on the left ground to a halt by noon, when the 3d Battalion ran into an increasing volume of fire from the same towering central ridges that had prevented any gains the previous day. On the right, in the 2/5 sector, Japanese machine gun and rifle fire from the mangrove swamp on the battalion's east flank made any advance very costly. Artillery and mortar fire had little effect until a call was made for air bursts about 30 feet above the swamp. This proved highly effective and permitted a rapid advance. Jumping off at 0700, 2/5 moved forward rapidly in the face of only scattered resistance, protected from enemy artillery observation by the canopy of tree tops and reached the road leading to the village of Ngardololok and the northeastern peninsula.

The mangrove-choked waters separating this peninsula from the mainland, however, pressed in so close to the road on both sides as to make the approach virtually a causeway. About 1040, a small patrol ventured across to test enemy reaction. When it returned safely without drawing any fire, an air strike was requested to pave the way for a crossing in force. To the Marines' disappointment, the carrier-based planes missed their target completely, and artillery concentrations had to be called down instead to soften up the Ngardololok area.

At 1335, a reinforced rifle company began crossing over the narrow approach route. Unknown to the battalion commander, the 5th Marines' CP had already ordered a second air strike to rectify the earlier abortive attempt. As the company negotiated the open causeway, U. S. Navy planes suddenly swooped down out of the skies to strafe the exposed troops. The Marines pushed on, despite heavy casualties, and established a firm bridgehead.

As if to compound the 2d Battalion's misfortunes that day, the unit was subjected twice more to misplaced American fire. An artillery concentration hit the battalion in the process of displacing forward, and later, mortar fire struck some elements as they crossed the causeway. Of the 34 casualties suffered by 2/5 on 18 September, almost all resulted from friendly fire.

The 3d Battalion's front, on the 18th, had been pinched down between the ridges and the sea to a size manageable by a single company. Accordingly, the

---

[12] *Harris ltr.*

other two companies displaced to positions on the right (south) flank of 2/5. By nightfall, the two battalions were dug in facing the Japanese installations at Ngardololok. The reserve 1st Battalion, which had been flushing out snipers in the rear, now moved up to support the next day's drive.

After dive bombers blasted the objective, the 2d Battalion attacked the remains of Ngardololok during the morning of 19 September. Only sporadic fire from scattered holdouts opposed the advance. As the 2d continued its push forward past the ruins, the 3d Battalion drove southward in the wake of artillery and mortar fire against extremely light resistance. In the following days, the 5th Marines systematically mopped up isolated enemy holdouts on the peninsula, which was secured on 21 September, and the off-shore islands, the last of which was seized on the 23d.

During this period of extensive patrolling, war dogs had about their only opportunity for effective use on Peleliu. Brought ashore on D-Day and sent up to the front lines, the dogs became extremely nervous under the constant shelling. Many even attacked their handlers and had to be destroyed. As a result, the dogs were brought back to the rear areas for night security duty at CPs, while their handlers served as stretcher bearers. When the war dogs operated with patrols of the 5th Marines, however, in a role for which they had been trained, their keen scent saved many Marine lives. On 20 September, for example, a Doberman-Pinscher scouting ahead of Company I's point detected an enemy ambush some 75 to 100 yards away. Once the dog alerted the Marines to their imminent danger, they were able to escape the trap laid by 20-odd Japanese armed with machine guns and other automatic weapons. The fruitful activities of the war dog platoon came to an untimely end when the 5th Marines reached northern Peleliu. An erratic salvo of white phosphorus shells landed in the area occupied by the platoon, and this unfortunate accident marked the end of its activity on the island.[13]

ASSAULT OF THE RIDGES[14]

Puller's 1st Marines jumped off in the general attack on the morning of 16 September and began a turning movement northward in coordination with the 5th Marines. The first problem of the 3d Battalion, on the left, was the long coral ridge that had blocked any successful advance on the previous day. It was not until noon, after the last fresh company of the regimental reserve, 1/1, was thrown into the struggle, that the riflemen, supported by two Shermans, were able to surge up the slopes and wrest a large portion of the high ground from the entrenched enemy.

With control of the commanding heights in their hands, the Marines were soon linked up with the survivors of Company K on the Point. These men had been isolated for some 30 hours, although reinforcements, consisting of shore party personnel and stragglers

---

[13] *Harris ltr.*

[14] Additional sources used for this section are: *1st Mar Hist; 1/1 UHist; 3/1 Rec of Events, 16-18Sep44; 2/7 WarD, 15-18Sep44;* Capt George P. Hunt, "Point Secured," *Marine Corps Gazette,* v. 29, no. 1 (Jan45) pp. 39–42, hereafter Hunt, "Point Secured."

on the beach, weapons, and supplies had been brought in over the water by an LVT early on the 16th. By nightfall, even though the mission of reaching phase line O-1 had not been accomplished by 3/1, the worst features of the tactical situation confronting the battalion—a frontline dotted with enemy-created wedges, and gaps between its own units—had been rectified.

Coordinating its attack on the right flank with that of 1/5, Honsowetz' 2d Battalion, 1st Marines, moved out in the wake of the preparatory fires across the northwestern portion of the airfield. When the advancing riflemen reached the building area, stiffening resistance from Japanese hiding among the ruins, plus a brief loss of contact with neighboring units, slowed the attack momentarily. Despite heavy casualties, however, the battalion overran the enemy defenders in savage hand-to-hand combat and began fanning out toward phase line O-2. The onrushing troops made good progress at first, but the Japanese bitterly resisted all efforts by the Marines to advance toward the important road junction linking the East and West Roads. Despite a substantial gain, the men halted for the night some distance short of phase line O-2, the West Road.

That night, the enemy made a determined effort to retake the Point regardless of cost. With this strategic elevation once again in their hands, the Japanese could set up their weapons and play havoc with the men, supplies, and vehicles crowded on the White Beaches. The counterattack came at 2200, when an estimated 500 enemy soldiers, following preparatory mortar and grenade fire, suddenly rushed Company K's positions on the coral outcropping. The defenders opened up with automatic weapons and hurled grenades, while supporting artillery and mortars blasted the terrain to the front.

In spite of this concentrated hail of fire, some 30 Japanese still managed to penetrate the frontlines. These attackers were dispatched in fierce fighting, while other enemy troops, attempting to flank the Point along the water's edge, were rooted out of the coral crevices by Marines employing thermite grenades and automatic weapons. By 0200, the counterattack subsided as swiftly as it had begun. The overwhelming fire superiority of the Marines had decided the issue. The light of dawn, remembered Captain Hunt, revealed 350 "more Japanese dead sprawled before our lines. Their rear units, horribly mutilated by our artillery and mortars, had been lugging a 40mm gun, for it lay in their midst, scarred by shrapnel, an abandoned symbol of their efforts to recapture the Point."[15] That morning, Company K was finally relieved, but it mustered only 78 men out of the 235 that the captain had led ashore on D-Day.

On 17 September, Colonel Puller had to put all three battalions in the line to press the attack, for his regiment had suffered over 1,000 casualties in just two days of battle. The 3d Battalion was on the left, the 1st in the center, and the 2d on the right, while 2/7 was in reserve. The last-mentioned battalion had finally landed the previous day to support its parent unit's drive south, but

---

[15] Hunt, "Point Secured," p. 42.

had been diverted north instead to support the more hard-pressed 1st Marines in their assault on the ridges.

Lieutenant Colonel Sabol's 3d Battalion pushed steadily ahead against light sniper fire for a gain of 700 yards, and only the danger of overextending itself prevented the battalion from advancing farther up the west coast that day. In the middle, the 1st Battalion's attack ran squarely into a heavily fortified group of mutually-supporting positions consisting of a huge reinforced-concrete blockhouse with four-foot thick walls and 12 pillboxes emplaced nearby. A hurried call to the battleship *Pennsylvania* brought 14-inch armor-piercing and high explosive shells slamming into this unmarred fortification that had somehow escaped the preparatory bombardment of the island. The shells breached the walls, and concussion killed the 20 enemy soldiers inside. Other supporting arms, meanwhile, had eliminated the surrounding pillboxes.

Resuming the advance, Major Raymond G. Davis' 1st Battalion surged forward across the road marking phase line O-2. Here, the terrain began sloping upward as the riflemen approached the foothills of the Umurbrogol Mountains. Since the entrenched foe to its front was pouring down a very heavy volume of fire that inflicted severe casualties, the battalion quickly regrouped and drove straight up the slopes. Aided by tanks, the infantrymen made good use of their bazookas to knock out 35 separate Japanese-infested caves before digging in for the night. Marine positions had been firmly established on the forward slopes of the first series of hills, notwithstanding the enemy commander's claim that this assault had been "repulsed by our timely firing."[16]

During its rapid advance to the right on 17 September, the 2d Battalion gained the distinction of being the first to encounter the Umurbrogol ridges, a misshapen conglomeration of soaring spires, sheer cliffs, and impassable precipices that was to become infamous in the weeks ahead. Some of the problems confronting the 1st Marines in its assault of this high ground were recorded by the regiment's history:

> Along its center, the rocky spine was heaved up in a contorted morass of decayed coral, strewn with rubble, crags, ridges and gulches thrown together in a confusing maze. There were no roads, scarcely any trails. The pock-marked surface offered no secure footing even in the few level places. It was impossible to dig in: the best the men could do was pile a little coral or wood debris around their positions. The jagged rock slashed their shoes and clothes, and tore their bodies every time they hit the deck for safety. Casualties were higher for the simple reason it was impossible to get under the ground away from the Japanese mortar barrages. Each blast hurled chunks of coral in all directions, multiplying many times the fragmentation effect of every shell. Into this the enemy dug and tunnelled like moles; and there they stayed to fight to the death.[17]

Early in the morning, the 2d Battalion surged forward to overrun the important road junction that the Japanese had defended so bitterly the previous day. Continuing up the East Road that ran along the base of the ridges, the exposed infantrymen came under increasing fire from enemy soldiers en-

---
[16] *Japanese CenPacOps*, p. 86.
[17] *1st Mar Hist*, pp. 11–12.

trenched on a 200-foot ridge to the left flank. This high ground, called Hill 200, paralleled the road and formed a threatening salient into the battalion's center. From these commanding heights, observers called down accurate artillery and mortar concentrations not only on the 2d Battalion, but also on the troops of the 5th Marines moving across level ground on the extreme right.

Orders came down from regiment for the troops advancing up the East Road to wheel left and take the ridge under assault. As the Marines attacked up the steep slopes, the Japanese unleashed a devastating fire of mortars and machine guns, while mountain guns and dual-purpose artillery pieces suddenly emerged from hidden positions to blast away at pointblank range before disappearing again into caves. Casualties mounted alarmingly, and many of the tanks and LVT(A)s brought up to support the infantry were knocked out by the accurate enemy fire. The Marines grimly continued climbing upward, however, and succeeded in clearing the crest of all defenders by nightfall. The men dug in quickly, for a slightly higher ridge to the west, Hill 210, still remained in the possession of the Japanese, who now brought a heavy and concentrated fire to bear on the newly-won Marine positions.

As this sustained enemy fire continued throughout the night, casualties became so heavy that a company from 2/7, the 1st Marines' reserve battalion, had to be rushed up the hill to bolster the depleted strength of the defenders. An overwhelming Japanese counterattack to retake this vital terrain probably was prevented only by the well-placed naval salvos on the enemy-held approaches to Hill 200. Elsewhere, however, the alert foe spotted the gap that developed between the 1st and 2d Battalions as they tied in their lines after dark. Infiltrating in force, the Japanese began exploiting their opportunity. Not until another reserve company from 2/7 fought its way forward into positions covering this void in the 1st Marines' line was the enemy finally contained.

During this same night, Colonel Nakagawa displaced his CP farther inland to a cave deep within his prepared final defensive perimeter in the Umurbrogol ridges. Such a move by the enemy commander underscored the tactical importance of the Marines' seizure of Hill 200. This accomplishment of the 2d Battalion removed a dangerous Japanese salient and replaced it with an American one jutting into the enemy-held terrain; the feat also eliminated the heavy flanking fire that had been hampering the progress of 2/1 and the 5th Marines. All that Colonel Nakagawa admitted to his superiors that night, though, was that "under protection of heavy naval gunfire, an enemy unit composed of two tanks and approximately two companies of infantry successfully advanced up to a high spot on the east side of *Nakayama* (Hill 200)."[18]

On 18 September, the same day that the 7th Marines finished its seizure of the promontories and the 5th Marines began its sweep up the northeastern peninsula, the 1st Marines returned to its bitterly-contested, yard-by-yard assault on the central ridges. Some of the

---

[18] *Japanese CenPacOps*, p. 87.

difficulties involved in fighting over this terrain, according to Lieutenant Colonel Spencer S. Berger, whose 2/7 joined the struggle on the Umurbrogols that day, were:

> ... there was no such thing as a continuous attacking line. Elements of the same company, even platoon, were attacking in every direction of the compass, with large gaps in between. When companies were asked for front lines they were apt to give points where the Company Commander knew or thought he had some men. It did not mean that he held a continuous unbroken line across his front. There were countless little salients and countersallents existing.[19]

Three days of continuous assault on fortified positions had so depleted Colonel Puller's rifle battalions—the 1st Regiment had suffered 1,236 casualties —that frontline replacements were absolutely essential, if the attack was to continue. To remedy the situation, Puller ordered the supporting units stripped of personnel to fill the gaps in his rifle platoons. Out of the 473 men jumping off in the 3d Battalion's zone on the 18th, for example, 200 were fresh from regimental headquarters. The 1st Pioneer Battalion also sent up 115 men to strengthen the assaults units. Just prior to the morning's attack, the 2d Battalion, 7th Marines relieved 1/1, which then passed into reserve.

The 3d Battalion moved forward on the left between the central ridges and the western coast against only scattered rifle fire, but was held to a day's gain of merely a few hundred yards because of the necessity of remaining tied in with 2/7. This battalion found the going slow in the center over the rugged coral ridges, where it cooperated with 2/1 in pinching out the enemy-held Hill 210 that jutted into the Marines' lines. The attackers stormed up both sides of this threatening salient, and their determined rushes finally carried the crest.

In 2/1's zone, the Japanese had been subjecting the riflemen on the northern slopes of Hill 200 to severe artillery and mortar fire in addition to savage counterattacks. By 1400, the battalion had withdrawn its men a short distance from its hard-won conquest of the previous day after reporting that its situation was desperate. Puller's reaction was typical. He instructed Lieutenant Colonel Honsowetz to hold at all costs. Marine mortars immediately placed a smoke screen on the hill to obscure Japanese vision, while Company B of 1/1 was ordered forward from its reserve area to assist.

This rifle unit aggressively assaulted the nearby enemy-held ridges in an attempt to divert fire from the sorely-pressed Marines on Hill 200. The closest ridge, Hill 205, was seized with light casualties, but when the riflemen attempted to press the attack toward the next row of commanding heights, they ran into the precipitous coral rampart that marked the perimeter of Colonel Nakagawa's final defensive positions. Unable to scale the almost sheer cliffs in the face of withering fire from Japanese entrenched on high ground both to the front and flanks, Company B was stopped cold. This failure terminated the day's action. On the extreme right of 2/1, meanwhile, some Marines had succeeded in moving along the base of Hill 200 to reach the ruined village of

---

[19] *Berger ltr.*

Asias and to tie in with the 5th Marines before halting for the night.

This day's assault pushed the 1st Marines' total casualties over the 1,500 mark, but the regiment had straightened its frontline, located the Japanese weakness along the western shore, and discovered the strongpoint of enemy resistance within the Umurbrogols. Puller would order an all-out attack the following morning in hopes of breaching Colonel Nakagawa's defensive positions among the ridges, but the high tide mark of the southern assault had been reached. Henceforth, the Marines were committed to a bitter war of attrition with a fanatical and tenacious foe, who had converted the jumbled coral cliffs, ravines, and precipices of the Umurbrogols into a nearly impregnable fortress.

CASUALTIES, CORPSMEN, AND CLIMATE[20]

To speed evacuation of the wounded during the assault, medical planners arranged for the empty amphibian vehicles to carry casualties on the return trip from the beach to the transfer line. Here, waiting boats finished transporting the injured Marines the rest of the way to the ships. Those LVTs and DUKWs evacuating men to whom minutes meant the difference between life and death made a beeline for the nearest transport still flying the signal flag that indicated empty beds, and then hurried back to the line of transfer to resume their primary task. So successfully did this humane plan work that wounded Marines were being treated on ships within an hour of the initial landing. An unfortunate drawback, however, was that the unexpectedly large number of casualties right from the start tied up an excessive number of amphibian tractors. As a result, the shortage of LVTs and DUKWs was intensified, and later waves of troops and supplies were delayed in being transported across the reef and onto the beach.

For support of the combat teams, Company A of the 1st Medical Battalion was attached to the 1st Marines, Company B to the 5th, and Company C to the 7th, while a surgical team from Company D was especially assigned to 3/5 for its later Ngesebus operation. These medical companies had come ashore early, but their equipment had been delayed in landing. Not until 21 September were any of them set up and operating with adequate hospital facilities. Prior to this date, the units aided the shore party in collecting and evacuating the wounded, and provided replacements for the RCTs' organic medical personnel, who had suffered severe losses.

Although 40 hospital corpsmen and 96 stretcher bearers accompanied each combat team, the high initial casualty rate quickly revealed a need for more. The stretcher bearers, fortunately, had received actual practice in first aid during the staging period, and they formed a nucleus of trained personnel when rear echelon troops were pressed into service. These men came from all supporting and garrison units for, as the

---

[20] Sources of medical data particularly consulted for this section include: *IIIAC Palaus Rpt*, Encl J, "Medical Report of Palaus Operation"; *1st MarDiv SAR*, Phase II, Anx D, "Medical."

CLOSE FIGHTING at edge of Peleliu airfield. (USMC 95260)

CASUALTY is hoisted aboard amtrac en route to hospital ship off Peleliu. (USMC 94940)

G-1 officer remarked, "I had no difficulty in obtaining volunteers for this important task, so anxious were the 'rear area' men to aid their infantry 'brothers.' "[21]

Over and above the toll exacted by the seemingly ubiquitous enemy fire, there were the many victims of the tropical island itself. "Peleliu is a horrible place,"[22] remarked a civilian correspondent, and Marines echoed his sentiments. The blazing sun, stifling heat, jagged coral, rugged terrain, and lack of readily available water all combined to make the island a living hell.

Heat exhaustion cases increased alarmingly as the fighting progressed, and stocks of salt tablets ashore quickly disappeared. Since they "were worth their weight in gold in preventing heat exhaustion,"[23] all salt tablets that the support ships could spare were sent ashore. Although several combat commanders believed that they lost as many men to the enervating heat as to enemy fire, no definite count of such casualties existed.[24] The high incidence of heat prostration cases, nevertheless, severely overloaded the limited medical facilities

and incapacitated valuable, trained Marines during the critical assault phase.

Compounding the unpleasantness of Peleliu was the unforgettable "sickening stench of decaying bodies which added to the difficulties under which the troops fought."[25] Not enough men could be spared during the first few days to collect and bury the dead whose bodies lay where they fell, exposed to the elements and insects. To prevent the spreading of disease by flies, three 15-men sanitary squads, equipped with knapsack sprayers, came ashore on D-Day and followed the combat teams, carefully spraying the newly-developed insecticide, DDT, on opened enemy supply dumps, bodies, uncovered human feces, and other fly-feeding and breeding places. Twelve days later when the tactical situation permitted, low-flying aircraft dusted all of Peleliu with DDT, while the malaria control unit operated a truck-mounted power sprayer in the swamps and other suspected areas.

Peleliu was the scene of the first large-scale combat testing of DDT as a sanitation control agent. All mosquito nets and jungle hammocks were treated with a combination of DDT and kerosene, as were tents and other personnel shelters that came into use later. Sanitation experts soon made the discovery, however, that while the new insecticide worked excellently against adult flies and mosquitoes, it proved ineffective in killing the larvae. As a result, flies continued to breed, despite the combined efforts of planes, trucks, and portable DDT sprayers. In fact, the swarms

---

[21] Col Harold O. Deakin ltr to CMC, dtd 10Mar50, in *Peleliu Comment File*. Negro Marines from the 16th Field Depot "were most proficient in this type of activity. All Unit Commanders praised their efficiency, zeal and cheerfulness in performing their duties." *1st MarDiv SAR*, Phase II, Anx D, p. 3.

[22] Robert Martin in *Time*, 16Oct44, p. 38.

[23] Col Richard P. Ross, Jr., memo to Maj Frank O. Hough, dtd 7Nov49, hereafter *Ross memo*.

[24] Most heat prostration cases were usually treated at the medical aid stations close to the front, where no records were kept.

---

[25] *Ross memo*.

of flies exceeded anything that American troops had seen to date. During the second week in October, a gradual decline in the fly population set in. Apparently, the exertions of the DDT sprayers had not been in vain. "Probably for the first time in the history of military operations," stated the corps after-action report, "there had been a negligible number of casualties that could be attributed to flies or mosquitoes."[26]

SUPPORTING THE DRIVE INLAND[27]

For the first few days on Peleliu, conditions for rendering effective logistic support to the assault units left much to be desired. The inadequate beach space for receiving the mountains of materiel required to keep the advance alive permitted little organization of the support area. Supply dumps, bivouac areas, artillery emplacements, and equipment were located helter-skelter on the first piece of unoccupied land. This random location of logistical activities made more difficult the tasks of coordinating and controlling resupply missions, undertakings which were frequently delayed because motor vehicles had severed vital telephone lines. Marines under enemy fire soon discovered that it was much faster to lay a new line than to search for a broken one. Adding to the cluttered appearance of the beachhead were the countless foxholes and shell craters that pockmarked the entire area.

When Rear Admiral John W. Reeves, Jr., responsible for the future base development of the Western Carolines Area, visited Peleliu shortly after D-Day, he was appalled by what he saw. The admiral at once requested through higher channels that certain artillery batteries be displaced immediately to allow supply dumps to occupy their permanent locations in accordance with the base development plan. General Rupertus, however, countered with the argument that these batteries firing from their present positions were essential in order to support the infantry and that it would be folly to tamper with an already critical tactical situation just to simplify some future garrison function. Since the recommendations of the ground commander are usually accepted during the combat phase, nothing ever came of Admiral Reeves' complaint.

As the assault troops pushed inland, regimental dumps displaced forward to support the attack. The Marines were fortunate in that the island's roads were capable, at least temporarily, of handling the division's transportation needs. For hauling supplies up to the front, each regiment had four LVTs, augmented by six 2½-ton cargo trucks once they became available.

---

[26] *IIIAC Palaus Rpt*, Encl J, "Medical Report of Palaus Operation," p. 5. One chaplain, however, clearly remembered "the havoc dysentery worked with the troops—almost equal to the heat and shells—and how everyone from the top down blamed it on the flies." LCdr Byron E. Allender ltr to CMC, dtd 8Feb50, in *Peleliu Comment File*.

[27] Additional sources used for this section are: *5th Mar Sup-EvacRpt*; Blackford, "Giants at Peleliu;" BuDocks, *Building the Navy's Bases in World War II: History of the Bureau of Yards and Docks and the Civil Engineer Corps 1940-1946*, 2 vols. (Washington: GPO, 1947), hereafter BuDocks, *World War II Hist.*

To facilitate unloading at the beach, a detachment of the 1054th Naval Construction Battalion (Seabees) began installing a pontoon causeway from Orange Beach 3 to the outer reef on 18 September, and the first LST unloaded over it on the following day. When additional pontoon causeways were added at the reef, the simultaneous unloading of three LSTs became possible. By 21 September, when the need for more unloading points became pressing, elements of the 1st Engineer Battalion and the 73d Seabees began work on access roads leading to the eastern and southern beaches. Two days later, both these beach areas were receiving LSTs for unloading.

On 19 September, the 33d Seabees started clearing the Peleliu airfield of all land mines, duds, debris, and shell fragments. Once the heavy engineering equipment began coming ashore, work on the repair of the existing fighter strip was immediately begun. Within 72 hours after having received the construction equipment on 20 September, the Seabees had cleared and leveled an operative strip, 260 feet by 3,875 feet, complete with runway lights.

The 1st Pioneer Battalion continued its shore party function, often unloading around the clock, until 28 September, when stevedores of the Island Command took over the beaches and supply dumps. While engaged in performing their assigned mission, the pioneers operated bulldozers on two different occasions to knock out enemy-held pillboxes; they supplied frontline troops directly from the shore dumps, often going to great lengths to locate vitally needed items; and once they even relinquished their own machine guns to fill an urgent infantry request.

Although during the initial phases of the landing no infantryman or artilleryman suffered from lack of ammunition —thanks to the acuity of the logistic planners and their innovations such as the waterborne supply beach—Marines found it difficult to build up desirable levels of 105mm and 81mm ammunition, as well as 60mm illuminating shells. Selective discharge of these needed items took place the day after the first ammunition resupply ship dropped anchor at Kossol Roads on 21 September. The high rate of ammunition expenditure continued, however, because of the strength of the enemy's defenses. The heavy fighting also resulted in many weapons being either damaged in combat or lost through carelessness. The 5th Marines, for example, had lost or damaged over 70 percent of its flamethrowers and bazookas by 17 September. In spite of the heavy fighting, which demanded large amounts of ammunition, weapons, and supplies, and the unforeseen beach congestion, which seriously hindered resupply operations, no real shortages of shells, weapons, or supplies developed during the first couple of weeks.

TACTICAL SUPPORT[28]

Until Marine artillery was emplaced ashore on Peleliu and could assume responsibility for providing direct fire support to the infantry battalions, carrier-based aircraft had to fill part of the gap. As early as 17 September, how-

---

[28] An additional source used for this section was *11th MarOpRpt*.

ever, the reduction of all targets, except those in defilade or on reverse slopes, became the exclusive province of the artillery, and, by the 21st, almost all air missions were of the deep support type. On the whole, Marines were satisfied with the kind of air support given them by the naval pilots, but felt that their attempts to strafe were "of little value, due to the fact that the strafing runs were begun and completed at too high an altitude; pullouts from such never were made under 1,800 feet."[29]

One other vexation was that some naval officers, prior to the landing, had led the Marines to expect too much from the use of napalm, considered at that time somewhat of a miracle weapon following its limited employment during the Marianas campaign. One briefing officer ever assured 1/7 that its assault to the south on Peleliu would encounter the infantryman's dream, "an objective stripped of concealing vegetation and devoid of live enemy soldiers."[30] The disappointment experienced by these Marines when they ran into some 1,500 elite Japanese troops who tenaciously resisted the southward advance can be imagined. Later, after the results of the first extensive use of napalm had been analyzed, the division recommended that the new weapon "should be used either on pinpoint targets or in such quantities that complete saturation of an area can be achieved. It is wasted when used in small quantities in area bombing."[31]

Carrier-based planes also provided aerial observation until Marine Observation Squadron-3 (VMO-3), whose first planes touched down on the partially repaired airstrip on 18 September, began operating ashore. The 11th Marines' battalions, in addition, had forward observers up with the advance infantry units. Since the officers coordinating the missions of air, naval gunfire, and artillery were all located at the division CP, each prospective target was assigned to the supporting arm best suited to reduce it.

For the first two weeks ashore, Marine artillery performed according to the operation plan, delivering preparatory, harassing, and interdicting fires as requested. When corps artillery came ashore on the second day, it was placed under control of the 11th Marines and tied in with the regimental fire direction center. Most artillery units massed their fires northward to support the assault on the ridges, but the 3d Battalion and a battery of the 3d 155mm Howitzer Battalion faced south to assist the 7th Marines' drive to the promontories. On 18 September, these units also shifted their fires northward against the entrenched Japanese amidst the central ridges. One battery of the 8th 155mm Gun Battalion, meanwhile, had taken up firing positions in anticipation of providing supporting fires for the 81st Infantry Division's landing on 17 September, but the expected call never came and this unit also faced about on the following day.

As a close support weapon on Peleliu, armor ranked just behind artillery, and far ahead of air or naval gunfire. "Tanks were so invaluable during the

---
[29] *1st MarDiv SAR*, Phase I, Anx L, pp. 4–5.
[30] *Worden ltr.*
[31] *1st MarDiv SAR*, Phase II, Anx L, p. 6.

first few days that tank units enroute to support designated units were repeatedly intercepted by other units in dire straits which would beg for tank assistance."[32] Whenever possible, this aid was given by the tankers before continuing on to their assigned destinations. Until the 155mm guns came ashore, the Shermans provided the only flat-trajectory, high-powered weapon that proved effective in sealing caves, blasting pillboxes, and reducing other fortifications. In fact, the tanks served as mobile artillery.

Because of the elaborate enemy underground defenses and the high value that Marines placed upon tank support, the Peleliu operation resulted in the longest continuous commitment in action experienced by any Marine tank battalion up to that time. The Shermans were seldom in reserve, even in the later stages, and often had to rearm several times daily. Their ammunition expenditure on D-Day, for example, was so high that an advance on the following day was possible only after shells were salvaged from damaged vehicles.

Throughout the campaign, supporting armor fought together with the assault troops as a team; only on three minor occasions did tanks ever advance without accompanying infantry. Because of the Shermans' better communication system and their constant presence near rifle units, division frequently made use of the tank radios to locate infantry elements or to pass on instructions to them.

Owing to mutual respect and admiration, the teamwork between the riflemen and the tankers was superb, and each went to heroic lengths to support the other. On one occasion, a rifle squad protecting the advance of a tank platoon melted away under enemy mortar fire until only two survivors remained, but these infantrymen doggedly kept on with their task of shepherding the Shermans. As if in an attempt to match the undaunted courage of their supporting infantrymen, the tankers reciprocated by risking both their bodies and their vehicles to aid hard-pressed Marines. Whenever the job could not be done any other way, the Shermans maneuvered into the most vulnerable positions, and crew members fought with part of their bodies protruding from the tanks' interiors to gain better observation. Indicative of the danger inherent in this practice was the high casualty rate among the tank battalion's officers. Eight out of the total 31 were killed, and only eight emerged from the long harrowing campaign unscathed. No Sherman was ever lost to close-in enemy assaults, however, for not even suicidal-minded Japanese, lugging bangalore torpedoes or demolition charges, ever succeeded in breaking through the protective screen of Marine riflemen.

The Marines especially valued the tanks for their ability to quickly and safely reduce enemy fortifications that proved impervious to either infantry weapons or assaults. With their heavy armored plates warding off the hail of deadly automatic fire from Japanese fortifications, the Shermans could move up to pointblank range. After firing three or four rounds of high explosives, the gunner would shift to white phosphorus shells, a few of which usually

---

[32] *Stuart ltr.*

silenced all enemy resistance. One tank crew actually destroyed 30 pillboxes and fortified positions within a single day's action.

Often, two Shermans would work in coordination with the thin-skinned LVT flamethrower to remove a particularly difficult position. After moving up and blasting the enemy fortification, the tanks would lay down covering fire while the flamethrower placed itself in between the protective hulls of the Shermans and burned out the target.

As an experiment, a small capacity flamethrower was installed in a Sherman, but the short range of the burst necessitated the tank's moving in at such close range that it became vulnerable to close-in enemy assaults, against which it was helpless since its bow machine gun had been removed to permit installation of the flamethrower. Primarily because of its lack of success in combat, this specially-equipped tank destroyed only a few enemy fortifications, and its assigned missions were more like battlefield experiments than anything else.

Another innovation tried by the 1st Tank Battalion on Peleliu was spaced armor. While still in the staging area, the tankers welded spare track over the turret and front slope plate of each Sherman, since earlier tests had demonstrated that this technique would increase the vehicle's resistance to both armor-piercing and large high-explosive projectiles. This unique use of spare track proved extremely effective and was officially credited with preventing the destruction of three tanks from direct hits by 75mm armor-piercing projectiles.

Without question, however, the most significant armored innovation on Peleliu was the flexible basis of tank employment. Previously, a tank company was attached to a rifle regiment and remained with it throughout the campaign regardless of whether the unit was in reserve or fighting over terrain unsuitable for tank employment. For the initial assault, Company A of the 1st Tank Battalion was attached to the 1st Marines, Company B to the 5th, and Company C to the 7th, but even after control reverted to the battalion commander on 16 September, the tank units still remained in direct support of the regiments. The radical departure from previous tank employment doctrine came when the insufficient number of Shermans within the division resulted in a widespread shifting of tanks and crews. Although the tank company commanders and liaison personnel remained permanently attached to the various regiments to insure continuity of liaison, the tank platoons were freely shifted from one rifle unit to another to replace battle losses, support a major effort, or take advantage of terrain suitable for tracked vehicle operations. The new policy proved its worth, since the maximum utilization of the limited number of tanks was realized.

The 1st Tank Battalion also experienced certain difficulties on Peleliu, for an "overoptimistic logistic concept of the Palau Operation resulted in an entirely inadequate amount of spare parts and maintenance equipment being taken forward."[33] Only by the salvaging of parts from damaged vehicles was the

---

[33] *1st MarDiv SAR*, Phase II, Anx J, p. 9.

average of 20 operative tanks maintained throughout the campaign. Moreover, the repair crews suffered considerable casualties while stripping the immobile tanks under the identical enemy fire that had knocked them out. "Additional spare parts," the tank battalion reported, "would have saved both men and time."[34] Just three tanks equipped with bulldozer blades and one tank retriever were landed, but they quickly proved invaluable. Besides serving to clear away debris and to fill antitank ditches, the tank-dozers were found to be quite useful in sealing up apertures of Japanese bunkers while the occupants were still active and firing.

Like the tankers, the combat engineers, including Headquarters and Service Company of the 1st Engineer Battalion, landed with the infantry regiments to which they were attached. Even after reverting to battalion control on 26 September, the engineers still worked closely with the assault troops. Often, details of combat engineers went forward of front lines to hack out trails, clear away mines and boobytraps, or blast enemy-held caves and fortifications. As the official report stated, demolitions proved to be "the greatest engineer problem."[35] One demolition team attached to 3/1 was credited with killing over 200 Japanese during a five-day period of neutralization of enemy pillboxes and caves. These demolition experts also cleared away coral heads that impeded the landing of amphibian vehicles, blasted water wells in the coral subsurface, deactivated duds and boobytraps, and cleared the beaches and access roads of all mines.

DEADLOCK AMIDST THE RIDGES[36]

By the fifth day of the assault, practically all those Japanese who were able to withdraw before the swift onslaught of the Marines had rejoined Colonel Nakagawa's main forces in the Umurbrogols. Here, according to General Inoue's master plan, the decisive struggle for Peleliu would be waged. In contrast to earlier Pacific campaigns, no large-scale *banzai* charge was contemplated. General Inoue had specifically warned the Peleliu Island Commander against wasting his battle strength in futile attacks; instead, Colonel Nakagawa was instructed to defend his hold on the high ground to the last man in an attempt to deny, or at least delay, the use of the airfield to the invading Americans. As long as some of the Japanese remained in their fortified positions, hidden high-velocity guns could bombard the airstrip, or suicide squads armed with high explosives could sally forth to wreak havoc on the runways. As a result, the advancing Marines were forced to assault each enemy emplacement individually, while Japanese artillery and mortar fire continued its rain of death and destruction along the front and to the rear.

At 0700 on 19 September, the attack was resumed along the entire 1st Ma-

---

[34] *Ibid.*
[35] *1st MarDiv SAR*, Phase II, Anx I, p. 3.

[36] Additional sources used for this section are: *1st Mar Hist; 1/1 UHist; 3/1 Rec of Events*, 19–23Sep44; *7th Mar R–2 Jnl*, 19–22 Sep44; *1/7 HistRpt*, 19–22Sep44; *2/7 WarD*, 19–22Sep44; *3/7 WarD*, 19–22Sep44.

rines' front. Colonel Puller had received no new directives; his regiment still had the assigned mission of seizing the high terrain up to phase line 0-2. The 3d Battalion, unmolested except by snipers, moved up the western coastal flats for some 400 yards before halting in order to retain contact with neighboring units advancing more slowly over the ridges. Here, 2/7, still under operational control of the 1st Marines, overcame stiff resistance to seize the forward slopes of Hills 200 and 260, for a day's gain of 300 yards. Company A of 1/1 passed through to press the attack, but it ran headlong into a sheer 150-foot cliff which, coupled with heavy enemy fire, stopped the assault cold. Only six men out of the entire rifle company managed to regain 2/7's lines without either being killed or wounded.

It was the 2d Battalion, however, that first tested the strength of Colonel Nakagawa's final bastion. After a 500-yard advance in the face of increasing enemy resistance, the foremost assault units encountered the same foreboding hill mass that had blunted the attack of Company B the previous day. This dominating piece of terrain became known as the Five Sisters, because it contained five peaks; they averaged 250 feet in height and were separated from each other by steep cliffs. The southern face was at first dubbed "Bloody Nose Ridge" by the Marines. No sooner had the battalion consolidated its forward positions than it launched a full-scale assault directly at the forbidding height.

Preparatory air and artillery strikes thoroughly plastered both the forward and reverse slopes of the hill mass, while all tanks and mortars attached to 2/7 were brought over to support the all-out effort of Honsowetz' battalion. Rushing forward in small groups to minimize casualties from the terrific enemy fire, the Marines grimly fought their way ahead, and their Shermans, mortars, and LVT flamethrowers ventured as far forward as possible to provide direct fire support. Despite the vigor and determination with which the riflemen pressed the assault, it collapsed completely by noon. Even the most pessimistic Marine present there that day did not dream that the defenders of the Five Sisters would frustrate all attempts to storm them for over two months.

Later in the afternoon, the attack was resumed. This time, the battalion commander committed all three of his rifle companies in a frontal assault, meanwhile attempting an enveloping movement from the east with Company C of 1/1, fresh from regimental reserve. If this force could seize Hill 100 (later to be christened Walt Ridge) whose summit dominated the East Road and adjoining swampy terrain, a springboard would be gained for an attack on the hill mass from the rear.

Captain Everett P. Pope led the 90 men of Company C through a swamp on the right flank of 2/1 to emerge on the East Road. No sooner had the group begun assault operations against two large pillboxes discovered near the base of Walt Ridge, than a Japanese machine gun opened up from the right flank across a small pond some 50 yards away. Pinned down without any hopes of reaching the enemy gunner, whose accuracy inflicted numerous casualties,

Captain Pope finally withdrew his men for another try along a different approach.

The concentrated Japanese fire, meanwhile, was exacting a stiff toll among the exposed men of the 2d Battalion as they struggled toward the towering Five Sisters. The losses within two of the rifle companies that afternoon became so great that they were combined in the field into a still-understrength company, even though a squad of men from the 4th War Dog Platoon had been thrown in as a reinforcement.

It was late afternoon before Company C, now supported by the division reconnaissance company, was in position to renew its assault on Walt Ridge. This time, Captain Pope planned to approach by way of a causeway over a large sinkhole and to continue up the East Road to the base of the objective. Armor was scheduled to spearhead the advance, but the first Sherman to venture onto the narrow causeway slipped off to one side, while a following tank also lost its traction and slid off the other side.

Since the partially-blocked route barred the approach of additional tanks, Captain Pope's men did the only thing left to them. Crossing the exposed causeway in squad rushes, the riflemen raced on to the base of the ridge, paused briefly to catch their breaths, and then assaulted directly up the slopes. With only machine gun and mortar fire supporting them, the climbers clawed and pulled their way up the rugged slides, and the swiftness of their attack took the enemy by surprise. The Marines carried the crest, but, to their disappointment, they immediately received extremely heavy fire from positions about 50 yards up the ridgeline, where the Japanese held a knoll that completely dominated the newly-won terrain.

Reluctant to abandon the summit that had cost them so many dead and wounded, the men of Company C held out in their isolated and exposed positions throughout the night, while the enraged foe hurled everything he had into the struggle in a desperate bid to oust the Marines from the vital crest. Machine gun bullets crisscrossed the entire ridgetop, and large-caliber shells and mortar rounds plummeted down from above with devastating effect. Using the darkness as a shield, Japanese infantry moved forward to launch one savage counterattack after another. Before dawn arrived to bring surcease to the besieged Marines, they had expended all of their ammunition and were forced to use their fists, broken ammunition boxes, and chunks of coral to hurl their assailants back down the slopes. Only Captain Pope and 15 men remained when the first light of morning revealed to the weary survivors that the enemy had moved up machine guns, which now opened with deadly effect. Since the Marines' positions were clearly untenable in the face of this new threat, permission was granted to withdraw.

That morning, 20 September, the 1st and 2d Battalions of Puller's regiment combined in a final all-out effort to retake Walt Ridge. Every available supporting arm, from LVT(A)s to 37mm guns, was brought up as far as possible, while regimental headquarters was stripped of personnel to bolster the depleted ranks of the assault units. Even a provisional company was formed of cooks, wiremen, and supply handlers, who manned 12 machine guns in support of the attack.

Somehow the weary Marines, already exhausted physically and mentally by five days of constant assault over rugged terrain and against fanatical resistance, summoned up enough reserve energy and courage to make another valiant attempt. One private remembered the ensuing assault that sixth day, when he and his comrades were waved forward toward the towering ridges by their sergeant:

> 'Let's get killed up on that high ground there,' he said. 'It ain't no good to get it down here.' As the men stumbled out for him, he said, 'That's the good lads.'
> The whole motley lot—a fighting outfit only in the minds of a few officers in the First Regiment and in the First Division —started up the hill. I have never understood why. Not one of them refused. They were the hard core—the men who couldn't or wouldn't quit. They would go up a thousand blazing hills and through a hundred blasted valleys, as long as their legs would carry them. They were Marine riflemen.[37]

Their bold rushes that day carried some of them to positions so advanced that the Marines killed in the fighting could not be removed for many more days. Their heroic sacrifice was in vain, however, for the seized ground proved untenable in the face of the concentrated and sustained enemy fire, which had already knocked out so many tanks and other supporting arms. "Despite the intense barrage, weapons which were not hit continued firing. The mortars glowed red, and machine guns blew up, but those that could, continued to fire."[38]

An accurate, if terse, account of the day's furious struggle was contained in Colonel Nakawaga's report to General Inoue that night:

> Since dawn, the enemy has been concentrating their forces . . . vainly trying to approach *Higashiyama* [Walt Ridge] and *Kansokuyama* [Hill 300] with 14 tanks and one infantry battalion under the powerful aid of air and artillery fire. However, they were again put to rout receiving heavy losses.[39]

That afternoon, the battered Marines of the 1st and 2d Battalions were relieved in their frontline positions by 1/7, while 3/7 replaced 2/7. The 3d Battalion, 1st Marines, still remained in its zone along the western coast for two more days, but the rest of the regiment had sustained too many losses and been strained too often to the breaking point during the battle of the ridges to be effective in any further assault effort.

On 21 September, two companies of the relatively fresh 1/7 moved up the East Road in column to attempt recapture of Walt Ridge. The lead unit, Company C, which was scheduled to make the assault, passed over the causeway, still partially blocked by the immobilized Shermans, and continued up the road

---

[37] Russell Davis, *Marine at War* (Boston: Little, Brown and Company, 1961), pp. 113, 114, used with permission.

[38] *1st Mar Hist*, p. 15.
[39] *Japanese CenPacOps*, p. 88.

to the point where it skirted the base of the objective. Here, supporting tanks, which had to bypass the causeway sinkhole, joined the advance.

As the leading elements of Company C came abreast of the ridge, enemy fire increased, and when the assault up the eastern slope began, the Japanese greeted the Marines with a mortar barrage that completely blanketed them. Soldiers in the caves above sprayed the scrambling Marines with automatic fire and lobbed grenades down on them, while artillery pieces, cunningly concealed on nearby high ground and impossible to spot, blasted the attackers. Weakened by excessive losses and unable even to hold the ground gained, the Marines evacuated the hillside and returned with their support unit, Company A, to the battalion lines, where Company B had remained poised all day.

On the same day, 3/7 assaulted over the ridges in the center. After a fast start, the progress, "for the rest of the day was slow and tedious and measured in yards."[40] Since it was evident that the only real gains would be made over the level ground, the battalions' zones were shifted, which narrowed 3/1's front and permitted this left flank unit to exploit the enemy's weakness in the area without breaking contact. Before 3/1 was relieved two days later, it succeeded in pushing a tank-infantry patrol forward 1,000 yards to reach the village of Garekoru without encountering serious opposition.

The next day, 22 September, the 3d Battalion, 7th Marines, attacked across the left portion of the ridges over terrain that steadily grew more difficult. The day's gain was a mere 80 yards, for skillfully concealed Japanese machine guns pinned the lead units down time and time again. In the center of the ridges, the 2d Battalion, whose exhausted troops had been brought out of reserve, remained on the defensive and did not attempt any offensive action. On the right, however, the 1st Battalion spent most of the day making careful preparation to seize the Five Sisters.

At 1445, after Marine artillery blasted the enemy front with heavy concentrations, Company B of 1/7 moved out in attack, followed by Company A in close support. Riflemen and supporting tanks made their approach to the objective under a screen of smoke laid down by Marine mortars, while Weapons Company blazed away at Walt Ridge in an attempt to confuse the enemy as to the direction of the attack. For the first 250 yards, the riflemen received only sniper fire; then hidden machine guns on the nearby ridges opened up with a murderous stream of fire.

By this time, the foremost Marines had begun venturing into the mouth of a draw, soon to be known as "Death Valley." Its steep walls on both sides were dotted with mutually-supporting enemy gun emplacements and rifle pits. The accompanying Shermans were barred from entering, for the floor of the declivity proved to be mined, but they fired white phosphorus and high-explosive shells into the caves lining the canyon's cliffs as the Marine riflemen pushed on. The Japanese gunners, however, with their clear fields of fire, exacted such a heavy toll that a platoon

---

[40] *3/7 WarD*, 21Sep44.

from Company A was rushed up to bolster the depleted ranks of the assault unit.

The Marines did not venture much farther into the funnel-like canyon before running into a sheer cliff that barred the way. At this point, the lead riflemen were actually within 100 yards of Colonel Nakagawa's CP and the last enemy stronghold to be reduced during the long campaign. Since the precipitous walls on all three sides made any infantry assault of the Japanese cave positions impossible, a withdrawal was ordered to prevent any additional losses from the deadly rain of fire that raked the Marines. The supporting company and its Shermans moved up under a cover of smoke to support the evacuation, and, by 1830, the entire force had withdrawn.

When darkness settled over the battlefield on 22 September, one phase of the Peleliu campaign had ended and another had begun. No longer would Marines, soon to be reinforced by Army troops from Angaur, suffer prohibitive casualties in fruitless frontal assaults on the ridges from the south. Instead, an end run around Colonel Nakagawa's devilishly-designed last-ditch positions would be made up the western coast in search of a better attack route to the final pocket of Japanese resistance.

Although the campaign was to drag on for another two months of bitter fighting, the 1st Marine Division in a week of constant assault had seized the vital airfield, the commanding terrain behind it, and all of the island south of the Umurbrogols. Ample room for the proper deployment of both division and corps artillery had been gained, and all hindrances to unloading over the beaches had been removed, leaving only the weather as an unknown factor.

All of Peleliu containing strategic value had been captured by the Marines, but the cost had been high. Casualties totaled 3,946. These heavy losses eliminated one regiment as an effective assault unit and severely depleted the strength of the other two. The 1st Marines, for instance, suffered 56 percent casualties and, among the nine rifle platoons of its 1st Battalion, not one of the original platoon leaders, and only 74 of the riflemen, remained. As a sergeant remarked upon relief, "This ain't a regiment. We're just survivors."[41]

---

[41] George McMillan *et al, Uncommon Valor: Marine Divisions in Action* (Washington: Infantry Journal Press, 1946), p. 58.

CHAPTER 5

Angaur and Ulithi [1]

ANGAUR: THE MEN AND THE PLAN

On D-Day, while the Marines fought tenaciously to secure a beachhead on Peleliu, the IIIAC landing force scheduled to seize Angaur participated in a feinting movement northward against Babelthuap. The convoy of transports and LSTs carrying the 81st Infantry Division, accompanied by a protective screen of destroyers, hove to off the coast of the huge enemy-held island about noon and began to engage in prelanding activities. Besides serving to confuse the Japanese as to the real target of the American attack, the force afloat provided a handy source of combat-ready troops in the eventuality that the Peleliu landing ran into trouble.

Though still untested in combat, the Army division had been training and preparing for this role for over two years. The insignia of the 81st was an angry wildcat, its nickname was the Wildcat Division, and the men referred to themselves as Wildcats.

Slated for the Pacific Theater and participation in Operation STALE-MATE, the Army division debarked in July 1944 at the Hawaiian Islands, its staging area. While the men topped off their stateside training with amphibious exercises, the staff planners busied themselves with the essential tactical and logistical preparations, coordinating them whenever necessary. The assigned target was Angaur Island, situated just south of Peleliu and possessing extensive low level areas which were considered ideal for the construction of a heavy bomber field.

Like the 1st Marine Division, the 81st found its planning complicated by the changing concept of Operation STALEMATE. The Navy plan for the invasion of the Palaus had called for seizure of Angaur first, to be followed almost immediately by the capture of Peleliu. General Julian Smith, in his dual capacity as Commanding General, Administrative Command, V Amphibious Corps, and Commanding General, Expeditionary Troops, took issue with this concept. He maintained that while Angaur was being attacked, the Japanese would have ample opportunity to reinforce Peleliu from Babelthuap, which was garrisoned by a force estimated at upwards of 25,000 troops. Initial seizure of Peleliu, on the other hand, would cut off Angaur from that source of reinforcement. The Navy accepted this revision of concept, but desiring Angaur for construction of a second airfield, continued throughout to

---

[1] Unless otherwise noted, the material in this section is derived from: 81st InfDiv Op Rpt, The Capture of Angaur Island, 17Sep–22Oct44, dtd 26Dec44, hereafter *81st InfDiv OpRpt—Angaur;* Historical Committee, *81st Infantry Division;* Smith, *Approach to the Philippines;* Morison, *Leyte;* Hough, *Assault on Peleliu.*

162

press for the earliest possible landing on that island.[2]

The plan continued to be revised through 16 September, at which time the last change became effective. On that date, RCT 323, then serving as IIIAC floating reserve, was designated the Ulithi assault force with orders to proceed immediately on its new mission. The Army officers responsible for planning the Angaur operation were at first handicapped by the lack of intelligence about the terrain and the enemy garrison. Fortunately, recently taken aerial photographs, as well as enemy documents captured on Saipan, reached the staff officers in time to help clarify the situation.

As finally evolved, the Angaur landing became a two-pronged assault utilizing two RCTs attacking over separate beaches. Red Beach was located on the northeastern coast of the island; Blue Beach was situated near the center of the east coast (See Map 6). Two thousand yards of rocky shoreline separated the two landing points. Single lines of advance from both beaches to the interior of the island led straight into the thick, tangled undergrowth of the rain forest. Even though these beaches were the least desirable of any on Angaur the decision of Army planners to land at the two widely separated points was based on sound tactical reasons. These were the absence of a fringing reef at the proposed landing sites and the presence of weaker enemy defenses than existed elsewhere on the island.

Major Ushio Goto, the Japanese commander on Angaur, did not have sufficient troops to defend all possible landing points. Even by concentrating his forces to cover only those beaches offering most advantages to an invader, he still had to spread his troops dangerously thin. To thwart the American assault, the major had only his *1st Battalion, 59th Infantry*, for General Inoue had withdrawn the remainder of the Angaur garrison to Babelthuap during the latter part of July in the belief that the larger island was the most likely objective of any Allied attack. Subsequent reinforcements from Babelthuap had brought the total Japanese strength on Angaur to 1,400 men. American intelligence overestimated enemy strength, and planners of the 81st Infantry Division expected to encounter no less than two Japanese battalions totalling 2,500 men. The decision to land two regiments in the initial assault was the direct result of this faulty intelligence.

The Japanese commander decided to rely upon the natural barrier provided by the rain forest and the distance between vital areas of the island to deter any Allied landing over Red and Blue Beaches. If the Americans chose to strike there, Major Goto expected to have ample time to concentrate and deploy his forces for a successful counterattack. The landing beaches selected for the assault were lightly fortified; the more favorable landing sites on Angaur featured elaborate defenses. These consisted of reinforced concrete pillboxes, supporting arms designed to provide clear fields of fire across the beaches, as well as mines, tetrahedrons, and barbed wire barricades. Major Goto had positioned the bulk of the island

---

[2] *Smith interview.*

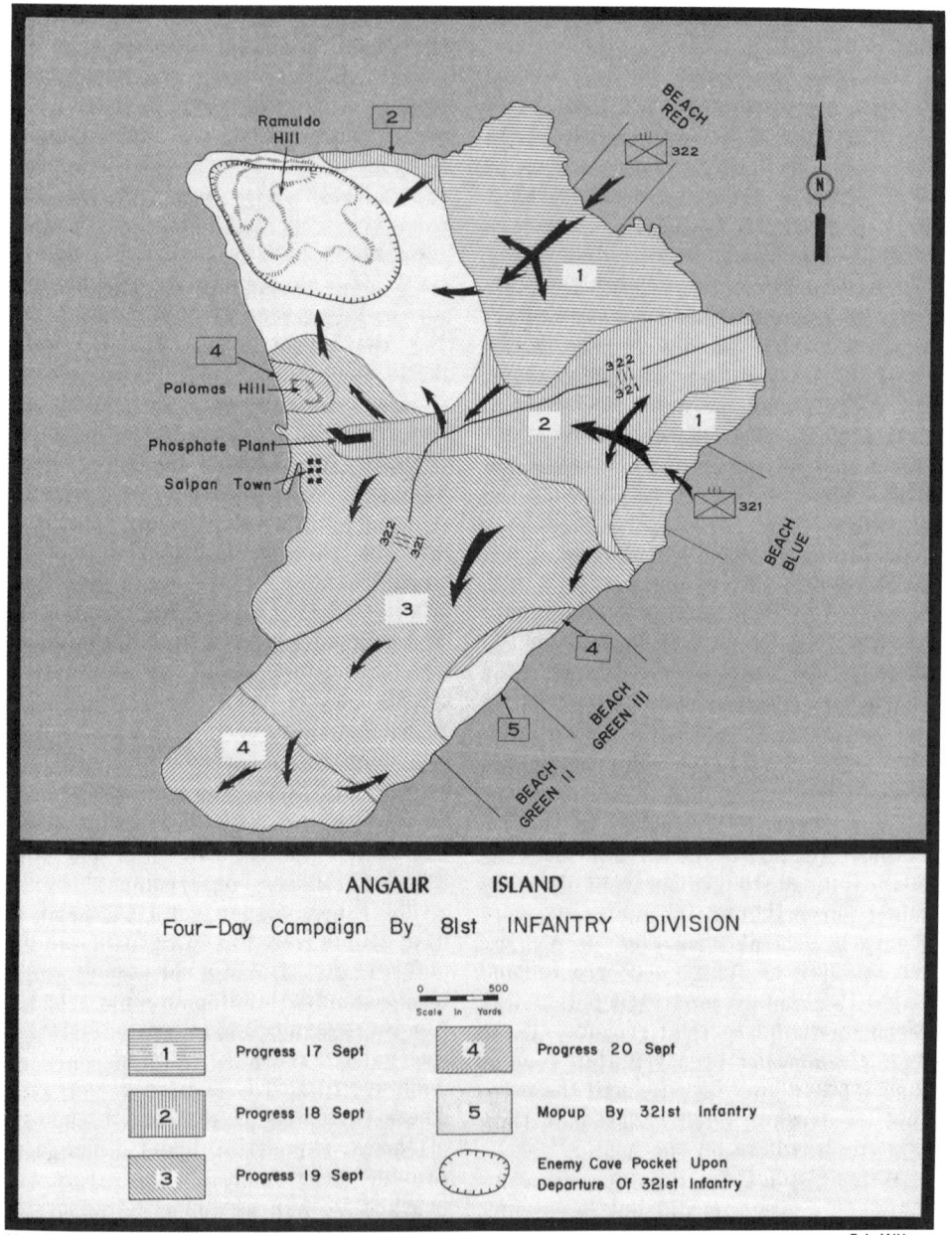

ANGAUR ISLAND
Four-Day Campaign By 81st INFANTRY DIVISION

1	Progress 17 Sept	4	Progress 20 Sept
2	Progress 18 Sept	5	Mopup By 321st Infantry
3	Progress 19 Sept		Enemy Cave Pocket Upon Departure Of 321st Infantry

Map 6

garrison within close supporting distance of the southern, western, and eastern beaches.

Upon completion of last-minute training, the 81st Division sailed from Hawaii on 12 August for Guadalcanal, where it arrived 12 days later. At Cape Esperance the infantrymen made two practice landings, attempting to simulate battlefield conditions on Angaur. In early September the Western Attack Force departed from Guadalcanal for the Palaus. Confidence prevailed among the infantrymen as they neared their first action. "The troops," commented the Army division history, "were as physically fit as any that ever set forth to war."[3] On the coral beaches of Angaur, in the crucible of combat, the truth of this statement was soon to be tested.

On the morning of 12 September, the Western Attack Force moved into position off the Palaus. While other ships proceeded with the task of softening Peleliu's defenses, the two battleships, four light cruisers, and five destroyers of the Angaur Attack Group, commanded by Rear Admiral William H. P. Blandy, began a deliberate and systematic bombardment of their objective. Every known or suspected enemy fortification on the small island was thoroughly blasted by the heavy naval guns, or bombed and strafed by carrier planes flying numerous strikes. Minesweepers and UDT teams, meanwhile, executed their prelanding missions off Red, Blue, and Green Beaches, the latter an alternate landing site.

Early on 15 September, the 1st Marine Division landed on Peleliu and embarked upon its task of wresting a secure beachhead from the defending force. Throughout the day, General Mueller and his men anxiously followed the progress of the assault, for its outcome would determine when the Wildcats would be released from their reserve mission for the Angaur landing. So confident was the Navy that Fox Day, the invasion of Angaur, would be on 16 September that, on the previous evening, in accordance with Navy custom, they fed the soldiers the best evening meal possible, including steak, chicken, frozen strawberries, and other delicacies.[4] The 15th passed, however, without the arrival of the expected order.

The next morning, 16 September, Marines advanced across the runways of the Peleliu airfield, prime objective of the assault. When General Rupertus failed to request reinforcements for his division by noon, higher commanders concluded that the need for the large Army reserve had passed. Moreover, Admiral Blandy had reported that the preliminary bombardments, hydrographic conditions, and UDT preparations all favored a successful landing on Angaur. During the afternoon of 16 September, the commanders of the Western Attack Force (Admiral Fort) and IIIAC (General Geiger) conferred and decided to release the 81st Infantry Division for a landing the following day. This order was issued at 1432, and the division command on board the APA *Fremont* immediately made last

---

[3] Historical Committee, *81st Infantry Division*, p. 65.

[4] *Ibid.*, p. 66.

minute preparations for the Angaur assault, then only 18 hours away.

THE WILDCATS SEIZE THEIR OBJECTIVE[5]

Before dawn on Fox Day, 17 September, the warships of the task group under Rear Admiral Blandy sent shells screaming towards Angaur. The fire support plan employed by the Navy provided for fire from 2 battleships, 4 cruisers, 5 destroyers, 9 LCI(G)s, and 4 LCI(M)s, the latter firing 20mm and 40mm guns, rockets, and mortars.[6] Heavy explosions soon rocked the island. Shortly after 0740, 40 fighter-bombers swept down out of the skies to bomb and strafe enemy positions behind the beaches. At 0810, precisely on schedule, the approach to the shore began. LCIs led the way, blazing away with guns, mortars, and rocket concentrations. The initial assault waves made the journey in LVTs, but following waves were boated in LCVPs and LCMs, for even LSTs could beach with dry ramps on the reef-free shores.

RCT 321 landed with two battalions abreast in columns of companies over Blue Beach at 0830, while RCT 322 did

likewise over Red Beach six minutes later. No entrenched Japanese infantry opposed the landing; the only enemy resistance consisted of sporadic mortar, machine gun, and rifle fire, which caused neither casualties nor damage.

As viewed through the eyes of the Japanese Army commander on Babelthuap, the American invasion of Angaur appeared to be fraught with disaster for the invasion force, and the situation at that island on 17 September was described as follows:

> Under the protection of bombing, strafing, and naval gunfire enemy craft, including battleships, approached as close as 100 meters off the coast and commenced firing. This has been going on since dawn. The enemy launched a landing party of 30 barges at 0800 along our northeastern coast line. However, the Angaur Unit was able to put the enemy to rout and start a state of confusion with the aid of the guns which had been planted there.[7]

Shortly thereafter the Japanese conceded that a second landing attempt was more successful and that by 0900 American forces in a strength of about 2,000 men had taken up positions on land, accompanied by a large group of tanks. The American losses for the first day of operations on Angaur were listed as 30 barges blown up and sunk, 20 barges destroyed, and 15 tanks destroyed, a somewhat unreasonable figure in view of the lack of initial Japanese opposition at the beaches.

The men of the invasion force remained blissfully unaware of the rout and disaster to which the Japanese headquarters staff at Koror had rele-

---

[5] Unless otherwise noted the material in this section is derived from: *81st InfDiv OpRpt—Angaur*; RCT 321 OpRpt, The Capture of Angaur Island, 1Jul–30Sep44, dtd 26Nov44, hereafter *RCT 321 OpRept—Angaur*; RCT 322 OpRpt, Angaur Island—Palaus Group, 1Jul–23Oct44, dtd 1Dec33, hereafter *RCT 322 Op Rpt—Angaur*; *Japanese CenPac Ops*; *Peleliu Comment File*; Historical Committee, *81st Infantry Division*; Smith, *Approach to the Philippines*; Morison, *Leyte*; Hough, *Assault on Peleliu*.

[6] Anx C, 81st InfDiv FO No. 7, dtd 5Aug44.

[7] *Japanese CenPacOps*, p. 87.

U.S. ARMY *81st Infantry Division invades Angaur Island. (USA SC 196034)*

"WILDCATS" *closing in on enemy pocket, Angaur. (USA SC 196033)*

gated them on paper. Rushing across some 20 yards of slightly inclined, rubble-strewn strips of sand to the crest of a low embankment at the edge of the jungle, the Army troops established a firing line. Then, with the beachheads secure, the men plunged headlong into the semi-dark, almost impenetrable undergrowth. Their immediate objective was Phase Line 0–1, some 300 yards inland. On the opposite side of Angaur, meanwhile, the transports carrying RCT 323, the IIIAC floating reserve, were feinting a landing off Saipan Town in hopes of confusing the enemy.

This ruse apparently succeeded. When Major Goto learned of the American landings, he dispatched a rifle company towards the eastern beaches to attack the Americans, but made no move to organize a large-scale counterattack. The Japanese commander's belief that the main assault would come over the southern beaches, where he had deployed the bulk of his troops, may have been further strengthened by the feint landing. At any rate, he did not attempt to shift any of his forces northward. To forestall any such move, American naval gunfire, as well as aerial bombing and strafing, repeatedly hit every potential assembly area on the island throughout the day. These interdictory fires might well have made any regrouping of the forces of Major Goto a disaster and prevented any sizeable counterattack from materializing. While the Japanese defense units prepared for combat, scouts were dispatched to observe the movements of the invasion force. In case the defense was unsuccessful in the daytime, a counterattack was planned for the coming night.[8]

The American assault regiments advanced slowly at first from Red and Blue Beaches. No roads penetrated the almost trackless jungle, whose floor was matted and choked with fallen trees, broken branches, and snarled vines. The sweat-drenched soldiers of the 322d, hacking and groping their way through the undergrowth, found the terrain a much more formidable obstacle than the intermittent mortar, machine gun, and sniper fire from an enemy hidden by the dense foliage. On the beaches, meanwhile, the buildup of men and materiel continued. Upon coming ashore, the medium tanks immediately headed for the frontlines over trails cleared for them by bulldozers. By noon it was apparent that despite the Wildcat's lack of familiarity with combat conditions, they had made a successful amphibious assault. They were now in a position to extend their grip on the island.

Although the advance of RCT 322 was progressing on schedule, the 321st had rough going from the very outset. The regiment encountered strongly held enemy fortifications on its southern flank near Rocky Point, on its northern flank near Cape Ngatpokul, and to its front as well. Expansion of the beachhead proved extremely difficult and time-consuming.

By late afternoon of Fox Day the accomplishments of his regiments failed to measure up to General Mueller's ex-

---

[8] IIIAC C-2 Rpt No. 7, dtd 21Sep44.

pectations. Not all of Phase Line 0-1, which extended from the northern shore of Angaur about 500 yards southwest of Cape Gallatin to a point roughly 250 yards southwest of Rocky Point had been seized. Furthermore, a 700-yard gap still separated the two regiments. Orders issued for the attack that afternoon were intended to rectify this situation. Before nightfall, General Mueller hoped to occupy more favorable positions and ordered his regiments to probe for a possible weak spot in the enemy defenses, particularly in the area separating the two beachheads. The 322d Infantry Regiment was to push forward to Phase Line 0-2, extending generally southward from a point about 400 yards west of 0-1 on the north shore to Green Beach on the eastern shore, with emphasis on achieving a juncture with RCT 321 as soon as possible.

By 1430 the general attack had been resumed, and the soldiers of both regiments pushed forward all along the line. In the vicinity of Blue Beach a combination of naval gunfire and bombing and strafing by supporting aircraft failed to eliminate the Japanese pillboxes impeding the advance of the 321st Infantry Regiment. The task of reducing them fell to the foot soldier. Gingerly picking their way over the rubble-strewn sand, riflemen gained positions from which they furnished protective fire until a portable flamethrower could be brought into action. Once the flaming tongue of napalm started licking at the gunport of a pillbox, demolition teams rushed forward to place their charges. No sooner had the walls of the fortification been breached than the riflemen began crawling towards the next pillbox. Though painfully slow, this method was effective. Dusk found some men of RCT 321 beyond Phase Line 0-1, but both flanks still lagged short of the first objective.

The advance of RCT 322 was progressing smoothly enough in the north, despite the failure of the two assault regiments to effect a juncture. Though RCT 322 managed to establish defensive perimeters along most of Phase Line 0-2 in its zone, it still had not been able to push patrols south far enough to join up with the adjacent unit. Out of necessity, both regiments bent their lines to form separate beachheads.

After a day of incessant pounding by American warships and planes, darkness came as a welcome relief to Major Goto and his men. This respite from the punishing interdiction fires gave the Japanese a chance to recuperate and to move to new defensive positions without fear of American interference. Like Colonel Nakagawa on Peleliu, the *Angaur Sector Unit* commander had received specific orders from General Inoue not to waste his men in any savage but short-lived *banzai* charges. Instead, Major Goto was to delay the capture of Angaur as long as possible. Once it had become clear beyond any doubt that the Americans were making their major drive over the northeastern beaches, Major Goto planned to withdraw his garrison forces from the southern part of the island and concentrate them in the hills that dotted the northwest portion of Angaur. Here, amidst the highest and most rugged coral ridges on the island, the Japanese garrison commander would make his final stand.

The Wildcats, weary both physically and emotionally from their first taste of combat, found little relief during the hours of darkness. Not only did small enemy patrols probe and jab at the perimeters of both regiments, but Japanese infiltrators continually attempted to penetrate the frontlines. To add to the confusion of the first night, the soldiers of the 81st, like all untried troops, engaged in indiscriminate firing at imagined targets.[9]

The next morning, in a predawn attack, a reinforced Japanese company smashed into the extreme southern flank of 1/321, forcing the Wildcats back some 50 to 75 yards. Nevertheless, the faltering lines soon rallied, and by 0618 division received word that the Japanese counterattack had been stopped. Any premature hope that the attack could now be resumed was doomed when it became apparent that the Japanese had broken off their initial counterattack only in order to regroup. Before long they struck again with renewed vigor and the men of the 1st Battalion were quickly initiated into the ferocity of close combat with a fanatical and determined opponent. The arrival of friendly aircraft and reinforcements after daybreak quickly turned the tide of battle for the beleaguered infantry and slowly the enemy attack subsided. This action marked the first time the 81st Infantry Division found itself in a defensive situation since going ashore.

While RCT 321 had been fully engaged in holding the ground it had taken the previous day, the 322d was not idle. At dawn a Japanese counterattack hit its lines, but on a somewhat smaller scale and with much less effect than the one that had hit the adjacent regiment. In launching these attacks Major Goto was complying without deviation with his orders from General Inoue "to carry out strong counterattacks, from previously planned and prepared positions in order to destroy the enemy that has landed, by dawn of the next day."[10]

Fortunately for the Wildcats, only one small group of enemy troops had moved into the gap separating the two regiments during the night, and they withdrew at daybreak without having fired a shot. This again represented a radical departure from previous Japanese tactics, which had required the Japanese to expend themselves as soon as possible after an American landing, often in a futile *banzai* charge. In fact, had the Japanese exploited their advantage and rushed men in force into this unprotected area, much damage might have been caused to the exposed beachheads, which by this time were crowded with supporting troops, supplies, and materiel. Such an attack would have been in keeping with the theory of General Inoue "that if we repay the Americans (who rely solely upon material power) with material power it will shock them beyond imagination. . . ."[11]

---

[9] "Stern measures were instituted to suppress the tendency toward trigger-happiness." Historical Committee, *81st Infantry Division*, p. 78.

[10] Palau Sector Group Headquarters; Palau Sector Group training order entitled "Training for Victory," dtd 11Jul44, Item No. 11,190 in CinCPac-CinCPOA Translations No. 3, dtd 7Nov44.

[11] *Ibid.*

Major Goto, however, had already taken steps to assure the success of his mission. According to his plans, the final and decisive battle for Angaur would be fought elsewhere on the island, in terrain of his choosing. Thus, for the moment, he had no intention of weakening his force unduly despite the confusion that could be created at the exposed beachheads by a well-timed and executed Japanese counterattack.

General Mueller's orders for the second day of operations on Angaur called for the attack to jump off at 0900. It so happened that neither regiment moved out on schedule. RCT 322 lagged behind mainly because of the confusion resulting from indiscriminate firing in the rear by nervous and inexperienced service troops that saw a Japanese lurking behind every bush and reacted accordingly. The 321st Infantry Regiment, on the other hand, was delayed by new counterattacks. At 0905 an attack hit the right flank of that regiment, but strafing and bombing runs called down by the air liaison officer quickly broke up the enemy effort. Half an hour later another counterattack struck the southern flank of the regiment. Well-timed and expertly delivered supporting fires from mortars, tanks, and an LCI lying off the beach permitted the Wildcats to hold their ground.

At 1045, RCT 321 finally jumped off with two battalions in assault. To the south, the 1st Battalion assaulted southwestward in the wake of the last abortive Japanese counterattack, only to be halted almost immediately by concentrated fire from enemy fortifications near Rocky Point. Here, to forestall any advance into the interior, the Japanese had constructed a near-perfect defensive system. It consisted of pillboxes, dugouts, rifle pits, and interconnecting trenches, all mutually supporting and capable of delivering fires both to the front and to the flanks. A frontal assault from the beachhead would be prohibitive both in time and in casualties, and so a flanking maneuver was set into motion.

The battalion started inland over the Southern Railroad,[12] and followed the tracks for some distance before swerving through the jungle to approach the heavily fortified beach positions from the vulnerable rear. Dense jungle, sniper fire, and a large number of antitank mines all combined to hamper the progress of the battalion. When darkness closed in, the advance elements, still attempting to negotiate the trackless wilderness, were pulled back along the rail embankment to establish a defensive perimeter.

In the north that day, 3/322 attacked on the left, the 2d on the right; the 1st went into reserve. Elements of the 3d Battalion were delayed somewhat by sniper fire and wild shooting to the rear by support troops. Finally, one company, preceded by a platoon of medium tanks, moved out along the roadbed of the Pacific Railroad against stiffening enemy resistance. Supporting armor, blasting every suspicious patch of terrain that might have hidden a Japanese position, knocked out several reinforced bunkers in the process. Within two hours, the riflemen had advanced some

---

[12] For the sake of simplicity, the various narrow-gauge railroad spurs on Angaur were named after railroad lines in the United States, but with the nomenclature all resemblance between the two ended.

500 yards to the junction of the Southern and the Pacific Railroads. By this time, supporting fires were falling dangerously close, so the soldiers pulled back along the railroad some 75 yards, and were there joined by Company L, which had advanced behind the lead unit.

At this point occurred one of these tragic events that only too often in World War II marred a campaign that was otherwise going well. Six Navy fighter planes suddenly swept out of the skies and subjected the exposed men to heavy bombing and strafing. The full brunt of the attack fell on 3/322. Before the men could take cover or the air strike could be called off, friendly aircraft had killed 7 and wounded 46. An investigation later determined that the incident resulted from an improper marking of the target area and was not the fault of the pilots. Upon learning of the extent of the damage, General Mueller requested all air attacks against Angaur be discontinued until further notice, but this measure, aside from assuring the nonrecurrence of such a blunder for several days, could not undo the damage that had been wrought. It should be noted that on Angaur the enemy may at times have instigated and exploited such incidents.

> Japanese machine gunners and snipers an Angaur used the sound of low-flying aircraft to mask their firing positions by firing only when planes passed close overhead. This led to reports from jittery troops that friendly planes were strafing them. The situation got so bad that even the air observer had to be ordered clear of the area.[13]

[13] Col Arthur T. Mason ltr to CMC, dtd 28Feb50, in *Peleliu Comment File*.

Despite the disorganization resulting from such severe casualties as those inflicted by the ill-timed air strike, the riflemen resumed their advance within half an hour. Pushing forward rapidly the men seized the Japanese phosphate plant north of Saipan by 1400, and during the remainder of the afternoon advanced to within 300 yards of the west coast of Angaur. Infantry-tank patrols, operating in generally open terrain, reached the northern limits of Saipan Town.

To the north of the RCT 322 zone, the 2d Battalion passed through the lines of the 1st, which then reverted to regimental reserve. Orders called for the battalion to outflank the rugged hills in the northwestern portion of the island and then to move southward along the western coast until it joined up with the 3d Battalion. The advancing Wildcats encountered only light resistance, but the terrain grew progressively more rugged. Before long the supporting armor had to be withdrawn, for the broken nature of the ground precluded the use of tanks. The infantrymen doggedly plodded onward, despite intense heat. One platoon, meeting no opposition, continued to Cape Pkulangelul, which formed the northwest tip of Angaur. The regimental commander, aware of the logistical problems involved in supporting such an advanced force, and the tactical difficulties resulting from having a weak unit occupy an exposed and vulnerable position, ordered a withdrawal to Phase Line 0–2.

The 18th of September featured the unloading of necessary supplies on a large scale. The previous day, during the confusion of the initial assault landing, beach congestion had resulted when following waves continued to dump their loads upon the already crowded beaches. As a result, a temporary halt had been called to the unloading and no attempt was made to land artillery until afternoon, when two field artillery battalions were put ashore. By morning of the 18th, all supporting artillery was in position and ready to fire.

From the intelligence reports received during the second day, General Mueller gathered that the main Japanese strength was still concentrated on southern Angaur. This belief, coupled with orders to seize the vital level area in the south to facilitate construction of the airfield, impelled the division commander to issue orders calling for a drive southward by both regiments on 19 September to overrun Saipan Town and to divide the enemy forces.

At 0730 on the 19th, following heavy preparatory fires, the two rifle regiments jumped off in a determined bid to split the island and its defending force. To the south, RCT 321 attacked with the 3d Battalion on the left, the 2d on the right, and the 1st in reserve. To the north, RCT 322 moved out with three battalions abreast, from left to right the 3d, the 1st, and the 2d. The two battalions on the right advanced southwestward in an attempt to seize all ground south of Phase Line 0–4, except for the rugged hills, which would be mopped up later by the 2d. Phase Line 0–4 extended eastward from the west coast about 600 yards north of Saipan Town to a point northeast of Saipan where it formed a juncture with Phase Line 0–3. The 2d Battalion also had the mission of preventing any escape by the Japanese along the northern coast. The 3d Battalion was to strike directly through Saipan Town and then occupy the area between Phase Lines 0–4 and 0–5, the latter extending southeastward from Saipan Town to Beach Green II on the southeastern shore of Angaur.

Supported by medium tanks, the two assault companies of 3/322 advanced rapidly from their nighttime positions near the phosphate plant. Only sporadic mortar, machine gun, and rifle fire opposed the advance into Saipan Town. The riflemen encountered a number of enemy pillboxes, bunkers, and other fortifications, but these defenses had been designed to prevent an attack by sea only. Since the Wildcats approached them from the rear, their reduction posed no great problem.

Following capture of the town, General Mueller conducted a personal reconnaissance of the front and ordered the drive to the south continued as rapidly as possible. Leaving small details to mop up any Japanese still lurking among the shattered buildings or hiding in caves along the edge of the water, the 3d Battalion started southwards along a railroad that paralleled the shore some 30 yards inland. The fast-moving soldiers encountered only small groups of enemy troops that were quickly bypassed and, by 1600, they had set up night positions on Cape Ngaramudel and the north shore of Garangaoi Cove.

The other two battalions of RCT 322 met little difficulty in advancing south to the phosphate plant. Here, the 1st Battalion found its zone already occupied by elements of the 2d and 3d Battalions and received orders to assemble as a regimental reserve. Subsequently, its mission was to guard the rear area against possible enemy infiltration. The 2d Battalion, on the other hand, reinforced with Company B of the 1st, launched an assault against the northwest hills. A rifle company quickly occupied Palomas Hill, also known as Lighthouse Hill, in the face of only negligible opposition and dispatched a patrol to reconnoiter to the front.

This patrol failed to make any headway, for devastating fire from cleverly concealed enemy positions on high ground poured down upon the advancing men. A flanking attempt by Company G, using the Western Railroad to advance from the east, was pinned down by heavy fire from Japanese entrenched in the Lake Salome area. Blocked in every forward movement and with daylight fading rapidly, the battalion pulled back to the phosphate plant to set up night positions.

To the south that day, in the RCT 321 zone, tank-infantry teams of the 2d Battalion overcame very light opposition and by 0900 had overrun Middle Village. Seizure of this settlement, some 400 yards east of Saipan Town, was contested only by occasional groups of Japanese infantrymen. Such weak resistance to the advance of the Wildcats encouraged the commanding officer of the 710th Tank Battalion to recommend an armored reconnaissance of southern Angaur.

When higher commanders concurred in his proposal, a company of medium tanks, each mounting six or more men, started rolling southward, skirting the western edge of a mangrove swamp in the southeast portion of the island. The remaining riflemen of the 2d Battalion followed more slowly on foot. Before the day ended, this tank-infantry reconnaissance force had completely circled the swamp area—even passing through the fortified eastern beach defenses that were still holding up the advance of the 3d Battalion. Surprisingly enough, this force did not at any time encounter serious opposition. Having reached their objective, the tanks took up positions behind the lines of the 2d Battalion, which extended across the island below the swamp to tie in with 3/322 near Garangaoi Cove.

While the above action was in progress, the 3d Battalion of RCT 321 passed through the lines of the 1st Battalion in the eastern part of Angaur to strike southward from the Southern Railroad. In the course of the morning, one column pushed forward along the coast, while the other, attempting a flanking movement inland, soon ran into the mangrove swamp. Negotiating this natural obstacle prove so difficult and time-consuming that the column turned eastward to rejoin the force assaulting along the beach.

Here, the same extensive fortifications that had blunted the previous attack barred the way to the south. No sooner had the Wildcats methodically reduced one group of the mutually supporting positions than they drew fire from additional defenses farther down the coast. By early afternoon, the attack had stalled. Even a substantial increase in mortar and artillery support failed to get the advance going again.

By this time, a gap had opened between the two assault battalions of

RCT 321. To fill this void, the 1st Battalion, previously held in reserve, plunged into the morass separating the two assault units. Somehow these men managed to move far enough ahead before nightfall to set up perimeter defenses some 600 yards inland from the 3d Battalion.

That night, as General Mueller surveyed the tactical situation confronting his troops, he had every reason to feel confident. Gains for the day had surpassed his expectations, a fact also recognized by General Geiger, who dashed off the following message upon his return from a visit to the frontlines on Angaur: "The advance of your Division today reflects a commendable aggressive spirit. Well done to all hands."[14] The day had also brought capture of the first Japanese prisoner, who identified his unit as the *1st Battalion, 59th Infantry Regiment, 14th Division*. According to this source, in June all Japanese troops, except for a garrison of more than a thousand, had departed for Babelthuap. If true, this intelligence was welcome news for the 81st Infantry Division, since the enemy strength was apparently less than had been anticipated. A heavy fight still lay ahead, however, before the entire island of Angaur could be secured.

There were, nevertheless, bright spots on the horizon. Already seized was the level terrain for the bomber strip, the main objective of the entire operation. It appeared unlikely that the Japanese would make any serious attempt to reinforce the Angaur garrison in view of the situation on Peleliu. There no longer could be any doubt of the issue on Angaur.

The first Marines to arrive on Angaur were members of a reconnaissance party of the 7th AAA Battalion, which landed on 19 September. Upon the arrival of the remainder of the battalion, the Marine unit was closely integrated in the Angaur Island defense plans, operating observation posts along the coast for waterborne targets in addition to being responsible for antiaircraft defense.

Still unaware of recent changes in Japanese defensive tactics, General Mueller, as a precautionary measure, alerted all his units to take the necessary steps to fend off any last-ditch *banzai* charges. The admonition of the division commander was to prove unnecessary. For the Japanese the time had now arrived to withdraw the major portion of their troops into the rugged, coral-ridged hills of northwest Angaur. Here the Japanese commander planned to exploit the natural terrain features to the utmost, forcing the Wildcats to root every last defending Japanese out of caves and dugouts while inflicting the heaviest casualties possible on the attacking force.

On the whole, the night of 19–20 September passed without any major incident. Division artillery blasted away at enemy positions; the ships offshore could fire only illuminating shells because of the proximity of friendly and opposing lines. Towards dawn, small, scattered remnants of the Angaur garrison began filtering through the American positions. These Japanese seemed

---

[14] Historical Committee, *81st Infantry Division*, p. 93.

intent solely upon escaping from the doomed southern portion of the island, however, and gaining the northwestern hills where Major Goto still retained control.

Early on 20 September all three battalions of RCT 321 resumed the final drive south to wipe out the two isolated pockets of enemy resistance still remaining there, while RCT 322 continued its assault against the Japanese-held hills to the north. The 322d was forced to divert one battalion northward to assume defensive positions along the second phase line between Lake Aztec and the north coast. This force had the mission of blocking any possible Japanese counterattack against Red Beach, which at the time was still congested with supplies and materiel. Since another of his battalions was stationed below Saipan Town, the regimental commander, Colonel Benjamin W. Venable, had only his 2d Battalion available for the assault.

The soldiers moved out and soon reoccupied Palomas Hill. Upon resuming the advance, the Wildcats found themselves attacking uphill over terrain that greatly favored the defenders, who were entrenched on the commanding heights to the front of the battalion. Every attempt by men of the 2d Battalion to push forward drew such heavy enemy mortar and machine gun fire that it had to be abandoned. Even a flanking maneuver to the east, making use of the Western Railroad, whose tracks cut through the ridges surrounding Lake Salome, failed when three self-propelled 75mm guns which were supporting the rifle company, emerged from the 50-yard-long railroad cut only to be knocked out by enemy action. Except for the recaptured ground at Palomas Hill no additional gains were made, and the men of the 2d Battalion dug in for the night in substantially the same positions they had held on the previous day.

Further south that morning, 2/321 with two additional rifle companies and two tank companies, quickly overran the heavily fortified southern beaches. Fortunately for the attackers, these positions, previously held in strength, were now defended by a mere handful of Japanese survivors. The only stiff opposition came from some pillboxes clustered near a tank barrier at the southeastern tip of Angaur. A flame-thrower-satchel charge team soon eliminated this threat. By 1100, after detailing one company to mop up any enemy personnel that had been overlooked, the reinforced battalion was able to throw its weight against the southeast beaches, where Japanese diehards had for some time delayed the advance of the 3d Battalion.

In the center, the 1st Battalion, now reduced to just one reinforced rifle company, resumed its attack through the mangrove swamp to take the southeast beach fortifications from the rear. The difficulties of maneuvering through the seemingly impenetrable terrain soon forced these men to abandon their efforts and rejoin the 3d Battalion in its assault along the coast. This drive south encountered only isolated stubborn resistance, for most of the beach defenses were found to be unmanned. The Japanese had evacuated their positions and fled north under cover of darkness. When the 2d Battalion completed regrouping and struck at the enemy pocket from the south, the last phase of the battle for Angaur began and the end of Japanese resistance was in sight. Only the inevitable mopping up by small details remained to be accomplished on southern Angaur. This was done the following day.

Earlier on 20 September, General Mueller had forwarded the following message to IIIAC: "All organized resistance ceased on Angaur at 1034. Island secure."[15] General Mueller made this statement because Major Goto no longer had the capability of posing a serious threat to the hold of the Army on Angaur. All necessary ground for the construction of the airfield and base installations had already been seized; an estimated 850 Japanese had been killed;[16] and the approximately 350 enemy troops that division intelligence figured were left had been compressed into the northwestern hills which were completely sealed off. What none of the Wildcats could visualize at this time, any more than the Marines on Peleliu, was that the elimination of such a relatively small and isolated pocket of enemy resistance would require an all-out effort by an entire infantry regiment, and that such an operation would drag on for yet another month.

The final Japanese defensive positions were located in the highest and most rugged portion of Angaur amidst the northwestern hill mass. Here the Japanese set up a well-conceived and constructed defensive system, utilizing the broken nature of the terrain to the utmost. Caves were dug, fire lanes cleared, and the artillery, mortars, antitank weapons, and machine guns sited in mutually supporting positions to exploit the defensive quality of the terrain and to thwart any infantry assault. Since practically every emplacement was hidden underground, the Japanese were for all practical purposes immune to naval gunfire, artillery, or air strikes. The attackers, on the other hand, could make little use of supporting armor, for the jumbled configuration of the ridges prohibited any closely coordinated tank-infantry assault. Only the most determined rushes by American riflemen could displace the entrenched enemy from his last-ditch positions.

Once again the enemy deployment and his complete knowledge of the forbidding terrain met every attack that the Wildcats could muster. The Japanese made effective use of machine guns, rifles, antitank guns, and mortars from concealed positions on commanding ground. These weapons were fired only when the chances that the shots would find their mark were good and when it appeared that the weapons and their crews would not be seen by the attacking infantrymen. Since the Japanese used smokeless and flashless powder, the locating of a weapon by even the most alert observer was practically impossible. In short, the northwest hills of Angaur had been transformed into a virtual fortress, a miniature version of Umurbrogol Mountain on Peleliu, whose reduction was also to prove difficult, costly, and time-consuming.

---

[15] Historical Committee, *81st Infantry Division*, p. 98.

[16] "This casualty figure was an overestimation. Probably fewer than 600 Japanese had been killed through the 20th, and Major Goto still had possibly 750 men with which to conduct an organized defense in the northwest." Smith, *Approach to the Philippines*, p. 518.

Reduction of the enemy redoubt fell to RCT 322, because on 21 September the tactical situation on Peleliu made necessary the transfer of RCT 321 to that island. Further, because of the restricted area of the pocket, there was room for only one rifle regiment to maneuver. Subsequently, for over a month, the men of RCT 322 were forced to fight, live, and die among the jumbled, jungle-cloaked coral ridges, spires, and cliffs of northwestern Angaur before the last enemy holdout had been either killed or captured.

Repeated attempts were made to avoid unnecessary bloodshed by inducing the Japanese to surrender. Such incentives were offered in the form of leaflets and broadcasts in the Japanese language over a public address system. The wording of these was approximately as follows:

> Japanese Soldiers: This island is surrounded by the American forces, and there is no reason for you to continue fighting against us. Further resistance is hopeless. Your communication and supply lines are cut. The Japanese Navy is far away. If you resist further, you will surely die by starvation and bombardment.
> If you cease fighting and come to us immediately, one by one, unarmed and with your hands up, you will receive food, clothing, and medical care.
> To die when encountered by a hopeless situation is neither heroic nor brave, and is only a useless death. Come over to us singly, unarmed, and with your hands up. We give you (time allotted) to come to us; otherwise we will be forced to take the only alternative action.[17]

Only a sprinkling of Japanese surrendered, one of them after the first broadcast, and another immediately following the second. On the whole, the results obtained were disappointing and it seemed that the Japanese required more demonstration of the power of the attacking force.

This was furnished in abundance, as day after day the Wildcats doggedly returned to the assault. Frequently they suffered minor reverses and losses. Progress at times could be measured in yards and remained agonizingly slow. Still, with each passing day and hour victory came ever closer within the reach of the tired, dirty but determined assault troops. First portents of success came towards the end of the first week in October when 183 natives emerged from the pocket, many of them in deplorable physical condition and in dire need of medical attention which was promptly furnished. By this time the protracted conflict had degenerated into minor patrol action with sniping, ambushing, and extensive boobytrapping employed by both sides. The true situation did not deter the Japanese from reporting as late as 10 October that "judging from the flarebombs and other indications, it is certain that our garrison units in the northwestern hills (of Angaur) are annihilating the enemy in close quarter combat."[18]

Four days later, however, the assault phase on Angaur came to an end, and the occupation period began for the island. For practical purposes, tactical operations were to continue long beyond this date. The 81st Infantry Division was to retain responsibility for eliminating the remaining isolated pockets of

---

[17] Historical Committee, *81st Infantry Division*, p. 111.

[18] *Japanese CenPac Ops*, p. 132.

enemy resistance. All other control concerning Angaur was passed on 14 October from General Mueller to the island commander, Colonel Ray A. Dunn, USA, whose mission it was to develop the island as a forward airbase. On the same date the Marine 7th AAA Battalion was relieved from attachment to the 81st Infantry Division and assigned to the Angaur Garrison Force, while still remaining under operational control of the division.

The indomitable Major Goto survived every American attack right up to the night of 19 October, when his luck finally ran out and he was killed. A few other Japanese, determined to escape from an untenable situation, decided to swim to Peleliu. One actually covered the seven-mile stretch before he was observed. The fate of those Japanese remaining on Angaur was now sealed, and on 21 October triumphant Wildcats overran the last remaining organized enemy position. This action terminated the tactical phase of the operation, even though a few Japanese stragglers inevitably remained. RCT 322 was withdrawn to the southern part of Angaur for rest and recuperation, leaving only a couple of supporting units in the area to seek out and annihilate whatever Japanese still lurked there.

It is interesting to note that following the break in Japanese communications between Angaur and Peleliu on 22 September, Colonel Nakagawa continued to report the heroic deeds of the Angaur garrison even after the men of RCT 322 had relinquished their combat duties for the less strenuous atmosphere of garrison life. It was not until mid-November that Nakagawa admitted that this continued resistance was just "his surmise."[19]

The Wildcats had accomplished the seizure of Angaur, killing an estimated 1,338 Japanese and capturing 59.[20] Losses sustained were 260 killed or dead of wounds and 1,354 wounded or injured as of 30 October 1944. An additional 940 Americans were temporarily incapacitated by battle fatigue, illness, or disease.[21]

The capture of Angaur was of prime importance because it eliminated a threat to Allied lines of communication that stretched across the western Pacific towards the Philippines. Angaur provided the Allies with another badly needed air base in a forward area. Construction of an airfield on Angaur had begun as early as 20 September, and the first aircraft touched down on the field on 15 October. It should be noted that since the island had not previously harbored any Japanese air installation the work had to start from scratch. First tasks were cutting back the jungle, filling swamps, and levelling very rough terrain.

From the Japanese point of view, the loss of Angaur and sacrifice of Major Goto's reinforced infantry battalion were more than offset by the advantages derived from this delaying action. There is evidence that General Inoue never considered Angaur as anything more than an outpost; hence his instructions to the garrison were to prolong the conflict as long as possible if attacked by a superior force. Goto's isolated battalion,

---

[19] *Japanese Ops in the CenPac*, p. 192.
[20] *81st InfDiv OpRpt*, Sec IX, p. 69.
[21] *Ibid.*, p. 112.

without the benefit of or any hope of obtaining air support or reinforcements, was able to deny the prime objective on the island, the projected site for the airfield, for several days in the face of a determined assault by two American regiments receiving all the support from the air and sea that could be mustered. When deterioration of the situation forced the inevitable Japanese withdrawal, Major Goto's skillful and tenacious defense of the hills in the northwestern portion of the island tied up an entire American infantry regiment for an additional month. The reward of the Japanese garrison for its tenacity was death, but death held little terror for many fatalistic Japanese.[22]

The men of the 81st Infantry Division emerged from the Angaur operation more combatwise and more certain of their ability to deal with a fanatical enemy. The lessons they had learned during the first combat action on Angaur were soon to serve the Wildcats well during the even more difficult and challenging mission awaiting them on Peleliu.

ON TO ULITHI[23]

The original concept of the STALEMATE II Operation envisioned the employment of a regimental combat team of the 81st Infantry Division to seize Angaur Island before the invasion of Peleliu got under way. Following the successful completion of this mission, it was planned that the division was to be further employed in operations against Yap, an island 258 miles northeast of the Palaus, with one RCT to be engaged in independent action under Navy control against Ulithi, an atoll about halfway between the Palaus and Yap.

Preliminary planning by the division for the consummation of this concept provided for the employment of RCT 322 on Angaur Island and RCT 321 on Ulithi Atoll. When revised estimates of enemy strength made it necessary to plan for the commitment of two RCTs on Angaur, RCT 321 was removed from consideration as the landing force to seize Ulithi and was reassigned to the Angaur assault. RCT 323 then was assigned the Ulithi operation; planning for it was begun on 1 August 1944.

As additional information about enemy strength in the Southern Palaus became available, it was apparent that the continued presence of elements of the 81st Infantry Division would be required in that area. As a consequence, on 22 August the division was relieved from participation in operations against Yap and Ulithi, and the mission of seizing the latter was assigned to a combat team of the 96th Infantry Division. Planning by the 81st Infantry Division for the Ulithi Operation ceased on that date. Further developments in the concept of the STALEMATE II Operation

---

[22] "To die is lighter than the birds' feathers," and "to die is like the blossoms of the cherry tree falling down." LtGen Sadae Inoue in *Worden ltr*.

[23] Unless otherwise noted, the material in this section is derived from: *81st InfDiv OpRpt—Angaur*; *81st InfDiv OpRpt—Ulithi Atoll and other Western Caroline Islands*; Marine Air Base Ulithi—Rpts and Correspondence re: Base Development Plans, dtd Oct44–Jul45; MAG–45, Rpt of Op, dtd 23Jan45, hereafter *MAG–45, Rpt of Op*; Historical Committee,

---

81st Infantry Division; Hough, *Assault on Peleliu*; Morison, *Leyte*; Smith, *Approach to the Philippines*.

involved abandoning the plan to capture the Yap Island Group and assigning the mission of seizing Ulithi to a combat team of the 77th Infantry Division.

On 15 September the Joint Chiefs of Staff decided to speed up the Pacific timetable of operations. Although the assault on the strongly-held Yap Island remained shelved, the seizure of Ulithi was to take place as scheduled. American planners particularly desired this atoll, since it possessed a spacious sheltered anchorage that was to serve as a forward base during the imminent invasion of the Philippines. On 16 September Admiral Halsey ordered Admiral Wilkinson to seize Ulithi "with resources on hand".[24]

The 77th and 96th Infantry Divisions, initially scheduled for the Yap-Ulithi assault, had been transferred to General MacArthur to form part of his invasion force for the Leyte landing. Only one uncommitted regiment, RCT 323, remained under Wilkinson's control.

On 16 September General Mueller was advised that one combat team of the division would constitute the landing force to capture Ulithi. RCT 323 was designated as the landing force.

This infantry unit was then serving as IIIAC floating reserve, the sole source of combat-ready troops in the event that the Marines ran into trouble on Peleliu or the Army required assistance on Angaur. Although the commander of the Expeditionary Troops, General Julian C. Smith, recommended to Wilkinson that the rifle regiment would be needed to ensure an early seizure of the hotly contested island, the admiral did not share this conviction.[25]

[24] Smith interview.

During the night following receipt of Halsey's directive, Wilkinson instructed General Mueller to ready RCT 323 for an immediate departure to assault Ulithi Atoll. The specific mission of the regiment was "to capture, occupy, and defend Ulithi Atoll in order to establish a fleet anchorage, seaplane base, and airbase thereat to support further operations against the enemy, and to commence development of the base until relieved."[26]

The Ulithi Attack Group was commanded by Rear Admiral Blandy and consisted of a cruiser, 9 destroyers, 3 patrol vessels, 12 landing craft, gunboats, 2 high-speed troop transports, and 5 attack transports and cargo vessels.

The final plan of operations presented to the Navy and approved by it provided for the landing of the reconnaissance detachment of RCT 323 on AMAZEMENT Island[27] prior to dawn of Jig Day minus 1. There the detachment was to establish a minor defense post in order to protect the Mugai Channel entrance into the Ulithi Lagoon, which was to serve as the transport area for the attack force (See Map 7). During the same day, a reconnaissance detach-

[25] "Navy officers sometimes have difficulty in understanding how idle troops can serve any useful purpose aboard ship while fighting is going on ashore." Smith interview.

[26] Attack Order No. A268-44, ComGroupOne, PhibsPac, dtd 15Sep44.

[27] Islands in Ulithi Atoll have been mentioned in the text by code name only. Code designations (in capital letters) were as follows: AMAZEMENT—Mangejang; KEENSET—Sorlen; LITHARGE—Mogmog; AMELIORATE—Falalop; ACETYLENE—Potangeras; AGGRAVATE—Fassarai; IDENTICAL—Asor.

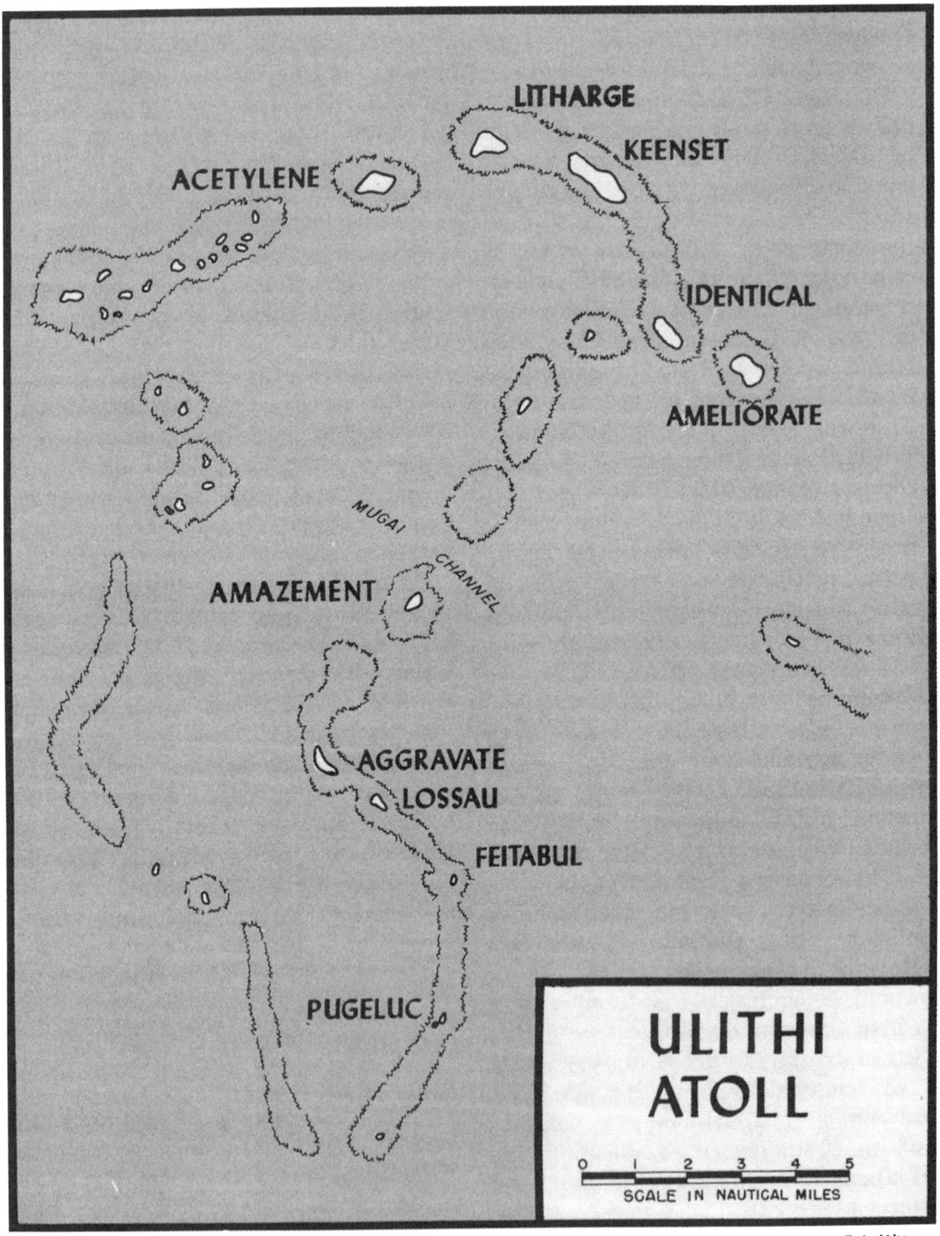

Map 7

E. L. Wilson

ment was to be landed on one of the southern islands of the atoll to remove a few natives for intelligence purposes.

On Jig Day a reinforced rifle company was to capture KEENSET Island to permit the emplacement of the combat team artillery in support of subsequent ship to shore operations against the northern islands of the atoll. The remainder of the BLT furnishing troops for the capture of KEENSET was to be prepared to capture LITHARGE Island. Upon completion of artillery registration firing and on order, a second BLT was to capture and defend IDENTICAL Island. During these operations, reconnaissance detachments were to reconnoiter and mop-up the small islands in the west central portion of the atoll.

On Jig Day plus 1, artillery and cannon-supported shore-to-shore operations were to be carried out against AMELIORATE and ACETYLENE Islands. Reconnaissance detachments were to be prepared to assist, on order, in reconnoitering and mopping up AGGRAVATE, LOSSAU, the remaining small islands to the south, and the islets eastward of the main atoll.

The Ulithi Attack Force proceeded as planned. Troops, equipment, and supplies had been combat loaded at Oahu, Hawaii in anticipation that RCT 323 would be employed as reserve in the Palau Operation or in an assault landing on Ulithi. Movement to the objective area was made in two echelons. The reconnaissance detachment, consisting of the Intelligence & Reconnaissance Platoon, 323d Infantry Regiment, reinforced with 24 enlisted men from one of the rifle companies, departed from the Palau area at 1330, 19 September. It arrived off Ulithi during the early morning of 21 September awaiting orders from the Commander, Ulithi Fire Support Group, under whose command the reconnaissance was to be effected. The remainder of the force departed at 1000, 21 September. Both echelons made the movement without incident.

The afternoon of 21 September saw the completion of final plans for the landing of a reconnaissance detachment on AMAZEMENT Island. Mission of this unit was to secure Mugai Channel for minesweeping and underwater demolition operations which were to be conducted in the lagoon on that date. It was decided that a preliminary offshore reconnaissance of the island was to be conducted that afternoon to determine the best beach for a landing. In the event that the reconnaissance was made without interference, troops would land that afternoon to seize the island.

The reconnaissance was carried out as planned and subsequently the reconnaissance detachment landed unopposed at 1515. A thorough search revealed no sign of recent habitation. Thirteen men stayed on the island, and the remainder returned to the ship.

During the early morning of 22 September, orders were issued to carry out a landing on AGGRAVATE Island for the purpose of removing a few natives for questioning. A detachment debarked in two rubber boats and proceeded towards the island. The entire shore was fringed with a coral reef extending out from the beach for about 150 yards. When the troops went ashore, they encountered two natives, who approached in a friendly fashion and agreed to accompany the troops back to the ship.

Their interrogation revealed that the Japanese garrison force had departed a few months earlier and that there were no Japanese on the atoll except for a crippled one on AMELIORATE Island. A thorough search of KEENSET Island failed to reveal any sign of recent occupation, though several Japanese graves were found. A search of LITHARGE Island likewise showed negative results.

During the morning of 23 September, elements of RCT 323 landed unopposed on AMELIORATE, which was officially declared secure at 1315. Once again no Japanese were found on the island, not even the reported cripple. A considerable number of inhabitants had taken refuge in a shallow cave in the northwestern part of AMELIORATE. After much coaxing about 30 natives were persuaded to return to their homes in the village. For the remainder of the day and throughout the next natives continued to leave their hiding places. In all, about 100 returned to the village.[28]

Occupation of IDENTICAL Island commenced at 1300, 23 September, when assault waves came ashore and found neither enemy nor natives on the island, though the bodies of two Japanese, apparently dead for several days, were discovered floating in shallow water. The seizure of LITHARGE and ACETYLENE Islands rounded out the operation, which was to become prominent for the absence of enemy resistance.

Ulithi Atoll contained a 300-berth anchorage and a seaplane base. Occupation of these Western Caroline islands provided still another base from which future operations against the enemy could be supported. The construction of an airstrip on AMELIORATE Island made possible fighter plane protection for the anchorage and afforded a base from which U. S. aircraft could continue neutralization of the nearby Japanese bases on Yap.

Together with Angaur and Peleliu Islands to the southwest and Guam, Tinian, and Saipan to the northeast, the capture of Ulithi Atoll completed a line of American bases that isolated Japanese holdings in the Central and South Pacific. The occupation of Ulithi Atoll further denied it to the enemy as a fleet anchorage, weather and radio station, and possible air and submarine base, in addition to precluding its use by the enemy to observe and report the activities of American forces in the sector.

By 25 September the unloading of all the support ships had been completed and Vice Admiral John H. Hoover, Commander, Forward Areas Western Pacific, took over the task of developing Ulithi Atoll into an advanced fleet base. Within a month after the capture of Ulithi, more than a hundred Navy craft from self-propelled types to lighters, floating drydocks, barges, landing craft, and seaplane wrecking derricks were en route to the island. During subsequent operations in the Philippines, the U. S. Pacific Fleet found Ulithi to be an extremely valuable base. Prior to the invasion of Okinawa, the island served as a staging area for fleet and amphibious forces. The atoll thus fulfilled a vital strategic role in the final phase of World War II.

---

[28] 81st InfDiv OpRpt, Ulithi, p. 17. According to Historical Committee, *81st Infantry Division*, no Japanese or natives were encountered on AMELIORATE.

CHAPTER 6

Securing the North: 23-30 September[1]

REINFORCEMENT FOR PELELIU[2]

Major General William H. Rupertus, commanding the 1st Marine Division, initially envisioned the Peleliu operation as a tough but short campaign. The landings took place on 15 September under weather conditions that were ideal except for excessive heat. Despite fanatical Japanese resistance, the Marines secured a firm foothold on the island. The 5th Marines seized the prime objective of the operation, the vital Peleliu airfield, on the second day of the assault, while the 7th Marines accomplished the mission of driving the Japanese from the southern part of the island. The 1st Marines had already encountered the fringes of the vast enemy defense system in the central ridges of Peleliu, and early optimistic reports soon gave way to a more somber perspective of the situation. During the first week of operations the 1st Marines had borne the brunt of the assault. There was little likelihood that the campaign would become easier or less costly as it progressed.

Even the most pessimistic predictions of the difficulties that the Marines were to encounter proved conservative when the full extent of the Japanese defensive system was revealed to the assault troops. By evening of 20 September, having made only minor gains, the 1st Marines found progress blocked by ridges honeycombed with elaborate Japanese defenses consisting of layers of caves, dugouts, and cleverly concealed emplacements. Worse still, in five days of incessant fighting, the regiment had sustained nearly 1,700 casualties or more than half its original strength. The 5th and 7th Marines had suffered fewer casualties, but their advance was also stymied by the heavily fortified ridges. To most division personnel, there appeared the sobering realization that the attack had bogged down in the incredibly tough and skillfully defended terrain. The division paid an extremely heavy price of nearly 4,000 casualties for the ground that had been seized. The heavy losses in personnel resulted in a corresponding reduction in the combat efficiency of the division, which as early as 18 September had dropped from "excellent" to "very good." By evening of 19 September, continued casualties and fatigue further reduced the efficiency of the 1st Marine Division.

On 21 September, General Geiger, accompanied by members of his staff, vis-

---

[1] Unless otherwise noted, the material in this chapter is derived from: *IIIAC Palaus Rpt; 1st MarDiv SAR; 1st MarDiv WarD, Sep44; 1st MarDiv D-2 Jnl; 1st MarDiv D-3 Periodic Rpt; Peleliu Comment File; Japanese CenPac Ops;* Smith, *Narrative;* Hough, *Assault on Peleliu;* Morison, *Leyte;* Smith, *Approach to the Philippines;* McMillan, *The Old Breed.*

[2] Additional sources used for this section are: *IIIAC C-3 Rpts; 3/1 WarD; Vandegrift Letters.*

ited the CP of the 1st Marines to obtain a clearer picture of the situation.

> It became rapidly apparent that the regimental commander was very tired, he was unable to give a very clear picture of what his situation was and when asked by the Corps Commander what he needed in the way of help he stated that he was doing all right with what he had.[3]

General Geiger and staff then proceeded to the division CP. After a look at the casualty reports, General Geiger told the division commander that, in his estimation, "the First Marines were finished."[4] In the course of the ensuing discussion with General Rupertus, General Geiger expressed the view that the 1st Marines should be relieved and replaced by an Army regiment. The division commander attempted to forestall such action by asserting that the island could be secured in another day or two without the employment of Army troops, a patently impossible solution in view of the overall tactical situation. In the end, General Geiger ordered preparations made for the evacuation of the 1st Marines to the Russells and for the immediate attachment of a regiment of the 81st Infantry Division to the 1st Marine Division.

Reluctance on the part of the Commanding General, 1st Marine Division, to use Army units was not limited to this instance. It may have been rooted in earlier experiences, which did not always result in harmonious relations with Army commanders.[5] On the other hand, General Rupertus may have distrusted a division that was new to combat and felt that the battle-hardened 1st Marine Division was capable of finishing the job it had undertaken without any help.

Prior to this latter incident [involving attachment of an infantry regiment to the 1st Marine Division], "the Corps Commander was disinclined to impose any particular line of action upon the division commander although more than once he had felt the urge to do so. Just what induced this reluctance on the part of General Rupertus was never understood by Corps. . . ." It is probable that he felt, like most Marines, that he and his troops could and would handle any task assigned to them without asking for outside help.[6]

At 1625, 21 September, IIIAC asked the Commanding General, 81st Infantry Division, if he could make a regimental combat team available for immediate movement to Peleliu to assist the 1st Marine Division in completing the seizure of the island. Within the hour General Mueller replied that the 321st Infantry Regiment was available as soon as it could complete its re-supply. Shortly thereafter, a group consisting of Rear Admiral George H. Fort, commander of the Western Attack Force, and Major Generals Julian C. Smith and Geiger arrived at division headquarters to confer with General Mueller. These four discussed the situation on Peleliu in detail and agreed on a general plan of movement for the 321st Infantry Regiment. Shortly before midnight, 21

---
[3] Col William F. Coleman ltr to CMC, n.d., in *Peleliu Comment File*, hereafter *Coleman ltr*.
[4] *Ibid.*
[5] MajGen William H. Rupertus ltrs to LtGen Alexander A. Vandegrift (CMC), dtd 7Dec43, 4Feb44, 18Feb44, and 24Mar44, in *Vandegrift Letters*.
[6] *Wachtler ltr*.

September, the reinforced regiment received orders directing its loading and movement to Peleliu.

The Assistant Division Commander of the 81st Infantry Division, Brigadier General Marcus B. Bell, was designated liaison representative to IIIAC, to coordinate details of the movement from Angaur to Peleliu and attachment of RCT 321 to the 1st Marine Division. On 22 September an advance detachment of the regiment arrived at Headquarters, 1st Marine Division, near the airfield, to complete the necessary arrangements for the reception and disposition of troops. On the same date, the Commanding Officer, 321st Infantry Regiment, Colonel Robert F. Dark, reported to General Geiger on board the USS *Mt. McKinley* and then proceeded to the 1st Marine Division command post on Peleliu.

The main body of the 321st Infantry Regiment embarked early on 22 September. Embarkation of all troops and loading of equipment, except for amphibian tractors, continued throughout the day and was finally completed by 1630. The ships stood off Angaur during the night of 22-23 September. Shortly after daybreak the amphibian tractors were loaded into LSTs. The force departed from Angaur at 1000 and two hours later reached Orange Beach, Peleliu. Attached to the regiment were an engineer battalion less one company, two medical companies less two platoons, an amphibian tractor company, and Company A, 710th Tank Battalion, an 81mm Provisional Mortar Platoon, and several detachments of service troops. Upon landing at Peleliu, the first elements of RCT 321 to reach the island proceeded to the western shore, where 2/321 relieved remnants of 3/1 between 1400 and 1500.

No advance for the 1st Marines had been ordered for 23 September. Patrols pushed 1,000 yards northward along the west coast without encountering serious opposition. The areas directly behind the Marine lines were harassed by mortar and sniper fire from the high ridges to the east. In a last skirmish prior to its relief, Company L, 3d Battalion, was able to inflict heavy casualties on a large body of Japanese moving up a draw across the front towards Company I. The enemy force was wiped out by combined artillery and mortar fire.[7]

The relief of the remainder of the 1st Marines was effected quickly. All maps, overlays, and other information pertaining to the terrain and enemy positions were turned over to the Army unit, which had no maps of the area.[8] The exhausted and depleted Marine regiment then moved out on foot or with such transportation as was available to a rest area on Purple Beach. There the units were reorganized and assigned defense sectors, which included the eastern coast of Peleliu and three islands offshore.

The men had hardly settled along Purple Beach before Colonel Puller informed them that they would go back into action after a three-day rest.[9] This was not the intention of the division, however, and the regiment retained its defensive mission until departure from Peleliu on the last day of September. Since coming ashore, the 1st Marines

---

[7] *1st MarHist*, 23Sep44.
[8] *3/1 WarD*, 23Sep44.
[9] McMillan, *The Old Breed*, p 319.

MEN AND SUPPLIES *arrive across 500-yard reef off Peleliu. (USMC 95606)*

81st INFANTRY DIVISION *troops join the battle of Peleliu. (USMC A96738)*

had suffered 1,672 casualties. In the 1st Battalion 71 percent of total strength had become casualties. Similarly, the casualty rate reached 56 percent in the 2d, 55 percent in the 3d, and 32 percent of authorized strength in regimental headquarters and Weapons Company.[10]

During the remainder of its stay on Peleliu, the depleted 1st Marines in its rest area was able to account for a few snipers and a number of Japanese stragglers attempting to flee through the shallow water from the large peninsula across the bay. In this manner the regiment remained in action against the enemy until the very last day of its stay on the island.

In relieving the 1st Marines near Ngarekeukl on the West Road, the 3d Battalion, 321st Infantry Regiment, moved into positions directly south of the 2d Battalion, which had occupied the lines previously held by 3/1. The 1st Battalion occupied an assembly area to the rear, where it was kept in regimental reserve.

CHANGE OF MAIN EFFORT[11]

The arrival of an additional regiment on Peleliu ushered in a new phase in the bitter contest for the island. Even though, in the estimate of the 1st Marine Division, about two thirds of the original Japanese garrison had been put out of action, organized resistance was far from over. Driving the Japanese defenders from the Umurbrogol ridges, as well as the remainder of the central ridge system, promised to be a costly and time-consuming task. From their positions in and on the hills, the Japanese were able to interdict all movement along the East and West Roads, which generally paralleled the island coastlines north of the airfield. Just north of Peleliu, the island of Ngesebus and its fighter strip were still in Japanese hands. Enemy strength in the remaining Palau islands still exceeded 25,000. As a result, the possibility of an enemy counterlanding was ever present. It had become abundantly clear that failure of the 1st Marine Division to score a breakthrough had resulted in a loss of momentum, which would have to be recovered before the Japanese hold on the island could be eliminated.

General Rupertus had for some time considered the possibility of launching a drive up the west coast of Peleliu to outflank the main Japanese defenses on the island. If successful, such an operation would open the dual possibility of attacking the Japanese center of resistance simultaneously from the north and south, and of crossing over a narrow body of water to Ngesebus to seize that island and its fighter strip.

In the minds of General Rupertus and his staff uncertainty prevailed as to Japanese intentions of sending reinforcements and materiel to Peleliu. Evidence on that score was conflicting. As early as 18 September two Japanese barges and one sampan had been observed unloading on the northwest coast of Peleliu. On the other hand, during the first week following the landing of the 1st Marine Division on Peleliu, repeated air searches of the islands to the north had shown no evidence of enemy movements to reinforce Peleliu.

---

[10] *1st MarHist*, 26Aug–10Oct44.

[11] Additional sources used for this section are: *IIIAC C-2 Rpts*; 1st MarDiv FO 3-44.

There was no uncertainty on Babelthuap, for the Japanese were ready to reinforce their hard-pressed garrison on Peleliu. This mission fell to the *2d Battalion, 15th Infantry Regiment*. From a military standpoint, General Inoue was not enthusiastic about sending this unit, because he believed that the Americans would attack Koror and Babelthuap once the operation on Peleliu had been concluded. His reason for reinforcing Peleliu was "for the sake of the garrison at Peleliu and to bolster the morale of the troops there."[12]

An advance detachment of the Japanese battalion left Babelthuap during the night of 22-23 September and stealthily headed for the northern tip of Peleliu. The Japanese felt that chances of detection were slight, for the first sustained rain since the beginning of the Peleliu operation fell throughout the night. The Marines on Peleliu likewise welcomed the rain:

> During our first days on Peleliu rain proved an aid to fighting troops rather than a hindrance; the sandy ground absorbing the water readily and preventing any problem of mud. Rainfall increased the available water supply and provided a welcome break in the energy-sapping heat.[13]

The Japanese were not to reach their destination undetected. At 0535, the destroyer *H. L. Edwards* spotted seven enemy barges about 1,000 yards northeast of Akarakoro Point at the northern tip of Peleliu, obviously headed for the island. The destroyer opened fire, sinking one barge before the remainder reached the beach. A combination of bombing and strafing, naval gunfire, and artillery hit the barges on the beach, and by 0845 the cruiser *Louisville* reported all barges destroyed.

The enemy version of this incident agrees only in part with the American account, adding that "despite receiving severe enemy air and artillery fire at a point two kilometers off the coast, they made a successful landing at 0520 hours under the command of 1st Lieutenant Murahori".[14]

Aware of the fact that at least some Japanese reinforcements were reaching Peleliu and still uncertain as to the extent to which the Japanese might support their garrison on the island, General Rupertus on 23 September faced a difficult tactical decision. If the enemy had any weak spot on Peleliu, it was bound to be situated between the central ridges and the western shore. It was here that General Rupertus decided to commit the 321st Infantry Regiment in a drive up the western coast of the island. Such an advance would take the regiment northward from Phase Line O-3 to O-4 (See Map 8). The line of departure for the attack was located about 1,000 yards north of Ngarekeukl. The drive was to continue until a point north of the village of Garekoru was reached. During the advance, the left flank of the regiment was to remain anchored on the beach, while the right was to extend about 250 yards east of the West Road into the ridges of the Umurbrogol. The 1st and 2d Battalions, 7th Marines, were to support the Army drive by pressing against the Japanese

---

[12] LtGen Sadae Inoue, IJA, interview with LtCol Waite W. Worden, in *Worden ltr*.
[13] *1st MarDiv SAR*, Ph II, Anx A, p. 7.

[14] *Japanese CenPacOps*, p. 109.

SECURING THE NORTH 191

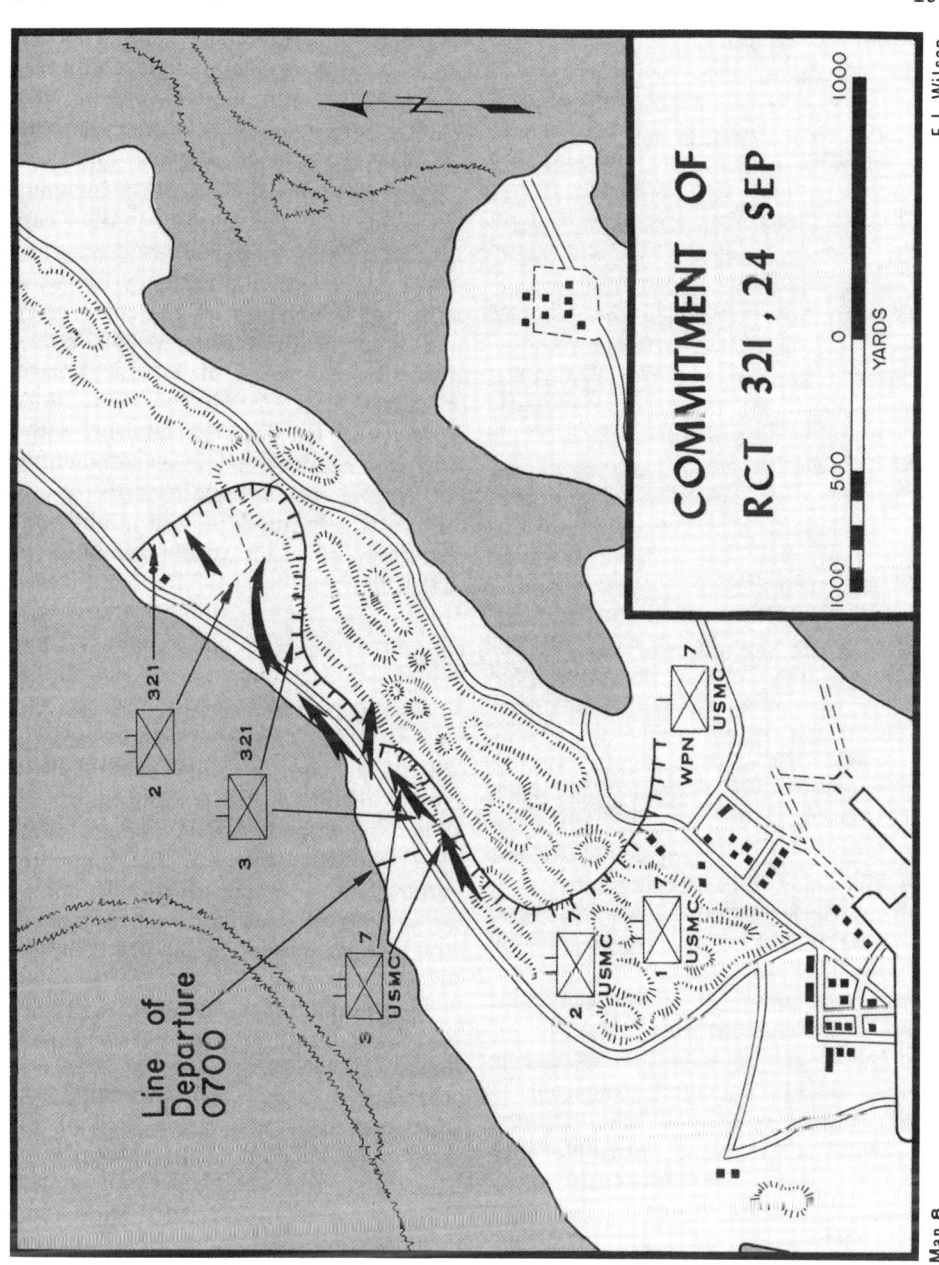

positions from the south and center, while 3/7 would advance to the right rear of RCT 321 over the high ground to cover the advance of the soldiers. If the situation called for bypassing the central Japanese defenses, the troops advancing northward were to remain on the lookout for any route that would permit the isolation of the Umurbrogol region from the north. The attack was to jump off at 0700, 24 September.[15]

The narrow coastal plain of western Peleliu, where RCT 321 was to operate during the drive to the north, varied in width between 50 and 750 yards. At the southern end of the West Road, where the soldiers relieved the 1st Marines, the coastal plain was about 500 yards wide. About halfway up the western coast of the island at a point where the coastal plain attained a width of 750 yards, was the village of Garekoru. Just south of the village an unimproved trail led eastward through the hills until it connected with the East Road. From its widest point near Garekoru the plain narrowed down to the north until its width near the northern tip of Peleliu was only about 50 yards.

Vegetation varied considerably on the west side of the island. To the south of Garekoru exposed coral was covered with dense tropical underbrush and trees. To the north of the village the soil and vegetation changed in character. The coral was gradually replaced by sand, and the tropical jungle gave way to coconut palms. From the point where the attack was to jump off on the morning of 24 September, slightly more than 6,000 yards separated the 321st Infantry Regiment from the northern tip of Peleliu. The broken, jagged coral cliffs dominating the western plain were honeycombed with Japanese defenses, which consisted of dugouts and caves extending from the very base to the tops of ridges, varying in elevation between 50 and 200 feet. Clearly, all the advantages of cover and concealment accrued to the defenders.

For the soldiers and men of the 7th Marines, the drive to northern Peleliu promised to be an arduous undertaking. Once again the stamina, aggressiveness, and raw courage of the men in the assault were to be pitched against the fanatical determination of a well provisioned foe who preferred death to surrender.

ISOLATING THE UMURBROGOL POCKET[16]

During the afternoon of 23 September, the 2d Battalion, 321st Infantry Regiment, occupied positions about 700 yards north of the airfield along the West Road. The 3d Battalion was echeloned closely behind it for immediate support. The 1st Battalion, designated as regimental reserve, was located in the vicinity of the regimental command post.

To obtain a more detailed picture of the tactical situation in his zone of attack, Colonel Dark dispatched patrols northward between the West Road and the seashore. Other patrols from 3/1 had previously reconnoitered this

---

[15] 1st MarDiv FO 3-44.

[16] Additional sources used for this section are: *IIIAC C-2 Rpts; 81st InfDiv OpRpts; 7thMar R-2 Jnl; VMF(N)-541 Hist; 2/11 SAR; 3/7 Rec of Events.*

ground, having advanced to Garekoru without meeting any heavy resistance. Nevertheless, the movements were observed by the Japanese occupying the ridges to the east of the road, whose fire on the patrols was without noticeable effect. At Garekoru the patrols encountered numerous land mines, aerial bombs emplaced as land mines, and a few defensive positions which were not being held in strength. At 1700, the patrols reported the entire area from Phase Line 0-3 to Garekoru free of Japanese.

The receipt of such an optimistic report impelled General Rupertus to advance his timetable for the drive, scheduled to get under way on the morning of 24 September. RCT 321 received orders to send one battalion forward at once with the mission to advance to Phase Line 0-4 and dig in for the night. The task was assigned to 2/321, which began to move north at 1730. One company, moving forward between the West Road and the coast, was able to advance unopposed under the cover of a low ridge. The Japanese on the central ridges promptly spotted the company advancing east of the road as it attempted to move over open ground. The unit drew such a heavy volume of rifle and machine gun fire that the advance promptly ground to a halt before it had made much headway. Even though it had not as yet drawn any enemy fire, the company on the left halted after an advance of 100 yards to maintain contact with the unit on its right. The fading hours of daylight found both companies withdrawing to their starting points, where they dug in for the night, after establishing a continuous line of defense.

Aside from the combat action along the western coast of Peleliu, several other developments had taken place on the island in the course of the day. On the beaches and at the airfield the combat engineers had continued the removal of bombs, mines, and duds. They cleared the main beach for about 1,000 yards, laid out perimeter roads around the airstrip, and constructed a road from the south end of the airfield to Scarlet Beach. Temporary repairs on the fighter strip were completed, as was a dispersal area for 9 night fighters and 24 day-fighter aircraft. Work had begun on the southwest half of the bomber strip and a temporary control tower was half finished. The urgency of work on the airfield was emphasized during the afternoon when a B-24, the first plane larger than a TBF to land on the Peleliu strip, made an emergency landing.

The relative quiet that settled over the island with the approach of darkness on 23 September was shattered by alerts that were sounded at 1823 and 1900. No enemy aircraft appeared, however, and no bombs were dropped. During an otherwise quiet night, an enemy mortar shell landed in the CP of 3/7, causing one casualty.

For the Japanese on Babelthuap the arrival of nightfall marked the time when the main body of the *2d Battalion, 15th Infantry Regiment* could begin its embarkation for Peleliu. Versions of what transpired as the Japanese approached the northern tip of Peleliu differ. According to the Japanese:

> The main body of our reinforcement force [*2d Battalion, 15th Infantry Regiment*] left the Palau Proper Islands on the

CORSAIR BEING READIED *for napalm attack on enemy positions in the Umurbrogol.* (USMC 100375)

JAPANESE RIDGE POSITIONS *on Peleliu under air attack.* (USMC 98401)

night of the 23d. Nine of our landing barges arrived safely, but six of them were shelled and burned when taking the wrong landing route. However, most of the personnel in those six barges were able to land by walking in the shallows.[17]

According to the American account of the action:

> ... during the night from 23–24 September, there was again considerable enemy barge activity to the north, with seven craft sighted in that area, attempting to reinforce the island. They were sighted at approximately 0330 on the morning of 24 September and were brought under our naval and artillery fire. LVT(A)s also were active in the northern waters, taking the barges under close-range fire. All the enemy craft were reported sunk.[18]

One of the units playing a major role in combatting the Japanese barges was 2/11, which at 0500 commenced firing on enemy barges approaching from the north and apparently heading for the northeastern tip of Peleliu. Destroyers also opened fire on the craft and kept them illuminated with star shells. An observer reported that the effect of the fire was excellent. He counted 8 or 10 barges sunk or damaged and saw many people swimming about the debris. Throughout the morning of 24 September, fire was placed on survivors who were attempting to wade ashore on Peleliu. The Japanese tendency to bunch up increased the effectiveness of the artillery fire. Final reports were that 11 barges had either been sunk or disabled.[19]

A prisoner of war, identified as a member of the engineer unit of the *2d Battalion, 15th Infantry Regiment*, shed further light on the incident. According to him, the barges intercepted off Peleliu the previous morning had carried most of the supplies of the *2d Battalion*, whereas the second echelon carried mostly troops. This prisoner estimated that 600 Japanese had gone ashore either on northeastern Peleliu or on small islands in the area.

Shortly before 0600, 24 September, an air, naval, and field artillery preparation was directed against the west side of the central ridges and suspected Japanese positions near Garekoru. At 0700, the 2d Battalion, 321st Infantry Regiment, jumped off in an attack designed to seize the area west of the central ridges to a line about 500 yards north of Garekoru. The 3d Battalion followed the attacking 2d in column. The beginning of the attack saw 3/7 echeloned to the right rear of the 2d Battalion, RCT 321, with the mission of screening the right flank of the advancing infantry.

This advance initially progressed on schedule as far as those elements moving through the coastal plain were concerned. Despite moderate small arms and mortar fire, the leading elements of 2/321 reached the junction of the West Road and a trail leading eastward by noon. (See Map 9). Fully aware of the importance of this juncture, the Japanese had established positions here that were more formidable than anything the infantrymen had encountered during the morning's advance. In a brief but violent action, the 2d Battalion overcame the Japanese at the road-trail

---

[17] *Japanese CenPacOps*, p. 109.
[18] *1st MarDiv SAR*, Anx A, p. 7.
[19] *2/11 AR*, 24Sep44.

ISOLATION OF UMURBROGOL

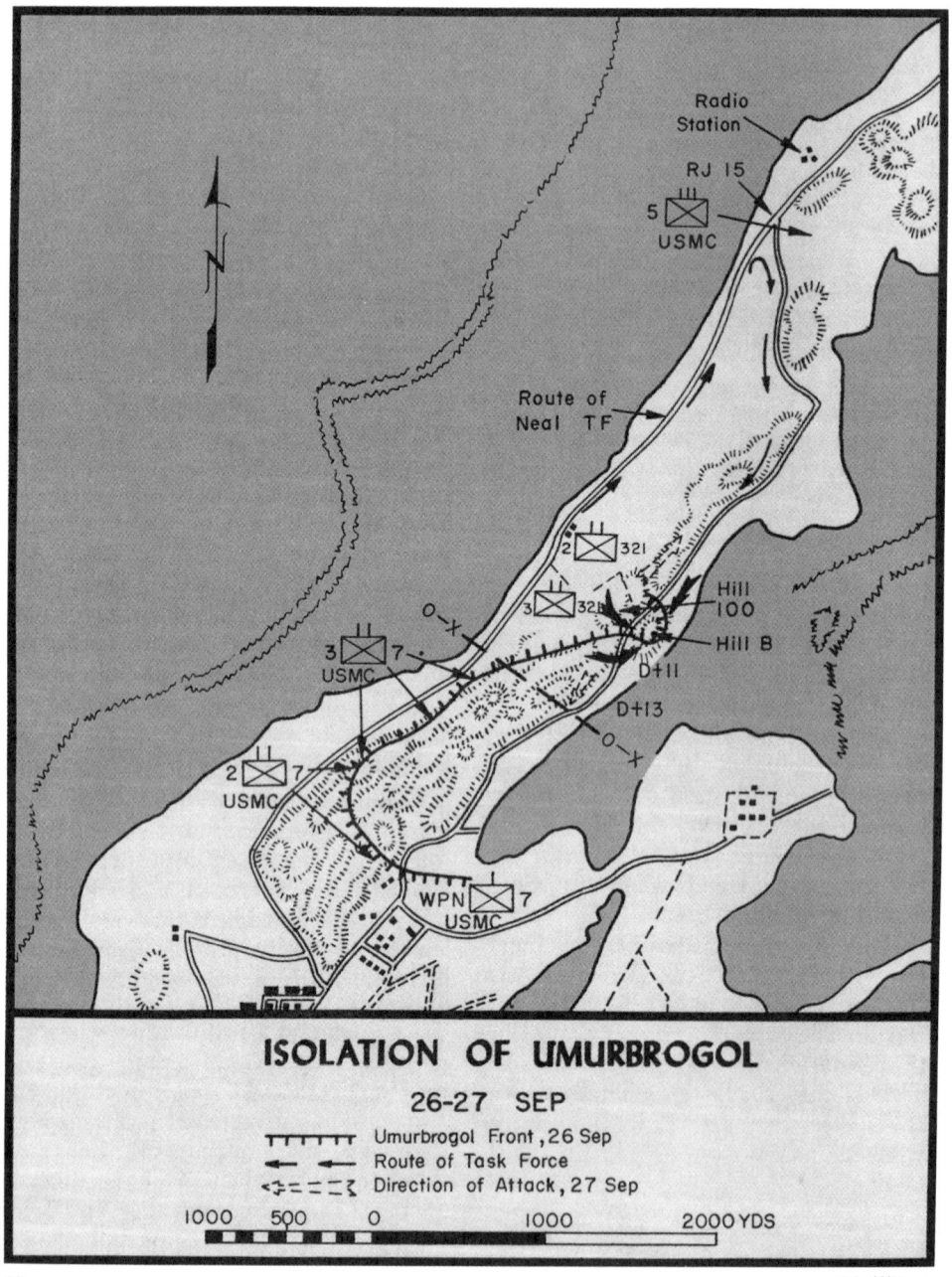

26-27 SEP

⊥⊥⊥⊥⊥	Umurbrogol Front, 26 Sep
← ←	Route of Task Force
⋖⋛≡≡⋛	Direction of Attack, 27 Sep

1000 500 0 1000 2000 YDS

Map 9

E.L. Wilson

junction. Ejection of the defenders from this strongpoint resulted in the capture of an antitank gun, three machine guns, and a naval gun. The 2d Battalion continued its advance up the road to Garekoru, leaving rear elements to explore the trail, which later was to assume major significance. In its rapid northward advance, the battalion reached Phase Line 0-4 to the north of Garekoru in midafternoon, when it halted, having reached the day's objective.

Elsewhere and particularly along the right flank, the advance did not proceed as envisioned. The rapid progress of 2/321 over the road had caused 3/7, moving over the ridges on the right, to fall behind. As a result, elements of 3/321 were sent up to the ridges to fill the gap. Soon, these elements ran into strong opposition along the low ridge that paralleled and dominated the road from a distance of 50 yards. In the face of strong opposition from this elevation, the infantry later pulled its right flank off the ridge and advanced up the coastal road. According to the Army version of the incident, withdrawal from the ridge occurred because the troops there wanted to maintain contact with the rest of the battalion.[20]

Regardless of the reasons leading to the withdrawal of troops from this vital terrain feature, it appeared likely that the Japanese might take advantage of the situation and reoccupy the ridge, a possibility that was glaringly apparent to the commanding officer of 3/7, who was anxiously watching this development.

It was perfectly obvious to anyone who stood on that ridge that its control by the Japs could have been disastrous to the whole effort. We had been ordered to maintain contact with them [RCT 321] by trailing their right flank in column along the crest of the ridge from the point where we had earlier tied in with 3/1. I myself was at this boundary when the movement by 3/321 commenced and I personally saw the whole thing. They moved forward along the ridge a few yards until they encountered the first enemy positions, then gave it all up as a bad idea, and bore sharply to their left front to the coastal road below. It was certainly not our mission to maintain the contact with them on the flat coastal road and turn the ridge over to the Japs. I therefore reported what I had seen immediately to CO, CT-7, as well as CO 3/321. The latter officer . . . promised that he would do everything within his power to get them back on the high ground. I watched several abortive efforts to do so before finally becoming convinced that if friendly troops were going to control the ridge that night it would have to be our I Company.[21]

At 1310, 3/7 informed regiment that Company K had been committed on the right of the battalion, while Company I had been committed on the left. In his report to the regiment Major Hurst emphasized that 3/321 had withdrawn from the hills towards the road, leaving an undefended gap on the left flank of 3/7, that the Japanese had occupied the hills, and that 3/7 was fighting to retake them.[22]

Five minutes later, while Company I was reoccupying the ridge, Captain Fer-

---

[20] Smith, *Approach to the Philippines*, p. 537.

[21] LtCol Edward H. Hurst ltr to CMC, dtd 15Mar50, in *Peleliu Comment File*, hereafter *Hurst ltr II*.

[22] *7th Mar R-2 Jnl*, 24Sep44.

guson, CO of the company, was killed.[23] Shortly before 1500, 3/7 reestablished contact with the Army units on the West Road. As a result of their taking the initiative to recapture the vacated ridge, the Marines eliminated a serious threat to the flank of the advancing Army units at a cost of 17 casualties.

In the course of the afternoon, the leading elements of 3/321 probed the central ridges north of the Marines in an attempt to discover a route leading eastward. One company of infantry was finally able to gain a foothold on the first ridge line east of the road and about 600 yards south of Phase Line 0-4. The main body of the battalion remained in the proximity of West Road during the night. At 1700, Company L, 3/7, relieved Company I, which went into bivouac as battalion reserve. At 1800, 3/7 dug in for the night on a 400-yard front with Company L on the left and Company K on the right.[24]

The 2d Battalion, RCT 321, reached Phase Line 0-4 by midafternoon of 24 September. For the remainder of the day, the battalion pushed aggressive patrols up the West Road. A strong combat patrol, supported by Marine and Army tanks, moved northward against negligible opposition for nearly 2,000 yards. At this point, the patrol had nearly reached Phase Line 0-5. From their vantage point the soldiers saw the extensive Japanese radio installations, which were situated about 600 yards north of Phase Line 0-5, and numerous Japanese pillboxes, caves, and other defenses along West Road. Before dark the patrol withdrew to Garekoru without having encountered serious enemy resistance.

In the meantime, Company G, the leading unit of the 2d Battalion, began organizing for defense to protect the north flank of the regiment. Hardly had this defense been established when, at 1700, the enemy counterattacked and forced the 2d Battalion to withdraw about 200 yards. The infantrymen promptly retook this ground. A second enemy counterattack shortly after 1800 disintegrated before it ever got started when effective artillery concentrations were placed on the assembly area.[25]

Aside from the activity which took place along West Road, the most far-reaching action on 24 September was destined to occur to the east of the road, and just south of the village of Garekoru, where the advancing infantry had earlier in the day discovered a poorly defined trail leading eastward into the enemy-held ridges. For lack of a better name, and because elements of RCT 321 had been the first to encounter it, the route was designated the "321st Infantry Trail."[26]

Since this trail could represent the only lateral link between the West and East Roads on Peleliu, its tactical importance was immediately apparent. From the point where it branched off from the West Road, the trail led through a stretch of swampland before ascending into the enemy-held ridges. Patrols cautiously followed the trail as it meandered into the high ground, encountering only negligible resistance. In

---

[23] *3/7 Rec of Events*, 24Sep44.
[24] *Ibid.*

[25] *81st InfDiv OpRpt*, 24Sep44.
[26] Historical Committee, *81st Infantry Division*, p. 139.

order to take advantage of what could prove a weak spot in the Japanese defenses, Colonel Dark dispatched an infantry company of 2/321 along the trail.

As the company advanced into the ridges, Japanese resistance stiffened, particularly on Hill 100, which dominated the route of advance and blocked the progress of the company to the east. Since this hill, which formed the northern bastion of the Japanese pocket in the Umurbrogol ridges, dominated not only the 321st Infantry Trail but also the East Road, its capture assumed major importance. In a brief but bitter engagement, the infantrymen seized the hill and then grimly held on against all Japanese attempts to retake it. Fully aware of the decisive importance of holding the hill and, if possible, of gaining further ground to the south, Colonel Dark diverted most of the 3d Battalion to the east. Soon three additional infantry companies were attacking eastward along the trail into the area south of Hill 100. Before nightfall, the 3d Battalion had seized an escarpment south of Hill 100 and established contact with 3/7 farther to the southeast.

By evening of 24 September, it appeared that the lack of momentum which had forestalled practically all forward movement for several days, had ended. From his new division command post in the former Japanese administration building at the northern edge of the airstrip, General Rupertus pondered his next move.[27] The advances made during the day had surpassed his expectations, and the tactical situation had radically changed for the better since morning. In addition, the sweep up the coast had brought a new high in the number of enemy prisoners, three being taken during the day.[28]

On the other hand, the successes achieved during the day were accompanied by difficult problems of evacuation and supply. Army engineers, already fully occupied in clearing Garekoru of mines and boobytraps, had to improve both the narrow West Road and the 321st Infantry Trail, a job that continued after darkness during the night of 24-25 September. The men on the escarpment south of Hill 100 faced an even greater predicament, since they had to manhandle all supplies going to their exposed positions. During the return trip the supply party encountered staggering difficulties in evacuating the wounded over the inhospitable terrain. Yet the advantages gained by the day's advance far surpassed all resulting problems.

Elsewhere on Peleliu, extensive work on the airstrip had progressed to the point where the short southeast-northwest runway was fully restored. Even though heavy fighting still was in progress about two thousand yards to the north, a large number of aircraft were able to land, including two C-46s, one C-47, four PBYs, and the first echelon of VMF(N)-541, consisting of eight Hellcats. Henceforth the night fighters would be available for night operations.[29]

For the continued operations the following day, 3/7 shifted Company I from

---

[27] *1st MarDiv SAR*, Anx A, p. 8.

[28] *Ibid.*
[29] *VMF(N)-541 Hist*, Feb44-Apr46.

battalion reserve to the left of Company L, a maneuver designed to extend the line held on the ridges an additional 250 yards to the north. The 1st Battalion was ordered to move up on the West Road, where it was to remain in Support of 3/321 until an opportunity arose to shift direction and advance southward into the central ridges.

There were no reports of night activity in any sector of the 1st Marine Division.[30] Lest an erroneous impression be created that everything on Peleliu was entirely quiet, some action continued intermittently throughout the night. At 2200, Japanese threw hand grenades in front of the 3/7 sector.[31] Also during the night, Japanese with demolitions fastened to their bodies, tried to infiltrate the 7th Marines lines. One Japanese, killed 10 feet in front of a halftrack, was found in the morning, a Molotov cocktail tied to one leg, explosives fastened to his back, and grenades stored in his pockets.[32]

The plan of operations for 25 September was to cut across the island near the 321st Infantry Trail. This maneuver would complete the isolation of Japanese forces in the Umurbrogol ridges. At 0700 elements of 2/321 jumped off from Hill 100 and in midmorning reached the edge of the East Road. Enemy resistance during this advance remained moderate and consisted primarily of rifle and machine gun fire from a key height across the East Road known as Hill B. The infantrymen paused in order to await the arrival of 3/321 for a combined drive across the road. When it attempted to expand the hold on the escarpment occupied the previous afternoon and to move onto East Road, the latter battalion ran into heavy fire from pillboxes and emplacements protected by steep walls and sheer cliffs guarding the northern approaches to the Umurbrogol defense system. There the drive of 3/321 bogged down and for the remainder of 25 September that battalion made no further gains. Any hope of a two-battalion assault against Hill B, which the Japanese were evidently holding in strength, had to be abandoned. For the remainder of 25 September, the Army troops near East Road remained in place.[33]

Despite the disappointing turn of events along the 321st Infantry Trail, progress appeared vastly more promising along the western coast of Peleliu. This applied primarily to developments along the West Road, where, at 0700, a strong Army combat patrol composed of infantry, tanks, and flamethrowers moved north from Garekoru village. The mission of this force was to destroy enemy installations that reconnaissance on the previous day had identified. This combat patrol advanced 1,200 yards, killing 30 Japanese and destroying four pillboxes and two large supply dumps before it reached Phase Line 0-5. The patrol arrived at its objective without sustaining any casualties.

Such weak resistance along the West Road indicated to General Rupertus that the enemy had concentrated his main strength in the central ridges of Peleliu. A swift drive to the north over

---

[30] *1st MarDiv SAR*, Anx A, p. 8.
[31] *7th Mar R-2 Jnl*, 24Sep44.
[32] *IIIAC C-2 Rpt*, 25Sep44.

[33] *81st InfDiv OpRpt*, 24Sep44.

West Road, coupled with a continuation of the RCT 321 drive to bisect the island, would result in the complete isolation of the Japanese in the central ridges while eliminating all enemy resistance in northern Peleliu. The possibilities that were now open to the division commander were greatly expanded, and General Rupertus decided that swift action was indicated. At 0945, division headquarters orally ordered the 1st Marines to take over the sector of the 5th in addition to its own. The 5th Marines was to pass through the lines held by 2/321 and attack towards the northern tip of Peleliu. Elements of the 321st Infantry Regiment engaged near East Road were to continue their attack eastward, but bypass the hard core of enemy resistance until movement up East Road became feasible. Then, in conjunction with the 5th Marines, they would launch a drive to the northern tip of the island.[34]

For the first time since the Marines had stormed ashore on Peleliu, all initiative had passed into the hands of the attacking force. The Japanese, holed up in their caves and dugouts, could still kill and maim; they were to inflict many more casualties before the fight for the island was over; but the road to the tip of the island was now open. Marines were moving up to eliminate any resistance that the enemy might still offer. Japanese hopes of receiving reinforcements were fading as more and more of the coastline in their hands had to be relinquished. The momentum of the American drive had been restored. At long last the beginning of the end of the costly and arduous operation was in sight.

DRIVE TO THE NORTH[35]

Orders to move to the western portion of Peleliu found the 5th Marines in static positions on Eastern Peleliu, where the regimental mission had been to prevent enemy counterlandings. The 1st Battalion was deployed in the vicinity of the radio direction finding station near Ngardololok, the 2d Battalion was holding the islands north of the north eastern peninsula, while the 3d Battalion, less one company, occupied defensive positions along Purple Beach. The 1st Marines completed the relief of the 5th shortly after noon and assumed command of the 5th Marines sector at that time. In order to expedite movement of the regiment to the West Road, the battalions moved out on trucks at 1300, with 1/5 in the lead, followed by 3/5 and 2/5.[36]

By 1600, the 5th Marines had executed the passage of the lines, and the regiment passed through Phase Line O-4 near Garekoru. As 1/5 continued its advance up the West Road, it encountered erratic resistance from what appeared to be Japanese holdouts. The level terrain was devoid of the dense jungle growth abounding elsewhere on Peleliu and offered ideal conditions for the movement of tanks and LVT flamethrowers accompanying the advance battalion. Aside from occasional Japanese sniper and mortar fire, the advance

---

[34] *81st InfDiv OpRpt,* 25Sep44.

[35] Additional sources used for this section are: *81st InfDiv OpRpt; 5th Mar URpts; 7th Mar War Jnl; 1/5 B-3 Jnl; 2/5 OpRpt; 2/11 SAR; 4/11 WarD, Aug–Nov44.*

[36] *5th Mar URpts,* 26Sep44.

continued for about 500 yards without interruption to Road Junction 15, where the West and East Roads met. This vital point was defended by a small Japanese force, which had installed itself on a ridge dominating the road forks.

Around 1700, as the Marines approached this point, the enemy opened fire, which served only to delay the Marines. When the firefight ended the Japanese had lost 20 killed. The battalion continued its advance for another 100 yards and seized the Japanese radio station, whose towers the forward elements of RCT 321 had spotted on the previous day. Having secured this objective, the battalion established night defenses north of the radio station from the beach to the high ground east of the West Road (See Map 10). For the remainder of the evening and throughout the night, the forward elements at the radio station were continuously and heavily engaged with the enemy. The 1st Battalion, 5th Marines, was the recipient of direct fire from two 70mm guns firing out of caves less than 300 yards away. The Marines drew additional fire from enemy artillery and mortars located on the northern tip of Peleliu, as well as from two 37mm guns on Ngesebus Island. Small arms fire from three directions converged on the battalion.[37]

To reduce the enemy artillery and mortar fire that was proving so troublesome to 1/5, the 11th Marines massed its batteries against suspected enemy artillery and mortar positions. Since direct observation was impossible, the regiment used a target list, firing on areas that looked promising on the basis of a chart and photographic inspection. Whenever such fire resulted in reduced enemy activity, continuous shelling at a slow, irregular rate was employed on the target throughout the night. This counterbattery fire proved very effective and helped the exposed battalion to maintain its forward positions.[38]

Nor was heavy mortar and artillery fire all that 1/5 had to contend with during the night of 25-26 September. The Japanese launched three counterattacks in the course of the evening against the hard-pressed Marines, but each of these attacks was repelled. At 0200, 26 September, a platoon of Company C took the initiative by launching a surprise counterattack, which resulted in the destruction of two particularly troublesome machine guns.[39]

Upon reaching Road Junction 15 in the wake of the advance of 1/5, the 3d Battalion pivoted to the southeast and headed down East Road, where it established night defenses on the road and along the western slopes of Hill 80. The latter hill, in itself an isolated terrain feature, owed its importance to its location, for it was the only link separating the Kamilianlul ridges to the south from the Amiangal ridges, which formed the northernmost hill mass on Peleliu.

Unlike the effective resistance that 1/5 had encountered near the radio station, the enemy that 3/5 came upon was either disorganized or unaware of the Marines' presence on the East Road. According to an eyewitness:

---

[37] Smith, *Narrative*, p. 83.

[38] Maj David R. Griffin ltr to CMC, dtd 13Mar50, in *Peleliu Comment File*, hereafter *Griffin ltr*.

[39] *1/5 B–3 Jnl*, 25Sep44.

SECURING THE NORTH

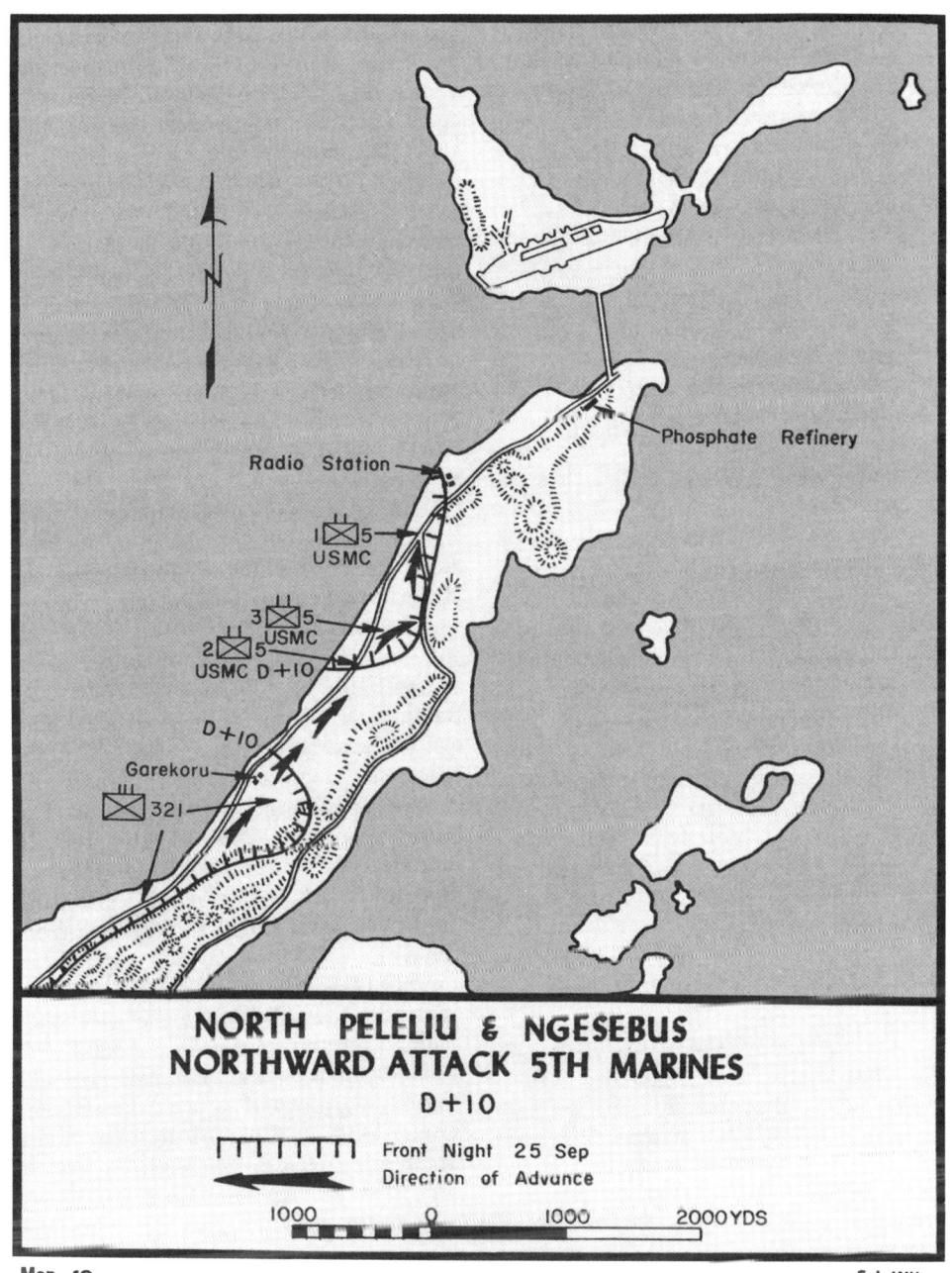

NORTH PELELIU & NGESEBUS
NORTHWARD ATTACK 5TH MARINES
D+10

Front Night 25 Sep
Direction of Advance

Map 10

E. L. Wilson

... darkness had fallen and I was engaged in tying in I Company with the adjoining Second Battalion Unit under the command of Capt. Albert J. Doherty. Captain Doherty and I were standing on the road with a small group around us discussing our situation when the word was passed from my outpost that enemy troops were approaching. We immediately took cover, not knowing how large a force it was or whether it was cognizant of our presence. The enemy was obviously unaware of the 5th Marines advance because they approached making a great deal of noise. When they reached the approximate position where Captain Doherty and I had been my men opened fire killing all of the enemy and sustaining no casualties. The enemy group consisted of about 12 Japanese Marines.[40]

Once again, on the evening of the second day of continuous forward movement, General Rupertus had cause to be pleased with the progress that had been made during the day. Even though the effort of the Army troops to isolate the central Japanese defenses had been temporarily halted, this lack of progress had been more than compensated for by the rapid advance of the 5th Marines up the West Road. Except for a critical shortage of hydrogen for flamethrowers, the flow of supplies was moving smoothly.[41]

Behind the front lines, the engineers were keeping pace with the advance of the combat troops. By evening of 25 September, 500 men of a naval construction battalion were engaged in shore party work. Improvement of roads by the engineers was continuing. This work helped largely to offset the complaint voiced by RCT 321 "that the presence of the 5th Marine Regiment on the west coast further complicated the traffic control problem."[42]

Work on the airstrip was also making good progress. The Engineer Group, consisting of elements of the 1st Engineer Battalion and the 33d and 73d Naval Construction Battalions, had dug out and refilled most soft spots and graded, rolled, and watered the entire strip. Radar units and control equipment were in operation. The airstrip tower had been readied for around the clock operation.

After a night of incessant harassment by the Japanese, 1/5 spent the early hours of 26 September in consolidating its positions around the radio station and preparing for continuation of its attack later in the day to the northern tip of Peleliu. Shortly after 0600, 3/5 jumped off for an attack against Hill 80 with Company K on the left and Company I on the right. The attack carried the hill and by 0830 the assault force reached a swamp bordering the east coast of Peleliu. This advance of the 3d Battalion was of major importance because it effectively cut the island in two.

The 1st Battalion, 5th Marines, ran into stiff opposition from the Amiangal ridges dominating northern Peleliu. The northern portion of the L-shaped hill system consisted of ridges running generally from northeast to southwest for about 1,000 yards; the southern leg extended from northwest to southeast. The southern leg of the ridges was not

---

[40] Maj John A. Crown ltr to CMC, dtd 13 Feb50, in *Peleliu Comment File*, hereafter *Crown ltr*.

[41] *1st MarDiv SAR*, Anx A, p. 10.

[42] *81st InfDiv OpRpt*, 25Sep44.

continuous but broken into four separate hills or knobs, designated from northwest to southeast as Hill 1, Hill 2, Hill 3, and Radar Hill, so named because it had at one time served as an enemy radar installation. These four knobs were to gain ill repute as Hill Row. The entire Amiangal ridge system was held in strength by the Japanese, particularly the portion paralleling the route of advance of 1/5. This part contained some of the most elaborate caves and tunnels on Peleliu.

The battalion had barely started out along the West Road when the enemy in and on Hill 1 opened up on the Marines with 37mm and 75mm guns as well as automatic weapons and mortars. This curtain of fire from the Amiangal ridges was reinforced by heavy fire from Ngesebus Island. All forward movement soon halted. Attacking eastward from the West Road, Company B assaulted the second knob, Hill 2, but also encountered opposition. Through sheer determination the company was able to gain a firm foothold on the hill by early afternoon. This accomplishment in effect served to outflank the Japanese on Hill 1, but Japanese resistance on the last mentioned hill continued throughout the day. An attempt by Company C to seize all of Hill 1 during the remaining hours of daylight was unsuccessful, and continuation of the assault had to await the following day.

During the bitter fighting in which 1/5 engaged during the night of 25-26 September and for most of the following day, 2/5 remained stationary on the southern flank of the regiment. At 1600 on 26 September, when it had become apparent that 1/5 could make no further progress, 2/5 was ordered to attack. The battalion advanced northward through the left wing of 1/5, carefully bypassing embattled Hill 1. In the course of its advance, the battalion drew heavy fire from Japanese emplacements in the plain, from the ridges on its right, as well as from Ngesebus. Enemy mortars proved especially troublesome. As a result of the heavy fire, Company F lost four of its supporting tanks before it had advanced very far beyond Hill 1.[43] Attempts by the artillery to give all possible support to the battalion were largely ineffectual. "We fired frequent missions throughout the day on these mortars; the reported effect was that the mortars were neutralized while we fired but that they were not destroyed. The enemy apparently withdrew into the caves during the period of our fire."[44]

As evening approached, the 5th Marines occupied a jagged front line. The 1st Battalion, though out of contact with the 2d, was tied in with the 3d on the right. The mission of the 3d Battalion was to support either the 1st or 2d Battalion in the event of a major Japanese counterattack. Further progress of the 2d Battalion was impeded by a large antitank ditch, which blocked the approach to the remnants of the Peleliu phosphate plant. The Japanese had converted the reinforced concrete foundation of the otherwise demolished structure into a major defensive installation. Exposed to the enemy fire from Ngesebus Island and plunging fire from caves and defensive positions from the hills,

---

[43] 2/5 OpRpt, 26Sep44.
[44] 2/11 AR, 26Sep44.

2/5 found itself in a very unenviable situation.

Further south on the island, at the juncture of the 321st Infantry Trail and the East Road, 26 September was to bring additional gains, though not without great difficulty. On the previous day, 2/321 had seized Hill 100 and advanced to the foot of Hill B, which dominated East Road and formed the last obstacle in the path of RCT 321's advance to the east coast. The mission of capturing this vital hill had been given to 3/321, which had been scheduled to launch the attack at 0700, with 2/321 in support. Even before 3/321 could get into its attack position along East Road it drew such furious fire from small arms, mortars, and automatic weapons in the northern strongpoints of the Umurbrogol Pocket that the movement bogged down.

When it became apparent around noon that the 3d Battalion would be unable to reach Hill B, the mission of seizing the hill was assigned to 2/321. To ensure the success of the attack, it was decided to launch a two-pronged assault against the hill. During the time that the 2d Battalion was organizing for the attack, a special task force composed of 7 medium tanks, 6 LVTs, 1 LVT flamethrower, and 45 riflemen, advanced northward over the West Road to its junction with East Road. There the column pivoted to the south, followed the East Road, and by 1500 had reached a point within 150 yards north of Hill B. Such a bold maneuver could not fail to attract enemy attention, and the column suddenly found itself under frenzied attack by 15 Japanese who, vastly outnumbered and outgunned, were promptly killed in the skirmish.

At 1600, when both attack forces had reached their jumpoff positions, the attack against Hill B commenced. White phosphorus mortar shells shrouded the hill in smoke, obscuring visibility of the defending force. The task force attacked from the north, while two companies of 2/321 attacked from the west and south. At the outset both attack forces encountered strong resistance, but in less than an hour the hill had changed hands and the entire Japanese force was wiped out. A number of Korean laborers, evidently less inspired than their taskmasters, preferred to surrender.

Despite the loss of Hill B, the Japanese took the initiative at least once during the day by attacking the command post of RCT 321 in force, after infiltrating the widely spaced Army and Marine lines. This surprise attack was launched by enemy troops armed with rifles and machine guns. The force created havoc momentarily but could not match the soldiers' fire. The Japanese then retreated, leaving 35 dead around the command post area.

Earlier that day, General Rupertus had felt that time for the capture of Ngesebus Island was ripe. "Improvement in our tactical situation led to the making of plans for an attack on Ngesebus to the north to be carried out the following day, but developments failed to warrant the pursuit of this action."[45]

Instead, an additional day was set aside for preparations for the assault on

---

[45] 1st MarDiv WarD, Sep44.

Ngesebus as well as consolidation of the hold the 5th Marines had gained on the northern portion of Peleliu. Despite heavy resistance, elements of RCT 321 in the center of the island and the 5th Marines in the north had reached the eastern coast. The Japanese on Peleliu, though still capable of prolonged resistance, were now divided into two distinct pockets whose elimination was merely a matter of time.

Also on 26 September, "a new high in the number of prisoners for a single day was obtained when six POWs were brought in, doubling our total for the operation."[46]

The night of 26-27 September was to be typical. The 11th Marines directed harassing fires against Japanese positions on the northern tip of Peleliu throughout the night.[47] The Japanese, in turn, shelled the area occupied by 3/321. Fighting also flared up in the center of the island where several Japanese were killed as they attempted to infiltrate the positions of 2/321 in the vicinity of Hill 100 and Hill B. The 7th Marines spent a generally quiet night, marked only by an exchange of hand grenades in the sector of 2/7. Weapons Company killed three Japanese during the night, one of them equipped with a machine gun. One of the Japanese dead carried the following message.

> American Brave Soldiers: We think you are much pity since landing on this island. In spite of your pitiful battle, we are sorry that we can present only fire, not even good water. We soon will attack strongly your army. You had done bravely your duty; now abandon your guns, and come in Japanese military with a white flag (or handkerchief) so we will be glad to see you and welcome you comfortably as we can well.[48]

The above Japanese offer found no takers among the soldiers and Marines on Peleliu. In fact, plans for the assault on Ngesebus were already completed. Naval demolition teams were busy offshore clearing the waters between Peleliu and Ngesebus in preparation for the coming assault.

At 0800, 27 September, another milestone in the Peleliu operation was reached when, in a simple ceremony, the American flag was raised in front of the division command post. Even while this ceremony was in progress, the 5th Marines was once again embroiled in fighting of the utmost severity, in which a battalion command post was just as exposed to enemy fire as any other forward position. This applied to the CP of 2/5, which on the morning of 27 September was located in the radio station near the northern tip of Peleliu. This building was very well constructed, but had been thoroughly worked over by artillery and air bombardment.

> The framework was still intact, however, and after clearing the dead Japs out, there were some rooms that were very suitable for a good CP. During the morning of the 27th several rounds of mortar fire were laid on the building with such accuracy that two of them went through the second story windows. Casualties were light but just knowing the Japs had the range on us wasn't so pleasant. Earlier that morning mortars were laid around

---

[46] *Ibid.*
[47] 4/11 WarD, Sep44.
[48] *7th Mar R-2 Jnl*, 27Sep44, also *1st Mar Div SAR*, Anx B, pp. 37-38.

the CP, with devastating effect, and caused light casualties. Major Gayle, for example, had men killed all around him but he was lucky and never got a scratch, just sand blown in his eyes, and the helmet blown full of holes. Lucky he didn't have the helmet on.[49]

The 2d Battalion was to find progress extremely rough for the remainder of the day. First, the erstwhile phosphate plant, which the Japanese had turned into a blockhouse, had to be secured in an area that bristled with snipers. The problem confronting Colonel Harris was a formidable one. The blockhouse in front of 2/5 could not be taken until the antitank ditch blocking the approaches to it had been seized. This was a job that the infantry could not tackle without armored support. The regimental commander decided to utilize all arms available in reducing these obstacles. First of all, Colonel Harris called naval gunfire and artillery in on Ngesebus and any other targets suspected of harboring artillery or mortar positions.

A medium tank, equipped with a bulldozer blade, was pressed into service to level the antitank ditch, and filled it by 0830. A LVT flamethrower then was able to come within effective range of the Japanese fortification. Moments later, when the flame and smoke had cleared, all resistance from this stronghold had ceased and more than 60 dead Japanese remained in the rubble. While this action was in progress, patrols from Company E seized a small, weakly defended ridge abutting the road from the east. The 2d Battalion thereafter resumed its advance northward along the road as well as over the adjacent ridge. Company F, at the head of the column, soon found itself embroiled in some of the most bitter and frustrating action of the entire campaign. Aside from receiving heavy Japanese artillery and mortar fire, the company faced a series of pillboxes and field fortifications on level ground, and layer upon layer of caves in the hillsides.

Even though they were not aware of it at the time, the men of the 5th Marines had come upon the most skillfully constructed defenses on Peleliu. The Japanese Army had utilized all of the many natural caves possessing tactical value, adapting them for the emplacement of heavier weapons with great ingenuity. On the other hand, Japanese naval troops had preferred to construct their own caves with the help of the *214th Naval Construction Battalion,* composed of men who had been professional miners and tunnel workers in civilian life. Since most of these Navy caves were located near the northern end of Peleliu, they proved a serious obstacle to the advance of the 5th Marines.

Sheer courage and heroism in themselves proved inadequate for the task. In the course of the morning of 27 September, Company F seized the two ridges forming the northwestern anchor of the Amiangal system and established observation posts on the crests. But this did not solve the problem of what to do about the Japanese occupying the caves about half way up the hill. Marine casualties mounted steadily, and evacuation of the wounded became more and more difficult. The assault on the ridges soon turned into a nightmare:

---

[49] *2/5 OpRpt,* 27Sep44.

The hill we were taking was honeycombed with caves, and we used everything in the book in closing them. (Hand grenades, five gallon cans of gas, composition C wrapped around 81mm WP mortar shells, flame throwers, and finally a 155mm gun).... During the assault the Japs still fired out of the caves, even throwing our own grenades out at us. It was hard to believe that a 70 lb. compo charge wrapped around a 81mm mortar shell, which when set off fairly rocked the OP on top of the hill, did not kill the Nips in the caves.[50]

Since the cave openings completely dominated the road leading past the northernmost ridge of Peleliu, the advance of the entire 2d Battalion ground to a halt. The first tank attempting to squeeze through the narrow gap between the hill and the northwestern shore was hit, and the Marines occupying the crest of the hill were powerless to cope with the caves underneath.

This seemingly insurmountable problem was solved late in the afternoon when the troublesome bottleneck was eliminated by means of an expedient involving a combination of arms. The solution was complicated but proved effective. First, artillery placed a continuous barrage on Ngesebus, while naval guns shelled Kongauru, an island northeast of Ngesebus and connected to the latter by a causeway. Joining the shoot were nine tanks which placed smoke shells on the closest Ngesebus beach from positions on the West Road. Every fourth artillery projectile fired against Ngesebus was a smoke shell. Five LVT(A)s, equipped with 75mm guns, then pushed out into the channel and fired point-blank into the mouth of the cave. Under this covering fire, the tanks, supported by Company G, moved up the road and beyond the cave. An LVT flamethrower was then employed against the cave. The lines of the 2d Battalion consolidated this gain and dug in for the night.[51]

The 1st Battalion also made important gains on 27 September. Most of the action for the day centered around Hill 1, which Companies B and C attacked at 0930. Once again the Marines were exposed to heavy fire from Japanese small arms and antitank guns emplaced in caves at the foot of the hill and on the slopes. After approaches for the supporting armor had been cleared, the rate of progress increased. In the course of the afternoon, 1/5 destroyed four 75mm and four 37mm guns, and a large number of automatic weapons. By 1700, having established a firm foothold on the hill, the Marines prepared to set up positions for the night. During the remaining hours of daylight, engineer demolition teams systematically eradicated every cave and each hollow even remotely resembling an enemy position.

In the course of 27 September, 84 Koreans and 7 Japanese were taken prisoner, a considerable increase over the previous total of 12 captured since the beginning of the operation.[52]

According to division intelligence estimates a total of 7,975 Japanese had been killed in 12 days of bitter fighting. Casualties for the 1st Marine Division were 768 killed, 3,693 wounded, and 273 missing in action, a total of 4,734.[53] Similarly, casualties for RCT 321 during the first week of its commitment on

---

[50] *2/5 Op Rpt*, 27Sep44.

[51] *5th Mar URpts*, 28Sep44.
[52] 1st MarDiv WarD, Sep44.
[53] *Ibid.*

Peleliu were 46 men killed, 226 wounded, and 7 missing, a total of 279.[54]

Even though a major portion of Peleliu was now in American hands, tenacious resistance could be expected to continue from the remaining enemy pockets. Aggressive action was needed, not only for the elimination of these pockets, but also to remove from the adjacent islands those Japanese still capable of rendering effective support to their compatriots on Peleliu.

SEIZURE ON NGESEBUS[55]

General Rupertus decided that Ngesebus Island was to be seized on 28 September, in a shore-to-shore operation executed with the assistance of all available supporting arms. The assault on the island was to be supported by a battleship, a cruiser, two destroyers, division and corps artillery, a tank company, a company of LVT(A)s, and a company of LVTs.

The mission of seizing Ngesebus was assigned to 3/5 about 1600, 27 September, when General Rupertus issued verbal orders to this effect to Lieutenant Colonel Lewis W. Walt, Executive Officer of the 5th Marines. Within the hour, members of 3/5 arrived at the 5th Marines command post to receive the attack order. Representatives of 1/7, held in reserve for the operation, also attended the meeting. The general plan of attack called for one hour of naval gunfire, air, and artillery preparation commencing at 0800. While the assault wave was covering the last 200 yards to the beach, Marine aircraft from the newly arrived VMF-114 would work the beach over. Sherman tanks were to form part of the first assault wave, flanked on either side by LVT(A)s and followed by LVTs loaded with the assault troops. The entire battalion was to embark in LVTs, and the waves were to land successively at two-minute intervals.[56]

H-Hour for the operation had been set to coincide with the lowest ebb of the tide to avoid water that would be too deep for the tanks, which could not be completely waterproofed.[57]

During the hours of daylight remaining on 27 September, 3/5, which had been held in reserve near Road Junction 15, relinquished its positions to 1/321 and assembled in preparation for the assault on Ngesebus. The Army battalion held a line extending from the junction in the north to Kamilianlul mountain, which was an extension of the Umurbrogol ridges north of the Wildcat Trail.

The curtain on the drama of Ngesebus opened on the morning of 28 September, when the massed fire of five artillery battalions from Peleliu, as well as heavy fire from warships and aircraft, blanketed the island. Near the northwestern shore of Peleliu, an impressive gathering of high-ranking officers had assembled to witness the operation. The group included such notables

---

[54] 321st RCT Unit Rpt 7, 30Sep44, Peleliu, as quoted in Smith, *Approach to the Philippines*, p. 549.

[55] Additional sources used for this section are: *5th Mar URpts;* VMF–114 WarD, Sep44; *2/11 SAR; 3/5 Rec of Events; Coleman ltr; Stuart ltr;* Smith, *Narrative*.

[56] LtCol Lewis W. Walt ltr to CMC, n.d., in *Peleliu Comment File*, hereafter *Walt ltr*.

[57] LtCol Arthur J. Stuart ltr to CMC, dtd 25Apr50, in *Peleliu Comment File*, hereafter *Stuart ltr*.

as Admiral Fort, and Generals Julian C. Smith, Geiger, Rupertus, Mueller, Oliver P. Smith, and Bell. The weather was cool and cloudy and interspersed with frequent rain squalls.[58]

For the Corsair pilots of VMF-114, air support for the Ngesebus landings represented a very interesting and original assignment. The operation marked the beginning of combat work for the squadron, which had reached Peleliu only two days earlier. At 0630, the Corsairs hit the airstrip on Ngesebus with 500-pound bombs and strafed the entire island as well as Kongauru to the northeast. "Strafing runs were made just a few feet off the deck and a hail of lead laid all over the island."[59] At 0840, 20 Corsairs preceded the landing craft and gave the island another heavy strafing. In the course of this attack, Japanese mortar positions were spotted and one specially prominent square blockhouse with an iron door was fired on and neutralized.

Whenever aircraft were not directly over the island, the artillery on Peleliu and naval guns offshore gave Ngesebus a heavy going over, starting at 0700 and concluding at 0905. Both quick and delay fuzes were used. Observers reported that the island was completely covered with fire.[60] In the course of the preliminary bombardment, naval gunfire ships pounded the northern portion of Ngesebus and continued to fire on that part of the island throughout the landing.

The 600-yard trip from Peleliu to Ngesebus proved generally uneventful, and the landing force proceeded as planned. Nevertheless, a few unforeseen contingencies arose that changed the sequence of events. Of the 16 tanks taking part in the operation, 3 failed to reach their destination after stalling and flooding in about three feet of water. The remaining tanks continued the crossing so cautiously that they could not keep up with the LVTs. In the end the infantry hit the beach long before the armor had completed the crossing. Another complication arose while the assault troops were en route to Ngesebus. Shortly after 0900, just as the assault waves departed Peleliu, spectators to the operation noticed that the naval gunfire had lifted and air attacks were slackening:

> Upon investigation as to why the naval gunfire did not support the attack, it developed that a great deal of confusion existed as to what the location of the troops would be at H-hour. The troops had planned this attack in the manner of land warfare and to them H-hour was the time of crossing the line of departure—in this case, the shore line of Peleliu. The Navy, planning as for an amphibious assault, considered H-hour to be the time the troops hit the beach on Ngesebus. Consequently, when H-hour arrived, the fire support ships assumed the troops were hitting the Ngesebus beach and lifted their fires, when actually the troops were just moving off Peleliu.[61]

This temporary lapse in preparatory fire did not result in any serious disadvantage to the men of 3/5, particularly since Marine aircraft, quickly sizing up the situation, jumped into the breach and resumed the relentless strafing of the southern beaches on Ngesebus. The planes halted their assault runs

---
[58] *1st MarDiv SAR*, Phase II, Anx A, p. 11.
[59] VMF-114 WarD, Sep44.
[60] *2/11 AR*, 28Sep44.

[61] *Coleman ltr*.

only when the assault force approached within 200 yards of the island.

The first wave hit the beach at 0911. Company K landed on the left, Company I on the right, and Company L followed in the rear as 3/5 reserve. The troops moved inland quickly and secured a beachhead against light resistance. Supporting LVT(A)s made short work of several pillboxes on the beaches. Companies I and K advanced to the northwest and linked up after crossing the airfield. To expedite the operation, the battalion commander committed Company L, which pivoted to the right and attacked towards the eastern shore of the island, encountering very little opposition in the process. The assault units suffered no casualties in the landing, while 50 of the enemy were killed or captured on or near the beaches.[62]

Within 12 minutes after the first assault wave had gone ashore on Ngesebus, the first tank lumbered across the beach. By 0930, all tanks and troop carriers except for three Shermans, had reached the island. Initial progress continued to be rapid, particularly in the zone of attack of Company L, which completed its mission of seizing the eastern part of Ngesebus within an hour and a half after going ashore. At 1300, a patrol of two tanks, three LVT(A)s, and one platoon of Company L landed on Kongauru Island off the northeastern tip of Ngesebus and secured the island against light resistance.

Companies I and K, attacking to the northwest, found the going considerably tougher in their zone of advance, particularly along the battalion left, where a series of ridges flanked the western shore of the island. There, the Japanese were offering determined resistance from caves and dugouts. Once again it became the unenviable task of the Marines to root the enemy out of these defensive positions, a job that was accomplished with the assistance of armor. In the midst of this operation, an enemy shell landed in the center of the battalion CP, wounding the battalion commander, Major John H. Gustafson, and a number of his men.[63]

By 1700, almost all of Ngesebus, except for a few hundred yards at the extreme northwestern tip of the island, was in American hands, though a few caves in the ridges still remained to be reduced. Because of the rapid progress made throughout the day, the presence of 1/7 was not required. The battalion reverted to division control as of 1500.[64]

The otherwise deadly serious business of seizing an enemy-held island was destined to feature at least one lighter episode. This was supplied by an aide to Major General James T. Moore, Commanding General of the 2d MAW. The aide, who also doubled as pilot, flew General Moore over Ngesebus Island in an L-5 observation airplane. In the course of this reconnaissance, the pilot observed a Japanese officer, equipped with sword and white gloves, directing the emplacement of a mortar. Upon completion of the flight and discharge of his passenger, the enterprising aide obtained several hand grenades and promptly headed back for a "bombing run" on the mortar position. The grenades were dropped with unobserved

---

[62] *3/5 Rec of Events*, 28Sep44.

[63] *Ibid.*

[64] *5th Mar URpts*, 29Sep44.

ASSAULT ON NGESEBUS ISLAND *as viewed from amphibious tank in third wave.* (USMC 97006)

MARINE ASSAULT TROOPS *advance into Ngesebus as oil dump burns in background.* (USMC 102051)

results, but the Japanese opened up on the L-5 with a machine gun. The pilot received a bullet in the leg, which was to put him out of action for the remainder of the Peleliu campaign.[65]

The 3d Battalion spent a relatively quiet night on Ngesebus. On the morning of 29 September, Companies I and K resumed the attack. Progress was normal until the two companies had nearly reached the northern tip of Ngesebus, when a 75mm gun opened up at point blank range. The Marines quickly destroyed this weapon and went on to overcome the rest of the resistance on the island. At 1500, 29 September, Ngesebus was declared secure.

An hour later, 2/321 relieved the Marines and completed mopping up. Having accomplished the mission on the island, 3/5 returned to Peleliu. The battalion had secured the island at a cost of 15 killed and 33 wounded.[66] In return, the Marines killed or captured 470 Japanese. Infantrymen of 2/321 were to account for another hundred of the enemy during the ensuing mop-up.[67]

After the capture of Ngesebus it became evident that the airstrip on the island was surfaced with sand so soft that the labor required to make the field operational was out of proportion to the benefits to be derived from it. As a result, no improvements were made to the airstrip, and the main advantage gained by the capture of the island was the final elimination of the bothersome fire from Ngesebus into the flanks and rear of the Marines advancing to the northern tip of Peleliu. At the same time, capture of the island deprived the Japanese of another possible staging area if they made another attempt to reinforce the Peleliu garrison.

MOPPING UP THE NORTH[68]

Throughout 28 September, the spectacular operation of 3/5 against Ngesebus held the limelight. For the two battalions of the 5th Marines remaining on Peleliu, it was business as usual as the drive continued to dislodge the Japanese from their elaborate defenses on the northern tip of the island.

On the morning of 28 September, the Japanese in the northern part of Peleliu still held a pocket slightly longer than 2,000 yards on fairly level ground, except for Hill 3 and Radar Hill, and some of the tunnels in the northern leg of the Amiangal ridges, where they still resisted in strength despite the fact that the Marines were firmly established on the crests (See Map 11).

The attack of 1/5 against Hill 3 was preceded by a mortar preparation lasting over an hour. At 0845, Company C jumped off. Approaching the hill from the north and west, bazooka and demolition teams crept forward and eliminated dugouts and caves one after the other. A Sherman tank rendered valuable support by firing directly into the cave openings. In this manner the tank knocked out a particularly annoying machine gun, which had been firing on the advancing Marines from the southeastern slope of Hill 3. Before noon, 1/5 had secured a foothold on the crest

---

[65] Smith, *Narrative*, p. 90.
[66] *3/5 Rec of Events*, 29Sep44.
[67] Smith, *Approach to the Philippines*, p. 548.

[68] Additional sources used for this section are: 1st MarDiv WarD, Sep44; *1st MarDiv SAR; 5th Mar URpts; 1/5 B–3 Jnl; 2/5 OpRpt*; Smith, *Narrative*.

SECURING THE NORTH

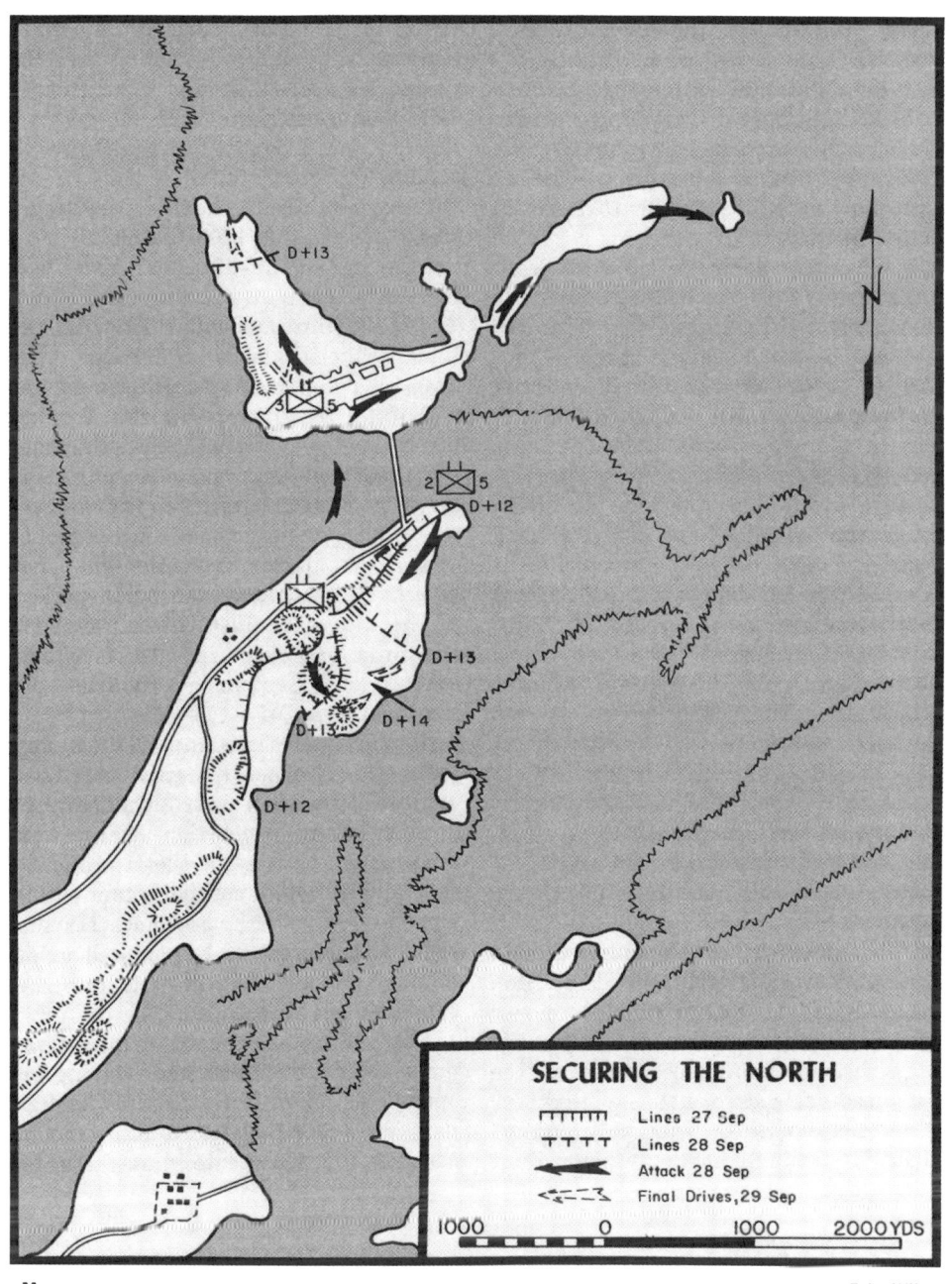

SECURING THE NORTH

⊥⊥⊥⊥⊥	Lines 27 Sep
⊤⊤⊤⊤	Lines 28 Sep
◄━━━	Attack 28 Sep
◄╌╌╌	Final Drives, 29 Sep

Map 11

E.I. Wilson

of the hill, though the Japanese still resisted in the caves below. Shortly before 1300, the enemy attempted to counterattack but was driven off by mortar fire. For the remainder of the afternoon Company C continued to consolidate its gains on the hill, capturing 15 Koreans in the process.[69]

At the very northern tip of Peleliu, 2/5 resumed its drive with the objective of seizing the flat ground to the north and east of the Amiangal ridges. Company G jumped off at 0700 and advanced through coconut groves near the eastern base of the ridges, where the Japanese had established elaborate fortifications. Despite heavy fire, the company continued its advance and by 1000 had killed 150 Japanese in the assault.[70] For the first time on Peleliu it was observed that some of the Japanese remained completely apathetic in the face of the Marine attack and did nothing either to attack the Americans or to defend themselves. Company G continued its advance southward until it was able to bring small arms fire to bear against Radar Hill, the last ridge of the Amiangal system still entirely in Japanese hands. Here the company halted the advance.

Throughout the day Companies E and F of 2/5 worked with the demolition men trying to neutralize the caves, which honeycombed the hills. When the caves became untenable, some of the Japanese decided to make a break for it. A chase ensued when a group of about 70 Japanese suddenly poured out of the hillside and headed for the reef. Marines of Company F gave chase with three LVTs, overtook the fleeing enemy, and killed those refusing to surrender.[71]

Since on 28 September the Japanese retained only two small islands of resistance on Peleliu, naval air support was secured as of 1800 that date. During the night of 28–29 September, fighting flared up in the center of Peleliu. There the Japanese launched what the 1st Marine Division designated "the first in a series of desperation raids" out of the Umurbrogol pocket against the lines of the 7th Marines. The regiment suffered light casualties in repulsing these assaults which at times closed to within bayonet range.[72] The Marines also drew mortar, machine gun, and rifle fire throughout the night.

The attack against the Japanese in the north of Peleliu reached its climax during 29 September, which also marked the end of large-scale operations in that part of the island. The 1st Battalion, 5th Marines, launched its assault against Radar Hill with flamethrowers, bazookas, and demolition charges. As anticipated, capture of the strongly defended hill could not be completed in one day. Even though the Marines reached the crest of Radar Hill on 29 September, a large cave underneath remained to be reduced.

East of the Amiangal ridges, Company G of 2/5 continued to mop up enemy remnants in this area. The company drew fire from caves in the ridges east of the phosphate plant. An ap-

---

[69] *1/5 B–3 Jnl*, 28Sep44.
[70] *2/5 OpRpt*, 28Sep44.
[71] *Ibid.*
[72] *1st MarDiv WarD*, 28Sep44.

proach to these ridges from the east did not appear feasible because a swamp separated the Marines from these hills. Tanks stationed in the coconut grove fired point blank with their 75mm guns at the mouth of one of the most troublesome caves, temporarily sealing it. On the western side, the Japanese had blasted from the inside and cleared openings to two caves that the Marines had sealed. As a result, the enemy was able to fire on both the east and west beaches.[73] Atop the ridges, Company F sealed four caves only to have the Japanese blast them open from the inside. To add to the vexation and frustration of the Marines operating near the northern tip of Peleliu, the Japanese suddenly fired into the rear of Company G from caves that had been sealed on the previous day. Company E finally assaulted these positions and chased some of the Japanese onto the reef, where riflemen on LVTs annihilated them in short order. Nevertheless, in these caves an undetermined number of Japanese remained, capable of causing additional trouble when it suited them.

For all practical purposes, organized enemy resistance on northern Peleliu, except for the grimly defended pocket in the high ground north of the airfield, came to a virtual end on 29 September.[74] The Japanese situation report for 29 September failed to indicate any great concern about events on northern Peleliu, mentioning only that ". . . on the front line, where our main forces are facing the enemy's main force, all is quiet; in fact, even some of our forces there are helping us out in the battle taking place in the north area of Peleliu."[75] Twenty-four hours later, the tenor of the Japanese report changed, for in reference to northern Peleliu, Colonel Nakagawa reported that ". . . after a fierce battle, the enemy was finally successful in occupying the area. Our surviving forces are attempting to dash southward, cutting through the enemy in order to join the main force."[76]

On the morning of 30 September, the 1st and 2d Battalions, 5th Marines, continued to mop up the northern leg of the Amiangal ridges and Radar Hill. At 1000, both battalions were ordered to withdraw to the vicinity of the radio station prior to being relieved by elements of the 321st Infantry Regiment.

This relief took place during the afternoon of 30 September. While the Marines, somber and weary after their prolonged struggle for northern Peleliu, were en route to Ngardololok for a well-deserved rest, few imagined that more than a sprinkling of Japanese had remained in the Amiangal ridges. As it turned out, those Japanese remaining on northern Peleliu dug their way out of previously sealed caves, reoccupied new positions, and in a number of instances forced the bewildered Wildcats to retake positions that the 5th Marines had previosuly secured.[77] At least two more days were required to end such resistance as remained in northern Peleliu, and even then isolated Japanese

---

[73] *2/5 OpRpt*, 29Sep44.
[74] 1st MarDiv WarD, 29Sep44.

[75] *Japanese CenPacOps*, p. 113.
[76] *Ibid.*
[77] Smith, *Approach to the Philippines*, pp. 546–547.

continued to exist in dugouts whose entrances were partially blocked by debris.

During the struggle for northern Peleliu, the 5th Marines had killed and captured over 1,170 Japanese. Elements of RCT 321 accounted for another 175 following their relief of the Marines.[78] The campaign for Peleliu during the last half of September had resulted in an estimated total of 9,076 enemy dead and 180 prisoners of war. During the same period of time, the 1st Marine Division had lost 843 killed, 3,845 wounded, and 356 missing, a total of 5,044 casualties.[79] Except for the Umurbrogol pocket the entire island of Peleliu was in American hands. The last phase of the bitter struggle for Peleliu was about to begin.

---

[78] *Ibid.*, p. 548.

[79] *1st MarDiv SAR*, Phase II, Anx A, p. 13.

CHAPTER 7

The Umurbrogol Pocket: 29 September-15 October[1]

PROBLEM AND SOLUTION[2]

The imminent conclusion of operations on northern Peleliu and the island of Ngesebus once again shifted the focus of attention to the center of Peleliu, where Colonel Nakagawa still held out in his final strongpoint, the Umurbrogol ridges. In this area, nature and the Japanese appeared to have conspired to block access to any force intent on seizing the fortress. The terrain was such that it was practically impossible to make an accurate measurement of the dimensions of the pocket, though the closest estimate described it as 1,900 yards north to south on its eastern side, approximately 1,200 yards long in the west, and, on the average, 550 yards wide from east to west. (See Map 12).

A scrutiny of the terrain in which the final operations on Peleliu took place clearly indicates the difficulties inherent in assessing the size of this relatively small pocket. The ridges of the Umurbrogol system were higher, longer, and more densely compressed than the hills occupying the northern portion of the island. Even though the highest elevation among the coral ridges was only about 300 feet, the sides of such hills were, as a rule, extremely steep and fissured. Many had razor-back summits devoid of any cover or concealment. Deep draws and gullies, the floors of which were often interspersed with coral boulders and outcroppings, were commonplace. The "chaotic jumble of steep coral ridges."[3] defies accurate description, though it has been said that:

> The exotic-sounding name Umurbrogol Mountain became associated with some of the most unpleasantly exotic terrain on the face of creation. . . . But words are inadequate, photographs not much better. One has to see it fully to believe it.[4]

A participant in the battle was to recall many years later:

> Our language just does not contain words that can adequately describe the horrible inaccessibility of the central ridge line on Peleliu. It was a nightmare's nightmare if there ever was one. Unfortunately, during the planning stage of the campaign we did not fully realize the nature of the ground so it caught us pretty much by surprise when we actually came upon it. Nothing in our planning studies and subsequent development of plans led us to realize how terrible it was. The maps

---

[1] Unless otherwise noted, the material in this chapter is derived from: *IIIAC Palaus Rpt; 1st MarDiv SAR;* 1st MarDiv WarD, Sep-Oct 44; *81st InfDiv OpRpt; 1st MarDiv D-2 Jnl; 1st MarDiv D-3 Jnl; Peleliu Comment File; Japanese CenPacOps;* Smith, *Narrative;* Hough, *Assault on Peleliu;* Morison, *Leyte;* Smith, *Approach to the Philippines;* McMillan, *The Old Breed;* Historical Committee, *81st Infantry Division.*

[2] Additional sources used for this section include: *CTF 32 AR; 1st MarDiv D-2 Rpts.*

[3] Smith, *Approach to the Philippines,* p. 551.
[4] Hough, *Assault on Peleliu,* p. 136.

219

220   WESTERN PACIFIC OPERATIONS

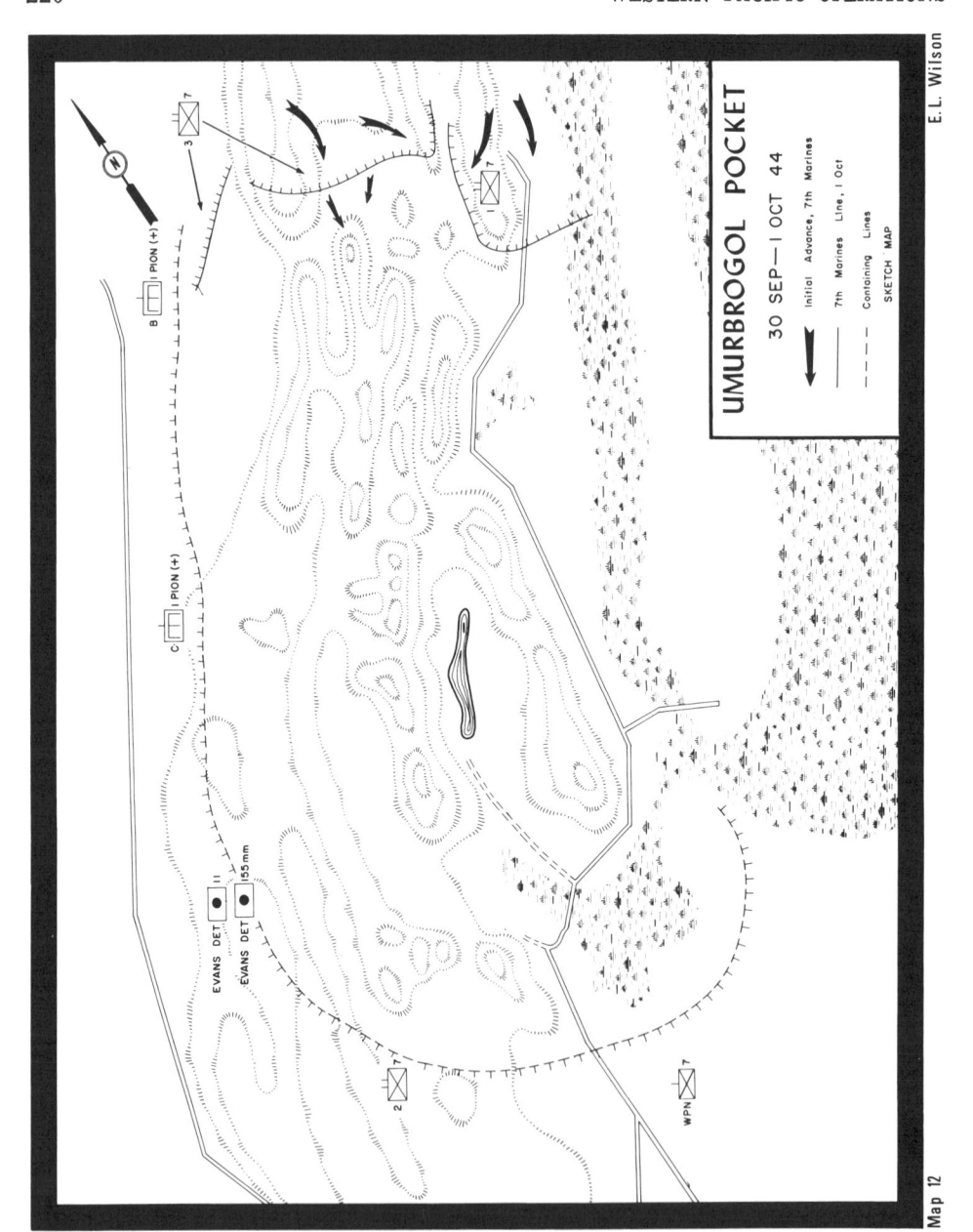

we had were lacking badly in accurate terrain configurations, and the relatively few aerial photos we at Corps Headquarters were permitted to receive did not give us much of a clue, probably because the vegetation hid the exact nature of the ground from our photo interpreters and the rest of us. So, we were somewhat unprepared for what actually existed. I think this led both naval and ground force commanders to make overly-optimistic predictions of the effectiveness of fires and capabilities of troops. The fact that the Marines and Army troops were able to capture the Umurbrogol Pocket at all is a tribute to sheer guts, tenacity, and unmatched bravery."

This, then, was the ground that the Japanese had pledged to defend to the death. Nature had done its share to aid the defending force, for the numerous hills in the pocket contained an undetermined number of caves, which the Japanese had skillfully exploited for the defense. These caves, mostly natural formations, lacked the size and sophistication of defenses on northern Peleliu, which had borne witness to the ingenuity and skill of Japanese naval engineers and miners. In contrast to the Navy, the Japanese Army had been primarily interested in adapting the terrain to defensive combat. As a result, the Army caves were constructed as covering or mutually supporting positions. Most of the Army caves were small; however, the few larger ones were ingeniously employed for the emplacement of heavy weapons. Out of the almost perpendicular coral ridges the Japanese had blasted a series of interconnecting caves, whose destruction

---

⁵ BGen William F. Coleman ltr to HistBr, dtd 9Jun66, in *Peleliu Comment File*.

was to prove by far the most difficult feature of the entire operation. The caves varied in size from simple holes, large enough to accommodate two men, to large tunnels with passageways on either side which were large enough to contain artillery, 150mm mortars, and ammunition. Some of the latter caves were equipped with doors that had been camouflaged.

All of the Japanese defensive positions, carefully chosen and well camouflaged, had excellent fields of fire. For all practical purposes they were immune to naval gunfire, bombardment by artillery and mortars, or bombing and strafing. Enemy small arms fire was particularly accurate, indicating thorough training in rifle marksmanship. Marines frequently were killed or wounded by enemy fire from positions 200–400 yards away.

The most outstanding landmarks and prominent elevations within the Umurbrogol Pocket were: Walt Ridge, occupying and dominating the southeast corner of the pocket, parallel to the East Road. Boyd Ridge, north of Walt, and separated from it by a depression which was 70 yards wide; an unnamed ridge which ran between Boyd Ridge and the 321st Infantry Trail; the Horseshoe or Horseshoe Valley, also known as Five Brothers Ridge. West of the Five Brothers was another valley, known variously as Main Valley, Little Slot, and finally as Wildcat Bowl. This depression was enclosed to the west by the China Wall, to the southeast by a jagged ridge known as Five Sisters. Another narrow depression, ominously designated as Death Valley, separated the Five Sisters and China Wall from the coral ridges dominating the West Road. Except for slight variations, all of the Umurbrogol ridges extended from northeast to southwest or from north to south.

While the situation of the Japanese in the pocket was serious, it was by no means desperate. Colonel Nakagawa was able to report on 28 September that his *Peleliu Area Unit* main force was about the size of two and a half battalions.[6] The Japanese garrison was not running short of food or ammunition, though individual prisoners occasionally reported a shortage of water. Such a lack of water was eliminated when heavy rains came to Peleliu on and after 28 September, in advance of far more severe weather that was shortly to hit the island. For the Japanese this rain was a godsend, and they trapped enough water in underground cisterns to last for months. Nor was the Umurbrogol Pocket as isolated as appeared at first hand, for unknown to the Marines, Colonel Nakagawa's command post maintained constant telephone communication over a sub-oceanic cable with General Inoue on Babelthuap. Throughout the prolonged operation on Peleliu, the existence of this cable was never suspected by the Americans.[7]

Though the Japanese in the pocket undoubtedly were aware that their annihilation was merely a matter of time, such realization did not affect an obviously high state of morale. During the last days of September, the 7th Marines attempted on several occasions to bring about the surrender of the enemy through leaflets and broadcasts over a public address system. In each instance, no positive results were attained, and the regiment was forced to report that the effect of propaganda leaflets had been absolutely nil. As a final resort, a prisoner was dispatched into the pocket to entice his compatriots to give themselves up. This maneuver produced mixed results. The first cave visited by this emissary, who was armed only with rations and cigarettes, was occupied by Japanese Army personnel who not only refused outright to consider his request but threw a hand grenade at him. Undaunted by such a discouraging reaction, the emissary visited a second cave, occupied by nine laborers. There a more friendly reception awaited him. The laborers listened and, emerging from the cave unarmed, surrendered to the Marines.

During the period from 22–27 September, the Japanese defending the Umurbrogol ridges had escaped the full wrath of the American assault, which at that time was directed against the northern portion of Peleliu and Ngesebus. In fact, no offensive operations were launched against the pocket during this period. The Japanese, on their part, remained generally quiet in the daytime and launched sporadic sorties against the American lines only under cover of darkness. During the lull in the fighting in this sector, elements of RCT 321 remained deployed along the northern fringes of the pocket near the 321st Infantry Trail, and the 7th Marines held the ridges adjacent to the West Road between the airfield and the trail. Korean laborers surrendering at the northeastern tip of the pocket near Hill

---

[6] *Japanese CenPacOps*, p. 112.
[7] Inoue interview, dtd Mar 50, in *Worden ltr*.

B on 27 September estimated that 3,000 Japanese remained in the Umurbrogol ridges.

In spite of the large number of Japanese remaining in a compact but extremely well-defended bastion the 1st Marine Division estimated on 29 September that:

> enemy resistance, except for the grimly-defined pocket in the high ground north of the airfield, came to a virtual end.... Despite continuing resistance, for all practical purposes, Palau Operation was completed![8]

On the following day, CTF 32 reported that Peleliu, Angaur, Ngesebus, and Kongauru had been captured and occupied, and that base development had been initiated and could proceed without enemy interference.

All hopes to the contrary, the bloodletting that marked the battle of Peleliu was far from over. Once again, tattered and grimy Marines would have to assault cave after cave with rifles, bayonets, and flamethrowers before the finish to one of the bloodiest operations of the war could be written. Conquest of the unyielding fortress could be achieved only through relentless and aggressive force applied against the weakest part of the pocket. Once this weak spot had been uncovered, aggressive action on the part of the Marines would do the rest.

THE 7TH MARINES ON THE OFFENSIVE[9]

Nearly a week had passed since the 1st Marines battered itself against Bloody Nose Ridge and the 7th Marines failed in the attempt to penetrate into the Umurbrogol from the southeast. As September drew to a close, the 1st Marines was preparing to leave Peleliu, handing to the 7th Marines and Army troops the task of overcoming whatever resistance remained on the island. The only gains made in the central area of Peleliu during the last week of September were in the north. There, men of the 321st Infantry Regiment had made a small advance southward from the trail bordering the pocket to the north. The Japanese still retained control of the dominating hills.

Even while operations on Ngesebus Island and in northern Peleliu were progressing in high gear, General Rupertus orally ordered 2/321 to move to Ngesebus to relieve elements of the 5th Marines on that island. On 29 September, 1/7 relieved the remainder of RCT 321 along the northern perimeter of the Umurbrogol pocket. The men of the 321st proceeded to the northern tip of Peleliu to assist the 5th Marines in subduing that portion of the island. The 7th Marines assumed responsibility for operations throughout the Umurbrogol pocket as of 29 September. The movement of troops took place while heavy rains and winds were buffeting the entire island, and roads turned into quagmires which impeded all movement. In fact, throughout 28 September and part of the following two days, the weather remained foul, and heavy rain squalls with strong westerly winds stopped unloading on the western

---

[8] *1st MarDiv SAR*, Phase II, Anx A, pp. 12–13.

[9] Additional sources used for this section are: *CTF 32 AR; 7th Mar R-2 Jnl; 1/7 Hist Rpt; 2/7 URpt; 3/7 WarD*, Sep-Oct44; *3/7 Rec of Events*.

beaches and retarded unloading on the eastern beaches.

On 29 September, the northern perimeter of the Umurbrogol Pocket ran slightly south of the 321st Infantry Trail, which it paralleled for about 400 yards. This line, designated as Phase Line X, passed through West and East Roads and angled southeastward from the 321st Infantry Trail to skirt Boyd Ridge in the northeastern tip of the pocket. Passing through extremely broken terrain, it was not a solid front line but a series of outposts deployed on the more elevated ridges. The most prominent terrain features directly south of this line were two hills known as Wattie and Baldy Ridges, which formed the northern anchor of the Japanese pocket. To the east of Walt Ridge, the extensive swamp bordering the pocket was considered so inaccessible to friend and foe alike that the Americans committed no troops in this area. Consequently, the ring of encirclement was manned only from the north, west, and south. In order to make as many men of the infantry battalions available for the assault as could be mustered, elements of the supporting arms helped hold the containing line.

Initially, the southern perimeter of the pocket was assigned to the 7th Marines Weapons Company, which moved into positions facing the mouth of the Horseshoe across the swamp. The company left flank skirted the base of Hill 300 and the Five Sisters. Along the west side of the pocket, a variety of units consisting of Marine artillerymen, engineers and pioneers, and personnel from amphibian tractor battalions manned a containing line, which extended for about 750 yards between the western terminus of Phase Line X and Bloody Nose Ridge. At night these lines were strongly reinforced by personnel from division headquarters. Along the northwestern edge of the pocket, 2/7 occupied containing lines, which had remained substantially unchanged since 21 September, when the battalion had first moved into these positions.

General Rupertus assigned the mission of reducing the Umurbrogol Pocket to 1/7 and 3/7. Both battalions were to attack southward from Phase Line X at 0800, 30 September. On the left, 1/7 was to attack along the East Road, secure the ridges dominating the road, and maintain contact with 3/7. While these preparations were being made, a company of the 710th Tank Battalion, together with units of the 1st Marines were readying for departure from Peleliu on 29 September.

An air strike against the pocket was scheduled for 1530, 29 September, aimed at shattering the complacency of the Japanese in the Umurbrogol. Because of inclement weather and poor visibility, it first appeared that the strike would have to be called off, but then it was decided to attack as scheduled, despite the weather. In a way, the strike, the first of many, was unique because the Corsairs were able to make the run from the airfield to Bloody Nose Ridge in only 15 seconds. Frequently the planes never even bothered to raise their wheels.[10] Over the pocket the aircraft released napalm bombs. Shortly thereafter, heavy explosions and a pall of smoke obscured the pocket, while

---
[10] Sherrod, *Marine Corps Aviation in World War II*, p. 257.

fires on the hillsides and in the depressions raged unchecked. This is how aerial warfare looked to the Marine aviators on Peleliu:

> After an observation hop to ascertain the facts about this incomparable cave country Major Stout's division was briefed at the division CP and took off at 1515 with 1,000 lb. bombs. The whole show could be seen right from our ready tent and from the tower top you could see right into the draw. Smoke bombs were used on the deck for a reference circle and Stout's flight laid them in without difficulty. It was a bit ticklish, but none landed or ricocheted outside the 400 yards area or the caves. . . . Sixteen planes returning from a bombing mission against Babelthuap took a good look at the damage done by Major Stout's flight in the horseshoe next to Bloody Nose Ridge and reported it was considerable.[11]

Regrettably, this impressive display of low-level bombing, though it must have rocked the Japanese in their caves, failed to diminish their capacity to resist. Prisoners captured later said that the only effect of the bombs was to make a big noise.[12] On the subject of air attacks, Colonel Nakagawa had only this laconic comment to make: "The enemy plan seems to be to burn down the central hills posts to ashes by dropping gasoline from airplanes."[13]

The disappointing results of this napalm strike and those that were to follow were probably due to the fact that the division concept of the proper employment of this weapon was in error. Based on incomplete reports of the Saipan operation, the 1st Marine Division felt that napalm would prove to be an excellent area weapon, highly effective in burning out areas of heavy foliage. There was no evidence to support this theory, and when used in this fashion, napalm was not effective.[14]

The night of 29–30 September was marked by numerous Japanese attempts to infiltrate the positions held by the 7th Marines. At approximately 2300, small enemy raiding parties, using hand grenades as their principal weapon, attacked company and battalion command posts, causing much confusion and a number of casualties. This infiltration was aided by a heavy rain which fell throughout the night. By 0100, four of the infiltrators had been killed in the 1/7 sector and quiet returned. At 0600, a Japanese occupying a foxhole within the battalion CP, was captured.[15] The 2d Battalion, in anticipation of enemy infiltration attempts during the night, had strengthened the perimeter with 85 men from the 1st Pioneer Battalion and stretcher bearers from the 16th Field Depot, but the enemy limited himself to harassing the Marine lines with mortar fire. Japanese infiltration attempts against 3/7 resulted in the death of one Marine, the wounding of three others, and the killing of four Japanese.[16]

That these were not haphazard or random attempts at infiltration is illustrated by a Japanese view of the raids, expressed by Colonel Nakagawa on 30 September:

> We are attempting to defeat the enemy by using our close-quarter combat tactics to the utmost. Last night two close-quarter combat units from the 15th Infantry Regi-

---

[11] *VMF–114 WarD*, Sep44.
[12] *2/7 WarD*, Sep44.
[13] *Japanese CenPacOps*, p. 131.

[14] *1st MarDiv SAR*, Phase II, Anx L, p. 6.
[15] *1/7 HistRpt*, 30Sep44.
[16] *3/7 WarD*, Sep44.

ment, 2d Battalion, put 70 enemy personnel on the casualty list. The enemy's total loss for last night's attack was one hundred and scores of casualties, and a great deal of provisions and ammunition was captured. Besides this, enemy losses may be greater for 10 close-quarter combat parties are still hidden in enemy territory.[17]

Company B of 1/7 jumped off at 0800 on 30 September and in little more than two hours accomplished its assigned mission to seize a ridge just west of the East Road, at the northeastern tip of the pocket. From this vantage point, the company was to support the attack by Company A as it headed down East Road for the next ridge 100 yards to the south. The heavy rain, which already had forced cancellation of an air strike earlier that morning, also interfered with the jumpoff of Company A, whose attack did not get under way until 1245. The intervening time was used to good advantage by an engineer demolition team, which sealed all of the caves in the area seized that morning. When visibility improved, Company A attacked down the East Road, supported by three tanks and a LVT flamethrower. Following a mortar barrage against the second hill, Company A was able to continue the advance down the East Road, even though it drew machine gun fire from enemy positions further south. One of the tanks and the LVT eliminated the enemy machine guns and the forward movement continued. As a result, an advance of 300 yards to the south was achieved. Company C, previously held in reserve, was committed to occupy the newly seized territory. At 1530, the 7th Marines halted the advance and set up a defensive perimeter for the night. In addition to the ground captured, the Marines had destroyed an enemy mountain gun[18] and a number of machine gun positions during the advance.

While 1/7 was pressing the attack down the East Road, 3/7 extended its line eastward in order to reduce the front of 1/7. Shortly before 1100, 3/7 received orders dividing it into two separate task organizations, one for the defense of the ridge line along the West Road and the other for support of the attack of 1/7 against the northern perimeter of the pocket. The commander of 3/7, Major Edward H. Hurst, took direct charge of a force consisting of Company L, one platoon of Company K, and part of Headquarters Company. The battalion executive officer, Major Victor H. Streit, was to employ the remainder of the battalion for the defense of the ridge line. During the afternoon, Company L aggressively patrolled forward of its lines, particularly against the hill designated as Baldy, but rain and fog made it necessary to withdraw the patrols for the night.[19]

In stationary positions parallel to the West Road, 2/7 occupied a ringside seat when at 0700, 30 September, VMF–114 carried out an air strike against the draws to the front of the 2d Battalion. The strike, conducted by 19 aircraft, attacked the horseshoe called "Death Valley," and dropped 20 half-ton bombs into an area only about 100 yards square. In the words of the aviators:

---

[17] *Japanese CenPacOps*, p. 114.

[18] *1/7 HistRpt*, 30Sep44.
[19] *3/7 WarD*, Sep44.

Again we were to bomb targets less than 1,100 yards from the airplane line. The Japs attempted to confuse our men by putting up white smoke against our colored smoke lines. However, it all went off well and 14 perfect hits were scored in an area skittishly small even for dive bombing with releases as low as 500 or 600 feet. Two bombs were duds and two bursts were made in the air after riccocheting off the ridge. Plenty of margin of safety and our bomb pattern adjudged satisfactory. After half the runs had been completed we got direct information from the regimental CP as to the exact position of each hit which made the balance of the bombing that much safer and more effective. A rain squall coming in from the north almost upset the show, but finally only delayed it for 10 minutes.[20]

Despite the accuracy of the air bombardment, the strike failed to achieve any conclusive results. Japanese resistance continued undiminished, and even before noon the 7th Marines Weapons Company reported that it was receiving rifle and machine gunfire from the area bombed earlier in the day.[21] Bombardment from the air was followed by a mortar barrage against the Japanese, who for the remainder of the day retaliated by subjecting 2/7 to heavy sniper fire. Snipers to the rear of the battalion, presumably members of the raiding parties that had infiltrated during the previous night, also harassed the supply lines of the battalion.[22]

Even though the gains made by the 7th Marines during 30 September appeared promising, there was increasing evidence that the battalions could not sustain the pace of the attack for long.

On the last day of September, for instance, the effective strength of 1/7 was only 90 men. Dysentery, as much as enemy action, was responsible for this reduction in combat strength. The men blamed the intestinal disorders on the presence of an excessive number of large flies, which allegedly had been drawn to the area by the presence of a large number of unburied Japanese dead.[23] To some extent, progress of 1st Division troops was slowed by growing combat fatigue and the shortage of personnel, the result of heavy casualties.[24] The combat efficiency of 3/7 also was estimated to be below 50 percent for the first time, the decrease being attributed in part to an increase in the sick rate.[25] The situation on Peleliu was perhaps best summed up by the division itself:

> The early days of October brought with them a change in the complexion of the combat activity that had occurred during the previous month on Peleliu. The campaign had now become a battle of attrition —a slow, slugging yard by yard struggle to blast the enemy from his last remaining stronghold in the high ground to the north of the airfield. This drive constituted within itself almost a separate operation, the rugged, almost impassable terrain requiring more time to clean out than previously had been spent in clearing all the southern Palaus.[26]

The morning of 1 October dawned inauspiciously with continuing unabated rain and high winds. Once again the 7th Marines prepared to advance into the Umurbrogol pocket from the north. The zone of action consisted of a series

---

[20] VMF–114 WarD, Sep44.
[21] *7th Mar R–2 Jnl*, 30Sep44.
[22] *2/7 WarD*, Sep44.

[23] *1/7 HistRpt*, 30Sep44.
[24] *1st MarDiv SAR*, Phase II, Anx A, p. 14.
[25] *3/7 Rec of Events*, p. 14.
[26] 1st MarDiv WarD, Oct44.

of precipitous coral ridges concealing an undetermined number of enemy well armed, adequately supplied, and with no apparent intention of surrendering. The seizure of Baldy Ridge was an essential step towards the further exploitation of the surrounding ridges.

At 0720 the left flank of Company L, 3/7, began to advance in an attempt to straighten the lines prior to a general attack on Baldy. The company gained about 75 yards during the first hour of the advance, but at this point the Marines were halted by heavy machine gun and small arms fire. Because of the precipitous slope and the strength of the enemy position on the peak, it was considered unwise to assault Baldy Ridge from the front, and 3/7 made no further progress for the remainder of the day.[27]

The 1st Battalion fared little better in attempting to link up with 3/7, though Company B reported visual contact at 1034. A friendly 155mm barrage against enemy positions on Baldy Ridge during the afternoon had to be lifted because shell fragments were landing in friendly lines.[28]

Aside from the limited advance of the 7th Marines on 1 October, the main activity for the day was the reorganization and movement of units. In the course of the morning, the 710th Tank Battalion relieved the Marine 1st Tank Battalion. The latter, together with the 1st Marines and 2/11, completed loading and stood by for departure. The next day the 1st Marines sailed for Pavuvu, the first echelon of troops to depart from Peleliu.[29]

At 0800, 1 October, 3/5 relieved 2/7 in the containing line along the southwestern perimeter of the Umurbrogol. In driving rain Companies E and G, 2/7 moved down to the West Road, where they were loaded into DUKWs and driven to the battalion bivouac area north of the airfield. Battalion headquarters and Company F returned via the trail running down Bloody Nose Ridge. After two continuous weeks in the line, the battalion was scheduled for a brief rest and hot food.[30] On the same day an additional squadron of Corsair fighters, VMF–122, landed on the island. Despite heavy rain and poor overall visibility, the American troop movements did not escape Japanese detection. Shortly before 2000, two enemy float planes approached Peleliu, dropped two bombs in the vicinity of Purple Beach and departed, causing neither damage nor casualties.[31]

In order to forestall a stalemate similar to the one that had previously checked the advance of the Marines into the Umurbrogol and because of the dwindling strength of his battalions, General Rupertus decided to launch a massive attack against the pocket on 3 October. Instead of continuing the lagging advance from the difficult terrain in the north of the pocket, the division commander planned to shift his main effort to the southeast and seize the remainder of the East Road and adjacent

---

[27] *3/7 Rec of Events*, p. 14.
[28] *1/7 HistRpt*, 1Oct44.
[29] 1st MarDiv WarD, Oct44.
[30] *2/7 WarD*, Oct44.
[31] *1st MarDiv SAR*, Phase II, Anx A, pp. 14–15.

ridges in the southeastern part of the pocket. Once the initial objective had been achieved, the enemy strongholds in the pocket were vulnerable to attack from the flanks.

On the basis of earlier observations, it was strongly suspected that Colonel Nakagawa maintained a highly flexible reserve which could be rushed at very short notice to any threatened point within the perimeter of the pocket. As a result, the attack of 3 October called for a coordinated series of efforts from different directions. The 2d Battalion, 7th Marines, attacking northward, was to seize Walt Ridge. Attacking southward, 3/7 had the mission of taking Boyd Ridge. Once having captured their objectives, both battalions were to shift their advance westward into the center of the pocket. To forestall a head-on collision between the two battalions, different jumpoff times were assigned. The 3d Battalion was to remain in position until 2/7 had seized the objective and could indicate its position with smoke.

While the Japanese were preoccupied with this new threat, 3/5 was to extend its front to the east and attack the Five Sisters in the southern portion of the pocket. The 5th Marines Weapons Company, supported by armor of the 710th Tank Battalion, was to move into Horseshoe Valley and up East Road in order to support the attack of 3/5. The depleted 1/7 was to relieve the regimental weapons company in the containing line during the morning of 3 October. The ranks of 3/7 were reinforced with an engineer company, a platoon of the regimental weapons company, and a detachment of 52 men from the 1st Amphibian Tractor Battalion. Two tanks and one LVT flamethrower were also attached to the battalion.[32]

During the remainder of 2 October, the units to take part in the attack on the following morning regrouped as scheduled. The 3d Battalion, 7th Marines relieved 1/7 along the northeastern perimeter of the pocket. To make additional manpower available for the attack, detachments of artillerymen took over the line previously held by 3/7.

Before effecting the relief of 1/7, Major Hurst, commanding 3/7, conducted a physical reconnaissance of the 1st Battalion lines. The relief commenced shortly after 1500 in driving rain and was not completed until 1845.[33] Major Hurst established his command post on a ridge adjacent to East Road about 300 yards behind the lines. At the CP of 2/7, preparations for the attack were also under way. Mindful of the heavy casualties that the Japanese had inflicted on 2/1 and 1/7 on 19 and 20 September in the same area, Lieutenant Colonel Spencer S. Berger, 2/7 commander, was taking every precaution to keep history from repeating. Initially, Berger conducted an aerial reconnaissance of the area, after which he and his staff carried out a ground reconnaissance. The intelligence officer reconnoitered the swamp to the east of East Road to ascertain whether a covered route of approach could be found. He soon discovered that it was not feasible to move a battalion through the mo-

---

[32] *3/7 Rec of Events*, p. 14.
[33] *1/7 HistRpt*, 2Oct44.

rass;[34] the approach would have to be made in single file over a narrow trail, which was fully exposed to observation and fire from the enemy in positions on the high ground. During the evening of 2 October, the battalion commander held a pre-attack conference at his command post, where he directed that all requests for mortar fire would go through a central fire direction center. For this attack a provisional rifle company was to be formed from the regimental weapons company and attached to 2/7.

Throughout the day, hostile eyes had observed unusual movements outside the pocket, and Colonel Nakagawa duly reported: "It seems that the enemy acted as if preparing for an attack on our surrounded garrison units in the central hills."[35] The Japanese did not have long to wait. At 0630 an intensive barrage by the 155mm guns and the massed fire of 81mm mortars of five battalions rocked the pocket, causing Colonel Nakagawa to report that "all through the night of the 2nd, the enemy fired 40,000 artillery shells from their positions on land and ships at our defense posts."[36] During the closing phase of the bombardment, the mortars fired smoke shells in order to screen the advance of 2/7.

Less than half an hour after it started, the preparatory fire ceased and Company G moved out in a single file across the swamp leading towards Walt Ridge. By 0730, having advanced under cover of the smoke, the first platoon had secured a foothold on the southern end of the ridge and was making good progress. Up to this point Japanese resistance had been negligible, but once the Marines gained the ridge, they began to draw heavy fire not only from their front but also from the Five Brothers to the west, across the Horseshoe. Company E was ordered to advance through the right of Company G and continue the attack. Both companies became pinned down by heavy enemy fire and when casualties mounted, tanks and halftracks attached to the weapons company moved into the Horseshoe to cope with the Japanese on the Five Brothers and the western slope of Walt Ridge. At the same time, LVT flamethrowers proceeded up the East Road to neutralize Walt Ridge from the east. At 0900, the advance bogged down when the Marines drew murderous crossfire upon reaching the top of a high vertical cliff, which was separated from the adjacent hilltop by a saddle. Two out of every four men attempting to get across were hit, including the commander of Company G. At this point, the supporting tanks discovered a large cave with a concrete front at the foot of one of the Five Brothers. The cave was promptly neutralized, and its 60 Japanese occupants were killed.

While the two companies held on to their precarious hold atop the southernmost slope of Walt Ridge, Company F, bypassing the scene of the most bitter fighting, advanced northward on the East Road and prepared to assault Walt Ridge at a point north of the saddle where the advance of the two remaining companies had bogged down. The leading elements of Company F had barely begun the climb when the company was ordered to pull back from the ridge and await further orders.

---
[34] *2/7 WarD*, Oct44.
[35] *Japanese CenPacOps*, p. 128.
[36] *Ibid.*

By this time, the tanks and halftracks supporting the infantry action in the Horseshoe were beginning to draw heavy mortar, artillery, and small arms fire. One halftrack was hit. Casualties mounted and it became increasingly difficult to evacuate the wounded. The tanks on the right flank along the crest reported that they were out of ammunition. The advance of the 2d Battalion had reached its limits. Having seized the southernmost crest of Walt Ridge, the 2d Battalion decided to consolidate, marking the northernmost positions with purple smoke, which signalled the 3d Battalion to begin the advance from the north.[37]

The attack by 3/7 began at 1020, when Companies K, I, and L moved out in that order. After crossing a ravine, which was covered by enemy small arms fire, a squad of Company K advanced 100 yards by 1130 and was halfway up a ridge paralleling the East Road. The rear half of the lead platoon was unable to get across the ravine because the enemy had stepped up his rate of fire. The remainder of the platoon detoured around the swamp to the east of the road and approached the ridge from that direction. By 1500, the entire company had gained the crest of Boyd Ridge. Accordingly, the battalion commander decided to send Company I through the swamp to effect a juncture with Company F of 2/7 and to build up a solid line on the left of Company K. Within the hour Company I established contact with Company F, but had to break it in order to stay tied in with Company K. In the end, Company I had to refuse its left flank, retaining only visual contact with Company F but remaining tied in with Company K on Boyd Ridge.

Following the successful capture of Boyd Ridge on 3 October by elements of the 3d Battalion, 2/7 continued its advance over the crest of Walt Ridge. At 1350 Company E moved through the right flank of Company G over a newly blasted trail, which the engineers had completed, while Company F advanced northward over the East Road. In mid-afternoon, Company F received the cheering news that elements of 3/7 were only 75 yards to their front. Shortly after 1600, the company tied in with 3/7 on the right and Company E of 2/7 to the left. At this point, elements of 1/7 relieved the exhausted men of Company G on top of Walt Ridge, and the company went into battalion reserve. Evening of 3 October found Companies B, E, and F on the crest of Walt Ridge, with Company F echeloned down the slope, where it tied in with the left of 3/7. Shortly before 1900, the attack was halted for the night. The provisional rifle company to the left of 2/7 was relieved by 1/7, which withdrew from positions forward of the causeway to the line previously held by the weapons company.[38]

In an action entirely separate from the operation taking place along the eastern perimeter of the Umurbrogol pocket, 3/5 attacked during the morning of 3 October from the south towards the Five Sisters with the objective of distracting the attention of the Japanese from the activities of the 7th Marines. Companies I and L ascended four out of the Five Sisters, while Company K,

---

[37] *2/7 WarD*, p. 18.

[38] *Ibid.*

supported by a tank, moved into Death Valley. There the difficult terrain, combined with increasing enemy resistance, prevented any further advance. In the course of the afternoon, 3/5 drew such heavy small arms fire from undetermined sources that the battalion withdrew and set up a line of defense about 100 yards from where it had jumped off in the morning.[39]

The multiple attacks of 3 October had resulted in the capture of Boyd and Walt Ridges as well as the opening of the East Road. Even then the road could not be considered safe for traffic as at least two sections of it remained under enemy fire. The 2d Battalion made these gains at a cost of 24 killed and 60 wounded against approximately 130 Japanese killed.[40] The 3d Battalion lost 4 killed and 25 wounded against 22 enemy dead.[41]

On 3 October the Japanese were not the only enemy that the Marines had to contend with, for the weather had also taken a turn for the worse. The onset of unfavorable weather was particularly detrimental to Marine aviation on Peleliu, as VMF-114 reported:

> No flights today of any kind. Two divisions stood by in the ready tent which nearly blew away in a 45 knot wind. Half of our maps were torn to shreds and the skipper came around with a dozen men to stake down the tent, before it was completely ruined. Huge breakers were pounding the beaches. Two LSTs tied up to what was once our pier on Orange Beach were pounding the coral and most of the shipping had been retired to Kossol Passage to ride out the storm. Most units ashore were put on two meals a day to stretch the food a little further. The water situation was not critical, but gasoline, bombs, and food were running short as nothing was being unloaded anywhere on the beaches.[42]

The discomfiture, which the inclement weather imposed on the Marines, promised to be a great boon for the Japanese on Babelthuap. Never slow to exploit an advantage, General Inoue and his staff felt that the time was ripe for another attempt to reinforce the Peleliu garrison.

> We prepared to move the three battalions remaining at Babelthuap and the one battalion at Koror, together with group headquarters, to Peleliu around 2–3 October. We learned through a report that a typhoon was headed in the direction of Palau and planned to move during the storm which we knew would neutralize the American carrier-based planes. However, the typhoon did not approach the Palaus, and we did not have an adequate number of barges, so we cancelled this plan.[43]

Not all of the 1st Marine Division casualties occurred at the perimeter of the pocket. Death also stalked the quiet sectors of Peleliu. A case in point was the West Road, which represented the more vital artery between northern and southern Peleliu. For several days prior to 3 October, a stretch of the road known as Dead Man's Curve had come under intermittent sniper fire from the ridges dominating the road from the east. The snipers had filtered out of the pocket

---

[39] *3/5 Rec of Events,* 3Oct44.
[40] *2/7 WarD,* Oct44.
[41] *3/7 Rec of Events,* p. 15.

[42] VMF-114 WarD, Oct44.
[43] Interrogation of Col Tokechi Tada, IJA, by 2d Lt James J. Wickel, AUS, 24May47, attachment to ltr, MajGen Paul J. Mueller, USA, to Director of Marine Corps History, dtd 9Aug50, in *Peleliu Comment File,* hereafter *Tada Interrogation.*

into the caves along the jungle-covered bluffs adjoining the road in the vicinity of Wattie Ridge. The 1st Division Military Police Company, responsible for traffic control on the West Road, was so depleted that it was unable to eliminate this menace.

During the afternoon of 3 October, Colonel Joseph F. Hankins, who occupied the dual position of Provost Marshal and commander of Headquarters Battalion, decided to take a personal look at the situation. Armed with an M-1 rifle, the colonel drove up the West Road in his jeep. Eye witnesses have testified as to what happened next:

> Colonel Hankins appeared at the curve in the road where the Military Police were regulating the one-way traffic. An LVT had become immobilized across the road directly in the open and two or three trucks were jammed up in the near proximity of this LVT. The men, under the heavy fire of small arms from the nearby cliff had deserted their vehicles and taken refuge on the reverse slope of the road. Colonel Hankins proceeded to the middle of the road in order to restore traffic to normal condition and had actually gotten the crews back on the vehicles when he was struck by a sniper's bullet and killed instantly.[44]

Colonel Hankins was the highest ranking Marine casualty sustained on Peleliu. Upon learning of the death of his provost marshal, General Rupertus pulled a company of 2/5 out of division reserve and ordered it into the high ground dominating Dead Man's Curve to eliminate the troublesome snipers once and for all. The company advanced for about 75 yards, supported by elements of the 11th Marines, and eliminated the snipers temporarily. It later became necessary to station three medium tanks at the curve with orders to fire in the general direction of the cliffs whenever sniper fire recurred.[45]

Colonel Nakagawa appeared generally unimpressed by the converging attacks of 3 October. He acknowledged receiving the heavy artillery preparation against the pocket but claimed that his garrison unit, by accurate firing and close quarter combat, had inflicted sufficient losses upon the Marines to force their withdrawal.[46]

On the morning of 4 October, strong winds and high seas continued unabated and nearly reached typhoon proportions.[47] Two LSTs, tied up at the Seabee-built causeway off Beach Orange 3, were driven ashore and no other craft was able to reach the beach from the supply ships. For American personnel on Peleliu, "the rains had a glooming effect. The lightless sky turned the whole island gray. Dust-coated dungarees turned stiff, hard and unpliable when they dried out, and when they were wet they were very heavy."[48]

Owing to the unfavorable weather and the extreme exertion of the previous day, the 7th Marines limited operations on 4 October to consolidating and expanding its positions. For the first time the East Road was open for supply and evacuation, though the Japanese still interfered with traffic from positions in the Horseshoe, in the draw between Walt and Boyd Ridges, and in a very

---

[44] Maj George J. DeBell ltr to CMC, n.d., in Peleliu Comment File, hereafter DeBell ltr.

[45] Smith, Narrative, p. 96.
[46] Japanese CenPacOps, p. 129.
[47] 1st MarDiv WarD, Oct44.
[48] McMillan, The Old Breed, p. 335.

narrow draw between Boyd Ridge and the adjacent ridge to the north.

Company I, supported by Company F of 2/7, mopped up in the draw separating Walt and Boyd Ridges, using tank support to good advantage. This movement resulted in a physical linkup of the 2d and 3d Battalions. The three knobs and a ridge to the right front still separated Company K atop Boyd Ridge from Baldy. The seizure of the three knobs and the adjacent ridge would permit an attack against enemy positions on Baldy from the rear.

Up to this point, the operations of 3/7 had followed a normal course. Yet a tragedy similar to the one that had befallen Captain Pope's men on 19 September was about to strike the 7th Marines. Once again all the necessary ingredients were present: fanatical Japanese silently lurking in caves, awaiting their opportunity to strike; eager Marines, determined to advance and wrest yet another ridge from the grasp of the defenders. The first act of the drama opened routinely enough, when at 1430 Company L prepared to seize the three knobs, a mission that was accomplished in less than an hour with unaccustomed ease. Instead of halting the attack for the day, Major Hurst, sensing a weak spot in the Japanese defenses, decided to press the advantage by seizing also Hill 120, which represented an ideal jumpoff position for an attack against Baldy Ridge from the flank and rear. A company of engineers relieved Company L on the three knobs. The latter company prepared to resume the assault.

At 1530 the company began the advance up the long axis of the ridge, paralleling the lines of Company K on Boyd Ridge barely 100 yards across the draw. Once again progress was uneventful. Shortly after 1600 the lead element, one platoon, reached the top of Hill 120, where it discovered and eliminated several Japanese positions.[49] Just when it appeared that capture of Hill 120 had been accomplished, the platoon on the ridge began to draw fire from Baldy Ridge and suffered several casualties. The men sought cover on the eastern slope of the crest, only to run into a hail of automatic weapons fire from enemy positions on the lower slopes of Boyd Ridge. As men were hit and fell, it became apparent that the platoon was caught in a merciless cross fire from which there was no cover or concealment. Neither was there any route of retreat, for Japanese along the lower reaches of Hill 120 and the three knobs contributed to the massacre. Enemy cannon and mortars joined in the cacaphony of death.

For the men trapped on the ridge, the only way out was down the face of the cliffs and out through the draw, but even then they would have to run the gauntlet of enemy fire. One of the first to be killed was the senior noncommissioned officer, a gunnery sergeant. Other Marines quickly shared his fate as Japanese bullets found their mark. In a matter of minutes, dead and wounded dotted the ridge and only a few men remained unhurt. The ferocity of the enemy fire did not spare the three corpsmen that had accompanied the platoon, for only one left the ridge alive. While searching for a way out, the pla-

---

[49] *3/7 WarD*, Oct44.

toon leader was hit and fell to his death in the gorge below.

Without any visible means of escape, the trapped men reacted instinctively. Unable to see their well-camouflaged assailants, the Marines fought back as best they could. Their predicament had not gone unnoticed. From the adjacent draw, Captain James V. Shanley, commanding Company L, known by the nickname "Jamo," was desperately seeking a means of rescuing his men. He ordered a tank up the narrow valley, but the terrain precluded the effective employment of armor. The tank eventually became a precarious shelter behind which some of the wounded could find cover. It could not take an effective part in the fighting and was helpless to stem the slaughter. From the crest of Boyd Ridge, men from Company K watched in silent rage the carnage taking place before their eyes. In desperation they began to hurl white phosphorus grenades into the gorge. Dense smoke mercifully began to obscure the scene of death and violence.

On the crest, the few men still able to maneuver did what they could to get the wounded off the ridge. There was no easy way out, and despite the smoke, Japanese bullets were still finding their marks. This is the picture that presented itself to an observer of the action:

> The wounded crawled behind rocks or just lay motionless, bullets hitting them again and again. Others cried pitifully for help and begged their comrades not to leave them there. Medical corpsmen worked bravely and efficiently, each of them dragging men to the ledge. One of them stood up to cry: "Take it easy! Bandage each other. Get out a few at a time...." He was shot and killed. Those men who could move threw away their weapons because they couldn't climb down the cliff speedily without using both hands. And as they climbed down, some were hit and fell to the ravine floor. Others slipped and fell, suffering severe cuts from the jagged and sharp coral.... One of the wounded who lay on the floor of the ravine tried to help another across the open draw to the safety of the tank. The lesser wounded put his arms around the other and the two hobbled across the open draw. They could not make it. They dropped helpless there in the open draw, and the Japanese opened fire on them.

This was more than Shanley could stand. Although a lieutenant tried to hold him, Jamo ran out from under cover into the draw, swept one of the men into his arms, carried him back to the tank, laid him down tenderly and ran out into the fire-swept open ground again for the other. He did not reach him. A mortar shell fell before Captain Shanley got there. Shrapnel tore through Shanley, wounding him mortally. When he saw Shanley fall, a second lieutenant, Shanley's exec, rushed out. He had just reached Jamo when the chug-chug of an antitank gun was heard. He fell at Jamo's side, dead.[50]

Only a few of the men made it across the draw. By 1820 it was all over. There were 11 men left out of the 48 that had ascended the ridge, and of these, only five from the leading platoon of Company L emerged from the draw unscathed.[51] Colonel Nakagawa's comment on the day's happenings was short and to the point:

> The enemy's plan seemed to be to attack Kansokuyama (main post of the southeastern part) with flame throwers as well as Suifuzan Hill (main post of the northern part). Our garrison unit by accurate firing and close quarter combat inflicted

---

[50] TSgt Jeremiah A. O'Leary, Jr., as quoted in McMillan, *The Old Breed*, pp. 329–331.
[51] 3/7 WarD, Oct44

losses upon the enemy who then withdrew.[52]

The disaster that had befallen Company L was to have further consequences, for it resulted in the evacuation of the summits of the three knobs and the withdrawal of Company I. At the end of 4 October, Companies I and L, 7th Marines, were down from an authorized strength of 470 Marines for the two units combined to a total of 80. The 1st Battalion could barely muster more than 100 men fit for duty; and the 2d Battalion reported in at 30 percent efficiency.[53] Clearly, the 7th Marines, owing to the heavy losses it had sustained, was no longer able to function as an effective combat unit on the regimental level. General Rupertus therefore ordered the 5th Marines to relieve the 7th on 5 October.[54]

Since D-Day, the 1st Marine Division had sustained a total of 1,027 Marines killed, 4,304 wounded, and 249 missing, a total of 5,580. The division estimated that it had killed slightly more than 10,000 of the enemy and had captured 214 Japanese and Koreans.[55] Both opponents were paying a premium price for possession of the uninspiring Umurbrogol ridges. The next chapter in the contest would be written with the blood of the 5th Marines.

THE 5TH MARINES IN THE FINAL ATTEMPT[56]

The relief of the 7th Marines by the 5th Marines took place during 5 and 6 October. As a result, there was relatively little action on Peleliu during this period. The 1st Battalion, 7th Marines, received orders at noon, 5 October, that it was to proceed aboard trucks to the bivouac area of 1/5 at Purple Beach. The battalion completed the move by 1530, and 1/5 took over the positions of 1/7 at the eastern perimeter of the Umurbrogol pocket.[57]

Throughout the remainder of 5 October, 2/7 engaged in continuous combat as the battalion prepared to eliminate additional caves along the East Road. Tanks supporting the infantry in this effort blasted caves on the East Road and in the draws, killing an estimated 50 Japanese in one cave alone. At 1655 the commander of 1/5, Lieutenant Colonel Robert W. Boyd, arrived at the 2/7 CP to make arrangements for the relief of the battalion and to look over the positions. The relief of 2/7 was effected on the morning of 6 October. The move did not proceed peacefully. Company F, en route to the West Road where trucks awaited the men, came under heavy fire from the draws on both flanks. Tanks had to be moved up to cover the men as they crossed the draws. While coming down the ridge, Company E drew enemy mortar fire and had several casualties. Once it had reached safety, the 2d Battalion proceeded to a rest area north of the Peleliu airfield.[58]

Relief of 3/7 by 2/5 was accomplished without incident at 0800, and the weary

---
[52] *Japanese CenPacOps*, p. 129.
[53] Smith, *Approach to the Philippines*, p. 556.
[54] 1st MarDiv FO 5/44, dtd 5Oct44.
[55] *1st MarDiv SAR*, Phase II, Anx A, p. 16.
[56] Additional sources used for this section are: *IIIAC C–2 Periodic Rpts; 1st MarDiv D–2 Rpts; 2/5 OpRpts; 3/5 Rec of Events; 1/7 HistRpt; 2/7 WarD, Sep-Oct44; 3/7 WarD, Oct44; 4/11 SAR*.
[57] *1/7 HistRpt*, 5Oct44.
[58] *2/7 WarD*, Oct44.

men of 3/7 moved into bivouac about 2,000 yards northeast of the airfield.[59] On the following day the battalion received orders from the regimental commander to provide garrison forces for the islands covering the northeast water approaches to Peleliu.[60]

For the 7th Marines, all heavy combat activity on Peleliu had come to an end. To the 5th Marines, responsibility for the final drive into the Umurbrogol was the continuation of heavy combat, which the regiment had by this time been involved in for more than three weeks. The severe losses, the unfavorable climate, and the primitive conditions that governed the Peleliu fighting had sapped their strength. As noted by a member of the 5th Marines regimental headquarters staff during most of the Peleliu operation, the regiment:

> ... had been the last outfit to leave New Britain. Many were veterans of Guadalcanal. The division had optimistically said that the 5th would be one of the first outfits to leave Peleliu, and yet after securing the northern end of the island everyone knew that we would be committed again. Now once again the 1st and 7th Regiment were for the most part gone or leaving and the 5th was back at it again. The men and the officers were superb during this last phase but very, very tired.[61]

This weariness was not confined to the Marines on Peleliu, for there is some evidence that the enemy was not entirely happy with conditions on the island. One Japanese sergeant recalled:

> Though we had much jungle training, we did not have the training to cope with the rocky terrain of this island. In addition, we were not used to the climatic conditions....[62]

Colonel Harold D. Harris, Commander, 5th Marines, decided to use a different approach in the conquest of the Umurbrogol ridges. All previous attempts to penetrate the pocket had encompassed an attack from the north, northeast, east, and southeast. Even though both the 7th Marines and RCT 321 had sought an approach from the vicinity of the 321st Infantry Trail, the objective in each instance had been possession and control of the East Road. The idea behind the new drive from the north and northwest was to nibble away at the Japanese positions in a slow but deliberate and inexorable advance, which in due time would achieve the desired result at a minimum cost in personnel and materiel.

Once the relief of the 7th Marines had been completed, 1/5 occupied a line parallel to the East Road. This line was approximately 1,200 yards long and included both Walt and Boyd Ridges. The 2d Battalion was deployed along the northern perimeter of the Umurbrogol pocket facing Baldy Ridge. Along the southern perimeter, 3/5 had reverted to regimental control and occupied a bivouac area south of the pocket between sorties against the Five Sisters. Along the western perimeter of the pocket, parallel to the West Road, supporting troops continued to man the containing

---

[59] *3/9 WarD*, Oct44.
[60] *Ibid.*
[61] Maj Donald A. Peppard ltr to CMC, dtd 13Nov49, in *Peleliu Comment File*, hereafter *Peppard ltr.*

[62] SgtMaj Masao Kurihara, IJA, written statement, n.d., attached to ltr, MajGen Paul J. Mueller, USA, to Director of Marine Corps History, dtd 9Aug50, in *Peleliu Comment File.*

line. Many of these men were volunteers that had come forward to lend a hand to their embattled comrades by bringing up supplies and serving as stretcher bearers. Others were noncombatant souvenir hunters who were turning out in such numbers as to become a major nuisance. The situation was quickly brought under control when the souvenir-hunters found themselves abruptly shanghaied into the lines by orders from higher authority.[63]

The first offensive action by the 5th Marines occurred within a half hour following the relief of the 7th Marines on the morning of 6 October. Company E of 2/5 attacked the northeastern perimeter of the pocket in substantially the same area where only two days previously Company L of 3/7 had met such a severe reverse. This time conditions favored the attacking force. The weather had cleared and the island was beginning to dry up after the prolonged drenching. The direction of the push was into the area west of the East Road, but unlike the abortive attempt of the 7th Marines, the efforts of the 5th were based on a firmer foundation and the rear of Company E was secure. The company advanced to the three knobs and seized two of them. (See Map 13.) Once again the Japanese let loose with everything they had. Even though any further advance was impossible in the face of such concentrated fire, the Marines managed to maintain their foothold on the two knobs, while bulldozers carved out an access road for gun and flame tanks once the drive to the south got under way. What amounted to a sheer cliff was thus demolished to facilitate a subsequent attack against a ridge which formed the western spur of Baldy.[64]

The tactical importance of this spur was twofold. First, as long as it remained in enemy hands the Japanese possessed a clear field of fire to the West Road. Second, at the center the spur connected with Baldy Ridge and thus constituted a direct route to this objective. As a result, capture of this spur was essential as an initial step towards the seizure of Baldy. The task of securing the spur fell to a platoon of Company G, 2/5 commanded by 2d Lieutenant Robert T. Wattie.

On the morning of 9 October Company G launched a frontal assault on Baldy. Lieutenant Wattie's platoon seized the spur which henceforth bore his name and became known as Wattie Ridge.

Lieutenant Wattie led his men southward along the crest of the spur for about 100 yards but drew such heavy fire that the position became untenable. At dusk the platoon was forced to withdraw from Baldy but retained possession of the two knobs that had been seized earlier in the day. The approach of night did not herald the end of the fighting for 2/5. Friendly mortar fire rocked the Japanese positions and covered the entire area from the three knobs to the top of Baldy. The Japanese retaliated by infiltrating. Hand grenades exploded all night long, but the morning of 7 October found the men of

---

[63] McMillan, *The Old Breed*, p. 337.

[64] Col Harold D. Harris interview with LtCol Gordon D. Gayle, Head, HistDiv, HQMC, 28–31Oct49, hereafter *Harris interview*.

THE UMURBROGOL POCKET 239

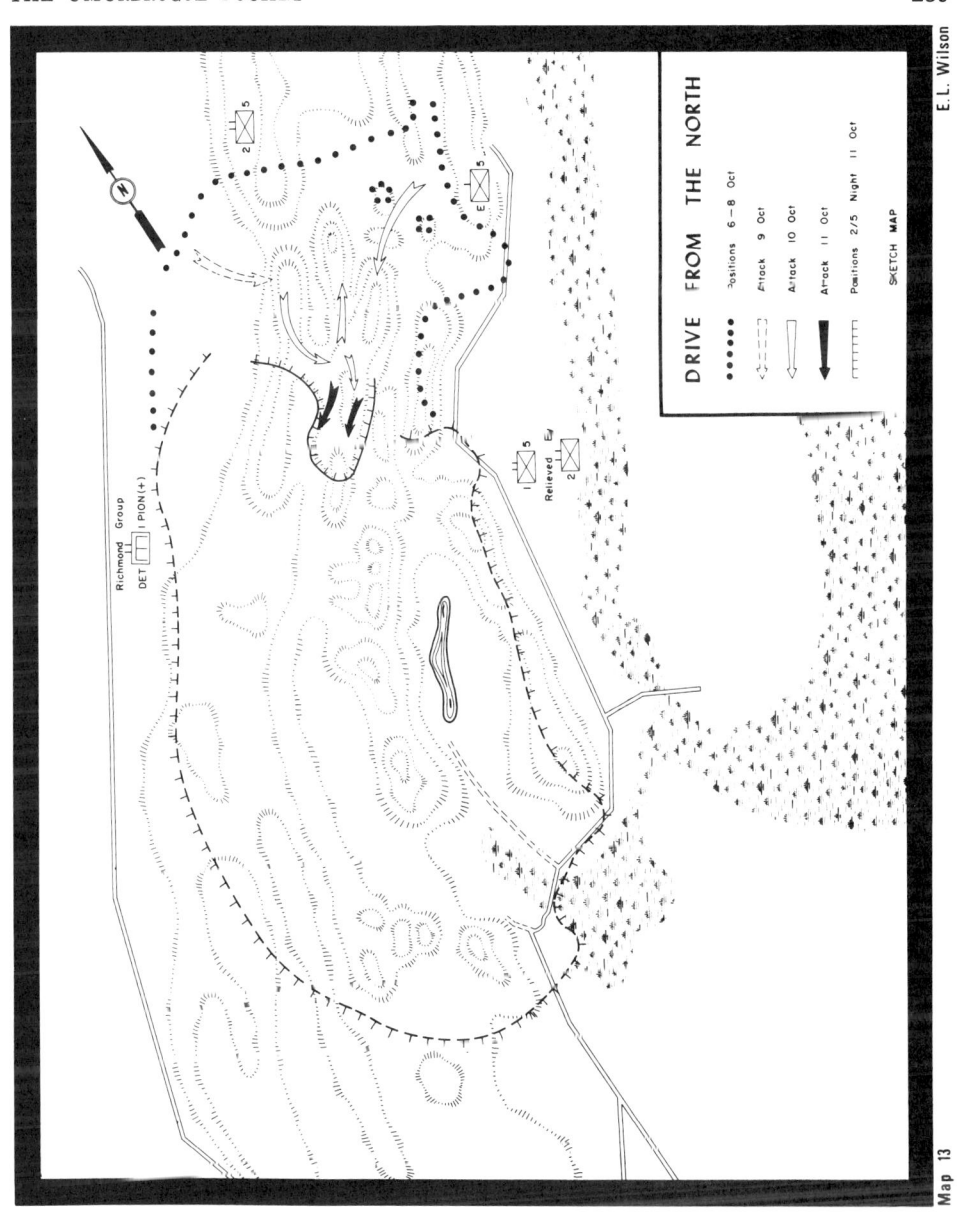

Map 13

2/5 still in possession of the ground seized the preceding day.[65]

There is evidence that the plan of Colonel Harris to have the 5th Marines move slowly and deliberately did not meet with approval at division headquarters, where the desire for a quick conquest of the island was still paramount.[66] It was not unnatural for the regimental commander to attempt to resist such pressure, of which, in his own words, there was plenty. On the division level the attitude prevailed that:

> ...troops frequently have a feeling that a constant and unreasonable pressure to hurry things up is being applied from above. Sometimes, if a pressure is not exerted a battle (especially an extremely bitter one) may be allowed to deteriorate into a stalemate simply because of the peculiarities of mass inertia....[67]

Any idea that the Japanese contained in the Umurbrogol were the disorganized remnants of the island garrison was dispelled by captured orders which were interpreted to show that, as late as 1 October, the enemy still was well organized and determined to take full advantage of his almost inaccessible positions. To the Japanese, the Marines appeared to be "exhausted" and "fighting less aggressively."[68] The Japanese retained a series of OPs, a mobile reserve of company strength, and close-combat units specializing in night infiltration and combat. These units had been organized specifically to destroy American tanks, LVTs, mortar positions, and other important targets. In addition, each unit within the pocket was charged with gathering and evaluating information, maintaining its own security, and carrying out liaison with higher, adjacent, and lower echelons. Japanese artillery and automatic weapons had standing orders to impede traffic on both the West and East Roads.[69] On 6 October, the 1st Marine Division estimated enemy strength at 300-600.[70]

Throughout 7 October, 3/5 kept the Japanese occupied in the southeastern perimeter of the pocket. Following a heavy preparation by mortars and 105-mm guns, Company I, supported by six tanks of the 710th Tank Battalion, advanced northward and entered the Horseshoe. Both infantry and tanks raked suspected enemy positions with fire, especially those along the lower slopes of Walt Ridge on the right and Five Brothers to the left. The Marines of 1/5 on the crest of Walt Ridge gave fire support to the advance. In the course of the day, a fire team of Marines was assigned to protect each tank. The armor was also supported by two LVT flamethrowers and a platoon of the 1st Engineer Battalion. The total advance of Company I for the day amounted to 200 yards. It represented the furthest inroad into the Umurbrogol pocket from this direction. The attack had successfully reduced Japanese cave positions that had thwarted earlier advances, though their seizure was only temporary. When the tanks ran short of ammunition later in the day and had to withdraw, the infantry also had to pull back. An attempt by Company I to bypass the

---

[65] *2/5 OpRpt*, 6Oct44.
[66] *Harris interview.*
[67] *Wachtler ltr.*
[68] *IIIAC C-2 Periodic Rpt* No. 22, 6Oct44.
[69] *Ibid.*
[70] *1st MarDiv D-2 Periodic Rpt.* 5-6Oct44.

Horseshoe and penetrate into the valley separating the Five Brothers from the China Wall, in the very heart of the pocket, drew such fierce resistance that the attack never really got off the ground.[71] Towards the end of the day, the battalion returned to its bivouac area north of the airfield.

In the 2/5 sector, the nibbling process continued. Patrols from Company E descended from the knobs and fired bazooka shells at the most prominent Japanese caves, while a 60mm mortar on the ridge north of Boyd Ridge registered on the terrain that the company would soon traverse. Two LVT flamethrowers and three tanks were attached to the battalion. Their effective employment in large measure would depend on the completion of a trail to higher ground where the armor could blast the Japanese positions within the pocket once the attack of 2/5 got under way.[72]

Another two days were to pass before Colonel Harris dispatched the 2d Battalion against the menacing crest of Baldy Ridge. During 8 October, pressure against the pocket was maintained by artillery fire from the north and south. Improvement in the weather enabled Marine aviation on Peleliu to participate once more in the devastation of the Umurbrogol Pocket. A shortage of aviation gasoline still prevailed because the severe storm had curtailed all logistical support. Rough seas and heavy surf precluded the use of landing craft. As a temporary expedient, gasoline in drums was floated over the reef and guided to the shore by swimmers.[73]

Peleliu-based aircraft stepped up their attacks on 8 October. Twenty aircraft of VMF-114 participated in the first strike, which began at 0700. Each Corsair carried a 1,000 pound bomb. The mission was repeated at 1300, and once again the sound of exploding bombs reverberated throughout Peleliu. The pilots of VMF-114 did not limit themselves to inflicting death and destruction on the Japanese; they also dropped leaflets to the cave-dwelling Japanese officers with the following message:

> Officers of the Japanese forces:
> As you can see if you look at the planes, the material and the ships, your best efforts are not impeding our work. American planes not only bomb you at will, but they also bomb Babelthuap and the other islands north of here. Perhaps you can see the flames. Your comrades to the north have all they can do to help themselves, so how could they help you?
> You honor and respect your men, but how can they honor and respect you if you make them die needlessly? Thousands of brave Japanese soldiers before you have realized the futility of death in such circumstances; they will live to raise families and help build a new Japan.
> You still have this choice—raise a white flag and come out unarmed. We will give you water, food, shelter, and medicine for your wounded.[74]

Even though Colonel Harris expressed satisfaction with the results of the two air strikes, the effect remained difficult to estimate "because with each aerial attack the Japs only burrowed deeper into their vast caves."[75] Just as before, the effectiveness of leaflets remained substantially nil. The Japanese did not entertain any thought of surrendering.

---

[71] *3/5 Rec of Events*, 7Oct44.
[72] *2/5 OpRpt*, 7Oct44.
[73] VMF–114 WarD, Oct44.

[74] *Ibid.*
[75] *1st MarDiv SAR*, Phase II, Anx A, p. 16.

A sign discovered in a Japanese dugout carried the message: "Defense to the death. We will build a barrier across the Pacific with our bodies."[76]

Along the northern perimeter of the pocket, the preparations for the capture of Baldy Ridge neared completion. Just off the West Road along the northwestern edge of the pocket, heavy weapons were emplaced near the command post of 2/5 to support the battalion attack. Major Gordon D. Gayle, commanding officer of 2/5, directed the fire of a battery of 105s against positions in and around Baldy Ridge and the hills to the south. The heavy shells, fired pointblank into the ridges, pulverized the coral until the very shape of the hills underwent considerable change.

Still worried about the possibility of Japanese counterlandings from Babelthuap, General Rupertus ordered a reinforced company of RCT 321 to seize the island of Garakayo, situated about 7,000 yards north-northeast of Peleliu. The soldiers, reinforced by 10 LVT (A)s from the 3d Armored Amphibian Battalion, were to land and annihilate or capture all enemy forces on Garakayo Island, and destroy enemy defenses.[77] After having seized and occupied the island, the soldiers were to establish an outpost. In addition to denying the use of Garakayo to the Japanese, the garrison was to prevent the movement of enemy forces from the north to reinforce Peleliu and Ngesebus and, at the same time, prevent the enemy from escaping northward from the two islands.

The Army troops landed on Garakayo as scheduled early on 9 October. There was little opposition. By late afternoon the soldiers had patrolled the entire coastline of the island and had reached some of the hills in the interior. The troops encountered numerous caves, observation posts, and machine gun emplacements showing signs of recent occupation but found them unmanned.[78] A total of five Japanese were found on the island and killed.

On Peleliu, the 5th Marines continued to probe the perimeter of the Umurbrogol pocket. There, elements of 2/5 succeeded in seizing a ridge west of Baldy and in knocking out a number of caves. Even though the Marines had to abandon some hard won ground, their artillery did seal some of the caves that had forced the withdrawal. Each Japanese position eliminated in this manner would reduce Marine casualties when the final capture of Baldy Ridge was attempted on the following day. The bulldozer that had started work on a trail into the Umurbrogol two days earlier continued to work until it had gone within the time allotted as far as it could—midway down the ravine between Boyd Ridge and Ridge 3, a semi-detached razorback south and slightly east of Baldy Ridge. In preparation for the attack scheduled on the following morning, VMF-114 carried out an additional air strike against the Japanese pocket.[79] The planes dropped twelve

---

[76] Gen Alexander A. Vandegrift and Robert B. Asprey, *Once A Marine: The Memoirs of General A. Vandegrift, United States Marine Corps* (New York: W. W. Norton & Company, Inc. 1964), p. 274, hereafter Vandegrift and Asprey, *Once A Marine*, used with permission.

[77] 1st MarDiv FO 8–44, dtd 10Oct44.

[78] *1st MarDiv D–2 Periodic Rpt*, 9–10Oct44.

MARINES OCCUPY RIDGE *in the Umurbrogol shrouded by smoke from aerial bombing and artillery fire. (USMC 95258)*

MARINE TANK-INFANTRY TEAM *advancing into the Peleliu ridges during final phase of the operation. (USMC 97433)*

1,000-pound bombs on target but failed to observe definite results.

The attack of 2/5 against Baldy Ridge jumped off on the morning of 10 October, preceded by an artillery barrage, which began at dawn and continued until shortly before 1100. At this time Company G jumped off with the mission of securing the southern spur of Baldy Ridge and advancing as far north as possible over the ridge. After a sharp skirmish with the Japanese defenders, the Marines carried the crest and swept northward until they had secured the entire ridge. Company E, jumping off shortly after noon, seized Ridge 120 southwest of the three knobs. This time the devastating fire that had cut Captain Shanley's company to ribbons was no longer in evidence, and the Marines were able to consolidate their gains. The importance of the terrain that had been seized was further underscored at approximately 1600, when 50 enemy troops came through the lines of Company G and surrendered.[80] Because Companies E and G were tied in only by fire during the coming night, heavy artillery and mortar fire was maintained throughout the night to cover the gap and discourage any enemy counterattack. A platoon from Company F joined Company G as reserve. The interdictory artillery fire in some instances was laid as close as 25 yards to Marine lines to keep the enemy from moving in and throwing hand grenades. No counterattack materialized.

In the course of 10 October a minor mystery was solved. For several days artillery shells from an unknown source had been landing on the southern tip of Peleliu. These had been reported as enemy shells whose place of origin was the subject of considerable speculation. The solution to the vexing problem turned out to be easier than anticipated: it was definitely established that the shells were our own, that they came from positions on the northern end of Peleliu, and that they had been directed into the Umurbrogol pocket. Apparently, some of the shells had ricocheted off the hills and continued on to the southern part of the island.[81]

The morning of 11 October saw the continuation of the slow, dogged advance that had marked the progress of the previous day. With nearly all of Baldy Ridge and Hill 120 in American hands, the way was open for an attack on Hill 140, which dominated the terrain between Baldy Ridge to the northeast and the Five Brothers to the south. In addition to representing the deepest inroad yet made into the heart of the Umurbrogol pocket, possession of Hill 140 would provide the Marines with a base they could use to fire directly not only on the northernmost of the Five Brothers, but also into the Horseshoe, and down the draw separating Walt and Boyd Ridges.

Preparatory to launching the attack on Hill 140, Company G seized the remainder of Baldy Ridge, though a few strongpoints still remained in enemy hands on the slopes. The advance continued until the Marines came up against a ravine separating Baldy Ridge from Hill 140. Along a parallel line to the east, Company E attacked along the

---

[79] *2/5 OpRpt*, 9Oct44.
[80] *Ibid.*

[81] *1st MarDiv D-2 PerRpt*, 9–10Oct44.

eastern slope of Ridge 3 until it encountered heavy small arms fire from enemy holdouts on the slopes of Baldy Ridge and the northern slope of Hill 140. Company G moved downhill, neutralizing one cave after another and thereby easing the situation of Company E, which was still exposed to heavy fire from Hill 140 to the southwest. At this point Colonel Harris committed Company F, which passed through the lines of Company E and attacked towards Hill 140 through a ravine separating Ridge 3 and the objective. The men bypassed the strongly defended northern slope of Hill 140 and attacked the formidable elevation from the west. The attackers made rapid headway, and by 1500 Company F had occupied the objective.

During the remainder of 11 October the Marines of 2/5 consolidated their newly won positions and eliminated many Japanese caves on the hillsides. In the words of the official report: "The enemy was very thick throughout our newly occupied areas, and the mopping up was a bloody procedure, 60 of the enemy killed in a very short time."[82]

The evening of 11 October found 2/5 in full control of the newly seized ground. Company E occupied Ridge 3, Company F remained on top of Hill 140, and Company G was firmly entrenched on Baldy. The drive of the 2d Battalion into the very heart of the Umurbrogol pocket not only achieved its objective but did so at a minimum cost in lives. In fact, the capture of Hill 140, one of the key bastions of the entire Japanese defense system, was attained at the cost

of 2 killed and 10 wounded. In commenting on the day's activities, Colonel Nakagawa did not mention the loss of his vital bastion in the northern part of his pocket; instead, he limited himself to the statement that ". . . all through the day there were heavy engagements with the enemy and our armies standing face to face. . . ."[83] Colonel Nakagawa was forced to admit in his report for the following day that the American drive had made progress. In keeping with the Japanese tendency of reporting only the brighter side of things, he added that ". . . the enemy penetrated our front lines but were repelled by night attack. . . ."[84]

To be sure, there was a Japanese counterattack against Hill 140 during the following night, combined with Japanese attempts to infiltrate the American positions. Nevertheless, conditions on Peleliu had undergone a radical change since the men of the 1st Marine Division had first attempted to enter the Umurbrogol. The situation had reversed itself and the Marines were in possession of the dominating heights, at least in the northern perimeter of the pocket. As a result, the Japanese counterattack made no headway, and at no time did it threaten the hold of the 5th Marines on the newly captured heights.

Important changes in the American command structure occurred on Peleliu on 12 October. Indirectly these resulted from the passing of control of operations in the Palaus scheduled for the next day, from the U. S. Third Fleet and Admiral Halsey to the Headquarters, Forward

---

[82] *2/5 OpRpt*, 11Oct44.

[83] *Japanese CenPacOps*, p. 141.
[84] *Ibid*.

Area Central Pacific (Task Force 57) under Admiral Hoover, scheduled for 13 October.[85] At 0800, 12 October, General Geiger moved his command post ashore on Peleliu and declared the assault and occupation phases of operations on the island ended.[86] "Its termination was to mark the passage of command from the task force afloat to an area commander. It did not signify that active combat had ceased. The battle on Peleliu was far from being over."[87] In accordance with this order RCT 321 and Garrison Force, consisting of the 16th Field Depot and other supporting units, passed under IIIAC control. RCT 321 assumed responsibility for the eastern arm of Peleliu, and the Island Garrison Force became responsible for the area south of the Umurbrogol pocket.

The capture of Hill 140 during the afternoon of 11 October and the penetration into the Umurbrogol pocket from the north was to mark the last offensive operation of 2/5 on Peleliu. In the course of the morning of 12 October, the weary Marines were relieved by 3/5. It became evident that the Japanese were becoming alert to the foothold that the Americans had gained in the Umurbrogol. The relief of 2/5 took place under heavy sniper fire. Before the movement was completed, 22 Marines had become casualties. The commanding officer of Company K, in attempting to familiarize himself with the company sector, was instantly killed by a Japanese sniper. The enemy exploited the confusion resulting from a relief of line units by reinfiltrating positions from which he had been driven the previous day. Company I drew heavy rifle and machine gun fire when it prepared to relieve Company F in the ridges above West Road (See Map 14).

Lest it appear that the initiative on 12 October rested entirely with the Japanese, one incident occurred that showed the Marines were equally adept in taking advantage of a situation and making improvisations when needed. Even prior to the capture of Hill 140, the Marines had speculated about the feasibility of getting a field piece up on this hill or on Wattie Ridge and using it to fire point-blank at Japanese positions on the Five Brothers, in the Horseshoe, and on the western base of Walt Ridge, where the Japanese caves had hitherto been immune to direct artillery fire. This immunity was to come to an end on 12 October. Getting a 75mm howitzer to the top of Hill 140 proved a laborious and time consuming process involving disassembly of the weapon, manhandling it up the hill to the forward position, and then reassembling it behind a protective layer of sandbags, all of which also had to be manhandled to the summit of the ridge. A participant in this action has described the operation as follows:

> The tube of the howitzer was, of course, the most difficult part to manhandle and at one spot I had a rope run through it and held it around a small tree paying it out as the men moved it along. Without this precaution, had either of the men carrying it been hit it would have fallen into the deep round hole that separated the southern end of Wattie's Ridge from Hill 140.

---

[85] IIIAC OpO 13-44, 13Oct44.
[86] IIIAC OPlan 12-44, dtd 10Oct44.
[87] Historical Committee, *81st Infantry Division*, p. 156.

THE UMURBROGOL POCKET 247

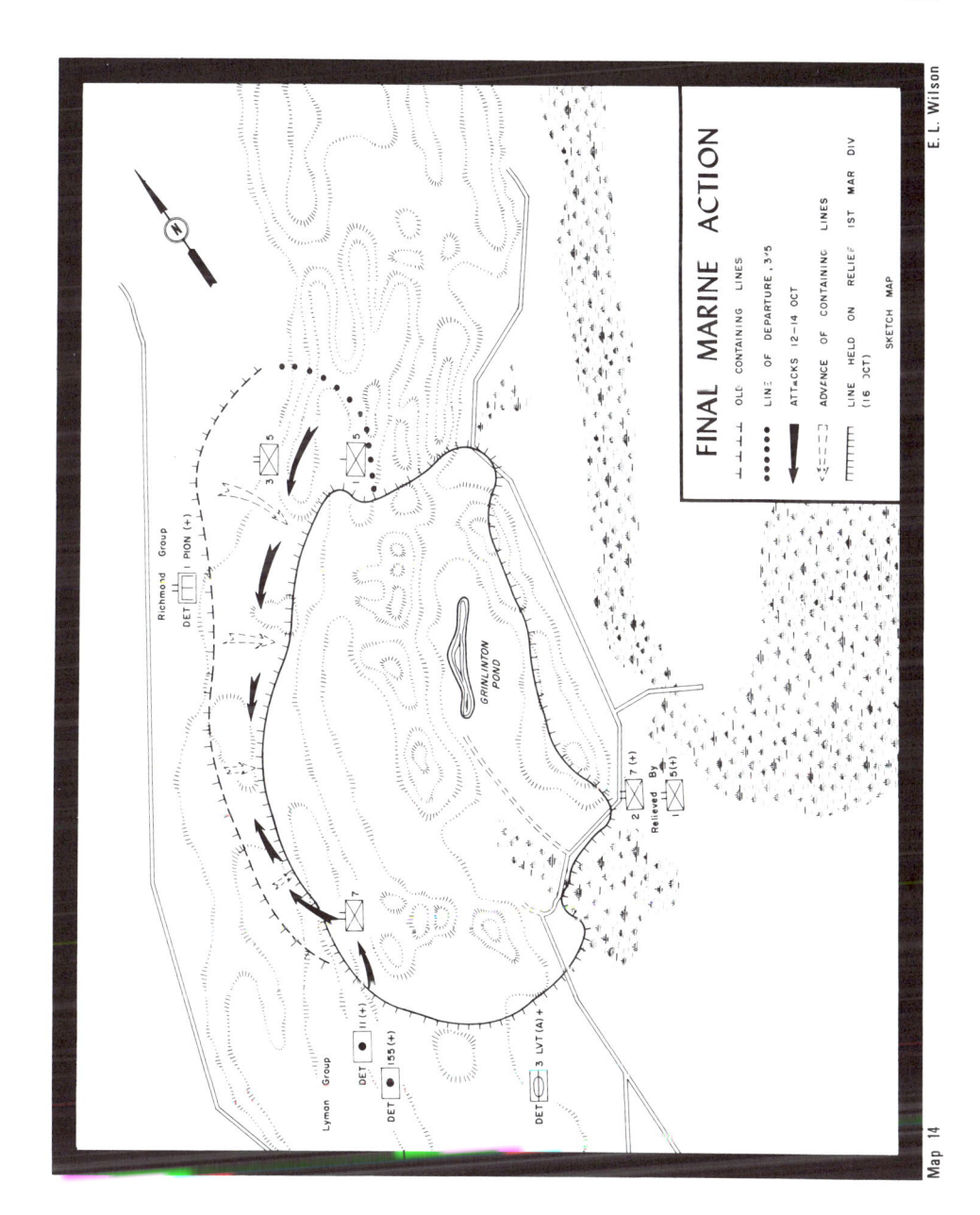

Map 14

After we had gained the summit of the hill we reassembled the piece and layed it on the entrance of a cave at the foot of Walt Ridge. However, we found it impossible to dig in the trail, so some rocks were piled around it and we fired our first shot. It took effect on the entrance to the cave but the piece recoiled so badly that one man was injured and a good deal of work had to be done before it could be fired again. When it became apparent that the piece could not be kept in place I communicated with LtCol Louis Reinberg, C.O. of the 4th Battalion, 11th Marines and requested him to send up sandbags the next morning. . . .[88]

Altogether, emplacement of the howitzer required seven hours. Once the difficulties in emplacing the piece had been overcome, the howitzer fired 11 rounds into the cave with good effect.[89]

A second howitzer went into position along the southeastern perimeter of the pocket near Walt Ridge, from where it was able to fire directly at the Five Sisters and the China Wall. The latter target offered interesting possibilities, since it was strongly suspected that Colonel Nakagawa's central hills command post was located there. Once the second howitzer had gone into position, the time had come to put the theory to the test. In the words of an eye witness and participant in the action:

> I spotted with binoculars and our first rounds routed out a covey of Nips around the top. Major Hank Adams reported to me later that about a dozen had been seen jumping and sliding off the east side of this hill to escape the shelling. One man was wounded after the howitzer fired about 40 rounds and it was deemed expedient to secure because of the danger of further casualties from close range sniper fire and because of the approaching darkness. The next morning Friday, October 13, I suffered two killed at daybreak at the banyan tree, both shot through the head by snipers across the canyon (75 yds). Consequently the howitzer was not reemplaced. This reaction further convinced me that we had picked on an important OP. This same point had been noticed earlier from a 155mm gun position near Buckley's old CP area. Nip officers in white gloves were observed several times through a captured high-power AA telescope, apparently examining the situation through binoculars.[90]

The artillery action on 12 October was to have an entirely unexpected effect on the final operations in the Umurbrogol. Intended originally only as a means of protecting the howitzers against small arms fire, the lowly sandbag soon evolved into an important tool of the infantry. The lack of cover and impossibility of digging-in had repeatedly forced the Marines to relinquish hard-won gains. Widespread use of the sandbag in protecting successive positions became a solution to the problem, though not the easiest one, since the interior of Peleliu contained no sand, and heavy sandbags had to be manhandled to the ridges in a cumbersome and laborious operation. During the final phase of operations on Peleliu the sandbag fulfilled a function as useful as that of any other offensive weapon, and in addition, provided the exposed infantrymen with a small sense of security.

---

[88] Maj George E. Bowdoin ltr to CMC dtd 9Feb50, in *Peleliu Comment File.*
[89] 4/11 WarD, Oct44.

[90] Col Edson L. Lyman ltr to CMC, n.d., in *Peleliu Comment File.*

On the morning of 13 October, 3/5 was the only unit of the regiment in the line with an offensive mission. The battalion was unruffled after a night of Japanese attempts to infiltrate and retake Hill 140. The Marines repulsed the enemy assault with little difficulty and the Japanese were forced to withdraw, leaving 15 dead behind them.[91] At 0915 another napalm air strike was directed against the Umurbrogol pocket. Although air and ground coordination functioned perfectly, no direct observation of the results of the bombing was possible. Following the bombing, Company K dispatched a patrol into the terrain just west of the containing line near the West Road in an effort to straighten the salient formed by Hill 140 and further constrict the pocket from a new direction which had not previously been explored because of the jagged and inaccessible terrain. Under a protective screen of artillery and mortar fire, the patrol advanced for 75 yards without meeting any resistance. Similarly, a patrol from Company I penetrated into the hills to a depth of 150 yards without encountering any Japanese. The absence of opposition in this previously unexplored area resulted in the preparation of plans for an attack into the pocket on the following day.

Puzzling as it was, the lack of Japanese opposition on 13 October did not signify that the Japanese on Peleliu no longer had the resources to put up a serious fight or impede any further advance by the Marines. To the contrary, on the evening of 13 October, Colonel Nakagawa reported his total strength as 1,150 military, including naval personnel. Nor were the Japanese bothered by a lack of arms, for they still possessed an arsenal of 13 machine guns, 500 rifles with 20,000 rounds of ammunition, 12 grenade dischargers with 150 rounds, 1 20mm automatic gun with 50 rounds, 1 antitank gun with 350 rounds, 1 70mm infantry howitzer with 120 rounds, 1,300 hand grenades, and 40 antitank mines.[92] Clearly, the elimination of the final pockets of Japanese resistance promised to be difficult.

At the same time, there were increasing indications that the days of the 1st Marine Division on Peleliu were numbered. Proof of this was a corps order placing the 321st Infantry again under control of the 1st Marine Division in order that comparatively fresh troops might relieve the 5th Marines, which was now quite exhausted, of the task of reducing the enemy pocket on Peleliu. The 5th Marines were to pass to corps control.[93] A division order called for the relief of the 5th Marines effective 0800, 15 October, by RCT 321. Effective 16 October, by which time two battalions of RCT 321 were expected to be in the line, control of all troops in the zone of action of the 5th Marines was to pass to RCT 321, whose mission was to continue the attack in the Umurbrogol pocket.[94]

The last full day of combat for the 5th Marines in the Umurbrogol pocket began with an air strike against the

---

[91] *1st MarDiv SAR*, Phase II, Anx A, p. 18.

[92] *Japanese CenPacOps*, p. 142.
[93] IIIAC OpO 13–44, dtd 13Oct44.
[94] 1st MarDiv FO 9–44, dtd 13Oct44.

Five Sisters. Following a heavy mortar preparation, Company I jumped off and attacked the western portion of the pocket, which had been undefended the day before. This time the Japanese were on the alert and subjected the Marines to heavy small arms fire, which slowed but did not halt the methodical advance. By late afternoon, after a gain of about 250 yards, the company had reached a point abreast of the northernmost two of the Five Brothers and roughly 150-200 yards west of the China Wall. Here, the Marines established a perimeter defense for the night.[95]

While Company I, 3/5, was advancing towards the south, Company C of 1/7 launched an attack from the southern containing line after having been attached to the 5th Marines. The company, supported by LVT flamethrowers, advanced west of the Five Sisters along an axis parallel to that portion of the containing line now manned by the 11th Marines. After a gain of approximately 125 yards, the advance came to a halt. As a result of the action on the part of 3/5 and 1/7, the containing line along the western perimeter of the pocket from north to south was shortened by about 400 yards. The Umurbrogol Pocket now had been reduced to an area approximately 400 yards by 500 yards.[96] Except for several small skirmishes with the Japanese elsewhere on Peleliu, the action on 14 October ended the participation of the 1st Marine Division in offensive operations on the island, though the final chapter in the conquest of Umurbrogol still remained to be written.

[95] *3/5 Rec of Events*, 14Oct44.
[96] *1st MarDiv D-2 Per Rpts*, 14-15Oct44.

RELIEF OF THE 1ST MARINE DIVISION[97]

The relief of units of the 1st Marine Division by elements of the 81st Infantry Division got under way on the morning of 15 October, when 2/321 took over the lines of 3/5 along the northern perimeter of the Umurbrogol Pocket. The maneuver of effecting the relief had already been set in motion on the previous day, however, when 2/5 relieved 2/321 on Ngesebus, Kongauru, and Garakayo Islands. The Army battalion, in turn, moved to an assembly area near the 321st Infantry Trail until it could carry out the relief of 3/5. In the course of 14 October, 1/323 had reached Peleliu from Ulithi. Upon arrival at Peleliu, the battalion was placed under the control of Colonel Dark, commanding officer of RCT 321. The mission of this battalion was to relieve the Marine units manning the containing line along the southwestern perimeter of the pocket. As the relief continued on 15 October, one month to the day since the Marines had first stormed ashore on Peleliu, 3/321 relieved 1/5 at the eastern perimeter on Walt and Boyd Ridges.

Until such time as preparations for the departure from Peleliu could be completed, the 5th Marines took up the defense of the northern portions of Peleliu, Ngesebus, and adjacent islands to the north. The 1st Battalion took up positions along the extreme northern portion of Peleliu; the 2d Battalion occupied Ngesebus, Kongauru, and Gara-

[97] Additional sources used for this section are: *1st MarDiv SAR; 81st InfDiv OpRpt; 1/7 B-2 & B-3 Jnl*, 15Sep/17Oct44, hereafter *1/7 B-2/3 Jnl; 3/7 WarD*, Oct44.

kayo; and the 3d Battalion deployed along the East Road, facing eastward toward the sea.

In the course of this major reshuffling of troops within a relatively confined area, it appeared at first glance as if at least one Marine unit had been forgotten. At noon on 16 October, when responsibility for operations against the Umurbrogol Pocket was transferred officially to Colonel Dark, 1/7 was still very much engaged in the northward drive on which it had embarked two days previously. During its last day of action in the Umurbrogol, the 1st Battalion sustained an additional seven casualties before being relieved by elements of 1/323 on the morning of 17 October.[98] Following its relief, 1/7 proceeded to Purple Beach preparatory to its embarkation in the transport *Sea Sturgeon*, which left Peleliu on 22 October and arrived at Pavuvu a week later.

The 2d Battalion, 7th Marines continued its mission of patrolling the islands northeast of Peleliu during the middle of October, and did not begin loading until the 26th. The defensive mission proved generally uneventful, and as a result, the men of the 2d Battalion enjoyed a well deserved rest.

Less fortunate than the other units of the 7th Marines was the 3d Battalion, which became involved in a hard and costly action on Peleliu. The operation began at 1840, 17 October, when General Rupertus committed Company I just south of the pocket in the area of Company E, 1st Medical Battalion, where a number of Japanese had infiltrated and reoccupied caves, from where they engaged in some very bothersome sniping. Company I arrived on the scene and entered into a brief firefight to dislodge him before nightfall. For the remainder of the night the company remained in the area to protect the service troops.[99]

At 0630, 18 October, Company L relieved Company I, which had gone into combat on such short notice the previous evening that it was not fully supplied with ammunition. Shortly after 1100 Company L reported that the enemy was infesting the area in considerably greater strength than had been anticipated and had holed up in 12 cave positions. In response to this information a tank was dispatched to support the attack of the infantry. Shortly before 1400, the tank struck a land mine or some other buried explosive and blew up, killing not only several members of the crew but also the Company L commander, who had been engaged in directing the tank fire on the enemy caves. During the remainder of the afternoon 37mm antitank guns were brought up to knock out the enemy positions, but some of the Japanese still resisted at nightfall. Company L was relieved by Army units on the morning of 19 October and reverted to regimental control.[100]

Even though RCT 321 had assumed responsibility for the continuation of the drive against the Umurbrogol Pocket as of 16 October, the 1st Marine Division retained overall responsibility for operations on Peleliu until the com-

---

[98] *1/7 B-2 Jnl*, 16–17Oct44.

[99] *3/7 WarD*, Oct44.
[100] *Ibid.*

mander of the 81st Infantry Division arrived on 20 October and took over. At 0800 on that date the responsibility for the ground defense of the southern Palaus and continuation of operations to destroy the remaining enemy forces on Peleliu passed from III Amphibious Corps to the 81st Infantry Division.[101] At 0830 General Geiger and his staff departed by air to Guadalcanal. General Rupertus, together with certain sections of division headquarters, departed Peleliu by plane at 2300.[102]

The 1st and 3d Battalions, 7th Marines, completed embarking on board the S. S. *Sea Sturgeon* on 21 October, left Peleliu the next day, and arrived at Pavuvu eight days later. The men of the 2d Battalion and 4/11 faced a somewhat more complicated situation in making their departure from Peleliu. They began loading on a Dutch merchantman on 26 October, but bad weather and other factors delayed the departure of the ship until "by dint of the Marines manning the winches and booms, we were able to load and depart on the 30th of October. We arrived home in Pavuvu 7 November."[103]

The departure of the 7th Marines left the 5th Marines and reinforcing elements as the last remaining Marine units on Peleliu. When General Mueller assumed command of operations on Peleliu on 20 October, the Marine regiment was organized as a task force under Brigadier General Oliver P. Smith, Assistant Division Commander, 1st Marine Division. For the remainder of its stay on Peleliu, the 5th Marines was attached operationally to the 81st Infantry Division, pending availability of transports to return the troops to the Solomons.

The 5th Marines did not see any additional fighting on Peleliu, but remained in its defensive positions until 26 October. The regimental command post was located in the ruins of the former radio station near the northern tip of Peleliu. Embarkation was delayed by the lack of suitable shipping, there were no attack transports available, and most of the freighters doing duty as resupply ships lacked accommodations for the men. Further, none of the ships had booms and winches strong enough to hoist some of the heavy equipment. Eventually the transport *Sea Runner* was able to take most of the 5th Marines on board, though a detail of 13 men with 15 vehicles of the 1st Motor Transport Battalion remained on Peleliu until 13 November. Detachments from the 1st Amphibian Tractor Battalion and the 3d Armored Amphibian Battalion also remained on Peleliu until then.[104]

For the men of the 1st Marine Division, a campaign had ended, which in the words of General Rupertus, was fought "in terrain which . . . was the worst I have even seen."[105] General Vandegrift described the campaign as "one of the hardest jobs that they have

---

[101] IIIAC OPln 14–44, dtd 18Oct44.
[102] *1st MarDiv SAR*, Phase II, Anx A, p. 20.
[103] *Berger ltr.*

[104] *1st MarDiv SAR*, Phase II, Anx A, p. 21.
[105] MajGen William H. Rupertus ltr to LtGen A. Vandegrift, dtd 18Oct44, in Vandegrift Letters.

handed them (the First Marine Division)."[106]

According to figures up to 20 October 1944 the 1st Marine Division, in wresting the heavily fortified and defended island from the Japanese, had sustained a total of 6,265 casualties. A total of 1,124 Marines were killed in action and dead from wounds, 5,024 were wounded in action, and 117 were missing. In the course of a sustained operation that lasted for over a month, the Marines had accounted for an estimated 10,695 enemy dead and 301 prisoners of war.[107]

---

[106] CMC ltr to MajGen William H. Rupertus, n.d., quoted in Vandegrift and Asprey, *Once A Marine*, p. 274.

[107] *1st MarDiv SAR*, Phase II, Anx A, p. 21.

CHAPTER 8

To The Bitter End[1]

Major General Mueller, commanding general of the 81st Infantry Division, took charge of the continuation of operations on Peleliu on 20 October. On this date, in addition to elements of the 1st Marine Division still on Peleliu, General Mueller commanded RCT 321, 1/323, which had recently arrived from Ulithi, the 710th Tank Battalion, and elements of the 154th Engineer Battalion. During the period 23 September to 20 October, RCT 321 had lost 98 men killed and 468 wounded, while killing more than 1,500 Japanese and capturing 108.

When the 81st Infantry Division assumed responsibility for the Umurbrogol Pocket, 3/321 was deployed at the eastern perimeter along the crests of Walt and Boyd Ridges with positions extending southward to the entrance of the Horseshoe; 2/321 occupied Hill 140 along the northern perimeter. The 1st Battalion was deployed along a line generally paralleling West Road. Manning the ring of encirclement along the southern perimeter of the pocket, in the vicinity of the Five Sisters and Death Valley, was 1/323 (See Map 15).

General Mueller's plan for the reduction of the Umurbrogol Pocket and for the final elimination of all Japanese resistance on Peleliu was to tighten the ring of encirclement slowly and methodically into a relentless vise that would stifle all further resistance at a minimum loss of life to his command. This idea was not an original one. In fact, it closely resembled the tactics that Colonel Harris, commanding officer of the 5th Marines, had advocated several weeks earlier. The latter regiment, now under control of the 81st Infantry Division, spent its final days on Peleliu on the northern portion of the island and on those islands to the north of Peleliu that had previously been garrisoned by RCT 321. The defense of the beaches along the southernmost sector of Peleliu was assigned to the 726th Amphibious Tractor Battalion. The 81st Infantry Division artillery, which also exercised operational control over 4/11, the 3d Field Artillery Battalion, and the 8th Field Artillery Battalion, was assigned the mission of supporting RCT 321 in the defense of Peleliu and adjacent islands.[2]

For the remainder of 20 October, the 81st Infantry Division engaged mainly in reconnaissance for an attack scheduled for the following morning. Following a napalm bomb strike at 0800, 21 October, against Japanese positions in front of 1/321, the battalion jumped off

---

[1] Unless otherwise noted, the material in this section is derived from: *81st InfDiv OpRpt;* Historical Committee, *81st Infantry Division;* Smith, *Approach to the Philippines;* Morison, *Leyte;* Hough, *Assault on Peleliu.*

[2] 81st InfDiv FO 22, 20Oct44.

TO THE BITTER END 255

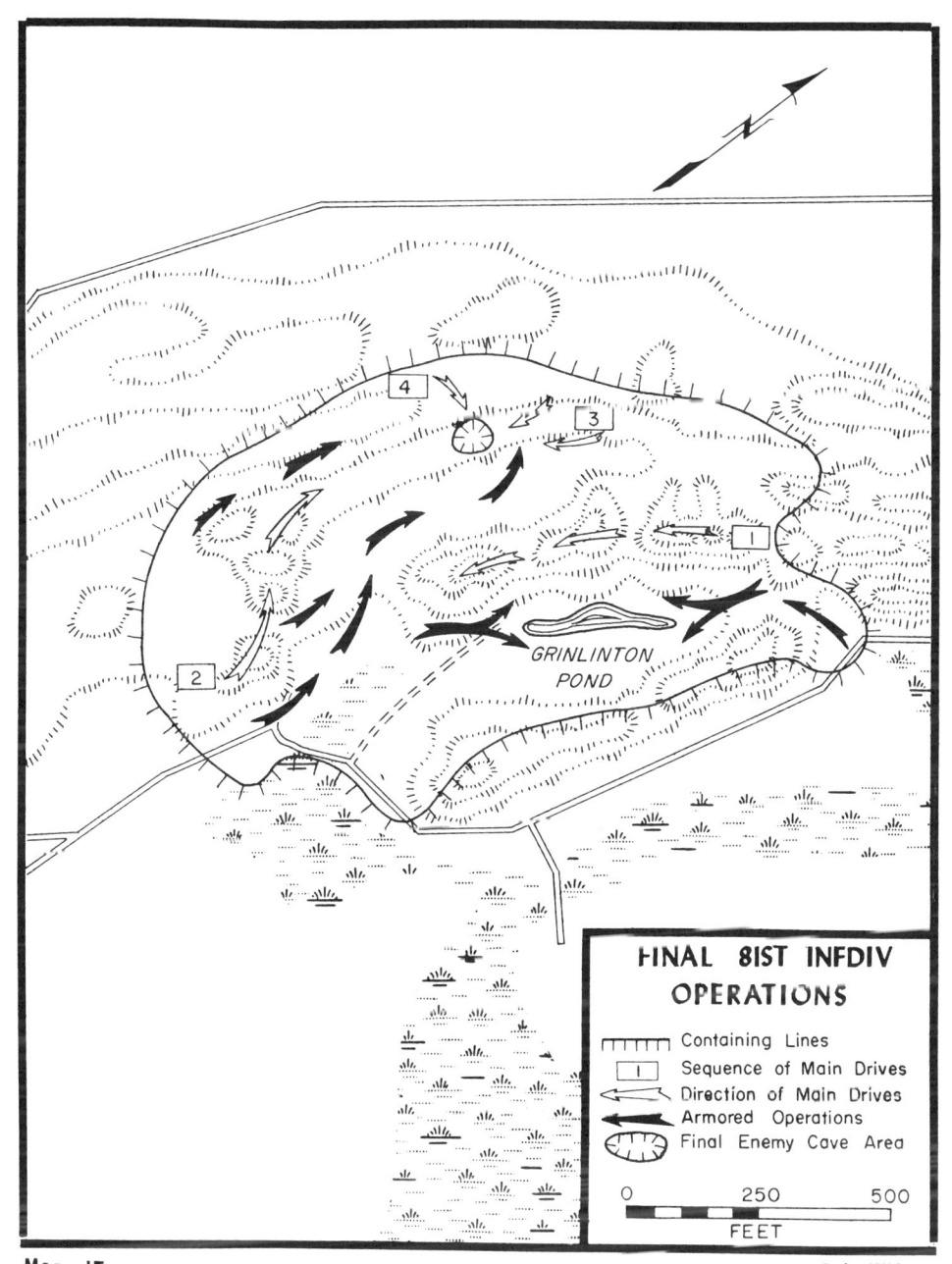

FINAL 81ST INFDIV
OPERATIONS

⊓⊓⊓⊓⊓ Containing Lines
☐ 1   Sequence of Main Drives
⟵   Direction of Main Drives
⬅   Armored Operations
◯   Final Enemy Cave Area

0   250   500
      FEET

GRINLINTON POND

Map 15   F. L. Wilson

from its positions along the northwestern edge of the pocket and advanced almost 100 yards towards the northern end of the China Wall and the northwest corner of the valley separating the China Wall from the Five Brothers. Subsequently, this valley was to become known as the Wildcat Bowl. During the afternoon, elements of the 2d Battalion seized the crest of the northernmost of the Five Brothers (hereafter referred to as Brother No. 1). Despite heavy fire from the enemy on Brother No. 3 and the northern end of the China Wall, the soldiers were able to consolidate their gains with the help of sandbags, which had to be manhandled up the ridge. They offered effective protection from Japanese small arms fire. During the night, the Japanese attempted to drive the soldiers from Brother No. 1, but were repulsed with grenades. A similar attempt, to scale the west wall of Walt Ridge and drive the soldiers from the crest, ended in failure. The Japanese were somewhat more successful in infiltrating a small group into the rear areas of 1/321 and 1/323, but aside from causing considerable excitement and confusion, the infiltrators did little damage and were forced to retreat.

Operations on 21 October began again when Corsairs of VMF-114 dropped napalm on Japanese positions in the vicinity of the Horseshoe. The frequent calls for air support from the Army division came as something of a surprise to the Marine aviators, who as early as 17 October had thought "that no further call would come for Napalm bombs—so short appeared our lines."[3]

But in the days that followed, calls for air support increased. The soldiers asked for unfused bombs to be dropped over specifically designated areas of the pocket. The napalm was subsequently fired by mortar shells. These tactics were successful, and machine gunners on the ground were able to destroy a good many Japanese trying to get away from the resulting inferno. In order to assist the aviators in pinpointing targets, the soldiers marked the end of the Horseshoe and its western approaches with smoke pots. Sixteen aircraft participated in this pinpoint bombing in the early morning and 12 more in the late afternoon. In the words of the Marine aviators: "We were using up a goodly supply of belly tanks, but everyone was being satisfied and Japs exterminated without commensurate losses to ourselves."[4]

During the morning of 21 October, 1/321 attacked southward upon completion of their air strike. Japanese automatic weapons from caves on the western slope of Brother No. 3 forced the soldiers to halt their advance after a gain of less than a hundred yards. A patrol from 2/321 attempted to capture Brother No. 1, but the attack faltered because of heavy enemy fire from the eastern slope of the hill. During the afternoon a combat patrol succeeded in seizing the northern part of Brother No. 1 and immediately sandbagged the position in anticipation of an enemy counterattack.

Meanwhile, men of 3/321, supported by tanks and flamethrowers, entered Horseshoe Valley from the south under

---

[3] *VMF-114 WarD*, Oct44.

[4] *Ibid.*

cover of a smoke screen laid down on the area between Walt Ridge and Brother No. 5. This force attacked Japanese lurking in caves along the base of the Five Brothers and Walt Ridge. Upon completion of their mission, the soldiers withdrew from the valley.

On 22 October, 2/321 seized Brothers No. 1, 2, and 3. The 3d Battalion launched another sortie in Horseshoe Valley supported by 2 tank platoons, 3 tank destroyers, and 2 LVTs equipped with flamethrowers. The combined infantry-armored force swept into the valley through the gap between Walt and Boyd Ridges and blasted caves along the bases of the remainder of the Five Brothers and the northeastern slopes of the Five Sisters. At least 34 Japanese were killed in this action, and others were sealed in caves. At the end of the day, the soldiers established a line of defense along the western base of Walt Ridge and during the night held this position against determined Japanese counterattacks in which an estimated 20 of the enemy were killed.

For the next two days, there was little change in the lines, though on 23 October 2/321 seized Brother No. 4 and fortified it with sandbag emplacements In an effort to confine the Japanese further, a company of 3/321 blocked the south exit from Horseshoe Valley, while another company occupied positions around Grinlinton Pond to deny the Japanese access to fresh water. The toughest resistance encountered during 23 October was in the zone of attack of 1/321, whose advance towards the very heart of the pocket ran into such heavy defenses that gains had to be measured in feet. The difficulties facing the battalion at this juncture were a combination of extremely unfavorable terrain and determined resistance. The division historian described the situation graphically:

> The limited avenues of approach to the Japanese positions and their strength made it necessary to construct sandbag fortifications along the route of advance as fast as the advance was made. In effect, the sandbags had to be used instead of armor in ground too rough and steep for tanks. Without sandbags the troops, on the sides and tops of ridges and peaks, were completely exposed to accurate enemy rifle fire. At times, it was necessary to push sandbags forward with poles so that a first layer could be placed which would protect the men who crawled forward to finish the work. Advance in this manner was slow and tedious but accomplished with a minimum of casualties.[5]

On 25 October, RCT 323, which had arrived from Ulithi, relieved the 1st and 2d Battalions, RCT 321. Control of operations against the Umurbrogol pocket passed from Colonel Dark to Colonel Arthur P. Watson, commander of RCT 323. The 1st Battalion, RCT 323, occupied positions at the western and southwestern perimeter of the pocket. The 2d Battalion took over the lines south of the Five Sisters. A company of 1/323 took up station on the Five Brothers, while the remaining two companies moved into sandbagged positions along the northwest perimeter of the pocket. The men of 3/321 remained in sandbagged emplacements along the base of Walt Ridge and Horseshoe Valley. Effective 25 October, 3/321 was attached for operations to RCT 323.

---
[5] Historical Committee, *81st Infantry Division*, pp. 175–177.

For the continuation of the attack against the Umurbrogol, two field artillery battalions and an engineer battalion would provide the necessary support.

During the remainder of 25 October the men of RCT 323 familiarized themselves with the terrain over which they were to operate. They also hauled supplies and strengthened defensive positions along the perimeter of the pocket. Two prisoners taken after nightfall revealed that 500-600 Japanese still remained in the pocket. Of this number, approximately half were sick or wounded and without medical care; the remainder were under orders to fight to the death.

In the course of 26 October, RCT 323 patrolled along the entire perimeter and blew caves in rear areas to prevent their reoccupation by the enemy. Shortly after noon a company engaged in searching out Japanese-occupied caves along the southern perimeter of the pocket suffered 4 killed and 29 wounded when a Japanese aerial bomb used as a land mine went off. A closer inspection of the area revealed that it was littered with aerial bombs, some of them cleverly booby-trapped by the Japanese. The night of 26-27 October was marked by numerous enemy probing attacks at various points within the perimeter. In a furious engagement at Brother No. 4, which the Japanese seemed determined to recapture, a hand grenade duel ended in the death of 30 Japanese. A party of seven Japanese hauling water from Grinlinton Pond was wiped out when soldiers from RCT 321 suddenly illuminated the area with improvised floodlights and opened fire with machine guns. The quantity of pyrotechnics expended at that time in an effort to foil Japanese attempts at infiltration led at least one observer to make this comment:

> Both day and night there was constant firing. At night the area was kept under constant illumination. I counted as many as three 60mm illuminating shells in the air at a time.[6]

During the period from 26 October to 1 November, operations on Peleliu stagnated because of heavy rain, fog, and poor visibility. The men of the 81st Infantry Division utilized this time to improve their positions further. According to Colonel Nakagawa, "our units were encouraged by the rain which fell all through the day of the 28th."[7] On the following day, the Japanese commander reported the strength of his garrison unit on Peleliu as approximately 590 men.[8] Throughout the period of inclement weather, there was little ground action in the daytime, though the Japanese became aggressive after nightfall. For several nights in succession the Japanese main effort was directed against the Americans on Brother No. 4, but the infantrymen repulsed every attack and held their positions.

Some unusual activity around and over Peleliu developed at the end of the month. During the night of 28-29 October, a Japanese landing craft carrying torpedo tubes was sunk just off Purple Beach, after it had fired a torpedo at the beach without doing any damage. It could not be clearly established what the mission of this craft

---

[6] Smith, *Narrative*, p. 117.
[7] *Japanese CenPacOps*, p. 162.
[8] *Ibid.*

had been. There were reports of additional enemy landing craft in the vicinity, though this information remained unconfirmed.[9]

Other evidence of unusual enemy activity from outside of the pocket persisted for the remainder of October. American surface craft sighted a midget submarine near Peleliu and speculation arose that the submarine, in conjunction with the landing barge sunk during the preceding night, might be attempting to evacuate personnel from the Umurbrogol pocket. Shortly after dark on 29 October and again on 31 October, Japanese float planes dropped parachutes to which were attached baskets and cylinders containing hand grenades and signal equipment. Most of the parachutes fell outside of the perimeter and were recovered by the Americans. When questioned about this incident after the end of World War II, Lieutenant General Sadae Inoue, IJA, commanding Japanese forces in the Palaus, volunteered the following information:

> General Murai had requested that radio batteries be sent because his were almost run down, and complete breakdowns were frequent. We knew his position was somewhere on the ridge running along the west coast of Peleliu but we didn't know the exact location.[10]

At night the interception of enemy aircraft over Peleliu was made difficult because of poor ground radar coverage. Nevertheless, on 31 October Major Norman L. Mitchell, a member of VMF(N)-541 intercepted and destroyed a Japanese floatplane over Peleliu Island. This was the only Japanese aircraft destroyed in the air by Marine aviation squadrons in the Palaus.[11]

Surprise encounters with isolated Japanese outside the Umurbrogol were not rare. In one instance, during the night 28–29 October, two enlisted men of VMF-114 thought that there was a "slant eyed gopher" outside their pup tent. In fact, the flaps were ripped open and buttons torn off. When the Marines reached for their weapons, the visitor became alarmed and fled. Another roving Japanese—or perhaps the same one—was spotted the following night near the airfield and killed when he failed to answer a challenge. A Japanese medical officer decided that continued resistance held little future for him and turned himself in to the Americans. This Japanese was "effusive, wanting to talk and to help—anxious to survive, he said, for the sake of science and research, to which he had always devoted himself. He spoke English fluently, although he had never been in the States."[12]

Because the Japanese were so unpredictable in their actions, General Mueller decided to take no chances. Beach defenses on Peleliu were manned at all times and certain units, including RCT 323 in the central combat zone, were required to furnish mobile reserve forces on call from division headquarters. Field and coast artillery units were prepared to fire antiboat missions

---

[9] VMF-114 WarD, Oct44.

[10] MajGen Paul J. Mueller, USA, ltr to DirMCHist, dtd 9Aug50, in *Peleliu Comment File*, Encl, 2dLt James J. Wickel, USA, interrogation of LtGen Sadae Inoue, IJA, dtd 23May47, hereafter *Inoue Interrogation*.

[11] *VMF(N)—541 Hist*, p. 7.

[12] *VMF-114 WarD*, Oct44.

and to assist in the beach defense in the event of an enemy landing. Amphibious patrols carried out repeated reconnaissance of the outlying islands. A number of observation posts, surface search radar stations, and searchlights were established on Peleliu and the outlying islands from which all approaches to Peleliu could be kept under constant observation. General Mueller established within the 81st Infantry Division a Ground Defense Headquarters with a mission of coordinating the activities of all organic and attached units in safeguarding Peleliu. The Ground Defense Headquarters received reports from all units charged with the operation of observation posts and radar stations and disseminated intelligence about the enemy and information about friendly ground, air, and naval forces.

When weather conditions improved on 1 November, General Mueller ordered the offensive against the Umurbrogol pocket to be resumed. Before an attack could be launched against the very heart of Japanese resistance, the area encompassing Wildcat Bowl and the China Wall, Hill 300, and the Five Sisters had to be secured.[13] The mission of seizing both objectives was assigned to 2/323. The attack was to begin on 2 November and would be preceded by an air strike and a 25-minute mortar preparation.

The 2d Battalion attacked at 0630. Resistance was surprisingly light and consisted only of sporadic sniper fire. Within two hours after jump-off, the soldiers had seized the top of Hill 300 and all of the Five Sisters. For the remainder of the day and part of the following night, the men consolidated the newly captured positions and erected sandbag fortifications. Japanese reaction remained feeble until shortly after midnight, when the enemy made an attempt to recapture the Five Sisters. The counterattack was repulsed, and 38 Japanese were killed in the action.[14]

Colonel Nakagawa, forced to concede that the situation for the Japanese on Peleliu was becoming more difficult, observed:

> Fifty days have elapsed since the enemy landed on Peleliu.... Part of this enemy unit which entered Mt. Kansoku and the southern extremity of Mt. Oyama were observed strengthening their positions

---

Horseshoe Valley appears as Mortimer Valley in Army records. For the sake of continuity, Marine designations are used in this narrative. Army designations are given only to identify those terrain features not previously named by the Marines. For the sake of simplicity, Japanese designations for terrain features in the Umurbrogol Pocket have been omitted from the narrative whenever possible, though they occasionally appear in quotations from Japanese records. The most frequently named hills were as follows:

Oyama	—northern portion of China Wall harboring Japanese command post on Peleliu
Nakayama	—central and southern portion of China Wall
Tenzan	—Five Sisters
Higashiyama	—Walt Ridge
Suifuyama or *Suifuzan*	—Boyd Ridge and northern perimeter of pocket
Kansokuyama	—Hill 300

[14] *81st InfDiv OpRpt*, p. 75.

---

[13] Army units on Peleliu frequently renamed ridges and valleys on Peleliu from earlier designations by the Marines. Army records refer to Hill 300 as Old Baldy, though the Marines had previously designed a ridge north of the Umurbrogol Pocket as Baldy Ridge.

TO THE BITTER END 261

with sandbags and wire entanglements. Our defense unit attacked this enemy unit every night but to no avail.[15]

At approximately noon, 3 November, 2/323 dispatched an infantry-tank patrol into Death Valley. This time the Japanese were prepared for the Americans, and the infantry was caught in the crossfire of enemy snipers hiding in the caves and holes along both sides of the valley wall. The advance halted, and the patrol returned to its starting point.

Lack of progress on the part of the Americans during 3 November did little to relieve the shortage that the Japanese inside the pocket were beginning to feel. Despite the rains of late October, there was an acute shortage of water, aggravated by the alertness of the Americans in preventing Japanese water-carriers from gaining access to Grinlinton Pond. For the first time since the beginning of the campaign, a shortage of ammunition was beginning to make itself felt, causing Colonel Nakagawa to cut the normal allowance of small arms ammunition by half. Even so, the Japanese commander glumly observed, "It was tentative as to whether it would last until 20 November."[16] The attrition in the Japanese ranks also had reached a critical point. Japanese personnel in the pocket still fit for combat numbered approximately 350. This figure included men that had suffered minor wounds. In addition to these, there were 130 heavy casualties incapable of taking part in combat.[17]

During the period 4–9 November, operations on Peleliu once again came to a virtual standstill. Heavy rains inundated the island, beginning on 4 November. Two days later a typhoon struck Peleliu and continued unabated until the morning of 8 November. During this time of enforced idleness, General Mueller ordered pack howitzers emplaced in the vicinity of the Five Sisters to support subsequent operations in Wildcat Bowl and along the eastern slopes of China Wall. Aside from isolated and feeble attempts to infiltrate the American lines, enemy activity within the pocket dropped sharply during this period. During the height of the storm a number of Japanese managed to slip out of the Umurbrogol Pocket and headed north, intent on escaping from the island. Members of RCT 321, stationed on the northern tip of Peleliu, spotted and killed a number of these infiltrators.

The ever-present danger of Japanese counterlandings on and around Peleliu was underscored once again on 9 November when a Japanese force estimated at 100 men stealthily crept ashore on Ngeregong, a small island about 9 miles northeast of the northern tip of Peleliu. A skirmish with a small Army force that was garrisoning the island ensued, following which the American soldiers withdrew under cover of 20mm and 40mm fire. For the remainder of the day, and throughout the following night, American patrol craft and destroyers shelled the island. In addition, a flight of 47 Navy aircraft bombed Ngeregong after dark. Most of the Japanese force had withdrawn to an adjacent island by this time, though one of the attacking aircraft was downed by enemy machine gun fire.

---

[15] *Japanese CenPacOps*, p. 181.
[16] *Ibid.*, pp. 181–182.
[17] *Ibid.*

During 10 November, 51 Navy aircraft dropped a total of 3,900 pounds of bombs on Ngeregong. As added insurance against similar Japanese incursions, General Mueller ordered his troops to seize Gorokottan Island, located halfway between northern Peleliu and Ngeregong. Gorokottan Island was seized on 11 November. No Japanese were found on the island. After extensive preparations, elements of the 81st Infantry Division recaptured Ngeregong Island on 15 November. The landing came as an anticlimax. There was no opposition, and the only evidence of recent Japanese occupation of the island consisted of three dead Japanese in an advanced state of decomposition and some enemy ordnance equipment.

The final drive into the Umurbrogol Pocket resumed on 13 November, when 1/323 and 2/323 launched simultaneous attacks into Death Valley. The 1st Battalion, attacking out of the ridges to the west of the valley, made few gains. The advance of 2/323 was somewhat more successful, and the soldiers gained about 75 yards while moving northward along the eastern ridge of the China Wall. Though the enemy was still offering bitter resistance, his time in the Umurbrogol was running out. Colonel Nakagawa gloomily informed his superior on Babelthuap that ammunition, food, water, and radio batteries were running low. In describing the action on 13 November, the Japanese commander reported:

> The enemy began attacking our defense line at Mt. Oyama. A part of the enemy force attacking from the west and south, the main force from the east. Our Defense Unit put up a stubborn resistance but the enemy force successfully penetrated the defense line. This enemy force attacked the men of our Defense Unit hidden in shelters with flamethrowers and guns.[18]

The Americans advanced slowly and steadily between 14 and 21 November, compressing the Umurbrogol Pocket. As a means of reducing the last Japanese defenses on Peleliu, ingenious soldiers set up fuel tanks in covered positions about 300 yards from the Japanese caves, then hooked up a hose to the tanks and poured oil into the most prominent enemy caves. This oil was ignited by white phosphorus hand grenades lobbed into the caves after the spraying. This method yielded good results and henceforth became an effective improvisation. As the drive through the Wildcat Bowl and Death Valley continued, flamethrowers, demolition teams, and armored bulldozers followed by tanks and LVTs, eliminated as many enemy caves as could be reached. Colonel Nakagawa, watching the Americans gradually approach his command post, reached some valid conclusions, observing:

> ... It is our guess that the enemy in the northern part of Mt. Oyama are planning to capture our Defense Unit Headquarters.... The enemy on the east side of Oyama Mountain penetrated our defense line and advanced towards the Defense Unit Headquarters, at the same time attacking our men, who were hidden in shelters, with flamethrowers. In this attack the casualties of our Defense Unit were heavy.... The men of our Defense Unit still capable of fighting number approximately 150. This includes light casualties.[19]

---

[18] *Japanese CenPacOps*, p. 197.
[19] *Ibid.*, pp. 197-198.

TO THE BITTER END						263

Up to this point, Major General Kenjiro Murai, advisor to Colonel Nakagawa, had remained completely in the background, though on occasion he acted as liaison between Colonel Nakagawa and General Inoue. In fact, General Murai remained so inconspicuous throughout the fighting that many Japanese were unaware of his presence on Peleliu. Once before, in early November, General Murai had attempted to obtain General Inoue's permission to launch an all-out attack against the Peleliu airfield. At the time, General Inoue had issued the following order:

> It is easy to die but difficult to live on. We must select the difficult course, and continue to fight because of the influence on the morale of the Japanese people. Saipan was lost in a very short time because of vain Banzai attacks, with the result that the people at home suffered a drop in morale.[20]

Now that the end for the Japanese on Peleliu was approaching, General Murai informed General Inoue that he was going to make a final, all-out attack against the Americans. Once again General Inoue dissuaded Murai from this course of action, pointing out that such an attack would only waste his men. Instead, General Murai was to hole up, play it safe, wait for the Americans to approach more closely, and then kill off as many as possible.[21]

Attrition of the Japanese remaining in the pocket increased at a rapid rate.

---

[20] MajGen Paul J. Mueller, USA, ltr to Dir, MarCorpsHist dtd 9Aug50, Encl, 2dLt James J. Wickel, USA, interrogation of Col Tokechi Tada, IJA, dtd 24May47, hereafter *Tada Interrogation.*

[21] Inoue interview, dtd Mar50, in *Worden ltr.*

During the night of 17–18 November the enemy made widespread attempts to escape from the pocket, and 33 were killed. By 20 November, Japanese resistance stiffened, and American combat patrols drew heavy fire from enemy snipers and machine guns in caves that had not been destroyed in previous attacks. Throughout the night and during the early part of the next day, the Wildcats attacked these caves. As a result, by noon of 21 November, patrols were able to operate without opposition throughout Wildcat Bowl and in the southern portion of Death Valley. On 22 November a company of infantry succeeded in scaling the north end of the China Wall; another company approached the Japanese command post from the west-northwest and gained 75 yards; a third company advanced 25–50 yards at the southern end of the China Wall. By the end of 22 November, the Japanese pocket had been reduced to an area approximately 285 yards in length from north to south and 125 yards wide. To enable tanks and LVT flamethrowers to bring their fire to bear on the last Japanese defenses in the center of the China Wall, engineers began the construction of a ramp up the east wall at the northern terminus of the Wildcat Bowl.

The battle for the last Japanese redoubt on Peleliu began in earnest on 22 November. Colonel Nakagawa reported that an enemy force was attacking the main point of the Japanese line with flamethrowers, and that his men were on the verge of collapse. The Japanese held on during 23 November, but by the next day the end had become imminent. As the Americans closed in on his command post, Colonel Nakagawa made his last report to Babelthuap, saying:

> Our Defense Units were on the verge of being completely annihilated. Therefore the unit destroyed the 2d Infantry regimental colors which they had in their possession. . . . All documents were burned. . . . Since 1800 the personnel left in this Defense Unit were Captain Nemoto and 56 men. This number split into 17 teams and decided to put on a last raid. . . . Splitting of men into 17 teams was completed at 1700 hours of the 24th. Following the Commander's wishes, we will attack the enemy everywhere. This will be the last message we will be able to send or receive.[22]

During the night 24-25 November both General Murai and Colonel Nakagawa committed suicide. The attempts of the remaining Japanese to break out of the tight ring of encirclement were doomed to failure, and the Wildcats killed 45 Japanese, including two officers. Additional Japanese were killed during the following days, though the men of RCT 323 noticed as early as the afternoon of 24 November that resistance had vanished almost completely. On 26 November, tanks and LVT flamethrowers moved up the newly finished ramp and began to fire on caves and other defenses along the center of the China Wall. On the morning of 27 November, eight rifle companies gingerly converged on the center of the China Wall. There was no resistance and only silence greeted the advancing soldiers. At 1100, Colonel Watson, commander of RCT 323, reported to General Mueller that organized resistance on Peleliu had come to an end. The enemy had fulfilled his determination to fight unto death.

Even the end of organized resistance on Peleliu did not mean that peace had finally returned to the island. During the weeks and months that followed, individual Japanese that had previously escaped annihilation were either captured or killed. There were bizarre overtones to an unusual operation. Both General Murai and Colonel Nakagawa were posthumously promoted to the rank of lieutenant general effective 31 December 1944.[23] On 13 January 1945, Major General Mueller turned over responsibility for ground defense of Peleliu to the Island Command. Five days later Japanese landing craft discharged troops at Purple and White Beaches. Mission of the Japanese landing force was to destroy aircraft, ammunition dumps, and the American headquarters on Peleliu. Even though the attackers succeeded in making their way inland, the attempt failed.[24] In a series of skirmishes reminiscent of the heavy fighting of the past months, the enemy had to be routed once again from caves by infantrymen of the Peleliu Ground Defense Force, supported by flamethrowers.

The Ground Defense Force, composed of elements of the 81st Infantry Di-

---

[22] *Japanese CenPacOps*, p. 200.

[23] Ltr, Japanese Demobilization Bureau, Repatriation Relief Agency to Headquarters, Supreme Commander of the Allied Powers, dtd 14Apr50.

[24] "This force failed to reach our planes, but was armed with spears and plenty of fire producing grenades." BGen M. B. Bell, USA, ltr to Head, HistBr, G-3 Div, HQMC, dtd 24Jun66, in *Peleliu Comment File*.

vision and the 12th Antiaircraft Artillery Battalion, was under the command of Marine Brigadier General Harold D. Campbell, the Island Commander. The action ended in the death of 71 and the capture of 2 Japanese.[25] Barely eight months later, Lieutenant General Inoue, Commanding the Japanese Forces in the Palaus, surrendered unconditionally to General Campbell's successor, Marine Brigadier General Ford O. Rogers. At the time of the Japanese surrender in the northern Palaus, 39,997 persons came under American control. This number consisted of 18,473 Japanese soldiers, 6,404 Navy personnel, 9,750 civilians, and 5,350 natives.[26] Following the Japanese surrender, personnel of the Peleliu Island Command assumed responsibility for the evacuation and repatriation of Japanese military and civilian personnel from the Palau Islands, though as late as February 1946 a thorough search of Babelthuap Island had to be carried out in order to apprehend and return all Japanese recalcitrants and stragglers attempting to avoid repatriation.[27]

It was thought that peace had finally returned to Peleliu on 21 April 1947, when a Japanese lieutenant and 26 men formally gave up in one of the last surrender ceremonies of World War II.[28] Around 1949 or 1950 a group of Peleliu natives went to hunt wild pigeons and wild chicken with .22 rifles and U.S. carbines on one of the islands three miles north of Peleliu. What they flushed out, in addition to birds, has been described by the principal of the Peleliu Elementary School:

> During this hunting there was a Japanese Army man who was at the time hiding in a cave of Ngercheu Island, who became frightened by the explosions of rifles and carbines. He then ran out from the cave to the seashore where an old Peleliu man by the name of Sisior was fishing nearby in his canoe. The Japanese ran up to him and asked him to save him from the enemy who were firing their guns in the forests and mountains. After the Japanese man came out his clothings were made out of rice sacks of Manila fiber. His beards have grown and hanged down to his hips. This man was captured and turned over to the District Administration to be sent to Japan.[29]

Five years later, a cave-dwelling Korean was seized on Peleliu by natives who had occasionally found food missing from their gardens. The Korean, a former civilian employee of the Japanese Navy, was likewise turned over to the authorities.[30] At the time of this writing, one can only guess that these were the last survivors of the Japanese garrison on Peleliu. Twenty years after the end of World War II, the debris of battle still litters the island, and a few Japanese may still be hiding in the Umurbrogol ridges, awaiting the command of the Emperor to fight their way to total extinction.

---

[25] Peleliu Island Command WarD, Feb45.
[26] *Ibid.*, Sep45.
[27] *Ibid.*, Feb46.
[28] McMillan, *The Old Breed*, pp. 340–341.

[29] Kulas Sengebau ltr to Head, HistBr, G-3 Div, HQMC, dtd 28Sep65, in *Peleliu Comment File*.
[30] *Ibid.*

CAMPAIGN LESSONS LEARNED[31]

A number of factors combined to set the Peleliu operation apart from the others that had preceded it and those that were to follow. First, there was a poorly developed staging area on Pavuvu with all the inherent disadvantages of muddy roads and inadequate water supply and camp facilities. Nevertheless, the 1st Marine Division did not recommend staging to another area from Pavuvu because the time required would have cut deeply into the training period. Another factor of great concern to General Rupertus was the shortage of materiel, which persisted during the division's stay on Pavuvu. Critical equipment, such as armored amphibians, amphibian tractors, flamethrowers, demolitions, BARs, bazookas, engineering equipment, tank and tractor spare parts, signal equipment, and waterproofing equipment did not reach the division until the last stages of the training schedule, and, in some instances, upon completion of loading.

At the time it embarked for the Peleliu Operation, the 1st Marine Division consisted of 843 Marine officers and 15,616 enlisted Marines, not including the rear echelon of 103 officers and 1,668 enlisted, which remained on Pavuvu. The division departed from the staging area with a five percent personnel overage, the first time that this Marine division embarked overstrength for an operation.[32] Prior to embarkation, changes were made in the assignment of medical personnel by increasing the number of hospital corpsmen organic to the infantry battalions from 32 to 40, which made it possible to attach two corpsmen to each platoon. Each infantry battalion assigned 32 men as stretcher bearers. These Marines were trained in casualty evacuation and first aid procedures. Normally, division bandsmen acted as stretcher bearers in combat. On Peleliu and later on Okinawa, however, the 1st Division band was trained to man part of the division CP defense perimeter and to serve as stretcher bearers. These assignments were expected to raise the efficiency of the combat troops and improve the morale of the fighting forces.[33]

Even during the planning phase of Operation STALEMATE, it was apparent that the 1st Marine Division was embarking on a campaign that differed from previous operations in the jungles of Guadalcanal and New Britain. The division initially would have to cross a 600–700 yard reef all along the prospective beachhead, a process that the 2d Marine Division had found costly in earlier Central Pacific operations. The division on Peleliu could expect to operate in terrain that was completely at variance with anything previously encountered, for Peleliu contained some of the most rugged and easily defended ground yet seen by American forces in the Pacific. Beyond the rugged terrain, the 1st Marine Division faced a determined enemy, who exploited almost

---

[31] Unless otherwise noted, the material in this section is derived from: *IIIAC OpRpt; 1st MarDiv SAR;* VMF–114 WarD, Sep44; Smith, *Narrative;* Isely and Crowl, *U. S. Marines and Amphibious War;* Sherrod, *Marine Corps Aviation in World War II.*

[32] *1st MarDiv SAR*, Phase I, Anx A, p. 2.
[33] *Ibid.,* Anx D, p. 2.

impregnable defenses to the utmost. In contrast to earlier campaigns, the Japanese on Peleliu conserved manpower and materiel. The traditional, reckless *banzai* charge, the final symbol of defiance in the face of certain death in earlier operations, had gone out of style. The enemy, well trained and dug in, no longer expended men and equipment in such heroic but useless gestures.[34]

The Japanese had prepared themselves thoroughly to repel a landing on the beaches. Careful planning of the static beach defenses was evident not only from their effectiveness but also from detailed sketches, which fell into American hands as the campaign progressed. Colonel Nakagawa made and rehearsed several plans for counterattacking assumed landings. He also reorganized several Japanese companies into special counterattack units. The Japanese commander further improvised a company trained to swim out to the landing craft and sink them with mines or destroy their occupants with hand grenades. One platoon of infantry had been trained to ride tanks into battle. Several teams of two or three men were taught to infiltrate and attempt to blow up American tanks or amphibian tractors. Among new Japanese weapons, a 150mm mortar was found on Peleliu. The Japanese had stored four of these mortars behind a hastily constructed position. In appearance, the weapon was an oversized 81mm mortar, similar to the American version. Fifty rounds of amunition were found.

There was no evidence that the Japanese ever made use of the new 150mm mortars on Peleliu. On the other hand, a new development in Japanese weaponry was observed with the capture of a 200mm rocket, which was eight inches in diameter and 43 inches in length. At least four of these new rockets were fired from an unknown position. Three of them exploded with minor effect. The fourth was a dud because the enemy failed to replace the shipping plug with the fuze. The rocket closely resembled an obsolete German type. It was fired electrically, probably from a simple launching platform or cage. The head consisted of 8 by 25-inch thin-walled explosive container filled with picric acid and flaked TNT, and an 18-inch propellant case closed by a tube plate. The propellant charge probably was black powder. There was no evidence of fins or of a gyro-stabilizing device. The rocket was easily observed as it wobbled in flight like a poor football pass. Its velocity was slow and its range was estimated to be less than 1,500 yards.[35]

The Japanese on Peleliu were adequately clothed, and scattered clothing dumps were found in the southern and extreme northern part of the island. Food, particularly canned fish, canned meat, and rice was abundant. Ammunition was plentiful for all weapons except the 200mm short-barreled naval gun and the 150mm mortar. Enemy supply dumps were small and well-dispersed. As on Saipan, the dispersal of supply dumps became a major disadvantage for the Japanese, for once they had been pushed back into small pockets, they

---

[34] *Ibid.*, Anx A, p. 1.

[35] *Ibid.*, Anx B, p. 24.

were effectively cut off from most of these dumps.

The enemy defensive plan for Peleliu was one of defense in depth in all sectors. All pillboxes and casemates were in logical commanding positions, and all were linked in a system of mutual support. When driven from his coastal positions along White and Orange Beaches, the enemy was able to fall back to prepared positions on the high ground to the north. Coastal installations on some of the beaches were protected by pillboxes and casemates, whose firing ports were sited for fire on the Americans attempting to wheel northward from the landing beaches. Even after the Marines had overrun the Japanese secondary lines and seized commanding ground, the enemy was able to withdraw to positions, both natural and prepared, that enabled him to continue organized resistance.

On the high ground separating White and Orange beaches, two casemates and a large number of pillboxes had been established in such a way that they provided a field of fire covering both beaches. Most of the Japanese defensive installations were in defilade from the sea, particularly the two casemates, which were 30 yards apart and sited to fire south on Orange Beach and north on White Beach. Inland from Purple Beach, the Japanese had dug into the coral and echeloned three casemates containing respectively one 75mm mountain gun, one 37mm gun, and one 25mm ground-mount automatic antiaircraft cannon depressed for horizontal fire. There were at least one casemate and six well-constructed pillboxes on the southern peninsula of Purple Beach. The casemate was equipped with a 37mm gun to cover the entrance to the southern mangrove swamp.

To further impede progress of the American landing force, the Japanese had buried numerous aircraft bombs on all paths leading inland from Purple Beach, as well as elsewhere on the island. The island also abounded in antitank ditches and obstacles. In the vicinity of the airfield, the Japanese used some scarecrows. They were made of fronds from coconut palms, with a coconut stuck on the top. The dummies were so constructed that the coconut was just visible over the parapet of the trench.

In view of their defensive preparations and high state of morale, it is not surprising that the Japanese felt that they had an excellent chance to beat off any American attack. For the Marines, Peleliu offered an opportunity to prove again the soundness of the amphibious doctrine developed over a period of many years. The very fact that an amphibious force was able to establish a beachhead in full view of the enemy on a heavily defended island in an operation lacking the element of surprise speaks for itself.

Preparations for the operation were thorough and extensive as every supporting arm and staff section applied the lessons previously learned at Guadalcanal and Cape Gloucester. Prior to D-Day, no amphibious scout patrols or reconnaissance landing parties went ashore on Peleliu. In their place, underwater demolition teams, attached to the naval task force, reconnoitered the reef and offshore waters near the landing beaches and destroyed obstacles and mines. Data pertaining to the reefs, water depths, tides, currents, and surf, location and nature of mines, obstacles, and barriers was promptly forwarded via radio dispatch to all ship and troop commanders in the 1st Marine Division convoy.

Few American offensive actions in the Pacific Theater were as dependent on the use of amphibian vehicles in assault and supply as was the operation at Peleliu. The crossing of the wide barrier reef surrounding the island was accomplished entirely by these vehicles. LVTs were practically the only means of getting American troops, equipment, and ammunition ashore during the initial landing. They continued to be the primary means of supply even after portions of the island had been secured. They were of great value in evacuating the wounded and performed excellent service in carrying water and ammunition to the front lines from beach supply dumps. DUKWs provided the primary transport for artillery, in addition to carrying 37mm guns, radio jeeps, and other equipment required for the assault. Even though 26 LVTs were knocked out by enemy fire on D-Day, the value of this amphibian to the landing force was inestimable. LVT(A)s saw extensive night patrol work in the waters to the north of Peleliu and were prepared to engage any barges or similar surface craft that might attempt to reinforce the enemy or evacuate him from the island.

Two types of LVTs, the LVT(2) and the LVT(4), were used at Peleliu. Of the two vehicles, the latter proved to be much more versatile and useful. No mechanical failures of the ramp were experienced; the position of the engine in the LVT(4) facilitated its maintenance, and the vehicle afforded more protection for the assault troops who disembarked from the rear. The only disadvantage observed in the LVT(4) was an inadequate cooling system which caused the engine to overheat.[35] From observations made during the Peleliu landings it became apparent that DUKWs should not be employed as assault vehicles unless they were provided with some armament. The DUKWs proved more vulnerable to enemy fire than the amphibian tractors and required ideal terrain to operate at peak efficiency. They were unsatisfactory as prime movers for amphibian trailers, but could be used to advantage in carrying small rolling stock, artillery, and in ship to shore movement where the reef was not too rugged or the enemy fire too heavy.

The landing of artillery on Peleliu was delayed by heavy enemy artillery and mortar fire on the beaches, which seriously depleted the number of LVTs available. As a result of the holdup, the firing batteries came ashore in a piecemeal fashion, though all 75mm batteries were in position by H plus 7. Reconnaissance for the 105mm howitzer battalions proved difficult because their prearranged position areas were still in enemy hands. On D-Day, the 3d Battalion, 11th Marines, was able to land only one battery, which fired southward in direct support of the 7th Marines. The remaining two batteries came ashore, but remained in DUKWs. Both batteries were dispatched to sea to re-

---

[35] *Ibid.*, Anx F, p. 1.

embark on LSTs for the night. During these two trips across the reefs, three DUKWs sank during the night, along with the 105mm howitzers and other material aboard. For the remainder of the Peleliu operation, 1st Marine Division artillery performed very satisfactorily, subject to a temporary shortage of ammunition and limitations imposed by the terrain. During the later stages of the campaign, high angle fire was out of the question because of the restricted area in which the Japanese were trapped.

During this period, batteries and single guns of all calibers were employed so that they could fire in several directions. These weapons were used for sniping at individuals and small groups of Japanese, as well as for closing caves, obstructing paths and roads, and interdicting the waterholes. It became evident during the very first day of the Peleliu operation that a need existed for a short-range, high-angle weapon that could be employed as artillery. Subsequently, wherever action was limited to a small pocket, this need became critical. The 60mm and 81mm infantry mortars proved inadequate. Furthermore, the latter was too unreliable to furnish the volume of controlled fire required under the circumstances. On the other hand, illuminating shells, fired from 60mm mortars, were called for by all units in unexpectedly great quantities. A new type of ammunition, it furnished needed illumination and appeared to provide a feeling of confidence and security to the troops of the using units.[36]

During the final reduction of the Umurbrogol Pocket, Army 4.2-inch mortars were used with great success; a 60mm shoulder mortar employed for the first time by the 1st Marine Division on Peleliu was not so well received. Despite its effectiveness in reducing caves and pillboxes, the latter weapon proved too heavy, and certain of its components exhibited structural weaknesses. The recoil of the mortar was so great that it became necessary to replace the gunner after two to four rounds had been fired.[37]

Difficulties were encountered with the offensive hand grenade, whose very name was considered a misnomer because of its relative ineffectiveness. The grenade was constructed to detonate on impact, but since it had no fragmentation effect, it was ineffective against materiel and useful against personnel only to a very limited extent. It was dangerous to handle, and two men of 1/1 had their hands blown off in the act of throwing a grenade of this type. Since fuzes for the grenade were supplied separately, it proved difficult to keep grenades and fuzes together in equal numbers.[38]

In contrast to the dubious performance of the shoulder mortar, another new weapon, the Navy Mk 1 flamethrower, proved vastly superior to anything of this type the 1st Marine Division had used on previous occasions. The weapon, modelled after the Canadian Ronson flamethrower, had been modified at the Navy Yard, Pearl Harbor, to

---

[36] *IIIAC OpRpt*, Encl H, p. 5.

[37] *1st MarDiv SAR*, Phase II, Anx A, p. 4.
[38] *IIIAC OpRpt*, Encl H, p. 6.

eliminate mechanical and technical difficulties. Prior to the Peleliu operation, the 1st Marine Division received three of these flamethrowers, together with four LVT(4)s for mounting the weapons. A fourth LVT(4) was used as a supply carrier for the flamethrowers. The new weapons were assigned to the 1st Amphibian Tractor Battalion. Initial tests indicated that the range of the flamethrower was 75 yards with gasoline and oil mixture, 150 yards with napalm. Duration of fire was 55 seconds for gasoline and oil mixture, and 80 seconds for napalm.[39] Because of the shortage and late arrival of pack-type or portable flamethrowers, no distribution of them was prescribed for the regiments. One method was to retain 19 portable flamethrowers and three bazookas under battalion control. To these were added a heavy demolitions unit. This group, called in some cases Battalion Weapons Platoon, was composed of 60 men drawn from the rifle companies. This left the companies 10 or 15 men understrength, but the rifle platoons were generally unimpaired in strength.

Flamethrowers were used tactically in pairs, operated by 5-man flamethrower groups. Two men were assigned to each flamethrower and the fifth man was group leader. Each group had a machine gun cart on which it mounted and transported two flamethrowers and refilling equipment consisting of two cylinders and two expeditionary water cans. Flamethrowers were waterproofed and rigged so that they could be dragged through surf and put into action in a few seconds. Assault companies each

---

[39] *1st MarDiv SAR*, Phase II, Anx A, p. 6.

had a flamethrower group to start with and received additional flamethrowers from the battalion. During the operational phase on Peleliu, flamethrowers, both portable and vehicle-mounted, played an extremely important part in eliminating troublesome caves, pillboxes, and other enemy obstacles.

Combat engineer units landed with the assault waves and proceeded under the control of combat team commanders. All organizational equipment was landed during the assault phase, though some difficulty was experienced in landing priority items, such as water purification and distillation units. Combat engineer companies performed demolition tasks as well as other normal functions. On occasion, regimental commanders used engineers as infantry.

Prior to the Peleliu landings, intelligence reports had indicated that water supply would be the greatest engineer problem and that there was no source of fresh water. On the basis of this information, additional distillation units were carried ashore and only five purification units. Subsequent to the landings, it became apparent that wells left by the enemy and those dug by the engineers were sufficient to provide for the needs of the 1st Marine Division. Water loaded in drums by the division quartermaster on Pavuvu was unpalatable because drums and cans previously had been used to store petroleum and had not been thoroughly cleansed before being filled with water. The condition of these containers, combined with condensation and rust, resulted in much misery to the Marines ashore during the first two days of the campaign. Heavy engineer equipment arrived on

Peleliu on D plus 4, though unloading was not completed for an additional six days. The 33d Naval Construction Battalion immediately began work on the existing fighter strip and by D plus 20 had also completed work on a bomber strip.

Armor played an important part on Peleliu, and its presence afforded considerable support to the Marines even in terrain that normally did not favor armored operations. Prior to the departure of the division from Pavuvu, .30 caliber machine guns were substituted for the .50 caliber guns on all tanks. As a result, the tank antiaircraft machine gun could be dismounted and used on the ground, while the .30 caliber regular ammunition was handy in an emergency. All tanks landed had been waterproofed by installation of standard deep water fording kits. As installation of these kits was an innovation unfamiliar to tank maintenance personnel, one tank was first waterproofed and tested. After two unsuccessful attempts, a correct procedure was established. During the third test the pilot tank remained in seven feet of water for 20 minutes with no leakage.

Another improvisation was made when it was found that the LCT ramp would frequently fly up as the tank ran off the LCT. In doing so, it ripped off the exhaust waterproofing on the rear of the tank. Two tongue-like metal extensions, each four feet long, 18 inches wide, and made of one-half inch steel plating were welded on the LCT ramp. These extensions were so placed that as the tank ran off the ramp, the vehicle tracks ran over the extensions. Thus the ramp was held down until the rear waterproofing was clear of the ramp. The commander of LCT Flotilla 6 effected this improvisation on all LCTs employed in the operation. Tank-infantry telephone extensions were improvised and mounted on the right rear bustle of all tanks. The telephone and cord were carried in a .30 caliber machine gun ammunition box welded on the rear armor face. The telephones were generally unsatisfactory in combat. Most of them soon became inoperative due to water damage, enemy fire, and lack of any self-winding feature necessary to retract the telephone extension.[40]

The 1st Tank Battalion resorted to an innovation during the assault on Peleliu. Each of the six LCTs, in addition to carrying five tanks, also had an LVT loaded on the rampway. The guide LVTs disembarked first, with a tank NCO aboard equipped with a portable radio for communication with the tanks. Each LVT led its tank platoon in column formation to the shore, detouring underwater potholes, shell craters, and coral obstacles. This innovation proved highly successful since no tanks were lost in crossing the reef due to underwater hazards, and the tank landing was accomplished without delay. Guide LVTs for tanks, as pioneered at Peleliu, were used in subsequent operations.[41]

Throughout the reef crossing, all tanks drew heavy artillery and mortar fire. Over half of the tanks received from one to four hits during the 10-minute reef crossing, though none was put out of commission. The fact that

---
[40] *Ibid.*, Anx J, p. 2.
[41] *Stuart ltr.*

the suspension systems and lower hulls were under water and therefore protected at this time no doubt prevented the loss of several tanks. All tanks were landed by H plus 18. This was much earlier than in any previous Marine operation. The early tank landing proved most wise, because tanks lent early impetus to the assault inland. The timely landing of tanks gave infantry commanders the means to destroy many direct fire weapons on the beaches, including gun emplacements and numerous beach machine guns.[42]

The 1st Marine Division had initially requested ships to land all of its tanks for the seizure of Peleliu, but the shipping made available permitted employment of only 30 tanks. Sixteen had to be left with the rear echelon. In the course of the Peleliu operation these tanks were badly needed, and the division was handicapped by their absence during the early phase of the operation, when a particular requirement for armor existed. The insufficient number of tanks that went ashore delayed complete seizure of the airfield. Tanks could have prevented additional casualties during the early days of the campaign.

For the fighting on Peleliu and Ngesebus tanks were used to support the general advance and destroy pillboxes, bunkers, and automatic weapons directly impeding the advance of the infantry. Tank-dozers proved valuable in filling antitank ditches and clearing logs and debris. Of the three tank-dozers landed, only one remained in operation throughout the campaign. A modified light tank, the E4-5 Mechanized Flamethrower, proved a good small-capacity weapon, but its use was limited. The tank was required to expose itself at a time when it was least able to protect itself because of the displacement of the bow machine gun. As a result, little use was made of the tank-mounted flamethrower in the reduction of bunkers and pillboxes, because its range was too short and its capacity too low to be really effective.

Tank supply and maintenance was a sore point during the Peleliu operation. The only tank supplies landed on D-Day were those that accompanied the tanks in the six guide LVTs. Additional ammunition and fuel, which was to have been landed by the second and third trip amphibians assigned to regimental combat teams, never arrived. Ammunition supply for tanks at the end of D-Day was critical, and only the salvaging of shells and bullets from 10 disabled tanks enabled the armor to resume the attack on the following day. An overly optimistic logistic concept of the Peleliu operation resulted in an entirely inadequate amount of spare parts and maintenance equipment being taken forward. As a result, the chief supply of spare parts were those that could be salvaged from completely knocked out tanks. Maintenance personnel suffered considerable casualties in stripping tanks in exposed positions. Maintenance was also handicapped by the fact that only one tank retriever was taken forward.

Of the 30 tanks that went ashore on Peleliu, only one remained completely unscathed; each of the remainder was put out of action at one time or another.

---

[42] *Ibid.*

The number of operational tanks never fell below 18 and averaged 20. All operational tanks were used continuously for 16 consecutive days of heavy combat. Only nine were a total loss. Tank reconnaissance personnel were landed with each assault infantry battalion headquarters, in advance of the tanks, and were intended to meet the tank unit commander and guide him to the landing team command posts. The tank reconaissance teams did not function in this manner. They either became casualties or were pinned down by the heavy fire falling on the beaches at that time. The tanks moved inland to positions offering maximum protection. Crews then dismounted long enough to remove waterproofing while tank officers oriented themselves to locate their infantry units. Time required to locate landing team command posts, become oriented, receive orders, and move up to join in the attack varied greatly between landing teams and ranged from five minutes to two hours.

On the whole, the medical planning for the Peleliu operation proved its worth. Medical companies varied from three to five percent above authorized strength in hospital corps personnel and medical officers. Organic medical units accompanied the 81st Infantry Division to Peleliu. Hospitalization for the soldiers was provided by 1st Marine Division medical companies. There were sufficient ambulances to carry the average daily number of casualties. On occasions when more transportation was required, cargo trucks were used. DUKWs proved invaluable for evacuating patients from inland medical facilities directly to ships.

In less than an hour from the time the first troops landed on Peleliu, casualties were being received aboard APAs from the beaches. The beach and shore party medical sections worked in close coordination. The latter remained on the beaches as aid and evacuation stations. They were consolidated when evacuation was discontinued on White Beach. When evacuation was begun on Purple Beach, a shore party medical section was established on the latter beach for evacuation.

Each Marine combat team had 96 men assigned as stretcher bearers. These personnel had previously received instruction in first aid and actual practice in the handling of litter cases in the staging area. Although this number was not sufficient to handle all litter cases, these men formed a trained nucleus to which additional personnel could be assigned. As far as the 1st Marine Division was concerned, before the operation was concluded, stretcher bearers were detailed from all supporting and garrison units—artillery, aviation, amphibian tractor, construction battalions, special CBs, and Navy communications units.[43]

On Peleliu there was practically no illness that could be directly attributed to flies or mosquitoes, though there was more than a lingering suspicion that their presence endangered the health of the troops. Mosquitoes were prevalent in the swamps adjacent to and north and northwest of the airfield, but were of the pest variety only. At the time the Marines went ashore on Peleliu,

---
[43] Col Harold O. Deakin ltr to CMC, dtd 10Mar50, in *Peleliu Comment File*.

there were few flies present. Three weeks later the fly population had reached proportions that made strenuous control methods essential. About two weeks after the initial landings, mild cases of gastro-intestinal disease appeared among frontline troops. Gradually the disorder spread to the rear echelon Marines. Even though the exact cause of this outbreak was never definitely established, the superabundance of flies on the island, caused by breeding in bodies, waste food, Japanese dumps, deposits of uncovered human feces, and non-flyproof latrines pointed to the source of the infection.

Maladies peculiar to the tropical climate causing acute discomfort were prickly heat and heat rash. Since water was scarce and dirt prevalent, scratching caused infection which spread rapidly. There were also numerous cases of multiple open sores, about the size of a dime which formed under the arms, around the belt, and on the inner parts of the legs.[44]

Prior to the actual landings, photographic intelligence was inadequate and until the end of August the photographs available were insufficient for beach defense study. Good photographs taken a week before the landing reached the task force while it was en route to the objective, but they were not made available to the troop commanders. Because of inadequate photography, maps were deficient, particularly insofar as the configuration of terrain was concerned. As an official Army Air Forces report was to put it later:

Whether or not more frequent and more careful photographic coverage of an island prior to the time of attack would reveal appreciably more than we now find is questionable. Certainly the number of suitable targets on the islands which have been located and listed for destruction were very few compared to the total which existed. Many of those which were undiscovered would have been effectively dealt with by the Navy's guns or by aerial bombardment. It is true, however, that photographic coverage, while complete, has been spasmodic. It is possible that had photographs been taken at more frequent intervals some of the defensive work would have been spotted in progress before work trails could have been covered and piles of spoil from the diggings had been dispersed.[45]

The Marines enjoyed certain advantages, however, in evaluating the enemy situation. American troops on Saipan had reaped a windfall with the capture of documents indicating that the total number of enemy troops on Peleliu exceeded 10,000 men.[46] The close similarity between the estimated figure of between 10,320 and 10,700 Japanese and the actual figure of about 10,900 was so striking that the IIIAC intelligence officer subsequently remarked "that the documents captured on Saipan provided a source of information which may be unparalleled in future operations."[47]

Unlike the campaign at Cape Gloucester, the 1st Marine Division

---

[44] LtCol Spencer S. Berger ltr to CMC, dtd 19Mar50, in *Peleliu Comment File*.

[45] Report No. 2, AAF Evaluation Board, Pacific Ocean Areas, (USAF Historical Archives File 138.6-2), p. 6, as cited in official USAF HistDiv comments, dtd 22Jun66, in *Peleliu Comment File*.

[46] Expeditionary Trps, ThirdFlt, Encl B to Palau Rpt; IIIAC, Encl C to Palau Rpt.

[47] *Ibid.*

captured few documents on Peleliu that were of immediate tactical value. Whether the dearth of captured documentary material was due to the fact that the Japanese had holed up in elaborate caves, many of which were sealed shut, or whether the enemy was becoming more security conscious was open to speculation. Nevertheless, a number of maps showing defensive sectors, the location of mine fields, and gun positions were captured. In one instance, the 7th Marines found a sketch showing the number and location of mines on a peninsula still in enemy hands. Subsequently, the same regiment turned in a captured ration statement for Japanese Army and Navy personnel stationed on Peleliu and Ngesebus. Since the document was dated 1 September, it provided excellent information about the strength of various Japanese units on Peleliu, which closely paralleled the intelligence previously obtained from documents seized on Saipan.[48]

Enemy materiel seized was not limited to documentary sources. Capture of the Peleliu airfield, for instance, yielded 130 aircraft, including spare parts and equipment. Even though these aircraft were not operational, an analysis of this materiel provided information of new developments, especially the discovery of a new model of the Type I medium bomber "Betty" and a model of another new medium bomber dubbed "Frances."[49]

American propaganda on Peleliu was generally ineffective because the Japanese maintained a high state of morale throughout the operation. A breakdown of enemy personnel captured on Peleliu up to 20 October showed that of the total of 302 captured, 92 were Japanese, including 7 Army, 12 Navy, and 73 laborers. The remainder of the prisoners was composed of non-Japanese laborers, including one Chinese, one Formosan, 206 Koreans, one prisoner who died before identification could be made, and two others whose physical and mental condition precluded identification.[50]

It was evident that most of the non-Japanese laborers, and in fact, some of the laborers of Japanese nationality, did not share an overpowering sense of loyalty to Japan and its military traditions. Many laborers stated that even though, as a rule, the American leaflets gave a time and place for surrendering, they felt that they could not get there safely and obtained better protection by remaining in their caves. One more reason has been advanced for the enemy's reluctance to surrender:

> ... the understandable but extreme bitterness of Marines in not wishing to take any prisoners but to kill every Jap sighted was just as much a factor in the prolonged resistance of the defenders as any fanatical, suicidal last ditch stand by the Japanese.[51]

That the above is not the isolated speculation of one individual was emphasized in an official report echoing the same sentiment:

> The lack of prisoners during the first several days was probably due as much to the bitterness of the fighting as to the ap-

---

[48] *1st MarDiv SAR*, Phase II, Anx B, p. 9.
[49] *Ibid.*, p. 25.
[50] *Ibid.*, p. 5.
[51] Capt Clyde L. Bozarth, MC, USN, ltr to CMC, dtd 13Mar50, in *Peleliu Comment File*.

parent reluctance of both troops and unit commanders to effect captures. It is believed that a more serious and sustained attempt to indoctrinate all personnel with the value and importance of taking prisoners would pay increasingly larger dividends as the war progresses.[52]

In one respect at least, the 1st Marine Division on Peleliu did not encounter the problems faced by other divisions on Guam, Saipan, and subsequently on Okinawa. This was in the field of civil affairs, where prior evacuation of natives from Peleliu by the Japanese proved advantageous to the Americans also. The Marines thus were relieved of the responsibility of controlling and caring for members of a civilian populace whose presence would have constituted a liability far in excess of any assistance they might have been able to render to the invasion force.

Signal communications on Peleliu did not present any undue problems, and the performance of radio and other signal equipment did not differ materially from that of other campaigns. During the first two days of the campaign, radio remained the primary means of communication, and both the SCR-300 and the SCR-610 performed excellently in corps and division nets. Two radio-equipped DUKWs were landed and operated moderately well until moisture affected the equipment and its performance became marginal. An experimental armored amphibian equipped with various types of communications gear was landed at H plus 90 minutes with the advance division message center. It was discovered at that time that the battery charging circuits were inoperative, and, as a result, no use of this equipment was made until D plus 10.[53]

One of the innovations in the field of communications on Peleliu was to encourage officers to talk directly over voice radio circuits, since this speeded communications and relieved crowded telephone circuits. Visual communication by blinker lamp was not used during the operation, nor were telegraph or teletype employed. In maintaining radio contact with tanks, frequency modulation equipment proved most rugged, reliable, and flexible. The only defect found in this equipment appeared to be its limited range. It became necessary to set up a relay station for transmissions from northern Peleliu to the vicinity of the airfield. When peaks intervened, the effective range dropped to as low as two miles.[54]

In connection with communications on Peleliu, the activities of the 4th Joint Assault Signal Company are of special interest. Upon arriving at the staging area at Pavuvu, the 10 communications teams, 9 shore fire control parties, and 13 air liaison parties were at once attached to battalions and regiments with which they were to operate. The greatest difficulty was experienced in the control of the communications teams which were attached to each battalion. The teams themselves worked well, although difficulty was experienced in coordinating them since they were not landed as a tactical unit. Air liaison parties and shore fire control parties worked very well, even though in many instances these teams went ashore too

---

[52] IIIAC OpRpt, Encl B, p. 2.

[53] 1st MarDiv SAR, Phase II, Anx F, p. 2.
[54] Ibid., Anx J, p. 10.

soon on beaches where assault troops were pinned down by fire.[55]

The quantity, quality, and thoroughness of naval gunfire are an extremely important factor in any amphibious assault. This held particularly true for a heavily fortified and strongly defended island like Peleliu. Because this particular phase of the Peleliu operation has since become the object of considerable controversy, a detailed discussion of naval gunfire support during the pre-landing phase appears in order.

The pre-bombardment of Peleliu had a threefold objective: to knock out enemy aircraft and artillery installations; to destroy as many enemy strongpoints as possible and to eliminate all enemy ships, barges, and small craft capable of reinforcing the enemy garrison from the north. To achieve these objectives, fires were scheduled not only against known enemy positions but also against areas that a study of the terrain and a knowledge of Japanese tactics would indicate enemy use for fortified positions, assembly areas, communications centers, or ammunition dumps.

The importance attached by the Navy to the STALEMATE operation was underscored by the personnages in attendance, whose presence has been described as follows by a naval historian:

> Peleliu was honored by the participation of a large number of flag and general officers. Vice Admiral Wilkinson and Major Generals Julian Smith and William Rupertus were on board Rear Admiral Fort's amphibious command ship *Mount McKinley*. General Geiger was on board *Mount Olympus*, to which Wilkinson shifted at Eniwetok. Rear Admiral Blandy and General Mueller were in *Fremont*. Rear Admiral Jesse B. Oldendorf in *Louisville* commanded a formidable fire support group of five battleships, five heavy cruisers, three light cruisers, and fourteen destroyers; and they had two more flag officers, Rear Admirals Ainsworth and Kingman, embarked. Rear Admiral Ralph Ofstie commanded between seven and eleven escort carriers to provide combat air and antisubmarine patrol, and Rear Admiral William D. Sample had a carrier division under him. Admiral Halsey dropped in on Peleliu 17 September; in the entire chain of command, only Admiral Nimitz stayed away.[56]

Surely, with such a large number of critical observers present, there was a great opportunity to show what preliminary bombardment could accomplish in support of an amphibious operation. Based on experience in similar operations, the Navy conducted the customary preliminary aerial and naval bombardment before the landing. As early as 6 September, fast carriers of Halsey's Third Fleet took the islands under aerial bombardment. After three days of bombing it was determined that the B-24 attacks had already inflicted serious damage on many of the enemy

---

[55] *Ibid.*, Anx E, p. 1.

[56] Morison, *Leyte*, p. 34. There appears to be some controversy as to who boarded what ship. According to other sources, Admiral Fort and Generals Geiger and Julian Smith, with the staffs of the higher echelons, were embarked in USS *Mount McKinley*, while General Rupertus and the bulk of the division staff embarked in USS *DuPage*; General O. P. Smith and the remainder of the staff were on the USS *Elmore*. Hough, *Peleliu Monograph*, pp. 21-22. This version is concurred in by the former chief of staff of IIIAC, LtGen Merwin H. Silverthorn (Ret) ltr to Head, HistBr, dtd 26Jun66, in *Peleliu Comment File*.

installations, and the carriers moved off towards the Philippines.

With the arrival of the task force off Peleliu on 12 September, the pre-bombardment of Peleliu began in earnest:

> The original plan had called for only two days of preparatory naval bombardment. Geiger objected that this was too little and asked for four. He finally got three for Peleliu and five for Angaur . . . Five old battleships, eight cruisers, and fourteen destroyers, most of them veterans of shore bombardment and under the command of Rear Admiral Jesse B. Oldendorf, USN . . . arrived off Palau on September 12. Oldendorf was handicapped in the execution of his mission both in the facilities he had on hand and in the size of his staff. His flag was an old battleship, not one of the new headquarters ships whose superior communications equipment had been one of the reasons for the increased effectiveness of naval gunfire support in the Marshalls and on Guam. Also he was short on staff personnel. In spite of many previous recommendations to the Bureau of Naval Personnel in Washington he had only a cruiser division staff, consisting of four officers. To add to his difficulties all of these but one were on the sick list during the preliminary bombardment.[57]

The ammunition expenditure in the tactical employment of naval gunfire amounted to 3,490 tons prior to H-Hour and 2,359 tons thereafter.[58] The naval bombardment obliterated much of the dense vegetation on the ridge immediately north of the airfield, subsequently to become known as Bloody Nose Ridge. What this naval gunfire could not and did not eliminate were the numerous Japanese defenses in caves and underground shelters, which enabled the enemy to remain safely underground until the bombardment lifted.

The Japanese on Peleliu did not at any time disclose their presence prior to the amphibious landing of the Marines. The total absence of Japanese counterbattery fire during the preliminary bombardment and the dense pall of smoke that soon hung over Peleliu like a shroud, combined to embue Admiral Oldendorf with a deceptive sense of optimism. In contacting Admiral Fort on the evening of 14 September, Admiral Oldendorf made the unfortunate remark that he had run out of targets. This statement, followed shortly by a rash prediction by General Rupertus of a short but tough campaign, subsequently cast a pall of disappointment, consternation, and bitterness that has at times tended to obscure the planning, effort, valor, and heroism which far surpassed interservice or interarm quibbling and reproach.

The bitterness of the Marines who had reason to assume that the landing would not be an extremely difficult one is understandable when it became apparent that some of the most important enemy defenses were still functioning during the amphibious assault. Typical of this feeling is the following comment, made long after the guns had become silent, though still filled with passionate reproach:

> There was never any question of the importance of the southwestern promon-

---

[57] Col Donald M. Weller ltr to Philip A. Crowl, dtd 22Mar50, as quoted in Isely and Crowl, *U. S. Marines and Amphibious War*, p. 402. RAdm Jesse B. Oldendorf ltr to Dir, MarCorpsHist, dtd 25Mar50, in *Peleliu Comment File*, hereafter *Oldendorf ltr*.

[58] *1st MarDiv SAR*, Phase II, Anx K, p. 4.

tory, the unnamed island, the left flank of the 1st Marines and the high ground to the north of the airfield, nor was there any question as to the necessity of knocking out enemy positions in those areas and the provisions for continuous support to be delivered. This fact was impressed upon the staff of RAdm Fort on many occasions.

Preliminary bombardment plans, air and naval gunfire, were made with the above consideration. Before the Advance Force sailed, great emphasis was placed on the necessity of thoroughly covering these areas. In this connection . . . the dispatch sent by Admiral Oldendorf was not only a surprise but was not understood by any of us on the Division Staff in view of the study, and requirements we had submitted, and the plans which had been so carefully prepared and agreed to as essential and necessary for the accomplishment of the Division mission. . . .

What happened on D-Day is a matter of history. . . . I have asked of the unit commanders many times for an explanation of just what happened. No one is certain of anything except that the enemy was not knocked out.[59]

In this connection, Rear Admiral Oldendorf's comments may be of interest, for they reflect the problems and difficulties which beset him at the time:

> My Gunfire Support Plan called for all known or suspected enemy strong points to be destroyed. . . . The preliminary bombardment was, I thought at the time, one of the most thorough that could be devised considering the lack of intelligence concerning enemy strong points. The prelanding gunfire support was, I thought, superior to anything which had been put on heretofore. My surprise and chagrin when concealed batteries opened up on the LVTs can be imagined. . . . Under these circumstances, no matter how many shells you fire or their caliber, you cannot destroy enemy gun emplacements on an island the size of Peleliu, unless the enemy will oblige by disclosing the position of his guns. . . . The best that can be done is to blast away at suspected positions and hope for the best.[60]

In commenting on naval gunfire at Peleliu, Rear Admiral George H. Fort deplored a tendency on the part of the Marines to set up the naval gunfire at Guam as the standard and to judge other operations by it. Instead, the "de luxe" bombardment of Guam, which had not been originally planned when the Marianas operation was first plotted, in the long run increased the difficulties of the Peleliu operation. Rear Admiral Fort expressed his views on this subject as follows:

> I think it is a grave error to set up the Guam operation as the standard for the future. It is erroneous to lead the Marines or other troops to expect any such support prior to landing. It never happened anywhere else and probably never will again. . . . The original plan was for two days' bombardment at Peleliu which was subsequently increased to three. Whereas this increase permitted somewhat more deliberate bombardment, it did not increase the weight of metal in the slightest. The same amount of ammunition was to have been used in the originally scheduled two days as was subsequently used in three. If Admiral Oldendorf broke off fire before he had used up his allowed ammunition on the grounds that there were no more targets, he was entirely correct. The idea which some people seem to have of just firing at an island is an inexcusable waste of ammunition.[61]

---

[59] LtCol Lewis J. Fields ltr to CMC, dtd 17Mar50, in *Peleliu Comment File*.

[60] *Oldendorf ltr*.

[61] RAdm George H. Fort ltr to BGen Clayton C. Jerome, dtd 20Mar50, in *Peleliu Comment File*, hereafter *Fort ltr*.

Many accounts of the Peleliu operation have dwelled so extensively on what was wrong with the prelanding bombardment that little has been said of naval gunfire support after the landings. Of this support in the hours following the landing on Peleliu, the following was noted:

> Naval gunfire support, by now an essential feature of amphibious assaults, was very little used on D-Day at Peleliu because of the confused nature of the fighting. Cruisers *Louisville, Portland* and *Indianapolis* were idle most of the day but Admiral Ofstie's eleven escort carriers flew 382 sorties on D-Day in support of the troops, besides making interdiction strikes on the airfield at Babelthuap and bombing enemy ships in Malakal and Koror harbors. No Japanese aircraft appeared in opposition.[62]

For the remainder of the Peleliu operation, naval gunfire provided close and deep support fire as well as harassing, interdiction, and night illumination fire. The lack of suitable observation points precluded the use of close supporting fires in many instances, so that they were not used as extensively as in other operations. Air spotting for deep supporting fire was used extensively in neutralizing enemy reserves, gun positions, supply and ammunition dumps, and observation and communication points. Air spotting proved to be one of the best and most effective means of fire control.

Harassing fire was used rather extensively. It was employed principally at night and was delivered in areas well clear of the front line. Ships firing night harassing fire also doubled for emergency call fire or illumination. Interdiction fire was employed in the areas at the north end of Peleliu and on the nearby island of Ngesebus to prevent enemy reinforcements from being brought up. Star shell illumination was used extensively. It was regulated, as were other fires, so that it would not illuminate friendly units and produce casualties among friendly troops. The rate of fire varied from 1 round per minute to 10 or 15 rounds per hour.[63]

One lesson that could be learned on Peleliu was that tanks could survive a pre-landing bombardment, and that naval gunfire and air could not prevent hostile tanks from closing on the landing force. "What the enemy achieved with thin-skinned, obsolete tankettes, a potential enemy possessing powerful tanks in great numbers might presumably also accomplish, thus posing a grave potential threat against a landing force."[64] On the other hand, no two tactical situations are exactly alike. During the Sicily operation, for instance, naval gunners were the major factor in breaking up a tank attack on the beaches near Gela.[65]

The 1st Marine Division did not have a Marine naval gunfire officer, and no officers in the division had been trained for such an assignment. As a result of its experiences on Peleliu, the 1st Marine Division recommended the selection of artillery officers for naval

---

[62] Morison, *Leyte*, p. 39.

[63] *1st MarDiv SAR*, Phase II, Anx K, p. 6.

[64] Stuart ltr.

[65] For a detailed account of this incident, see Samuel Eliot Morison, *Sicily-Salerno-Anzio (January 1943–June 1944)—History of United States Naval Operations in World War II*, v. IX, (Boston: Little, Brown and Company, 1902), pp. 103-104.

gunfire training. Another recommendation was the addition of a division naval liaison officer with a team, and three regimental naval gunfire liaison teams to the JASCO. Naval gunfire was stopped during practically every air strike. The 1st Marine Division felt that this practice should be the exception rather than the general rule, if in the opinion of the commanding officer such fire did not endanger friendly aircraft.[66]

Aside from a temporary halt to the unloading of supplies during periods of stormy weather, the Peleliu operation was not beset by any major supply difficulties. The pioneer battalion, using one company of engineers, formed the framework for the division shore party. The commanding officer of the pioneer battalion was the division shore party commander. The shore party was responsible for handling supplies on and behind the beach and for processing casualties recovered from division units.

Initially, the operation of the shore party was decentralized, *i.e.* a detachment of the regimental shore party went in with each assault battalion. When the infantry regimental headquarters landed, the regimental shore party commander took over and consolidated battalion shore party operations for the regimental beach. In turn, the division shore party commander took over shore party operations on all beaches and determined what beaches were to continue as supply beaches. Operations of the shore party were closely coordinated with those of the naval beach parties. By the time that all assault troops, equipment, and supplies had gone ashore, the 16th Field Depot, a supply agency of the Island Command, took over the supply dumps. Subsequently, the field depot also supplied those components of the 81st Infantry Division operating on Peleliu.

The distribution and forwarding of supplies caused little difficulty, because distances were extremely short and amphibian tractors and DUKWs, in many instances, were able to move directly from the water to regimental dumps. During the last days of September, bad weather caused unloading difficulties. When the ration level reached four days' supply, the troops were put on two meals per day, and MAG–11 flew in 42,000 Ten-in-One Rations.[67] The rugged ground in which the troops had to operate caused excessive wear and tear on clothing. When organizational supplies became exhausted, a total of 1,000 suits of utilities, 5,000 pairs of socks, and 1,000 pairs of shoes were flown in from Guam.[68]

The attachment of a field depot unit to the 1st Marine Division was an innovation that worked extremely well. As expressed by the Commanding Officer, 1st Service Battalion:

> . . . this subjected the depot to the direct orders of the Division Commander and resulted in excellent assistance and cooperation without the necessity of dealing with them through a Corps Headquarters. All the difference between ordering and asking.[69]

All air strikes immediately preceding D-Day and for 13 days thereafter were

---

[66] *Ibid.*, p. 9.

[67] Smith, *Narrative*, p. 77.
[68] *Ibid.* p. 78.
[69] Col John Kaluf ltr to CMC, datd 7Mar50, in *Peleliu Comment File.*

flown by Navy pilots from fast and escort carriers. The 1st Marine Division was able to make certain recommendations and requests for air strikes against specific and important targets to Commander Support Air after the arrival of the Western Attack Force in the staging area. These requests and recommendations were followed as closely as possible within the limitations of the already existent air plan. This was the only opportunity offered the division to participate in or make recommendations regarding planning for air support.[70]

As a result of planned missions and call missions requested by battalion, regimental, and division air teams, over 300 missions were flown from D-Day through 28 September. During this period of time, carrier-based aircraft dropped 620 tons of bombs of all types including napalm. After D plus 13 it was felt that carrier-based air could no longer be profitably employed, so naval air support was secured at the end of 28 September.[71]

The efficiency of naval air support was readily apparent while fighting was in progress in the level terrain on the southern portion of Peleliu, where it was relatively easy to spot targets and mark and distinguish front lines. When the fighting moved into the rugged hills on the northern half of the island, the effectiveness of air support diminished greatly. This decrease was due to the difficulty in marking friendly and enemy terrain, inaccuracy of available maps, and the control of all missions directly from the headquarters ship. In no instance was any battalion air liaison party permitted to control or direct missions, even though by reason of its forward location, the party was in possession of the latest information. On the basis of these experiences, the 1st Marine Division recommended that in subsequent operations, the battalion and regimental air liaison teams be allowed to control aircraft directly from the ground. The advantage of this was obvious, since the man on the spot would be able to coach the strike on the target better than an air control officer on board the headquarters ship.[72]

In contrast with the more effective aerial bombing, the strafing missions carried out by support air were considered to have little or no value. Naval aircraft began and completed strafing runs at too high an altitude: they seldom made pullouts under 1,800 feet.[73]

The ineffectiveness of such procedure was particularly apparent during the pre-landing attacks on the Peleliu beaches and subsequent strafing runs in the hills. On the basis of this experience, the 1st Marine Division felt that at most, such strafing could result in keeping the enemy pinned down for the duration of the strafing run.

The employment of VMF-114 on Peleliu on and after 28 September put an end to the deficiencies of the avail-

---

[70] According to Navy sources, the selection of Pavuvu as a camp for the 1st Marine Division was an important factor in impeding close joint planning for air support. The stepped-up time schedule was also involved. Eller ltr.

[71] 1st MarDiv SAR, Phase II, Anx T, p. 1.

[72] Ibid., p. 8.

[73] Some Navy squadrons, such as VC-21 based on Marcus Island, reported pullouts from strafing runs ranging from 700 and 1,000 feet. See Eller ltr.

able air support. The close support given by the Corsairs flown by Marine aviators proved extremely effective during the landing on Ngesebus. The effectiveness of subsequent bombing missions against the Umurbrogol Pocket was limited only by the difficult terrain and the relative invulnerability of underground Japanese defenses to aerial attack. General Rupertus, often reticent and sparing in praise, found the close air support furnished by VMF-114 to be "executed in a manner leaving little to be desired."[74]

The Peleliu operation was unique in that it featured the first Marine aviation support of a Marine landing since Bougainville. It was also the first time since Guadalcanal that the 1st Marine Division had received close air support by Marines. Peleliu, in addition, had the distinction of featuring the very first Marine air support of a Marine amphibious operation in the Central Pacific.

Results of the napalm strikes carried out during the Peleliu operation were generally disappointing, probably because of an erroneous concept about the proper employment of this weapon. This lack of understanding of the capabilities and limitations of napalm is best illustrated by the following account:

> A few days before D-Day, while we were at sea, our regimental intelligence officer spoke at a conference of all officers of BLT 1/7. We had been told that a certain aircraft carrier, loaded with napalm bombs, was to plaster the southwestern peninsula (our battalion objective) to burn out the Japs with this sticky, inflammable substance. But until the date of this conference, the report had come in that the fuses for these bombs had not arrived. At the conference, however, we were told that the fuses had finally arrived, had been delivered to the carrier by air, and at that very moment were being affixed to these wondrous bombs. The Intelligence Officer announced with some excitement and eloquence, and with sincere belief in what he was saying, that these remarkable bombs, even though they may not splatter each Jap, gave such intense, prolonged heat that they would literally suffocate any holed-up Jap because of their huge appetite for oxygen. Furthermore, this peninsula would be denuded of vegetation. Now, what infantryman would not relish an objective stripped of concealing vegetation and devoid of live enemy soldiers? Incredible as it may sound now, it was generally believed to be quite truthful. We had not seen these bombs. Napalm was a war wonder. And there is the human tendency to enfold any and all optimism at a time like this. This information . . . was quickly disseminated to the troops and was received with cheers.[75]

The capture of Peleliu and Angaur was very costly in American lives. At the end of the Peleliu operation the 1st Marine Division (Reinforced) listed its casualties sustained on Peleliu as 1,121 officers and men killed in action, 5,142 wounded in action, and 73 missing in action.[76] For the period of 23 September to 27 November 1944, the 81st Infantry Division listed its casualties on Peleliu as 277 killed in action or dead of wounds and 1,008 wounded or injured in action.[77] Casualties of the 81st Infantry Division on Angaur for the period of 17 September-30 October 1944, were 260 killed or died of wounds and 1,354 wounded or injured in action.[78]

---

[74] Quoted in Sherrod, *Marine Corps Aviation in World War II*, p. 257.

[75] *Worden ltr.*
[76] *1st MarDiv SAR*, Phase II, Anx G, p. 2.
[77] *81st InfDiv OpRpt*, Peleliu, Anx F, p. 109.
[78] *81st InfDiv OpRpt*, Angaur, Anx P, p. 112.

Subsequent tallies show certain revisions and deviations from the earlier findings. A later figure for Marine casualties on Peleliu lists 1,252 as dead (killed in action, died of wounds, and missing presumed dead) and 5,274 wounded.[79] In a later compilation, casualties of the 81st Infantry Division on Peleliu, Angaur, and the smaller islands off Peleliu totalled 542 killed and 2,736 wounded or injured in action.[80] The subsequent revisions of figures contained in the earlier official after-action reports are the result of additional information not included in earlier reports. This would include a number of wounded who subsequently died of wounds sustained in the operation.[81]

The exact number of Japanese killed on Peleliu will presumably never be known, though a reasonably close figure can be obtained through the process of deduction. Even prior to the landings on Peleliu, Japanese strength on that island had been estimated at between 10,320 and 10,700. If the 302 Japanese captured are deducted from a median of 10,500, it follows that at least 10,200 of the enemy must have died on the island, even when allowance is made for a small number that may have escaped to Japanese-held islands to the north. Since an additional 600 Japanese went ashore on Peleliu while operations there were in progress, a total of 10,900 could be considered a reasonably conservative figure, which is generally supported elsewhere.[82]

PELELIU IN RETROSPECT[83]

More than two decades have passed since the 1st Marine Division assaulted Peleliu. From those that had participated in the campaign, there has been no lack of superlatives in its description. A former Commandant of the Marine Corps has called it ". . . one of the least publicized and most difficult campaigns of World War II." [84] The official U.S. Army history calls the Palaus operation ". . . one of the bloodiest battles of the war." [85] In commenting on the Peleliu campaign, Admiral Fort expressed himself as follows:

---

[79] Hough, *Assault on Peleliu*, p. 183.

[80] Smith, *Approach to the Philippines*, p. 573.

[81] Differences in casualty reporting and accounting systems have resulted in a further variance. Based on the most recent official Marine Corps statistics available at the time of this writing, 1,794 Americans died on Peleliu and adjacent islands during the Peleliu Campaign and approximately 7,800 were wounded or injured in action.

[82] The Army version of the Peleliu Operation lists over 11,000 Japanese killed on Peleliu, and 2,600 more on Angaur and the smaller islands off Peleliu. Smith, *Approach to the Philippines*, p. 572. Morison, in *Leyte*, p. 46, cites the same total of 13,600 Japanese killed on Peleliu and vicinity. Speaking of Peleliu Island alone, Isely and Crowl estimate a total of 10,695 enemy dead up to 20 October 1944, in *U. S. Marines and Amphibious War*, p. 411. In the light of the documentary material available and other evidence, the figure of 7,000 personnel on Peleliu (Army and Navy combined) advanced by General Inoue in a postwar interview appears far too low to be credible. Inoue interview in *Worden ltr*.

[83] Unless otherwise noted, the material in this section is derived from: Smith, *Narrative*; Vandegrift and Asprey, *Once A Marine*; Craven and Cate, *The Pacific*; Isely and Crowl, *U. S. Marines and Amphibious War*; Halsey and Bryan, *Admiral Halsey's Story*; Morison, *Leyte*; Smith, *Approach to the Philippines*.

[84] Vandegrift and Asprey, *Once A Marine*, p. 274.

[85] Smith, *Approach to the Philippines*, p. 573.

I think those who have taken the trouble to investigate are in general agreement that the capture of Peleliu was the most difficult amphibious operation in the Pacific War. . . . I believe that the Palaus operation has been underestimated. Were it not for the untimely deaths of Generals Geiger and Rupertus so soon afterwards, I feel sure that they would have helped to clarify the situation. Iwo Jima was done by the so-called Central Pacific "First Team" and received widespread publicity and acclaim. As General Geiger once said, "The only difference between Iwo Jima and Peleliu was that at Iwo Jima there were twice as many Japs on an island twice as large, and they had three Marine Divisions to take it while we had one Marine Division to take Peleliu."[86]

The above statement, made by the commander in direct tactical control at Peleliu and Angaur, bears closer scrutiny. It not only lends emphasis to what others have said about the severity of the fighting on Peleliu, but also adds a new note with respect to the numerical adequacy of the force committed. General Geiger's comment, as quoted by Admiral Fort, leaves little doubt that he was referring to a failure to provide an adequate reserve for the 1st Marine Division. Of three regiments employed to assault Peleliu, only one battalion remained in division and another in regimental reserve. Had the 81st Infantry Division been committed on Peleliu when it became apparent that Japanese resistance there did not permit the speedy conquest of the island, the landing on Angaur could have been postponed until completion of operations on Peleliu. This conclusion is supported by General Inoue, who subsequently stated ". . . it was estimated that at least three American divisions would land on either the southern or the eastern beaches. . . ."[87]

In view of the heavy American casualties on Peleliu, opinion has been divided whether the gains derived from the capture of the island were worth the heavy cost in American lives. Comments from historians and military leaders alike question whether the results were worth the effort. In the words of one historian:

> . . . doubts are easily raised in the light of the fact that eleventh-hour changes in plans for subsequent operations—notably the invasion of the Philippines—made it impossible to fit the Palaus into the operational role originally planned for them. . . . Nevertheless, with the information available to them in the summer and early fall of 1944, Admiral Nimitz, General MacArthur, and the Joint Chiefs of Staff all believed that only by securing the Palaus could the Allies dominate Japanese bases in the western Pacific and insure the safety of forces moving toward the Philippines.[88]

Among the military leaders who felt strongly that Peleliu should not have been invaded, Admiral Halsey perhaps is best qualified to voice his opinion, for it was he who opposed the operation from the very outset. In commenting on Peleliu, Admiral Halsey had this to say:

> I had been weighing this operation ever since it had been broached to me, early in May, at a conference with King and Nimitz in San Francisco, and the more I weighed it, the less I liked it. Ulithi had a useful anchorage, but I saw no need for any of the other islands. Yap's only value was as a minor staging

---

[86] *Fort ltr.*

[87] *Inoue Interrogation.*
[88] Smith, *Approach to the Philippines*, pp. 573-575.

point for aircraft. The Palaus threatened the route between New Guinea and the Philippines, but although they also offered an anchorage—Kossol Roads—and several sites for airfields, I felt that they would have to be bought at a prohibitive price in casualties. In short, I feared another Tarawa—and I was right.[89]

By far the most outspoken comment comes from another naval officer who was deeply involved in the Peleliu Operation. In reviewing the campaign he forthrightly came to the conclusion that:

> ... if military leaders (including naval) were gifted with the same accuracy of foresight that they are with hindsight, undoubtedly the assault and capture of the Palaus would never have been attempted.[90]

On the surface, the above comments carry considerable weight, the more so if it is considered that the airfields on Peleliu and Angaur, the primary objectives of the assault, ultimately played only a minor part in the liberation of the Philippines. The airfield on Angaur was not ready for use by bombers until 21 October, the day after American forces had landed on Leyte, and it was 17 November before the first bomber mission was flown against a target in the Philippines from a field in the Palaus.[91]

What, then, were the advantages, if any, that accrued to the United States through the capture of Peleliu and Angaur? First, the seizure of these islands prevented their use as bases by enemy aircraft and submarines. By late November, Angaur-based bombers rendered vital support to American forces on Luzon. Beyond that, some 43,000 Japanese were effectively neutralized in the northern Palau islands, where they remained until their unconditional surrender at the end of the war, of no more use to the Empire or the beleaguered Japanese forces in the Philippines than if they had been stationed at the North Pole. Ulithi Atoll in American hands provided an excellent fleet anchorage and assumed major importance during subsequent operations in the Pacific Theater, particularly as a staging area for forces destined for Okinawa.

In retrospect, it appears idle conjecture whether an invasion of the Philippines could have been successful had there been no invasion of the Palau Islands. Military planning is based on a sound appraisal of strategic and tactical factors. It is a logical process of reasoning by which a commander considers all the circumstances affecting the military situation and arrives at a decision which determines the course of action he should take to accomplish his mission. On the basis of the information available to the planners of STALEMATE II during the spring and summer of 1944, the situation called for an operation against Peleliu, Angaur, and adjacent islands. Changes in the basic plan were instituted as necessary to conform to changes in the overall situation.

Peleliu vindicated the amphibious doctrines developed by the Marine Corps in many years of careful study and analysis. The operation proved once again that an amphibious assault on a

---

[89] Halsey and Bryan, *Admiral Halsey's Story*, pp. 194-195.
[90] *Oldendorf ltr.*
[91] Craven and Cate, *The Pacific*, p. 372.

heavily fortified island was feasible. In a way it closely resembled previous landings in the Gilberts and Marshalls and gave a preview of things to come on Iwo Jima and Okinawa. At least one source has commented that ". . . the most valuable contribution to victory of this costly operation was to prepare the Army and Marine Corps for what they would experience at Okinawa."[92]

The operation against Peleliu had one more similarity with the Battle of Tarawa. At the conclusion of both campaigns, the Marine Corps received considerable criticism because of the high number of casualties. The truth applying to the cost of such operations has been set forth so aptly by a former Commandant of the Marine Corps that his reply to similar criticism after Tarawa bears repeating in this context:

> . . . A landing attack is recognized by all military experts as being the most difficult and costly of all forms of attack. Losses at Tarawa were heavy, and losses will be heavy in future attacks of this nature. . . .
> . . . In the case of a heavily defended small island such as Tarawa . . . the defender can concentrate his forces against any landing attempt. . . . The attacker attempts to "soften" resistance by naval gunfire and aerial bombardment. Where the defenses are very strongly constructed, as at Tarawa, the gunfire and aerial bombardment have only partial effect. Many of the hostile installations will remain operative and fire from them must be faced.
> No one regrets the losses in such an attack more than does the Marine Corps itself. No one realizes more than does the Marine Corps that there is no royal road to Tokyo. We must steel our people to the same realization.[93]

In the overall picture of a global conflict, Peleliu was merely a stepping stone towards the ultimate objective, a battle not slated for fame in the outside world, yet an event that left its permanent mark on the men who fought it. In conclusion, it seems fitting to quote an echo from the past; words uttered long ago in a different war, and on another battlefield, yet singularly appropriate in this context. Let it be said of the once cruel and inhospitable soil of Peleliu that ". . . the brave men, living and dead, who struggled here, have consecrated it, far above our poor power to add and detract. . . ."

---

[92] Morison, *Leyte*, p. 47.

[93] Statement by General Alexander A. Vandegrift to Senator Walsh, 15Dec44, as quoted in Vandegrift and Asprey, *Once a Marine*, pp. 235–236.

PART IV

Marines in the Philippines

CHAPTER 1

Background and Planning [1]

Even though relatively few Marines participated in the liberation of the Philippines, the support they furnished and the services they performed were out of proportion to their small numbers. Marine artillerymen under the command of Brigadier General Thomas E. Bourke supported Army troops on Leyte; Marine pilots commanded by Colonel Clayton C. Jerome bombed and strafed assigned targets and flew fighter missions throughout the campaign, under the overall direction of General MacArthur's air commander, Lieutenant General George C. Kenney. Even more important were the accomplishments of the pilots who developed, crystallized, and refined the doctrine and techniques for the close air support of ground troops. On Leyte, Luzon, Mindanao, and other islands, Marine pilots convinced skeptical Army ground commanders that aviation was capable of rendering valuable and effective support to the frontline troops. These pilots proved their worth by assisting in the capture of objectives and helping to meet the operational timetable. It was here, in the rain, mud, and jungle of the Philippines, that Marine aviation put the new doctrine of close air support to the test.

No individual can be more closely identified with the liberation of the Philippines than General Douglas MacArthur. During the darkest days of the war the general had pledged his return to the Philippines. From the time that General MacArthur left Corregidor in 1942 to take over the new Allied command formed in Australia, the liberation of the Philippines dominated his thoughts. Only a short time after establishing General Headquarters, Southwest Pacific Area (SWPA), in Brisbane the general initiated planning for that return. More than two years were to pass before these plans were fulfilled.

During this period of time, the command setup in the Pacific Theater underwent several changes. As early as the Guadalcanal campaign, General MacArthur had wielded strategic control over most of the Solomons. Inasmuch as the SWPA commander at the time was preoccupied with operations in eastern New Guinea, Admiral Halsey

---

[1] Unless otherwise noted, the material in this section is derived from: Maj Charles W. Boggs, Jr., *Marine Aviation in the Philippines* (Washington: HistDiv, HQMC, 1951), hereafter Boggs, *Marines in the Philippines;* Isely and Crowl, *U. S. Marines and Amphibious War;* *The War Reports of General of the Army George C. Marshall, General of the Army Henry H. Arnold, and Fleet Admiral Ernest J. King* (Philadelphia and New York: J. B. Lippincott Company, 1947), hereafter *War Reports* with appropriate originator; USSBS, *Pacific Campaigns;* Morison, *Leyte.* Where location citations for documentary sources for this part are missing, the material is in the files of the Reference Branch, Historical Division, HQMC.

291

was given control over the entire Solomons chain in addition to the operational command he already exercised at Guadalcanal.[2]

Initially, the JCS viewed the importance of liberating the Philippines with skepticism. A compromise between the JCS and General MacArthur resulted in a two-pronged campaign in the Pacific during 1943 and 1944. Admiral Nimitz' forces in the Central Pacific received priority in their drive through the Marshalls, the Marianas, and the Carolines while General MacArthur's forces moved northward along the New Guinea coast.

A JCS directive of 12 March 1944[3] guided operations in the Pacific Theater for the remainder of the year. As it became apparent that the Japanese power in the Pacific was waning and the two-pronged advance continued, the Joint Chiefs decided that the entire Pacific timetable should be advanced. This revision was based on a sound premise. The campaign in the Marshalls, in February 1944, had brought speedy results. Carrier strikes, in mid-February 1944, against the fortress of Truk proved that Japanese air and naval strength was far weaker than had been assumed. In the end, General MacArthur had been able to advance the target date for the Admiralties operation by a full month.

The 12 March directive was of crucial importance to General MacArthur.

Even though it fell short of his expectations by not giving him full priority for his return to the Philippines, the directive did authorize the capture of supporting bases and provided for the movement of MacArthur's forces into Mindanao, the southernmost of the Philippine islands. General MacArthur's air commander, General Kenney, was "dumbfounded" to learn that the Joint Chiefs seemed to attach more importance to Nimitz' Central Pacific drive than to any other campaign in the Pacific Theater.[4] Despite the limitations imposed on further operations in the Southwest Pacific by this change in strategy, the SWPA staff continued to plan for the most ambitious action possible under the circumstances.

In late March 1944, Admiral Nimitz visited General MacArthur in Brisbane for a planning conference. The immediate subject under discussion was the Hollandia operation, though it was inevitable that the two military leaders would also bring up the invasion of the Philippines.[5] As a result of this conference, MacArthur and Nimitz set up, subject to JCS approval, an operations schedule which called for SWPA forces to land on Mindanao on 15 November 1944.

The Joint Chiefs in March 1944 did not make any provisions for operations in the Philippines following the invasion of Mindanao. Strategy in the Pacific for 1944 called for SWPA forces to move gradually northwest along the New Guinea coast, occupy the islands northwest of the Vogelkop Peninsula,

---

[2] JCS 238/5D, 28Mar43 had placed operations in the Solomons under Halsey's direct control subject to MacArthur's "general directions," as cited in Boggs, *Marines in the Philippines*, p. 1.

[3] JCS 713/4, 12Mar44. *Ibid.*, p. 5.

[4] Kenney, *Reports*.

[5] *Ibid.*, p. 377.

and seize a foothold on Mindanao. American forces in the Central Pacific were to advance towards Japan by way of the Marianas and westward towards the Philippines by way of the Palaus.[6]

While MacArthur's and Nimitz' forces were drafting plans to implement the 12 March directive, the Joint Chiefs conducted a complete reappraisal of the situation in the Pacific and concluded that operations there could be further accelerated. As a result of these deliberations, the Joint Chiefs sent American commanders in the Pacific three alternate proposals for consideration and comment. One of these was revolutionary in that it suggested bypassing the Philippines in favor of Formosa. The other two dealt with advancing target dates and bypassing presently selected objectives. Neither MacArthur nor Nimitz favored the new proposals, and both commanders insisted that the operations as proposed by MacArthur in RENO V were sound.[7] Nimitz considered it important to take reasonable shortcuts and exploit favorable situations as they arose. He felt that complete control over sea and air was absolutely essential in major assault operations. Naval superiority was assured, but an invasion of Formosa could succeed only if Japanese airfields on Luzon were first neutralized by land-based aircraft. CinCPac felt that aircraft carriers should not be used to support prolonged operations ashore but should be utilized to carry out strategic missions.[8]

General MacArthur strongly opposed any direct operations against Japan unless air bases were first secured on Luzon. Admiral King, on the other hand, insisted that Formosa should be seized before the Japanese had a chance to reinforce it. In the end General MacArthur won his point, but not until the President had intervened. A new operations schedule called for Southwest Pacific forces to occupy Morotai on 15 September, followed by the invasion of Mindanao on 20 December. Once these two objectives had been secured, the forces of the Southwest Pacific and Central Pacific commands would jointly assault either Luzon or Formosa and Amoy off the China coast.

On 15 June 1944 General MacArthur, as Supreme Commander, Southwest Pacific Area, reassumed control of the area west of 159 degrees East Longitude and south of the Equator. This reacquisition included most of the Solomon Islands west of Guadalcanal. Admiral Halsey relinquished the title of Commander, South Pacific (ComSoPac) to Vice Admiral John H. Newton and returned to sea as Commander, Third Fleet. Due to this change in boundaries, MacArthur regained not only the area he had previously controlled but all units located there.

---

[6] For a detailed account of the roles of Admirals Nimitz and Halsey and Generals MacArthur and Sutherland in altering these plans, see Morison, *Leyte*, pp. 13–15.

[7] The RENO plans provided for the approach to and recapture of the Philippines. They had originated within General MacArthur's SWPA headquarters.

[8] USSBS, Military Analysis Division, *Employment of Forces Under the Southwest Pacific Command* (Washington: U. S. Government Printing Office, 1946), p. 36.

TARGET: PHILIPPINES[9]

The Philippines consist of more than 7,000 islands of varying size with a land area of roughly 115,000 square miles. Located only 500 miles off the mainland of Asia, the Philippines occupy a strategic position in the Pacific in relation to southeast Asia, China, and Japan. The islands extend from the vicinity of Formosa in the north to Borneo and Celebes in the south, a distance of 1,150 miles. Astride the trade routes from Japan and China to southeast Asia and the former East Indies, now known as Indonesia, the islands are centrally located within 700 miles of Formosa and Hong Kong and 1,500 miles from Singapore; only 1,800 miles separate Tokyo from Manila, the capital of the Philippines.

Among the islands within the archipelago, Luzon ranks foremost in size and population. Next in size is Mindanao, followed by a large group of islands in the center of the archipelago commonly known as the Visayas, consisting of Samar, Panay, Cebu, Leyte, Negros, and a number of unnamed smaller islands. (See Map 16).

A tropical climate prevails throughout the Philippines, with alternating wet and dry seasons, though these are not so pronounced on Mindanao and southern Luzon as in other areas of the archipelago. Monsoon winds hit the islands from the southwest between June and September; northeasterly winds prevail from October through April. Mountains with elevations up to 10,000 feet are common in the Philippines; these ranges are often surrounded by narrow coastal plains culminating in sand beaches at the shoreline.

In 1941 the population of the Philippines numbered 17,000,000. Manila had 684,000 inhabitants and was the largest city in the archipelago. The people of the Philippines are predominantly of Malayan origin, though about 30,000 Japanese and 117,000 Chinese also resided in the islands. A peculiar language problem exists throughout the archipelago in that no less than 65 dialects are spoken there, and even though certain similarities exist, natives from different parts of the Philippines frequently find it difficult to communicate with each other.

Spain had gained a foothold on the islands in 1565, when Spaniards established their first permanent settlement in the Philippines on Cebu. Spanish possession of the archipelago continued until 1898, when the United States wrested the islands from Spain. As a result of lengthy foreign domination, a curious mixture of Oriental and Occidental cultures blended, resulting in the adoption of Islamic religion and Moslem customs in the south; Christianity and European culture were predominant in the remainder of the islands. When the United States gained possession of the Philippines, a small percentage of the population spoke Spanish. By the outbreak of World War II, it was

---

[9] Unless otherwise noted, the material in this section is derived from: Louis Morton, *The Fall of the Philippines—The War in the Pacific—U. S. Army in World War II* (Washington: OCMH, DA, 1953), hereafter Morton, *Fall of the Philippines;* LtCol Frank O. Hough, Maj Verle E. Ludwig, and Henry I. Shaw, Jr., *Pearl Harbor to Guadalcanal—History of U. S. Marine Corps Operations in World War II,* v. I (Washington: HistBr, G–3 Div, HQMC, 1958), hereafter Hough, Ludwig, and Shaw, *Pearl Harbor to Guadalcanal.*

BACKGROUND AND PLANNING

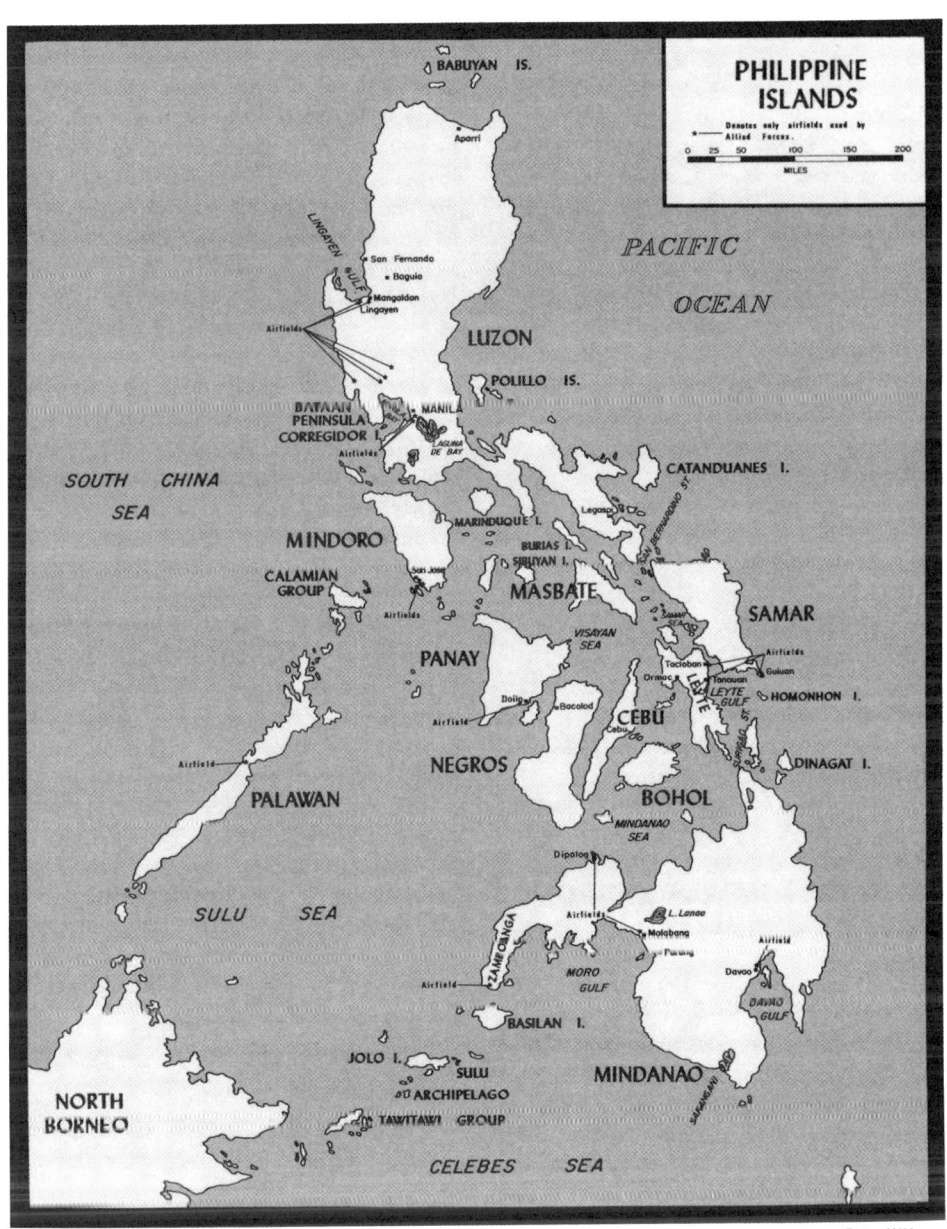

Map 16

estimated that about one quarter of the population spoke English.

The Philippines were predominantly devoted to agriculture; principal crops were rice, sugar, corn, hemp, and tobacco. Mining for gold, silver, and other metals was carried on in mountain areas but never achieved major importance before the outbreak of the war.

The dispersal of the islands over a large area and the resulting decentralization reduced the need for roads and railroads; inter-island commerce depended primarily on coastal shipping. The only exception to the sparse rail and road net was Luzon, where routes of communication were somewhat more adequate to support military operations. Prior to World War II there were only 50,000 motor vehicles in the Philippines. Principal towns and cities in the archipelago are linked by telephone, telegraph, and radio. Transcontinental telephone and telegraph lines radiate from Manila to provide communications with the remainder of the globe.

Manila owed its importance as capital of the Philippines to its proximity to Manila Bay, one of the best natural harbors in the Far East. Several small islands at the approach to the bay split it into two channels. The largest and most strategically located island is Corregidor, whose defense in World War II was to become a classic of heroic efforts.

Following the acquisition of the Philippines and the pacification of the islands, the United States maintained a permanent garrison in the archipelago. This force numbered about 10,000 men in the mid-thirties, when a Commonwealth Government was established. Up to this time the defense of the Philippines had been a purely American responsibility. Even though the 10,000-man force was a U.S. Army unit, half of the garrison consisted of Filipinos. Except for this force and a Philippine Constabulary organized at the turn of the century, the Filipinos did not have any military tradition that could serve as a basis for a national army.

During the summer of 1935, General Douglas MacArthur, then Chief of Staff of the U.S. Army, became military advisor to the new Philippine government at the request of the first President of the Philippines, Manuel L. Quezon. General MacArthur's mission was to establish a national army to consist of 10,000 regulars and a reserve of 400,000. Since these figures were to be reached in 1946, at the time that the Philippines were to gain independence, progress in setting up the Army was slow. When war suddenly came to the archipelago, the combined American and Filipino forces were unable to stem the determined Japanese onslaught; the fall of the islands became inevitable despite the solidarity and heroism of Americans and Filipinos fighting side by side. As the fortunes of war changed and Japanese power in the Pacific receded, the Philippines once again figured prominently as another milestone on the long, hard road to Tokyo in Allied planning for the conquest of Japan.

ENEMY SITUATION, DISPOSITION, AND PLANS[10]

By the end of June 1944, the Japanese military situation had greatly deterio-

---

[10] Unless otherwise noted, the material in this section is derived from: USSBS, *Pacific Campaigns;* Military History Section, FEC, Japanese Monograph No. 50, Central Pacific Air Operations Record, 1953, (OCMH), here-

rated. Serious Allied interference with Japanese sea commerce, and piercing of the outer circle of the defenses ringing Japan had underscored the seriousness of the situation. Far from slackening, Allied operations in the Pacific were still gaining momentum, and Japan was faced with the threat of becoming separated from those islands in the South and Southwestern Pacific that constituted a major source of oil. According to Admiral Soemu Toyoda, Commander in Chief of the Japanese *Combined Fleet*.

> ... the biggest cause of fall in production, especially in aircraft and air materiel, was the effect of your bombing on the plants—factories—in Japan proper; but as regards the effects on our war strength on the whole, I think the greatest effect was felt after all by the lack of ships and consequent inability to bring material from the south.[11]

United States control of the Central Pacific forced the Japanese to establish a line of defense extending from Japan proper through the Ryukyu Islands, Formosa, the Philippines, and finally to Timor, Java, and Sumatra. Since the Japanese expected the decisive battles of the war to be fought near the Japanese homeland, *Imperial Japanese Headquarters* initiated four contingency plans in anticipation of decisive operations. These plans, designated *Sho* or *Sho-Go* Operations,[12] visualized four possible Allied operations during the summer and autumn of 1944. *Sho*-1 envisioned a decisive battle in the Philippine Islands by the end of August; *Sho*-2, a decisive campaign in the Formosa area and Ryukyus at about the same time; *Sho*-3 and 4, decisive battles in various parts of Japan proper by late October.

Since *Sho*-1 and -2 were considered the most imminent, the Japanese gave full priority to strengthening their defenses in these areas. The Army and Navy agreed that an all-out land defense in the Philippines would be made only if Luzon was invaded. In the event of an American invasion of the Central or Southern Philippines, only air and naval forces would seek decisive action.

The defense of the Philippines from American attack received priority in the minds of the Japanese high command. Reinforcements were dispatched to the northern part of the archipelago by the Japanese Army, which harbored a distrust of the capabilities of the Navy in stemming the American tide of victory. Once the Americans had committed themselves to a specific objective in the Philippines, a mobile counterlanding force was to throw back or at least delay the invader.

By summer of 1944, the Japanese Fleet was hopelessly outnumbered and outclassed, yet ready to fight wherever American forces were landing. The Japanese were fully aware that land-based forces in the Philippines did not stand a chance at success unless they were backed up by the *Combined Fleet*. For

---

after *Japanese CenPac Air Ops Rec;* James A. Field, Jr., *The Japanese at Leyte Gulf* (Princeton and London: Princeton University Press, 1947), hereafter Field, *Japanese at Leyte.*

[11] USSBS, NavAnalysisDiv, *Interrogation of Japanese Officials,* 2 vols. (Washington: GPO 1946), Interrogation No. 378, Adm Soemu Toyoda, IJN, II, p. 313, hereafter *Toyoda Interrogation.*

[12] The Japanese word "*Sho-Go*" stands for "Conquest" or "Victory Operation."

this reason, there was no choice but to gamble the entire fleet. In the words of Admiral Toyoda:

> If things went well we might obtain unexpectedly good results; but if the worst should happen, there was a chance that we would lose the entire fleet; but I felt that that chance had to be taken.... There would be no sense in saving the fleet at the expense of the loss of the Philippines.[13]

During the late summer of 1944, the *Fourteenth Japanese Area Army* under the command of Lieutenant General Shigenori Kuroda was charged with the ground defense of the Philippines. This army consisted of about 260,000 men stationed throughout the archipelago. (See Chart 2). Under the overall command of the *Fourteenth Area Army*, the *Thirty-Fifth Army* was to defend the Visayas and Mindanao. The Japanese *Combined Fleet*, under Admiral Toyoda, consisted of a *Striking Force*, the *First Mobile Fleet*, as well as the *Second, Third, Fifth*, and *Sixth Fleets*. Japanese air defense of the Philippines was furnished by the *First Air Fleet* of the Imperial Navy and the *Fourth Air Army*. Subsequently, the *Second Air Fleet* was moved from Formosa to the Philippines and joined with the *First Air Fleet* and the *Fourth Air Army* to form the *First Combined Air Force* under Vice Admiral Shigeru Fukudome. At that time Japanese air strength in the Philippines consisted of 400 aircraft, two-thirds of which were operational.[14]

The plan evolved by *Imperial General Headquarters* for the defense of the Philippines called for the commitment of 10 divisions and 5 brigades. The main force, consisting of 5 divisions and 2 brigades, was to be stationed on Luzon. Four divisions and two brigades were to defend the southern Philippines. One division and one brigade stood by in China and Formosa, ready for immediate movement to the Philippines once an American landing became imminent.

In the end, lack of cooperation between the Japanese armed services resulted in a compromise, which really failed to please any of the Japanese commanders involved.[15] The *Fourth Air Army*, in loose cooperation with the Army and Navy, planned to annihilate the Americans when the invasion force hit the Philippines. Army and Navy aviation units were to destroy American landing fields and carrier-based

---

[13] *Ibid.*, pp. 280-281.
[14] Craven and Cate, *The Pacific*, p. 346.

[15] "Small manpower and large area to defend, that is how we planned to wage the fight on Luzon Island alone, but if we gave the American Air Force a chance to gain a foothold on islands other than Luzon, these would seriously interfere with Japanese operations on land, sea, and air. So the Japanese decided to fight for any part of the Philippines. If Americans landed in Central or Southern Philippines or North, then the Japanese air and sea forces would have to bear the brunt of battle in an entirely different kind of fighting from ground operations on Luzon. This is something that the armed forces could not understand, that they had to have coordination. About air defense, Navy aviation wanted to fight American carriers and part of the Army air power would be used for this purpose. Army aviation was to concentrate on convoys and when Americans had landed and constructed air bases on land, then the Japanese were to attack there." Official Japanese comment, War History Office, Defense Agency of Japan, Mr. Susumu Nishiura ltr to Head, HistBr, G-3Div, HQMC dtd 16Dec66, in *Philippines Comment File*.

BACKGROUND AND PLANNING

JAPANESE COMMAND ORGANIZATION
DEFENSE OF THE PHILIPPINES AS OF 1 OCTOBER 1944

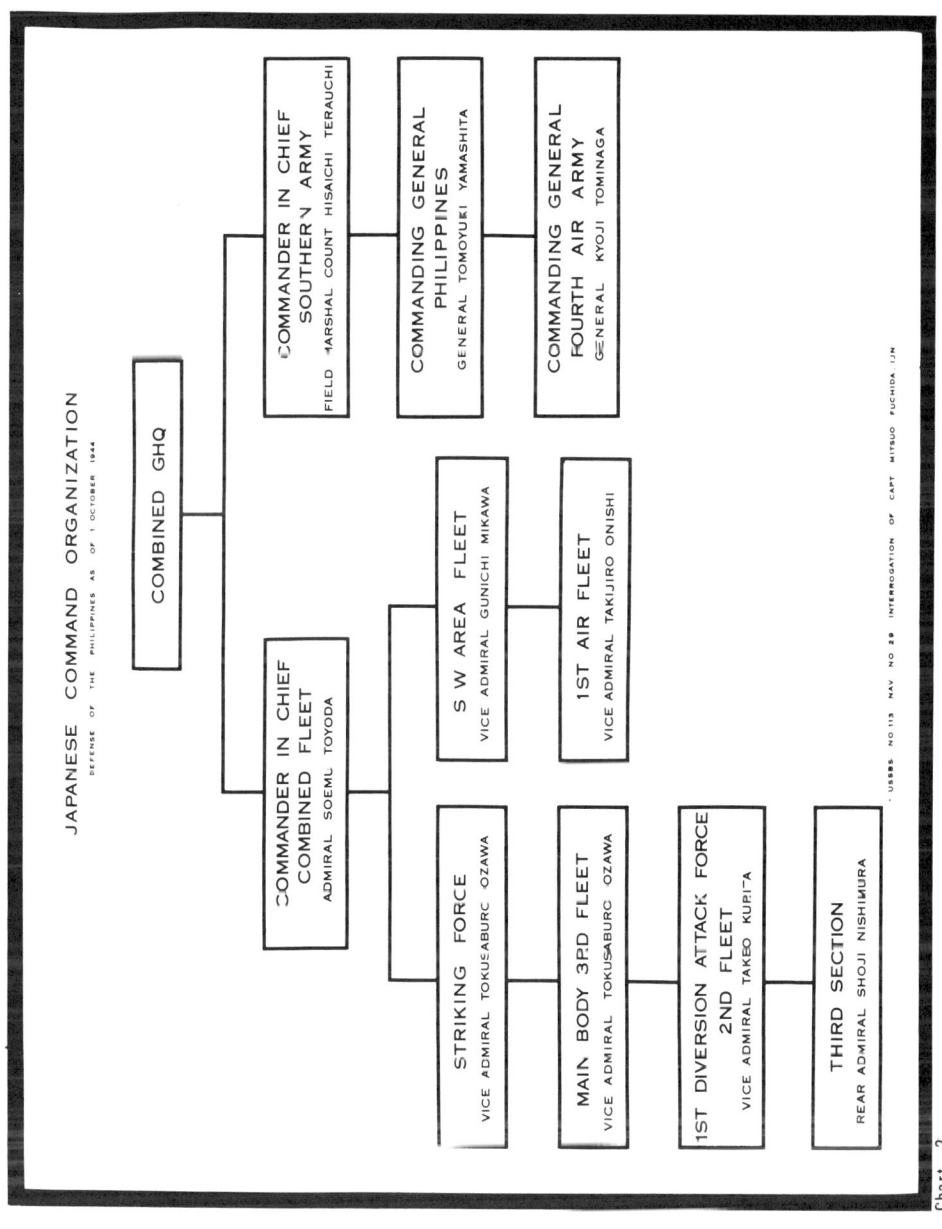

COMBINED GHQ

- **COMMANDER IN CHIEF SOUTHERN ARMY** — FIELD MARSHAL COUNT HISAICHI TERAUCHI
  - **COMMANDING GENERAL PHILIPPINES** — GENERAL TOMOYUKI YAMASHITA
  - **COMMANDING GENERAL FOURTH AIR ARMY** — GENERAL KYOJI TOMINAGA

- **COMMANDER IN CHIEF COMBINED FLEET** — ADMIRAL SOEMU TOYODA
  - **SW AREA FLEET** — VICE ADMIRAL GUNICHI MIKAWA
  - **1ST AIR FLEET** — VICE ADMIRAL TAKIJIRO ONISHI
  - **STRIKING FORCE** — VICE ADMIRAL TOKUSABURO OZAWA
  - **MAIN BODY 3RD FLEET** — VICE ADMIRAL TOKUSABURO OZAWA
  - **1ST DIVERSION ATTACK FORCE 2ND FLEET** — VICE ADMIRAL TAKEO KURITA
  - **THIRD SECTION** — REAR ADMIRAL SHOJI NISHIMURA

USSBS NO 113 NAV NO 29 INTERROGATION OF CAPT MITSUO FUCHIDA IJN

Chart 2

aircraft. Fighter units, based in the central and southern Philippines, were to be committed against the American main force. Japanese heavy bombers were to attack the American convoys; the fighters could be alternately employed against American aircraft or shipping.

A study of batttle lessons learned in previous campaigns had led the Japanese planners to conclude that a fight for annihilation at the beachhead did not hold much promise, and for this reason a resistance in depth similar to the one on Peleliu was projected. On 9 October, General Tomoyuki Yamashita assumed command over the *Fourteenth Area Army,* in place of General Kuroda, who was not deemed sufficiently aggressive to cope with the defense of the Philippines.

In preparation for the American invasion of the Philippines, the Japanese Navy planned to concentrate its strength for a decisive action in defense of Japan proper and of the chain of islands linking Japan with the southern islands. Once the Americans struck at any of these vital areas, the Japanese Navy was to fight a decisive battle with all the strength it could muster. The overall mission was to intercept and destroy the Americans within the operational sphere of Japanese land-based aircraft.

Even before the American invasion of the Philippines got under way, however, the Japanese suffered heavy losses in Army aircraft, carriers, and carrier-based planes. As a result, land-based Japanese aircraft would have to bear the brunt of the American attack. The timing of the American invasion of the Philippines also was a factor that caused concern to the Japanese. Admiral Toyoda expressed his sentiments in the following words:

> I expected your offensive against the Philippines would commence around August or September; that is not to say that we were prepared at the time to meet that offensive, for the reason that our forces, both Army and Navy, had lost practically all their supporting aircraft at the various operations and it took anywhere from four to five months to replenish the lost aircraft.[16]

When the Allied invasion came on 20 October 1944, uncertainty paralyzed the enemy and prevented him from taking immediate counteraction at the time when troops were en route to the shore and American shipping was extremely vulnerable to air attack. Admiral Toyoda delayed alerting his forces until American warships were actually observed entering Leyte Gulf. Several days were to pass before the Japanese Navy could pit its still formidable might against the U.S. Third and Seventh Fleets.

PLANNING TO RETURN[17]

The only Marines to participate in ground action in the Philippines were approximately 1,500 Marine artillerymen under the command of Brigadier General Thomas E. Bourke. The attachment of this Marine force, which consisted of the corps artillery of the V Amphibious Corps (hereafter VAC) to the Army XXIV Corps had a strange

---
[16] *Toyoda Interrogation,* p. 316.
[17] Unless otherwise noted, the material in this section is derived from: Sherrod, *Marine Corps Aviation in World War II;* Halsey and Bryan, *Admiral Halsey's Story.*

background. During the campaign in the Marianas (Operation FORAGER), most of the corps artillery of XXIV Corps had been detached to VAC.

In view of the circumstance, CinCPOA decided to attach elements of VAC artillery to the XXIV Corps for the Yap operation. Initially, Headquarters Battery, VAC artillery, three 155-mm gun battalions, two 155mm howitzer battalions, and one Army field artillery observation battalion were to support the assault on Yap. The three gun battalions were to include one Army and two Marine battalions; the two 155mm howitzer battalions were to consist of one Marine and one Army battalion each. Subsequently, because of a shortage of shipping, one Marine gun battalion was deleted.

While planning for the Yap operation was still in progress, the VAC units slated for attachment to the XXIV Corps were stationed in Hawaii, as was Headquarters, XXIV Corps. When the invasion of Yap was cancelled and planning for the recapture of Leyte got underway, the VAC artillerymen, still under the command of General Bourke, remained attached to the XXIV Corps.

The revamping of the command structure in the Southwest Pacific did not fail to leave an imprint on the organization of aviation units in the theater. Under the overall control of SWPA, Lieutenant General George C. Kenney had been commanding Allied Air Forces and the U.S. Fifth Air Force. Transfer of the U.S. Fifth and Thirteenth Air Forces, the 1st Marine Aircraft Wing, and other Allied aviation units to SWPA made a revision of the air command structure necessary. General Kenney exercised a dual command over Allied Air Forces and the next lower echelon, the Far East Air Forces. (See Chart 3). The latter command consisted of the Fifth and Thirteenth Air Forces; units of the Royal Australian and the Royal New Zealand Air Forces, Aircraft Seventh Fleet (U. S. Navy), and Aircraft Northern Solomons with the 1st Marine Aircraft Wing came under Allied Air Forces.

Under the peculiarities of the command structure in the Pacific, it was more commonly the rule rather than the exception for a commander to exercise a dual function. Aircraft Northern Solomons (AirNorSols) was no exception. The headquarters, first established by Admiral Halsey in his capacity as ComSoPac, was a composite of Marine, Navy, New Zealand, Australian, and U.S. Army Air Forces units then based in the Solomons. Major General Ralph J. Mitchell, USMC, commanded AirNorSols and the 1st Marine Aircraft Wing (1st MAW) simultaneously from his headquarters at Torokina, Bougainville Island. In addition to Marine aviation units, all remaining Allied aviation in the Solomons came under General Mitchell's command. Many of Mitchell's aviators were experienced and battle-hardened; others were new arrivals from the States getting their first taste of combat.

As early as May 1944, General Mitchell had made the rounds of various headquarters in Brisbane, Australia, in order to sell an idea. In addition to approaching General MacArthur, General Mitchell also conferred with the Commander of the Seventh Fleet, Vice Ad-

ORGANIZATION OF AIR COMMAND SWPA
15 JUNE 1944

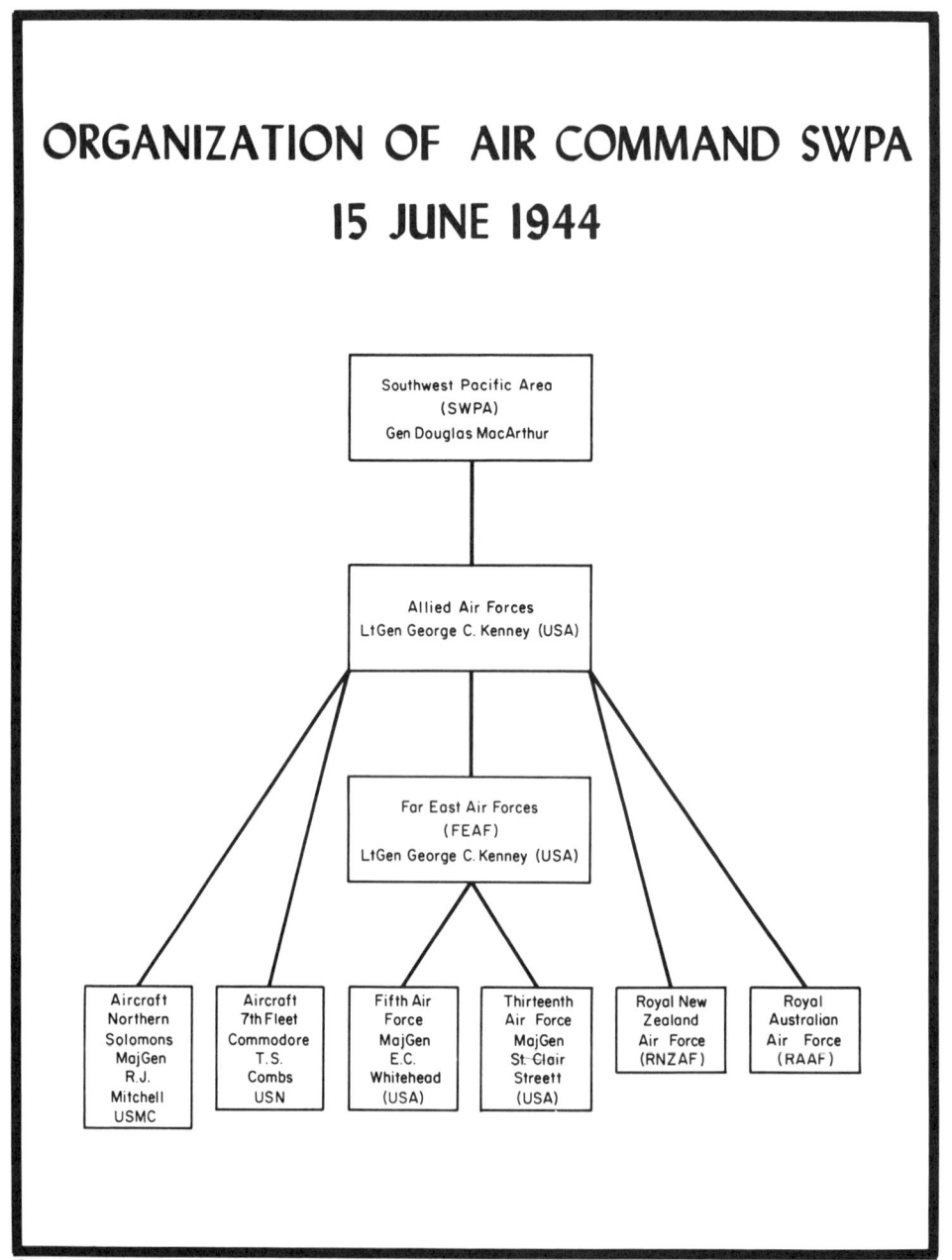

```
                    Southwest Pacific Area
                           (SWPA)
                    Gen Douglas MacArthur
                            |
                            |
                    Allied Air Forces
                LtGen George C. Kenney (USA)
                            |
           ┌────────┬───────┼───────┬────────┬────────┐
           │        │       │       │        │        │
                        Far East Air Forces
                            (FEAF)
                  LtGen George C. Kenney (USA)
```

| Aircraft Northern Solomons MajGen R.J. Mitchell USMC | Aircraft 7th Fleet Commodore T.S. Combs USN | Fifth Air Force MajGen E.C. Whitehead (USA) | Thirteenth Air Force MajGen St. Clair Streett (USA) | Royal New Zealand Air Force (RNZAF) | Royal Australian Air Force (RAAF) |

CHART 3   K.W. WHITE

miral Thomas C. Kinkaid, and General Kenney. The Marine general was attempting to draw the attention of SWPA Headquarters to the fact that under his command, a large number of well-trained and experienced aviation units were not being utilized to best advantage, even though they were eager to participate in operations farther west.[18] Japanese air power in the Northern Solomons and on New Britain was no longer in evidence and many of the aviators felt that they were beating a dead horse.

Initially, these entreaties appeared to fall on deaf ears. A ray of hope for the restive Marine aviators appeared briefly and flickered out when General Kenney directed AirNorSols to support the planned U.S. Army XIV Corps drive from the Solomons to New Ireland, then called off the move because shipping and forward airfields were not available. The Marine aviators pounded Rabaul and Kavieng without much enthusiasm, still trying to find ways and means to get some real action.

Just when it appeared that the eager Marine aviators would be forced to sit out the remainder of the war as actors in a sideshow, fate intervened and a radical change in the situation occurred. On 12 September Admiral Halsey's Third Fleet struck the Central Philippines. In three days of almost continuous air attacks, averaging 1,200 sorties per day, pilots of the Third Fleet downed 173 enemy aircraft, destroyed an additional 305 on the ground, sank 59 ships, probably sank another 58, and inflicted heavy damage on installations, at the cost of 9 aircraft. The implications of this victory were at once apparent to Admiral Halsey, who felt that:

> ... we had found the central Philippines a hollow shell with weak defenses and skimpy facilities. In my opinion, this was the vulnerable belly of the imperial dragon. The time might be ripe not only to strike Manila, but perhaps to mount a far larger offensive. Specifically, I began to wonder whether I dared recommend that MacArthur shift to Leyte the invasion which he had planned for Mindanao, and advance the date well ahead of the scheduled November 15.[19]

Admiral Halsey made his recommendation, and on 15 September the Joint Chiefs of Staff decided to bypass Mindanao in favor of Leyte. Five days later, Far East Air Forces announced that seven dive bomber squadrons of the 1st Marine Aircraft Wing would be committed against Luzon. On 10 October, Brigadier General Claude A. Larkin, Deputy Commander of the 1st MAW, summoned Colonel Lyle H. Meyer, commanding officer of MAG-24, and informed him that the group was to get ready to provide air support to Army ground forces in the Philippines. Later information revealed that the remaining three dive bombing squadrons of the wing would become attached to another headquarters, but accompany MAG-24. MAG-32 was sent from Pearl Harbor, and Colonel Clayton C. Jerome, Chief of Staff to the Commander, AirNorSols, took command.

It appeared that Marine aviators were finally back in a shooting war again. The major impact of the new

---

[18] MajGen Ralph J. Mitchell memo to MajGen Field Harris, dtd 26Mar46.

[19] Halsey and Bryan, *Admiral Halsey's Story*, p. 199.

mission fell on MAG-24, whose operations officer, Lieutenant Colonel Keith B. McCutcheon, had to come to grips with planning for effective support of ground troops. The job promised to be far from easy. As Lieutenant Colonel McCutcheon himself expressed it:

> When Marine Air Group 24 was informed early in October 1944, that it would give close support to an Army Corps in the Philippines, it was completely unprepared to fulfill its mission. Efforts were made immediately to assemble all the available literature on the subject but it became clearly apparent that the existing instructions were published piecemeal in many forms and much of the data was contradictory. . . .[20]

In developing a new concept of close air support, Lieutenant Colonel McCutcheon was able to utilize the tools that had been previously tested by others. For instance, the radio gear that was to play such a significant role in the maintenance of ground-air communications had been obtained early in 1942 by Major Peter P. Schrider who at the time served as Air Officer for the Amphibious Training Command at Quantico under General Holland Smith. With the assistance of other aviators, communication experts, and supply personnel, Schrider, anticipating a future need for a forward air controller, experimented with portable and jeep-mounted radio equipment for direct contact with supporting air. These tests, which were conducted in the Chesapeake Bay area, included the employment of front line marking panels.

Subsequently, the experiences gained were used with success in the training of Army battalions in amphibious operations.[21]

In his efforts to set forth his doctrine of close air support, Lieutenant Colonel McCutcheon had the full support of Colonel Jerome, Commanding Officer of MAG-32. The latter, in the words of one of his contemporaries, represented

> . . . the firm guiding hand behind all this endeavor. It was Colonel Jerome who set the general policy for implementation of close air support and who, through imagination, persuasion, salesmanship, and sheer force of personality brought his various commands so satisfactorily into the overall combat picture. . . .[22]

The time for the formulation of a clearcut doctrine for close air support had arrived; once such a procedure had been devised, it would remain for Marine aviators to test it in the crucible of combat.

TRAINING FOR CLOSE AIR SUPPORT[23]

The changed combat mission of the 1st Marine Aircraft Wing immediately raised a number of questions in the minds of responsible Marine planners. Foremost among these was the question of the techniques that should be

---

[20] LtCol Keith B. McCutcheon, "Close Support Aviation," in Marine Aviation in Close Air Support File, HQMC-DivAvn, Aug-Nov 45, hereafter *McCutcheon Rpt*.

[21] Col Zebulon C. Hopkins ltr to Head, Hist Br, G-3 Div, HQMC, dtd 2Nov66, in *Philippines Comment File*.

[22] LtGen Vernon J. McCaul ltr to Head, Hist Br, G-3 Div, HQMC, dtd 5Nov66, in *Philippines Comment File*.

[23] Unless otherwise noted, the material in this section is derived from: 1st MAW Hist and WarD, Jul-Dec44; Records of Committee on History and Doctrine of Close Air Support, DivAvn, HQMC, 8Nov45, hereafter *CAS Recs*.

employed to give the most effective support to the infantry while still keeping within the generally accepted bounds of caution to avoid endangering the lives of friendly forces.

Though generally favored as a necessity, close air support had previously been employed on the basis of spur of the moment decisions, and with varying degrees of success. On Guadalcanal, Marine and Army pilots had given an excellent account of themselves in providing effective close support—so close, in fact that prior to taking off on a mission they could frequently get a look at the target from the ground. But long before World War II, back in 1927, Marine aviators had taken credit for the first organized dive bombing attack and possibly the first low-altitude attack ever launched in support of ground troops. On that occasion, Marine aviators in Nicaragua had first dived out of column from 1,500 feet and pulled out at about 600 feet. In subsequent dives the Marines started their run at 1,000 feet and pulled out at 300.[24]

During the New Georgia campaign, close air support for ground troops suffered from a lack of air-ground coordination. The simple truth was that the friendly ground troops were afraid of the bombers. At the time, close air support meant bombing and strafing about 1,000 yards in front of friendly lines, but under conditions of jungle warfare the front lines were frequently only a few yards apart. The difficulties encountered by Marine aviators attempting to provide close support on New Georgia have been described as follows:

The use of aircraft in close support of ground troops proved to be impractical. The dense jungle encountered made the location of enemy positions suitable for air attack impossible until friendly troops were too close to the prospective target for safety. As 200 to 300 yards was a good day's advance, it was not practical to withdraw sufficiently to use air attacks. . . . Frequently troops could not locate their own position on the map, much less the position of the enemy.[25]

During the Bougainville campaign in 1943, close air support was still regarded with more than casual suspicion, once again for the reason that ground troops had occasionally been bombed by the planes they had requested. On 13 December 1943, in an attempt to dislodge the enemy from "Hellzapoppin' Ridge," one of the attacking aircraft missed the target and instead hit friendly troops 600 yards away, killing two men and wounding six. Despite this mishap, close air support was redeemed when Marine aviators, attacking with delayed-fuze bombs, greatly aided the ground troops in seizing the obstinately defended ridge. Marines who fought at Bougainville had this to say about the air support they had received:

It was the air attacks which proved to be the most effective factor in the taking of the ridge. Lieutenant Colonel Butler, Executive Officer of the 21st Marines, was ordered to plot and direct the strikes. He flew with the flight leader to spot the enemy positions, with which he was now thoroughly familiar.

The two final strikes proved to be the most successful examples of close air support thus far in the Pacific war. The

---

[24] Sherrod, *Marine Corps Aviation in World War II*, p. 25.

[25] Headquarters New Georgia Air Force (Forward Echelon, MAW-2) SAR, 29Jun–13Aug43, as cited in Sherrod, *Marine Corps Aviation in World War II*, p. 151.

planes, flying at times only fifty feet above the ground, bombed and strafed the enemy as close as 75 yards from the Marines' positions. The Japanese, who held out so desperately against infantry and artillery attack, were almost completely destroyed. Following the second air strike the 1st Battalion, Twenty-First Marines smashed through the last resistance with bayonet and grenade on the afternoon of December 18.[26]

The above action marked the first time that Marine aviators received credit for a support mission that was beyond the capabilities of the artillery. After Bougainville, there was an extended lull as far as Marine air support for Marine ground forces was concerned. Peleliu offered a welcome opportunity to further improve ground-air coordination, though conditions on that island severely limited the effectiveness of air support; the Ngesebus operation offered an even more graphic illustration of what close support during a shore-to-shore landing could accomplish.

The Navy had partially solved the problem of controlling support aircraft through shipborne radio systems, which greatly reduced the time required to coach aircraft to their targets. Since this method was geared to carrier-based air support, the Marine divisions employed air liaison parties to transmit requests for aerial support and to direct air strikes. The Marine concept of close air support differed from that of the Army or the Navy in that it was felt that members of the air liaison parties, stationed in the front lines, should maintain direct communications with the attacking aircraft instead of having the information channelled through intervening echelons.

Under the supervision of Lieutenant Colonel McCutcheon, operations officer of MAG-24, a detailed doctrine for air support organization was drawn up. Aside from special equipment and conditions that could be expected in the Philippines, the doctrine was based on the premise that close air support is an additional weapon to be employed at the discretion of the ground commander. He may employ it against targets that cannot be reached by other weapons or in conjunction with the ground weapons in a coordinated attack. It should be immediately available and should be carried out with deliberation and accuracy and in coordination with other assigned units.[27]

In addition to outlining the requirements for communications equipment, the establishment of radio nets, and the implementation of procedures that would ensure accurate and efficient air support when and where needed, the doctrine put forth the following points:

> 1. Air support does not supplant any of the other existing weapons and it cannot be considered a general competitor of either field or naval artillery.
>
> 2. Aircraft provide a mobile platform for transporting projectiles to the enemy, but if the same target is within artillery range, the latter can deliver a heavier and more accurate volume of fire per unit of time than aircraft.

---

[26] Robert A. Aurthur and Kenneth Cohlmia, *The Third Marine Division* (Washington: Infantry Journal Press, 1948), p. 78.

[27] LtCol Keith B. McCutcheon, "Close Air Support SOP," *Marine Corps Gazette*, v. 29, no. 8 (Aug45), pp. 48-50.

3. When the infantry commander is bogged down and he makes an estimate of the situation, he must weigh clearly the advisability of using aircraft in preference to artillery. Unless the attack is coordinated closely, the planes will not do enough damage to warrant the cessation of fire by the artillery for the necessary length of time.[28]

Once the doctrine of close air support had been formulated, it remained for MAG-24 to implement it by training personnel for the impending mission. Beginning on 13 October, only three days after Colonel Meyer had received word of the new mission of MAG-24, its pilots, crews, communications personnel, air combat intelligence officers, and operations officers on Bougainville were subjected to an intensive ground school course. This course, which lasted until 8 December, covered all phases of close air support ranging from organization and tactics of U.S. and Japanese infantry units to map reading, communications, artillery spotting, and target identification. Similarly, personnel were also familiarized with the geography and history of the Philippines, as well as the peculiarities of the Philippine climate.

Lieutenant Colonel McCutcheon, who supervised the training, handpicked his instructors and finally emerged with a cadre of wing and group intelligence officers, and specialists from the Seventh Fleet intelligence section and the staff of two Army divisions stationed on Bougainville at the time. One of the Army units, the 37th Infantry Division, scheduled joint training problems with the Marine aviators. All pilots were able to observe a ground exercise conducted by an infantry battalion simulating an attack on a Japanese pillbox installation. To these exercises, MAG-24 added planes in close support with their own air liaison parties on the ground. No live bombs were dropped during the training exercises, but the infantry actually fired all of its weapons. Altogether, about 500 Marine pilots and gunners attended the course; a final examination and critique determined the effectiveness of the training.

Concurrently with the training program, a series of conferences were scheduled with representatives of the Fifth Air Force to coordinate planning for the Philippine operation. In the course of these conferences it was brought out that the Fifth Air Force would furnish the support air parties, but Fifth Air Force did not contemplate using direct communication between the air liaison parties and the aircraft engaged in a close air support mission. The Navy concurred with the Army Air Forces in this matter. As far as Lieutenant Colonel McCutcheon was concerned, the only logical way to conduct close support was to train and utilize Marine air liaison parties, which actually constituted a combination of the air liaison party and the support air party.

The Army Air Forces agreed with a statement expressed by the British Field Marshal Sir Bernard L. Montgomery:

> . . . that though a tactical air force must be integrated with the ground force,

---

[28] *Ibid.*

it must not be tied in piecemeal lots to ground units. Its function was massed, theatre wide blows and deep penetrations to fill the gap between tactical and strategic operations.[29]

According to the interpretation by MAG-24, Marshal Montgomery was correct, though close support aviation was not identical with tactical aviation and there was a decided difference in the employment of the two. MAG-24 had no intention of attaching units to divisions piecemeal; it did plan to maintain close control of its aircraft when engaged in close support. If Marine liaison parties were not to be permitted to maintain that control, then the group would send out its own personnel to exercise it in accordance with the SOP that had been very carefully developed for close support by Marine aviation.

MAG-24 planned to attach air liaison parties to infantry units down to the battalion level. Utilizing radio-equipped jeeps (AN-VRC-1), air liaison personnel functioned like forward observers. The ALP could keep pace with advancing command posts and still remain in constant communication with aircraft. The radio equipment could be used to operate on Very High Frequencies (VHF) with the SCR-542 for short-range communications or with the SCR-193 on the lower frequencies (HF) where longer distances had to be covered. If, for any reason, the air liaison officer had to leave his jeep, he could still use a portable transceiver[30] or field telephone, the latter to keep in touch with the jeep radio operator, who in turn relayed messages to the aircraft.

A guide for the successful employment of close air support had now been established. Out of a hazy idea had grown a plan, which evolved into a concept. At maturity it became a doctrine that Marines could translate into action. In the short time available, all possible training that would assist Marine aviation personnel in the air and on the ground to put the theory into practice, had been given. The stage was set for the ultimate test.

---

[29] Field Marshal Sir Bernard L. Montgomery in TIME Magazine, v. 44, no. 7, p. 28, 14Aug44, cited in *McCutcheon Rpt*, p. 9.

[30] A radio capable of transmitting and receiving, usually compact because part of the circuit is alternately used for either function. Each ALP was provided with a TBX portable HF radio set to meet the initial communication needs of the party.

CHAPTER 2

The Leyte Landings [1]

The seizure of Peleliu and Morotai provided Allied forces in the Pacific with important air bases and airfield sites. Above all, control of these islands protected General MacArthur's flanks during the impending invasion of the Philippines. The accelerated timetable for operations in the Pacific called for landings on Leyte on 20 October 1944. Under the overall command of General MacArthur, the Seventh Fleet, under Vice Admiral Thomas C. Kinkaid, was to transport and establish the ground assault force ashore. Lieutenant General Walter Krueger, Commanding General of the Sixth Army, was to command the ground forces. The Third Fleet, in conjunction with the Seventh Fleet, was to provide air support until Army Air Forces units could begin to initiate operations from airfields on Leyte.[2]

By far the most important mission assigned to Admiral Halsey's Third Fleet was the preinvasion neutralization of Japanese air power on Okinawa, Formosa, Northern Leyte, and the Visayan Islands in the Central Philippines. Admiral Kinkaid's Seventh Fleet was directly responsible for providing air cover for the invasion ships and for furnishing direct air support for the landings until land-based aircraft could assume those functions. The Fifth Air Force, based on New Guinea, was to destroy the enemy air forces in the Celebes Sea, neutralize Japanese air power in Mindanao, and give such protection to ships as it was able to provide. The Thirteenth Air Force, also stationed on New Guinea, and elements of the Royal Australian Air Force were slated to play a supporting role in neutralizing Japanese air along the east coast of Borneo and in assisting upon request the Fifth Air Force in the southern Philippines. Additional Army Air Forces units in China and the Central Pacific would furnish long-range support.

The island of Leyte, lying in the Visayas Group of the Central Philippines, is 115 miles in length and varies in width from 15 to 40 miles. The main mountain range runs the entire length of the island from north to south, leav-

---

[1] Unless otherwise noted, the material in this section is derived from: Seventh Flt Rpt of Op for the Capture of Leyte Island Incl AR of Engagements in Surigao Strait and off Samar Island on 25Oct44, hereafter *Com, Seventh Flt AR, Leyte*; 4th Marine Air Wing Operations Report, Leyte, dtd 11Nov44, hereafter *4th MAW OpRpt;* M. Hamlin Cannon, *Leyte: The Return to the Philippines—The War in the Pacific—U. S. Army in World War II* (Washington: OCMH, DA, 1953), hereafter *Cannon, Leyte;* Saburo Hayashi and Alvin D. Coox, *Kōgun—The Japanese Army in the Pacific War* (Quantico, Va.: Marine Corps Association, 1959), hereafter *Hayashi and Coox, Kōgun.*

[2] For a detailed account of command relations during this period, see Morison, *Leyte,* pp. 55–60.

309

ing a wide coastal plain along the east coast. At the outbreak of Word War II, the population of 916,000 lived chiefly in the coastal areas, where cultivation of available ground was intense. Crops consisted mainly of coconut, corn, hemp, and rice. The area in which the invasion force was to operate initially did not contain any heavy jungle and was reasonably clear of thick undergrowth. Some difficulty was expected from swamps and marshy ground, which bordered the intricate network of rivers flowing eastward from the mountains to the coast. All beaches in the invasion area were hard sand, with no reefs or obstacles offshore.

The Sixth Army troops for Operation KING II, code name for the invasion of Leyte, were composed of the X and XXIV Corps and the 6th Ranger Battalion. The X Corps included the 1st Cavalry Division and the 24th Infantry Division; the XXIV Corps consisted of the 7th and 96th Infantry Divisions. In reserve were the 32d and 77th Infantry Divisions at Hollandia and on Morotai and Guam Islands. The two divisions were prepared to embark for the objective area three days after the invasion date.

The Sixth Army had the mission of seizing and occupying Leyte, establishing control of western and southern Samar until the conquest of that island could be completed, and of destroying other hostile garrisons in the Visayas. The operation was to be carried out in three phases, beginning with capture of the entrance to Leyte Gulf. Large scale amphibious landings along the coast of eastern Leyte between Tacloban and Dulag were to usher in the second phase. Initial objective of the invasion force was the seizure of airfields and potential airfield sites in this area. The third and final phase of the operation envisioned the destruction of Japanese forces on Leyte and southern Samar. Within the scope of this overall plan, X Corps was to seize the area between Tacloban and Palo and launch a drive to the northern tip of the island. The XXIV Corps was to land near Dulag to the south of X Corps and advance westward across Leyte. A regimental combat team was to invade southern Leyte and secure Panaon Straits.

The first phase of the plan was readily accomplished on 17 and 18 October, when the islands barring access to Leyte Gulf were seized. There was no enemy resistance. Following a two-day naval bombardment, the main landings got under way on the east coast of Leyte between Dulag and Tacloban on 20 October. (See Map 17). The combined American beachhead was about 18 miles long. Except for Japanese mortar and artillery fire, enemy resistance at the beaches was light. X Corps seized the Tacloban airfield on A-Day and captured the town of Tacloban on the following day. From Tacloban, the corps advanced in a northerly and northwesterly direction. Elements of the XXIV Corps secured Dulag airfield on 21 October, then swerved westward and seized three airfields near Burauen. Troops of the XXIV Corps pivoted south along Leyte Gulf, seized Abuyog on 29 October, then swerved westward, and, cutting across the island, secured Baybay on the west coast of Leyte.

THE LEYTE LANDINGS

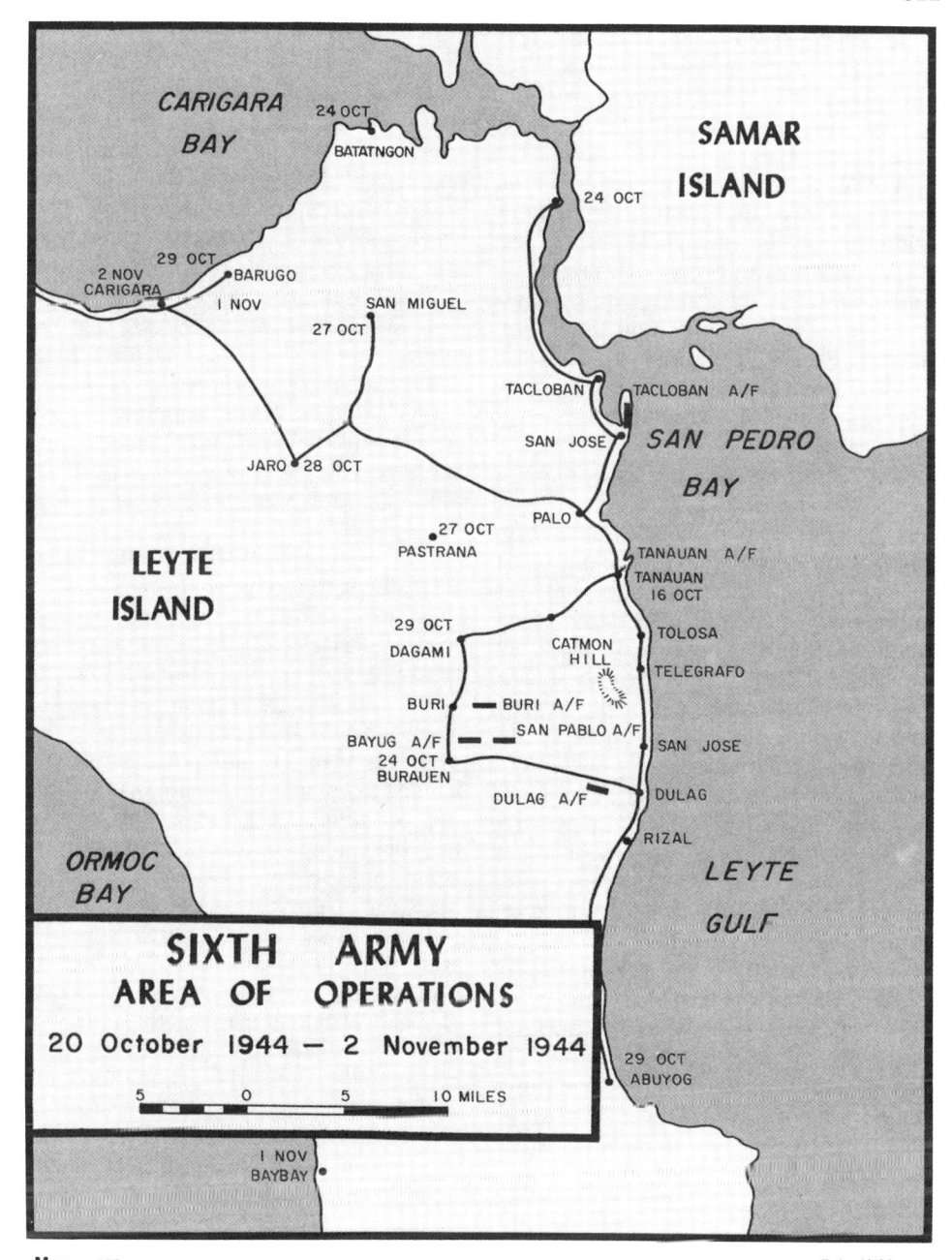

SIXTH ARMY AREA OF OPERATIONS
20 October 1944 – 2 November 1944

Map 17

E.L. Wilson

Japanese reaction to the American landings on Leyte consisted of a hurried activation of *Sho* No. 1. On 23 October, a Japanese fleet headed for Leyte to seek battle in a last-ditch attempt to halt the Americans. A decoy carrier force was to divert the Americans, while the two other surface forces, protected by Japanese aircraft on Luzon and Samar, were approaching Leyte Gulf through Surigao and San Bernardino Straits. The Japanese aimed at nothing less than the complete destruction of American shipping near the landing beaches.

The resulting major naval engagement, which lasted from 23-26 October, has become known as the Battle for Leyte Gulf.[3] The Japanese came close to achieving their objective, but not quite close enough. By evening of 26 October, the Japanese had lost four carriers, three battleships, six heavy and four light cruisers, nine destroyers, and a submarine. "For all practical purposes, the Japanese Navy, as a navy, had ceased to exist."[4] American naval losses in this battle, consisting of three small escort carriers, two destroyers, and one destroyer escort[5] were heavy but not crippling. Responsible Japanese commanders subsequently blamed in large part the loss of the Battle of Leyte Gulf and the defeat in the Philippines on Japanese weakness in land-based air, "October saw the end of the Japanese air forces in the conventional sense; what had once been a formidable weapon was transformed perforce into a sacrificial army of guided missiles."[6]

The Battle for Leyte Gulf was to have an interesting aftermath for at least a few Marine aviators. During the summer of 1944 General Mitchell, commander of the 1st MAW, had been unsuccessful in getting a combat assignment for his wing for the planned invasion of the Philippines. Even though Marine aviation was not assigned any part in the Leyte landings, a few aviators were assigned as observers during the invasion of Leyte. As a result, General Mitchell and three members of his staff took part in the landings and went ashore on A-Day with elements of the Fifth Air Force. On 25 October, while the Battle of Leyte Gulf was still in progress, more than a hundred U.S. naval aircraft, whose carriers had been sunk or severely damaged, were forced to land at Tacloban and Dulag airfields. The field at Tacloban was in deplorable shape; amphibious vehicles had churned up the ground, converting it into a veritable sea of mud and even though repairs had been started, the field was in no condition for the emergency landings by Navy aircraft.

Fortunately, General Mitchell and his staff were at Tacloban airfield at this crucial time. As an experienced aviator General Mitchell realized that the only place for safe landings was to the right of the field, where the original sod was still firm. The wing commander promptly seized a pair of signal flags, ran to the end of the strip, and, acting as a landing signal officer, assisted the Navy planes in making a safe landing. At

---

[3] For a detailed description of this battle, see Morison, *Leyte*, pp. 168–343.
[4] USSBS, *Pacific Campaigns*, p. 286.
[5] Cannon, *Leyte*, p. 92.
[6] *Ibid.*, p. 283.

NAVY PLANES *from carriers sunk or damaged during the Battle for Leyte Gulf find refuge at Dulag airfield, Leyte, 25 October 1944. (USMC A700601)*

RADAR-EQUIPPED NIGHT FIGHTERS *of VMF(N)–541 over Leyte. (USMC A700605)*

the Dulag airstrip, about 20 miles south of Tacloban, the Navy pilots were not quite so lucky, and 8 out of the 40 aircraft attempting to land cracked up. There were no bombs, ammunition, or gasoline at Dulag, and barges had to transport those items there to enable the aircraft to become operational again by the following day.[7]

Difficulties with soft and muddy airstrips apparently were not limited to the Americans; a Japanese account of the Leyte operation mentions "a marked increase in the number of crippled planes because of poor maintenance of the air fields. . . . It became impossible for the supply to catch up with the losses."[8]

Marine aviation, aside from General Mitchell's providential presence at Tacloban, did not play a direct part in the Leyte landings or the early phase of the Leyte campaign. Nevertheless, about 1,500 Marines were deeply involved in the operation from its outset and were to contribute materially to the liberation of the island.

SUPPORTING ARTILLERY[9]

The Marines that took part in the Leyte landings were elements of the VAC Artillery, which had been attached to the XXIV Corps earlier in 1944, while still at Hawaii. The Marine complement consisted of the 5th 155mm Howitzer Battalion under the command of Lieutenant Colonel James E. Mills; the 11th 155mm Gun Battalion, under the command of Lieutenant Colonel Thomas S. Ivey, and Headquarters Battery, led by Captain George K. Acker. Army field artillery battalions in the XXIV Corps were the 198th Field Artillery Battalion (155mm Howitzer), the 226th Field Artillery Battalion (155mm Gun), and the 287th Field Artillery Battalion (Observation).

The Marine artillery elements assigned to the XXIV Corps, as well as the 226th Field Artillery Battalion, had been formed from former seacoast artillery units; though familiar with heavy artillery, the men had received only rudimentary field artillery training. Prior to the departure of these units from Hawaii, the Marine artillery had undergone intensive field artillery training. Embarkation of personnel from Hawaii was accomplished between 6 and 14 September 1944.

The two Marine artillery battalions and the headquarters battery were embarked in the LSV USS *Monitor* and the LSV USS *Catskill*. General Bourke, on board the amphibious command ship USS *Mount Olympus*, served as XXIV Corps Artillery Officer as well as its coordinator for naval gunfire, air strikes, and artillery support. Equipment for the artillery battalions was carried by the cargo ship USS *Auriga*. The ships arrived at Eniwetok in the

---

[7] Kenney, *Reports*, p. 459.
[8] Hayashi and Coox, *Kōgun*, p. 127.
[9] Unless otherwise noted, the material in this section is derived from: A History of the X Corps in the Leyte-Samar Philippine Islands Operation, dtd 6Jan45, hereafter *CG X Corps Hist;* VAC Arty SAR, Leyte, dtd 6Jan45, hereafter *VAC Arty SAR;* VAC Arty OpRpt, Leyte, dtd 28Dec44, hereafter *VAC Arty OpRpt;* 5th 155mm HowBn SAR, dtd 28May45, hereafter *5th 155mm HowBn SAR;* Woodbury Rpt; Maj Edwin J. St. Peter Rpt, Leyte, dtd 7Dec44, hereafter *St. Peter Rpt;* Maj Justin G. Duryea Rpt, Leyte, dtd 13Nov44, hereafter *Duryea Rpt.*

Marshalls on 25 September and three days later sailed for the final staging area at Manus Island in the Admiralties, where they arrived on 3 October. A Marine observer attached to the 5th 155mm Howitzer Battalion shed an interesting sidelight on the manner in which the troops learned of their objective:

> Two days out of Pearl Harbor (17Sep44), a PBY bomber dropped dispatches containing information changing the target from STALEMATE II to KING II. This information was not disseminated to the troops when we arrived at Eniwetok on 25 September 1944, but upon arrival at Manus Island (Admiralty Group) on 3 October 1944, said information was passed on to the lower command echelon. As a result, the name and date of the landing on Leyte Island was known even to the enlisted personnel while the ships of the convoys were still in the last staging area. Unfortunately this information was common talk among all hands and no great attempt, in general, was made to preserve the secrecy necessary in an operation of this kind.[10]

On 14 October the invasion fleet departed Manus Island for Leyte. The ships in which the corps artillery was embarked arrived in the transport area off Leyte during the morning of 20 October. Naval bombardment of the objective began at approximately 0745 and continued for two hours. Shortly before 1000, Sixth Army units began the invasion of Leyte. X Corps, on the right of the Sixth Army front, landed on the northern part of the invasion beaches; XXIV Corps, consisting of the 7th Infantry Division on the left (south) and the 96th Infantry Division on the right (north) established a southern beachhead. The landings did not take place earlier in the day because the ships could not risk a passage through minefields at night. In the words of a Marine observer with the 96th Infantry Division:

> ...the landing was perfect. LCI rocket boats and gun boats preceded the first waves of (amtracs) to the beach and laid down heaviest concentration of rocket, 40mm and 20mm fire used to date on a beach in the Pacific. All troops landed on schedule and proceeded inland without opposition. Not many more than 15 mortar shells landed in the water or on the beaches, and in the entire division only 2 dead and 14 wounded were suffered in getting ashore.[11]

As units of the X and XXIV Corps were going ashore and setting up beachheads, the artillerymen remained on board their ships. Reports from the beachheads indicated that the Japanese tactics differed completely from those encountered in the Central Pacific. The Japanese no longer concentrated their resistance on the beaches but defended the interior of the island. Owing to the large land area, the Japanese had the problem of properly utilizing their limited manpower. The Japanese *16th Infantry Division* with attached service troops was charged with the defense of Leyte. The division was disposed with the *33d Infantry* to the north, in the zone of the X Corps, the *9th Infantry* to the south opposite the XXIV Corps, and the *20th Infantry* in reserve between Dulag and Tanauan. It was estimated that there were 20,000 Japanese on Leyte, including between 5,000 and 10,000 labor and service troops mostly employed in airfield construc-

---

[10] *St. Peter Rpt*, p. 2.

[11] *Duryea Rpt*, p. 1.

tion and maintenance in the area around Tacloban, San Jose, Burauen, and Dagami.[12]

As the Sixth Army beachheads were established and expanded, it became evident that the Leyte landings had come as a complete surprise for the enemy. The beaches on which the 96th Infantry Division landed were undefended, though two Japanese antitank guns in the landing area of the 7th Infantry Division succeeded in knocking out five medium tanks. Aside from this action, the assault troops did not encounter any enemy interference until they had advanced several hundred yards inland. Few defensive installations were found on the beaches and those that were encountered were makeshift and indicative of hasty construction. Though some 75mm artillery and sporadic mortar fire hit the beaches, the enemy made no attempt to mass his fire. No Japanese tanks were in evidence near the invasion area. The biggest obstacle for the first 3,000 yards inland from the beaches was the terrain, which was so swampy and muddy that the advance had to be held up for a day in order to get supplies to the front lines.

On the morning of 21 October, General Bourke ordered all corps artillery units to dispatch advance parties to meet him at Blue One Beach, which was situated just north of Dulag. Owing to communications problems, word of this order reached only the 5th 155mm Howitzer Battalion and the Army 287th Field Artillery Battalion in time. As a result, representatives of these two battalions were the only ones to meet General Bourke before nightfall on 21 October. The remaining hours of daylight were utilized in reconnoitering and selecting initial positions. Advance parties from the 11th 155mm Gun Battalion, the Headquarters Battery of the VAC Artillery, and the Army 226th Artillery Battalion went ashore after nightfall but did not select their positions until the morning of 22 October. At this time General Bourke requested XXIV Corps to land the entire corps artillery.

The Army 198th and 226th Field Artillery Battalions and the 287th Field Artillery Observation Battalion went ashore without undue difficulty. The two Marine artillery battalions and the headquarters battery, on the other hand, ran into a major problem almost at once. The USS *Auriga* (AK-98) which carried the equipment of the Marine units, had been ordered to begin unloading on A-Day by the Commander, Transport Division 28, who had failed to coordinate his operation with either the Commanding General of the XXIV Corps or General Bourke. As a result, when advance parties of the artillery units reached the beach on A plus 1, half of the vehicles and weapons, as well as some ammunition, had already been landed, even though no artillerymen were present on the beach to dispose of this materiel. Equipment was scattered over several beaches and some of the heavy guns had been landed in areas in which no suitable firing positions could be obtained. As a result, positions further inland had to be reconnoitered.

By A plus 3 all of the Marine artillery was ashore, in position, and supporting the XXIV Corps. The first positions

---

[12] *CG, X Corps Hist*, p. 5.

occupied by the artillery were on a narrow rise about a quarter of a mile inland from the seashore. From here, the artillery was able to support the infantry which advanced northward from the invasion beaches towards an enemy-held hill that was nearly 400 feet high. By this time, the artillery units were well organized, and earlier problems associated with the landing had been overcome. Following in the wake of the infantry advance, the 5th 155mm Howitzer Battalion moved first to positions halfway between Dulag and Burauen and subsequently into the area between Burauen and Dagami. The 11th 155mm Gun Battalion followed within a few days, together with the advance echelon of Headquarters Battery. By evening of 22 October, the 226th Field Artillery Battalion occupied positions on the western outskirts of Dulag and was assigned the mission of reinforcing the fires of the 7th Infantry Division artillery, as the division advanced toward Dulag, Burauen, and Dagami. On the following day the 198th Field Artillery Battalion was assigned the mission of supporting the fires of the 96th Infantry Division Artillery to the north and northwest of San Jose. The 287th Observation Battalion established positions along the highway north of Dulag. By 24 October all units under the command of General Bourke were in position and firing in support of the XXIV Corps.

Since the Japanese were holding terrain to the west that was considerably higher than that held by the invasion force, the enemy had the advantage of superior observation. For the Americans, ground visibility was so poor that aerial observation assumed an unusual importance. Artillery spotter aircraft soon became the backbone of artillery observation. At the time of the landings some planes were brought in over the beach in a partially disassembled condition, put together, and flown to an airstrip from a narrow, sandy road paralleling the beach. Others took off from their carriers and completed the flight without undue difficulty, except for one plane, whose pilot got lost in a rainstorm and landed in enemy territory on the southern tip of Samar. The pilot, a field artillery officer, kept a cool head, which was badly needed since he carried with him parts of the operation plan. He carefully buried the important document, hid his aircraft as best he could, and, with the assistance of natives, found his way back to the American lines. Subsequently, accompanied by a rescue party, the pilot returned to the scene of the mishap, dug up the papers, repaired the plane, and flew it back to Dulag Field on Leyte.[13]

The observation planes available to the XXIV Corps Artillery consisted of 12 Type L-4 artillery spotter aircraft; a total of 13 pilots comprised the flying personnel; a dozen observers were available to carry out visual observation. The XXIV Corps furnished the pilots and planes; the observers were Marines from the artillery battalions or the Air Section of VAC Artillery Headquarters as well as Army personnel from their artillery battalions. The spotter aircraft also handled such special assignments

---

[13] BGen Bert A. Bone ltr to CMC, dtd 5Apr51, hereafter *Bone ltr* in *Philippines Comment File*.

as reconnaissance, search, and photographic missions for the XXIV Corps.

During the first few days of the Leyte operation, Japanese air action consisted of several raids each day. The enemy did not focus his attention on the troops but concentrated his air attacks against American shipping, beach supply dumps, and airfields. In the 96th Infantry Division area, these raids were executed by only two or three planes at a time. Since the beaches were jammed with ammunition, gasoline dumps, and other supplies for nearly 200 yards inland, the Japanese were bound to hit something. "In one raid, over 50 percent of the 7th Division ammunition and gasoline stores were burned up by the one bomb dropped, not to mention other supplies."[14] Beginning on 24 October the tempo of enemy air attacks picked up.

Aside from the destruction of materiel, the enemy air raids had an effect that could hardly have been anticipated by even the most optimistic Japanese. This unexpected byproduct was the confusion they had caused. A Marine observer attached to the Army described the result in the following words:

> Air raid warning systems had not been installed. The confusion caused by green troops having first enemy planes and then friendly planes fly over caused them to fire at all planes even when the markings were easily distinguishable. All that was necessary was for one gun to open fire, then all guns would fire even down to troops armed with M-1s and carbines. I personally saw one TBF shot down by our own fire and several others fired on.[15]

The indiscriminate firing against aircraft did not end there. According to another Marine observer, the gun crews of liberty ships and small boats were the worst offenders, probably because of poor recognition training. In any event, before the confusion died down, "they even shot down one cub artillery-spotting plane."[16]

By nightfall of 22 October, the 5th Howitzer Battalion and the 226th Field Artillery Battalion were in position ready to fire although the 5th Battalion had only 10 of its 12 pieces emplaced. The Headquarters Battery was also in position with communications to all units at this time. The 287th Observation Battalion had surveyed sufficient terrain to permit the division and the corps artillery to tie in to a common control. The initial area assigned to the 5th and 11th Battalions required the construction of a corduroy road across a small swamp. Both battalions worked on the construction of this road, but the 5th Battalion, which moved into position first, found access so difficult that the corps artillery commander ordered the 11th Battalion to occupy a different area. The battalion moved into its new position during the late afternoon and night of 23 October.

Marine artillerymen on Leyte came close to being actively involved in the Battle of Leyte Gulf. While that battle was reaching a climax, it appeared for a time that the Japanese Central Force would penetrate the screen of warships protecting the American transports. In the words of General Bourke:

> I was ordered by General Hodge, the XXIV Corps Commander, to turn the two 155mm Gun Battalions toward Leyte Gulf and prepare for the defense of the Beach-

---

[14] *Duryea Rpt.*, p. 3.
[15] *Woodbury Rpt.*, p. 5.

[16] *Duryea Rpt.*, p. 4.

head in that direction, against elements of the Japanese Fleet then believed to be approaching. As these battalions were originally trained in Coast Defense Methods this was readily accomplished.[17]

As the battle developed, the Japanese did not succeed in breaking through to the beachhead, and the corps artillerymen on Leyte never got a crack at the Japanese Navy. Instead, until 1 November, the XXIV Corps artillery continued to fire reinforcing missions for the division artillery in the beachhead. The marshy ground had a more adverse effect on the siting of positions and efficiency of artillery support than did the tactical situation. More often than not, cross country movement of medium and heavy artillery became impossible and positions had to be selected along roads or in the vicinity of airfields. On numerous occasions, positions to cover target areas could not be selected without frequently shifting the weapons. The 198th Field Artillery Battalion, as late as 1 November, was forced to occupy positions about 1,200 yards behind the front line because of unfavorable terrain. As a result, for several days the artillerymen drew intermittent small arms fire and attracted infiltrators.

On 1 November, the Marine howitzer battalion followed the infantry advance and displaced inland into the area between Burauen and Dagami. On the same day, the 198th Field Artillery Battalion was assigned the mission of reinforcing the fires of the 96th Infantry Division Artillery in support of operations west and northwest of Dagami. A few days later, the Marine gun battalion and the forward echelon of Headquarters Battery moved into the same general area as the Marine howitzer battalion. The immediate establishment of a fire direction center situated along the road between Burauen and Dagami enabled the artillery to fire massed concentrations along the entire XXIV Corps front. On 4 November, the 226th Field Artillery Battalion was detached to operational control of the X Corps and displaced to that sector.

Heavy rains in November immobilized almost all vehicular traffic in the Burauen-Dagami area. A static period developed along the entire corps front. At this time the artillery battalions often found themselves very close to the front, so that local perimeter defense assumed major importance. Heavy infantry weapons were sited with emphasis on air defense during the day and ground defense at night. At various times all artillery battalions came under enemy air attack, particularly the Marine battalions stationed near newly captured airfields. The 5th Howitzer Battalion claimed two enemy aircraft shot down and the 11th Battalion claimed one; the Army 226th Battalion also took credit for two aircraft downed.[18]

Local defense of artillery units consisted of manned positions around each

---

[17] LtGenThomas E. Bourke ltr to CMC, n.d., hereafter *Bourke ltr*, in *Philippines Comment File*. "The 11th Gun Battalion, near the beach, found itself swinging its guns around to fire on dug-in Japanese positions on Catmon Hill from which the beach and rear area installations were receiving fire. They also had to swing around 180 degrees, prepared to fire at sea." Col James E. Mills ltr to Head, HistBr, G-3 Div, HQMC dtd 7Nov66, in *Philippines Comment File*, hereafter *Mills ltr*.

[18] *VAC Arty SAR*, p. 7.

battery and barbed wire when possible.[19] Each artillery battalion was bothered from time to time by infiltrating snipers, who attempted to neutralize the batteries by small arms fire which was normally delivered as the artillery pieces fired. In this way the enemy hoped to escape detection by local security details. In some instances at night it became necessary to load the pieces and have the cannoneers take cover before firing. During the night of 24 October, the 226th Artillery Battalion was attacked by about 35 Japanese equipped with automatic weapons, explosive charges, magnetic mines, and grenades. Part of Battery A was temporarily neutralized, and one piece was disabled by an explosive charge. After a heavy exchange of fire the enemy force was scattered. The Japanese left 26 dead around the battalion sector. Remnants of this patrol evidently remained in the swamps around the battalion for some time, and for the next few nights sniping on the artillery position continued.

Since much enemy activity along the front occurred at night, the corps artillery had to maintain intermittent harassing and interdiction fires during the hours of darkness. It soon became evident that after personnel had been provided for all firing installations, the number of men available for local security was scanty. Nevertheless, the artillerymen performed their missions and despite poor roads, bad weather, and enemy harassment, lent effective support to the advancing infantry units.

In general, the corps artillery missions were the usual interdiction, harassing, and deep supporting fires. Each time a counterbattery mission was fired, air observation was utilized to locate and adjust upon the target. During daylight hours, fires consisted usually of registrations and adjustment on sensitive areas as a basis for night fires. Targets of opportunity were fired on as they appeared. Upon occasion, close supporting fires at night were requested by division artillery during periods of enemy activity.

The Japanese employment of artillery on Leyte was such that it was seldom used to maximum effect. In the words of the U. S. Army history of the Leyte campaign:

> The gunnery techniques were "remarkably undeveloped" and inefficient, the pieces being used singly or in pairs and only rarely as batteries. Their fire was never massed. The gun positions generally were well constructed but they were frequently selected with such high regard for concealment that the fields of fire were limited.[20]

By 2 November the Sixth Army ground offensive on Leyte had attained initial objectives. Advancing up the Leyte Valley, U. S. Army troops had advanced to Dulag, Burauen, Dagami, and Tanauan, reaching the west coast of Leyte on 1 November. Though initially slow to react, the Japanese did not by any means consider their situation on the island hopeless. While the

---

[19] "The 5th Battalion was in such a forward position that it had to maintain extensive patrol activity to the front and flanks of its position. There were a few patrol encounters with small scattered groups of the enemy. This battalion did not encounter enemy harassment or sniping which is attributable to the patrol activity." *Mills ltr.*

[20] Cannon, *Leyte*, p. 252.

Battle of Leyte Gulf was still in progress and American attention was focused on the naval operation, several Japanese infantry battalions from the western Visayas landed at Ormoc on the west coast of Leyte. On 26 October, an additional 2,000 men comprising the *41st Infantry Regiment* from Mindanao went ashore.

These reinforcements were only driblets of what was shortly to turn into a torrent of men and supplies. On 1 November, the Japanese *1st Division*, coming from Shanghai on troop transports escorted by destroyers and coast defense vessels, reached Ormoc and went ashore with about 12,000 men and equipment. Unloading was virtually completed before the convoy was discovered. Within two weeks after A-Day, the Japanese had landed some 22,000 reinforcements.[21]

To deprive the Japanese of their main port of debarkation on Leyte, General Krueger decided to launch two converging drives against Ormoc. X Corps was to move south through the Ormoc Valley; XXIV Corps was to advance northwards from Baybay. At the conclusion of this drive the Japanese remaining on Leyte would be forced to move into the mountains west of the Ormoc Valley, where effective organized resistance was all but impossible. In the XXIV Corps area, the 96th Infantry Division was to eliminate about 6,000 Japanese in the hills west of Dagami during the time that the 7th Infantry Division was consolidating its gains between Abuyog and Baybay.

Meanwhile, the Japanese continued to pour reinforcements into Leyte. In fact, "the idea of a mobile counterlanding force to reinforce the invaded area, had been an integral part of the Japanese Sho plan."[22] Between 23 October and 11 December 1944, the Japanese landed substantial reinforcements in nine echelons, until a total of some 30,000 men had gone ashore.[23] At the same time, strong enemy aircraft reinforcements arrived from Formosa. As November came to a close, the Japanese resistance on Leyte stiffened, aided by heavy rainfall, which impeded the progress of the Sixth Army's mechanized equipment. By mid-November it had become clear to both opponents that the struggle for Leyte would be long and costly; the idea of an easy victory for either opponent had vanished once and for all.

In an attempt to gain the initiative, the Japanese resorted to some unorthodox tactics. During the early hours of 27 November, three enemy transport aircraft came in low over Leyte Gulf. The aircraft made no attempt to black out and had all their lights on. When one of the planes crash-landed just 25 yards offshore near the bivouac of an amphibian tractor battalion, one of the guards jumped on the wing to offer assistance. Hand-grenade throwing Japanese emerging from the plane quickly convinced the guard that his help was not wanted. Two of the enemy were subsequently killed by small arms fire. Three others vanished into a swamp, where about a dozen others soon joined them.

---

[21] Sixth Army Report of Leyte Operation, pp. 34–40, as cited in Craven and Cate, *The Pacific*, p. 377.

[22] USSBS, *Pacific Campaigns*, p. 287.
[23] *Ibid.*

The second air transport crashed while attempting to land on Buri airstrip and all of the occupants were killed. The third airplane crash-landed north of Abuyog across a small river from a bivouac area occupied by troops of the 11th Airborne Division. According to a history of that division:

> An antiaircraft machine gun crew, which outfit is forgotten now, was in position on the alert for enemy aircraft. When the plane landed and came to a halt, they called across the small river: "Need any help?" "No, everything OK," someone yelled back, and the machine gun crew went back to watching the skies for enemy aircraft.[24]

The presence of stronger Japanese reinforcements on Leyte soon had an effect on the tactical situation of the XXIV Corps Artillery, particularly those units stationed in the Burauen area, where three out of the four airfields on Leyte were situated. During the early morning of 6 December, an estimated 100 Japanese infiltrated the area adjacent to Headquarters Battery, 287th Observation Battalion, in an apparent attempt to advance towards Buri airfield. Two days were to pass before the enemy infiltrators were eliminated.

At dusk on 6 December, enemy planes bombed Buri airfield, which harbored the corps artillery air sections totalling 30 officers and men, and laid a heavy smoke screen over the surrounding area. Shortly after the bombing, a force of about 150 Japanese parachuted into the vicinity of the field. The Marines of the air sections were armed with individual weapons and two machine guns, one of which had been salvaged from a wrecked plane. In the course of the morning, enemy attacks gradually drove friendly troops from their positions. As these men fell back on the position held by the Corps Artillery air sections, an additional 175 antiaircraft gun crews and service troops were hastily organized for defense by Marine Captain Eugene S. Roane, Jr., Assistant Corps Artillery S-2 and Air Observer, who was the senior officer present at the time of the Japanese attack.

Fighting for Buri airfield continued until 8 December. During the afternoon of that day, the antiaircraft personnel comprising part of the defensive force were ordered off the field. Having lost a large segment of their strength by this reshuffling of troops, the Marines were forced to pull back to the infantry perimeter. While fighting for the airfield was in progress, liaison pilots and observers from corps artillery repeatedly took off from and landed on the field under fire to evacuate wounded and bring in supplies and ammunition. All planes were hit by enemy small arms fire, which wounded one pilot and a mechanic. On 9 December the remaining personnel of the Corps Artillery Air Section were evacuated from Buri airfield.[25]

Some of the enemy paratroops dropped on 6 December landed near the position of the 5th 155mm Howitzer Battalion. For the next four days and nights, Marines of the battalion found themselves dodging enemy bullets and hand grenades. The tactics employed

---

[24] Maj Edward M. Flanagan, Jr., *The Angels, A History of the 11th Airborne Division, 1943–1946* (Washington, D. C., 1948), p. 34.

[25] *VAC Arty SAR*, p. 9.

by the Japanese consisted of remaining inactive during the day and emerging at night to lob grenades into the battery positions. For the most part such attacks were sporadic, lasting no more than one hour at a time and repeated four to five times each night. At this particular time, most of the equipment and men were at the beach preparing to load on board ship to depart Leyte, and those Marines who remained to encounter the enemy paratroops were members of cleanup details consisting of about 50-75 men whose nights were made even more unpleasant by the hard rain which filled the foxholes with cold water. Fortunately for the Marines, it was possible to trace the grenade trajectory by the glow of the fuze, enabling them to fire at the source. Before the action ended, the artillerymen had killed 23 of the Japanese and accounted for one more who preferred to commit suicide.[26] The remaining Japanese were driven from Buri airfield on 10 December.

At 0800 on 11 December, following the arrival of the XXIV Corps Artillery from Saipan, the V Amphibious Corps Artillery was relieved of all missions in support of the XXIV Corps. The 5th and 11th Battalions and Headquarters Battery sailed from Leyte on 13 December for Guam. General Bourke departed from the island by air for Guam on the same day.[27] During their attachment to XXIV Corps, the Marine artillerymen lost 2 officers and 7 enlisted men killed, 3 officers and 31 enlisted men wounded in action, and 1 Marine missing.[28]

---

[26] *5th 155mm HowBn SAR,* 6-10Dec44.

[27] BGen Thomas E. Bourke ltr to CMC, dtd 28Dec44, Encl to *VAC Arty SAR.*

[28] *VAC Arty OpRpt,* p. 16.

Though the battle for Leyte was still far from over, the Marine artillerymen had contributed their share to ultimate victory.

ENTER MARINE AIR[29]

During the early days of the Leyte operation, the Navy furnished all air support for the U. S. ground troops. The Battle for Leyte Gulf made it necessary for the escort carriers to use all available aircraft for offensive and defensive missions. Incessant rains and mud on Leyte impeded the development of airfields. The advent of Japanese suicide attacks[30] against American ships in Leyte Gulf caused losses that badly hurt the Navy escort groups.

Alien as the spirit of self-destruction may appear to Occidental eyes, the idea of sacrificing an airplane and pilot to destroy an Allied ship was effective and entirely practical from the Japanese point of view. Overwhelming American superiority in both personnel and materiel forced the Japanese to adopt this step. The effectiveness of *kamikaze* attacks in Leyte Gulf was further increased by American difficulties with shore-based radar, which left supporting units in the Gulf exposed to increasing threat of suicide attack.[31] Among the many statements made during and after World War II on the subject of the *kamikaze,* perhaps the most poignant one came from a Navy commander, who philosophized as follows:

---

[29] Unless otherwise noted, the material in this section is derived from MAG-12 WarDs, Nov-Dec44.

[30] Designated as *Kamikaze* in Japanese naval terminology and called *Tokko* by the Japanese Army.

[31] Morison, *Pacific Campaigns,* p. 280.

Every time one country gets something, another soon has it. One country gets radar, but soon all have it. One gets a new type of engine or plane, then another gets it. But the Japs have got the *kamikaze* boys, and nobody else is going to get that, because nobody else is built that way.[32]

Despite the initial success of the Japanese ramming attacks and the losses they were able to inflict on American shipping at Leyte, such bizarre tactics could not offset American superiority, nor could they accomplish a turning of the tide in the strategical situation. No other tactic could have illuminated more clearly the weakness of the Japanese Air Force. A dispassionate and objective analysis of the overall impact of the *kamikaze* tactic came to the conclusion that with the first *kamikaze* attack:

...the Japanese may be said to have abandoned the air war; from this time on they made little attempt at reviving their air force. Macabre, effective, supremely practical under the circumstances, supported and stimulated by a powerful propaganda campaign, the special attack became virtually the sole method used in opposing the United States striking and amphibious forces, and these ships the sole objectives.[33]

The exploits of Japanese *kamikaze* pilots could not change the fact that Japanese air operations in the Philippines were beset by severe difficulties. Foremost among these was the speed employed by the American invasion forces in seizing the Japanese airfields on Leyte. Even though the numerical weakness of American land-based aircraft initially permitted the Japanese to land substantial reinforcements, the arrival of additional aircraft and the completion of airfields on the island were bound to shift the balance in favor of the Americans. For the Japanese, there was a marked increase in the number of crippled aircraft because of the poor state of Japanese airfields in the Philippines. Only about 10 Japanese aircraft reached the battle zone towards the end of October. At that time the daily attrition rate was 20–25 aircraft.[34] It became impossible for Japanese aircraft production to catch up with the losses.

Throughout November, the fast carriers hit Luzon in order to reduce the heavy flow of Japanese aircraft reinforcements that were being sent to the Philippines from Formosa. No fewer than 700 enemy aircraft and 134,000 tons of Japanese shipping were destroyed in this manner.[35] The Japanese Air Force was unable to compensate for such heavy losses. In the words of the former Military Secretary to the Japanese Minister of War:

Aerial operations in the Philippines were conducted in the form of an aircraft-replacement race, instead of combat between hostile aircraft carriers. At the time, moreover, there existed such a tremendous difference in the air-replacement capabilities of the Japanese and the Americans that there was scant opportunity for the former to win the decisive battle for Leyte—even if various other conditions were temporarily favorable.[36]

During the initial phase of the Leyte campaign, the Japanese Air Force had the upper hand. FEAF aircraft were too few in numbers to do more than

---

[32] Cdr John Thach, quoted in Sherrod, *Marine Corps Aviation in World War II*, p. 273.
[33] USSBS, *Pacific Campaigns*, p. 286.
[34] Hayashi and Coox, *Kōgun*, p. 127.
[35] USSBS, *Pacific Campaigns*, p. 287.
[36] Hayashi and Coox, *Kōgun*, p. 127.

provide a defense against enemy air attacks. Tacloban was the only operational strip on Leyte, though the Dulag airfield was used on occasion for emergency landings. Before the first Army Air Force planes could land at Tacloban on 27 October, 2,500 feet of steel matting had to be laid in two days. The advent of the rainy season and the arrival of three typhoons, accompanied by heavy rains, further complicated airfield construction. As a result, the arrival of sorely needed light and medium bombers had to be postponed repeatedly. On several occasions engineers engaged in airfield construction had to be diverted to road maintenance.

By the end of November, all of Leyte except the Ormoc Bay area and the northwest coast of the island was in American hands. The continuous flow of Japanese reinforcements threatened to cause a military stalemate, even though Sixth Army had seven divisions ashore and the Navy had driven the Japanese fleet from the waters surrounding Leyte. The Tacloban airstrip received unwelcome attention by the Japanese, who made several determined attempts to render the strip useless for the Americans. On 4 November, 35 enemy aircraft raided the airfield, killing 4 men, wounding 30, and destroying 2 P-38s and damaging 39 others.[37] Two *kamikazes* crashed into two air transports bringing in the ground echelon of a bombardment group, killing 92 men and wounding 156 others. Additional American aircraft at the Tacloban field fell victim to Japanese air attacks later in the month.

Even though Allied air power had begun to count by mid-November and an increasing number of Japanese ships engaged in shuttling reinforcements to Leyte were sent to the bottom, air operations on Leyte continued to be hamstrung by the lack of base facilities. "FEAF could meet the demand for planes and combat crews, but they could not operate without surfaced strips. By 30 November, only 182 fighters were on Leyte, and an average of only 111 had been operational daily during the preceding week."[38]

No immediate relief for the shortage of airfields on Leyte was in sight. Facilities completed at Bayug and Buri were closed down by bad weather shortly after they had become operational; poor drainage, faulty soil bases, and poor access roads finally forced Fifth Air Force to abandon Buri and San Pablo airstrips. Construction of an all-weather airfield at Tanauan between Tacloban and Dulag began during the latter part of November, but until completion of this strip the lack of air facilities on Leyte was bound to reduce the effectiveness of American air power. Fifth Air Force expended its strength in a struggle to gain air superiority; the insufficient number of aircraft available on Leyte precluded the employment of aircraft for close support missions until late in the campaign.

By 27 November, Admiral Kinkaid had become increasingly restive under the continued *kamikaze* attacks, which continued to exact a heavy toll among American ships. Admiral Halsey's carriers had already stayed in the Philippines almost a month longer than had

---

[37] Craven and Cate, *The Pacific*, pp. 374–375.

[38] *Ibid.*, p. 383.

been planned and the Admiral itched for action against the Japanese mainland. General MacArthur was dissatisfied with the air defense of Leyte and suggested to Admiral Nimitz an exchange of night fighter squadrons. The Marine night fighters were better able to cope with the Japanese night bombers, which were too fast for the P-61 Black Widow fighter plane, built by Northrop, used by the Army night fighter squadron on Leyte. VMF(N)-541 was to be shifted from Peleliu to Leyte, relieving a Fifth Air Force squadron that in turn was to move to the Palaus.

For General Mitchell's Marine aviators, the old adage that "all good things come in bunches" was about to prove true. Hardly had the word of VMF(N)-541's transfer to Leyte been passed when Admiral Halsey intervened in order to get the Marine aviators more fully committed in the Philippines. The Admiral described this development in the following words:

> I had under my command in the South Pacific a Marine Air Group which had proved its versatility in everything from fighting to blasting enemy vessels. I knew that this group was now under MacArthur's command, and I knew, too, without understanding why, that when Kenney was not keeping it idle, he was assigning it to missions far below its capacity. Kinkaid's complaint of insufficient air cover prompted me to take a step which was more than a liberty; to a man of meaner spirit than MacArthur's, it would have seemed an impertinence. I called these Marines to his attention. He ordered them forward, and within twenty-four hours of their arrival, they had justified my recommendation.[39]

[39] Halsey and Bryan, *Admiral Halsey's Story*, p. 231.

Admiral Halsey's recommendation to General MacArthur bore immediate fruit. As November drew to a close, VMF(N)-541 on Peleliu and four Marine fighter squadrons of MAG-12 in the Solomons stood ready to move to Leyte when the word was received.

Marine Night Fighter Squadron 541 was placed on standby alert for departure to Leyte on 28 November. Under the command of Lieutenant Colonel Peter D. Lambrecht, the squadron had spent over two months on Peleliu. Equipped with Grumman "Hellcats," more formally known as F6Fs, the squadron specialized in night intercept operations. To this end, the "Hellcats" were equipped with special radar devices, and all of the pilots had received thorough training in the squadron specialty.

Three days later, General Mitchell ordered Marine Aircraft Group 12 (MAG-12), commanded by Colonel William A. Willis, to move four of its fighter squadrons, VMF-115, -211, -218, and -313 to Tacloban by 3 December for duty with the Fifth Air Force.[40] To expedite the movement, General Mitchell requested Fifth Air Force to make C-47 transports available to airlift men and materiel of the ground echelons to Tacloban. This request was granted; similarly, the Seventh Fleet promised logistic support for the ground echelon at its destination.

Early on 2 December, 85 Corsairs from MAG-12, escorted by PBJs from

[40] MAG-12 WarDs, Nov-Dec44. At this time VMF-115 was commanded by Maj John H. King, Jr; VMF-211 by Maj Stanislaus J. Witomski; VMF-218 by Maj Robert T. Kingsbury III; and VMF-313 by Maj Philip R. White.

MAG-61, left the Solomons for Leyte. After refuelling at Hollandia and other islands, 82 fighters reached Peleliu on 3 December, only a few hours after VMF(N)-541 had left for Tacloban. The remainder, having developed mechanical trouble, required repairs before they could catch up with the main flight. The night fighters of VMF(N)-541 flew the 600 miles from Peleliu to Leyte without incident and landed at Tacloban during the morning of 3 December; in the course of the afternoon, 66 Corsairs and 9 escorting patrol bombers touched down on the same airstrip; 16 Corsairs had remained at Peleliu with mechanical troubles, none of them serious.[41]

Marine aviators had come to the Philippines in strength to fly cover for convoys, execute fighter-bomber strikes against enemy shipping in Visayan waters and ground installations on southern Luzon, and fly ground support missions on Leyte. Above all, they helped to deny the ports of western Leyte to the enemy during his desperate attempts to reinforce his troops and made him pay dearly for attempting to run the aerial blockade.

CORSAIRS AND HELLCATS ON LEYTE[42]

Marine aviators arriving at Tacloban were quick to discover that facilities at the airfield left something to be desired. One author gave the following graphic description:

> Tacloban strip was now the none-too-happy base of 87 Marine planes. Although the invasion had taken place six weeks before the first Marine flyers got there, work on the airfield had progressed but little. Severe storms lashed the east coast of Leyte during the October-January northeast monsoon, and stories about the mud at Tacloban are still legendary.[43]

One of the aviators of MAG-12 has described the arrival of the Air Group as being attended "by some of the worst conditions of overcrowding, lack of space, and inadequate operational facilities, not even excluding Guadalcanal in August of 1942."[44]

On the day of their arrival at Tacloban, six Hellcats of VMF(N)-541 flew their first mission in the Philippines by covering PT boats in Surigao Strait and providing air cover over Ormoc Bay. Bad weather on 4 December precluded flight operations; instead, Marine aviation personnel set up and improved the camp site located about 300 yards west of the southern end of the Tacloban strip.

Marine pilots in the Philippines drew their first blood on 5 December, when a Hellcat on predawn patrol between Bohol Island and southern Leyte shot down an enemy fighter. Not to be outdone by the nightfighters, the Corsair pilots also claimed a Japanese fighter on the same day.

---

[41] MAG-12 WarD, Dec44.

[42] Unless otherwise noted, the material in this section is derived from: Dec44 WarDs of MAG-12, VMF-115, VMF-211, VMF-218, VMF-313; Boggs, *Marines in the Philippines; Philippines Comment File*; Smith, *The Approach to the Philippines*; Morison, *Leyte*; Craven and Cate, *The Pacific*; Halsey and Bryan, *Admiral Halsey's Story*; Cannon, *Leyte*.

[43] Sherrod, *Marine Corps Aviation in World War II*, p. 276.

[44] Maj Roy T. Spurlock ltr to CMC, dtd 7Feb51, in *Philippines Comment File*, hereafter *Spurlock ltr*.

This was only the beginning of what was to prove an exciting, demanding, and fruitful operation for the Marine aviators. For the remainder of the month, the biggest assignment for the nightfighters, alternately known as the "Bateye Squadron," was to intercept Japanese aircraft that preferred to execute raids at dusk, dawn, and during the night. Some difficulty was experienced initially because the ground controllers guiding the night fighters were Army personnel using procedures that differed from those followed by Marine controllers, though in time coordination improved. Crowded conditions at Tacloban and deficiencies in radar coverage and performance did not make the task of the Hellcat pilots easier.

The day-fighter squadrons of MAG-12 soon discovered that the mission they had so thoroughly trained for—that of close support for ground troops—did not materialize at once. There were daily missions of raiding enemy airfields, providing air cover for friendly convoys, rescues, and attacks against Japanese troops and communications. The most important contribution of Marine fighters in the Leyte operation resulted from the tactical situation, which made it necessary for Marine pilots to play an active part in stemming the steady enemy flow of reinforcements to Leyte by attacking Japanese ships.

Marine fighters of VMF-211 struck their first blow against Japanese shipping on the morning of 7 December, when a dozen Corsairs went out in search of seven Japanese vessels reportedly en route to Ormoc Bay. By the time the Corsairs spotted the ships at anchor at San Isidro Harbor, Japanese fighters were flying cover for the convoys. Eight Marine fighters engaged the Japanese aircraft; four Corsairs went after the enemy ships and damaged one destroyer, which caught fire and subsequently ran aground. In the course of this action, three Corsairs were shot down.

The action continued during the afternoon, when Corsairs of VMF-211, -218, and -313 with Army fighters as escorts, returned to San Isidro and sank three cargo ships, a troop transport, and a destroyer. While this action was in progress, Ormoc Bay became a hotbed of activity for both belligerents, for a convoy carrying the Army 77th Infantry Division was approaching to land the division several miles south of Ormoc.

That plenty of air action resulted from the attempts of both Americans and Japanese to put troops ashore near Ormoc on the same day is not surprising. Nor could it be expected that the Japanese would stand by idly as the American convoy approached the shores of Leyte. Beginning at 0820, and practically without interruption, Japanese air attacks hit the American ships in Ormoc Bay. Fifth Air Force aircraft did all they could to protect the friendly vessels, but more than once enemy aircraft broke through this cover and a curtain of antiaircraft fire put up by the ships. The enemy air attacks continued for more than nine hours and included numerous *kamikaze* runs that found their mark. A destroyer and high-speed transport were so badly damaged that they subsequently had to be sunk by gunfire.[45] In addition, a landing ship was hit near the beach and had to be abandoned, and a destroyer, an LST, and a high-speed transport were damaged.

On 11 December, the Japanese made a final attempt to reinforce their garrison on Leyte. In the course of the morning, a Japanese convoy of six cargo ships and transports and four destroyers and escorts was observed heading for Leyte. The four Marine dayfighter squadrons put 27 Corsairs into the air, which intercepted the Japanese ships about 40 miles west of Panay Island. Each plane carried a 1,000 pound bomb armed with a 4–5 second delay fuze. Pilots of VMF–313, commanded by Major Joe H. McGlothlin, dive-bombed a troop transport, scoring a hit amidships with two bombs. VMF–115, led by Major John H. King, scored a hit on a cargo ship, setting it on fire. The eight Corsairs from VMF–211 in the group did not score any direct hits on the convoy but instead became embroiled in a dogfight with more than a dozen enemy fighters and downed four of them. During the bombing run, the Corsairs drew heavy antiaircraft fire, which was intense but inaccurate. Pilots of VMF–218 did not have a chance to observe the results of their bombing because they suddenly found themselves under attack by seven enemy fighters. In a running fight, two of the Japanese fighters were downed; another one disappeared in a cloudbank, trailing black smoke. When the action ended, the score was two enemy ships severely damaged and six aircraft downed, with one more probable.

During the afternoon of 11 December, 30 additional Marine aircraft, accompanied by Army P–40s, attacked the same convoy. Pilots of VMF–313 sank one large troop transport, a cargo vessel, and a destroyer and set two freighters on fire, at a cost of four Corsairs hit by antiaircraft fire, two of which were badly damaged. VMF–211 sank two destroyers and a troop transport at a cost of two aircraft. Aviators of VMF–115 scored a direct hit on a large cargo ship and left another listing and burning, at the cost of two aircraft. VMF–218 set the remaining destroyer on fire and scored hits on a large troop transport with unobserved results; one Corsair was lost in that operation.

Throughout the action, Japanese antiaircraft fire was unusually intense. Equally noteworthy were the tactics employed by the Marine pilots to counter it. While the Army aircraft released their bombs at altitudes between 2,000 and 10,000 feet, the Corsairs attacked at masthead level. One of the Marine pilots, speaking of the P–40s, somewhat caustically remarked:

> They accomplished nothing except to make interesting splashes in the water and wake up the Japs. AA immediately became very intense. As the last Army bombs were falling our Corsairs were in position and coming in fast and low. The Japs never saw us coming until we started to shoot (we received no fire until past the screening destroyers).[46]

Elsewhere off Leyte, the situation was reversed, and Corsairs of MAG–12 found themselves protecting American

---

[47] Cannon, *Leyte*, p. 283.

[46] Capt Rolfe T. Blanchard ltr to CMC, n.d., in *Philippines Comment File*, hereafter *Blanchard ltr*.

ships in Leyte Gulf from enemy air attacks. During the afternoon of 11 December, 4 Corsairs of VMF-313 spotted 16 Japanese fighters, carrying 500-pound bombs under each wing, headed for an American convoy passing through Surigao Straits. The Marine aviators, diving through friendly antiaircraft fire, engaged the enemy fighters, shot down five, and drove the remainder from the area, but not before two Japanese suicide planes had sunk a destroyer. Even though the timely intervention of the Corsairs prevented far greater damage to the convoy, the Marine aircraft received considerable damage from friendly antiaircraft fire.[47]

While the Corsairs of the Marine day-fighter squadrons were busy attacking Japanese ships, protecting American shipping, and patrolling, the Hellcats of VMF(N)-541 also did their share of fighting. Early on 12 December, the nightfighters intercepted a number of unidentified aircraft on their radar screens while flying cover for a convoy near Ormoc Bay. Just as a Japanese flight of 33 torpedo bombers, dive bombers, and fighters approached the American convoy, the Hellcats intercepted them and broke up the formation. Even though some of the enemy bombers inevitably got through to the target, the outnumbered Marine aviators kept the enemy off balance. As a result, all of the enemy bombs missed the convoy. During the battle it became evident that the Japanese evaded air combat whenever possible, though the Marines were greatly outnumbered.

When the battle ended, the night fighters of VMF(N)-541 had destroyed 11 enemy aircraft and damaged 1, with no losses to themselves.[48]

War is not only the realm of suffering, as Clausewitz has put it, but is equally the sphere of the unexpected. Frequently, the perversity of weather or terrain can do greater harm than enemy action. For MAG-12, the predawn hours of 13 December spelled tragedy. At 0530, under conditions of extremely poor visibility, six Corsairs of VMF-313, accompanied by two Hellcats, set out on a mission to escort a friendly convoy. Because of bad weather and poor runway conditions at the Tacloban airfield, one of the Corsairs crashed during takeoff. In a tragic sequence of events, the plane smashed into a jeep, injuring its two occupants, one of whom was the group intelligence officer, who lost his left arm and suffered numerous other injuries. With scarcely diminished force, the plane hit an ambulance and a crash truck in front of the operations building, killing four men. The flaming inferno spread by the wrecked aircraft and vehicles prevented the remainder of the flight from taking off.[49]

Shortly afterwards, another Corsair, which had previously taken off crashed between Leyte and Samar for undetermined reasons. The pilot, in attempting to bail out, was struck in the face by the vertical stabilizer and killed. Far luckier was the pilot of one of the Corsairs who, following another strike against enemy shipping, was last re-

---

[47] MAG-12 WarD, Dec44.

[48] VMF(N)-541 WarD, Dec44.
[49] MAG-12 WarD, Dec44.

ported attempting a water landing. When no further word from him was received, he was initially presumed missing in action. Days later, after an odyssey that included ditching in the water, rescue by natives who thought he might be a German, and a feast on candy bars, whose wrappers bore the legend "I shall return," the pilot made it back to Tacloban, not much the worse for wear.[50]

Before the day was over, the 13th lived up to its reputation in yet another way. Even though 35 Corsairs of MAG-12 covered a friendly invasion convoy bound for Mindoro Island, a Japanese suicide plane arrived over the convoy at a time when the Corsairs were not on duty. The *kamikaze* selected none other than the flagship *Nashville* as his victim. The plane crashed into the ship, killing 129, including the chiefs of staff of both the naval force and the ground force commander, as well as the commanding officer of the 310th Bombardment Wing. In addition, four men were missing in action. Twenty-eight of the 41 Marines in the ship's detachment perished in the disaster.

Better days were to follow. The invasion of Mindoro Island, located just south of Luzon and 200 miles northwest of Leyte, promised to secure better airfields without the mud, which had so greatly plagued ground troops and aviators alike. At the same time, construction of a new airfield at Tanauan, about 45 miles west of Tacloban, promised to provide some relief for the overcrowding that had characterized MAG-12 operations at Tacloban. Though Japanese air power over Luzon remained strong, enemy air strength over Leyte was rapidly diminishing by mid-December. During the latter half of that month, ground operations on Leyte went into their final phase. Corsairs and Hellcats met fewer and fewer of their opponents in aerial combat until enemy resistance in the air all but ceased. For the Marine aviators on Leyte, the demise of the Japanese air strength did not mean the end of a mission but merely a change in emphasis. The type of operation for which they had been trained so zealously before coming to the Philippines, the support of ground troops, still had to be put into practice.

GROUND SUPPORT MISSIONS AND CLOSING PHASE[51]

Marine pilots on Leyte flew their first ground support missions on 10 December, when they struck at enemy bivouac areas at Ormoc and San Isidro on the west coast of the island. The results of both raids were generally unobserved, though fires subsequently swept the target areas. On 17 and 19 December, Corsairs again hit Japanese ground targets. On these occasions, 12 aircraft of MAG-12 bombed and strafed Japanese supply installations at Palompon, on the northwest coast of Leyte.[52] For the remainder of the month, Japanese airfields on Negros and Panay Is-

---

[50] Sherrod, *Marine Corps Aviation in World War II*, pp. 281-282.

[51] Unless otherwise noted, the material in this section is derived from: MAG-12 WarD, Dec44; VMF(N)-541 WarDs, Dec44-Jan45; Boggs, *Marines in the Philippines*; Philippines Comment File.

[52] MAG-12 WarD, Dec44.

lands as well as on Mindanao and Luzon became primary targets of the Marine aviators.

Even though such attacks ultimately contributed to Japanese demoralization and defeat in the Philippines, this type of air support was a far cry from the close support tactics for which the Marines had trained. At no time during the Leyte operation did MAG-12 ever receive an assignment commensurate with its capabilities of giving close air support to ground troops. The Joint Assault Signal Companies, equipped with air-ground signal communication facilities, were not used for direct air-ground control. Pilots were briefed on their missions prior to takeoff and targets assigned on the day preceding an air strike. Once the flight became airborne, no further control was exercised from the ground.

It must be recalled that Marine aviation on Leyte came under the overall command of the Fifth Air Force and for this reason operated under the procedures and guidelines set forth by the AAF. Even though Marine and Army Air Forces pilots flew numerous missions over Leyte together, important differences in doctrine and training continually cropped up. Army aircraft on bombing missions, when subjected to enemy attack, tended to jettison their bombs and engage the enemy fighters. In so doing, they tended to abandon their primary mission; the Corsair pilots, on the other hand, kept their bombs and continued on despite enemy interference. As one of the Marine aviators on Leyte put it:

> The reason the Marine air strikes against enemy shipping were markedly more successful than the Army strikes was due simply to more thorough briefing and planning and vastly better air discipline.

The thought was instilled in the minds of all Marine pilots that the assigned mission came first. Time after time Marine flights on combat air patrol would give up chasing bogeys who escaped from their assigned patrol area, rather than leave their assigned area, even though they could hear Army patrols on the same type of mission, merrily chasing Japs all over the Visayan Sea.[53]

For the remainder of December 1944 the Corsairs of MAG-12, in close teamwork with two Army fighter groups, bombed a series of villages on Luzon and attacked railway bridges, trains, and other railroad facilities. On Leyte, the fate of the Japanese was sealed when, on 25 December, elements of the Army's 77th Infantry Division went ashore at Palompon and seized the last port on Leyte under Japanese control. The enemy units remaining on Leyte were now completely cut off without any further hope of receiving reinforcements or evacuating the island. In their customary style, the Japanese fought on for another five months in a battle to the bitter end, but the die was cast. On 26 December, operations on Leyte passed into the hands of the Eighth Army, commanded by Lieutenant General Robert L. Eichelberger. The Sixth Army now prepared for the next vital step in the liberation of the Philippines, the invasion of Luzon, scheduled for 9 January 1945.

For the fighter squadrons of MAG-12, the latter part of December brought at least some relief from the squalid conditions under which they had op-

---

[53] *Ibid.*

erated at crowded Tacloban airfield. Beginning on 21 December, and continuing through the 27th, the four dayfighter squadrons moved from Tacloban to the newly completed airstrip at Tanauan. This move once and for all brought to an end the congestion and mud that had been the trademark of Tacloban. The runway at Tanauan consisted of Marston matting, which had been placed over sand; despite the noisy vibration of the metal, landings were considerably safer than they had been at Tacloban.

As 1944 drew to a close, the role that Marine aviation was destined to play in support of ground operations on Leyte, had been partly fulfilled. In less than four weeks of operations, the fighter pilots of MAG-12 had flown a total of 264 missions. They destroyed 22 enemy ships and accounted for a total of 40 enemy aircraft. The price paid by the Marines for their exploits during the Leyte operation was 9 pilots killed and 34 aircraft lost.[54]

The night fighters of VMF(N)-541, during their stay on Leyte, also established a record worthy of mention. During the month of December, the squadron carried out 312 individual combat flights, totalling 924 combat hours. When, on 11 January, the Hellcats returned to Peleliu, they had accounted for 22 aircraft destroyed in the air, 5 destroyed on the ground, plus several probables. The night fighters had also destroyed four small surface craft loaded with enemy personnel.[55]

For their performance on Leyte, the nightfighters received a Letter of Commendation from Fifth Air Force and V Fighter Command, praising the squadron for making "an important contribution to the control of the air that is now assured our forces."[56]

As planning for General MacArthur's accelerated drive through the Philippines gained momentum, additional Marine aviation units stood poised to play their part in the liberation of the islands. For the enemy, the damage inflicted by Marine squadrons during the Leyte campaign was only a forerunner of what was to follow. The full impetus of the Marine doctrine of close support for the ground forces was yet to be tested in battle. The day for this test was fast approaching.

---

[54] MAG-12 WarD, Dec44.

[55] VMF(N)-541 WarD, Dec44–Jan45.

[56] Ltr of Commendation, BGen Paul D. Wurtsmith, CG, V Fighter Cmd., n.d., as shown in VMF(N)-541 WarD, Dec44–Jan45, pp. 16-17.

CHAPTER 3

The Luzon Campaign[1]

Except for a prolonged mopping up operation, the Leyte campaign was completed on 26 December 1944. The next step in the liberation of the Philippine Islands, scheduled for 9 January, was the invasion of Luzon at Lingayen Gulf, about 150 miles north of Manila. The lack of air bases on Leyte had already made necessary a postponement of the Luzon operation, initially scheduled for 20 December. The need to build airstrips on Mindoro Island just south of Luzon, from which land based aircraft could support the invasion, contributed further to the delay.

In many respects, the plan advanced for the seizure of Luzon resembled that employed for Leyte. Once again, the Sixth Army was to execute the landings, supported by the Third Fleet. Allied Naval Forces, under the command of Admiral Kinkaid and Allied Air Forces under General Kenney were to support the operation. In addition to the Fifth and Thirteenth Air Forces under SWPA, the Fourteenth Air Force in China and the Twentieth Air Force in the China-Burma-India Theater were to lend strategic support to SWPA operations in the Philippines. The immediate objective of the Luzon campaign was seizure of the plain of Central Luzon and Manila, the annihilation of Japanese forces on the island, and denial of the northern entrance to the South China Sea to the enemy.

As preparations for the Luzon invasion were going into full swing, additional Marine aviation units were en route from the Solomons to the Philippines, an indication of the expanded role that Marine aviation was to play in the liberation of the islands. As early as 7 December, General Mitchell had alerted MAG-14, then based in the Solomons, for movement to the Philippines. Under the command of Colonel Zebulon C. Hopkins, the group consisted of VMFs-212, -222, -223 and VMO-251, subsequently redesignated a fighter squadron.[2] For the remainder of December, despite the early alerting order, MAG-14 sat out the month in the Solomons, awaiting the conquest of Samar by the 1st Cavalry Division and

---

[1] Unless otherwise noted, the material in this chapter is derived from: 1st MAW WarD, Dec44; VMF-212 WarDs, Oct44-Feb45; VMF-222 WarDs, Oct44-Mar45; USSBS, *Pacific Campaigns*; Robert Ross Smith, *Triumph in the Philippines—The War in the Pacific—U. S. Army in World War II* (Washington: OCMH, DA, 1963), hereafter Smith, *Triumph in the Philippines*; Samuel Eliot Morison, *The Liberation of the Philippines, Luzon, Mindanao, the Visayas, 1944–1945—History of United States Naval Operations in World War II*, v. XIII (Boston: Little, Brown and Company, 1959) hereafter Morison, *Liberation of the Philippines*.

[2] The names of squadron commanders during this time period have been included in the Marine Task Organization and Command List which forms an appendix to this volume.

the construction of an airstrip near the town of Guiuan on southeastern Samar. By the last week of December, the Seabees of the 61st and 93d Naval Construction Battalions had completed facilities at Guiuan to handle at least one squadron of MAG-14. On 30 December the flight echelon of VMO-251 departed Bougainville, and by way of Emirau, Owi, and Peleliu, reached Samar on 2 January. By mid-January, the remaining squadrons of MAG-14 had installed themselves at Guiuan, under conditions as primitive as those which MAG-12 had encountered on Leyte barely a month previously.

As 1944 neared its end, ground echelons of the squadrons of MAGs-24 and -32 were en route to yet unspecified objectives in the Philippines, though it appeared certain that their destination could be none other than Luzon. Following a Christmas service at Headquarters, General Mitchell made a brief speech to the assembled Wing Headquarters personnel. "His pronouncement that his Headquarters would be on its way to a forward area in a matter of weeks was enthusiastically received."[3]

Marine aviation based on Leyte was to play only a very limited role in support of the landings on Luzon. Two weeks prior to the assault on the main island and the days following the landings, Corsairs of MAG-12 struck at highway and railroad bridges in order to restrict enemy mobility and disrupt the Japanese transportation system. Because of frequent bad weather, the Corsairs occasionally were unable to reach the objectives assigned to them and instead attacked such targets of opportunity as trains and vehicular traffic. Japanese air activity was negligible throughout this period and air-to-air combat occurred infrequently, with "the remaining operational Japanese aircraft being either so widely dispersed as to be unavailable on short notice, or else being held in reserve for suicide attacks against the most dangerous enemy, the expected approaching fleet."[4]

The approach of that fleet was not a figment of the enemy's imagination, for on 3 January the minesweeping, shore bombardment, and escort carrier groups headed north through the Sulu Sea toward Lingayen Gulf. At the same time that the Seventh Fleet was departing from Leyte Gulf, the fast carriers of Halsey's Third Fleet struck hard at Formosa and the Ryukyus in order to forestall any Japanese attempt to reinforce the Luzon garrison. These air strikes, in which VMFs-124 and -213 from the carrier *Essex* participated, resulted in the destruction of over 100 enemy aircraft, despite extensive Japanese attempts at dispersal and camouflage.[5]

As the invasion fleet headed for Luzon, the officers and men on board the transports and escort ships were under no delusions as to the enemy's strength. In mid-December, a SWPA intelligence

---

[3] 1st MAW WarD, Dec44.

[4] USSBS, *Pacific Campaigns*, p. 288.

[5] For a detailed account of Marine aviators on carriers, see Benis M. Frank and Henry I. Shaw, Jr., *Victory and Occupation —History of U. S. Marine Corps Operations in World War II*, v. V (Washington: HistBr, G-3 Div, HQMC, 1969), Part III, Chap 2, section entitled "Marine Air on Carriers," *passim*.

estimate had identified a tank division, five infantry divisions, six independent mixed brigades, and two separate infantry regiments on Luzon. By the end of the month, MacArthur's intelligence estimate figured enemy strength at a total of 152,000 troops of all categories. The Japanese were expected to commit all available air strength against the Allied invasion fleet and against any beachhead that might be established on Luzon. Japanese air strength in the Philippines was estimated at 400-500 aircraft, most of them stationed on Luzon.

As the main body of the Luzon Attack Force moved out of Leyte Gulf, the huge convoy posed a challenge which the enemy could not ignore. Beginning on 4 January, the remnants of the Philippine air garrison launched a series of *Kamikaze* attacks that soon began to take a toll of Allied ships. A suicide plane crashing into the escort carrier *Ommaney Bay* started a chain reaction of gasoline explosions which resulted in the abandonment and sinking of the ship. Another escort carrier barely escaped the same fate. On the following day the Japanese attacks against the convoy reached a new high when seven *Kamikazes* crashed into Allied ships and inflicted heavy damage on an escort carrier, two cruisers, and a destroyer, though none of these ships were sunk.[6] On 6 January the fury of the enemy onslaught from the air reached a climax. One of the ships attacked was the USS *New Mexico*, which was carrying Colonel Clayton C. Jerome, who was charged with the direction of the Marine aviation effort on Luzon. As the officer helplessly watched, a *Kamikaze* crashed the bridge of the *New Mexico*, causing 30 fatalities, including the captain of the ship, and wounding 87 men.[7] Before the day ended, an additional 15 Allied vessels were struck by suicide attacks. Even though only one ship sank as a result of this assault from the air, damage to the ships struck varied from moderate to extensive. Loss of personnel for 6 January alone totalled 167 killed and 502 wounded.[8]

As it became apparent to General MacArthur that land-based Allied aircraft could not keep all of the enemy airfields on Luzon neutralized, he diverted the fast carriers of the Third Fleet from Formosa and committed them against Japanese airfields on central Luzon. During a two-day period, on 6 and 7 January, repeated strikes by Navy and Marine carrier-based aircraft of the Third Fleet resulted in the destruction of more than 100 enemy aircraft.[9]

This blow, combined with strikes by land-based Allied aircraft on Leyte and Mindoro, broke the back of the massive Japanese onslaught against the invasion convoy, though this was not immediately apparent to American commanders, who were openly worried about the situation. From the Japanese point of view, the *Kamikaze* attacks were not as effective as had been hoped. Orders issued to the suicide pilots to concentrate their attacks on Allied transports were not followed, and com-

---

[6] USSBS, *Pacific Campaigns*, p. 288.

[7] Morison, *Liberation of the Philippines*, p. 105.

[8] *Ibid.*, App IV, p. 325.

[9] USSBS, *Pacific Campaigns*, p. 289.

bat vessels were instead singled out for attack. No one can estimate what would have happened, had the Japanese decided to rush air reinforcements from Formosa to Luzon. After 7 January the massive Japanese air effort tapered off, though:

> ... suiciders continued to appear in two's and three's for a week or more, but the battle in the Gulf, weird as it was and impressive as a testimony to the effectiveness of this form of attack, marked the end of the Japanese air forces in the Philippines. On 8 January the Naval Air Commander left for Singapore and his staff for Formosa, while the Commanding General of the 4th Air Army retired without his army to the hills of Luzon.[10]

Following in the wake of the harrowing voyage of the invasion convoy from Leyte Gulf to Lingayen, the Sixth Army landings of 9 January came as something of an anticlimax. Contrary to an earlier intelligence estimate at MacArthur's headquarters, which assumed that "a large and potentially dangerous concentration of Japanese forces held the region immediately east, northeast, and southeast of Lingayen Gulf,"[11] and deduced the presence of "at least two infantry divisions in position to defend Lingayen Gulf and environs,"[12] the landings were in fact unopposed. The X and XIV Corps went ashore and by nightfall had secured positions 3-5 miles inland along 15 miles of shoreline of southern Lingayen Gulf. (See Map 18).

The first Marines to go ashore on 10 January were Colonel Jerome, Lieutenant Colonel McCutcheon, operations officer of MAG-24, and the colonel's driver, a Marine corporal. As the three Marines consolidated their "beachhead," they immediately set out in search of a strip which could be developed for the use of Marine aviation. A prewar field near Lingayen soon was so crowded with Army aircraft that selection of another strip was deemed desirable. An undeveloped site about 15 miles east of Lingayen appeared promising and was selected. Work on the strip had barely begun when, on 14 January, it became apparent that heavy graders had destroyed the thin crust of top soil and with it any chance of a solid undersurface. Colonel Jerome forthwith decided to abandon this site and instead selected an expanse of rice fields between Dagupan and Mangaldan about six miles to the southwest.

The selection of such a locale may at first glance appear a poor choice, though Colonel Jerome explained his action in the following words:

> The Mangaldan strip was only a rice paddy. But if the hills of a rice paddy are knocked down without tearing out the roots they make a fine, flat surface which, when oiled, will serve as an airstrip about 12 inches above the water level. Rains would eventually raise the level of the muck but Colonel Jerome, an old Philippines hand from the twenties, figured three dry months were due and that was all he needed at Mangaldan, and recommended that the Army engineers build there.[13]

And build they did. On this occasion Army engineers employed light bulldozers and built a 6,500-foot east-west runway. While this work was in prog-

---

[10] Ibid.
[11] Smith, Triumph in the Philippines, p. 27.
[12] Ibid., p. 28.

[13] Colonel Clayton C. Jerome interview by Robert Sherrod, cited in Sherrod, Marine Corps Aviation in World War II, p. 299.

338   WESTERN PACIFIC OPERATIONS

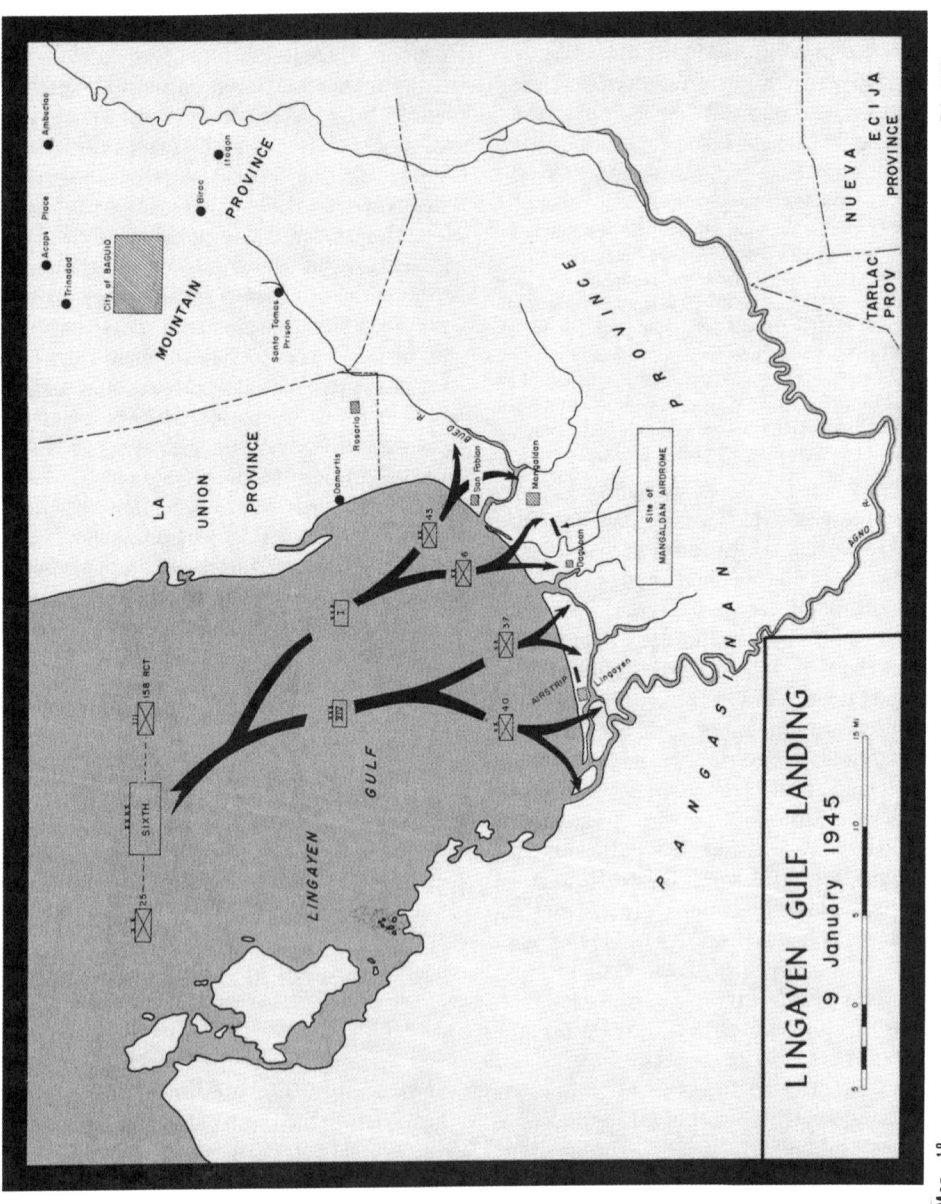

LINGAYEN GULF LANDING
9 January 1945

Map 18

ress, Colonel Meyer, commanding officer of MAG-24, who had been in charge of the movement of the ground echelon, arrived at Lingayen with 14 pilots and 278 enlisted men. Before leaving for the Marine airstrip at Mangaldan, the Marines assisted Sixth Army in unloading and laying steel matting on the Lingayen airfield, which earned them a commendation from General Krueger, the Sixth Army commander. In mid-January additional men and supplies arrived at San Fabian, five miles north of Mangaldan, where all hands helped in constructing a camp and such other facilities as were required for full-scale operation of the strip.

As work on the Mangaldan airstrip neared completion, Colonel Jerome was designated Commander, Air Base, Mangaldan, and at the same time Commander, Marine Aircraft Groups, Dagupan (alternately abbreviated as MAGs-Mangaldan or MAGsDagupan). The first aircraft of MAGs-24 and -32 arrived at Mangaldan on 25 January, and combat operations began two days later. By the end of the month, 7 squadrons consisting of 472 officers and more than 3,000 men, and 174 Douglas Dauntless divebombers (SBDs) had reached Mangaldan. These squadrons were VMSBs-133, -142, -236, -241, -243, -244, and -341.

Before long, the splendid isolation in which the Marine aviation squadrons had hoped to operate was shattered with the arrival of 250 Army Air Forces planes which were also stationed at the field. The Army aircraft and personnel, as well as the Marines, were under the operational control of the 308th Bombardment Wing of the Fifth Air Force. Colonel Jerome retained complete responsibility for the operation of the base and camp facilities, though he had not envisioned at the outset that before long Mangaldan airfield would become one of the busiest airports in the Western Pacific.

The arrival of two Marine air groups on Luzon and preparations for close support of Sixth Army ground troops on the island during most of January tended to overshadow the activities of MAGs-12 and -14 on Leyte and Samar. During the month of January, MAG-12 flew 306 missions, most of them in support of the Lingayen operation, while MAG-14 flew 1,590 sorties.[14]

Following completion of an improved landing strip at Tanauan on Leyte, operations of MAG-12 could be carried on under somewhat more normal conditions than had been the case on the overcrowded and treacherous Tacloban strip. For the Marines of MAG-14 stationed at Guiuan strip on southeastern Samar, problems grew from the lack of dispersal areas, adequate taxiing strips, and a field lighting system. These conditions inevitably resulted in a number of operational accidents; during January alone, MAG-14 lost 19 aircraft from this cause.

A spectacular accident, somewhat akin to the disaster that had struck at Tacloban on 13 December, marred operations at Guiuan on the morning of 24 January. During takeoff, a Corsair blew a tire, went out of control, and smashed into the revetment area shared

---

[14] Sherrod, *Marine Corps Aviation in World War II*, p. 289.

jointly by VMFs-212 and -222. Within a matter of seconds the tents housing the intelligence section, oxygen, and other supplies were completely destroyed. In a desperate effort to rescue the pilot, Marine aviation personnel rushed to the blazing wreck, reaching it just as the plane exploded. The explosion snuffed out the lives of 11 Marines, including the pilot; more than 50 Marines were injured, many of them seriously.[15]

The occurrence of such accidents was unavoidable under existing conditions. By late January, the military situation in the Philippines had radically changed in favor of the Allies. Massive *Kamikaze* attacks had hurt the huge Allied invasion fleet headed for Luzon, but had failed to interfere with the actual landings. In effect:

> The submarine blockade, four months of carrier strikes overwhelming the Japanese air garrisons and destroying their merchant shipping, the destruction of their fleet in the great battle of October, and the attrition of their surviving air, of their transport, and other installations... made possible the invasion of Luzon under militarily ideal circumstances. Unopposed on the beaches, our troops went ashore to fight a campaign at their leisure against an enemy disorganized and demoralized, badly equipped and badly supplied, isolated beyond hope of remedy; a campaign in which every aircraft in the sky was friendly.[16]

A large number of the friendly aircraft sweeping ahead of and clearing the path for the advance of the Sixth Army were the dive bombers of the Marine air groups based at Mangaldan, and a historical account of the Army sweep through Luzon also becomes the story of Marine aviation close support.

CLOSE AIR SUPPORT ON LUZON[17]

The overall Japanese plan for the defense of Luzon provided for the *Fourteenth Area Army* to halt or delay the advance of American forces into Central Luzon (See Map 19). Such tactics were designed to forestall additional American advances towards the Japanese homeland or other islands scheduled for invasion. On the whole, the outlook for the Japanese did not appear promising. At a time when MacArthur's headquarters estimated Japanese strength on Luzon at 152,000, the *Fourteenth Area Army* had only about 90,000 men there; the remainder consisted of 25,000 airmen and 20,000 naval personnel. The defense was further hampered by an extremely meager supply of arms and ammunition. Poor transportation facilities, the lack of effective antitank weapons, and a shortage of rations added to the precariousness of the Japanese foothold on Luzon. Increased activity on the part of American-led Philippine guerrillas also began to prove bothersome to the Japanese.

---

[15] VMF-212 and VMF-222 WarDs, Jan-Feb45.
[16] USSBS, *Pacific Campaigns*, p. 289.

[17] Unless otherwise noted, the material in this section is derived from: Marine Aviation in Close Air Support File; (HistBr, G-3 Div, HQMC), hereafter *Marine Close Air Support File*; McCutcheon Rpt; Philippines Comment File; Maj Bertram C. Wright, USA, *The First Cavalry Division in World War II* (Tokyo: Toppan Printing Company, Ltd., 1947) hereafter, Wright, *1st CavDiv Hist*; Hayashi and Coox, *Kōgun*; Sherrod, *Marine Corps Aviation in World War II*.

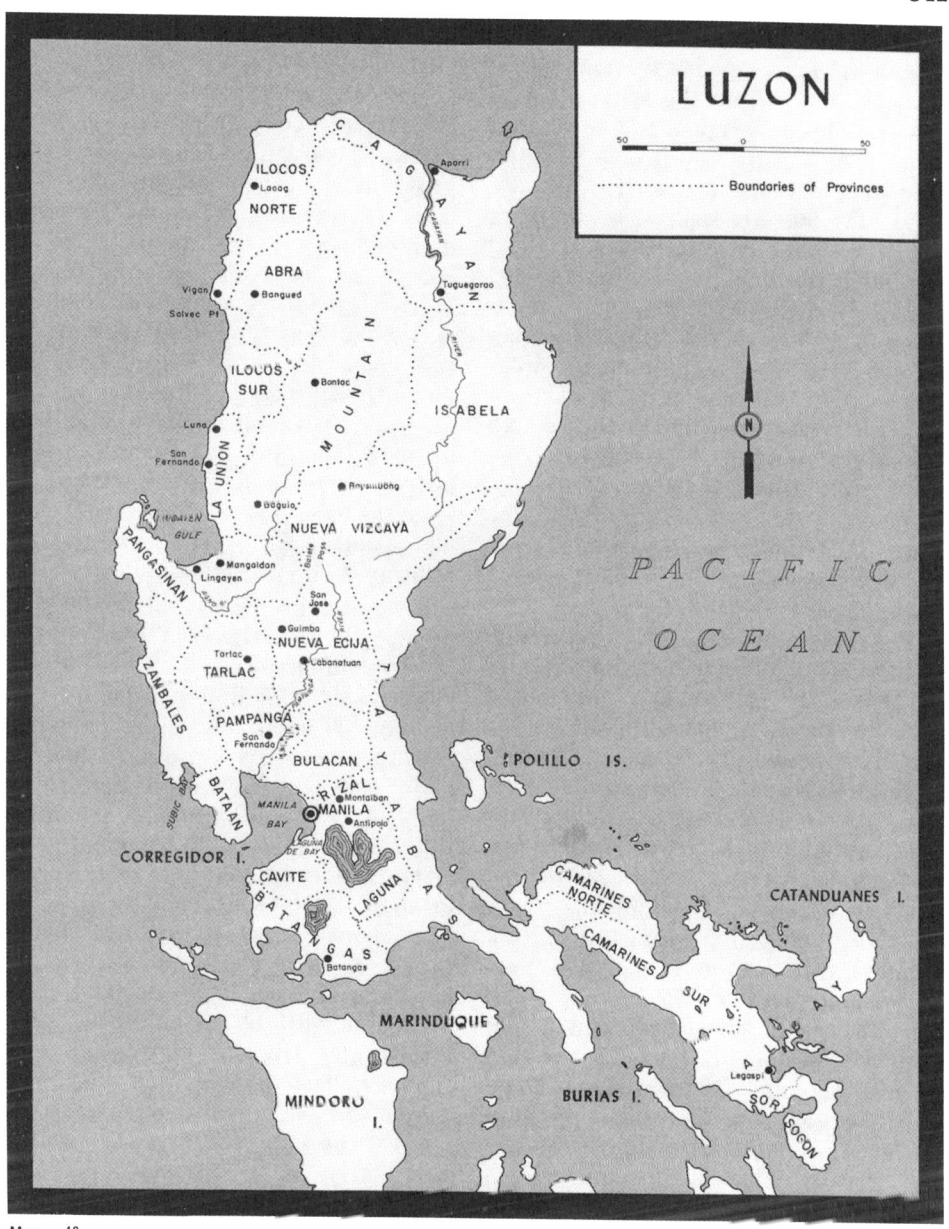

Map 19

These disadvantages did not prevent the enemy from offering determined resistance, but during the latter part of January Sixth Army made important gains. The I Corps had driven 50 miles southeast of Lingayen Gulf to Talevera. (See Map 20). By the end of January, the XIV Corps had seized Clark Field and Fort Stotsenburg and was advancing westward into the Zambales Mountains. Elements of the XIV Corps had in fact reached a point only 25 miles from Manila. Other units landed on western Luzon near Subic Bay on 29 January and pushed eastward. Two days later, American paratroopers descended on Batangas Peninsula to the south of Manila. The stage was set for the envelopment of the capital of the Philippines.

Following the completion of the airstrip at Mangaldan, the Marine aviators of MAGs-24 and -32 had anticipated immediate close support operations for the Sixth Army advance across Luzon. It quickly became apparent, however, that the missions assigned to the Marines differed little from those flown on Leyte by MAG-12, and were directed against targets far behind the front lines. Beginning on 27 January, Marine aviators from Luzon raided San Fernando and Clark Field; in four days' time they had flown 255 sorties and dropped 104 tons of bombs, at the cost of one aircraft. The missions flown were assigned the evening preceding the attacks; moreover, control of the air strikes followed a cumbersome chain of command which led through the Army Air Forces 308th Bombardment Wing all the way to the Sixth Army, a far cry from strikes directed on target from jeep-mounted air liaison parties in the front lines.

Nevertheless, the dive bombers of the two Marine aircraft groups on Luzon performed creditably during the early phase of their employment on the island. The use of the Douglas Dauntless dive bombers by the Marines was unique in at least one respect, for the Marine squadrons were the only units still flying that type of aircraft during this phase of the war. The Army had discontinued use of dive bombers as early as 1942, and during the summer of 1944 the Navy had turned to more heavily armed and faster aircraft. Despite the valiant service the dive bomber had rendered for Marine aviation from Midway to Bougainville, due to the accuracy obtained with the aircraft in pinpointing targets, the SBD was rapidly becoming obsolete. This was due particularly to its limited combat radius of only 450 miles. The Luzon campaign was to become its swan song and the plane was scheduled for retirement at the end of the Philippines campaign. But Marine aviators in their outmoded aircraft were to have one more chance to show what they could do with the dive bombers in which they had so carefully trained in the Solomons. The opportunity was not long in coming.

It came with the arrival of the Army 1st Cavalry Division on Luzon on 27 January. The division had fought on Samar and Leyte before moving to Luzon. On the following day, the cavalrymen moved to an assembly area near Guimba, 35 miles inland from Lingayen, where the division was assigned to the XIV Corps. When General MacArthur visited the troopers on 31 January, he gave them an electrifying order, which was to:

> ...go to Manila. Go around the Nips, bounce off the Nips, but go to Manila. Free the internees at Santo Tomas. Take Malacanan Palace and the Legislative Building.[18]

To sustain this daring 100-mile dash through enemy territory, the 308th Bombardment Wing alerted all seven Marine squadrons on Luzon to provide a screen of nine planes from dawn to dusk over the 1st Cavalry Division.[19] Here was an assignment that the Ma- Lieutenant Colonel McCutcheon formu lated his doctrine of close air support back in the Solomons. For the first time, Marines would be able to fly close support with their own ALPs functioning right in the front lines. The teams, working closely in conjunction with the ground force commander, could call for air support when opposition was encountered, guide the aircraft to their targets, observe the effects of bombing or strafing, and correct any pilot errors without delay. For the dive bomber squadrons of MAGs-24 and -32, this was the long-awaited chance to prove their value to the ground forces.

At 0001 on 1 February, a specially organized "flying column" under the command of Brigadier General William C. Chase set out on the dash to Manila. There was an element of risk involved in the venture, for at such short notice the cavalrymen had not been able to reconnoiter routes of advance. Intelligence concerning the enemy was vague. The only transportation available consisted of vehicles organic to the 1st Cavalry Division and attached units. The advance, carried out over primitive roads, began in a complete blackout; the columns crossed rivers and rice paddies. At dawn the troopers approached Cabanatuan, their first major objective. There, the enemy offered determined resistance which continued throughout the day.

Despite enemy opposition, the column was not long delayed, and the high degree of mobility of the task force began to pay off. Included in the force were reconnaissance, antitank, medical, field artillery, tank, engineer, and infantry heavy weapons units, all working together to form a balanced striking force. Mindful of the mission they had received from General MacArthur, the cavalrymen did not waste any time on a costly frontal assault but, approaching Cabanatuan, converged on the town from three directions. Bypassing the Japanese stronghold, the main body of the task force continued on towards

---

[18] General MacArthur to MajGen Verne D. Mudge, (USA), cited in Wright, *1st Cav Div Hist*, p. 126

[19] "The 308th Bomb Wing did not want to authorize the 1st Cavalry Division to levy requests on us directly. Since the Division could not tell a day ahead exactly when and where targets would occur we suggested to them that they submit a request for nine aircraft to be overhead on station continuously from dawn to dusk. These arrangements were made by Captain Francis B. "Frisco" Godolphin of MAG–24. He visited the 1st Cavalry and ran into a staff officer who had been a student of his at Princeton University. Liaison was thus firmly established. The Division requested the aircraft from the 308th Bomber Wing. The 308th flagged us. We took it from there." MajGen Keith B. McCutcheon ltr to Head, HistBr, dtd 21Oct66, in *Philippines Comment File*, hereafter *McCutcheon ltr*.

Manila. The tactic of bypassing the Japanese wherever possible was followed on successive days, for:

> The mission of the 1st Cavalry Division was not to become embroiled in a large scale battle with the enemy, however, but rather to dash through him using such force as was necessary to get to Manila where the internees were waiting for liberation.[20]

During the three day sweep to Manila, the nine Marine dive bombers screening the advance and flanks of the column maintained a continuous vigil during the daylight hours. The planes were not utilized for bombing or strafing as the troops were able to cope with whatever resistance was encountered. Even though this state of affairs was disappointing to the pilots, "the very presence of the planes contributed greatly to the advance of the Division. The planes in effect were the flank guards and were used for observation and recco missions to provide information to the ground units on the status of roads, bridges, etc."[21]

From the very outset of the operation, an excellent relationship prevailed between the Marine air liaison parties attached to the task force and the cavalrymen. The Marine ALP consisted of two radio jeeps and a radio truck, manned by personnel of MAGs-24 and -32. Each jeep carried a Marine officer and one enlisted man, while the communications officer of MAG-24 and two enlisted men manned the radio truck.[22]

Indicative of the matter-of-factness and cordiality which the Marine ALP received from the cavalry troopers is the reception accorded them by General Chase, who was in charge of the expedition. When informed of the presence of a radio jeep carrying two Marines, he merely ordered the occupants to stay beside him and his jeep at all times. Since the jeeps travelled well forward and were very useful in getting information from the planes direct to the unit commanders, it was not long before a battalion or regimental commander became a passenger in one of the radio jeeps.[23]

It was apparent that the simplicity of the Marine air-ground communications setup appealed to General Chase, as did the idea of literally having nine SBDs at his fingertips. Droning overhead in a lazy circle, the dive bombers were ready to pounce downward to stop any threat to the flanks of the column. Subsequently, the Marines were to learn to their astonishment that the 308th Bombardment Wing had also attached a formidable air liaison party to the "flying column." This party consisted of:

> ...a DUKW (complete with Filipino houseboy), a weapons carrier, a jeep, 27 men and 2 officers ... but its equipment was such that it couldn't keep up with the advance or semiexposed positions.

---

[20] Wright, *1st CavDiv Hist*, p. 127.
[21] *McCutcheon Rpt*, p. 8.
[22] With General Chase and the 1st Brigade was the radio jeep with Captain McAloney, driven by radio operator PFC P. E. Armstrong. With General Hugh Hoffman and the 2d Brigade was Captain Godolphin and his driver-radio man, Technical Sergeant R. B. Holland. In the radio truck, travelling with General Mudge and division headquarters were Captain Titcomb, Staff Sergeant A. A. Byers, and Staff Sergeant P. J. Miller. Captain Samuel H. McAloney ltr to CMC, n.d., in *Philippines Comment File*.
[23] *Ibid*.

THE LUZON CAMPAIGN 345

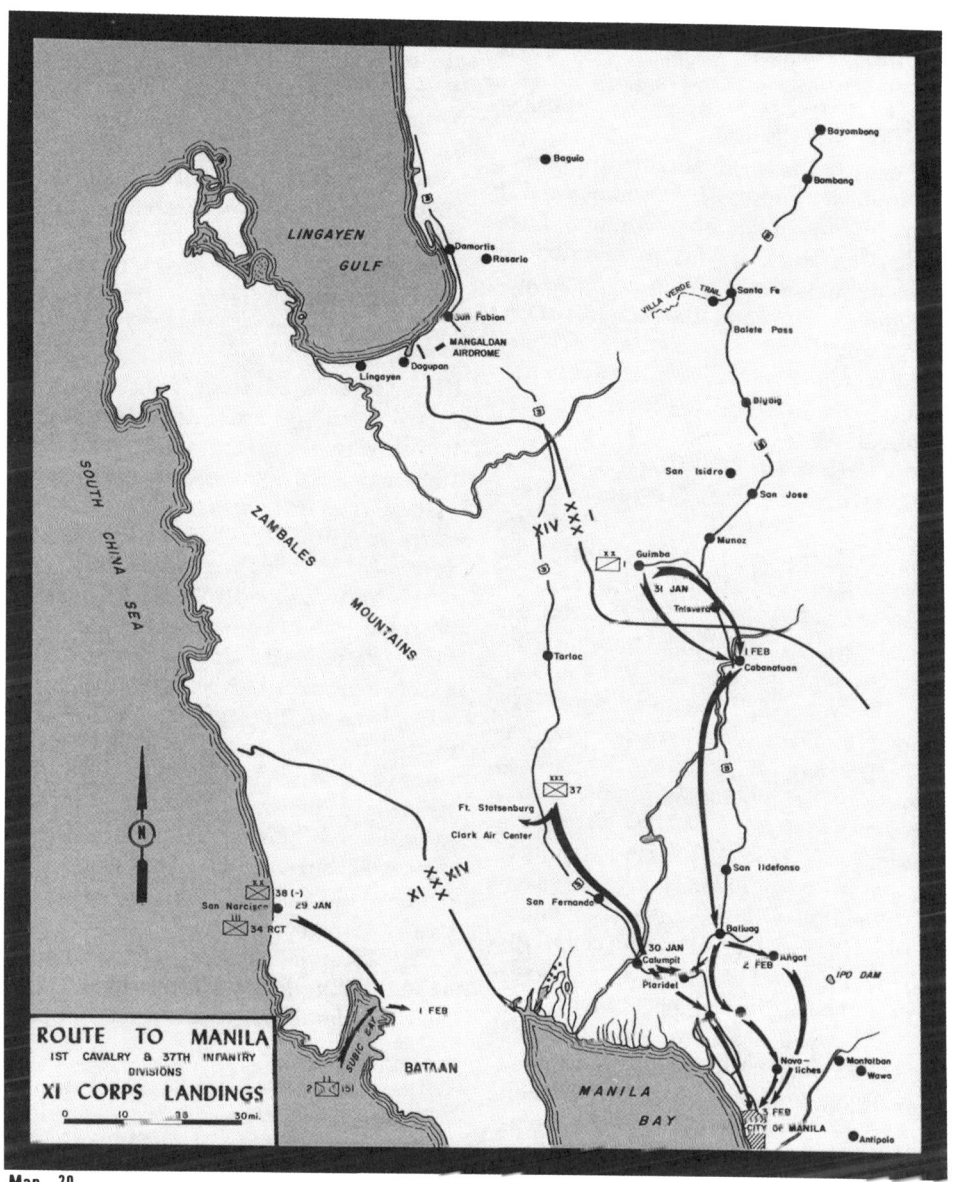

Map 20. ROUTE TO MANILA — 1ST CAVALRY & 37TH INFANTRY DIVISIONS — XI CORPS LANDINGS

Besides, for air support through that channel, requests would have to be forwarded and approved first by Division, then Corps, then Army and finally by 308th Bomb Wing.[24]

For three days the Marine dive bombers rode shotgun over the exposed left flank of the advancing column. Tirelessly, the Marine aviators searched an area 30 miles ahead and 20 miles behind the advance ground patrols, reporting all enemy troop movements that could conceivably interfere with the cavalrymen's ever lengthening lines of communications.

Aside from the nine SBDs flying over the task force, other Marine aviators bombed and strafed ahead of the column. On 1 February, while fighting at Cabanatuan was still in progress, two separate nine-plane flights attacked ahead of the cavalrymen in air strikes directed against Angat and San Jose del Monte, where enemy troops were known to have concentrated. On the following day, aircraft of VMSBs-133, -142, and -241 bombed and strafed San Ildefonso just ahead of the "flying column." Later on 2 February, after having passed through Baliuag, vanguards of the column linked up with elements of the 37th Infantry Division near Plaridel and crossed the Angat River, where strong opposition was encountered.

To the southeast of Baliuag, near Santa Maria, the cavalrymen encountered a well-entrenched enemy battalion occupying high ground which commanded the road and the river valley. In a situation where a costly firefight appeared unavoidable, the Marine aviators distracted the Japanese through a ruse which had worked once before during the capture of Hellzapoppin Ridge on Bougainville.[25] Since friendly troops were too close to enemy positions for a conventional dive bombing and strafing attack, "the dive bombers of MAG-32 made several strafing passes at the Japs without firing a shot . . . and enabled the squadron to slug its way into the defensive position and rout the occupants."[26]

The end of the second day of the drive towards Manila found the vanguard of the column within 15 miles of its objective. As the cavalrymen continued their advance south along Route 5, they ran into a road junction just north of Novaliches which was heavily defended by the Japanese. This junction, quickly dubbed "The Hot Corner," protected the approaches to a vital bridge in the path of the column. When the Marine aviators reported that this bridge was still intact, the cavalrymen rushed the Japanese defenses at the road junction and made for the bridge. Braving a hail of enemy fire, a Navy mine disposal officer ran onto the span and cut a burning fuze to a large mine which would have blown the bridge to bits within seconds.

At 1835 on 3 February, the vanguard of the "flying column" crossed the Manila city limits. The cavalrymen slipped

---

[24] *Ibid.*

[25] For a detailed account of the battle for Hellzapoppin' Ridge, see Henry I. Shaw, Jr., and Maj Douglas T. Kane, *Isolation of Rabaul—History of U. S. Marine Corps Operations in World War II*, v. II (Washington: HistBr, G–3 Div, HQMC, 1963), Part III, Chap 6, section entitled "Hellzapoppin' Ridge and Hill 600A," *passim.*

[26] Wright, *1st CavDiv Hist*, p. 128.

into the city just as dusk was settling. Guided by two Filipinos, the troopers began to roll past the Chinese Cemetery, where they became embroiled in a running battle with the enemy who sought cover behind the tombstones. The column kept moving through the darkness toward Santo Tomas University. Shortly before 2100, the 3,700 emaciated and tattered internees huddled inside the compound heard the clanking of tank treads.

> Indistinct voices floated up to the internees leaning out of the windows bent on missing nothing. A flare was sent up. Its light showed the time to be 8:50 P.M. Everything was quiet.
>
> A voice cut through the darkness: "Where the hell is the front gate?" The Americans had arrived for sure.[27]

Thus ended the 100-mile dash of the 1st Cavalry Division to Manila. In 66 hours after setting forth from Guimba, the task force had reached its objective, though driving the enemy out of Manila was to prove a costly and time-consuming process which was not due to be completed until 3 March.

For the part they had played during the dash for Manila, the Marine aviators received generous praise from the cavalrymen. The 1st Cavalry Division history evaluated the contribution of the Marines as follows:

> Much of the success of the entire movement is credited to the superb air cover, flank protection, and reconnaissance provided by the Marine Air Groups 24 and 32. The 1st Cavalry's audacious drive down through Central Luzon was the longest such operation ever made in the Southwest Pacific Area using only air cover for flank protection.[28]

---

[27] *Ibid.*, p. 125.
[28] *Ibid.*, p. 127.

Major General Verne D. Mudge, commanding the 1st Cavalry Division, was equally unsparing in his praise. Commenting on the support received from Marine dive bombers, the general had this to say:

> On our drive to Manila, I depended solely on the Marines to protect my left flank against possible Japanese counterattack. The job that they turned in speaks for itself. I can say without reservation that the Marine dive bombers are one of the most flexible outfits that I have seen in this war. They will try anything once, and from my experience with them, I have found out that anything they try usually pans out in their favor. The Marine dive bombers of the First Wing have kept the enemy on the run. They have kept him underground and have enabled troops to move up with fewer casualties and with greater speed. I cannot say enough in praise of these men of the dive bombers and I am commending them through proper channels for the job they have done in giving my men close ground support in this operation.[29]

General Chase remarked "that he had never seen such able, close and accurate air support as the Marine fliers were giving him,"[30] and this was ample praise, indeed, from the man who had fearlessly led his "flying column" into the heart of Manila.

Events in the progressing Philippines Campaign did not permit the Marine aviators to rest on their laurels, and other missions, equally as challenging as the drive to Manila, awaited them.

---

[29] Statement of MajGen Verne D. Mudge, USA, n.d., in *Marine Close Air Support File*, p. 9.
[30] *Ibid.*, p. 3.

SUPPORTING GUERRILLAS[31]

The excellent record which the Marine aviators of MAG-24 and -32 established in rendering close support to the 1st Cavalry Division on Luzon did not end with the liberation of Manila. While fighting for the capital of the Philippines continued throughout February and into the early days of March, another unusual assignment awaited the Marine pilots. Once again they were called upon to provide close air support, but in this instance the support was for Filipino guerrilla bands which were attempting to drive the Japanese invaders from Philippine soil.

The insurgent movement dated back to the early days of World War II, when U.S. Army officers organized remnants of cut-off Filipino forces into guerrilla bands. At the time that American resistance on Bataan ended, two U.S. Army officers, Major Russell W. Volkmann and Captain Donald D. Blackburn escaped and made their way to Northern Luzon, where they reported for duty to Colonel Martin Moses, the senior U.S. Army officer in that area.[32] It was estimated that "five regiments of these natives roamed the mountains and jungles of Northern Luzon,"[33] though a more conservative breakdown in the official Army history lists guerrilla strength on Luzon prior to the Lingayen landings at about 8,000 men, of whom only 2,000 were well armed.[34] This figure subsequently increased to more than 20,000 men.

Following the Luzon landings, Sixth Army took official cognizance of these insurgents by organizing them under the designation of United States Armed Forces in the Philippines (USAFIP or USFIP), North Luzon (NL). By any standard, the equipment of the guerrillas was primitive and consisted primarily of small arms. They had no artillery, only a few mortars, and very few machine guns.

From the Japanese point of view, even prior to the Lingayen landings, the guerrillas had already become annoyingly active. The *Area Army* was apprehensive lest all the natives become partisans whenever U.S. troops landed on Luzon. From the middle of November 1944, the Japanese therefore began to suppress the armed guerrillas. The outnumbered and ill-equipped insurgents proved no match for the Japanese, for they were not organized to engage major Japanese units in a sustained effort. At the outset it appeared unlikely "that Volckmann's or any other guerrilla unit, would ever become effective combat organizations."[35]

Increasing guerrilla strength and successes prompted General Krueger to reassess the role that the insurgents

---

[31] Unless otherwise noted, the material in this section is derived from: MAG-32 WarDs, Jan44-Jun45; Wright, *1st CavDiv Hist;* Sherrod, *Marine Corps Aviation in World War II;* Hayashi and Coox, *Kōgun.*

[32] BGen Russell W. Volkmann, USA, ltr to Head, HistBr, G-3 Div, HQMC, dtd 21Nov66, in *Philippines Comment File,* hereafter *Volkmann ltr.*

[33] Sherrod, *Marine Corps Aviation in World War II,* p. 307.

[34] Smith, *Triumph in the Philippines,* p. 466.

[35] *Ibid.* The above is disputed by General Volckmann who claims that after January 1944 the Japanese forces presented very little overall threat to USAFIP. *Volckmann ltr.*

were to play on Luzon. In the course of February more and more of the irregulars were equipped with arms and uniforms. In addition to harassing the Japanese, guerrillas also were increasingly active in reporting Japanese troop movements and gun positions on northern Luzon by means of radio equipment controlled by Colonel Volckmann. The rapid growth of the guerrilla forces on northern Luzon permitted an expansion of the role that the irregulars were to play. In addition to harassing raids, sabotage, and intelligence, the guerrilla mission was enlarged until in due time Colonel Volckmann's insurgents were able to substitute for a full combat division.

By mid-February 1945, Sixth Army was aware of the close support work that Marine aviation had been doing on Luzon. Since the Marines had trained ALPs which had already been successful in coaching dive bombers to their targets near Manila, the 308th Bombardment Wing decided to attach Marines to Colonel Volckmann's guerrillas to direct close support missions. Once again, the Marine aviators were confronted with a situation that even a few months previously no one could have anticipated. On 20 February, four officers from MAG-24 and -32 held a preliminary conference with Colonel Volckmann, the purpose of which was to plan methods of giving close air support to the guerrillas on northern Luzon.

As a result of this meeting, three officers, three enlisted men, a radio jeep, and a radio truck were loaded on an LCT and put ashore on northwestern Luzon about 50 miles behind the enemy lines and attached to Colonel Volckmann's guerrilla headquarters at Luna, where they arrived on Washington's Birthday. From the point of view of Marine aviation, the assignment promised to be of more than casual interest, for:

> ...there the airplane could prove itself as a weapon against enemy troops because there was no confusing it with the field artillery and naval gunfire. If a dead Japanese was found who hadn't been drilled by a .30 caliber bullet, the chances were he owed death to the close-support airplane.[36]

The first mission awaiting the Marine ALP was the elimination of Japanese entrenched on a ridge just east of the enemy-held port of San Fernando. The ridge ran from north to south; in the hands of the guerrillas this terrain feature would afford control over the port city from the east. The trouble was that the Japanese were well dug in on the ridge and held the highest parts of it. The terrain was devoid of cover and with no supporting weapons to assist them, the Filipinos were stymied.

The arrival of the ALP offered new possibilities, which were realized at once. The resourceful guerrillas cut a trail from the north to the top of the ridge. Under cover of darkness, they dragged the radio jeep up to the top, where it was concealed behind a rise in the ground about 50 yards from the front line. A remote control was run from the jeep to a good observation post at a high point just behind the dug-in troops. The radio truck remained a few miles to the rear at a

---

[36] Sherrod, *Marine Corps Aviation in World War II*, p. 308.

location where it could function as a direct link between the jeep and MAGs-Dagupan 50 miles to the south. In order to eliminate any chance of having an air strike hit friendly troops, cloth panels were displayed to mark the front line, a procedure that had already been tested and adopted prior to World War II.

The first strike aircraft to arrive were 12 Army planes, which were guided to the ridge and flew over its entire length until the pilots had a clear picture of the front lines. What followed next has been described in the following words:

> All was now set for the strike. Running from north to south at a minimum altitude in three plane sections, the planes released 100-pound parafrags [fragmentation bombs dropped by parachute, fuzed to go off instantaneously on contact] to hit less than 200 yards beyond the front line panels, and at minimum intervals on down the ridge. The result was a complete plastering of the entire ridge and the Jap entrenchments for 1,000 yards ahead of the Filipinos. At the completion of the bomb runs the planes returned and made very low altitude strafing runs, starting in hardly 100 yards ahead of the guerrillas and raking the ridge for a little over 1,000 yards. After three or four live runs were made by the planes everything was set for the troop advance.[37]

Following a prearranged signal, the guerrillas charged out of their holes while the aircraft, forewarned of the forward movement of friendly troops by radio, skimmed over the heads of the insurgents in dry runs. The Filipinos advanced 1,000 yards to a high point on the ridge without incurring a single casualty, encountering only dead Japanese and seizing a quantity of abandoned materiel en route. About 50 Japanese attempting to withdraw from the ridge were spotted and strafed by the Army aircraft.

Once the aircraft left the area, however, the Japanese rallied and began to inflict casualties. Once more, the Marine radio truck called for air support. On this occasion five Marine dive bombers carrying 500-pound general purpose bombs pounded and strafed the Japanese positions on the center of the ridge. Again the Japanese were forced to pull back from the hill, but on this occasion the radio jeep "talked" the dive bombers onto houses in the valley where a number of the enemy had been observed taking refuge. Both houses and occupants were eliminated after final corrections had been made by dry runs on specific buildings.

On 26 February, as the fight for San Fernando continued, the guerrillas encountered difficulty in driving well dug-in Japanese from Reservoir Hill, an elevation just north of the city. Once again, using the same tactics previously employed in driving the enemy from a hilltop at San Fernando, Army and Marine aircraft bombed and machine-gunned the Japanese on the hill, knocking out individual pillboxes during the attack. While aircraft buzzed over their heads, the guerrillas occupied the hill. Later that day the Japanese counter-attacked with artillery support and re-captured the height. As a result, on 28 February, the Marine dive bombers and Army fighters had to repeat the entire performance, though on this occasion

---

[37] Samuel H. McAloney, "Air Support," in *Marine Corps Gazette*, v. 29, no. 11, (Nov 45), pp. 38–43, hereafter McAloney, "Air Support."

napalm was added to burn down bamboo thickets. This measure was effective, and guerrilla capture of Reservoir Hill proved permanent.

In many other instances too numerous to mention here the coaching of air strikes by Marine ALPs in the front lines was similarly successful. In one instance, the air strikes killed 137 out of 150 enemy troops. As to the remainder, the guerrillas reported: "Of the 13 who were still alive, we have killed seven and are hunting the other six in the woods."[38] As the guerrilla movement on Luzon grew in size and insurgent operations increased in momentum, the Marines continued to give such close air support as was required. On 1 March, one of the Marine officers serving as a member of the ALP with USAFIP, Captain Jack Titcomb, was killed by a sniper's bullet "while asking for more planes for a strike, microphone in hand."[39]

Between 5-31 March, a total of 186 missions were flown in support of guerrillas on Northern Luzon. As the guerrilla operations spread to other islands in the archipelago, the Marines provided additional ALPs where needed, as well as the necessary close support. In each instance, the results obtained were the same. The Japanese either died in place or were forced to pull back. Of one position where the Japanese had decided to stick it out, a report of the position after it had been pasted by close support aircraft described it as "a stink hole of dead."[40]

On northern Luzon, guerrilla operations finally reached proportions where Colonel Volckmann's force was able "to substitute for a full division, taking the place of the regular division that Krueger had planned to send up the west coast in a series of shore to shore operations, an undertaking that by mid-February, USAFIP(NL) successes had rendered unnecessary."[41]

Once again, as in close support of regular forces, the versatility of Marine aviation had vindicated Lieutenant Colonel McCutcheon's doctrine. Before the liberation of the Philippines was completed, Marine aviators were to make further important contributions to the campaign.

FINAL MARINE AVIATION ACTIVITIES ON LUZON[42]

The arrival of the 1st Cavalry Division in the city of Manila in early February did not mean the end of fighting for the capital of the Philippines. An additional month was required before the last Japanese resistance was wiped out. In the mountains northeast of the city, about 80,000 Japanese were holed up in caves and pillboxes. The Japanese line of defense known as the *Shimbu* Line, generally extended for about 25 miles, from north to southeast. The

---

[38] *Ibid.*, p. 40.
[39] Comment of Capt. Samuel H. McAloney, as cited in Sherrod, *Marine Corps Aviation in World War II*, p. 310.
[40] McAloney, "Air Support," p. 41.
[41] Smith, *Triumph in the Philippines*, p. 467.
[42] Unless otherwise noted, the material in this section is derived from: MAG-24 WarD, Mar45; MAG-32 WarDs, Feb-Mar45; *Marine Close Air Support File*; Boggs, *Marines in the Philippines*; Sherrod, *Marine Corps Aviation in World War II*.

50,000 Japanese comprising the *Shimbu Group,* firmly entrenched in excellent defensive positions, posed a threat not only to the city of Manila but also to the vital reservoir on which the city depended for its water supply.

Even though Marine aviators had given an excellent account of themselves in supporting the 1st Cavalry Division Drive to Manila and in assisting guerrillas in northwestern Luzon, a number of Army commanders still were unaware of the type of air support available to them or otherwise remained skeptical. It became incumbent upon the Marine aviators to make their capabilities known to high-ranking Army officers. As commander of the Marine air base at Mangaldan, Colonel Jerome approached Major General Innis P. Swift, Commander of I Corps, and the Commanding General of the XIV Corps, Major General Oscar W. Griswold, urging these commanders to make maximum use of close air support. In the final analysis, the division commanders had to be convinced that close support would materially help the infantry.

The task of making the rounds of infantry divisions fell to officers of Colonel Jerome's staff. The efforts of these officers to sell Marine close support to the division commanders did not always fall on fertile ground. One of the division commanders, Major General Edwin D. Patrick, USA, commanding the 6th Infantry Division was particularly hard to convince. Captain James L. McConaughy, Jr., one of the assistant MAG-32 intelligence officers, summed up the division commander's attitude as follows: "He (the general) was scared of airplanes; that is, scared of their accuracy and lack of ground control. He was polite but absolutely firm."[43]

On 8 February, when the 6th Infantry Division and the 1st Cavalry Division faced formidable Japanese defenses east of Manila, the division commander experienced a change of heart. General Patrick happened to be visiting the 1st Cavalry Division zone of attack when General Mudge, commander of the cavalry division, called for an air strike to help his troops seize a ridge from which the Japanese were pouring heavy machine gun and mortar fire on his troops. When the leader of the air strike arrived overhead, the Marine air liaison officer instructed him to hit the Japanese on the reverse side of the hill in order to preclude any chance of hitting friendly troops. As the two division commanders watched, the target was marked with white phosphorus smoke. Shortly thereafter, the first bomb hit near the crest of the ridge, on the reverse slope. As seven dive bombers in succession unloaded their bombs on the target, "the cavalrymen cheered like football fans."[44] After the dust had settled a patrol gingerly moved up to the crest of the ridge. There was no opposition. What was left of 8 machine gun and 15 mortar emplacements offered mute testimony to the effectiveness of close air support. Three hundred enemy dead lay nearby. In

---

[43] Capt James L. McConaughy, Jr., ltr to Robert Sherrod, dtd 13May48, as cited in Boggs, *Marines in the Philippines,* p. 84, hereafter *McConaughy ltr.*

[44] Sherrod, *Marine Corps Aviation in World War II,* p. 304.

addition, the troopers picked up 11 unmanned heavy machine guns.

Two days later, in the biggest strike of the Luzon campaign, 81 aircraft from VMSBs-241, -142, -243, -244, and -341 attacked Japanese oil dumps, antiaircraft artillery positions, and a number of towns serving as enemy strongpoints. Once again, with the help of guerrilla-supplied information, the bombs landed square on target.

By this time General Patrick required no further urging. When the 6th Infantry Division launched an attack against the *Shimbu* Line on 24 February, the division commander saw to it that Marine aviators were coached to the target by an air liaison officer. The first bombs hit targets 1,000 yards from the friendly troops, but on subsequent runs bombs were dropped within 500 yards or less from the American lines. All the tricks of the trade, including dummy runs while the infantry advanced, were employed.

General Patrick was so impressed with this performance that henceforth he not only began to insist on close air support but also required all units of his division to submit accurate evaluations of air strikes. As they arrived, such evaluations bore additional witness to the value of Marine air support.

One of the regiments of the 6th Infantry Division, the 1st Infantry, staunchly refused to have anything to do with air support—Marine or otherwise. Colonel James E. Rees, the regimental commander, had been leery of aircraft ever since 4 February when Fifth Air Force B-25s, making an unscheduled strafing run across the regimental front, had killed 2 and wounded 25 of his men near San Jose north of Manila.[45] However, on 28 February a situation arose which made it incumbent upon the regimental commander to call for the assistance of Marine aircraft. During the heavy fighting then in progress at the *Shimbu* Line to the east of Manila, most of a group of 15 or 20 men withdrawing from high ground near Mount Mataba lost their footing and tumbled into a 40 foot ravine. Eventually a lieutenant and a dozen men wound up in the ravine, which was covered by enemy fire. The men refused to abandon the lieutenant whose leg was injured and who was unable to walk. A member of the Marine ALP in the vicinity has described the situation as follows:

> There were Japs a couple of hundred yards away, though because of the terrain it might take them an hour to reach the stranded party. We said we could help. After a very thorough briefing, all by radio, the regimental commander said the lead plane could drop one wing bomb. It was beautiful to watch. We were on a high cliff on one side of the valley and it was a clear day. The first drop was dead on. The colonel was impressed and allowed that we could let the lead plane come in again and drop his belly and other wing bomb. It took the SBD 20 minutes to climb up again. His second dive was fantastically accurate, too, and the colonel said he was convinced, so the other eight planes followed the squadron leader down. The bombing was fantastically successful—the farthest one of 27 bombs being 30 yards off the target. They got the party out thanks to this discouragement to the Nips and from then on this colonel couldn't get enough planes for his regiment. Liter-

---
[45] 6th InfDiv Jnl and Jnl File, 4Feb45; 1st InfRpt Luzon, pp. 23–24 as cited in Smith, *Triumph in the Philippines*, p. 198.

ally, he asked for nine flights (nine planes each) as a standing, daily order.[46]

One of the bystanders closely observing the air strikes was General Patrick, commander of the 6th Infantry Division. In a letter of commendation, the division commander had this to say about Marine air support and this incident:

> The close air support given this Division by the 308th Bombardment Wing and Marine Air Group, Dagupan (MAGD), in the operations now being conducted in the Marakina Watershed area has been outstanding. The advance of our troops over difficult mountainous terrain against a well-armed determined enemy is being made possible in no small part by such air strikes.
>
> Particularly noteworthy have been the skillfully coordinated and accurate air strikes of the SBD's of the MAGD based at Mangaldan Field. In one strike made on 28 February against Mt. Mataba, these Marine pilots dive-bombed a pinpointed target located between two friendly forces with accuracy comparable to that obtained by field artillery. The courage, patience, and willingness displayed by these men deserve high praise.[47]

Throughout the month of February, while bitter fighting continued in and around Manila, Marine aviation remained much in evidence in the Philippine capital. In addition to providing close air support to the ground troops, SBDs of MAGs-24 and -32 divebombed Nichols Field, attacked docks and buildings on Corregidor, struck at derelict shipping that served as enemy nests of resistance in Manila Harbor, and otherwise harassed the Japanese at every turn. Marine aviators, never loath to improvise when the situation called for it, soon took advantage of one of the broader Manila avenues:

> Within three days after the American entry into Manila, the 1st Cavalry Brigade had established itself in the vicinity of Quezon City, a suburb in the eastern outskirts of Manila. A widened Quezon boulevard turned into a makeshift airstrip, became a familiar roosting spot for SBDs. Especially did it facilitate pilot forays to front lines for ground liaison duty or observation. A MAGSDAGUPAN skeleton crew later was maintained on the "strip" to service Marine planes landing there, and two jeeps were kept on hand for transportation forward.
>
> * * * * * * *
>
> The boulevard-strip, as an emergency landing field during these (close support) operations, had something more than incidental utility. For a time, an average of one SBD per day had reason to seek refuge there because of damage from antiaircraft fire, mechanical difficulties or fuel shortage.[48]

For the remainder of February and during early March the SBDs gave close support to the 6th, 25th, 37th, 38th, 40th, and 43d Infantry Divisions, as well as the 1st Cavalry and the 11th Airborne Divisions. In the case of each division the Marine aviators found acceptance once the quality of their air support had become recognized. Far from being content to rest on their laurels, Marine aviators continued to perfect air-ground coordination of air strikes. One innovation tested on 19 February was the use of an airborne coordinator. A single plane, piloted by the air coordinator, reported to the

---

[46] *McConaughy ltr.*

[47] MajGen Edwin D. Patrick ltr to CO, 308th Bombardment Wing; CO, Marine Air Group, Dagupan (MAGD) Thru: CG, XIV Corps, dtd 1Mar45, in *Marine Close Air Support File.*

[48] Boggs, *Marines in the Philippines,* p. 90.

U.S. ARMY 37TH INFANTRY DIVISION *troops move up Highway 5 on Luzon after Marine dive bomber attack on enemy hill positions.* (USMC A700603).

MARINE DIVE BOMBERS *returning from close air support mission for Sixth Army troops on Luzon.* (USMC 109092)

SAP and ALP prior to arrival on target of the strike flight. Ground radio tendered him all target and friendly troop identification and, upon the arrival of the flight over the target, he would make a marking run on the objective for their benefit. This run could be followed by an immediate attack.

Aside from an occasional air alert, the air base at Mangaldan escaped enemy attack throughout the month of February. Early on 2 March, the Japanese struck back in retaliation for all the indignities Marine aviation had heaped upon them since the invasion of Luzon. At 0200 a Japanese twin-engine bomber (commonly known as Betty), flying at a high altitude, was picked up by the searchlights. While every antiaircraft gun in the area opened up on this lone intruder, almost all personnel stood up in their foxholes to watch the action. Exploiting the diversion, two additional Bettys came over the camp area at an altitude of 300 feet or less and dropped nearly 300 antipersonnel bombs on the unsuspecting Marines. The casualties caused by this air attack were 4 dead and 78 wounded.[49] Among the officers wounded were Colonel Lyle H. Meyer, who had assumed command of MAGs-Dagupan on 19 February, and Lieutenant Colonel Wallace T. Scott, operations officer of MAG-32.

Around a dozen 500-lb. bombs struck the east end of the airfield and burrowed deeply into the ground, but did not explode. A direct bomb hit on an SBD resulted in the total loss of the aircraft; another SBD had a wing torn off by shell fragments. Damage to the telephone switchboard, sick bay area, ordnance and quartermaster tents, and other base facilities was extensive. Nevertheless, the raid did not disrupt flight operations, and squadrons carried out their assigned strikes as usual while the ground echelon went about the business of restoring the camp.

The progress of operations on Luzon and operations planned for the southern Philippines resulted in a reshuffling of Marine aviation units at MAGsDagupan. As early as mid-February Colonel Jerome received word that MAG-32 would be used in the Mindanao campaign and that the ground echelon of the air group would accompany Army assault forces into Zamboanga on 10 March. For the Zamboanga operation, one additional tactical squadron was transferred to MAG-32, bringing the strength of the air group to four squadrons. By 20 February the ground echelon of MAG-32 had moved to the vicinity of San Fabian, and departed in LSTs on 23 February. Some members of the MAG-32 headquarters staff left Mangaldan during the last two days of February by air transport.

Even though the landings at Zamboanga took place on schedule on 10 March, the flight echelon of MAG-32 remained on Luzon until 24 March, the last aircraft of the air group departing from the island on the 26th. MAG-24, now reduced to three squadrons, remained at Mangaldan. For the ground echelon of MAG-24, the departure of MAG-32 planes and pilots represented a major relief, since the movement of the ground echelon of MAG-32 on 23 February had imposed on the MAG-24

---

[49] MAG-24 WarD, Mar45.

ground crews the necessity of servicing both air groups. Combat operations of MAG-24 continued unchanged until 2 April, when the squadrons were ordered to halt operations and prepare for movement to Mindanao. As the ground echelon of MAG-24 was in the process of boarding ship on 7 April, Sixth Army called for the resumption of combat operations. Torrential rains and extremely heavy mud precluded operational use of Mangaldan until 10 April, when nine aircraft bombed the Japanese near Balete Pass. Four days later, it became evident that rain and mud were washing out the airfield, and all operations ceased as of that date. The flight echelons of the three squadrons moved south to Clark Field. On 20 April MAG-24 joined MAG-32 on Mindanao.

During the time they operated on Luzon, the Marine aviators of MAGs-24 and -32 had flown a total of 8,842 combat missions. The SBDs fired over one and a half million rounds of .30 and .50 caliber ammunition and dropped 19,167 bombs. Between 27 January and 14 April, the Marines flew an average of 1,000 sorties per week.[50] The ground crews at MAGsDagupan kept an average of 81 percent of the SBDs in a state of combat readiness; in many instances individual aircraft were flown up to nine hours per day.

Marine Corps files are replete with letters of commendation from Army corps and division commanders who witnessed the performance of Marine aviators on Luzon. In praising the achievements of Marines on Luzon, General Walter Krueger, commanding the Sixth Army, had this to say:

> In the crucial stages of the Luzon Campaign . . . this support was of such high order that I personally take great pleasure in expressing to every officer and enlisted man . . . my appreciation and official commendation for their splendid work.
>
> Commanders have repeatedly expressed their admiration for the pin-point precision, the willingness and enthusiastic desire of pilots to fly missions from dawn to dusk and the extremely close liaison with the ground forces which characterized the operations of the Marine fighter groups. By constant visits of commanders and pilots to front line units in order to observe targets and to gain an understanding of the ground soldier's problems, by the care which squadron commanders and pilots took to insure the maximum hits, and by the continuous, devoted work of ground crews in maintaining an unusually high average of operational crews, the 24th and 32d Marine Air Groups exemplified outstanding leadership, initiative, aggressiveness and high courage in keeping with the finest traditions of the Marine Corps.[51]

---

[50] Figures taken from Marine Corps statistics as cited in Sherrod, *Marine Corps Aviation in World War II*, p. 311.

[51] General Walter Krueger ltr to CO, 1st MAW, dtd 16May45, in *Marine Close Air Support File*.

CHAPTER 4

Southern Philippines Operations[1]

The beginning of March 1945 saw American forces firmly entrenched in the Philippines. On Leyte, military operations were all but completed and the objectives of the Leyte campaign, the establishment of a solid base for the reconquest of the Philippines, had been achieved. Japanese emphasis on the defense of Leyte had adversely affected the enemy capability of making a decisive stand on Luzon, the strategic nerve center of the Philippines. Unable to stem the American advance, the *Fourteenth Area Army* on Luzon resorted to the operational stratagem of "confining the American forces to Luzon despite inferior strength . . . and holing up in the mountainous districts of Luzon."[2] Aside from tying down sizable American forces in what was at best a prolonged delaying action, the enemy was unable to seriously upset the American timetable. In four months of operations, the U. S. Sixth and Eighth Armies had also seized Samar and Mindoro, as well as some of the smaller islands in the Visayan and Samar Seas.

Barely a month after the campaign on Luzon had begun, General MacArthur decided that the time had come to move into the southern Philippines. The general deemed the recapture of Palawan, Mindanao, and other islands in the Sulu Archipelago essential for two reasons. First, bypassing the southern Philippines would leave their inhabitants at the mercy of Japanese garrisons for an undetermined period of time, a situation clearly inconsistent with United States interests in the area. Secondly, theater strategy required early seizure of the islands for ultimate use as air and naval bases, as well as for serving as a steppingstone in the projected conquest of Borneo and other Japanese-held islands in the Dutch East Indies, the area presently part of Indonesia.

The plans developed for the recapture of the Southern Philippines were known as the VICTOR operations. They were numbered I through V and called for the following schedule:

VICTOR I (Panay) 18Mar45
VICTOR II (Cebu, Negros,

---

[1] Unless otherwise noted, the material in this chapter is derived from: Eighth Army Operational Monograph on the Palawan Operation (VICTOR III) n.d., hereafter Eighth Army, *Palawan Ops* (NARS, WWII Recs Div); Eighth Army Operational Monograph on the Zamboanga-Sulu Archipelago Operation (VICTOR IV), n.d., hereafter Eighth Army, *Zamboanga-Sulu Archipelago Ops* (NARS, WWII Recs Div); *Marine Close Air Support File;* Hayashi and Coox, *Kōgun*; Boggs, *Marines in the Philippines;* Robert L. Eichelberger and Milton Mackaye, *Our Jungle Road to Tokyo* (New York: The Viking Press, 1950), hereafter Eichelberger and Mackaye, *Jungle Road to Tokyo*, quoted with permission; Smith, *Triumph in the Philippines;* Sherrod, *Marine Corps Aviation in World War II.*

[2] Hayashi and Coox, *Kōgun*, p. 132.

Bohol) 25Mar45
VICTOR III (Palawan) 28Feb45
VICTOR IV (Zamboanga and
  Sulu Archipelago) 10Mar45
VICTOR V (Mindanao) 17Apr45

On 6 February 1945, General MacArthur ordered Eighth Army to prepare operations against Palawan, Mindanao, and other islands in the Sulu Archipelago. Lieutenant General Robert L. Eichelberger, the army commander, had available for the southern Philippine operations Headquarters, X Corps, five infantry divisions, and a regimental combat team of parachutists. On 17 February, Eighth Army issued a plan of operations for the reoccupation of the southern Philippines.[3] The first of the operations was VICTOR III. Landings by the 41st Infantry Division were to be carried out on 28 February at Palawan and on 10 March at Zamboanga, the western extremity of Mindanao. The Thirteenth Air Force was to provide air support for the two operations in addition to its mission of supporting Eighth Army on those Philippine islands that were located south of Luzon.

Far East Air Forces planned to have Marine aviation units participate in the liberation of the southern Philippines. To this end, MAG-12 and -14, stationed on Leyte and Samar respectively, were to reinforce the Thirteenth Air Force; the Marine dive bomber units of MAGs-24 and -32, which had performed so well on Luzon, were to be shifted south to Mindanao as soon as they had completed their mission of supporting the Sixth Army. MAGs-12, -14, and -32

were to provide direct air support during the landings on Zamboanga and in the subsequent ground operations.

The 41st Infantry Division had the task of seizing the town of Zamboanga in an amphibious assault. Due to its peculiar location in relation to the remainder of Mindanao, Zamboanga province was virtually separated from the island except for a narrow isthmus. There, inaccessible mountains and dense jungle formed a major terrain obstacle. During the conquest of Mindanao, Eighth Army expected to rely on the assistance of a sizable guerrilla force. Organized in 1942 and supplied and trained by the Americans since then, this native force could be of immediate assistance to the invasion troops. The guerrillas, under the command of Colonel Wendell W. Fertig, numbered over 33,000 by February of 1945; 16,000 of them were armed.

Similar guerrilla organizations of varying size existed on the islands of Negros, Cebu, and Panay. Bohol, Palawan, and other islands in the Sulu Archipelago harbored small guerrilla units that were relatively ineffective. Prior to the assault on the southern Philippine islands, the primary mission of the insurgents was to furnish intelligence; once the invasion of an island was imminent, the guerrillas were to cut enemy lines of communications, clear beachheads, and box in the Japanese to the best of their capabilities.

The Japanese garrison on eastern Mindanao consisted of the *30th* and *100th Infantry Divisions*; the *54th Independent Mixed Brigade*, consisting of three infantry battalions as a nucleus, with attached naval units, was deployed on

---
[3] Eighth Army FO No. 20, dtd 17Feb45.

CURTIS "HELLDIVERS" *armed with rockets and bombs, replace SBDs of VMSB-244.* (USMC A700606)

FILIPINO GUERRILLAS *at Malabang Airstrip, Mindanao.* (USMC 117638)

Zamboanga Peninsula. The *55th Independent Mixed Brigade,* composed of two infantry battalions, occupied Jolo Island in the Sulu Archipelago. The *102d Division* was spread over Panay, Negros, Cebu, and Bohol; half of the division had been previously sent to Leyte. The Japanese in the southern Philippines were under the command of the *Thirty-Fifth Army* headed by Lieutenant General Sosaku Suzuki. The latter's attempts to evacuate most of his forces from Leyte to the southern islands was frustrated by the vigilance of American aircraft and torpedo boats; in all, only about 1,750 of the 20,000 Japanese on Leyte eventually made it across to Cebu Island during the early months of 1945. The Japanese commander was able to make good his escape to Cebu in mid-March, only to perish at sea a month later while en route to Mindanao, when the vessel on which he was embarked was sunk off Negros by American aircraft.

There were more than 102,000 Japanese in the southern Philippines, including 53,000 Army troops, nearly 20,000 members of the Army air forces, 15,000 naval personnel, and 14,800 non-combatant civilians. Despite this imposing figure, there were only about 30,000 combat troops. Moreover, the enemy garrisons were spread over numerous islands. Even though they were aware of the existence of guerrilla units, the Japanese felt that they were firmly in control of the situation. There was a sense of optimism—quite unfounded as it turned out—that the Americans might bypass the southern Philippines as they left Japanese garrisons unmolested on other islands in the Pacific. The sentiment among the Japanese was one of general unconcern; even if the Americans decided to venture into the southern Philippines, they would probably be content to seize only the principal ports. The overall attitude of the Japanese garrisons in the southern Philippine islands was perhaps best summed up by a U. S. Army historian, who described the situation as follows:

> The Japanese in the Southern Philippines, therefore, apparently felt quite secure if not downright complacent. Such an outlook would be dangerous enough if shared by first-class troops; it was doubly so when held by the types of units comprising the bulk of the forces in the southern islands. . . . Most of the Japanese units in the Southern Philippines had enough military supplies to start a good fight, but far from enough to continue organized combat for any great length of time. . . . As was the case in Luzon, the Japanese in the Southern Philippines, given their determination not to surrender, faced only one end—death by combat, starvation, or disease.[4]

What could happen when Japanese complacency was shattered was clearly illustrated on Palawan Island in mid-December 1944. Up to the autumn of 1944, the Japanese garrison numbering somewhat more than 1,000 men, had led a relatively peaceful existence, except for an occasional ambush by Filipino insurgents. Since the summer of 1942, about 300 American prisoners of war had worked on the construction of an airfield on Palawan. This field was eventually destroyed by American air attacks before it ever became of any major use to the enemy. As the pace of the campaign quickened and an invasion

---
[4] Smith, *Triumph in the Philippines,* pp. 586-680.

of Palawan appeared imminent in mid-December, the Japanese garrison panicked and carried out a brutal massacre of the unarmed American prisoners of war. Many of them, huddled in trenches or shelters, were soaked with gasoline and burned to death, while others were bayoneted or shot in the stomach. A few of the Americans were able to escape their tormentors and eventually found their way back to American-held islands, where word of the atrocity was spread. But for most of the prisoners of war on Palawan, the eventual liberation of the island two months after the massacre came too late.[5]

ZAMBOANGA[6]

Marine aviation did not play any part in the conquest of Palawan, though the Thirteenth Air Force carried out extensive bombing and strafing operations during the two days preceding the landing. Results of these air attacks were limited by the absence of enemy installations and defenses. The landing itself was unopposed and the two airstrips on the island were seized within hours after the first troops had gone ashore. The Japanese garrison withdrew to the hill country in the interior and from there offered sporadic opposition, which continued well into the summer. Even

---

[5] For a detailed account of this incident, see Eighth Army, *Palawan Ops*, pp. 44–48.

[6] Additional sources for this section include: 1st MAW WarDs, Jan-Mar45; MAG–24 WarDs, Jan-Mar45; *TG 78.1 AR, Zamboanga, Mindanao, Philippines;* VMF–115 WarD, Mar45; VMB–611 WarD, Jul44-Nov45; *Philippines Comment File;* William F. McCartney, *The Jungleers, A History of the 41st Infantry Division* (Washington: Infantry Journal Press, 1948), hereafter McCartney, *41st InfDiv Hist.*

though work on airstrips near Iwahig and Puerta Princesa began at once, neither strip was ready for use by fighter and transport planes until 18 March. By that time, it was too late to provide air support for the invasion of Zamboanga, for that operation had already been launched on the 10th.

Participation of Marine aviation units in the VICTOR operations had already been decided upon in the course of February. Under the overall direction of the Thirteenth Air Force, MAGs–12, –14, –24, and –32 were slated to move south to Mindanao. The initial mission of MAGs–12, –14, and –32 was to provide direct air support to the 41st Infantry Division during the invasion of Zamboanga. General Kenney authorized the 1st MAW to reinforce the four Marine air groups with additional wing units from the northern Solomons.

The imminent liberation of the southern Philippines necessitated the employment of even more Marine aircraft. From his headquarters at Bougainville in the Solomons, General Mitchell, commander of 1st MAW and Commander Aircraft, Northern Solomons, controlled all aircraft in the area, except for a few Australian tactical reconnaissance planes. Since by late February of 1945, only few Marine squadrons were still operating in the Solomons, it was planned that responsibility for air operations in the Solomons-Bismarck Archipelago would in time be transferred to the Royal New Zealand Air Task Force.

In preparation for the invasion of Zamboanga, Marine air units from bases scattered between the northern

Solomons and the Philippines began to stage. Control of the staging was complicated by the fact that a number of aviation units had been broken up. As a result, by late February, the headquarters and service squadrons of MAG-12 still had not caught up with the air group, nor had the ground echelons of VMF-115, -211, -218, and 313 joined their flight echelons, which were engaged in combat operations on Leyte. The situation of MAG-14 was similar, with ground echelons of VMF-212, -222, -223, and -251 still en route to the Philippines in late February, even though the flight echelons of these squadrons had been operating from Samar since early January. MAG-61, commanded by Colonel Perry K. Smith, was still stationed on Emirau Island, north of the Solomons, where it was both undergoing final training in medium altitude bombing and employed for tactical operations against the Japanese on New Britain, New Ireland, and Bougainville. Like other Marine air groups, MAG-61 suffered from overdispersal. The headquarters and service squadrons, as well as VMB-413, -433, -443, and the flight echelon of VMB-611 were stationed on Emirau; VMB-423 occupied Green Island; the ground echelon of VMB-611 had departed Hawaii in late September 1944 and since then had remained aboard ship off Leyte, Samar, and Lingayen before finally going ashore on Mindoro on 25 February.

Additional Marine air units sent to assist in operations in the southern Philippines were Air Warning Squadrons 3 and 4 (AWS-3 and -4). The latter arrived off Leyte on 4 March from Los Negros in the Admiralty Islands, while the former, coming from Bougainville, reached Mindoro on the 20th. As the date for the invasion of the Zamboanga Peninsula drew closer, a personnel change occurred when on 25 February, Colonel Verne J. McCaul relieved Colonel William A. Willis as commanding officer of MAG-12. General Mitchell charged Colonel Jerome of MAG-32 with overall command of Marine air units of MAGs-12, -24, and -32 scheduled to move to Zamboanga for participation in operations against Mindanao and the Sulu Archipelago. From the island of Samar, MAG-14 was to support operations on Panay, Cebu, and Mindanao.

Before the assault against Zamboanga could be launched, steps had to be taken to assure that the primary objectives of the operation were met. The prime purpose of the seizure of the peninsula was to gain control of Basilan Strait which constitutes one of the two main approaches to Asia from the southwest Pacific. The peninsula featured good landing beaches and airfields protected by inaccessible mountains. The airstrips were located along the southeast coast near Zamboanga Town. Possession of Zamboanga would enable the Americans to establish additional air and naval bases for continued operations in the southern Philippines, particularly against eastern Mindanao.

On Zamboanga, as on other enemy-occupied islands in the Philippines, Filipino insurgents had gradually taken over small areas; on Mindanao, Negros, and Cebu half a dozen airstrips were in Filipino hands. When necessary, these airstrips were used by Army transport

WESTERN PACIFIC OPERATIONS

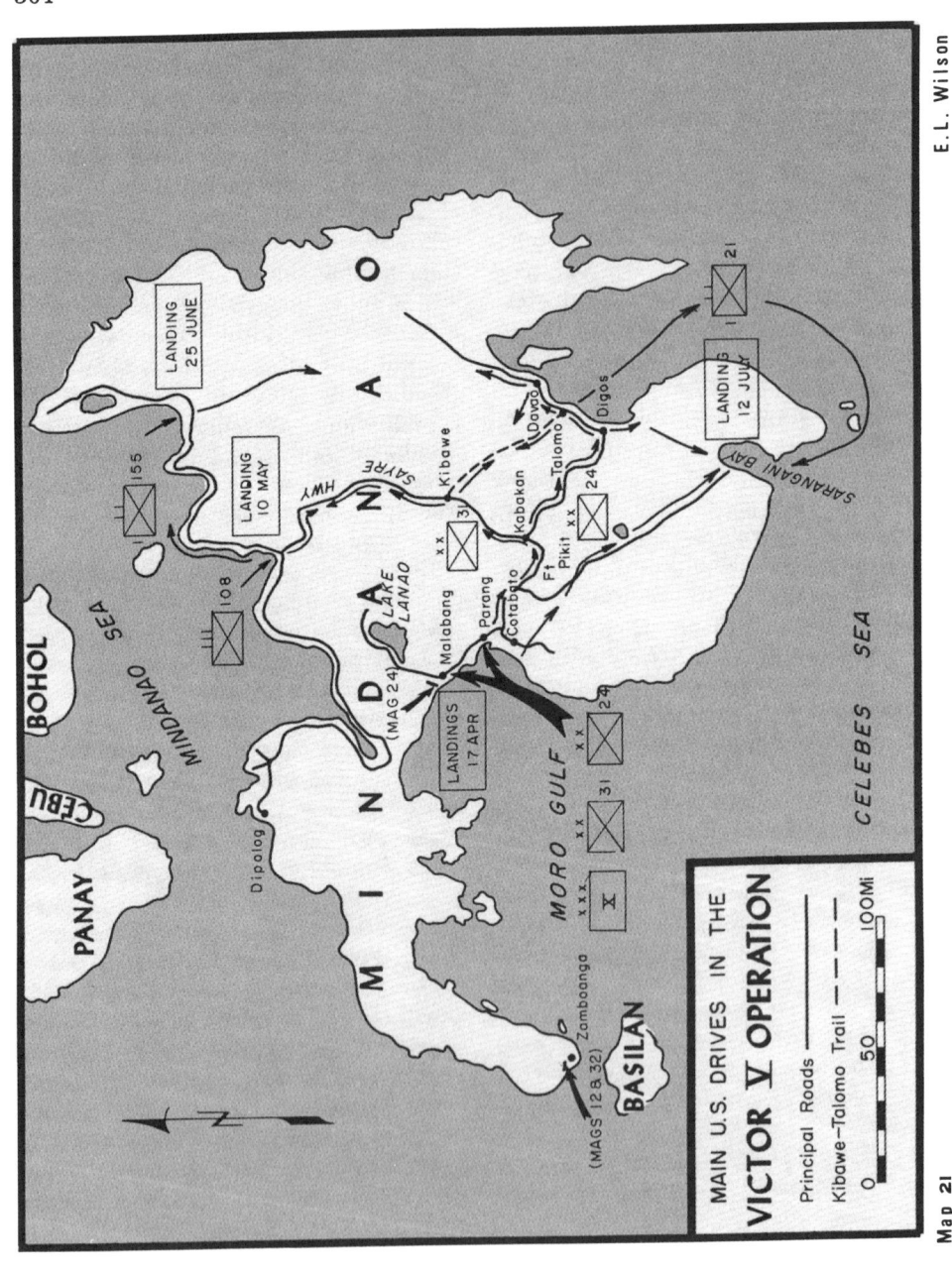

MAIN U.S. DRIVES IN THE
VICTOR V OPERATION

Map 21

aircraft, escorted by Marine Corsairs, to furnish the natives with supplies. About 150 miles to the northeast of Zamboanga Town, near the northern tip of the peninsula, the guerrillas were in possession of an airstrip near the town of Dipolog. (See Map 21). This airfield had been used since 1943 by Allied aircraft to supply guerrilla forces on the Zamboanga Peninsula.

As preinvasion plans for the assault against western Mindanao neared completion, Far East Air Forces reported on 2 March that the airfield on Palawan Island would not be completed in time for VICTOR IV, and it was decided to move one fighter squadron to Dipolog. Before the arrival of the fighters, however, it became necessary to provide adequate protection for the airfield. In a rapid change of original plans, and in order to forestall any Japanese attempt to seize the airfield from the guerrillas, two companies of the 24th Infantry Division, reinforced with two heavy machine gun platoons and one 81mm mortar section, were airlifted to Dipolog on 8 March, two days before the actual invasion date. The mission of this force was to defend the airfield, though they were not to take offensive action unless it became necessary to do so in maintaining uninterrupted air support.

This Army force, however, was not the first American contingent to arrive at Dipolog, for as early as 2 March MAG-12 ordered an advance echelon consisting of two officers and six enlisted men to move to the airstrip to prepare it as a staging base for guerrilla support missions in northwestern Mindanao. This move was completed on the following day. On 7 March, two Corsairs arrived at Dipolog in order to support the guerrillas. By 9 March, a total of sixteen Corsairs were stationed at the field, all of them engaged in support of guerrillas or in flying missions in support of the imminent invasion. As far as was known to Eighth Army, "this was the first time that aircraft have operated from airdromes before securing them by an assault landing. The use of guerrilla-held airstrips proved to be a marked advantage in this operation."[7]

There were bizarre overtones to the activities of Marine aviators operating from an enemy-held island, as outlined in the following account:

> Two planes from Dipolog reconnoitered the road from Dipolog to Sindangan. On the road about a mile north of Siari they sighted about 200 troops dressed as natives but all were carrying arms. The troops at the head of the column were carrying a large American flag. The planes buzzed the troops and the troops waved back. They also sighted four bancas (dugout canoes) about thirty to forty feet long just off Lanboyan Point. Upon returning to Dipolog and reporting their sightings, guerrilla headquarters informed them that the troops sighted were Japs, not guerrillas, and that the bancas were also Jap controlled.[8]

In a quick response to this information, the two Marine aviators took off again, and headed back to the scene of the earlier sightings. Five dugout canoes, under sail and occupied, were the first to be strafed. The planes then went after the troops and caught up with the column, which was plodding

---

[7] Eighth Army, *Zamboanga-Sulu Archipelago Ops.*, p. 31.
[8] MAG-12 WarD, Mar45.

along the road, still carrying the American flag. When the aircraft began to circle for a strafing run, the troops dropped the flag and headed for the bushes. The two pilots strafed the troops on the road, five pack carabaos, as well as bushes on either side of the road, using about 4,000 rounds of ammunition in the process. The foliage prevented any observation of results.

While Marine aircraft were operating with impunity from Dipolog under the very noses of the Japanese, an amphibious force under the command of Rear Admiral Forrest B. Royal, Commander of Naval Task Group 78.1, was en route to Mindanao. The invasion convoy carried the 41st Infantry Division, commanded by Major General Jens A. Doe, charged with making the assault landing. The prime mission of the naval task group was to transport the division from its staging areas on Mindoro and Leyte to the Zamboanga Peninsula and keeping it supplied after the landings. A secondary mission was the protection of the assault force against hostile naval action, although intelligence indicated that only motor torpedo boats and submarines would be encountered.

Included in the assault force were staffs and ground echelons of MAG–12 and –32, as well as AWS–4. The ground echelon of MAG–32, loaded in six LSTs, had left Luzon on 23 February and proceeded to Mindoro for staging. Ground crewmen of MAG–12 had boarded LSTs at Leyte and headed to Mindoro for staging. AWS–4 staged directly from Leyte Gulf on 8 March and joined the invasion convoy as it headed for western Mindanao. Among the Marines headed for Zamboanga were the forward echelons of MAGs–12 and –32 consisting of operations, intelligence, and communications personnel under the command of Colonel Jerome.

The Thirteenth Air Force had commenced the preinvasion bombardment of the Zamboanga Peninsula as early as 1 March. From 4-8 March, the Army Air Forces concentrated on the destruction of enemy aircraft, personnel, and supplies in areas adjacent to Japanese airfields in Borneo, Davao, and Zamboanga. Planes from MAG–12, based at Dipolog, and Army aircraft provided air cover for the assault force as the ships approached the Zamboanga Peninsula. No opposition was encountered in the air.

Early on 10 March, a task force consisting of two light cruisers and six destroyers moved into Basilan Strait just off the southern tip of the Zamboanga Peninsula. This force began an intense bombardment of the beachhead area, which included a stretch of the coastline from Caldera Point to Zamboanga City and inland for a distance of 2,500 yards. As incessant air strikes hit the landing beaches and adjacent area to the north, the first infantrymen went ashore. The beaches, though heavily fortified, were not defended in strength and only moderately heavy machine gun fire greeted the assault units. Japanese defensive positions, although superior in layout and construction to any previously encountered in the Philippines, were in many instances unmanned.

By midmorning, the advancing infantrymen seized the first airstrip near Zamboanga Town. At noon, the 163d

Infantry Regiment, supported by a tank company, stood poised to assault the town itself. Except for a number of mines and booby traps that remained to be cleared, Zamboanga Town was firmly in American hands by late afternoon.

The initial objective of the Marine aviation personnel taking part in the landings was San Roque airfield, situated northwest of Zamboanga Town and only a mile inland from the invasion beaches. Heavy resistance encountered by the men of the 41st Infantry Division near the village of San Roque delayed capture of the airfield until 12 March, though Colonel Jerome and his staff were able to reconnoiter the strip on the day of the first landings. Personnel from MAGs-12 and -32 began unloading shortly before noon of J-Day, even though by this time the Japanese were shelling the beaches with artillery and mortars.

The 41st Infantry Division did not succeed in driving the Japanese entirely from the San Roque airstrip area until the afternoon of 13 March. At this time, the 973d Aviation Engineer Battalion moved in on the heels of the advancing infantry and work began around the clock to ready the field for operations. Upon arrival at San Roque airfield, the Marines promptly redesignated it as Moret Field in commemoration of a Marine aviator, Lieutenant Colonel Paul Moret, formerly commanding VMTB-131, who had been killed when a transport on which he was a passenger crashed on New Caledonia in 1943.

While work on Moret Field was in progress, aircraft from Dipolog flew patrol missions over the beach area and executed air strikes in support of the infantry. As the soldiers advanced into the foothills to the north of Moret Field, Japanese resistance stiffened; elaborate booby traps also took their toll among the Americans. On 13 March the 163d Infantry Regiment suffered 83 casualties when the Japanese blew up a hill north of Santa Maria to the north of Zamboanga Town.[9] Apparently the enemy had decided to explode a hidden bomb and torpedo dump and detonated it electrically when American troops had advanced up the hill in strength.

Japanese demolition experts also succeeded in throwing a scare into the Eighth Army commander following his inspection trip to Zamboanga. Just as General Eichelberger was preparing to return to the USS *Rocky Mount* and was passing through Zamboanga Harbor on a barge, the Japanese decided to give him a farewell salute. As the general himself described the incident:

> Apparently enemy field glasses still accurately observed the harbor. Anyway, a detonator somewhere let loose a naval mine which sent a cascade of water ten stories high. It just missed my boat; after swallowing hard, I found myself intact and went aboard the cruiser. A Navy flying boat picked me up shortly after and took me back to Leyte in very stormy weather.[10]

During the time that Moret Field was being readied for operations, the Japanese remained passive in the air. The only exception occurred on 13 March, when a single enemy aircraft made two strafing runs over the field and dropped a bomb with negligible effect. Moret Field became operational on 15 March

---

[9] McCartney, *41st InfDiv Hist*, p. 147.
[10] Eichelberger and Mackaye, *Jungle Road to Tokyo*, p. 207.

with the arrival of eight Corsairs of VMF–115. By the 18th, the flight echelons of VMF–211, –218, and –313 had reached Zamboanga. The Army Air Forces 419th Night Fighter Squadron, equipped with P–61s, was also based at Moret Field.

As early as 12 March, Thirteenth Air Force had designated Colonel Jerome as Commander Air Groups, Zamboanga, Mindanao, hereafter referred to as Marine Aircraft Groups, Zamboanga (MAGsZam). Initially, Colonel Jerome's command included MAGs–12 and –32, though a month later MAG–24 joined the two air groups on Mindanao. One member of MAG–24, Lieutenant Colonel McCutcheon, had accompanied Colonel Jerome to Moret Field for the express purpose of establishing an organization similar to the one previously used at MAGsDagupan on Luzon.

As the infantry continued the advance into the interior of the Zamboanga Peninsula, enemy harassment of Moret Field decreased until it stopped altogether. The Corsairs of MAG–12 began to lend close air support on 17 March, when Captain Samuel H. McAloney, intelligence officer of MAG–32, was designated as commander of the support air party with the 163d Infantry Regiment. The primary mission of MAGsZam was close support of ground troops, though Marine Corsairs also maintained continuous convoy over friendly shipping in the Sulu Sea.

Marine organization for close air support at MAGsZam was simpler than it had been on Luzon, since Marine aviation had sole responsibility for the operation of Moret Field. In addition, the regiments of the 41st Infantry Division requested air support directly from MAGsZam. The support air parties with the infantry consisted of a captain, one or more first lieutenants, two or more radio operators, and two or more radio technicians. Air-ground communication was carried on with two types of mobile radio gear. A large van with high frequency (HF) equipment with an effective range of more than 100 miles was used; where only distances of less than 15 miles had to be covered, more compact equipment was employed. The use of the van or jeep depended on the distance of the air support parties from MAGsZam, though there were many occasions when the two vehicles, working as a team, were employed. The radio jeep, in view of the limited range of its radio equipment, maintained contact with the communications van; the latter, in turn, acted as a relay with MAGsZam.

On the level below the air support party was the air liaison party consisting of a Marine aviator, a radio operator, and a technician. The liaison party was equipped with a radio jeep, maps and aerial photographs of the area in which it was to operate, as well as a field telephone which could be used in conjunction with the radio. Air-ground liaison was helped by the presence of AWS–4 at Moret Field. The latter unit, redesignated the 76th Fighter Control Center, had ample communications facilities. Beyond its mission of watching for approaching enemy aircraft and assisting friendly aircraft in getting back to the field, personnel of the air warning squadron employed their radio

LSTs *land Marine aviation personnel and supplies on Zamboanga. (USMC 116824)*

U.S. ARMY *41st Infantry Division honors Marine aviation for air support received in the Southern Philippines. (USMC 116887)*

and radar equipment in supplementing the existing ground-air communications setup.

Marine aviators on the Zamboanga Peninsula flew their first air support missions at very close range, since the objectives invariably were located just a few miles from the runways of Moret Field. In a situation similar to that on Peleliu, Marine aviation personnel could watch the entire action from the runway. It was not unusual for a member of the air liaison party to scan the frontline before a mission, accompanied by the flight leader. The two Marines would then discuss the situation with the commander of the Army battalion involved, and the flight leader thus could receive a direct briefing as to the type of air support desired by the ground troops.

As the Japanese were driven back into the hills of Zamboanga, and Moret Field was further extended, additional aviation units began to arrive. The mission of the Marine dive bomber squadrons on Luzon came to a close on 23 March and VMSB-142 and -236 reached Moret Field on the following day. Despite an otherwise uneventful flight of the SBDs from Luzon to Zamboanga, this flight was to culminate in the death of two Marine aviators:

> Fate decided this by the toss of a coin. Squadron procedure had two pilots assigned to one plane. Prior to departing from Luzon, it was decided to toss a coin to see who would fly to Zamboanga. Lt. Charles C. Rue and Lt. Charles F. Flock tossed, and Rue won the toss. On the flight down from Mangaldan, Rue broke an oil line and made a crash landing, on the supposedly guerrilla held air strip on Panay. Planes in the flight observed Rue and his gunner get out of their plane and wave to a group of men who came out of the jungle at the edge of the strip. About six weeks later, when the Army invaded Panay, it was learned through interrogation of prisoners, that Rue and his gunner had been beheaded the day after they were taken prisoner.[11]

Between 18 and 24 March, MAGsZam aircraft carried out their primary mission of supporting the 41st Infantry Division advance. Among the first air strikes was an attack by eight aircraft against the enemy dug in at Capisan, 3,500 yards north of Zamboanga Town. The planes dropped instantaneously fused 1,000 pound bombs on the assigned area, but results of the attack were unobserved. While strafing the entire area, the Marines drew light but accurate machine gun fire which damaged two of their aircraft. In a second strike on the same day, eight aircraft, each carrying a 175-gallon napalm fire bomb, attacked a ridge north of Zamboanga Town, where the enemy was dug in. Six napalm bombs covered the area; two failed to release; one of these was jettisoned over the water and the other was returned to base. After the strike, ground observers reported that the area of the target was well burned out and appeared lifeless and deserted.

As the Japanese were driven back into the inhospitable interior of Zamboanga, Marine aviators continued to carry out similar missions. In an innovation of close air support techniques, a support air party officer on 21 March relayed target information from an L-4 spotter plane to the air liaison party in a radio jeep on the ground; the lat-

---

[11] 1stLt Charles F. Flock ltr to CMC, n.d., in *Philippines Comment File*.

ter, in turn, coached the planes to the target. Positions indistinguishable from a fast moving Corsair thus could be easily pinpointed. The observer in the Cub plane remained over the target after the strike and reported excellent results. This was later verified by the commanding officer of the 1st Battalion, 162d Infantry Regiment, who reported that the enemy had withdrawn from the bombed area, blowing up two ammunition dumps and firing one warehouse on their way.

On 22 March, 16 Corsairs executed a concentrated attack on Japanese troops dug in on top of an L-shaped ridge 500 yards northwest of Masilay. The infantry had failed in the attempt to take the ridge on the preceding day. The planes dropped 13 quarter-ton bombs over the target without being able to observe the results of the bombing. However, when 2/162 resumed its advance, the infantrymen did not encounter any enemy opposition on the ridge. The battalion commander subsequently reported that an enemy pillbox had received a direct bomb hit and 63 Japanese dead had been counted by nightfall.

The remainder of March saw the continued advance of 41st Infantry Division troops into the interior of Zamboanga. As early as 26 March, MAG-32, in discussing the development of Moret Field, was able to make the following note:

> This lower end of Zamboanga Peninsula has taken on a bustling, business-like air, and with the air strip in full operation, camps being built, engineering sheds being rushed to completion, mess halls going up, all Marine units are functioning at top speed to establish all the elements of a fully equipped advance Marine Air Base.[12]

Except for the presence of an Army Air Forces night fighter squadron and a few Navy PBYs used for rescue work, Moret Field continued to remain under Marine control. Eventually, the field was to house a total of 299 aircraft: 96 F4Us, 151 SBDs, 18 PBJs, 18 SB2Cs, 2 F6Fs 1 FM, 2TBFs, 5 R4Ds, and 6 Army P-61 "Black Widow" night fighters.[13]

Operations at Moret Field soon were going into high gear and MAGsZam aircraft extended their operations to adjacent islands in the Sulu Archipelago. Between 8 and 22 March, the guerrilla-held strip at Dipolog was occupied by a group of Marine ground personnel and an Army security detail. The grass strip even boasted a temporary fighter control center. Aircraft from MAGsZam became frequent visitors to Dipolog, flying in one day with supplies for the guerrillas, staying overnight, and returning to Moret Field on the following day.

On 27 March word was received at Moret Field that a force of about 150

---

[12] MAG-32 WarD, Mar45.

[13] Figures cited from Sherrod, *Marine Corps Aviation in World War II*, p. 316. Aircraft designations for abbreviations used above are as follows:

SBD — Douglas Dauntless dive-bomber
PBJ — Mitchell, North American medium bomber, identical to the Army Air Forces B-25
SB2C — Curtiss dive-bomber, "Helldiver"
F4U — Vought fighter-bomber, "Corsair"
F6F — Grumman fighter, "Hellcat"
FM — Martin fighter, "Wildcat"
TBF — Grumman torpedo-bomber, "Avenger"
R4D — Douglas utility or cargo plane, "Skytrain"

Japanese, armed with two grenade launchers, one light machine gun, two automatic rifles, and more than a hundred rifles was headed towards Dipolog and had advanced to within about 11 miles of the field.[14] The guerrilla force of 400, commanded by Army Major Donald H. Wills, was armed but had never been in action before. Because of the potentially menacing situation, all American personnel were ordered to evacuate Dipolog on 27 March and left the field in the course of the day.

MAGsZam dispatched four aircraft to Dipolog to investigate conditions there. Though somewhat at variance in minor details with the official record, the comments of the division leader are of interest:

> We sent a division of Corsairs to Dipolog in response to a request for air support. The tone of the message received at Zamboanga was that Dipolog was in imminent danger of falling, which we learned was not the case when we got there. The 500 to 600 Filipino guerrillas who opposed the Jap force were evidently keenly interested in avoiding a fight with the Japs. Major Wills evidently figured an air strike might boost their morale and damage the enemy at the same time.
> The lack of maps or photos of any kind, as well as no way to mark targets and no communication with the troops all combined to dictate the method we used. Sharpe [1st Lieutenant Winfield S. Sharpe], as the smallest man in the division, was elected to sit on Major Wills' lap.[15]

Shortly thereafter, the aircraft took off. Sitting on the Army major's lap,

Lieutenant Sharpe led the four Corsairs in six strafing runs over the enemy positions while Major Wills pointed out the targets. The Japanese received a thorough strafing and were forced to pull back several miles. Having expended their ammunition, the Corsairs returned to Dipolog where Captain Rolfe H. Blanchard, the division leader, and Lieutenant Sharpe spent the night while the remaining two aircraft returned to Moret Field. Following his return to MAGsZam on 28 March, Captain Blanchard discovered that squeezing two men into the narrow confines of a Corsair cockpit did not meet with the wholehearted approval of his superiors. In the flight leader's own words:

> I don't recall what happened to Sharpe for this incident, but I was mildly reprimanded by Lieutenant Colonel Leek of MAG-12, who acted as MAGSZAM Group Operations Officer, together with Lieutenant Colonel McCutcheon until the latter's departure from Moret Field and I learned (reliability of source unknown) that Major Wills was awarded the Silver Star.[16]

The existence of a Marine aviation group with two operations officers requires an explanation, which since the end of World War II has been furnished by Colonel Leek, who made the following comment:

> The operations organization as it existed had been set up by LtCol Keith B. McCutcheon who, although the operations officer of MAG-24, had accompanied Colonel Jerome from Dagupan for the express purpose of placing into effect a command operations organization similar to the one at Dagupan. Once the organiza-

---

[14] VMF-115 WarD, Flight Rpt No. 27, 27-Mar45.
[15] Capt Rolfe H. Blanchard ltr to CMC, n.d., in *Philippines Comment File*.

[16] *Ibid.*

tion was functioning, LtCol Frederick E. Leek who had taken the advance echelon of MAG–12 into Zamboanga relieved LtCol McCutcheon. Although personnel were pooled, responsibilities can never be shared. LtCol Leek as senior of the two group operations officers functioned as MAGSZAM operations officer until he was detached, at which time (17May45) he was relieved by LtCol Wallace T. Scott of MAG–32.[17]

On 29 March, a ceremony was held in front of the operations tower on Moret Field. While the 41st Infantry Division band played, Colonel Jerome, with officers of the Marine air groups at attention behind him, received a plaque from General Doe, commanding the 41st Infantry Division. The plaque itself was spectacular in its own right Six feet high by four feet, it was trimmed with captured Japanese naval signal flags. Mounted on it was a Japanese light machine gun, still showing the scars of battle. Below that was an enemy battle flag of white silk with the red "Rising Sun" of Nippon. Beneath it were listed the islands nearby which the division had invaded with Marine air support. At the top of the plaque were the words: "In Appreciation-41st Infantry Division."

Even more impressive for the Marines were the words of the Army division commander which accompanied the award. In addition to commending the air groups for the support of ground operations, General Doe had this to say:

The readiness of the Marine Air Groups to engage in any mission requested of them, their skill and courage as airmen, and their splendid spirit of cooperation in aiding ground troops have given this Division the most effective air support yet received in any of its operations.[18]

On 30 March, the already formidable Marine establishment at MAGsZam was further strengthened by the arrival of the flight echelon of VMSB-611 under the command of Lieutenant Colonel George H. Sarles. Prior to its arrival at Moret Field, the squadron had been stationed on Emirau Island in the St. Matthias Group. VMSB-611 was equipped with 16 Mitchell medium bombers (PBJs). Each of these aircraft was capable of carrying eight rockets, a bombload of 3,000 pounds, and anywhere between eight and fourteen .50 caliber machine guns. The bombers further contained airborne radar, an instrument panel for the pilot and copilot, as well as long-range radio and complete navigation equipment. The profusion of electronic gear made the PBJs particularly adaptable to operating at night and under conditions of poor visibility.

The versatility that Lieutenant Colonel Sarles expected from his pilots and planes became evident during intensive training on Emirau. His copilot, who remained with the squadron commander in preference to having a crew of his own, made this following comment about his commanding officer:

He wanted us to be able to play the role of fighters where fighters were needed, or bombers, of photographers, skip bombers,

---

[17] Colonel Frederick E. Leek ltr to CMC, dtd 29Jan51, in *Philippines Comment File.* Upon being relieved, Lieutenant Colonel McCutcheon returned to MAG–24 and there became involved in planning for the Malabang landing. He went ashore at Malabang and set up operations for a third time. *McCutcheon ltr.*

[18] Sgt E. Payson Smith, Jr., Marine Corps combat correspondent rpt, as cited in MAG-32 WarD, Mar45.

and indeed it seemed on some occasions that he thought we were capable of dive bombing. During the Philippine campaign we strafed, bombed, skip bombed, fired rockets, photographed, flew observers, were sent on anti-sub patrols, were sent up at night as night fighters, and bombed at medium altitudes. In fact, one member of VMB-611 shot down with his fixed guns, and using his bombsight as a gun-sight, a Japanese twin-engine light bomber, a "Lily."[19]

Shortly after their arrival at Moret Field, the PBJs began to fly long-range reconnaissance patrols over Borneo and Mindanao. They searched the seas for enemy submarines and photographed future landing sites in the Sulu Archipelago. Pilots of VMB-611 struck at enemy truck convoys and airfields at night and harassed the Japanese with nuisance flights. Use of the Mitchells made it possible for MAGsZam to conduct operations against the enemy around the clock.

Progress of the 41st Infantry Division advance across the Zamboanga Peninsula was a costly and time-consuming process. Operations on the peninsula continued until the latter part of June, which saw the end of coordinated enemy resistance, though infantrymen and guerrillas continued to ferret enemy stragglers out of the inaccessible hills and jungles long after that date. At the same time that Japanese resistance on Zamboanga was gradually reduced, a number of operations, many of them supported by Marine aviation, were executed in the southern Philippines. For many of the enemy, the illusion that the islands which they garrisoned might be bypassed by the Americans, was effectively destroyed.

SOUTHERN VISAYAS AND SULU ARCHIPELAGO[20]

The invasion of the Zamboanga Peninsula on 10 March 1945 represented only the first step in an entire series of amphibious landings designed to drive the Japanese out of the southern Philippines. Six days after the 41st Infantry Division set foot on Zamboanga, a company of the 162d Infantry of that division crossed Basilan Strait and went ashore on Basilan Island, 12 miles south of Zamboanga Town. Other islands in the vicinity were quickly captured against negligible enemy resistance.

Capture of Basilan Island marked the arrival of the first American troops in the Sulu Archipelago, a chain of islands extending southwestward from Mindanao toward Borneo. Even while the drive against the Sulu Archipelago got under way, two other divisions of the Eighth Army were assaulting additional islands in the central Philippines, particularly those islands surrounding the Visayan Sea. The assault on these islands—Panay, Negros, Cebu,

---

[19] 1st Lieutenant Willis A. Downs ltr to CMC, dtd 23Jan51 in *Philippines Comment File.*

[20] Additional sources for this section include: Eighth Army Operational Monograph on the Panay-Negros Occidental Operation (VICTOR I), n.d., hereafter Eighth Army, *Panay-Negros Ops* (NARS, WWII Recs Div); Eighth Army Operational Monograph on the Cebu-Bohol-Negros Oriental Operation (VICTOR II), n.d., hereafter Eighth Army, *Cebu-Bohol-Negros Ops* (NARS, WWII Recs Div); *Philippines Comment File;* VMF-222 WarDs, Apr45-Jul46; VMF-223 WarDs, Apr45-Jul46; VMSB-236 WarDs, Mar-Apr45.

and Bohol—began with the invasion of Panay on 18 March when the 40th Infantry Division landed on the latter island unopposed. Following a brief destroyer bombardment the first assault wave hit the beach—to be greeted on shore "by men of Colonel Peralta's guerrilla forces, dressed in starched khaki and resplendent ornaments."[21]

The landing on Panay marked the beginning of the VICTOR I operations. Air support for the landings was provided by planes from three Marine fighter squadrons of MAG 14 based on Samar. Twenty-one Corsairs of VMF-222 patrolled over the beachhead during the day of the landings, though the enemy remained just as passive in the air as on the ground. The squadron's only attack mission for 18 March was the strafing of six barges in the Iloilo River.

Pilots from VMF-251 searched the waters adjacent to the Panay beachheads for enemy shipping, but failed to find any trace of enemy activity. VMF-223 had the mission of neutralizing any Japanese air effort on adjacent Negros Island while the landings were in progress. The Corsairs swept down on six enemy airstrips on Negros during the day and destroyed two Japanese fighters. No lucrative targets ever materialized for the eager Marine aviators on Panay; the enemy kept to the woods and offered only weak resistance to the advancing infantry. The occupation of Panay largely resembled a major mop-up operation; just as most of the American forces on Panay had refused to surrender to the Japanese in 1942, so now the Japanese commander, Lieutenant Colonel Ryoichi Totsuka, marched the 1,500 troops under his command into the hills, where they remained until the end of the war. By the end of June, U.S. Army casualties on Panay were about 20 men killed and 50 wounded.

On 26 March, VICTOR II got under way when the Americal Division landed on Cebu Island, about five miles southwest of Cebu City. Preceded by a devastating naval bombardment, leading waves of LVTs rolled onto the beach, where a nasty surprise awaited them. The first wave was abruptly halted when ten of the 15 landing vehicles were disabled by land mines. Several men were killed and others were severely injured as they stepped on mines while dismounting.

> It was soon discovered that the existing beach defense was the most elaborate and effective yet encountered in the Philippines, even though the covering fire from prepared defenses was limited to small arms and mortar fire. The entire length of the landing beach bristled with mines ranging in size from 60mm mortar shells to 250-pound aerial bombs.
> Subsequent waves of infantry unloaded on the beach, but made no attempt to move forward into the mined area. All along the shore, between the minefield and the water's edge, men were crowded shoulder to shoulder, two and three deep. As they moved up and down the beach, unsuccessfully trying to find a clear opening, it became apparent that organization was breaking down and adequate control was lacking.[22]

Eventually, the confusion on the beachhead subsided, and despite the

---

[21] Eighth Army, *Panay-Negros Ops*, p. 37.

[22] Eighth Army, *Cebu-Bohol-Negros Ops*, pp. 41-42.

lack of an adequate number of engineers, the troops pushed through after lanes were finally cleared. Behind the minefield, 50 yards inland in the palm groves, the assault force encountered continuous barriers; antitank ditches, log fences and walls, timber sawhorses, and steel rail obstacles all designed to block the advance of tracked or wheeled vehicles. Together with the minefields, these obstacles were covered by well-prepared firing positions which included concrete pillboxes having walls from seven inches to three feet thick, emplacements walled with one to four coconut logs, barbed wire, and a network of trenches.

Strangely enough, the presence of such formidable defenses did not induce the Japanese to vary their recently instituted strategy of withdrawing from the beach area and resisting the American invasion troops with a force only strong enough to be of nuisance value. The enemy reaction to the American assault on Cebu proved no exception to his earlier practice. Even the few Japanese who were left to man the prepared positions had been forced to abandon them by the intensive and concentrated bombardment of the beach area by American naval guns. "Had these installations been manned by even a small but determined force, the troops massing behind the mine field would have been annihilated and the eventual victory would have become far more costly."[23] As it was, enemy casualties on or near the invasion beaches the first day were 88 killed and 10 captured;

American losses were eight killed and 39 wounded.[24]

As infantrymen of the Americal Division consolidated their beachhead on Cebu and advanced northward toward Cebu City, the Japanese began a hasty evacuation of the town. Throughout 26 March, Marine aviators of MAG-14 attacked enemy motorized columns and dismounted infantry headed for the hills northwest of Cebu City. Planes from VMF-222, -223, and -251 strafed the enemy with .50 caliber machine guns, destroying about 20 trucks and inflicting an undetermined number of casualties.

Japanese resistance on Cebu followed a familiar course. Unable to stem the American advance and severely harassed by American air, the enemy withdrew into the hills, from where he offered prolonged resistance. By late June numerous Japanese were still able to hide out in the hills, living a hunted existence, but ineffective as fighting groups.

Meanwhile, the American drive through the southern Philippines continued. Two days after the invasion of Cebu, troops of the 40th Infantry Division invaded Negros Island in a shore-to-shore operation from Panay. As on Cebu, the enemy withdrew into the hills, harassed by Marine aircraft and Filipino guerrillas. By mid-June, the Japanese on Negros no longer constituted an organized fighting force. A number of stragglers remained to lead a precarious existence, in which a struggle for survival in the hills was paramount.

---

[23] *Ibid.*, p. 44.

[24] *Ibid.*, p. 45.

The isolation in which the remaining enemy troops in the southern Visayas found themselves is best illustrated by their ignorance of the end of the war. American leaflets dropped over enemy-held areas on Cebu by order of Major General William H. Arnold, commanding the Americal Division, informed the Japanese holdouts that the war was over and promised them fair treatment in accordance with the rules of the Hague and Geneva Conventions. On 17 August the Japanese replied with the following message:

> We saw your propaganda of 16th August 1945, do not believe your propaganda. We request that you send to us a Staff Officer of General Yamashita in Luzon if it is true that Imperial Japanese surrendered to the Americans.[25]

A further exchange of communications proved fruitless. The Japanese radio equipment on Cebu was out of order, and the holdouts had no way of getting direct information from Tokyo. Orders were issued to the effect that officers and men would be punished if they believed the American propaganda. The situation was clarified however, on 19 August, when the Japanese were able to repair one of the radio receivers and learned that Japan was in fact defeated. "There was no longer any doubt in their minds; their country was really defeated, so their only course of action was to surrender themselves to the Americans."[26] On Cebu, two lieutenant generals, a major general, and an admiral surrendered, as did the remaining Japanese garrison of 9,000 men. The Americal Division and attached units had killed another 9,300 Japanese on Cebu and about 700 more on nearby Bohol and eastern Negros at a cost of 449 men killed and 1,872 wounded in action.

Throughout the VICTOR I and II operations in the southern Visayas, aircraft of MAG-14 gave all possible support to the ground troops. In addition to guerrillas who directed the Marine pilots to their targets, Army support air parties also were in operation on all of the newly invaded islands. The Thirteenth Air Force on Leyte directed MAG-14 by means of daily assignment schedules to report in for control to various support air parties. The Army Air Forces on many occasions furnished air coordinators in B-24s, which led the flights to the targets and pinpointed objectives. Despite poor weather, planes of MAG-14 flew a total of more than 5,800 hours during the month of April alone, an average of almost nine hours per day per plane.[27]

By early May, the need for air support in the central Philippines had decreased and MAG-14 was transferred to the 2d Marine Aircraft Wing on Okinawa. The air group ceased combat operations on Samar on 15 May. Once more, Marine aviators had made a material contribution to the liberation of the Philippines. In paying tribute to the accomplishments of these Marine aviators, General Eichelberger expressed himself as follows:

---

[25] G-2 Periodic Rpt, HQ, Americal Div, dtd 18Aug45, as cited in Eighth Army, *Cebu-Bohol-Negros Ops*, p. 131.
[26] Ibid., p. 132.

[27] Boggs, *Marines in the Philippines*, p. 119.

Marine Air Group Fourteen rendered an outstanding performance in supporting overwater and ground operations against the enemy at Leyte, Samar, Palawan, Panay, Cebu, and Negros, Philippine Islands. This group provided convoy cover, fighter defense, fire bombing, dive bombing and strafing in support of ground troops. The enthusiasm of commanders and pilots, their interest in the ground situation and their eagerness to try any method which might increase the effectiveness of close air support, were responsible in a large measure for keeping casualties at a minimum among ground combat troops.[28]

Concurrently with operations in the southern Visayas, the drive into the Sulu Archipelago, a continuation of VICTOR IV, also gained momentum. On 2 April, elements of the 41st Infantry Division invaded Sanga Sanga in the Tawi Tawi Group at the extreme southern end of the Sulu Archipelago, 200 miles south of Zamboanga and 30 miles east of the coast of Borneo. The invasion force encountered only light opposition and, later in the day, launched a shore-to-shore assault against adjacent Bongao Island.

Both assault operations were supported by Marine aircraft. On 1 April, both islands had been heavily bombed and napalmed by Corsairs of VMF-115 and -313. The next day, on board the destroyer USS *Saufley,* Colonel Verne J. McCaul, commanding MAG-12, served as support air commander. The control room of the destroyer contained three air support circuits. One of these controlled the combat air patrol; another circuit was available for air-sea rescue operations; a third was utilized for direction of support missions on the beach. In the course of both landings, as Marine fighters and bombers circled overhead, a radio jeep went ashore with the assault troops. This jeep contained the Marine air-ground liaison team headed by Captain Samuel McAloney as support air controller. As soon as the Marine team reached the beach, Captain McAloney took charge of the direction of the strike planes.

During the Bongao landings, 44 dive bombers from MAG-32 dropped 20 tons of bombs on the island. SBDs of VMSB-236 attacked an enemy observation post and troop concentrations. While the dive bombers were bombing such enemy objectives as they could locate, Corsairs from VMF-115 and -211 flew combat air patrol over Sanga Sanga. The Marine fighters attacked an enemy radio station with unobserved results. The Corsairs provided air cover for the invasion force until 8 April, when targets suitable for aerial bombing or strafing were no longer in evidence.

Even as the occupation of Sanga Sanga and Bongao Islands was progressing, bypassed Jolo Island to the north was drawing a lot of attention from the Marine aviators, who carried out daily raids. As early as 4 April, SBDs of VMSB-236 carried General Doe, commanding the 41st Infantry Division, and a member of his staff to Jolo Island on a reconnaissance mission. Following several reconnaissance flights by the division commander, all officers and senior noncommissioned officers of RCT 163 made similar flights over their landing beaches and zones of advance. This was possible because

---

[28] Eighth Army, Office of the CG, ltr, dtd 25Jun45, as cited in Boggs, *Marines in the Philippines,* pp. 120–121.

of the large Marine aircraft group at Zamboanga and the lack of Japanese air strength.

Jolo, situated 80 miles southwest from Zamboanga, was within easy range of Moret Field. Moro guerrillas had seized the initiative from the Japanese prior to the American landings. As a result the Japanese had been forced to withdraw into the interior, where they established their defenses on five mountains named Bangkal, Patikul, Tumatangas, Dato, and Daho.

On 9 April, elements of the 41st Infantry Division landed on Jolo Island in a shore-to-shore operation from Zamboanga. The Marine landing party, consisting of 5 officers and 11 men, was headed by Captain McConaughy. Lieutenant Colonel John Smith was support air commander and Captain McAloney was support air controller. The team was equipped with a radio-equipped truck and two similarly equipped jeeps. During the landing near Jolo Town, the Marine air liaison party was compelled to disembark the radio-equipped jeeps in four feet of water, because the Landing Ship, Medium (LSM), carrying these vehicles could not get close enough to the beach. The unexpected baptism in salt water played havoc with the radio gear, which had to be disassembled, carefully cleansed with fresh and sweet water, dried with carbon tetrachloride from fire extinguishers, and finally reassembled before it could be put back into operation. The radio truck landed somewhat later at a different beach without undue complications.

In the face of light enemy opposition, the 41st Infantry Division pressed onwards into the interior of the island.

Two of the Japanese hill strongholds, Mt. Patikul and Mt. Bangkal, were seized within 24 hours after the initial landings. The infantry advance was executed under a constant umbrella of Marine fighters and dive bombers. On the very first day of the Jolo operation, Marine aviators pummeled the enemy with 7,000 pounds of napalm, nearly 15 tons of bombs, and 18,200 rounds of ammunition.[29] In one day, Marine aviators knocked out nine enemy gun positions, razed two radio shacks and towers, and knocked out seven enemy-occupied buildings and personnel areas.

The infantry advance into the interior of Jolo Island met its first strong resistance at the approaches to Mt. Dato. Nevertheless, this enemy strongpoint fell on 12 April. Mt. Daho, six miles southeast of Jolo Town, loomed as the next major obstacle in the path of the advancing infantry. This formidable strongpoint with an elevation of 2,247 feet was of historical significance, for about four decades earlier Americans had fought the Moros on this mountain. It was estimated that about 400 *Special Naval Landing Force* troops were entrenched on Mt. Daho, equipped with nine dual 20mm guns, as well as heavy and light machine guns.

The attack against Mt. Daho began on 16 April, when infantrymen and Filipino guerrillas ran into a veritable hail of fire from the Japanese defenders, who were using connecting trenches, pillboxes, and dugouts to best advantage. The preliminary bombardment of the Japanese strongpoints by aircraft and artillery proved inade-

---

[29] MAG-12 WarD, Apr 45.

quate and the advance stalled. For the next four days, artillery and Marine aviation took turns in softening up the enemy, who obviously was determined to make his last stand here. On 18 April, 27 SBDs of VMSB-243 and 18 SBDs of VMSB-341 from Moret Field dropped over 21 tons of bombs on the enemy under the direction of the Support Air Party. On the following day, 47 SBDs of VMSB-236 and 18 SBDs of VMSB-243 continued the neutralization of the enemy on Mt. Daho. Of the results achieved, the ground forces reported: "Of 42 bombs dropped this morning, 35 were exactly on the target. Remainder were close enough to be profitable."[30]

By 20 April it seemed that Mt. Daho was ripe for a direct assault. As the infantrymen edged their way up the hill, they were halted by a hail of fire which killed 3 men and wounded 29.[31] Once more, the attack was halted as artillery and supporting aircraft shelled, bombed, and strafed the obstinate holdouts. In the course of 21 April, 70 SBDs dropped more than 15 tons of bombs on enemy positions at Mt. Daho. As night fell, the artillery began to saturate the target area.

Early on 22 April, 33 SBDs from VMSB-142, -243, and -341 and four rocket-firing Mitchell bombers (PBJs) of VMB-611 attacked Japanese positions on Mt. Daho. Again, the infantry jumped off for the attack on the stronghold. This time, the attack carried the hill. Speaking of the final assault, the division historian made the following comment:

The combined shelling and bombing was so effective that the doughboys were able to move forward at a rapid pace without a single casualty. The area was found littered with bodies of 235 Japs and it was believed that many more had sealed themselves into caves and blown themselves to bits. This broke the Jap stand in this sector and the few enemy troops that escaped from Mt. Daho wandered aimlessly in small groups and were easy prey for roving guerrilla bands.[32]

Fighting on Jolo Island continued until well into the summer of 1945, but the capture of Mt. Daho had broken the backbone of the enemy defense. Control of Jolo provided the Americans with the best port in the Sulu Archipelago; it also marked the completion of the drive into the archipelago.

MINDANAO[33]

One more operation was required to bring all of the southern Philippines under Allied control. This operation was VICTOR V, the seizure of Mindanao, southernmost and second largest island in the Philippines. This island, measuring 300 miles from north to south and about 250 miles from east to west at its widest point, had a population of nearly two million just before the outbreak of World War II. Even

---

[30] MAG-32 WarD, Apr45.
[31] McCartney, *41st InfDiv Hist*, p. 152.

[32] *Ibid.*, p. 153.
[33] Additional sources for this section include: CG, X Corps, History of X Corps on Mindanao, 17April-30June45, hereafter *X Corps Mindanao Hist;* VMSB-241 WarD, May45; VMB-611 WarDs, Jul44-Nov45; John A. DeChant, *Devilbirds—The Story of United States Marine Corps Aviation in World War II* (New York and London: Harper & Brothers, 1947), hereafter DeChant, *Devilbirds*.

though the Zamboanga Peninsula technically is part of the Mindanao mainland, "the peninsula, for purposes of military planning, was not considered part of Mindanao at all."[34] Hence, because of the forbidding mountain barrier separating eastern Mindanao from the Zamboanga Peninsula, a separate invasion of the eastern portion of the island had to be instituted despite the presence of American forces on Zamboanga since 10 March 1945.

Prior to the VICTOR V operation, enemy strength on Mindanao, less Zamboanga, was estimated at 34,000. Of this number, 19,000 were combat troops; 11,000 were service troops; an estimated 3,000-5,000 poorly armed Japanese civilians, conscripted residents of Mindanao, made up the rest of the garrison.[35]

Responsibility for the Mindanao operation was assigned to the X Corps, commanded by Major General Franklin C. Sibert. Capture of the island was to be carried out by the 24th and 31st Infantry Divisions, which were to invade the west coast of Mindanao near Malabang and Parangon 17 April 1945. Task Group 78.2, under the command of Rear Admiral Albert G. Noble, furnished the amphibious lift, convoy escort, and naval gunfire support for the X Corps en route from staging areas on Mindoro, Leyte, and Morotai to Mindanao.

Despite the impressive size of the Japanese garrison on Mindanao, the invasion force could count on assistance from guerrilla forces on the island, which "were the most efficient and best organized in the Philippines."[36] These Filipinos were commanded by Colonel Wendell W. Fertig, a former American engineer and gold miner, who had turned guerrilla after the fall of the Philippines and built up an effective insurgent force. Fertig had maintained radio communications with MacArthur's headquarters ever since the summer of 1942 and, from 1943 onwards, had been the recipient of supplies brought in first by submarine and later by air or small vessels. The presence of an insurgent force in the enemy rear began to pay dividends even before the first X Corps troops landed on Mindanao. Prior to the invasion force's move towards the island, Colonel Fertig's guerrilla force had been attacking the Japanese garrison at Malabang, with the support of Marine aircraft from Moret Field.

By 5 April, following the expulsion of the enemy from Malabang and vicinity by the guerrillas, Marine aircraft started to operate from the Malabang airstrip. "As the front lines were then less than a half mile from the airstrip, Marine pilots visited ground observation posts for briefing, and after studying enemy defenses, flew a mere 800 yards before releasing their bombs on primary hostile targets."[37]

Nor were these Marine air strikes in support of the guerrillas all the Japanese had to worry about. For six days prior to the American landings on Mindanao, heavy bombers hit Cagayan, Davao, Cotabato, Parang, and Kubacan, some of the more important towns

---

[34] Eichelberger and Mackaye, *Jungle Road to Tokyo*, p. 216.
[35] *X Corps Mindanao Hist.*, p. 6.
[36] Eichelberger and Mackaye, *Jungle Road to Tokyo*, p. 217.
[37] *X Corps Mindanao Hist.*, p. 53.

on the island. At the same time medium bombers struck Surigao, Malabang, Cotabato, and the Sarangani Bay area. Dive bombers hit pinpointed targets, while fighters carried out several sweeps daily over the roads and trails throughout the island.

The official Army history has described the situation of the Japanese in the immediate area of the contemplated landings as follows:

> By the 11th of April the last Japanese had fled toward Parang and the guerrillas had completed the occuption of the entire Malabang region. On 13 April Colonel Fertig radioed Eighth Army that X Corps could land unopposed at Malabang and Parang and that the Japanese had probably evacuated the Cotabato area as well.[38]

In addition to the assistance furnished to the guerrillas on Mindanao by aircraft from MAGsZam, the Thirteenth Air Force, reinforced by elements of the Fifth Air Force and the Royal Australian Air Force Command, had carried on a continuous air offensive of neutralizing enemy air, ground, and naval forces, and to prevent Japanese reinforcements and supplies from reaching the objective area. Fifth Air Force, commanded by Major General Ennis C. Whitehead, had the specific mission of providing aerial reconnaissance, photography, and providing air cover for the convoys and naval forces. The Allied Forces had done their job well. As the time for the invasion of Mindanao approached, little was left of the 1,500 enemy aircraft once assumed to have been stationed on Mindanao. The actual measure of the destruction of the Japanese Air Force was evident by the number of Japanese aircraft that were to make an appearance over the island during the VICTOR V operation. Throughout the campaign, only five enemy aircraft were sighted over Mindanao. Even though the enemy controlled two dozen airstrips on the island, American air supremacy was complete.

As soon as possible after X Corps had gone ashore on Mindanao, MAG-24 was to be flown from Luzon to the Malabang airstrip, situated 150 miles east of Moret Field. Upon its arrival on Mindanao, MAG-24 was to operate under the direction of Colonel Jerome as part of MAGsZam in an organizational scheme closely resembling that previously existing on Luzon.

Since the guerrillas appeared to be in firm control of the Malabang area, the landing force sent to Malabang was reduced from a division to one battalion. Instead, the main assault was made at Parang, 17 miles to the south. This decision, which involved changing the entire assault plan at sea, was reached after Lieutenant Colonel McCutcheon of MAG-24 had personally reconnoitered the Malabang area several days before the landings. The Marine aviator conferred with guerrilla leaders on the ground and, accompanied by one of them, Major Rex Blow, an Australian who had been captured by the Japanese at Singapore and who subsequently had found his way to the Philippines, flew back to Zamboanga. These two men proceeded by small boat to join the Mindanao-bound invasion convoy on the afternoon of 16 April. "Information these two men furnished

---

[38] Smith, *Triumph in the Philippines*, p. 621.

to the X Corps commander, firmed the decision to land at Parang rather than Malabang."[39]

The landings at Parang proceeded without incident early on 17 April, following an unnecessary two-hour cruiser and destroyer bombardment. Fighters, dive bombers, and medium bombers from Moret Field maintained vigil over Parang and Malabang. Incessant sweeps over the highways of Central Mindanao kept the movement of enemy troops to a minimum. An Army Air Forces air support party, in direct contact with the Marine pilots, directed the aircraft to targets that included enemy supply dumps, troop concentrations, and installations. Eighteen dive bombers of VMSB-341 and 17 SBDs of VMSB-142 circled over the beachheads, subject to call by the support air party. At the same time, 20 Corsairs of VMF-211 flew combat air patrol over the beaches; another 10 Corsairs from VMF-218 protected the cruiser force offshore.

First Marine unit ashore at Parang was AWS-3, which landed at noon and set up radio equipment on the beach. VMSB-244 personnel landed at Parang along with the main body of X Corps. The remainder of the Marine aviation units landed later in the day three miles north of Malabang Field. Movement of personnel and equipment to the airstrip was impeded by heavy rains, muddy roads, and bridges which had been demolished by guerrillas or the withdrawing enemy. In the words of the U.S. Army X Corps commander: "As to bridges, they had been destroyed by guerrillas time and again until I don't believe there was a highway bridge intact in the whole island."[40]

With the help of Army engineers, Malabang Field was readied for the flight echelon of MAG-24. When the first planes of MAG-24 arrived from Luzon on 20 April, the pilots and crews found an engineering line already set up and a camp area beginning to take shape. First of the dive bomber squadrons to arrive was VMSB-241, followed by VMSB-133 and -244 during the following two days. The Marines renamed the airstrip Titcomb Field in honor of Captain John A. Titcomb who had been killed while directing an air strike on Luzon.

On 21 April, AWS-3, meanwhile redesignated as the 77th Fighter Control Center, assumed fighter direction and local air warning responsibility from the control ship. The air warning squadron's radio and radar equipment operated around the clock; personnel monitored two radar search sets, in addition to eight different radio channels at various frequencies in the high frequency and very high frequency bands.[41]

---

[39] Boggs, *Marines in the Philippines*, p. 126.

[40] MajGen Franklin C. Sibert, USA, ltr to Head, HistBr, G-3 Div, HQMC, dtd 24Oct66, in *Philippines Comment File*.

[41] HF band is an arbitrary designation for frequencies in the radio spectrum between 3 and 30 megacycles; VHF comprises that part of the spectrum between 30 and 300 megacycles. Over the years, the concept of what constitutes high, very high, ultra high, and extremely high frequencies had undergone

The advance of the 24th and 31st Infantry Divisions towards the east coast of Mindanao near Davao and towards the southeastern tip of the island towards Sarangani Bay made good progress in the days following the invasion. On 22 April, MAG-24 initiated operations from Titcomb Field to support the advance of the Army divisions, one day ahead of schedule. Technically, MAG-24 came under the control of MAGsZam. In practice, because of the distance between Moret and Titcomb Fields, MAG-24 operated practically as a separate unit. Night fighters and local combat air patrols for Titcomb Field were made available by MAGsZam to MAG-24 from aircraft stationed at Moret Field.

The operations of MAG-24 on Mindanao differed considerably from those of Marine aviators elsewhere in the Philippines. The X Corps retained control of the air support strikes because of the distances support aircraft had to fly to provide support and the existence of two separate Marine air groups, not including elements of the Thirteenth Air Force which furnished heavy strikes. The circumstance that the two infantry divisions were operating in widely separated zones, plus the necessity of close coordination with the guerrillas, all combined to make a centralized control indispensable.

---

considerable change. During the early years of radio, frequencies above two megacycles were generally considered useless for communications. During World War II, frequencies up to 600 megacycles were used, primarily for radar in the high end of the spectrum.

To facilitate close control over air strikes, support air parties were attached to X Corps and the two infantry divisions. The support aircraft officer worked closely with the division air officer and provided communications facilities for direct support requests. In addition to the support air parties, the Army 295th Joint Assault Signal Company (JASCO) made available 12 forward air control teams equipped with short-range radio gear mounted in jeeps for air-ground communication. These teams were apportioned between the two infantry divisions for the primary purpose of directing close support strikes.

The technique employed on Mindanao was unusual in other respects. Due to the organizational setup, a constant air alert was maintained overhead to minimize the delay between requests for air support and the actual strikes. JASCO teams were used throughout the Mindanao campaign. With the support air parties thus reinforced, there was no need to shuffle the JASCO teams from one line unit to the other as strikes were required. Instead, a battalion commander could request air support with reasonable assurance that the strike would be carried out without undue delay.

As the two infantry divisions of X Corps advanced across Mindanao, SBDs from Titcomb and Moret Fields ranged ahead of the Army troops, driving the enemy from roads and villages in the path of the American advance. Despite demolished bridges and sporadic resistance, the advance of the ground forces proceeded ahead of schedule. On 27 April, the 24th Infantry Division seized

SOUTHERN PHILIPPINES OPERATIONS

Digos on the east coast of Mindanao and pivoted northward towards Davao; the capital city of the island fell on 3 May, after the infantry had covered a distance of 145 miles in 15 days. The 31st Infantry Division, advancing northward through the Mindanao Valley seized Valencia on 16 May and Malaybaley several days later.

Marine aviators employed napalm bombs for the first time on Mindanao on 30 April, when they were dropped on an enemy held hill near Davao. The results of this attack were such, that, according to an official Army account:

> From this time on, fire from the air was available, with strikes as large as thirty-two 165 gallon tanks being dropped on a target. In several instances, entire enemy platoons were burned in their positions and in other cases, flaming Japanese fled from positions, only to encounter machine gun fire from ground troops.[42]

On 8 May, three SBDs of VMSB-241 and eight dive bombers from VMSB-133 flew a spectacular strike against an enemy strongpoint west of Sayre Highway opposite Lake Pinalay. At this point, elements of the 124th Infantry Regiment, 31st Infantry Division, were encountering heavy enemy resistance. Since the weather was closing in, and the opposing forces were only about 200 yards apart, there was a great risk involved to the friendly troops in obtaining close support. Nevertheless, such support was forthcoming in what the Marine pilots subsequently termed "the closest support mission yet flown by VMSB-241."[43] Yellow panels were employed to indicate friendly positions. The target was marked with smoke, and nine SBDs, in a neat example of precision bombing, unloaded nearly five tons of bombs within the 200 yard area. The Japanese position was completely eliminated. The grateful commander of 3/124 requested the Marine ground controller to radio the following message to the Marine pilots:

> Jojo (133) and Dottie (241) flights gave finest example of air-ground coordination and precision bombing I have ever seen. Debris from the bombs fell on our men but none was injured.[44]

As the 24th Infantry Division approached Davao, the normal combat air patrol was increased from three to six aircraft. At the same time, an intensive effort was under way to break up the Japanese defensive positions near the city. As a result, the pace reached between 150 and 200 sorties a day. The largest number of strikes in one day involved 245 aircraft, dropping 155 tons of bombs.[45] Attempts by Marine aviators to have close air support gain the acceptance of the ground troops had by this time come full circle. As early as the drive through the Sulu Archipelago, one observer noted:

> . . . the sight of the jeeps with their Marine insignia was a matter of course to the infantrymen. Close air support was no longer novel or a matter of unusual interest to the soldiers. It was always there. It always worked. It was now just a part of the first team.[46]

Far from having to fight for acceptance, some Marine pilots on Mindanao found that "the infantry was apt to call

---

[42] *X Corps Mindanao Hist.*, p. 56.
[43] VMSB-241 WarD, May45.
[44] *Ibid.*
[45] *X Corps Mindanao Hist.*, p. 56.
[46] De Chant, *Devilbirds*, p. 197.

for planes to hit a pin-point target that any hard-driving rifle squad could have taken. However, such enthusiasm was much preferred to indifference."[47]

During the latter part of May, Japanese resistance in the mountains east of the Sayre Highway stiffened appreciably. Even though, by this time, the X Corps operations on Mindanao had entered the mop-up and pursuit phase, rough terrain and poor trails in the mountainous regions of the island hampered the advance of the infantry. At the same time, heavy rains curtailed aerial observation of Japanese activity. As American troops advanced farther into the mountains, the enemy began to fight doggedly for every inch of ground.

In order to drive the Japanese from one of their strongholds, Marine dive-bomber pilots tried out yet another tactic on 1 June. This new method involved the saturation bombing of a very small area. No less than 88 SBDs attacked an enemy troop concentration and gun positions with a variety of bomb loads, including napalm. No enemy fire greeted the advancing infantrymen, who had expected to encounter stubborn resistance.

The stage for the biggest air strike on Mindanao was set when, on 19 June, a 31st Infantry Division artillery spotter aircraft observed large contingents of enemy troops moving into the Umayam River Valley in northern Mindanao. On the following morning, additional liaison aircraft flew over the area and reaffirmed the presence of enemy concentrations, but unfavorable weather precluded any offensive action from the air. On 21 June, all Marine aircraft that could be spared were requested to hit this area. Airborne coordinators in artillery spotter planes directed 148 dive bombers and fighter bombers to the target. During a four-hour period, the planes unloaded 75 tons of bombs on bivouac areas, supplies, buildings, and marching troop columns. Because of inclement weather, observation of results was limited; nevertheless, a number of large fires were clearly visible, bodies were observed floating in the river, and individual Japanese could be seen fleeing before the strafing aircraft. Subsequent reports indicated that about 500 Japanese were killed in this attack.

Despite bad weather and occasionally fanatical enemy resistance in the mountains of central and northern Mindanao, the handwriting was on the wall for the Japanese remaining on the island. On 30 June, General Eichelberger declared the eastern Mindanao operation completed and reported to General MacArthur that organized opposition on the island had ceased. Actually, isolated Japanese units were to continue fighting right up to the end of the war, and during the period 30 June through 15 August, American and Filipino guerrilla units killed 2,235 Japanese in addition to the more than 10,000 enemy killed on Mindanao prior to 30 June.[48] U.S. Army casualties through 15 August had numbered 820 killed and 2,880 wounded.[49] Among the Marine aviators who did not survive the Mindanao operation was Lieutenant Colonel Sarles, the energetic commander of VMB–611,

---

[47] Ibid.

[48] Smith, *Triumph in the Philippines*, p. 647.
[49] Ibid., p. 648.

whose PBJ failed to pull up after a low level attack on the Kibawe Trail in northern Mindanao on 30 May.[50]

During the period of 17 April through 30 June, Marine aviators flew a total of 10,406 combat sorties in support of X Corps, and dropped a total of 4,800 tons of bombs. Nearly 1,300 five-inch rockets were fired in low level attacks against Japanese installations during the same period.[51] From the first strategic attack until the final Japanese defeat, more than 20,000 sorties of all types of aircraft were flown in support of the Mindanao Campaign.[52]

On 12 July, Marine aviators in the Philippines carried out their last major support mission of the war when they flew cover for an amphibious landing team of the 24th Infantry Division at Sarangani Bay in southern Mindanao. With few exceptions, Marine and Allied aircraft had exhausted all profitable targets by mid-July. As far as the liberation of the Philippines was concerned, Marine aviation had fully achieved the objective it had set for itself: close air support that was consistently effective, and a menace only to the enemy.

CONCLUSION OF PHILIPPINE OPERATIONS[53]

By late April 1945 the main objectives of American operations in the Philippines had been accomplished: MacArthur's forces had seized strategic air bases which could be used to deny the enemy access to the East Indies; at the same time, American forces had gained control of bases in the Philippines from which an invasion of Japan could be mounted. In addition, the Allied advance through the Philippines had freed the majority of Filipinos from Japanese occupation. In a futile attempt to stem the American advance through the Philippines, the Japanese had sacrificed more than 400,000 of their troops.[54] When the war ended, more than a 100,000 Japanese—including noncombatant civilians—still remained in the archipelago. While the main body of American troops were preparing for an assault against Japan proper, the remnants of erstwhile proud Japanese garrisons in the Philippines were reduced to impotence and forced to forage for scraps to keep themselves alive, hunted by Americans and Filipinos alike.

For Marine aviators in the Philippines, the summer of 1945 brought changes both in personnel and equipment. On 1 June, Colonel Lyle H. Meyer turned over the command of MAG–24 to Colonel Warren E. Sweetser, Jr.[55] Two days later, after 26 months' service in the Pacific Theater, General Mitchell relinquished his command of the 1st Marine Aircraft Wing and AirNorSols

---

[50] VMB–611 WarD, May45.
[51] *X Corps Mindanao Hist.*, p. 57.
[52] *Ibid.*
[53] Additional sources for this section include: 1st MAW WarDs, 1945; Robert Debs Heinl, Jr., *Soldiers of the Sea—The United States Marine Corps, 1775–1962* (Annapolis: United States Naval Institute, 1962), hereafter Heinl, *Soldiers of the Sea*; George Odgers, *Air War Against Japan, 1943–1945—Australia in the War of 1939–1945*, series 3, Air, v. II (Canberra: Australian War Memorial, 1957), hereafter Odgers, *Air War Against Japan.*
[54] Smith, *Triumph in the Philippines*, pp. 651–652.
[55] MAG–24 WarD, Jun45.

to Major General Louis E. Woods who, as a lieutenant colonel, had organized and commanded the wing at Quantico during the summer of 1941. General Woods was to recall:

> ... I arrived at Headquarters, AirNorSols before lunch and about 3 p.m. I received immediate orders to proceed to Guam and report in person to Admiral Nimitz. I left later that night so that I would arrive in Guam at about seven o'clock when his Headquarters opened. I reported to him personally, was briefed by him, and ordered by him to proceed at once to Okinawa and relieve General Mulcahy. I doubt if I was in command of AirNorSols more than five hours.[56]

Upon his arrival on Okinawa, General Woods took over the 2d Marine Aircraft Wing. Colonel Harold C. Major, who had succeeded General Woods in command of the 1st Wing, held the post for only four days. On 10 June, Brigadier General Lewie G. Merritt arrived on Bougainville to take command. Two months later to the day, General Merritt, in turn, was relieved by Major General Claude A. Larkin, who was initially scheduled to take the 1st Wing into Kyushu once the invasion of the Japanese home islands got under way.

Other Marine aviators who had been instrumental in gaining acceptance for Marine close air support operations were caught up in the reshuffling of personnel. On 4 July, Colonel Jerome turned over his command of MAG-32 and MAGsZam to Colonel Stanley E. Ridderhof and returned to the United States. Six weeks later, on 17 August, Colonel Verne J. McCaul assumed command of MAGsZam.

The rapid turnover of personnel was accompanied by a similar reshuffling of Marine aviation units. On 1 August, the dive bomber squadrons of MAG-32, VMSB-133, -236, and -241 were decommissioned. Three days later, Headquarters of the 1st MAW and MAG-61 (including VMB-413, -423, -433, and -443), were ordered by Far East Air Forces to proceed from Bougainville to Zamboanga. Two weeks after the Japanese surrender, MAGsZam was dissolved; operational control of Moret Field and the air defense of Mindanao was turned over to the Army Air Forces 13th Fighter Command, effective 1 September. The end of the war saw numerous Marine aviation units in the process of being decommissioned; only a few Marine squadrons were to remain in the Philippines. The 1st Marine Aircraft Wing would shortly move to Okinawa, and from there into China.

Even as units and personnel in the Philippines were undergoing major changes, the SBDs, long the mainstay of Marine dive bombing, were also making their exit. On 16 July, in a formal ceremony at Titcomb Field, Colonel Warren E. Sweetser, commanding MAG-24, bid farewell to the Douglas Dauntless dive bombers, which had rendered such faithful service to the Marine Corps from the first day of the war to almost the end. Several days later, the SBDs were ferried to Cebu for final disposition by the Navy.[57] Only VMSB-244, equipped with the

---

[56] LtGen Louis E. Woods ltr to Head, HistBr, G-3 Div, HQMC, dtd 25Nov66, in *Philippines Comment File*.

[57] 1st MAW WarD, Jul45.

new SB2C Helldivers, remained operational within MAG-24.

For the 1st MAW and Marine aviation in general, the employment of Marine aircraft in the Philippines marked the end of a lengthy period in which the Marines had believed, with some validity, that they were being left out of major operations in the Pacific Theater. In this feeling they were not alone, for Australian flying units expressed similar discontent at being assigned missions against long bypassed Japanese which they considered costly and nonessential.[58]

For Marine aviation, the Philippines campaign represented a unique opportunity to improve on a doctrine of air support that had been born long ago in the jungles of Central America. Earlier in World War II, there had been air support provided to ground forces by Marines. However, this air support had left something to be desired; a doctrine had not yet been evolved and techniques were yet to be refined. One Marine observer put it into the following words:

> Although there had been jury-rigged, prearranged airstrikes on Guadalcanal (some even involving depth charges as bombs), effective close air support never developed, nor did subsequent air support ventures in the undistinguished New Georgia campaign provide much encouragement.[59]

On Bougainville, it was Lieutenant Colonel John T. L. D. Gabbert, air officer of the 3d Marine Division, who began to study ways to make close air support more effective. Marine aviators proved at Hellzapoppin' Ridge what their close support capabilities were. Prior to the invasion of the Philippines, Lieutenant Colonel McCutcheon with the benefit of improved radio equipment that had meanwhile become available, adapted his own and Gabbert's experiences as a further step in evolving a sound doctrine of Marine style aviation close support. That this technique, so often vindicated towards the end of the Second World War, really worked is attested to by many letters of commendation and gratitude from commanders of ground forces benefiting from such support. Though the Marine doctrine has come under attack from various quarters, during World War II and since, the comments of the ground forces themselves provide the most eloquent testimony in its favor. On this subject, the official U.S. Army history of the Philippine campaign has this to say:

> Ground combat units that at one time or another had close support from both U. S. Army and U. S. Marine Corps Aviation were virtually unanimous in preferring the latter, at least during the earlier months of the campaigns. Later, when Fifth Air Force units became more experienced in close ground support activity and began to work more closely with the ground combat forces, confidence in the Army's air arm grew. Nevertheless, the campaign ended with almost all ground units still hoping for an improved, more effective air-ground liaison system insofar as Army air echelons were concerned, and also seeking methods by which to establish a closer, more effective working relationship between the Army's ground and air units.[60]

---

[58] For a detailed discussion of this situation, see Odgers, *Air War Against Japan*, pp.386–390.

[59] Heinl, *Soldiers of the Sea*, p 300.

[60] Smith, *Triumph in the Philippines*, p. 655.

Towards the end of the campaign in the Philippines, more than 30 letters of gratitude and commendation were directed to Marine aviation units from General MacArthur down to Army division commanders.[61] Perhaps General Eichelberger has summed it up best when he made the following comment, after the war, on the subject of close air support:

> There were four groups of Marine fliers who, in the interest of the integration of the services, were attached to the Thirteenth Air Force. During the central and southern Philippines campaign I had personal contact with the 12th, 14th, and 32nd Groups, and that was enough to convince me. These fliers had been trained by the Marine Corps with ground troops for the *specific purpose* of supporting ground troops. Their accomplishments were superb in the Zamboanga and Mindanao campaigns. The Marine liaison officers were always in front lines with the infantry commanders, and they were familiar with the forward positions as was the infantry. By radio they guided in the planes, and often the target of the strike was no more than three hundred yards ahead of the huddled doughboys.
>
> Colonel Clayton C. Jerome commanded these air men, and their accurate bombing and strafing earned them the gratitude and friendship of the 24th, 31st, and 41st Infantry Divisions. Nothing comforts a soldier, ankle-deep in mud, faced by a roadblock or fortified strongholds, as much as the sight of bombs wreaking havoc on stubborn enemy positions. It puts heart into them.[62]

The success of Marine aviators in the Philippines was not without sacrifice; 58 officers and 42 men of aviation units committed in the archipelago were killed in action; 46 officers and 81 Marines were wounded; and a total of 22 officers and 28 Marines died in operational aircraft accidents, from disease or accidents, or were missing.[63]

In the evolution of Marine aviation, the experiences gained by Marine pilots in the Philippines marked an important milestone. Close air support of ground forces became an accepted factor in ground operations. Techniques pioneered in the Philippines would require further refinement as new equipment became available; but Marine aviators had proven once and for all that their concept of close air support was correct and workable.

---

[61] Copies of these letters are contained in *Marine Close Air Support File.*

[62] Eichelberger and Mackaye, *Jungle Road to Tokyo,* p. 250.

[63] Figures furnished by Marine Records Section, HQMC, in a Special Aviation Rpt on 19Nov47, cited in Boggs, *Marines in the Philippines,* App. III, p. 152.

PART V

Marine Aviation in the Western Pacific

CHAPTER 1

Mounting the Offensive [1]

The movement of Marine aviation into the Central Pacific followed the general pattern of operations that earmarked the turning of the tide as the Guadalcanal campaign neared a successful conclusion. In late February 1943, U.S. Army troops, supported by Army Air Forces and Marine squadrons based at Henderson Field, landed in the Russell Islands. By May, an airstrip had been completed on Banika from which Marine dive bombers, as well as Army and Navy aircraft, stepped up the air war against enemy fields along the chain of islands extending up to Bougainville.

Invasion of the New Georgia Group in the Central Solomons on 30 June by a joint Marine-Army force was supported by squadrons of MAG-21. In addition to providing close air support to the ground troops, it became a prime mission of Marine aviation to reduce Japanese air strength in the Solomons and at the same time neutralize and isolate Japanese strongpoints that had been bypassed in favor of seizing more weakly defended islands farther to the enemy's rear. This strategy was successfully applied to recently established enemy airfields on New Georgia that had been designed to support the five major air bases ringing Rabaul, which were neutralized from the air for more than a year. Similarly, the capture of Vella Lavella Island effectively isolated an enemy garrison of 10,000 on Kolombangara Island 20 miles to the southeast. (See Map 22).

Once the success of such island-hopping tactics had been established, it was a foregone conclusion that they would be applied in the Central Pacific which was the logical next step in the American drive towards the Japanese

---

[1] Unless otherwise noted, the material in this chapter is derived from: DivAvn, HQMC, Pers and Loc Status Sheets, Mar43-Dec46, hereafter DivAvn, *Status Sheets*, with date; 4th MBDAW WarDs, Dec42-Mar46; MAG-13 WarDs, Jan43-Sep44; MAG-15 WarDs, Jan43-Dec45; MAG-22 WarDs, Apr43-Dec44; MAG-22 Hist, Mar42-Apr47; MAG-31 WarDs, Feb43-Jul46; VMF-111 WarDs, Jun43-Nov45; VMF-113 WarDs, Jan43-Jul45; VMF-151 WarDs, Apr43-May45; VMF-224 WarDs, May42-Jun44; VMSB-231 WarDs, Jun43-Jul45; VMF-241 WarDs, Apr42-Dec44; VMF-241 Hist, Mar-Dec43; VMF-311 WarDs, Sep43-Aug45; VMSB-331 Hist, Feb43-Dec44; VMJ-353 WarDs, Jun43-Jun44; VMF-422 WarDs, Jun43-Dec44; VMF-422 Hist, Jan43-Apr47; VMF(N)-532 Hist, Apr43-May47; Richard W. Johnston, *Follow Me!—The Story of the Second Marine Division in World War II* (New York: Random House, 1948), hereafter, Johnston, *2d MarDiv Hist;* Masatake Okumiya, Jiro Horikoshi, and Martin Caidin, *Zero!* (New York: E. P. Dutton & Co., Inc., 1956), hereafter, Okumiya, Horikoshi, and Caidin, *Zero!,* quoted with permission; Capt. Carl W. Proehl, *The Fourth Marine Division in World War II* (Washington: Infantry Journal Press, 1946), hereafter Proehl, *The Fourth Marine Division;* DeChant, *Devilbirds;* Sherrod, *Marine Corps Aviation in World War II.*

393

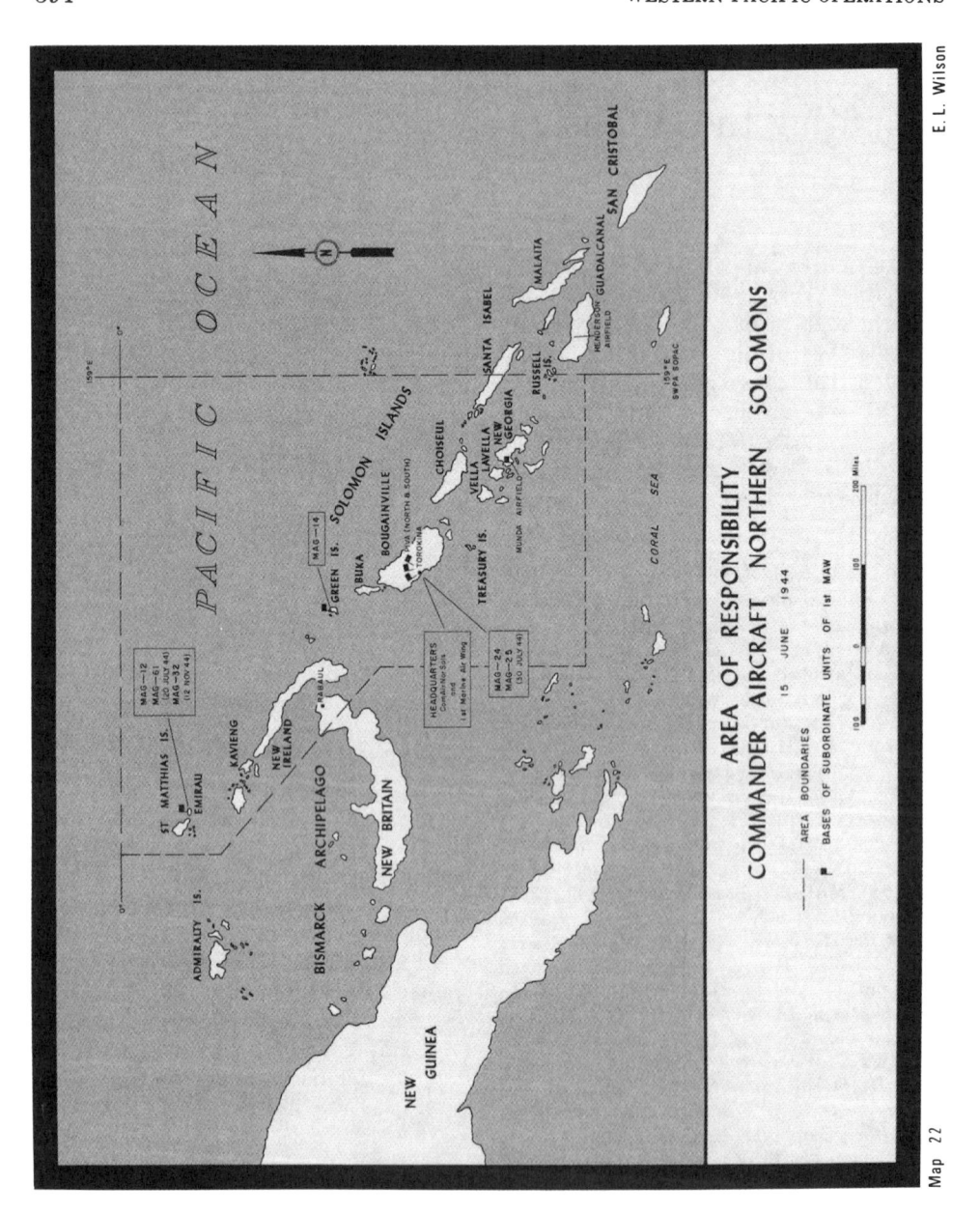

394 WESTERN PACIFIC OPERATIONS

Map 22

home islands. United States strategy for operations in the Central Pacific called for the seizure of the Gilbert Islands, to be used as a stepping-stone towards the Marshall Islands, the Marianas, and in time, the Carolines. The offensive in the Central Pacific was to begin on 20 November 1943 with an attack against the Gilberts. Operations in the Central Pacific were to be conducted under the command of Admiral Chester W. Nimitz. In emphasizing Navy sentiment towards the employment of Marines for assault missions of this type, Admiral Ernest J. King, Commander in Chief of the United States Fleet, expressed his conviction "that they were singularly appropriate for assaults on atolls, where no extended ground operations would follow the landings. In this kind of warfare you either take an island or you do not take it."[2]

Marine aviators took part in preliminary movements towards the Gilberts as early as 25 August 1943, when the 2d Marine Airdrome Battalion (Reinforced) moved into Nukufetau, a small atoll in the Ellice Islands. With the help of naval construction battalions, Marines constructed a fighter strip in Nukufetau, where VMF-111 landed on 20 October. Following this, the Seabees cut down 50,000 coconut trees to make room for a bomber strip. On 7 November, Navy Bomber Squadron 108 (VB-108) arrived on the strip, followed a week later by VMSB-331. Subsequently, a U.S. Army Air Force B-24 squadron also was based on this field.[3]

On 31 August, the 16th Naval Construction Battalion, together with a detachment of the 7th Marine Defense Battalion (Reinforced) had gone ashore on Nanomea, the northernmost of the Ellice Islands, situated about 400 miles southeast of Tarawa. A Marine fighter squadron, VMF-441, arrived on the island in late September. After an uneventful stay, the Marine squadron relinquished Nanomea in December to two Army Air Forces heavy bomber squadrons.

In connection with the Gilberts operation, it should be noted that the primary purpose for the expenditure of lives and materiel was not the elimination of Japanese garrisons on Tarawa and other islands in the group, but the further use to which the islands could be put in pursuit of the overall American strategy in the Pacific. To this end, initial possession of the Gilbert Islands, and subsequent seizure of the Marshalls would provide the United States with a base for an attack against the Marianas. In effect, the island groups and atolls in the Central Pacific represented unsinkable aircraft carriers. It was hoped that the airplane—capable of spanning ever-greater distances and of carrying an increasing bomb load—would be the medium that could isolate the enemy on the ground, knock him out of the sky, and when within launching distance of the Japanese homeland, could curtail and in time eliminate his capacity to wage war.

The epic assault by the 2d Marine Division on Tarawa in the Gilberts was

---
[2] King and Whitehill, *A Naval Record*, p. 481.
[3] Col J. Frank Cole ltr to Head HistBr, G-3 Div, HQMC, dtd 1Sep67, in *Marine Aviation Comment File*, hereafter *Cole ltr*.

destined to write an indelible page in the history of the Marine Corps. Heavy resistance and unusual beach and tidal conditions resulted in 20 percent casualties among the 15,000 Marines in the assault force.[4] Nevertheless, after three days of ferocious fighting, the 2d Marine Division was in firm control of Betio Island.

Marine aviators were not directly involved in air operations at Tarawa and at Makin Island either prior to or during the amphibious assault. Such aerial support was the task assigned to Army Air Forces pilots and carrier-based Navy aviators. Bombers of the Seventh Air Force, flying from recently occupied Nanomea and from Funafuti in the Ellice Islands, 660 miles east of Tarawa, were charged with denying the enemy the use of his airfields on Tarawa, Makin, Mille, Jaluit, Maloelap, and Nauru. Between 13 and 19 November 1943, they dropped 63.3 tons of bombs on Tarawa, in addition to flying missions against the other islands in the Gilberts and the Marshalls. On 18 November, naval planes dropped more than a hundred tons of bombs on Tarawa; nearly 70 additional tons were dropped on the following day. Altogether, approximately 900 carrier-based naval aircraft supported the operation in the Gilberts. The pilots flew 2,284 sorties in missions designed to neutralize Japanese air bases, provide direct support of ground operations, oppose enemy air efforts, and create diversions on adjacent islands.

Japanese efforts to assist their hard-pressed garrisons in the Gilberts consisted of air and submarine activity. Neither arm proved capable of seriously interfering with the American assault, though on 20 November one Japanese aircraft scored a torpedo hit on the light carrier *Independence*, which had to withdraw for repairs. Four days later, the enemy submarine *I–175* torpedoed and sank the escort carrier *Liscome Bay*, but even this serious loss failed to stem or even delay the tide of events in the Gilberts.

For Marine aviators, hampered by the short range of their aircraft, the Gilberts operation consisted of executing search and patrol missions and generally fulfilling a base defense mission. When, on 23 November, the smoke of battle lifted over newly captured Betio, the time had come to bury the dead, clear up the debris of battle, and take stock of what had been accomplished. Of the valor of the Marines, who had seized the island, little remained to be said; long rows of casualties awaiting burial spoke for themselves. The enemy's fanaticism in holding the atoll to the last also required little comment. In view of the 3,000 tons of naval shells hurled at Betio, an island less than half a square mile in size, and the relative ineffectiveness of this bombardment, Admiral Nimitz expressed the view that "heavier support of this kind is not to be expected in the Central Pacific Campaign, but increased efficiency in that support is to be expected."[5]

Following the Tarawa operation in

---

[4] Shaw, Nalty, and Turnbladh, *Central Pacific Drive*, Pt II, pp. 23–114.

[5] CinCPac forwarding ltr of 15Dec43 on ComCenPacFor rpt dtd 10Dec43, cited in Isely and Crowl, *U. S. Marines and Amphibious War*, p. 230.

late 1943, General Holland Smith recommended that Marine aviators be assigned to escort carriers, where they would play a part in furnishing direct air support in any future amphibious operation involving a Marine division. In the event such an assignment was not feasible, the Navy aviators given this mission would have to receive special indoctrination and training in close support tactics.

At the time, the climate was not yet ripe for the changes recommended, partly because the Navy already had its carriers earmarked for other employment and partly because not all of the Marine officers grappling with this important issue were pushing in unison for the same objective. In this connection, criticism may be directed against those both within the Navy and within the Corps who simply failed to see a need for putting Marine aviation on carriers. In the words of at least one authority on this subject:

> High-ranking Marine officers—aviators and non-aviators alike—showed a remarkable lack of foresight in failing to insist that their flyers be put on escort carriers at this time. It is easy to say that "Ernie King would never have stood for it," or "Admiral Whoosis doesn't believe in Marine aviation." But it was the job of the Marine Corps to find the right "persuaders."
>
> The truth is that the top Marine aviators didn't pay enough attention to (1) close support, (2) amphibious landings, (3) a combination of the two. They were too deeply interested in shooting enemy planes out of the wild blue yonder, so they lost sight of their primary mission.[6]

The story of how, following lengthy negotiations in 1944, Marines finally did get carriers assigned to them, has been well told elsewhere in this series.[7] In any case, during operations in the Central and Western Pacific in 1944 and early 1945, the absence of such close air support by Marines as had been envisioned was bound to have a profound and long-lasting effect on the role that Marine aviation could be expected to play during this phase of the war. One authoritative account of the campaign summed up the situation in the following words:

> The decision, however, prevented Marine pilots from supporting their comrades and army troops ashore in the Marshalls and the Marianas. Marine pilots in the Central Pacific before Tarawa served important defensive missions, but after that battle, since their craft were of short range, they watched the war leave them far behind. Their principal function in that section of the globe was bombing by-passed atolls.[8]

On 26 November, while the last enemy defenders were being hunted down on the northern islands of Tarawa Atoll, a Marine transport plane piloted by Major Edmund L. Zonne, executive officer of VMJ–353, landed on the newly reconditioned Japanese airstrip on Betio. This was the first Marine aircraft to touch down on the freshly captured island. At the same time, naval

---

[6] Sherrod, *Marine Corps Aviation in World War II*, p. 235.

[7] For a detailed account of Marine air on carriers, see Denis M. Frank and Henry I. Shaw, Jr., in *Victory and Occupation—History of U. S. Marine Corps Operations in World War II*, v. V (Washington: HistBr, G 3 Div, HQMC, 1969) pt. III, Chap. 2, section entitled "Marines on Carriers," pp. 410–429, hereafter Frank and Shaw, "Marines on Carriers."

[8] Isely and Crowl, *U. S. Marines and Amphibious War*, p. 231.

construction battalions and Army engineers began work on airfields on Makin and Apamama Islands. Scheduled flights to the latter two islands got under way in mid-December, when both airstrips became the terminals of regular passenger flights.

Christmas Day of 1943 witnessed the forward displacement of the 4th MBDAW, commanded by Brigadier General Lewie G. Merritt, who on 5 October had succeeded General Campbell as wing commander. The forward echelon of the wing moved from Funafuti in the Ellice Islands to Tarawa; a week later, on 2 January 1944, the rear echelon displaced from Tutuila in Samoa to Funafuti. In August 1943, when General Campbell had first brought the wing to Tutuila, he had under his command the forward echelons of VMJ-353 and VMF-224, as well as MAG-13, consisting of Headquarters Squadron 13 and Service Squadron 13, VMF-111, -151, -241, and -441. Five squadrons of Fleet Air Wing 2 were attached to his command for operational control.

Increasing Marine aviation strength in the Central Pacific was reflected in the organization of the 4th MBDAW at the beginning of 1944. General Merritt had under his command MAG-13, headed by Colonel Lawrence Norman; MAG-31, commanded by Colonel Calvin R. Freeman; and units of Fleet Air Wing 2, which was headed by Rear Admiral John Dale Price, with headquarters at Kaneohe, Hawaii. MAG-13, based on Funafuti, consisted of its headquarters and service squadrons and VMSB-151 and -331. In addition to headquarters and service squadrons, MAG-31, based on Wallis Island on the western fringes of Samoa, was comprised of VMF-111, -224, -311, -422, and -441. Units of Fleet Air Wing 2 in the Samoa-Gilberts-Ellice area consisted of three scouting squadrons, two patrol squadrons, four bombing squadrons, and a photographic squadron.

Marine aviators arriving in the South and Central Pacific often found the accommodations awaiting them little to their liking, as indicated by the history of one bombing squadron, whose author had this pungent comment to make:

> Wallis Island in French Samoa is by no stretch of the imagination the Pearl of the Pacific. It has gained the reputation—at least among the personnel of this squadron —as about the best spot on God's earth to keep away from. The health conditions were far from favorable and the quarters were not very satisfactory, being in part tents and in part huts constructed by the natives without floors or similar improvements. The recreational facilities—such as they were—consisted of a movie theater at a distance which invited only the most ambitious, and half a dozen books and a dart game which our predecessors had left behind. There were no electric lights, the water supply lasted for about half an hour a day, and the food was made up almost entirely of C rations. And to top matters off it was either so dusty you couldn't breathe or so muddy you couldn't walk, and always present was the tropical mosquito responsible for giving at least half the complement Dengue fever at one time or another. But despite the personal difficulties that everybody had to contend, our planes were kept in the air and the patrols went out on schedule and an intensive training program was undertaken.[9]

After only about three weeks on Wallis Island, the first ground echelon departed on 13 November for Nukufetau

---
[9] VMSB-331 Hist, op. cit., p. 3.

in the Ellice Islands. By 28 November, all of VMSB-331 had settled down on Nukufetau. The island was described as "a coral atoll about the size of a ten cent piece and when the tide was in gave us around 9 cents change. The health conditions were as good as those at Wallis had been bad. There were no mosquitoes and no diseases and the worst we had to contend with were tribes of rats."[10]

Two days following its arrival on Nukufetau, VMSB-331, commanded by Major Paul R. Byrum, Jr., dispatched a detachment of six SBDs and maintenance personnel to Tarawa to lend a hand in air patrols and possible air strikes. One such strike materialized on 21 December, when 5 SBDs, together with a dozen Army B-24 bombers and 15 of the new Navy F6F Grumman fighters as escorts, attacked enemy shipping at Jaluit in the Marshalls. In the course of this strike, the squadron claimed credit for sinking a 6,000- or 7,000-ton cargo ship in the Jaluit lagoon. Postwar accounts have made it appear more likely that the enemy ship sunk on this occasion was a 1,912-ton converted water tender already immobilized in a previous raid by naval aircraft from the *Yorktown*. In any case, the men of VMSB-331 considered the sinking of an enemy vessel during their first combat mission a promising omen. This air strike turned out to be the only offensive mission executed by any unit under the 4th MBDAW until March 1944.

The attack inflicted little damage on the Japanese in the Marshalls. Possibly, the greatest significance can be found in the presence of the F6F Grumman fighters. This new Grumman fighter, otherwise known as "Hellcat," made its debut during the Gilberts Operation. Like the Corsair, the F6F was powered by a Pratt & Whitney 2,000-horsepower air-cooled radial engine. This airplane quickly won the grudging admiration of Japanese aviators, one of whom expressed this opinion of the Hellcats' capabilities:

> There is no doubt that the new Hellcat was superior in every respect to the Zero except in the factors of maneuverability and range. It carried heavier armament, could outclimb and outdive the Zero, could fly at higher altitudes, and was well protected with self-sealing fuel tanks and armor plate. Like the Wildcat and Corsair, the new Grumman was armed with six 12.7mm machine guns, but it carried a much greater load of ammunition than the other fighters. Of the many American fighter planes we encountered in the Pacific, the Hellcat was the only aircraft which could acquit itself with distinction in a fighter-vs.-fighter dogfight.[11]

Following their capture by the Americans, Tarawa, Makin, and Apamama Islands immediately were converted into a springboard for the aerial offensive against the Marshall Islands. By late December, no less than four airfields in the Gilberts had become operational, and B-24s had begun staging missions through Tarawa. As 1943 drew to a close, bombers of TF 57 dropped 550 tons of bombs on the Marshalls and 28 tons on Nauru, an island 525 miles west of the Gilberts. Japanese

---

[10] *Ibid.*, pp. 4-5.

[11] Okumiya, Horikoshi, and Caidin, *Zero!*, p. 222.

antiaircraft fire was frequently intense and hostile fighters also took a toll of American bombers. Enemy land-based aviation in the Marshalls, however, was unable to cope with the development and operation of American bases only 300 miles to the south; during the latter part of December 1943, and throughout January 1944, the Japanese raided the new American bases in the Gilberts on more than 30 occasions. With only one exception, the Japanese air attacks occurred at night. Total damage inflicted at the four airfields consisted of 33 aircraft destroyed, 9 planes damaged, 5 men killed, and a number of men wounded. In early December 1943, the arrival on Tarawa of VMF(N)-532, commanded by Major Everette H. Vaughan, severely hampered the after-dark raids of the enemy air marauders. Major Vaughan's night fighters were the first planes of this type to reach the Central Pacific, though a sister squadron, VMF(N)-531, had already begun to fly night patrols from Banika in the Russell Islands in September 1943.

Throughout January 1944, preparations for the imminent invasion of the Marshall Islands continued at a brisk pace. By the 13th, the 4th Marine Division had arrived in Hawaii en route to the Marshalls from the west coast of the United States. The Marine division, as well as the Army's 7th Infantry Division, departed Hawaii on 22 January en route to Kwajalein. A total of 297 ships, not including fast carrier task groups or submarines, transported about 54,000 troops to their objectives. A force of three cruisers, four destroyers, and two minelayers stood by to neutralize enemy bases at Wotje and Taroa. Landings were scheduled for 31 January.

As in the case of Tarawa, Marine aviation was not scheduled to play an active part in the amphibious phase of the assault. Once again, the Marine squadrons based in the Gilbert and Ellice Islands were assigned patrol and logistic missions. After the initial objectives in the Marshalls had been seized, Marine air squadrons were to relocate rapidly to them. In line with this forward movement, MAG-13 was to displace to Majuro. The destination of MAG-31 was Roi Island, at the northern tip of Kwajalein Atoll. During the first two weeks of January, VMF-111 under Major J. Frank Cole, VMF-224, commanded by Major Darrell D. Irwin, VMF-441, headed by Major James B. Moore, and VMF-113 under Major Loren D. Everton joined MAG-31, as did VMF(N)-532.[12]

Six planes of the latter squadron, comprising its forward echelon, were the first aircraft to land on the newly activated field at Roi, led by the squadron commander, Major Vaughan. The latter was to comment later:

> I was the first American pilot to land on Roi as I led the unit there via Makin Island. The story was carried by United Press and appeared in the San Diego Union saying that I was the first American pilot in the Central Pacific to land an

[12] "After Roi was bombed and supplies and space were limited, the ground echelon of VMF-111 was returned to Makin Island to join the air echelon waiting there. VMF-111 remained on Makin bombing bypassed islands in the Marshalls. A typical day would see planes take off from Makin, bomb Mille, rearm and refuel at Majuro, and strike again on the return to Makin." *Cole ltr.*

aircraft on pre-war-held Japanese territory. I had been instructed to let Colonel Calvin Freeman make the first landing but when I arrived in the vicinity of Roi with my group of aircraft low on fuel, the Colonel was not in the area so, I proceeded to land. (I heard much about it later when he did arrive!)[13]

In order to further strengthen Marine aviation in the Central Pacific, MAG-22, under the command of Lieutenant Colonel James M. Daly, was scheduled to come under General Merritt's 4th MBDAW in early February 1944. The air group had been stationed on Midway Island ever since 1 March 1942, and following the epic defense of that island, had led a relatively peaceful and isolated existence there, engaged in routine patrols and occasional search and rescue missions.

Into the period preceding the invasion of the Marshall Islands falls the saga of VMF-422, destined to become the "Lost Squadron." VMF-422, commanded by Major John S. MacLaughlin, Jr., had been part of MAG-22 until 15 December, when it was detached from the air group and flown to Hawaii in transport aircraft. Upon arrival there, the ground echelon was attached to the task force staging for the invasion of the Marshalls. On 17 January 1944, the flight echelon consisting of 27 pilots and 3 enlisted men together with 24 newly issued Corsairs, boarded the escort carrier USS *Kalinin Bay* and departed for the Gilbert Islands on the following day. Once the escort carrier arrived within 50 miles of Tarawa, the squadron was to launch its aircraft and fly to Hawkins Field on Betio Island for further orders from Admiral Hoover, who had assumed direct operational command of garrison aircraft effective 11 January.

On the morning of 24 January, the aircraft were catapulted as planned practically within sight of Tarawa and shortly thereafter landed on Hawkins Field. The three spare pilots, as well as the three enlisted men who were to service the planes, went ashore by boat. Upon its arrival on Betio, the squadron received orders from Admiral Hoover to proceed to Funafuti, pending further assignment within the scope of Operation FLINTLOCK, the invasion of the Marshalls.

At 0945 on 25 January, 23 of the Corsairs left for Funafuti on a two-leg trip of a 700-mile flight; a stopover was scheduled at Nanomea, the northernmost of the Ellice Islands, about 463 miles south-southeast of Tarawa. One aircraft remained behind at Hawkins Field because of starter trouble. The flight departed Betio Island under good weather conditions without any navigational escort. Major MacLaughlin, the squadron commander, led the fighter formation of three flights. Estimated time of arrival at Nanomea was 1225.

Flying at an altitude of 2,000 feet, the squadron encountered the first of two severe weather fronts only 15 minutes before reaching Nanomea. The front rapidly developed into a violent tropical storm, reaching from sea level to over 13,000 feet. Because the torrential downpour greatly restricted visibility, the squadron commander ordered the planes to descend to a water level

---

[13] Col Everette H. Vaughan ltr to Head, HistBr, G-3 Div, HQMC, dtd 28Sep67, in *Marine Aviation Comment File*.

course and to follow it through the disturbance. When the flight emerged from this front, it discovered that three Corsairs had lost formation and had disappeared from sight. Radio contact was maintained with these pilots, but they had been hopelessly separated from the formation and were on their own. Of the three, Captain John F. Rogers disappeared without a trace. The second, Lieutenant John E. Hansen, was able to get bearings towards Funafuti from one of the other pilots and actually reached his destination. The third, Lieutenant Walter A. Wilson, landed on an island, where natives looked after him until he was taken off by a destroyer, the USS *Hobby*.

The remaining 20 pilots established their position as being over Nui Island, about halfway between Nanomea and Funafuti. At this point, one of the Corsairs piloted by Lieutenant Christian F. Lauesen developed engine trouble and made a water landing. The flight circled over him and observed that he was afloat by means of his "Mae West" life preserver; the pilot's life raft, however, was not to be seen. While the remainder of the pilots continued the flight, one of the group, Lieutenant Robert C. Lehnert, circled the castaway pilot until his own plane ran out of gas and Lehnert was himself forced to bail out. After hitting the water, Lehnert conducted a futile search for Lauesen with whom he intended to share his life raft. Lauesen was never seen again and Lehnert himself remained adrift for two days before he was rescued.

At 1245 Major MacLaughlin informed the remainder of the flight that he had made contact with the Funafuti beam[14] and that they would proceed there. At this time, the squadron encountered a second squall which, if anything, was worse than the first. As the storm increased in violence, the flight again reported navigational difficulty. Simultaneously, something went haywire with the squadron commander's radio receiver. Failing to contact Major MacLaughlin by radio, Captain Cloyd R. Jeans flew across the squadron commander's bow and attracted his attention. Aware of the malfunctioning of his receiver, Major MacLaughlin turned over command of the flight to Captain Jeans and ordered the latter to lead the flight back to Nui Island. Shortly thereafter, Major MacLaughlin was observed to fly a course tangent to the rest of the flight. He disappeared in the thick overcast and was not sighted again, despite the efforts of his wingmen to keep him in view.

Led by Captain Jeans, the flight made a 45 degree turn off its original heading of 180 degrees and reversed course towards Nui. In an effort to avoid the squall, some of the pilots broke formation and quickly became confused as to their positions. Lieutenant Earl C. Thompson disappeared into the tropical storm and was not seen thereafter. At 1500, Lieutenant Robert P. Moran, one of the 16 remaining participants in the flight informed Captain Jeans that contact with Nanomea had been established. This link lasted for only five

---

[14] Beam—a directional radio signal transmittted in quadrants from a radio range station audible as a continuous tone or whine as long as an aircraft proceeds directly on the proper course, but audible as dot-dash or dash-dot as it veers to the left or right.

minutes, for Lieutenant Moran's plane ran out of fuel. The pilot parachuted but became entangled in his shroud lines and drowned in the heavy surf off Nui Island.

For the 15 remaining pilots, the confusion was compounded by the fact that the aircraft were not flying at identical speeds. In summing up the disastrous flight, the squadron history was to describe the plight of VMF-422 in this manner:

> Some elements of the formation were compelled to fly full throttle to maintain contact with the flight leaders, as the latter maintained normal cruising speed. However, the density and violence of the storm prevented flying a standard formation, resulting in maneuvers at full throttle one instant and retarded throttle the next. Several pilots soon reported being low on fuel. Those who maintained good formation had sufficient gas to have possibly reached Funafuti.[15]

At 1530 two of the remaining pilots informed Captain Jeans that they were running short of fuel and had to land. One of them, Lieutenant William A. Aycrigg, set his plane down in the water and was seen to be riding in his life raft. The other pilot ditched seven miles away. At this point, Captain Jeans decided that the remaining aircraft should hit the water together, because it appeared that most of the planes would shortly run out of fuel, though several pilots reported having sufficient gasoline to remain airborne for another hour. The flight then formed a traffic circle and made water landings. Of the two pilots that had run out of fuel at 1530, Lieutenant Aycrigg vanished in the vastness of the Pacific and was never found. The pilot of the second aircraft, Lieutenant Theodore Thurnau, was rescued by the USS *Welles* on 28 January.

The remainder of the flight landed and, with one exception, each pilot got his life raft and survival equipment out of the plane before it sank. One pilot lost all of his clothing and equipment extricating himself from his plane and had to take refuge on board one of the other rafts. By this time, the other 12 pilots had joined and had started to pool their equipment for equal sharing among the survivors. The rafts were secured together by the cord hand holds but in the extremely heavy seas some of these holds were torn off. Eventually, the rafts had to be held together by hand.

The drifting aviators quickly noticed that their new environment was hardly more secure than the turbulent air had been. In fact, there appeared a new kind of hazard:

> A number of sharks were observed, some making passes at the sea anchor or scraping against the boats—which added nothing to the peace of mind of the occupants. Facetious names were given to the most persistent of these animals, one being readily identifiable by a notched dorsal fin. Their persistence in scraping against the boats grew to such an extent that one of them was finally shot, whereupon all dispersed. To the now familiar statement, "There are no atheists in foxholes," may it also be added that there are no atheists in rubber boats! Frequent "prayer meetings" and songfests helped to bolster morale.[16]

The odyssey of VMF-422 ended during the afternoon of 27 January, when

---

[15] VMF-422 Hist, *op. cit.*, Anx B, Flight Echelon, p. 3.

[16] *Ibid*, pp. 6-7.

a search plane sighted the group. The pilot, eager to be of assistance, landed in the heavy sea and damaged his plane while taxiing to pick up the survivors. The rescuer, himself now marooned, radioed for help. About two hours later, the USS *Hobby* arrived and picked up the 12 pilots of VMF-422 as well as the rescue pilot and eight members of his crew. Upon coming on board, the survivors of VMF-422 were pleasantly surprised to find Lieutenant Wilson, one of the first three pilots that had become separated from the squadron during the first squall, waiting for them. The destroyer had picked him up from his island refuge, which "he left rather reluctantly because of his royal treatment by the natives."[17] A thorough search of the area by the USS *Hobby* and other ships failed to yield any sign of Lieutenant Thurnau. The defunct rescue plane was sunk by naval gunfire. All of the rescued pilots were suffering from immersion, sunburn, and general weakness, though only the pilot that had lost his clothing had to be hospitalized.

On 29 January the 14 castaways were placed ashore at Funafuti, where they were met by Lieutenant Hansen. The latter was the only one to have flown his aircraft to Funafuti. Of 23 Corsairs and pilots that had left Tarawa, only one plane had reached its destination. In addition to the loss of 22 aircraft, the episode cost the lives of 6 pilots.

A board of investigation, subsequently convened to probe the disaster, determined that faulty communications and human error were largely responsible for the mishap.[18] Radio aids data were incomplete in that voice calls for the bases were not listed and range bearings for the Funafuti range were not given. Operations towers on various fields in the Gilbert and Ellice Islands were monitoring a radio frequency different from that used by the squadron. It was further brought out that no one at Hawkins Field had cleared the flight in the first place. Nothing was sent to Nanomea telling of the flight until that base requested information. The final touch of irony was added when it became known that Nanomea had been plotting the planes by radar since 1225 of 25 January at a distance of between 10 and 70 miles. Inasmuch as Nanomea had not been advised of the flight, the control tower personnel assumed that bombers were passing through the area.

In connection with the VMF-422 disaster, it may be of interest that the Japanese suffered an almost identical mishap earlier in the war, with even more serious consequences. After the war, a leading enemy air ace was to make the following comment on flying conditions and long-distance fighter hops:

> In the vast reaches of the Pacific the distance between each small outcropping of land can assume terrifying proportions. Without radar, indeed, without even radios in our Zero fighters, we dared not risk the loss of most of our planes. Our experience in such matters had been tragic. Early in 1943, several squadrons of Army fighter planes, manned by pilots

---

[17] *Ibid.*

[18] "At least two senior officers in the 4th Defense Wing received letters of reprimand because of this disaster." LtGen Louis E. Woods ltr to Head, HistBr, G–3 Div, HQMC, dtd 2Nov67, in *Marine Aviation Comment File,* hereafter *Woods ltr.*

who had absolutely no experience in long-distance flying over the ocean, left Japan for a base to the south. En route, they encountered severe weather conditions, but refused to turn back. Almost every plane disappeared in the endless reaches of the Pacific.[19]

Meanwhile, the invasion date for the Marshalls was drawing near. Fast carrier task groups of Task Force 58, commanded by Rear Admiral Marc A. Mitscher, began preinvasion attacks against the Marshalls on 29 January 1944. Launched from 12 carriers, 700 aircraft began to carry out simultaneous attacks against enemy airfields on Roi, Kwajalein, Wotje, and Taroa (also known as Maloelap). (See Map 23). In the words of an official report, "simultaneous attacks by this force were so successful in achieving surprise and destroying their targets that by evening on 29 January there was not an operational Japanese aircraft east of Eniwetok."[20]

The American landings on 31 January were executed on schedule. Japanese planners had expected an invasion of Jaluit, Mille, or Wotje and had reinforced those garrisons, as well as the one at Maloelap. That the Americans would strike at Kwajalein, in the heart of the Marshalls, came as a complete surprise to the enemy, whose reinforcement of the atolls under attack was not quick enough to stem the tide. Roi-Namur was secured by noon of 2 February. Two days later, all Japanese resistance on Kwajalein Island came to an end. Majuro Atoll fell into American hands without opposition, having been abandoned by the Japanese before the invasion force reached the objective.[21]

Elimination of Japanese air power in the Marshalls was of crucial importance for the continuation of the American drive in the Central Pacific. The widely held view that the Japanese had fortified the Marshalls long before the outbreak of World War II proved to be erroneous. The Japanese had built an airstrip on Roi during the 1930s, but had undertaken little else to fortify the Marshalls until 1941. By the end of that year, the enemy had constructed airstrips on Maloelap and Wotje; the latter island also served as a seaplane base. On Mille, the Japanese completed an airstrip towards the end of 1942, but for the remainder of that year, the total number of aircraft stationed on the four atolls did not exceed 65. As the end of 1943 approached and the invasion of the Marshalls became imminent, the Japanese built up their air strength to about 130 aircraft, which Admiral Mitscher's preinvasion bombing and strafing promptly destroyed.

The first Marine aviation personnel to go ashore in the Marshalls were members of the forward echelon of VMSB-231, which reached Majuro on 3 February 1944. The airstrip on the island became operational on 19 February and two days later the flight echelon, led by the squadron commander, Major Elmer G. Glidden, Jr., took off from the escort aircraft carrier *Gambier Bay* and landed on the island. On 26 February, VMSB-

---

[19] Sakai, Caidin, and Saito, *Samurai!*, pp. 199–200, quoted with permission.

[20] USSBS, *Pacific Campaigns*, p. 193.

[21] For a detailed account of Marine operations in the Marshalls, see Shaw, Nalty, and Turnbladh, *Central Pacific Drive*, Pt 3, v. III, pp. 117–227.

Map 23

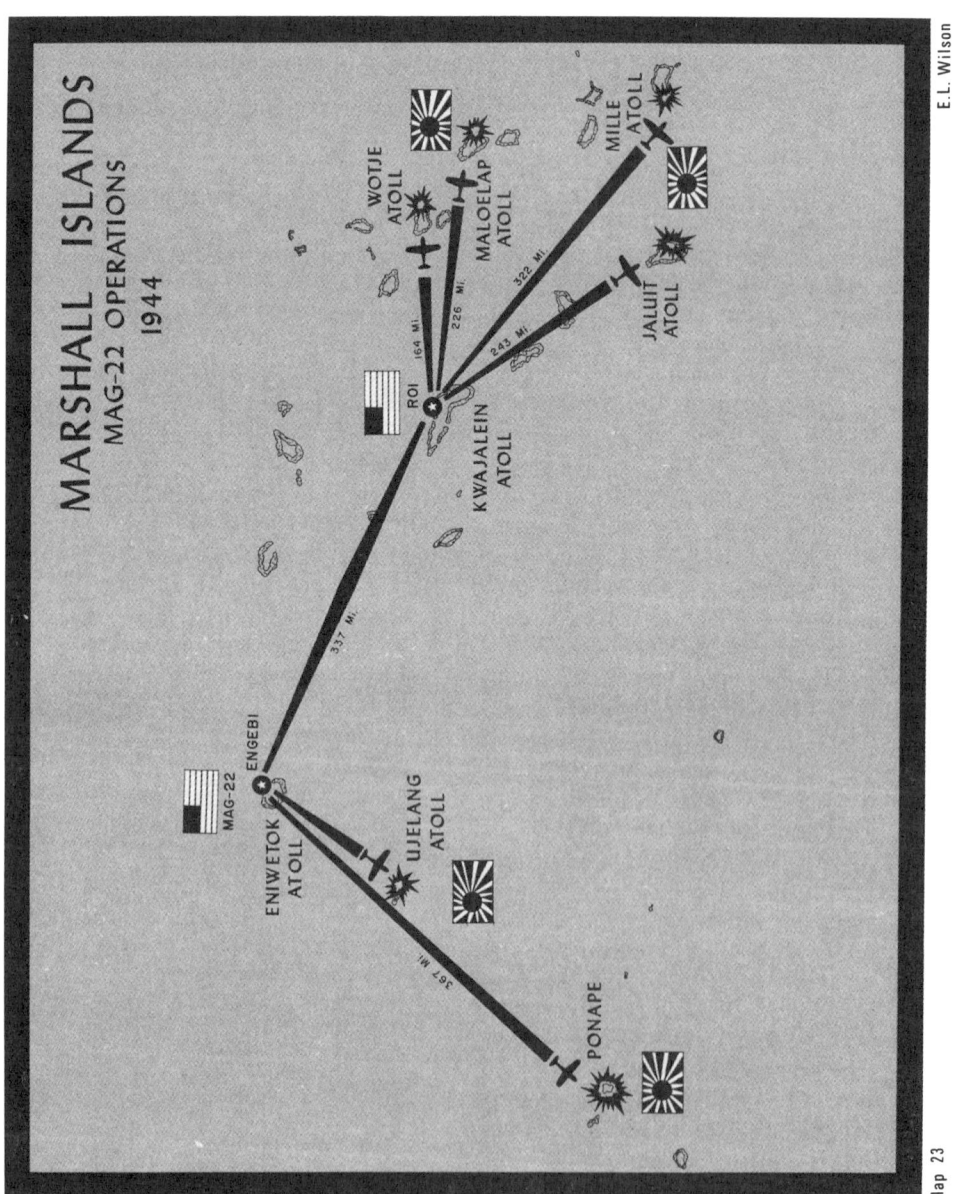

331 arrived on Majuro. Both of the MAG-13 squadrons were given the mission of neutralizing the enemy on those Marshall islands that had been bypassed.

On 7 February, Colonel Calvin B. Freeman's MAG-31 moved to Roi right on the heels of the ground action. Only five days had elapsed since the 4th Marine Division had completed the conquest of Roi and Namur Islands and barely 48 hours had gone by since the 7th Infantry Division had eliminated the last enemy resistance on Kwajalein Island, 50 miles to the south. The daring advance into the heart of the Marshalls and Gilberts had brought an area one thousand miles long and including at least seven Japanese strongpoints under the control of the United States. Accruing to the American forces as a result of the Gilbert-Marshalls operations were additional benefits, summed up in an official postwar analysis:

> Continuous operation of United States carrier task forces in the area, unchecked by Japanese land-based aircraft, forced the Japanese Fleet to abandon Truk as a major base. Between 3 and 10 February 1944 all units of that fleet except a few cruisers and destroyers of the Area Defense Forces withdrew to Palau and the Empire leaving United States forces in the Central Pacific unopposed except by garrison troops and a decimated Japanese air force.[22]

Even though the Japanese no longer considered Truk as a safe anchorage for large segments of the *Combined Fleet,* they nevertheless were determined to hold it to the last. A buildup of enemy strength on Truk began in early 1944 and continued throughout the year. The Japanese Army sent troops to the island, which soon bristled with pillboxes, minefields, and coast defense and antiaircraft artillery. Navy torpedo boats and rocket launchers supplemented the Japanese defenses on the island. In line with the policy of avoiding, if possible, a direct assault on enemy islands known to be strongly fortified, the JCS decided on 12 March 1944 to bypass and neutralize Truk. Keeping the Japanese on Truk off balance was a job delegated to long-range Army Air Forces and Navy bombers in the Marshall and Admiralty Islands. Cancellation of a direct assault on Truk left Marine aviation without an important part, which, according to initial plans, Marine fighters and dive bombers were to have played in the conquest of the Japanese stronghold. It appeared as if Marine pilots, eager to participate in the advance into the Carolines, would instead be relegated to riding herd on a large number of Japanese marooned on various islands in the Gilberts and Marshalls. This was hardly the type of mission that would appeal to young aviators eager to test their skill in aerial combat with the enemy.

The fledgling Marine fliers should not have been disenchanted with their assignment, for bypassed Japanese had shown themselves to be cunning and dangerous opponents. This fact was brought home to the ground echelon of MAG-31 only five days after its arrival on Roi-Namur. Shortly before 0300 on 12 February, about a dozen enemy bombers, based on Ponape Island in the Carolines, hit Roi in a devastating surprise raid. Immediately preceding the bombing, Japanese scattered large quantities of narrow tinfoil strips in the air,

---
[22] USSBS, *Pacific Campaigns*, p. 194.

which rendered the American radar equipment practically useless. These metallic pieces, known as window or chaff, had first been successfully used by the British Royal Air Force over Germany earlier in the war. The enemy raiders, believed to be seaplanes, came over in four flights of three planes each with about five-minute intervals between flights. The bombs dropped were 500 pounders, antipersonnel bombs, and magnesium incendiaries. One of the first bombs dropped by the enemy scored a direct hit on the biggest bomb dump on the island. In the words of a 4th Marine Division historian, ". . . a moment later the whole island was an exploding inferno. To elements of the Twentieth Engineers and Seabees, who were still on Roi, the holocaust was more terrible than anything they had gone through in capturing the island."[23]

Even more graphic in his description of the resulting inferno was a combat correspondent who commented:

> Tracer ammunition lit up the sky as far as we could see and for a full half hour red-hot fragments rained from the sky like so many hail-stones, burning and piercing the flesh when they hit. A jeep exploded in our faces a few yards away. Yet half an hour after the first bomb hit, several hospitals and first aid stations were functioning with all the efficiency of urban medical centers."[24]

The bombardment from the ammunition dump continued for four hours. When it was all over, nearly half of the air group equipment, which had just been unloaded, lay destroyed about the area. Individual equipment, personal effects, and the clothing of approximately 1,000 officers and men were also lost. There were casualties as well. Five enlisted personnel of MAG-31 were killed in the course of the attack. Six officers and 67 enlisted men were wounded; they were evacuated to Hawaii, ironically enough on the same ships that had brought them to the Marshalls. An additional 10 officers and 67 enlisted men were wounded, but not seriously enough to require evacuation.[25]

After 14 February, MAG-31 took positive action to prevent similar attacks. On that date, the air group commander, Colonel Freeman, reached Roi with 10 F4U-1s of VMF-224 and 6 F4U-2s of VMF(N)-532 from Tarawa via a refueling stop at Makin Island. Day and night combat air patrols were instituted at once. Seven additional night fighters of VMF(N)-532 arrived on Roi on 23 February. Two Douglas Skytrain aircraft (R4Ds) brought radar equipment and crews to the island to improve the defense against surprise air attacks.

The drive into the Marshall Islands continued to gain momentum. On 18 February, coinciding with a devastating attack of TF 58 against Truk, two battalions of the 22d Marines seized Engebi Island, in the northern portion of Eniwetok Atoll. On the following day, a combined force of soldiers and Marines went ashore on Eniwetok. Three days later, the 22d Marines seized Parry Island after a stiff fight.

Shortly after the assault troops had landed, Marine aviation personnel came ashore. Among those to land on Eniwetok was the ground echelon of the ill-

---

[23] Proehl, *The Fourth Marine Division*, p. 34.
[24] Marine combat correspondent Bernard Redmond, cited in *Ibid.*

[25] MAG-31 WarD, Feb44.

fated VMF-422. Between 17 and 27 January, this echelon had left Hawaii en route to the Marshalls with elements on board the escort carrier *Kalinin Bay*, and the transports *President Monroe, Island Mail,* and *Cape Isabel*. On February 6, six days after the invasion of the Marshalls, the ground personnel of VMF-422 on board the *Island Mail* were ordered ashore on Kwajalein. There, they were detailed to stevedore duties; some of the men worked continuously for 48 hours at this task. Others actually participated in the occupation of the island when scattered resistance flared up in some shattered blockhouses and some of the working parties came under small arms fire. Several members of VMF-422, ordered to collect and bury the enemy dead, discovered that not all of those slated for burial had been rendered harmless. Booby traps attached to some of the bodies made the Marines' task not only unenviable and odious, but dangerous as well. In this connection, the official account of the activities briefly states that "officers in charge were quick to recognize dangers to enlisted personnel and the unit was quickly reorganized into small groups with NCO's enforcing rigid discipline."[26]

The remaining personnel of the fighter squadron's ground echelon on board the *Kalinin Bay*, the *President Monroe*, and the *Cape Isabel* stayed on their ships which were peacefully anchored off Kwajalein Island. On 7 February, this interlude came to an end when the squadron was advised that it would proceed with a new task force in attacking and garrisoning Engebi Island on Eniwetok Atoll. Squadron gear was transferred from the *Island Mail* and the *Cape Isabel* in two days. While this work was in progress, Army troops boarded the *President Monroe*, adding greatly to the congestion already prevailing on that ship.

On 18 February, after an uneventful two-day journey, the ground echelon of VMF-422 approached Eniwetok Atoll. The arrival of the convoy at the objective led an observer to note:

> Mine sweepers led a mighty column through Deep Passage, assault troops little dreaming that Parry and Japtan Islands, flanking the entrance into the lagoon, would soon be the scene of the most bitter fighting. The *Tennessee* and *Colorado* led the attack columns into the lagoon, proceeding directly to the site of the airfield, Engebi Island, fifteen miles away. The normally khaki colored decks appeared deserted as all hands were ordered below. Troops decorating the rails of transports would be easy prey for hidden Jap marksmen. Despite protestations, officers being in the majority, all recalcitrants were summarily ordered from the weather decks. The importance of guarding against fire from beach positions was forceably demonstrated when a squadron mechanic was seriously wounded by sniper fire as the ship lay at anchor off Engebi Island.[27]

The preinvasion bombardment of Engebi continued throughout 17 February. Early on the following morning, assault units landed on the island and after a six-hour battle, brought all organized resistance to an end, though enemy pockets of resistance were to remain active for several days. On the evening of 19 February, one month to the day since embarking at Pearl Harbor, the VMF-422 echelon on board the

---

[26] VMF-422 Hist, *op. cit.*, Anx A, Ground Echelon, p. 6.

[27] *Ibid.*, p. 8.

President Monroe went ashore. The joy these men felt at having dry land under their feet once again was somewhat diminished as, in the gathering dusk, they bedded down in shell holes and craters on the nearly flat island. Less than a quarter of a mile away, the enemy was still giving battle from remaining pockets of resistance. On several occasions during that long night, small arms fire swept the bivouac of the newly arrived aviation personnel, and a mortar lobbed several rounds into the area.

Throughout the night, the men of VMF-422 on Engebi saw, or at least thought they saw, silhouetted enemy remnants moving from one place of shelter to the next. A squadron security detail fired at fast-appearing and -disappearing shadows without being able to determine who or what was actually transpiring all around them. Some of the doubts as to whether there were still any Japanese around were dispelled on the morning of 20 February, when a Japanese was found occupying a foxhole within the squadron bivouac area. This enemy soldier did not offer any resistance, and after capture, assisted in the apprehension of another 15 troops and laborers.

In the bright light of day, the men of VMF-422 had an opportunity to assess the newly won real estate. The appearance presented by Engebi "on the morning after" made many of them wish that they were back on board ship, as expressed by one of those present:

> The unsuspecting initiates were confronted with a disturbing scene as they looked over the newly won island. Enemy dead were grotesquely strewn over the landscape. Duds varying from fourteen inch shells to grenades littered the battleground. All types of enemy ordnance and material, as well as Marine, were scattered over the scarred surface of Engebi. Souvenir seeking was held down to a minimum with repeated warnings of the attendant dangers proving an effective measure. All hands immediately set to work and before the sun reached its high point on the 20th of February, temporary shelters had been erected with many a bomb crater serving as an expedient foxhole.
>
> In the ensuing twelve days, the bivouac area came to be familiarly known as "Jungle Town." It compared favorably with the ramshackle abodes ineptly constructed by wayward citizens in city disposal areas. The procedure included the digging of a three foot deep foxhole, large enough to fence in a necessary cot, and then elaborately camouflaged with Jap corrugated tin. A plentiful supply was on hand. Lightweight Jap lumber, ponchos and remnants of enemy tents were often added to embellish temporary shelters. All these precautions were but slight protection against the hot sun and irritating dust. The well tanned individual fared best as the white skinned Marine suffered from heat blisters which were aggravated by the salt water, the only medium, if temporary, of keeping clean. Guadalcanal veterans readily admitted that this was the roughest going yet.[28]

In addition to being exposed to the unfavorable climate and poor living conditions on Engebi, enlisted personnel were detailed to working parties, which on occasion manhandled supplies for 36 consecutive hours. Some of the men assigned to such details considered themselves fortunate, for they were on occasion able to obtain a hot meal on board ship, a welcome change from the K rations dispensed ashore. Other work details were engaged in the construction of a squadron living area. There was

---
[28] *Ibid.*, pp. 10-11.

MOUNTING THE OFFENSIVE

an ever-present possibility of evening air raids. To at least one observer it appeared that "the likelihood of evening air raids spurred the men on and as the moon became larger on the horizon the tempo increased. Fortunately, no attacks were launched until our unit was squared away in its new area. It was a gesture for which all hands were thankful."[29]

While the ground echelon of VMF-422 worked to make Engebi habitable, additional Marine aviation units began to arrive on the island. Among the first to reach Engebi was the headquarters of MAG-22 under Colonel Daly, who reached the island on 20 February. The same day witnessed the arrival of AWS-1 (Air Warning Squadron 1), with 9 officers and 218 men. The air warning squadron had moved to Engebi directly from the West Coast. Ten days after setting up its radar equipment on the island, the squadron began to function as a fighter-director unit. On 27 February, VMF-113, coming from Kwajalein, took up station on Engebi. On the same day, eight night fighters of VMF(N)-532 were transferred from Roi to Engebi. Two days later, on the last day of the month, the flight echelon of VMSB-151, commanded by Major Gordon H. Knott, arrived on Engebi following a five-day flight from Wallis Island, roughly 2,000 miles to the southeast. The other half of the squadron remained on Roi Island to fly patrols and cover landings on some of the smaller Marshall islands. That part of the squadron stationed on Engebi was assigned to reef and submarine patrols.

The rapid buildup of Marine air strength on Engebi did not fail to escape enemy attention, and on the night of 8-9 March the Japanese struck. AWS-1 detected the approaching enemy bombers on the radar scope and alerted the night fighter on patrol. A second night fighter was launched, but neither aircraft succeeded in intercepting the enemy. The enemy flight, skillfully using cloud cover and jamming the radar instruments with tin foil, was aided by a stroke of luck, for the first string of bombs, dropped shortly after 0400, rendered the radar equipment inoperative. The VHF equipment, essential for ground-air communication, was destroyed next. As if sensing that they were immune from interception, the Japanese carried out the raid in a leisurely fashion and remained overhead for two hours. During this time, the enemy hit a squadron bomb storage area; the resulting blast was to cause the most damage. Next, a small fuel dump less than 50 yards from the squadron area was hit and burst into flames. The illumination produced by this fire provided the enemy with the light necessary to pinpoint other targets. Antiaircraft fire was meager and ineffectual. As a parting gesture, one of the bombers strafed the north end of the bivouac area.

An assessment of the damage from this air attack showed that, in addition to the bombs detonated and the fuel destroyed, four tents had burned down and many others had been perforated by bomb fragments. For some unaccountable reason, several aircraft parked off the recently completed runway remained undamaged. The raid de-

---

[29] *Ibid.*, p. 12.

stroyed large supplies of machine gun ammunition and quartermaster items. Casualties to Marine aviation personnel included 3 killed and 21 wounded.[30]

On 4 March, the 10 fighter and 4 bomber squadrons under the 4th MBDAW began the first of a long series of attacks against Wotje, Maloelap, Mille, and Jaluit Atolls, which were still garrisoned by the Japanese. The enemy, who no longer had any aircraft left, nevertheless, put up a curtain of antiaircraft fire and scored hits on nearly half of the attacking planes of Majuro-based VMSB-331, the squadron carrying out the first bombing mission. Since most of this surprisingly accurate antiaircraft fire had come from Jaulit, VMSB-231, on the following day, made the enemy antiaircraft defenses on that island its special objective.

Continued enemy resistance on the bypassed atolls was particularly surprising in view of the severe pounding inflicted on them over a four-month period by Army, Navy, and Marine aircraft. During the spring and early summer of 1944, the bombing of the four bypassed islands in the Marshalls became a joint enterprise, for in addition to the squadrons of the 4th MBDAW, land-based Navy aircraft and bombers of the Seventh Air Force flew strikes against the islands. Even before Marine aviation became involved in flying missions against Wotje, Maloelap, Mille, and Jaluit, carrier aircraft alone had flown more than 1,650 sorties against the same objectives.

During March 1944, planes from 4th MBDAW squadrons flew a total of 830 sorties against enemy bases in the Marshalls and eastern Carolines. These 830 sorties were flown in 87 missions; during March enemy antiaircraft fire downed three aircraft. On 18 March, eight Corsairs of VMF-111, based on Makin Island, bombed antiaircraft gun emplacements on Mille Island. This raid marked the first time that the F4U was used as a fighter-bomber in the Marshalls. Together with an attached Navy F6F squadron, 4th Wing aircraft, including F4Us equipped with improvised bomb racks, dropped 419,000 pounds of bombs on enemy installations. Of this total, 75,000 pounds were 1,000 pound bombs carried by Corsairs. The F4Us carried out 11 bombing raids during March and the results obtained in these raids indicated that the Corsair could be used safely and efficiently as a dive bomber.[31]

All of the strafing and bombing missions flown against the Marshall Islands during March were marked by the complete absence of the enemy in the air. No Japanese fighters were in evidence to intercept air attacks against those bypassed islands. The situation changed temporarily on 26 March, when six Corsairs of VMF-113, led by Major Loren D. Everton, were escorting four B-25s of the Army Air Forces' 48th Bomber Squadron for a strike against Ponape, in the eastern Carolines, 370 miles southwest of Eniwetok. This was the island from which the devastating enemy air attack of 8 March against Engebi had originated. During the later attack, the Marine aviators encountered 12 Zero fighters over Ponape. In the en-

---

[30] 4th MBDAW WarD, Mar44.

[31] *Ibid.*

suing melee, eight of the enemy fighters were destroyed in the air; three were listed as probably destroyed, and a fighter was destroyed on the ground. None of the Corsairs sustained any damage. This aerial encounter marked the last time for the remainder of 1944 that the enemy dispatched fighters to intercept Marine aviators. For the remainder of 1944, except for occasional night heckling raids, enemy air activity in the Marshalls and Carolines remained completely passive.

Unable to put up any effective resistance in the air against American fighters and bombers, the Japanese decided to strike back against American airfields in the Marshalls during the night of 14 April, possibly for a repeat performance of the damaging raid previously executed against Engebi in March. Once again, Engebi was to be the target of the Japanese attack. As a flight of 12 enemy bombers approached their objective, night fighters of VMF(N)-532 were waiting for them. This is how the squadron history recorded the air action that took place:

> During this night operation, Lieutenant Edward A. Sevik was able to reach 20,000 feet in ten minutes. He was vectored on to a bogey, made visual contact, identified the aircraft as enemy, and at fourteen minutes after takeoff, had fired at it and seen it explode. Captain Howard W. Bollman also successfully intercepted and shot down one of the enemy bombers. Lieutenant Joel E. Bonner, Jr. was not so fortunate. Although the bomber he intercepted was probably destroyed it was able to damage Lieutenant Bonner's plane to the extent that it became necessary for him to jump.[32]

---

[32] VMF-532 Hist, *op. cit.*, p. 11.

Lieutenant Bonner was subsequently rescued by the destroyer-escort USS *Steele*. Another night fighter flown by Lieutenant Frank C. Lang completed several interceptions, but all of his targets turned out to be cleverly designed decoys, which the enemy bombers had ejected over the target. Made of tin foil or other thin metallic material, the "Gismos," as they were called by Marine pilots, caused the radar gear on the ground as well as that used in the F4U night fighters, to pick up images.

One night fighter pilot, Lieutenant Donald Spatz, received incorrect directions from a fighter control unit on Eniwetok and instead of heading back to his field, went out to sea and did not return. In addition to the downing of two enemy bombers and the probable destruction of a third, the successful night-fighter operation resulted in all of the enemy bombs being dropped into the water. On this occasion, personnel on Engebi did not suffer any casualties and there was no damage to materiel.

The 4th MBDAW was further augmented when on 1 April, MAG-15, commanded by Lieutenant Colonel Ben Z. Redfield, reached Apamama Island, where VMJ-252 and 353 were attached to the air group. This brought the total strength of 4th MBDAW to 4 air groups with 15 flying squadrons and an attached naval squadron. During the month of May, Marine aviators stepped up their attacks against the remaining bases in the Marshall Islands. Once again, Wotje, Mille, Jaluit, and Maloelap Atolls were subjected to attack as continuously as weather conditions permitted. In addition to daily dive-bombing and strafing attacks by aircraft of the 4th Air Wing, Jaluit and Wotje Atolls were subjected for one day each to mass attack by the concentrated strength of all available squadrons of the Wing. Army and Navy aviation units carried out additional attacks against these islands. Night harassment of the enemy-held atolls also got under way. The primary purpose of these missions was to keep planes over the target at all hours of the night to drop bombs singly. In this way, the enemy was compelled to remain on the alert and prevented from sleeping.

Use of the F4U-1 fighter as a bomber, begun in March by squadrons of the 4th Wing for the first time in the Central Pacific, increased during May. Results obtained were gratifying; the elimination of a concrete power plant, three reinforced magazines, and a radio station on Wotje Island, and the destruction of a radio station on Aineman Island could be directly attributed to low-level bombing by the F4U. Altogether, during the month of May 1944, General Merritt's wing dropped 949,805 pounds of explosives on enemy positions. The F4Us alone dropped 514,765 pounds of this total and fired approximately 722,000 rounds of .50 caliber ammunition in strafing runs. During the same period, the SBDs dropped a total of 435,040 pounds of bombs on enemy installations.[33]

In mid-May Brigadier General Thomas J. Cushman succeeded General Merritt as wing commander. The numbers of missions flown by units of the 4th MBDAW hit a peak in July and August 1944 both in sorties flown and in the tonnage of bombs dropped. By July all Marine squadrons using Corsairs were equipped with the necessary bomb racks and were taking part in dive-bombing and low level bombing attacks. Total tonnage of bombs dropped during the month by 4th MBDAW aircraft amounted to more than 700 tons. The F4Us dropped over 300 tons of this total and fired approximately 448,250 rounds of .50 caliber ammunition in strafing attacks; SBDs dropped a total of nearly 400 tons.[34] In August 1944, the bombing reached a peak of 1,200 tons of explosives dropped on the bypassed atolls in the Marshalls; of the total, 650 tons were released by F4Us and 546 tons by SBDs.[35]

In September the neutralization missions against the remaining enemy-held islands in the Marshalls continued but on a reduced scale. In accordance with an order from the Commander of Shore-Based Aircraft, Forward Area, Major General Willis H. Hale, USA, who in turn was subordinate to the Commander, Forward Area, Central Pacific, Vice Admiral Hoover, the number of squadrons sent on strikes was limited to four per day. As a result of this ceiling on the number of squadrons that could be employed each day and numerous cancellations of strikes due to inclement weather, the total number of sorties flown during the month dropped to about 61 percent of the August total. Tonnage of bombs dropped similarly decreased by about 38 percent.

Compared to what it might have cost

---

[33] 4th MBDAW WarD, May44.

[34] 4th MBDAW WarD, Jul44.
[35] *Ibid.*, Aug44.

in human lives had a direct attack been launched to seize the bypassed islands, the cost in pilots and planes expended in keeping these islands neutralized to the end of the war was relatively small. Between the beginning of the employment of Marine aviation against the Marshalls and the end of 1944, the squadrons of the 4th MBDAW lost 29 pilots, 2 gunners, and 57 aircraft due to enemy action. As the summer of 1944 turned into autumn, the observation, harassment, and neutralization of the bypassed islands were extended beyond the Marshalls to Kusaie, Ocean, Nauru, and Wake Island.

As far as much-bombed Wotje, Maloelap, Mille, and Jaluit in the Marshalls were concerned, visual observation and official photographs indicated that the garrison forces there were capable of repairing the airfields. This capability might enable the enemy to fly in aircraft for supply, evacuation, and reconnaissance. Even though such a possibility was remote, it nevertheless could not be overlooked. At the same time, Marine aviators had to be on a continuous lookout for enemy submarines, which might attempt to supply or evacuate the bypassed bases.

To the north, Wake remained a threat. Even though no shipping or land plane activity had been noted there for some time, reconnaissance had revealed the use of seaplanes, probably for supply or evacuation. The possibility that the Japanese might use Wake Island as a base from which to stage an attack against American bases in the Marshalls could not be excluded. Ponape and Nauru, while largely neutralized, also remained potential threats, especially as staging points for reconnaissance aircraft.

For many of the Marine aviators, the daily bomb runs over the bypassed enemy garrisons gradually became a monotonous undertaking. On the other hand, the effectiveness of the air strikes in keeping the enemy neutralized in this area was also obvious. A report by the 4th MBDAW stated:

> The constant hammering is obviously wearing the Japanese down, for their anti-aircraft fire is steadily getting lighter. There has been no fire from heavy guns for some time, so these obviously have been destroyed. The Japanese now defend themselves with 20, 40 millimeter, and .50 caliber fire. Just what the conditions are on the Japanese Islands, where probably no supplies from home are obtained, is not known for certain; but there can be no doubt that supplies are running low, and the time will come when they will be left without ammunition, weapons, and the necessities of life.
>
> All this, however, isn't a harmless game. The besieged Jap garrisons still have their light anti-aircraft weapons and sufficient ammunition left to make it hot for the Marine birdmen each time they come. Indeed, the Japanese have been getting so much practice in anti-aircraft fire that the Japs remaining in the Marshalls and Gilberts are probably the most proficient anti aircraft gunners in the world today. Many of the Marines' planes have been shot down, and many pilots have been killed. Again and again planes have returned to their bases after being struck, and the pattern of Japanese bullet holes has been in the dead center of the airplane. Such remarkable hits have been made so many times that it is obviously not a matter of luck.[36]

---

[36] Capt C. C. Beach memo to LtCol Brayton, 4th MAW, dtd 2Jan45, Encl to 4th MAW WarD, Nov44.

Aside from providing the Japanese antiaircraft crews with gunnery practice, Marine aviators relieved some of the monotony of their missions by trying out new methods of attack, experimenting with new types of bombs, and by improvising new uses for their aircraft. On 22 April 1944, Major Everton, commanding VMF-113, led three F4Us in a long distance flight to cover landing operations on Ujelang Atoll. Nine hours and 40 minutes after takeoff, the Corsairs returned to their home base. Another long-distance bomber mission flown in October was to set a new record for the fighter-bombers of the 4th MBDAW. For the record, this occasion was noted in the following words:

> A notable event of the month was the bombing of Ponape Island on the 5th by Corsair fighter-bombers of the Fourth Marine Base Defense Aircraft Wing—an attack which set a new distance record for Pacific fighter-bomber operations. When this strike was made and the planes completed the long over-water round trip of 750 miles without loss or damage of any kind or injuries to personnel, the event was heralded as the longest fighter-bomber mission ever carried out by such planes with normal bomb loads. By the end of the month such attacks had become routine.[37]

Another important event during the month of October was the first employment of napalm by aviators of the 4th MBDAW; it was used on the 28th in an attack against Emidj Island in Jaluit Atoll. This was the first of a series of attacks to determine the effectiveness of napalm against enemy installations in the bypassed Marshall Islands. The first raid, carried out by 17 Corsairs of VMF-224 and 21 Corsairs of VMF-441, was considered promising; jettisonable gas tanks loaded with napalm, dropped on enemy automatic weapons positions, found their mark; as the raiders departed from the area, four large fires, started by the napalm bombs, were still burning brightly.

Before the year 1944 came to an end, several changes in personnel took place within the headquarters of the 4th MBDAW. General Cushman, who on 15 May 1944 had relieved General Merritt as Commanding General, 4th MBDAW, was succeeded on 20 August by Major General Louis E. Woods. Shortly before the end of 1944, there had also been a change in the designation of the air wing, long overdue in the opinion of many Marine aviators. In keeping with the more offensive mission of the air wing during the latter part of 1944, the 4th MBDAW on 10 November 1944 was redesignated as the 4th Marine Aircraft Wing.

The neutralization of the bypassed Marshalls continued for the remainder of 1944. Momentous events had taken place elsewhere in the Central Pacific, where the Marianas and some of the islands in the Palaus had been seized. In early 1945, the invasion of Iwo Jima was imminent. In the southwestern Pacific, the campaign in the Philippines was well underway. On land, on sea, and in the air, the Japanese had sustained major reverses. The general course of the war affected the operations of the 4th Marine Aircraft Wing. Effective 23 January 1945, bombing attacks against the enemy-held islands in the Marshalls and adjacent areas

---

[37] 4th MBDAW WarD, Oct44.

were virtually terminated by a change of policy ordered by the Commander in Chief, Pacific Ocean Areas. Pursuant to this order, such attacks were no longer to be made except where expected results would justify the expenditure of personnel, fuel, and explosives.

Beyond any doubt, this order was issued in the knowledge that by the beginning of 1945, the isolated enemy bases, which had been under almost constant attack since the invasion of the area by American forces a year ago, had been battered into virtual impotence. Most of the enemy installations had been knocked out by air power alone. Fixed antiaircraft positions for the most part had been destroyed, and shore defense positions blasted to rubble. Bivouac areas had been gutted and the hapless surviving Japanese were virtually forced underground.

Following the implementation of the new policy, Marine aviators were able to devote considerable attention to the destruction of enemy submarines, which became active in the vicinity of the Marshalls during the first week of February, when six verified enemy submarine sightings were made. Countermeasures promptly instituted by air and naval units presumably prevented the enemy from attacking any of the numerous convoys that were passing through the area at the time. Four of the submarines were declared sunk, though ultimately the Marine aviators failed to receive credit for these sinkings. Nor was Marine aviation employed solely against enemy submarines during the turn of the year, for Marine aviators continued their attacks against enemy shipping in the bypassed atolls. In February 1945, 23 small boats were destroyed by Marine aircraft; the following month, search planes attacked and sank 17 small boats of various categories, damaged three more, and attacked six with unobserved results.

The month of February also saw the inauguration of a new phase of warfare in the Marshalls—a war of psychology, an experimental but well-organized campaign in which exhortations to give up and showers of propaganda leaflets replaced the bombs that had reduced the bypassed Japanese bases to a shambles. This campaign was directed initially against the remaining enemy forces on Wotje Atoll. In a novel series of flights, a psychological warfare plane cruised over the islands of this atoll, broadcasting music, news, and messages to the Japanese holdouts. After every flight of this aircraft, planes of VMF-155, commanded by Major John E. Reynolds and subsequently Major Wayne M. Cargill, dropped propaganda leaflets by the thousands. Initial results of the propaganda campaign were meager, though the leaflets may have served to undermine flagging enemy morale.

On 27 February, a transport plane carrying its crew and a number of passengers, including Lieutenant General Millard H. Harmon, Commander, Strategic Air Forces, Central Pacific Area, was lost en route from Kwajalein to Oahu, Hawaii. The disappearance of this plane, for which no explanation was ever found, set in motion an air and sea rescue effort in which all available aircraft participated around the clock. The extended search failed to turn up any wreckage of the plane.

During the month of March, Marine

aviators based in the Marshalls devoted increased attention to interdiction of inter-island traffic between the bypassed islands. To this end, search and patrol craft blasted all forms of surface craft encountered, attacking a total of 39 boats of various categories ranging from small skiffs and rowboats to sizeable power launches. Of this number, 22 were destroyed, 13 were damaged, and 4 were attacked with unobserved results. At the time, American commanders in the Marshalls could only estimate the results of the prolonged isolation on the Japanese marooned on the bypassed islands, though the toll taken by disease and starvation was estimated to be high. That death and hunger were stalking these islands is shown in the diary of a Korean, who was a member of the Japanese force garrisoning Aur Atoll. The diary shows the progressive reduction in strength from 367 men on 1 January to 308 by the end of the month; nearly all of them died of malnutrition. Representative of the diet to which the Japanese were reduced by this time are the following entries:

18 January—
Breakfast: Rice and bush leaves.
Dinner: Rice and bush leaves, and canned fish.
Supper: Fried rice, canned fish and salt.
Every two men must catch a rat for food.
This kind of food is not good for our health.
Another new kind of food is added to our diet: earthworm. We began eating earthworm in supper last night.

19 January—
Breakfast: Rice and bush leaves.
Dinner: Too bad, nothing to eat.
Supper: Rice, salt, and rats.[38]

March of 1945 saw the first concrete evidence of a deterioration of morale on the part of enemy holdout garrisons in the Marshalls. On 24 March, several Japanese on Wotje Atoll surrendered after verbal exhortations from a plane manned by psychological warfare personnel. The Japanese on Wotje were clearly undernourished and otherwise in poor physical shape. Four days later, 5 Koreans, 1 Japanese, and 2 natives from Mille Atoll surrendered to the crew of LCI–392 after persuasion over a megaphone. Upon interrogation, these gaunt, emaciated, and almost dazed men asserted that hunger was the factor which had led them to turn themselves in. Even the enemy personnel appeared happy to have been taken prisoner.

The month of April saw the use of rockets by 12 Helldivers (Curtiss SB2C scout-bombers) of VMSB–331 against Wotje Island. Of 89 rockets fired against two enemy gun positions, 67 landed in the target area and scored six possible direct hits. Seven rockets failed to function properly and had to be brought back to base. On the 27th, a significant development occurred when three Japanese chief petty officers were taken into custody on Mille Atoll. Following their capture, the prisoners contended that many others would have capitulated if high seas had not prevented them from doing so. As in the

---
[38] Anx D to CTG 96.1 Shore Based Air Force WarD for period 1–30Apr45, 4th MAW WarD, Apr45.

MARINE DIVE BOMBERS *based in the Marshalls en route to target in the bypassed islands.* (USMC 118399)

U.S. PERSONNEL *tour Mille Island after 18 months of continuous bombing by 4th Marine Aircraft Wing.* (USMC 134062)

preceding month, Marine aviators devoted particular attention to interdicting enemy inter-island food supply traffic. Nineteen small craft of various categories ranging from 10-foot rowboats to 30-by-50 foot barges were hunted and strafed. Four of these craft were sunk or completely demolished, 3 were left inoperable, and 12 were damaged in varying degrees.

From the spring of 1945 to the end of the war in the Pacific Theater, the Japanese hold on the islands they still occupied in the Marshalls grew progressively weaker. On 6 May, the destroyer-escort USS *Wintle*, a minesweeper, and *YMS-354*, infantry landing craft LCIs -392, -394, -479, -491, and -484 together with appropriate air cover evacuated 494 natives from Jaluit Atoll. The Japanese attempted to prevent the evacuation, but were unable to do so. In the course of the operation, the enemy killed a Navy lieutenant, inflicted a bad arm wound on a native scout, and sprayed one of the landing craft with .50 caliber bullets, injuring an enlisted man. On the following day, an additional 84 natives were evacuated from the atoll.

On 11 May 1945, Brigadier General Lawson H. M. Sanderson succeeded General Woods in command of the 4th Aircraft Wing. During the summer of 1945, the neutralization of the bypassed Marshall islands entered a new phase when, in response to the combined strike and psychological warfare campaign, 42 Japanese and Koreans surrendered. On 2 July, search planes located a Japanese hospital ship, the *Takasago Maru*, on an eastward course and tracked it. At the same time, the destroyer *Murray* departed from Eniwetok with two Japanese language interpreters to investigate the ship. On the following day, the *Murray* stopped the enemy vessel, which was bound for Wake Island to evacuate sick personnel. After boarding the ship, the Americans conducted a search which failed to uncover any violations of international law; as a result, the enemy ship was permitted to proceed to Wake Island. On 5 July, when the hospital ship was on its return voyage, a renewed search indicated that the vessel had picked up 974 patients at Wake, nearly all suffering from serious malnutrition. Medical personnel on board the *Murray* estimated that 15 percent of the Japanese would not survive the return trip to Japan.[39] The ship was permitted to proceed on its voyage by order of Admiral Nimitz over Admiral Halsey's objections.

In his memoirs, Admiral Halsey made this comment on the incident:

> That made me mad. Although Japan had never signed the Geneva Convention, she professed to observe it; yet I had suspected throughout the war that she was using her hospital ships for unauthorized purposes. This was an instance. Battle casualties are legitimate evacuees; malnutrition cases are not. For three years we had been blockading the bypassed Jap islands in an attempt to force their surrender. The starving men on the *Takasago Maru* had constituted a large part of the Wake garrison; their evacuation meant that Wake's scanty provisions would last that much longer. I sent a destroyer to intercept the ship and escort

---

[39] 4th MAW WarD, Jul45.

her to Saipan, and I intended recommending either that all but her battle casualties be returned to Wake, or that an equal number of Japs be sent there from our Saipan prison camps as replacements. CINCPAC directed me to let her proceed, and I had to comply.[40]

When, on 15 August, Japan accepted the Allied demand for an unconditional surrender, CinCPOA issued an order calling for the cessation of all offensive operations against the Japanese except for the continuance of searches and patrols. On 22 August, the Japanese commander of Mille Atoll surrendered his forces unconditionally. The remaining Japanese strongholds in the Marshalls capitulated following the signing of the formal surrender documents in Tokyo Bay on 2 September.[41]

---

[40] Bryan and Halsey, *Admiral Halsey's Story*, p. 258.

[41] For information concerning Marine surrender and occupation duties in the Pacific islands following the war, see Frank and Shaw, *Victory and Occupation*, pp. 449–463.

CHAPTER 2

Marine Aviation in the Marianas, Carolines and at Iwo Jima[1]

THE MARIANAS[2]

While Marines of the 4th MAW were engaged in neutralizing enemy strongholds in the Marshalls, American military operations in the Central Pacific were accelerating. By June of 1944, Operation FORAGER, the invasion of the Marianas, had gotten under way. For the operation, Admiral Raymond A. Spruance, commanding the Fifth Fleet, had assembled more than 800 ships, a far cry from the total of 82 ships that had been available for the Guadalcanal landings barely two years earlier. A similar increase in aircraft strength available for FORAGER was notable. Shore-based aircraft for the invasion of the Marianas totalled 879 planes; 352 belonging to the Marine Corps, 269 to the U.S. Army, and 258 to the Navy. Marine aircraft consisted of 172 fighters, 36 night fighters, 72 dive bombers, 36 torpedo bombers, and 36 transport aircraft.[3]

Despite the large number of Marine shore-based aircraft in the Gilberts and Marshalls, air operations in the Marianas were carried out largely by the Navy carrier planes. Previous attempts by exponents of Marine aviation to have

---

[1] Unless otherwise noted, the material in this chapter is derived from: 2d MAW Hist, Jul41-Sept46; 4th MBDAW WarDs, Dec42-Nov44 and 4th MAW WarDs, Nov44-Mar46; MAG-11 WarDs, Oct42-Oct44 and MAG-11 Hist, Aug41-Dec49; MAG-21 WarDs and Hist, Feb43-Dec44, hereafter *MAG-21 Hist;* MAG-25 WarDs, Aug42-Jun46; MAG-45 OpRpt, 8Jan45; MBDAG-45 WarDs and Hist, Feb-Oct44; VMO-2 WarDs and Hist, Nov43-Jul46 hereafter *VMO-2 Hist;* VMO-4 WarDs, Mar44-Oct45 and Hist, 20Dec43-31Dec44, hereafter *VMO-4 Hist;* AWS-5 AR and WarDs, Mar-Jul44; VMF-114 WarDs, Jul43-Apr47; VMF-121 WarDs, Oct42-Dec44 and Hist, May41-Jul44; VMTB-131 WarDs, Dec41-Sep42 and Jan44-Nov45; VMF-216 WarDs, Jun43-Mar46; VMF-217 WarDs, Jul43-May46; VMF-225 WarDs, Jan43-Mar47; VMF-225 Hist, Jan43-Dec49; VMTB-232 WarDs, Jul43-Feb45; VMTB-242 WarDs, Jul43-Nov45; VMTB-242 Hist, Jul43-Jul45; VMF-252 WarDs, Apr42-Jan44; VMF-321 WarDs, Sep43-Jan46; VMF(N)-532 WarDs, Dec43-Jul46 and VMF(N)-532 Hist, Apr43-May47; VMF(N)-541 Hist, Feb44-Dec49; VMB-612 WarDs, Aug-Dec44 and VMB-612 Supp and Hist, Oct43-Aug45; VMR-952 WarDs and Hist, Jul44-Jul46, hereafter *VMR-952 Hist;* Isely and Crowl, *U. S. Marines and Amphibious War;* King and Whitehill, *Fleet Admiral King;* Sherrod, *Marine Corps Aviation in World War II;* Heinl, *Soldiers of the Sea;* Morison, *Victory in the Pacific.*

[2] Additional sources for this section include: Major Carl W. Hoffman, *Saipan—The Beginning of the End* (Washington: HistDiv, HQMC, 1950), hereafter Hoffman, *Saipan;* Major Carl W. Hoffman, *The Seizure of Tinian* (Washington: HistDiv, HQMC, 1951), hereafter Hoffman, *Tinian;* Major Orlan R. Lodge, *The Recapture of Guam* (Washington: HistBr, G-3 Div, HQMC, 1954), hereafter Lodge, *Guam;* USSBS, *Pacific Campaigns.*

[3] Aircraft figures above cited in USSBS, *Pacific Campaigns,* p. 235.

Marine flyers operate from carriers had not yet reached fruition. The invasion of Saipan on 15 June found Navy aviation in full control of the skies. During the epic air battle of the Philippine Sea, which was to become known as the "Marianas Turkey Shoot," the Navy destroyed 476 enemy aircraft, nearly all of them in the air. Between 22 and 24 June, 73 Army Air Forces Thunderbolt fighters (P-47s) were catapulted from the Navy carriers USS *Natoma Bay* and USS *Manila Bay* 60 miles off Saipan and landed on Aslito airfield. These planes gave valuable assistance to the Navy in furnishing close support for the troops on Saipan, where bitter fighting was in progress.[4]

At the end of the Saipan operation, numerous voices were raised in criticism of the close support the hard-pressed Marine divisions had received on the ground. The most frequent complaint was that excessive time was required before a much needed air strike was actually executed. Many of the requested missions had to be cancelled because the infantry had already advanced beyond the targets before the first airplane appeared over the battlefield. An evaluation of close air support on Saipan summed up the situation this way:

> . . . as compared with the assistance given to the fighting troops by naval ships, close air support was decidedly inferior. In the early part of the operation, close support missions were flown exclusively by navy planes, and only toward the end of the operation were army aircraft . . . employed for this purpose. At no time

were specially trained Marine pilots available for this kind of work.[5]

Responsible officers of the 4th Marine Division attributed deficiencies in close air support on Saipan to inadequate training of pilots, overcrowding of radio circuits between troops on the ground and units controlling the air strikes, involvement of too many echelons in the control of air strikes, and poor coordination between aviation, naval guns, and artillery. Following the Saipan operation, General Holland Smith once again urged that air groups be designated and trained as direct support groups and be assigned to CVE-type carriers (escort aircraft carriers, hereafter referred to as CVEs), and that Marine aviation provide air groups for this specialized duty.

At the same time, General Vandegrift, Commandant of the Marine Corps, initiated action designed to get Marine aviation assigned to carriers. Following discussions with the Chief of Naval Operations and a conference at Pearl Harbor in August 1944, attended by General Vandegrift and ranking naval leaders, the placement of Marine aircraft on carriers was authorized. On 21 October, Marine Carrier Groups, Aircraft, Fleet Marine Force, Pacific, was established as a tactical command with headquarters at Santa Barbara, California. Colonel Albert D. Cooley was appointed commanding officer of the Marine Carrier Groups, which consisted of Marine Base Defense Aircraft Group 48 (MBDAG-48) at Santa Barbara and MAG-51 at Mojave. In early November, the two groups were re-

---

[4] For a detailed account of Marine ground operations on Saipan, see Shaw, Nalty, and Turnbladh, *Central Pacific Drive*, pp. 231–428.

[5] Isely and Crowl, *U. S. Marines and Amphibious War*, p. 333.

designated as Marine air support groups. Each group consisted of four carrier air groups, each with an 18-plane fighter squadron and a 12-aircraft torpedo bomber squadron. The Marine air support group was scheduled for assignment to a CVE division of six carriers. Each carrier air group was to be stationed on a CVE. The Marine air support group staff was to function in the flagship as part of the admiral's staff for directing operations of the carrier air groups in support of ground troops in a target area.

It was not envisioned that the Marine squadrons would furnish all close air support. Instead, Marine aviation was to provide close air support for Marine divisions when the situation permitted. Though carrier-based Marine aviation was not yet a reality during the Marianas campaign, the framework for such an organization was rapidly being laid.

Lest it be thought that Marine aviation was completely left out of operations on Saipan, it must be mentioned that some Marine aircraft did take off from carriers and perform a very useful mission in support of the ground action. These were airplanes of VMO-2, commanded by Major Robert W. Edmondson, and VMO-4, under Captain Nathan D. Blaha. Most of the small artillery spotter monoplanes flew off the carriers USS *Fanshaw Bay* and USS *White Plains* on 17 June, landed on Yellow Beach and the dirt strip at Charan-Kanoa, and subsequently, on 22 June, moved to Aslito airfield.

The flying personnel of VMO-2 soon noticed that combat situations varied considerably from textbook theory, as related in the squadron history:

From the first hops on, it was realized that use of our planes could not be employed the way it was originally intended. Theoretically, we were to remain at all times behind our front lines, never going deep into or even over enemy territory and all artillery firing and adjustment was supposed to be done behind our own pieces. Very little time was needed for us to realize that this method was impractical and relatively ineffective. Due to the rugged mountainous terrain, observation was practically impossible from such a position. Consequently, we found it necessary not only to go behind enemy lines, but deep into enemy territory to scout and pick out targets, and to remain there while fire was conducted on these targets so proper adjustments could be made and the effect of the fire on the targets could be observed. Therefore, most all of our flying was done over and forward of our front lines for the remainder of the Saipan and Tinian operations.[6]

The monoplanes of VMO-2 continued their spotting missions until the end of the Saipan operation on 9 July 1944. None of the pilots or planes was lost, though enemy antiaircraft fire hit many of the aircraft; two of them had their gas tanks damaged but both returned safely to their base. On the night of 26 June, enemy bombers raided the squadron area and dropped numerous antipersonnel bombs, wounding some of the Marines on the ground.

Considerably less lucky in the course of the Saipan operation were the men of VMO-4, whose mission in support of the 4th Marine Division was identical to that executed by VMO-2 for the 2d Division. The first two planes of VMO-4 left the *White Plains* 150 miles offshore on 19 June and arrived safely at

---

[6] VMO-2 Hist, *op. cit.*, p. 8.

the Charan-Kanoa strip. The remaining aircraft, in crates, were brought ashore two days later; by 22 June, eight squadron planes were in operation. From this point on, and for the duration of its employment on Saipan, bad luck appeared to dog the squadron. Six days after reaching Saipan, VMO-4 had already lost a substantial number of its original aircraft. Two planes were damaged beyond repair by enemy fire; another had to be scrapped after it collided with a vehicle during takeoff. Loss of the fourth plane resulted in the death of the pilot as well.

The misfortunes of VMO-4 did not end there. On the night of 26 June, the squadron area was bombed. This raid, from which the men of VMO-2 had escaped relatively unscathed, had a far more serious effect on the sister squadron. Three enlisted men of VMO-4 were killed and three officers and men were wounded. Among the seriously injured was the squadron commander, who had to be evacuated and was succeeded by Lieutenant Thomas Rozga.[7]

Another Marine aviation unit on Saipan was Air Warning Squadron 5 (AWS-5). On 17 April 1944 the squadron, commanded by Captain Donald D. O'Neill, had been divided into three detachments for operations with V Amphibious Corps. One of these was assigned to the Northern Troops and Landing Force, the other two to the 2d and 4th Marine Divisions. The initial mission of these detachments was to provide an early air raid alert for the headquarters to which they were attached and to record all enemy air activity observed. On the morning of D plus 2, 17 June, the squadron went ashore on Saipan. As fighting on the island progressed, the detachments displaced forward with their radar equipment in line with the advance of the two Marine divisions. While conducting a reconnaissance for a new site to be occupied on 29 June, a lieutenant and five men were taken under enemy machine gun fire. The lieutenant was killed and a corporal subsequently was reported as missing.

On 12 July, after the battle for Saipan had come to an end, a dozen aircraft of VMF(N)-532 joined the Army Air Forces night fighters already stationed on the island. An advance echelon of 7 officers and 32 enlisted men had been flown to Saipan a week earlier. Beginning 10 July, in addition to patrolling over Saipan, the squadron maintained one night fighter on station over Guam between the hours of 1930 and 0530.

The invasion of Guam on 21 July found MAG-21, commanded by Colonel Peter P. Schrider, offshore awaiting the seizure of the Orote Peninsula. The air group had been detached from the 2d MAW on 4 June and subsequently was attached to the 4th MBDAW. After 30 days at sea, the aviation Marines were eager to go ashore and get an airfield operational on the peninsula. Due to the heavy and prolonged fighting in this particular part of Guam, the forward echelon of MAG-21 was still ship-bound a week after D-Day. Two days later, a work detail of 50 men finally went ashore to assist in the restoration of the old airstrip. The initial job was to clear the strip of shell fragments and Japa-

---

[7] VMO-4 Hist, *op. cit.*, pp. 11–12.

nese dead in various stages of decomposition. There remained to be done another extremely unpleasant job, which fell to the bomb disposal officer of MAG-21: clearing the area of mines, unexploded bombs, and the booby traps around the designated bivouac area.

From the time that the first Marines of MAG-21 started to restore the airstrip, and for many weeks thereafter, they were constantly harassed by enemy snipers and bypassed stragglers who lurked in the underbrush at night and infested the coral caves on both sides of the strip. Mechanics of the air group captured several Japanese; hundreds remained to be killed or captured on Orote Peninsula.

By 31 July, a 2,500-foot section had been added to the coral strip, which had already been cleared. The strip was ready for operations and several Marine officers planned to have the first American plane to land on Guam be one from VMO-1, commanded by Major Gordon W. Heritage, whose craft were poised on the escort carriers USS *Sangamon* and USS *Suwanee*.[8] This plan was frustrated when, during the afternoon of 31 July, a Navy torpedo bomber from the USS *Chenango* attempted a landing on the newly constructed strip shortly before the Marine observation planes were scheduled to arrive. The importance of the occasion was not lost on the numerous observers gathered to witness this memorable event, which was recorded for posterity in these words:

Sniper fire cracked across Orote Air-

---

[8] Col Frederick P. Henderson ltr to CMC, dtd 21Nov52, as cited in Shaw, Nalty, and Turnbladh, *Central Pacific Drive*, p. 525n.

field as the first American plane attempted to land on the captured strip, and the Marine reception committee lay pinned to the deck at the moment the Grumman torpedo bomber began its cautious approach toward the former Jap airbase. Halfway down the strip, mangled and charred Jap bodies lay in grotesque mounds before a fallen redoubt of concrete. The stench of 3,000 other dead Japs was over the scorched peninsula . . . a bullet-riddled wind sock flapped wearily in the hot breeze from across Apra Harbor. The noise of battle from the smoky mountain sides beyond the harbor rode on the same wind.

The word passed quickly. In a few minutes the strip was lined with curious spectators. But as Navy Lieutenant (jg) Edward F. Terrar, Coffeyville, Kansas zoomed the field, the sharp whine of bullets cut the air overhead, and the onlookers scrambled for cover without thought of dignity. Unmindful of the commotion on the ground, the Navy pilot dropped his flaps, cut his throttle and came on. His wheels touched lightly once, bounced harder a second time, and as the plane leaped on the third impact, he opened the gun and roared back into the air for a second try.

As he circled for another approach, the Marines on the ground weighed curiosity against prudence. But even the sniper was caught up in the drama of the situation. As suddenly as they had begun, the shots ceased. The TBF settled in again, but this time it greased the runway all the way, and pulled up to an easy stop as Marines swarmed around on every side. The time was exactly five o'clock; American aviation was on Guam.[9]

The stay of this American aircraft on Guam was very shortlived. Three minutes after landing, heavy sniper fire forced the torpedo bomber to take off. Minutes later, without major fanfare, a "grasshopper" of VMO-1, piloted by

---

[9] *MAG-21 Hist*, pp. 33–34.

the squadron commander, Major Gordon W. Heritage, landed on the airstrip as previously scheduled. As it developed, neither the torpedo bomber nor the VMO-1 spotter planes were the first American aircraft to touch down on Guam following its recapture. That honor fell to an Army liaison aircraft assigned to the 77th Infantry Division Artillery, which had taken off from an improvised airstrip elsewhere on the island at 1310 of the 30th.[10]

Work on the field continued at a furious pace through 4 August, by which date all but 150-200 yards at the west end of the strip had been completed. Except for unloading parties working on board ships, most of the MAG-21 headquarters and service squadron personnel moved into a new bivouac area at the east end of the field. Initially, the lot of these men was not an easy one. For one thing, the new "shelter-half camp" lacked mess and sanitary facilities. The air group history gives a vivid account of conditions prevailing at Orote airstrip at this time:

> In the camp, unavoidably in some respects, the men lived for more than a month in filth. The group did not bring with it ready-made heads or sanitation facilities. Men ate canned rations for some time before stoves could be set up and hot rations served. Worse than the mosquito that pestered Marine aviation men in the South Pacific, far worse was the big, fat ordinary variety of houseflies that swarmed over everything on Guam the first month. Of course, as the dead were gradually buried and ration cans properly disposed of, the fly began to disappear.

But the men were only on Guam a few days when dengue fever and dysentery began to take their toll. Dengue fever, with its symptoms very much like malaria, doesn't hang on and recur like malaria, but its original effects are much more painful. Every section of the MAG was hit seriously by dengue in those first few weeks. As soon as hot food was served, when dead Japs had all been buried, and when plenty of fresh water was available, dengue and dysentery slowly disappeared. After the first month and a half, cases dropped appreciably.[11]

On 4 August, Marine aviation returned to Guam in force. MAG-21 squadrons, flying in from the aircraft carrier USS *Santee*, safely touched down on the airstrip just before noon. The first squadron to land was VMF-(N)-534 flying Grumman Hellcats, led by the squadron commander, Major Ross S. Mickey, followed by VMF-216, -217, and -225. As the squadrons touched down, the planes were moved to the edge of the runway for parking since revetment areas had not yet been completed. At 0600 on 7 August, VMF-225 took off from Orote Field to make the first regular combat air patrol flown by Guam-based aircraft.

Barely a week after Orote Field had become operational, distinguished visitors arrived on board a large C-54 Skymaster transport. The dignitaries included Admiral Chester W. Nimitz, Commander in Chief, Pacific Fleet, and Lieutenant General Alexander A. Vandegrift, Commandant of the Marine Corps. Awaiting them at the field were Lieutenant General Holland M. Smith, Major General Roy S. Geiger, Major General Henry L. Larsen, Brigadier

---

[10] 77th InfDiv Arty AAR, 21Jul-10Aug44, as cited in Shaw, Nalty, and Turnbladh, *Central Pacific Drive*, p. 525.

[11] *Ibid.*, pp. 37-38.

General Pedro A. Del Valle, and other ranking Marine and naval officers on the island.

Even though pilots and ground crews had landed on Guam with high hopes of engaging the enemy in combat, they soon learned to their disappointment that no enemy airmen were going to challenge American domination of the skies over the island. For a few months following the capture of Guam, there were several air alerts, but no enemy bombs were dropped. There were no operational accidents in more than 6,000 takeoffs and landings during the first month. Orote airfield had the distinction of becoming the first all-Marine airfield in the Pacific Theater.

Situated only 1,500 miles from Tokyo, the new base dispatched fighters and bombers to attack Japanese-held Pagan Island, 200 miles north of Guam, and Rota, only 55 miles to the northeast and halfway to Saipan. The establishment of Orote airfield represented a long and ambitious step forward in the two-year story of developing American air power in the Pacific. Just two years earlier, Marine pilots had flown into embattled Henderson Field on Guadalcanal to establish a precarious foothold in the southern Pacific. Almost a year later, in August 1943, Marine aviators were the first to land on Munda airstrip on New Georgia. That advance of only 181 tortuous miles had followed a year of bitter fighting in the South Pacific. By August 1944, American forces had advanced boldly into the Marianas—1,100 miles west of the Marshalls and halfway along the 3,000-mile road from the Solomons to the Japanese homeland.

In flying strafing and bombing missions against the enemy-held island of Rota, the pilots of MAG–21 initially concentrated their attacks on the enemy airfield. Continuous bombing, on the average of once a day for four consecutive months, kept the enemy field in a chronic state of disrepair. The run to Rota and return required barely an hour and at least one pilot cracked: "Sighted Rota, sank same, and got home in time for lunch."[12]

For a while it appeared that the bomb runs to Rota were a picnic, and Marine aviators came to look upon the island as something akin to a practice range—a place to discharge a dull, routine, and necessary, but not overly hazardous, task. Enemy antiaircraft fire initially was feeble. As weeks turned into months, the enemy antiaircraft gunners marooned on the island apparently derived some benefit from tracking the daily low level sweeps of the Marine pilots. In any case, as time went on, the raiding aircraft began to get hit. Some managed to limp back to their base, others were shot down outright. In contrast to their earlier nonchalance, the pilots learned to respect Rota. When vegetable gardens were subsequently spotted on the island, the Corsair squadrons were dispatched to destroy them and so to deprive the enemy holdouts of a much-needed food supply. The tactics used were simple but effective. Several fighters dropped belly tanks of aviation gasoline on the targets. Planes following closely behind the belly-tank-bombers would then

---

[12] *Ibid.*, p. 47.

strafe the fuel-soaked fields with incendiary bullets.

Another enemy-held strongpoint frequently on the receiving end of Marine fighter bombers was Pagan. Ever since the American invasion of the Marianas, the enemy had tried to keep the Pagan airstrip operational, but these efforts were frustrated by continuous air raids. Taking off with a heavy gas load, carrying belly tanks and a pair of thousand pound bombs apiece, the Corsairs repeatedly attacked the enemy airfield on Pagan in the face of fairly heavy antiaircraft fire. Enemy aircraft caught on the ground were raked by strafing fighters, and in time the field became well pockmarked with bomb craters. In keeping the enemy airstrips on Rota and Pagan Islands in daily disrepair, the Corsairs of MAG-21, acting as fighter-bombers, played a vital part in protecting the new B-29 Superfortress bases on Saipan, Tinian, and Guam from enemy air action.[13]

On 7 September 1944, Colonel Schrider, commanding MAG-21, was succeeded by Colonel Edward B. Carney, who remained in command until late March 1945. By late November, MAG-21 consisted of VMF-216, -217, -225, -321, VMTB-131 and -242, VMO-1 and -2, VMF(N)-534, VMR-253, VMB-612, and AWS-2. The complement of the group at this time included 529 officers and 3,778 enlisted personnel. Aircraft of the group included 113 fighters (98 F4Us and 15 F6Fs), 15 night fighters (F6F-Ns), 39 torpedo bombers (TBFs and TBMs), 15 medium bombers (PBJs), 14 transports (R4Ds), 22 observation planes (OYs), and a solitary amphibious utility plane (J2F-6).[14] As 1944 drew to a close, most veteran pilots of the MAG-21 fighter squadrons either had or were in the process of returning to Pearl Harbor and the continental United States for training on aircraft carriers.

THE CAROLINES[15]

The occupation of the Marianas by U.S. forces during the summer of 1944, coupled with further advances in the southwest Pacific, opened the door to the seizure of the Philippine Islands. The logical step before retaking the Philippines was the seizure of the western Carolines, whose possession would not only provide the final stepping-stone to the Philippines but also protect the right flank of the invasion force. By this time, the Japanese were facing a strategic situation that had greatly changed to their disadvantage, for American forces were strongly em-

---

[13] The first B-29 arrived on Saipan on 12 October 1944 while final paving and other construction was still incomplete. Facilities were not substantially operative until April 1945. On Guam, the newly constructed airfields did not become operational for B-29s until late February 1945. On Tinian, the first two runways were completed in January 1945, the third in late February, and the fourth in early May. The first runway of West Field became operational on 22 March 1945, the second on 20 April. Craven and Cate, *The Pacific*, pp. 515-520.

[14] Figures on personnel and materiel taken from *MAG-21 Hist*, p. 50.

[15] Additional sources for this section include: 2d MAW WarD, Jan-Apr43; *IIIAC Palaus Rpt*; Hough, *Assault on Peleliu*; Smith, *Approach to the Philippines*; Fane and Moore, *The Naked Warriors*.

placed on their inner line of defense. The fall of Saipan in the overall Japanese view of the war was a disaster comparable to the German defeat at Stalingrad during the winter of 1942-43. For many Germans the loss of the *Sixth Army* at Stalingrad meant the war could no longer be won; many Japanese reached the same conclusion following the loss of Saipan. While, for the time being, no political repercussions in Germany followed in the wake of the military debacle, the loss of Saipan proved a sufficient disaster to topple the cabinet of General Tojo. In announcing the fall of Saipan to the nation, the latter was forced to admit that "Japan was facing an unprecedented national crisis."[16]

As early as 10 May 1944, Admiral Nimitz had designated the commander of the Third Fleet, Admiral Halsey, to head the invasion of Peleliu and Angaur under the code name Operation STALEMATE. A second phase of the operation called for the capture of Yap and Ulithi. The seizure of Yap was subsequently shelved, and the island remained in enemy hands until the end of the war. The invasion date for Peleliu and Angaur was set for 15 September. While planning for STALEMATE was in progress, Army Air Forces bombers frequently attacked enemy installations in the Palaus. As in previous invasions, the target was out of range of land-based fighter aircraft, and direct air support for the Peleliu beachhead would have to be furnished by naval aviation. The Navy had already struck at enemy defenses on Peleliu in March 1944, when carrier-based planes had dropped 600 tons of bombs on the island in a two-day raid. Preinvasion air strikes were designed to eliminate any enemy aircraft left in the Palaus. Once the Marines of the III Amphibious Corps had seized the Peleliu airfield, the main objective of the operation, Marine aviation was to be based on the island.

The task of bringing Marine aviation to Peleliu was turned over to the 2d MAW, commanded by Brigadier General Harold D. Campbell. The air wing, consisting of MAGs-11 and -25, had spent considerable time in the Pacific Theater. Some of its squadrons had participated in the Battle of Midway and in operations on New Georgia. On 30 June 1944, the headquarters of the 2d MAW moved from Efate, in the New Hebrides, to Espiritu Santo, where it joined the remainder of the squadrons attached to the wing. One week later, Major General James T. Moore took over as wing commander. Upon his arrival at Espiritu Santo, General Moore found the wing fully engaged in preparing for Operation STALEMATE. Commanding officers and loading officers of VMF-114, -121, -122, and VMF(N)-541 were reporting to the 1st Marine Division at Guadalcanal with embarkation data for the impending operation.

It is perhaps not surprising that officers of the 2d MAW should show a greater than average interest in shipborne movement to a new objective. Many of them remembered or had heard of the saga of the liberty ship S.S. *Walter Colton*, which in January 1943 had transported part of the wing headquarters to the South Pacific. At the

---

[16] USSBS, *Pacific Campaigns*, p. 220.

time, what had begun as a routine three-week voyage when the ship pulled out of San Diego Harbor on 8 January, had turned into a seemingly interminable odyssey for the aviation Marines on board. No one to this date has determined what factor was responsible for the strange voyage of the *Colton*, but something went awry along the way. The wing historian subsequently was to describe the sequence of events in the following words:

> Instead of proceeding directly to Guadalcanal, the *Colton* received a change of orders directing her to Noumea; then, running ahead of schedule, she failed to pick up radioed orders from Pearl Harbor which directed her to Espiritu Santo instead. Dropping anchor in Noumea Harbor, the ship and passengers learned they were not expected there. Several days later they steamed on, arriving February 4 at Espiritu. Apparently the ship was not expected there either, for during the following 2½ months while crew and passengers fretted to be moving, and the Squadron's materiel lay useless in her hold, the ship remained tied up in that big port without orders for further movement.
>
> Major Wilfrid H. Stiles and several other officers and enlisted personnel got off the *Colton* on February 6, and were flown to Guadalcanal. Others followed at later dates, but some of those who left the States on that ship never were detached from her until she reached Auckland, New Zealand, late in April.
>
> The result was that the ship never reached Guadalcanal, nor did she reach Efate, where the material aboard also could have been used. Until she sailed for Auckland where the cargo finally was taken ashore, she remained at Espiritu Santo.[17]

No such long voyage was planned

---

[17] 2d MAW WarD, Jan-Apr43.

for the ground personnel of Marine squadrons attached to the 2d MAW, and ground elements of the air wing went ashore on Peleliu on 15 September only one hour behind the assault waves. During the early phase of the operation, enemy resistance was so fierce that aviation Marines were used as stretcher bearers, ammunition carriers and riflemen.[18] Six Marines of the 2d MAW were killed and 11 wounded while aiding the ground troops during the early part of the operation.

The unfinished Japanese airfield on Peleliu was captured on 16 September; roughly a week later it became operational. On 24 September, General Moore, with part of his staff, arrived by transport and set up his headquarters as Air Commander, Western Carolines (Task Group 59.6). In this capacity, he headed a combined Army-Navy-Marine staff in addition to personnel of the 2d Wing, to direct the operations of all aircraft based on Peleliu, Angaur, and Ulithi. Garrison Air Force, Western Carolines, whose largest component was the 2d MAW, had a threefold task. It had to provide air defense for all ground troops and convoys in the Western Carolines, furnish air support for the ground troops in the vicinity of Peleliu Island; and neutralize the remaining enemy bases in the Western Carolines.

The first Marine aircraft to operate on Peleliu Island were the spotter planes of VMO-3, commanded by Captain Wallace J. Slappey. The ground echelon of the observation squadron

---

[18] For the complete history of ground operations on Peleliu, see Part III of this volume.

went ashore on Peleliu on 17 September and built a small airstrip about 500 feet long, just south of the main airfield. The first planes touched down on the following day, the remainder arriving on the 19th. On that day artillery spotting got under way and continued for the remainder of the month. The difficult and jagged terrain on the island required aerial observation 90 percent of the time. Most spotting was directed at seeking out previously unidentified natural fortifications, which had remained hidden from view beneath heavy vegetation. Despite the volume of fire directed against such fortifications, positive destruction of the enemy could not be determined because of the depth and strength of these positions. All enemy positions, buildings, and dumps of any kind that were exposed or built above ground level were either destroyed or left burning.

In addition to artillery spotting, the squadron assisted the infantry by executing numerous reconnaissance flights at extremely low altitudes over the front lines, seeking enemy gun positions that were holding up the advance. Other flights maintained a patrol over enemy-held islands to the north, looking for activities in general and barge movements in particular. Spotter aircraft also aided in directing amphibian tractor patrols to enemy troops trying to escape from the island. The pilots, not content with passively spotting targets, carried hand grenades and mortar shells along on many flights and dropped these on enemy troops and buildings. On occasion, planes returned from flights with holes from small arms fire and shell fragments. During the Peleliu operation, two OY-1 spotter aircraft were lost. The first loss occurred on take-off from the CVE on the day that the spotters were launched from the carrier off Peleliu. The second aircraft was shot down behind enemy lines. In both instances the flying crews were rescued.

On 24 September, the first eight F6F night fighters of VMF(N)-541, which had staged from Emirau through Owi Island, off New Guinea, arrived on Peleliu. Two days later, the Corsairs of VMF-114, commanded by Major Robert F. Stout, touched down. The Marine Corsairs wasted no time in assisting the ground troops in blasting the enemy out of his strongpoints. Details of these missions have been described elsewhere in this volume, but for the purposes of an overall description of Marine aviation activities on Peleliu there were two types of missions that deserve particular mention. One feat was the dropping of 1,000-pound bombs by Corsairs on enemy caves less than a mile from the Peleliu airstrip. The other was the employment of napalm, beginning on 12 October, against enemy caves and dugouts.

Japanese air power in the Western Carolines never posed any serious threat to Marine aviation. Enemy strips at Babelthuap and Yap were kept out of commission by repeated attacks of Marine fighters and torpedo bombers. By the end of October, Garrison Air Force, Western Carolines, had complete control of the air. The capture of Ulithi and adjacent islands provided Marine aviation with additional airfields. As a result, by the end of 1944, 11 squadrons were operating from fields on Peleliu,

Angaur, and Ulithi. As early as 17 November, Army bombers based on Angaur and attached to General Moore's task group were able to bomb enemy-held objectives on Luzon.

The only instance of direct air support for ground troops during the Peleliu operation occurred on 28 September, when the Corsairs of VMF-114 supported the landing of 3/5 on Ngesebus, an Island adjacent to Peleliu. This isolated instance of direct air support was only a forerunner of what Marine aviation was to accomplish several months later in the Phillppines. Nevertheless, even on this occasion, spectators to the operation, including Generals Smith, Geiger, Rupertus, and Moore, were highly impressed with the results obtained. The commander of the 1st Marine Division, General Rupertus, complimented the squadron commander, Major Robert F. Stout, on the performance of his pilots. Major Stout was destined not to survive the war; he was killed by enemy antiaircraft fire over Koror on Babelthuap Island on 4 March 1945, one of 16 pilots and 2 crewmen to lose their lives in bombing the remaining enemy-held islands in the Palaus and on Yap.

Following the capture of Ulithi on 21 September 1944, MBDAG-45, commanded by Colonel Frank M. June, was charged with the responsibility of providing air defense for the biggest anchorage in the western Pacific. The air group, subsequently redesignated as MAG-45, landed on Falalop Island on 8 October. The 51st Naval Construction Battalion, assisted by the group, completed a 3,500-foot airstrip within three weeks. On 22 October, the ground cchelons of VMF-312 and VMTB-232 arrived at Ulithi from Espiritu Santo in the New Hebrides and joined the air group at Falalop. Two days later, VMF-312 was administratively attached to Commanding General, Aircraft, Fleet Marine Force, Pacific. Operational control remained with the commanding officer of MAG-45 until the ground echelon departed from Ulithi on 19 November.

On 29 October, the flight echelon of VMF(N)-542, led by Major William C. Kellum, reached Falalop and began flying local combat air patrol around the clock on the following day. The second day of November witnessed the arrival of the flight echelon of VMTB-232, led by Major Menard Doswell III, from Peleliu. On the 4th, a division of six Avengers of this squadron carried out a reconnaissance of Yap Island. By 14 November VMTB-232 had begun a regular antisubmarine patrol, with two-plane sections flying two-hour flights around the atoll from dawn to dusk. Two days later, the Avengers launched the first of many strikes against the Japanese airstrip on Yap.

Even though the enemy field on Yap had been heavily pounded from the sea and air long before the arrival of Marine aviation on Ulithi in early October 1944, it remained a constant threat to Allied bases and shipping in the Western Carolines. Well entrenched enemy ground troops on Yap made it necessary to neutralize the enemy strongpoint from the air, for there was always the danger that the strip might be hastily repaired and used as staging point for a surprise air assault on the Ulithi base and anchorage. There was a further possibility that the enemy might use Yap as a refuelling station for submarines. Even though Marine pilots did not expect aerial opposition over Yap, they did encounter antiaircraft fire of sufficient intensity to cause them to maintain a minimum altitude of 6,000 feet.

Proof that the enemy was aware of the presence of American shipping at Ulithi anchorage was furnished on the morning of 20 November, when enemy submarines, the *I-36* and *I-47*, released five midget subs. One of these torpedoed the USS *Mississinewa*, a fleet oiler loaded with more than 400,000 gallons of aviation gas. The ship sank at her berth in the lagoon with a loss of 50 officers and men.[19] Immediate countermeasures taken by hunter-killer teams under the atoll commander, Commodore Oliver O. Kessing, resulted in the destruction of all five midgets, two of which fell victim to Marine Corps aircraft. Nevertheless, both the *I-36* and the *I-47* were able to make good their escape.

In general, tactical operations of MAG-45 from 30 October 1944 through the end of the year consisted of routine strikes and reconnaissance of Yap, Sorol, and Fais, and regular dawn to dusk antisubmarine patrols, all executed by Avengers of VMTB-232. VMF(N)-542 flew the regular combat air patrols, using the Falalop strip and its facilities, but depending on its own maintenance crews for service. On such missions, naval aviators were briefed by the Marine group operations and intelligence officers.

IWO JIMA[20]

As Marine aviation began to expand its operations to the Western Carolines, a development important to the future of Marine air was taking place far from the Pacific scene of action. After prolonged discussions and long delays, Marine Carrier Groups, Aircraft, Fleet Marine Force, Pacific was finally established on 21 October 1944 as a tactical command.[21]

Training of Marine pilots for carrier qualification had already started during the summer of 1944. Even though about 15 percent of the aviators assigned to Marine Carrier Groups, FMFPac, had seen combat action, few had ever landed on a carrier. On 3 February 1945 the first carrier, the *Block Island*, was assigned to MASG-48. Three other carriers were furnished at one-month intervals. It was hoped that by late 1945, when the invasion of Japan itself was to get under way, eight carriers would be available to the Marines.[22]

The invasion of Iwo Jima, Operation DETACHMENT, came too early to en-

---

[19] Morison, *Leyte*, p. 51.

[20] Additional sources for this section include: MajGen Holland M. Smith, ConfRpt, TF 56, "Air Operations in Support of the Capture of Iwo Jima," n.d., hereafter Smith, *Iwo Jima Special Air OpsRpt*; S. E. Smith, *The United States Navy in World War II* (New York: William Morrow & Company, 1966), hereafter Smith, *U. S. Navy in World War II*; Vice Admiral E. P. Forrestel, *Admiral Raymond A. Spruance, USN—A Study in Command* (Washington: GPO, 1966), hereafter Forrestel, *Admiral Spruance*; Okumiya, Horikoshi, and Caidin, *Zero!*; Leckie, *Strong Men Armed*.

[21] Sherrod, *Marine Corps Aviation in World War II*, p. 329.

[22] *Ibid.*, p. 331.

able Marine aviation to furnish close air support from its escort carriers. Each one of the 11 escort carriers taking part in the operation was manned by Navy pilots. Nevertheless, Marine aviators were to be given at least a limited opportunity to strike a blow both directly and indirectly in support of the Iwo Jima operation, one against the island itself, the other in the diversionary attack against the Japanese mainland.

While the program to put Marines on carriers was being slowly implemented stateside, a crisis arose in the field that was to hasten this development in an entirely unforeseen fashion. The appearance of Japanese suicide planes during the Leyte campaign in the autumn of 1944 had created an instant need for additional fighters based on the big carriers of the Third Fleet. The employment of Marine fighters and pilots was decided upon as an immediate expedient; by the end of 1944 the first of the Marine fighter squadrons were to fly from the decks of five of the big carriers in major operations involving a fast carrier task force.[23]

On 28 December 1944, VMF-124, under the command of Lieutenant Colonel William A. Millington, and VMF-213 under Major Donald P. Frame, went aboard the USS *Essex* at Ulithi. After a series of air strikes against Formosa and Luzon from 3-9 January 1945, Admiral Halsey's Third Fleet moved into the South China Sea, from where air strikes were launched against Indochina, Hong Kong, and Formosa. Effective 27 January, having returned to Ulithi, the Third Fleet was redesignated the Fifth Fleet and Admiral Spruance took over the tactical command from Admiral Halsey.

On 10 February, TF 58 sortied from Ulithi bound for Tokyo, 1,500 miles to the north. Three additional large carriers, each with two Marine fighter squadrons on board, joined the Fifth Fleet, so that in the end Admiral Spruance disposed over eight Marine fighter squadrons on four large carriers. The air attack on Tokyo was to precede the invasion of Iwo Jima by troops of the V Amphibious Corps by three days. Following their attacks against the Japanese capital, the Marine squadrons of TF 58 were to furnish air support at Iwo Jima on D-Day, which was set for 19 February.

Following the air strikes against Japan, which were carried out under unfavorable weather conditions, TF 58 was approximately 100 miles from Iwo Jima on D-Day, and prelanding strikes were launched against the landing beaches and adjacent areas. The initial sweep against the Iwo defenses was executed by a flight of 24 Marine Corsairs and an equal number of Navy Hellcats. Under the command of Colonel Millington of VMF-124, this flight attacked the flanks and high ground along the landing beaches with napalm, rockets, and machine gun fire. Five minutes before the first Marines hit the shore, the flight attacked the landing beach in low-level attacks. The contribution of Marine aviation in direct support of

---

[23] For additional details on this subject matter, see Frank and Shaw, "Marines on Carriers," *op. cit.*

the Iwo landings was relatively small in numbers, for on D-Day a total of more than 600 aircraft, including those of the Navy and Army Air Forces, were engaged in reducing enemy defenses and supporting the assault. Carrier-based Marine aviation continued to fly in close support of the assault troops until 22 February, when Corsairs from the *Wasp* flew a ground support mission as part of a 23-plane flight. After that date, air support for the embattled Marines on the island was turned over to Navy escort carrier planes and Army P-51s, who did the best job under the circumstances.

Marine aviation contributed to operations on Iwo Jima in other ways. First to become engaged in the aerial assault against the island were the Mitchell medium bombers (PBJs) of VMB-612 commanded by Lieutenant Colonel Jack R. Cram. From early December 1944 until the end of January 1945, this squadron, based in the Marianas, flew night sorties against enemy shipping in the Volcano and Bonin Islands and seriously disrupted the flow of enemy supplies to these islands. Once the Marines had landed on Iwo, artillery spotter aircraft of VMO-4, commanded by Lieutenant Thomas Rozga, and VMO-5, headed by Lieutenant Roy G. Miller, lent valuable support to ground operations. For the Marines, whether on the ground or in the air, Iwo was to be an extremely difficult operation; the spotter aircraft were to share the dangers and tribulations of the campaign along with the remainder of the assault force.

The difficulties of the observation squadrons had begun in December 1944. The Commanding General, V Amphibious Corps, directed the pilots of VMO-4 in Hawaii to test a special piece of equipment, dubbed "Brodie gear," which had been designed by the U. S. Army to launch the small observation aircraft from an LST. The device, which resembled a giant slingshot, consisted of two projecting beams, a cable, arresting gear, and a loop. Hooks were fitted on the planes, and on 21 December 1944 tests were begun using LST *776* as a base. Initial tests were unsatisfactory and resulted in the loss of several spotter aircraft.

The experimentation did not end here, however. With added experience it became evident that launching the small spotter aircraft from an LST in this fashion was possible, though three planes fell overboard and sank before the feasibility of such launchings was established. For more than a week following the invasion of Iwo Jima, LST *776* with Brodie gear and observation planes on board remained offshore. By 26 February, when the first strip on Iwo had been secured, two spotter aircraft of VMO-4 on board the aircraft carrier *Wake Island* took off and reached the new field while it was still under mortar and artillery fire. A plane of VMO-5 reached the strip on the following day. By the last day of February, all of the planes that had made the voyage on aircraft carriers were ashore.

When the first of the observation planes on board LST *776* was finally launched with the help of the Brodie gear on 27 February, it fell into the water. Another attempt made on 1 March was at least partially successful. Of the four planes of VMO-4 launched that day, two received a dunking; the remainder made it to Maple Field No. 1 on Iwo Jima.[24]

Pilots and planes of the two observation squadrons eked out a hazardous existence even after their arrival on the island. While stationary on the airstrip, the small aircraft were frequently hit by enemy fire. VMO-4 spotted for the 3d and 4th Marine Divisions; VMO-5 supported the 3d and 5th Marine Divisions. When VMO-4 completed its mission on Iwo after 19 days, the pilots had flown more than 200 missions. Of the squadron's seven planes, six had been so badly damaged that they had to be scrapped. VMO-5 pilots flew 379 missions in support of the divisions on the ground; their spotter aircraft incurred heavy damage similar to those of VMO-4. One pilot was shot down behind the enemy lines and lost.

The story of Marine aviation in the Central Pacific would be incomplete without mention of the Marines that were members of the Transport Air Group, an organization responsible for hauling passengers and equipment all over the Pacific area.

VMR-952 was organized on 15 June 1943 under MAG-15. At the time of the squadron's activation, it was commanded by Major Harry F. Baker, who in early July was replaced by Major Malcolm S. Mackay. One of the first problems facing the newly commissioned squadron was the replacement of its time-honored R4D Douglas Skytrain transports with the little heard of and lesser known R5C, the Curtiss "Commando," the largest twin-engined plane then in production. The squadron history described the early weeks of the unit's existence at an airfield in California as follows:

> An area was pointed out along the taxiway at Camp Kearney Field; tents were erected, a field telephone was installed, and the three "commandos" then belonging to the Marine Corps were rolled onto the check line.
>
> This was an occasion! Although a few of the squadron's new recruits could boast of a little experience with the "Commando" (they had flown and maintained the three first planes for the short time that they were attached to Marine Aircraft Group 15), the majority of the personnel from the pilots to the mechanics had never been in one. Their time in the R4D had been brief enough, but now this. Never had they been confronted with so large a portion of the unknown at one showing. Amazement soon gave way to curiosity and the quest for knowledge began anew.[25]

In February 1944, the squadron was transferred to Hawaii, where it became attached to Marine Air, Hawaiian Area, working directly under the supervision of that headquarters. The initial mission of the transport squadron was to keep open the lines of communication and supply between Hawaii and Midway, Johnson, and Palmyra Islands. Weekly and semi-weekly flights were made to each island with special additional flights when the need arose. VMR-952 transported personnel and equipment and escorted single engine aircraft to facilitate their movements. Pilots of the transport squadron carried out overwater flights which extended to New Caledonia in the Southwest Pacific

---

[24] RAdm E. M. Eller, Navy HistDiv, ltr to Head, HistBr, G-3 Div, HQMC, dtd 28Sep67, in *Marine Aviation Comment File.*

[25] VMR-952 Hist, *op. cit.,* p. 2.

and included stops at Espiritu Santo and Guadalcanal, as well as at Tarawa, Kwajalein, Majuro, and Eniwetok, in the Central Pacific.

In August 1944, the squadron moved to Emirau, in the Bismarck Archipelago, where it remained until Christmas Day, when it shifted to Guam. Following the capture of the Peleliu airfield in mid-September, transport aircraft of VMR-952 made frequent stops on Peleliu, bringing in urgently needed equipment and departing with wounded. On 4 October 1944, two of the big Curtiss transports, carrying 43 wounded, left Peleliu, inaugurating the first air evacuation of battle casualties from the island.[26] On the following day, three more flights took out an additional 63 casualties.[27] During the extended Peleliu campaign, the planes delivered large quantities of welcome fresh food to the island.

Three Marine transport squadrons and a similar Army Air Forces unit participated in the Iwo Jima operation. These four were VMR-253, -353, and 952, as well as the 9th Troop Carrier Squadron. The Army Air Forces squadron dropped supplies to Marine ground forces on Iwo on 28 February. On the following day, pilots of VMR-952 arrived with urgently needed mortar shells, spare parts for machine guns, blood plasma, and mail. On 3 March, the commanding officer of VMR-952, Lieutenant Colonel Mackay, flew from Guam to Saipan and then to Iwo Jima, where he piloted the first plane to land on the slightly more than 3,000 feet of runway. After the unloading of its 5,500 pounds of mortar ammunition, the aircraft returned to Guam. The next day, a crippled B-29 bomber, returning from a raid on Japan, was the first of many in like condition to make an emergency landing on the Iwo strip.

On each return flight from Iwo, the air transports evacuated casualties. Before the Iwo operation ended, VMR-952 had made 79 trips to the island and evacuated 625 wounded. The remaining air transport squadrons also contributed to the operation. VMR-353, for example, carried out 8 flights during the month of March 1945; and VMR-253 evacuated 100 casualties in 20 flights.

In a direct ratio to the growth of American air power in the Pacific theater was the decline of Japanese air strength. Aside from a growing shortage in raw materials and aviation fuels, there was a breakdown in planning and aircraft production all along the line. As seen from the "enemy side of the hill," the technical and administrative factors that hampered production were explained as follows:

> The urgent need of the combat air corps forced the Army and Navy to place in production several types of experimental aircraft which lacked the required test flights and design modifications. Airplanes were rushed from the experimental hangars to the production line, with the result that the planes were dispatched to the front lines before we could determine the missions which they could most effectively perform. Our engineers lacked the time necessary to prepare maintenance manuals and texts; thus the front-line mechanics, plagued with primitive working conditions, were forced to service airplanes about which they understood little. The confusion of the maintenance crews

---

[26] VMR-952 WarD, Oct44.
[27] Ibid.

inevitably caused equipment malfunction and breakage on a prohibitive scale.[28]

Along with the decline of older equipment and failure of new and better models to replace aircraft that were becoming more and more obsolete as the American war effort swung into full action, there was a corresponding drop of morale in the ranks of Japanese pilots. This did not in any way lessen the enemy pilot's determination to do his duty to the death. Nevertheless, even the enemy was well aware of the human factor involved, though few, if any, positive steps were taken by the Japanese military leadership to ease the lot of their aviators. Enemy flyers, sizing up their adversaries, could see with their own eyes the great value that Americans placed on retaining experienced pilots and air crews. Japanese flying personnel, whose quality and quantity were both in a severe state of decline, avidly observed:

> ... after every mission the Americans sent out flying boats to the areas in which their planes had fought, searching for and rescuing air crews which had been shot down and stood a good chance of surviving aboard life rafts. Every lumbering flying boat, normally an easy catch for our fighter planes, went out on its search mission with nine to twelve escort fighters. Although their duties were extremely hazardous, the crews of these flying boats performed their missions gallantly, and there arose few occasions during the war when groups of men so consistently exposed themselves to multiple dangers. Our pilots could not fail to be impressed with these daring search missions and, despite the fact that enemy pilots manned the flying boats, our men regarded them as unusually courageous.[29]

In contrast with the all-out American attempts to salvage downed air crews was the attitude of the Japanese naval command, which held that the possible loss of a large flying boat could not be risked to effect the rescue of one air crew. A former Japanese naval aviator who participated in and survived action over Midway, Guadalcanal, New Guinea, and Santa Cruz, expressed the following thoughts on the subject of rescue and survival:

> I pondered this situation more than once. For this apathy toward rescuing downed pilots was not merely the attitude of the high command ... our own combat men, the flying mates of the same men who were shot down and adrift at sea, would not, even under orders, take any unnecessary chances to save their lives. Lest this attitude be misconstrued as indicating that our men lacked compassion for their friends, it should be added that they would not expect otherwise should they be the ones to be shot down. Any man who was shot down and managed to survive by inflating his liferaft realized that his chance for continued survival lay entirely within his own hands. Our pilots accepted their abandonment stoically. At any rate, the entire Japanese Navy failed to evince any great interest in rescue operations of this nature.[30]

Along with the men fighting on the ground, and the flying personnel of the other services, Marine pilots in the Central Pacific made their contribution to the overall war effort. The day of close air support that Marines were to deliver in the Philippines had not yet dawned when operations in the Central Pacific

---

[28] Okumiya, Horikoshi, and Caidin, *Zero!*, p. 357.

[29] *Ibid.*, p. 311.
[30] *Ibid.*, p. 312.

got under way. But the Marine air arm left its milestones across the vast reaches of the Central Pacific. Often relegated to arduous but monotonous duty, Marine pilots defied death and disease in areas that did not rate headlines and that are all but forgotten today. They braved the dangers of combat or, if captured, humiliation, torture, and oftentimes death, at the hands of a remorseless enemy. Many survived against all odds the ravages of an equally cruel sea. Others fell victim to flying accidents. All of them, together with those who survived, had an equal share in bringing the war across the Central Pacific to the enemy's doorstep, paving the way for final victory.

PART VI

Iwo Jima

CHAPTER 1

Background to DETACHMENT[1]

The autumn of 1944 saw the Allies poised for a major thrust both in Europe and in the Pacific. On the European Continent, the Allies had liberated almost all of France and stood ready to advance into Germany; in fact, the German western border and the heavily fortified Siegfried Line had already been breached; on the Eastern Front, the Russians had recaptured almost all Russian territory, had driven deep into the Balkans, and were engaged in cutting off sizable German forces in the Baltic countries after an advance into East Prussia. It was evident that Germany, now fighting by herself, having been abandoned by nearly all of her former allies, could stave off the collapse of the Third Reich for only a limited time.

In the Pacific Theater, the year of 1944 had gone badly for the Japanese also. Starting with the American offensive against the Gilberts in November 1943, the inexorable advance across the Pacific had taken American forces 3,000 miles westward by the end of the year. The conquest of Saipan, more than any other reverse, had brought home to Japanese leaders the realization that there no longer was any chance of a Japanese victory. Loss of the Marianas, accompanied by the Battle of the Philippine Sea which all but destroyed Japanese naval aviation, left the Japanese home islands open to American attack. Capture of Peleliu and Ulithi protected the American right flank for a thrust into the Philippines. By late October 1944, American forces had not only gained a foothold on Leyte, but had also inflicted disastrous punishment on the *Imperial Navy* during the Battle for Leyte Gulf.

The beginning of 1945 saw American forces in possession of most of Leyte and with a solid foothold on Luzon. The enemy naval forces, rendered largely impotent by the reverses they had suffered during the previous year, were no longer able to interfere successfully with American operations in the Philippines, whose liberation had become merely a matter of time.

The Allied advance by early 1945 had carried friendly forces deep into enemy territory in a line extending from an area east of the Kurile Islands southward and westward to a point separating the Mariana and Volcano Islands,

---

[1] Unless otherwise noted, the material in this chapter is derived from: LtCol Whitman S. Bartley, *Iwo Jima: Amphibious Epic* (Washington: HistBr, G-3 Div, HQMC, 1954), hereafter Bartley, *Iwo Monograph*; Iwo Jima Comment File (HRB, HistDiv, HQMC), hereafter *Iwo Comments*; Smith, *Approach to the Philippines*; Capt. Clifford P. Morehouse, *The Iwo Jima Operation* (Washington: HistDiv, HQMC, 1946), hereafter Morehouse, *Iwo Jima Campaign*; Morison, *Victory in the Pacific*; Isely and Crowl, *U. S. Marines and Amphibious War.*

thence westward to the Philippines, where the line turned to the southeast and continued southwestward towards New Guinea and Australia (see Map I, Map Section). Even though many thousands of enemy troops remained on bypassed islands such as New Britain, Kavieng, Wake, Marcus, and Yap, these erstwhile Japanese strongholds had been so effectively isolated and neutralized by American air power and submarines that they remained merely a nuisance. With the capture of the Mariana Islands during the summer of 1944, the United States had obtained a strongpoint from which the further assaults towards the Japanese home islands could be launched. As an added steppingstone towards the ultimate invasion of Japan, an advance from the Marianas to the Ryukyus appeared logical. It was also considered necessary to secure a foothold in the Nanpo Shoto. The island finally selected for invasion within the Nanpo Shoto was barely more than a speck of dust and volcanic ashes in the Pacific. Little known to the outside world until 1945, its name was destined soon to be on the lips of thousands of men and women throughout the free world and Japan. That island was Iwo Jima.

HISTORY AND IMPORTANCE OF THE BONIN ISLANDS[2]

From the entrance to Tokyo Bay, a chain of islands, known as the Nanpo Shoto, extends southward for about 750 miles to within 300 miles of the Mariana Islands. The Nanpo Shoto consists of three major groups of islands: the Izut Shoto, the Bonin Islands, also known as the Ogasawara Gunto, and the Volcano Islands, known to the Japanese as the Kazan Retto. Among the latter group of islands lies Iwo Jima, located about 670 miles south of Tokyo, 700 miles north of Guam and nearly halfway between Tokyo and Saipan.

Iwo Jima, translated into English, means Sulphur Island, named for the sulphur deposits that extend to the very surface of the island. Iwo's shape has alternately been compared to that of a pork chop, a dripping ice-cream cone, or an elongated sea shell of the type commonly found on ocean beaches of the mid-Atlantic and southern United States. From northeast to southwest, the island measures less than five miles across; the width varies from approximately two and a half miles in the northern part to only one-half mile in the southern portion. Altogether, Iwo Jima occupies less than eight square miles.

There was little about Iwo Jima or the remainder of the Volcano-Bonin Islands to make them attractive to foreigners in search of areas that could be colonized. In the mid-Sixteenth Century a Spanish navigator sighted the Volcano Islands but thereafter Europeans paid little attention to them. As the century drew to a close, a Japanese explorer dis-

---

[2] Additional sources for this section include: Amphibious Forces South Pacific G–2 Study, *Information on Iwo Jima (Kazan Retto)*, n.d.; *Encyclopedia Britannica*, 1944 Edition, "Ogasawara Jima" and "Volcanic Islands"; Foster R. Dulles, *America in the Pacific* (New York: Houghton Mifflin Company, 1932); Philip T. Terry, *Terry's Japanese Empire* (New York: Houghton Mifflin Company, 1914); Willard Price: *Japan's Islands of Mystery* (New York: John Day Company, 1944).

covered the Bonin Islands and found them to be uninhabited. They remained this way until the early part of the Nineteenth Century, when an assortment of British and American whaling captains sailed into the waters surrounding the islands. A group of colonists, consisting of Englishmen, Portuguese, Italians, Hawaiians, and an American named Nathaniel Savory, who hailed from New England, set out from Hawaii and settled on Chichi Jima under British sponsorship.

In 1853, Commodore Matthew Perry stopped at Chichi Jima and, impressed by the possible use of the island as a coaling station for U. S. Navy vessels, urged the government to purchase a strip of land on the island on which warehouses could be erected. Congress at the time showed little interest in such a venture, and in the end the project was abandoned.

While none of the European powers showed any interest in the largely barren and forbidding island of Iwo Jima, the Japanese had different ideas. Shortly after Perry's visit to Japan in 1853, the Japanese sent officials and colonists to the Volcano-Bonins. Eight years later, Japan laid formal claim to these islands. By 1891, following increased colonization, all of the islands in the Nanpo Shoto had come under the direct jurisdiction of the Tokyo Prefecture and thus became an integral part of the Japanese homeland. A ban on foreign settlement all but stamped out outside influence in the islands with only one exception: on Chichi Jima, the descendants of Nathaniel Savory and his group still celebrated Washington's Birthday and the Fourth of July; on these occasions they proudly displayed Old Glory, an act hardly in keeping with Japanese policy.[3]

By 1943, Japanese colonization of Iwo Jima had resulted in the settlement of almost 1,100 Japanese civilians on the island. Most of these Japanese were either employed at a sugar mill located in the northeastern portion of the island or a sulphur mine and refinery located in the same general area. The inhabitants of Iwo Jima lived in five villages or settlements scattered over the northern half of the island. The northernmost of these was Kita, located in the north central part of Iwo. The village of Nishi was situated in the northwestern part of the island, while Motoyama, the largest built-up area on Iwo, was located in close proximity to the sulphur mine and refinery. The remaining two villages, Higashi and Minami, were located in the northeastern part of the island. (See Map 24).

Only the northern part of Iwo Jima had soil permitting some gardening. Vegetables, sugar cane, and dry grains were raised for local consumption. Rice and all other manufactured consumer items had to be obtained from Japan proper. The inhabitants of Iwo were able to supplement their diet through fishing. In this connection it must be pointed out that one of the most serious impediments to large-scale settlement of the island was the total absence of any source of fresh water, such as a lake or a river. Since the island also lacked wells, water had to be obtained

---

[3] Maj John N. Rentz interview with HistBr, G–3 Div, HQMC, dtd 29Nov51, in *Iwo Comments*.

Map 24

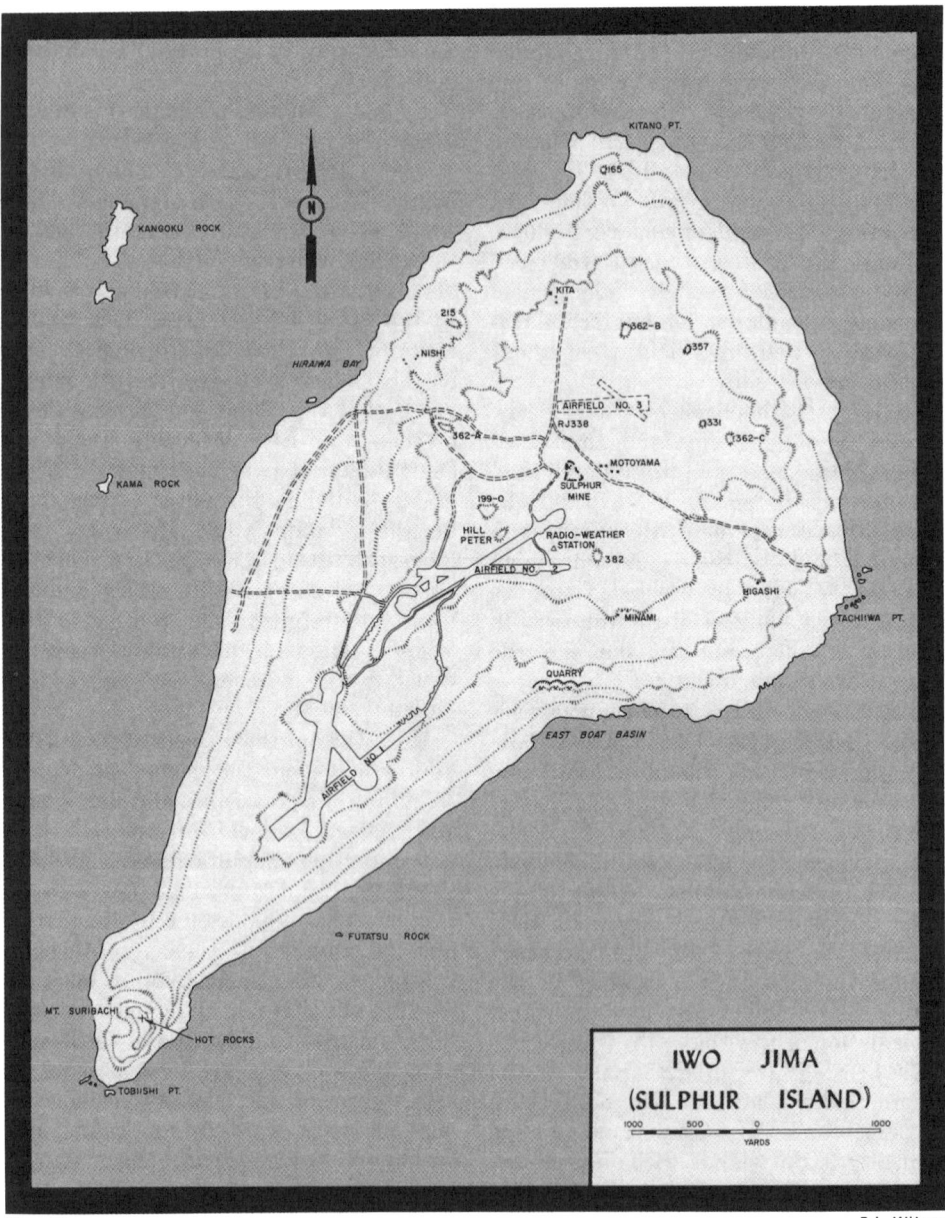

exclusively from rain carefully collected in concrete cisterns. At times, Iwo Jima was supplied with potable water by tankers. Some effort was also made to augment precious water supplies through the distillation of sea water.

While the northern part of the island was hardly designed to become a tourist attraction, the southern half of Iwo Jima was ugly beyond description. Near the narrow southern tip of Iwo, dominating the entire island, stands Mount Suribachi, an extinct volcano, which rises to an elevation of about 550 feet. To the north of Suribachi, inland from the beaches, the ground terraces successively upward to form a broad tableland occupying most of the central section of the island. The area between the northern base of Suribachi and the dome-shaped northern plateau is covered by a deep layer of black, volcanic ash so soft and so much subject to drifting that even walking becomes a problem. Wheeled vehicles cannot negotiate such ground; tracked vehicles can move across it only with difficulty.

The northern plateau consists of several elevations; the highest of these is Hill 382, located just east of Motoyama Airfield No. 2, halfway between Motoyama and Minami; two other hills reach a height of 362 feet. Much of this terrain consists of rough and rocky ground, interspersed with deep gorges and high ridges. Sulphur vapor permeates the entire area with a characteristic smell of rotten eggs. The ground itself is hot in this part of the island; the veils of vapor only serve to accentuate the impression of a ghostly landscape.

The beaches of Iwo Jima from Kitano Point, the northernmost tip of the island, to Tachiiwa Point, two miles to the southeast, are steep and narrow with many rocky shoals offshore. They border terrain that rises sharply towards the northern plateau. Rough and broken ground is typical of all beaches on northern Iwo Jima, in numerous instances with cliffs that drop off sharply towards the water's edge. Beaches along the southwestern and southeastern shores of the island vary in depth from 150 to 500 feet and generally are free from rocks offshore. The terrain would be level, rising gradually towards the interior, if it were not for the existence of sand terraces created by the action of waves. These terraces, which differ in height and width, are undergoing a constant change depending on the surf and winds. Surf conditions at Iwo are unfavorable, even under normal conditions. The island does not possess any anchorage or other inlets to protect ships from the fury of the sea. Steep beaches bring breakers close to the shore, where they can mete out severe punishment to small craft that are inward bound or beached. Winds hitting the shore from the sea serve to increase the fury of the waves.

The climate of Iwo Jima is subtropical with a cool season extending from December through April and a warm season from May through November. Temperatures are moderate, with an average ranging between 63 and 70 degrees during the cool period and 73 through 80 degrees during spring, summer, and autumn. Annual rainfall averages 60 inches, with February the driest month and May the wettest.

The desolation of the island is further accentuated by the sparse vegetation.

A few coarse grasses and gnarled trees are engaged in a perennial struggle for survival. An officer in the *Imperial Japanese Army,* formerly stationed on Iwo, has described it as an "island of sulphur, no water, no sparrow, and no swallow."[4] The only living thing on Iwo, aside from the Japanese, was a bird resembling the American rail, a wading bird related to the cranes, but of medium size.

The above description of Iwo Jima, hardly complimentary in essence, may easily give rise to the question how an island of such poor proportions could assume the strategic importance that both the Japanese and Americans placed on it by the summer of 1944. At least one American, speaking to a Navy Chaplain, expressed the sentiment that "after God got through making the world, he must've took all the dirty ash and rubble left over and made Iwo Jima."[5] Yet the island was destined to witness one of the epic amphibious assaults of World War II, followed by a month-long running battle that cost the assault force heavily in men and equipment and at the same time resulted in the complete destruction of the enemy garrison. The factors that made this otherwise worthless pile of rock and black sand such a prize to friend and enemy alike, require a detailed explanation. Only then can the struggle between 23,000 Japanese and an assault force initially of 60,000 men, combatting each other at closest quarters on this inhospitable island, be readily understood.

JAPANESE DEFENSIVE PREPARATIONS IN THE BONIN-VOLCANO ISLANDS[6]

Japanese military interest in the Volcano-Bonin Islands first arose in 1914, coincident to the outbreak of World War I. Even though the Japanese home islands were never threatened during that war, which Japan entered on the side of the Allies, a few defenses were prepared on Chichi Jima, an island in the Bonin-Volcano Group about 175 miles north-northeast of Iwo Jima. On 10 August 1920, the *Chichi Jima Branch, Army Fortification Department,* was formally established, followed by the construction of fortifications beginning in June 1921. As a result of the Naval Arms Limitation Agreement, concluded on 6 February 1922, work on the fortifications was halted.[7] Since all of the action had occurred elsewhere, the Japanese garrison on Chichi Jima led a peaceful existence and never fired a shot in anger.

During the postwar period and

---

[4] Major Yoshitaka Horie, IJA, "Explanation of Japanese Defense Plan and Battle of Iwo Jima," dtd, 25Jan46.

[5] Capt Raymond Henri, USMC, *Iwo Jima —Springboard to Final Victory* (New York: U. S. Camera Publishing Corporation, 1945), hereafter Henri, *Springboard to Final Victory.*

[6] Additional sources for this section include: Smith and Finch, *Coral and Brass*; Richard F. Newcomb, *Iwo Jima* (New York, Chicago, and San Francisco: Holt, Rinehart, and Winston, 1965), hereafter Newcomb, *Iwo Jima,* quoted with permission; Richard F. Newcomb notes for *Iwo Jima,* hereafter *Newcomb notes;* Heinl, *Soldiers of the Sea;* Sakai, Caidin, and Saito, *Samurai!;* Hayashi and Coox, *Kogun;* Capt Raymond Henri, et al, *The U. S. Marines on Iwo Jima* (Washington: The Infantry Journal, 1945), hereafter Henri et al, *Marines on Iwo Jima.*

[7] War History Office, Defense Agency of Japan ltr to Head, HistBr, G–3 Div, HQMC, dtd 21Aug69 in *Iwo Comments,* hereafter *Japanese Defense Agency Comment.*

throughout the twenties and thirties, the status of Chichi Jima did not undergo any appreciable change. Though a small garrison remained on the island, no additional installations were constructed. On Iwo Jima, the presence of any military installation was even less conspicuous, though by 1937 a wooden sign had been erected by the *Imperial Navy*, bearing a legend in both Japanese and English, clearly cautioning the careless trespasser from recording or photographing such installations as he might encounter on the island.

At the time of the Japanese attack on Pearl Harbor an Army force of about 3,700–3,800 men garrisoned Chichi Jima. In addition, about 1,200 naval personnel manned the Chichi Jima Naval Base, a small seaplane base, the radio and weather station, and various gunboat, subchaser, and minesweeping units.[8] On Iwo Jima, the *Imperial Navy* had constructed an airfield about 2,000 yards northeast of Mount Suribachi. Initially stationed on this field were 1,500 naval aviation personnel and 20 aircraft.[9]

In the wake of the American seizure of the Marshalls and devastating air attacks against Truk in the Carolines during February 1944, the Japanese military leadership was forced to conduct an agonizing reappraisal of the military situation. All indications pointed to an American drive towards the Marianas and Carolines. To counter such a move, it became necessary to establish an inner line of defense extending generally northward from the Carolines to the Marianas, and from thence to the Volcano-Bonin Islands. In March 1944, the *Thirty-First Army*, commanded by General Hideyoshi Obata, was activated for the purpose of garrisoning this inner line. The commander of the Chichi Jima garrison was placed nominally in command of Army and Navy units in the Volcano-Bonin Islands.

Following the American seizure of most of the Marshalls, both Army and Navy reinforcements were sent to Iwo Jima. Five hundred men from the naval base at Yokosuka and an additional 500 from Chichi Jima reached Iwo during March and April 1944. At the same time, with the arrival of reinforcements from Chichi Jima and the home islands, the Army garrison on Iwo Jima had reached a strength of over 5,000 men, equipped with 13 artillery pieces, 200 light and heavy machine guns, and 4,552 rifles.[10] In addition, the defense boasted 14 120mm coast artillery guns, 12 heavy antiaircraft guns, and 30 25mm dual-mount antiaircraft guns.[11]

The loss of the Marianas during the summer of 1944 greatly increased the importance of the Volcano-Bonins for the Japanese, who were fully cognizant

---

[8] *Japanese Defense Agency Comment.*

[9] To the Japanese, this first of two airstrips on Iwo Jima to be completed prior to the American invasion was known alternately as Chidori Airfield or Motoyama Airfield No. 1. A second airfield, located about 2,000 yards northeast of the first one, in the very center of the island, was known to the Japanese as Motoyama No. 2. A third airfield north of the village of Motoyama was still under construction at the time of the American landings.

[10] CinCPac-CinCPOA Item No. 9652, "A Report from the Chief of Staff of the Thirty-First Army to the Chief of Staff, Central Pacific Fleet," dtd 31May44.

[11] *Ibid.*

that the loss of these islands would facilitate American air raids against the home islands. Such raids, beyond any doubt, would raise havoc with the entire Japanese war production program, and deal a severe blow to civilian morale. Final Japanese plans for the defense of the Volcano-Bonins were overshadowed by the fact that the *Imperial Navy* had already lost most of its naval strength and no longer constituted a major factor in frustrating possible American landings. Moreover, aircraft losses throughout 1944 had been so heavy that, even if war production was not materially slowed by American air attacks, combined Japanese air strength was not expected to increase to 3,000 aircraft until March or April of 1945. Even then, these planes could not be used from bases in the home islands against Iwo Jima because their range did not exceed 550 miles; besides, all available aircraft had to be hoarded for possible use on Formosa and adjacent islands where land bases were available in close proximity.[12]

In a postwar study, Japanese staff officers described the strategy applied in the defense of Iwo Jima in the following terms:

> In the light of the above situation, seeing that it was impossible to conduct our air, sea, and ground operations on Iwo Island toward ultimate victory, it was decided that in order to gain time necessary for the preparation of the Homeland defense, our forces should rely solely upon the established defensive equipment in that area, checking the enemy by delaying

---

[12] USA, FEC, HistDiv, "Operations in the Central Pacific"—Japanese Studies in World War II (Japanese Monograph No. 48, OCMH), p. 62.

tactics. Even the suicidal attacks by small groups of our Army and Navy airplanes, the surprise attacks by our submarines, and the actions of parachute units, although effective, could be regarded only as a strategical ruse on our part. It was a most depressing thought that we had no available means left for the exploitation of the strategical opportunities which might from time to time occur in the course of these operations.[13]

Even before the fall of Saipan in June 1944, Japanese planners knew that Iwo Jima would have to be reinforced materially if it were to the held for any length of time, and preparations were made to send sizable numbers of men and quantities of materiel to that island. In late May, Lieutenant General Tadamichi Kuribayashi was summoned to the office of the Prime Minister, General Hideki Tojo, who informed the general that he had been chosen to defend Iwo Jima to the last. Kuribayashi was further apprised of the importance of this assignment when Tojo pointed out that the eyes of the entire nation were focused on the defense of Iwo. Fully aware of the implications of the task entrusted to him, the general accepted. By 8 June, Kuribayashi was on his way to his toughest and final assignment, determined to convert Iwo Jima into an invincible fortress that would withstand any type of attack from any quarter.

The Japanese could hardly have selected an individual better qualified to lead the defense of Iwo Jima. As a member of a *Samurai* family, the 54-year-old Kuribayashi already had a distinguished military career behind him at the time he received the Iwo as-

---

[13] *Ibid.*

signment. In the 30 years in which he had served the Empire, the general had seen much of the world. During the late twenties, as a captain, Kuribayashi had spent two years in the United States performing attache duties. In the course of his travels in America, he gained a keen appreciation of American economic power, as expressed in a letter to his wife:

> The United States is the last country in the world that Japan should fight. Its industrial potentiality is huge and fabulous, and the people are energetic and versatile. One must never underestimate the American's fighting ability.[14]

Following his travels in the New World, Kuribayashi served in the Japanese cavalry. In August 1936, as a lieutenant colonel, he commanded a cavalry regiment. For the next two years, by then a colonel, he served in the Ministry of War. In 1940, he was promoted to brigadier general and given command of a cavalry brigade. Following the Pearl Harbor attack, he participated in the occupation of Hong Kong as chief of staff of the *Twenty-Third Army*. In 1943, General Kuribayashi, by then a major general, was recalled to Tokyo, where he commanded the *Imperial Guards* until his appointment as commander of the Iwo Jima Garrison.[15]

General Kuribayashi arrived on Iwo Jima between 8 and 10 June. As a result, he was on the island when TG 58.1 and TG 58.4, consisting of seven

[14] Tadamichi Kuribayashi ltr to Yoshii Kuribayashi, as cited in Newcomb, *Iwo Jima*, pp. 8–9.

[15] For a detailed breakdown of General Kuribayashi's military assignments, see *Japanese Defense Agency Comment*; Hayashi and Coox, *Kōgun*.

aircraft carriers under the command of Rear Admiral Joseph J. Clark, unleashed their first strike against the Bonins, which resulted in the destruction of 10 Japanese fighters in the air and a possible 70 planes on the ground in two days of operations. In addition, 21 seaplanes were destroyed on Chichi Jima. On 24 June 1944, the American carriers under Admiral Clark again struck at Iwo. This time, 80 Japanese fighters rose to challenge the intruders. When the smoke of battle over Iwo cleared nearly half of the Japanese fighters had been destroyed. One of the Japanese fighter pilots who survived the fierce dogfights over Iwo Jima that day commented:

> The loss of forty planes and pilots in a single action staggered me. Equally disturbing was the sight of our inexperienced pilots falling in flames, one after the other, as the Hellcats blasted our outmoded Zeros from the Sky. How much like Lae the battle had been! Except that now the obsolescent planes were Zeros, and the inexperienced pilots were Japanese. The war had run full circle.[16]

The loss of the 40 sorely needed fighters on 24 June was not the only disaster that befell Rear Admiral Teiichi Matsunaga, commanding the Japanese naval forces on Iwo. Not one of 20 torpedo bombers he sent out against the American carriers returned to the island. A third wave of 41 aircraft dispatched against the task force not only failed to inflict any damage on the carriers, but in the process nearly half of the Japanese planes were shot out of the sky.

On the evening of 2 July, Japanese radio monitors on Iwo Jima noted a sudden increase in their adversary's

[16] Sakai, Caidin, and Saito, *Samurai!*, p. 213.

radio traffic. Though the Japanese were unable to decipher the code, the strength of the signals indicated to experienced monitors that an American force was in fairly close proximity to Iwo Jima. Early the following morning, American carrier-based aircraft once again raided the island. While the 40 Japanese fighters remaining on Iwo took to the air to intercept the attacking American planes and soon became engaged in heavy dogfights, a squadron of bombers pounced on the island and bombed the airstrip in five waves. Not a single fighter opposed them, since all of the Zeros had been diverted by the American fighters. At the end of the day it became apparent that once again the Japanese had lost half of their remaining fighters, which left only 20 of the original 80. The air battle over Iwo continued on 4 July. At the end of the day, only nine Zeros, most of them badly damaged, returned to Iwo. This left Japanese aviation on the island with nine damaged fighters and eight torpedo bombers which had somehow escaped the holocaust in their revetments.

On the following day, this remnant of Japanese naval aviation on Iwo was dispatched on a final mission: to seek out the American naval task force and destroy as many carriers as possible. The fighter pilots were admonished to stay with the eight torpedo bombers and avoid combat with intercepting American fighters at all costs. It was made clear to both fighter and bomber pilots that they were engaged in a one-way mission from which they were not expected to return. When the attack force approached Admiral Clark's carriers it proved no match for the intercepting fighters. The slow, sluggish Japanese bombers, heavily loaded with their torpedoes, were shot down one after the other by the attacking Hellcats. One of the few Japanese pilots to survive this action reported that in less than a minute seven of the bombers had been destroyed by American fighters. Late on 5 July, four dispirited Japanese fighter pilots and one bomber pilot returned to Iwo.

In addition to the annihilation of virtually all Iwo-based aircraft, another ordeal was in store for the Japanese garrison. On the day following the unsuccessful bombing mission, a U. S. naval force boldly appeared within sight of the island and subjected the Japanese to a naval bombardment from point-blank range. What it felt like to be on the receiving end of such a bombardment has been recorded by one of the Japanese:

> For two days we cowered like rats, trying to dig ourselves deeper into the acrid volcanic dust and ash of Iwo Jima. Never have I felt so helpless, so puny, as I did during those two days. There was nothing we could do, there was no way in which we could strike back. The men screamed and cursed and shouted, they shook their fists and swore revenge, and too many of them fell to the ground, their threats choking on the blood which bubbled through great gashes in their throats. Virtually every last structure on Iwo Jima was torn to splintered wreckage. Not a building stood. Not a tent escaped. Not even the most dismal shack remained standing. Everything was blown to bits. The four fighter planes which had returned from our last sortie were smashed by shells into flaming pieces of junk.[17]

---

[17] *Ibid.*, p. 235.

For several days the survivors of the bombardment remained in a state of shock from their ordeal and frantic calls for reinforcements went out in view of what appeared to be an imminent invasion of the island. When several Japanese transport ships appeared on the horizon, the garrison rejoiced, only to fall into deeper gloom and frustration when American submarines torpedoed these ships before their very eyes. Lookouts posted atop Mount Suribachi scanned the ocean for signs of the approaching invasion fleet, and false alarms were frequent.

Much to the surprise of the Japanese garrison on Iwo, an American invasion of the island did not materialize during the summer of 1944. There was little doubt that in time the Americans would be compelled to attack the island. General Kuribayashi, who had personally witnessed Admiral Clark's second air strike against Iwo, as well as the naval bombardment in early July, was more determined than ever to exact the heaviest possible price for Iwo when the invaders came. Without naval and air support, it was a foregone conclusion that Iwo could not hold out indefinitely against an invader possessing both naval and air supremacy.

As a first step in readying Iwo for a prolonged defense, the island commander ordered the evacuation of all civilians from the island. This was accomplished by late July. Next came an overall plan for defense of the island. Lieutenant General Hideyoshi Obata, Commanding General of the *Thirty-First Army*, early in 1944 had been responsible for the defense of Iwo prior to his return to the Marianas. At the time, faithful to the doctrine that an invasion had to be met practically at the water's edge, Obata had ordered the emplacement of artillery and the construction of pillboxes near the beaches. General Kuribayashi had different ideas. Instead of a futile effort to hold the beaches, he planned to defend the latter with a sprinkling of automatic weapons and infantry. Artillery, mortars, and rockets would be emplaced on the foot and slopes of Mount Suribachi, as well as in the high ground to the north of Chidori airfield.

A prolonged defense of the island required the preparation of an extensive system of caves and tunnels, for the naval bombardment had clearly shown that surface installations could not withstand extensive shelling. To this end, mining engineers were dispatched from Japan to draw blueprints for projected underground fortifications that would consist of elaborate tunnels at varying levels to assure good ventilation and minimize the effect of bombs or shells exploding near the entrances or exits.

At the same time, reinforcements were gradually beginning to reach the island. As commander of the *109th Infantry Division*, General Kuribayashi decided first of all to shift the *2d Independent Mixed Brigade*, consisting of about 5,000 men under Major General Kotau Osuga, from Chichi to Iwo. With the fall of Saipan, 2,700 men of the *145th Infantry Regiment*, commanded by Colonel Masuo Ikeda, were diverted to Iwo. These reinforcements, who reached the island during July and August 1944, brought the strength of the garrison up to approximately 12,700 men. Next came 1,233 members of the *204th Naval Construction Battalion*, who quickly set to work constructing concrete pillboxes and other fortifications.

On 10 August, Rear Admiral Toshinosuka Ichimaru reached Iwo, shortly followed by 2,216 naval personnel, including naval aviators and ground crews.[18] The admiral, a renowned Japanese aviator, had been crippled in an airplane crash in the mid-twenties and, ever since the outbreak of the war, had chafed under repeated rear echelon assignments. More than pleased with finally having been granted a combat assignment, Ichimaru penned a poem which began:

> Grateful to his Majesty for giving me
> A chance to fight on the foremost front.
> I depart with buoyant heart,
> Filled with joy and exultation.[19]

Next to arrive on Iwo were artillery units and five antitank battalions. Even though numerous supply ships on route to Iwo Jima were sunk by American submarines and aircraft, substantial quantities of materiel did reach Iwo during the summer and autumn of 1944. By the end of the year, General Kuribayashi had available to him 361 artillery pieces of 75mm or larger caliber, a dozen 320mm mortars, 65 medium (150mm) and light (81mm) mortars, 33 naval guns 80mm or larger, and 94 antiaircraft guns 75mm or larger. In addition to this formidable array of large caliber guns, the Iwo defenses could boast of more than 200 20mm and 25mm antiaircraft guns and 69 37mm and 47mm antitank guns. The fire power of the artillery was further supplemented with a variety of rockets varying from an eight-inch type that weighed 200 pounds and could travel between 2,000–3,000 yards, to a giant 550-pound projectile that had a range of more than 7,500 yards.[20] Altogether, 70 rocket guns and their crews reached Iwo Jima. As a result of American attacks against Japanese shipping, a number of artillery pieces were lost. Others reached Iwo, but their crews, travelling on other ships, drowned en route. In several instances, guns and crews arrived intact, only to discover that vital optical sights, shipped on other vessels, had been lost. Large shipments of barbed wire, essential for the defense of Iwo, never reached the island; the ships carrying this vital commodity were sunk en route.

In order to further strengthen the Iwo defenses, the *26th Tank Regiment*, which had been stationed at Pusan, Korea after extended service in Manchuria, received orders for Iwo. The officer commanding this regiment was Lieutenant Colonel Baron Takeichi Nishi. Like Kuribayashi, he was a cavalryman, had travelled extensively abroad, and in the 1932 Olympics at Los Angeles had won a gold medal in the equestrian competitions. The regiment, consisting of 600 men and 28 tanks, sailed from Japan in mid-July on board

---

[18] For a breakdown of Japanese naval units on Iwo Jima, see *Japanese Defense Agency Comment*.

[19] Newcomb, *Iwo Jima*, p. 14.

[20] Information on the Japanese artillery buildup on Iwo Jima was compiled from data contained in CinCPac-CinCPOA Bul 152-45, dtd 1Jul45, pp. 38, 76, 80, 84; CinCPac-CPOA Bul No. 6-45, Supplmt 4, dtd 4Jun45; VAC IntelRpt, Iwo Jima, p. 18.

the *Nisshu Maru*. As the ship, sailing in a convoy, approached Chichi Jima on 18 July 1944, it was torpedoed by an American submarine, the USS *Cobia*. Even though only two members of the *26th Tank Regiment* failed to survive the sinking, all of the regiment's 28 tanks went to the bottom of the sea. It would be December before these tanks could be replaced, but 22 finally reached Iwo Jima. Initially, Colonel Nishi had planned to employ his armor as a type of "roving fire brigade," to be committed at focal points of combat. The rugged terrain precluded such employment and in the end, under the colonel's watchful eyes, the tanks were deployed in static positions. They were either buried or their turrets were dismounted and so skillfully emplaced in the rocky ground that they were practically invisible from the air or from the ground.

For the remainder of 1944, the construction of fortifications on Iwo also went into high gear. The Japanese were quick to discover that the black volcanic ash that existed in abundance all over the island could be converted into concrete of superior quality when mixed with cement. Pillboxes near the beaches north of Mount Suribachi were constructed of reinforced concrete, many of them with walls four feet thick. At the same time, an elaborate system of caves, concrete blockhouses, and pillboxes was established. One of the results of American air attacks and naval bombardment in the early summer of 1944 had been to drive the Japanese so deep underground that eventually their defenses became virtually immune to air or naval bombardment.

While the Japanese on Peleliu Island in the Western Carolines, also awaiting American invasion, had turned the improvement of natural caves into an art, the defenders of Iwo literally developed it into a science. Because of the importance of the underground positions, 25 percent of the garrison was detailed to tunneling. Positions constructed underground ranged in size from small caves for a few men to several underground chambers capable of holding 300 or 400 men. In order to prevent personnel from becoming trapped in any one excavation, the subterranean installations were provided with multiple entrances and exits, as well as stairways and interconnecting passageways. Special attention had to be paid to providing adequate ventilation, since sulphur fumes were present in many of the underground installations. Fortunately for the Japanese, most of the volcanic stone on Iwo was so soft that it could be cut with hand tools.

General Kuribayashi established his command post in the northern part of the island, about 500 yards northeast of Kita village and south of Kitano Point. This installation, 75 feet underground, consisted of caves of varying sizes, connected by 500 feet of tunnels. Here the island commander had his own warroom in one of three small concrete-enclosed chambers; the two similar rooms were used by the staff. A communications blockhouse protruded above the ground level. This structure was 150 feet long, 70 feet wide; the roof had a thickness of 10 feet with walls five feet wide. The blockhouse was manned by 70 radio operators who worked in shifts.

Farther south on Hill 382, the second

highest elevation on the island, the Japanese constructed a radio and weather station. Nearby, on an elevation just southeast of the station, an enormously large blockhouse was constructed which served as the headquarters of Colonel Chosaku Kaido, who commanded all artillery on Iwo Jima. Other hills in the northern portion of the island were tunnelled out. All of these major excavations featured multiple entrances and exits and were virtually invulnerable to damage from artillery or aerial bombardment. Typical of the thoroughness employed in the construction of subterranean defenses was the main communications center south of Kita village, which was so spacious that it contained a chamber 150 feet long and 70 feet wide. This giant structure was similar in construction and thickness of walls and ceilings to General Kuribayashi's command post. A 500-foot-long tunnel 75 feet below the ground led into this vast subterranean chamber.[21]

Perhaps the most ambitious construction project to get under way was the creation of an underground passageway designed to link all major defense installations on the island. As projected, this passageway was to have attained a total length of almost 17 miles. Had it been completed, it would have linked the formidable underground installations in the northern portion of Iwo Jima with the southern part of the island, where the northern slope of Mount Suribachi alone harbored several thousand yards of tunnels.[22] By the time the Marines landed on Iwo Jima, more than 11 miles of tunnels had been completed.[23]

A supreme effort was required of the Japanese personnel engaged in the underground construction work. Aside from the heavy physical labor, the men were exposed to heat varying from 90 to 120 degrees Fahrenheit, as well as sulphur fumes that forced them to wear gas masks. In numerous instances a work detail had to be relieved after only five minutes. When renewed American air attacks struck the island on 8 December 1944 and thereafter became a daily occurrence until the actual invasion of the island, a large number of men had to be diverted to repairing the damaged airfields.

While Iwo Jima was being converted into a major fortress with all possible speed, General Kuribayashi formulated his final plans for the defense of the island. This plan, which constituted a radical departure from the defensive tactics used by the Japanese earlier in the war, provided for the following major points:

a. In order to prevent disclosing their positions to the Americans, Japanese artillery was to remain silent during the expected prelanding bombardment. No fire would be directed against the American naval vessels.

b. Upon landing on Iwo Jima, the Americans were not to encounter any opposition on the beaches.

c. Once the Americans had advanced about 500 yards inland, they were to be taken under the concentrated fire of automatic weapons stationed in the vicinity of Motoyama airfield to the north,

---

[21] POW Interrogation Rpt, Iwo Jima, 3d MarDiv G-2 Language Sec, dtd 2Mar45.
[22] *VAC C-2 Rpt*, Encl H.

[23] *Japanese Defense Agency Comment.*

as well as automatic weapons and artillery emplaced both on the high ground to the north of the landing beaches and Mount Suribachi to the south.

d. After inflicting maximum possible casualties and damage on the landing force, the artillery was to displace northward from the high ground near the Chidori airfield.

In this connection, Kuribayashi stressed once again that he planned to conduct an elastic defense designed to wear down the invasion force. Such prolonged resistance naturally required the defending force to stockpile rations and ammunition. To this end the island commander accumulated a food reserve to last for two and a half months, ever mindful of the fact that the trickle of supplies that was reaching Iwo Jima during the latter part of 1944 would cease altogether once the island was surrounded by a hostile naval force.

Opposition to General Kuribayashi's unorthodox defense plan, which reflected changes in earlier Japanese military doctrine, was not long in developing. It must be noted that the defensive form of combat in itself was distasteful to the Japanese, who early in the war had been loath to admit to themselves that the *Imperial Army* would ever be forced to engage in this form of combat. In fact, "so pronounced was their dislike for the defensive that tactical problems illustrating this type of combat were extremely rare."[24] According to standard Japanese doctrine, the object of the defensive was to inflict on the superior hostile forces such losses by firepower—disposed appropriately on the terrain and behind man-made works—that the initial disparity of forces became equalized to the point of eventually permitting the defense force to go over to the offensive.

As far as the objective in defending Iwo Jima was concerned, General Kuribayashi's plan adhered closely to the prevalent doctrine. It was the manner of execution that aroused the displeasure of some of his subordinates, for during the period following the American capture of Guadalcanal and up until the end of the fighting on Saipan, it had become almost standard procedure for the Japanese to defend the beaches in an attempt to drive the invader back into the sea. Once the position of the defending force on an island had become untenable, a brave *banzai* charge, in which the defenders sought victory in death, usually terminated all organized resistance. Kuribayashi's intent of conserving his manpower and not staking all on a defense of the beaches or futile *banzai* charges was the epitome of the revised Japanese doctrine, already employed at Biak in the Southwest Pacific, to some extent in the Palaus, and very extensively on Luzon in the Philippines.

The most vociferous opposition to General Kuribayashi's plan of defense, strangely enough, came from his own chief of staff, Colonel Shizuichi Hori, a former instructor at the Japanese Military Academy. The latter was strongly supported by General Osuga, commander of the *2d Independent Mixed Brigade*. In an unusual display of solidarity between Army and Navy, Captain Samaji Inouye, commanding the *Naval Guard Force*, sided wih the two

---

[24] MilIntelDiv, WD, Handbook on Japanese Military Forces, TM–E 30–480 (Washington, 1944), p. 99.

Army dissidents. According to one source who was stationed on Iwo during the summer of 1944:

> Arguments raged in July, August, and September. Arguments were not confined to Iwo command alone, but taken to Tokyo's Army and Navy staffs. In August Tokyo asked Nazi German General Staff's opinion. Germany replied that waterfront repulse was unfeasible under overwhelming American shelling and bombings according to German experience. It was not that German reply was the decisive factor. But anyway, supporters of the waterfront idea gradually dwindled. Kuribayashi made some compromise and the hot arguments ended in September.[25]

Finally, in December 1944, General Kuribayashi decided to restore unity to his command. He dismissed Colonel Hori as chief of staff of the *109th Division* and replaced him with Colonel Tadashi Takaishi. General Osuga, commander of the *2d Independent Brigade,* was succeeded by Major General Sadasue Senda, an experienced artilleryman who had seen combat in Manchuria and China. Altogether, a total of 18 officers were replaced.

During the final months of preparing Iwo Jima for the defense, General Kuribayashi saw to it that the strenuous work of building fortifications did not interefere with the training of units. As an initial step towards obtaining more time for training, he ordered work on the northernmost airfield on the island halted. In an operations order issued in early December, the island commander set 11 February 1945 as the target date for completion of defensive preparations and specified that personnel were to spend 70 percent of their time in training and 30 percent in construction work.

Despite intermittent harassment by American submarines and aircraft, additional personnel continued to arrive on Iwo until February 1945. By that time General Kuribayashi had under his command a force totalling between 21,000 and 23,000 men, including both Army and Navy units.[26]

General Kuribayashi made several changes in his basic defense plan in the months preceding the American invasion of Iwo Jima. The final stratagem, which became effective in January 1945, called for the creation of strong, mutually supporting positions which were to be defended to the death. Neither large scale counterattacks, withdrawals, nor *banzai* charges were contemplated. The southern portion of Iwo in the proximity of Mount Suribachi was organized into a semi-independent defense sector. Fortifications included casemated coast artillery and automatic weapons in mutually supporting pillboxes. The narrow isthmus to the north of Suribachi was to be defended by a small infantry force. On the other hand,

---

[25] Interview of Capt Tsunezo Wachi, IJN, Former CO, Iwo Navy Garrison, from Feb-Oct44, by Fred Saito, 25Jan64, in Saito ltr to Richard F. Newcomb, 25Jan64, p. 5, in *Newcomb Notes.*

[26] Available sources disagree as to the exact strength of the Iwo Jima garrison. Bartley, in *Iwo Monograph,* App VI, pp. 230–231, places Japanese strength on 19Feb45 at 20,530–21,060. Morehouse, in *Iwo Jima Campaign,* App C, p. 159C, estimates enemy strength at 21,000–22,000. A Japanese postwar report that mentions a figure of 17,500 Army and 5,500 Navy personnel is cited in Hayashi and Coox, *Kogun,* p. 137. Japanese postwar sources place the total of Japanese troops on Iwo Jima at 20,933, consisting of 13,586 Army and 7,347 Navy. *Japanese Defense Agency Comment.*

this entire area was exposed to the fire of artillery, rocket launchers, and mortars emplaced on Suribachi to the south and the high ground to the north.

A main line of defense, consisting of mutually supporting positions in depth, extended from the northwestern part of the island to the southeast, along a general line from the cliffs to the northwest, across Motoyama Airfield No. 2 to Minami village. From there it continued eastward to the shoreline just south of Tachiiwa Point. (See Map 25). The entire line of defense was dotted with pillboxes, bunkers, and blockhouses. Colonel Nishi's immobilized tanks, carefully dug in and camouflaged, further reinforced this fortified area, whose strength was supplemented by the broken terrain. A second line of defense extended from a few hundred yards south of Kitano Point at the very northern tip of Iwo across the still uncompleted Airfield No. 3, to Motoyama village, and then to the area between Tachiiwa Point and the East Boat Basin. This second line contained fewer man-made fortifications, but the Japanese took maximum advantage of natural caves and other terrain features.

As an additional means of protecting the two completed airfields on Iwo from direct assault, the Japanese constructed a number of antitank ditches near the fields and mined all natural routes of approach. When, on 2 January, more than a dozen B-24 bombers raided Airfield No. 1 and inflicted heavy damage, Kuribayashi diverted more than 600 men, 11 trucks, and 2 bulldozers for immediate repairs. As a result, the airfield again became operational after only 12 hours. Eventually, 2,000 men were assigned the job of filling the bomb craters with as many as 50 men detailed to each bomb crater. The end of 1944 saw American B-24 bombers over Iwo Jima almost every night while U. S. Navy carriers and cruisers frequently sortied into the Bonins. On 8 December, American aircraft dropped more than 800 tons of bombs on Iwo Jima, which shook the Japanese up but did very little real damage to the island defenses. Even though frequent air raids interfered with the Japanese defensive preparations and robbed the garrison of much badly needed sleep, progress of the work was not materially slowed.

Despite the air raids, which became a daily occurrence in December, and increasing isolation from the homeland, morale remained high among members of the Iwo garrison. Japanese national holidays, such as the birthday of Emperor Meiji on 11 February, were celebrated with rice cake and an extra ration of *sake*. At the same time, the Iwo Jima defenders, gathered in small groups near their battle stations, listened to a Tokyo broadcast in which a song, especially dedicated to the defense of Iwo, was released to the public. Many of the men wore white headbands, similar to the ones worn by *kamikaze* pilots, to demonstrate their determination to die in defense of the island. Inside the pillboxes, for all to see and burn into their minds, were copies of the "Courageous Battle Vow," which pledged all to dedicate themselves to the defense of Iwo, and to fight to the last with any and all weapons at hand. The pledge appropriately ended with the following words:

Each man will make it his duty to kill

Map 25

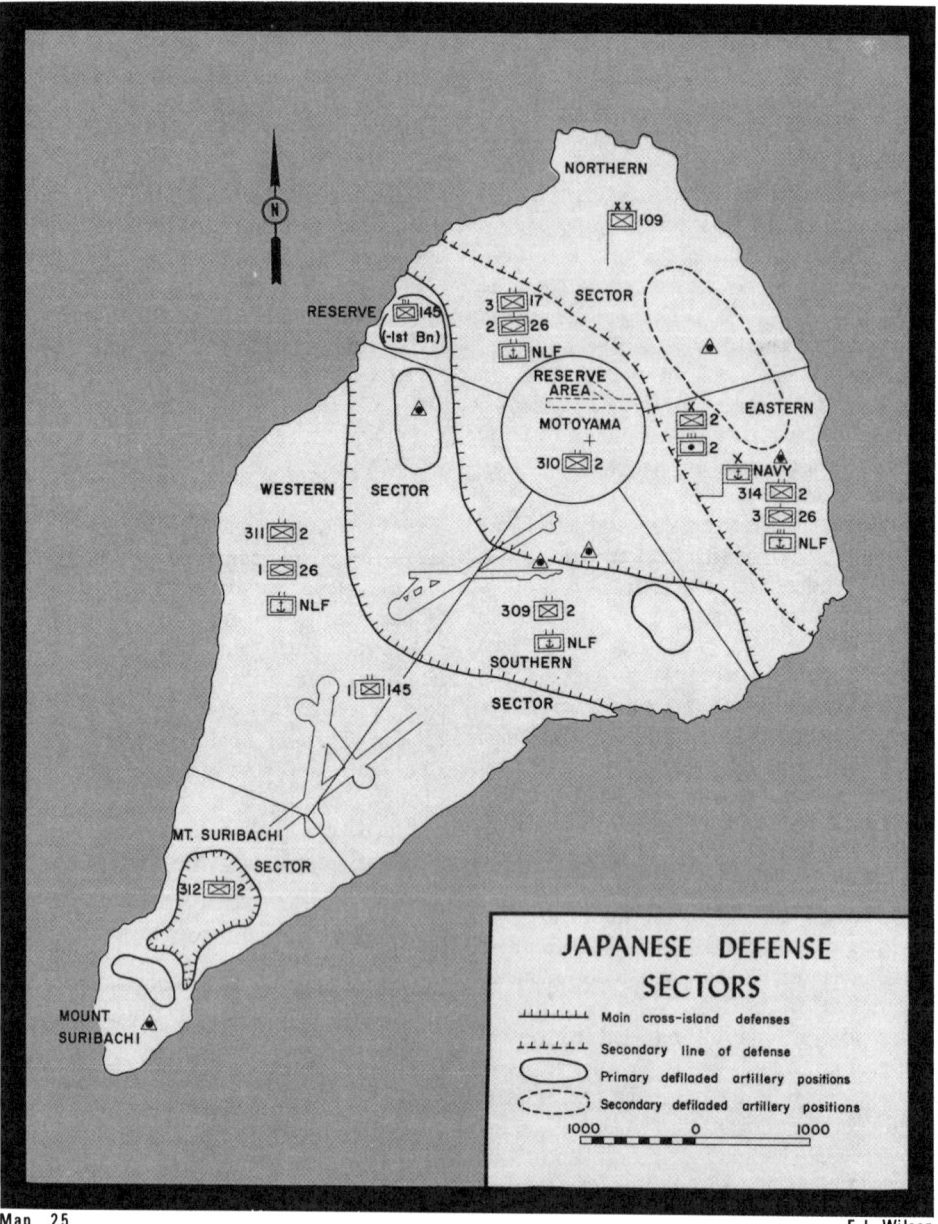

ten of the enemy before dying. Until we are destroyed to the last man, we shall harass the enemy by guerrilla tactics."

As early as 5 January 1945, Admiral Ichimaru conducted a briefing of naval personnel at his command post in which he informed them of the destruction of the Japanese Fleet at Leyte, loss of the Philippines, and the expectation that Iwo would shortly be invaded. Exactly one month later, Japanese radio operators on Iwo reported to the island commander that code signals of American aircraft had undergone an ominous change. On the 13th, a Japanese naval patrol plane spotted 170 American ships moving northwestward from Saipan. All Japanese troops in the Bonin Islands were alerted and occupied their battle positions. On Iwo Jima, preparations for the pending battle had been completed, and the defenders were ready.

---

[27] 4th MarDiv Translations, Iwo Jima, 21 Feb45.

CHAPTER 2

Offensive Plans and Preparations[1]

Preliminary planning for the seizure of an objective in the Volcano-Bonin Islands began as early as September 1943, when the Joint War Plans Committee, a planning agency of the Joint Chiefs of Staff, advocated such a move.[2] However, because of impending military operations in the Gilberts, Marshalls, and Marianas no further preparation for any operations against the Bonins were made until the summer of 1944. The successful completion of the Saipan operation in July brought the continuation of operations in the Central Pacific into sharper focus. In a conference held in Washington by top echelon U. S. military leaders from 13-22 July 1944, the senior members of the Joint War Plans Committee presented to the Joint Chiefs the possible courses of action in continuing the war against Japan. Plans for the bombing of the Japanese home islands figured prominently in these discussions. In this connection, the use of the Marianas as a base for long-range bombers was again discussed, as well as the need for seizing the Bonins to facilitate such air operations.[3]

In the course of a visit to Hawaii in mid-July 1944, Admiral Ernest J. King discussed with Admiral Chester W. Nimitz some of the decisions which the Joint Chiefs had reached. He apprised Nimitz of the fact that the Army Air Forces had been ordered to set up four B-29 groups in the Marianas for long-range bombing. In time, 12 groups of B-29s were to be based in the Marianas. In this connection, King brought up the desirability of establishing bases in the Bonins to furnish fighter escorts for the B-29s. With oper-

---

[1] Unless otherwise noted, the material in this chapter is derived from: USPacFlt OpO 1-45, dtd 10Jan45; Fifth Flt OPlan No. 13-44, dtd 31Dec44; ComPhibPac OPlan A25-44, dtd 8Dec44; CinCPOA OPlan 11-44, dtd 25Nov44; VAC OPlan 3-44, dtd 23Dec44; TF 51 OPlan A25-44, dtd 27Dec44; TF 52 OPlan A101-45, dtd 1Jan45; VAC AR, Iwo Jima, Anx A, OPlan (Alt) 4-44, dtd 31Dec44, and OPlans and Orders, 20Feb-22Mar45; 4th MarDiv OPlan 49-44, Iwo Jima, dtd 26Dec44; 4th MarDiv OPlan 50-44, Iwo Jima, dtd 4Jan45; 5th MarDiv OPlan 2-44, Iwo Jima, dtd 31-Dec44; 3d MarDiv OPlan 1-45, Iwo Jima, dtd 22Jan45; *Iwo Comments*; Craven and Cate, *The Pacific*; Robert A. Aurthur and Kenneth Cohlmia, *The Third Marine Division* (Washington: Infantry Journal Press, 1948), hereafter Aurthur and Cohlmia, *The Third Marine Division*; Proehl, *The Fourth Marine Division*; Howard M. Conner, *The Spearhead—The World War II History of the Fifth Marine Division* (Washington: Infantry Journal Press, 1950), hereafter Conner, *The Fifth Marine Division*.

[2] JWPC 91/D, dtd 13Sep43, "Seizure of the Bonins," in Bartley, *Iwo Monograph*, p. 19.

[3] Early planners for operations against Iwo Jima and Chichi Jima referred to these islands as being part of the Bonin Islands even though they are actually located in the Volcano Group.

462

ations in the Carolines and the Philippines scheduled within the next few months, both naval commanders felt that no forces should be diverted to the Bonins at this time. Nevertheless, King instructed Nimitz to prepare plans for an assault against the Bonins, although he considered such an operation unwise unless it was shortly followed by an invasion of Japan.

Planning for an amphibious assault against the Bonins was inextricably interwoven with the development of the B-29 long-range bomber of the U. S. Army Air Forces, and for this reason an explanation of the development and characteristics of this aircraft appear warranted. The B-29 had its origin in 1939, when General H. H. Arnold, then Chief of the Army Air Corps, ordered the experimental development of a four-engine bomber with a range of 2,000 miles. As eventually developed, the B-29 or "Superfortress" had a wing span of slightly more than 141 feet, a length of 99 feet, and four Wright engines with turbo-superchargers developing 2,200 horsepower each at sea level. The giant bomber was armed with a dozen .50 caliber machine guns and a 20mm cannon mounted in the tail. The B-29 had a service ceiling of 38,000 feet and near that altitude had a maximum speed of 361 miles per hour. Without a load, the aircraft was estimated to have a range of 4,400 miles; it could move 3,500 miles when carrying a bomb load of four tons.[4]

During the latter half of 1944, about 100 B-29s operated from airfields in China under the Army Air Forces XX Bomber Command. This command, for all practical purposes, constituted an experimental organization, designed to serve as a prototype for similar units to be activated later. Its mission was three-fold: to test the B-29 under combat conditions; to formulate and refine a tactical doctrine; and to perfect the administrative structure to support the B-29 strikes. By mid-October 1944, China-based B-29s had flown a total of 10 missions against a variety of industrial targets ranging from Bangkok in southeast Asia to Manchuria and the home islands.

Meanwhile, the progress of the American offensive in the Central Pacific had resulted in the capture of the Marianas. Preparations got under way for a sustained bomber offensive against the home islands by Marianas-based B-29s. It was anticipated that the first airfield in the Marianas capable of accommodating the big B-29s would be operational by October 1944. In connection with the initiation of very long-range bombing of the Japanese home islands from B-29 bases in the Marianas, the Volcano-Bonin Islands, situated halfway between the Marianas and Tokyo, assumed major strategic importance. As part of this island group, Iwo Jima appeared the logical choice for invasion because it was the only island suitable for the construction of airfields of sufficient size to handle the new Superfortresses. In this connection, it was not intended to use Iwo as a base or staging area for the B-29s, but as a forward air station from which fighters could fly escort missions for the big bombers. At the same time, crippled

---

[4] Craven and Cate, *The Pacific*, pp. 8-9.

B-29s limping back from raids over Japan would be able to make emergency landings on the island instead of ditching into the Pacific. Even while the battle for Saipan was in full swing, 500 of the giant bombers were ready for combat.

As increasing attention focused on bases in the Marianas, the strategic importance of the B-29 bases in China waned. As early as September 1944, General Arnold had seriously considered transferring the XX Bomber Command to a more profitable site. Japanese gains in China ultimately forced the abandonment of the B-29 bases and transfer of the B-29 combat groups and their supporting units to the Marianas.

In July 1944, the Army Air Forces advised the Joint Staff Planners that Iwo was a potential base for fighter planes, since Tokyo would be within the range of P-51 Mustangs based on Iwo.[5] On 12 August, the Joint War Plans Committee recommended the seizure of the Volcano-Bonins, listing as major reasons their availability for bases from which fighter cover could be provided to support the air effort against Japan; denial of these strategic outposts to the enemy; furnishing air defense bases for American positions in the Marianas; and providing fields for staging heavy bombers against Japan.[6]

In a study of naval personnel requirements prepared by the Joint Planning Staff in late August 1944, a list of projected operations included an assault against the Volcano-Bonin Islands with a target date of mid-April 1945. It was estimated that three divisions would be required for these operations.[7] While planning an invasion of Formosa, Admiral Nimitz also was attracted to the Volcano-Bonin Islands. In September 1944, he informed Lieutenant General Holland M. Smith, Commanding General, Fleet Marine Force, Pacific, that the 2d and 3d Marine Divisions should be retained in the Marianas as an area reserve for Formosa. In addition, they were to make up the bulk of the landing force once an attack was mounted against Iwo Jima.

By this time, key service commanders were beset by serious doubts with respect to a major operation against Formosa. Lieutenant General Millard F. Harmon, Commanding General, Army Air Forces, Pacific Ocean Areas, advocated that Formosa be bypassed in favor of the Volcano-Bonins and Ryukyus. His superior, Lieutenant General Robert C. Richardson, Jr., Commanding General, Army Forces, Pacific Ocean Areas, likewise failed to see any advantage in seizing Formosa and expressed himself in favor of advancing through the Nanpo Shoto. Admiral Nimitz felt that the capture of Formosa could serve a useful purpose only if it was a preliminary step towards subsequent landings on a coast of China, where recent Japanese military gains made such a move of questionable value.

Despite an increasing rejection of Formosa as an invasion target by the military leaders concerned, Admiral

---

[5] AAF Memo to JPS, dtd 21Jul44, "Fighter Escort for VLR Bombers," in Bartley, *Iwo Monograph*, p. 20.

[6] JWPC 91/3, dtd 12Aug44, "Plan for the Seizure of the Bonins," as cited in *Ibid*.

[7] JLC 67/4m "Memorandum of Request, Naval Personnel Requirements," dtd 23Aug44, as cited in *Ibid*.

King, Commander in Chief of the U.S. Fleet, consistently adhered to the projected operation against that island, at least until early October 1944. However, on 11 and 12 July, when Admirals King and Nimitz visited Saipan, King asked Admiral Raymond A. Spruance what objective he would recommend for his next operation. Spruance replied that he would like to take Okinawa.[8]

Admiral Spruance has described his participation in the early planning and the final change of objectives in the following words:

> After the completion of the Marianas Operation I turned my command over to Admiral Halsey on 28 August 1944 and returned to Pearl Harbor early in September. On reporting to Admiral Nimitz, he advised me that my next operation would be the capture of Formosa and Amoy. I said that I thought Iwo Jima, followed by Okinawa, would be preferable, but was told that the orders from Cominch called for Formosa.[9]

Following this conversation, Admiral Spruance went on leave. He was about to return to Pearl Harbor during the latter part of September, when he was ordered to attend a conference between Admiral King and Admiral Nimitz which was to be held towards the end of the month at San Francisco. Admiral Spruance recalled the focal points of this meeting as follows:

> At this Conference Admiral Nimitz presented a paper—prepared, I believe, by Captain Forrest Sherman, U.S.N., head of Fleet War Plans Division—recommending the substitution of Iwo Jima and Okinawa for Formosa and Amoy. The reason for this change was that Lt.Gen. S. B. Buckner, U.S.A., Commander 10th Army, who was to command the Landing Force for Formosa, said that he had insufficient Service Troops for an objective so large as Formosa; but that he could take Okinawa. Admiral King, after considerable discussion, was convinced of the necessity for the change and so recommended to the JCS who approved it.[10]

The Joint Chiefs of Staff lost little time in issuing a new directive on 3 October ordering Admiral Nimitz to provide fleet cover and support for General MacArthur's forces in the occupation of Luzon, scheduled for 20 December 1944; to occupy one or more positions in the Nanpo Shoto, with a target date of 20 January 1945; and to occupy one or more positions in the Nansei Shoto by 1 March 1945.[11]

Subsequently, delays encountered in operations in the Philippines affected planning for the Iwo Jima and Okinawa Operations, which were designated DETACHMENT and ICEBERG, respectively. Target dates had to be readjusted to 19 February for the Iwo operation, and to 1 April for the invasion of Okinawa.

On 7 October Admiral Nimitz and his staff issued a staff study for preliminary planning, which clearly listed the objectives of Operation DETACHMENT. The overriding purpose of the operation was to maintain unremitting military pressure against Japan and to extend American control over the Western Pacific. In American hands, Iwo Jima could be turned into a base from which

---

[8] Admiral Raymond A. Spruance ltr to CMC, dtd 5Jan52, in *Iwo Comments*.
[9] *Ibid.*
[10] *Ibid.*
[11] JCS 713/19, 30Oct44, "Future Operations in the Pacific," in Bartley, *Iwo Monograph*, p 88.

we could attack the Japanese home islands, protect our bases in the Marianas, cover our naval forces, conduct search operations of the approaches to the Japanese home islands, and provide fighter escort for very long-range operations. Three tasks specifically envisioned in the study were the reduction of enemy naval and air strength and industrial facilities in the home islands; the destruction of Japanese naval and air strength in the Bonin Islands, and the capture, occupation, and subsequent defense of Iwo Jima, which was to be developed into an air base.

On 9 October, General Holland Smith received the staff study, accompanied by a directive from Admiral Nimitz ordering the seizure of Iwo Jima. This directive designated specific commanders for the operation. Admiral Spruance, Commander, Fifth Fleet, was placed in charge as Operation Commander, Task Force 50. Under Spruance, Vice Admiral Richmond Kelly Turner, Commander, Amphibious Forces, Pacific, was to command the Joint Expeditionary Force, Task Force 51. Second in command of the Joint Expeditionary Force was Rear Admiral Harry W. Hill. General Holland Smith was designated Commanding General, Expeditionary Troops, Task Force 56.

It was not accidental that these men were selected to command an operation of such vital importance that it has since become known as "the classical amphibious assault of recorded history."[12] All of them had shown their mettle in previous engagements. One chronicler of the Iwo Jima operation put it in the following words:

> The team assigned to Iwo Jima was superb—the very men who had perfected the amphibious techniques from Guadalcanal to Guam. Nearly every problem, it was believed, had been met and mastered along the way, from the jungles of Guadalcanal up through the Solomons, and across the Central Pacific from the bloody reefs of Tarawa to the mountains of the Marianas.[13]

For General Smith, who was 62 years old, the Iwo Jima operation was to be his last. In mid-October 1944, Smith issued a letter of instruction designating Major General Harry Schmidt, Commanding General, V Amphibious Corps, as Commander of the Landing Force, Task Group 56.1. General Schmidt, 58 at the time, was a veteran of nearly 26 years of military service, who had commanded the 4th Marine Division during the invasion of Roi-Namur in the Marshalls and during the Saipan operation in the Marianas. His experienced staff, headed by Colonel William W. Rogers,[14] was responsible for the preparation and execution of all Landing Force plans for the operation. When completed, plans for the execution of the landing had to be submitted by the commander of the landing force to General Smith for the latter's approval. On 20 October 1944, VAC received a directive from FMFPac, assigning troops to the corps for training, planning, and operations. Initially, the

---

[12] Isely and Crowl, *U. S. Marines and Amphibious War*, p. 432.

[13] Newcomb, *Iwo Jima*, p. 27.

[14] Promoted to brigadier general for duty as corps chief of staff about 1 Mar 1945. MajGen William W. Rogers ltr to HistBr, G–3 Div, HQMC, dtd 26Jun69 in *Iwo Comments*, hereafter *Rogers ltr*.

corps was to be ready in all respects for combat by 15 December.[15]

The major units assigned to the Landing Force were the 3d, 4th, and 5th Marine Divisions. The 3d Marine Division had already distinguished itself on Bougainville in the Solomons and on Guam in the Marianas. While planning for Operation DETACHMENT was in progress during the late autumn of 1944, the division was still reorganizing on Guam after the heavy fighting for that island and was actively engaged in rounding up or dispatching Japanese that continued to infest the island. At the age of 47, the division commander, Major General Graves B. Erskine, was one of the youngest generals in the Marine Corps with a well-established reputation for toughness. Joining the Marine Corps Reserve in 1917 as a second lieutenant, Erskine had distinguished himself in France during World War I. Following the war, he had seen service in Haiti, the Dominican Republic, Nicaragua, and China.

At the time of the Pearl Harbor attack, he served as Chief of Staff of the Amphibious Corps, Atlantic Fleet. In 1942, he was assigned as Chief of Staff of the Amphibious Corps, Pacific Fleet, under Holland Smith, who was then a major general. After taking part in the amphibious training of Army troops for the Kiska and Attu operations in the Aleutians, Erskine became Deputy Corps Commander and Chief of Staff of the V Amphibious Corps when it was organized in 1943. He had an active part in planning the seizure of Tarawa and accompanied the assault forces which took Kwajalein, Saipan, and Tinian. When the Fleet Marine Force, Pacific, was organized after the capture of Saipan, General Erskine became Chief of Staff of that organization. Promoted to the rank of major general in October 1944, he assumed command of the 3d Marine Division at that time.[16]

The 4th Marine Division, commanded by Major Clifton B. Cates, also had seen considerable action. During the invasion of Roi-Namur in the Marshalls, it had been the first Marine division to go directly into combat from the United States.[17] In less than a year's time, the division had taken part in three landings. In addition to the Roi-Namur operation, the 4th had also made assault landings on Tinian and Saipan. The forthcoming invasion of Iwo Jima would be the division's fourth landing in less than 13 months.

General Cates had assumed command of the division on 12 July 1944, when General Schmidt became the Commanding General of the V Amphibious Corps. Cates already had a long and distinguished Marine Corps career behind him, having served in France during World War I as a company grade officer. During his 20 months of service with the 6th Marines he had been wounded in action twice and had earned the Navy Cross, in addition to other decorations. At Guadalcanal early in World War II, he had commanded the 1st Marines, one of the two assault regiments that landed on the island.

---

[15] VAC AR, App 3 to Anx B, GenStaff Sec Rpts, dtd 31Mar45, p. 3.

[16] For further details concerning the operations of the 3d Marine Division and its commanders, see Aurthur and Cohlmia, *The Third Marine Division*.

[17] Proehl, *The Fourth Marine Division*, p. 15.

In contrast to the 3d and 4th Marine Divisions, the 5th Division had not seen combat as a unit prior to the Iwo Jima operation. Organized at Camp Pendleton, California, on 11 November 1943, the division was commanded by Major General Keller E. Rockey. Like his counterparts in the 3d and 4th Marine Divisions, General Rockey had seen combat action at Chateau Thierry in 1918. Even though the 5th Marine Division had no previous combat experience, nearly half of the men comprising the unit had served with other combat units. In speaking of the division after the end of World War II, General Rockey made the following comment:

> From its earliest days to the hour of its disbandment, I found the 5th to possess and maintain a high standard of military performance and an esprit exceptionally fine. And when the 5th Division entered combat, it acted from the first hour like a unit of veterans. It fought that first fight with the utmost vigor, courage, and intelligence.[18]

At the time that final plans and preparations for Operation DETACHMENT were being made, the 3d Marine Division was still stationed on Guam, following the recent recapture of that island. As commander of VAC, General Schmidt had also located his command post on that island. The 4th Marine Division, upon completion of operations on Saipan and Tinian in the Marianas, had returned to its permanent camp site on Maui in Hawaii. In August 1944, the 5th Marine Division had moved from California to Hawaii, where it underwent final training. The close proximity in which the 4th and 5th Marine Divisions found themselves in Hawaii during the latter part of 1944 was to have a favorable effect on joint planning between the divisions. When General Schmidt moved VAC headquarters to Pearl Harbor on 13 October, the major planning staffs concerned with Operation DETACHMENT, except for the 3d Marine Division, now were functioning close to each other, a circumstance that resulted in better coordination of efforts.

Of the three divisions scheduled to participate in DETACHMENT, the 3d Marine Division was the only one still actively engaged in military operations during the planning phase for Iwo Jima. Even though Guam had been officially declared secure by 10 August 1944, Marines continued to round up or annihilate stragglers until mid-December. The situation on Guam was not without effect on the planning for Iwo Jima and resulted in one of the changes in the basic operations plan. As General Holland Smith was to reminisce at a later time, with reference to the status of the 3d Marine Division:

> It had been proposed to hold the division in reserve, alerted at Guam. On further study, I considered it much sounder for this division to arrive with the other troops in the target area on D-Day, available as a floating reserve. This decision proved sound because we ran into a larger garrison and far stronger defenses than we had anticipated.[19]

General Schmidt issued the first blueprint for Operation DETACHMENT on 19 October 1944, to be used as a guide by subordinate commanders. On the following day, General Smith directed him to have the VAC ready for

---

[18] Conner, *The Fifth Marine Division*, Preface.

[19] Smith and Finch, *Coral and Brass*, p. 242.

Operation DETACHMENT by 15 December.[20]

During the two remaining months of 1944, VAC evolved tactical and logistical plans in joint conferences with all commanders concerned. As increasing intelligence became available, alternate plans were drafted and changes were incorporated into the original plan.[21] All commanders issued tentative drafts of their respective operation plans, and continual adjustments were made to achieve maximum support with the forces available and to organize the most effective assault force possible. Planning remained flexible right up to D-Day, which itself was postponed twice because the naval forces required for the invasion of Iwo Jima were still engaged in the Philippines. As a result, on 18 November D-Day was postponed to 3 February 1945; on 6 December, an additional postponement to 19 February became necessary.[22]

When Admiral Spruance assumed command of all forces assigned to the Central Pacific Task Force on 26 January, CinCPOA Plan 11-44 was in full effect. Designated for the beach assault were the 4th and 5th Marine Divisions, less the 26th Marines, which was to be held in Landing Force reserve. For training purposes prior to the operation, the 26th Marines would remain with the 5th Division. The 3d Marine Division was to stage on Guam and would remain as reserve on board ship in the objective area until D plus 3.

The VAC scheme of maneuver for the landings was relatively simple. The 4th and 5th Marine Divisions were to land abreast on the eastern beaches, the 4th on the right and the 5th on the left. When released to VAC, the 3d Marine Division, as Expeditionary Troops Reserve, was to land over the same beaches to take part in the attack or play a defensive role, whichever was called for. The plan called for a rapid exploitation of the beachhead with an advance in a northeasterly direction to capture the entire island. A regiment of the 5th Marine Division was designated to capture Mount Suribachi in the south.[23]

Since there was a possibility of unfavorable surf conditions along the eastern beaches, VAC issued an alternate plan on 8 January 1945, which provided for a landing on the western beaches. However, since predominant northerly or northwesterly winds caused hazardous swells almost continuously along the southwest side of the island, it appeared unlikely that this alternate plan would be put into execution.[24]

The eastern beaches over which the landings were to be made extended for about 3,500 yards northeastward from Mount Suribachi to the East Boat Basin. (See Map 26). For purposes of organization and control of the invasion force, these beaches were divided into seven

---

[20] For Task Organization of VAC Landing Force, see App G.

[21] Final drafts for Operation DETACHMENT were published on the following dates: CinCPOA OPlan 11-44, 25Nov44; VAC OPlan no. 3-44, 23Dec44; Joint Exped Force OPlan no. A25-44, 27Dec44; and ComFifthFlt OPlan no. 13-44, 31Dec44.

[22] *TF 56 AR*, Encl B, G-3 Rpt, Planning and Ops, Iwo, dtd 27Mar45.

[23] VAC OPlan no. 3-44, dtd 23Dec44, in *TF 56 AR*, Encl A, p. 5.

[24] VAC OPlan no. 4-44, dtd 8Jan45, in *TF 56 AR*, Encl A, p. 6.

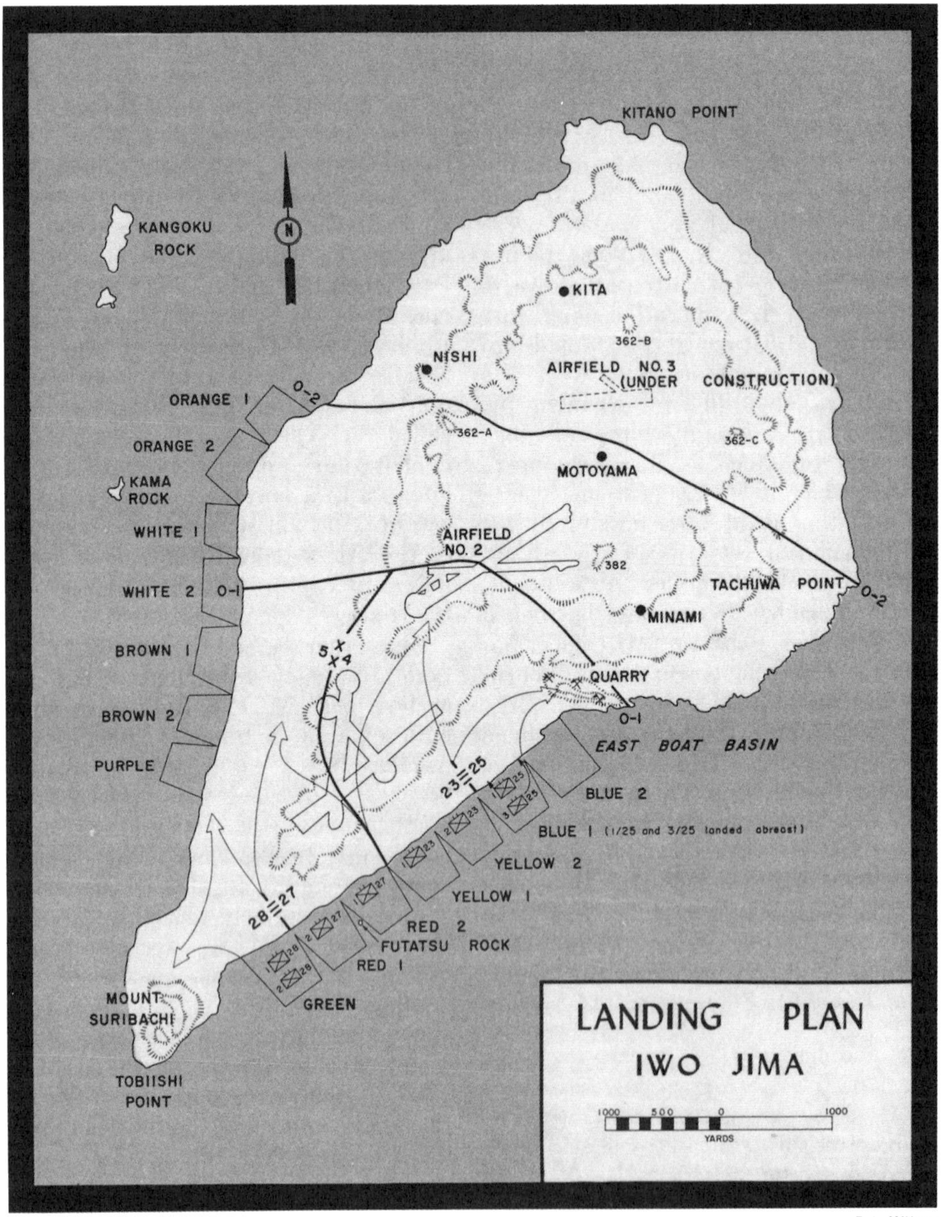

Map 26

E. L. Wilson

500-yard segments, which, from left to right, were designated as Green, Red 1 and 2, Yellow 1 and 2, and Blue 1 and 2. The 5th Marine Division, landing over Green, Red 1, and Red 2 beaches, was to advance straight across the island, which at this point formed a narrow isthmus, until it reached the west coast. At the same time, it was to hold along the right, while part of the division wheeled to the south to capture Mount Suribachi. The 4th Marine Division had the specific mission of moving into the center of the isthmus, while its right flank swerved to the north to seize Motoyama Plateau, the high ground above the East Boat Basin. Unless this vital ground to the north of the invasion beaches and Mount Suribachi to the south—terrain features which overlooked the beaches and permitted the enemy to fire at the exposed Marines at will—were quickly seized, the landing force could be expected to take very heavy casualties.

Once the southern portion of Iwo Jima had been secured, the two divisions could join in a combined drive to the north. At this time, the 3d Marine Division, initially in Expeditionary Troop Reserve on board ships near the beachhead, could be disembarked and landed to assist in maintaining the momentum of the VAC attack.

The detailed scheme of maneuver for the landings provided for the 28th Marines of the 5th Marine Division, commanded by Colonel Harry B. Liversedge, to land on the extreme left of the corps on Green 1. On the right of the 28th Marines, the 27th, under Colonel Thomas A. Wornham, was to attack towards the west coast of the island, then wheel northeastward and seize the 0-1 Line. Action by the 27th and 28th Marines was designed to drive the enemy from the commanding heights along the southern portion of Iwo, simultaneously securing the flanks and rear of VAC. As far as the 4th Marine Division was concerned, the 23d Marines, commanded by Colonel Walter W. Wensinger, was to go ashore on Yellow 1 and 2 beaches, seize Motoyama Airfield No. 1, then turn to the northeast and seize that part of Motoyama Airfield No. 2 and the 0-1 Line within its zone of action. After landing on Blue Beach 1, the 25th Marines, under Colonel John R. Lanigan, was to assist in the capture of Airfield No. 1, the capture of Blue Beach 2, and the 0-1 Line within its zone of action.[25] The 24th Marines, under Colonel Walter I. Jordan, was to be held in 4th Marine Division reserve during the initial landings. The 26th Marines, led by Colonel Chester B. Graham, was to be released from corps reserve on D-Day and prepared to support the 5th Marine Division.

Division artillery was to go ashore

---

[25] The initial VAC LanFor plan had called for the use of Blue Beach 2 as a landing beach. Because of the proximity of Blue 2 to the commanding high ground on the right, and in order to provide a safety factor while maintaining adequate neutralization fires on this high ground during the landing, the 4th Marine Division had requested that the landing of the 25th Marines be limited to Blue 1. This permission was granted, and the 25th Marines was ordered to land on Blue Beach 1 and seize Blue 2 as quickly as possible to enable succeeding units and supplies to use this beach. *4th MarDiv OpRpt*, Iwo Jima, dtd 18May45, Sec. I, p. 2.

on order from the respective division commanders. The 4th Marine Division was to be supported by the 14th Marines, commanded by Colonel Louis G. DeHaven; Colonel James D. Waller's 13th Marines was to furnish similar support for the 5th Marine Division.

The operation was to be so timed that at H-Hour 68 LVT(A)4s, comprising the first wave, were to hit the beach. These vehicles were to advance inland until they reached the first terrace beyond the high-water mark. The armored amphibians would use their 75mm howitzers and machine guns to the utmost in an attempt to keep the enemy down, thus giving some measure of protection to succeeding waves of Marines who were most vulnerable to enemy fire at the time they debarked from their LVTs. Though early versions of the VAC operations plan had called for tanks of the 4th and 5th Tank Battalions to be landed at H plus 30, subsequent studies of the beaches made it necessary to adopt a more flexible schedule. The possibility of congestion at the water's edge also contributed to this change in plans. In the end, the time for bringing the tanks ashore was left to the discretion of the regimental commanders. Company A of the 5th Tank Battalion attached to the 27th Marines was scheduled to land on the Red Beaches at the prearranged time of H plus 30 minutes.[26]

In the event that the landings took place on the western beaches of Iwo, the alternate plan made provision for a company of the 24th Marines, reinforced by a platoon of armored amphibians from the 2d Armored Amphibian Battalion, to seize Kangoku Rock, a 600-yard-long island lying about 2,200 feet northwest of Iwo Jima. The island could be used as an artillery site and for this reason a contingency plan was prepared to land the 105mm howitzers of 4/14 there.

INTELLIGENCE PLANNING[27]

The scheme of maneuver for the Iwo Jima operation, as well as the preliminary planning, was largely based on available intelligence. Enemy documents seized on Saipan during the summer of 1944 gave a fair indication of enemy strength in the Volcano-Bonin Islands. Captured Japanese maps, supplemented by aerial photographs obtained by U.S. Navy carrier pilots during the air strikes of June and July 1944, were utilized in the preparation of situation maps and beach studies. During the planning phase for the operation, pilots of Navy Photographic Squadrons 4 and 5 and the Army Air

---

[26] *5th MarDiv AR*, Sec. VII, p. 10.

[27] Additional material in this section is derived from: Amphibious Forces Pacific, Information on Iwo Jima, n.d., hereafter *PhibForPac G-2 Rpt*; Hq, US Army Forces, POA, IntelRpt, n.d.; Nanpo Shoto Info Bulletin No. 122-44, Supplmt 1, dtd 10Oct44; CinCPac-CinCPOA Bulletin No. 9-45, dtd 10Jan45; TF 56 AR, Encl C, Rpt of Intelligence, Iwo Jima, dtd 1Apr45, hereafter *TF 56 G-2 Rpt*; TF 51 AR, Iwo Jima, 27Dec44-26Mar45, hereafter *TF 51 AR*; VAC C-2 Special Study of Enemy Sit, Iwo Jima, dtd 6Jan45, hereafter *VAC G-2 Study*; VAC Rpt on Beaches, Iwo Jima, dtd 30Oct44; VAC Estimate of Enemy Sit and Strength, dtd 7Mar45; VAC G-2 Jnl, 11Jan-24Mar45; 4th MarDiv D-2 Tactical Study, Iwo Jima, dtd 20Jan65, hereafter *4th MarDiv G-2 Study*; 5th MarDiv D-2 Study, Iwo Jima, dtd 16Nov44, hereafter *5thMarDiv G-2 Study*.

Forces 28th Photographic Reconnaissance Squadron flew 371 sorties. Liberators of the Seventh Air Force obtained additional photographic coverage of the island in the course of their bombing missions.

Significantly, during the preparatory phase, representatives of the 3d, 4th, and 5th Marine Divisions, the Commander, Amphibious Forces, Pacific, and VAC combined their efforts in preparing a Joint Situation Map which was completed on 6 December 1944. Representative officers from Navy and Marine units were ordered to report to Photographic Interpretation Squadron 2, based on Guam, in late January 1945. There, the most recent photographs were available. On the basis of the most current information then available, a final enemy installations map was prepared that was to play a major part in the pre-D-Day naval and aerial strikes, as well as during the actual assault phase.[28]

Between 29 November and 2 December 1944, the submarine USS *Spearfish* conducted a reconnaissance off Iwo Jima. Approaching as close to the island as he could without being detected, the submarine commander gave a running account of the view that presented itself to his eyes as he watched through his periscope. This commentary was transcribed. So close did the submarine approach the shore of Iwo that at one point the skipper spotted a cave going into the base of Mount Suribachi "with a dejected looking individual sitting right in the entrance sunning himself."[29] Additional observations included construction work at various parts of the island, an armored car in motion, and various earthworks and blockhouses on different parts of the island. The submarine reconnaissance failed to discover any guns or emplacements on the slopes of Mount Suribachi itself, nor could individual pillboxes be identified, though a number of caves were visible.[30]

Beach studies indicated that movement over the loose sand would be difficult for wheeled vehicles; tracked vehicles were not expected to bog down. Partially buried gasoline drums, observed at the edge of the water both on the eastern and western beaches, gave rise to considerable speculation. It was thought that these drums might be wired for electrical ignition, so that burning gasoline would run out over the water to check landing craft, or that they would ignite at the moment the amphibious tractors or tanks reached land to raise a wall of fire before them. It was also possible that the drums had been converted into mines, equipped with pull-type detonators, with attached trip wires, which would ignite when either personnel or tanks came into contact with the wire.[31]

In any case, Marines were warned to expect the widespread employment of antitank mines and obstacles, combined with "close quarter attack units" using hand-placed charges. No change in

---

[28] Extracts from CG, VAC Landing Force Rpt, Iwo Jima, 013/124, Ser. 02848, dtd 20May45, p. 9.

[29] USS *Spearfish* ReconRpt, Iwo Jima, 1Dec44, p. 4.

[30] *Ibid.*, p. 2.

[31] 1st Supplement to Nanpo Shoto Info Bulletin No. 122-44, dtd 10Oct44; CinCPac-CinCPOA Bulletin No. 9-45, 10Jan45, p. 10.

Japanese artillery tactics was anticipated. Even though the presence of a large number of artillery pieces on the island was a foregone conclusion, there was no reason to believe that the Japanese would employ massed fires in larger than battery concentrations.

From a thorough study of aerial photographs and a captured map showing the scheme of the enemy's defense, it was known that the Japanese had established an elaborate defense in depth. Gun positions were sited to place withering fire on the selected beaches; defensive works such as pillboxes, blockhouses, antitank trenches, and mines were located where they could repel the American advance once the invasion force had landed. Numerous antiboat gun positions as well as coast defense guns were discovered. Unless these guns were neutralized, it was more than likely that the enemy would use them to fire on the leading waves and transport areas of the invasion force.

Planners for the invasion of Iwo Jima further deduced from documents captured on Saipan that the enemy would adhere to his older tactics of attempting the destruction of the invasion force before an adequate beachhead had been established. The most likely time for this counterattack was considered the early morning of the day following the initial landing.[32]

Further study of aerial photographs and captured documents indicated that Iwo had probably been divided into four defense sectors with one infantry battalion manning each sector. Since the Japanese were believed to have nine infantry battalions on the island, this would leave five battalions to be held in reserve. Photographs taken in January 1945, as the invasion date was drawing closer, indicated that the number of field fortifications, pillboxes, and covered artillery positions was increasing despite intensive aerial bombardment. A most significant development noted in these photographs was the construction of a line of defense across the island from a point near Hiraiwa Bay on the northwest coast to high ground north of the East Boat Basin.

During the period from 3 December 1944 to 10 February 1945, it was noted that the number of enemy coast defense guns on the island increased from 3 to 6; the number of dual purpose guns rose from 16 to 42. Automatic antiaircraft guns showed an increase from 151 to 203, and covered artillery positions rose from 39 to 67. There was a decrease in openly emplaced artillery, antitank and antiboat guns, and machine guns, but in the words of the Expeditionary Troops G-2, Colonel Edmond J. Buckley, the apparent reduction in observed machine guns could be offset by the heavy increase in field fortifications, including blockhouses and pillboxes. The blockhouses could contain fixed artillery, and, in numerous instances, their construction was such as to permit mobile artillery pieces to be wheeled into them. It also appeared likely that each pillbox was equipped with one or more machine guns, whose presence could not be ascertained by aerial observation.

Prelanding reconnaissance had shown that the Japanese had established nu-

---

[32] *VAC C-2 Study*, p. 17.

merous antiboat gun positions, as well as coast defense guns. It was imperative that these guns be neutralized. Such neutralization, of course, depended upon the ability of the invasion force to detect targets and destroy them by naval gunfire and aerial attack prior to H-hour.[33]

Even though planners of the Iwo Jima invasion were generally correct with reference to the enemy's intentions and capabilities, their intelligence estimate erred in two important respects. First among these was an underestimation of enemy strength on the island. Intelligence officers had estimated that the Iwo garrison numbered between 13,000 and 14,000 troops.[34] Names and background of Japanese commanders in the Bonins were known, though the intelligence estimate mistakenly assumed that General Kuribayashi exercised overall command of the Volcano-Bonin Defense Sector from his *109th Division Headquarters* on Chichi Jima, and that a Major General Osuka was in charge of the defense of Iwo Jima. Information on the Japanese naval guard and air base units on Iwo was lacking.

The second serious shortcoming of preinvasion intelligence was the mistaken assumption that the enemy defensive tactics to be expected on Iwo Jima would conform to tactics employed in earlier operations. In describing Japanese capabilities, the intelligence estimate voiced the following expectations:

> The enemy may be prepared to attempt small local counterattacks prior to the establishment of our beachhead in order to annihilate our forces at the beach. His doctrine specifies that the enemy must not gain a foothold on shore and that in order to combat this all troops must be prepared to attack with the mission of splitting our forces and destroying them by local counterattacks.[35]

At the latest, the enemy could be expected to throw all available reserves against the beachhead prior to dawn on D plus 1.

In addition to their task of accumulating and analyzing all information available to them about the enemy's strength, capabilities, and dispositions during the planning period, American planners were faced with the formidable problem of maintaining complete secrecy with reference to the movement of such a large force as was to take place in the Iwo Jima assault. This was not an easy undertaking in view of the tremendous size of the force assigned to capture and develop the island. Admiral Turner's command alone consisted of 495 ships, including, among others, 4 command ships, 8 battleships, 12 aircraft carriers, 19 cruisers, 44 destroyers, 43 transports, 63 LSTs, and 31 LSMs. The addition of Task Force 58, together with supply and auxiliary ships, brought the invasion fleet to more than 800 vessels. The Marine assault troops numbered 70,647 officers and men.[36] This force was further augmented by Marine and Army garrison units, as well as three Army amphibian truck companies in the assault phase, and Navy personnel assigned to shore duty, bringing the total of the expeditionary force to 111,308 men.[37] If one further adds the crews of Turner's

---

[33] *VAC C-2 Study*, p. 17.
[34] *Ibid.*, p. 3.

[35] *Ibid.*, p. 17.
[36] *TF 51 AR*, pt. I, p. 4.

ships and of Task Force 58, more than 250,000 men on the American side were involved in the Iwo operation.[38]

Intelligence officers had a few bad moments on 22 December 1944, when a Pearl Harbor newspaper printed two pictures of Iwo Jima under aerial attack. The pictures bore a startling resemblance to pictures and maps of "Island X," which VAC had issued for training purposes. In order to prevent the Japanese from learning of the assembly and destination of the invasion force, General Schmidt recommended a counterintelligence diversion. Word was spread in the bars and hotels of Honolulu that the command would shortly depart for an attack on Formosa. Whether the diversion had any effect in deceiving the enemy could not be determined.[39]

A serious breach of security occurred on 14 February 1945, while the invasion convoy was en route to the objective. In the course of a radio transmission, someone in the vicinity of Saipan was overheard making the following statement:

> We are going to Iwo Jima. It's a Jap island not far from here. The B-29s bomb it from here every day. It's about 600 miles from Japan. We'll make it hot for them Japs when we get there. We're leaving for there in the next day or so.[40]

Such a breach of security was more than enough to make experienced intelligence officers quake in their boots. The intelligence officer of Amphibious Group 2 reported the incident to VAC. There is no indication that this information ever reached the Japanese, though under different circumstances this compromise of vital information could have had disastrous consequences.

LOGISTICS AND ADMINISTRATION[41]

Another major responsibility accruing to the staff of the VAC was logistical planning, which had already begun even before VAC staff officers reached Pearl Harbor on 13 October. Special staffs of FMFPac conducted preliminary conferences and executed logistical planning for the assault on Iwo Jima. As in other areas, logistics required the harmonious teamwork of different levels of command, and between the armed services.

The Quartermaster, U. S. Army Forces, Pacific Ocean Areas, was responsible for supplying rations (Class I) to all personnel taking part in the operation, as well as clothing, special equipment, and supplies (Class II), and ammunition (Class V), for participating Army troops. Fuel and lubricants (Class III) were to be supplied

---

[37] *Ibid.*
[38] Newcomb, *Iwo Jima,* pp. 27-28.
[39] *VAC G-2 SAR, Iwo Jima,* 30Apr45, p. 8, in *VAC AR,* Anx B, GenStaffSecRpts.
[40] *Ibid.*

[41] Additional material in this section is derived from TF 56, AdminO 1-44, 8Nov44; VAC C-1 PersRpts, Iwo Jima, 20Feb-24Mar45, hereafter *VAC G-1 Rpt;* VAC C-4 Jnl, 29Jan-21Feb45; 3d MarDiv D-1 Jnl, 14Feb-12Apr45; 3d MarDiv Breakdown of Ammunition and Fuel, Iwo Jima, 1Feb45; 3d MarDiv C-4 Jnl, 23Feb-8Apr45; 3d MarDiv G-4 Log, 8Dec44-9Aug45; 3d MarDiv G-4 Periodic Rpts, 3Jan-20Mar45; 4th MarDiv AdmO 44-44, 24Dec44; US PacFlt Logistics Plan for Land-Based Forces, 14Oct44.

by the Navy's Service Force, Pacific. The Supply Service, FMFPac, was to furnish ammunition (Class V) and special supplies, and equipment (Class IV) for the Marines. The latter supplies were to be distributed initially by the 6th Base Depot in Hawaii and the 5th Field Depot on Guam.

Administrative planning, including service and support to the VAC Landing Force, was the responsibility of the G-4 Section, V Amphibious Corps. Prescribed levels for Class I supply were two days' rations for the assault troops plus a 30-day backup supply. Water was to be carried in cans, drums, or other organizational equipment at the ratio of two gallons per man per day for five days.[42] Class II and IV supplies were to be stockpiled for 30 days. Ammunition for ground forces (Class V) was to be provided in quantities of seven units of fire (U/F) for artillery, mortars, and antiaircraft guns, and five units of fire for all other types of weapons.[43]

Special preloads on LSTs were made to provide a balanced initial supply of rations, fuel, and ammunition for the assault troops. These supplies were loaded in LST tank decks and were designed to provide initial priority combat supplies close in to beaches on D-Day and D plus 1. A total of 38 LSTs were to be preloaded at Pearl Harbor, Hilo, and Guam prior to the embarkation of the assault units. In addition, 42 2½-ton Amphibian Trucks (DUKWs) were to be preloaded at Pearl Harbor with assorted small arms and mortar ammunition, rations, fuel, medical supplies, and flamethrower fuel. These vehicles were scheduled to provide an early replenishment supply on the beaches on D-Day.

Resupply plans and preparations were performed by the Marine Supply Service. Initial resupply ships were to be loaded at Oahu with 30 days Class I, II, and IV supplies and 15 days Class III supplies (except for aviation gasoline) for two reinforced Marine divisions and for all garrison troops estimated to be located on Iwo Jima at D plus 35. Class V was to be loaded in this shipment on board one ammunition ship at the rate of 9 U/F for one Marine division, 7 U/F for one 155mm howitzer battalion, 8 U/F for one Army heavy antiaircraft battalion, 4 U/F for one Army light antiaircraft battalion, and 90 tons of engineer and Chemical Warfare Service demolitions.

The Commander, Forward Area, Central Pacific was instructed to hold available in the Marianas for shipment on call in an emergency, a stock of 30 days supplies of Classes I, II, III, and IV and two units of fire for one reinforced Marine division and one reinforced Army division. Supplies were to be provided by the Commanding General, Pacific Ocean Areas, the Commanding General, FMFPac, and ComServPac. ComAirPac was to maintain a 45-day stock of aviation supplies, except for Class V, in floating storage in the forward area for Navy and Marine aircraft employed in that area. Aviation supplies at Guam and on Roi-Namur were to be held available for emergency shipment. ComGenPOA was to maintain

---

[42] VAC G-4 SAR, Iwo Jima, dtd 30Apr45, p. 2, hereafter *VAC G-4 SAR*.

[43] A unit of fire is a predetermined quantity of ammunition a weapon can be expected to fire in an average day of combat.

a 45-day stock of aviation supplies in floating storage in the forward area for Army aircraft. ComServPac was to provide the necessary storage if space and facilities assigned to ComGenPOA proved inadequate. ComServPac was to shift Service Squadron 10 to Ulithi to furnish support to fleet units and emergency supply for land-based forces. Elements of the above squadron were to be located in the Marshalls and Marianas for support of small task forces.

Pre-packaged supplies were stockpiled by the VAC Air Delivery Section on Saipan for emergency deliveries by air. If needed, the Commander, Expeditionary Troops, could draw from similar stockpiles in Hawaii and elsewhere in the Marianas. For the Iwo Jima operation, VAC organized the 8th Field Depot, commanded by Colonel Leland S. Swindler. The depot was designed to serve as the nucleus of the shore party organization; the depot commander had a dual designation as Shore Party Commander of the Landing Force, in which capacity he was responsible for coordinating the activities of the division shore parties.

Since Iwo Jima was not surrounded by reefs, all types of landing craft could proceed directly from the transport area to the beachhead without becoming involved in time-consuming transfer operations that had been characteristic of many previous landings in the Central Pacific. This circumstance led VAC to authorize subordinate units to mount up to 50 percent of their supplies on pallets.[44]

Planners of the Iwo operation were aware of the fact that the soft volcanic ash along the beaches, as well as the steep terraces en route inland, would impede the movement of wheeled vehicles. To insure a steady flow of supplies from the beaches inland, runner sleds were improvised that could be loaded with needed items and pulled inland by tracked vehicles. Another improvisation designed to overcome the soft sand or volcanic ash was the use of Marston matting at the beaches. Even though this material was originally used for the construction of airfield runways, it likewise could be employed to great advantage in bridging strips of sand along the beaches that would otherwise be impassable.

In addition to the large variety of supplies and equipment normally used for an amphibious operation, VAC employed two items for the first time. One was the two-wheeled Clever-Brooks 3½-ton amphibion trailer, the other the M-29C light cargo carrier, subsequently known as the "Weasel." This boat-like, tracked vehicle resembled a miniature LVT without ramps. The amphibian trailers reached the three assault divisions during November and December 1944.[45] The Weasels arrived in November and were subjected to extensive tests which revealed that the cargo carriers were capable of excellent performance under conditions anticipated at Iwo.

---

[44] Pallets was the designation for wooden platforms on which supplies were strapped or fastened. Palletization facilitated loading and unloading when cranes and other lifting devices were available to handle such convenient but heavy loads.

[45] The 3d Marine Division was issued the trailers in November; the 4th and 5th Marine Divisions received theirs in December.

Three Army and two Marine DUKW companies were assigned to VAC for the operation, as were the 31st and 133d Naval Construction Battalions.[46] In addition, a Marine engineer battalion, a topographic company, an Army bomb disposal company, and the 62d Naval Construction Battalion were attached to VAC and placed under operational control of the Corps engineer. These units would be responsible for clearing minefields, bomb disposal, road construction and maintenance, water supply, and the restoration of airfields on Iwo Jima. Following the beach assault, and as soon as conditions permitted, the 62d Naval Construction Battalion was to begin to ready Motoyama Airfield No. 1 for observation and fighter aircraft. Target date for completion of this assignment was D plus 7. The 31st Naval Construction Battalion was to restore Airfield No. 2 for use by the B-29 bombers. Making the latter field operational for this purpose involved not only restoration of facilities that were already in existence, but called for extension of existing runways to 7,000 feet to accommodate the giant aircraft. Airfield No. 2 was to become operational at D plus 10.[47]

In view of the size and scope of the impending operation, the handling and evacuation of casualties required special planning. Initially, it was assumed that seizure of the objective would require 14 days. It was estimated that five percent of the assault force would become casualties on each of the first and second days; three percent on the third and fourth days; and one and one-half percent on each of the remaining 10 days. It was further estimated that 20 percent of all casualties would be dead or missing.[48]

For the evacuation of casualties from Iwo Jima, two hospital ships, the *Samaritan* and the *Solace* were assigned, as well as the auxiliary hospital ship *Pinckney*, and LSTs *929*, *930*, *931*, and *1033*. These LSTs, especially equipped to handle casualties close to the beach, were to be stationed 2,000 yards offshore and serve as evacuation control centers. There, the casualties would be logged, given additional emergency treatment, and transferred to other ships for further care. One of the LSTs was equipped with a blood bank.

As in so many other instances of operations in the Pacific Theater, the adaptation of existing equipment to a new use was due to the efforts of one individual who not only conceived the idea but also had to sell it at the right time and place. In this instance the conversion of LSTs for the evacuation of casualties was the brainchild of Lieutenant Commander George J. Miller, Medical Corps, USNR, who prepared blueprints of the LSTs showing the plan of operating tables, beds, and other equipment. In December 1944 he presented his idea to several high ranking naval medical officers who initially vetoed it. In the end, the persistent lieutenant commander was able to sell the idea to an even higher ranking personage who immediately recognized the

---

[46] The 133d Naval Construction Battalion was attached to the 4th Marine Division, the 31st to the 5th Marine Division.

[47] VAC OPlan 3-44, dtd 23Dec44, Anx M, Eng Plan.

[48] VAC Surgeon, SAR, Iwo Jima, dtd 24Mar 45, hereafter *VAC MedRpt*.

merit of the plan and gave his unqualified approval of it.[49]

In addition to the hospital ships and the specially converted LSTs, long range dispositions had to be made from Iwo Jima for the reception of casualties. In addition to the hospitals that were to be set up on the island itself, once the situation following the landings had stabilized to some extent, 5,000 beds were available in hospitals on Saipan and Guam. Air transportation of casualties was scheduled to begin as soon as airstrips were ready to accommodate transport planes.[50]

These preparations only give a bare outline of the time and effort required to bring logistics and administration into line with the operational planning. At least one account has briefly summed up the diverse items involved and the thought that had to be given to their transport and storage:

> It was necessary to think of everything —pencils, blood, toilet paper, 'this item,' said the orders, 'will be stowed under tarpaulin at the rear of all landing vehicles to protect it from spray,' matches, gasoline, socks, bullets, wooden crosses (prepainted), water, welding rods, garbage cans, splints, food, spark plugs, blankets, flares, dog food, maps, holy water, smoke pots, paint, shoelaces, fingerprint ink, batteries, rock-crushers, bulbs, cigars, asphalt machines, carbon paper. The Fifth Division alone carried 100 million cigarettes and enough food to feed Columbus, Ohio, for thirty days.
>
> Ships began loading as early as November, every parcel stenciled, weighed, sized, and stowed in a particular spot. Marked photos showed where the cemetery would be located, orders specified the exact depth of burial and space between bodies (3 feet from centerline to centerline of body, fifty bodies to a row, 3 feet between rows.) The graves registration team would land on D-Day, equipped with its own bulldozers to bury the bodies exactly 6 feet deep. Then men would mound each grave with a special wooden form.[51]

Nor was the multiplicity of supplies all that the planners had to consider; there was one more commodity whose importance transcended all others. This was the flow of men towards the scene of action to replace those who would become casualties. During the last months of 1944, long before the first Marines were scheduled to hit the beaches of Iwo Jima, the complex machinery of administration was already set in motion when six replacement drafts embarked from the United States to join VAC. Each draft was composed of about 1,250 officers and men. Each of the three Marine divisions slated to participate in the operation received 2,500 replacements, some of whom were incorporated into the divisions before they left their staging areas. The bulk of the replacement units was kept intact; their personnel were assigned to shore parties, to be employed on the beaches until they were needed to replace combat losses.[52]

Launching an amphibious operation on the scale of the contemplated assault

---

[49] "This use of LSTs saved many, many lives of wounded men who received treatment on the LSTs. If they had not received this treatment and had had to be taken from the beach all the way to the hospital ships, many would have died before they reached the ships." BGen John S. Letcher ltr to Head, HistBr, G-3 Div, HQMC, dtd 12Jun69, in *Iwo Comments*, hereafter *Letcher ltr*.
[50] *VAC G-1 Rpt*, p. 13.

[51] Newcomb, *Iwo Jima*, p. 37.
[52] *VAC G-1 Rpt*, pp. 13–15.

against Iwo Jima required far more than merely assembling men and materiel and shipping them to the objective. The real planning effort had only begun at the point when the objective had been decided upon and the means to seize it were being made available. The efforts of various arms and services had to be combined until the gigantic machine of war functioned as an instrument of precision. Each man, each weapon, each unit, every ship, tank, and airplane had a very definite part in the scheme of things. In this respect, an assembled invasion armada can be likened to an orchestra. The finest musicians, well skilled in their profession and equipped with the best instruments that money can buy, still must learn to work with one another. Few among the audience are aware of the tremendous effort that went into writing the score, the seemingly endless rehearsals, the continuous and often painful planning and rehoning that must take place before all meshes into an integrated whole.

It is no different with the orchestra of war. A plan is made, followed by the assembly of men and supplies. Only then can the vital and difficult process begin of forging the whole into an instrument of such power and precision that it continues to function even in the face of the most adverse conditions that climate, weather, and enemy opposition can impose. When the curtain rises, the spectator is awed by the booming of the big naval guns, the columns of dirt and smoke rising over the objective from naval shells or aircraft dropping their lethal cargo, as rockets swoosh towards the target. Once this orchestra has begun to play, any flaw still remaining can be measured in the lives of assault troops who are separated from the enemy bullets and shells by no more than a few cubic feet of air, often protected only by the thickness of a uniform.

The forging of the precision instrument of war, under way months before Marines went ashore on Iwo, determined in large measure how many men of the landing force would go on to seize the objective and return home; the number whose fragile and mangled bodies would be carried off Iwo for salvage and repair; and those destined to remain on the island forever.

CHAPTER 3

The Preliminaries[1]

In his capacity as Commanding General, VAC Landing Force, Major General Harry Schmidt was directly responsible for the preparation and training of all units placed under his command for the Iwo Jima operation. Such training, in addition to a routine program, not only featured the participation of VAC units in tests and demonstrations of new types of amphibious equipment such as the Clever-Brooks amphibian trailer and the M-29C cargo carrier (Weasel), but also familiarized personnel with new weapons and techniques scheduled for employment during Operation DETACHMENT. Division training programs stressed attacks against fortified positions; the reduction of pillboxes; detection, marking, and removal of mines; and the employment and coordination of supporting arms.

During the last two weeks of November, the 4th Marine Division carried out amphibious maneuvers on Maui, and a field exercise on the division level. Two command post exercises followed. The 5th Marine Division conducted training exercises at Camp Tarawa on Hawaii Island. At Hilo, the men practiced the embarkation and debarkation of troops and loading and unloading of equipment onto LSTs. The artillery battalions of the 13th Marines went to Maume beach for special loading exercises with DUKWs, LSTs, and LSMs. Using the big amphibious trucks, the artillerymen learned how to load and unload their howitzers and practiced moving in and out of the great jaws of the LSTs, causing at least one Marine to comment: "This reminds me of Jonah and the whale."[2]

Within the 5th Marine Division, the 28th Marines, scheduled to spearhead the assault, received special training.

---

[1] Unless otherwise noted, the material in this chapter is derived from: *TF 51 AR;* TF 52 AR, Iwo Jima, 10–19Feb45, 22Feb45, hereafter *TF 52 AR;* TF 54 AR, 10Feb-10Mar45, hereafter *TF 54 AR; TF 56 AR;* VAC Landing Force AR, Iwo Jima, Oct44–Mar45, 13May45, hereafter *VAC AR; PhibGru 2 AR;* 3d MarDiv AR, Iwo Jima, 31Oct44–16Mar45, 30Apr45, hereafter *3d MarDiv AR;* 5th MarDiv AR, Iwo Jima, 19Feb-26Mar45, 24Mar45, hereafter *5th MarDiv AR;* ComPhibPac TrngO A29–44, Iwo Jima, 18Dec44; TF 31 Rpt of Trng, 31-Jul44; TF 52 OpO No. A105–45, 3Feb45; TG 53.2 AR, Iwo Jima, 31Oct44-4Mar45; TransDiv 32 AR, Iwo Jima, 10Feb-6Mar45; TransDiv 45 AR, 27Jan-19Feb45, hereafter *TransDiv 45 AR;* 3d MarDiv EmbO 1-44, 18Dec44; 3d Mar Div EmbO 1-45, 19Jan45; 3d MarDiv TrngO 1-45, 5Jan45; 4th MarDiv TrngOs, 27Oct44-22Jan45; 4th MarDiv Trng Memo 82–44, 10-Dec44; 5th MarDiv TrngO 64-44, 31Dec44; *Iwo' Comments;* Conner, *The Fifth Marine Division;* Craven and Cate, *The Pacific;* Smith and Finch, *Coral and Brass;* Heinl, *Soldiers of the Sea;* Isely and Crowl, *U. S. Marines and Amphibious War;* Morison, *Victory in the Pacific;* Proehl, *The Fourth Marine Division;* Newcomb, *Iwo Jima.*

[2] Conner, *The Fifth Marine Division*, p. 21.

Each battalion of that regiment conducted exercises that involved landing on beaches resembling those of Iwo, right down to soft volcanic ash. The maneuvers also included the envelopment of a hill that could pass for a fairly close duplicate of Mount Suribachi. Without those in the ranks being aware of it, elements of the division actually executed the scheme of maneuver called for in the Iwo operations plan. The division conducted three command post exercises in Hawaii, including one problem calling for the coordination of air, naval gunfire, and artillery support.

On Guam, the men of the 3d Marine Division trained for the impending operation in accordance with the mission assigned to them. Training stressed the phases a reserve unit had to pass through upon landing and moving up into the interior of the island. Since the division was not scheduled to take part in the amphibious assault, no assault landing exercises were conducted. The 3d Division was to utilize the shore party facilities of the two assault divisions preceding it ashore.

The replacement drafts did not join their divisions until late November. Even though the replacements had received basic individual training in the United States, they had to learn basic small unit tactics and had to exercise in them before qualifying as combat ready. Since the men were to serve with shore parties prior to being assigned to combat duty, they also had to be initiated into cargo-handling duties.

Owing to the advanced state of training in the divisions and the high level of experience of their Marines, VAC training directives were concerned with refinement of combat techniques and provision for supervision and support of divisions and corps troops. Otherwise, training was left to the divisions. A late delivery of DUKWs caused some delay in training the newly activated amphibian truck companies with their vehicles. Considerable retraining was required to familiarize tank crews and maintenance personnnel with the operation and servicing of new M4A3 Sherman tanks.

Upon the conclusion of amphibious exercises, the Hawaii-based assault forces began staging on 24 December 1944; by 9 January, all troops had embarked. Individual units proceeded to Oahu, where they assembled with other elements of the Joint Expeditionary Force for rehabilitation. This period lasted from 19-26 January 1945. During this time, all men received some liberty ashore and took part in supervised recreation.

From 27 December 1944 to 8 January 1945, the 4th Marine Division moved on board its transports off Maui. The 5th Marine Division loaded at Hawaii from 25 December to mid-January. The men of the 3d Marine Division on Guam were not scheduled to begin embarkation for another month.

Final rehearsals for the remainder of the landing force were held in the Marianas during the second week of February. Also participating in these rehearsals were aircraft and ships of the Amphibious Support Force (TF 52), commanded by Admiral Blandy, and the Naval Gunfire and Covering Force (TF 54), under Rear Admiral Bertram J. Rodgers. The final exercises had the primary aim of testing coordination between the attack force and the supporting arms. Shore fire control parties actually landed on Tinian and tested communications in connection with a simulated bombardment. Sea conditions made it impractical to boat the troops during that part of the exercises conducted on 12 February; on the following day, however, the troops debarked, waves were formed, and landing craft were taken to within 300 yards of the beaches on the west coast of Tinian.

On 15 February, the combat-loaded LSTs (tractor groups) departed for the target area; during the afternoon of the following day, Transport Squadrons 15 and 16, carrying the landing force assault troops moved out, screened by cruisers and destroyers. On the same day, ships carrying the 3d Tank Battalion, corps engineers, naval construction battalions, one corps artillery and two U. S. Army antiaircraft artillery battalions left Guam. On 17 February, Transport Squadron 11 departed Guam, carrying the 3d Marine Division as Expeditionary Troops Reserve. During the voyage to Iwo Jima, RCT 26 was released from Corps Reserve to the 5th Marine Division. RCT 21, which was embarked in Transport Division 32, left Guam on the evening of 16 February, to be released from Expeditionary Troops Reserve to Corps Reserve when it reached Iwo in midmorning of 19 February.

As the invasion fleet silently moved towards the objective, Admiral Turner's flagship, the USS *Eldorado,* carried a distinguished passenger, who on 15 February had boarded the ship with such little fanfare that a large number of the crew initially was unaware of his presence. It was James V. Forrestal, Secretary of the Navy, intent on witnessing the imminent operation as an observer. Dressed in khakis without insignia of any kind, he might easily have been mistaken for one of the civilian war correspondents on board the command ship.[3]

The Japanese were aware of the armada's departure from Saipan almost as soon as it had gotten under way. Whether the fleet was spotted by an enemy aircraft or submarine has never been clearly established, though at least one source credits a naval patrol plane with having reported on 13 February that 170 ships were moving northwest from Saipan.[4] As a result, all Japanese troops in the Volcano-Bonins were placed on a state of alert.

The reaction to the news that an American invasion force was moving towards the Bonins or the Volcano Islands was nothing short of explosive in the home islands, where emotions had already been whipped to a fever pitch:

> Uniformed schoolboys stormed into Perry Park at Kurihama, near Yokohama, the site where Commodore Perry had come ashore nearly a century before to reopen Japan to the Western world. The boys, rallying under the banner of the Imperial Rule Assistance Youth Corps, rushed the granite shaft and in a frenzy of patriotism toppled it to the ground and spat upon it.[5]

No such hysteria gripped General Kuribayashi and his Iwo Jima garrison. The Japanese defenses on the island had progressed as far as they ever would. In the time available to fortify

---

[3] Smith and Finch, *Coral and Brass,* p. 251.
[4] Newcomb, *Iwo Jima,* p. 59.
[5] *Ibid.*

the island, all that could possibly be done had been accomplished. Filled with great fighting spirit, reverence for the Emperor, and determination to drive the invaders back into the sea, the enemy sat in his dugouts and waited.

PRELIMINARY AIR AND NAVAL BOMBARDMENT[6]

Actually, the battle for Iwo Jima had opened long before the first ships of the American invasion fleet hove into view off the island. Following the first large-scale carrier raid of June 1944, regularly scheduled air strikes against the target began in August. Air operations against Iwo passed through two stages. First, there was the strategic phase prior to 16 February 1945, carried out mainly by Marianas-based B-24 bombers of the Seventh Air Force.

---

[6] Additional material in this section is derived from: FMFPac, Naval Gunfire Section, Rpt on NG Support in Operations, hereafter *FMFPac NGS*; FMFPac, Naval Gunfire Section, The Bargaining Phase, Iwo Jima Bombardment, 24Oct44-20Jan45, hereafter *Iwo Preliminary Gunfire Requirements*; FMFPac, Naval Gunfire Section, Preliminary Rpt on NGF in Iwo Jima Operation, 1Apr45; Amphibious Forces, U. S. Pacific Flt, Amphibious Gunnery Bulletin No. 1, Capture of Iwo Jima, 11Mar45; Fifth Flt, NGF Support, Exp Trps Rpt, 16Jun45, hereafter *Fifth Flt NGF Rpt*; TF 56, Sp Rpt on Air Ops in Support of the Capture of Iwo Jima, n.d.; *VAC AR*, Anx C, Apps 2 and 3, NGF and Air Rpts, 30Apr45 and 30May45, hereafter *VAC NGF and Air Rpts*; Col Robert D. Heinl, Jr. "Target Iwo," *U. S. Naval Institute Proceedings*, v. 89, no. 7, (Jul63), pp. 71–82, hereafter, Heinl, *Target Iwo*; Col Donald M. Weller, "Salvo-Splash! —The Development of NGF Support in World War II," *U. S. Naval Institute Proceedings*, Pt 1, v. 80, no. 8 (Aug54), pp. 839-849, Pt 2, v. 80, no. 9 (Sep54), pp. 1011–1021.

Beginning on 8 December, and continuing for 74 consecutive days, the bombers rained death and destruction on the Volcano-Bonin Islands. Iwo Jima received special attention.[7] Marine PBJs (B-25 medium bombers) of VMB-612 participated in this bomber offensive from early December 1944 until the last days of January 1945. Operating from the Marianas under the Army Air Forces VII Bomber Command, the Marine aviators flew night missions over the Volcano-Bonin Islands with special emphasis on the disruption of enemy shipping, since it was known that the Japanese, vulnerable to American air attack during the daytime, were making a frantic effort to rush supplies to Iwo and nearby islands at night.

As of 31 January 1945, all air missions were executed in accordance with the Iwo Jima Air Support Plan.[8] During the last three weeks preceding the invasion, B-24s from the Marianas flew 30 sorties a day or more against the island.[9] The overall purpose of the bombing was to neutralize the airfields and installations on Iwo, destroy gun positions and fixed defenses, and unmask additional targets.[10] Initially, the

---

[7] AAF POA, Rpt of Participation in the Iwo Jima Op, 1945, p. 75.
[8] CTF 51 OPlan, A25–44, dtd 27Dec44.
[9] *TF 51 AR*, Pt V, Sec E, pp. 17–18.
[10] "While it was true that the runways were not kept out of operation for any length of time, it was also true that after 2 January 1945 no enemy air raids were made from Iwo Jima fields against the B-29 bases in the Marianas. The B-24s used large quantities of 100-pound bombs and fragmentation bombs, which obviously were not intended to destroy fixed defense installations such as blockhouses, pillboxes, etc. The B-24 targets on Iwo Jima specified in VII Bomber Command mission

land-based missions against Iwo were executed under the Commander, Task Force 93, Lieutenant General Millard F. Harmon, USA. As the invasion date neared, the bomber raids were conducted in accordance with requests from the Commander, Joint Expeditionary Force.

Beginning 16 February, air attacks against Iwo increased in frequency until a daylight attack hit the island at least once every 24 hours. In addition, Iwo was exposed to night harassing missions and fighter sweeps. Photographic reconnaissance flights attempted to obtain a last-minute picture of enemy defenses prior to the invasion.

At numerous times prior to D-Day, aerial photographic reconnaissance attempted to estimate the effectiveness of both aerial and naval bombardment of the target with particular emphasis on the study of selected target areas which had been the subject of specific strike requests. Among the last of these studies was one submitted to the Chief of Staff (C/S) of VAC on 9 February 1945. The first paragraph of this report poignantly stated:

> Photographic coverage of Iwo Jima to 24 January 1945 indicates that damage to installations resulting from bombing strikes between 3 December 1944 and 24 January 1945 was, on the whole, negligible. These strikes have apparently not prevented the enemy from improving his defensive position and, as of 24 January 1945, his installations of all categories had notably increased in number. The island is now far more heavily defended by gun positions and field fortifications than it was on 15 October 1944, when initial heavy bombing strikes were initiated.[11]

This information was corroborated in a special memorandum submitted by the G-2 to the C/S on 13 February.[12] This memorandum compared the enemy's static defenses between 3 December 1944 and 10 February 1945, and noted significant increases in the number of heavy weapons and field fortifications, particularly blockhouses and pillboxes.

A further evaluation of the constant bombing indicated that it was not altogether ineffective: the destruction of aircraft on the ground and the temporary neutralization of the Iwo airfields was accomplished. On the other hand, gun emplacements, blockhouses, pillboxes, shelters, and other strong points proved far less vulnerable owing to the thorough preparation of such installations against attack from the air and naval gunfire. The rugged terrain with its countless caves afforded excellent protection from high level bombing.[13]

Even the bomber attacks against the Iwo Jima airfields could not prevent their use by the enemy for any appreciable length of time. In evaluating the effectiveness of the air strikes, the Army Air Forces had to concede "that at no time were all of Iwo's strips rendered inoperational and no single strip was

---

reports for February 1945 were generally AA defenses and radio/radar installations." Dr. Robert F. Futrell ltr to Head, HistBr, G-3 Div, HQMC, dtd 7Jul69, hereafter *Air Force Comment*, in *Iwo Comments*.

[11] Encl C, Extract from Bomb Damage Assessment, G-2 Rpt no. 2, 9Feb45, p. 4, in *TF 56 AR*.
[12] State of Enemy Defenses, Iwo Jima, dtd 13Feb45, in *ibid.*, p. 5.
[13] TF 56 SplRpt, Air Operations in the Support of the Capture of Iwo Jima, n.d., p. 3.

out of service for a whole day: the destructive Christmas raid on Saipan was run the day after a heavy air-sea bombardment of Iwo.[14]

As D-Day for Operation DETACHMENT approached, the Army Air Forces stepped up the assault against Iwo. Between 1 and 16 February, Seventh Air Force bombers flew 283 daylight sorties, dropping 602 tons of bombs and 1,111 drums of napalm; in the same period, B-24s flew 233 night snooper missions, dropping 504 tons of bombs. On 12 February, 21 B-29s of the 313th Bombardment Wing dropped 84 tons of bombs on carefully pinpointed gun emplacements on Mount Suribachi as well as on antiaircraft positions and radio and radar installations elsewhere on the island. Again results were disappointing because the bombers flew at moderately high altitudes and frequently released their bombs by radar because of cloudy weather. In any case, the bomber crews found it extremely difficult to score square hits on the cleverly concealed and deeply dug-in targets. Napalm was dropped for the purpose of burning off the camouflage, but this method was unsuccessful, partly because of inaccurate drops and partly because the rocks and ashes used as cover would not burn.

In view of the failure of the bombing assault to inflict crippling damage on the Japanese on Iwo, the preliminary naval gunfire bombardment of the island, a vital and indispensable prelude to the operation, was bound to grow in importance. The very nature of an amphibious assault against a strongly fortified enemy bastion, largely devoid of the element of surprise, made it mandatory for the preliminary gunfire to eliminate a sizable portion of the enemy defenses. Without this shore bombardment, the very success of the assault could become imperiled or severe casualties could result among the Marines slated to go ashore. It was in this vital realm of naval gunfire support that Marine and Navy leaders of the Iwo expedition failed to achieve complete accord; the former, represented by General Holland Smith, had seen in previous assaults what fire from an enemy not sufficiently subdued could do to Marine assault waves nearing the shore of a well-defended island.

General Smith's anxiety increased the closer D-Day approached. This experienced Marine leader compared Iwo to a worm that became stronger the more it was cut up, for the island seemed to thrive on the American aerial bombardment. The leader of the expeditionary troops was to recall his feeling of what was ahead:

> My own study of early air photographs indicated that a situation of an incredible nature existed on the island. It was plain that Iwo Jima had fortifications the like and extent of which we had never encountered. Mindful of Tarawa, where most of the fortifications were above ground and were still standing when the Marines landed, my opinion was that far more naval gunfire was needed on an island five times the size of Tarawa, with many more times the number of defenses, most of them deep under ground.
>
> I could not forget the sight of Marines floating in the lagoon or lying on the beaches at Tarawa, men who died assaulting defenses which should have been taken

---

[14] Hist Air War POA, III, Anx to p. 129, pp. 143–150, p. 159. AAF Eval Bd POA, Rpt no. 7, cited in Craven and Cate, *The Pacific*, pp. 584–585.

PREINVASION BOMBING of Iwo Jima by the U.S. Seventh Air Force. Note Mt. Suribachi in left foreground. (USAF 54717 AC)

AERIAL VIEW OF IWO JIMA LANDINGS as assault waves head for the shore. Mt. Suribachi looms in the background. (USN 80-G-415308)

out by naval gunfire. At Iwo Jima, the problem was far more difficult. If naval guns could not knock out visible defenses, how could they smash invisible defenses except by sheer superabundance of fire?[15]

General Smith and his staff were in agreement that the softening up of Iwo Jima would have to be preceded by an especially lengthy period of intense naval gunfire. The type of guns, as well as the amount and type of ammunition required to do a thorough job, hinged on the intelligence on the kind and number of targets. Based on such intelligence, the number of ships to be employed in the bombardment force could be computed with some degree of accuracy. The guaranteed destruction of a target required visual identification by a spotter on board ship or in the air, followed by precision adjustment. In addition to competence in surface gunnery, the men directing this shore bombardment required special training and experience. On the basis of previous operations at Tarawa, Guam, Saipan, and Peleliu, Marine planners knew that the process of preliminary gunfire could not be hurried.

As early as September 1944, the staff of VAC, supported by members of Fleet Marine Force, Pacific, had begun the preparation of detailed planning for the naval gunfire required for the assault on Iwo Jima. This planning was carried out under the direction of Lieutenant Colonel Donald M. Weller, who had been designated Naval Gunfire Officer for both VAC and FMFPac. Since, even at this early stage of the planning effort, it was known that Iwo Jima represented one of the most heavily fortified strongpoints on earth, Marine planners stipulated that a force of battleships and cruisers would require 10 days to reduce point targets on the island that could bring direct fire to bear on either of the two landing beaches then under consideration. On 24 October 1944, VAC submitted to Admiral Turner its naval gunfire requirements, which called for a preliminary bombardment force of seven battleships, seven heavy cruisers, and two light cruisers.[16]

Meanwhile, Admiral Turner's gunnery officers had also worked on the naval gunfire requirements for Operation DETACHMENT. Their conclusions differed materially from those of the Marines. In this respect, the naval officers' viewpoint was influenced by a number of factors that unintentionally were to work to the disadvantage of the Marine assault force. Foremost among these was the consideration that the initial surface bombardment had to be closely coordinated with the first carrier attack against Tokyo by the Fast Carrier Force (TF 58). Admiral Spruance initially had planned that a carrier strike on Tokyo was to coincide with the opening of the prelanding bombardment of Iwo Jima. Once the naval bombardment started, all tactical surprise at Iwo would be lost. The longer the prelanding bombardment continued, the more it became likely that enemy aircraft from the home islands would interfere with the landings. A two-day carrier strike against Japan would detract enemy attention from Iwo. At the same

---

[15] Smith and Finch, *Coral and Brass*, pp. 243–244.

[16] CG, VAC ltr to ComPhibPac, dtd 24Oct44, in *Iwo Preliminary Gunfire Requirements*.

time, naval aviation could strike a blow at the enemy's aircraft manufacturing plants, which thus far had escaped crippling damage from landbased aircraft. Sustained air attacks would be required to reduce enemy aircraft production. Admiral Spruance observed, nevertheless, that he could see no object in combatting these aircraft around the perimeter if accurate bombing could wreck the factories that produced the enemy planes. As a result, carrier aircraft were to be employed against a strategic, rather than a tactical objective.[17]

Somewhere in the course of the naval planning process, the air strike against Honshu began to loom ever larger in importance until what had started out as a diversionary maneuver began to turn, in the minds of the naval planning staff, into the major attraction. More and more emphasis was placed on the importance of the naval air strike against Japan; the imminent assault on Iwo gradually began to recede further into the background. Naval planners, in reaching their own conclusions as to what could be made available by way of preliminary gunfire, had to consider limitations on the availability of ships, difficulty in replenishing ammunition, and a tight schedule that made it necessary to launch and complete the Iwo operation with all possible dispatch to avoid any delay in the assault on Okinawa, which was to follow closely at the heels of Operation DETACHMENT.

The two widely varying viewpoints of Marine and Navy naval gunfire planning staffs soon found their expression in the times recommended for preliminary naval gunfire by the Navy commanders and those of the Marine landing force. The initial VAC request for naval gunfire not only asked for a minimum of 10 days' bombardment, but also stipulated that D-Day be made dependent on "the successful prosecution of the destruction of enemy defensive installations."[18]

Marine Corps naval gunfire requirements, strongly endorsed by General Holland Smith, were forwarded to the Commander, Amphibious Forces, Pacific Fleet. The expectation was that the Navy would generally concur with what was considered a carefully prepared and reasonable estimate of the naval gunfire required to ensure the quick seizure of the objective with a minimum of casualties. To the surprise and consternation of Marine planners, Admiral Turner informed VAC on 15 November that "a methodical and thorough bombardment would be instituted by the Amphibious Support Force on Dog minus three."[19]

Faced unexpectedly with a reduction of the vital naval gunfire support from 10 days to 3, General Schmidt had a special staff study prepared, consisting of detailed tabulations, and an appended interpretation and evaluation of these very detailed statistics. As a concession, the study pointed out that the overall time for preliminary fires of all types, including support of Underwater Demolition Team (UDT) and minesweep-

---

[17] Forrestel, *Admiral Spruance*, p. 171.

[18] CG, VAC ltr to ComPhibPac, dtd 24Oct44, *op. cit.*, p. 6.

[19] ComPhibPac ltr to CG, VAC, dtd 15Nov44, in *Iwo Preliminary Gunfire Requirements*.

ing operations, as well as the systematic preparatory missions, should not be less than nine days.[20]

Admiral Turner countered the VAC recommendations with a letter that praised the Marine planners and at the same time dashed icy water on any hopes that VAC would receive anything approaching the nine days of naval gunfire. In Turner's words:

> ... the preliminary Naval Gunfire Estimates for the assault of Iwo Jima given in the basic letter are much the best such analysis ever submitted to this command. It is desired not only to meet the wishes expressed in the letter as far as limitations of ships, ammunition, and time permit, but also to furnish even more support than asked for, up to the limit of naval capabilities.[21]

Attached to the basic letter were comments supporting the naval viewpoint. Once again, the efforts of VAC to obtain what it considered a minimum amount of naval gunfire preparation had been thwarted. Nevertheless, General Schmidt was not yet ready to accept the inevitable. By way of another proposal, this one a severe compromise, he asked that the preliminary bombardment begin on D minus 4.

In this request, the Commading General, VAC, was strongly seconded by General Holland Smith, who pointed out that from lessons learned in previous operations and from continued study and analysis of Operation DETACHMENT, he considered four full days for the preliminary bombardment the absolute minimum necessary for success. General Smith went on to warn that unless the strong Japanese defenses were destroyed or at least neutralized, casualties far beyond any heretofore suffered in the Central Pacific had to be expected; in fact, the success of the entire operation might be jeopardized.[22]

On 30 November, it appeared that Admiral Turner was willing to go along with four days of naval gunfire, provided both that the Commander Fifth Fleet agreed, and that the fast carrier strike force could deliver its blow against Japan on D minus 4.[23] Upon being apprised for the recommended extra day of naval gunfire, Admiral Spruance disapproved the request. The rejection was based on three reasons. First, Spruance insisted that the initial surface bombardment had to coincide with the initial carrier attack upon the Tokyo area. Second, the Commander, Fifth Fleet, thought that the situation on Iwo Jima differed from that previously encountered on Saipan for the reason that by D-Day the enemy personnel and fixed defenses at Iwo would have been under heavy shore-based air attack for a considerable period of time. According to Spruance, this prolonged air bombardment, which was not undertaken at Saipan, had to be considered at least as effective as the recommended additional day of ship bombardment. Third, the admiral pointed out that there would be no early opportunity for

---

[20] CG VAC ltr to CG, FMFPac, dtd 8Nov44, in *ibid*.

[21] ComPhibPac ltr to CG, VAC, dtd 26Nov44, in *ibid*.

[22] CG, FMFPac ltr to ComPhibPac, dtd 26-Nov44, in *ibid*.

[23] ComPhibPac ltr to ComFifthFlt, dtd 30Nov-44, in *ibid*.

replacement of naval ammunition, a large proportion of which had to be saved for support on D-Day. There was a limit to the quantity of ammunition available for pre-D-Day bombardment and no advantage was seen in delivering that quantity in four days rather than in three.[24]

Still, the last word on the subject of naval gunfire support had not yet been spoken, and during the first week of January the Marines tried again. On the 2d, General Schmidt once again pleaded for an extension of the preliminary bombardment period. On this occasion, he suggested that either the time allotted for the preliminary bombardment be increased or the fire be concentrated against the main landing beaches, leaving other parts of the island for later. Once again, General Holland Smith supported the VAC request adding that since the overall time element was an important factor in the capture of Iwo Jima, a preliminary bombardment of sufficient time would actually reduce the duration of the operation. Smith reiterated that the effects of the horizontal bombing attacks on the objective had thus far been negligible and that the final result of the air offensive against the island could not be expected to measure up to the benefits derived from an additional day of naval bombardment. The Commanding General, FMFPac, warned that only an adequate, methodical preliminary bombardment could reduce the island defenses to a point where a quick capture was assured. The preliminary bombardment then planned not only would increase the overall time necessary to complete the operation, but also would require an unnecessary expenditure of lives during the initial assault phase.[25]

In his memoirs, General Smith conceded with some bitterness that his warning did not fall on fertile ground:

> Limited, against our better judgment, to only three days' preliminary bombardment there seemed nothing to do but make the best of the situation . . . Thus we were defeated—a group of trained and experienced land fighters, our full realization of the necessity for naval gunfire based on many previous island operations—again overridden by the naval mind. Finding ourselves in this dilemma, we had tried our best to enlighten the high command, feeling that our judgment would be respected, but naval expediency won again.[26]

Even while the duration of the preliminary naval bombardment was still under discussion, the force required to deliver this fire was being organized. The Amphibious Support Force (TF 52), commanded by Rear Admiral Blandy, consisted of a Gunfire and Covering Force (TF 54) under Rear Admiral Rodgers; a Support Carrier Group (TG 52.2) under Rear Admiral Calvin T. Durgin; a Mine Group (TG 52.3), commanded by Rear Admiral Alexander Sharp; an Underwater Demolition Group (TG 52.4), commanded by Captain B. Hall Hanlon; Gunboat Support Units One and Two (TUs 52.5.1 and 52.2.2), headed by Commander Michael J. Malanaphy; and an Air Support Unit (TU 52.10), under Captain Elton C. Parker.

---

[24] ComFifthFlt, ltr to ComPhibPac, dtd 2-Dec44, in *ibid*.

[25] CG, FMFPac ltr to ComFifthFlt, dtd 6Jan45, in *ibid*.

[26] Smith and Finch, *Coral and Brass*, pp. 246–247.

The limitation of the preliminary bombardment to three days placed a heavy burden on the support ships of TF 54, whose mission it was to knock out or neutralize the most powerful and menacing enemy defenses prior to D-Day. There were no less than 724 Type A and B priority targets [27] to be destroyed during 16, 17, and 18 February. The mission was to be executed by 6 battleships, 4 heavy cruisers, 1 light cruiser, and 16 destroyers. The battleships were the *Tennessee, Idaho, Texas, New York, Nevada,* and *Arkansas;* the *Chester, Salt Lake City, Tuscaloosa,* and *Pensacola* made up the heavy cruiser force; the light cruiser was the *Vicksburg.* The *Arkansas, Texas,* and *Nevada* were veterans of the Normandy invasion in June 1944; the *New York* had seen previous service during the invasion of North Africa in 1942. Two new battleships, the *North Carolina* and the *Washington,* each equipped with 16-inch guns, were the most powerful ships initially slated to take part in the preinvasion bombardment. They were withdrawn, however, to take part in the strike of Task Force 58 against Tokyo.

On board the AGC *Estes* were Admiral Blandy and his staff, responsible for all operations against Iwo during the preassault period. Lieutenant Colonel Weller was also on board the *Estes,* heading the Marine gunfire team. Marines under his command were stationed on board each ship participating in the preassault firing. The bombardment plan incorporated lessons learned in the European and Pacific Theaters of Operations. Iwo Jima had been divided into numbered squares and each square was assigned to a specific ship. (See Map 27). Every target was numbered, and on board the *Estes* was a master card index which consisted of a card with appropriate information for each target. Carrier pilots, with special training as gunfire spotters, were ready to take to the air from the carrier *Wake Island* to act as eyes for the bombardment ships. An elaborate radio net had been set up to coordinate the efforts of the various gunfire teams. Since area bombardment had been found wasteful and inefficient in previous operations, all fire support units had been ordered to fire only when specific targets could be identified and the effects of the shelling could be observed from the air.[28]

Early on 16 February, just as Admiral Mitscher was launching his planes against the Japanese homeland, Admiral Blandy's bombardment fleet appeared off Iwo Jima in plain view of the Japanese garrison. Aware of the approach of the invasion force, General Kuribayashi had on the previous night dispatched to Tokyo an urgent request for the *Imperial Japanese Fleet* to come out and engage the American forces. The reply to his urgent plea was negative; the *Imperial Fleet* would not

---

[27] Target priorities for the preliminary bombardment were: *Priority A:* Installations threatening ships, aircraft, and UDT operations (coast defense and antiaircraft guns, artillery emplacements and antitank guns). *Priority B:* Installations threatening the landing force in the ship to shore movement (blockhouses, covered artillery, pillboxes, machine guns, and command posts). *Priority C:* Installations such as caves, ammunition and fuel dumps, and bivouac areas.

[28] Adm W. H. P. Blandy ltr to CMC, dtd 20Jan53, in *Iwo Comments.*

494   WESTERN PACIFIC OPERATIONS

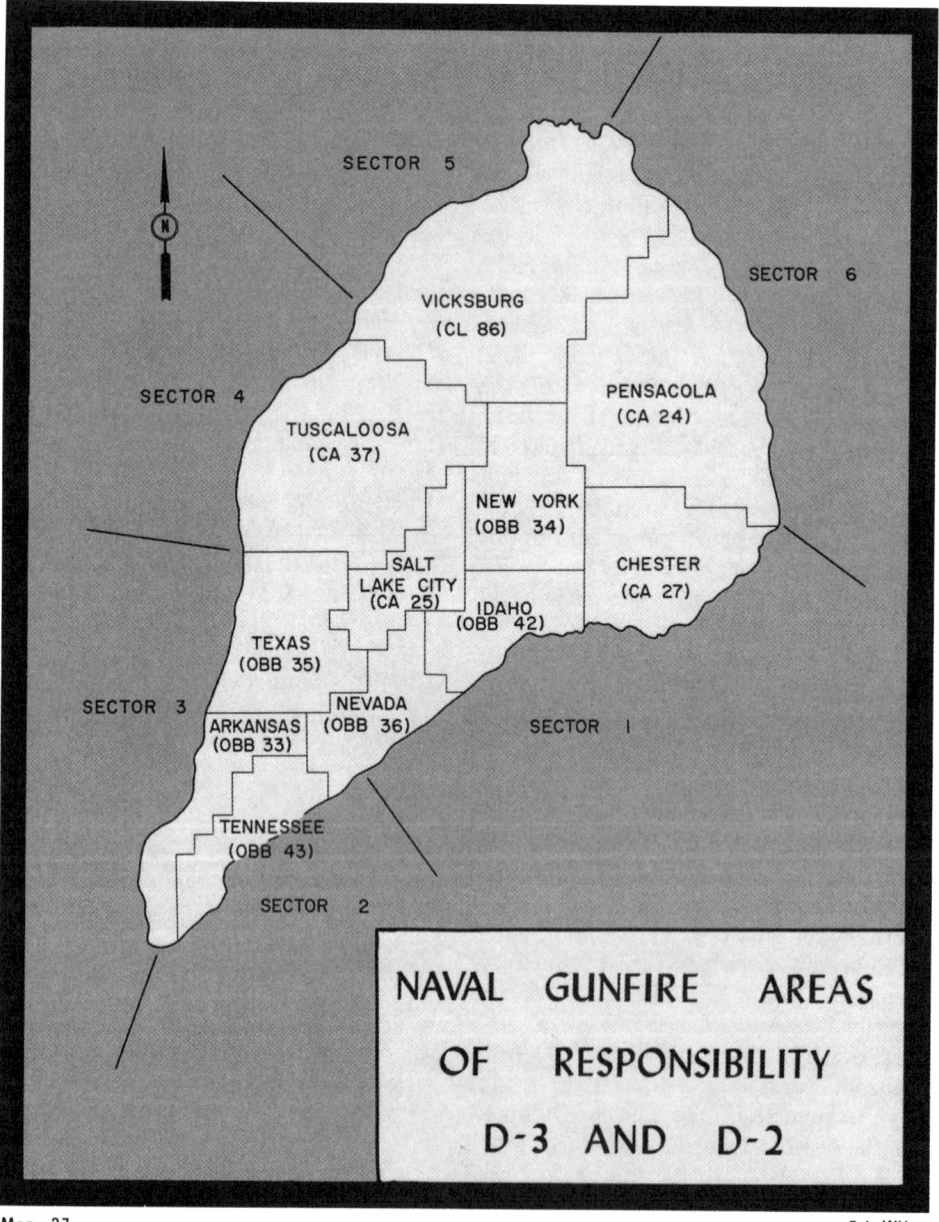

NAVAL GUNFIRE AREAS OF RESPONSIBILITY D-3 AND D-2

Map 27 — E.L. Wilson

Sectors 1–6 shown around the island. Ships and areas:
- VICKSBURG (CL 86)
- PENSACOLA (CA 24)
- TUSCALOOSA (CA 37)
- NEW YORK (OBB 34)
- SALT LAKE CITY (CA 25)
- CHESTER (CA 27)
- IDAHO (OBB 42)
- TEXAS (OBB 35)
- NEVADA (OBB 36)
- ARKANSAS (OBB 33)
- TENNESSEE (OBB 43)

come out now, but on 1 April, when it would sally forth and push the Americans back all the way to the mainland.[29]

The shore bombardment began at 0800, with support vessels following the minesweepers. It became apparent almost at once that prevailing weather conditions precluded the execution of scheduled firing. A low ceiling made it impossible for observers and spotters to perform their duties. Each ship fired in its assigned sector only when the weather permitted. On those infrequent occasions, intensive antiaircraft fire from the island forced observation planes to maintain an altitude above 3,000 feet, too high for an accurate assessment of the effects of the naval gunfire.

Despite the unfavorable weather, the air offensive against Iwo continued on D minus 3, though on a vastly reduced scale. Eight Navy fighters attacked Airfield Number 1 with rockets, while other carrier aircraft attacked gun emplacements on Mount Suribachi. During the afternoon, 42 B–24 bombers arrived from the Marianas, but by this time the overcast had thickened, so Admiral Blandy ordered them back home with their bombs still aboard. Altogether, on 16 February, carrier aircraft from Rear Admiral Calvin T. Durgin's Support Carrier Group (TG 52.2) flew 158 sorties. Until the airfields on Iwo were secured, carrier-based aircraft would have to furnish all the close air support for the combat troops ashore.[30]

During the afternoon of the 16th, little more was accomplished as far as the destruction of primary targets on Iwo Jima was concerned. During one tense moment, the pilot of one of the spotter planes from the *Pensacola*, an OS2U Kingfisher, reported that there was a Zero on his tail. To everyone's surprise, the much faster Zero missed the slow moving target, and as he roared by, the pilot of the spotter plane fired into the Japanese fighter's tail, causing the plane to crash. The appearance of this Zero marked the only aerial opposition the Japanese offered throughout the day.

During the late afternoon, members of UDT 13 proceeded in small boats to Higashi Rock, about 1½ miles off the eastern beaches, where they placed a marker which flashed at two-second intervals, to be used as a guide for the assault troops. The Japanese observed the men on the rock and fired at them, but failed to inflict any casualties. Their mission completed, the frogmen withdrew. At 1800, the bombardment ships sailed further out to sea for the night. An undetermined number of the several hundred priority targets on Iwo had been destroyed by the first day's bombardment. Poor visibility precluded an accurate assessment of the results. It was not an auspicious beginning for the Marines.

Six hundred miles to the north, Admiral Mitscher's Fast Carrier Force had also gone into action on the 16th. From a launching position only 60 miles off the Japanese mainland, TF 58 unleashed its carrier planes against the Tokyo area in the early morning hours, spe-

---

[29] Newcomb, *Iwo Jima*, p. 67.
[30] USS *Makin Island* Action Report, Iwo Jima, 10Feb–11Mar45, pp. 2–3.

cifically against aircraft plants that previous Army Air Forces B–29 raids had failed to obliterate. Despite a low ceiling and bad weather, the carrier pilots, in two days of pounding the Japanese homeland, inflicted heavy damage on enemy war plants. In addition, TF 58 claimed 341 enemy planes shot down, 190 destroyed on the ground, at a cost of 60 aircraft lost in combat and 28 operationally.[31] When weather conditions deteriorated on 17 February and temperatures dropped so low that a considerable number of guns of carrier aircraft froze, Admiral Mitscher cancelled further strikes. After recovering its planes, TF 58 began retiring towards Iwo Jima during the afternoon of the 17th, a day sooner than had been planned. During the night from 17–18 February, destroyers of TF 58 en route to the landing force objective destroyed several small enemy picket boats and rammed a fourth. In passing Chichi Jima and Haha Jima to the north of Iwo, carrier planes attacked the airfield on the former and destroyed several small vessels offshore. TF 58 approached Iwo Jima during the afternoon of the 18th and prepared to lend direct support to the landings scheduled for the morning of the 19th.

The activities of Admiral Blandy's bombardment force off Iwo Jima on 17 February were to be of decisive importance, particularly in view of the fact that little damage on the Japanese defenses had been inflicted by the shelling of the previous day. All indications were that the second day of the prelanding bombardment would be more successful than the first, for the morning's weather had brought clear skies and excellent visibility. The schedule for 17 February called for fighter sweeps against Chichi Jima, minesweeping off Iwo Jima, and beach reconnaissance by Underwater Demolition Teams, closely supported by the large ships, destroyers, and LCI gunboats. During the early afternoon, B-24s were slated to give the island another going over.

Shortly after 0800, a dozen minesweepers approached to within 750 yards of the island, searching for mines and obstacles and probing the reefs and shoals. The tiny wooden vessels drew small arms fire from Mount Suribachi, but refused to be deterred from their mission. No mines or shallows were discovered. At 0840, the battleships *Nevada, Idaho,* and *Tennessee* moved to within 3,000 yards from shore to provide close support for the UDT team operations scheduled for 1100 that morning. The three vessels opened fire at almost point blank range. It quickly became apparent that the Japanese did not intend to take this bombardment lying down, and the covering fire support vessels drew heavy fire from enemy shore batteries. First to receive a hit was the *Tennessee*, which had four men injured shortly before 0900, though the ship itself suffered no damage.[32]

Around 0930, the *Pensacola* came close in under the cliffs of the east coast of Iwo in order to provide cover for the minesweepers. Even though the Japa-

---

[31] TF 58 OpRpt, 10Feb–4Mar45, hereafter *TF 58 OpRpt*; cf. ComAirPac "Analysis of Air Operations, Tokyo Carrier Strikes, Feb45," dtd 28Apr45, cited in Morison, *Victory in the Pacific*, p. 25.

[32] *TF 52 AR*, p. A-38.

nese had received specific orders to hold their fire, the temptation for one gun crew of having such a juicy target pass within 1,500 meters of its gun proved too much; the enemy gunner opened fire at the heavy cruiser with the 150mm gun. The first round was 50 yards short. The *Pensacola* took immediate evasive action, but by this time the Japanese had the range and in a matter of three minutes scored six hits on the vessel. The shells wrecked the combat information center, set fire to a plane on the starboard catapult, punctured the hull, and killed 17 and wounded 120 of the ship's crew.[33] Among the dead was the executive officer. Despite the heavy damage and the extensive casualties, the *Pensacola* continued to fire as she withdrew to extinguish the fire and repair damage. She continued to carry out her mission, ceasing fire from time to time while casualties were being operated on and given blood transfusions.[34]

Shortly before 1100, nearly 100 UDT swimmers headed for the island. The hazardous mission of these daredevil frogmen was to check beach and surf conditions, look for underwater obstacles both at the approaches to the landing beaches themselves and on the beaches, and to destroy any such impediments while in plain view of the enemy. As the swimmers neared the island, they came under heavy mortar and small arms fire. Covering them were 12 LCIs, stationed about 1,000 yards offshore, from where they directed a steady barrage of rockets and 40mm gunfire against the beaches. This fire, and particularly the launching of the rockets, presumably led the enemy to believe that an assault against Iwo Jima was under way. In any case, contrary to the orders they had received to hold their fire until the assault force had landed, Japanese heavy artillery to the north of the eastern beaches and at the foot of Suribachi opened fire on the lightly armored gunboats. In the course of this uneven contest, which continued for 45 minutes, the LCIs absorbed a severe pounding. An official report noted:

> The personnel of these little gunboats displayed magnificent courage as they returned fire with everything they had and refused to move out until they were forced to do so by material and personnel casualties. Even then, after undergoing terrific punishment, some returned to their stations amid a hail of fire, until again heavily hit. Relief LCI(G)s replaced damaged ships without hesitation.[35]

During the furious though unequal exchange of fire, all of the 12 gunboats were hit. The Japanese damaged LCI *474* so badly that the crew had to abandon the ship; when it capsized later, friendly shells sent it to the bottom. Intensive fire from destroyers and fire support ships, and a smoke screen laid by white phosphorus projectiles, were used to cover this operation. Fire support ships took on board casualties from the LCI(G)s as they withdrew. Altogether, 7 men had been killed and 153 wounded in the LCIs; the destroyer *Leutze* also had received a direct hit which killed 7 and wounded 33. Only 6 of the 12 gunboats, LCIs *438*, *449*,

---

[33] *TF 51 AR*, Pt V, Sec H, MedRpt, Table II, p. 6.
[34] *U. S. Fleet OpRpt*, Iwo Jima, pp. 1–13.
[35] *Ibid.*

450, 466, 457, and *469* made it back to Saipan under their own power.

By 1220 all of the frogmen, with one exception, had been recovered; the fate of the missing man was to remain unknown. The members of the four UDT teams had accomplished their mission. Their reconnaissance had disclosed that there were no underwater or beach obstructions or minefields. Beach and surf conditions were found to be favorable for a landing. In fact, some of the swimmers actually had crawled out of the water to collect soil samples for examination on board ship.[36]

While the badly damaged LCIs were withdrawing out to sea, the *Nevada* delivered a heavy and concentrated counterbattery fire against the enemy artillery positions until 1240. At the same time, the battleship *Tennessee* and two others, the *Idaho* and the *Nevada,* put down a smoke screen along the entire eastern beach area to cover the withdrawal of the frogmen. The smoke screen also obscured the view of supporting destroyers and battleships, which experienced difficulty in picking out enemy weapons because of the smoke screen over the water and the dust kicked up by shells bursting on the island.

The work of the UDTs was not completed with the exploration of the eastern beaches; a reconnaissance of the western beaches was scheduled for the afternoon of the 17th. As elements of the UDTs were preparing for the second reconnaissance, heavy bombardment ships began to pound top priority targets on the east coast. The heavy enemy fire from hitherto unsuspected positions had brought home to officers conducting the preliminary bombardment the fact that a large amount of damage remained to be inflicted on the enemy installations. Admiral Blandy revised ammunition allotments upward to permit heavier concentrations of fire against the eastern beaches, particularly those areas sheltering the recently spotted enemy coast defense guns. Admiral Rodgers, commanding the Gunfire and Covering Force (TF 54), recommended to Admiral Blandy that all available fire power be brought to bear against top priority installations around Mount Suribachi and on the high ground north of the eastern beaches. This recommendation was approved, and for the remainder of the 17th, Fire Support Units One and Two, including the *Nevada, Idaho, Tennessee, Vicksburg,* and *Salt Lake City* executed close range fire missions against those areas.

The UDT reconnaissance of the western beaches got under way at 1615, under the protection of three battleships and a cruiser. Once again, the swimmers drew Japanese automatic weapons and rifle fire, but on this occasion there were no casualties and at 1800 the frogmen, having completed the reconnaissance, returned to their APDs. One mine was discovered and destroyed. No minefields or water obstacles blocked the approach to the western beaches. Both beaches and surf conditions were thought to be suitable for landing. Twenty-two Marines from the reconnaissance companies of the 4th and 5th Marine Divisions had accompanied the

---

[36] *TF 52 AR,* Pt C, p. 1,; Cdr D. L. Kauffman, USN, ltr to HistBr, HQMC, dtd 13Jan53, in *Iwo Comments.*

THE PRELIMINARIES

UDT teams on both beach reconnaissance exploits. Upon completion of these missions, the Marines returned to their units on board command ships at sea. The intelligence collected by the reconnaissance men provided assault unit commanders with current information about the area they were soon to encounter.

As a result of good weather throughout 17 February, aviation also carried out destructive raids on Iwo Jima during the day. Carrier pilots flew a total of 226 sorties, not counting search and patrol missions. The main targets of these attacks were dual-purpose guns and antiaircraft automatic weapons around the airfields and beach areas. Napalm dropped by eight Navy fighters during the day had only limited success. Some of the bombs did not release; others failed to ignite upon hitting the ground. In any case, there was little left to burn on Iwo. The Japanese did not remain passive in the face of the continuous air attacks, for heavy antiaircraft fire met the attacking planes. A force of 42 Army Air Forces B-24 bombers dropped bombs from an altitude of 5,000 feet, scoring hits in the target area. As far as could be ascertained, however, this bombing inflicted little or no known damage to enemy installations.[37]

Late on the 17th, it became apparent that the Japanese really believed that they had repulsed an invasion of Iwo earlier that day. Radio Tokyo reported that the American landings had been frustrated and that five warships, including a battleship, had been sunk.

In a similar vein, Admiral Soemu Toyoda, Commander in Chief of the *Combined Fleet*, sent the following message to Rear Admiral Ichimaru on Iwo:

> Despite very powerful enemy bombings and shellings, your unit at Iwo coolly judged the enemy intentions and foiled the first landing attempt and serenely awaits the next one, determined to hold Iwo at any cost. I am greatly elated to know that, and I wish you to continue to maintain high morale and repulse the enemy, no matter how intense his attacks, and safeguard the outer defenses of our homeland.[38]

Even as the Japanese were rejoicing at the thought of having driven an assault force back out to sea, the top echelon of the American invasion force met in Admiral Blandy's cabin on board the *Estes*. The atmosphere was not a joyful one, for only one more day remained, and two days of bombardment had inflicted comparatively little damage on enemy installations on shore. In fact, following two days of heavy shelling, the Iwo defenses looked more formidable than ever. In Blandy's presence, Commander W. P. Chilton, the gunnery officer, and Lieutenant Colonel Weller, representing the landing force, discussed what should be done. Weller urged that on the last day remaining, all available fire-power be brought to bear against the defenses commanding the beaches. Admiral Blandy approved this recommendation at once.[39]

According to the modified plan drawn up on the evening of 17 February, four

---

[37] *TF 52 AR*, Encl I, p. 1.

[38] Adm Soemu Toyoda msg to RAdm Toshinosuke Ichimaru n.d., in Newcomb, *Iwo Jima*, pp. 82-83.

[39] *VAC NGF and Air Rpts*, p. 15.

battleships, the *Tennessee, Nevada, New York,* and *California,* as well as the heavy cruiser *Chester,* were to concentrate their entire armament of 5–, 8–, and 14–inch guns in a blanket bombardment of the landing areas. The ships received permission to fire all unexpended ammunition, except that needed for D-Day, provided the weather permitted it.

Promptly at 0745 on the morning of the 18th, Admiral Rodgers ordered his Gunfire and Covering Force to "close beach and get going."[40] These ships immediately moved to within 2,500 yards offshore and opened fire. In line with Blandy's special order, the *Tennessee* and *Idaho* were to concentrate their fire against the batteries sited at the foot of Mount Suribachi, as well as against the coast defense guns emplaced on the rim of a quarry about 400 yards north of the East Boat Basin. In executing this vital mission in somewhat less than five hours, the *Tennessee* expended a total of 333 rounds; the *Idaho* fired 280 rounds during the same period of time.[41]

Unfortunately, the weather on 18 February was not nearly so favorable as on the preceding day. Visibility, only fair throughout most of the day, was reduced to poor during the frequent light rains on D minus 1. Despite the handicap imposed by poor observation, the massive bombardment was having its effect. When the last day of the preparatory fire ended shortly before 1830, vital enemy installations had sustained massive damage. Among 201 major targets in the main landing area, 11 coast defense guns, 22 out of 33 five-inch dual-purpose guns, 16 of 20 large blockhouses, and nearly half of the 93 pillboxes had been destroyed or heavily damaged.

While Iwo was receiving a final going over by the bombardment group, Seventh Air Force bombers arrived over the island after a long flight from the Marianas. Once again the weather failed to cooperate, and the air strike had to be cancelled. Naval aviators of the Support Carrier Group, commanded by Rear Admiral Calvin T. Durgin, flew 28 sorties against positions flanking the landing beaches. These were the last of 612 sorties flown by carrier planes against ground targets on Iwo Jima prior to D-Day. Only three of the naval aircraft fell victim to enemy ground fire, and their air crews were rescued.[42]

Late on 18 February, a low-flying enemy plane was to strike a brief but vicious blow against the invasion force. At 2130, the *Blessman* (APD-48) was hit by an enemy bomb which exploded in the troop space above the forward fireroom. In addition to serious material damage, 2 of the courageous frogmen of UDT 15, who had emerged from the hazardous beach reconnaissance missions of the previous day unharmed, were killed, and 20 were wounded. The crew of the *Blessman* suffered 11 wounded.[43] This attack on the evening of 18 February was the only action by enemy aircraft to inflict any damage on American units at or near Iwo during the preinvasion operations.

---

[40] *TF 52 AR,* p. 11.
[41] *VAC NGF and Air Rpts,* p. 15.
[42] *TF 52 AR,* Encl D, p. 9.
[43] *TF 51 AR,* Pt IV, p. 13; *TF 52 AR,* Encl H, p. 1.

THE PRELIMINARIES

All that remained now before Marines would hit the Iwo beaches the following morning was the execution of the D-Day fires in preparation for the landings. This pre-H-Hour bombardment would be the Navy's final opportunity to pound the enemy defenses before the assault. In fact, when the heavy support units withdrew from Iwo on the evening of the 18th, the softening-up phase had already come to an end. On the eve of D-Day, Admiral Blandy sent this message to Admiral Turner:

> Though weather has not permitted complete expenditure of entire ammunition allowance and more installations can be found and destroyed with one more day of bombardment, I believe landing can be accomplished tomorrow as scheduled if necessary. I recommend, however, special attention before and during landing to flanks and East Coast of island with neutralizing fire and white phosphorus projectiles immediately available if required.[44]

The final night before the landings was one of deep soul-searching for General Holland Smith, who found that "the imminence of action and the responsibility for the most appalling operation we had yet undertaken weighed heavily."[45] This veteran Marine commander was filled with apprehension by the gravity of the coming battle. Weeks earlier, Smith recalled, when the Navy had overruled the Marines' request for nine days of preparatory gunfire and then withdrew two of the 16-inch gun ships to provide antiaircraft fire for Task Force 58, Admiral Spruance had told him: "I regret this confusion caused in your carefully laid plans, but I know you and your people will get away with it."[46] Smith realized even then that any curtailment in the duration and volume of preparatory naval gunfire would be paid for with the lives of many Marines. Years later, the general was to recall:

> I felt certain we would lose 15,000 men at Iwo Jima. This number was the absolute minimum calculated in our plans made at Pearl Harbor, although some of my officers wistfully predicted a lower figure. So far as the Marines were concerned, we had made every preparation humanly possible to capture the island as expeditiously and as economically as possible. We were to land 60,000 assault troops, and the estimate that one in every four would be dead or wounded never left my mind.
>
> I was not afraid of the outcome of the battle. I knew we would win. We always had. But contemplation of the cost in lives caused me many sleepless nights.[47]

As night descended upon Iwo Jima and its surrounding dark waters on the evening of the 18th, the preliminary bombardment phase came to an end. Early on the 19th a new phase, the assault, would begin. The invasion of Iwo Jima would take place without modification of the carefully laid plans.

---

[44] CTF 52 msg to CTF 51, NCR 60303, dtd 18Feb45, as cited in Bartley, *Iwo Monograph*, p. 49.

[45] Smith and Finch, *Coral and Brass*, p. 253.

[46] *Ibid.*, p. 247.

[47] *Ibid.*, pp. 253–254.

CHAPTER 4

D-Day on Iwo Jima[1]

PRE H-HOUR BOMBARDMENT[2]

Early on 19 February, the assault ships of Task Force 53 under Admiral Hill arrived off Iwo Jima and joined Admiral Blandy's Amphibious Support Force. As dawn rose over Iwo Jima, more than 450 ships of the Fifth Fleet lay offshore, the largest armada ever assembled thus far for a military operation in the Pacific Theater.

Included in Admiral Hill's Attack Force were the troop ships carrying the 4th and 5th Marine Divisions. The huge vessels headed towards the transport area about 10,000 yards offshore. On board the ships, 50,000 Marines ate a hearty breakfast and went topside for a glance at the island which they would shortly assault. There was little to see. Almost totally obscured by the darkness, the island appeared as a shadowy mass of land, dominated by Mount Suribachi which "gave thousands of straining eyes aboard ship only periodic glimpses of its sharp, vertical-cone."[3]

It was apparent by early morning that the landing force would encounter favorable weather. The sea was relatively smooth and surf conditions were satisfactory. The sky was clear; visibility was virtually unlimited, and the temperature was 68 degrees. Wind velocity was eight to ten knots from the north.

Promptly at 0640, the heavy support ships launched the pre-H-Hour bombardment, as Admiral Rodgers' Gunfire

---

[1] Unless otherwise noted, the material in this chapter is derived from: U. S. Flt Ops Rpt, 16Feb-16Mar45; *TF 51 AR*; *TF 52 AR*; *TF 56 AR*; TF 56 G–3 Jnl, 26Jan-14Mar45, hereafter *TF 56 G–3 Jnl*; TG 53.2 AR, 19Feb-4Mar45, hereafter *TG 53.2 AR*; *PhibGru 2 AR*; *VAC AR*; *VAC G–2 Rpts*; VAC C–3 Jnl, 25Jan-27Mar45, hereafter *VAC C–3 Jnl*; VAC C–3 PerRpt, 19Feb-26Mar45, hereafter *VAC C–3 Rpt*; VAC C–4 Jnl, 6-13Mar45, hereafter *VAC C–4 Jnl*; 4th MarDiv OpRpt; 4th MarDiv G–2 PerRpts, 19-25Feb45, hereafter *4th MarDiv G–2 Rpts*; 4th MarDiv D–3 PerRpts, 8Feb-17Mar45, hereafter *4th MarDiv D–3 Rpts*; 4th MarDiv D–4 PerRpts, 3Jan-19Mar45, hereafter *4th MarDiv D–4 Rpts*; *5th MarDiv AR*; 5th MarDiv G–1 Jnl, 19Feb-26Mar45, hereafter *5th MarDiv D–1 Jnl*; 5th MarDiv D–2 PerRpts, 19Feb-26Mar45, hereafter *5th MarDiv D–2 PerRpts*; 5th MarDiv D–3 Jnl, 19Feb-26Mar45, hereafter *5th MarDiv D–3 Jnl*; 5th MarDiv D–4 Jnl, 19Feb-26Mar45, hereafter *5th MarDiv D–4 Jnl*; *Iwo Comments*; Bartley, *Iwo Monograph*; Sherrod, *Marine Corps Aviation in World War II*; Craven and Cate, *The Pacific*; Proehl, *The Fourth Marine Division*; Conner, *The Fifth Marine Division*; Newcomb, *Iwo Jima*; Morehouse, *The Iwo Jima Campaign*; T. Grady Gallant, *The Friendly Dead* (New York: Doubleday and Company, Inc., 1964), hereafter Gallant, *The Friendly Dead*, quoted with permission.

[2] Additional material in this section is derived from: *Fifth Flt NGF rpt*; *Iwo Preliminary Gunfire Requirements*; *TF 53 AR*; *TF 56 AirRpt*; *TF 56 Preliminary NGF Rpt*; *VAC NGF and Air Rpts*; Henri et. al., *Marines on Iwo Jima*.

[3] Conner, *The Fifth Marine Division*, p. 43.

and Covering Force hurled tons of high explosives into the island. This was the last chance to silence the heavy enemy guns that dominated the boat lanes and beaches, and the gun crews of the *North Carolina, Washington, New York, Texas, Arkansas,* and *Nevada* turned-to with grim determination. As shell bursts flicked flame, smoke, and chunks of Iwo into the air, it appeared as if the bombardment were intended to blow the very island out of the sea. Even the dead crater of Mount Suribachi seemed to come to life as it steamed from successive hits along its lip. Blasts, following one another in close succession, rocked the beaches, the airfields, and the northern portion of Iwo with its numerous hills and gullies.

In addition to the heavy gunfire ships, the gunboat and mortar support groups participated in the preparatory fire. The latter groups consisted of 42 LCI gunboats. Twelve of the LCIs were armed with 4.5-inch rockets and 40mm guns; 18 carried 4.2-inch mortars, and 9 were equipped with 5-inch rocket launchers.[4] The LCIs joined the bombardment by the big ships at 0730 and, throughout the morning, expended nearly 10,000 rockets and large quantities of mortar ammunition while showering the slopes of Mount Suribachi and the high ground to the north of the beaches with rocket and mortar fire.

At the same time, initial preparations for boating the assault force got under way. LSTs and troop transports eased into the areas assigned to them and prepared to discharge their cargo of troops and equipment. The transports lowered the landing craft, which circled as they waited to be boarded by the Marines. On the tank decks of the LSTs, the engines of the LVTs were started, and Marines took their places in the vehicles assigned to them to await the launching signal. The signal was given at 0725; less than half an hour later, 482 amtracs were churning the water, ready to carry eight battalions into battle.[5]

The prelanding bombardment proceeded exactly as scheduled. A few minutes after 0800, the naval guns lifted their fire and 120 fighters and bombers of TF 58 swept over the island in two waves. The aircraft concentrated their attack against the slopes of Mount Suribachi, the landing beaches, and the high ground to the north of the landing beaches. Following the bombing and strafing by the first wave, the second arrived over the island and unleashed napalm, rockets, and machine gun fire against the defenders. Included in the second wave were 24 Marine F4U Corsairs under the command of Lieutenant Colonel William A. Millington, commanding VMF-124 on board the *Essex*.

The squadron commander led his flight over Iwo Jima to attack the flanks and high ground along the landing beaches. From H minus 45 to H minus 35, the planes remained over the island and launched their attacks in accordance with a plan previously worked out between Millington and Colonel Vernon E. Megee, Commander of the Landing Force Air Support Control Unit and Deputy Commander, Aircraft, Landing Force. Prior to the mission,

---

[4] *VAC NGF Rpt,* pp. 25–26.

[5] Bartley, *Iwo Monograph,* p. 51.

Megee had admonished the fighter squadron commander to "go in and scrape your bellies on the beach"[6] and that is precisely what Millington proposed to do.

While these air strikes were under way, the gunfire support ships moved closer to the shore and assumed positions from which they would deliver the final neutralization fires. A strike by 44 Army Air Forces bombers had also been scheduled prior to H-Hour, but over half of the Liberators failed to complete the trip from the Marianas; only 15 arrived to drop 19 tons of 100-pound bombs on the eastern defenses of Iwo.[7]

At 0825, the naval bombardment resumed. Since only a half hour remained before the first assault wave would hit the beaches, all available fire was directed against the landing sites. As the last phase of the pre-assault bombardment got under way, air bursts were employed to annihilate any Japanese that might be caught out in the open. The naval gunners subsequently shifted to impact rounds as time for the approach of the first assault wave grew near. During the final 15 minutes of the bombardment, the naval vessels offshore blasted the invasion beaches with everything they had. The thunderous roar of the 16-inch guns was supplemented by the sharper bark of the 5- and 8-inch guns of the destroyers and cruisers. Rocket craft unleashed their fire, and mortar boats shelled inland to a depth of about 1,000 yards. As the assault troops approached the shore, the naval bombardment shifted ahead to provide the mightiest preinvasion shelling thus far experienced in the Pacific Theater. In less than 30 minutes, more than 8,000 shells smashed into the beach area.

In other amphibious assaults in the Pacific Theater, naval gunfire had sometimes lifted too far inland when the troops came ashore. This lack of adequate fires close to landing areas had resulted in heavy casualties early in the operation, notably at Saipan. In order to prevent this situation from arising at Iwo Jima, VAC recommended the use of a rolling barrage reminiscent of the massive artillery concentrations of World War I. Such a barrage had to be precisely timed to keep the fire just ahead of the advancing troops; infantry commanders had to exercise maximum care to keep their men from advancing faster than the scheduled time for lifting the barrage forward. The rolling barrage was to be delivered by the 5-inch batteries, whose gunners were to maintain a 400-yard margin of safety ahead of the friendly troops. If, for any reason, the attack bogged down and did not move forward as rapidly as anticipated, certain prearranged fires were to be repeated.[8]

Only minutes remained to H-Hour. None of the officers responsible for the preliminary bombardment could fathom the effect of the damage inflicted on the enemy defenses; at best they could hope that the naval bombardment and the aerial bombing and strafing had seriously diminished the enemy's ability

---

[6] Colonel Vernon E. Megee, as quoted in Sherrod, *Marine Corps Aviation in World War II*, p. 347.

[7] Craven and Cate, *the Pacific*, pp. 591–592.

[8] *VAC NGF and Air Rpts*, p. 23.

to frustrate the imminent landings. The Marines about to hit the hostile beaches would be the first to know for certain how strongly the enemy could still react to their amphibious assault.

THE AMPHIBIOUS ASSAULT[9]

For the Marines in the assault waves, D-Day had started with the traditional meal of steak and eggs. Shortly after 0800, while naval shells were rocking Iwo, the amphibian tractors carrying eight Marine battalions to the Iwo beaches were churning in the water. A line of departure had been established about two miles offshore and parallel to the beach. At each end of this line, a control vessel was stationed to mark its boundaries. A central control vessel occupied the middle of the line. Along the line, at regular intervals, small vessels marked the boat lanes. The assistant division commanders, Brigadier General Franklin A. Hart for the 4th Marine Division, and Brigadier General Leo D. Hermle for the 5th, stationed themselves at each end of the line of departure as observers.

Boated and circling, the first three waves were ready to cross the line of departure by 0815. It was from here that the Marines watched the island take a severe pounding from the naval shelling and cheered as the supporting aircraft unloaded their lethal cargo over the island. The men approaching Iwo Jima were fully aware of what lay ahead; there had been no attempt at concealing the fact that a tough and costly battle awaited them. Men of the 4th Marine Division were going in with the prayer of their commander, General Cates, that as many of them as possible might be spared. General Schmidt felt that it would be a bitter but short fight.

The men in the assault waves hoped that the Navy could come up to its expectation of knocking out all defenses on the beaches, as well as most other targets further inland. Their mood varied from incredulity that any of the defenders could survive the heavy naval bombardment to skepticism born out of past experience. Many Marines remembered how many of the Japanese had survived similar bombardments on Tarawa, Guam, and Peleliu. There was also some wishful thinking; smaller islands in the Volcano-Bonins had been known to sink into the ocean, and there was hardly a Marine in the convoy who did not hope that Iwo might put on such a disappearing act under the weight of the explosives pouring upon it.[10]

At precisely 0830, the central control vessel dipped her pennant, releasing the first assault wave. Sixty-eight LVT-(A)s of the 2d Armored Amphibian Battalion, commanded by Lieutenant Colonel Reed M. Fawell, Jr., crossed the line of departure and headed for the beaches. While hundreds of naval shells whistled overhead, the first wave followed the gunboats that poured rockets and 40mm shells into the beach before

---

[9] Additional material in this section is derived from: *TransDiv 45 AR*; 2d Armd Amtrac Bn AR, 17Apr45; 1st SP Bn UJnl, 19-24-Feb45; 2d SP Bn UJnl, 19Feb-3Mar45; 5th SP Rgt. AR, n.d.; LSM Gru 13 AR, 19Feb-14Mar-45, hereafter *LSM Gru 13 AR*; 31st NCB AR, 9Mar45, in *5th MarDiv AR*, Anx U, hereafter *31st NCB AR*; 1st JASCO OpRpt, 5Apr45.

[10] Henri *et al, Marines on Iwo Jima*, p. 34.

turning right and left respectively to positions from where they continued to support the flank battalions.

The operations plan had allowed 30 minutes for each assault wave to travel the 4,000 yards from the line of departure to the beaches. Following the first, successive waves crossed the line at 250- to 300-yard intervals. The second assault wave, consisting of 1,360 Marines in LVTs, crossed the line of departure two minutes behind the first wave. Eight more waves formed behind the first two, to be landed at five-minute intervals. The plan called for 9,000 men to be ashore in somewhat less than 45 minutes.

When the leading wave had reached a point 400 yards offshore, the naval bombardment shifted to the interior of the island and to the flanks. At the same time, Lieutenant Colonel Millington's fighters streaked down in magnificent strafing which continued relentlessly as the LVT(A)s approached the beaches. In accordance with their orders, the pilots, who earlier that morning had executed the napalm and rocket strike against Iwo, now hit the beaches in daring low-level attacks. Just as the first wave came ashore, the planes shifted their strafing runs about 500 yards inland.

The ship-to-shore movement of the assault waves was carried out according to schedule. The first wave landed between 0859 and 0903; the second and third waves came ashore at two-minute intervals. The defenders remained strangely silent as the first assault troops approached the beaches, and the initial waves were not subjected to any enemy antiboat fire during the final approach to the objective. For some of the Marines, a small sliver of hope began to emerge that the heavy bombardment had reduced the enemy to impotence.

Up to the point where the first LVT(A)s emerged from the water and ground forward, the entire maneuver had been executed with parade-ground precision. For the incoming Marines, the only indication of the enemy's presence on the island thus far had been confined to the air. One moment, a 5th Marine Division observation aircraft was circling lazily overhead; the next, enemy antiaircraft fire scored a direct hit and the small airplane spiralled into the surf. The first tractors had no sooner reached the beach and commenced heading inland than it was discovered that the 15-foot terrace directly behind the beach blocked their fields of fire. The height and steepness of the terrace was the first unpleasant surprise that the Marines were to encounter on Iwo. A second one was not long in coming. As the Marines of the 4th and 5th Divisions swarmed from their vehicles, it became evident that the composition of the volcanic sand was not what had been expected. Instead of sand with sufficient consistency to support at least tracked vehicles and men on foot, Marines of the landing force, many of them weighted down with more than 100 pounds of weapons and other gear, found themselves floundering in a sea of soft volcanic ash that all but precluded their ascending that 15-foot seawall. Almost immediately, the Marines sank up to their ankles into the loose ash that tugged at their feet and made all forward movement a strenuous undertaking.

ASSAULT TROOPS *of the 4th Marine Division go ashore on Iwo Jima. (USMC 110109)*

MARINES OF 2/27 *hit the beach in the shadow of Mt. Suribachi. (USMC 111688)*

Some of the amphibian tractors never slackened their speed upon reaching the beaches but pushed their way straight inland, up the first terrace and beyond it until they had advanced between 50 and 75 yards. Those LVT(A)s failing to negotiate the incline headed back out to sea, where they turned around and fired inland. At 0907, the third wave of 1,200 men went ashore, followed about five minutes later by another 1,600 men of the fourth wave. Successive assault waves followed closely behind the first ones. There still was no organized enemy opposition though a few isolated artillery and mortar shells began to fall in the surf as the later waves neared the shore. Except for a number of land mines, the beaches were found clear of man-made obstacles.

The eight battalions of the 4th and 5th Marine Divisions that landed abreast on the southeastern shore of Iwo Jima were 1/28, commanded by Lieutenant Colonel Jackson B. Butterfield, and 2/28, commanded by Lieutenant Colonel Chandler W. Johnson, on Green 1; 2/27, under Major John A. Antonelli, on Red 1; 1/27, under Lieutenant Colonel John A. Butler, on Red 2; 1/23, commanded by Lieutenant Colonel Ralph Haas, on Yellow 1; 2/23, under Major Robert Davidson, on Yellow 2; 1/25, headed by Lieutenant Colonel Hollis U. Mustain, on Blue 1; and 3/25 under Lieutenant Colonel James Taul, on the southern edge of Blue 2.

As the men headed inland, the Japanese gradually came to life. The first among the landing force to feel the enemy reaction were the men of Major Davidson's 2/23 on Yellow 2 in the 4th Division sector. A moderate amount of mortar fire hit the beach within two minutes after the first wave had landed. Within 15 minutes, Marines on the Yellow and Blue beaches were reporting heavy enemy mortar fire. To the south, on the Red Beaches and Green 1, 5th Division Marines started to advance inland against initially light opposition. By 0930, 1/28 had moved 150 yards inland. Ten minutes later, the battalion reported receiving heavy mortar fire from the left flank. By the time the advance had covered 300 yards, the men were sprinkled, showered, and ultimately deluged by mortar and artillery fire from Mount Suribachi, as well as from the high ground to the north of the landing beaches. The loose, slipping sand offered poor cover; foxholes filled in almost as fast as a man could shovel, and urgent requests for sandbags began to fill the air waves. By 0935, Green 1 and the Red Beaches were on the receiving end of a heavy mortar barrage. Marines moving inland drew intense machine gun and rifle fire from well-concealed pillboxes, blockhouses, and caves as soon as they left the protective cover of the first terrace.

While the Marines advancing into the interior of Iwo were being swamped by enemy fire that was still increasing both in volume and accuracy, congestion among the additional waves along the shore began to mount. The Japanese meanwhile had begun to concentrate their fire on LVTs and landing craft on and near the beaches. Enemy mortars and artillery soon scored numerous direct hits on the hapless vessels. Jeeps and trucks emerging from those landing craft that had been fortunate enough to survive the trip ashore rolled out on the beaches only to become bogged down in the treacherous volcanic ash even before they had cleared the ramp. Many of the small craft, their bows pinned to the beach, broached and swamped.

Despite the enemy fire, congestion at the water's edge, and initial confusion accompanying the landings, men and supplies continued to pour ashore. Within an hour and a half from the time that the Marines of the first wave had set foot on the island, all of the eight assault battalions were ashore. At 1005, three LSMs carrying 16 tanks of Lieutenant Colonel Richard K. Schmidt's 4th Tank Battalion hit the Yellow Beaches. The tanks encountered considerable difficulty in getting ashore. Even then, their troubles were far from over, and three tanks struck mines less than 150 yards in from the water.

While the naval barrage was still providing cover, the four newly landed Marine regiments prepared to reorganize and begin the push inland. From north to south these regiments were the 25th Marines, commanded by Colonel John R. Lanigan, and the 23rd Marines under Colonel Walter W. Wensinger, both belonging to the 4th Marine Division. The 5th Marine Division was represented by the 27th Marines, led by Colonel Thomas A. Wornham, and the 28th Marines under Colonel Harry B. Liversedge.

THE ADVANCE INLAND[11]

As troop strength built up ashore, the time had come to put the basic plan of attack into effect. Along the northern part of the beachhead, the 25th Marines was to advance towards a quarry just north of the East Boat Basin, which formed the eastern anchor of the O-1 Line denoting the objectives to be seized by the end of D-Day. This line, bisecting Motoyama Airfield No. 2, curved across the center of the island to the western shore at a point approximately 1,200 yards west of the airfield. Moving inland from the Yellow Beaches, the 23d Marines was to advance across the northern portion of Motoyama Airfield No. 1 towards Airfield No. 2. To the 27th Marines fell the task of advancing inland in a northwesterly direction, slicing across the southern tip of Airfield No. 1 and then pivoting more to the north, to reach a point west of Airfield No. 2. The 28th Marines had the mission of isolating Mount Suribachi and assaulting this formidable obstacle. To this end, the 1st Battalion, landing at H-Hour, was to cut across the narrow neck of the island, a distance of only 700 yards. The 2d Battalion was to

---

[11] Additional material in this section is derived from: 13th Mar UJnl, 19Feb-21Mar45, hereafter *13th Mar UJnl;* 23d Mar OpRpt,

9Apr45, 4th MarDiv OpRpt, Anx F, hereafter *23d Mar OpRpt;* 24th Mar OpRpt, 19Feb-18Mar45, Anx G to 4th MarDiv OpRpt, hereafter *24th Mar OpRpt;* 25th Mar UJnl, 18Feb-23Mar45, hereafter *25th Mar UJnl;* 25th Mar OpRpt, 15Apr45, 4th MarDiv OpRpt, Anx H, hereafter *25th Mar OpRpt;* 28th Mar UJnl, 19Feb-26Mar45, hereafter *28th Mar UJnl;* 5th Tank Bn AR, Feb-Mar45, hereafter *5th Tank Bn AR;* 1/13 UJnl, 19Feb-17Mar45, hereafter *1/13 UJnl;* 1/24 OpRpt, 20Apr45, hereafter *1/24 OpRpt;* 2/24 AR, 19Feb-16Mar45, hereafter *2/24 AR;* 1/27 UJnl, 19Feb-18Mar45, hereafter *1/27 UJnl;* 2/27 UJnl, 19Feb-23Mar45, hereafter *2/27 UJnl;* 3/27 UJnl, 19Feb-23Mar45, hereafter *3/27 UJnl;* 471st Amph Truck Co (Army) OpRpt, 17Mar45, hereafter *471st Amph Trk Co OpRpt.*

advance about 350 yards inland, then turn southward towards Mount Suribachi.

At 0935, 2/28 started to land on Green 1 behind 1/28. Its mission was to take up positions facing Mount Suribachi, protecting the left flank of the landing force. By this time, heavy mortar and artillery fire was enveloping the beaches, making reorganization of the companies difficult.

As the 1st Battalion launched its 700-yard sprint for the western shore with Companies B and C abreast, accurate enemy small arms fire from concealed positions began to rake the advancing Marines. It soon became evident that the advance would prove costly. The intensity of the enemy fire all but precluded a coordinated movement. Men advanced in small groups, heedless of security to their flanks; some units were temporarily pinned down by an enemy who remained largely invisible. Between the bursts of artillery and mortar shells all around them, the Marines strained to get a glimpse of the defenders. What they saw was not reassuring, for halfway across the island a maze of mutually supporting blockhouses and pillboxes extended across the entire front.

In a situation where movement threatened to bog down in the heavily fortified area, the courage of individual Marines kept the attack rolling. Among the first to distinguish himself was Captain Dwayne E. Mears, commanding Company B. Armed with only a pistol, the company commander personally assaulted a pillbox that was retarding the advance of his company. Despite a wound that later proved to be fatal, Captain Mears continued to attack successive enemy positions until he became too weak to move.[12] On the right, Captain Phil E. Roach led the advance of Company C across the island, carefully maintaining the same rate of progress as Company B. While assaulting a heavily fortified position, Captain Roach also became a casualty. Many men who found themselves separated from their platoons during the dash across the island formed small groups that continued to advance independently, thus helping to preserve the momentum of the attack.

The success of the 28th Marines' attack owed much to the support provided by the 60mm mortars which maintained continuous fire against groups of Japanese that had been flushed out of their emplacements. This fire kept the enemy on the run and out in the open, where he presented a visible target to the advancing riflemen. Lieutenant Richard H. Sandberg, commanding Company A's mortar platoon, spotted an enemy 90mm mortar squad and concentrated his fire on the Japanese until they were forced to abandon their weapon. Even more remarkably, in the heat of the engagement this platoon leader was observed firing a 60mm mortar with amazing accuracy, though it was without a base plate.[13] Before noon, Lieutenant Sandberg became a casualty and had to be evacuated.

At 1035, elements of Company B reached the western shore of Iwo. Enemy fire had inflicted so many casualties and made control so difficult that

---

[12] *5th MarDiv AR*, Anx S, p. 2.
[13] *Ibid.*

D-DAY ON IWO JIMA

THE INVASION OF IWO JIMA *as seen through the eyes of a Japanese artist. (USA SC 301128)*

DOBERMAN PINSCHER *of the 6th War Dog Platoon and handler approach enemy cave. (USAF 58252 AC)*

only the platoon leader, Lieutenant Frank J. Wright, and four men of the 1st Platoon, Company B, made it all the way across the island. Lieutenant Wesley C. Bates, leading the 2d Platoon, and six of his men reached the western beach around 1100 and joined forces with Lieutenant Wright.

Even though elements of the 1st Battalion had now crossed the island, bypassed enemy positions continued to offer fierce resistance. Company A, which had landed in 1/28 reserve and faced south towards Mount Suribachi to protect the battalion's left flank, was now relieved by 2/28 and joined the remainder of the 1st Battalion in mopping up. Because of the heavy casualties 1/28 had sustained, Colonel Liversedge requested the release of 3/28, the division reserve, to his control. General Rockey granted this request. The battalion, boated and prepared to land on any 5th Division beach, received the order to land at 1210. Ten minutes later the first boats crossed the line of departure. As the leading wave approached the shore, heavy fire from Mount Suribachi and the high ground north of the landing beaches was directed at the boats. This unit suffered many more casualties during the ship-to-shore movement than had the 1st and 2d Battalions. Shortly after 1300, all elements were ashore, though it was not until late afternoon that the battalion was able to edge its way into the line. Following a naval gunfire preparation, and with adequate air support, the 2d and 3d Battalions were to jump off jointly at 1545 to attack south towards Mount Suribachi.

For such an attack, the support of armor was necessary. Company C of the 5th Tank Battalion was therefore ordered to land in direct support of the 28th Marines. This company had 14 Sherman M-4 tanks, two flametanks, one tankdozer, and one retriever. When they landed on Red One Beach about 1130, the tanks found it rough going because soft sand and storm terraces made exit difficult and the first terrace was mined. By the time additional elements of the 5th Tank Battalion got ashore, the beach was congested by stranded wheeled vehicles disabled by enemy fire. The increasing concentration of men and equipment in a restricted area was beginning to cause considerable confusion.

An eye witness had this to say about Company C's arrival on Iwo Jima:

> An infantryman picked up one of the first tanks to land and started to guide him off the beach; the route he used was marked with white tape. When the tank reached the top of the first terrace, he was guided to the right, across the tape and immediately struck a horn mine. One casualty was suffered, the driver having both legs broken, the remainder of the crew was badly shaken up. The interior of the tank was so badly damaged no attempt was made to repair it. Later it was turned into spare parts.[14]

Altogether, eight of the battalion's tanks were unable to get off the beaches. Five threw tracks, one hit a mine, one stuck in the sand, and one stalled.[15] Even less fortunate were other sup-

---

[14] Co C, 5th Tank Bn AR, Encl C, p. I, to *5th tank Bn AR.*
[15] *5th Tank Bn AR*, p. 4.

porting arms units, such as the regimental rocket section of RCT 28 which landed during the morning. Enemy artillery smashed three of the four truck-mounted rocket launchers immediately after landing. When the remaining launcher finally got into action and opened fire, a terrific explosion rocked the target area bringing loud cheers from Marines nearby.[16]

The tanks of Company C eventually exited the beach by a road between Red Beach 1 and 2, arriving in the zone of action of 1/28 about 1400. Lieutenant Colonel Butterfield's battalion at the time was pinned down, suffering casualties from Japanese fire coming from pillboxes and blockhouses bypassed earlier. It was decided to use the entire tank company in cleaning up the area. Because of minefields and tank traps, the tanks advanced in a column which came under antitank fire immediately after moving out. Armor-piercing shells penetrated the turrets of two tanks, each of which suffered three casualties. Shortly thereafter, the enemy scored a hit on a third tank, rendering the turret inoperative. The tankers ultimately knocked out the hostile gun. This completed their mission with 1/28.

About 1600, the tanks formed up to support 2/28 and 3/28 in the planned attack towards Mount Suribachi but enemy fire was so heavy that the attacking battalions could not get into their proper positions. The 3d Battalion, commanded by Lieutenant Colonel Charles F. Shepard, Jr., was unable to get into jumpoff positions alongside the 2d Battalion. The tanks of Company C had moved out about 200 yards when it was observed that the troops on the right were not moving. By the time the 3d Battalion did get on line, it was considered too late to launch the attack, and Shepard's men began to dig in for the night.

Shortly before 1700, 2/28 launched an attack of its own, supported by tanks of Company C. By 1730, the battalion had advanced only 150 yards and even this slight gain, obtained at the cost of many casualties, had to be relinquished when 2/28 was ordered to fall back and tie in with the 3d Battalion for the night. The tanks of Company C thereafter found themselves in the unusual role of remaining forward of the lines, firing at pillboxes and covering the infantry units as they prepared for the night. Company C was released from this assignment about 1845. One tank, bogged down in a shell crater, had to be abandoned after the crew removed the gun mechanism and destroyed the radio. The company withdrew to a point about 300 yards from the front lines and dug in for a first night marked by almost continuous mortar fire.

At the same time that the 28th Marines was advancing inland from Green Beach, Colonel Wornham's RCT 27 was preparing to advance inland from Red 1 and 2, where 2/27 and 1/27 had landed abreast. On the left, 2/27 pushed inland, initially meeting only scattered resistance. Both battalions advanced rapidly against stiffening resistance, bypassing numerous enemy positions along the way. By 1130, 1/27

---

[16] LtCol Oscar F. Peatross ltr to CMC, dtd 23Dec52, in *Iwo Comments*.

was infiltrating the southern end of Motoyama Airfield No. 1 and consolidating along the western edge of the field. Company C had passed the field and occupied a line extending for about 250 yards from its southwestern part to the northwest. The 2d Battalion was generally abreast of the 1st, maintaining contact with it. The 27th Marines also was receiving its share of enemy mortar and artillery fire, and casualties mounted as the advance continued. Among those wounded at this time was the executive officer of the regiment, Colonel Louis C. Plain, who was hit in the arm and subsequently evacuated.

The support of armor was needed to overcome the stubborn enemy resistance, so Company A of the 5th Tank Battalion was attached to 1/27. Earlier that morning, this company had been the first tank unit ashore, landing on the Red beaches at 0925. In attempting to get off the beaches, four tanks broke their tracks in the loose sand; the engine of another Sherman malfunctioned so that it could no longer move. The remaining tanks finally found a way off the beach and proceeded towards Motoyama Airfield No. 1. With their support, 1/27 was somewhat better able to reduce the strongly defended enemy positions, although the presence of armor in the front lines proved a mixed blessing to the hard pressed Marines who found that the Shermans attracted enemy antitank fire. Even with tank support, however, the 1st Battalion was unable to make any significant advance for the remainder of the day.

It was a different story with Major Antonelli's 2d Battalion, hell-bent on driving to the opposite side of the island. Moving inland from Red Beach 1, the battalion ran into heavy fire from light machine guns and rifles; progress was further impeded by the enemy's use of hand grenades.

About 50 yards inland, the battalion encountered its first pillbox, one of many carefully camouflaged in this area. In accordance with their orders to cross the island as quickly as possible, Companies E and F bypassed many enemy installations, eliminating only those directly in their path. Assault teams equipped with flamethrowers and hand grenade-throwing riflemen neutralized the Japanese inside while engineer teams blew up the pillboxes with explosive charges.

Leading a machine gun platoon of 1/27 past the southern end of Motoyama Airfield No. 1 was Gunnery Sergeant John Basilone, know as "Manila John" and famous for his exploits on Guadalcanal in October 1942 that had won him the Medal of Honor. On Guadalcanal he had thwarted a Japanese assault by alternately firing two machine guns and a pistol. His presence on Iwo Jima was his own choice; he had previously turned down a commission in favor of remaining an enlisted man. As Manila John rushed for the west coast of Iwo, a few steps ahead of his men, a mortar shell suddenly burst close behind him, mortally wounding this great fighting Marine and four of his men.

Although the 1st Battalion, 27th Marines could not advance to the north, 2/27 was able to push its attack westward and seized the cliffs overlooking the west coast by mid-afternoon. The regimental reserve, 3/27 under the command of Lieutenant Colonel Donn J. Robertson, had landed at 1130 and, moving up behind 2/27, assisted in mopping up positions bypassed by the 2d Battalion.

Despite heavy Japanese shelling of the entire beachhead on D-Day, additional units arrived on shore throughout the day. At 1500, 1/26, commanded by Lieutenant Colonel Daniel C. Pollock, completed its landing and moved into an assembly area about 300 yards inland from Red Beach 1. Shortly thereafter, the battalion was attached to the 27th Marines and ordered to take up defensive positions behind 2/27. Company B, 5th Tank Battalion, began landing on Red Beach 1 at 1300. As in the case of the armor that had landed earlier, the tanks encountered trouble in getting off the beach, but by 1600 they had reached the western side of the island, where they were attached to the 27th Marines.

Meanwhile, the 26th Marines, under Colonel Chester B. Graham, had spent most of the day on board ship in corps reserve. Just before 1000, General Schmidt released the regiment, less the 1st Battalion, to its parent division; the 21st Marines of the 3d Marine Division became the corps reserve. The 26th Marines was ordered to proceed to the line of departure shortly after 1100, but the crowded condition of the beaches and limited space inland precluded a landing until late afternoon. It was 1730 before Colonel Graham's regiment finished coming ashore over Red Beach 1. The regiment moved into an assembly area just south of Motoyama Airfield No. 1, where it took up defensive positions.

The four artillery battalions of the 13th Marines, commanded by Colonel James D. Waller, were also preparing to go ashore. Reconnaissance parties sent to the beaches as early as 1030 had discovered that the previously selected battery positions were still in enemy hands. As a result, 3/13, under Lieutenant Colonel Henry T. Waller, did not reach the island until 1400. Half an hour later, 2/13, commanded by Major Carl W. Hjerpe, went ashore, to be followed at 1645 by 1/13 under Lieutenant Colonel John S. Oldfield. Major James F. Coady's 4th Battalion reached Iwo between 1930 and 2000. The darkness and enemy fire took their toll of 4/13. Three DUKWs swamped; their cargo, consisting of two guns and badly needed radio equipment, was lost.

Major Hjerpe's 2d Battalion had been scheduled to land on Red Beach 2, but just as the first DUKWs approached the shore, they were hit by a heavy enemy barrage. One 105mm howitzer was destroyed by enemy fire; another was slightly damaged. The landing of 1/13 took place under more favorable conditions. One hour after landing, despite the same beach conditions that had slowed up the other battalions, the first battery was in position and ready to fire, a state achieved by the entire battalion at 2245. Last to go ashore, 4/13 was able to emplace eight howitzers by 0440 on D plus 1; two of the 105s and other equipment did not reach the position until later in the morning because their access road was blocked by crippled LVTs.

Landing four artillery battalions on beaches that were still exposed to incessant enemy fire was a hazardous undertaking. When the DUKWs of the Marine 5th and the Army 471st Amphibian Truck Companies reached the beaches with their cargo of 75mm and 105mm guns, they found it difficult to negotiate the deep sand. The wheeled vehicles could not get over the steep terrace behind the beaches until bulldozers and LVTs were pressed into service to pull them over the crest. Inland, the cargo was unloaded amidst heavy mortar and machine gun fire, while many furiously working artillerymen used their helmets and whatever else they could lay hands on to dig gun pits.

The arrival of the artillery on Iwo Jima underscored the fact, if any such emphasis was required, that the Marines had come to stay. To the men pinned down by heavy enemy fire, the presence of friendly artillery had additional implications:

> The 13th's guns got over the south beaches somehow, and up the terraces. Within thirty minutes the crack of artillery, clearly recognizable to the foot soldiers, gave heart to the men on both fronts. Sergeant Joe L. Pipes' "Glamor Gal" was first to fire on Suribachi. At about the same instant, Sergeant Henry S. Kurpoat's 75 let go from behind Yellow 2, firing north.
>
> They never settled the argument over which gun fired first, and it really didn't matter. Other guns were right behind them. The Marines shouted as the shells went over them. Dukws of the Army's 471st Amphibian Truck Company, their Negro drivers pressing ashore through the wreckage, landed the field pieces of the 13th Marines in a steady column.[17]

Most of the artillery managed to get ashore. From that time on, the Japanese no longer had it all their way, though they retained the capability of inflicting major punishment on the assault force for some time to come.

The experience of the 13th Marines is typical of what was accomplished on D-Day and of the difficulties all Marines were to encounter on Iwo Jima. The 3d Battalion, going ashore at the northern end of Green Beach, went into position close to the water's edge. Within 20 minutes, one section of the 105mm guns was registered; by 1745, all guns were in position and ready to support the 28th Marines.

Throughout D-Day, reinforcements poured ashore as the organizational component of the landing force began to build up. At 1430, General Hermle went ashore with the ADC group and a headquarters reconnaissance party and established an advanced 5th Division command post. The assistant division commander, the first American general officer to set foot on the island, crossed Motoyama Airfield No. 1 while it was still under heavy enemy fire and gained first-hand information from units in the front lines.

The picture that presented itself to the observer at the beaches during the afternoon of D-Day was not a pretty one:

> At the water's edge amtracs, LCMs and LCVPs were hit, burned, broached, capsized, and otherwise mangled. The loose, black volcanic cinders, slid past the churn-

---

[17] Newcomb, *Iwo Jima*, p. 119.

ing tires of wheeled vehicles, miring them axle-deep; the steep terraces blocked egress from the beach and extensive minefields took a heavy toll. Debris piled up everywhere.

Wounded men were arriving on the beach by the dozen, where they were not much better off than they had been at the front. There was no cover to protect them and supplies of plasma and dressings ran low. The first two boats bringing in badly needed litters were blown out of the water. Casualties were being hit a second time as they lay helpless, under blankets, awaiting evacuation to ships.[18]

A similar situation prevailed on the 4th Marine Division beaches. There also, men's feet sank to the ankles in the loose, coarse, volcanic ash and jeeps sank to the hubcaps. Trucks could not operate at all, and supplies had to be manhandled from the water's edge to the front. On the congested beaches, the enemy laid down a sustained fire along the water's edge that at times caused heavier casualties among Seabees and engineers and in evacuation stations than those suffered by combat units. One account likened operating in such terrain to "trying to fight in a bin of loose wheat."[19]

While 5th Division Marines struggled for the southern portion of Iwo Jima, fierce action developed on the northern beaches, where General Cates' 4th Division had gone ashore. Precisely at H-hour, Colonel Walter W. Wensinger's 23d Marines had landed on the Yellow beaches with two battalions abreast. The 1st Battalion, commanded by Lieutenant Colonel Ralph Haas, landed over Yellow 1; the 2d Battalion, under Major Robert H. Davidson, landed to the right over Yellow 2. As in the 5th Division sector to the south, RCT 23 encountered little initial resistance until the two assault companies reached the second terrace. At this point, they began to draw heavy and accurate fire from the front and flanks, where the enemy was very much alive and firmly entrenched in pillboxes, ditches, and spidertraps. Squarely astride the regiment's front were two huge blockhouses and 50 pillboxes. Even though the blockhouses had sustained massive damage from the pre-landing bombardment, they still afforded cover for the enemy. Before an advance inland could get under way, the formidable enemy obstacles had to be eliminated, a task requiring the employment of armor.

Shortly before 1000, Company C of the 4th Tank Battalion was dispatched from the line of departure for Beaches Yellow 1 and 2, in three LSMs, carrying a total of 16 tanks. The first tank to leave LSM 216 bogged down after getting off the end of the ramp. Discharge of the armor from the remaining landing ships proceeded more smoothly, but after moving inland less than 150 yards from the water's edge, three tanks were immobilized by mines or the terrain.[20] After attempting for half an hour to recover the tank that had bogged down just off the ramp, LSM *216* withdrew to the line of departure. At 1100, another attempt was made to land the tanks, this time on Yellow 1, but none succeeded in getting ashore. Instead, LSM *216*, having received a number of hits, proceeded to the hospital LST to

---

[18] Conner, *The Fifth Marine Division*, p. 53.
[19] Proehl, *The Fourth Marine Division*, p. 149.

[20] *4th MarDiv OpRpt*, Anx F, p. 9.

discharge casualties. At 1245, LSM *216* finally succeeded in landing its tanks on Yellow 1. These tanks proceeded inland, but were unable to locate a route to the hard pressed 2/23. Nor was such a route ever found on D-Day.

Thus, only 1/23 received any tank support on 19 February, and due to difficult terrain and heavy enemy resistance, this support was relatively ineffective. Colonel Wensinger eventually requested that two tank retrievers be landed to assist the assault tanks which were in trouble along the beach. Some progress was made, but the nature of the terrain and heavy mortar and artillery fire from the flanks severely hindered retrieving operations.

RCT 23 had to fight its way forward with limited armored support. A hail of shells and small arms fire took a heavy toll of casualties. It was generally agreed that of all the unpleasant beaches on Iwo that day, those of the 4th Division were the hottest. At 0930, 1/23 reported that its forward elements had advanced 250 yards inland. Continued progress was slow. Ten minutes later, 2/23 sent word that it had advanced inland a similar distance, but that its leading elements were pinned down by machine gun fire from pillboxes to its front and flanks.

At noon, 1/23 had advanced 500 yards further inland to within 200 yards of Airfield No. 1. The advance of the 2d Battalion, still meeting intensive resistance, was lagging. In fact, 2/23 had made only 250 yards since its earlier report. The absence of tank support for the 2d Battalion was beginning to make itself felt; at the same time, it became apparent that such support would not be available for some time. In view of this situation, the regimental commander decided to land 3/23, the reserve battalion, commanded by Major James S. Scales. The battalion received orders at 1300 to land along Yellow 1 Beach, move 200 yards inland, and support the attack of 2/23 with 81mm mortars.

Upon going ashore, the reserve battalion came under very heavy mortar and artillery fire. Fortunately, none of the landing craft received direct hits during the approach to the beach. Once they had come ashore, it was a different story; enemy shells could not help but hit something on the congested beaches, and casualties and destruction of materiel caused serious disorganization.

More trouble for the landing force on the beaches was in the offing, and for a time it appeared as if nature had joined hands with a stubborn and determined enemy to thwart the invasion of Iwo. At the same time that the intensity and accuracy of enemy fire on the beaches reached a climax, the surf began to rise. As LVTs bogged down or were hit, the congestion and confusion on the beaches grew immeasurably. But no real trouble developed until the arrival of the LCVPs. As the light boats hit the beaches, the surf broke over them, broaching some and swamping others. Other boats, some already disabled, piled in behind the first ones and were soon hurled on the beach by the waves.

Despite this combination of unfavorable surf and deadly resistance, Marines continued to advance inland, though often every yard gained was paid for in blood. In the zone of attack of RCT 23, tanks finally reached the front lines during the afternoon. The left flank of 1/23 had advanced to the edge of Airfield No. 1 shortly after 1400, but heavy antitank fire forced the armor to beat a hasty retreat behind the revetted edge of the field. In order to get 3/23 off the congested beaches, Colonel Wensinger ordered the battalion to pass through 1/23 and carry the attack across the airfield. This order was partly carried out despite casualties and confusion, and, by 1700, 3/23 had reached the airfield boundary. The 2d Battalion derived little benefit from the arrival of armor in its zone of attack, where enemy mines, the soft volcanic ash, and accurate enemy fire precluded effective tank support. By 1730, Company F was barely able to reach the apron of Airfield No. 1, and there halted its advance for the remainder of the night.

As a result of the heavy resistance encountered by the 23d Marines, General Cates shortly after 1400 committed two battalions of the division reserve, the 24th Marines, commanded by Colonel Walter I. Jordan. The 1st and 2nd Battalions were to be attached to the 25th and 23d Marines respectively. At 1615, 2/24, under Lieutenant Colonel Richard Rothwell, was ordered to land on Yellow Beach 2 to relieve 2/23. Shortly before 1700, the battalion landed and moved inland about 700 yards to the front line. By 1800, it had relieved 2/23 and dug in for the night just short of the airfield, tying in between 2/23 and 1/25.

Among all of the Iwo beaches, the one most exposed to enemy fire was Blue Beach 1, the northernmost of the invasion beaches, located right below a cliff that was held by the enemy in great strength. It was the unenviable task of the 25th Marines to secure the Blue Beaches. The regiment, under Colonel John R. Lanigan, landed two battalions abreast over Blue Beach 1 and the southern edge of Blue Beach 2. As on the remaining beaches, the first waves, landing shortly after 0900, reported only light enemy fire until the troops disembarked and moved approximately 25 yards from the LVTs, when they came under very heavy machine gun, mortar, artillery, and rocket fire.

At 0935, 1/25, commanded by Lieutenant Colonel Hollis U. Mustain, reported that the battalion was still under heavy fire of all types but had moved inland 300 yards.[21] Half an hour later, 3/25, under Lieutenant Colonel Justice M. Chambers, reported that elements of the battalion had moved 350 yards northeastward along the beach and that the battalion's left flank was inland 400 yards and in contact with 1/25. The continuous, well-aimed enemy fire caused some disorganization along the beach and the men sought cover in large bomb craters along the shore. Casualties were heavy. By midafternoon, Company K had lost eight officers; Company L had lost five by 1630, and Company I lost six.[22]

At 1020, Company A, 4th Tank Battalion, which had been attached to 3/25, went ashore on Blue Beach 1. Almost at once the enemy concentrated the fire

[21] *4th MarDiv OpRpt*, Anx H, p. 1.
[22] Colonel Justice M. Chambers ltr to CMC, dtd 5Nov52, in *Iwo Comments*.

of his mortars, artillery, and antitank guns on the tank landing ships (LSMs). All three of the LSMs were hit and damaged while unloading. The enemy fire could not prevent the LSMs from landing, but caused a delay in launching the tanks. After having discharged the tanks, the LSMs retracted from the beach. A tank dozer cut a road from the first terrace inland from Blue Beach 1, but became a total loss when it hit a mine and turned into a sitting target for Japanese mortars and artillery.

The remaining tanks formed a column and gingerly proceeded inland for about 100 yards. At that time, the column came to a halt when it encountered an enemy minefield. Though immobilized for the time being, while engineers cleared the mines, the tanks supported the Marine riflemen with their 75mm guns, which fired on enemy positions and pillboxes behind the beach and in the cliffs to the north.

Meanwhile, the withering enemy fire had inflicted very heavy casualties on the 25th Marines, which doggedly continued its advance against a continuous mortar barrage and intense rifle and machine gun fire both from the front and the flanks. By noon the attack of the two assault battalions had become so channelized that a 100-yard gap had opened between 1/25 and 3/25. At this time, Colonel Lanigan decided that it was imperative for RCT 25 to seize the high ground northeast of Blue Beach 2. To this end, he ordered Lieutenant Colonel Lewis C. Hudson to land 2/25, which constituted the regimental reserve, on Blue Beach 1. The battalion was to attack in a column of companies astride the boundary between 1/25 and 3/25, seize the high ground to the northwest near a quarry, and assist the advance of 3/25.[23]

By 1400, 2/25 had moved one company into the line between the other two battalions and a coordinated attack to the north got under way. From the very outset, the regimental attack moved slowly because of heavy enemy resistance. The 3d Battalion advanced for about 300 yards along the beach, then headed for the quarry about 400 yards north of the East Boat Basin. On the battalion's left, elements of 2/25 and 1/25 advanced 100 yards, but were driven back by intense small arms fire. By 1730, casualties and disorganization of 3/25 had assumed such proportions that Colonel Lanigan requested and received permission to commit one company of 1/24. An hour later, 2/25 and 3/25 had seized the high ground on top and inland of the quarry, but this advance had been paid for with extremely heavy casualties. At 1900, Lieutenant Colonel Chambers reported that the combat strength of 3/25 had diminished to only 150 men.[24]

In order to compensate for the heavy losses his regiment had sustained on D-Day, and because the Japanese were expected to counterattack along the right flank of the regiment, Colonel Lanigan requested from division the use of one company of 3/24, the division reserve, which was in position directly behind 3/25. This request was denied, but the regimental commander received permission to use one more company of 1/24. As a result, Company B of 1/24

---

[23] *4th MarDiv OpRpt*, Anx H, p. 2.
[24] *Ibid.*

was attached to 3/25. Units began digging in at 1700 and firm contact was established along the front of RCT 25 except on the left flank where a 75-yard gap remained. This gap was covered by fire and observation during the night. In the course of the evening, the depleted 3/25 was relieved by 1/24 and took up defensive positions to the rear of 1/24. The relief, which took place under occasional enemy fire, was not completed until close to midnight.

The last battalion of the 24th Marines to go ashore was 3/24, under Lieutenant Colonel Alexander A. Vandegrift, Jr. The battalion landed before 1900 and moved inland a short distance from Blue Beach 2. All of the 4th Marine Division's infantry battalions were now ashore, and Marines were busily making preparations for an enemy counterattack they felt sure would develop during their first night ashore.

As in the 5th Marine Division sector on the southern beaches, additional units reached Iwo on the northern beaches during D-Day. With most of the infantry ashore, the time had also come for the artillery regiment of the 4th Division, under Colonel Louis G. DeHaven, to land on the island. Reconnaissance parties from the artillery battalions had already debarked early in the afternoon in order to select positions for their batteries. In doing so, they faced difficulties similar to those encountered by the 13th Marines on the southern beaches. The front lines had advanced more slowly than planned; no routes had been cleared to enable the DUKWs to carry artillery pieces inland. One of the first members of the reconnaissance teams to become a casualty was Lieutenant Colonel Robert E. McFarlane, commanding the 3d Battalion.

At 1405, General Cates ordered 1/14 under Major John B. Edgar, Jr. to land in direct support of the 25th Marines; Major Clifford B. Drake's 2/14 was to lend direct support to RCT 23. Upon hitting Blue Beach 1, the DUKWs of the 4th Amphibian Truck Company with their cargo of 75mm Pack Howitzers of 1/14, became immobilized at once. They quickly bogged down and settled in the volcanic ashes. Bulldozers attempting to get the DUKWs mobile again tugged and strained, but more often than not cables snapped and towing cleats sheered. One howitzer was lost when the DUKW in which it was loaded sank immediately after being discharged from its LST.[25] Nevertheless, by 1715 the 1st Battalion had succeeded in getting 11 howitzers into position after wrestling them up the terraces by hand. Half an hour later, all batteries of 1/14 were registered and ready to fire.

An even more difficult feat was to get the 105mm howitzers of 2/14 ashore. Because of the increased weight of these guns, it proved impossible to manhandle them up and over the terrace. The only feasible expedient was to keep each howitzer in the DUKW and then attempt to get the loaded DUKWs over the terrace. Surf conditions, the slippery sand, and continuous enemy fire combined to make this movement a miserable undertaking that took hours to complete. None of the DUKWs received a direct hit, though several casualties resulted from near misses.

---

[25] *14th Mar OpRpt*, App. 6, p. 3.

Shortly before dusk, all 12 howitzers of Major Drake's 2/14 were in position near Yellow Beach 1.

The 3d Battalion, under Major Harvey A. Feehan, was ordered to launch its DUKWs shortly after 1500. At this time, for unknown reasons, several DUKWs could not be started and more than an hour elapsed before all of the vehicles were in the water. Because of the congestion ashore and approaching dusk, Colonel DeHaven decided that the 3d and 4th Battalions were to delay going ashore until the following day, and 3/4 was reembarked on board the LST. During the reembarkation, a howitzer and a DUKW were lost when the amphibian truck's motor failed as it headed back up the ramp.

As D-Day on Iwo Jima came to an end, Marines all along the VAC front lines braced for a major Japanese counterattack they felt sure would come before the night was over.[26] The carnage which had taken place on the island on D-Day differed from anything the Marines had encountered elsewhere in the Pacific Theater during World War II. Despite the enemy presence, which made itself felt everywhere and continuously on the island, and to which the numerous dead and wounded could attest, few of the men who had landed on Iwo that day had actually seen a live Japanese. No prisoners had been taken that first day, and only an occasional enemy corpse was visible.

Nevertheless, a steady flow of American casualties from the front to the beaches underscored the ferocity of the enemy resistance. Along the surf line, the litter of war continued to pile up in an almost unimaginable jumble: smashed landing craft surged upward and forward with every wave, crashing headlong into trucks, crates, and bodies at the edge of the water. Nearby, the wounded were gathered in small groups sitting or lying, just as exposed to the incessant enemy shelling as anyone else on the island and even more helpless in the face of it. For the remainder of D-Day, and into the night, boats approached Iwo Jima, loaded with reinforcements and supplies; having unloaded these, they took on a new cargo: the wounded, for whom surgeons would be waiting in transports and hospital LSTs especially prepared for this purpose.

FIRST NIGHT ON IWO JIMA[27]

As D-Day on Iwo Jima came to an end and darkness descended over the island, Marines could take well justified pride in having seized a solid foothold on a heavily fortified bastion, where both the advantage in terrain and troop disposition rested with the defending

---

[26] "It was realized by VAC that there was much confusion and congestion on the beaches as D-Day wore on, but it was considered essential to avoid confusion afloat also, and Divisions were requested to get as many troops ashore as possible on D-Day, and to prepare for the anticipated banzai attack that night. We had more troops on the island by nightfall than the enemy had all told." *Rogers ltr.*

[27] Additional material in this section is derived from: 28th Mar AR, 19Feb-26Mar45, in *5th MarDiv AR*, Anx S, hereafter *28th Mar AR; 28th Mar UJnl;* VAC Rpt on Night Operations, Iwo Jima, 12Aug45, hereafter *Iwo Jima Night Ops Rpt.*

garrison. Even though the advance nowhere came near to reaching the 0-1 Line, VAC had succeeded in getting six infantry regiments and six artillery battalions—nearly 30,000 men and thousands of tons of equipment—ashore. (See Map 28).

From General Holland Smith down through the ranks, it was generally believed that according to their earlier tactics, the Japanese would throw all the manpower they had against the vulnerable Marines during their first night ashore. The enemy was known to have a large reserve force of infantry and tanks available for such an all-out counterattack.[28] None of the intelligence personnel of VAC could suspect at the time that General Kuribayashi planned to conserve his manpower and would find other means to decimate the Marines that were crowded into the narrow beachead.

The burden of battle was not only borne by the Marine assault units who had gone ashore on D-Day. Throughout the day, the supporting arms of the Amphibious Support Force had done all they could to assist their hard pressed comrades in arms. Carrier pilots of TF 58 and the escort carriers of TF 52 flew missions as long as daylight prevailed; airborne observers and spotters kept a continuous vigil over the target area. More than 600 aircraft flew 26 missions in the course of the day, including strikes prior to H-Hour, dropped 274,500 pounds of bombs, not including more than 100 napalm bombs. Offshore, naval guns continued to shell enemy positions on Iwo in response to Marine requests. Gunfire support ships shelled enemy gun emplacements on the high ground north of the beaches and did their best to destroy the concealed enemy mortars whose fire was causing so many casualties on the beaches.[29]

The heavy enemy fire on the beaches, as well as unfavorable surf conditions, precluded the landing of all but highest priority cargo on D-Day. In order of importance, this cargo was limited to ammunition, rations, water, and signal equipment. Once this equipment had been unloaded on the beaches, the shore party teams could do little more than stack the supplies. LVTs and weasels carried these supplies inland and returned with a cargo of wounded.

As night fell, most of the transports and other vessels retired from Iwo, but some of the command ships, preloaded LSTs, and hospital LSTs remained behind. The work of stacking supplies on the beach and terraces continued after nightfall. Offshore, mortar boats concentrated their fire against the enemy positions on the high ground overlooking the 4th Marine Division beaches. Bulldozers continued hauling vehicles inland, and whenever possible, pulled equipment out of the sand. Under cover of darkness, critical items, especially 81mm ammunition, were brought in. The 81mm shells that had been hand-carrried ashore with these mortars had lasted for only one hour after the mortars opened fire. With the 81mm mortars out of ammunition, the assault battalions lost the services of a large

---

[28] *VAC G-2 PeriRpt No. 1, dtd 19Feb45.*

[29] *TF 54 OpRpt*, p. 13.

524   WESTERN PACIFIC OPERATIONS

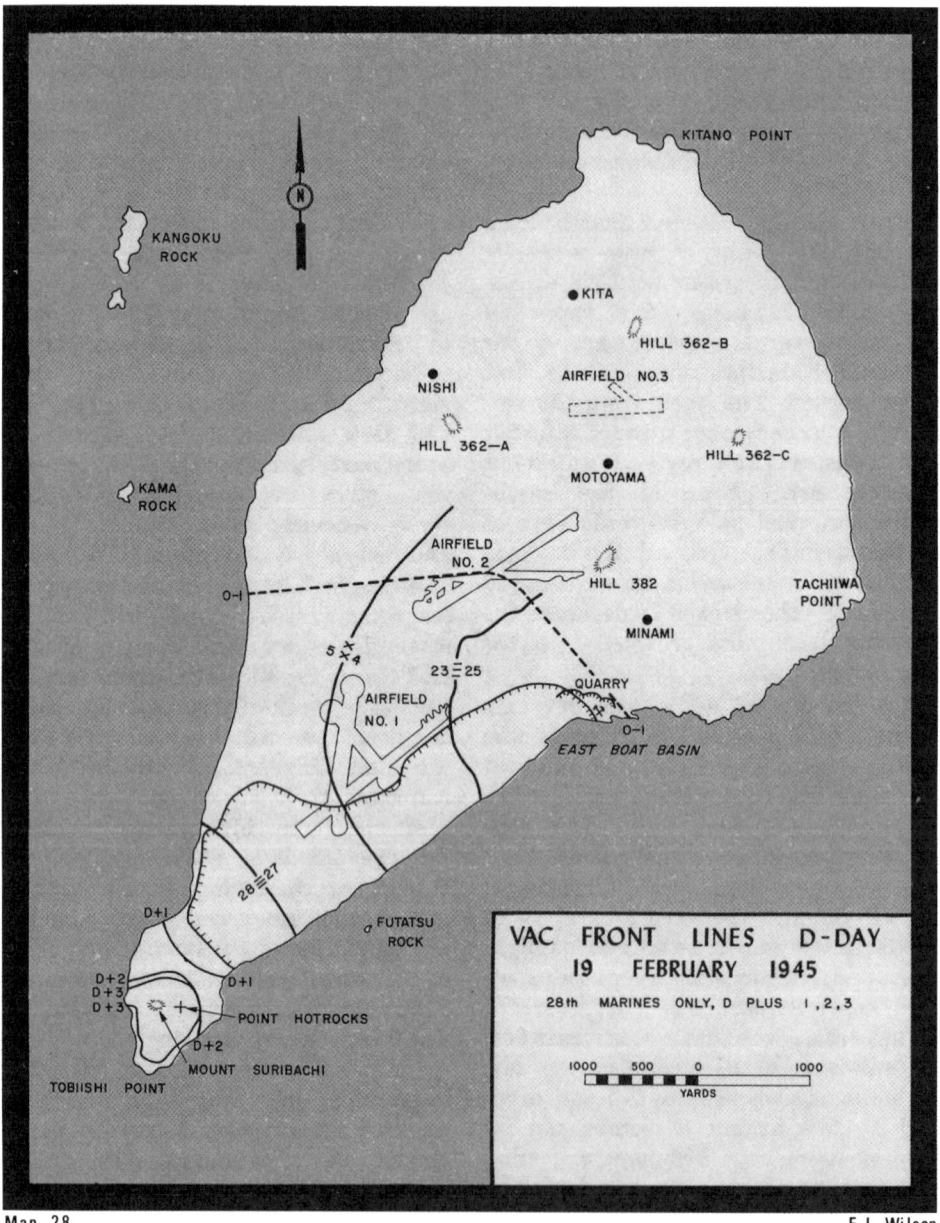

Map 28

portion of high trajectory weapons support during most of the violent action on D-Day.[30]

While the Marines anxiously awaited the big *banzai* charge that would finally bring the enemy out into the open, General Kuribayashi cannily began to employ his plan which would destroy the Americans and their supplies on and near the beaches without his risking many of his own men. In short, his plan consisted of a few attempts at infiltration, while at the same time stepping up the fire of his deadly artillery and mortars against the crowded American beachhead. As the night progressed, the rain of enemy shells mounted in intensity, as did the number of American casualties.

By 2300, the enemy shelling of the Yellow and Blue Beaches had become so heavy that both beaches were ordered closed. Elsewhere, it proved to be a sleepless night for most of the Marines on Iwo. On the southern beaches, a few vessels still attempted to bring in cargo, as runners crawled in and out of command posts, bearing reports and orders. Other men were shuffling around in the darkness looking for their units and their equipment. Because of the disorganization of units, it proved impossible at this time to obtain an accurate account of D-Day casualties, though it was known that they were heavy. It was to be determined later that 501 Marines had died on this first day of the invasion; 1,775 had been wounded in action; an additional 47 died of wounds, and 18 were missing in action;

99 of the assault force suffered from combat fatigue.[31]

Despite the heavy casualties, on the evening of D-Day VAC still rated the combat efficiency of the assault force as very good to excellent.[32] As the day ended, the 5th Marine Division had established a beachhead approximately 1,500 yards wide and 1,000 yards in depth, dividing the enemy forces in the northern and southern part of the island and effectively isolating Mount Suribachi. The 4th Marine Division had reached a line extending northward and inland from Blue Beach 2 for about 200 yards on low ground, then from the Quarry on top of the ridge for about 300 yards, then south across the low ground which led off the beach towards Motoyama Airfield No. 2, and from there to a line which was roughly a projection of the main runway of Airfield No. 1. It was clear that the landing had been successful. The Marines were dug in and occupied positions that were difficult but tenable. Supplies were scanty but sufficient for immediate needs.

As the night progressed, there was movement of all kinds on and around Iwo Jima. Offshore, transports carrying the 3d Marine Division were arriving in the reserve area 80 miles southeast of the island. Amidst the steady thump-

---

[30] Lieutenant Colonel Fenton J. Mee ltr to CMC, dtd 15Dec52, in *Iwo Comments*.

[31] Casualty figures taken from statistics prepared by the Casualty Section, HQMC. It should be noted that in the confusion of D-Day, casualties were thought much more severe than was actually the case. 1/28 alone reported 600 missing. However, many of these men had returned by D plus 2. They had been fighting with other companies and in some cases other regiments. *28th Mar AR*, p. 17.

[32] *VAC AR*, Anx B, Encl A, p. 12.

ing and crashing of the enemy artillery and mortar shells deluging the 30,000 Marines that had gone ashore, there was stealthy movement as some of the enemy, their guns near Mount Suribachi rendered useless by American air and naval bombardment, moved through the lines and headed for northern Iwo. The enemy had lost a good part of his artillery, and within three hours after H-Hour, all of the heavy guns on the slopes of Mount Suribachi had been silenced.

There were several enemy attempts at infiltration. Shortly after 2300, a barge carrying 39 Japanese approached the west coast of Iwo and prepared to land them. The enemy was spotted by alert riflemen of 1/28, who picked the Japanese off one by one as they tried to get ashore, until all had been killed.[33] On the east coast of Iwo a member of a naval construction unit had a strange experience. He was watching a log in the surf which the current bore south along the shore. Suddenly, the log made a sharp turn. The Seabee fired 13 rounds and at dawn found a riddled Japanese body at the water's edge.

What it felt like to be a member of the VAC assault force during that first eerie night on Iwo Jima has been graphically described as follows:

> Bunched in foxholes along the perimeter, the Marines took turns on watch, fighting to stay awake, waiting, waiting for the crazy *banzai*. Now and then, shouting and ragged fire broke out in hysterical patches as the rocks and bushes seemed to move in the eerie light of the star shells. Still the rush didn't come.[34]

---

[33] *28th Mar AR*, p. 17.
[34] Newcomb, *Iwo Jima*, p. 135.

Japanese artillery kept pounding the American positions. Shortly after midnight, the enemy scored a direct hit on the command post of 1/23 on Yellow Beach 1, killing Lieutenant Colonel Haas and the regimental operations officer, Captain Fred C. Eberhardt. Minutes later, one of the giant spigot mortar shells, which many Marines first thought to be a P-61 night fighter because of the peculiar sound it made while passing over, came wobbling down from the north and exploded on one of the Green Beaches near Mount Suribachi. Around 0400, the 25th Marines ammunition and fuel dump went off with a terrifying roar. Two full boatloads of 81mm mortar shells, gasoline, and flamethrower fuel exploded, caving in foxholes for yards around.

Initially, these disasters were attributed to lucky enemy hits on these vulnerable targets. It remained for a Japanese postwar history to clear up this point. According to the Japanese version:

> Instead of all-out desperate banzai charges, Kuribayashi organized small packs of prowling wolves—three or four in a pack—which sneaked in at night to enemy depots or concentration of fuel and ammunition and attacked with demolition charges and hand grenades. This new tactic again proved quite successful at the nights of February 19 and 20. For instance, heaps of 81mm mortar shells of the 4th Marine Division blew up at the southern coast; flamethrower fuel and gasoline at the same coast also burned.[35]

---

[35] Excerpts from Masanori Ito, *Fall of the Imperial Army* (Teikoku Rikugun No Saigo) v. IV, pp. 55–110), in *Newcomb Notes*, hereafter Ito, *Fall of the Imperial Army*.

As dawn rose over the island on 20 February, less than 24 hours had passed since the first Marines hit the Iwo beaches. A newspaper correspondent, looking at the scene surrounding him, made this comment:

> The first night on Iwo Jima can only be described as a nightmare in hell. About the beach in the morning lay the dead. They died with the greatest possible violence. Nowhere in the Pacific have I seen such badly mangled bodies. Many were cut squarely in half. Legs and arms lay 50 feet away from any body. All through the bitter night, the Japs rained heavy mortars and rockets and artillery on the entire area between the beach and the airfield. Twice they hit casualty stations on the beach. Many men who had been only wounded were killed.[36]

It appeared that General Kuribayashi's strategy was paying off. There had been no *banzai* that first night; but from dusk to dawn Japanese shells had steadily killed off Marines on the congested beaches at no cost to the enemy. As the new day dawned, it would be up to the tired Marines to strip the enemy of his excellent observation posts and firing positions, their only means of eliminating the deadly fire in which the entire landing force was engulfed.

---

[36] Robert Sherrod, as cited in *Ibid.*, pp. 136–137.

CHAPTER 5

The Struggle for Suribachi [1]

SECURING THE BASE [2]

Dawn on 20 February saw VAC Marines engaged in two distinct operations. One was the capture of Mount Suribachi whose forbidding slopes glowered down on the Americans on the exposed ground beneath. The other was a prolonged drive to the north, intended to seize the vital airfields and eliminate all enemy resistance.

The story of the capture of Suribachi is basically that of the 28th Marines. After landing on D-Day, Colonel Liversedge's men were facing southward, prepared to tackle the mountain, while the remainder of the 5th Division and all of the 4th had wheeled to the right to complete the capture of Airfield No. 1, and then continue the advance to the northeastern part of Iwo.

The assault on the extinct volcano promised to be difficult. To some of the Marines, gazing at the mottled, bare mountain, "Suribachi resembled the head of a fabulous serpent, with fangs ejecting poison in all directions from its base."[3] Between Colonel Liversedge's men and the base of Suribachi lay a wasteland of broken rock and stubble. This wasteland, guarding the one approach to the volcano, was studded by hundreds of caves, pillboxes, blockhouses, bunkers, spider traps, mines, and every other conceivable defense. It was in the slow and costly approach to the mountain that many Marines were to die or be wounded.

On the mountain itself, 1,600 Japanese were occupying well-camouflaged defensive positions with orders to hold out to the very end. That the Marines had cut the southern portion of Iwo off from the northern part on D-Day had little effect on General Kuribayashi's dispositions and plans. The wily enemy commander had foreseen that the island defenses would be split early in the operation. In relation to his overall defensive plan, Mount Suribachi was

---

[1] Unless otherwise noted, the material in this chapter is derived from: *TF 51 AR; TF 56 AR; VAC AR; VAC G-2 Rpts; 5th MarDiv AR; 5th MarDiv D-2 PerRpts; 5th MarDiv D-3 Jnl; 5th MarDiv D-4 Jnl;* 28th Mar R-2 Jnl, 19Feb-25Mar45, hereafter *28th Mar R-2 Jnl; 28th Mar UJnl; 28th Mar AR;* 2/28 OpRpt, 19Feb-26Mar45, hereafter *2/28 OpRpt;* 5th Tk Bn AR; 5th Tk Bn UJnl, 19Feb-26Mar45, hereafter *5th Tk Bn UJnl;* 5th EngBn OpRpt, 9Mar45, hereafter *5th Eng Bn OpRpt;* Bartley, *Iwo Monograph; Iwo Comments;* Henri et al, *Marines on Iwo Jima;* Conner, *The Fifth Marine Division;* Newcomb, *Iwo Jima; Newcomb Notes;* Morehouse, *Iwo Jima Campaign;* Morison, *Victory in the Pacific;* Isely and Crowl, *U. S. Marines and Amphibious War.*

[2] Additional material in this section is derived from: Richard Wheeler, *The Bloody Battle for Suribachi* (New York: Thomas Y. Crowell Company, 1965), hereafter Wheeler, *Suribachi,* quoted with permission.

[3] Isely and Crowl, *U. S. Marines and Amphibious War,* p. 488.

528

37MM GUN *firing on Japanese positions on the slopes of Mt. Suribachi. (USMC 110139)*

DEBRIS OF BATTLE *litters two beaches on D plus 2. (USMC 110252)*

but one of several semi-independent defense sectors capable of resisting the American assault with their own resources.

Colonel Liversedge's plan of attack was for the 28th Marines to surround the base of the mountain, maintain a steady pressure on enemy positions that could be identified in the cliffs, and seek out suitable routes to the summit. The regiment was to advance towards Suribachi with the 2d Battalion on the left, the 3d on the right, and the 1st in reserve. H-Hour was 0830, 20 February.[4]

At first light, carrier planes attacked the mountain with bombs and rockets. Napalm was dropped at the foot of the slopes, since most of the enemy fire seemed to come from that area. A destroyer stood offshore close to the west coast to support the advance of the 3d Battalion; a minelayer stood off the east coast to assist 2/28. The weather had changed for the worse; a light rain was falling and it had turned chilly. Four-foot waves were pounding the beach and the wind from the south was rising.

As Colonel Liversedge's men waited to jump off, they felt far from rested. The exertions of the previous day had been followed by a night of continuous enemy bombardment. The sense of gloom and foreboding felt by many men on the morning of D plus 1 was due not only to lack of sleep and the weather, but to the nature of the objective. Mount Suribachi itself imposed a mental hazard on the assault troops similar to that faced by the Allies in Italy a year earlier when they suddenly found themselves confronted by Mount Cassino. The impact of such a terrain feature, known to be held in strength by the enemy, can be formidable. As one account of the Iwo operation was to report:

> On this day, and increasingly as days went by, Suribachi seemed to take on a life of its own, to be watching these men, looming over them, pressing down upon them. When they moved, they moved in its shadow, under its eye. To be sure, there were hundreds of eyes looking at them from the mountain, but these were the eyes of a known enemy, an enemy whose intent was perfectly clear. In the end, it is probable that the mountain represented to these Marines a thing more evil than the Japanese.[5]

The assault of the 28th Marines against Suribachi began on schedule, preceded by a bombardment of the mountain by destroyers, rocket gunboats, and artillery. This bombardment destroyed a few enemy emplacements and at the same time unmasked many concrete structures buried in the scrub and rocky ground leading to the base of Suribachi. It soon became evident that the caves on the lower slopes and at the base of the mountain were as formidable as its pillboxes and blockhouses. The caves had from two to five entrances with interconnecting tunnels. Prior to the invasion they had served as air raid shelters and living quarters. They were linked with supply and command caves containing food, water, and ammunition. From the entrances to the caves, 6-inch guns, protected by five-foot walls, pointed down the island.

---

[4] *5th MarDiv AR*, Sec VIII, p. 19.

[5] Conner, *The Fifth Marine Division*, p. 57.

Almost immediately, the advancing Marines came under heavy fire from small arms, mortars, and artillery. Working against the success of the attack was the lack of needed tank support. The 5th Tank Battalion had been scheduled to support RCT 28. Even though eight tanks were available, no fuel or ammunition was at hand. The tankers finally salvaged some from disabled tanks and divided it up. During this redistribution, the enemy put a heavy mortar barrage on the vehicles, forcing them to move to another position. Almost immediately, the mortar fire shifted to the new position. This occurred three times; there was no place where the tankers could move that was not under direct enemy observation.

During the morning, the Marines advanced only 50 to 70 yards. Support from aircraft and ships helped, as did the artillery support from 3/13. However, even the best efforts of these combined arms failed to neutralize enemy fire, particularly that coming from the well-camouflaged pillboxes hidden in the scrub around the base of the mountain. Once the Marines advanced into these formidable enemy defenses, they would be too close for support from aircraft and artillery. Assault demolition teams, using flamethrowers and explosive charges, would have to do the job. Once again, the continuation of the advance depended on the skill and bravery of the individual Marine.

At 1100, the tanks were finally ready to support the advance. The 37mm guns and 75mm half-tracks of the regimental weapons company were also moved up in support. In the face of bitter enemy resistance, only split-second teamwork by every unit could gain any ground. The procedure employed was for infantry and tanks to take each pillbox under fire, while a flamethrower team worked up to one of the entrances. After several bursts of flame had been squirted at the fortification, the remainder of the assault squad closed in to finish the job with grenades. Once the occupants had been eliminated, engineers and demolition teams blasted the positions to ensure that they would not be reoccupied by the Japanese after nightfall. Whenever the rugged terrain permitted, flamethrowing tanks were employed against the pillboxes.

By 1700, RCT 28 had laboriously moved 200 yards closer to the objective, at the cost of 2 officers killed and 6 wounded, and 27 men killed and 127 wounded.[6] The advance had taken the Marines of 2/28 and 3/28 close to the base of the mountain; in the course of the afternoon, they had closed off nearly 40 caves with demolitions. As the men prepared to dig in for the night, they found themselves surrounded by the debris of the heavy enemy coastal guns which the naval bombardment had smashed prior to and during D-Day. Moving towards Mount Suribachi along the western shore of Iwo, 3/28 killed 73 of the enemy. The Japanese corpses presented an encouraging sight in an operation where, thus far, little had been seen of the enemy, dead or alive.

---

[6] *28th Mar AR*, 19-20Feb45, p. 18.

FLAME THROWERS *in action at the base of Mt. Suribachi. (USMC 110599)*

LONE MARINE *protects flank of patrol headed for summit of Mt. Suribachi. (USMC A419741)*

As the 28th Marines pressed their assault, the enemy situation on Suribachi steadily deteriorated. The American naval and air bombardment on D-Day had knocked out all of the 140mm guns. Inside the mountain, the commander of the Suribachi Sector, Colonel Kanehiko Atsuchi,[7] pondered his mounting casualties and dispatched a message to General Kuribayashi asking the latter's permission to go out and seek death through a *banzai* charge, rather than sitting it out in his present position. Shortly thereafter, the advancing Marines found and cut the buried cable linking Suribachi with the northern sector. Colonel Atsuchi never received a reply from the island commander, either because communications were now disrupted or simply because General Kuribayashi felt that his sentiments regarding the outdated *banzai* charge were sufficiently well known to his subordinates to require no repetition.

Some postwar Japanese sources, emphasizing that Atsuchi was actually in charge, have implied that the island commander was not happy with having entrusted Atsuchi, then 57 years old, with command of the crucially important batteries on Suribachi.[8] One of the Japanese officers, initially stationed on Iwo, who was familiar with the enemy command organization, later was to refer to the *Suribachi Sector* commander as "a poor superannuated amateur," adding "that it was the Army's mistake to send such an aged and rusted character to Iwo, who was simply a misfit for leading many people."[9] Other accounts were somewhat more charitable towards Atsuchi. In any case, there can be no doubt that a *banzai* attack was precisely what General Kuribayashi did not want. He much preferred to force the Americans to fight for the mountain foot by foot, and to inflict heavy losses as a price for seizing the strongly defended elevation.

Loss of telephone communications with the command post in the northern part of Iwo did not mean that Atsuchi's men had been abandoned by their comrades. As darkness fell, the Japanese on Suribachi fired white and amber flares as a signal that artillery and mortar support were desired from the northern sector. For the second night in succession, artillery and mortar fire from Suribachi and northern Iwo pounded the Marine positions. American guns, ashore and afloat, answered this barrage, as the din of battle echoed and resounded well into the night.

As on the eve of D-Day, the men of the 28th Marines peered into the dark-

---

[7] Mistakenly referred to as Navy Captain Kanehiko Atsuchi in Ito, *Fall of the Imperial Army*, pp. 55–110. There is some disagreement as to who was in charge at Mount Suribachi. According to one Japanese source, Major Nagahiko Matsushita, commanding the *10th Independent Antitank Battalion*, was the unit commander in the Mount Suribachi area, while Colonel Atsuchi (also spelled Atsuji) was dispatched from the *109th Division* headquarters to provide operational guidance. *Japanese Defense Agency Comment.*

[8] Major Yoshitaka Horie comments on Iwo Jima operation, in Fred Saito ltr to Richard R. Newcomb, dtd 27Jan64, in *Newcomb Notes.*
[9] *Ibid.*

ness, ever watchful for signs of an enemy counterattack. Tired eyes strained to the south in an effort to detect enemy activity, but for the second night the expected counterattack failed to develop. Division orders for D plus 2 called for a continuation of the 28th Marines attack towards Mount Suribachi. Despite enemy artillery and mortar fire, the tired men tried to obtain what little sleep they could get in anticipation of the rigors that awaited them on the following day.

On the morning of 21 February, the rough weather of the previous day showed no signs of abating. The wind had risen to 19 knots from the northeast and six-foot waves were pounding the landing beaches. Since the distance between the forward elements of the 28th Marines and the base of Mount Suribachi was still significant for air strikes, naval gunfire, and artillery support, the combined force of air and artillery was again brought to bear against the Japanese before the Marines jumped off.

Prior to the scheduled jumpoff at 0825, 40 aircraft struck at the enemy with bombs and rockets, and, strafing within 100 yards of the forward Marine lines, concentrated against an area inaccessible to tanks. This was the closest air support thus far provided and possibly the last, since another day's advance would bring the men too close to their objective.

The 1st Battalion was assigned a one-company front on the regimental right. When the regiment jumped off for the attack at 0825, the units and boundaries assigned to it were identical to those of the previous day. Once again, the tanks were unable to meet H-Hour because of delays in rearming and refuelling, and the attack had to get under way without them.

Under cover of fire from warships and land-based artillery, the 1st Battalion attacked towards Mount Suribachi along the west coast. Because the terrain there precluded effective employment of tanks, their absence at the beginning of the attack was immaterial. On the left, it was a different story; even with naval gunfire support no gains were made until the tanks arrived. By 1100, the attack gained momentum when armor, 37mm guns, and half-tracks mounting 75mm guns, as well as rocket detachments, joined in pounding the enemy positions. By noon, the 1st Battalion had reached the western base of Suribachi.

During the advance it became apparent that the enemy was particularly vulnerable to the heavy explosive blast of the rockets and retaliated by concentrating his fire on the rocket launching trucks which were unprotected by armor-plate. When caught in such a concentration of fire, the crews withdrew to cover and ran up singly to load the rocket platform. When the order to fire was given, one Marine would scamper forward, dive under the truck, then reach his arm around the side to push the firing button. The resulting explosion when the rocket hit the target usually meant that the Marines had one less enemy position to contend with.

Advancing in the center, the 3d Battalion encountered heavy resistance from the same positions that had blocked the advance on the previous day. Nevertheless, the attack of this battalion also was gaining momentum by 1100. Within the hour, an enemy counterattack struck the front of 3/28; this action failed to halt the advancing Marines, and by 1400 the forward elements had reached the foot of Mount Suribachi. There, 3/28 spent the remainder of the day.

The attack of the 2d Battalion down the eastern shore also got under way slowly. At first, there was little resistance and for a few moments, the hulking natural fortress remained quiet, but enemy reaction was not long absent. First came the crack of rifles and the chatter of machine guns. The chatter turned into a heavy clatter and bullets began to snap and whine around the advancing Marines. Some of them found their mark. Then the Japanese began firing their deadly mortars. Some of the Marines could see the high arc of the mortar rounds. Soon the area was blanketed by roaring funnels of steel and sand. The noise and fury increased until the hearing of the attacking Marines was numbed and their thinking impaired. It seemed as if the volcano's ancient bowels had suddenly come to life and the men were advancing into a full-scale eruption. One of the Marines, speaking of the holocaust, was to remark later:

> It was terrible, the worst I can remember our taking. The Jap mortarmen seemed to be playing checkers and using us as their squares. I still can't understand how any of us got through it.[10]

Not all of the attacking Marines did get through the lethal curtain of fire, but there were enough of them to carry the advance forward. The feelings of these men, as they faced what seemed to them almost certain death, were expressed by one of their number who lived to tell about it:

> We were now part of a real hell-bent-for-leather attack, the kind the Marines are famous for. But there was nothing inspiring about it. None of our ex-raiders shouted "Gung Ho!" . . . and none of our southerners let go the rebel yell. We felt only reluctance and enervating anxiety. There seemed nothing ahead but death. If we managed somehow to make it across the open area, we'd only become close-range targets for those concealed guns. I myself was seized by a sensation of utter hopelessness. I could feel the fear dragging at my jowls.
>
> It is in situation like this that Marine Corps training proves its value. There probably wasn't a man among us who didn't wish to God he was moving in the opposite direction. But we had been ordered to attack, so we would attack. Our training had imbued us with a fierce pride in our outfit, and this pride helped now to keep us from faltering. Few of us would have admitted that we were bound by the old-fashioned principle of "death before dishonor," but it was probably this, above all else, that kept us pressing forward."[11]

Two uncommon acts of heroism, among many, were to occur during the day, indicative of the caliber of the men who had gone ashore on Iwo Jima. The first one was unpremeditated, nor was there time for lengthy thought. It took place in 2/28 when Private First Class Donald J. Ruhl deliberately threw himself on a hand grenade that had landed

---

[10] Wheeler, *Suribachi*, p. 108.

[11] *Ibid.*, p. 100.

next to him and his platoon guide, Sergeant Henry O. Hansen, sacrificing his own life in order to save the sergeant. The second involved the rescue of two Marines who lay wounded for more than 24 hours at the eastern base of Mount Suribachi. A hospital corpsman had been keeping them alive by creeping up to them and treating their wounds under fire. One of the wounded was breathing through a glass tube in his neck. Since evacuation by land was out of the question because of enemy fire, a group of Marines, headed by Staff Sergeant Charles E. Harris, manned a raft, landed it on the rocky shore in a heavy surf, and succeeded in evacuating both men under the noses of the enemy. Both casualties survived the ordeal.

By evening of 21 February, the 28th Marines occupied a line which formed a semicircle just north of Mount Suribachi. The 1st Battalion was halfway around the mountain on the western shore; 2/28 had advanced an equal distance along the eastern base of the mountain; the 3d Battalion was squarely facing the volcano in the center of the semicircle. During this third day ashore, the 1st Battalion had advanced 1000 yards, the 2nd Battalion 650 yards, and the 3d, 500 yards. These gains were made at a cost of 34 Marines killed and 153 wounded. Due to these heavy additional casualties, by evening of 21 February the combat efficiency of the 28th Marines had declined to 75 percent.[12]

Much of the success of the day's advance had been due to the tank support available on D plus 2. Altogether, seven tanks supported the advance towards Mount Suribachi. Two of them were put out of action by the enemy and one by the terrain. One ran over a mine, one was hit by antitank fire, and one broke a track. About 1630, after the advance halted for the day, the tanks were released. To avoid any delay when the attack resumed on the following morning, the tanks were rearmed and refueled before dark. Despite the damage sustained by the three vehicles, the tankers engaged near Mount Suribachi had suffered no casualties on this third day of the invasion.[13]

As the afternoon of 21 February wore on, a cold rain began to fall on Iwo, greatly increasing the discomfort of the Marines holding positions around the base of Suribachi. Behind them, and all around them were the remnants of the main defenses guarding the volcano. Some of the pillboxes and bunkers had been crushed like matchboxes by naval gunfire; others had been seared black by napalm flames. The entire area was pervaded by the smell of death and burned flesh, where flamethrowers had done their deadly work. The expenditure of flamethrower fuel had reached such proportions that a temporary shortage developed — overcome only when versatile Weasels carried additional supplies to the front lines.

In the gathering dusk, many Marines could clearly hear the enemy talking inside the mountain. They succeeded in killing a large number of Japanese by pouring gasoline down the fissures and setting it aflame. Inside the volcano, Colonel Atsuchi was dying from a shell

---

[12] *28th Mar AR*, 20-21Feb45.

[13] Co C, *5th Tk Bn AR*, p. 3.

fragment wound incurred during the day.[14] His last order was that a squad of men attempt to break through to General Kuribayashi's headquarters to report the situation on Suribachi. Many of the enemy felt extremely bitter at their own lack of air support while American aircraft filled the sky. Nevertheless, enemy morale remained unshaken and nearly all were determined to go down fighting.

Actually, air support for the Japanese garrison on Iwo was closer at hand than anyone, friend and foe alike, might have suspected. At dusk, as the Marines were digging in for the night, the enemy made one effort from the air. About 50 *kamikazes* had left an airfield near Tokyo early in the day and, after refuelling at Hachijo Jima in the Bonins, headed towards Iwo Jima. Each member of the Special Attack Unit had but one objective: to hurl his aircraft and himself at the invasion fleet that was gathered around Iwo.

Radar equipment on the *Saratoga*, about 35 miles northwest of the island, picked the aircraft up when they were still 100 miles away, but they were first mistaken for friendly planes. At 1700, interceptor aircraft reported that the approaching formation was Japanese and that they had downed two of the intruders. Shortly thereafter, two *kamikazes* struck the *Saratoga* and set her on fire. These fires had barely been put out when another Japanese plane grazed the flight deck and crashed overboard, its bomb blowing a hole in the flight deck. Nevertheless, shortly after 2000, the *Saratoga* once again was able to recover planes. Losses were 123 killed and missing and 192 wounded; in addition, the carrier lost 36 planes by burning and jettisoning, and six by water landings in the choppy seas.[15] The *Saratoga*, once her fires had been extinguished, limped back to Pearl Harbor for repairs.

Another carrier, the *Bismarck Sea*, was in position 20 miles east of Iwo when, shortly before 1900, a *kamikaze* hit the ship square abeam. Gassed planes on board caught fire and ammunition exploded in the rapidly spreading blaze. As a 22-knot wind fanned the fires, it became necessary to abandon ship. Following a tremendous explosion, the *Bismarck Sea* turned over and sank. Many of the men who had gone overboard were picked up by the escort vessels; others succumbed to the cold waters. Altogether, 218 men of the *Bismarck Sea* were lost, out of a crew of 943 officers and men.[16]

Other ships attacked by the *kamikazes* were the escort carrier *Lunga Point*, which fought off four torpedo bombers without loss; the net tender *Keokuk*, set afire, losing 17 men killed and 44 wounded; and LST *477* carrying artillery for the 3d Marine Division. The LST was struck a glancing blow by a *kamikaze*, which failed to do any major damage. None of the Japanese pilots survived the attack.

As 21 February came to an end, the hospital ship *Samaritan* sailed from

---

[14] Official Japanese sources claim that Colonel Atsuchi was killed during the daylight battle on 20 February. *Japanese Defense Agency Comment.*

[15] Morison, *Victory in the Pacific*, p. 54.
[16] *Ibid.*, p. 55.

Iwo Jima to Guam. Her cargo consisted of 623 seriously wounded Marines. The care given to these wounded was in stark contrast to the little attention the Japanese received from their own medical personnel. Japanese defense plans for Iwo Jima had made no provision for the evacuation of any wounded. Those Japanese who were wounded either crawled back or were carried to aid stations behind the lines. There, they might be placed in niches in the walls of tunnels, where their comrades would look after them as best they could. Some of the Japanese bound up their wounds and remained with their units, either to fight again if physically able or else perform other work behind the lines.

For the Marines dug in around the base of Mount Suribachi, another restless night was in the offing. The rain was still coming down, increasing their discomfort. Some of the Japanese inside the mountain were moving around and talking, but no *banzai* charge developed. Enemy artillery and mortar fire continued to fall in the area, though its effect was not as deadly as during the preceding night. The enemy confined himself to two attempts at infiltrating the American lines in the 28th Marines sector. Men of the regiment's 81mm mortar platoon killed some 60 Japanese in front of 2/28 during one of these efforts. Company C accounted for 28 more who, in accordance with Colonel Atsuchi's final orders, attempted to infiltrate north along the western beaches.

The following morning, 22 February, began with all the earmarks of a miserable day. The cold, hard rain had turned Iwo's loose soil and cinders into a sloshy gumbo. At 0800 the enemy scored a mortar hit on the regimental CP which killed the regimental surgeon, Lieutenant Commander Daniel J. McCarthy. The rain, driven from the southeast by a strong wind, not only caused great discomfort to the Marines, but the wet volcanic ash clogged automatic weapons, which could fire only single rounds. Nevertheless, the 28th Marines continued their attack at the foot of Mount Suribachi. Because of the bad weather and the Marines' proximity to the mountain, no air support was available, and artillery support was severely curtailed. Once again, it became the task of individual Marines to pick a path through the rubble, blasting and burning their way through the enemy defenses. The Japanese within the mountain and isolated pillboxes around the base still resisted with heavy mortar and small arms fire.

Once again, seven tanks of Company C, 5th Tank Battalion, supported the attack of the 28th Marines. Two were attached to 2/28 to work around the east side of Suribachi; three were sent to 1/28 to advance around the right, and two remained in support of 3/28 in the center. The heavy rainfall that continued throughout the day severely limited the operation of the tanks. At one time during the afternoon, the rain became so heavy that the crews, unable to see where they were going, had to be guided by men on foot.

Poor weather and enemy resistance to the contrary, 22 February marked the day on which Mount Suribachi was neutralized and surrounded. The men of 3/28 cleared out the base of the north face of the volcano during the day and sent a patrol around the west coast down to Tobiishi Point, Iwo Jima's southernmost extremity. There, the men of 3/28 encountered a patrol from 2/28 which had advanced down the east coast. By 1630, the 28th Marines halted operations for the day. One sergeant of Company I who scrambled part way up the north face of Mount Suribachi reported seeing no Japanese. He asked whether he should continue up the mountain, but Colonel Liversedge felt that it was too late in the day, and the final advance to seize the mountain was delayed until the following morning.

By the end of D plus 3, the fight for Mount Suribachi was virtually over. Substantial numbers of the enemy, perhaps 300 in all, still occupied caves and other places of concealment within the volcano. But in the course of the 28th Marines' advance, hundreds of the enemy had been killed, and the pernicious power of the fortress was now broken. As Marines, shivering from the cold and wetness, huddled at the foot of Suribachi, the enemy survivors within debated whether they should stay or attempt to fight their way north. Only half of them decided to remain and fight it out. The remainder crawled out into the murky darkness and tried to make their way north through the American lines. Most of them fell victim to accurate fire from alert Marines, determined to halt any infiltration. About 20 of the enemy made it across the lines and reached General Kuribayashi's headquarters near Motoyama in the northern part of the island where they were reassigned.

For the Marine survivors of the drive to Mount Suribachi, the final act in the drama was about to open. The time had come to start climbing. On the evening prior to that venture, no one could guess what the following day would bring.

SEIZING THE HEIGHTS[17]

Friday, 23 February, marked the day on which the Marines climbed to the top of the craggy 550-foot rim of Mount Suribachi. The steep slopes of the mountain fortress all but precluded a converging ascent from various directions. When it was discovered that the only practical route to the crater lay up the north face of the mountain, in the zone of the 2d Battalion, Lieutenant Colonel Johnson became directly involved in planning the climb. The battalion commander's decision was to send several small reconnaissance patrols to the top before ordering a platoon-size combat patrol to make the ascent.

At 0800, Sergeant Sherman B. Watson of Company F led a four-man patrol up the mountain. On top of Suribachi this patrol encountered a battery of heavy machine guns with ammunition stacked alongside around the rim of the crater. There was no sign of the enemy. The bald, gray rock was now surrounded by silence; the caves and underground chambers seemed devoid of life. Uprooted blockhouses and pillboxes offered mute testimony to the destructive power of the heavy naval

---

[17] Additional material in this section is derived from: 5th EngBn UJnl, 19Feb-24Mar45, hereafter 5th EngBn UJnl; Maj Yoshitaka Horie (IJA) Rpt, Iwo Jima, dtd 11Feb46, hereafter Horie Rpt.

guns; most of the tunnels on the slopes were closed and smoking. Unaccustomed to the silence, the men wondered why they drew no fire. They slid and scrambled down Suribachi to report to the battalion commander.

Even before the first reconnaissance patrol returned from its climb, Lieutenant Colonel Johnson dispatched two three-man patrols from Companies D and F at 0900 to reconnoiter other suitable routes up the mountain and probe for enemy resistance. None drew any fire. While the small reconnaissance patrols were still executing their mission, Colonel Johnson assembled the combat patrol that was slated to seize Mount Suribachi in force and hoist the American colors over the mountain. The 3d Platoon, Company E, was selected for this mission. The Company executive officer, 1st Lieutenant Harold G. Schrier, led the patrol. A member of the patrol was to recall later:

> The 25 men of the 3d Platoon were by this time very dirty and very tired. They no longer looked nor felt like crack combat troops. Although they had just had a relatively free day, their rest had been marred by a chilling rain. They hardly yearned for the distinction of being the first Marines to tackle the volcano. But the colonel didn't bother to ask them how they felt about it.[18]

Lieutenant Schrier assembled the platoon at 0800 and bolstered its thin ranks with other men of Company E until it totalled 40 men. Before starting the ascent, he led the men back around the base of Suribachi to battalion headquarters just northeast of the base. Johnson's final orders were simple and to the point: the patrol was to climb to the summit, secure the crater, and raise the flag. As the patrol prepared to move out, the battalion commander handed Schrier a folded American flag that had been brought ashore by the battalion adjutant, 1st Lieutenant George G. Wells. The flag, measuring 54 by 28 inches, had been obtained from the *Missoula*, the transport that had carried 2/28 from its staging area to Iwo Jima.

Forming an irregular column, the patrol headed straight for the base of Suribachi. They moved at a brisk pace at first. When the route turned steep and the going became more difficult, the patrol leader dispatched flankers to guard the vulnerable column against surprise attack. The men, heavily burdened with weapons and ammunition climbed slowly, stopping occasionally to catch their breath. At times, the route became so steep that they moved upward on their hands and knees. Along the way, they passed close to several cave entrances, but the caves appeared deserted and no resistance developed. The only Japanese encountered were the dead. Friendly eyes were observing the patrol's laborious ascent: Marines near the northeast base of Suribachi and men of the fleet, who, cognizant of the drama unfolding before them, were watching through binoculars.

Higher and higher the patrol picked its way, avoiding heavily mined trails and keeping men out on the flanks to thwart any enemy ambush. Within half an hour after leaving battalion headquarters, the patrol arrived at the rim of the crater. There, Schrier called a halt while he sized up the situation. He

---

[18] Wheeler, *Suribachi*, p. 128.

THE STRUGGLE FOR SURIBACHI

MEN OF THE 28TH MARINES *raise Old Glory on Mt. Suribachi, morning of 23 February 1945 (USMC 112720)*

spotted two or three battered gun emplacements and several cave entrances, but no sign of the enemy. He signalled the men to start filing over the rim. As the patrol entered the crater, the men fanned out and took up positions just inside the rim. They were tensed for action, but the caves along the rim and the yawning floor below remained silent.

While half the patrol deployed around the rim, the remainder pressed into the crater to probe for resistance. Part of their mission had been executed. It now remained for them to locate something to serve as a flagpole. Scouting along the rim of the crater, a couple of men located a 20-foot section of pipe. Lashing the flag to one end, they thrust the other into soft ground near the north rim. At 1020, the Stars and Stripes rose over the highest point of the island, where it fluttered in a brisk wind. Small though it was, the flag was clearly visible from land and sea, proof that Suribachi had fallen.

Far below, on the sandy terraces and in foxholes, still exposed to deadly fire from enemy artillery and mortars in the north of Iwo Jima, exhausted and unshaven men openly wept, while others slapped each other on the back and shouted. Out at sea, ships' whistles, horns, and bells rang out in jubilation. On deck of the hospital ship *Solace*, badly wounded Marines raised themselves on their elbows to look up at the tiny speck on the summit.

Not far from the CP of the 28th Marines, a group of men stood on the beach near the surf. They had just stepped ashore from a Higgins boat to become fascinated spectators of the most dramatic moment of the Iwo operation. Deeply moved by the sight was Secretary of the Navy Forrestal, accompanied by General Holland Smith and an assortment of Navy and Army personnel including two admirals. Turning towards General Smith, Forrestal said gravely: "Holland, the raising of that flag on Suribachi means a Marine Corps for the next 500 years."[19]

Atop the mountain, the men of Lieutenant Schrier's patrol had little time for rejoicing. The sight of the American flag waving over Suribachi was too much for the remnants of Colonel Atsuchi's garrison to take lying down. Sergeant Louis R. Lowery, a Marine photographer, had just clicked the shutter of his camera, taking pictures of the flag raising on the rim of the crater, when two Japanese charged out from a cave near the summit. One of the Japanese, running towards the flag and waving his sword was promptly shot down. The other heaved a hand grenade at the Marine photographer who escaped injury or death by vaulting over the rim and sliding about 50 feet down the mountain before his fall was broken. His camera was smashed, but the negatives inside remained safe. The second Japanese was also killed. Other Japanese, frenzied by the sight of the American flag, started to emerge from caves near the crater and met the same fate.

Three hours later, a larger flag, almost twice the size of the first one, was raised over Mount Suribachi. It was the raising of this second flag, obtained

---

[19] Smith and Finch, *Coral and Brass*, p. 261.

from LST 779, that resulted in photographer Joe Rosenthal's picture of the flag raising that became perhaps the most famous photograph of World War II and that has since served as an inspiration to countless Americans.

Proportionate to the elation of Americans at the fall of Suribachi, the Japanese on Iwo Jima and elsewhere felt great consternation. Upon receiving the news of the fall of the volcano, one Japanese staff officer, once himself stationed on Iwo, but subsequently reassigned to Chichi Jima, later recalled that "he was bursting with emotion."[20] Equally shocking to this officer was the fact that the mountain fortress had fallen in only three days. According to the Japanese timetable, Suribachi was to have been held for at least two weeks.[21]

For the remainder of the afternoon, 2/28 continued to mop up on and around Mount Suribachi. Marines annihilated enemy snipers and, together with the engineers, blasted shut a large number of cave entrances. Many Japanese were sealed in and though undoubtedly some later managed to dig their way out of these tombs, an unknown number succumbed from their wounds or were asphyxiated. A few Japanese who survived the fall of Suribachi managed to get back to their own lines in the northern part of Iwo where they faced yet another ordeal. As the survivors from Suribachi entered the Japanese lines, the following incident took place, to be remembered long after by a Japanese petty officer who survived the operation:

I remember a very dramatic scene I saw February 24, 1945. A Navy lieutenant, whose name I don't recollect, and several of his men—all blood stained wearing torn uniforms, reached the command post and said they broke through the enemy encirclement of Suribachi and managed to reach the command post for a report. When I showed the lieutenant up to Captain (IJN) Inouye's desk, Inouye became furious and bellowed: "Why did you come, you son of a bitch? Wasn't your assignment to hold that fortress at any cost? Shame on you to come here. Shame, shame, shame! Don't you know what shame is? I tell you that you are a coward and deserter!" His aides tried to calm the Captain down. But Inouye was madder and howling more profanity, and finally said: "Under any military regulations, a deserter is executed summarily. I shall condescend myself to behead you."

So the Captain drew his sword and pulled it up. The wounded lieutenant knelt down silent, immobile. Presently, the aids clung to the captain and physically wrested his sword away. Inouye burst into tears, mumbling: "Ugh, ugh, Suribachi's fallen! Suribachi's fallen!" The aides took the lieutenant away to the sick bay for first aid treatment.[22]

While the reinforced platoon of Company E scaled Suribachi, part of the same company patrolled down around the eastern end of the island until it made contact with elements of 1/28 advancing down the west side.[23] Temporary contact between patrols in this

---

[20] Horie Rpt, p. 8.
[21] Ito, Fall of the Imperial Army.
[22] Fred Saito interview with Riichi Koyatsu, former Intendance Petty Officer 3/c, in Saito ltr to Richard F. Newcomb, dtd 10Feb64, in Newcomb Notes.
[23] "My recollection is that, on my way down the mountain (I was up there between the two flag raisings) I met the rest of E Company, its commander at its head, marching up with the second flag." BGen Robert H. Williams ltr to Head, HistBr, G–3 Div, HQMC, dtd 25Jun69, in Iwo Comments.

THE SECOND FLAG RAISING, *afternoon of 23 February 1945. (USMC 113062)*

area had already been made on the previous day. The two patrols met near Tobiishi Point at 1015, just a few minutes before the first flag raising. There was no enemy resistance, though a mine killed two men of 1/28.

To garrison the summit of Mount Suribachi during the coming night, 40 men from Company E remained on the crest; the rest of the regiment occupied positions around the base of the mountain. During the night, 122 Japanese were killed trying to infiltrate the American lines. Many of them had demolitions tied to their bodies and probably were trying to blow up Marine command posts and artillery positions along with themselves.[24]

During one predawn breakthrough attempt early on 24 February, 30 grenade-throwing Japanese assaulted the command post and aid station of 1/28. Personnel of battalion headquarters, corpsmen included, used whatever weapons were at hand to kill the infiltrators while protecting wounded Marines who lay helpless on stretchers amidst the turmoil.

There were to be no easy victories on Iwo Jima, and the cost of seizing Mount Suribachi was high. The operation from D plus 1 to D plus 4 cost the 28th Marines 519 casualties. Of these, 3 officers and 112 men were killed and 21 officers and 354 men were wounded.[25] These figures do not include the 385 casualties sustained by the regiment on D-Day.[26]

It proved impossible to obtain an accurate figure of Japanese killed on and around Suribachi, though 1,231 enemy were counted and hundreds more were sealed inside caves and blockhouses.[27] Except for a handful of men that succeeded in getting through to northern Iwo, the entire garrison of Mount Suribachi was virtually killed to a man. In the days following the fall of the fortress, an occasional Japanese might succeed in digging his way out of a cave or tunnel that had been blasted shut, only to be shot by the alert Marines stationed on and around the mountain for the purpose.

Working together with the infantry, members of the 5th Engineer Battalion had destroyed 165 concrete pillboxes and blockhouses, some with walls 10 feet thick. They had blasted 15 strong bunkers and naval gun positions; destroyed thousands of enemy shells, grenades and land mines; and had sealed 200 caves, some of them three stories high and equipped with heavy steel doors. In addition, the supporting troops evacuated several hundred wounded Marines and bulldozed 1,500 yards of roads and tank paths up to the crater.

Immediately after it was secured, Mount Suribachi was put to practical use. The 14th Marines rushed echo and flashranging equipment to the top in order to spot Japanese artillery and fortifications in the northern end of the island from this vantage point, which thus was turned into a vital observation post. Colonel Liversedge's regiment remained in corps reserve in the Suri-

---

[24] *28th Mar AR*, p. 22.
[25] *5th MarDiv AR*, Sec VII, pp. 17–22.
[26] *Ibid.*, p. 17.

[27] Conner, *The Fifth Marine Division*, p. 68.

bachi area for the next five days, picking off occasional enemy survivors, salvaging arms and equipment, and training new replacements.

As vital and dramatic as the capture of Mount Suribachi was, it marked but one step in the conquest of the stubbornly defended island. A grim and deadly battle was being fought to the north. Few Marines at this stage suspected the strength of the enemy defenses and the cost to be exacted in advancing to the northern end of the island. For the Marines on Iwo, the capture of Suribachi marked the end of a beginning; for General Kuribayashi's well entrenched main force it was the beginning of the end.

CHAPTER 6

Drive to the North [1]

CAPTURE OF AIRFIELD NO. 1 [2]

While the 28th Marines was engaged in the epic assault on Mount Suribachi during the first four days of the invasion, a bloody slugging match involving the main body of General Schmidt's VAC was developing to the north. The battalions in line for the offensive were, from west to east, 1/26, 3/27, 3/23, 2/24, 1/25, 2/25, and 3/25. Two companies of 1/24 were attached to the latter battalion. The seven battalions were deployed along a 4,000-yard front extending from the western shore just north of Mount Suribachi northeastward across the southern end of Airfield No. 1. From there, the line followed the eastern fringes of the field and then pivoted sharply to the east, meeting the coast at the East Boat Basin. (See Map II, Map Section).

It had already become evident on D-Day that, despite extensive naval gunfire and air support, numerous enemy positions had survived the preliminary bombardment completely unscathed. At this juncture, the depth of the enemy defense system on the island was still a matter of conjecture. The dramatic drive of the 28th Marines towards Mount Suribachi had initially captured the limelight; but it was in the central and northern part of Iwo that General Kuribayashi had concentrated the bulk of his forces. The wily enemy commander had left nothing undone to make his defenses in the northern and central sectors impregnable. In this, he was aided by the topography of the island, for the entire area comprised a weird looking array of cliffs, ravines, gorges, crevices, and ledges. Jumbled rock, torn stubble of small

---

[1] Unless otherwise noted, the material in this chapter is derived from: *TF 51 AR; VAC AR; VAC C-1 PerRpts; VAC G-2 Rpts; VAC C-3 Jnl; VAC C-3 PerRpts;* 3d MarDiv AR, 19Feb-25Mar45, hereafter *3d MarDiv AR;* 3d MarDiv D-2 Jnl, 14Feb-27Mar45, hereafter *3d MarDiv D-2 Jnl;* 3d MarDiv G-3 Jnl, 6Feb-3Apr45, hereafter *3d MarDiv G-3 Jnl;* 3d MarDiv G-1 PerRpts, 14Feb-11Apr 45, hereafter *3d MarDiv G-1 PerRpts;* 3d MarDiv D-1 Jnl, 14Feb-12Apr45, hereafter *3d MarDiv D-1 Jnl; 4th MarDiv G-2 Rpts; 4th MarDiv D-3 Jnl; 4th MarDiv D-3 Rpts; 4th MarDiv OpRpt; 5th MarDiv D-1 Jnl; 5th Mar Div D-2 PerRpts; 5th Mar Div D-3 Jnl; 5th MarDiv AR;* 5th MarDiv Casualty Rpts, 17Feb-26Mar45, hereafter *5th MarDiv Casualty Rpts; 5th TkBn AR; Iwo Comments;* Bartley, *Iwo Monograph;* Morehouse, *Iwo Jima Campaign;* Newcomb, *Iwo Jima; Newcomb Notes;* Aurthur, Cohlmia, and Vance, *The Third Marine Division;* Proehl, *The Fourth Marine Division;* Conner, *The Fifth Marine Division;* Morison, *Victory in the Pacific;* Isely and Crowl, *U. S. Marines and Amphibious War.*

[2] Additional material in this section is derived from: 1/24 OpRpt, 19Feb-18Mar45, hereafter *1/24 OpRpt;* 2/24 AR, 19 Feb-16Mar45, hereafter *2/24 AR;* 25th MarRgt UJnl, 18Feb-23Mar45, hereafter *25th MarRgt UJnl;* 26th MarRgt UJnl, 19Feb-26Mar45, hereafter *26th MarRgt UJnl;* 3/27 UJnl, 19Feb-23Mar45, hereafter *3/27 UJnl.*

trees, jagged ridges, and chasms sprawled about in a crazy pattern. Within this maze, the enemy sat deeply entrenched in hundreds of carefully constructed positions, ranging from blockhouses to bunkers, pillboxes, caves, and camouflaged tanks. All fields of fire were well integrated.

One of the reasons for the failure of American naval gunfire and aircraft to neutralize or destroy an appreciable number of enemy positions prior to the landings was the masterful use of camouflage by the enemy. So skillfully had the Japanese hidden their positions that American ships and aircraft failed to detect them. Even those that were spotted and became targets of American naval gunfire and bombs frequently escaped major destruction because of their structural strength.

In the northern part of Iwo Jima, just as in the south, the first night ashore proved to be a restless one. Damage and casualties to the 1/23 command post on Yellow 1, as well as the explosion of the 25th Marines ammunition dump during the early morning hours, have already been recounted. Elsewhere, it was a similar story. At 0230, about 500 Japanese formed in front of the 27th Marines but were dispersed by artillery fire from the 13th Marines. Shortly after 0700, the enemy scored a mortar hit squarely on the command post of 2/25 above Blue Beach 1. The battalion commander, Lieutenant Colonel Lewis C. Hudson, Jr., the executive officer, Major William P. Kaempfer, and the operations officer, Major Donald K. Ellis, were badly wounded. The commander of Company B, 4th Tank Battalion, who had stopped by to obtain further details about the impending attack, scheduled to be launched within the hour, was killed. The executive officer of 3/25, Lieutenant Colonel James Taul, took over the command of the 2d Battalion.

The initial objective of the assault on D plus 1 was to seize the 0–1 Line extending eastward from Iwo's west coast to the southern tip of Airfield No. 2, whence it curved southward in the form of a horseshoe and continued generally east to the coast northeast of the East Boat Basin. In order to reach the 0–1 Line, VAC units would have to complete the northward pivot from west to east, which had already begun on D–Day. Units along the left flank of VAC and those in the center were to sweep across Airfield No. 2 and straighten the sagging portions of the line until they had advanced generally abreast of the 25th Marines, with 1/24 attached, which occupied the hinge position on the right.

For many of the Marines preparing to jump off on the morning of D-plus 1, daylight brought with it a most depressing sight. At least one observer was to record:

> ... it was not until the next morning, when Marines along the airfield could look back on the beach, that the full extent of our losses was apparent. The wreckage was indescribable. For two miles the debris was so thick that there were only a few places where landing craft could still get in. The wrecked hulks of scores of landing boats testified to one price we had paid to put our troops ashore. Tanks and half-tracks lay crippled where they had bogged down in the coarse sand. Amphibian tractors, victims of mines and well aimed shells, lay flopped on their backs. Cranes, brought ashore to unload cargo, tilted at

DRIVE TO THE NORTH

insane angles, and bulldozers were smashed in their own roadways.

Packs, gas masks, rifles, and clothing, ripped and shattered by shell fragments, lay scattered across the beach. Toilet articles and even letters were strewn among the debris, as though war insisted on prying into the personal affairs of those it claimed.

And scattered amid the wreckage was death. An officer in charge of an LCT had been hit while trying to free his boat from the sand and was blown in half; a life preserver supported the trunk of his body in the water. Marines, killed on the beach, were partially buried under the sand as the tide came in. Perhaps a hand stretched rigidly out of the sand, and that was all.[3]

In the face of all this death and destruction, the battle continued and, following an intensive artillery, naval gunfire, and air preparation, the VAC attack to the north jumped off as scheduled at 0830. Along the 1,000-yard front in the 5th Division zone of attack, Colonel Wornham committed 1/26 and 3/27 abreast, keeping 1/27 and 2/27 in reserve. General Rockey had designated the 26th Marines, less 1/26 which had been attached to RCT 27, as division reserve, standing by in positions near the southwestern tip of Airfield No. 1.

The advance of 1/26, commanded by Lieutenant Colonel Daniel C. Pollock, and 3/27, under Lieutenant Colonel Donn J. Robertson, soon was seriously slowed down by numerous enemy pillboxes and land mines; even more deadly was the well-aimed enemy mortar and artillery fire and particularly a heavy concentration of air bursts from Japanese antiaircraft guns fired from their minimum angle of elevation. West of the airfield, Colonel Wornham's men had to move through relatively open terrain that offered neither cover nor concealment from an enemy who enjoyed both excellent observation and fields of fire. Supported by Companies A and B of the 5th Tank Battalion, the 5th Division Marines moved forward steadily, taking heavy losses as they advanced. At 1800, when Colonel Wornham ordered the two battalions to halt and consolidate, the advance had gained 800 yards. However, 1/26 on the left had to pull back about 200 yards to more favorable ground for night defense. As D plus 1 came to a close, the two 5th Division battalions dug in along an east-west line extending from the northwestern edge of Airfield No. 1 to the west coast. For the night, 2/27 backed up 1/26 while 1/27 dug in behind 3/27 to provide a defense in depth.

For the attack on D plus 1, the 4th Marine Division committed two regiments abreast. On the left of the division zone of attack, the 23d Marines, with 2/24 attached, jumped off at 0830 and almost immediately encountered intense enemy machine gun, mortar, and artillery fire. In attempting to pinpoint the source of this fire and silence it, Colonel Wensinger's men temporarily lost contact with Lanigan's 25th Marines. Even though the terrain in this area was unfavorable for the employment of armor, a reinforced platoon from Company C, 4th Tank Battalion was able to support the advance of the 23d Marines. By noon, an aggressive attack had carried past the northern fringes of Airfield No. 1. This thrust breached an important portion of the Japanese defensive system and at the same time

---
[3] Proehl, *The Fourth Marine Division*, pp. 152–153.

reduced a number of well-concealed pillboxes and infantry strongpoints. The attacking Marines also had suffered severe casualties. Movement, both on the airfield flats and on the slopes from the beaches, was almost entirely under enemy observation, and the Japanese made the most of their favorable situation.

During the afternoon, the 23d Marines continued the advance. However, minefields and increasingly rough terrain all but precluded effective armored support. The enemy directed deadly rocket, artillery, and mortar fire against the advancing Marines, and after the morning's gains little more ground was taken for the remainder of the day. Altogether, in crossing the airfield, Colonel Wensinger's men had advanced roughly 500 yards. At 1630, the reserve of the 23d Marines, consisting of 1/23 and 2/23, moved forward to positions along the seaward edge of the airfield to form a strong, secondary line of defense. The 23d Marines linked up with the 27th Marines on the left and the 25th Marines on the right before nightfall.

The attack of Colonel Lanigan's 25th Marines on D plus 1 was to be carried out by three battalions abreast. On the left, 1/25 under Lieutenant Colonel Hollis U. Mustain, was to make the main effort; the 2d Battalion in the center, commanded by Lieutenant Colonel James Taul, was to seize the high ground directly to its front and, after taking it, give fire support to 1/25. On the extreme right flank, the attached 1/24 under Major Paul S. Treitel, was to remain in place until 1/25 and 2/25 could come abreast. Because of heavy casualties sustained on D-Day, 3/25 was pulled out of the lines and held in regimental reserve.

The 25th Marines jumped off on schedule. Tanks of Company B, 4th Tank Battalion, supported the attack, but the exceptionally rough terrain made this support practically worthless. In addition, each time that a tank reached a firing position, it immediately attracted accurate enemy mortar and artillery fire. Crossfire from enemy machine guns mounted in concealed emplacements, combined with a heavy volume of well-aimed rifle fire, seriously interfered with the advance of Colonel Lanigan's regiment and inflicted heavy casualties.

In discussing the advance on D plus 1, a survivor of the Iwo battle later was to remark:

> There was no cover from enemy fire. Japs deep in reinforced concrete pillboxes laid down interlocking bands of fire that cut whole companies to ribbons. Camouflage hid all the enemy installations. The high ground on every side was honeycombed with layer after layer of Jap emplacements, blockhouses, dugouts, and observation posts. Their observation was perfect; whenever the Marines made a move, the Japs watched every step, and when the moment came, their mortars, rockets, machine guns, and artillery, long ago zeroed-in—would smother the area in a murderous blanket of fire. The counterbattery fire and preparatory barrages of Marine artillery and naval gunfire were often ineffective, for the Japs would merely retire to a lower level or inner cave and wait until the storm had passed. Then they would emerge and blast the advancing Marines.[4]

The deadly effectiveness of the enemy fire was not limited to the front lines. At

---
[4] *Ibid.*, p. 153.

1100, Japanese artillery scored a direct hit on the aid station of 1/25, killing six Navy corpsmen and wounding an additional seven. It was apparent that General Kuribayashi had so sited his artillery that all the beaches and routes into the interior of the island were covered. Japanese gunners could search out various supply dumps, evacuation stations, and command posts at will. Normally, LVTs had the task of bringing supplies to the front lines. In the zone of attack of the 25th Marines, however, even these versatile vehicles were unable to get through and work details from units in reserve had to manhandle critically needed materiel.

Colonel Lanigan's Marines continued to press the attack throughout the afternoon of D plus 1, but progress was woefully slow. At 1600, the exhausted men were cheered by the arrival of friendly aircraft which, it was hoped, might lend some impetus to the advance. This joy, however, soon, turned into terror when .50 caliber machine gun bullets, rockets, and bombs from a friendly air strike hit men of Company B, 1/24, standing upright on the southern slope of the quarry about 400 yards inland from the eastern shore. This strike, neither called for nor controlled by 1/24, was delivered without a preliminary run and placed on the front lines despite the fact that yellow front-line marking panels had been displayed prior to and during the attack. In consequence of this error, 1/24 suffered five killed and six wounded.[5] As if attempting to advance under heavy enemy fire and being strafed, bombed, and rocketed by friendly aircraft were not enough, the hapless company also was shelled by naval gunfire and found friendly artillery registering on its positions.[6] This misguided naval gunfire, consisting of two complete salvos fired by an unidentified cruiser, landed in the front line of 1/24 and resulted in approximately 90 casualties.[7]

By 1800, 1/25 and 2/25 had made gains of 200-300 yards. The left flank of 1/25, on the other hand, had been unable to move at all throughout the day because of extremely heavy fire received from the left front in the zone of action of the 23d Marines. At 1800, orders were issued to all units to consolidate, dig in, and establish firm contact with each other.

As night descended over bitterly contested Iwo Jima on 20 February, the capture of Airfield No. 1 had been completed and the 4th Division front had advanced between 200 and 500 yards. For these gains, the Japanese had exacted a heavy price. As the second day ended, the 5th Marine Division had lost 1,500 men killed and wounded and the 4th Division about 2,000.[8] The first prisoners, a total of three, had been taken during the day, but two of them died. A total of 630 enemy dead had been counted, but it was assumed that many others had been killed.

Early on D plus 1, General Schmidt had ordered the corps reserve, the 21st Marines, commanded by Colonel Hartnoll J. Withers, to boat and prepare to

---

[5] *4th MarDiv OpRpt*, Anx H. p. 4.

[6] *4th MarDiv OpRpt*, Anx G, p. 121.

[7] LtCol Paul S. Treitel ltr to CMC, dtd 5Feb53, in *Iwo Comments*.

[8] Newcomb, *Iwo Jima*, p. 146.

land on order. The regiment began debarking before noon, in rain and rough water. Dozens of men missed the drop into the bobbing boats and after they had been fished out, the boats went to the rendezvous area. There the LCVPs circled for six hours, the Marines cold, wet, and miserable. The congestion at the beaches which was steadily increasing, combined with a rising surf that made landing conditions hazardous, precluded their landing. In the end, General Schmidt ordered the regiment back to its transports to be landed later when conditions had improved.

At the same time, on D plus 1, there was a desperate need for artillery, whose landing could not be postponed. As a result, the 4th Marine Division landed the 3d and 4th Battalions of the 14th Marines during the day. Shortly after 1000, 3/14 had launched all of its DUKWs, but the landing was delayed by enemy fire. Finally, in midafternoon, the amphibian trucks carrying 3/14 began to land over the southernmost portion of Yellow 1. The battalion's 105mm howitzers moved into positions prepared by the 3/14 reconnaissance party just inland from the boundary separating Yellow 1 and Red 2. Around 1730, the howitzers opened fire and reinforced the fires of the 1st Battalion of the division artillery.[9]

The landing of the 105s of 4/14 turned into a disaster. The first DUKW to emerge from LST *1032* remained afloat only for a moment. Then waves surged over the side, the engine stopped, and the DUKW sank, taking the 105 down with it. Seven more DUKWs waddled out of the LST and sank in succession. As a result, a total of eight 105s were lost, as well as a dozen officers and men. It was subsequently determined that motor failure of the DUKWs was caused by water in the gasoline, and by insufficient freeboard resulting from extremely heavy loads and choppy water. Thus, 4/14 had lost 8 out of 12 howitzers before firing a round on Iwo Jima.[10]

The disaster for Lieutenant Colonel Youngdale's battalion did not end here. The remaining four DUKWs headed for the beach late in the evening and two of them broached at the surf line while attempting to go ashore at 2230. Out of a dozen DUKWs and howitzers, only two finally made it to shore. The guns, having gone into position, began firing northward into the inky darkness.

In order to offset the critical artillery shortage, some of the big 155mm howitzers also were ordered to land. In late afternoon, LST *779* forced its way through the wreckage littering Red Beach 1 and discharged Battery C of the 2d 155mm Howitzer Battalion. Despite extremely difficult beach conditions, the four howitzers were hauled up the steep bluffs by tractors and were in position by 1840 in the 5th Marine Division sector near the west coast. The two remaining batteries of Major Earl J. Rowse's battalion were not landed for another two and four days respectively. Even those artillery battalions that did make it ashore encountered unusual problems from the

---

[9] *14th Mar OpRpt*, App. 3, pp. 8–10.

[10] *14th Mar OpRpt*, App. 5, p. 3.

very outset. Before the 28th Marines put the Japanese artillery on Mount Suribachi out of action, artillerymen firing to the north received enemy fire from the south that proved more troublesome than enemy rounds from the front.[11]

ADVANCE TOWARDS THE 0-1 LINE[12]

At the cost of heavy casualties, the Marines at the end of D plus 1 controlled nearly one-third of Iwo Jima and occupied a two mile-wide beachhead extending along the landing area and 2,000 yards up the southwest coast. Motoyama Airfield No. 1 was completely in American hands. Marine lines stretched in an east-west direction from the west coast opposite the end of the airstrip, past the end of the airfield, with a slight curve to the quarry. Just beyond that point the line curved at right angles to face east with the right flank resting on the shore along the ridge facing the East Boat Basin. The 0-1 Line had not yet been reached at any point, but positions were well knit and more artillery and serviceable tanks were available for support. Even though

---

[11] LtCol Roland J. Spritzen ltr to CMC, dtd 7Nov52, in *Iwo Comments*.

[12] Additional material in this section is derived from 13th MarRgt UJnl, 19Feb-21Mar45, hereafter *13th MarRgt UJnl*; 14th MarRgt OpRpt, 22Feb-14Mar45, hereafter *14th MarRgt OpRpt*; 5th EngBn UJnl, 19Feb-24Mar45, hereafter *5th EngBn UJnl*; 5th Shore Party Rgt AR, 19-28Feb45, hereafter *5th Shore Party Rgt AR*; 2/26 UJnl, 19Feb-26Mar45, hereafter *2/26 UJnl*; 3/26 UJnl, 19Feb-26Mar45, hereafter *3/26 UJnl*; VAC Transl of Jap Docs, Iwo Jima, hereafter *VAC Translations*.

enemy resistance on 20 February was even heavier than that encountered on D-Day, both Marine divisions were holding the ground they had seized.

Beach conditions remained extremely difficult throughout the day, both because of a high surf and the continuous enemy artillery fire. The shore party battalions were raked by artillery, mortar, and small arms fire as they desperately attempted to clear the beaches and unload incoming landing craft. They stacked supplies well above the high-water mark, but gear piled up there faster than it could be moved inland. In order to cope with this crisis, the entire logistical plan of establishing shore-party dumps had to be abandoned. Without pausing on the beaches, incoming amtracs—the only vehicles that could climb the terraces and reach firm ground unassisted—waddled up the slopes into the front lines, where they delivered ammunition, rations, and water directly to the combat units. The tractors freed weapons and vehicles that had bogged down and hauled supply-laden DUKWs over the terraces, thus enabling the latter vehicles to move supplies right up to the front lines. In addition to the vehicles shuttling back and forth between the beaches and the lines, Marine working parties hand-carried ammunition forward in order to alleviate critical shortages.

In view of the overall situation, it became apparent to Generals Smith and Schmidt at the close of D plus 1, that the strength of enemy resistance dictated the necessity of employing the 3d Marine Division, still afloat, before long. The requirement of furnishing food and ammunition to an additional 20,000 Marines would impose an added strain on available beach facilities, but the dwindling combat strength of the two Marine divisions already on the island left no other choice. As a result, the 21st Marines of the 3d Marine Division were again ordered to land on D plus 2, to be placed at the disposal of General Cates.

The night of 20-21 February was punctuated by loud explosions as the Japanese exchanged artillery fire with the Americans. At the same time, U.S. Navy gunfire support ships and LCIs mounting 4.2-inch mortars delivered counterbattery and harassing fires. Early in the evening, around 2000, a group of Japanese was observed massing opposite the 27th Marines. Immediate fire by the 13th Marines and attached corps artillery killed a number of the enemy and dispersed the rest. Shortly before 0500, about 100 Japanese attempted to pierce the lines of the 4th Marine Division in the 1/25 sector, but were driven off with heavy losses.

As 21 February dawned, 12 destroyers, 2 cruisers, 68 aircraft, and 33 howitzers took turns at battering the enemy-held portion of Iwo before VAC resumed the attack on D plus 2. At 0810, both the 4th and 5th Marine Divisions jumped off. On the left flank of VAC, the 27th Marines met immediate and violent resistance from the enemy's main defensive positions, which consisted of a belt of caves and concrete-and-steel emplacements. This defense system had a depth of a mile and a half and extended from the west coast to the east coast of Iwo. It featured innumerable pillboxes and around 1,500 caves.

The terrain in the 27th Marines' zone of advance was suitable for the employment of armor; elements of the 5th Tank Battalion moved forward just ahead of the infantry. By 1340, 1/26 on the left and 3/27 on the right had advanced nearly 1,000 yards and had reached a point just south of the 0-1 Line. Because of the relative speed of the advance and heavy enemy shelling, a sizable gap had developed by this time between the 4th and 5th Marine Divisions. Company B, 1/27 was committed from regimental reserve to fill this gap between 3/27 and the 23d Marines. Under continuous enemy fire, the 5th Marine Division spent the remainder of the afternoon reorganizing, evacuating casualties, and consolidating its lines. In the course of the afternoon, General Rockey and his staff came ashore and established their headquarters near the southern end of Airfield No. 1.

At the same time that the 5th Marine Division jumped off on D plus 2, the 23d and 25th Marines continued their attack. The 23d, with 2/23 on the left and 2/24 on the right slowly pushed forward with 1/23 and 2/23 following at a 600-yard interval. Almost immediately, the advancing Marines encountered severe mortar, machine gun, and artillery fire, as well as a number of minefields. The advance through the minefields and against numerous pillboxes was very time-consuming and costly. Engineer units went forward to remove the mines. The only significant advance made was on the left flank in the 23d Marines zone of advance, where slightly defiladed areas permitted local and restricted envelopment. But even the progress of the 23d Marines averaged only slightly more than 100 yards during the entire day. After reestablishing contact with the 27th Marines on its left, the 23d dug in for the night shortly before 1800.

On the extreme right, the 25th Marines attacked with 1/25, 2/25, and 1/24 in line, and 3/25 in reserve. Even though the enemy had laid minefields in front of the 25th Marines, the terrain here was so rocky and irregular that the enemy had not been able to mine all avenues of approach. Tanks of Company A, 4th Tank Battalion, supported the advance of 1/25 and 2/25, while tanks of Company B fired on pillboxes and dugouts on the cliff facing 1/24, driving the enemy from the heights of the quarry and cliff areas. Howitzers of 1/14 placed counterbattery and supporting fire across the regimental front. Resistance in the center of the regimental zone gradually weakened and fair progress was made on the right along the shore of the East Boat Basin. Altogether, the 25th Marines gained from 50-300 yards in the course of the morning. Casualties were heavy throughout; at 1000, while checking his frontline positions, Lieutenant Colonel Hollis U. Mustain, commanding 1/25, was killed by enemy shellfire. The battalion executive officer, Major Fenton J. Mee, assumed command.

The irregular advance of units over difficult terrain caused a serious gap to develop between the 1st and 2d Battalions, 25th Marines; in midafternoon Colonel Lanigan committed his 3d Battalion between the two. Since all units were under heavy enemy fire, 3/25 encountered major difficulty in moving into the line. By 1700, the move had been accomplished and the regiment consolidated for the night. Similarly, in order to fill a sizable gap between the right flank of the 5th Marine Division and the left flank of the 4th, 1/27 was moved into position along the 5th Division's right flank. Lines of General Rockey's division had to be extended about 400 yards into the 4th Division zone of attack.

Throughout the day, the two-divisional advance towards Airfield No. 2 received effective air and naval gunfire support. More than 800 aircraft flew direct support missions with a total of 32 strikes carried out by 14-20 planes each. Eleven destroyers stood by offshore to provide direct support and illuminating fires for VAC; 1 destroyer, 2 LCI mortar support units, and 2 cruisers fired deep support missions.[13] Naval gunfire and artillery air spotters continued to use carrier-based aircraft, since Airfield No. 1 was still unable to accommodate VMO units.

A pressing need for reinforcements made it necessary to land more troops on Iwo as soon as possible. Improved beach and landing conditions on the morning of D plus 2 finally permitted the 21st Marines of the 3d Marine Division to come ashore. The regiment, commanded by Colonel Hartnoll J. Withers, was ordered to land at 1130 over the Yellow Beaches; it was to be attached to the 4th Marine Division to assist in the capture of Airfield No. 2.[14] Colonel Withers landed his battalions through-

---
[13] *VAC AR*, Anx B, p. 16.
[14] *4th MarDiv OpRpt*, Sec IV.

out the afternoon of 21 February. Despite a heavy surf, the regiment did not incur any casualties and by 1800 all three battalions and the regimental command post were ashore. After being attached to the 4th Marine Division, RCT 21 assembled near the edge of Airfield No. 1.

Shortly after noon, the assistant commander of the 4th Marine Division, Brigadier General Hart, also went ashore in order to report on beach conditions and select an appropriate site for the division command post. Finding the beaches under heavy fire and littered with the debris of the invasion, General Hart recommended that division headquarters remain afloat at least until 22 February. The assistant division commander also recommended, after consultation with the regimental commanders, that the 21st Marines, instead of relieving the 25th Marines as previously planned, would relieve the 23d Marines on D plus 3. His recommendation was approved.

As 21 February drew to a close, VAC held a very irregular line which passed between the two airfields. When units consolidated their positions for the night, a total of eight battalions was facing the enemy across the island. The slow Marine advance during D plus 2 had forced the Japanese back yard by yard. Once again, for the gains made in the course of the day, VAC Marines had paid with heavy casualties. During the first 58 hours ashore, the landing force had sustained more than 4,500 casualties, and combat efficiency of the 4th Marine Division had been reduced to 68 percent.

The night from 21-22 February proved to be a bad one for men of the landing force, who felt extremely uncomfortable in the cold drizzle. Within the overall scope of General Kuribayashi's prohibition of any major *banzai* charges, the Japanese did all within their power to make their unwanted guests as miserable as possible.

At dusk, enemy aircraft attacked American shipping offshore and scored hits on the outer ring of the warships surrounding Iwo Jima. Taking advantage of the commotion resulting from the sudden air attack, the enemy executed local counterattacks and infiltration against both the 4th and 5th Divisions. Along the left front of VAC, an enemy counterattack in undetermined strength hit the 27th Marines at 2100. No penetration resulted from this attack, which was stopped within the hour. At 0245, the exhausted men of Colonel Wornham's regiment repulsed an attempted infiltration. An hour later, the enemy tried his luck once again, and at 0400, RCT 27 reported 800 enemy massing in front of its lines.[15] As the long night finally ended, the regiment's lines were still intact, though an undetermined number of the enemy had managed to infiltrate.

It also proved to be a restless night for Marines of the 4th Division. Shortly before midnight, an enemy force of about 200 men massed on Airfield No. 2 and headed for the lines of 3/23. Before this attack could get organized, the enemy was hit by naval gunfire and artillery and was forced to withdraw.

---

[15] *5th MarDiv AR*, p. 21.

During the long night, the 25th Marines reported that an enemy aircraft had bombed Blue Beach behind its lines. Almost as steady as the rain was the volume of enemy mortar and artillery fire that covered the Marine front lines, beaches, and rear areas throughout the night.

D plus 3 was, if anything, even worse than the three days that had preceded it. A cold, heavy rain pelted the island, coating Marines and their weapons with a sort of grayish paste on top of the layer of volcanic ash they had already acquired. The front lines of VAC, on the morning of 22 February, bent back in the form of a horseshoe in the center of the 3,400-yard line, where elements of the 23d Marines still were 1,200 yards short of the 0-1 Line. Fatigue and heavy casualties both had left their imprint on the men in the lines, and the three days and nights of incessant, nerve-shattering action were beginning to have an adverse effect on combat efficiency. Without rest or sleep, subsisting solely on a diet of K rations and water, occasionally supplemented by unheated C rations, the men were beginning to show a marked drop in morale.

In order to provide added impetus for the attack on this fourth day of the operation, both Generals Rockey and Cates decided to relieve some of the frontline units, notably the 23d and 27th Marines. Along the left flank of VAC, the 26th Marines under Colonel Chester B. Graham moved out at daybreak with the mission of relieving the 27th Marines and continuing the attack to the north. Once RCT 26 had passed the lines, 1/26, which previously had been attached to RCT 27, was to revert to its parent regiment. The 27th Marines reserve, 2/27, would become attached to the 26th Marines.

At 0500 the 21st Marines prepared to relieve RCT 23 with the attached 2/24. Upon being relieved, the 23d Marines, less two mortar platoons, was to be held in VAC reserve near the northeastern edge of Airfield No. 1. The mortar platoons were to remain in position to support the attack of RCT 21. The 25th Marines, with 1/24 attached, was to remain on the 4th Division right, while the 24th Marines, less 1/24, would continue in division reserve.

The relief of the 27th Marines took place in a heavy downpour of rain, which turned the ground into gumbo. Mortar fire, coming from the higher ground ahead and in the center of the island, fell as steadily as the rain, and both combined to create confusion and disruption. The 26th Marines, with 2/27 attached, passed through the lines of the 27th Marines with the mission of attacking to the northeast, following the western contour of the island. At the same time to the right, the 21st Marines moved in on the left of the 4th Marine Division.

The zone of attack of the 5th Division extended from the western beaches to a formidable terrain obstacle which ran from northeast to southwest down the west center of the island, curving west across the division's front near Airfield No. 2. This obstacle was a bluff almost 100 feet high, whose slopes dropped almost vertically towards the American lines. The high ground above the bluff provided the enemy with perfect observation into the division area and enabled him to effectively block any advance from both the front and the right flank.

At 0835, following preparatory naval gunfire and air strikes, both divisions jumped off. In the zone of attack of the 5th Marine Division the 26th Marines attacked with three battalions in the line. Almost immediately, the advancing Marines drew heavy fire from the front and right flank. Enemy shells and bullets were no respectors of rank; around 0940, Lieutenant Colonel Tom M. Trotti, commanding 3/26, and his operations officer, Major William R. Day, were killed by a mortar shell. Captain Richard M. Cook, commanding Company G, took over until noon, at which time Major Richard Fagan, the division inspector, assumed command. Despite heavy losses, the 26th advanced for about 400 yards. In the course of the day, the weather turned from bad to worse. Rain was falling in torrents and visibility became extremely poor. Because of the heavy rain, no air support could be made available. The poor weather even handicapped the tanks, whose drivers could see but a few yards ahead.

During the afternoon it became apparent that the attack by 3d Division Marines against the bluff itself had stalled, leaving the 26th Marines exposed to heavy fire from the front, the right flank, and the right rear. In addition, the Japanese were beginning to launch several thrusts against the regiment's left flank and center. As if to mock Colonel Graham's drenched and dispirited Marines, Japanese artillery and mortars on the bluff directed heavy fire into the 26th Marines' lines. At 1400, the exhausted and severely mauled Marines were forced to relinquish the 400-yard gain they had made earlier in the day and pulled back to the line of departure. Japanese mortar and artillery fire harassed the men for the remainder of the afternoon during the withdrawal and continued after the Marines had occupied defensive positions for the night.

In the sector occupied by the 4th Marine Division, things had gone little better during D plus 3. At 0500, the 21st Marines began the relief of the 23d. The newly arrived 3d Division Marines faced very rough going from the outset. In the heavy downpour and continuous enemy fire, the relief of the 23d Marines required nearly six hours. Even before the relief was completed, Colonel Withers committed his 1st and 2d Battalions, commanded by Lieutenant Colonel Marlowe C. Williams and Lieutenant Colonel Lowell E. English, respectively, against an intricate network of mutually supporting pillboxes on the high ground between the two airfields. The 3d Battalion, under Lieutenant Colonel Wendell H. Duplantis, remained in reserve.

As the 21st Marines advanced northward, with 1/21 on the right and 2/21 on the left, it had to push its attack uphill against mutually supporting pillboxes and bunkers with mined approaches. These pillboxes were well protected on the flanks and only direct hits by large caliber weapons appeared to have any effect on them. In the taxiways between the airfields, bunkers blocked the advance, and the area adjoining the runways of Airfield No. 2 was dotted with pillboxes that were covered with sand and often protruded only a foot or so above the ground. This was the beginning of the enemy main line of resistance. The restricted nature of the area and the excellent defensive system precluded any maneuver but a frontal assault.

Bad weather and a well-entrenched enemy who took full advantage of the terrain with prearranged fires, presented the 21st Marines with an exceedingly brutal introduction to Iwo Jima. By afternoon of D plus 3, 2/21 had advanced 250 yards in places; 1/21 had gained about 50 yards. Casualties had been out of all proportion to the gains made. Lieutenant Colonel Williams was wounded by a mortar shell but refused evacuation until nightfall, at which time he turned command of 1/21 over to the battalion executive officer, Major Clay M. Murray.[16] At about 1700, the attack halted for the day and all units began to prepare positions for the night.

To the right of the 21st Marines, the 25th, with three battalions and the attached 1/24 in the line, was to have attacked on D plus 3 in order to straighten its regimental front in conjunction with the advance of the 21st Marines. Once the lines had been straightened out, both the 21st and 25th Marines were to launch a coordinated drive to the north to seize the O-1 Line. Failure of the 21st Marines to make any sizable gains had an adverse effect on operations of the 25th Marines, which was unable to launch a full-scale attack. Nevertheless, in the course of the morning, 1/25 advanced about 200 yards, only to find its left flank completely exposed. As a result, the advance had to be halted until the battalion could tie in firmly with the 21st Marines. In the center of the 25th Marines line, the 3d and 2d Battalions found themselves marking time. The only cheerful note for the day was sounded when 3/25 requested and received rocket support against a hill some 800 yards northwest of the quarry. Two salvoes fired against enemy positions on this hill drove about 200 Japanese from their emplacements. Caught out in the open by well-placed machine guns of 3/25, a large part of the enemy force was wiped out.

Around 1530, the Japanese struck back. While leaving his forward observation post, Lieutenant Colonel Chambers was severely wounded by enemy machine gun fire, when a bullet struck his left collarbone. Since Lieutenant Colonel James Taul, the battalion executive officer, had assumed command of 2/25 on 20 February, when the commander of 2/25 had been wounded and evacuated, Captain James C. Headley assumed command of 3/25.

The 2d Battalion of the 25th Marines, meanwhile, remained largely stationary during the day. Even so, it took its share of casualties. In midmorning, the Japanese laid a heavy and accurate mortar barrage on the battalion lines; an attempted enemy counterattack was quickly smashed. At 1830, Japanese were observed moving towards the bat-

---

[16] Major Murray himself was wounded on the following day and forced to turn command of the battalion over to Major Robert H. Houser, who led 1/21 for the duration of the Iwo operation. LtCol Robert H. Houser ltr to CMC, dtd 3Apr53 and Col Marlowe C. Williams ltr to CMC, dtd 9Feb53, in *Iwo Comments*.

talion lines. Before an attack could get under way, infantry heavy weapons fire and artillery support from the 14th Marines dispersed the Japanese.

At the right end of the VAC lines, 1/24 spent most of the day in mopping up along the east coast above the landing beaches. Major Treitel's men blasted caves and pillboxes in an attempt to reduce the heavy enemy mortar and sniper fire originating in the bluffs around the quarry. In its operations during D plus 3, the battalion fared better than the 25th Marines on its left and casualties were comparatively light. At 1700, the battalion consolidated its positions and established contact between units.

The ferocious battle raging between the airfields took its toll not only of men but also materiel. Thus, at the end of D plus 3, the 4th Tank Battalion reported that 11 of its tanks had been destroyed and 8 were under repair, leaving 28 operational.[17] The 5th Tank Battalion reported 34 tanks operational, 4 under repair, and 13 destroyed.

Even though the advance towards the north of Iwo had made little headway during 22 February, the command organization and activities on the Iwo beaches became somewhat better coordinated. Headquarters of the 9th Naval Construction Brigade, commanded by Captain Robert C. Johnson, CEC, USN, was set up ashore, and initial work was started on preparing Iwo to serve as a giant aircraft carrier. In the course of the day, burials began in the Fourth Division cemetery halfway between Yellow 1 and Airfield No. 2.

Burials in the 5th Division cemetery, located just south of the airfield, had already commenced during the afternoon of D plus 1.[18] Provision was made for those Marines who died on board ship to be buried at sea, provided that this took place in water more than 100 fathoms deep.

Evacuation of the numerous casualties became a critical problem on D plus 3 because of poor beach conditions. LST *807* voluntarily remained on the beach under fire and acted as a hospital ship during the hours of darkness, while the remaining LSTs withdrew for the night. As darkness descended over the battle area, a steady stream of casualties arrived on the *807*, where doctors performed emergency operations in the wardroom. Before morning, more than 200 casualties had been treated on the LST; of this number only 2 died.[19]

At sundown on 22 February, Task Force 58 set sail for its second raid against Tokyo. On board the *Indianapolis*, Admiral Spruance accompanied this strike force. A task group of this fast carrier force, TG 58.5, consisting of the *Enterprise*, two cruisers, and Destroyer Squadron 54, remained at Iwo to provide night fighter protection. The departure of TF 58 materially reduced the availability of aircraft for direct ground support; overall responsibility for providing this type of support for the Marines ashore now fell on the small carriers of the carrier support force under Admiral Durgin, in addition to its mission of conducting air searches for survivors, providing anti-

---

[17] *VAC AR*, p. 18.

[18] *VAC C–1 PerRpts*, p. 21.
[19] *5th Shore Party Rgt AR*, p. 6.

submarine and combat air patrols, and strikes against nearby Chichi Jima. As a result, the close air support for Marines fighting on the ground would henceforth have to be curtailed due to the shortage of aircraft.[20]

Marines shivering from wetness and cold in the front lines, faced another restless night. The Japanese began to probe the American lines shortly after dusk. Following an extremely heavy mortar and artillery barrage around 1800, a strong enemy force attacked the northernmost lines of the 26th Marines and succeeded in driving back the outposts. The enemy counterattack was brought to a halt after heavy casualties had been inflicted upon the attacking force. During the early morning hours, enemy swimmers, who had infiltrated across the western beaches into the 5th Division area, had to be eliminated. Similarly, in the zone of action of the 4th Marine Division, there was sporadic enemy activity throughout the night. Around 0500, an estimated 100 Japanese attempted to infiltrate the lines of 2/25 and 3/25. Even though these enemy efforts were thwarted, the intermittent firing served to keep the weary Marines from getting some much-needed sleep. In addition to all this activity, Japanese artillery continued to hit friendly positions along the corps front, inflicting further casualties and adding to the sense of uncertainty.

Despite the continuous harassment by enemy infantry and supporting arms, VAC plans called for the continuation of the attack on 23 February. The objective for D plus 4 was to be the 0-2 Line. Jumping off at 0730, the 4th Marine Division was directed to make the main effort on its left against Airfield No. 2. Since the strongly defended bluffs on the far left of the 4th Division's zone of advance dominated all of western Iwo, VAC authorized the 5th Marine Division to advance beyond the boundary separating the two divisions if such an advance promised to neutralize or eliminate these prominent obstacles.

At 0730 on 23 February, the VAC attack continued in the direction of Airfield No. 2 and the 0-2 Line. The 26th Marines, with 2/27 attached, moved forward against very heavy fire from the front and the right flank. After advancing for about 200 yards against bitter opposition, the regiment found the ground untenable and withdrew to its jumpoff positions. Shortly before noon, enemy artillery scored a direct hit on the command post of 2/26. The battalion commander, Lieutenant Colonel Joseph C. Sayers, was wounded and had to be evacuated. Major Amedeo Rea, the battalion executive officer, assumed command. For the remainder of D plus 4, the 26th Marines attempted to advance, but it was driven back each time by heavy enemy fire. At the end of the day, the battalions dug in for the night in about the same positions they had occupied during the preceding night.

In the center of the VAC line, where the 4th Marine Division with the attached 21st Marines was to make the main effort against Airfield No. 2, events took a similar turn. Because of the importance of this airfield General Kuribayashi had assigned the *145th*

---

[20] *VAC Air Support Summary*, p. 2.

Regiment commanded by Colonel Masuo Ikeda to defend this vital objective. This regiment was considered the best Japanese outfit on Iwo Jima; its 47mm antitank guns were sited to fire straight down the runways. In fact, the Marines were now encountering the enemy main defense line, which began in the west at the rocky cliffs to the north of the western beaches, stretched east across the island to skirt the southern end of Airfield No. 2, and terminated in the cliffs at the northern end of the eastern beaches. This line was organized in depth with all types of heavy weapons within and behind it, capable of delivering fire upon both the isthmus and beach areas. It was also heavily organized with a series of mutually supporting pillboxes, bunkers, blockhouses, tunnels, and other dug in positions. In addition, all approaches to the airfield were mined; enemy dead, saki bottles, helmets, and ammunition dumps were found booby trapped.

It became the lot of the 21st Marines to advance into this cauldron of enemy fire. Typical of the fighting which this regiment was to see at the approaches to Airfield No. 2 on D plus 4 were the experiences of some of the members of this unit:

> Major Clay Murray taking over 1/21 for his first day, figured that if he could find the weakest point and destroy it he could then knock off the supporting positions one by one. He lifted the telephone to give an order and a machine gun burst smashed the phone in his hand. Two bullets tore through his left cheek and out his open mouth, taking five teeth with them, and the rest of the burst sheared the knuckles of his left hand and ripped open his left ear. Major Robert H. Houser became 1/21's third commander in two days.
>
> Private First Class George Smyth, 18, of Brooklyn, had never seen such Japanese. They were six footers, and they never retreated. Smyth's buddy fell beside him, a pistol bullet through his head, dead center. It came from a captured Marine .45. On the other side, a Japanese came down with his sword, both hands grasping the hilt. The Marine put up his right hand to ward off the blow, and his arm was sliced down the middle, fingers to elbow. As Smyth ran forward, a Japanese disappeared before him into a hole. Smyth dropped at the hole to finish him off, but the Japanese was already rising from a tunnel behind him. Smyth turned just in time to kill him. The ground was giving Ikeda's men every advantage, and they were using them all.[21]

In the end, 1/21 was unable to make any gains for the day and had to consolidate for the night in its jumpoff positions. The 2d Battalion, now commanded by Major George A. Percy, had already become engaged in a sharp firefight at daybreak and, as a result, did not jump off until 0935. The heavy curtain of enemy fire prevented any advance until a second artillery preparation had neutralized some of the known targets on Airfield No. 2. The assault companies reached the southwest approaches to the airfield, but every effort to get troops onto the field itself failed, despite heavy support from naval gunfire and a rocket barrage. Finally, some of the advance elements succeeded in crossing the lower end of the northeast-southwest runway following an air strike, only to be driven back later by

---

[21] Newcomb, *Iwo Jima*, pp. 175–176.

heavy machine gun and direct antitank fire. The 21st Marines consolidated its lines for the night at the southern edge of the field. For all practical purposes, gains for the day were nil, though the regiment had sustained heavy casualties.

On the right flank of the 4th Marine Division zone of attack, the 24th Marines, now in line with three battalions abreast, was to make the only sizable gains for the day. Advancing against moderate to heavy enemy resistance, Colonel Jordan's men gained as much as 300 yards. Since units along the regiment's left flank failed to advance, the regiment halted around 1500 and dug in for the night.

Even though two air strikes, artillery, and naval gunfire had supported the VAC attack on D plus 4, gains made for the day remained negligible. Before the morning attack opened, the *Idaho* had fired 162 rounds of 14-inch fire within 400 yards of the Marine lines; the *Pensacola* fired 390 rounds of 8-inch ammunition, all apparently without seriously affecting the enemy's power to resist. Discouraging as this tenacious enemy defense was to the frontline troops, there was a brighter side to the picture along the beaches, where, almost imperceptibly, order was beginning to emerge out of chaos. More exits from the beaches were being opened, permitting a steady flow of supplies inland. On 24 February, 2,500 rounds of 81mm mortar ammunition, of which there had been a critical shortage, were brought ashore, as were 25 tanks of the 3d Marine Division. When an eastward shift of the wind made it apparent that Iwo's eastern beaches would have a high surf on the following day, preparations were made to shift the unloading of cargo to the western beaches in the 5th Division sector for the next few days.

At the same time that supplies were coming ashore at a more steady pace, the command organization on Iwo Jima also became more stabilized. During the morning of D plus 4, General Cates came ashore and established his command post just east of the northwest-southwest runway of Airfield No. 1. Now that the headquarters of both the 4th and 5th Marine Divisions had been set up on the island, General Schmidt made an inspection of activities ashore while an advance party of the VAC Landing Force under the corps chief of staff made preparations for the establishment of a command post.[22] In the course of a meeting between General Schmidt and the division commanders it became apparent that more pressure against the enemy would have to be applied if any appreciable progress was to be made on the following day. In consequence, an intermediate objective south of the O-2 Line was established. The new line roughly corresponded at both ends with the O-1 Line; however, in the center it protruded nearly 800 yards to include all of Airfield No. 2. On 24 February, a concerted attack was to be launched against the bluffs that stood squarely in the center of the VAC line. The assault was to be preceded by the heaviest concentration of aerial bombardment, naval gunfire, and artillery

---

[m] *VAC AR*, p. 20.

that could be mustered. Tanks of the 3d, 4th, and 5th Marine Divisions were to support the main effort. Lieutenant Colonel William R. Collins, Tank Officer of the 5th Marine Division, was charged with responsibility for coordinating the armored support. At the same time, the remainder of the 3d Marine Division, except for the 3d Marines, was to land and move into position, prepared to take over the center of the VAC line on the following day.[23]

As D plus 4 drew to a close, one phase of the Iwo Jima campaign had ended. The Stars and Stripes had been hoisted above Mount Suribachi; Task Force 58 had already pulled out on the previous day, and Secretary of the Navy Forrestal departed for Guam during the late afternoon of 23 February. The Marines of VAC had established a solid foothold ashore, and there no longer was any chance for the Japanese on the island to dislodge them. Yet the most bitter and bloody part of the campaign was just about to begin. No one knew this better than the Japanese who, poised in their massive defenses, somberly awaited the American onslaught. During the night from 23-24 February, Admiral Ichimaru cabled to Admiral Toyoda his apologies for not having annihilated the Marines at the water's edge, adding:

> Real battles are to come from now on. Every man of my unit fully realizes the importance of this battle for the future of the nation and is determined to defend this island at any cost, fulfilling his honorable duty.[24]

Even as the Japanese naval commander was composing this message, small groups of Japanese once again attempted to infiltrate the lines of both the 4th and 5th Marine Divisions. In the 5th Division sector the enemy attempted to infiltrate both from the north and the south. In addition, the enemy shelled the rear areas and beaches during the night, thus assuring another miserable night for the Marines, who were dug in as best they could on the fringes of the enemy's main defense line.

On Saturday, 24 February, Iwo Jima resembled a giant beehive as the strong winds of the previous day diminished and moderate wind and surf under partly cloudy skies favored the unloading of men and supplies. On the beaches, a steady stream of men, machines, and supplies was pouring ashore, heedless of sporadic enemy mortar fire that was still hitting the beaches. At 1000, General Schmidt landed and assumed command ashore; shortly after noon, the VAC command post opened near the western beaches.[25] On Airfield No. 1, men of the 31st Naval Construction Battalion began the hazardous job of restoring the field. With riflemen covering them, they had to crawl up the runways on hands and knees, probing for mines and picking out shell fragments. Hidden Japanese still sniped at the Seabees and enemy artillery occasionally shelled the runways, but the work continued without interruption. By midafternoon, the 9th Marines, commanded by Colonel Howard N. Kenyon, and Headquarters,

---

[23] *Ibid.*
[24] Newcomb, *Iwo Jima*, p. 176.

[25] *VAC AR, Anx B*, p. 21.

3d Marine Division, had come ashore.[26] General Erskine established his command post at the northern tip of Airfield No. 1, preparatory to taking over the central zone of action on the following day.

On the northern front D plus 5 got under way with a terrific bombardment of enemy positions just north of Airfield No. 2 from air, ground, and sea. Beginning at 0800, the *Idaho*, stationed off the western beaches, began to hurl 14-inch salvoes at the heavily fortified area abutting the field; standing off the eastern beaches, the *Pensacola*, still bearing the scars of her previous duel with enemy artillery on Mount Suribachi, was firing her heavy guns against enemy positions lying east of the *Idaho's* target area. This destructive naval bombardment continued for more than an hour. At 0845, howitzers of the VAC artillery joined the bombardment in conjunction with the division artillery, which laid down a powerful preparation directly in front of the VAC line. At 0900, the naval bombardment ceased as aircraft from the escort carriers arrived over Iwo Jima to saturate the target area with bombs and rockets. Following the powerful preparation, VAC opened its attack at 0910 with the 26th Marines on the left, the 21st Marines in the center, and the 24th Marines on the right.

The Corps attack order[27] had placed the axis of the main effort in the zone of action of the 5th Marine Division. For all practical purposes, however, tanks advancing on Airfield No. 2 in the zone of advance of the 21st Marines, were to deliver the main stroke. Once this attack had gained impetus, the combined force of infantry, armor, and artillery was to be brought to bear against the enemy. The concentration of overpowering force at one point, in accordance with the maxims of war, could produce significant results.

It was evident from the outset that the success or failure of the day's operation would hinge largely on the performance of the tanks of the three Marine divisions, which had been placed under the overall control of Lieutenant Colonel Collins. The approach of the tanks to the front lines ran into considerable difficulty almost from the outset. The original plan for the employment of armor had stipulated that the 5th Division tanks, followed by those of the 3d Division, were to proceed to Airfield No. 2 by way of the westernmost taxiway which led from Airfield No. 1 to the second field. Tanks of the 4th Marine Division were to head for No. 2 airfield over the eastern taxiway.

This plan proved impossible to carry out when Company A, 5th Tank Battalion, which spearheaded the advance along the western route, ran into horned mines, buried aerial torpedoes, as well as heavy antitank fire. The first tank in the column struck a mine and was disabled. Shortly thereafter, the second tank in line, which had proceeded some distance beyond the first, ran over a buried aerial torpedo which demolished the vehicle and killed four members

---

[26] "When the balance of the 3d Division less 3d Marines was released to VAC, a separate beach was assigned by contracting the 4th and 5th Division beaches at the junction, allowing some 700 yards for the 3d." *Rogers ltr.*

[27] OpO 4–45, dtd 23Feb45, in *VAC OpRpt*, Anx A.

of the crew.[28] In the midst of the confusion resulting from the explosion of the aerial torpedo, heavy artillery and mortar fire immediately hit the remaining tanks in the column, four of which were put out of action momentarily, though two of them were repaired under fire. Since the enemy had effectively blocked their route of advance, the remaining tanks returned to the bivouac area and prepared to advance on Airfield No. 2 by way of the eastern taxiway. There, the advancing armor also encountered mines and spent most of the morning in clearing a lane. Eventually, a dozen tanks reached the fringes of Airfield No. 2 and, having arrived there, opened fire on enemy emplacements to the north of the field.

Because of the delayed arrival of the supporting armor, the 26th Marines did not jump off until 0930 when, with three battalions abreast, it advanced making the main effort on its right in coordination with the assault by the 21st Marines. Progress was slow, and many tanks fell victim to mines and accurate enemy antitank fire. For the men of the 21st Marines, who were denied the expected armored support during the early part of the day, the going was extremely rough, and the regiment had to advance into intense enemy fire. Shortly after 1000, both Companies I and K lost their commanding officers in a matter of minutes. Nevertheless, and despite high casualties, the advance continued. By noon, elements of Company K, 21st Marines, had crossed the field and were attacking enemy positions on an elevation just north of the junction of the two runways.

It was rough going for the attacking Marines of 3/21 all the way, as they charged across Airfield No. 2 and uphill against a well-defended belt of interconnected pillboxes, trenches, tunnels, and antitank gun positions. Twice they were driven off the ridge, but they attacked again. Once within the enemy positions, the Marines assaulted Colonel Ikeda's men with rocks, rifle butts, bayonets, knives, pistols, and shovels. Around noon, just as it appeared that the ridge had been secured, heavy artillery fire began to hit the forwardmost elements of 3/21 and the attack ground to a halt. Nevertheless, a gap had been made in the enemy line and through this gap tanks, bazookamen, mortarmen, and machine gunners were now able to advance.

The attack of 2/21 encountered considerable difficulty in moving towards Airfield No. 2 in its zone of advance. The arrival of supporting armor at 1000 proved to be a mixed blessing, since the armor attracted a heavy volume of artillery and mortar fire that pinned down the assault companies. When the supporting tanks tried to advance over the runways, Colonel Ikeda's antitank guns soon put a stop to this effort. Nevertheless, by inching northward around the end of the runway, elements of 2/21 were nearly abreast of the 26th Marines on their left shortly after noon. This advance served to erase the deep bulge which the enemy positions had previously made into the Marine lines.

At 1330, as soon as the 21st Marines

---

[28] Co A, *5th Tank Bn AR*, p. 2.

had consolidated the morning's gains, a second deadly preparation of naval gunfire and artillery, similar to that which had preceded the jumpoff in the morning, rained down on the Japanese positions north of Airfield No. 2. As aircraft joined in the preparation, the 26th and 21st Marines launched a coordinated tank-infantry attack against the high ground to the north of the airfield. Once again, vicious hand-to-hand combat broke out. By 1415, Companies I and K of 3/21 had occupied the high ground across the east-west runway and tied in with each other. The supporting tanks now were able to operate on the western half of both runways, from where they directed their fire against enemy gun emplacements and pillboxes. The enemy responded with heavy antitank fire and mortar barrages. The latter did little damage to the tanks, but proved extremely detrimental to the infantry advancing alongside the armor. By the time the attack halted in late afternoon, the most forward elements of the 21st Marines had to withdraw to the southern edge of the east-west runway. Companies I and K of 3/21, on the other hand, were determined to hold their hard-won positions north of the airfield and remained in place. Badly needed supplies for these men had to be brought up after dark across the airfield.

At the same time that the 21st Marines swept northward across the airfield during the afternoon, the 26th Marines, with 2/26 and 3/26 abreast, also jumped off. Colonel Graham's men moved forward without significant difficulty over the ground directly in front of the regiment until they pulled abreast of the forward lines of the adjacent 21st Marines. From that point on, they drew continuous fire from cave positions to their right front. As the Marines approached, the Japanese on the high ground lobbed down grenades on the exposed assault force. The Marines retaliated with flamethrowers and white phosphorus grenades. By 1600, 3/26 had advanced about 400 yards beyond the forward lines of the 21st Marines and secured for the day. The 1st Battalion, 26th Marines, was pulled out of reserve and moved up to positions along the foot of the ridge line on the right boundary which the 5th Marine Division shared with 2/21. As in the case of the 21st Marines, RCT 26 had paid for the day's advance with heavy losses. The enemy did not spare the stretcher bearers who were forced to run a gantlet of fire as they attempted to carry wounded Marines to the rear, and losses among these men were heavy.

The most difficult fighting and terrain, with the least gains on D plus 5 fell to Colonel Jordan's 24th Marines on the very right flank of the VAC line. Following the thunderous preparation prior to H-hour, the 24th Marines, with 2/25 attached, jumped off. Both 2/24 and 3/24 attacked alongside the 21st Marines towards Airfield No. 2. Initially, the two battalions made good progress and by 1100, 2/24 was approaching the eastern end of the east-west runway.

At this point the advancing Marines found themselves confronted by a nondescript hill which ran along the south east edge of the east-west runway. For lack of a better name, in accordance with military custom, this otherwise insignificant elevation was designated as Charlie-Dog Ridge, so named after the map grid squares in which it was located. To the southeast, a spur of this ridge culminated in a semicircular rise of ground soon to become infamous as the "Amphitheater." There, the Japanese had constructed some of the most formidable defenses on the island. The approach to this terrain feature from the south came squarely under the guns emplaced on the ridge. To the east, the route led across a weird series of volcanic outcroppings and draws.

Just before 1130, as the Marines were preparing to assault Charlie-Dog Ridge, only 150 yards from the eastern end of the east-west runway, the enemy on the ridge fired at point-blank range with heavy machine guns, rifles and antitank guns. At the same time, 2/24 and 3/24 were hit by antiaircraft airbursts and mortar and artillery fire that stopped them cold. The 24th Marines was approaching the core of General Kuribayashi's central island defense system, featuring Hill 382, highest elevation on northern Iwo just beyond the airfield, as well as the Amphitheater, Turkey Knob, and Minami village. A sensitive enemy nerve had been exposed, and the Japanese reacted accordingly. Once the pinned-down men had taken the measure of what confronted them, they called for support from the 105mm howitzers of the 14th Marines and brought fire from their 81mm and 60mm mortars to bear against the firmly entrenched enemy. While these weapons peppered the enemy positions, Marines of 2/24 were able to move four machine guns into positions offering a clear field of fire on some of the enemy emplacements on Charlie-Dog Ridge. At the same time, men of the weapons company moved a 37mm gun close to the front and succeeded in knocking out a number of enemy emplacements.

Under cover of this barrage, the Marines were able to inch their way forward. For the remainder of the afternoon, assault squads, burning and blasting their way to the top of the ridge, led the way, followed by the remainder of Company G. As elsewhere along the VAC line, casualties were heavy; at 1500, the mortars of 3/24 fired 80 white phosphorus smoke shells to screen the evacuation of wounded. Shortly after 1600, just as it appeared that all the enemy resisting on Charlie-Dog Ridge could be mopped up before nightfall, the Japanese unleashed a tremendous mortar barrage which drove 2/24 and 3/24 off the ridge that had been taken at such heavy cost. One of the mortar shells exploded in the command post of 3/24, killing three men and wounding the battalion commander, Lieutenant Colonel Alexander A. Vandegrift, Jr., the son of the Commandant. Wounded in both legs, the battalion commander had to be evacuated and the battalion executive officer, Major Doyle A. Stout, assumed command.

On the right of the 24th Marines, the 1st Battalion had also jumped off for the attack on D plus 5. However, from the very outset, the progress of 1/24 was seriously impeded by the broken terrain, which prevented the battalion from playing any part in the main effort taking place to its left. Instead, Major Treitel's men crept and crawled forward, while an unseen enemy, operating from cleverly concealed emplacements and caves, poured a steady stream of fire into the attack force. In its attempt to keep the advance from bogging down altogether, 1/24 had the assistance of five LVT(A)s which had been attached to the regiment for fire support. Three of the vehicles went up the coast road a short distance beyond the East Boat Basin and fired on targets designated by infantry commanders; the remaining two fired inland from the water, giving the hard pressed infantry all possible support. At 1700, Colonel Jordan ordered all units of his regiments to consolidate for the night. During the day, the left flank of RCT 24 had advanced about 500 yards; the center approximately 50 yards, and the extreme right flank about 100 yards, thus straightening the line in the regimental sector.[29]

On the whole, 24 February had been a gruelling day for all VAC units. As the day closed, General Schmidt was able to report that gains of 200 to 1,000 yards has been made in the attack and that the VAC objective had been reached on both flanks.[30] The price for the gains made in men and materiel continued to be very heavy. Since D Day, the enemy had destroyed 32 friendly tanks.[31] As D plus 5 ended, American casualties on Iwo Jima had risen to 7,758, an increase of 5,388 since the end of D-Day. During the five-day drive to Airfield No. 2, 773 Marines had died; 3,741 had been wounded, of whom nearly 300 subsequently were to succumb to their injuries; 5 were missing, and 558 were suffering from combat fatigue.[32] The combat efficiency of the 4th Marine Division at the end of the day had been reduced by casualties and battle fatigue to an estimated 60 percent.[33] The 5th Marine Division with a total of more than 3,000 casualties, had fared little better. The 26th Marines, in particular, had sustained very heavy losses. By evening of D plus 5, Colonel Graham's regiment had lost 21 officers and 332 enlisted men.[34]

Nevertheless, the Japanese were beginning to feel the impact of the VAC assault. Late on 23 February, the commander of the *309th Independent Infantry Battalion* had already reported to Major General Sadasue Senda, commanding the *2d Mixed Brigade*, that communication to all units had been severed, and that his command post had been surrounded for the last three days and harassed by hand grenades and flamethrowers through the entrance. "Nevertheless," the battalion commander concluded, "the fighting spirit of all men and officers is high. We shall continue to inflict as much damage as possible upon the enemy until we are all annihilated. We pray for final victory and the safety of our country".[35]

Japanese intentions for the continued

---

[29] *4th MarDiv OpRpt*, Anx G, p. 11.
[30] *TF 51 AR*, 24Feb45.
[31] *Ibid.*

[32] Bartley, *Iwo Monograph*, p. 98.
[33] *4th MarDiv D-3 PerRepts*, 23-24Feb45.
[34] *5th MarDiv AR*, Anx Q, p. 7.
[35] Capt. Awatsu Rpt to *2d Mixed Brigade*, 23Feb45, in *4th MarDiv Translations*, Iwo Jima, dtd 25Feb45.

defense of Iwo Jima were correctly formulated in a 4th Marine Division intelligence report which concluded that "lack of a large scale enemy counter-attack to date was an indication of conservation of forces for a continued stubborn defense in depth."[36] Since the enemy had a sizable force left, an eventual counterattack could not be discounted. In fact, since the high ground held by the Japanese now was jeopardized, a counterattack by a large enemy force was a dangerous probability. In any event, the enemy was certain to continue his harassment of the invasion force with artillery and through air attacks launched from nearby islands. The scales of battle had not yet tilted fully in favor of the American assault troops. It was clear to all involved that much heavy fighting lay ahead before all of Iwo Jima was conquered.

---

[36] *4th MarDiv G-2 Rpts*, 23Feb45, p. 4.

CHAPTER 7

3d Marine Division Operations on Iwo Jima[1]

ADVANCE IN THE CENTER[2]

By the end of the first week on Iwo Jima, VAC had made important gains, though far more slowly than had been anticipated. The key to seizing the remainder of the island north of the two completed airfields was the flat, high ground in the center of northern Iwo, commonly known as the Motoyama Plateau. The plateau itself was relatively level and unmarked by ravines. To the east and west, the ground was broken, descending to the shore in a very irregular pattern of gullies, canyons, and arroyos. The extensive shelling this part of the island had received prior to and since the landings had done nothing to improve the terrain, which was beginning to look like a lunar landscape. Cliffs, often with a sheer drop down to the waterline, were characteristic of the coast along the northwestern, northern, and northeastern shore of the island.

The frontal assault northward from Airfield No. 1 towards the second airfield had thrown the Marines squarely against the most heavily fortified part of the island. There was no way to bypass this area. On the west coast, the 5th Marine Division was confronted with one ridge after another. In each instance, men fought their way up the slope and over the top, only to run into another ravine with another ridge beyond. To the east, the 4th Marine Division was attempting to maneuver on a battlefield devoid of all cover. Where trees once had grown, all that remained was shattered rock, tangled brush, and defiles running to the sea. In the midst of this desolation, three terrain features stood out, each a formidable

---

[1] Unless otherwise noted, the material in this chapter is derived from: *VAC AR*; *3d MarDiv AR*; 3d MarDiv Staff Memos, 23Jan–17Mar45, hereafter *3d MarDiv Staff Memos*; *3d MarDiv G–1 PerRpts*; *3d MarDiv D–2 Jnl*; 3d MarDiv G–2 PerRpts, 14Feb–4Apr45, hereafter *3d MarDiv G–2 PerRpts*; 3d MarDiv G 3 PerRpts, 16Feb 27Mar45, hereafter *3d MarDiv G–3 PerRpts*; 3d MarDiv G–4 Jnl, 16Feb–8Apr45, hereafter *3d MarDiv G–4 Jnl*; 3d Mar AR, 5Nov44–8Mar45, hereafter *3d Mar AR*; 9th Mar URpts, 26Feb–4Apr45, hereafter *9th Mar URpts*; 9th Mar UJnl, 24Feb–11Mar45; 9th Mar AR, 24Feb–4Apr45, hereafter *9th Mar AR*; 12th Mar AR, 25Feb–16Mar45, hereafter *12th Mar AR*; 21st Mar UJnl, 24Feb–16Mar45; 1st ProvFldArty Gru G–1 Jnl, 9Jan–15Mar45; *Iwo Comments*; Bartley, *Iwo Monograph*; Morehouse, *Iwo Jima Campaign*; Newcomb, *Iwo Jima*; *Newcomb Notes*; Aurthur and Cohlmia, *The Third Marine Division*; Isely and Crowl, *U. S. Marines and Amphibious War*; Benis M. Frank, *A Brief History of the 3d Marines* (Washington: HistBr, G–3 Div, HQMC, 1963), hereafter Frank, *Brief History of the 3d Marines*.

[2] Additional material in this section is derived from: 1/9 AR, 15Jan–6Apr45, hereafter *1/9 AR*; 2/0 AR, 24Feb 7Apr45, hereafter *2/9 AR*; 3/9 UJnl, 24Feb–18Mar45; 3/21 URpts, 25Feb–12Mar45, hereafter *3/21 URpts*; 3d TkBn AR, 7Nov44 27Mar45, hereafter *3d TkBn AR*.

571

obstacle in itself: Hill 382, highest elevation in northern Iwo; a bald knob designated as Turkey Hill, and the southeastern extension of Hill 382, known as the Amphitheater.

Since an advance up either coast did not appear promising the only way for VAC to take the remaining two-thirds of the island was to go up the high ground in the center. Since, from D plus 6 onward, the three Marine divisions on Iwo Jima fought jointly but in clearly defined areas, the narrative henceforth will deal separately with the day-to-day progress of each division as it forged a laborious trail across the island.

Fully aware of the limitations imposed upon the assault force by the terrain, General Kuribayashi had established his most elaborate defenses across Motoyama Plateau, right in the path of the 3d Marine Division. A detailed description of the plateau, therefore, appears in order:

> ... dangling ledges, and caves carved by nature as well as the Japanese. Fissures of steam spewed from cracks in the ground, and evil-smelling sulphur fumes vied with the repulsive odor of decomposing bodies. Everywhere were Japanese defenses, grottoes, bunkers, blockhouses, pillboxes, deep caves, antitank ditches and walls, minefields, and a profusion of flat-trajectory antitank guns, dual purpose automatic antiaircraft weapons, and small arms, all backed by lethal mortars and rockets firing from reverse slopes. At a loss for words to describe this devil's playground, correspondents and officers writing their action reports sometimes recalled a Goya sketch or Dore's illustrations for Dante's *Inferno*.[3]

In the midst of this rubble, Major General Sadasue Senda had deployed his *2d Independent Mixed Brigade,* consisting of the *310th, 311th,* and attached *315th Independent Infantry Battalions,* plus an artillery and an engineer battalion. The top of Hill 382 harbored remnants of a thoroughly demolished radar station; on the far bluff of the Amphitheater, cave mouths and tunnel entrances could be seen, yet not a single gun barrel was visible. But, according to one account,

> ... at every turn and fold in the rock were crosslanes of fire for machine guns and mortars, automatic weapons and rifles, light artillery, and rapid-fire cannon. Behind them were the men, some with sabres or pistols, bamboo lances, and sacks of grenades, waiting.[4]

Since there was no way to bypass the strongest enemy defenses on the Motoyama Plateau, an advance into this veritable hornets' nest became unavoidable. The enemy had to be driven from the high ground in the center of Iwo Jima to permit opening up the western beaches. VAC was working under a tight deadline to clear the beaches, get the airfields back into operation, and unload with all possible dispatch so that ships could be made available for Operation ICEBERG, the invasion of Okinawa, now only five weeks away.

The same urgency applied to driving the Japanese from the high ground in the northeastern portion of the island, which enabled the enemy to place observed fires on VAC reserve areas and rear installations. Even though the Japanese had interfered with the American buildup on Iwo Jima, they had

---

[3] Isely and Crowl, *U.S. Marines and Amphibious War*, pp. 489–490.

[4] Newcomb, *Iwo Jima*, p. 188.

not done so to the extent that they were capable. Probably, they feared that such activity, if carried too far, would expose their guns and mortars to aerial observation, and that these mainstays of the defense would fall victim to American artillery and naval gunfire.

One of the problems facing General Schmidt at the end of D plus 5 was maintaining control of his advance up the island. Fresh in his mind was his experience on Saipan, where the 4th Marine Division had advanced so rapidly that at one point it was left with a 3,000-yard gap on its flank.[5] Similarly, on Iwo Jima, if one division advanced significantly beyond the others, troops for flank security would have to be made available, and the exposed division could expect to receive fire from every direction. Even though the VAC commander was aware of the necessity of executing a frontal assault across the center of the Motoyama Plateau, he was determined, for the time being, to push the VAC front forward all along the line in what may appear to have been "a partial violation of the military principles of mass and economy."[6]

In any case, as of 25 February, General Schmidt still favored a coordinated advance across the island. Since the 4th and 5th Marine Divisions, which had thus far borne the brunt of the fighting, were already seriously depleted in men and materiel, General Schmidt decided to commit the 3d Marine Division for the assault against the enemy's main defenses in the center of the island. Of the 3d Division's three infantry regiments, the 3d, 9th, and 21st Marines, the latter had already been landed and attached to the 4th Marine Division on 21 February. Three days later, the 9th Marines, commanded by Colonel Howard N. Kenyon, had gone ashore, together with division headquarters, leaving only the 3d Marines afloat. Attached to the infantry were units of the 12th Marines, the 3d Tank Battalion, the 3d Pioneer Battalion, and the 3d Engineer Battalion.

By the end of D plus 5, three battalions of the 9th Marines had moved into assembly areas ready to join in the attack. Elements of the 12th Marines, under Lieutenant Colonel Raymond F. Crist, Jr., also came ashore on the 24th, followed by more batteries on the following day. It was 1 March before all of the 3d Division artillery had been landed. Several factors were responsible for the slow debarkation of the artillery. Foremost among these were the lack of landing ships and adverse beach conditions. Having anticipated that his troops would be employed piecemeal, General Erskine had decentralized his artillery while combat loading. Most of the men and equipment of the 3d Division were embarked in attack transport and cargo vessels. It had been planned to put them ashore as needed in landing craft, DUKWs, and amphibian tractors borrowed from the 4th and 5th Marine Divisions.

Participation in the drive to the north by the 3d Marine Division could not wait until all of the division artillery had come ashore. As a result, only one battery of the 12th Marines, and 1/14

---

[5] General Harry Schmidt ltr to CMC, dtd 28Oct52, in *Iwo Comments*.
[6] Isely and Crowl, *U.S. Marines and Amphibious War*, p. 491.

in direct support and 4/13 in a reinforcing role, would be available on the morning of D plus 6.

As of 0700, 25 February, the task of clearing the critical central portion of the Motoyama Plateau fell to General Erskine and his 3d Marine Division. The division's route of advance lay across Airfield No. 2, through the remains of Motoyama Village to Airfield No. 3, which was still largely unfinished. As soon as the 21st Marines was returned to its parent division, General Erskine passed the 9th Marines through the 21st to continue the attack, while the latter unit went to the rear to rest and reequip. On D plus 6, the line of departure for the 9th Marines skirted the southwest edge of Airfield No. 2, protruded across to the high ground due north of the center of the field, and then receded to the southern edge, where the regiment tied in with the 4th Division. On the left, 2/9, commanded by Lieutenant Colonel Robert E. Cushman, Jr., faced heavily defended positions along a line of bluffs that extended northward from the western edge of the airfield and the high ground just north of the east-west runway. On the right 1/9, under Lieutenant Colonel Carey A. Randall, was face to face with a low but strategically placed hill subsequently to become known as Hill PETER. (See Map III, Map Section).

Preparations for the 3d Marine Division attack on D plus 6 were similar to those of the previous day. A battleship and two cruisers fired for 20 minutes before the jumpoff. The naval bombardment was followed by a 1,200-round preparation fired by the VAC artillery. More than half of these shells hit the enemy in front of the 3d Marine Division, where the main effort was to be made. Carrier planes pounded the enemy positions with 500-pound bombs just prior to the jumpoff.

As soon as the attack got under way at 0930, both the 1st and 2d Battalions of the 9th Marines moved out, with 2/9 making the main effort. Lieutenant Colonel Cushman's men almost immediately drew heavy fire from enemy emplacements to their front and left flank and made little progress. The 1st Battalion made some headway and one platoon actually advanced to the base of Hill PETER, but was unable to hold the position. Since the main effort was to be made on the left, 26 tanks from Companies A and B, 3d Tank Battalion, under Major Holly H. Evans, had been attached to the 2d Battalion. Prior to the attack, Lieutenant Colonel Cushman had weighed the idea of having his infantry ride the tanks across the airfield. In view of the heavy enemy mortar and machine gun fire, this idea had to be abandoned, and the tanks moved out across the airstrip 200 yards ahead of the infantry. Almost immediately, the three leading tanks were hit by enemy antitank fire; two of them flamed, the third was immobilized. The heavy enemy mortar fire directed against the tanks did little damage to the vehicles but inflicted heavy losses on the infantry following in their wake. As the agonizingly slow advance of the 2d Battalion continued, nine tanks were knocked out before some of the enemy installations could be destroyed.

By 1400, the situation had reached a comparative stalemate. Both assault battalions had made slight gains, the biggest one being made by 1/9, which in five hours of bitter fighting had advanced 100 yards. The battalions were now separated by a sizable gap which had developed during the intense fighting. As a result, at 1430, the 3d Battalion, commanded by Lieutenant Colonel Harold C. Boehm, was ordered to pass through the right of 2/9 and attack to the north until it had bypassed the center of resistance that had thwarted the advance of 2/9.[7] Once this had been accomplished, 3/9 was to effect a junction with the 26th Marines of the 5th Marine Division.

As soon as 3/9 began its advance, it started to receive a hail of rifle and automatic weapons fire from the front and the left flank. At the same time, the mortar and artillery fire increased in volume and accuracy. Casualties mounted with alarming speed. Unless the high ground to the battalion's front was quickly seized, the attack was in danger of bogging down. As the Marines crept ahead, the Japanese adjusted their artillery to keep pace with the advance. Within minutes, the two commanders of the assault companies were killed; many more officers and men became casualties. By 1700, losses had become so heavy that units were beginning to show signs of disorganization; the riflemen could not penetrate the curtain of fire thrown up by the enemy and some of the ground previously seized was being ceded.[8] Despite the confusion of battle, Lieutenant Colonel Boehm succeeded in reestablishing contact with adjacent units, so that shortly after 1900 the situation had again stabilized and contact existed between all units along the regimental front. As D plus 6 came to a close, the 9th Marines had gained little ground, but, at any rate, the line had moved north of Airfield No. 2 at all points except for the extreme right tip. The regiment had seized a foothold on the rising ground north of Airfield No. 2 from where, on the following day, the attack could be continued.

Three additional batteries of the 3d Division artillery came ashore during 25 February and were ready to fire by 1700. The newly arrived units were organized into a provisional battalion under 1/12, and 1/14 was relieved of supporting the regiment. Additional help for the 9th Marines during the day had been furnished by the 21st Marines, which had fired heavy machine guns, 37mm guns, and light mortars at the stubborn enemy defenses. The 81mm mortars of the 21st Marines also had been attached to the 9th Marines during the day, but reverted to control of the parent regiment in late afternoon.

At 0800 on 26 February, the 9th Marines resumed the assault, following a

---

[7] In commenting on this order, the CO, 3/9 had this to say: "2/9 reported being pinned down by heavy enemy fire—unable to move—and it was through this kind of fire that 3/9 was expected to execute a 'passage of lines'; a poor decision at best!" Col Harold C. Boehm ltr to Head HistBr, G-3 Division, HQMC, dtd 17Jul69 in *Iwo Comments*, hereafter *Boehm ltr*.

[8] "The losses of key and seasoned personnel in this...attack manifestly reduced the battalion's effectiveness in later situations." *Boehm ltr*.

45-minute artillery preparation. The 1st and 2d Battalions attacked abreast, with 3/9 and newly attached 3/21 in reserve. The men of Colonel Kenyon's regiment knew that they were now up against the enemy's main defenses. In front of the regimental zone of attack, Hill PETER and 225 yards to the northwest, Hill OBOE, formed the most important obstacles to the advance.

Once again, the 1st and 2d Battalions bore the full brunt of the day's fighting. At the cost of heavy casualties, slight gains were made in the high ground beyond Airfield No. 2. The 3d Battalion remained in position, returning to regimental reserve after the attack jumped off. For the remainder of the day, 3/21 occupied a defensive position just north of the east-west runway. Several aircraft were on station throughout the day and executed four missions for the ground troops. Tanks were also available to support the assault. Naval gunfire was employed against deep targets spotted by aircraft; infantry units called for supporting fire against suspected gun and mortar positions. The effects of this support could not be accurately gauged by the assault units, for enemy resistance continued unabated. With respect to the air support received during this critical phase of the operation, the 3d Marine Division had this comment:

> The number of planes on station daily for support of three divisions was eight fighters and eight torpedo bombers, a decidedly inadequate number. An average of two and a half hours was required before a mission could be executed. . . . Support aircraft, like artillery, should not be frittered away in the execution of piecemeal missions but should be employed in mass in support of the main effort of the ground forces.[9]

In his operation order for 27 February, General Schmidt ordered the 3d Marine Division to continue the assault. The corps artillery was directed to devote half of its fire in support of this main effort, while the remaining 50 percent was to be equally divided between the 4th and 5th Marine Divisions.[10]

At 0800 on D plus 8, the 3d Marine Division continued its attack, which was preceded by a 45-minute artillery preparation in which corps artillery fired 600 rounds. Once again, the 9th Marines, with the 1st and 2d Battalions abreast and 3/9 and 3/21 in reserve, jumped off. The 1st Battalion on the right immediately encountered devastating enemy mortar, artillery, and small arms fire from well concealed emplacements on and around Hills OBOE and PETER. On the left, 2/9 made an initial advance of approximately 150 yards. The increased employment of armor, particularly in the 2/9 zone of advance, aided the attack materially, even though 11 tanks were knocked out. The infantry, using flamethrowers and rocket launchers to good advantage, made small gains throughout the morning. The 2d Battalion finally reached the base of Hill OBOE, while 1/9 took the top of Hill PETER and began working down the northern slope. At this point, 1/9 was pinned down by fire from well-concealed enemy positions on the reverse slope of the hill. Heavy fire from Hill OBOE also caused the advance of the 2d Battalion to grind to a halt.

---
[9] *3d MarDiv AR*, p. 48.
[10] VAC OpO 6–45, dtd 25Feb45.

Just as it appeared that the remainder of the day would pass without any major gains being made, the unexpected occurred. Following a 10-minute preparation by the entire 3d Division artillery, reinforced by the corps artillery, 1/9 and 2/9 jumped off in a coordinated attack. This time, the coordination of all arms brought results, and the Japanese, stunned by the massed artillery fire, were temporarily unable to halt the Americans. Following the preparation, the 2d Battalion moved forward rapidly for a distance of 700 yards. The 1st Battalion overran Hill PETER, continued down the reverse slope and drove up to the crest of Hill OBOE. Now that most of the enemy fire from the two important hills had been silenced, Lieutenant Colonel Cushman's 2nd Battalion moved forward rapidly for approximately 1,500 to 1,700 yards. For the first time since the beginning of the attack, the lines of 2/9 now were abreast of those of the 1st Battalion.

Thus, after three days of ramming headlong into the main enemy defenses, the 9th Marines had scored a major advance. All of Airfield No. 2 and the commanding terrain to the north were now in American hands, even though enemy troops, many of them bypassed in their caves, continued to offer stubborn resistance. Mopping up operations in the area would require two more days, but General Erskine's men were now coming out on the Motoyama Plateau, with relatively level terrain ahead. As D plus 8 came to an end, yet another phase of the heavy fighting for Iwo Jima had been brought to a close, at least in the 3d Marine Division zone of advance. In summing up the overall results of this phase, the 9th Marines listed gains of 800-1,200 yards. Beyond that, the regiment stated that highlighted in this fighting were:

... the skill, determination and aggressiveness displayed by our troops; the unprecedented tenacity and defensive resourcefulness displayed by the enemy (in the left of the 2d Battalion 77 large pillboxes were counted); the decisive aid rendered infantry troops by tanks; and finally, the excellent coordination of all supporting units with infantry maneuvers.[11]

ADVANCE TO MOTOYAMA VILLAGE[12]

On Wednesday, 28 February, the 3d Marine Division continued its drive to the north. The last day of February marked the tenth day since the Marines first had stormed ashore on Iwo Jima. Optimistic forecasts to the contrary, somewhat less than half of the island had been taken thus far. No one ashore doubted that fighting of the utmost severity still lay ahead.

Since the 5th Marine Division on the left also had made gains during the last days of the month, the center and western portion of the VAC front now was approaching the O-2 Line. As a result, in his operation order for 28 February, General Schmidt established an O-3 Line. This line started on western Iwo about 1,000 yards south of Kitano Point, then curved southeastward, generally following the northern and northeastern contour of the island

---

[11] *9th Mar AR*, p. 5.

[12] Additional material in this section is derived from: *VAC Arty Rpt*; 21st Mar URpts, 26Feb-26Mar45, hereafter *21st Mar URpts*.

until it reached the eastern shore just north of the eastern terminus of the O-2 Line near Tachiiwa Point.

Before dawn on D plus 9, the 21st Marines, with the 3d Tank Battalion and the 81mm mortar platoons of RCT 9 attached, relieved the 9th Marines. Enemy snipers and machine gunners interfered with these movements, but by 0815 the relief was essentially completed and the 9th Marines passed into division reserve.

Following a 30-minute preparation by the division artillery, reinforced by corps artillery, the 21st Marines continued the attack at 0900 with the 1st Battalion on the left and 3/21 on the right; the main effort was to be made by 1/21. The artillery preparation was followed by a seven-minute rolling barrage which lifted 100 yards every minute to extend 700 yards beyond the front lines. The 1st Battalion advanced about 500 yards when it was stopped by hostile mortar and small arms fire. On the right, 3/21 also made good progress, closely following the barrage and, within a half hour after the jump-off, had gained 400 yards. As the morning wore on, elements of 3/21 became intermingled with 4th Division troops near the division boundary.

Shortly after launching its attack, Company I of 3/21 was to have an eerie experience. As the men moved forward in the wake of the rolling barrage:

> ... Company I was confronted with tanks rising from the earth. These were Colonel Nishi's tanks, flushed at last from what had appeared to be hillocks. They churned forward, throwing off mounds of dirt, shrubbery, and rocks, and firing rapidly. The Marines faltered in shock before the heavy fire, and for moments the battle teetered. Captain Edward V. Stephenson, who had fought at Guam with great valor, rushed forward and rallied his company. Massing flamethrowers and bazookamen, he led a counterattack that smashed the tanks. Three were destroyed on the ground, and planes caught two more of them with 20mm fire.[13]

Now there were only three tanks left out of the 22 which Colonel Nishi had been able to obtain the previous December, all of which had been carefully dug in. Shortly before noon, the attack bogged down all along the 3d Division front. At this time, 3/9 was attached to the 21st Marines and by VAC order, 4/13 reverted to the 5th Division control, after having been attached to General Erskine's division for several days.

At 1300, following a five-minute preparation by the corps and division artillery, the 1st and 3d Battalions of the 21st Marines launched a coordinated attack. The 1st Battalion bogged down almost at once, but 3/21, following closely behind an artillery barrage, advanced rapidly and seized the remnants of Motoyama Village and the high ground overlooking Airfield No. 3. The advance of 3/21 created a gap between the left of the 3d Battalion and the right of 1/21; into this gap, 2/21 was committed at 1530 with orders to attack. (See Map IV, Map Section). Following a five-minute preparation, the battalion moved out in an attempt to outflank the enemy positions which were holding up the advance of 1/21. Because of the heavy fire it received as it moved up to the line of departure, 2/21 was unable to launch its attack on time and consequently did not closely follow the

---

[13] Newcomb, *Iwo Jima*, pp. 203–204.

rolling barrage. As a result, only small gains were made. At 1700, when the assault troops halted for the night, units held a winding but continuous line across the division front.

As night fell over the battle-scarred island, it appeared that the 3d Marine Division had burned and blasted its way through the center of the Japanese main line. To either side of the 3d Division, however, neither the 4th nor the 5th had kept pace with General Erskine's men. As a result, the VAC operation order for 1 March made a change in the quantity of supporting fires that would be made available. The lion's share of artillery support no longer would go to the 3d Marine Division; instead, the corps artillery henceforth was to divide its fires equally among the three divisions.

General Erskine believed that this division, in breaking through the enemy's main defenses in the center of Iwo Jima, had not received all of the neutralizing support it should have had. In commenting later on the Iwo Jima operation, he stated:

> ... that the zone of action assigned this division was the most suitable for making the main effort as it extended along the high ground in the center of the island. Had the bulk of all supporting weapons been allotted to this division instead of being more or less equally distributed between all three divisions, it is believed that penetration would have been effected sooner at less cost.[14]

---

[14] *3d MarDiv AR*, p. 38. In connection with this report the VAC chief of staff was to comment that: "It was essential that no substantial gaps occur, therefore it was necessary for the 4th and 5th Divisions to advance also, which necessitated adequate support"; and "Half of the Corps artillery was assigned to

By morning of 1 March, all battalions of the 12th Marines were ashore. For the remainder of the operation, until the 3d Marine Division reached the northeast coast, Erskine's *modus operandi* remained the same. He brought all the fire power available to him to bear against the enemy. Neutralization furnished by his own guns and by the corps artillery, when available, enabled him to push forward. As soon as he sensed a weak spot in the enemy defenses, he exploited the situation by committing reserves at the flanks and through the gaps that were created as his two assault regiments moved forward. The advance across Motoyama Plateau did not leave room for any additional maneuver.

The tactics employed by General Erskine during this critical phase of the operation have been explained as follows:

> Erskine's zone of action was sufficiently narrow and his reserve sufficiently deep to permit him to employ these tactics more readily than could the other division commanders who were operating on wider fronts and across more difficult terrain. Cates and Rockey were equally competent, but the Third Division was in the pivotal position.
>
> These tactics saw Erskine's men advance across the second airfield and up onto the Motoyama Plateau, through the stench of the sulphur refinery, and beyond the shambles that was Motoyama Village. No longer could the Japanese sit atop the central ridge and place observed fire on every inch of lower Iwo. The Third Division had cut its way through the main line of resistance into the guts of Iwo

---

the 3d Division as well as the bulk of the naval gunfire support, in addition to elements of the 12th ashore, and at least standby support from the 13th and 14th." *Rogers ltr.*

Jima. The evening of the 28th found these Marines looking down on the third airfield. It was believed that penetration to the coast would be easy, and the final airfield was quickly overrun, but then the secondary line of resistance was struck, and again the assault slowed and halted.[15]

At 0830 on 1 March, the 21st Marines continued the assault with 2/21 and 3/21 abreast, the latter making the main effort. Once again, the attack was preceded by a heavy artillery preparation. The 12th Marines fired a 15-minute preparation in support of the attack, reinforced by VAC artillery. Direct support destroyers fired a half-hour preparation from 0800 to 0830, deepening the fires of the 12th Marines. The heavy artillery preparation was followed by a rolling barrage which lifted 100 yards every eight minutes for 300 yards. The 1st Battalion remained behind on the left flank to mop up the enemy pocket that the regiment had bypassed on the previous day.

As the two battalions jumped off, the 2d Battalion, which had attacked to the north on 28 February, pivoted on its right and advanced towards the northeast. Initially, both battalions made good progress, particularly 2/21 which was receiving effective tank suport. As a result, the 21st Marines was moving well ahead of elements of the 5th Marine Division to the left. In order to protect the left flank of 2/21 and seize the left boundary of the division's zone of action, at the same time encircling the enemy pocket, 3/9 was committed in support of 1/21 in the course of the morning.

The 3d Battalion, 9th Marines, advanced against light resistance and prior to 1500 had arrived at the division's left boundary. By this time 1/21, attacking generally north to mop up the pocket of resistance to its front, had eliminated it and also had reached the boundary of the division to the left of 3/9. By VAC order, at 1500, the boundary between the 3d and 5th Marine Divisions was adjusted to shift the position held by 1/21 to the 5th Division sector. The latter division was ordered to extend to the northeast and relieve 1/21.

In mid-afternoon, 2/21 and 3/21 were unable to advance further in view of effective enemy opposition. After having broken through the center of the first line of resistance, Marines of General Erskine's division now had to advance into even more nightmarish terrain whose outstanding features are described below:

> Beyond the low-lying final airfield, the ground rose again sharply into a saddle, and then fell off to the sea. The high points of the saddle were two additional hill masses of almost identical height, which represented the northwestern and southeastern corners of the Motoyama tableland. These terrain features were intermingled with caves and bunkers in deep criss-crossing crevices, and were studded with huge standstone boulders, many outcroppings, and defensive weapons of all calibers and types. Their height gave the enemy full observation of the Marines to the east of the third airfield, and Erskine found it impossible to snake between them. The job was all the more difficult since there were no feasible ridge lines which could be followed onto their summits. On the contrary, just to the northwest of the right point of the saddle, commanding direct approaches to the high

---

[15] Isely and Crowl, *U.S. Marines and Amphibious War*, p. 494.

ground in the center, was a third heavily fortified hill, almost as high as the other two.[16]

The three hills were situated in such proximity that the two on the right fell into the zone of advance of the 3d Division, while a portion to the left was just beyond the division boundary. Since the capture of this high ground was deemed essential for the further advance of General Erskine's division, it was shifted from General Rockey's zone to that of the 3d Marine Division. Even so, the Japanese would be able to delay any advance on General Erskine's left until the 5th Division had been able to pull up alongside. The center of the secondary line of resistance thus would have to be broken by a frontal assault against the southeastern hill mass.

Several days were to pass before this second line could be cracked. In the meantime, General Erskine, "his available infantry substantially weakened by the furious fighting of late February,"[17] had little choice but to continue the assault. Thus, at 1545 on 1 March, he decided to launch a coordinated attack with both regiments abreast, while the 9th Marines took over a portion of the zone of action of the 21st Marines, with 3/21 and a tank company attached. The 3d Tank Battalion, less one company, was to remain attached to the 21st Marines. The attack actually got under way at 1645, the 9th Marine passing 1/9 through 3/21, which took up a reserve position in the vicinity of Motoyama Village. The 2nd Battalion, 9th Marines, went into reserve.

[16] Isely and Crowl, *U.S. Marines and Amphibious War*, p. 496.
[17] *Ibid.*

The afternoon attack was preceded by a five-minute preparation fired by the division artillery and direct support destroyers, followed by a rolling barrage. Enemy resistance remained heavy, particularly in front of the 9th Marines, and little ground was gained. When lines were consolidated shortly after 1800, General Erskine had contact with both adjacent divisions. Even though the afternoon attack had brought little gain, some progress had been made during the day, and the 21st Marines, in the course of the morning, had advanced 500 yards to deepen the breach in the heavily fortified enemy defense line. On the evening of 1 March, the two 3d Division regiments faced northeast from positions about 600 yards east of Motoyama Village, along a line running north across the western portion of Airfield No. 3.

The peculiarities of the terrain within the 3d Marine Division's zone of attack dictated some changes in the division boundary. While Hill 362B did not physically block the advance of the 21st Marines, the division left flank was completely exposed to it. The decision to attack this hill was made on the evening of 1 March and permission to do so was obtained at that time. This decision departed from convention in that in attacking and seizing the hill, 3/9 which was still attached to the 21st Marines, would attack north across the division boundary to seize the ground vital to the division's progress.[18]

[18] *Boehm ltr.* There were three hills with an elevation of 362 feet on Iwo Jima. In order to avoid confusion, they were designated as A, B, and C. Hill 362A was located in northwestern Iwo in the 5th Division sector. Hill

On the morning of 2 March, the 3d Marine Division continued its attack with the 21st Marines and the 9th Marines abreast. The 21st Marines attacked with 3/9 attached on the left and 1/21 on the right, while the 9th Marines attacked with 2/9 on the left and 1/9 on the right. The attack, which jumped off at 0800, followed a 15-minute artillery and naval gunfire preparation. Again, a rolling barrage preceded the assault units. Tanks, using direct fire, participated in the advance.

Almost immediately, the 9th Marines ran into heavy small arms, mortar, artillery, and antitank gun fire. The supporting tanks were able to destroy one enemy gun and several emplacements; at the same time, it was becoming apparent that Colonel Kenyon's men were facing an exceptionally strong and well-organized enemy position.

The 21st Marines, advancing in a column of companies, made only small gains before the attack bogged down by heavy machine gun and antitank gun fire from Airfield No. 3. Only 3/9, supported by tanks firing directly on emplacements, was able to move forward. By 1300, 3/9, advancing against strong enemy resistance, had secured a foothold on the rising ground in front of Hill 362B. By this time, the battalion had advanced beyond the units on its right and left regardless of flank security. Using 60mm and 81mm mortars, the Marines slowly moved up to a ridge that would serve as the final jumpoff position for a direct attack on the final objective.

As a result of heavy enemy resistance, the attack came to a standstill in early afternoon. A new assault, following a powerful artillery preparation, was launched at 1530. Eight artillery battalions took part in this preparatory fire. As had become customary by this time in 3d Marine Division attacks, the original preparation was followed by a rolling barrage. But even with such powerful support, the infantry was unable to score any notable gains. At 1730, the commanding officer of 2/21, Lieutenant Colonel Lowell E. English, was wounded, and the executive officer, Major George A. Percy, took over command. In tying-in for night defense, one company of 2/21 had to be pulled back a short distance from its exposed position. A slight withdrawal also became necessary for 3/9 to more favorable night positions.

As D plus 11 drew to a close, there had been some significant progress on the division left, but little gain elsewhere. The attack of 3/9 had driven a 700-yard salient into the enemy lines, and the battalion had occupied positions on the lower slopes of Hill 362B.[19] At the same time, 2/21 had advanced northeast along the left boundary. However, the 9th Marines had gained almost nothing against the enemy stronghold in the right of the 3d Division zone of advance. In their exposed positions, the

---

362B, also in the 5th Division sector, was in the north-central portion of the island. Hill 362C, located to the northeast, was in the 3d Division zone.

[19] "This enabled the 5th Division to occupy the hill with little difficulty the following day, which they hadn't previously been able to do at all. The majority of enemy gun emplacements on the 362B hill mass had been destroyed." *Boehm ltr.*

3d Division Marines were to spend a restless night. Throughout the hours of darkness, the enemy remained very active in the broken terrain in front of the 21st Marines. Since Airfield No. 3 was still covered by enemy fire, it was not possible to occupy a continuous line.

During the night 2-3 March, luck played into the hands of the 3d Marine Division. An enemy sketch of the defensive area facing the division, particularly the zone of action of the 9th Marines, fell into General Erskine's hands. This map had been captured by the 21st Marines and was immediately forwarded to the division command post, where it was translated. The captured sketch bore out the belief that the 9th Marines was in contact with a strongly organized enemy position, if there had been any doubt left. General Erskine now hoped that he might find a soft spot in the enemy defenses, through which a wedge could be driven, somewhere between the enemy holding up the 9th Marines and the strong enemy defenses near Hill 362B.

The VAC operation order for 3 March called for elements of the 5th Marine Division to relieve 3d Division units near Hill 362B by 1000. In line with this relief, General Erskine planned to adjust the boundary between his regiments so that the zone of attack of the division was again equally divided. In consequence, the 21st Marines once again would be attacking northeastward.

At 0800 on 3 March, the 3d Marine Division resumed the attack with the same formation but with a new boundary between the regiments. The assault was preceded by a 10-minute preparation by the division artillery and direct support destroyers, followed by a rolling barrage. Almost immediately, the 9th Marines drew such heavy fire that it was unable to advance. In the zone of action of the 21st Marines, 3/9 maintained its position while waiting to be relieved by elements of the 5th Division. This relief was accomplished in the course of the day, but the maneuver was complicated by the fact that both the relief force and 3/9 became embroiled in time-consuming fire fights with the enemy.

In the zone of action of the 21st Marines, 2/21 advanced slowly under heavy fire and shortly before noon secured a foothold on Hill 357. At this time it was believed that no major resistance remained in front of 2/21, though it was still receiving heavy fire from the high ground to its left in the zone of action of the 5th Marine Division. General Erskine decided to change the direction of attack by assigning a new boundary between regiments in order to attack the flank of the enemy defensive area opposite the 9th Marines. Accordingly, an attack to the southeast was launched at 1500 with the main effort on the left.

At this time, 1/21 was pulled out of reserve and moved to the rear of 2/21 with orders to launch a drive towards the southeast with the mission of seizing Hill 362C. At the same time, 2/21 was to advance northeastward to the 0-3 Line. The 3d Battalion was to remain in 9th Marines reserve, but could not be committed without General Erskine's specific permission.[20]

---

[20] *3d MarDiv AR*, p. 12.

The afternoon assault followed a five-minute artillery and naval gunfire preparation. The 1st Battalion, 21st Marines, initially made rapid progress and advanced for about 250 yards to its front. The 2d Battalion seized the high terrain on Hill 357 along the eastern edge of the Motoyama Plateau, but was unable to continue its drive because of heavy flanking fire from hills in the 5th Marine Division zone of action. The movements of 1/21 were facilitated by a platoon of tanks attached to the 21st Marines which, from positions in the vicinity of Motoyama Village, effectively supported the battalion's attack by placing direct fire on targets in front of 1/21.

In resuming its attack during the afternoon of 3 March, the 9th Marines once again ran into a stone wall and no gains were made. In an attempt to make some progress, Colonel Kenyon committed tanks singly and in small groups in the broken terrain. The armor did what it could and, in fact, reduced a number of enemy emplacements and some guns. Nevertheless, the tanks were unable to breach this enemy position sufficiently to permit an advance by the infantry.[21] The Japanese emplacements, cleverly hidden in the chaotic jumble of torn rocks, could not be detected, because enemy artillery, mortars, and small arms firing from these positions were using smokeless powder as a propellant. In addition, the heavier weapons were not as active as they had been on previous days, but the fire from antitank guns and machine guns was devastating.

At 1800, the attack halted and the assault battalions consolidated for the night as best they could. In the zone of action of the 21st Marines, 2/21 and 1/21 made physical contact, but an open flank remained on the right of the 21st adjoining the 9th Marines. The gap was 250 yards wide and covered by fire. It would not take the combat-wise Japanese long to note the existence of this gap and take advantage of it.

Most of the action in the 3d Division zone of attack on D plus 12 had taken place in the northern half of the zone, where the 21st Marines had seized nearly all of the high ground northeast of the airfield. Beyond that, they had launched a drive to the southeast to envelop the enemy to the south. The 9th Marines, having made little headway, remained in substantially the same positions it had occupied all day.

At this point, an assessment of the situation from the Japanese point of view appears in order. In seeking to block General Erskine's drive to the sea, the Japanese resisted at every hill, rise, and rock. Every fold in the earth was cut with trenches and tank traps and covered by mortar and machine gun fire. Artillery had been sited across the unfinished runways of Airfield No. 3, and the roads and edges of the field were strewn with mines. From Hill 362B, north of the airfield, the fire came straight down into the flanks of units moving east. As one account of the battle was to sum up the situation:

> The enemy was making a last organized stand, and doing it well. This was Kuribayashi's order. He had estimated that losses on both sides had been about equal until the end of February. He felt these early days of March to be the crucial ones

---

[21] *Ibid.*

and believed that if he could apply enough force, possibly even a counterattack, the Americans might fall back, or at least halt. If not victory, he would buy time, which is all he really hoped for.[22]

During the night of 3-4 March, General Kuribayashi decided that the time was ripe for a limited counterattack. How the Japanese learned of the existence of the gap between the 21st and 9th Marines is not clear, but at approximately 0300, 4 March, an estimated 200 enemy troops attempted to infiltrate the eastern end of Airfield No. 3 between 2/9 and 1/21. After a sharp fire fight, the brunt of which was borne by the left company of 2/9, the enemy was repulsed with 166 casualties; 2/9 also had heavy losses. Reports indicated that some of the enemy infiltrators had succeeded in crossing the lines and were observed moving along the airfield. Patrols were sent to intercept this enemy force and 3/21, which ordinarily would have moved out for the attack at dawn of 4 March, was directed to remain in place and continue patrolling until after daybreak, when the situation could be clarified. Around dawn, patrols of 3/21 killed two or three of the enemy and the situation was found to be under control.[23]

The VAC attack on 4 March had been scheduled to jump off at 0815. General Erskine initially had issued orders for 3/21 to be released to the 21st Marines. The battalion was to have moved prior to daybreak, passing through 1/21 and continuing the attack to the southeast to seize Hill 362C. In view of the confusion caused by the enemy infiltration, General Erskine had to secure permission from VAC to delay the 3d Division attack until 3/21 could complete its mopping up and get into position to attack. The battalion started to move shortly before 0700, at which time it reverted to its parent regiment. In crossing the area to the northwest and north of Airfield No. 3, the battalion drew heavy fire from enemy mortars and small arms. Extremely poor visibility further delayed and hindered preparations for the passage of lines, so that 3/21 did not reach its positions until 1100.

Forty minutes later, the division attack jumped off, again preceded by an artillery preparation and a rolling barrage. The same scheme of maneuver used on the previous day was employed, except that 3/21 passed through 1/21. Once again, the 9th Marines was unable to penetrate the enemy positions to its front. Similarly, the 21st Marines encountered heavy resistance, including direct fire from artillery pieces that were difficult to locate; little progress was made. Still unable to advance because of hostile flanking fire from the high ground to its left in the zone of action of the 5th Division, 2/21 suffered heavy casualties.

In the course of the morning, elements of the 5th Marine Division relieved 3/9, which, together with 1/21 withdrew to reserve positions near Motoyama Village. One company of 1/21 was employed to cover the gap between the 9th and 21st Marines when lines were consolidated for the night. At 1800, the units dug in with assault battalions just east of Airfield No. 3 and Motoyama Village. All of the assault battalions

---

[22] Newcomb, *Iwo Jima*, p. 218.
[23] *3d MarDiv AR*, p. 12.

of the 3d Marine Division were tied in with each other, as well as with 5th Division units on the left and the 4th Division on the right.

Late in the afternoon of D plus 13, a welcome dispatch from VAC reached the exhausted troops of all three Marine divisions.[24] Except for limited adjustment of positions, no attacks were to be launched on 5 March. Instead, present positions were to be held and one battalion of each regiment was to be rested, reorganized, and prepared to resume the assault on the following day, when all three divisions were to launch a coordinated attack.

On 5 March, the 3d Marine Division held an irregular line with 2/21, 3/21, 1/9, and 2/9, while the other two divisions spent the day receiving replacements and equipment to strengthen their tired and depleted units for the attack on 6 March. Two companies of the 21st Marines were pulled back from their positions on the line to rejoin the 1st Battalion in an assembly area north of Airfield No. 2. The men of 3/9 remained in position as division reserve between the northeast-southwest runway and Motoyama Village.

The day of rest and rehabilitation passed without any major ground action, though artillery duels took place and naval guns continued their harassing fires throughout the day. One air strike was conducted in the area of Hill 362C. It appeared as if even the Japanese welcomed a respite, as shown by their lack of aggressiveness. On their part, the men of VAC also were badly in need of a rest. Their condition on 5 March has been described in the following words:

> All were tired and listless, their key personnel were largely casualties, and it was little short of miraculous that they could advance at all. Some gained comfort and a much-needed lift from a powerful drink called "Suribachi Screamer," sick bay alcohol and fruit juice. But even where units were pulled back in corps or division reserve, there was only relative quiet and rest, because night infiltration and minor counterattacks were constant; and day and night, Japanese appeared from overrun caves and tunnels, necessitating mopping up of seized ground.[25]

In military operations enemy opposition often surpasses all expectations. According to this maxim, after seeing most of its carefully scheduled and supported attacks frustrated day after day, VAC may have tended to overestimate the extent of the resistance of which the enemy on Iwo Jima was still capable. Actually the position of the Japanese during the first week of March was far from reassuring. According to at least one account:

> The fact was the island defenders were in a bad way. Most of their artillery and tanks had been destroyed, and 65 percent of the officers had been killed. On Saturday, March 3, General Kuribayashi estimated that he had 3,500 effectives left. Communications had broken down to the point that General Senda was virtually isolated in the east. Captain Inouye still commanded a small remnant of sailors near Airfield No. 3. Admiral Ichimaru was in the north, in touch with Kuribayashi but no longer having effective control over Inouye. In the northern corner of the island, no organized force remained —only small groups of survivors of individual units, acting locally and almost

---

[24] VAC Dispatch, 1624, 4Mar45.

[25] Isely and Crowl, *U.S. Marines and Amphibious War*, p. 97.

independently. Spirit was still strong, however, and in no unit was there the thought of surrender.[26]

VAC orders called for a resumption of the attack on 6 March. Since any further advance by 2/21 was dependent directly on the progress made by the adjacent 5th Division, the 2/21 attack was to be coordinated with that of General Rockey's men. The advance of 2/21 was so timed that the battalion would move out at 0800, one hour ahead of the remainder of the 3d Division, which would launch its assault in conjunction with that of the 4th Division. Except for the staggered timing, no other changes were made in the previous scheme of maneuver.

At 0600 on 6 March, 3/9 was attached to the 21st Marines in preparation for the attack. For ten minutes prior to the jumpoff of 2/21, three battalions of the 12th Marines, three battalions of the 14th Marines, and one battalion of the corps artillery laid down a heavy preparation, which was further supplemented by naval gunfire. However, no sooner had 2/21 attacked than it became apparent that the artillery preparation had been totally ineffective. The advance bogged down almost at once in the face of heavy enemy mortar and small arms fire coming from the high ground in the zone of action of the 5th Marine Division.

Prior to the jumpoff of 3/21 and the 9th Marines, three battalions of the 12th Marines and one battalion of the corps artillery fired two five-minute preparations, which were further supplemented by naval gunfire which continued for an hour and a half. A rolling barrage was also fired in support of the attack. Nevertheless, despite all this expenditure of ammunition, results remained negligible. As soon as the remainder of the 3d Division attacked at 0900, it drew such heavy fire from enemy small arms, mortars, artillery, and antitank guns that any advance was all but out of the question.

A second push was ordered for 1440, again preceded by a heavy artillery preparation. This time 1/21, having passed through 3/21, was able to score some gains against continued bitter enemy resistance, slowly advancing for 200 yards before lines were consolidated at 1800 for the night. Once again, the progress made was completely out of proportion to the ammunition and effort exerted. During the two preparatory fires on the morning of 6 March, 11 artillery battalions had expended 2,500 rounds of 155mm howitzer ammunition and 20,000 rounds of 75mm and 105mm shells.[27] In addition, a battleship and cruisers had fired an additional 50 rounds of 15-inch and 400 rounds of 8-inch ammunition. Carrier-based aircraft had bombed and strafed the Japanese positions, all apparently without eliminating the enemy's power to resist.

There was one bright note on this otherwise very discouraging day. During the bitter fighting, two platoons of Company G, 3/21, fought their way to the top of a ridge. Before enemy fire drove them off, they were able to get a glimpse of the sea, just 400 yards away. It was an inspiring view, for it indicated

---

[26] Newcomb, *Iwo Jima*, p. 224.

[27] *VAC Arty Rpt*, pp. 14–15.

DRIVE TO THE SEA[28]

On the evening of 6 March it was apparent that the Japanese positions on northern Iwo would not yield to the tactics that had been thus far employed. At the same time, General Erskine was keenly aware of the heavy losses that were draining the offensive strength of his division. As a result, despite the known risk inherent in such an operation, he ordered an attack against Hill 362C under cover of darkness. It was hoped that employment of the element of surprise would yield results where all other conventional means had failed. Instead of attacking at 0730 on the morning of 7 March, as specified in VAC orders issued late on 6 March,[29] General Erskine requested and received permission to jump off at 0500. The 21st Marines was to make the main effort. Its objective was to seize Hill 362C, while the 9th Marines was to advance for about 200 yards in the darkness as a diversionary measure. Actual seizure of Hill 362C was to be executed by Lieutenant Colonel Boehm's 3/9, which was attached to the 21st Marines.

In reconstructing the events leading to this attack and the preparations made, Lieutenant Colonel Boehm later was to comment:

> The order for the attack on Hill 362C, received verbally over the telephone from Colonel Eustace Smoak, executive officer of the 21st Marines, was simply to attack at 0500, using the present front lines of 1/21 as a line of departure, maintain maximum secrecy and silence, and seize the hill. My complaint that I had never seen the ground was countered by the assurance that Major Bob Houser, CO 1/21, would give me all the details on the lay of the land to the front, point out the objective, etc. etc., "Don't worry about a thing, Houser's been observing the ground all afternoon, he'll give you all the dope."
> I had my company commanders meet me at the K Company CP, which was nearest 1/21's disposition, briefed them, then took them to the 1/21 CP. Major Houser accompanied us up to a point about the center of his lines, pointed to a hill mass about 300 yards to the front and said that was Hill 362, my objective. I told him it didn't seem possible that his position was so close to the hill. He assured me that it was, and his company commanders determinedly agreed, so we went back a short distance and, under cover, consulted a map. He confidently indicated the position of his front lines and, although highly skeptical, I had no alternative but to accept his description as an accurate picture.[30]

There was a good chance that the surprise attack would succeed. As a rule, during previous World War II operations in the Pacific Theater, Marines had not carried out night attacks. Aside from night patrols, Americans had not ventured in front of the lines after dark on Iwo Jima. To prevent the enemy from learning of the proposed attack, special precautions had to be taken. No mention of the attack was

---

[28] Additional material in this section is derived from: 3d EngBn URpts, 26Feb-9Apr45, hereafter *3d EngBn URpts;* 3d Amtrac Bn, AR, dtd, 18Mar45, hereafter *3d Amtrac Bn AR.*

[29] VAC OpO 14-45, dtd 6Mar45.

[30] *Boehm ltr.*

made in any radio traffic, nor was the assault to be preceded by any artillery preparation, except for white phosphorus shells fired around the objective five minutes before the jump-off. The men were ordered to move as quietly as possible. No one was to fire until it became certain that the enemy had discovered the main body of the assault force.

The assault companies moved out of their assembly areas at 0320 for the line of departure. A light rain was falling throughout the night, and the darkness that engulfed everything on the island was broken only by the naval gunfire illumination, which ceased before the attack was launched.

Minutes before H-Hour, the situation at the 3d Marine Division command post was tense. Even though there was a good chance that surprise would be achieved, there had been no opportunity for Lieutenant Colonel Boehm's battalion to carry out any detailed prior reconnaissance. In the inky darkness, his men would be stumbling into the unknown. The risks inherent in the venture were only too apparent. The atmosphere prevailing at General Erskine's command post during these crucial minutes has been recaptured as follows:

> In the Division CP, the staff checked watches; it was 0430. Every few minutes someone would look outside through the foul and rainy weather. If a burst of fire or a stray round was heard, faces tensed. At 0450, the illumination slacked and ceased. Five more minutes, and there followed the familiar crack and swish of an outgoing harassing concentration from the artillery. You could set a watch by the 12th Marines. Then at King hour, a star-shell burst. Hadn't all illumination been checked? Get the naval gunfire officer! It was a 4th Division ship, he reported, and lunged to the field phone and radio. Meanwhile, word came back that the attack had jumped off. Still no sound. Were they moving at all? Had the steaming earth swallowed them?[31]

It had not. At 0500, the assault companies climbed out of their holes and silently headed southeastward towards Hill 362C assumed to be 250 yards away. The surprise attained was total and 3/9, catching the enemy asleep in his emplacements, took a heavy toll with flamethrowers and automatic weapons. Shortly after 0530, a Japanese machine gun came to life. It was quickly silenced by a flamethrower, and Lieutenant Colonel Boehm's battalion continued its slow but determined advance towards the objective. By this time, sporadic enemy resistance was making itself felt, but still the advance continued.

Shortly before daybreak, around 0600, 3/9 reported that it had taken Hill 362C. Japanese were being killed out in the open with flamethrowers as they stumbled out of their caves. The battalion had advanced 400 yards with no resistance whatever for the first 40 minutes, and only a smattering of it afterwards. Just when it appeared that complete success had been attained, the light of day revealed a somewhat different and sobering picture. It became apparent that on the basis of the instructions received from 1/21 the preceding evening, 3/9 had captured Hill 331 instead of Hill 362C. The real

---

[31] Maj Robert D. Heinl, Jr., "Dark Horse on Iwo," *Marine Corps Gazette*, v. 29, no. 8 (Aug 45), p. 58.

objective still lay 250 yards ahead. Apparently, the battalion's jumpoff positions had been somewhat further back than anyone had realized.

Determined to strike while the iron was still hot, Lieutenant Colonel Boehm called for artillery support and continued to press the attack against the real objective. By this time, the element of surprise had been lost. Jumping off at 0715, 3/9 savagely slashed its way forward from Hill 331 towards 362. The advance progressed over broken and treacherous ground, which exposed Lieutenant Colonel Boehm's men to fire from the front, the flanks, and the rear. Bitter fighting continued throughout the morning, and in approaching the objective, Marines had to eliminate caves and bunkers one by one with flamethrowers, rockets, and demolition charges. At 1330 3/9 reported that it had captured the objective.[32] This report proved correct, and a major obstacle in the path of the 3d Marine Division's advance was thus eliminated. In outlining the activities of 3/9 on 7 March, the battalion commander was to make this comment:

> Most notable in the night attack was the fact that, although nearly all the basic dope was bad, the strategy proved very sound, since it turned out that the open ground taken under cover of darkness was the most heavily fortified of all terrain captured that day, and the enemy occupying this vital ground were taken completely by surprise (actually sleeping in their pillboxes and caves).... It should be kept in mind, however, that a stroke of luck went a long way toward making the attack a success.[33]

---

[32] *3d MarDiv AR*, p. 15.
[33] *9th Mar AR*, Encl C, p. 11.

While 3/9, as part of the 21st Marines, was to make the most spectacular gains for the day, the remainder of the 9th Marines was to see some of the most bitter fighting of the Iwo operation. While 3/9 was attacking southward towards Hills 331 and 362C, 1/9 and 2/9 attacked eastward, also in the general direction of Hill 362C. By daybreak the 9th Marines, with the 2d Battalion on the left and the 1st Battalion on the right, had advanced about 200 yards. However, at first light of day the enemy, consisting of Baron Nishi's *26th Tank Regiment,* awoke to the presence of the intruders and put up a fierce opposition. The 2d Battalion, which had already advanced into the enemy fortifications, began to draw heavy fire from the front, flanks, and rear. For all practical purposes, the two battalions were cut off and casualties were heavy.

By midmorning it became apparent that the 9th Marines could not break through the resistance it faced from the front, and General Erskine shifted the regimental boundaries so that the advance of the 21st Marines would pinch out the 9th. Around noon, 1/9 regained some freedom of movement and attempted to establish contact with elements of 3/9 atop Hill 362C. This attempt which, if successful, would have caught Baron Nishi's men in a giant vise, failed. Instead, elements of 2/9 were themselves surrounded and unable to move in any direction. Tanks sent forward in support of 2/9 were unable to get through, though they did relieve some of the pressure on the surrounded units. At dusk on 7 March, elements of 2/9 were still pinned down.

It would be 36 hours before two companies of Lieutenant Colonel Cushman's battalion would be able to extricate themselves from the encirclement.

Just about that length of time would be required before the first Marines of the 3d Division reached the coast. It would not be an easy advance for the men of 2/21, 1/21, and 3/9 who would continue the drive for the sea, while Marines of 3/21 and 2/9 would continue to chip away at a stubborn pocket of enemy resistance that still showed no sign of disintegrating.

On the morning of 8 March, D plus 17, the men of the 3d Marine Division resumed the attack, this time with conventional tactics. The attack was preceded by a 10-minute artillery preparation. Destroyers offshore supported the division and corps artillery with a half-hour bombardment. Once again, a rolling barrage was employed. The 21st Marines jumped off with the 1st and 2d Battalions abreast, 1/21 on the right. The advance of 2/21 had to be coordinated with that of the adjacent 5th Marine Division.

This time, the Japanese were wide awake and the 21st Marines received heavy flanking fire from the sector of the adjacent division, as well as from the zone of action of the 9th Marines, whenever an attempt was made to move down to the cliff overlooking the beach. Nine tanks from the 3d Tank Battalion supported 2/21 as best they could by shelling caves and pillboxes in the rugged terrain over which the battalion had to advance. To the right of 2/21, the 1st Battalion was making slow progress and by evening had advanced 300 yards through what was believed to be the final organized enemy defenses before the coast was reached.

In the zone of action of the 9th Marines, 3/9 attacked eastward from Hill 362C, passing 3/21, which had been attached to it, and moving through the right of 1/9. The intermediate objective of 3/9 was the edge of the plateau overlooking the beach; the final objective was the beach itself. Despite tenacious enemy resistance, the battalion advanced some 400 yards beyond Hill 362C towards the beach. At times it appeared that, despite the ferocity of the battle, enemy resistance was less organized and assumed the dimensions of a "last ditch" fight.[34] In order to assist the battalion in its drive through the broken terrain, in which sandstone buttes abounded, a destroyer fired into the draws that led down to the sea; an air strike also was directed into the same general area. By late afternoon, 3/9 had seized the intermediate objective and was ordered to hold up the advance on the high ground.

Meanwhile, the attack of the remainder of the 9th Marines had bogged down in the inaccessible terrain in which the Japanese had holed up. Remnants of Colonel Nishi's force were making their last stand here, fighting from caves and emplacements in the sandstone with all they had. The materiel at their disposal was still formidable: well concealed antitank guns, and dug-in tanks, equipped with 37mm and 47mm guns. As a result, no coordinated advance was possible. Small teams of

---

[34] "This is exactly what it was, but with the inevitable 'handwriting on the wall' they fought like Hell." *Boehm ltr.*

men, rushing from one standstone butte to another, fought Indian style, blasting away at the enemy defenses here and there, but nowhere could the pocket be dented.

The following day, 9 March, saw the continuation of the 3d Division drive to the sea. Once again, 3/9 jumped off following the customary preparation and advanced towards the beach. While still very much in evidence, enemy resistance was becoming more sporadic. By late afternoon, 3/9 had penetrated down to the beach, both 3/9 and 1/21 dispatching patrols to the water's edge. In support of the two battalions, an air strike was directed against an obstinate enemy pocket in the zone of action of the 5th Division. In addition, a destroyer offshore, with the 3d Division naval gunfire officer on board, fired on caves and enemy positions in the beach area.

Once again, the 9th Marines, with 3/21 attached, hit a stone wall of resistance. Even though tank support was available, the terrain severely limited the employment of armor. The enemy was not slow to take advantage of this situation. He first fired a number of air bursts over one of the tanks in order to disperse the infantry. Once this had been accomplished, he dispatched a demolition detachment under cover of a smoke screen which put the tank out of action with a demolition charge and a Molotov cocktail. Neither 2/9 nor 3/21 were able to score any sizable gains during the day.

Ever since the 3d Marine Division had entered the fight for Iwo Jima and begun its drive through the center of the island, General Erskine had been deeply disturbed by his losses and their adverse effect on his division's combat efficiency. He strongly felt that some of these casualties could have been avoided and subsequently made this statement:

> Infantry battalions were now definitely beginning to feel the presence of the large number of replacements, manifested by a sharp drop in combat efficiency. These men were found to be willing but very poorly trained, especially in basic individual conduct. The faulty teamwork, resulting from lack of small unit training, was also a definite hindrance to the operation of the infantry battalions. Many needless casualties occurred in these replacements because of a lack of knowledge of the proper use of cover and concealment.[35]

The situation described by General Erskine resulted from an organizational innovation employed for the first time in the Marianas and subsequently on Iwo Jima. Six replacement drafts, totalling 7,188 officers and men, all of them recent arrivals from the United States, had been attached to the three divisions. It had been planned to feed these replacements into the combat units as warranted by casualties, in hopes that such a steady flow would guarantee a high degree of combat efficiency. Prior to being channeled into the combat units, these men were to supplement the shore party, thus serving a dual purpose. The basic thought behind this procedure may have been sound, but:

> ... unfortunately, this plan did not work out nearly so well as had been hoped. Like most replacement drafts, these had been sent overseas with inadequate combat training, the idea being that they would complete this in the field. But the

---

[35] *3d MarDiv AR*, p. 17.

necessity of mastering shore party duties prevented this, with the result that most of them had to be broken in during actual battle by the units into which they had been incorporated. This was hard on all hands, and there were times during the later stages when it appeared that progress was being hindered rather than helped by the presence of the new men.[36]

In reviewing the handling of replacements during the Iwo Jima operation, the former VAC chief of staff was to comment:

1. These replacements were the only ones available. VAC could do nothing about additional training.
2. If not used for shore party duty, separate troops would have been required for that, necessitating additional shipping.
3. Shore party requirements should be reduced as the advance continued. In fact some pioneers were used later as frontline troops.
4. Duty with the shore party in itself necessitated some training in self protection, which should have proved useful at the front.[37]

In any case, by evening of 9 March, General Erskine had achieved his primary mission which was to break through to the northeastern shore of the island. The initial approach to the beach had been made by elements of Company A, 21st Marines, who were later joined by 3/9. By nightfall the 3d Division Marines held nearly 800 yards of shoreline, thus cutting the area still in enemy hands into two separate sectors. At the northern tip of the island, near Kitano Point, General Kuribayashi would continue to offer stubborn opposition. This last vestige of enemy resistance would be eliminated only after protracted fighting by elements of both the 3d and 5th Marine Divisions. Upon reaching the northeast coast after their arduous and costly advance through the center of Iwo, elated 3d Division Marines sent back a canteen filled with sea water to General Schmidt, marked "for inspection, not consumption."

Another milestone in the prolonged battle for Iwo Jima had been reached. In the words of one historical narrative:

> Not as dramatic an incident as the flag raising on Suribachi, this was far more significant. The enemy in the bulge of the island was split, and Americans controlled the terrain approaches from the Motoyama tableland down the deep ravines to the cliffs and to the sea.[38]

General Kuribayashi and the remnants of his garrison still held one square mile in the north of the island, determined as ever to sell their lives as dearly as possible. Small though tenacious pockets of resistance remained in the southeastern portion of Iwo. But an end to the terrible slaughter was finally in sight.

---

[36] Hough, *The Island War*, p. 335.
[37] Rogers ltr.
[38] Isely and Crowl, *U.S. Marines and Amphibious War*, pp. 497–498.

CHAPTER 8

Airfield Development and Activities Behind the Lines

RECONSTRUCTION OF THE AIRFIELDS[2]

[1] Unless otherwise noted, the material in this chapter is derived from U. S. Pacific Fleet, Base Development Plan, Iwo Jima, *TF 51 AR; TF 52 AR; TF 56 AR; TF 56 TQM Rpt; TF 56 Air Rpt; TF 56 Med Rpt*, dtd 28Mar45; *VAC SAR; VAC C-1 PerRpts; VAC C-3 Rpt; VAC C-4 Jnl; VAC Logistics Rpt; VAC NGF and AirRpts; 3d MarDiv G-1 PerRpts;* 3d MarDiv G-4 Per Rpts, 27Feb-1Apr45; 3d MarDiv G-4 Jnl, 23Feb-8Apr45, hereafter *3d MarDiv G-4 Jnl; 4th MarDiv D-4 Rpts; 5th MarDiv Casualty Rpts; 5th MarDiv D-1 Jnl;* 5th MarDiv SerTrps UJnl, 19Feb-8Mar45, hereafter *5th MarDiv SerTrps UJnl; 5th SP Rgt AR; ComPhibGru 2 AR; Iwo Comments;* Bartley, *Iwo Monograph;* Newcomb, *Iwo Jima;* Sherrod, *Marine Corps Aviation in World War II;* Craven and Cate, *The Pacific;* Gallant, *The Friendly Dead;* Carter, *Beans, Bullets, and Black Oil;* Smith and Finch, *Coral and Brass;* Brooks E. Kleber and Dale Birdsell, *The Chemical Warfare Service: The Technical Services—U. S. Army in World War II—Chemicals in Combat* (Washington: Office of the Chief of Military History, Department of the Army, 1966), hereafter Kleber and Birdsell, *Chemicals in Combat;* Leo P. Brophy and George J. B. Fisher, *The Chemical Warfare Service: The Technical Services—U. S. Army in World War II—Organizing for War* (Washington: Office of the Chief of Military History, Department of the Army, 1959), hereafter Brophy and Fisher, *Organizing for War;* David E. Lilienthal, *The Journals of David E. Lilienthal, The Atomic Years, 1945-1950,* v. II (New York: Harper and Row, 1964), hereafter Lilienthal, *The Atomic Energy Years;* Department of the Navy, *Building the Navy's Bases in World War II,* v. II (Washington: U. S. Government Printing Office, 1947); William Bradford Huie, *From Omaha to Okinawa* (New York: E. P. Dutton & Company, Inc., 1945).

[2] Additional material in this section is derived from: *31st NCB AR:* 1st JASCO OpRpt, Iwo Jima, 27Nov44-19Mar45, hereafter *1st JASCO OpRpt;* 2d Sep Eng Bn URpts, 25-Feb-26Mar45, hereafter *2d Sep EngBn URpts;* 3d JASCO AR, Iwo Jima, 7Nov44-16Mar45, hereafter *3d JASCO AR;* 2d Bomb Disposal Co. UJnl, Iwo Jima, 19Feb-22Mar45, hereafter *2d Bomb Disposal Co UJnl.*

While three Marine divisions were inching their way northward against tenacious resistance, an equally difficult battle was being fought to the rear of the combat troops. Aside from the Japanese who, particularly during the early days of the operation, were able to blanket any part of the island with artillery and mortar fire, the biggest enemy was the time factor. The basic premise on which the entire operation had been planned was to secure the two southernmost airfields on the island as quickly as possible, and it was for this purpose that Marines up front were hourly giving their lives. Unless the airfields could be quickly put into operation, the sacrifice of these Marines would serve little, if any, purpose.

On D plus 5, men of the 31st Naval Construction Battalion, commanded by Lieutenant Commander Dominick J. Ermilio, began work on the southern airfield. This job initially had been assigned to the 133d Naval Construction

594

Battalion under Lieutenant Commander Raymond P. Murphy, but the battalion had suffered such heavy casualties on D-Day that it was still undergoing reorganization four days later. While, to the north, the battle for Airfield No. 2 was in progress, the Seabees, with riflemen covering them, were crawling up the runway of No. 1 Airfield on hands and knees, probing for mines and picking up the most jagged shell fragments that could wreak havoc with the rubber tires of aircraft.

Throughout the day, the Seabees and elements of the VAC 2d Separate Engineer Battalion, commanded by Lieutenant Colonel Charles O. Clark, sifted the dirt on the runways, often under enemy sniper and artillery fire. By late afternoon of 25 February, the engineers had filled, bladed, and rolled 1,500 feet of the north-south runway of Airfield No. 1, which was then ready for use by small aircraft. This was the scene that took place at the airfield on the following day:

> Down on Airfield No. 1 the first planes came in, two little OY-1s of the 4th Division (VMO-4), their wheels kicking up spurts of dust as they touched down. Dirty engineers and Seabees lined the runway and cheered as the little spotter planes rolled to a stop. The Grasshoppers (Stinson Sentinels), or "Maytag Messerschmitts," stayed only a few minutes and then took off again, to fly over Turkey Knob and the Amphitheater to spot targets for the 4th Division. As they left, the first of the 133d Seabees' rollers and scrapers climbed up onto the runway. After a week of fighting, and heavy casualties, and reorganization, the 133d was ready to start on the job it had come for.[3]

[3] Newcomb, *Iwo Jima*, pp. 193-194.

Once the first spotter aircraft had flown in from the escort carrier *Wake Island*, others followed in rapid succession. By 1 March, 16 planes of VMO-4 and -5 had reached the island. Since the airstrip was still under enemy artillery and mortar fire, many of the small planes sustained damage which had to be patched up in frantic efforts. Of the seven aircraft which VMO-4 brought ashore, six eventually were so badly damaged that they had to be surveyed after the end of the operation.

Completion of the first 1,500-foot strip of Airfield No. 1 was but the initial step in the restoration of the entire field. The 2d Separate Engineer Battalion was charged with the reconstruction of the north-south and northwest-southeast runways, while the 62d Naval Construction Battalion, commanded by Lieutenant Commander Frank B. Campbell, was responsible for rebuilding the northeast-southwest runway. Quarries available on the island yielded an excellent sand-clay fill that could be used for the construction of roads and was widely utilized in rehabilitating and extending Airfield No. 1. In fact, it was the use of this material that had made possible the early completion of the short strip for the land-based observation planes.

Good progress was made in restoring the airfield, except for the hours of darkness and those times when the enemy took the field under fire. On the last day of February, Airfield No. 1 invited emergency landings by carrier aircraft. This offer was promptly accepted by a damaged torpedo bomber. From this time on, the popularity of

HOLY COMMUNION *during Mass atop Mt. Suribachi. (USMC 110322)*

FIRST MARINE OBSERVATION PLANE *lands on Motoyama Airfield No. 1 (USMC 110595)*

the airfield among carrier pilots rapidly increased. By 2 March, a 4,700-foot runway had been completed and the first air transport, a R4D of Air Evacuation Squadron 2, departed with 12 wounded Marines on board. Noting increased activity on the newly restored airfield, the enemy concentrated his artillery fire on the strip. For the remainder of the day, the field remained inoperative, but subsequent evacuation flights became an almost daily occurrence without any further serious enemy interference.

A new milestone was reached during the afternoon of 4 March, when a B-29 bomber, returning from an air attack against the Japanese homeland, made a forced landing, refueled, and continued on its return flight. This was only the first of hundreds of the giant B-29s which were to make emergency landings on the island for the remainder of the war.

As early as 28 February, planes of the Army Air Forces 9th Troop Carrier Squadron had dropped more than 9,000 pounds of supplies near the western beaches. Beginning 1 March, airdrops were made over the southern airfield. The cargo dropped consisted of badly needed 81mm mortar shells, medical supplies, radio gear, and mail. Work on the two short runways was completed on 4 March. On this date, the first Marine transport, a R5C, piloted by Lieutenant Colonel Malcolm S. Mackay, commanding VMR-952, landed on the island. The aircraft, carrying 5,500 pounds of badly needed mortar shells and ammunition from Guam, had stopped at Saipan before continuing the flight to Iwo. Once Airfield No. 1 had become operational, a variety of aircraft could be brought into the island. The value of Iwo Jima was further enhanced when, on 12 March, the 5,800-foot strip was completed. By this time, landings and takeoffs on Airfield No. 1 had become a daily occurrence.

In addition to the aircraft using the southern airfield for bringing in supplies and evacuating the wounded, fighter planes were needed to assist the ground forces fighting on Iwo. Their mission was both an offensive and a defensive one. On the one hand, the fighters had to give the closest support possible to Marines fighting on the ground. Their second mission, of no less importance, was to make continuous sweeps over Japanese islands in the vicinity of Iwo to preclude any reinforcement of the Iwo garrison, and at the same time to eliminate any Japanese air power still remaining in the Bonins. Above all, the enemy had to be prevented from interfering with the progress of the Iwo ground operation or with the numerous supply ships standing by offshore.

During the first two weeks of the Iwo Jima operation, Colonel Vernon E. Megee acted as the Commander, Landing Force Air Control Unit. In this capacity, he came ashore on 24 February but did not assume control of support aircraft until 1 March, at which time he also became Commander Air, Iwo Jima. The establishment of these functions ashore greatly facilitated coordination and control of fire support for VAC,[4] particularly since Colonel Megee, using forward observers, developed a

---

[4] *TF 51 AR*, Pt V, Sec E, p. 15.

system of close air support controlled from VAC Headquarters.[5]

This proved to be a very busy time for the representative of Marine aviation, who was to reminisce later:

> You see, I had a dual status there really. In fact, I stayed Commander there even —let me see, we were supposed to have an Air Force Brigadier for that job but he never showed up until a couple of weeks after the landing and during the interim I was the Air Commander, Iwo Jima.... And I had air defense responsibility and the logistical responsibilities during that time so I was like the proverbial paper hanger with the itch.[6]

On 6 March, Brigadier General Ernest Moore, USA, arrived on Iwo to assume his duties as air commander. With him came an initial complement of 28 P-51 Mustang fighters and 12 P-61 Black Widow night fighters of the 15th Fighter Group. On 8 and 9 March, the forward echelon of VMTB-242 ar-

---

[5] *Rogers ltr.*

[6] Gen Vernon E. Megee interview with HistDiv, HQMC, dtd 17May67 (Oral History Collection, HistDiv, HQMC), p. 32. According to USAF historical sources, "On 10 January 1945 General Moore recommended that Colonel Megee (as Landing Force Commander, Air Support Control Unit) would continue to act as the Landing Force Aircraft Commander during the assault phase at Iwo until the arrival of the designated Landing Force Aircraft Commander, namely Moore. He stated that Colonel Magee concurred in the plan since it would provide unity and continuity of command. Moore also pointed out that he would be needed on Guam to get aircraft prepared to go forward as scheduled, and it would be more important for him to do this than to be on Iwo during the assault phase.... On 6 March, General Moore led the air echelon of the 15th Fighter Group to Iwo Jima, and upon arrival there promptly assumed the Air Commander duty. *Air Force Comment.*

rived from Tinian. This squadron, commanded by Major William W. Dean, began to fly air defense missions around Iwo Jima day and night. Based on the southern airfield, the bomber squadron also relieved carrier aircraft of antisubmarine patrol missions. After 23 days of well executed and strenuous operations, the Support Carrier Group departed from Iwo.[7]

On 11 March, 15 of the Iwo-based P-51 fighters launched their first attack against nearby Chichi Jima. This was only the first raid of many to follow. Throughout the assault and occupation phase, Army Air Forces bombers based in the Marianas conducted day and night raids against Haha and Chichi Jima with two raids being directed against enemy positions on Iwo Jima in general support of our forces. Aircraft from the Support Carrier Group, while it was still in the Iwo area, in addition to their numerous daily local commitments, also flew several strikes against Haha and Chichi Jima. Once the southern airfield became operational, an increasingly large number of B-29s sought refuge on the island while returning from raids over Japan, often in a precarious condition. By 14 March, D plus 23, 24 of the giant bombers had made emergency landings on the island,[8] often under the very noses of the enemy still holding out in northern Iwo.

Even as Airfield No. 1 was becoming operational and the number of aircraft using its facilities increased, first steps were under way to restore the second

---

[7] *TF 56 AR*, Encl F, p. 4.

[8] *ComPhibGru 2 AR*, pp. 9–10.

B–29 SUPERFORTRESS, *the first of many, makes emergency landing on Iwo Jima.* (USAF 57013 AC)

4TH MARINE DIVISION *observation post near wrecked enemy aircraft at northern end of Motoyama Airfield No. 1.* (USMC 110251)

airfield. Since the field, shortly to become known as the Central Airfield, was still under enemy fire during the latter part of February and early March, little could be done by way of actual reconstruction. As a first step, an abundance of mines and booby traps, which the enemy had left behind, had to be cleared, an unenviable task that was handled by the 2d Bomb Disposal Company, a Marine unit specializing in the removal of mines and duds. The company had already performed a similar job creditably at the southern airfield before restoration could get under way. By 16 March, the Central Airfield had been restored to a point where it also became operational. It featured one strip graded to 5,200 feet, another to 4,800 feet.[9]

As the assault phase on Iwo Jima came to a close, attention turned to the execution of plans for the development of the island as an important air base. To this end, once the objective was secured, a naval construction brigade was organized and additional construction units were employed. Original plans for the development of Iwo Jima had called for three airfields and installations to accommodate the garrison. The fields were to be designed to handle up to 90 B-29s daily, as well as five groups of escort fighters. The Central Airfield was to be utilized for staging Superfortresses en route from the Marianas to Japan. Airfields No. 1 and 3 were to serve fighters and smaller bombers. Alternate plans, however, were more ambitious than the earlier ones and eventually it was anticipated that the Central Field would be turned into one huge complex featuring two B-29 strips, two fighter strips, and a combat service center. It was finally decided that once the island was secured, the North and Central Fields would be combined, covering more than four square miles, just about half of the surface of the island.[10]

In rebuilding the Iwo Jima airfields, the engineers ran into complex and exasperating problems. Because of the recent volcanic origin of Iwo, laying out the runways or putting in subsurface gasoline lines became a very difficult undertaking when steam pockets or sulphur laden crevasses were encountered. Construction of runways on the volcanic rock also posed a major problem and it became necessary to put the naval construction units on a schedule of two 10-hour shifts daily.[11]

By mid-July, the first B-29 runway had been paved to its full length of 9,800 feet. The second strip had been graded to 9,400 feet by the end of the war but was never resurfaced. The old runway, running from west to east, became a 6,000-foot fueling strip. The fighter strip on Number 1 Airfield was eventually paved to 6,000 feet and was equipped with 7,940 feet of taxiways and 258 hardstands. The rough terrain in the area of the northern strip delayed construction, so that by the end of the war it had been paved to 5,500 feet for the use of fighters; in addition, some 10,000 feet of taxiway had been graded. Two large tank farms and facilities at each field took care of the supply of fuel.

---

[9] Craven and Cate, *The Pacific*, p. 595.

[10] *Ibid.*, p. 596.

[11] *Ibid.*, p. 521.

The utilization of Iwo Jima as a fighter base was to be greatly affected by the overall war situation. The reduction of enemy air strength in Japan proper proceeded so rapidly during the late spring and early summer of 1945 that in time fighter escorts from Iwo were no longer required for the B-29s. Nevertheless, some 1,191 escort sorties were to be flown from Iwo, as well as 3,081 strike sorties against enemy targets in Japan.[12] The primary use to which the airfields on the island were put was as an intermediate landing point, particularly for big B-29s in distress. By the time the war came to an end, about 2,400 of the giant bombers had made emergency landings on Iwo runways, involving a total of 25,000 airmen.

LOGISTICS, REAR INSTALLATIONS, AND NEWS COVERAGE[13]

A combination of enemy fire, deep volcanic ash, and heavy surf resulted in grave supply problems during the Iwo Jima operation. The early phase, in particular, became a nightmare for the Navy beach parties and the Marine shore parties. In the days following the initial landings, the main emphasis was on meeting the urgent requirements of the combat troops. The supplies brought ashore in LVTs and DUKWs often were sent directly inland without any rehandling on the beaches. For the first five days, until roads capable of supporting wheeled vehicles could be utilized, LVTs, DUKWs, and the versatile Weasels took care of transporting the bulk of supplies from the beaches to the inland dumps.

The landing of ammunition and supplies took place under extremely difficult conditions. Heavy swells caused extensive broaching of landing craft. With each wave, boats were picked up bodily and thrown broadside of the beach, where succeeding waves swamped and broached numerous landing craft. Other craft in succession hit the wrecks already beginning to pile up on the beaches until considerable wreckage had accumulated. The LSTs and LSMs sent to the beaches once the beachhead was secured also had great difficulty in keeping from broaching. Tugs were in constant attendance to tow them clear. Since unloading continued day and night, the beach parties had to work around the clock.

In order to facilitate getting supplies to the combat troops, Marston matting and armored bulldozers were utilized on the beaches. The matting was of tremendous value in overcoming the obstacle created by the soft volcanic ash on the landing beaches. The armored bulldozers, equipped with steel plates to protect both the driver and the machine, were employed on the beaches to level sand terraces and carve out

---

[12] *Air Force Comment.*

[13] Additional material in this section is derived from: *3d EngBn AR*; 3d Pioneer Bn URpt, 25Feb-26Mar45, hereafter *3d Pioneer Bn URpt*; 4th MedBn OpRpt, Iwo Jima, 19Feb-Mar45, hereafter *4th MedBn OpRpt*; 4th Ser Bn OpRpt, Iwo Jima, 27Dec44-19Mar45, hereafter *4th SerBn OpRpt*; 5th Eng Bn UJnl, Iwo Jima, 19Feb-24Mar45, hereafter *5th EngBn UJnl*; 5th MedBn UJnl, Iwo Jima, 27Feb-18Mar45, hereafter *5th MedBn UJnl*; 5th Pioneer Bn UJnl, Iwo Jima, 7-23Jul45, hereafter *5th Pioneer Bn UJnl*.

exits. When fighting shifted to the northern part of the island, several bulldozers were used to cut roads through the rocky gorges characteristic of northern Iwo, notably in the 5th Marine Division zone of advance.

In discussing the value of the Marston matting and the armored bulldozers, the Commander of the Attack Force Beach Party Group, Captain Carl E. Anderson, USNR, pointed out that these two items of equipment:

> ... contributed materially to the success of the landing and the moving of heavy equipment off the beaches, which could not have otherwise been accomplished without almost insurmountable hardship.[14]

The pioneer battalions were the basic component of their respective division shore parties. The 133d and 31st Naval Construction Battalions provided equipment operators and cargo handlers for the 4th and 5th Marine Divisions. In addition, the Army's 442d and 592d Port Companies, assigned to the 4th and 5th Divisions respectively, and Marine service and supply units were given special tasks within the shore party organizations. Invaluable service was also rendered by the three Army DUKW companies which, like the port companies, were Negro units. Replacement drafts furnished the largest source of labor for ships platoons and shore details, though their subsequent integration into the depleted combat units left much to be desired. As of D plus 3, units of the 8th Field Depot went ashore and were assigned to assist the divisional shore parties, which were becoming depleted from casualties and fatigue.

There were slow but steady signs of progress. On D plus 6, the day that General Erskine launched his drive up the center of Iwo, engineers of the 5th Marine Division began the operation of the first water distillation plant on the West coast. Cognizant of the geological characteristics that were peculiar to the island, the engineers drove intake pipes into the natural springs. The water emerging from the ground was so hot that it had to be cooled with sea water. One of the first amenities of civilization, the hot shower, thus became a welcome arrival on the island.

On the same day, the VAC Shore Party assumed control of all shore party activities, a further indication that the situation on the beaches was stabilizing. The general unloading of cargo ships on the eastern beaches now got under way. As large quantities of supplies began to reach the shore, it soon became evident that additional beaches on the west coast of the island would have to be utilized. Preliminary surveys had indicated that conditions on the west coast were suitable for beaching LCTs and smaller craft. By D plus 8, beach exits and roads had been constructed on western Iwo. Simultaneously, a number of beaches, designated as Purple, Brown, White, and Orange, were established.

The Japanese, increasingly compelled to watch the beehive of activity along the eastern shore in helpless frustration, saw an opportunity to interfere with operations on the western beaches. On 1 March, an ammunition resupply ship, the *Columbia Victory*, was ap-

---

[14] RAdm Carl E. Anderson ltr to CMC, dtd 26Nov52, in *Iwo Comments*.

proaching the west coast with a cargo of artillery ammunition when mortar fire from Kama and Kangoku Rocks, as well as northwestern Iwo, bracketed the vessel. One shell exploded so close to the ship that it wounded one man and caused light damage to the vessel. Anxious eyes were watching the Japanese artillery fire, including those of Generals Holland Smith and Schmidt, who viewed the action from VAC headquarters on the west beach. More than the loss of a ship was involved. If the *Columbia Victory's* cargo of ammunition blew up, the entire west coast of Iwo could go with it, along with thousands of Marines working on the beaches. Keenly aware of the danger, the cargo ship reversed course and, miraculously evading additional near misses, headed back out to the open sea.[15]

As a result of enemy interference, the western beaches could not be opened until D plus 11, when Purple 2 went into operation. By 3 March, all assault shipping had been unloaded and retired from Iwo Jima, and Garrison Force Zero began to discharge its cargo. This element consisted of troops of the garrison force, commanded by Major General James E. Chaney, USA. The Zero echelon had been embarked in additional shipping to arrive at the objective on call after the assault ships, but prior to the first echelon garrison ships.[16] General Chaney, together with his staff and elements of the Army's 147th Infantry Regiment and men of the 7th Fighter Command, had already gone ashore on D plus 8 as the advance echelon of Army ground and aviation troops that would play an important part in garrisoning the island. Meanwhile, the Army 506th Antiaircraft Battalion, having landed on D plus 6, was firing its 90mm guns at Kama and Kangoku Rocks off the west coast, from which the enemy had harassed the *Columbia Victory*. Men of the 5th Marine Division advancing up the west coast had already become the target of mortar and rocket fire from these islets.

While the Marines in the front lines were pitting their bodies against a cruel and remorseless enemy, the battle to save lives was being waged with equal devotion in the rear. American skill at improvisation, coupled with determination and medical know-how, were destined to save many lives. On Purple Beach on the west coast, a Navy evacuation hospital opened on the evening of D plus 6 with a capacity of 200 beds. At the 4th Marine Division hospital, located at the northern tip of the southern airfield, 17 doctors, operating in four surgical teams, worked around the clock. The Army's 38th Field Hospital, consisting of 22 officers and 182 enlisted men, came ashore on 25 February. Working together with the Navy medical facilities, it was to make a major contribution in providing medical care to the wounded in the days to come. Hospital facilities on Iwo were further supplemented when the 5th Marine Division Hospital went into operation at the southern tip of Airfield No. 1.

In order to provide the best possible care for the wounded, time was of the essence. This applied particularly to the

---

[15] ComInCh 1–9.
[16] *TF 56 TQM Rpt*, p. 6.

availability of blood at the company medical aid stations. Blood plasma had been used in earlier operations, where its life-saving capabilities had already become legend. On Iwo Jima fresh whole blood, recently drawn on the west coast of the United States, packed in ice and airlifted directly to the scene of action was used with excellent effects. Initially, whole blood was flown in by seaplane to a base established near Mount Suribachi at the southeastern tip of Iwo. Use of the seaplane base continued until 8 March, at which time it was decommissioned and the seaplanes, which had also been used to conduct rescues at sea, were returned to Saipan.

Once the southern airfield became operational, whole blood was flown into Iwo by casualty evacuation planes. Up to D plus 25, a total of 960 pints had been flown in. Additional supplies of blood plasma were obtained from the hospital ships. Before the Iwo operation came to a close, the Landing Force had used up 5,406 pints of whole blood. The total used for the care of the Iwo casualties up to this date amounted to 12,600 pints.[17]

Before the Iwo Jima operation ended, Army and Marine air transports, consisting of C-46s and C-47s, airdropped 78 tons of supplies and delivered another 40 tons by air freight. The cargo planes involved were from the Army Air Forces 9th Troop Carrier Squadron and Marine VMR-253, -353, and -952.[18]

On D plus 9, the hospital LSTs, which thus far had provided emergency treatment for the wounded, were released and left the area, fully loaded with casualties. At this time, shore-based medical facilities took over the task of caring for the wounded. Serious cases were subsequently evacuated directly from the beach to hospital ships and transports. By D plus 14, more than 9,500 casualties had been evacuated to rear areas by transports and hospital ships, not counting another 125 evacuated by air.[19] Plans called for the evacuation of the wounded to Saipan, where 1,500 beds were available and to Guam, which had beds for 3,500.[20] From the Marianas, the casualties were to be transported to Hawaii by such surface ships as were available and by air as the condition of the men permitted.

Part of the activities carried on in the rear involved the collection and burial of the dead. This task was performed by service troops, often under extremely hazardous conditions, since the dead were in close proximity to the front lines. Carrying parties often became the target of enemy small arms and mortar fire. The ever present specter of death on Iwo Jima was to give rise to this description by a veteran of the battle:

> As the struggle in the dust of Iwo Jima, in the rocks and ravines, continued night and day, the act of war became a monotony of horror, a boredom of agony and death; it became a way of life, a task, a burden,

---

[17] HQ FMFPac MedRpt, Iwo Jima, dtd 28-Mar45, p. 19, hereafter *FMFPac MedRpt.*
[18] *VAC Logistics Rpt.* Encl A, pp. 16-23.

[19] Bartley, *Iwo Monograph,* p. 113.
[20] *TF 56 MedRpt,* p. 3.

a work that was repetitious, galling to the body and mind.

Death was so commonplace as to be without interest to the living, for the living were resigned to it. They no longer expected to survive. Fear was not of death, but of mutilation. And there was no end to this; no end to mutilating wounds.[21]

Because of the heavy casualties during the Iwo operation, burial of the dead posed a special problem. Disposition of the dead was the responsibility of the 4th Marine Division burial officer, Captain Lewis Nutting, who occupied a dual position as VAC burial officer. Headquarters personnel, and especially members of the division band, performed this sad but necessary duty, which in time became a never-ending chore, as outlined here:

> All day long, men carried litters to the field and placed them in neat rows. Two men passed along the rows, taking fingerprints, if the right index finger remained. Other men picked up one dog tag from each body, leaving the other for burial. If there were neither hands nor dog tags, and often there were not, the teams tried to establish identification by means of teeth, scars, tattoos, birthmarks, clothing stencils, jewelry, or uniform marks. Sometimes there was so little left that it was necessary to ascertain which section of the battlefield the body came from in order to determine to which unit the man had belonged.
>
> When a row was ready, the bodies were wrapped in blankets or ponchos and placed in a trench. The bulldozer covered them with 6 feet of Iwo Jima sand, and a grader spread clay on top to keep it from blowing away. The sounds of battle off to the north were ignored. Since D plus 3, Captain Nutting's unit had suffered five casualties of its own. Even in the cemetery there was no security.[22]

The Japanese, on their part, appeared reluctant to abandon their dead on the field, presumably not for sentimental reasons but in order to keep the advancing American forces from becoming aware of the true extent of the enemy losses. As a result, frequently under cover of darkness, Japanese carrying parties sneaked into the battle area and removed the dead. Where the disposition of bodies proved impractical, the enemy burned his dead or buried them in pillboxes.

As the campaign progressed, the efficiency of the landing force organization increased. Improved coordination of air, naval gunfire, and artillery was achieved through the VAC artillery officer, Colonel John S. Letcher, who already had worked out detailed guidelines back in Hawaii with the 4th and 5th Marine Divisions.[23] In close teamwork with members of the Landing Force Air Support Control Unit and the corps air and naval gunfire officers, Letcher screened requests for supporting fires with members of the three division artillery regiments. Some of the members of this coordinating group continued to function on board the *Auburn* even after corps headquarters had gone ashore on 24 February. On the other hand, Colonel Letcher left the

---

[21] Gallant, *The Friendly Dead*, p. 164.

[22] Newcomb, *Iwo Jima*, pp. 254–255.

[23] For a detailed account of the procedure laid down for obtaining various types of artillery and air support, and the sequence in which such type of support was to be requested by the infantry, see Letcher ltr.

155MM GUN *on Iwo Jima at moment of firing. (USMC 110636)*

MARINE ROCKET TRUCKS *furnishing fire support for advancing infantry. (USMC 111100)*

Auburn at 1430 that date and half an hour later went ashore, where he remained until the operation had ended.

Along with the demands of the situation, there were changes in the organization of the shipping that stood by off Iwo Jima. A new type of logistic vessel, the small craft tender, was introduced here. This vessel was a self-propelled barracks ship, later designated as the APB. Two of these vessels were employed at Iwo Jima on an experimental basis. Actually, the vessels were LSTs converted to meet the needs of the numerous small craft employed around the island with insufficient endurance for long voyages and long periods at objectives. In order to effectively support the small craft, the converted LSTs each carried about 225 tons of frozen and dry provisions, 120,000 gallons of water, and about 235,000 gallons of fuel; they had berthing facilities for 40 transient officers and 300 men, a sick bay for 14 patients, and messing arrangements for 750 men on a round-the-clock basis. The ships serviced by these tenders at Iwo included destroyers, destroyer escorts, destroyer minesweepers, landing ships, minelayers, patrol and landing craft, minesweepers, submarine chasers, and rescue tugs. From 19 February through 7 March, the two APBs refueled and rewatered 54 vessels and reprovisioned 76.[24]

The above does not by far represent the total accomplishment of the two vessels, whose performance was to lead to the following observation:

> Perhaps the best thing of all was the way the tenders mothered the landing boats and their crews. Many of these were caught at the beach when their own ships moved out of sight. Many were temporarily disabled, some lost. These tenders berthed a total of 2,500 officers and men, and fed 4,000 on the scale of one man, 1 day. It was a great help to a tired and hungry boat crew to have a place to eat and sleep. The tenders did not carry landing-craft spares or repair facilities. The principal part of the maintenance and repair work at Iwo was done by 3 landing ships (dock), 3 repair ships, 1 diesel repair ship, and 1 landing-craft repair ship. The job was no small one, totaling work on 30 landing ships (tank), 3 destroyers, 5 attack transports, 1 net ship, and numerous landing boats. It has been said that every small boat used in landing on beaches had sustained damage of some sort, many of them more than once. The LSDs worked 24 hours a day on repairs. The divers of the repair ships practically lived in diving suits from sunrise to 10 or 11 o'clock at night clearing propellers and doing underwater repair and salvage work.[25]

An account of developments on and around Iwo Jima would not be complete without mention of the 3d Marines. This regiment, commanded by Colonel James A. Stuart, constituted the Expeditionary Troops Reserve. As early as D plus 9, 28 February, both Generals Schmidt and Erskine had requested commitment of this reserve to lend impetus to the lagging drive up the center of the island.[26] This request was made at a time when the landing

---

[24] Carter, *Beans, Bullets, and Black Oil*, p. 290.

[25] *Ibid.*, pp. 290–291.

[26] CTG 56.1 Dispatch to CTF 56, 1732, 28 Feb45.

force already had sustained crippling casualties, and the loss of manpower, coupled with exhaustion of the men, was beginning to seriously impair the combat efficiency of all three Marine divisions committed on Iwo Jima. Despite the energetic efforts on the part of VAC to get the 3d Marines landed, General Holland Smith felt compelled to repeat the argument of Admiral Turner, Commander of the Joint Expeditionary Force, that the number of troops already ashore was sufficient to complete the capture of the island and that the employment of an additional regiment would only add to the congestion.[27] This contention was to be strongly disputed by the VAC operations officer who was to make this comment:

> It was my considered opinion while on Iwo Jima, having visited all parts of the island in our hands, and keeping in close touch with the situation, that the 3d Marine Regiment could have been landed without in any way overcrowding the island. Commitment of this well trained and experienced regiment would have shortened the campaign and saved us casualties.[28]

The pros and cons of committing the 3d Marines were to spark a controversy that has remained unresolved more than two decades later. Members of the landing force still consider with bitterness that "commitment of a fresh regiment at that time would have cheered up the exhausted troops ashore and would have permitted the final capture of Iwo Jima in much less time and with far fewer casualties."[29] According to one analysis of the situation:

> The consequences of using battle replacements rather than landing the infantrymen of the Third Regiment and shortening the fronts of the units in the line are, in retrospect, evident. Completing the assault was delayed. Key personnel in the front lines were unduly exposed, and casualties relative to the resistance encountered began to increase both among regular infantrymen and among the battle replacements.[30]

In almost all respects, the conversion of Iwo Jima into an American military base was influenced by the small physical size of the island. There were no buildings, roads, wooded areas, fields, or streams. But above all, there was little room in the rear area, such as there was. Always close to the front lines and never more than two or three miles to the rear, the airfields, gun positions, supply dumps, and troops occupied virtually every inch of the island.

The lack of space in the rear had its effect as much on the location of medical facilities as it did on the headquarters of the three divisions operating on the island and VAC headquarters. The medical organizations dispersed their units into such areas

---

[27] According to the VAC chief of staff: "I was present when General Smith discussed this with General Schmidt, and to the best of my recollection General Smith stated categorically that Admiral Turner would not release the 3d Marines unless General Schmidt stated that he could not capture the island without them. This, of course, General Schmidt could not do." *Rogers ltr.*

[28] LtGen Edward A. Craig ltr to Head, HistBr, G–3 Division, HQMC, n.d., in *Iwo Comments*, hereafter *Craig ltr*.

[29] *Rogers ltr.*

[30] Isely and Crowl, *U. S. Marines and Amphibious War*, p. 528.

AIR VIEW OF *Iwo Jima beachhead on D plus 11. (USMC 112223)*

SHORE PARTIES *prepare to haul supplies to the front line. (USMC 109635)*

as were allotted "and with the help of the ubiquitous bulldozer literally dug themselves a place on the island."[31] Portable plywood operating rooms were set up in holes in the ground and covered with tarpaulins to keep out the dust and cold. The engineers built roofs over sunken water reservoirs which made good operating rooms. Ward tents were set up in airplane revetments or simply in long trenches bulldozed in the ground. The electric lights went in, the field surgical units were set up, the blood bank moved ashore, and by the time the transports left, a system of excellent surgical facilities was in operation.

In his memoirs, General Holland Smith recalled his impression of the command posts on Iwo Jima which he had occasion to inspect:

> I went ashore every second day, calling on Harry Schmidt at V Corps Headquarters, or on Rockey, Cates, and Erskine at their Command Posts, and going forward to watch the progress of the fighting. None of these Command Posts was the Hotel Splendide the invading general seizes for himself and his staff in fictional war. Cates' post, overlooking the sea near the fortified quarry, was a knocked-out Japanese pillbox, where the smell of decomposing enemy dead, buried in the ruins, grew more loathesome every day. Erskine, just south of Motoyama Airfield Two, occupied an abandoned Japanese gun emplacement, with a tarpaulin slung over a 4.7-inch dual purpose gun. Over on the left, Rockey had a ramshackle place up against a cliff, where the Japanese had been flushed out recently.[32]

Supply of the landing force was a highly complex operation. Thus, the average daily expenditure of artillery ammunition right up to the final phase of the campaign, exceeded 23,000 rounds daily. Enough ammunition of various types was unloaded across the beaches to fill 480 freight cars, plus enough food to feed the entire city of Columbus, Ohio, for an entire month.[33] Expressed in definite numbers, for the naval bombardment alone the total of ammunition actually expended came to a staggering 14,650 tons. This amount was divided into 2,400 rounds of 16-inch, weighing 2,280 tons; 5,700 rounds of 14-inch, 3,640 tons; 1,440 rounds of 12-inch, 520 tons; 11,700 rounds of 8-inch high capacity, 2,020 tons; 8,400 rounds of 6-inch high capacity, 440 tons; 152,000 rounds of 5-inch high capacity, 4,160 tons; 17,700 rounds of 5-inch star, 300 tons; 12,000 rounds of 5-inch, 270 tons; 10,000 rounds of 4-inch, 145 tons; and 70,000 rounds of 4.2 mortar, 875 tons.[34]

In addition to ammunition, an amazing quantity of fuel and other items were to be required for the capture of the five-mile long island. These included: 4,100,000 barrels of black oil, 595,000 barrels of diesel oil, 33,775,000 gallons of aviation gasoline, and 6,703,000 gallons of motor gas; plus about 28,000 tons of various types of ammunition; 38 tons of clothing; more than 10,000 tons of fleet freight; more than 7,000 tons of ship supplies of rope, can-

---

[31] *FMFPac MedRpt*, p. 21.
[32] Smith and Finch, *Coral and Brass*, p. 267.
[33] CG FMFPac, Arty Anx to Encl G, Iwo AR; *New York Times* Editorial, 25Feb45, p. 8E, columns 2-3, as cited in Isely and Crowl, *U. S. Marines and Amphibious War*, p. 517.
[34] Carter, *Beans, Bullets, and Black Oil*, p. 289.

vas, fenders, cleaning gear, and hardware; approximately, 1,000 tons of candy; toilet articles, stationary, and ship's service canteen items; and about 14,500 tons of fresh, frozen, and dry provisions.[35]

General Holland Smith himself was to remark later "that the amount of effort that had gone into the capture of the barren island was staggering. The Navy had put more ammunition on Iwo Jima than anywhere else in the Pacific. Marine artillery expended 450,000 shells and we used huge quantities of mortar shells, grenades, and rockets."[36]

Closely connected with the expenditure of ammunition by shore-based artillery and naval gunfire was the Air Support Control Unit, in charge of the combat air and antisubmarine patrol. The unit was composed of Marine and Navy officers and Marine enlisted technicians and operators. Here the cramped space available on Iwo Jima was an advantage. In this case, the unit was located only 75 feet from the Landing Force Command Post. As a result of this proximity, troop requests for air support could be handled much more expeditiously than before.

For the coordination of artillery fire and air strikes, a brief of each air strike was broadcast over the Corps Artillery Fire Direction Control Net. Each air strike was given a number and information obtained on number and type of aircraft, direction of approach and retirement, minimum altitude, and other pertinent data. Each artillery battalion thus was able to control its fire so that it did not interfere with strikes. A complete cessation of artillery fire became necessary only once or twice when aircraft delivered a low-level napalm attack.[37]

Progress in developing the island did not stop with the construction of new facilities. In some instances, the very shape of the island had to be changed to meet the requirements of the new occupants. Even Iwo's most outstanding landmark, Mount Suribachi, was to be affected by these changes. The Army garrison troops planned to get various trucks housing radar, weather, and navigational equipment for the coming assault against the Japanese home islands on top of the mountain. Before such plans could be realized, it became necessary to construct a road to the top, a project that had never been realized by the Japanese. On D plus 15, construction of a two-lane road, 35 feet wide, got under way, winding its way up and around the mountain for nearly a mile. Early the following morning, the first bulldozer drove into the crater at the top of Suribachi. The Japanese, a number of whom were still living inside the mountain after surviving the battle for Suribachi, were powerless to interfere with the road construction. They stole out of their caves only at night in search of food and water and were methodically eliminated when spotted.

In the midst of the multitude of supporting headquarters and units operating on the island, there was a special complement of men, neither wholly military or civilian, whose job it was

---

[35] *Ibid.*, p. 291.
[36] Smith and Finch, *Coral and Brass*, p. 275.
[37] *ComPhibGru 2 AR*, Pt 5, pp. 1–2.

to photograph the action on the island or write about it. They were representatives of American and Allied news services, radio networks, and local newspapers. The news reporters were given the widest possible latitude in covering the operation and thus could be found among the invasion force, in the landing boats, and occasionally in the foxholes.

In addition to the accredited civilian correspondents, each of the military services had its own news writers and photographers, including a special Navy film crew which recorded the entire operation on color film. Radio teletype equipment was set up on the beaches for the benefit of the press, and a Navy floatplane was made available to carry copy, photographs, and newsreels directly to Guam, where this material was processed and flown back to the United States. Another precedent was established when, on D plus 7, Admiral Turner and General Holland M. Smith were interviewed on Iwo Jima in a live broadcast while the battle was still raging on the island.

The events on the battlefield received wide coverage and distribution in American newspapers and magazines. None of the ferocity of the fighting was withheld from the American public. As casualties mounted and the full impact of the cost in lives expended to secure the island began to hit home, plaintive voices arose to question the need for such a bloodletting. Then as now, sincere and serious-minded Americans, appalled witnesses to the savage fighting they could not stem, groped for a way out, at least a more inexpensive way to subdue the enemy. Among the expedients suggested was the employment of toxic gas.

THE CASE FOR AND AGAINST CHEMICAL WARFARE[38]

Unknown to the public at large, the employment of chemical warfare agents in the Pacific Theater had already undergone active consideration while the Iwo operation was still in the planning stage. Through collaboration with the Office of Strategic Services, forerunner of the Central Intelligence Agency, a special report had been compiled on the subject of gas warfare on Iwo Jima.[39] Its primary feature was the recommendation that Japanese transmitters on the island be jammed. Once the enemy's communications had been rendered inoperable and he was isolated, the entire island was to be inundated with gas. In late June 1944, the director of Research and Development, OSS, had made a special trip to Hawaii to discuss the project with Admiral Nimitz.

The difficulties of employing gas warfare were twofold, both technical and moral. During the early part of World War II, the United States had thought

---

[38] Additional material in this section is derived from: Frederic J. Brown III, *Chemical Warfare, A Study in Restraint* (Princeton: Princeton University Press, 1968), hereafter Brown, *Chemical Warfare*.

[39] A chapter dealing with this matter, known as the Lethbridge Report, appears in the recollections of Stanley P. Lovell, former Director of Research and Development, OSS, in his memoirs entitled: *Of Spies and Strategems* (Englewood Cliffs, N. J.: Prentice-Hall, 1963), pp. 70–78.

of the use of toxic gases only as a retaliatory measure. In this connection, the 100-pound mustard-filled bomb was considered by chemical warfare officers as the most suitable munition for retaliation. The peak stock of this item attained in the Pacific Theater in July 1944 was 15,244 bombs with 541.2 tons of toxic filling. In the words of a chemical warfare service officer:

> This supply was token only. If, for example, this entire supply had been used on Iwo Jima, which had an area of seven and one-half square miles, it would only have contaminated a little more than half, or four and one half square miles. Considering the vapor effect of mustard and the fact that the entire island would not have been regarded as a target, the stock would have been sufficient for one contamination. In the opinion of most chemical officers one contamination would have been enough to end all enemy resistance on the island. The question of resupply for other objectives would then arise.[40]

The second difficulty in employing chemical warfare against the Japanese could be found in the attitude of most of the nation's civilian and military leaders. In fact, military reluctance to use this weapon had its origin in the experiences of the American Expeditionary Forces in World War I. In connection with the possible employment of toxic gas on Iwo Jima, General Holland Smith made this comment:

> I am not prepared to argue this question. Certainly, gas shells smothering the island, or gas introduced into caves and tunnels would have simplified our task, but naturally the use of this prohibited weapon was not within the power of a field commander. The decision was on a higher level. It was in the hands of the Allied Powers, who alone could authorize its use in a war which would have assumed even more frightful proportions had gas been allowed.[41]

In the end, it was the Chief Executive of the United States who had a final voice in approving or disapproving the entire plan. Regardless of their divergent political views, both Herbert Hoover and Franklin D. Roosevelt in the years between the two world wars had been in favor of eliminating gas as a military weapon. In 1937, when vetoing a bill that would have changed the designation of the Army Chemical Warfare Service to that of Chemical Corps, the President had expressed his views on this subject in no uncertain terms:

> It has been and is the policy of this Government to do everything in its power to outlaw the use of chemicals in warfare. Such use is inhuman and contrary to what modern civilization should stand for.[42]

One of the official Army histories dealing with chemical warfare has pointed out in this connection that "gas warfare had no advocates in high places."[43] While this may have been true during the early years of World War II, there is some evidence that, as of early 1945, the atmosphere in Washington has begun to shift in favor of chemical warfare.[44] Another reason for increased

---

[40] Kleber and Birdsell, *Chemicals in Combat*, pp. 269-270.

[41] Smith and Finch, *Coral and Brass*, p. 276.
[42] Veto msg of Bill S.1284, as cited in Brophy and Fisher, *Organizing for War*, pp. 21-22.
[43] Kleber and Birdsell, *Chemicals in Combat*, p. 653.
[44] In Brown, *Chemical Warfare*, the author attributes this change to three factors. Germany's imminent collapse, removing the last

American readiness to accept initiation of chemical warfare towards the final phase of the war may be found in the extremely heavy American casualties sustained in the Western Pacific. None other than General of the Army George C. Marshall was to testify after the war had ended that "following the terrible losses at Iwo Jima, he was prepared to use gas at Okinawa."[45]

It is interesting to note that, at the same time that American views towards the employment of gas offensively became more aggressive, the Japanese policy shifted in the opposite direction. With the loss of the Marianas in the spring and summer of 1944, the home islands had suddenly become extremely vulnerable to American chemical attack. In the firm belief that the United States would not initiate gas warfare, and since Japanese ability to retaliate was in any case too low, Japan, in mid-1944:

> ... decided to discontinue production of toxic agents and to recall all stocks of gas munitions from the hands of troops in the field. Thus, in mid-1944, the Japanese started a policy of disarmament. Readiness spiraled downward until hostilities ended.[46]

Thus we are faced with the strange spectacle of a hostile nation, pledged to fight to the death, and confronted by an immense military machine, dismantling its limited chemical warfare apparatus as operations reached their climax. Stranger still, Japanese reasoning apparently was based on the declared policy of the United States not to initiate gas warfare. The Japanese failed to consider that, given different time and circumstances, such a policy might be subject to change.

With present knowledge, not available to Allied planners in 1944, it becomes clear that by the time the Iwo Jima operation got underway, Japan was no longer in a position to retaliate with chemical means in response to Allied action, with one minor exception.[47] All that prevented the employment of gas on Iwo Jima was the President's aversion to gas warfare. Even though the United States had not signed any international instrument outlawing such warfare, national policy clearly limited the conditions under which toxic gas might have been introduced. In consequence of this policy, heavy casualties to the contrary, Marines would continue to assault Iwo Jima with rifle, hand grenade, and flamethrowers until all resistance had been overcome.

In a matter of roughly three weeks from D-Day, Iwo Jima had been transformed from a strongpoint in the Japanese defense system to an important American air base of strategic and tac-

---

Axis possibility of retaliating with gas against an Allied population; President Roosevelt's death; and the over-riding importance of bringing the war against Japan to a speedy conclusion.

[45] Quoted in Lilienthal, *The Atomic Energy Years*, p. 199.

[46] Brown, *Chemical Warfare*, p. 260.

[47] "The Japanese troops on Iwo Jima had been supplied with glass containers—I suppose they could be called gas grenades—which was liquid hydrogen cyanide. These containers of clear glass were a little larger than a baseball. When the container was broke the liquid released cyanide gas. These could have been effective if they had been used inside pillboxes or caves or other closed spaces." Letcher ltr.

tical importance to the overall air offensive against Japan. The capture and development of the island denied its use to the enemy and at the same time it served as an emergency haven for aircraft returning from raids against Japan. In American hands, Iwo Jima represented an advance base for search and reconnaissance. It further provided a base within fighter range of Japan. Furthermore, the island could be utilized as a staging point for bombers, permitting greater bomb loads in lieu of gasoline, though the island was not much used for this purpose.[48] Iwo Jima could also become a refuelling stop for short-range aircraft en route to bases closer to Japan yet to be seized before the general assault against the Japanese homeland got underway later in the year.

This, then, was the significance of the fiercely contested island. This is why General Kuribayashi had decided to adopt those tactics that would prove most costly to the invasion force and that would cause the most delay in the conversion of the stronghold to American use. After three weeks of bitter fighting, his intention has been partially realized as far as taking a toll in American lives was concerned. But, just behind the front lines, bulldozers were shifting earth, changing the very landscape of the island; communications were humming, and heedless of tenacious Japanese holed up in the northern part of the island, the task of reconstruction was proceeding at an ever-increasing pace.

---

[48] Craven and Cate, *The Pacific*, p. 597.

CHAPTER 9

The 5th Marine Division Drive on the Left [1]

ADVANCE UP THE WEST COAST [2]

As the battle for Iwo Jima neared its climax, the full force of three Marine divisions was employed to reduce the main enemy defenses near the Central Airfield. General Erskine's drive up the center of the island to the northern shore has already been narrated. In addition to the men of the 3d Marine Division who fought and died at such landmarks as Hills OBOE and PETER, Motoyama Village, and Hill 362C, Marines of the adjacent 4th and 5th Divisions were making similar sacrifices to the east and west respectively. In the sectors of the latter two divisions the landmarks may have varied in some respects. They were to bear names like Hill 362A, 362B, Nishi Ridge, and Bloody Gorge. Men of the 4th Division would suffer at places appropriately named the Meat Grinder, the Amphitheater, and Turkey Knob. For all of them the enemy remained the same: fanatical, utterly devoted to his mission, bent on the destruction of the invaders who had dared violate sacred Japanese soil.

An attack by the 5th Marine Division on 24 February had resulted in sizable gains by the 26th Marines, which by the end of the day advanced 400 yards north of the 3d Division ele-

---

[1] Unless otherwise noted, the material in this chapter is derived from: ComPhibPac AR, Iwo Jima, 12Jan-26Mar45, dtd 19May45, hereafter *ComPhibPac AR*; *TF 51 AR*; *TF 56 AirRpt*; *TF 56 G-3 Rpt*; *VAC AR*; *VAC G-2 Rpts*; *VAC C-3 Jnl*; *VAC C-3 Rpt*; *VAC NGF and AirRpts*; *VAC Translations*; *5th MarDiv AR*; *5th MarDiv D-1 Jnl*; 5th MarDiv D-2 Jnl, Iwo Jima, 19Feb-27Mar45, hereafter *5thMarDiv D-2 Jnl*; *5th MarDiv D-2 Per Rpts*; *5th MarDiv D-3 Jnl*; *5th MarDiv Casualty Rpts*; 1st ProvFldArtyGru G-1 Jnl, 9Jan45-15 Mar45, hereafter *1st ProvFldArtyGru G-1 Jnl*; *13th Mar UJnl*; *13th Mar AR*; *26th Mar UJnl*; 26th Mar AR, Iwo Jima, 1Jan-26Mar45, dtd 20Apr45, hereafter *26th Mar AR*; 27th Mar UJnl, Iwo Jima, 19Feb-22Mar45, hereafter *27th Mar UJnl*; 27th Mar AR, Iwo Jima, 19Oct44-23Mar45, dtd 18Apr45, hereafter *27th Mar AR*; *28th Mar UJnl*; *28th Mar AR*; *28th Mar R-2 Jnl*; *Horie Rpt*; *Iwo Comments*; Bartley, *Iwo Monograph*; *Newcomb Notes*; Morehouse, *Iwo Jima Campaign*; Morison, *Victory in the Pacific*; Henry et al, *U. S. Marines on Iwo Jima*; Isely and Crowl, *U. S. Marines and Amphibious War*; Conner, *The Fifth Marine Division*; Smith and Finch, *Coral and Brass*; Robert Leckie, *Strong Men Armed*; Newcomb, *Iwo Jima*.

[2] Additional material in this section is derived from: *5th TkBn UJnl*; *5th TkBn AR*; *2/26 UJnl*; 2/26 Obs Rpt, Iwo Jima 18Feb-23Mar45, hereafter *2/26 ObsRpt*; 2/26 AR, Iwo Jima, 19Feb-27Mar45, dtd 18Apr45, hereafter *2/26 AR*; *3/26 UJnl*; 3/26 AR, Iwo Jima, 19Feb-26Mar45, dtd 19Apr45, hereafter *3/26 AR*; *1/27 UJnl*; 1/27 AR, Iwo Jima, 19Feb-23Mar45, dtd 20Apr45, hereafter *1/27 AR*; *2/27 UJnl*; 2/27 AR, Iwo Jima, 10Nov44-23Mar45, dtd 17Apr45, hereafter *2/27 AR*; *3/27 UJnl*; 3/27 AR, Iwo Jima, 10Nov44-23Mar45, dtd 10Apr45, hereafter *3/27 AR*.

ments on its right. The gains were made at a heavy cost; 21 officers and 332 enlisted men became casualties on D plus 5.[3] In order to give the 9th Marines a chance of straightening the lines, the 26th Marines was ordered to remain in place on 25 February.

On the morning of D plus 6, the 5th Marine Division held a line extending for 1,200 yards from west to east. From the left to right, 2/27 held the cliffs overlooking the western beaches; the center of the line, protruding into enemy territory, was held by 2/26; to the right of this battalion, the line slanted southward, held by 3/26 with one attached company of 1/26. (See Map V, Map Section). It had become evident by this time that the high ground in the zone of action of the adjacent 3d Marine Division exerted a paramount influence on the further advance of the 5th Division. No major progress could be expected until General Erskine's division had driven the enemy from this high ground in the center of the island.

While the 26th Marines consolidated its positions on 25 February, the adjacent 9th Marines of the 3d Division attacked northward along its joint boundary with the 5th Marine Division. On this day, the 9th Marines failed to make any noteworthy gains, and the situation along Colonel Graham's right flank remained substantially unchanged. Throughout the day, heavy enemy fire from the right front raked the positions occupied by the 26th Marines, greatly interfering with supply and evacuation. Nevertheless, the men of the 5th Division were to get one break during the day. Around 1500, one of the spotter planes reported enemy artillery moving north along a road following the contour of the island on northern Iwo. Three batteries of the 13th Marines immediately adjusted on the target and fired nearly 600 rounds. At the end of this fire mission, the observer reported that three artillery pieces had been destroyed, several prime movers were burning, and an ammunition dump was ablaze.[4] This was the only time during the Iwo Jima campaign that the enemy ever offered such a choice target. Hereafter, Japanese artillery deployed to new firing positions only at night.

On D plus 7 General Rockey's division resumed the attack. Following a 45-minute artillery and naval gunfire preparation, the 26th Marines jumped off in the main effort. Almost immediately, the attack ran into heavy resistance. The enemy poured fire from small arms, machine guns, and mortars into the ranks of the advancing Marines. At the same time, heavy artillery and mortar fire from the northern part of the island hit the assault troops. As the Marines closed with the enemy, hand grenade duels ensued.

During the advance, the nature of the terrain underwent a subtle change. Thus far, General Rockey's division had been operating in soft, sandy, and open terrain. As the 26th Marines moved northward, the level ground gave way to heavily fortified cliffs. Essentially, the 5th Marine Division now entered a difficult complex of ridges. In each case, the attack had to be carried up one

---

[3] Conner, *The Fifth Marine Division*, p. 81.

[4] *13th Mar AR*, p. 13.

slope, across the top, and then down into another ravine beyond. Above the ridges, there loomed a major enemy bastion, Hill 362A, just south of Nishi Village. This terrain feature impressed the advancing Marines because its sinister presence overshadowed all other obstacles in the area. The hill was rugged and rocky, devoid of all vegetation on its southern slopes. To the north, as yet unseen by the Americans advancing from the south, there was a sheer drop of about 80 feet. The Japanese had exploited this formidable obstacle to the utmost. The entire hill bristled with caves of varying sizes, many of them serving as mortar and machine gun emplacements. The elevation enabled the enemy to observe western Iwo all the way south to Mount Suribachi, and thus exposed to his view all American activity in the front lines, as well as on the western beaches.

Despite fierce enemy resistance, the 5th Marine Division attack on 26 February moved steadily towards Hill 362A, still about 800 yards away, whose very prominence made it a natural objective. The three battalions in the main effort were the 2d and 3d Battalions, 26th Marines, commanded respectively by Major Amedeo Rea and Major Richard Fagan, and 2/27 under Major John W. Antonelli. Because of heavy automatic weapons fire from an enemy strongpoint consisting of pillboxes and caves, the advance of 2/26 was so slowed that in two hours gains of only 50 yards were registered. Tanks of Company B, 5th Tank Battalion, took a hand in the fighting. At 1000, Company F of 2/26, thus far held in reserve, was committed. With the support of armor, the infantry launched a spirited attack against the stubborn enemy position. The efforts of this company were quickly crowned with success. For the first time since 2/26 had come ashore, the battalion came face to face with the usually elusive and unseen enemy. In the resulting pitched battle, the Japanese came out second best. Those of the enemy who sought to flee were killed out in the open. Catching the ordinarily well entrenched enemy for once in such a vulnerable position greatly boosted the morale of the Marines engaged in this action, "for no man likes to fight something he cannot see, and the sight of running Japs was, if nothing else, reassuring."[5]

Advancing on the right and supported by tanks of Company A, 5th Tank Battalion, 3/26 gained about 100 yards, smashing fortifications as it went along and destroying numerous guns in the ravines that led down from the plateau perpendicular to the route of advance. Gains made by the adjacent 9th Marines helped 3/26 in its forward movement.

To the left of the 26th Marines, 2/27 initially made rapid progress, gaining 400 yards during the first two hours. For the remainder of the day, the battalion stayed in place in order to permit 2/26 to come abreast. The terrain in the zone of advance of 2/27 precluded the employment of tanks. Instead, 20 LVT(A)s of the 2d Armored Amphibian Battalion, under Lieutenant Colonel Reed M. Fawell, Jr., supported the battalion attack from the sea. The 75mm fire from the armored

---

[5] Conner, *The Fifth Marine Division*, p. 85.

SOLIDLY EMPLACED *tank of the Japanese 26th Tank Regiment after capture.*
(USAF 70317 AC)

MARINE COMBAT PATROL *moves through jagged terrain in northern Iwo Jima.*
(USMC 142316)

amphibians knocked out several enemy caves, but in the choppy seas their fire began to endanger friendly troops and, as a result, they were ordered to cease fire.[6]

When action halted on the evening of 26 February, the lines of the 5th Marine Division still formed an arc whose apogee extended some 400 yards into enemy territory. Gains for the day amounted to roughly 300 yards. Most important of all, the day's advance had netted the 26th Marines two Japanese wells, the last ones believed to be under enemy control. Henceforth, the Japanese would have to rely on such water as they had been able to store or on rainfall.

Enemy reaction to the loss of this vital resource was not long delayed. Following a rainy afternoon, the skies cleared. In bright moonlight, a company-size force of Japanese assembled and started to move down the west coast, presumably with the intention of recapturing the two vital wells. Men of the 26th Marines spotted a sizable enemy force heading for one of the wells near the cliffs south of Hill 362A. The Japanese represented a splendid target in the moonlight. Both artillery and naval gunfire racked the enemy force and dispersed it before it reached any of the wells.

In another incident during this restless night, at the observation post of Company D, the company commander, Captain Thomas M. Fields, and a member of his staff observed three Japanese walking boldly within 25 feet of them with picric acid satchel charges. The two officers routed the enemy with hand grenades, killing one of the intruders.[7] This was only one example of the enemy's boldness in approaching or penetrating the American lines. Marines up front could never be sure of who or what was approaching them in the darkness. One of the early incidents which occurred on D plus 2, involved the compromise of the password "Chevrolet" in the area then occupied by Company F, 2/26. A sentry challenged a moving figure, who gave the correct password. Not satisfied with the pronunciation of "Chevrolet," the sentry repeated his challenge. Once again the password was mispronounced. The sentry fired and killed the intruder, who the next morning was identified as Japanese.[8]

Confrontations of this type tended to increase the vigilance of Marines on Iwo Jima. At times, such alertness was carried to the extreme and, a few nights later, resulted in a humorous incident involving the same company. During the night of 25-26 February, Company F, 2/26, seized a Navajo Indian, who was mistakenly identified as Japanese.[9] His poor English, made worse by a bad case of fright, made his position pre-

---

[6] *5th MarDiv AR*, Anx M, pp. 12, 15.

[7] *2/26 AR*, p. 8.

[8] *Ibid.*, p. 6.

[9] On Iwo Jima, as in other military operations in the Pacific Theater during World War II, the U. S. Marine Corps employed specially trained Navajo communicators or "talkers," whose language was not known to the Japanese and thus not open to enemy translation. In tactical situations where time was of the essence, precious minutes were gained since radio voice transmissions could be used without coding or decoding.

carious for a while. Fortunately, he escaped physical harm; his ordeal ended when he was finally identified by another Navajo Marine.

At 0630 on 27 February, the 27th Marines, with 1/26 attached, relieved the 26th Marines. Ninety minutes later, following a half-hour preparation by the 13th Marines, reinforced by corps artillery, Colonel Wornham's men jumped off with 2/27 on the left, 1/27 in the center, and 3/27 on the right. The 1st Battalion, 26th Marines, remained in regimental reserve. Shortly before the jumpoff, truck-mounted launchers of the 3d Rocket Detachment showered the area directly in front of the lines with a heavy barrage of 4.5-inch rockets, then pulled back before the enemy could retaliate. At the same time, naval gunfire was brought to bear against Hill 362A, followed by carrier aircraft which bombed and rocketed the hill.

Moving forward in the center, 1/27 gained 200 yards before running straight into a heavily defended cluster of pillboxes. A half-track was able to knock out one of these strongpoints with its 75mm gun before its crew was hit by well-aimed small arms fire. A decision to move up 37mm guns for support could not be implemented because no suitable positions could be found. Consequently, the task of reducing the formidable obstacle once again fell to small flamethrower-demolition teams who would reduce one pillbox after another in the slow, dangerous, but time-proven method.

During the afternoon, when the company advancing on the left of the 1st Battalion encountered a heavily fortified area, the call went out for tanks. The arrival of a flamethrower tank, in particular, was eagerly awaited. When it finally reached the scene of action, accompanied by other armor, it received a mortar hit and was disabled before it had a chance to take part in the engagement. Nevertheless, the remaining Shermans lent effective support. They fired with everything they had and then moved forward in concert with the infantry. In the course of this advance, several more enemy pillboxes, as well as a dug-in tank, were put out of action. Once the momentum of the attack had been regained, the Marines moved forward for an additional 200 yards until they halted shortly after 1900.

Advancing on the left of the 27th Marines, the 2d Battalion faced not only a determined enemy, but extremely difficult terrain. The cliff on the high ground adjacent to the west coast beaches was honeycombed with caves and emplacements, most of them sheltering mortars and machine guns. In such terrain the employment of tanks was out of the question; furthermore, the few existing routes of approach were heavily mined. Once again, the full burden of the attack fell on small infantry and demolition teams, each one advancing more or less independently, taking its losses as it eliminated one enemy strongpoint after another. Of necessity, such a movement is slow and extremely exhausting, yet steady gains were made and by late afternoon, 2/27 had advanced 500 yards.

On the right of the division line, 3/27 moved against a ridge which guarded the approach to Hill 362A.

Company G launched a frontal assault against this ridge and was promptly thrown back. A group of 30 men attempting to outflank this position was initially repulsed; a second try appeared more promising. As the Marines advanced up the slope they were hit by a hail of hand grenades thrown by the enemy from the reverse slope. Ten Marines were killed on the spot, including Gunnery Sergeant William G. Walsh, who dived on a hand grenade which landed in a hole where he and several of the men had taken cover. As other elements of the company reached the scene, the enemy was driven from the reverse slope, and the ridge remained in friendly hands.

As D plus 8 came to a close, the 5th Marine Division had gained roughly 500 yards through the heart of the enemy main line of resistance in some of the heaviest fighting in which any Marine unit on Iwo Jima was to take part. Losses throughout the day had been heavy, some units being harder hit than others. In one instance, Company A, 1/27, occupied a ridge only to discover that it was exposed to heavy enemy rifle and machine gun fire. The company suffered additional casualties from enemy hand grenades, thrown from bypassed positions in the flanks and rear. For all practical purposes, the Marines of Company A on top of the ridge were cut off. The 1st Platoon, in particular, was hard hit. By the time the company was relieved by Company B, 8 men had been killed and 50 wounded.[10] While the Company A losses were unusually heavy, they serve as an indication of the 5th Marine Division's losses since D-Day. By noon of D plus 8, the division had sustained 32 officers and 530 men killed, 134 officers and 2,360 men wounded, and 2 officers and 160 men missing in action, a total of 168 officers and 3,058 men.[11]

The 5th Marine Division had now reached the 0-2 Line across its entire zone of advance, though the lines on the evening of D plus 8 were not perfectly straight. Not all of the action occurred in the front lines. Continuous vigilance was required to clear the enemy out of the previously captured ground. Japanese kept appearing seemingly out of nowhere. Only later was it determined that they could move at will through a carefully constructed system of tunnels. As a result, before a day's attack could get under way, some mopping up remained to be done in the rear area. Despite the gains made by the 27th Marines on 27 February, an even more difficult operation awaited 5th Marine Division units on the following day.

THE ASSAULT ON HILL 362A[12]

On the morning of D plus 9, the last day of February, the 5th Marine Divi-

---

[10] Conner, *The Fifth Marine Division*, pp. 86-87.

[11] *5th MarDiv AR*, App 3, Sec VIII, p. 15.

[12] Additional material in this section is derived from: 5th Eng Bn AR, Iwo Jima, 19Feb-26Mar45, dtd 13Apr45, hereafter *5th EngBn AR;* 1/26 AR, Iwo Jima, 15Nov44-26Mar45, dtd 19Apr45, hereafter *1/26 AR;* 1/28 AR, Iwo Jima, 19Feb-26Mar45, n.d., hereafter *1/28 AR;* 2/28 OpRpt; 2/28 AR, Iwo Jima, 19 Feb-26Mar45, dtd 10Apr45, hereafter *2/28 AR;* 3/28 AR, Iwo Jima, 19Feb-26Mar45, n.d., hereafter *3/28 AR.*

sion was squarely up against Hill 362A, the highest elevation on western Iwo. The hill loomed forbiddingly above the Marines huddled at its approaches. Around the base of this hill mass, rocky outcrops dominated every approach. The Japanese had fortified each one of these rocky spurs, which afforded excellent fields of fire. For the attack on 28 February, the 27th Marines had been ordered to seize an intermediate objective between the 0-2 and 0-3 Lines.

Initially, the mission of taking Hill 362A had been entrusted to 3/27, while 1/27 was to simultaneously attack an irregular line of ridges extending from the objective down to the western beaches. During the night, 1/26 had relieved 2/27 and was committed along the left flank of the regiment along the beaches. Following a 45-minute preparation by artillery, naval gunfire, and rockets, and supported by carrier-based aircraft, the 27th Marines jumped off at 0815 for what was to develop into one of the bloodiest encounters on the island.

From the outset, the enemy offered stubborn resistance all along the regimental front. Advancing in the center and on the right of the regimental line, 1/27 and 3/27 encountered some of the heaviest small arms fire yet directed against them. The 1st Battalion called for and received tank support as it had on the previous day, but the terrain in the zone of advance of 3/27 precluded the employment of armor, and the battalion had to rely strictly on its own fire power. Advancing gingerly across 200 yards of difficult terrain, the two assault battalions reached the foot of the hill around noon.

At this point, the attack began to bog down. In accordance with General Kuribayashi's orders, the Japanese remained in their positions and fought to the bitter end. Those who were bypassed continued to fire into the rear of the advancing Marines. At such close range, the enemy snipers were extremely effective and inflicted heavy casualties on the assault force. In the course of the afternoon, several patrols from 3/27 probed the defenses on the hill itself, seeking for a way to seize it. A patrol from Company I actually made it up the southwest slopes to the crest of the hill around 1630. However, since cohesion between 1/27 and 3/27 had been lost, the patrol had to be recalled in late afternoon and Company I pulled back about 100 yards, where it tied in with elements of the adjacent 21st Marines on the left of the 3d Marine Division.

Far from being content with halting the Marine advance, 50-100 enemy troops sallied forth from positions on Hill 362A during the late afternoon and counterattacked the 3/27 lines. The brunt of this blow fell upon Company H, which engaged in desperate hand-to-hand fighting with frenzied Japanese before the latter were driven off.

By nightfall, men of the 27th Marines were still stalled at the foot of Hill 362A, which towered above them, seemingly as impregnable as ever. After a day of extremely bitter action, which had cost numerous casualties, the overall regimental gain had been about 300 yards. To the left, 1/26 had sent out advance detachments along the beaches, but the northward movement of any large body of troops was seriously impaired by the enemy's possession of the adjacent high ground.

The night from 28 February to 1 March turned out to be a very quiet one for the exhausted 5th Division Marines in the front lines. Four listening posts had been established by 2/26 along the beaches to frustrate any enemy intentions of landing reinforcements on the island. Each listening post had been augmented with one dog and its handler from the 6th War Dog Platoon. Eventually, things became so quiet that even the dogs found it difficult to remain awake.[13]

Elsewhere on Iwo Jima, it was a different matter. In the southern part of the island, in the vicinity of Mount Suribachi where they had been positioned ever since that elevation was captured, the 28th Marines was preparing to move north to join the 5th Division drive. At midnight, the enemy began shelling the positions of the corps artillery and those of the 13th Marines. This bombardment continued at some length. Shortly after 0200, the 5th Marine Division ammunition dump blew up with a tremendous roar, blazing fiercely for the remainder of the night. At least 20 percent of the division small arms ammunition supply was lost in the conflagration, along with large quantities of heavier ammunition. One of the exploding shells landed in the corps artillery fire direction center but caused no casualties, though it did wreak havoc with the telephone wire.[14]

In the course of the operation, VAC Headquarters itself came under fire a number of times from mortars and artillery. This shelling resulted in several casualties. On at least two occasions, all work in the operations tents of the various staff sections came to a stop and officers and men piled together on the ground as shells landed nearby.[15]

In the midst of the commotion caused by the exploding ammunition dump, the island's air alert system went off. The nerves of personnel in the southern part of the island were further strained when exploding white phosphorus shells were mistaken for gas shells and someone gave the gas alarm at 0300. Within ten minutes, the gas alarm was cancelled; not so the air alert, which continued until 0430.[16]

As it turned out, there was some substance to the air alert. No enemy planes appeared over Iwo Jima during the night, but shortly before 0300 an enemy aircraft, skimming in low over the water, dropped a torpedo near the destroyer *Terry* a few miles north of Kitano Point. The destroyer took evasive action and barely avoided getting hit by the torpedo. However, a few hours later, while passsing the northernmost point of Iwo Jima, the ship came under fire from enemy shore batteries, which scored hits on the main deck and forward engine room. Eleven destroyer crewmen were killed and 19 wounded before the *Terry*, assisted by the *Nevada* and *Pensacola*, made good her escape. In addition to the loss in lives, the ship had suffered substantial damage.[17] Another vessel, the destroyer *Colhoun*, an-

---
[13] *26th Mar AR*, App. 4, p. 9.
[14] BGen John S. Letcher ltr to CMC, dtd 13Mar53, in *Iwo Comments*.
[15] *Craig ltr*.
[16] *VAC OpRpt*, p. 28.
[17] Morison, *Victory in the Pacific*, p. 64.

chored off the northeastern coast of Iwo to repair damage sustained in a collision, took several hits from enemy shore batteries which wrecked a torpedo tube, exploded the air flask of a torpedo, and caused other extensive damage. One man was killed and 16 were wounded in the course of this action.[18]

At 0630 on 1 March, the 28th Marines, with the 5th Tank Battalion and 3/27 attached, moved forward through the 27th Marines in order to continue the attack on Hill 362A. Between 0745 and 0830, the objective and surrounding area received a heavy shelling from all four battalions of the 13th Marines and the corps' 155mm howitzers. Offshore, a battleship and two cruisers joined in the bombardment. The volume of fire was such that it was deemed best, in the interests of coordination, to exclude aircraft from the preparatory fires. They would have ample opportunity to support the attack later in the day.

Shortly before 0900 the 28th Marines jumped off with the 1st, 2d, and 3d Battalions from right to left. The attack moved ahead slowly under heavy enemy mortar and small arms fire. To Colonel Liversedge's men, the dogged defense of Hill 362A was reminiscent of the action at the base of Mount Suribachi. The scheme of maneuver called for 1/28 and 2/28 to attack around the right and left of Hill 362A respectively and link up on the north side of the hill. Meanwhile, 3/28 was to advance up the west coast to the left of 2/28.

By 1030, both the 1st and 2d Battalions had reached the top of the ridge and the ridgeline running east and west of Hill 362A. As they attempted to advance beyond the crest, they discovered that a steep drop of nearly 100 feet into a rocky draw confronted them. To make matters worse, heavy fire from small arms, automatic weapons, and mortars hit the advancing Marines from the adjacent ridge to the north, subsequently to become known as Nishi Ridge. The draw itself ran parallel to the ridge line and was bisected by an antitank ditch that ran perpendicular to the hill. Covering the ditch were cleverly constructed positions in the face of the steep cliff, inaccessible from the top. Beyond the antitank ditch and the draw, the ground leveled off for about 200 yards before again rising sharply to form Nishi Ridge.

In order to keep the attack moving, Lieutenant Colonel Jack B. Butterfield, commanding 1/28, sent his reserve, Company A, around the right of Hill 362A. This maneuver proved unsuccessful and the company came under such withering fire, accompanied by a shower of grenades, that it was stopped short in its tracks. During this assault the company commander was killed. A similar attempt by Company B to get into the draw proved equally unsuccessful, and the company commander was wounded. In this jumble of rock, both companies suffered heavy casualties. Among these was Corporal Tony Stein of Company A, who had already made a name for himself on D Day. He set out with 20 men to clear the ridge of snipers. Only seven men returned from

---

[18] Ibid.

this mission. Among the men of Company B killed near the base of Hill 362A this day were three who had raised the American flag on Mount Suribachi; one of them had taken part in the first and the two others had participated in the second flag raising.

Throughout the day, 10 regular tanks and 2 flame tanks of Company C, 5th Tank Battalion, gave all possible support to 2/28 to the extent that the terrain permitted, with fire on the cliffs and the high ground to the front. Shortly after noon, two platoons of tanks spearheaded an attack along the left flank of the battalion; subsequently, one platoon was withdrawn and shifted to the right of the zone of action of 2/28, just north and west of Hill 362A. Even with the support of tanks, 2/28 proved unable to advance. The battle raged hot and heavy at close quarters; in one instance, one of the tanks bogged down, surrounded by 30-40 Japanese, some of them occupying a cave only 10 feet from the tank. Fighting as infantry, the tank crew was able to make a harrowing escape after disabling the gun and radio.

For the remainder of the afternoon of D plus 10, the 1st and 2d Battalions, 28th Marines, remained stalled along the crest of Hill 362A and at the base of the hill, where the enemy still held out in caves. In the course of the afternoon, the boundary of General Rockey's division was extended about 200 yards to the east to facilitate the advance of the adjacent 3d Marine Division. As a result, General Rockey committed 3/26 on the right of the 28th Marines.

Shortly before 1900, 3/26 relieved 1/21 and established contact with 3/9 on the right and 1/28 on the left. At the same time, 2/26 displaced forward as 28th Marines reserve.

While the 1st and 2d Battalions, 28th Marines, were making little progress in the extremely difficult and well defended terrain, 3/28 was making a steady advance with two companies abreast near the west coast. The battalion moved forward against moderate resistance until its assault elements on the left were ahead of those on the right, at which time they drew heavy fire from the right front. The battalion had gained about 350 yards and since the regimental attack to the right had stalled, 3/28 halted its advance.

By the end of 1 March, Hill 362A and a rocky ridgeline extending to the west coast had been seized. In all, elements of the 5th Division held a 1,000-yard front, which was exposed to heavy artillery and mortar fire from positions to the north. In order to obtain better observation over the northwestern coast of Iwo Jima, artillery observers were placed on board an LCI(G) which cruised up and down the northwest shore. This expedient was successful and several enemy positions were located and silenced.[19]

At the end of 1 March, the 5th Marine Division had taken a total of 12 prisoners; it was estimated that 3,252 of the enemy had been killed in the 5th Division area of responsibility.[20] Casualties sustained by the division to this

---

[19] *5th MarDiv AR*, pp. 23–24.
[20] *Ibid.*, p. 24.

date were 48 officers and 952 men killed, 161 officers and 3,083 men wounded in action, and 2 officers and 47 men missing.[21] The capture of Hill 362A and the ridges on either side of it in a one-day operation had cost the 28th Marines alone 224 casualties.[22]

While General Rockey's men were engaged in reducing Hill 362A, the adjacent 3d Marine Division had penetrated the enemy defense system in the center of the island and had pivoted to the northeast. This move threatened to open a widening gap between the 3d and 5th Marine Divisions. As a result, for 2 March, General Schmidt directed the 5th Marine Division to make the main effort on the right while maintaining contact with General Erskine's men. In order to carry out the newly assigned mission calling for an expansion of his boundaries, General Rockey committed the 26th Marines to the right of the 28th. For the continuation of the 5th Division attack on D plus 11, the fire of the 13th Marines was augmented by half of the corps artillery fires.[23]

At 0800 on 2 March, the 26th Marines jumped off along the division boundary with 3/26 in the assault. As the battalion moved forward, a gap arose on the left, and Companies D and F of 2/26 were committed to regain contact with 1/28. In the zone of advance of the 26th Marines the Japanese made maximum use of cleverly concealed positions, whose approaches were mined. Progress was correspond-

ingly slow. Even though the terrain did not favor the use of armor and abounded in antitank obstacles, 3/26 requested tank support, and tanks from Company A, 5th Tank Battalion, spearheaded the attack.

Companies D and F of 2/26 were in the midst of blasting their way into and through the enemy defenses when the battalion had to shift to the right to close a new gap that had developed between the 3d and 5th Divisions. In executing the shift, the two companies had to disengage under heavy fire; they were further harassed by mortars and minefields. A solid line was finally formed in late afternoon just before nightfall. In order to fill the void created when the two companies of 2/26 were shifted to the northeast, it became necessary to commit 1/26.

When fighting came to an end on D plus 11, 3/26 had gained 500 yards. (See Map VI, Map Section). Responsible for these gains to a large measure were the division engineers, who moved alongside the assault units to clear minefields and open supply roads in the rear. In front of the 26th Marines, the enemy had mined the approaches to his pillboxes and permanent fortifications; without the help of the engineers, the advance of Colonel Graham's regiment on D plus 11 would have been doomed to failure.

In the left of the 5th Division zone of advance, the 28th Marines jumped off at 0800 with its three battalions employing the same scheme of maneuver as on the previous day. The 1st and 2d Battalions were to attack around both sides of Hill 362A and join on the north side for a coordinated assault against

---

[21] *Ibid.*
[22] Morehouse, *Iwo Jima Campaign,* p 53.
[23] VAC OpO 10–45, dtd 1Mar45.

the next elevation 200 yards to the north. This obstacle, extending westward from the plateau almost to the water's edge, was squarely in the path of the 28th Marines. Beyond were the stark remains of what had once been a small hamlet called Nishi. From it, the elevation took its name: Nishi Ridge.

As the two battalions jumped off, they encountered undiminished resistance. Every time the Marines moved into the depression north of Hill 362A, they drew heavy fire from both the front and the rear. Tanks from Company B, 5th Tank Battalion, tried to give effective support, but were severely limited in their movements by the antitank ditch extending across their front.

As a result, the 28th Marines made only little progress. The 13th Marines gave all possible support to the infantry, concentrating its fire on enemy mortar positions identified from the air and through forward observers. Finally, elements of the regimental weapons company succeeded in setting up three .50 caliber machine guns to cover the caves that honeycombed the northern slopes of Hill 362A. Friendly mortar fire saturated the defile in front of the infantry.

Eventually, armored bulldozers of the 5th Engineer Battalion got close enough to the antitank ditch to fill in a portion of it. This permitted the tanks to move out and advance for 200 yards until the terrain narrowed and precluded any further forward movement. Caught in this type of cul de sac, the tank crews fought with the enemy at closest quarters. At 1400, tanks of Company C relieved those of Company B, which was beginning to run out of ammunition.

En route to the front lines, the tanks of Company C, including a flame tank, blasted and burned enemy positions in the steep northern face of Hill 362A, from which the enemy was still firing into the rear of the advancing infantry.

The enemy made numerous attempts to destroy the supporting armor with satchel charges. Apparently, the appearance of tanks in close support of the infantry in terrain that all but precluded the effective employment of armor confounded the Japanese. One of the officers on General Kuribayashi's staff was to make the following comment on this subject:

> When American M-4 tanks appeared in front of Osaka Yama (Hill 362A), Lieutenant General Kuribayashi was very anxious to know how to dispose of this tank. Even our 47mm antitank gun could not destroy it, and at last came to the conclusion that bodily attacks with explosives was the only way to destroy it.[24]

Actually, the Japanese island commander may have overestimated the structural strength of the M-4 tank, which was indeed vulnerable to 47mm antitank fire. Nevertheless, the Shermans were indispensable on Iwo, and without them the assault might have failed. Ideally, a tank with heavier armament and a lower silhouette, as well as improved traction, would have been more desirable, but at the time of the Iwo Jima operation only the Shermans were available to the Marines engaged in the assault.

While the tanks were keeping the enemy to the rear occupied, Company E, 2/28, charged across the exposed terrain north of Hill 362A to the foot

---

[24] *Horie Rpt*, p. 8.

of Nishi Ridge. Enemy reaction to this move was immediate and, in the words of the regimental report, "All Hell broke loose"[25] as the Japanese fought back from the cliff line to the north, from Hill 362A, and from a blockhouse in front of and to the east of Hill 362A. Combined with the heavy enemy artillery and mortar fire was a counterattack by a large group of Japanese against 1/28. This attack was repulsed with 129 Japanese killed.

Losses among the Marines of 2/28 also were beginning to mount. Shortly after 1400, Lieutenant Colonel Chandler W. Johnson, commanding 2/28, was hit squarely by an artillery shell as he was inspecting the front lines. The battalion commander was killed instantly and the battalion executive officer, Major Thomas B. Pearce, Jr., assumed command. For the remainder of the afternoon, reserve units mopped up in the vicinity of Hill 362A, whose northern face was giving the advancing Marines infinitely more trouble than the southern slopes had.

While bitter fighting was raging along the center and eastern portion of the division line, 3/28 was advancing along a narrow front near the west coast. Movement in this area was seriously impeded by numerous caves and heavy enemy artillery and mortar fire. The caves were attacked and slowly neutralized with 37mm guns, heavy mortars, and demolition charges; a total of 68 were blasted during the day. At 0900 and again around noon, shells falling within the battalion zone of advance gave off a green-yellowish gas which induced vomiting and caused severe headaches to some of the men exposed to it. A brief gas scare resulted until it became apparent that only those men in the immediate proximity of a shell burst were affected; symptoms lasted only for a short time. In the end, the ill effects were ascribed to the presence of picric acid fumes.[26]

At 1700, VAC ordered the lines to be consolidated for the day. In the 5th Division zone of advance, fighting continued until nightfall, some of it at very close quarters. For the night, 5th Division Marines were generally dug in at the base of Nishi Ridge; on the far right, the 2/26 lines extended to the northeast along the division boundary where they tied in with 3/9 near Hill 362B. The biggest advance for the day had been made by the 26th Marines, which had gained 500 yards. There were indications that the regiment was moving into a different type of defensive position than had been previously encountered. There were fewer concrete fortifications and more rock barriers and tank ditches. Even though the enemy was resisting as fiercely as ever, he was abandoning some of his equipment. Items captured on D plus 11 were a generator truck found behind one ridge and a large searchlight behind another.

As night fell, the enemy made several attempts to infiltrate the 5th Division lines. About 50 Japanese sallied forth near Hill 362A and some of this force succeeded in getting into the Marine positions. Once the Marines became aware of their presence, bitter

---

[25] *996th Mar AR*, p. 27.

[26] *Ibid.*

hand-to-hand fighting ensued, in the course of which knives, sabers, pistols, and hand grenades were liberally used. The alertness of the Marines in dealing with the infiltrators led General Kuribayashi to report that "the lookout of American forces has become very strict and it is difficult to pass through their guarded line. Don't overestimate the value of cutting-in attacks."[27]

On the evening D plus 11, the battle of Hill 362A was over, but an even bigger challenge was to confront General Rockey's men for the following day: the capture of Nishi Ridge and Hill 362B.

NISHI RIDGE, HILL 362B AND BEYOND[28]

On the morning of D plus 12, the 5th Marine Division resumed the attack with basically the same formations it had employed on the previous day. From the very outset, both the terrain and enemy resistance combined to make it a difficult day. The 26th and 28th Marines were to make the main effort. In the path of the 28th Marines lay a series of gorges and ridges; in front of the 26th Marines the terrain was heavily mined; in addition, from strongly held Hill 362B, the enemy was able to sweep the area with fire. New roads would have to be dozed out before tanks could move in to support the advance.

The attack jumped off at 0745. Supported by 75mm half-tracks, 37mm guns, and a reinforced tank platoon, 1/28 and 2/28 in the regimental center moved out and almost immediately ran into heavy mortar and small arms fire. As the two battalions inched forward, the men soon came to close grips with the enemy and numerous hand grenade duels were fought. Within two hours after the jumpoff, Nishi Ridge had been seized and the battalions prepared to move into the rugged terrain beyond. As the advance gained momentum, the 28th Marines swept down from Nishi Ridge into the remnants of Nishi Village, and by late afternoon had reached a point about 200 yards beyond, despite mounting casualties, for enemy resistance never slackened. At the close of the day, when the fury of the battle receded, 1/28 made further gains which brought it ahead of the other two battalions. Since morning, 1/28 had gained 500 yards, while 2/28 had scored gains of only 150 yards, as had 3/28 along the coast.

By far the most spectacular fighting and resultant gains were made in the zone of advance of the 26th Marines. The mission assigned to the 26th Marines for D plus 12 had been to advance northeastward to relieve elements of the 3d Marine Division near Hill 362B. The line of departure for 2/26 and 3/26 formed an inverted horseshoe with 3/26 on the left and 2/26 on the right. The two battalions moved out rapidly, even though both began taking casualties almost at once. Company B

---

[27] *Horie Rpt.*, p. 9.

[28] Additional material in this section is derived from: *133d NCB AR;* 2/13 UJnl, Iwo Jima, 19Feb-27Mar45, hereafter *2/13 UJnl;* 2/13 AR, Iwo Jima, 27Oct44-21Mar45, n.d., hereafter *2/13 AR;* 3/13 UJnl, Iwo Jima, 19-Feb-17Mar45, hereafter *3/13 UJnl;* 3/13 AR, Iwo Jima, 27Oct44-21Mar45, n.d. hereafter *3/13 AR;* 4/13 AR, Iwo Jima, 27Oct44-21Mar-45, dtd 7Apr45, hereafter *4/13 AR.*

of the 5th Tank Battalion supported the 2d Battalion by covering the left flank of Company F. Just as it had done on D plus 7 when first committed in the assault, this company smashed into the enemy defenses with great force and aggressiveness. Since, at the outset, the terrain was comparatively level and thus favored the employment of armor, the company commander was able to radio instructions to the armor through a tank liaison man assigned to the command post of 2/26. The assault swept on for about 300 yards before the open terrain changed into the deep gorges and rock formations characteristic of northern Iwo Jima. In these rocky badlands the battle continued, frequently man against man. The Japanese fiercely contested the advance behind every rock and boulder but could not stop it. In some of the most bitter fighting of the entire operation, every weapon at hand was brought into play.

By the time the forceful advance came to a halt, Company F had advanced more than 600 yards to the high ground to its front. Even then, the Japanese grimly contested every foot of the freshly seized ground, and numerous hand grenades continued to harass the Marines from cleverly hidden caves and gullies whose presence had hitherto been unsuspected. But the enemy was mortal, and bazooka shells accurately fired into such defensive positions usually eliminated this resistance in short order.

The 600-yard advance of 2/26 eliminated the horseshoe and for all practical purposes, straightened the line. With the severe threat to its left flank gone, 3/26 was able to launch an advance of its own, which resulted in a 200-yard gain. While Company F was tackling the enemy at close quarters, Companies D and E launched an attack northeastward along the division boundary in order to seize Hill 362B and relieve 3/9. The relief was completed by 1430 and the two companies, from positions just southwest of the hill, prepared for the assault.

When it came, at 1600, the battle for the hill proved to be a bloody one. Using rocket launchers, flamethrowers, demolitions, plus a goodly amount of sheer courage and will, the two companies forced their way to the top. The southern and western slopes of the hill were honeycombed with caves and pillboxes, each of which required an individual assault. By the time the crest of the hill was reached, both company commanders and many of their men had become casualties.

The advance made by the 5th Marine Division on 3 March was almost spectacular under the conditions in which the battle was fought. The cost of seizing this ground was correspondingly high. On D plus 12, the 26th Marines alone had 281 casualties.[29] Total losses for the 5th Marine Division on 3 March were 9 officers and 127 men killed or dead of wounds, and 15 officers and 357 men wounded.[30] As of D plus 12, total casualties for the division since D-Day numbered 4,960 officers and men.[31]

---

[29] *26th Mar WarD*, Mar45.
[30] *5th MarDiv Casualty Rpts*, dtd 25Jun45.
[31] *Ibid.*

As the fury of the battle receded on the evening of D plus 12, the 5th Division lines extended from the west coast at a point roughly 200 yards north of Nishi Village along the northern edge of Motoyama Plateau to the crest of Hill 362B. All along the front, the casualty rate had reached alarming proportions and it became necessary to send men from headquarters and weapons companies into the line as riflemen to bolster the tired and depleted units. Not all of the 5th Marine Division men were able to get much rest that night. In the sector of the 28th Marines, there were relatively few attempts at infiltration. It was another story in the 26th Marines area, where the enemy infiltrators appeared more aggressive and crowded the 26th Marines throughout the night. Almost all of the nearly 100 would-be infiltrators were killed.

Following an artillery preparation and rocket barrage, the 5th Marine Division resumed the attack on the morning of D plus 13. As the men jumped off in the same formation they had employed on the previous day, they were hit by intensive fire from small arms and mortars. Once again, the Marines advanced into terrain dotted with interconnected caves. The lines were now so close to each other that artillery support could be used only on special occasions. Because of a low cloud ceiling, the air support which had been scheduled for the day had to be cancelled.

The low clouds soon gave way to intermittent showers, which did little to lift the morale of the men who were still exhausted in spirit and body from the rigors of the preceding days' combat and lack of sleep caused by the continuous Japanese infiltration attempts of the previous night. The rugged terrain seriously limited the use of 75mm half-tracks and 37mm guns. With Japanese lurking all around them, the crews of these vehicles felt progressively more exposed to enemy fire. Beyond that, the enemy was beginning to take a toll in vehicles with mines, skillfully emplaced in the few avenues of approach available to the supporting armor.

Perhaps the biggest difference between the success attained on D plus 12 and the fighting on the following day was the fact that the attacks were not closely coordinated. Once again, the brunt of the battle was borne by small detachments, moving more or less haphazardly against those enemy caves and pillboxes that were unmasked. As a result, only small gains were made, even though in this jungle of rocks the bravery of the individual Marine continued undiminished. As on the previous day, losses were heavy and many of the combat units were operating at half strength or less. The enemy was noticeably more aggressive in the daytime than he had been before, and the 26th Marines beat back several counterattacks executed in company strength. Nowhere did the Japanese succeed in breaking through the 5th Division lines, but the counterattacks served to take additional steam out of the drive of the fatigued Marines, and net gains for the day remained practically nil. As one account of the day's operations put it, "The only successful move, in fact, was made by Division headquarters which moved from its original location near the eastern beaches to a position north of Airfield No. 1 on the west side of the island.[32] At about this time, General Kuribayashi shifted his headquarters from the center of Iwo Jima to a large cave in the northwestern section of the island, between Hiraiwa Bay and the ruins of Kita Village, where he prepared to make his final stand.

General Schmidt's order to his three divisions that 5 March was to be utilized for reorganization, resupply, and preparations for the resumption of the attack on the following day reached 5th Division units during the afternoon of 4 March. At a time when physical strength and fighting spirit were beginning to flag, this order was more than welcome. Logically, the day of rest would be used, above all, to funnel replacements into the depleted ranks of the frontline units. The exigencies of combat had already necessitated sending some men with specific and critical skills, such as demolition personnel and bazooka or flamethrower operators into the lines prior to 5 March. On the whole, except for small emergency details, replacements were sent forward when the combat battalions were out of the lines. Replacements, no matter how willing and well trained, always tended to present something of a problem before they were wholly integrated. The reasons for this were outlined in the following report:

> Reports from infantry units indicate that the average replacement, upon being assigned to a rifle unit and immediately subjected to the type of fierce fighting encountered, was initially bewildered and terrified resulting from a mental attitude of his being "alone," and not knowing his leaders and companions on the battlefield. This lack of a sense of security, even when among battle-experienced troops, was brought about by his separation from contact with those with whom he had previously trained and not yet having become assimilated into a fighting team. Those who did not readjust themselves quickly had a high percentage of casualties since in their bewilderment they usually carelessly exposed themselves.[33]

For the resumption of the attack on 6 March, General Rockey directed 1/26 to relieve 1/27 and ordered the 27th Marines into reserve. At the same time, the 28th Marines was to reorganize so that 3/28 would take over the sector of 2/28. This would leave all three battalions of the 26th Marines in the line, the 28th Marines holding a front with 3/28 on the left and 3/27 on the right, and the 27th Marines, less the 3d Battalion, in reserve.

In accordance with VAC orders, combat activity by 5th Division units was limited to local attempts to straighten the lines during the morning. Throughout the day, artillery and naval gunfire were brought to bear on suspected enemy positions, and carrier aircraft flew 18 missions. Within the 26th Marines sector, a few tanks engaged in reducing caves and other strongpoints that were directly menacing the front lines. Those tanks not actually engaged with the enemy received badly needed maintenance in the bivouac areas.

Despite general inactivity on the part of the Japanese infantry, the 5th

---

[32] Conner, *The Fifth Marine Division*, p. 95.

[33] *5th MarDiv AR*, Anx A, p. 14.

Division suffered casualties through enemy action even on this day of rest. One of the tanks operating near the 26th Marines lines ran over a mine and was disabled, another was hit by enemy antitank fire. Japanese mortars continued to harass the Marines throughout the day, particularly when the enemy observed troop movements near Road Junction 338 northwest of Motoyama Village. Even though this junction was situated in the 3d Marine Division area, it constituted a supply road for the 26th Marines and other 5th Division units.

A particularly unfortunate incident occurred shortly after the relief of 1/27 by 1/26. The 1st Battalion, 27th Marines, was in the process of moving to an assembly area in the vicinity of Road Junction 338 when an enemy shell hit the jeep carrying the battalion commander, Lieutenant Colonel John A. Butler, who had been observing the relief. The battalion commander was killed, and two other men in the vehicle were wounded. Later that afternoon, Lieutenant Colonel Justin G. Duryea, the operations officer of the 27th Marines, took over command of 1/27.

While all three Marine divisions on Iwo remained in place and prepared to continue the assault, several important changes occurred to the rear, indicative of what had been accomplished and how much remained to be done. At the foot of Mount Suribachi, the 133d Naval Construction Battalion put into operation six portable water distillation units. The processed water was sent to the front and there was enough to furnish three canteens per day per man, a vast improvement over what had been previously available. As early as 3 March, the situation from a naval viewpoint had become relatively quiet. Unloading and evacuation progressed favorably over both the eastern and western beaches. It thus became possible for all of the assault shipping including the Defense Group and the Joint Expeditionary Force Reserve to retire to rear areas.

On the morning of D plus 15, it was business as usual for all three assault divisions on Iwo. The only change from the norm was that the heaviest artillery barrage thus far fired preceded the attack. Shortly before 0700, 11 artillery battalions, a total of 132 guns ranging from 75mm to 155mm in caliber, unleashed a tremendous bombardment of enemy positions in northern Iwo, followed by a rolling barrage. Offshore, a battleship, two cruisers, three destroyers, and two landing craft added their fire to that of the land-based artillery, which in little more than an hour expended 22,500 shells, some of them falling within 100 yards of the Marines waiting to jump off. At pretimed intervals, carrier planes strafed, rocketed, and bombed the enemy positions. The portion of the island still in Japanese hands literally rocked under the punishment being meted out, and it appeared that little could withstand such an extensive pounding.

As soon as they jumped off at 0800, the Marines of the 5th Division, as well as those of the two remaining divisions, discovered to their dismay that the barrage had done little to soften up enemy resistance. When the artillery fire lifted, the Japanese, little the worse for wear, contested the advance of General Rockey's men from prepared bunkers, pillboxes, and caves. Marines attempting to advance north from Hill 362B immediately drew heavy rifle, machine gun, and mortar fire interspersed with white phosphorus shells. It was almost as if the heavy bombardment had never happened. The broken terrain all but precluded close tank support and, instead of a big push, the advance could be measured in yards. The vigorous drive to the 0–3 Line that had been envisaged could not materialize under such conditions and the attack soon bogged down. By the end of the day, the 26th and 27th Marines had gained between 50 and 100 yards; the 28th Marines' advance bogged down altogether.

The only progress made could be measured, not in yards, but in the number of enemy caves and emplacements destroyed. Engineers operating with the 28th Marines were able to seal off numerous caves. As in preceding days, the Japanese harassed the advance from the front, flanks, and rear. Casualties were correspondingly heavy. The type of vicious close in fighting the Marines were engaged in during this period was reflected in the nature of the casualties evacuated to the rear. In the words of one observer:

> At the Fifth Division hospital, Lieutenant Evans was noticing a change in the type of wounds coming in. They were bad ones, from close range sniper or machine gun fire. The earlier wounds, mostly from mortar bursts, had been numerous and ragged, but not so penetrating. The whole blood was being used as little as twelve

days after it was given on the West Coast, but often it could not help.[34]

After the heavy volume of artillery fire on 6 March, expended with such little effect, VAC limited the use of ammunition, particularly for harassing missions. In his orders for 7 March,[35] General Schmidt directed the 5th Marine Division to seize the high ground overlooking the sea with the main effort to be made in the northeastern portion of the division zone of action. Within this zone, the main effort was to be carried out by the 27th Marines, while the 26th and 28th Marines were to execute limited objective attacks.[36]

THE DRIVE TO THE SEA[37]

Just as General Erskine's division on the right jumped off for a surprise attack without an artillery preparation early on 7 March, so the 26th Marines, less 2/26 in VAC reserve, duplicated the maneuver on a minor scale. Jumping off 40 minutes prior to H-Hour without an artillery preparation, 1/26 and Company H, 3/26, set about to reduce the stubborn enemy defenses that had thwarted the regiment's advance on the previous day. After overcoming moderate resistance, the battalion reached a 30-foot knoll just north of Nishi Village. As Marines wearily surrounded this hill, enemy fire all but ceased. The sudden stillness was broken only when

---

[34] Newcomb, *Iwo Jima*, p. 247.
[35] VAC OpO 14–15, dtd 6Mar45.
[36] 5th MarDiv OpO 13–15, dtd 6Mar45.
[37] Additional material in this section is derived from *1/13 UJnl; 1/13 AR, Iwo Jima, 27Oct44-21Mar45*, dtd 5Apr45, hereafter *1/13 AR*.

demolitions men blasted and closed one cave entrance, while machine gunners made short work of several of the enemy who rushed out of a rear entrance. Marines of Company H ran towards the top of the hill in a suspicious silence that was most unnatural for Iwo, until about 40 had gathered on the crest. Then the unbelievable occurred:

> ... The whole hill shuddered and the top blew out with a roar heard all over the island. Men were thrown into the air, and those nearby were stunned by the concussion. Dozens of Marines disappeared in the blast crater, and their comrades ran to dig for them. Strong men vomited at the sight of charred bodies, and others walked from the area crying. The enemy had blown up his own command post, inflicting forty-three Marine casualties at the same time.[38]

All that remained of the ridge was a mass of torn, twisted, and burning rock and sand. Smoke emerged from a ragged hole so large that it might well have harbored a good sized apartment building. Many of the men, not directly injured by the blast but stunned by the concussion, were staggering around in a daze. It remained for the commander of Company H, Captain Donald E. Castle, to gather the remnants of his men and lead them in a renewed attack.[39]

---

[38] Newcomb, *Iwo Jima*, p. 252.

[39] This was the first time that men of the 5th Marine Division had become involved in a disaster of this type. A similar incident, on a somewhat smaller scale, involved 2/24 of the 4th Division on Roi-Namur in November 1943. Then, a large blockhouse used to store aerial bombs and torpedo warheads blew up as the Marines surrounded it. At the time, in an instant, the battalion suffered more than half of its total battle casualties for the operation. Proehl, *The Fourth Marine Division*, p. 29.

Meanwhile, 3/26 had also jumped off and almost at once ran into such heavy resistance that continuous fighting at close range, which lasted until nightfall, produced a gain of only 150 yards. Once again, even this meager advance had to be paid for with heavy casualties.

The 5th Marine Division main effort on D plus 16 was made by 2/27, supported by a company of 1/27. Following a 15-minute preparation by a battery of the 13th Marines, the battalion jumped off for an attack that was coordinated with elements of the 21st Marines operating beyond the division boundary. The objective was a stretch of high ground squarely astride the regimental zone of advance. Initially, good progress was made until the forward elements entered a draw directly in front of the first of a series of ridges. At this point, enemy machine gun fire, coming from two directions, raked the exposed men, who sought in vain to pinpoint the well-camouflaged positions. Casualties mounted as a 37mm gun was arduously manhandled to a forward position, from where it engaged the hidden machine guns with undetermined results.

Throughout the day, fighting raged at close quarters, each side making generous use of hand grenades. In the end, the overall gain for the 27th Marines on D plus 16 was 150 yards, similar to the ground seized by the 26th. Even such a limited advance, executed against a firmly entrenched enemy force that contested every foot of ground with knee mortars, grenades, and deadly accurate sniper fire, was a major accomplishment. The task of the Marine infantrymen might have been greatly eased had tank support been available. As it was, the broken terrain was altogether impassable for armor. During the afternoon, platoon-sized elements of 2/27 attempted to outflank some of the enemy positions, only to be caught by heavy flanking fire that all but isolated them from the main body. A withdrawal became possible only with the help of a smoke screen. Fighting continued throughout the afternoon and individual enemy caves were assaulted and taken. But there was no way of telling how many hidden tunnels led into these caves, or how long it would take the enemy to restock them with new men and weapons after the Marine assault squads had moved on.

The only sign of progress of the 5th Marine Division on 7 March occurred on the division's left wing. There, in the zone of advance of the 28th Marines near the west coast, 3/28 and 3/27 dispatched combat patrols before the main body launched a general attack. These patrols moved out at 0900, met with little resistance, and reported this fact back to the regiment. One hour later, without any special artillery preparation, the main body moved out. There was scattered resistance, but not enough to delay the forward movement as 3/28 and 3/27 struck out in a northeasterly direction. In this instance, the extremely difficult terrain proved to be much more of an obstacle than the sporadic resistance encountered. In order to maintain the momentum of the attack, numerous caves were bypassed, to be mopped up later by 1/28 and 2/28. Mortar and rocket fire was directed well ahead of the advancing Marines; additional fire support came from a destroyer offshore.

By 1530, the two battalions had advanced about 500 yards over and through rocky gorges in terrain that was passable only for men on foot. Included in the ground taken this day was Hill 215, located about 500 yards northeast of Nishi Village, only 750 yards from the northern shore. The relative absence of enemy resistance in this sector was to be the most surprising development of the day's operations. In addition to making the longest advance yet in the 5th Division zone, the attacking units killed nine of the enemy in this area and captured one.[40] According to the battalion action report, "a little further advance might have been made, but the positions for the night would have been weak, so the defenses were laid out in the area indicated."[41]

From the time the advance halted for the day until dusk, all three battalions of the regiment dug in for the night in the vicinity of Hill 215, while some of the Marines were engaged in mopping up in the immediate vicinity of the hill In the midst of this activity, few Marines paid much attention to the fact that a stiff breeze had begun to blow from the north towards the American lines. This nonchalance changed to

---

[40] *3/28 AR*, 7Mar45.
[41] *Ibid.*

near-panic when this ill wind was found to be:

> ... bringing with it eye-smarting sulphur fumes and smoke from a burning enemy ammunition dump. Unit commanders, always alert to the possibility of the enemy's employing poison gas, sounded an alert which brought hundreds of gas masks into use. The alarm soon passed, however, and CT 28 went on with its reorganizing.[42]

The 5th Division advance on D plus 16 had moved the lines forward from 500 yards in the west to 150 yards along the boundary with the 3d Marine Division, where resistance had been the stiffest. In support of the day's operations, naval gunfire had played a significant part. Following the tremendous expenditure of ammunition by the shore-based artillery on 6 March, VAC had restricted the use of the corps 155mm howitzers to "deliberate destructive fires against known enemy targets."[43] The resulting gap in artillery support had been taken up by naval gunfire. All naval gunfire control parties received instructions to expend 500 rounds per ship. On the basis of data furnished by the corps intelligence section, the 5th Division intelligence officer, Lieutenant Colonel George A. Roll, assigned target priorities.[44] Additional support was obtained through air strikes, even though the shrinking enemy perimeter and the proximity of the lines made such support a rather risky undertaking. Altogether, 119 carrier aircraft flew 147 sorties. The employment of napalm bombs was somewhat less than successful: of 40 carried, 7 failed to release; of the 33 released, 7 failed to ignite.[45] An additional 67 500–pound bombs, 170 100–pound bombs, and 426 rockets were not subject to technical failures, but no estimate as to their effectiveness against a well dug-in enemy could be obtained.

The night of 7–8 March was characterized by relatively light enemy activity, though it was far from quiet. In the zone of action of the 5th Marine Division, the Japanese kept things lively with small arms and knee mortar fire and hand grenades. Enemy patrols probed the Marine lines at various points. The only determined attempt at infiltration occurred in front of 1/26, where approximately 25 Japanese tried their luck. The attempt ended in dismal failure when the enemy, tripping flares in his stealthy approach, became a good target and was mowed down by the alert Marines.

The operations order issued by General Schmidt for D plus 17 was simple and to the point. Instead of naming phase lines to be reached in the coming day's assault, the VAC commander directed all three divisions "to capture the remainder of the island."[46] For General Rockey's division, these orders meant that the main effort would continue to be made on the right by the 27th Marines, advancing to the northeast coast along the division boundary parallel to the movements of the adjacent 3d Marine Division.

The terrain over which the 27th Marines was to advance featured a series

---

[42] Conner, *The Fifth Marine Division*, p. 101.
[43] VAC OpO 14–45, dtd 6Mar45.
[44] 5th MarDiv D/3 PerRpt No. 17, dtd 7Mar45.

[45] *VAC AirRpt, Encl* A, p. 5.
[46] VAC OpO 15–45, dtd 7Mar45.

of interconnected caves and tunnels. All approaches to these defenses were heavily defended. Colonel Wornham planned to meet this challenge by having trails bulldozed into enemy terrain, over which the infantry could advance into close proximity of the enemy. Once there, Marines could reduce the Japanese fortifications at close range with time proven methods. As added insurance, tanks would support the infantry advance over the newly bulldozed trails.

At the first glint of dawn, prior to the jumpoff of 2/27 scheduled for 0750, Shermans of the 5th Tank Battalion slowly crawled forward from their bivouac area over a previously reconnoitered route. In the rough, unfamiliar terrain, the tanks moved slowly and did not reach the front until 0930. Meanwhile, 2/27 had launched its assault on schedule, but little progress was made until the tanks arrived. The armor immediately commenced cleaning out pillboxes and emplacements, permitting the infantry to move in close to caves in order to seal them. The enemy opposed the Marines with accurate small arms fire, grenades, and mortar fire. Despite this opposition and the heavily mined terrain, elements of 2/27 by 1030 had gained 100 yards. Company E, 2/27, reported killing 75 Japanese during the first two hours.[47]

On the battalion left, Companies D and F attempted an advance without tank support and were soon halted by heavy machine gun and mortar fire. A 15-man crew from Battery B, 13th Marines, manhandled a 75mm pack howitzer and 200 rounds of ammunition close to the lines to provide badly needed fire support. This unorthodox employment of artillery raised the eyebrows of the 1/13 intelligence officer, impelling him to leave this statement for posterity:

> We thought this morning that this battalion had done everything it was possible for an artillery unit to do. We had landed under machine gun, artillery, and mortar fire; gone into position at night; repelled Jap pre-dawn counterattack on D plus 1; fired countless counterbattery missions; had snipers in our position area; participated in regimental missions; fired T.O.T. missions; had our observers on land, on sea, and in the air, and we hauled ammo all night. But today we detached No. 4 Baker and sent it forward to knock off some Jap pillboxes. A report came back that their fire on pillbox was very effective. This was a new twist but the same result—Japs destroyed.[48]

The infantry received additional support from rocket launcher crews who blasted the Japanese in their holes and buried them alive. Despite the punishment doled out to the enemy, neither company made much progress, and gains were limited to less than 100 yards.

In the center of the division line, the 26th Marines failed to make even that much progress. With 1/26 and 3/26 still in the assault, Colonel Graham's men found themselves facing a complex system of pillboxes and interconnected caves among the debris that was all that had remained of Kita Village. In the midst of such forbidding defenses, the regimental attack barely got off the ground and, at the end of another exhausting day, the regiment was still in

---

[47] 2/27 AR, p. 12.

[48] 1/13 G-2 memo, dtd 8Mar45, in *1/13 UJnl*.

substantially the same position it had occupied prior to the jumpoff. A gain of 400 yards laboriously carved out by 1/26 during the day had to be relinquished at dusk because it was untenable.

The 28th Marines on the division left nearly equalled the previous day's advance. Moving along the coast against initially weak enemy resistance, 2/28 actually advanced another 500 yards. Once again, opposition became more stubborn on the regiment's right where 1/28 gained a respectable 300 yards. Both battalions covered the initial 100 yards before serious resistance developed, both from the front and the rear. Within the limitations imposed by the terrain, the attached 75s and 37mm guns of the weapons company supported the regiment, as did the 81mm mortars. Ahead of the advance, naval gunfire attempted to neutralize enemy positions near the coast, while carrier planes struck twice at Hill 165, one of the last significant obstacles separating the 5th Division Marines from the northern shore. For these carrier aircraft, 8 March was the last day of support for the ground forces. Effective 9 March, such close support would become the responsibility of the Army Air Forces.

The violent battle of attrition raging in the craggy terrain of northern Iwo on D plus 17 was to have more than its share of personal drama in the informal setting of war. Tragedy struck within the setting of Company E, 2/27, which in the course of the morning had already scored an advance of 150 yards through engineer-tank-infantry teamwork. Only a jumble of rocks separated the Marines of Company E from the sea, but hidden behind every crag and in every crevice was an enemy determined to block any and all egress by the advancing Marines to the sea just east of Kitano Point.

As bitter close fighting raged in this inaccessible area, one man began to stand out among the rest of Company E. He was 1st Lieutenant Jack Lummus, a former gridiron star at Baylor University, now determined to overcome the final obstacle barring his men from the sea. Rushing forward at the head of his platoon, the lieutenant was knocked down by an exploding grenade. He got to his feet, shook off some of the dust, and rushed an enemy gun emplacement. A second grenade exploded, knocking him down again and shattering his shoulder. Undaunted, the platoon leader got up, rushed a second enemy position and killed all of its occupants. As his men watched, Lummus continued his rush. When he called to his platoon, the men responded, now moving forward with a deadly purpose. As the attack gained momentum, the entire company began to move, hesitantly at first, then with growing speed and assurance.

Lummus was still at the head of his men, viciously slashing at the enemy in his path, when the incredible happened:

> Suddenly he was in the center of a powerful explosion obscured by flying rock and dirt. As it cleared, his men saw him, rising as if in a hole. A land mine had blown off both his legs, the legs that had carried him to All-American football honors at Baylor University. They watched in horror as he stood on the bloody stumps, calling them on. Several men, crying now, ran to him and, for a moment, talked of shooting him to stop his agony.

But he was still shouting for them to move out and the platoon scrambled forward. Their tears turned to rage, they swept an incredible 300 yards over impossible ground, and at nightfall they were on a ridge overlooking the sea. There was no question that the dirty, tired men, cursing and crying and fighting, had done it for Jack Lummus.[49]

Lieutenant Lummus died later that day and was subsequently awarded his country's highest decoration. Even in death his triumph over the enemy and the slaughter that was Iwo Jima was complete. His devotion to duty and personal sacrifice had supplied the impetus for the wild charge.[50] A mixture of love and compassion for their leader, mixed with anger and frustration, had supplied the spark to an explosive mixture which set off a reaction that, for all practical purposes, was the American equivalent of the traditional enemy *banzai* charge.

Throughout D plus 17, tanks of the 5th Tank Battalion supported the infantry assault units as best they could. Tanks of Company B, backing up 2/27, advanced into an important enemy bivouac area replete with ammunition dumps, motor vehicles, and trailers. In the course of this advance, tankers observed at least 100 of the enemy killed, many of them wearing U. S. Marine uniforms.[51] Eleven regular tanks and two flame tanks of Company C, 5th Tank Battalion, moved out in support of 2/28 but soon were unable to keep up with the infantry advance when the engineers, who were checking the road for mines, were pinned down by sniper fire. As a result, tank support was limited to four rounds of 75mm and half a load of flame fuel in this area for the entire day. At about 1300, one platoon with a flame tank was dispatched to the center of the division zone of advance to support 1/26. Even though the area allegedly had been checked by the engineers, two of the tanks hit mines causing considerable damage to both. These tanks had to be abandoned after the guns and radio had been disabled.[52]

As fighting came to a close on the evening of 8 March, the 5th Marine Division had slashed deeply through the enemy lines and was within reach of the northern shore. It had rained intermittently throughout the day and the men were utterly exhausted. However, the enemy was in little better shape, as indicated by the following report submitted by General Kuribayashi on the day's action:

> Troops at "Tamanayama" and Northern Districts are still holding their position thoroughly and continue giving damages to the enemy. Their fighting situation believing their country's victory looks god-like.[53]

Two hours later, the Japanese commander conceded:

> I am very sorry that I have let the enemy occupy one part of the Japanese territory, but am taking comfort in giving heavy damages to the enemy.[54]

On the evening of D plus 17, the 5th Marine Division stood within reach of victory, but more than two weeks of bitter fighting over the island's most

---
[49] Newcomb, *Iwo Jima*, p. 256.
[50] *27th Mar AR*, p. 13.
[51] *Co B, 5th Tk Bn AR*, p. 7.
[52] *Co C, 5th Tk Bn AR*, p. 7.
[53] *Horie Rpt*, 1800, 8Mar45.
[54] *Ibid.*

treacherous terrain in northwestern Iwo would be required before Japanese resistance within the division zone of action was broken. During 9 and 10 March, there was no forward movement, and General Rockey's men, with extreme exertion, were able to extend the division left flank about 40 yards. At this point, the 28th Marines came under intensive fire from the high ground that extended southeast from Kitano Point. This fire brought the drive to the northeast to an abrupt halt in front of a long, low ridgeline overlooking a deep gorge. This canyon was to become the final enemy pocket of resistance on Iwo Jima, where General Kuribayashi and the remnants of his garrison would fight to the bitter end. In the northeastern portion of the island, between Tachiiwa Point and Minami, in the 4th Marine Division sector, a second pocket occupied mostly by naval personnel, would soon become depleted following a reckless *banzai* charge.

By noon of D plus 18, within sight of the sea to the north, General Rockey's Marines still faced an uphill battle in some of the worst ground on Iwo. There, the ridges and gorges were so steep as to be almost impassable even for men on foot. As in more accessible areas, caves and dugouts abounded. This phase of the fighting, in the face of undiminished enemy opposition, is referred to in the official records as "a battle of attrition".[55] For a number of days to come, the advance could be measured in feet instead of yards.

As on the previous day, another human drama, again involving the 27th Marines, was to be enacted in the front lines on 9 March. During the early afternoon, Lieutenant Colonel Duryea, commanding 1/27, and Major Antonelli, commanding the adjacent 2d Battalion, went forward to check their lines. They were headed back to the rear when:

> . . . Duryea called to his runner, who was sitting on a rock, and the youngster replied "I'm coming Colonel." He took one step and was blown to bits. He had set off the detonator of a 6-inch naval shell buried in the ground to catch a tank.
>
> A huge fragment of the shell tore off Duryea's left arm at the elbow and another smashed his left knee. Antonelli fell, blinded by sand. Duryea, still conscious, could not see his left leg, doubled under him and thought he had lost it. Thinking an attack was under way he shouted to the others, "Come here, come here. Don't go away." He tried to roll over to get the pistol under his right hip, but could not.
>
> A captain ran to get corpsmen, and they bundled Duryea and Tony Antonelli into stretchers. Duryea's left leg dangled off the side, and a bullet pierced it, breaking it.[56]

With the two battalion commanders out of commission, the executive officers of the two battalions, Major William H. Tumbelston and Major Gerald F. Russell, assumed command. The detonation had also wounded the company commander and another officer of Company E, as well as the intelligence officer of 2/27. Major Antonelli, despite his eye injuries and a broken eardrum, refused evacuation until he had issued orders for the resumption of the attack. Subsequently, the indomitable battalion

---

[55] *5th MarDiv AR*, p. 26.

[56] Newcomb, *Iwo Jima*, pp. 262–263.

commander walked out of the division hospital and returned to his unit until Colonel Wornham personally ordered him to return to the hospital. The following day, Antonelli was back at the battalion command post, where he remained during the daylight hours for another week until Colonel Wornham requested his evacuation from the island to prevent further injuries.[57]

Aside from routine operations on 9 March, two developments occurred. One was indicative of progress made in developing Iwo Jima as an air base. The other showed to what extent the combat units had been depleted. During the difficult fighting along the north coast, Army Air Forces P-51s went into action for the first time, strafing and bombing the enemy-held gorges in precision attacks that drew admiration from the Marines on the ground.[58] Nevertheless, this impressive air support failed to break enemy resistance or morale, and the results remained inconclusive.

At noon of 9 March, General Rockey decided to bolster the dwindling combat strength of his infantry units by sending personnel from the supporting arms to the front. On the morning of 10 March, 100 men of the 13th Marines joined 3/28 as riflemen. About the same number reinforced 3/26. The 11th Amphibian Tractor Battalion furnished 55 men for 3/27 and slightly more than 100 men from the 5th Motor Transport Battalion joined 1/28.

While the Marines were still able to reinforce their frontline units, such expedient was denied to General Kuribayashi. In the narrow strip of coast separating the 5th Division from the sea, the northern pocket had been compressed into an area less than one square mile in size. Caught in this pocket were General Kuribayashi and his division headquarters, elements of the *2d Battalion* of Colonel Ikeda's *145th Infantry Regiment*, remnants of the *2d Battalion, 17th Independent Mixed Regiment* and a conglomeration of stragglers from other units. Altogether, Japanese Army and Navy strength in northern Iwo came to approximately 1,500 men.[59]

At 0800 on 10 March, the 5th Marine Division continued its attack against enemy opposition that was undiminished in ferocity. On the division left, the 28th Marines made an advance of 200 yards before it was stopped by fire from a ridge running generally southeastward from Kitano Point. The 26th Marines gained roughly 100 yards in almost impossible terrain. The 27th Marines destroyed numerous enemy caves and pillboxes in close-in fighting, but progress was minimal. By the end of D plus 19, after another day of heavy and costly fighting, the lines of the 27th Marines were substantially the same as they had been that morning.

Throughout the day, the 5th Marine Division attack was supported by shore-based and naval gunfire, as well as air

---

[57] Conner, *The Fifth Marine Division*, p. 108.
[58] On 10 March, the VAC air officer reported: "The precision low altitude work of the P-51s was particularly pleasing to the ground troops." *VAC Air Rpt*, Encl A, p. 6.

[59] *Horie Rpt*, p. 10.

strikes. Once again, the effectiveness of this support could not be accurately gauged by the exhausted Marines on the ground. It was obvious by this time that it was becoming increasingly difficult to make effective use of these supporting arms because of the rapidly diminishing area held by the enemy. At the same time, the bombs and heavy gunfire directed in heavy concentrations against a shrinking pocket were bound to hurt the enemy. This is best confirmed by the messages emanating from General Kuribayashi's headquarters on the evening of 10 March. Beginning on a fairly confident note, the Japanese commander reported that, "even though American attacks against our northern districts are continuing day and night, our troops are still fighting bravely and holding their positions thoroughly."[60] Changing to a more plaintive note, General Kuribayashi continued:

> . . . 200 or 300 American infantrymen with several tanks attacked "Tenzan" (northern Iwo in the 5th Division sector) all day. The enemy's bombardments from one battleship (or cruiser), 11 destroyers and aircraft are very severe, especially the bombing and machine gun firing against Divisional Headquarters from 30 fighters and bombers are so fierce that I cannot express nor write here.
>
> Before American forces landed on Iwo Jima, there were many trees around my Headquarters, but now there are not even a grasp of grass remaining. The surface of the earth has changed completely and we can see numerous holes of bombardments.[61]

In its two-week drive up the coast of western Iwo Jima between 25 February and 10 March, General Rockey's division had covered about 3,000 yards from the vicinity of the Central Airfield to a line that ran from west to east across the base of the northern tip of the island. In the course of this advance the division had sustained more than 4,000 casualties.[62]

Indicative of the severity of enemy opposition is the minute number of prisoners taken by D plus 19. Altogetheer VAC had seized 111 prisoners since D-Day. Of this figure, only 67 were Japanese, the remainder consisting of Korean labor troops.[63] At the same time, 8,073 enemy dead had been counted in the 5th Marine Division sector.[64] On the evening of 10 March, no one could guess how much more blood would be shed before the battle for Iwo Jima was over.

---

[60] *Ibid.*, 1930, 10Mar45.

[61] *Ibid.*

[62] These losses consisted of 830 killed in action, 2,974 wounded, 263 died of wounds, 5 missing in action, and 220 cases of combat fatigue, a total of 4,292 casualties.

[63] A breakdown of this total by divisions is as follows: the 3d Marine Division had captured 49; the 4th Marine Division 28, and the 5th Marine Division, 34. Bartley, *Iwo Monograph*, p. 148.

[64] 1/13 G–2 memo, dtd 11Mar45, in *1/13 UJnl.*

CHAPTER 10

The 4th Marine Division Drive on the Right[1]

ADVANCE INTO THE MEAT GRINDER[2]

The first six days of the Iwo Jima operation had taken the 4th Marine Division to the eastern portion of the Central Airfield and Charlie-Dog Ridge, which had been secured at heavy cost on 24 February. As of D plus 6, it became the division's mission to seize and hold that part of Iwo that lay east of the Central Airfield and to the south of Hill 362C. The ruggedness of the terrain over which General Cates' Marines would have to advance equalled or outdid that encountered by the 3d and 5th Marine Divisions.

As might be expected, the enemy had made maximum use of the natural terrain features by digging caves, constructing blockhouses, and tunnelling between ridges until the entire area was honeycombed with defense installations rivaling every other sector on the island. Among a large number of nondescript ridges and canyon-like depressions, the following stood out and formed cornerstones of the main line of defense in the northeastern part of the

---

[1] Unless otherwise noted, the material in this chapter is derived from: *TF 51 AR; VAC AR; VAC G-2 Rpts; VAC C-3 Jnl; VAC C-3 Rpts; VAC NGF and Air Rpts; VAC Translations; 4th MarDiv D-2 PerRpts; 4th MarDiv OpRpt; 4th MarDiv D-3 Jnl; 4th MarDiv D-3 PerRpts; 4th MarDiv D-4 PerRpts; 4th MarDiv OpOs*, Iwo Jima, 24Feb-9Mar45; *4th MarDiv Translations;* 4th MarDiv Dispatch Summaries, Iwo Jima, 19Feb-15Mar45; 4th MarDiv Support Gp OpRpt, Iwo Jima, 28Dec-44-17Mar45, dtd 4Apr45, hereafter *4th MarDiv Support Gp OpRpt;* 1st ProvFldArtyGp G-1 Jnl; *23d Mar OpRpt; 24th Mar OpRpt; 25th Mar UJnl; 25th Mar OpRpt;* 25th Mar Strength and Casualty Rpt, Iwo Jima, 19Feb-26Mar45; 25th Mar R-2 PerRpts, Iwo Jima, 22Feb-16Mar45, hereafter *25th Mar R-2 PerRpts;* 14th Mar WarD, 28Dec44-5Apr45; *14th Mar OpRpt;* 14th Mar R-3 Rpts, 22Feb-14Mar45, hereafter *14th Mar R-3 Rpts; Iwo Comments;* Bartley, *Iwo Monograph;* Morehouse, *Iwo Jima Campaign;* Horie *Rpt;* Morison, *Victory in the Pacific;* Isely and Crowl, *U. S. Marines and Amphibious War;* Newcomb, *Iwo Jima; Newcomb Notes;* Hayashi and Coox, *Kogun;* Henri et al, *Marines on Iwo Jima;* Proehl, *The Fourth Marine Division;* Leckie, *Strong Men Armed.*

[2] Additional material in this section is derived from: 2/14 OpRpt, Iwo Jima, 15Jan-13Mar45, n.d., hereafter *2/14 Op Rpt;* 4th TkBn OpRpt, Iwo Jima, 19Feb-18Mar45, dtd 18Apr45, hereafter *4th TkBn OpRpt;* 1/23 OpRpt, Iwo Jima, 31Dec44-16Mar45, n.d., hereafter *1/23 OpRpt;* 2/23 OpRpt, Iwo Jima, 31Oct44-16Mar45, n.d., hereafter *2/23 OpRpt;* 3/23 OpRpt, Iwo Jima, 18Jan45-16Mar45, dtd 12Apr45, hereafter *3/23 OpRpt;* 1/24 OpRpt, Iwo Jima, 11Feb-18Mar45, dtd 20Apr45, hereafter *1/24 OpRpt;* 2/24 OpRpt, Iwo Jima, 27Oct44-18Mar45, dtd 10Apr45, hereafter *2/24 OpRpt;* 3/24 OpRpt, Iwo Jima, 1Jan45-17Mar45, dtd 20Apr45, hereafter *3/24 OpRpt;* 2/25 OpRpt, Iwo Jima, 13Jan-17Mar45, dtd 16Apr45, hereafter *2/25 OpRpt;* 3/25 OpRpt, Iwo Jima, 22Nov44-17Mar45, n.d., hereafter *3/25 OpRpt;* 2d ArmdPhibBn, Iwo Jima, 10Feb-13Mar45, n.d., hereafter *2d PhibBn OpRpt.*

645

island: Hill 382, just east of the Central Airfield (*Nidan Iwa* to the enemy), situated about 250 yards northeast of the east-west runway. About 600 yards south of Hill 382, just west of the remains of Minami Village, was an unsightly elevation which was to become known as "Turkey Knob." Even though its height was not impressive, it sheltered a large communications center made of reinforced concrete. The top of this hill afforded an unobstructed view of the entire southern portion of the island. To the southwest, the high ground gave way to a depression soon to become infamous as the "Amphitheater."

On the evening of D plus 5, units of the 4th Marine Division held a line, facing east, extending from the Central Airfield southward to the coast to the vicinity of the East Boat Basin. From their lines, the men could see Hill 382, the highest point in northern Iwo, second in size only to Mount Suribachi. The hill was readily identifiable from the remnants of a radar station, where the skeleton of a radio tower pointed starkly skyward. The Japanese had hollowed out a sizable portion of the hill, which was bristling with field pieces and antitank guns. The guns themselves were housed in concrete emplacements, often protected by as many as 10 supporting machine guns. Some of Colonel Nishi's tanks, mounting 47mm and 57mm guns, backed up these formidable defenses.

The concrete blockhouse on Turkey Knob was so soundly constructed as to make it virtually immune to bombing and naval gunfire. The Knob dominated a broad, rocky area of a deceptively innocent appearance, the Amphitheater. Prior to the naval bombardment, this area had been covered by heavy vegetation and resembled a slight depression in rolling terrain. The true extent and cohesiveness of this major enemy defensive area had not as yet revealed itself to the 4th Division Marines. To them, it looked just like a slight hollow in rolling terrain, though in reality "the Amphitheater was a veritable large scale booby trap, containing three tiers of deep prepared positions facing their advance."[3]

The failure of the advancing 4th Division units to be aware of what awaited them on the rocky, cave-studded terrain of northeastern Iwo Jima was not due entirely to a lack of intelligence. Observers had studied the terrain in the zone of advance of the division from battalion observation posts, from a vessel close to the shoreline, and from one of the reconnaissance planes of VMO-4. A detailed intelligence report compiled on the basis of such observation noted:

> The volcanic, crevice lined area is a tangled conglomeration of torn trees and blasted rocks. Ground observation is restricted to small areas. While there are sundry ridges, depressions, and irregularities, most of the crevices of any moment radiate from the direction of Hill 382 to fan out like spokes generally in a southeasterly direction providing a series of cross corridors to our advance and eminently suitable for the enemy's employment of mortars. The general debris caused by our supporting fires provides perfect concealment for snipers and mortar positions. From the air, caves and

---

[3] Morehouse, *Iwo Jima Campaign*, p. 61.

tracks are observed everywhere, but the enemy's camouflage discipline is flawless and it is the rarest occasion that an Aerial Observer can locate troops.[4]

The enemy force charged with the defense of the Meat Grinder, which consisted of Hill 382, Turkey Knob, and the Amphitheater combined, was the *2d Mixed Brigade* under Major General Sadasue Senda. This force consisted of five infantry battalions,[5] an artillery battalion, an engineer battalion, and a field hospital. Prior to D-Day, the *2d Mixed Brigade Engineers* had consolidated the three terrain features into a closely integrated defense system, complete with extensive communications and electric lights. Marines of the 4th Division, preparing to move into northeastern Iwo, faced the most extensive and powerful defenses on the island.

In the course of 25 February, General Cates' men prepared to advance into the eastern bulge of Iwo Jima. Early on D plus 6, the 21st Marines which had been attached to the 4th Division, reverted to General Erskine and the boundary between the 21st and 24th Marines became the left boundary of the 4th Division. At the same time, the 23d Marines reverted from VAC reserve to the 4th Division and prepared to attack after passing through the left of the 24th Marines. Plans for the assault on D plus 6 called for 3/23 to move out with 1/23 following 600 yards behind. The 2d Battalion, 23d Marines, was to

remain in reserve. In the adjacent sector, the 24th Marines, with 2/25 attached, was to continue the advance with 3/24 on the left and 1/24 on the right. The 2d Battalion, 24th Marines, was to become regimental reserve as soon as it had been relieved by 3/23. The 25th Marines, less 2/25, was to remain in division reserve. The division main effort was to be made on the left, where the 23d Marines was to maintain contact with the adjacent 3d Marine Division.

The attack jumped off at 0930. (See Map VII, Map Section). Almost immediately, Colonel Wensinger's 23d Marines, advancing in a column of battalions, encountered heavy mortar and machine gun fire from pillboxes, bunkers, and caves. Progress was accordingly slow. Enemy antitank guns and mines, as well as unfavorable terrain, made it impossible to move armor to the front in the 4th Division zone of advance. The adjacent 3d Division was requested to permit tanks of the 4th Tank Battalion the use of an approach route leading through 3d Division terrain to the Central Airfield. Permission was granted shortly before 1300. Once the Shermans had taken up firing positions along the left boundary of the 23d Marines, they were able to lend effective support to the infantry, destroying antitank weapons, pillboxes, and enemy machine gun emplacements. Once these defenses had been eliminated, an armored bulldozer of the 4th Engineer Battalion was able to clear a route of advance for the tanks in the zone of action of the 23d Marines. Throughout the day, 3/23 continued to meet heavy resistance as it gained a

---

[4] *4th MarDiv D-2 PerRpt* No. 62, dtd 5-Mar45.

[5] *309th, 310th, 311th, 312th,* and *314th Independent Infantry Battalions.*

foothold on the high ground at the northeastern edge of the Central Airfield and pushed eastward along Charlie-Dog Ridge. Heavy and accurate enemy mortar fire that blanketed the runways of the airfield made it extremely difficult for Colonel Wensinger's Marines to maintain contact with the adjacent 9th Marines.

The 24th Marines, with 2/25 attached, made only little progress on 25 February, slowed by difficult terrain, mortar fire, and interlocking bands of fire from automatic weapons in pillboxes, bunkers, and caves. Prior to the jumpoff, artillery, naval gunfire, and carrier aircraft attempted to soften up the Amphitheater and Minami Village. While the air strike was in progress, 81mm mortars fired 200 rounds into this area. Offshore, LVT(A)s of the 2d Armored Amphibian Battalion attempted to support 1/24, but rough seas soon made their withdrawal necessary.

Enemy resistance in front of 3/24 came from the Amphitheater, while 1/24 found its advance contested by strong enemy defenses to its front. Five tanks of Lieutenant Colonel Richard K. Schmidt's 4th Tank Battalion eventually got into position to support the attack, but the rough terrain severely limited the movement of armor. Having gained roughly 100 yards, the two battalions were halted by heavy enemy fire that took a steady toll among officers and men. Among those mortally wounded in the course of the morning was the commander of Company A, 1/24. The battalion intelligence officer was wounded and evacuated.

For the remainder of the afternoon, neither regiment made any significant gains. An air strike against the high ground facing 3/24 in the early afternoon temporarily reduced the volume of the enemy mortar fire and enabled Major Stout's men to move forward a few additional yards. In midafternoon, 2/24, which had spent most of the day in regimental reserve, was ordered to relieve 1/24 on the regiment's right. This relief, ordered at short notice, was executed without casualties.

On the evening of D plus 6, the 4th Marine Division was poised for the attack into the enemy's strongest line of defenses in the division's zone of advance. At this stage, even before the division had launched a direct assault into what came to be called the Meat Grinder, its combat efficiency had already been reduced to an estimated 55 percent by casualties and battle fatigue.[6] Yet General Cates and the men under his command were unflagging in their determination to see the difficult job through. In commenting on the limited gains of 25 February, the division sized up the situation as follows:

> The combination of terrain skillfully employed to the best advantage by the enemy, terrain unsuited for tank employment, the locations of installations in areas which were defiladed from our artillery, and the stubborn fight to-the-death attitude of the defenders had temporarily limited the advance of this Division; but the Division prepared to continue the attack.[7]

At 2200 on D plus 6, the rear command post of the 4th Marine Division closed on the USS *Bayfield*. In the course of the evening, support ships fired night

---

[6] *4th MarDiv OpRpt,* 25Feb45.
[7] *Ibid.*

missions. During the night, there was little activity in the 4th Marine Division sector. A small enemy patrol attempted to infiltrate into the 3/24 area, but all of the Japanese were either killed or dispersed. The enemy fired sporadically into the division sector with rockets, mortars, and artillery.

The 4th Division attack on the morning of 26 February was preceded by a coordinated preparation fired by the corps and division artillery and naval gunfire support ships. Following the shelling, the 4th Marine Division resumed the attack at 0800 with five battalions abreast. Once again, on the division left, Colonel Wensinger's 23d Marines attacked with 1/23 on the left and 3/23 on the right. On the division right, Colonel Lanigan's 25th Marines, which had relieved the 24th Marines earlier that morning, advanced at 0830 with all three battalions. The half hour delay in the jumpoff of the 25th Marines was caused by the necessity of returning 2/25 from 24th Marines' control and moving the battalion to the line of departure.

The division attack encountered the same difficulties that had stymied its progress on 25 February. Enemy resistance from well organized and mutually supporting positions continued undiminished. In front of the 23d Marines, the enemy occupied a maze of pillboxes, bunkers, and caves. All avenues of approach were protected by successive minefields, which made it almost impossible to commit armor in support of the infantry. On the other hand, enemy tanks dug in on the slopes of Hill 382 had a clear field of fire into the advancing Marines. One of the enemy medium tanks, armed with a 57mm gun, occupied a stationary position in a crevice, from where it could fire at will along the entire length of the main runway of the Central Airfield. Three 47mm antitanks guns were emplaced in the northern portion of Charlie-Dog Ridge, which also afforded an unimpeded field of fire at the same runway.

Despite bitter opposition, Colonel Wensinger's Marines continued to push the attack throughout the day. Elements of 1/23, commanded by Lieutenant Colonel Louis B. Blissard, drew heavy and accurate fire not only from Hill 382, but also from the adjacent 3d Division zone, where the enemy still occupied strong positions to the north of the Central Airfield. To the right of 1/23, the 3d Battalion, commanded by Major James S. Scales, met equally heavy fire, but managed to fight its way forward, eliminating well-emplaced and dug-in pillboxes and blockhouses through the use of flamethrowers, rockets, and demolition teams.

By late afternoon, the 23d Marines had gained about 300 yards and seized the southwest slopes of Hill 382. This advance partially denied the use of this vital hill to the enemy. At 1700, the regiment was ordered to consolidate, but one hour later Major Scales' men were still engaged in close combat with the enemy and vicious fighting at close quarters continued until well into the evening. In addition to receiving fire from the front and flanks, the Marines occupying precarious positions on the slopes of Hill 382 also drew scattered sniper fire from the rear, which did little to ease the minds of the exposed Marines. When heavy enemy mortar and rocket fire began to hit the southwestern slopes in the afternoon, it became necessary to withdraw all units to the foot of Hill 382.

The 25th Marines was to find the going equally rough on D plus 7. Following a rolling artillery barrage, Colonel Lanigan's regiment, with 3/24 attached, jumped off with 1/25, under Major Fenton J. Mee on the left, 2/25 under Lieutenant Colonel James Taul in the center, and 3/25 commanded by Captain James C. Headley, on the right.

Initially, the advance of 1/25 and 3/24 into the Amphitheater proceeded slowly but steadily against enemy small arms fire. After an advance of about 150 yards, the terrain became extremely difficult. At the same time, Japanese machine guns and mortars unleashed such a deluge of fire from well prepared and camouflaged positions near Minami Village that the men were effectively pinned down. Tanks of Company A, 4th Tank Battalion, attempted to reduce enemy pressure on the infantry but succeeded only in drawing additional artillery and mortar fire which resulted in the destruction of two Shermans just east of the airfield. In the jumbled terrain, artillery forward observers were unable to direct effective counterbattery fire against the enemy. Two spotter aircraft from VMO-4, which had just reached the island, made an attempt to spot the bothersome enemy mortar and artillery positions from the air, but this effort was also unsuccessful due to skillful enemy camouflage.

With the left and center of the 25th Marines pinned down, Company C of 1/25 made an attempt at 1400 to send a platoon, supported by three Shermans, around the right flank to envelop enemy defenses on Turkey Knob. This attempt ended in dismal failure when the Japanese became aware of the maneuver and shifted their mortar fire. The barrage caught the men out in the open and killed several, including the platoon leader. The survivors of this ill-fated platoon were able to withdraw only under cover of a smoke screen.

Along the division right flank, 3/25 made a slow but steady advance against heavy machine gun and rifle fire from the high ground on the left and caves and pillboxes to the front. As Company L slowly moved forward, Company I, supported by two medium tanks and by LVT(A)s offshore, was systematically mopping up near the East Boat Basin. In the wake of Company L's advance followed Company K, using demolition charges and flamethrowers on every position that might possibly shelter enemy troops that had been bypassed.

As D plus 7, 26 February, came to a close, the 4th Marine Division held a very irregular line somewhat resembling the wings of a seagull. On the left, the 23d Marines had gained roughly 200 yards. In the center of the division line, where 1/25 was directly in front of Turkey Knob and the Amphitheater, gains were at best 75 yards. The most progress for the day had been made by 3/25 on the right which by late afternoon had seized a line of cliffs east of the East Boat Basin for an overall gain of nearly 500 yards. One more accomplishment accrued to 3/25: in mopping up the area near the East Boat Basin, the battalion wiped out the last nest of snipers that had interfered with shore party activities on the beaches below. Even though the unloading was still carried on under the muzzles of the enemy artillery and rockets from northern Iwo still were capable of hitting any point on the island, at least the bothersome sniper fire had been eliminated.

The 4th Marine Division intelligence report for D plus 7 outlined the severity of the resistance that the division had encountered, particularly in front of Hill 382 and Turkey Knob, and noted "that the enemy is now fighting to the death in pillboxes, foxholes, and trenches ... and is not retreating as he apparently formerly had done."[8]

The enemy unit to which this report referred was the *309th Independent Infantry Battalion*. On D-Day, this battalion had been stationed near the Southern Airfield and since then it had fought a delaying action, gradually withdrawing northeastward under superior pressure. On D plus 7, the attack by the 23d Marines had severely mauled the battalion and pushed it southeastward, where it found itself in the path of the 25th Marines' advance. As a result, when the day ended, the battalion had been for all practical purposes annnihilated.

After a day of exhausting action, 4th Division Marines were in for a restless night. Enemy mortars and artillery kept both the division's front and rear areas under steady fire, paying special attention to the division artillery positions. Beyond any doubt, the accuracy of the enemy fire was aided by bright moonlight which emerged after an afternoon of intermittent rain. Less accurate, but equally disturbing to the peace of mind of 4th Division Marines, were the huge rockets wobbling over their positions and exploding far to their rear. In the midst of this bedlam, there was small arms fire from the enemy side.

Small groups of Japanese attempted to infiltrate all along the division perimeter. Around 0530, the sound of tank engines was heard in front of the 23d Marines and there were indications that the enemy was preparing to counterattack. An artillery preparation into the presumed enemy assembly area restored silence. Offshore, support ships furnished harassing fires and illumination. Aside from the enemy probes, no major attack developed and it was assumed that the artillery barrage had dispersed the possible counterattack. Indicative of the bitterness of the action that continued through the long night is the fact that in the area in front of 1/25 alone, 103 enemy dead were counted after daybreak.[9]

Dawn on 27 February, D plus 8, marked the beginning of the second day of the concerted 4th Division assault into the Meat Grinder. The lineup of units for the attack was substantially the same as on the previous day. From left to right, the five battalions committed were 1/23 and 3/23, and all three battalions of the 25th Marines. The 24th Marines, except for the 3d Battalion which was still attached to the 25th Marines, continued in regimental reserve.

The assault was preceded by a 45-minute preparation of the corps and division artillery. Even though, at this

---

[8] *4th MarDiv D-2 PerRpt*, 26Feb45.

[9] *25th Mar OpRpt*, p. 8.

particular time, the corps artillery was giving priority to supporting General Erskine's 3d Division, Colonel Letcher, commanding the 1st Provisional Field Artillery Group, ordered his 155mm howitzers to expend 300 rounds as part of the preparation. For the remainder of the day, the corps artillery was authorized to fire up to 25 percent of the general support missions for General Cates' division. The 4th Division objective for D plus 8 was capture of Hill 382 and advance to the 0-2 Line.

Following a thunderous artillery preparation, the 4th Division attacked at 0800. On the division left, the two battalions of the 23d Marines resumed the assault on Hill 382. While 1/23 attacked northeastward in order to envelop the hill from the north, the 3d Battalion resumed the assault up the southwestern slopes. Since the Japanese atop the hill enjoyed a perfect view of the American lines, smoke was employed to screen the reorganization and movement of frontline companies in the 3d Battalion area. The enemy was not deceived, however, and almost immediately, the advancing Marines came under such severe fire that forward movement was all but impossible. Nevertheless, throughout the morning, 3/23 launched repeated assaults up the southwestern slopes of the hill without making any substantial headway. Strong and determined enemy resistance from the high ground effectively pinned Major Scales' men down. Two of Colonel Nishi's tanks, emplaced in the recesses of Hill 382, further added to the volume of the enemy fire. A new technique resorted to by the Japanese at this time was firing rifle grenades in volleys, which took a further toll of casualties among the exposed Marines.

By noon, the Japanese were still fully in control of the hill. The 1st Battalion, 23d Marines. was slowly gaining ground to the northwest of Hill 382. Once he had bypassed the objective from the north, Lieutenant Colonel Blissard, the battalion commander, planned to attack up the reverse slope. Both battalions, but especially 3/23, had sustained losses that had reduced them to little more than company strength; some of the companies had shrunk to platoon size. Nevertheless, the assault continued. In order to assist 3/23 in its frontal assault, 2/14 fired a 30-minute preparation beginning at noon, against Hill 382. Following this barrage, the exhausted men of 3/23 jumped off. This time, some progress was made, as Marines threw grenades and satchel charges into the caves and other strongpoints still held by the obstinate defenders. Once the Marines had advanced within striking distance of the two tanks, they were able to finish them off with bazooka fire. Slowly and painfully, the assault force fought its way up the hill.

Additional support for Major Scales' men arrived in two forms. First, shortly after 1400, Lieutenant Colonel Blissard's battalion, having bypassed the hill, commenced an attack up the reverse slope. Secondly, almost at the same time, engineers with a tank dozer began to carve out a path over which some of the Shermans could come within striking distance. Once they had gone into position, the supporting tanks took the

Japanese on the higher reaches of Hill 382 under effective fire. This badly needed support, arriving at a crucial time, reversed the situation. The Japanese on the hill found themselves virtually cut off. The deadly fire of the Shermans forced them to stay under cover. As Major Scales' men approached the top of the hill, they discovered that the top had been hollowed out and that it contained a solid wall of artillery and antitank gun positions.

Here, among the ruins of the radar station, the men of 3/23 came to grips with the Japanese in vicious close combat in which no quarter was asked or given. Just when it appeared that the Japanese would be driven off, a heavy artillery and mortar barrage hit the advancing Marines. With darkness approaching, 3/23 still had not gained a solid foothold on top of Hill 382, and rather than risk an envelopment during the night, 3/23 was ordered to consolidate on ground that would permit solid contact with adjacent units to the left and the right. As a result, Major Scales' men withdrew from the hill and spent the night in practically the same positions from which they had launched their attack on the morning of D plus 8.

Progress on 27 February was little better to the right of the 23d Marines, where the 25th Marines, with 3/24 attached, jumped off at 0800. On the regimental left, the advance of 1/25 hinged on the progress made by 3/23. If the latter succeeded in seizing the crest of Hill 382, 1/25 was to advance north through part of the 3/23 zone of attack, then pivot southeastward to envelop Turkey Knob while 2/25 was to attempt an envelopment from the south. When it became evident by 1500 that the advance of 3/23 was progressing much more slowly than anticipated, Major Fenton J. Mee, commanding 1/25, ordered the battalion forward, even though Hill 382 still had not been taken. The attack, supported by tanks and preceded by a rocket barrage, initially gained 150 yards across open terrain but came to a halt before cover on the far side could be reached when heavy mortar and antitank fire, as well as intense machine gun fire, hit the assault force. In addition to inflicting heavy casualties on the infantrymen, the Japanese also succeeded in putting two of the three tanks supporting the attack out of action and damaging the third. Shortly after 1700, it had to be conceded that the commanding ground which formed the day's objective could not be reached before nightfall, and the battalion pulled back to its jumpoff positions.

In the regimental center and on the right, 2/25 and 3/25, attacking due east gained between 200 and 300 yards. After having reached ground that was favorable for night defense, both battalions were ordered at 1600 to halt for the day. Since it was still considered possible that the enemy might attempt a flanking attack from the sea, elements of 3/25 were held in reserve near the East Boat Basin with the specific mission of defending that area against any further attack from the ocean.

As D plus 8 ended, an analysis of the progress made that day showed clearly that the gains made were minimal. Summing up the situation at Hill 382, the 4th Division noted with some disgust that "it was envisaged that the capture of this terrain freak would be a costly and a time-consuming job."[10]

THE BATTLE OF ATTRITION[11]

For 4th Division Marines, the night from 27-28 February proved to be a restless one. Throughout the darkness, both the front and rear areas came under heavy mortar fire. For a while it appeared that the enemy had singled out the division command post for special punishment, and no less than 15 heavy shells hit the CP prior to 2200.[12] At the same time, the enemy fired on the beach area with either 20mm or 40mm automatic weapons. Offshore, ships of Task Force 54 furnished normal harassing and illumination fires. The enemy probed various sectors in the 4th Marine Division lines, but no counterattack developed.

Shortly before 0100, the 23d Marines reported that enemy cargo parachutes were dropping into the enemy lines about 400 to 600 yards ahead of them. Strangely enough, none of the enemy planes had been picked up by the American radar on and around Iwo Jima. Nevertheless, the visual sightings were sufficient to spur American artillery into vigorous action. Concentrated artillery and naval gunfire into the drop zone,

---

[10] *4th MarDiv OpRpt*, p. 25.

[11] Additional material in this section is derived from: 1/14 OpRpt, Iwo Jima, 27Jan-15Mar45, dtd 27Mar45, hereafter *1/14 OpRpt;* 3/14 OpRpt, Iwo Jima, 13Jan-13Mar45, dtd 27Mar45, hereafter *3/14 OpRpt;* 1/25 OpRpt, Iwo Jima, 27Dec44-17Mar45, dtd 19Apr45, hereafter *1/25 OpRpt;* 1st JASCO OpRpt, Iwo Jima, 24Aug44-18Mar45, hereafter *1st JASCO OpRpt.*

[12] *4th MarDiv OpRpt*, p. 26.

though unobserved, was expected to have resulted in the destruction of most of the supplies that had been airlifted to General Senda's *2d Mixed Brigade*, elements of which were still holding the crest of Hill 382. The cargo received by the Japanese that night consisted of medical supplies and ammunition, dropped with paper parachutes from planes based elsewhere in the Bonins. Some of these supplies, still attached to the flimsy parachutes, were recovered several days later when Marines entered the drop zone.

Objectives for the continuation of the attack on the last day of February, D plus 9, remained unchanged though some of the regimental boundaries within the 4th Division underwent a slight change. On the left, the 23d Marines was to continue the assault on Hill 382; in the center, 1/25 and 2/25 were to continue their envelopment of Turkey Knob, while 3/25 along the coast was to advance to the 0-2 Line.

At 0815, following a 45-minute artillery preparation, the assault battalions of the 4th Marine Division jumped off. On the left, the 23d Marines, reinforced with one company of the 24th Marines, resumed the attack with 1/23 on the left and 2/23 on the right after the latter battalion had relieved 3/23. The 2d Battalion, under Major Robert H. Davidson, attempted an advance into the area between Hill 382 and Turkey Knob, while 1/23 again assaulted the hill from the east. Following the jumpoff, 2/23 advanced about 200 yards before it came under increasingly heavy mortar and automatic weapons fire from concealed bunkers and pillboxes. The 1st Battalion likewise drew fire from automatic weapons and mortars, which brought its advance to a virtual standstill. The 3d Battalion spent most of the morning reorganizing and did not start its push up the southwestern slopes of Hill 382 until later in the afternoon.

As a result, the only battalion of the 23d Marines to make any appreciable gains in the course of the morning was 2/23. At 1300, following a 10-minute preparation, 1/23 launched a coordinated attack with the 21st Marines of the adjacent 3d Marine Division. This joint venture resulted in a 300-yard advance of 1/23 near the division boundary. Other elements of 1/23, attacking Hill 382 from the east, destroyed two of Colonel Nishi's dug-in tanks and continued the ascent to a point where they could take the enemy on top of the hill under fire. By midafternoon, Hill 382 was virtually surrounded; the noose around the Japanese was further tightened when two companies of 3/23 were committed to reinforce the lines of the two assault battalions.

Despite the punishment he was taking, the enemy atop Hill 382 continued to fight as if nothing out of the ordinary were happening around him. In addition to resistance coming from the hill itself, the Marines of the encircling force drew heavy mortar, rocket, and artillery fire from enemy positions hidden in the jumbled rocks to the east of the hill. Behind the American lines, the supporting weapons did all they could to support the attack of the infantry against Hill 382. In addition to firing preparations before the jumpoff, the 14th Marines shelled the area ahead of the infantry in an attempt to silence enemy small arms and automatic weapons. Corps and division observers teamed up in an effort to pinpoint as many as possible of the cleverly hidden enemy mortar, artillery, and rocket positions, a slow and time-consuming process that did not always produce immediate results.

The difficult terrain, combined with Japanese expertise in mining the approaches to the front lines and the excellent marksmanship of the enemy antitank gun crews, severely curtailed the use of tanks in close support of the infantry. Nevertheless, individual tanks were able to move forward to deliver overhead fire, which was helpful but still lacked the volume necessary to be really effective. Finally, it was decided that the 4.5-inch rockets of the 1st Provisional Rocket Detachment might provide the massed firepower needed. Initially, whenever the rocket trucks went into action, they invariably attracted immediate counterbattery fire from the enemy entrenched on the dominating heights blessed with the advantage of unlimited observation. In order to compete effectively at such a disadvantage, the rocket launcher crews employed hit-and-run tactics. Rocket trucks would whip into position, fire their launchers, and take off to pre-designated assembly points in the rear with all possible speed. If a particularly intensive barrage was desired, six trucks and launchers would fire once, reload with rockets carried on the vehicles, fire a second salvo, and then head for the rear. In this way, a double ripple of 432 rounds could be delivered in somewhat less than five minutes.[13]

---

[13] *4th MarDiv OpRpt*, Anx C, p. 27.

By late afternoon of 28 February, it became evident that despite the deteriorating situation of enemy troops on the crest of Hill 382, capture of this objective would not be completed in the remaining hours of daylight. As a result, the 23d Marines remained active well into the night in an attempt to consolidate its lines for night defense. The 1st Battalion, in particular, found it extremely difficult to close the gap on the left with the 21st Marines. This was finally accomplished under sniper fire from enemy pockets that has been bypassed in the adjacent 21st Marines' zone of advance during the day. Gains made by the 23d Marines on D plus 9 totalled about 300 yards on the left and 200 yards on the right.

As Colonel Wensinger's regiment vainly struggled to complete the capture of Hill 382 on D plus 9, the adjacent 25th Marines faced its own ordeal in its drive to seize Turkey Knob, the Amphitheater, and the area separating the Knob from the east coast. At 0815, the regiment, with 3/24 attached, jumped off in the same formation it had maintained on the previous day. Two companies of the 1st Battalion, plus one company of 3/24, were to attempt an envelopment of Turkey Knob from the north, while another company was to advance along the low ground southwest of the Knob and attack eastward around the Amphitheater until it could link up with the northern pincers.

Following the usual preparation, elements of the 1st Battalion moved into the wooded area just north of Turkey Knob and advanced some 50 yards. At this point, the enemy unleashed a tremendous mortar and artillery barrage; heavy machine gun fire from the front and the left flank began to rake the Marines. Prompt counterbattery fire called for by observers with the 1st Battalion failed to silence the enemy batteries. By noon, the situation of 1/25 in the woods had become critical and the battalion was suffering heavy casualties. Nevertheless, Major Mee, the battalion commander, ordered his men to hold the woods in order to enable the southern pincers to complete the envelopment of Turkey Knob. As Company B, which was to make the envelopment, started its encircling movement, supported by two Shermans, the enemy on the high ground east of the objective started to shower the force with hand grenades, at the same time raking them with accurate machine gun fire. One of the tanks soon hit a mine and was disabled; the other managed to pull back.

At the fury of the enemy fire increased and casualties mounted, the attack of Company B stalled. By 1645 it was readily apparent that continuation of the attack in the face of such heavy enemy resistance during the limited daylight remaining would serve no useful purpose, and both pincers of 1/25 pulled back to their respective starting positions. In the fading daylight, two tanks made their way forward to a point northwest of Turkey Knob and from this vantage point opened fire against the enemy communications center atop the hill. The 75mm shells, to all appearances, did little damage to the concrete structure and the shelling was ineffective.

To the right of 1/25, the 2d Battalion attempted to extend its left flank to support the advance of the southern pincers of 1/25. To this end, it had to seize the high ground directly to its front. Enemy fire, most of it coming from pillboxes to the left of the battalion zone of advance, pinned down the infantry. The difficult terrain made it impossible for the Shermans and half-tracks to give close support to the infantry. The attack soon stalled. At noon, the battalion commander, Lieutenant Colonel Taul, decided to improvise in order to get the attack moving again. He requested and received permission to have a 75mm pack howitzer rushed forward, to be used as a direct assault weapon. A DUKW was used to transport the howitzer to a position just behind the front lines. There, the gun was dismantled and the various pieces were gingerly hand-carried into the zone of advance of 2/25, where the piece was carefully reassembled. Once this feat had been accomplished, the pack howitzer pumped 40 rounds at the concrete structure atop Turkey Knob. Most of the shells bounced harmlessly off the thick concrete walls and did little, if any, damage to the communications center. However, it was not altogether a wasted effort for the battalion reported that while "the direct result to the enemy was not readily apparent, the morale effect on the men of this battalion was of considerable value because after the howitzer was fired our lines advanced approximately 75 yards by 1900."[14] Two hours later, under cover of darkness, the pack howitzer was again disassembled and returned to its parent organization.

On the right of the 25th Marines' zone of advance, 3/25 jumped off on the morning of D plus 9 at the same time as the other battalions of the division. Moving eastward roughly parallel to the east coast, the battalion had gained about 100 yards by 1000. At that time, the advance of the adjacent 2d Battalion began to bog down, and 3/25, which was pacing itself by the progress of the unit on its left, also halted the attack. Since 2/25 on the left failed to make any further progress for the day, neither did 3/25. At 1800, units of the 25th Marines were ordered to consolidate for the night.

In summing up the results of the day's operations, the 4th Marine Division felt that, even though the enemy was still clinging to the crest of Hill 382 and Turkey Knob, the day's limited advance had outflanked these enemy strongpoints. The feeling was that 4th Division Marines could henceforth bypass the Amphitheater and continue the drive along the east coast of Iwo Jima. Despite the small gains made on D plus 9, the division intelligence officer felt that the central defensive core of resistance had been cracked. He affirmed the possibility of an enemy counterattack, but assumed that the Japanese would be least likely to mount any major counterattack in the zone of action of the 4th Division because of the difficult terrain.[15] Events were to prove this forecast only 50 percent correct.

Throughout 28 February, the assault battalions had received a variety of assistance from the supporting arms. Off-

---

[14] 2/25 OpRpt, p. 8.

[15] 4th MarDiv D-2 PerRpt No. 57, dtd 28-Feb45.

shore, gunfire support ships furnished call-fire missions, while smaller craft fired mortars in support of 2/25 and 3/25. During the afternoon a destroyer approached the east shore and began shelling enemy positions on the high ground in front of the 2/25 zone of advance. Air support extended to the entire 4th Division sector, though half of the napalm bombs dropped in front of the 25th Marines in the course of the morning failed to ignite. A second strike, this time in support of the 23d Marines, took unduly long to be executed. When the aircraft did arrive, they went into action against the wrong target area.[16]

The night from D plus 9 to D plus 10 turned out to be another restless one for Marines of the 4th Division. The enemy concentrated his artillery fire against rear installations of the 5th Marine Division and scored several lucky hits on the ammunition dumps of that division. The resulting explosions coming from the rear did little to reassure the men of any of the three divisions. Some enemy mortar and artillery fire also fell in the 4th Division area, causing further disruption of sleep. Alert Marines of 3/23 frustrated several enemy attempts to infiltrate their lines, and 29 enemy dead were found in front of the lines on the following morning. Around 2200, the 25th Marines noticed that the enemy in company strength was massing for a counter attack near the coast in the 3/25 area. Naval gunfire and shore-based artillery promptly fired on and dispersed this assembly.

[16] *4th MarDiv D-3 PerRpt* No. 55, dtd 28-Feb45.

Division orders for 1 March called for continuation of the attack against Hill 382 and Turkey Knob. Beginning at 0530, the 24th Marines was to relieve the depleted units of the 23d, with 2/24 relieving 1/23 and 1/24 taking over the 2/23 sector.[17] The relief was completed by 0630 without major incident and, following a 45-minute naval gunfire and corps artillery preparation, the attack against the key enemy defenses resumed. For 10 minutes prior to H-Hour, set for 0830, the division artillery blasted enemy positions in the division zone of advance.

On the division left, the 24th Marines jumped off, with the 2d Battalion, commanded by Lieutenant Colonel Richard Rothwell on the left and 1/24, under Major Paul S. Treitel, on the right. Almost immediately, 2/24 was hit by heavy artillery and mortar fire. In order to keep his battalion from getting bogged down, Lieutenant Colonel Rothwell requested supporting fire. Shortly after 0930, carrier aircraft dropped napalm about 600 yards in front of 2/24. The aerial assault was followed within the hour by a fire concentration against the same area by the corps artillery; this fire was followed by naval gunfire. This counterfire had a salutary effect and enemy opposition diminished to the extent that elements of the battalion, in the course of the afternoon, were able to make gains of 150 yards.

While part of 2/24, notably Company F, was engaged in attacking northeastward along the boundary with the 3d Marine Division, at times even cross-

[17] 4th MarDiv OpO 10-45, dtd 28Feb45.

ing the boundary, the gains made by General Erskine's men on 1 March exceeded those of the 4th Division and, in consequence, a gap developed along the boundary. Colonel Walter I. Jordan, commanding the 24th Marines, at 1430 had to commit two companies of 3/24 into the gap in order to regain contact with the 3d Division along the left flank.

Somewhat farther to the south, the battle for Hill 382 continued with undiminished fury. The reduction of the battered strongpoint fell to Company G, 2/24, which assaulted the hill with flamethrowers, bazookas, grenades, and whatever else was at hand. Just as elements of the 23d Marines had previously fought their way to the top to engage in close combat with the defenders, only to be driven off, so it was with the determined Marines of Company G, 2/24. The viciousness of the fighting that ensued has been depicted in these words:

> At one time, Company G of 2/24 was astride the top, but still there was no quarter. The attackers fought with rifles and grenades, with flamethrowers and satchel charges. Still the defenders would not give up, even though their own fire fell on them from the ridges further east. These were the men from Kumamoto in Kyushu, a historic battlefield of the 1877 Civil War, and they would not give up. Not even when Major Kenro Anso died, burned from head to foot by a flamethrower. He led the 3d Battalion, 145th Regiment, in defense of the hill. So great was his inspiration that at his death he was promoted two full ranks to colonel.[18]

As the afternoon wore on, the battle for control of the hill continued without letup. While hand grenades flew back and forth, assault squads were blowing cave entrances, and flamethrowers were incinerating such Japanese as showed themselves. Lieutenant Colonel Rothwell, escorted by his company commanders, appeared on the scene in order to conduct a personal reconnaissance, select positions for the coming night, and make plans for the attack on D plus 11. Despite heavy fire that was coming from nearly every direction, the reconnaissance party completed its inspection and the battalion commander left the hill unscathed. As the day ended, the remnants of Major Anso's battalion clung to the crest of Hill 382, still full of fighting spirit despite the loss of their commander.

Along the southern slopes of the hill and near its base to the southeast, the fighting on D plus 10 waxed just as bitterly as it did at the top. Here, 1/24 was attempting an envelopment of Hill 382 from the south against heavy fire coming not only from the top of the hill but also from a patch of woods directly in front and the high ground beyond. As men of the 1st Battalion inched ahead, two tanks attached to Company C provided covering fire. Just before noon, the company commander was wounded and casualties mounted to a point where smoke had to be employed to screen evacuation of the wounded.

Following a heavy artillery and mortar concentration, and led by a new commander, Company C resumed the attack at 1300. Within minutes, the new commander was wounded and had to be replaced. Despite all enemy opposition, the company continued its dogged advance and by 1700, when it began to

---
[18] Newcomb, *Iwo Jima*, p. 212.

consolidate its positions, it had seized some of the high ground to the southeast of Hill 382.

The biggest gains for the 24th Marines on D plus 10 were to accrue along the 4th Division boundary, where 2/24 made an advance of 400 yards to the east. To the right, the dogged attack of 1/24 to the high ground southeast of Hill 382 culminated in a gain of 200 yards. This forward movement, flanking Hill 382 from two sides, all but surrounded the enemy atop the hill, though this made little, if any, difference to Japanese determined to die there. Of added importance to the further advance of the 24th Marines was the fact that from the high ground southeast of Hill 382, Company C was able to look down on the ruins of Minami Village. Thus it appeared that the day's advance had served not only to outflank most of Hill 382, but a portion of Turkey Knob and the Amphitheater as well.

To the south, the 25th Marines, attacking in the same formation employed in previous days, also was in for a hard day's work. The regiment's plan was ambitious: to execute a double envelopment of Turkey Knob, supported by two companies of 3/23 which relieved elements of 3/24 that had been attached to 1/25 for the past two days. As the 1st Battalion moved out, supported by the companies of 3/23, it crossed an open area prior to entering the woods to its front. Upon reaching the edge of the woods around 1000, 1/25 encountered the same conditions that had halted the advance on the previous day. Once again, Major Mee's men were hit by heavy mortar, artillery, and machine gun fire, which caused the advance to bog down. Despite counterbattery fire and aerial spotting, it proved impossible to put the enemy mortars out of action, nor were the aerial observers able to spot to the cleverly concealed enemy artillery positions.

Fighting for the woods raged throughout 1 March, as Marines of 1/25 pressed the attack. It was an unequal contest with the enemy possessing the advantage of cover, concealment, commanding terrain, and superior fire power. In the end, the assault units of 1/25 had to pull back to their jump-off positions. As the tired men began their withdrawal the enemy, in a final gesture of defiance, subjected them to a heavy mortar and rocket barrage, which caused additional casualties. The withdrawal was accomplished with the help of a smoke screen, which also made it possible to evacuate the casualties. Shortly after 1600, the Japanese added insult to injury by subjecting Colonel Lanigan's command post to a severe shelling.

Since the remaining two battalions of the 25th Marines were pacing themselves in relation to gains to be made by the 1st Battalion, they remained more or less in place when it became apparent that the attack of 1/25 had bogged down. Nevertheless, 2/25 did succeed in gaining 100 yards along its left. For the most of the day, the division reconnaissance company was attached to 2/25 in order to mop up the rear area. From the 3/25 area, a tank was able to destroy two enemy machine guns, but no additional ground was taken. Indicative of the artillery support furnished to the 25th Marines by 1/14 on D plus 10 are the following figures. The battalion fired 4,640 rounds for 135 missions, of which 94 were harassing, 31 were aimed at targets of opportunity, 6 were for preparation, and 4 were fired at miscellaneous targets.[19] The figures listed above do not include the defensive fires, which 1/14 started at 1640, and harassing fires which continued throughout the night.

As D plus 10 came to a close, the 4th Marine Division could book only very limited gains for itself. After five days of continuous assault into the Meat Grinder, all three of the mutually supporting cornerstones of the enemy defense system, Hill 382, Turkey Knob, and the Amphitheater were still in enemy hands, and, with the exception of Hill 382, firmly so. With the heaviest assaults still ahead, the combat efficiency of the 4th Division on the evening of 1 March remained at 55 percent.[20]

The night from 1-2 March passed with few untoward incidents, except in front of 2/24, where small groups of the enemy made various attempts at infiltration, keeping the battalion in a general state of unrest. All of the 4th Division units came under sporadic enemy mortar and artillery fire that hit the lines and rear area in a seemingly haphazard fashion. By way of response, the corps and division artillery replied to each enemy salvo with immediate counterbattery fire, the results of which could not be readily determined.

Early on 2 March, General Cates' division again resumed the battle of attrition in the Meat Grinder. Though none of the weary 4th Division Marines was aware of it that morning, the final battle for the Meat Grinder was about to begin. The main effort was to be made by the 24th Marines against Hill 382, while farther south the 23d and 25th Marines were to assault the Amphitheater and Turkey Knob from the north and south. If the heavy enemy fire against Hill 382 from these two staunch bastions of the enemy defense system could be eliminated, the hill itself could be taken.

Following a 25-minute artillery preparation fired by the corps artillery from H-Hour minus 30 to minus 15, and again from minus 10 to H-Hour, the assault resumed. On the morning of D plus 11, there was one change in the preparatory fires. Precisely at H-Hour, 0800, the division artillery unleashed an intensive preparation, followed by a rolling barrage.

On the division left, the 24th Marines with 3/24 on the right, 2/24 in the center, and 1/24 on the left moved out for the attack. The 3d Battalion, commanded by Major Doyle A. Stout, advanced eastward along the division boundary northeast of Hill 382 and, while keeping contact with 3d Division elements on its left, advanced about 300 yards. As the battalion fought its way forward, enemy opposition stiffened until all further movement became impossible.

It was in the regiment's center and on its right that the most desperate fighting for the day was to occur. It

---
[19] *1/14 OpRpt*, p. 16, dtd 1Mar45.
[20] *4th MarDiv OpRpt*, p. 30.

fell to 2/24 to launch an assault against Hill 382 from the northeast, while 1/24 enveloped the hill from the south. At the time they jumped off, the men of 2/24 had spent an even more restless night than had other units in the division. The front lines on Hill 382 had been active throughout the night. Hand grenade duels and hand-to-hand fighting frequently erupted with small groups of the enemy that filtered out of recesses in the hill in front of the Marine positions, between them, and even to the rear. In fact, two Marines had received saber cuts during the nocturnal fighting.[21] Nevertheless, the battalion attacked Hill 382 with vigor, even though it was immediately subjected to heavy machine gun, rifle, mortar, and artillery fire. Since Lieutenant Colonel Rothwell's men constituted the main effort, four Shermans and a section of the 1st Provisional Rocket Detachment furnished support, in addition to the division artillery. As the tanks and rocket launchers blasted the area ahead of 2/24 with shells and flame, they were spotted by the enemy and taken under such heavy fire that the armor had to pull back. The rocket launchers were able to fire three missions before they, too, had to be withdrawn.

By 1100, the frontal assault on Hill 382 was beginning to bog down in the face of interlocking enemy machine gun fire, as well as heavy mortar fire. The importance that the Japanese attached to the defense of the hill was underscored not only by the severity of the mortar fire but also by the unusually large caliber of mortar shells employed. As elsewhere on Iwo Jima, the artillery and naval gunfire furnished in support of the attack was of little benefit to the infantrymen slowly inching their way up the reverse slope of Hill 382, exposed to everything the enemy was capable of throwing at them with little else but their own organic weapons to answer.

As the attack was on the verge of bogging down, Lieutenant Colonel Rothwell assembled his company commanders a short distance behind the lines and decided that one platoon of Company E, accompanied by two tanks, was to make an attempt to outflank the stubborn enemy defenders from the right. At this time, a platoon of Company E, commanded by 2d Lieutenant Richard Reich, had already reached the top of the hill and was locked in close combat with the enemy underneath the radar antenna at the same spot which already had seen vicious close fighting when the 23d Marines was attempting to seize the hill. As Major Roland Carey, commanding Company E, attempted to relay the orders for the flanking movement to his men, he was hit by machine gun fire and had to be evacuated. The executive officer, Captain Pat Donlan, took over and prepared to see that his predecessor's orders were carried out.

Just as Captain Donlan was in the process of orienting his platoon leaders and issuing orders for the flanking movement at the battalion command post, he was hit by a fragment of a mortar shell exploding nearby. As one of the platoon leaders, 1st Lieutenant Stanley Osborne, prepared to relieve

---

[21] *2/24 AR*, p. 16.

THE 4TH MARINE DIVISION DRIVE ON THE RIGHT 663

him, another large mortar shell scored a square hit on the command post with devastating results:

> Osborne was killed instantly, Donlan's right leg was blown off below the knee, and two other officers were wounded, one mortally. Reich, still holding under the radar screen, was in command. He was the only officer left in Company E.[22]

Despite the loss of five of its officers, Company E continued the assault on Hill 382. When elements of Company F, commanded by Captain Walter Ridlon, joined forces on the hill with Company E, the doom of the defenders was sealed. By 1530, 2/24 reported the objective secured.[23] Colonel Jordan, the regimental commander, had by this time apparently grown somewhat leery of optimistic reports concerning the capture of this particular objective, and in consequence, in describing the action of 2 March, the 24th Marines reported only "that small gains were made throughout the day all along the line except in the vicinity of Hill 382 where the bitter opposition continued."[24] The regiment did not officially record the capture of Hill 382 until the following day.

There was some truth to the comment that enemy opposition at Hill 382 continued, even though the Marines were now in possesssion of the crest. In the words of one account of the action on 2 March, "the hill was overrun, but it was not subdued."[25] A clue to this seeming contradiction may be found in a 4th Division report for D plus 11, which introduces a new element in assessing the progress made by 2/24 on 2 March by pointing out:

> It appears that there are underground passageways leading into the defenses on Hill 382 and when one occupant of a pillbox is killed another one comes up to take his place. This is rather a lengthy process.[26]

And that is precisely the way it turned out. For the remainder of D plus 11, 2/24 mopped up the objective and consolidated its positions atop the hill. Because of the underground tunnels linking various pillboxes and strongpoints on the slopes of Hill 382, "the mopup proved to be an almost interminable process."[27] In fact, sealing the caves around Hill 382 and the elimination of isolated enemy holdouts would require several additional days. But for all practical purposes, one of the three strongpoints of the enemy defense system in the 4th Division zone of advance had been eliminated, which left the remaining two, Turkey Knob and the Amphitheater, somewhat more vulnerable to attack.

Operations on D plus 11 to the south of Hill 382 also differed from those of preceding days. While the enemy atop Hill 382 was treated to an exceptionally heavy preparation on that day, precisely the opposite was the case in the 25th Marines zone of advance. There, Colonel Lanigan decided to employ the element of surprise and launch an attack at 0630 without the benefit of any artillery preparation. During the early stages of the action, while the

---

[22] Newcomb, *Iwo Jima*, p. 215.
[23] *2/24 OpRpt*, p. 188.
[24] *24th Mar OpRpt*, p. 15.
[25] Newcomb, *Iwo Jima*, p. 216.

[26] *4th MarDiv D–3 PerRpt* No. 57 dtd 2Mar45.
[27] Morehouse, *Iwo Jima Campaign*, p. 66.

enemy was still off guard, 1/25 was to infiltrate and seize the high ground north of Turkey Knob. Elements of 1/25 and 3/23, the latter having been attached to the 25th Marines, were to execute an envelopment from the northwest and the south.

The infiltration got under way at 0630 and proceeded on schedule for about 20 minutes. However, the Japanese soon recognized the multiple threat facing them and at 0650 unleashed a devastating rocket and mortar barrage against the assault forces. As Marines hit the ground to escape the lethal shell fragments, enemy machine guns opened up at close range and raked the area in which the assault force was pinned down. All need for further secrecy having disappeared, Marine artillery and mortars retaliated, and eight Shermans moved forward in support of the attack. Once again, the large blockhouse atop Turkey Knob drew most of the supporting fire. A large number of 75mm shells and no less than 1,000 gallons of flamethrower fuel were hurled against this impressive obstacle, but no immediate effects of this fire became apparent. The blockhouse appeared to be unoccupied after the tank attack, but it was assumed that the enemy would feed replacements into it through tunnels as soon as the fury of the American assault diminished.

Under cover of the heavy supporting fire, the envelopment of Turkey Knob continued, though progress was slow. By 1430, the two pincers of the double envelopment were only 65 yards from each other, and for a while it appeared that the movement might still succeed. However, as soon as the enemy became aware of this latest development, he threw a tremendous barrage against Company B, 1/25, which had been inching its way north to the high ground from positions south of the Amphitheater. This murderous rocket and mortar fire, interlaced with a heavy volume of small arms fire, inflicted over 30 casualties on the company and forced its withdrawal.[28]

In the center of the 25th Marines line, 2/25 was to extend its left flank to assist 1/25, and for this purpose one company of 3/23 was attached to the battalion. Since no appreciable gains were made by 1/25 during the day, the 2d Battalion remained in place and spent the day in mopping up enemy stragglers and reducing such fortifications in its zone as the enemy still occupied or had reoccupied. Similarly, 3/25, nearest the coast, remained in position during the early part of the day. Enemy mortar fire into these positions caused several casualties, leading Captain James C. Headley, the battalion commander, to make this comment:

> Throughout this period of time we were suffering casualties from enemy mortar fire and our failure to advance while suffering casualties had a depressing effect upon the morale of the troops.[29]

During the late afternoon of 2 March, elements on the right of 2/25 and the 3d Battalion finally were given permission to advance to the high ground directly to their front. Surprisingly enough, the enemy did not contest this advance, and the 25th Marines gained

---
[28] *25th Mar OpRpt*, p. 12.
[29] *3/24 OpRpt*, p. 11.

300 yards, enabling the regiment to consolidate on the freshly taken high ground.

By evening of D plus 11, the 4th Division line protruded both in the north and in the south, hanging back only in the center where the Amphitheater and Turkey Knob remained to be taken. Overall, important progress had been made during the day with the seizure of Hill 382 and the unexpectedly easy advance near the coast during the latter part of the day. The fighting for Hill 382 had been costly for 2/24, in particular, which summed up the day's fighting as follows:

> Today's fighting more intense than any other day up until now. Enemy resistance very heavy. Many pillboxes and strong emplacements to the direct front. Many officers, NCO's and experienced personnel were casualties. Leadership now an acute problem. Enemy installations knocked out during the day's advance: 8 machine guns; 15 cave entrances, from which fire was being received, were sealed; one 47mm gun in bunker knocked out. No count of enemy dead, estimated to be over 100.[30]

Throughout 2 March, Marines on the ground had received excellent support from the sea as well as from the air. Two battleships and one cruiser furnished general support, while destroyers and gunboats deployed near the eastern bulge of the island to shell the rocky draws leading down to the sea. Carrier-based aircraft carried out six strikes against enemy positions in front of the 4th Division. The pilots and observers of VMO-4 flew five missions, including a rather unorthodox one in which a division public relations photographer took pictures from an altitude of 1,000 feet. This improvisation became necessary because "the sustained bombardment of Iwo Jima had so torn the face of the land that pre-D-Day maps were by now of little use in terrain appreciation.[31]

The night from 2–3 March passed without major incidents. It almost appeared as if the Japanese were beginning to feel the results of the prolonged battle of attrition. Along the 4th Marine Division lines, the only action occurred in front of 2/24, where the enemy attempted an infiltration. Once the presence of the intruders had been discovered, a lively firefight ensued. It ended when the enemy withdrew, leaving behind 20 dead. Four Marines of 2/24 were killed in this action.[32]

For the continuation of the assault on 3 March, General Cates made certain changes in the disposition of his forces. At 0500, the 23d Marines relieved the 25th and just before H-Hour, set for 0630, 1/23 passed through 1/25. The 2d and 3d Battalions, 25th Marines, were attached to the 23d and retained their positions in the center and on the right. There were no changes in the 24th Marines' sector, where Colonel Jordan's men were preparing to continue the attack, except that Company L, 3/24, suffered 22 casualties while relieving elements of the 9th Marines near the division boundary.[33]

In an attempt to use the element of surprise, the 4th Marine Division attack

---

[30] 2/24 OpRpt, p. 189.
[31] 4th MarDiv OpRpt, Sec IV, p. 32.
[32] Ibid.
[33] 24th Mar OpRpt, p. 16.

was not preceded by any preparatory fire. On the division left, the 24th Marines jumped off against formidable new defenses in its zone of advance, the bulk of which appeared to be concentrated on the high ground to the northeast of Hill 382, and in the vicinity of Minami Village. Initial resistance was heavy, and mortar, artillery, machine gun, and rifle fire hit the assault companies as soon as they began to move out. Directly in front of 2/24 were pillboxes and reinforced concrete emplacements, including one emplacement containing a high velocity gun.

Immediately following the jump-off, corps and division artillery began to pound these defenses with some effect. The regiment, with 3/24, 2/24, and 1/24 from left to right, slowly advanced against the enemy positions to its front. Some progress was made until the lines advanced to a point close enough to work on enemy emplacements with demolitions and flamethrowers. Once this close-in fighting got under way, fierce action ensued and the assault slowed to a crawl. The terrain consisted of numerous hillocks, mounds, and shallow cross-corridors with vertical sides. Covered reinforced concrete and sand-covered log machine gun and rifle emplacements with firing ports covering the front and both flanks blocked the advance. It soon became apparent that the line of defense to the north and east of Hill 382 had a depth of over 300 yards.

The difficulties accompanying an advance into prepared positions of this type were only too apparent. Due to the character of the terrain, these defenses were well protected from the supporting artillery fire. Tanks and flamethrower tanks, in particular, encountered major problems in getting into position. Once there, their fields of fire were limited so that they could effectively concentrate only on a few emplacements. As the infantry approached the enemy positions, the very close support needed could be furnished only by 60mm and 81mm mortars emplaced within 50 yards of the front lines. A shortage of ammunition limited the employment of the 81mm mortars, so that these weapons were fired only periodically and when dire necessity made their close supporting fires indispensable.

As usual, the infantry bore the brunt of the fighting. Marines, equipped with demolitions, portable flamethrowers, a variety of small arms, bazookas, and smoke and fragmentation grenades, maneuvered into position in small groups and attempted to neutralize the enemy positions one by one. It was a slow, tedious, and costly process calling for able leadership on the part of squad and fire team leaders, a number of whom were killed or wounded and had to be evacuated.

By late afternoon, the center of the 24th Marines had advanced 350 yards, with smaller gains along the northern and southern flanks. Throughout the day, the Shermans of Company B, 4th Tank Battalion, gave as much support to the regiment as the difficult terrain allowed. Rocket launchers employed their now customary hit and run tactics to escape counterbattery fire from the enemy mortars and artillery.

When Colonel Jordan's regiment consolidated on D plus 12, the 3d Battalion on the left had tied in with elements of the 9th Marines, while 1/24 on the right held a narrow front with only Company B in the line. After another day of fatiguing combat, the men were even more exhausted than on the previous day. Their condition was graphically outlined in a 2/24 report for the day:

> Men very tired and listless, lack leaders. Close support by effective close support weapons, such as tanks and 37mm weapons not possible except in rare instances, due to terrain limiting fields of fire. Tank support is seldom sufficient to warrant the casualties resulting from the counter-mortar fire.[34]

Bitter fighting also marked the day's operations to the south of the 24th Marines, where the enemy still retained a strong hold both on the Amphitheater and Turkey Knob. There, 1/23 was to make the main attack southeastward above the Amphitheater and link up with units on the left of 2/25. If completed, this envelopment would result in reduction of Turkey Knob and encirclement of the well-dug in enemy troops in the Amphitheater. In order to support the attack, Company C, 4th Tank Battalion and a platoon of the 4th Engineer Battalion were attached to 1/23.

Following the artillery preparation which came after the jump-off, the enemy initially appeared stunned and, in the words of the regimental report, "the initial phase of the attack progressed favorably."[35] However, progress on the regiment's right soon lagged when Marines drew fire from the concrete blockhouse atop Turkey Knob. In addition, the enemy had mined the routes of approach. Any attempt to remove these antipersonnel mines was frustrated by deadly accurate sniper fire. Nevertheless, by 1400 the attached engineer platoon had cleared a path over which flame tanks and infantry demolition teams were able to get within effective range of the blockhouse. As a result of the combined teamwork of these arms, the blockhouse atop Turkey Knob was partially reduced in a slow and costly assault that continued during the latter part of the afternoon. By evening of 3 March, however, when units consolidated for the night, the Japanese were still firmly in control of Turkey Knob.

While 1/23 was battling for possession of the Knob, the remaining two battalions of the 23d Marines remained in position, except for Company K, 3/23, which, supported by tanks and 75mm halftracks, assaulted stubborn enemy defenses along the southwestern portion of the Amphitheater. Towards the end of the day, Company I was moved into a gap south of the Amphitheater between 1/23 and 2/25. The 2d Battalion of the 23d Marines remained in corps reserve for the day; it occupied an assembly area between the Southern and Central Airfields and could be moved anywhere within the Corps zone of action as required. For the remainder of D plus 12, 2/25 and 3/25 remained in their respective positions on the division's right, while 1/25 in division reserve underwent reorganization and

---

[34] *2/24 OpRpt*, p. 191.
[35] *23d Mar OpRpt*, p. 14.

rehabilitation, and got some badly needed rest.

Throughout the day, the slight but nevertheless important gains made by the 4th Marine Division had been achieved with the help of the supporting arms. Within the division, 2/14 had furnished direct support to the 23d Marines, while 1/14 had reinforced the fires of 2/14. The 24th Marines had been directly supported by 3/14, while 4/14 was in general support. The 4th Tank Battalion had furnished such assistance as the difficult terrain permitted. By the end of 3 March, 36 tanks were operational, 12 had been destroyed, and 8 had been damaged.[36] Ships of TF 54 continued to provide supporting fire, but the use of such support was restricted because of safety factors dictated by the location of the front lines.

At the end of D plus 12, the combat efficiency of the 4th Marine Division was estimated to be 50 percent. All units were ordered to consolidate at 1700, prepared to continue the attack on the following day. With the capture of Hill 382, one of the main props of the enemy's defensive system in the 4th Division sector had been knocked out, and despite heavy losses, it could be assumed "that the Division was now fighting in the rear of the highly prepared defensive area in which the operations for the past three days had been conducted."[37]

The night from 3-4 March passed without major incident in the 4th Marine Division zone of operations, except for the sector occupied by the 24th Marines. There, small groups of the enemy attempted unsuccessfully to infiltrate the lines of 3/24. The enemy placed heavy artillery and mortar fire into the 24th Marines area throughout the night, causing moderate casualties. Four destroyers provided illumination during the night.

At 0730, 4 March, the 4th Marine Division continued its attack with no change in its formation or direction of advance. Prior to the jumpoff, the corps and division artillery fired a half-hour preparation, which was further supplemented by naval gunfire. In contrast to the preceding days, the weather on D plus 13 was overcast and showers began to fall in the morning. Because of the leaden skies and the limited visibility, all air strikes had to be cancelled. It also was a very poor day for aerial observation.

On the ground, the battle of attrition continued. On the division left, the 24th Marines attacked in a generally southeasterly direction. The direction of advance was to be parallel to the corridors. Once again, the assault turned into a step-by-step affair, as usual combined with heavy casualties and little gain. Such progress as could be made was achieved with the assistance of the Shermans, which were employed with good effect against the numerous pillboxes and caves. Good results were also obtained from the flamethrower tank which scorched the enemy defenses. Even though the regiment advanced only about 100 yards, the steady destruction of the formidable enemy defenses sooner or later was bound to have a concrete effect. Indicative of the regiment's effort is the fact that 2,200

---
[36] *4th MarDiv OpRpt*, p. 34.
[37] *Ibid.*

pounds of explosives were employed on D plus 13 to blow cave entrances and exits.[38]

On the division right, the 23d Marines, with 2/25 and 3/25 still attached, 1/23 in line, and 2/23 in corps and 3/23 in division reserve, made small gains in the 1/23 zone of advance. The two attached battalions of the 25th Marines on the regiment's right had to sit it out in their positions, much against their will. As the division was to report the day's activities:

> BLT's 2/25 and 3/25 could have advanced within their zones, but such an advance was not deemed advisable because it would have overextended the lines. The terrain in front of this RCT was the most difficult yet encountered; observation was limited to only a few feet, and it was impossible to support the attack with anything heavier than normal infantry weapons.[39]

By evening of 4 March, the combat efficiency of the 4th Marine Division had dropped to 45 percent, the lowest yet since the Marines had gone ashore on Iwo Jima. The enemy was still offering stubborn resistance from closely integrated positions, and General Cates' men were more exhausted than ever. This circumstance, combined with the murky skies, the discomfort created by the rain, and the ever present enemy snipers in front of, behind, and between the lines should, by all normal yardsticks, have reduced the morale of the wet and tired Marines to a new low.

Yet, strangely enough, this was not the case. There was no definite indication that the enemy's morale was sagging, and in his battered positions in the Amphitheater, he was clinging to every foot of ground as resolutely as ever. Nevertheless, there was a quiet feeling of optimism that perhaps, after all, the enemy might be beginning to crack. Perhaps it was brought about by the decrease in the accuracy of the enemy artillery and mortar fire resulting from the accurate counterbattery fire furnished by the corps artillery. It was also possible that the loss of Hill 382 and the severe mauling that Turkey Knob had taken by this time had deprived the enemy's artillery observers of their choice observation sites.

The battle of attrition being waged all over northern Iwo Jima was beginning to affect the enemy's power to resist, even though his spirit was as high as ever. In recognition of the bitter struggle waged by General Kuribayashi against overwhelmingly superior American forces, his superiors in Tokyo sent a message addressed both to him and Admiral Ichimaru, expressing Japan's admiration for the battle they were waging. Ichimaru replied: "The enemy is hitting us hard, but we will hit back."[40] For his part, General Kuribayashi had earlier stated defiantly "I am not afraid of the fighting power of only three American divisions, if only there were no bombardments from aircraft and warships. This is the only reason why we have to see such miserable situations."[41]

Looking at the overall situation on Iwo and the decimated remnants of his garrison, consisting of only 3,500 ef-

---

[38] *Ibid.*, p. 35.
[39] *Ibid.*

[40] *Ibid.*, p. 225.
[41] *Horie Rpt.*, p. 9.

fectives, General Kuribayashi saw clearly that his time was running short. In desperation, he signalled Tokyo for help on the evening of 4 March, calling for air and naval support. "Send me these things, and I will hold this island", he said. "Without them I cannot hold."[42] But there was no response from the Japanese mainland, which itself was reeling underneath the intensified American bombing attacks. In view of total American air superiority in the Bonins and a mighty American fleet patrolling the surrounding waters, Iwo Jima was, indeed, isolated. The defenders of Iwo Jima had the full sympathy of almost the entire population of Japan, whose attention was riveted on the fierce battle in progress there. On its part:

> ... the Army High Command had meanwhile been conducting earnest investigations into the possibility of mounting an effective attack against the U. S. naval forces which were swarming around Iwo Jima. Air power on hand was small, however, while overwater flight training was inadequate; hence a massive effort could not be staged.[43]

As for the Japanese Navy contingent on Iwo Jima, Admiral Ichimaru did not even bother to radio for help. Admiral Toyoda, Commander in Chief of the Imperial Navy, had sent word that the Navy would be ready for the next expected American thrust by the end of April, but that all plans depended on the outcome at Iwo. The message ended with these words: "I regret that except for full submarine support and some air support, we cannot send reinforcements to Iwo. However, in view of overall requirements, I earnestly hope you will maintain calm and fight staunchly by any means."[44]

The meaning of this was clear and Admiral Ichimaru, who had never expected reinforcements in the first place, accepted the inevitable. Clearly, the Iwo garrison was on its own, and its prolonged death throes would, in any case, be a lonely business.

REORGANIZATION AND CONTINUATION OF THE ATTACK[45]

In accordance with General Schmidt's order that 5 March was to be a day of rest and rehabilitation for all VAC units, no offensive action was planned in the 4th Division sector on D plus 14. Instead, the division was to reorganize so that by noon it would have one regiment, less one battalion, available to continue the attack on a limited front on the following day. The general direction of the attack on 6 March was to be eastward. (See Map VIII, Map Section).

The regiment which General Cates selected for the main effort was Colonel Wensinger's 23d Marines. In order to relieve this regiment from its other duties, the area on the division's right reverted to the 25th Marines. The 2d and 3d Battalions of the 25th Marines, hitherto attached to the 23d, reverted to

---

[42] Quoted in Leckie, *Strong Men Armed*, p. 456.
[43] Hayashi and Coox, *Kogun*, p. 138.

[44] Quoted in Newcomb, *Iwo Jima*, p. 207.
[45] Additional material in this section is derived from: 4th SerBn OpRpt, Iwo Jima, 27Dec44-19Mar45, dtd 2Apr45, hereafter *4th SerBn OpRpt*; 4th MedBn OpRpt, Iwo Jima, 19Feb-15Mar45, n. d., hereafter *4th MedBn OpRpt*.

the parent regiment. The 1st Battalion, 25th Marines, relieved 1/23 in almost identical positions held by 1/25 on 2 March. Since 3/23 was still heavily committed along the southern fringes of the Amphitheater, where it was mopping up previously bypassed enemy defenses and overcoming other stubborn pockets of resistance, Colonel Lanigan combined the division reconnaissance company, which had been attached to his regiment as of 0700 on 5 March, with Company L, 3/25, into a provisional battalion, commanded by Major Edward L. Asbill, executive officer of 1/25. In the northern portion of the division sector, three companies of the 24th Marines were pulled out of the line and stationed in the regimental rear area, where they were to form a strong regimental reserve. In order to further bolster the 25th Marines, Company B of the 2d Armored Amphibian Tractor Battalion was attached to the regiment. This company was to patrol the beach areas north of the 3/25 sector and fire on targets along the beach.

The reorganization within the 4th Division area of responsibility was completed by noon of 5 March, as scheduled. During the entire period of reorganization, beginning on the evening of 4 March, the enemy did not initiate any offensive action, though his supporting arms remained active. During the night from 4–5 March, only sporadic fire hit the 4th Division zone, with the exception of the 24th Marines' area. There, heavy mortar and artillery fire was received almost incessantly during the hours of darkness. Throughout D plus 14, the 14th Marines continued to fire on targets of opportunity and executed harassing fires. A total of 17 missions employed air observation. VMO–4 flew 10 tactical observation missions. One pilot was wounded and evacuated. By late afternoon of 5 March, the squadron had four aircraft that were still operational. In addition to the artillery fire provided by the 14th Marines on D plus 14, elements of TF 54 fired call fire missions throughout the day.[46]

It had, for all practical purposes, been a quiet day on Iwo Jima. There had been no gains since there had been no offensive action. Yet, as this day of rest ended, "there had been more than 400 casualties on the line where there was no fighting. The men got ready for the next big push."[47]

Following the day of rest, the VAC offensive resumed on the morning of 6 March. In order to obtain the maximum results from extensive massed preparations, General Schmidt had ordered his divisions to attack in echelon. Each attack was to be preceded by an intensive artillery and naval gunfire preparation, in which the corps and division artillery, as well as the medium and heavy guns of the fire support ships, were to join.[48] Altogether, not including the naval gunfire, 12 artillery battalions would unleash a devastating curtain of fire against the enemy garrison that still blocked the path of the VAC advance. They would first fire for approximately 30 minutes at the western portion of the front, then shift the preparation for a little over half an

---

[46] *4th MarDiv OpRpt*, p. 39.
[47] Newcomb, *Iwo Jima*, p. 244.
[48] VAC OpO 13–45, dtd 5Mar45.

hour to the eastern half. Within the overall assault, the 4th Marine Division was to jump off at 0900, H plus 60 minutes, with the main effort on its left in conjunction with the adjacent 9th Marines of the 3d Marine Division.

At 0845, the coordinated fire of the 132 guns and the naval gunfire shifted to support the second phase of the VAC attack along the eastern portion of the front. The shore-based artillery alone had expended 22,500 shells ranging from 75mm to 155mm in a little over an hour. In the zone of action of General Cates' division, the full force of the barrage was brought to bear on the left in the zone of action of the 23d Marines. There, prior to 0600, the 23d Marines, less 1/23, had moved into position. In preparation for the assault, 2/23 had relieved 3/24 without enemy interference. The weather promised to be fair with good visibility; only a slight haze obscured observation in the early dawn.

Following the earth-shaking artillery preparation, which gave way to a rolling barrage, 2/23 jumped off at H-Hour, followed by the 3d Battalion at a 400-yard interval. As the assault battalion advanced eastward towards the high ground to its front, it became apparent that the heavy volume of artillery fire had not incapacitated the Japanese who emerged from their dugouts little the worse for wear and, in the extremely rugged terrain, put up a spirited fight for every yard of the way and defended each cave, pillbox, and emplacement with the greatest tenacity.

As the advance gained momentum, in the face of accurate fire from rifles and automatic weapons to the front, the assault companies moved forward about 50 yards. On the left, where the terrain favored the employment of armor, Company G, 2/23, supported by four tanks, gained 300 yards. As the company prepared to move into a gap that had arisen between it and Company F, the enemy caught Company G in a murderous mortar barrage that caused numerous casualties and wounded the company commander. Fierce fighting continued throughout the day. At 1800, when 2/23 dug in for the night, Company G on the left still was 350 yards in front of the line of departure; the remainder of the 2d and 3d Battalions, 23d Marines, had gained approximately 100 yards during the day.

To the right of the 23d Marines, 2/24 and 1/24 jumped off abreast at H-Hour. Almost immediately, Colonel Jordan's Marines found themselves in the same type of terrain that had impeded the movements of the 23d Marines to the north. The ground was characterized by a series of jagged ridges and heavy undergrowth, both favoring the defending force. Despite support from gunfire ships and three heavy air strikes, enemy resistance continued undiminished. After a day of exhausting and costly fighting, the regiment gained 150 yards on the left and even less on the right.

Since the Amphitheater and Turkey Knob had, for all practical purposes, already been bypassed prior to D plus 15, no frontal assault was launched against these positions, which still formed a deep salient in the 4th Division lines. Because of these protruding enemy positions, the 23d and 24th Marines north of this salient attacked in an east-south-

THE 4TH MARINE DIVISION DRIVE ON THE RIGHT

easterly direction, while the 25th Marines to the south were attacking generally to the northeast. As a result, it appeared that all the 4th Division thrusts on 6 March were directed generally towards the remnants of Higashi Village.

For the three battalions of the 25th Marines, it was another day of waiting for the left wing of the division to move forward. Since no decisive gains were made by the 24th Marines, 2/25 and 3/25 stayed in position and conducted mop-up operations within their respective areas. The only forward movement took place in the 1/25 sector, where Marines continued chipping away at enemy fortifications to the east of Turkey Knob near Minami Village, supported by flame and medium tanks and 75mm half-tracks. Once the armor had completed its mission, the tanks were pulled back in order to prevent their exposure to the expected enemy counterbattery fire.

By evening of 6 March, it was evident that the momentous artillery preparation which had so promisingly ushered in the resumed offensive had failed utterly in crushing the enemy's will or capacity to resist. At the time it consolidated for the night, the 4th Marine Division held a line extending for roughly 2,470 yards. A gap of 400 yards still separated the division's left flank from the right of the adjacent 3d Division.

Once again, despite meager gains, the division's losses on D plus 15 had been heavy. The division D-3 report for the day estimated combat efficiency at 40 percent and added that "the result of fatigue and lack of experienced leaders is very evident in the manner in which the units fight."[49] Conversely, the enemy seemed to adapt himself readily to the changing conditions on Iwo Jima by making widespread use of American equipment. Thus it was discovered during the day that five enemy bodies in front of the 4th Division lines were fully dressed in Marine uniforms. One Japanese who decided to give American food a try was to record in his diary: "I tasted Roosevelt's rations for the first time, and they were very good." No doubt, the frequently maligned originator of the American combat rations would have been pleased with this compliment.

The night of 6-7 March turned into a veritable hell for many 4th Division Marines. The continuous and exhausting action in preceding days had been enough to wear down many of them, both physically and mentally. Instead of the rest which they so badly needed and desired, the men were kept in a state of upheaval all night by Japanese activity which, according to the official report, was "sporadic but costly".[50]

At 2130, several enemy mortar shells fell in the lines of 2/23, wounding approximately 30 men. While confusion engulfed this hard-hit battalion, the action shifted to the right flank of the 4th Division. There, shortly after 2200, enemy were reported moving in front of 3/25. Immediate artillery fire was brought to bear on the enemy assembly, which was dispersed. Up to this time,

---

[49] *4th MarDiv D-3 PerRpt* No. 61, dtd 6Mar45.
[50] *4th MarDiv OpRpt*, p. 40.

all had remained quiet in front of 1/25, but as the night continued, an estimated 40–50 Japanese infiltrated the battalion sector and sneaked into the foxholes occupied by Major Mee's men. An occasional bursting hand grenade punctured the quietness of the night— a solitary rifle shot, a deep grunt or groan, and then stillness again. It was not until morning that an accurate tally of the 1st Battalion's losses was possible. Then it became evident that 1/25 had lost one officer and 12 men killed; the enemy had lost an estimated 50 men.[51] Conversely, 1/24 reported that this had been the quietest night in its sector.

Just as it appeared that this long night was nearing its end, disaster struck once more, this time in the 2/23 area. Shortly after 0500, one of the big, inaccurate enemy rockets wobbled its way into the 2/23 command post with devastating results. The battalion commander, Major Robert H. Davidson, was badly shaken up by the blast and suffered a severe concussion; the communications chief was killed, and the battalion executive officer, the operations officer, the adjutant, and two clerks were wounded. With practically all the headquarters staff officers out of action, a skeleton staff was quickly formed at regimental headquarters under Lieutenant Colonel Edward J. Dillon, the regimental executive officer, who proceeded to 2/23 around dawn and took over the battalion.

H-Hour for D plus 16 had been set for 0730. The 4th Division was to continue the assault in the same direction and with the same lineup of units as on the preceding day. There was to be no preliminary artillery or naval gunfire preparation, though neutralization fire against known enemy mortar and artillery positions was scheduled between 0800 and 0830. Because of the disruption caused by the enemy rocket hit on the command post of 2/23, H-Hour was postponed for an additional half hour.

Promptly at 0800 the 4th Division attack resumed, with the battered 23d Marines, less 1/23, in the main effort. The supporting neutralization fire appeared to be having a salutary effect, since there was little response from the enemy supporting arms. As a result, 2/23, attacking along the 4th Divison boundary, was able to make slow gains in the course of the morning, particularly along the regimental left. In the center and on the right, on the other hand, enemy resistance was as bitter as ever, and there the advance quickly ground to a halt. By shifting the focal point of the assault quickly between companies, comparable to a boxer who hits his opponent with a low blow and then follows with a haymaker to the uncovered chin, the 2d Battalion was able to catch the Japanese off balance long enough to make a gain of 150 yards within an hour after jumpoff. Following this limited success, strong enemy positions were encountered all along the battalion front and for the remainder of the day progress was minimal. Enemy resistance on 7 March consisted primarily of heavy machine gun fire and extremely accurate rifle fire from concealed positions in the rocky ridge for-

---

[51] *Ibid.*

mations and draws along the front. The virtual absence of enemy artillery fire at the 23d Marines' front was noticeable, though the regiment still drew intermittent fire from enemy mortars.

The 24th Marines resumed the attack with 2/24 and 1/24 on the line and almost immediately encountered heavy opposition, particularly on the right where intense machine gun and mortar fire halted the advance of the 1st Battalion before it really got moving. For the remainder of the morning, the regimental advance could be measured in yards as small demolition teams blasted and burned the enemy out of his well concealed and strongly-held positions. At 1245, the 14th Marines fired a five-minute preparation which signalled a renewal of the attack. Employing the same tactics used during the morning, and with considerable air support, the regiment scored a gain of 50 yards before 1700, when the lines were consolidated for the day.

On the division right, Colonel Lanigan's 25th Marines continued mopping up the numerous stragglers in its rear area. On the regiment's left, the 1st Battalion, supported by regular and flame tanks, destroyed enemy emplacements to its front, while the Provisional Battalion continued the systematic reduction of stubborn enemy defenses in the bypassed Amphitheater and Turkey Knob. Even though the 25th Marines did not seize any new ground on D plus 16, its strategic location along the division right would shortly change its mission into a defensive one. As the 23d and 24th Marines very slowly and inexorably continued their east-south-eastward advance towards Tachiiwa Point on the east coast, they threatened to envelop Captain Inouye's forces, which would be compressed in an area bounded by the sea in the east and the 25th Marines to the south. For all practical purposes, the northern wing of the 4th Division formed a hammer while the stationary 25th Marines would serve as the anvil. In all respects, this type of maneuver closely resembled the large-scale German antipartisan operations in Russia where precisely such tactics often led to success.[52]

In anticipation of increased pressure once this pocket was compressed, Colonel Lanigan took preparatory measures to enable his regiment to cope with any threat posed by the Japanese whose encirclement was imminent. Engineers attached to the regiment laid antipersonnel mines across the front. Barbed wire was strung out along the line. The men sited machine guns, 37mm cannon, and 60mm mortars, waiting for the Japanese to be driven against the regimental line. For the time being, the mission of the 25th Marines would be a defensive one.

Activity during the night from 7-8 March was not comparable to that of the preceding night and along the 4th Division lines consisted mainly of mortar and small arms fire. Some of the enemy mortar shells fell into the positions of 1/24 and in front of the 25th

---

[52] For further information on this subject, see Department of the Army Pamphlet No. 20-244, Edgar M. Howell, *The Soviet Partisan Movement* (Washington: Department of the Army, Office of the Chief of Military History, Aug 1956).

Marines. At 0300, 3/24 returned to the parent regiment and two hours later relieved 2/24 in the line.

On D plus 17, the division main effort changed from the left to the center, and the direction of the attack shifted to the southeast. Within the shrinking area left to the Japanese on Iwo Jima, the designation of phase or objective lines had become superfluous, and General Schmidt's operations order for 8 March was essentially "to capture the remainder of the island."[53] No one familiar with the yard-by-yard struggle expected enemy resistance to cease on this day, or for a number of days to come, but the tenor of the order gave a vague assurance that there was to be an end to the bloodletting. Facing the Marines of all three divisions were only the jumbles of rock and the sea, and a dwindling number of highly motivated Japanese determined to sell their lives as dearly as possible.

H-Hour on 8 March had been set for 0750. However, in accordance with corps orders, the 4th Marine Division jumped off at 0620, 90 minutes ahead of the 3d and 5th Divisions. The jump-off was carried out without any artillery preparation, though for half an hour following it the 14th Marines and the corps artillery fired successive concentrations in support of the attack. In the zone of advance of the 23d Marines, there was initially only light resistance, the enemy apparently being confused by the early morning attack. Even though opposition stiffened in time, gains were made in the center of the regimental zone of advance, as 2/23 drove southeastward in the general direction of Tachiiwa Point.

The 24th Marines, with 3/24 on the left and 1/24 on the right, jumped off on schedule, but encountered far stronger resistance than the 23d Marines to the north, mostly from enemy units concealed in perfectly fortified positions. Enemy opposition was characterized by extremely heavy fire from small arms, knee mortars, and mortars of larger calibers. Gains made during the day were negligible, though at the end of the day the regiment was tied in with the 23d Marines on the left and the 25th Marines on the right. Throughout the day, 2/24 remained in division reserve.

On the right flank of the division, the three battalions of the 25th Marines remained in position and continued to strengthen the regimental lines in the event that the enemy decided to counterattack as he was driven into a corner. Behind the lines, various elements of the regiment and the division reconnaissance company continued to mop up; enemy stragglers were also rounded up in the vicinity of Minami Village.

In the course of D plus 17, Shermans of the 4th Tank Battalion gave such support as was feasible to the regiments of the 4th Division, though the movement of armor was restricted largely to the few existing trails, most of them in the 23d Marines' area. There, several tanks ran into a minefield and three were destroyed. During the time required to clear the minefield, the remaining tanks remained in place. In the course of an air strike, an auxiliary gas tank filled with napalm was dropped erroneously into the friendly lines. It

---

[53] VAC OpO No. 15–45, dtd 7Mar45.

landed directly behind one of the Shermans, and napalm splashed all over the tank. Even though the outer surfaces of the Sherman caught fire, the crew was able to evacuate the vehicle and put out the blaze with a portable fire extinguisher. There were no casualties and the mishap failed to put the Sherman, at this point somewhat the worse for wear, out of action.[54]

When the regiments of the 4th Division secured for the night around dusk of 8 March, the combat efficiency of the division was still clinging to a precarious 40 percent, but even this figure fails to convey the excessive number of key personnel, the driving force of any unit, that had been sent out of the lines suffering from wounds or battle fatigue. The weather had turned cloudy and cold, and the men of General Cates' division shivered in their foxholes while attempting to rest their weary bodies for the continuation of the struggle that would await them in the morning.

THE ENEMY STRIKES BACK[55]

In the gathering dusk and during the early evening of 8 March, something was beginning to stir in front of the 23d and 24th Marines. At first, there was only the blur of muted voices and movement, nothing definite that would indicate anything out of the ordinary was brewing. But then the intensity of the enemy mortar, artillery, and rocket fire against the two Marine regiments increased, followed at 2300 by large-scale infiltration of the 2/23 and 3/24 sectors.

Had the Marines compressing the Japanese naval force into the pocket near Tachiiwa Point been able to look into the enemy lines, and had they been able to gauge the background and volatile temperament of the Japanese Navy captain commanding the 1,000-odd men about to be trapped, certain inevitable conclusions would have become apparent almost at once. Captain Samaji Inouye, commanding the *Naval Guard Force* on Iwo Jima, was a *Samurai*, a noisy, swashbuckling extrovert, a champion swordsman, who was prone to boast of his prowess as a fighter, lover, and drinker in front of his subordinates.[56]

It was totally incompatible with Inouye's character that he would sit back in his dugout and idly watch his force being encircled. Also, he had felt deeply emotional about the loss of Mount Suribachi and, in his grief at the American capture of this landmark, he had nearly decapitated the hapless survivors of the force that had straggled into his lines following the fall of the mountain. For the Japanese, ever since the attack on Pearl Harbor, the eighth day of each month had a special significance, and Inouye was only too well aware that 8 March would be his last. He planned to make it a memorable one for all concerned.

Late in the evening, at 2200, he gathered the remainder of his troops, a mixture of survivors from many Navy

---

[54] *4th MarDiv OpRpt*, p. 43.

[55] Additional material in this section is derived from: 4th EngBn OpRpt, Iwo Jima, 18Feb-19Mar45, n.d., hereafter *4th EngBn OpRpt*.

[56] A fascinating account of Inouye's background and mentality is contained in a letter from Fred Saito to Richard F. Newcomb, dtd 5Feb64, in *Newcomb Notes*.

units on Iwo Jima. It was anything but a uniformly equipped force:

> ... many men had only bamboo spears, but some had hand grenades and rifles. There were a few machine guns, and some men strapped land mines across their chests, determined to blow up some Marines with themselves.[57]

What Captain Inouye had in mind was, of course, an all-out charge against the American lines. But, short of killing Americans, there had to be a definite purpose to the assault. Still preoccupied with the loss of Mount Suribachi, where the Stars and Stripes fluttering on the summit had kindled his anger anew every day, the Captain announced to his assembled force the objective of the imminent assault was Suribachi itself. En route, after breaking through the American lines, the men were to blow up as many American planes as they could on the airfields.

Judged by the standards employed earlier in the war on islands like Guadalcanal, and particularly when compared to the desperate Japanese all-out charge on the Garapan Plain at Saipan, what Inouye had planned could best be described as a mini-*banzai*. His objective was unrealistic, the Marines to his front were too alert, and above all, he lacked the approval of his superiors for the action he was about to take. As the attack got under way, the following situation developed:

> The band started south, not in a wild charge, but crawling slowly and quietly. One group got within 10 yards of 2/23's command post, where Lieutenant Colonel Dillon was still in command, before the alarm was given. Then the sailors lobbed grenades and charged, shrieking "Banzai!"

[57] Newcomb, *Iwo Jima*, pp. 257–258.

In a moment there was chaos. The Marines threw up flares and star shells lighted the sky. Machinegun fire, rifles, and mortars began to cut into them, but still the Japanese came on. Some of them carried stretchers and shouted "Corpsman, corpsman" in fair English. Finally the hordes faltered and broke, and no one knew where Captain Inouye was. He had last been seen running and shouting, his sword waving in the air.[58]

According to an account of Inouye's orderly, who became separated from the captain in the melee, Inouye charged ahead with loud shouts, followed by his men. As accurate Marine fire raked the ranks of the charging Japanese, Inouye shouted "*Banzai, Banzai,*" at the top of his voice, and that was the last heard of him. As one of the Japanese was to comment regretfully later: "It's a pity he could not reach the American position for a full display of his final swordsmanship."[59]

As the Japanese charged the boundary between the 23d and 24th Marines, it was inevitable that some of them would get through the Marine lines. There was vicious fighting throughout the hours of darkness. Some of the action eventually extended to the 24th Marines and, on a smaller scale, to the 25th. Company E, 2/23, continued to bear the brunt of the counterattack, expending 20 cases of hand grenades, 200 rounds of 60mm illumination shells, and an unknown quantity of machine gun, BAR, and rifle ammunition.[60] Company E faced a critical situation around 0100, when ammunition began to run out. Finally, additional loads

[58] *Ibid.*, p. 258.
[59] Saito ltr to Newcomb, 5Feb64, in *Newcomb Notes.*
[60] *2/23 OpRpt*, p. 33.

were sent forward in a jeep and trailer, which brought the badly needed supplies forward over an enemy infested road, with the aid of 60mm illumination. The jeep drew several rounds of enemy small arms fire but was able to deliver its badly needed cargo. Fire support ships expended 193 star shells during the night, thus lessening some of the confusion that accompanied the action. In the flickering light the chewed-up volcanic ground became visible, filled with wriggling forms. Artillery fire soon blanketed the area and many of the would-be infiltrators halted in their tracks.

But many of the attackers did get into the Marine lines and, in the words of one account:

> The night became alive with the noise and lights of a determined fire fight. Red tracer bullets shot across the flats. Jap rockets hurtled through the air, leaving a quarter-mile trail of golden sparks. Star shells of yellow and green hung in the sky.
> The battle kept up all night. Individual men in foxholes didn't know what was happening. They waited for Japs to appear and killed them as fast as they came. Men with telephones whispered into their instruments and tried to discover how strong the enemy attack actually was. Machine guns chattered incessantly. Grenades popped.[61]

As day dawned over Iwo Jima on 9 March, the area in and around the 2/23 positions, and to a lesser extent in front of the 24th Marines, showed the signs of horrible carnage. Mopping up continued until noon. A body count of enemy dead revealed approximately 650 at the focal point of the attack, while another 150 were discovered in the adjacent sectors. Among those who perished in the counterattack was Captain Inouye, who died as he had wished to die. The counterattack cost the Marines 90 men killed and 257 wounded, a large number of men to lose in one night's bitter fighting; yet beyond any doubt the cost would have been higher had it been necessary to ferret the enemy out of his dugouts one by one.

To the Japanese survivors of the slaughter, the arrival of daylight brought little comfort. Stripped both of the protective cover of darkness and leadership on which all of them so much depended, the 200 sailors that had survived the abortive *banzai* huddled in small groups, wondering what to do next. It was apparent to all that getting to Mount Suribachi or any of the airfields was far beyond their capabilities. A lieutenant finally gathered them together and those who could crawled away from the place of carnage, constantly harassed by the Marines hunting for them. As to their further operations:

> Their fighting was over. Each night the lieutenant sent out patrols of three to five men. They never returned. Others went into caves, and some died of wounds, of sickness, or of thirst. Some drank urine and died.
> The lieutenant lasted until April 29, the Emperor's birthday, when he told the others, "We will steal a B-29 and fly to the homeland. You others do as you please after we're gone." He left, accompanied by the chief Navy medical officer, an ensign, and a petty officer.[62]

There was to be one more sequel to Captain Inouye's counterattack: Obviously aware of General Kuribayashi's

---

[61] Henri et al, *Marines on Iwo Jima*, p. 291.

[62] Newcomb, *Iwo Jima*, p. 259.

orders to stay in place and fight as long as possible, he had neglected to inform his superior, Admiral Ichimaru, of his intentions. As a result:

> ... on the night of Inouye's last charge, Admiral Toyoda again messaged Admiral Ichimaru, praising the brave acts of the Navy men and again begging them to hold out as long as possible. Ichimaru did not know that Inouye had already sacrificed the last of the Japanese Navy force on Iwo Jima.[63]

For the men of the 4th Marine Division, Captain Inouye's abortive counterattack at one stroke eliminated a large segment of the enemy force holding the eastern part of the island. With just about all of this force out of the way, there no longer was any central direction of Japanese forces in the east. Major General Senda, with a force of undetermined strength, was still assumed to be blocking the 4th Division's path between Higashi Village and the coast. Enemy remnants were still in control of Turkey Knob, and a few other pockets of resistance still existed, but by this time the enemy's capability to resist was drastically reduced.

Even though the mopup of survivors of the counterattack continued throughout the morning of 9 March, the 4th Division continued its attack in accordance with previously laid plans. At 0700, following a 10-minute preparation, the 4th Division jumped off. Once again, the division employed the same scheme of maneuver it had used in previous days, with the 23d Marines on the left, the 24th Marines in the center, and the 25th Marines on the right. The 23d Marines, with 2/23 in the assault,

[63] *Ibid.*, pp. 259-260.

was able to advance in the center and to its right against resistance that lacked the bite of the preceding days. However, the left of the regiment drew heavy fire from a ridge near the division boundary about 500 yards north of Higashi. By 0900, the ridge had been seized in direct assault, and the battalion slowly but persistently forced its way forward. At 1500, 1/23 reverted to the regiment. Ordered to consolidate at 1700, Colonel Wensinger's men continued the attack to improve their positions and did not halt until half an hour later. Gains for the day were a respectable 300 yards. As the regiment dug in, it maintained contact with the 3d Marine Division on the left and the 24th Marines on the right.

In the remaining division sectors, enemy opposition was as strong as ever, and, in consequence, no additional ground was seized in the center and on the right of the division. To some extent, lack of progress in the center was due to depletion of manpower, which made it necessary to shuffle companies from one battalion to another in order to bring the assault battalion up to effective strength. As part of the reorganization of 1/24, Lieutenant Colonel Austin R. Brunelli, the regimental executive officer, assumed command of 1/24, relieving Major Treitel. Because of the heavy resistance on its left flank, the 25th Marines, less 3/25 but with 2/24 attached, remained in position.

During the night from 9-10 March, there was a relative lack of enemy activity. A small amount of light and medium mortar fire at infrequent intervals harassed the 4th Division lines during the night, and infiltration attempts remained on a large scale. In order to counter the threat still posed by groups of the enemy operating in the division rear, the Provisional Battalion, which had been mopping up in the Amphitheater and around Turkey Knob, was disbanded and its mission taken over by 2/25. At the same time, a 4th Provisional Battalion, consisting of 37 officers and 498 enlisted men, was organized from units of the Division Support Group. This unit, under the command of Lieutenant Colonel Melvin L. Krulewitch, had special responsibility for mopping up behind the division lines and retained this mission until 12 March, when it was disbanded.[64]

At 0800 on D plus 19, the 4th Marine Division continued its attack after a coordinated corps and division artillery preparation, which changed into a rolling barrage as the men moved out. On this day, which was to be full of significant developments for General Cates' men, the assault was made essentially by the 23d and 25th Marines. The 24th Marines reverted to division reserve. The 1st Battalion, 24th Marines, was pulled out of the line and replaced by 3/25. The 3d Battalion, 24th Marines, remained in its previous zone of action but was attached to the 23d Marines, while 2/24 remained attached to the 25th Marines.

The 23d Marines, with 2/23 on the left and 3/24 on the right launched a vigorous attack that encountered only light opposition on the right. The enemy, entrenched in the rocky ridges along the left boundary of the division, replied with accurate and effective mortar and small arms fire which reduced gains of 2/23 in this sector. Throughout the regimental zone of advance, small but determined groups of the enemy tried to impede the advance. Since the Japanese no longer held a solid line on commanding ground, the Marine assault elements were able to bypass such nests of resistance, leaving their annihilation to teams of engineers, tanks, and infantry, which blasted and scorched such obstacles with demolitions and flamethrowers.

As the regimental attack gained momentum, an enormous amount of ground was taken by Iwo standards. By 1500, Colonel Wensinger's men had advanced no less than 700 yards and were within 500 yards of the east coast. Having reached commanding ground in this area, the regiment halted in midafternoon. Patrols from 2/23, dispatched during the remainder of the afternoon, reached the coast near Tachiiwa Point without encountering any enemy opposition. A short distance to the south, elements of 3/24 reconnoitered to within 100 yards of the coast without making contact with the enemy.

On the division right, the 25th Marines, with 2/24 and the Reconnaissance Company attached, completed the relief of 1/24 by 0600. Following this relief, 3/25 took over the sector of 1/24. In order to complete the encirclement of those enemy remnants still holding out in the Amphitheater and on Turkey Knob, 3/25 was shifted to the north of the enemy salient, where, together with 1/25, it would attack to the southeast parallel to the axis of advance of the 23d Marines. Along the southern per-

---

[64] *4th MarDiv Support Gp OpRpt*, pp. 17–18.

imeter of the salient, 2/25 and 2/24 were to advance generally to the northeast or east respectively, which would enable 2/25 to effect a linkup with those units of the regiment attacking towards the coast from the northwest.

Jumping off at H-Hour on 10 March, 3/25 and 1/25 attacked towards the high ground to their front from where the enemy still offered moderate to heavy opposition. It soon became apparent that the 3d Battalion would be able to move faster than 1/25 and, in consequence, 3/25 was ordered to continue regardless of its flanks. As the attacks of 3/25 and 2/25 converged, the distance separating the two units dwindled until, shortly after noon, the two battalions linked up. Overall gains for the 25th Marines on D plus 19 were 600 yards. More important than the yardage gained was the fact that Turkey Knob was at last completely surrounded and all resistance remaining could now be eliminated. As the 25th Marines consolidated for the night, its left flank was tied to the 23d Marines about 800 yards from the coast while the stationary right flank was still anchored on the beach to the south.

The significance of the 4th Division's movements and gains on 10 March was summed up in one historical narrative in these words:

> It was now evident that the Japanese counterattack had marked the turning point in the battle. Although bitter and costly fighting continued for six more days, particularly in the 25th Regiment's zone, organized resistance was now dying out in the 4th Division area.
>
> During the 14-day period covered in this chapter, the 4th Division, in constant head-on assault, fought its bloody way from Charlie-Dog Ridge past Hill 382, the Amphitheater, Turkey Knob, through Minami and formidable defenses northeast of 382, almost to the coast. The slow but relentless movement of this division front can be compared to the closing of a giant door. The right flank, which advanced less than 1,000 yards, acted as a hinge while the rest of the division (the door) turned upon it and attacked northeast, east, and southeast to close and sweep trapped enemy toward the sea.[65]

The 4th Division assault on eastern Iwo Jima thus had broken the back of enemy resistance by 10 March. In the wake of the division's advance, there remained a staggering number of casualties, whose bodies and minds bore ample witness to the ferocity of the fighting. Between 25 February, when General Cates' men first attacked the Meat Grinder and 10 March, when they were within a stone's throw of the coast, the division had sustained 4,075 casualties. A total of 847 Marines had been killed or were dead of wounds; 2,836 had been wounded; 1 was missing, and 391 were suffering from combat fatigue.[66]

As the three Marine divisions slowly approached the coastline in their respective zones of advance, it became apparent to all on the island that time for General Kuribayashi and his garrison was running out. In Japan, anxious eyes were watching the contest of wills being waged for possession of Iwo Jima. To the military observers, the outcome was a foregone conclusion. But the nation's morale was precariously

---
[65] Bartley, *Iwo Monograph*, p. 176.
[66] *Ibid.*, p. 177.

perched on the faint hope that General Kuribayashi's masterful defense of the island would give the business-minded Americans food for thought about the cost of a full-scale invasion of the home islands. Thus, in Japanese eyes, the prolonged defense of Iwo Jima pursued not only the immediate tactical objective, but a vastly more far-reaching strategic one.

Few of the surviving members of that garrison had any illusions left about the outcome of the war. One Japanese captured in the 4th Division area late on 9 March was better qualified than most others to comment on the overall situation. A peacetime editor and publisher of one of the large metropolitan newspapers of Japan, he remarked that "this is not a winning war for Japan—she cannot win, but she is trying her darndest to lessen her defeat."[67]

That time was running out on the mainland as well was strongly reemphasized on the evening of 9 March, when more than 300 B-29s mounted one of the biggest air raids of the war against Tokyo. This attack severely devastated the enemy capital, serving notice to all Japanese that they were now open to American attack both from sea and air; that henceforth the citizens of Tokyo were as exposed to American explosives as General Kuribayashi's diminishing garrison on Iwo Jima.

---

[67] Interrogation of Leading Private Yutaka Oyanagi, 10Mar45, by 1stLt G. A. Hoeck, 4th MarDiv Preliminary POW Interrogation Rpt #15, 10Mar45, in *4th MarDiv Translations*.

CHAPTER 11

Final Operations on Iwo Jima[1]

ELIMINATION OF THE POCKETS— 3D MARINE DIVISION AREA[2]

On 11 March 1945, operations on Iwo Jima entered their final phase. No longer under any central direction, three more or less clearly defined enemy pockets fought a battle to the death in the zone of advance of each of the three Marine divisions. As the pockets became more constricted, the nature of the fighting changed, mostly because the terrain no longer permitted the employment of naval gunfire, air support, and in the end even artillery. Eventually, as Japanese resistance neared the end, tanks and half-tracks furnished the heavy supporting fire needed to root out the last of the obstinate enemy defenders.

On D plus 20, the only major opposition in the zone of advance of the 3d Marine Division extended along the division's rough boundary, where enemy remnants still occupied a ridgeline paralleling the coast to the east of Kitano Point. (See Map IX, Map Section). A second center of resistance farther south, to the east of Motoyama Village, southeast of the Northern Airfield, and southwest of Hill 362C was a pocket which had already been under attack for several days prior to 11 March. Named after the commander of 2/9, Lieutenant Colonel Cushman, this pocket was honeycombed with caves and emplacements cut into sandstone. The pocket itself was ringed by antitank guns and Colonel Nishi's dug-in light and medium tanks, equipped with 37mm and 47mm guns. The most prominent occupant of the pocket was Colonel Nishi, who had thus far survived the ferocious fighting on the island.

[1] Unless otherwise noted, the material in this chapter is derived from: *TF 51 AR; VAC SAR; VAC G–2 Rpts; VAC C–3 Jnl; VAC Translations; 3d MarDiv AR; 3d MarDiv D–2 Jnl; 3d MarDiv G–2 PerRpts; 3d MarDiv G–3 PerRpts; 4th MarDiv OpRpt; 4th MarDiv D–3 Jnl; 4th MarDiv D–3 PerRpts; 4th MarDiv Translations; 5th MarDiv AR; 5th MarDiv D–1 Jnl; 5th MarDiv D–2 Jnl; 5th MarDiv D–2 PerRpts; 5th MarDiv D–3 Jnl; 5th MarDiv Casualty Rpts; Horie Rpt;* Bartley, *Iwo Monograph; Iwo Comments;* Morehouse, *Iwo Jima Campaign;* Newcomb, *Iwo Jima; Newcomb Notes;* Morison, *Victory in the Pacific;* Henri et al, *Marines on Iwo Jima;* Isely and Crowl, *U.S. Marines and Amphibious War;* Leckie, *Strong Men Armed;* Smith and Finch, *Coral and Brass;* Aurthur and Cohlmia, *The Third Marine Division;* Proehl, *The Fourth Marine Division;* Conner, *The Fifth Marine Division;* Hayashi and Coox, *Kogun.*

[2] Additional material in this section is derived from: *9th Mar URpts; 9th Mar UJnl; 9th Mar AR;* 21st Mar AR, Iwo Jima, 23Jan–16Mar45, dtd 10Apr45, hereafter *21st Mar AR; 21st Mar UJnl; 21st Mar URpts; 1/9 AR; 2/9 AR; 3/9 AR;* 1/21 AR, Iwo Jima, 29Jan–26Mar45, dtd 6Apr45, hereafter *1/21 AR;* 2/21 AR, Iwo Jima, 30Jan–24Mar45, dtd 12Apr45, hereafter *2/21 AR;* 3/21 AR, Iwo Jima, 15Jan–16Mar45, dtd 11Apr45, hereafter *3/21 AR; 1/23 OpRpt; 3d TkBn AR.*

684

On 11 March, 1/9 and 3/9 were to execute a converging attack from the high ground near the east coast into the northeastern fringes of the pocket. Once the two battalions had linked up, they were to launch a concerted drive into the pocket from the east. In the course of the morning, the 1st Battalion assaulted a ridge overlooking the pocket and blasted its way to the top, demolishing caves and other positions as it went along. The advance was supported by Shermans from the 3d Tank Battalion, whose fire either destroyed such enemy defenses as could be spotted or at least kept the occupants of strongpoints underground to permit the approach of demolition teams. The 3d Battalion was forced to assault similar terrain during the morning without tank support, which did not arrive until an armored bulldozer had carved out a road for the Shermans during the early afternoon. In mid-afternoon, shortly after 1500, the two battalions linked up. For the remainder of the day, elements of both battalions mopped up along the east coast, outposted the beach, and established defensive positions on the high ground east of Hill 362C.

Even though no solid line of containment surrounded the pocket from the west or southwest, there was no activity on the part of the Japanese trapped within, aimed at either evading the encirclement or launching a direct assault against the Marines approaching them. Instead, the enemy followed the orders issued by General Kuribayashi to the letter. Remaining within their relatively secure pillboxes, dugouts, caves, and stationary tanks, the Japanese contested every foot of ground, continuing to make the Marines pay an exorbitant price for every yard gained.

In order to support the advance of 3/21, a 7.2-inch rocket launcher, mounted on a sled, was attached to the battalion. This improvisation was the idea of the VAC ordnance officer, who had four of the rocket launchers mounted on sleds when it was found that these weapons did not fit the M4A3 tank with which VAC was then equipped. The sled mount appeared to be the answer to the problem of getting this powerful supporting weapon into terrain which was impassable for tanks. Each rocket launcher, equipped with 20 tubes, was capable of delivering 640 pounds of TNT in a salvo. Effective range of the launcher was 250 yards. A volley of rockets, exploding within a narrow area, could be expected to have a gruesome and highly demoralizing effect upon the enemy.

As 3/21 approached the confines of the pocket, meeting very heavy resistance all the way, a rocket launcher was towed into action by a tank of Company C, 3d Tank Battalion. Altogether, 10 volleys were fired into the pocket with undetermined results. Only too soon did it become apparent that the efficiency of the launchers did not match the visual effect created by the exploding rockets. When the dust settled, the enemy still sat securely in his defenses, little the worse for wear. An official report of this action was to note with discouragement: "Nearly 200 of the 7.2-inch rockets were thrown into this pocket and still our infantry was unable to go in and occupy the ground."[3]

Elsewhere in the 3d Division zone of advance, General Erskine was able to pull 2/21 out of the line for a much needed rest after elements of the 27th Marines of the 5th Division had moved behind the left flank of that battalion. To fill the gap thus created, 1/21 extended its lines northward and tied in with the adjacent 5th Division. At the same time that 1/9 and 3/9 were converging on Cushman's Pocket from the northeast, 3/21, then attached to the 9th Marines, was approaching the pocket from the southwest.

For the remainder of 11 March, 3d Division engineers and riflemen blasted caves and dugouts. Because of the proximity of the battle lines, General Erskine's division did not receive any artillery support that day, though 1/12 stood by for call fires if needed. Similarly, there was no air support for the same reasons, except that aerial observation was used to report the movements of 3d Division units. After nightfall the Japanese, employing hit-and-run tactics, emerged from their hideouts and stealthily approaching the Marine positions, hurled a few hand grenades, and then attempted to disappear as quietly as they had come. Such tactics succeeded only infrequently, and many of the infiltrators did not survive to tell of their exploits.

On the evening of 11 March, 3/21 was facing eastward with a frontage of 200-300 yards, while 1/9 and 3/9 were facing westward with a frontage of about 600 yards. A distance of 500-600 yards separated 3/21 from the two battalions of the 9th Marines. The 2d Battalion, 9th Marines, was in division reserve just east of Motoyama Village, where it was engaged in mopping up the enemy units on the southern fringe of the pocket. At the same time, the battalion formed a line some 400 yards long which acted as a stop-gap for any enemy troops seeking to escape westward from the encirclement.

Early on 12 March, compression of Cushman's Pocket continued, with 1/9 and 3/9 again hammering from the east while 3/21 formed the anvil along the western fringes. Lieutenant Colonel Boehm's 3d Battalion, advancing westward, apparently hit one of the developing weak spots in the enemy lines and made fair progress. The 1st Battalion to the south, on the other hand, ran into heavy resistance and was unable to keep pace with 3/9. Finally, an armored bulldozer carved out a path over which the Shermans could move to the front lines. Once the tanks had arrived there, eager infantrymen accurately pinpointed the enemy position for the tankers, and, in the words of the official report, "successful work in eliminating these positions was done by the tanks."[4]

In the zone of advance of the 1st and 3d Battalions, 9th Marines, extreme difficulty was encountered with the terrain which alternately featured steep banks and gulches filled with soft volcanic ash. The tankers constantly had to be on the alert for Japanese in the vicinity who were only too eager to seek death if there was a chance of

---

[3] *3d TkBn, AR,* 11Mar45.

[4] *Ibid.,* 12Mar45.

blowing up an American tank along with themselves. Tanks bogged down in the difficult terrain proved irresistible objectives for suicidal Japanese, not to mention their attractiveness as stationary targets of opportunity for the remaining enemy antitank guns. In addition to the above, the tankers found it very difficult to maintain direction since their movements were directed over the radio through remote control. Many of the enemy positions were so carefully camouflaged that as often as not Marines were almost on top of them before they were spotted. Once again, flamethrowers and demolitions proved their worth in this type of fighting. Progress was made on D plus 21, but in the rear of Cushman's Pocket, specifically along the crest of the ridge overlooking the east coast of Iwo Jima, resistance remained stubborn.

On the following day, 13 March, the pocket was further compressed when 1/9 and 3/9 continued their drive. Once again, the progress of the attack was impeded by caves, pillboxes, emplaced tanks, stone walls, and trenches. So masterfully had these defenses been camouflaged that "only those immediately in front of the troops could be located. . . . Out of about 150 of these positions (by later count), we knew roughly twenty or thirty of them."[5] Nevertheless, despite the initial advantage accruing to the defenders, the Marine incursion into the pocket could not be stopped. Sherman tanks, particularly those equipped with flamethrowers, lent the necessary emphasis to the advance of the two battalions. The flame tanks proved most effective in reducing a number of troublesome concrete emplacements. Still operating in very rough terrain, the Shermans moved only short distances at a time, and then only with the aid of an armored bulldozer.

As far as the 9th Marines was concerned, the performance of the Shermans was of crucial importance. The regimental commander, Colonel Kenyon, considered them "to be the most formidable supporting weapon at our disposal . . . tank support was the deciding factor in this action."[6]

By the end of D plus 22, Cushman's Pocket had shrunk to a mere 250 yards. The diminishing size of the pocket enabled the withdrawal of two units from the encircling force. On the morning of 13 March, 1/21 relieved those elements of 3/21 that were engaged on the line, and the latter battalion reverted to its parent regiment. Having cleared its zone of action by evening of the same day, 3/9 was pulled out of this area early on 14 March and shifted to the vicinity of Hill 362, where it commenced a systematic mop-up.

The morning of 14 March marked the beginning of the final drive aimed at eliminating Cushman's Pocket. The main burden of the attack now rested on 1/9, which pressed forward throughout the morning and by midafternoon had gained about 100 yards. Once again, the use of armor proved decisive in eliminating the stubborn enemy defenses. A flame tank belonging to Company B, 3d Tank Battalion, was hit

---

[5] Aurthur and Cohlmia, *The Third Marine Division*, pp. 246–247.

[6] *9th Mar AR*, p. 6.

by a rifle grenade which caused a small explosion inside the vehicle, wounding the driver and assistant driver.

At 1530, 2/9 reverted from division reserve to regimental control. Shortly before 1800, the battalion passed through 1/9 and launched an attack into the enemy position which by this time had already shrunk to about 150 square yards. Shermans of the 3d Tank Battalion played a dominant role in reducing whatever stubborn resistance remained, but a flame tank borrowed from the 5th Marine Division outdid all others. This tank was able to shoot a flame about 125 yards and, according to the official report, it "proved to be the weapon that worked when all others failed. Its long flame range and the area covered by one burst were the contributing factors to its remarkable success."[7] By the time the Shermans and flame tanks had roamed through the pocket, blasting and burning everything in their path, enemy resistance became sporadic and gradually began to flicker out. The stage was now set for the infantry to move in and finish the job.

What might have turned into a routine chore of mopping up turned instead into a rather protracted operation requiring all the skill the attacking force could muster. The action that 2/9 saw for the remainder of 14 March was subsequently described with the statement: "Inconclusive hand to hand fighting ensued until dark."[8] Hidden within this sentence, however, was a factor which was to be brought out elsewhere, namely the combination of physical and mental exhaustion that was taking its toll among Marines on Iwo Jima at this phase of operations as surely as had shells and bullets of the enemy. Few Marines who had made the initial landing were left during the final phase of the fighting. Their places had been taken by willing though inexperienced replacements, whose performance in combat left much to be desired. As one Marine historian was to put it:

> By this stage in the operation a large percentage of infantry troops were replacements who lacked the combat training and experience that prepared and conditioned men for closing with the enemy. Therefore, the skill and efficiency of assault Marines showed marked deterioration after three weeks of personnel attrition of original D-Day troop strength. During the final days of 3d Division efforts to smash remaining pockets, armor support made success possible. Gun tanks, armored bulldozers, and flame-throwing Shermans combined their operations to give the exhausted infantry a very effective and much needed assist.[9]

In dealing with the same subject matter, the battalion report was to state succinctly: "Almost all of the infantry were replacements. They lacked entirely the will to close with the enemy."[10] Needless to say, this statement was not intended as an indictment of the men involved, but of the replacement system which forced men to join strange squads and platoons whose teamwork was dissipated by heavy casualties. For the individual Japanese, who fought to the end among friends,

---

[7] *Ibid.*, p. 7.
[8] *2/9 AR*, p. 3.

[9] Bartley, *Iwo Monograph*, p. 181.
[10] *2/9 AR*, p. 3.

death was an infinitely less lonely and impersonal affair than for the average Marine replacement.

While bitter fighting continued in Cushman's Pocket, where one enemy position after the other was eliminated, a different type of action took place just to the east of the pocket on one of the ridges overlooking the east coast. Initially, this ridge had been seized on D plus 16 in the conventional manner —direct attack with flamethrowers, small arms, and demolitions—by 3d Division Marines, who blasted this objective like hundreds of others and then moved on, leaving behind blackened and battlescarred cave entrances that looked sinister even in broad daylight. Several days passed and the front lines had moved on to the north when this desolate ridge came to life again.

The first indication that something was going awry in this so-called rear area came when a heavy Japanese machine gun, hidden somewhere in the previously cleared ridge, opened up on an unsuspecting Marine carrying ammunition and killed him. Other Marines near the ridge soon became startled victims of the enemy fire from the ridge which grew in intensity as small arms joined the machine gun. The next victims were stretcher bearers and their wounded burden. Eventually, tanks and demolitions men arrived and the dangerous, time-consuming job of clearing the ridge had to be repeated. To quote one report:

> Despite their preponderance of weapons the Marines found that there were too many holes. They would attack one only to be shot at from another one half a dozen feet away. Moreover, the ridge was not a straight wall but, in many places, curved like an S. Entranceways protected each other, so that Marines would be hit in the back from holes guarding the one they were assaulting. The inter-connecting tunnels inside the ridge also allowed the Japs to play deadly tag with the Marines. They would shoot out of one hole. By the time Marines got close enough to that hole, the Japs had left it and were shooting from another one twenty yards away and higher up in the wall. The Marines had to post guards at every hole they could see in order to attack any one of them. The tunnels also curved and twisted inside the ridge. The Japs could escape the straight trajectory weapons and grenades thrown into the cave entrances, merely by running back into the interior.[11]

Finally, flamethrowers squirted their lethal liquid into the caves, which became boiling infernos. A number of the Japanese who had reoccupied the ridge were incinerated. Others, their clothing and bodies aflame, tried to escape, only to fall prey to accurate Marine bullets. In desperation, some of the enemy trapped inside the ridge blew themselves up with hand grenades. Before long:

> ... the scene became wild and terrible. More Japs rushed screaming from the caves. They tumbled over the rocks, their clothes and bodies burning fiercely. Soon the flamethrowers paused. A Marine lifted himself cautiously into view. There were no shots from the caves. A Jap with his clothes in rags hunched himself out of one hole, his arms upraised. The Marines stood up behind the rocks and waved to him to come out. The Jap indicated that there were more who would like to surrender. The Marines motioned him to tell them to come out.[12]

In all, 40 men emerged from the ridge, many of them Koreans. Marines

---
[11] Henri et al, *Marines on Iwo Jima*, p. 231.
[12] *Ibid.*, p. 232.

shouldered their weapons as the prisoners were marched to the rear. The tanks left the erstwhile battlefield and quiet descended over the area. Yet this peaceful interlude was soon to be shattered again a few hours later when the Japanese, moving through underground tunnels, reoccupied the ridge. One of the first victims proved to be Sergeant Reid Chamberlain, a Marine with an unusual background. As a member of the U.S. Army, he had witnessed the fall of Bataan and Corregidor, but instead of surrendering to the enemy, he had turned his activities towards the organization and training of Filipino guerrillas. He received a commission in the U.S. Army and returned to the United States, where he promptly resigned his commission and enlisted in the U.S. Marine Corps.

En route to the forward positions of the 21st Marines, Sergeant Chamberlain was walking past the long, rocky ridge, unaware that there were any enemy in the vicinity. Suddenly, there were several shots, one of which hit the sergeant in the head. This incident took place in front of several Marine news correspondents, some of whom also drew enemy fire. When help arrived for the sergeant, it was too late. As one of the correspondents present was to put it later, speaking of the enemy:

> In an instant they had claimed one of our best men. Chamberlain's wonderful war record had ended abruptly. After so many heroic deeds, it seemed an added tragedy that he was killed while doing nothing but walking. There was nothing anybody could do about it.[13]

---

[13] *Ibid.*, pp. 250–251.

Efforts to employ flamethrowers against the ridge during the fading hours of daylight proved unavailing, since all of these weapons were committed in the front lines. At dusk, elements of the 9th Marines bivouacked on the ridge, which had become dormant again. Apprised of the situation, the commanding officer posted sentries behind the rocks facing the ridge, ready to fire on anything that moved.

Hardly had dusk settled over the area, when there was stealthy movement on the slopes of the ridge as individual Japanese emerged from previously undetected cracks and holes. Marines opened fire on these blurred silhouettes. The results of this fire became quickly evident as some of the Japanese who had been hit groaned with pain, others jerked spasmodically and then lay silent while the remainder, realizing that they were trapped, attempted to burrow their way back into the ground. A few who managed to get back under cover committed suicide.

Shortly before midnight there was a tremendous blast which hurled huge pieces of rock through the air and shook the entire area. Some of the Marines were buried in volcanic ash and debris up to their necks and had to be dug out. Others were hit by chunks of concrete that rained down throughout the area. The ridge itself became a mass of fire and disintegrating matter. While the Marines were still engaged in assessing what had happened and trying to aid each other as best they could, Japanese began to emerge from their holes on the ridge, some of them dazed, others carrying antipersonnel mines tied around their waists. A group of five Japanese, running along the wall of the ridge, was spotted by the light of the flames and all were instantly killed.

At dawn it became apparent that, despite the explosion and subsequent bitter fighting, the Marines had suffered only one serious casualty. There might have been more if men, who found themselves buried in debris and volcanic ash, had not been rescued by fellow Marines before they were smothered. It was subsequently discovered that the enemy had used land mines and aerial bombs to blow up the ridge.

On 15 March organized resistance in the 3d Division sector had just about ended. General Erskine's division was ordered to relieve elements of the 5th Marine Division on the right of that division and attack to the northwest.[14] Early on 16 March, D plus 25, the 21st Marines took over an 800-yard sector on the right of General Rockey's division. The boundary between the two divisions now extended from a point 400 yards east of Hill 362B to the northern tip of Iwo Jima near Kitano Point.

Following the relief of 3/27 and 2/26 by the 1st and 2d Battalions of the 21st Marines, that regiment prepared to attack to the north in conjunction with elements of the 5th Marine Division. A 20-minute preparation by the 3d and 5th Division artillery, as well as the 155s of the corps artillery, preceded the jumpoff, which was scheduled for 0815, and continued for 10 minutes following H-Hour. The rolling barrage, which marked the final phase of the preparatory fire moved only 50 yards ahead of the assault units and then moved forward at 100-yard intervals in conjunction with the advance. In addition to the shore-based artillery, a destroyer offshore shelled northern Iwo for nearly an hour and then stood by to deliver call fires. Fighters stationed on the Southern Airfield were available for air support, but the restricted area in which the final operations on Iwo Jima took place precluded their employment.

The attack of 1/21 made good headway against only light resistance. On the other hand, 2/21 encountered heavy small arms fire and extremely difficult terrain, both of which combined to retard its advance. Japanese, fighting from caves and spider trap positions, offered their customary obstinate resistance. Some of them, obviously bent on suicide, charged tanks or groups of Marines with grenades and demolition charges. For the most part, such sorties were marked more by fierce fanaticism than cool logic, and most of them failed before the human bomb could inflict much damage on the Marines or their armor. During the early afternoon both battalions reached the coast near Kitano Point. From that point, it became a matter of mopping up such enemy as remained in caves and other shelters.

By the end of 16 March, General Erskine's men had completed the elimination of Cushman's Pocket and, at the same time, had completed their mission in helping out the 5th Marine Division. This action, for all practical purposes, ended combat operations of the 3d Marine Division on Iwo Jima. Late on D plus 25, General Erskine announced

---

[14] VAC OpO No. 23-45 with changes, dtd 15Mar45.

that all enemy resistance in the zone of action of his division had ceased.[15]

In fact, even though Cushman's Pocket had been overrun, Colonel Nishi, commanding the *26th Tank Regiment,* was still inside with about 450 men, all that had remained of his command. Of these, 300 were wounded and few of them were able to move on their own. From their underground hideout, the Japanese could hear their erstwhile comrades, now prisoners of war and working for the Americans, calling on Colonel Nishi to surrender. But such appeals fell on deaf ears. Early on 19 March, with only two days' food supply remaining, Colonel Nishi ordered his men to make a final charge against the Americans. Only 60 were able to heed his call. Sometime between 19 and 22 March, Colonel Nishi died. Whether he was felled by an American bullet or by his own hand has never been clearly determined though his widow finds solace in the thought "that he died at the foot of the northern cliffs, and that ocean waves have scattered his remains."[16]

4TH MARINE DIVISION MOPUP[17]

Following its impressive gains on 10 March, which had taken some of its assault units to the vicinity of the east coast, the 4th Marine Division continued the attack on the following morning. Jumping off with the 23d and 25th Marines at 0730, the division continued its advance to the coast. (See Map X, Map Section). On the left the 23d Marines reached its objective rapidly, overrunning such enemy resistance as flared up in its path. In the wake of the regiment's advance, engineers sealed caves and constructed a road. In late afternoon, 1/23 relieved 2/23 and pulled back to the same positions held during the preceding night. Combat patrols were dispatched into the beach areas to search out enemy stragglers or holdouts.

The advance of the 25th Marines did not progress as smoothly as that of the 23d. Almost immediately after the jumpoff, Colonel Lanigan's regiment ran into heavy fire from rockets, mortars, and small arms. As a result, little ground was gained. An explanation of the stubborn resistance came during the afternoon when the interrogation of a captured Japanese revealed that about 300 of the enemy were holed up in caves and tunnels directly in front of the regiment. The prisoner further volunteered that a Japanese brigadier general was trapped inside the pocket.[18]

In describing the area of the pocket, 4th Division records had this to say:

> It was at once apparent that this area was the final defensive position of the enemy in this zone. The terrain in this area was not normal in any respect; it could be classified only as a terrain freak of nature. However, it was well suited for the construction of cave positions, and the Japanese had utilized this advantage to

---

[15] *3d MarDiv G-3 PerRpt* No. 31, dtd 16-Mar45.

[16] Newcomb, *Iwo Jima,* p. 267.

[17] Additional material in this section is derived from: *23d Mar OpRpt; 24th Mar OpRpt; 25th Mar UJnl; 25th Mar OpRpt; 14th Mar OpRpt; 1/23 OpRpt; 2/23 OpRpt; 2/24 OpRpt; 1/25 OpRpt; 2/25 OpRpt; 3/25 OpRpt.*

[18] *4th MarDiv D-2 PerRpt* No. 68, dtd 11-Mar45.

FINAL OPERATIONS ON IWO JIMA 693

the fullest extent. Their scheme of maneuver was to hold up the advance as long as it was possible, and to inflict as many casualties as they could before they were forced to adopt their usual suicidal tactics.[19]

The terrain itself consisted of a series of deep crevices and steep ridges that extended generally to the southeast towards the coast. Smaller gullies cutting through the area created a maze of compartments and cross compartments. The rough rocky outcroppings and scrubby vegetation that had survived the extensive shelling provided the Japanese with excellent cover and concealment.

That the elimination of this small but tough pocket of resistance would be a difficult and time-consuming operation had already become apparent to 4th Division Marines by the end of 11 March. The presence of one of the big fish in the pocket, General Senda, commander of the *2d Mixed Brigade,* made it virtually certain that the remnants of that unit would fight to the bitter end with undiminished fanaticism.[20]

Even though there was only a marginal possibility that General Senda might be persuaded to surrender, intelligence personnel of the 4th Marine Division decided on 12 March that such an attempt was worth the effort. A prisoner of war volunteered to lead a detail of Marines to the vicinity of General Senda's presumed hideout during the early morning of D plus 21. Under sniper fire, which eventually caused a casualty, Marines set up an amplifier-speaker system over which an appeal to surrender was to be broadcast. For more than two hours the psychological warfare team failed in its efforts to start a power generator which would have provided the electricity needed to drive the amplifier. A second motor-driven power plant failed to start and due to this technical breakdown the entire operation had to be called off. Whether General Senda might have heeded the appeal promising and guaranteeing him and his men the best of treatment, remains doubtful. Certainly none of the other Japanese commanders approached in this fashion on Iwo Jima proved responsive.

Following the two-hour delay engendered by the abortive surrender appeal, Marines of the 4th Division launched their attack into the pocket at 0900 with 2/25, 3/25, and 2/24. The scheme of maneuver called for 2/25 to attack down the draws toward the coast while 3/25 and 2/24 were to support the attack with heavy weapons fire. This fire, furnished by bazookas, antitank grenades, and 60mm mortars, had to substitute for artillery support. As of 12 March, the limited area occupied by the enemy in the 4th Division zone no longer constituted a practicable target area, and orders had been issued to secure all 4th Division artillery.

The Japanese, firmly entrenched in ravines, caves, and pillboxes, resisted in their customary tenacious fashion, with the result that only minimal progress was made. The character of the terrain precluded the employment of tanks,

---

[19] *4th MarDiv OpRpt,* p. 50.
[20] For a detailed breakdown of General Senda's military career, see *Japanese Defense Agency Comment.*

forcing Marines to flush the enemy out of his emplacements one or two at a time. In addition to the slow progress, this type of fighting was, as usual, expensive for the attacking force. By evening of 12 March, the combat efficiency of General Cates' division had dropped to a new low of 36 percent.[21].

The drive to eliminate General Senda's pocket continued on 13 and 14 March along the same lines as on the 12th. Progress throughout remained agonizingly slow, due to the depletion of personnel as much as enemy resistance. While the pocket was being reduced, the 23d Marines began a systematic mopping up of its area from the beach towards the regimental rear. At the same time, the regiment took care of other urgent business, notably the evacuation of the friendly dead, the burial of enemy dead, and the general policing of the area.

By 15 March, the slow and deliberate advance of the 25th Marines was beginning to bear dividends. Even though the enemy continued to offer desperate resistance, there were signs that his power to resist had been considerably reduced. Since 2/25 had become so depleted in strength that it required relief, 2/24 was ordered into the line. A provisional company composed of headquarters personnel and members of the 81mm mortar platoon of 1/25 was organized to take over the area previously held by 2/24. Colonel Lanigan ordered his men to press the attack into the pocket regardless of contact. At the same time, flame tanks stationed on the road paralleling the east coast of Iwo fired northwestward into the inaccessible draws with good effect.

This drive on D plus 24 resulted in a net gain of 200 yards. More important, it scored a deep penetration of the left flank of the pocket, where General Senda had established his strongest positions. In the midst of this bitter fighting, repeated attempts were made to induce the surrender of the Japanese, but none of them fell on fertile soil. The destruction of one cave after another, together with their occupants, continued.

Increased evidence that the pocket could not hold out much longer was received during the night of 15-16 March, when a group of 50-60 Japanese attempted to break out of the encirclement. Six of the enemy were killed and the remainder were driven back into the caves from which they had emerged. When the 25th Marines resumed the attack at 0630 on 16 March, the Marines drew rifle and machine gun fire, and hand grenades exploded all around them. Nevertheless, the Japanese now fought without any real organization and such resistance as was offered came from small, isolated groups. By midmorning, the assault battalions had fought their way through to the beach road and Colonel Lanigan declared all organized resistance in his zone of action ended as of 1030.[22]

General Senda's body was never found; prisoners volunteered that he had committed suicide on 15 March. As the din of battle receded, all that remained in the hotly contested area were the torn and battered terrain, large

---

[21] *4th MarDiv OpRpt*, p. 53.

[22] *Ibid.*, p. 58.

numbers of enemy dead, and the scarred and blackened cave entrances. In six days of bitter fighting, General Senda's pocket had finally been reduced. The Japanese had fought practically to extinction. The 4th Marine Division had paid for the ground with 833 casualties.

5TH MARINE DIVISION DRIVE TO KITANO POINT[23]

Elimination of the enemy centers of resistance in eastern Iwo Jima left only one area in the hands of the Japanese. This was to be the final enemy pocket of resistance in the very northern part of the island, where General Kuribayashi with about 1,500 men was preparing to make his final stand. The Japanese pocket, squarely in the path of the 5th Marine Division's advance, occupied approximately one square mile between Kita Village and Kitano Point on the northwest coast. Not by coincidence, it also comprised the worst ground on the island.

The badlands of northern Iwo, as this area may well be called, consisted of thousands of soft sandstone outcroppings. Here, the Japanese had dug in with their customary efficiency. Each underground position had been provided with multiple entrances and exits to protect the defenders against fire and to permit their escape if one or more of the entrances were sealed. These defenses had been dug to such a depth that flamethrowers could neither burn out their occupants nor exhaust the supply of oxygen available within this defensive system.

In addition to the excellent cover, the Japanese also had the advantage of effective concealment. Their uniforms blended closely with the color of the sandstone. They were familiar with the maze of tunnels that criss-crossed the entire area and could find their way around in the darkness as well as in the daytime. Fighting this type of defensive action, General Kuribayashi could continue to hang on with the austere means at hand. He had no logistics problem, for anything that had to be moved, be it men or supplies, travelled underground. Such vital supplies as ammunition, food, water and medicine all had been stockpiled underground long before the first Marines began to approach the northern portion of the island. In addition to his extensive preparations for combat, General Kuribayashi had seen to it that the knowledge of the entire defense layout was limited to very few of his men, most of whom were told only enough to be familiar with the immediate defenses in their vicinity. As a result, few of the enemy knew anything about the command setup of their own forces and most of them did not know the precise location of Kuribayashi's command post.

For General Rockey's men, the battle for northwestern Iwo meant a continuation of previous difficulties aggravated by worsening terrain. Once again, they would have to seize the forward face of a ridge, fight their way across the crest, then continue to fight their way down the reverse slope, all the while drawing fire from the front, the flanks, from the

---

[23] Additional material in this section is derived from: *TF 56 OpRpt; 26th Mar AR; 27th Mar UJnl; 27th Mar AR; 28th Mar R-2 Jnl; 28th Mar AR; 13th Mar AR; 1/26 AR; 2/26 AR; 3/26 UJnl; 3/26 AR; 3/27 UJnl; 3/27 AR.*

ENEMY POSITIONS *near Nishi Village under fire. Note burning M-4 tank at left.* *(USMC 142316)*

PRISONER *captured by 5th Marine Division near Hill 165 is escorted to the rear for interrogation.* *(USMC 114881)*

rear, and, in some instances, even from below. The latter circumstance was perhaps the most demoralizing, as pointed out by one participant in the fighting:

> Perhaps worst of all, every Marine commander fighting through this sandstone jungle knew that underneath him were healthy Japanese who would be out that night to harass his rear, steal his supplies, either recover or booby-trap their own dead, and booby-trap his dead if he couldn't get them out first.

And so the battle for Iwo Jima was ending as it had begun, at close quarters with Marine forces stripped of the advantages of their fire power, fighting an enemy who had been indoctrinated since childhood that the greatest honor he would ever know was to die for his Emperor. He could not be threatened out of his position by encirclement or by superior force; he could not be induced to surrender because of his hopeless position—tactically or strategically, he had to be killed.[24]

The 5th Marine Division drive into the biggest enemy pocket remaining on the island got under way on 11 March. The attack was preceded by a 10-minute preparation, which continued until 20 minutes after the jumpoff. The half-hour barrage, fired by the 12th, 13th, and 14th Marines, as well as the corps artillery, provided an impressive spectacle but once again, in accordance with previous experience, was generally ineffective against enemy personnel who huddled in well-protected cave positions.

As the division attacked, with the 27th Marines on the right and the 28th on the left, the men faced a double foe: the Japanese and the terrain, each being equally formidable. The 27th Marines, with 1/26 attached, was able to carve out limited gains of 200 yards and to continue the systematic destruction of enemy cave positions. This was the job of small infantry-demolition teams, which operated more or less on their own, blasting their way forward as they went along. Operating on the division left, the 28th Marines encountered similar difficulties as Marines assaulted individual strongpoints guarding a rocky gorge to the front. The significance of this gorge, which was approximately 200 yards wide and 700 yards long, was not yet apparent to Colonel Liversedge's Marines. However, it was clear that the Japanese had taken great precautions to effectively cover all approaches leading into the gorge with rifle and machine gun fire.

While the enemy generally remained underground and invisible throughout the day, the entire division front erupted into action shortly after nightfall and remained that way throughout the night. Small groups of Japanese continuously attempted to infiltrate the Marine lines. A few were successful in reaching the 81mm mortar positions of 3/27. Seven of the infiltrators were killed in this attempt, one of them wearing a Marine uniform and equipped with an M-1 rifle.[25] Around 2100, an enemy concentration opposite the 28th Marines was broken up by an artillery and mortar barrage which killed 26 of the enemy. Sporadic rifle fire and grenade duels continued for the remainder of the night.

The arrival of daylight on D plus 21 returned the initiative to the Marines, who, once again, carried the battle to the enemy. On this occasion, the day

---

[24] Conner, *The Fifth Marine Division*, p. 107.

[25] *5th MarDiv AR*, p. 26.

started off with several air strikes against enemy positions just south of Kitano Point. One of the 500-pound bombs aimed at a blockhouse missed its target, only to fall into the mouth of a cave, where a tremendous explosion caused not only this entrance, but various others connected to this cave system, to belch fire and smoke. A similar incident occurred during the early afternoon, when a 500-pound bomb hit a cave entrance and created a violent explosion with smoke observed coming out of caves 200-300 yards away.

For the remainder of the day, the course of the fighting mirrored that of D plus 20. The enemy continued to resist from caves, emplacements, and spider foxholes, frequently holding his fire until Marines had approached to within a few feet of his positions. With the support tanks, the 27th Marines made slow progress against a network of pillboxes and prepared positions. In the course of this advance, between 15 and 18 pillboxes were destroyed, but overall progress still had to be measured in a few yards. The Japanese also had learned a few tricks in recent operations and, in order to escape American air strikes and artillery fire, attempted to hug the Marine lines. Backbone of the Japanese defense were his machine guns, rifles, and knee mortars, all of which continued to exact a continuous toll in Marine lives for each foot of the advance.

During the afternoon of 12 March, Company B of the Amphibious Reconnaissance Battalion scouted Kama and Kangoku Rocks, situated close to the northwestern shore of Iwo Jima. Intermittently throughout the campaign, Marines advancing up the west coast had been harassed from suspected Japanese positions on these two islands. There was no doubt that even if the enemy had not permanently stationed artillery there, they harbored keen-eyed observers who had helped to harass shipping approaching the western beaches during the early phase of the operation. As the Marines neared the two islands on 12 vehicles furnished by the 2d Armored Amphibian Battalion, they were greeted by silence. It was decided that a landing on the island would be made at 0900 on the following morning.

These landings, carried out by 6 officers and 94 men, proceeded without incident. The Marines went ashore first on Kama Rock and subsequently on Kangoku, the larger island. On the latter, there was evidence of previous enemy occupancy in the form of several caves and stone emplacements, but no Japanese were present to offer any resistance. Having completed its mission, the reconnaissance company withdrew from the islands.

In a report issued on 12 March, the 5th Marine Division intelligence officer estimated that at least 1,000 Japanese were still defending the northern end of Iwo Jima and concluded: ". . . there is no shortage of manpower, weapons, or ammunition in the area the Japanese have left to defend."[26] Actually, the battle was beginning to reach General Kuribayashi's very doorstep. As one account was to relate it:

> On March 13, a patrol from the 26th Regiment came very near to Kuribayashi, peering into the cave in which he sat, near

---

[26] *5th MarDiv D-2 PerRpt* No. 22, dtd 12-Mar45.

the eastern end of the Gorge. The General's orderly quickly blew out the candles and wrapped the General in a blanket. "Thank you," Kuribayashi said, and walked deeper into the cave. The Marines, one carrying a flamethrower walked a little way into the cave then turned and went out. The orderly sighed.[27]

While the Japanese on northern Iwo Jima had been suffering badly in the battle of attrition that was now reaching its climax, the Marines of all three divisions had hardly fared any better. As assault troops of General Rockey's division were beginning to close in on the final enemy pocket, the men wearily attacking the ridges above the gorge were tired to the point of exhaustion and many of them found it difficult to remain on their feet. Few veterans of the early battles were left, and death had reaped a grim harvest among the men who had gone ashore on the island 22 days before. Companies were now reduced to platoon size. Most of the aggressive and experienced small unit leaders had long since become casualties. Gaps in the decimated ranks had been filled with replacements who lacked combat experience that would enable them to fight and survive.

On 14 March it became apparent that the slow, step-by-step advance of the 27th Marines finally had cracked the strong enemy positions along the northeastern coast of Iwo Jima. Since the main ridge lines in this area ran from the center of the island to the sea on the west coast, General Rockey decided that the most practical direction of attack henceforth would be from east to west. As a result, the 28th Marines was ordered to hold its present line while the 27th Marines was to shift its direction of attack westward. In the center of the division line the 26th Marines took over a two-battalion front and was ordered to attack northward with 3/26 on the left and 2/26 on the right.

Enemy resistance was less obstinate on D plus 23 than it had been during the preceding days and the 27th Marines, with 2/26 attached, gained up to 600 yards. The attack was supported by tanks which were able to assist the infantry after armored tankdozers had carved routes of approach to the front lines for them. The official report, speaking of the flame tanks, pointed out:

> ... this was the one weapon that caused the Japs to leave their caves and rock crevices and run. On many occasions the Japs attempted to charge our flame tanks with shaped charges and other explosives. Few of these attempts were successful.[28]

Other developments on Iwo Jima on 14 March gave clear evidence that the end of the long battle was approaching. In mid-morning, five Army Air Forces planes bombed and strafed Japanese positions in front of 3/27 for what proved to be the last air support mission over Iwo Jima. The diminishing size of General Kuribayashi's pocket rendered all further air support impractical. Limited support until the end of the operation would continue to be furnished by artillery and destroyers, and even these supporting arms soon found it difficult to furnish fire in the small area still remaining under enemy control.

While compression of the northern pocket was under way, a ceremony was

---

[27] Newcomb, *Iwo Jima*, pp. 270–271.

[28] *5th MarDiv AR*, p. 27.

taking place at 0930 on 14 March at General Schmidt's headquarters. It was not an elaborate proceeding; in fact, its stark simplicity underscored the significance of the long awaited event. In the presence of flag and general officers of the fleet and landing force, assembled around a flagpole erected in these stark surroundings, the official flag raising on Iwo Jima was held. Among those present were General Holland Smith, Admirals Turner and Hill, and Generals Schmidt, Erskine, Cates, Rockey, and Major General Chaney, representing the Army Garrison Force.[29] After the reading of an official proclamation in which the United States officially suspended the powers of government of the Japanese Empire and took over the occupation of the island, the flag was raised at the same time that the one on top of Mount Suribachi was taken down. Upon completion of the ceremony, General Holland Smith and his staff departed from the island by air.[30]

The night from 14-15 March was marked by continuous enemy activity directed against the 5th Division lines. Around 0200, close to 100 Japanese attempted to infiltrate the positions of 3/27. In the ensuing firefight, 15 of the enemy were killed, most of them by mortar fire.[31] Around the same time, a small number of Japanese approached the lines of 2/26 and started tossing hand grenades. At dawn, the action shifted to 3/26, where 30 of the enemy were discovered attempting to enter caves southwest of Kitano Point. Half of this group were killed, the remainder committed suicide.[32]

The 5th Division attack continued on 15 March. On the right, the 27th Marines advanced 400 yards and reduced enemy resistance in this sector to sporadic small arms fire. In the center, the 26th Marines made smaller but equally significant gains, carving out an advance of 200 yards. On the division left, in front of the 28th Marines, enemy reaction remained determined and formidable. At this time, enemy resistance was still centered in two areas: the steep draw that extended northwest to the sea across the front of the 28th Marines and the strong core of resistance in front of the 26th Marines, just east of the draw.

Within the diminishing pocket, General Kuribayashi and the surviving members of his staff were still in radio contact with the Japanese on Chichi Jima. They were also able to listen to the "Song of Iwo Jima," especially broadcast from Tokyo for the Iwo Jima garrison. Already on the morning of 15 March, General Kuribayashi had announced that the situation was very dangerous and that his strength was down to 900 men.[33] By the evening of the following day, his strength had been reduced to 500. Clearly, the end was

---

[29] The VAC chief of staff recalled that "while the ceremony of raising the flag was in progress near VAC headquarters, the ground was shaking around us from the bombardment of the unsecured area by nearby Corps artillery." *Rogers ltr.*
[30] *TF 56 OpRpt*, pp. 10–11.
[31] *5th MarDiv AR*, p. 27.

[32] *Ibid.*
[33] *Horie Rpt*, p. 10.

drawing near. General Kuribayashi summoned the commander of the *145th Infantry Regiment*, Colonel Ikeda, to see how much longer resistance could continue. When the regimental commander informed him that it would all be over in another day or so, General Kuribayashi admonished him to be certain that the regimental colors were burned lest they fall into American hands.

Behind the Marine lines, additional signs of progress were becoming evident as the naval construction engineers put the final touches on the restoration of the Central Airfield. Even though the runways remained unpaved, they were usable and the field was about to become operational. Additional gasoline storage facilities had been completed, and the carpenters of the 5th Division were already busily engaged in building crates in which the division's equipment would be shipped. At the southern end of Iwo Jima, a dirt road leading to the top of Mount Suribachi had been completed and it was now possible to make the trip up by jeep or bulldozer.

Reduction of the northern pocket continued on 16 March. During this final phase of the operation, General Rockey's division was supported by elements of the 3d Marine Division, which passed through the 27th Marines and took over a sector on the right of the 5th Division. Attacking to the north, General Erskine's men reached the north coast shortly before 1400.

The 26th Marines, with 3/28 attached, attacked with three battalions abreast. The advance progressed slowly against heavy rifle fire, as it proceeded over rugged and rocky ground, where all movement was extremely difficult. However, it was a sign of the progress that had already been made that the volume of enemy machine gun fire had greatly diminished, as had the number of caves that were encountered. Nevertheless, there was still an abundance of spider foxholes and positions in the rocky outcrops which permitted the enemy to inflict a deadly fire from close range. In the course of the day, the 26th Marines advanced 200 yards. The 28th Marines remained in position along the southern rim of the rocky gorge and continued the reduction of enemy defenses to its immediate front and flanks. Losses of the 5th Marine Division at this time consisted of 89 officers and 1,993 men killed, 249 officers and 5,710 enlisted men wounded, and 3 officers and 128 men missing. Combat efficiency was estimated at 30 percent.[34] The division had sustained a total of 8,162 casualties in 25 days of fighting.

At 1800 on 16 March, Iwo Jima was officially declared secured. Three hours earlier, the 13th Marines had fired its last rounds, since the regiment's guns could no longer furnish supporting fires in the limited area comprising the remaining pockets of resistance. It now became incumbent on the mixed 3d and 5th Division assault forces to complete the occupation of the island with all possible dispatch, a task easier contemplated than accomplished.

Following its relief by the 21st Marines on 16 March, the 27th Marines re-

---
[34] *5th MarDiv AR*, p. 28.

organized its badly depleted units into three battalions, each consisting of two rifle companies and a headquarters company. A composite battalion, consisting of a headquarters company and four rifle companies, was formed under the command of Lieutenant Colonel Donn J. Robertson. A small remainder of the 27th Marines stayed in division reserve until the end of the operation. The unit mopped up in the rear area and prepared to leave the island. The composite battalion, numbering 460 men, subsequently was to be attached to the 26th Marines, where it would participate in eliminating the final enemy positions on northern Iwo Jima.

All of the records dealing with this final phase of the operation emphasize the state of exhaustion in which the men found themselves. According to one account:

> That the Division still moved forward at all was a credit to the men and their leaders, but the fearful strain of days in the line was showing up in every unit. Men were getting careless, exposing themselves to fire when they were tired. Too, many of the men now were replacements, men who fought gallantly and brought credit to themselves and the Division, but who were not, nevertheless, as highly trained as the Division's original men had been and for that reason probably took slightly heavier losses.[35]

A sustained effort was made on the part of General Rockey's division to keep up morale. Baked goods and fruit juice were sent to the units in the line; the wounded were evacuated and the dead buried with all possible dispatch. A division newspaper was circulated among the frontline units, and such articles of clothing and toilet articles as were available were sent up to the lines. Some of the more lucky Marines even enjoyed the luxury of hot showers. But, despite such amenities, the report concludes "Iwo Jima remained an unclean, evil little island, an island that these men would never forget, however much they would have liked to."[36]

Despite their ebbing strength and often only through the application of sheer will power, those men of the 3d and 5th Marine Divisions still able to move on their feet and carry a weapon now entered the final phase of the battle for Iwo Jima. Fought in a narrow corner of the island, the final struggle would prove every bit as difficult as the early phase of the operation: death came no easier now than in the beginning.

With the end clearly approaching and under steadily increasing pressure from the advancing Marines, General Kuribayashi on 16 or 17 March left his headquarters, housed in a large dome-shaped concrete structure, and moved to a cave occupied by Colonel Ikeda and Admiral Ichimaru, the remaining senior officers of the Iwo Jima garrison following the death of Major General Senda and Captain Inouye in the 4th Division sector. From this cave, situated near the southeastern end of the gorge, the Japanese officers could do little but exhort their men to continue resistance to the last. This cave was still linked to Chichi Jima by radio, and thus the final days of Japanese resistance on Iwo Jima have become a matter of record.

---

[35] Conner, *The Fifth Marine Division*, p. 113.

[36] *Ibid.*, p. 114.

BATTLE FOR THE GORGE AND FINAL OPERATIONS[37]

The final battle for Iwo Jima began on 17 March, D plus 26, when 1/26 reached the north coast and pivoted to the southwest towards the gorge which had already been blocked by the 28th Marines for the past few days. (See Map XI, Map Section). It was here that General Kuribayashi had determined to make his final stand, and he had chosen his final position with great care. The gorge, 700 yards long and 200-500 yards wide, would have been difficult to approach even under normal conditions. Outcrops of rocks subdivided the ravine into minor draws that greatly impeded all movement. The Japanese commander had taken care to insure that all routes of approach leading into the gorge were covered by machine gun and rifle fire from positions that were all but invisible to the approaching Marines.

Units of the 5th Marine Division preparing to offer the coup de grace to the final enemy position on the island would have to use their last strength in attaining this objective. A brief breakdown of casualties in this connection speaks for itself:

> Our own losses at this time had been extremely heavy. The average battalion which landed with 36 officers and 885 enlisted, now had about 16 officers and 300 enlisted from the original battalion. Most of the company commanders, platoon leaders, and squad leaders had become casualties and many platoons were commanded by Corporals or PFC's. Assault squads were depleted.[38]

Plans for reducing the final pocket called for the 28th Marines, with elements of the 5th Pioneer Battalion and the division reconnaissance company attached, to occupy a blocking position along the southern rim of the pocket while the 26th Marines, in conjunction with 3/28 and 3/27, was to advance into the gorge from the north and east. Because of the depleted strength of the units and the condition of the men, assigned zones of action were relatively narrow. In their drive against the pocket on 17 March, 3/26 and 3/28 made slight gains in the northeastern perimeter of the pocket, but once again their progress could be measured in yards.

A drama of a different sort was enacted on the island on D plus 26. On the preceding day, prisoners captured by General Erskine's men had conveyed to their captors the whereabouts of General Kuribayashi and his staff, and, acting upon this information, General Erskine decided to make an attempt to induce these officers to surrender. Realizing that a direct appeal to General Kuribayashi would be fruitless, General Erskine instead dispatched a message to Colonel Ikeda, commanding the *145th Infantry Regiment*. The message was handed to two prisoners of war who, carrying cigarettes and rations, proceeded into the gorge, fully aware of the importance of their mission. As they trudged off on this unusual errand, the pair was handed a walkie-talkie over

---

[37] Additional material in this section is derived from: *1/28 AR; 2/28 AR; 3/28 AR;* 5th Pioneeer Bn UJnl, 7–23Mar45; U. S. Army Forces in the Pacific Ocean Areas Rpt, Iwo Jima, Feb–Mar45, dtd 4Feb46; *VAC Shore Party AR;* Clive Howard and Joe Whitley, *One Damned Island After Another* (Chapel Hill: The University of North Carolina Press), 1946.

[38] *5th MarDiv AR*, p. 29.

which they were to maintain contact with the 3d Division Language Section.

As they slowly continued on their journey, the two emissaries crossed lines and soon made contact with groups of Japanese, apparently without arousing anyone's suspicion. Several radio messages were received by 3d Division personnel indicating that the prisoners were getting close to their objective. At this point, the couriers stopped all further transmissions. One of them, who had incurred a leg wound, dropped out, but the other continued and six hours after embarking on his bizarre mission, reached the headquarters cave. There, he turned the message over to one of the sentries who passed it on to the regimental commander. Upon learning that Ikeda had taken the message in to General Kuribayashi, the prisoner lost his nerve and beat a hasty retreat.

As soon as he had rejoined his fellow courier, the radio trasmissions to the 3d Division resumed and the Marines were informed that the two were on their way back. Upon reaching the Marine lines at the rim of the gorge, the prisoners thought themselves safe and were more than slightly disturbed at the rude reception accorded to them by 5th Division Marines, who were unaware of General Erskine's psychological warfare effort. The situation was finally straightened out before the two messengers came to any harm, though it took some convincing of the skeptical 5th Division Marines that the two Japanese were indeed working for General Erskine.

The practical results of this surrender attempt, as in previous instances, were nil. None of the high-ranking Japanese officers on Iwo Jima surrendered, and the battle of attrition continued to take its slow and agonizing course. Even though nearly all of the Japanese on Iwo Jima, under General Kuribayashi's dynamic leadership, would fight to the end, there were some who heeded the repeated appeals to surrender. American planes dropped propaganda leaflets, and the artillery fired shells filled with surrender leaflets and passes. For the Japanese soldier on Iwo Jima, surrender was not an easy matter. He could count on being executed by his own people if caught with American propaganda on his person. Surrender might mean that he could never again return to his homeland and face his compatriots. And, last but not least, he had no guarantee that the Marines would honor their promise of fair treatment once he turned himself in to them. No wonder that the Japanese were hesitant to take the final and irreversible step in view of the uncertainty surrounding it. A sampling of 65 prisoners of war showed that 53 had been influenced in their decision to give up by some contact with American propaganda. The remaining 12 had been deterred by fear of their officers and distrust of the Marines and were captured under different circumstances.[39]

Meanwhile, the Marines continued to close in on General Kuribayashi's pocket. With the end in sight, the Japanese garrison commander addressed this order to his men on 17 March:

    1. The battle situation came to the last moment.

---

[39] *VAC G-2 Rpts*, pp. 19, 20.

2. I want my surviving officers and men to go out and attack the enemy tonight.

3. Each troop! Go out simultaneously at midnight and attack the enemy until the last. You all have devoted yourself to His Majesty, the Emperor. Don't think of yourself.

4. I am always at the head of you all.[40]

Strangely enough, there was no unusual activity during the night from 17-18 March, and nothing even resembling a *banzai* charge occurred. From this point onward, the information concerning the last days of the enemy's battle for Iwo Jima becomes increasingly hazy. Most of what has remained passed through the hands of the Chichi Jima garrison, which continued to receive radio messages from Iwo that were filed and subsequently turned over to the Americans. Thus, early on 17 March, Chichi Jima was notified that "the *145th Infantry Regiment* fought bravely near 'Hyoriuboku' holding their regimental flag in the center." Later in the day, Colonel Ikeda sent this cryptic message: "Here we burnt our brilliant Regimental Flag completely. Good bye."[41]

Iwo Jima became the scene of a wild celebration on the evening of 18 March. It had nothing to do with the fact that the enemy was finally cornered in the northwestern portion of the island and his elimination now was but a matter of days. Instead, someone had leaked word that Germany had surrendered, and this item of news, entirely unfounded and nearly two months premature, spread all over Iwo Jima like wildfire. As a result:

...for about an hour the island was the happiest spot on earth. Antiaircraft and other units in rear areas opened up a jubilant barrage with machine guns, antiaircraft guns, carbines, rifles, and pistols.[42]

Before it was over, units all over the island and the ships offshore had the news. An end to the celebration came only when Condition Red was declared, a warning that enemy planes were in the area. As one account has it, "The Fifth Division hospital treated three casualties from 'the German war' and there were certainly others."[43] Following the excitement, Marines on Iwo Jima returned to the more normal routine of routing individual Japanese and thwarting the enemy's infiltration attempts.

As the advance continued on 19 March, enemy resistance became centered around General Kuribayashi's erstwhile headquarters. The structure proved completely impervious to the 75mm tank shells and likewise defied all attempts to demolish it with 40-pound shaped charges. It would take the assaulting Marines two days to destroy the surrounding positions and then commence a direct assault on the command center. Engineers with bulldozers sealed an entrance on the north side of the structure and several air vents. Finally, four tons of explosives, divided into five charges, proved sufficient to destroy this stubborn center of resistance. Just who and how many among the Japanese perished within has never become known. However, the garrison commander and the high-ranking officers were safely tucked away in Colonel Ikeda's cave, and reports continued to reach Chichi Jima, though

---

[40] *Horie Rpt*, p. 11.
[41] *Ibid.*
[42] Conner, *The Fifth Marine Division*, p. 117.
[43] Newcomb, *Iwo Jima*, p. 281.

communications daily became more sporadic.

Around 17-18 March, General Kuribayashi sent his final message to Imperial General Headquarters, in which he apologized to the Emperor for his failure to hold the island. The message was accompanied by a poem in which the garrison commander promised:

> My body shall not decay in the field
> Unless we are avenged;
> I will be born seven more times again
> To take up arms against the foe.
> My only concern is
> Our country in the future
> When weeds cover here.[44]

About the same time, but in a less poetic and more down-to-earth fashion, Admiral Ichimaru penned a rather vituperative letter to none other than President Roosevelt, charging the latter with a lack of understanding for Japan's problems and accusing the white race, and the Anglo-Saxons in particular, "of monopolizing the fruits of the world, at the sacrifice of the colored races."[45]

Meanwhile, reduction of the pocket continued unabated. Tanks moved up to the front lines over paths cleared by the tank dozers which themselves frequently came under attack by individuals or small groups of Japanese bent on suicide. The slow but steady Marine advance into the gorge was carried out under the command of the assistant division commander, General Hermle, whom General Rockey had entrusted with operational control of all units engaged in the final mop-up at the gorge. From an observation post affording a clear view of the gorge, General Hermle directed the operation that would bring organized enemy resistance in this sector to an end.

On Chichi Jima, Major Horie learned with astonishment on 21 March that General Kuribayashi and his men were still fighting. The durable garrison commander reported that his cave was under direct attack by tanks and demolition teams. Of American attempts to induce his surrender he mentioned disdainfully that "they advised us to surrender by a loud-speaker, but we only laughed at this childish trick and did not set ourselves against them."[46] Major Horie radioed to Iwo Jima the information that, effective 17 March, the Imperial government had promoted Kuribayashi to the rank of full general, Ichimaru to vice admiral, Inouye to rear admiral, and Nishi to full colonel. The two latter promotions were made posthumously, though most likely all of them were intended that way.

On D plus 30, 21 March, the 26th Marines, with 3/27 and 3/28 attached, continued the assault as 1/26 and 3/27 advanced into the gorge. At the rim, 3/28 held its positions. Fighting on this day, as on the preceding ones, was exceedingly bitter. The Japanese refused to yield; in fact, there no longer was any place for them to go but stand their ground and die. Thus, the Marines had to eliminate them one by one. As on an earlier occasion, it was noticed that many of the enemy were wearing Ma-

---

[44] Newcomb, *Iwo Jima*, p. 272.

[45] Admiral Ichimaru ltr to President Roosevelt, n.d., in Morehouse, *Iwo Jima Campaign*, pp. 172–173. This letter was found by Marines in a cave in the northern part of Iwo Jima; the original reposes in the museum of the U.S. Naval Academy, Annapolis, Md.

[46] *Horie Rpt*, p. 11.

rine uniforms and firing M-1 rifles. In the course of the day's advance, elements of 1/26 made gains of 200 yards down the gorge, but beyond that point required the support of flame tanks. It developed that the terrain did not permit their employment, so that portable flamethrowers were used until the Japanese shot the liquid out of the tanks. When his equipment was hit, one of the operators became a human torch and burned to death; another was just barely saved from suffering the same fate.

As D plus 30 ended, 1/28 had gained 400 yards at the edge of the cliff, while 2/28, after one of its patrols had eliminated 20 of the enemy, moved forward 100 yards to the very edge of the cliff. On this day, Major Horie received a message from Iwo Jima, informing him: "We have not eaten nor drunk for five days. But our fighting spirit is still running high."[47] The end was now very near, yet the battle for Death Valley, a name Marines had given to the gorge, continued. In a situation where the orthodox arms and tactics of warfare proved unavailing, other means had to be improvised. In the words of one account:

> The Marines tried everything in the book, and a good many things that weren't, to clean the Japs out of the gorge. Explosives were lowered over cliffs by rope to blast the Japs from their caves. Drums of gasoline were emptied into canyons and set afire. Over-sized rockets were hauled up to the front on bulldozers and used to blow the Japs off hillsides. Aerial observers dropped grenades on enemy positions from their low-flying grasshoppers.

[47] *Ibid.*, p. 12.

For four days men of the 5th Division tried to take Death Valley by direct assault. They failed, because any man who set foot in the gorge was dead.[48]

Still, some progress was apparent as one enemy defensive position after another was whittled away. On 22 March, 3/27, supported by tanks, tank dozers, and flame tanks, gained another 300 yards. On the following day, D plus 32, Major Horie received one final message from Iwo Jima which said: "All officers and men of Chichi Jima, good-bye."[49] For three more days, Horie tried to communicate with Iwo Jima, but there was no answer and it was assumed that all resistance on the island had ended. This fact had already been mournfully announced over Tokyo Radio by the Japanese Prime Minister, who bemoaned the fall of the island as "the most unfortunate thing in the whole war situation."[50]

By 24 March, the backbone of enemy resistance in Death Valley had been broken, and the size of the pocket was down to a square of 50 by 50 yards. On the following day, D plus 32, exhausted Marines of 3/26 and 3/28 moved down into Death Valley and completed the task of mopping up, sealing caves and squeezing the enemy into an area that was no longer defensible. Still, individual Japanese held out until 25 March, when death-tired remnants of the 26th, 27th, and 28th Marines staggered into the gorge and silenced what remained of enemy resistance. At

[48] Henri *et al, Marines on Iwo Jima*, p. 303.
[49] *Horie Rpt*, p. 12.
[50] Radio address by Premier Kuniaki Koiso, 17Mar45, as cited in Newcomb, *Iwo Jima*, p. 274.

1045 on D plus 34, the gorge was declared secured and fighting on northern Iwo officially came to an end.

Withdrawal of Marine units from Iwo Jima got under way on 17 March, when the VAC artillery completed embarkation. Artillery of the three divisions reembarked on subsequent days, except for 4/12, which stood by for several days, prepared to deliver fire on request. On 18 March, the 3d Marine Division relieved the 4th and General Cates closed his CP on Iwo Jima. On the same day, men of this division embarked. Two days later, the ships carrying the division departed from the island en route to their rehabilitation area in Hawaii. The arrival of the 147th Infantry Regiment on 20 March brought Army troops into the picture. The regiment was attached to General Erskine's division for operational control. As early as 7 March, General Chaney had assumed responsibility for base development and antiaircraft defense of all Iwo ground installations. He had delegated the air defense of Iwo Jima to General Moore effective that date. At 0800 on 26 March, General Chaney took over as Iwo Jima garrison commander, in effect assuming operational control of all units stationed on the island. General Moore continued as Air Defense Commander.

Just as it appeared that Iwo Jima was about to become a garrison, rather than a fiercely contested battlefield, the Japanese decided to strike a last blow against the invaders who by this time had victory all but within their grasp. Mopping up operations up to this time had continued daily in northern and central Iwo, and day and night individual Japanese had either been killed or captured. As a precautionary measure, a LCI(G) patrolled off the northwest beaches to prevent the escape of any of the enemy by water during the hours of darkness.

Early on 26 March, a force of between 200 and 300 Japanese moved down from the area near the Northern Airfield over a trail skirting the western coast of the island and launched a full-scale attack against Marine and Army units encamped near the western beaches. Far from executing a howling *banzai* charge, the Japanese launched a well-organized attack which was carried out in echelon from three directions. Carefully calculated to achieve the maximum confusion and destruction, the Japanese set about to do their deadly work in silence. Beginning at 0515, and for more than three hours, the enemy ranged through the Marine and Army bivouacs, slashing tents, knifing sleeping airmen, and throwing grenades at random.

The units engaged and partly overrun were the 5th Pioneer Battalion, elements of the 8th Field Depot, comprising the VAC Shore Party, the 98th Naval Construction Battalion, elements of the 21st Fighter Group, the 465th Aviation Squadron, and the 506th Antiaircraft Artillery Gun Battalion. In the darkness, the fighting was confused and terrible. The chief difficulty, that of distinguishing between friend and enemy, was compounded by the fact that many of the attackers were armed with BARs, M-1 rifles, .45 caliber pistols, and one even with a bazooka. Other Japanese charged with their swords, a sure indication that a sizable part of the assault force consisted of officers.

FINAL OPERATIONS ON IWO JIMA 709

OFFICER BIVOUAC AREA *of the 21st Fighter Group following the Japanese attack of March 1945. Note bullet-marked tents. (USAF 47590 AC)*

GENERAL VIEW *of parking area on Motoyama Airfield No. 1 after its restoration. (USAF 57620 AC)*

At the height of the attack, the Japanese penetrated to the Army 38th Field Hospital, where they tore out the telephone lines, slashed tents, and machine-gunned ambulances. In the midst of the prevailing turmoil, officers of the 5th Pioneer Battalion organized the first resistance, and there were instances of great personal heroism and sacrifice. Initially, a firing line was established in some foxholes. Subsequently, as the din of battle increased, other Marines arrived on the scene and Army flame tanks began to go into action. The 5th Pioneers organized a skirmish line and, for the first time, the enemy was forced to give ground. Joining in the action was anyone who had a weapon, including airmen, Seabees, Army medical personnel, and members of the Corps Shore Party. In fact, the performance of the latter Marines earned them a special commendation from their commanding officer who stated:

> The Corps Shore Party Commander is highly gratified with the performance of these colored troops, whose normal function is that of labor troops, while in direct action against the enemy for the first time. Proper security prevented their being taken unawares, and they conducted themselves with marked coolness and courage. Careful investigation shows that they displayed modesty in reporting their own part in the action.[51]

When it was all over, 196 Japanese littered the area of the 5th Pioneer Battalion alone; 66 of the raiders were killed in the adjacent areas and a total of 18 were captured. Rumor had it that General Kuribayashi had led the attack, and the efficiency with which it was carried out would lend some substance to the report. The 40 swords gathered up on the field of battle after the action gave evidence of the high percentage of officers and senior noncommissioned officers that participated. Years after the war, a Japanese who had been taken prisoner during this final attack and who had been subsequently repatriated, was to claim that one-legged Admiral Ichimaru had taken part in the charge. But a body count following the battle and examination of the bodies failed to identify either Kuribayashi, Ichimaru, or Ikeda, and their exact fate has never been determined.

The final Japanese attack also proved costly to the Americans in terms of casualties. The 5th Pioneers lost 9 killed and 31 wounded in this action; units of the VII Fighter Command had 44 killed and 88 wounded.[52] At just about the time that the last of the enemy raiders were being killed off on western Iwo, the capture and occupation phase of the Iwo Jima operation was announced completed. As of 0800, 26 March, the Commander Forward Area, Central Pacific, Vice Admiral John H. Hoover, assumed responsibility for the defense and development of the island. General Schmidt closed his CP and departed from Iwo Jima by air shortly after noon. The remainder of his headquarters embarked on the USS *President Monroe*.

Embarkation of the remaining Marine units followed a schedule long

---

[51] Shore Party AR, dtd 30Apr45, in *VAC AR*, App 10, Anx C, p. 13.

[52] *VAC G-3 PerRpt* No. 35 dtd 26Mar45; *5th Pioneer Bn AR*, Iwo Jima, 27Mar45, p. 2.

worked out in advance. Thus, elements of the 3d Marine Division began to embark on 27 March, when the 21st Marines and the division CP went aboard ship. The remainder of General Erskine's men departed on the return run of ships carrying garrison forces to Iwo. On 4 April, the Army's 147th Infantry Regiment, commanded by Colonel Robert F. Johnson, assumed full responsibility for the ground defense of the island and the 9th Marines prepared to embark. The last unit of General Erskine's division left Iwo on 12 April and arrived on Guam six days later. During the final phase of the operation between 11 and 26 March, the Marines had sustained a total of 8,885 casualties.[53] Total Marine casualties for the Iwo Jima operation came to 25,851.[54]

The total number of Japanese who died in the defense of Iwo Jima has never been definitely established, but nearly the entire garrison went down fighting. As of 26 March, the Marines had taken only 216 prisoners,[55] a large number of whom were Korean laborers. Nor did the fighting and dying on the island end with the departure of the VAC Landing Force. Aggressive patrols and ambuscades by the 147th Infantry Regiment continued throughout April and into May, resulting in additional Japanese killed and captured. Isolated enemy strongpoints continued to hold out and had to be reduced, some of them more than once.

During the first week of April, in an incident reminiscent of the unexpected enemy attack of 26 March, about 200 Japanese materialized just above the East Boat Basin, where they attempted to rush an infantry command post. This battle continued all night and all of the attackers were killed, but not before they had succeeded in exploding 6,000 cases of dynamite, which rocked the island and caused a number of casualties.[56] Nor was this the end. Also during the month of April, Army troops stumbled upon the field hospital of the *2d Mixed Brigade*, located 100 feet underground on eastern Iwo Jima. The surrender of the hospital proved to be somewhat complex, as outlined by this account:

> A language officer appealed to the Japanese to come out. After a long discussion, the senior medical officer, Major Masaru Inoaka, called for a vote. The ballot turned out sixty-nine for surrender, 3 opposed. Of the three nays, Corporal Kyutaro Kojima immediately committed suicide. The others came out, including two more medical officers, Captain Iwao Noguchi and Lieutenant Hideo Ota. Captain Noguchi, beset by remorse that he had lived while so many died, later emigrated to Brazil, unable to accept life in Japan.[57]

For the remainder of April and May, members of the 147th Infantry Regi-

---

[53] Broken down by divisions, these casualties were as follows: 3d Marine Division: 147 killed, 60 died of wounds, 505 wounded, and 53 combat fatigue; 4th Marine Division: 139 killed, 87 dead of wounds, 412 wounded, and 52 combat fatigue; 5th Marine Division: 467 killed, 168 died of wounds, 1,640 wounded, 3 missing, and 122 combat fatigue. Above figures derived from HQMC postwar statistics.

[54] A detailed breakdown of Marine casualties by unit is shown in Appendix H.

[55] *VAC G–2 PerRpt* No. 35, dtd 9Apr45.

[56] Headquarters, Army Garrison Force G–2 Weekly Rpt No. 2, dtd 8Apr45, as cited in Morison, *Victory in the Pacific*, pp. 69–70.

[57] Newcomb, *Iwo Jima*, p. 287.

ment accounted for 1,602 Japanese killed and 867 captured.[58] As the fighting and dying gradually subsided, the utilization of the island as a forward base went into high gear. But even as bulldozers tore across ground that had previously been so bitterly contested and aviation gas was beginning to reach Iwo in large quantities, three large Marine Corps cemeteries remained to offer a mute eulogy to the men who had fought and died there. Arriving on Iwo Jima on 20 April 1945, one eminent Navy historian counted 5,330 graves in the Marine Corps cemeteries, but, in his own words:

> . . . there were about 31,000 soldiers, Air Force ground crews and Seabees on the island, very much alive, healthy and in high spirits. Army officers said they wouldn't trade Iwo for any South Pacific island.[59]

There were many who would pay tribute to the heroism of the Marines who captured this key bastion of the Japanese inner defense ring, bristling with the most powerful defenses a clever and crafty enemy could devise. None of them put it better than Admiral Nimitz, Commander in Chief of the Pacific Fleet and Pacific Ocean Areas, who made this comment:

> The battle of Iwo Island has been won. The United States Marines by their individual and collective courage have conquered a base which is as necessary to us in our continuing forward movement toward final victory as it was vital to the enemy in staving off ultimate defeat.
>
> By their victory the Third, Fourth and Fifth Marine Divisions and other units of the Fifth Amphibious Corps have made an accounting to their country which only history will be able to value fully. Among the Americans who served on Iwo Island uncommon valor was a common virtue.[60]

---

[58] Headquarters, 147th Infantry Regiment, Report of Operations Against the Enemy, Iwo Jima, dtd 11Jun45, as cited in Bartley, *Iwo Monograph*, p. 193.

[59] Morison, *Victory in the Pacific*, p. 70.

[60] Pacific Fleet Communique No. 300, dtd 17Mar45.

CHAPTER 12

Summary[1]

The battle of Iwo Jima requires a detailed analysis because it was unique in certain respects. First, it featured the employment of three Marine divisions (less one regiment) under a single tactical Marine command, the largest body of Marines committed to combat in one operation during World War II. Secondly, enemy resistance under General Kuribayashi was such that American casualties sustained in this operation exceeded those of the Japanese. Out of the savage struggle for eight square miles of inhospitable island emerged convincing re-affirmation of the fact that once air and naval superiority had been gained over and around an objective, Marines could make a landing, gain a foothold, and extend it until the enemy was driven into a severely restricted area. There, he could be annihilated, regardless of the size and number of his guns or the quality of his defense. The then Secretary of the Navy, James V. Forrestal, gave voice to his "tremendous admiration and reverence for the guy who walks up beaches and takes enemy positions with a rifle and grenades or his bare hands."[2] Yet it would be folly to assume that sheer courage alone, even when coupled with material superiority, was the decisive factor that led to certain, if bloody, victory. Even Admiral Spruance's statement, that "in view of the character of the defenses and the stubborn resistance encountered, it is fortunate that less seasoned or less resolute troops were not committed,"[3] only touches on one important facet within the overall picture.

The reason Marines were able to prevail against a firmly entrenched enemy, who knew in advance of the impending attack, can be found in detailed and meticulous planning. The plans for the Iwo Jima operation possibly were the most far-reaching for any operation in the Pacific area up to this time in World War II. Preparations extended not only to American bases in the Marianas, the Marshalls, and the Hawaiian Islands but all the way back to the mainland of the United States, "from whence came hundreds of new ships to transport the troops to the

---

[1] Unless otherwise noted, the material in this chapter is derived from: *Fifth Fleet OpRpt; TF 51 AR; TF 52 AR; TF 53 OpRpt; TG 53.2 AR; TF 56 AR; VAC AR; VAC NGF Rpt; 3d MarDiv AR; 4th MarDiv OpRpt; 5th MarDiv AR; 1st Prov FdArty Gp AR;* Shaw, Nalty, and Turnbladh, *Central Pacific Drive;* Bartley, *Iwo Monograph; Iwo Comments;* Morehouse, *Iwo Jima Campaign;* Craven and Cate, *The Pacific;* Forrestel, *Admiral Spruance;* Morison, *Victory in the Pacific;* Isely and Crowl, *U S. Marines and Amphibious War;* Sherrod, *Marine Corps Aviation in World War II;* Heinl, *Soldiers of the Sea.*

[2] Quoted in *The New York Times,* dtd 26-Feb45, p. 1, col 6, as cited in Bartley, *Iwo Monograph,* p. 210.

[3] *Fifth Flt OpRpt,* p. 8.

713

objective. Most of these ships were under construction less than six months before the target day, and some of the smaller ones existed at that time only in blueprint form."[4] In fact, with one exception, the transports carrying the 4th and 5th Marine Divisions to the objective were either under construction or being commissioned as late as 31 October 1944.[5] It is typical of the long-range planning preceding Operation DETACHMENT that many of the participating vessels had to be transferred from the European Theater to the Pacific prior to the invasion.

At Iwo Jima, as in similar operations, two command ships were employed so that, in the event one command ship became a casualty, the commander aboard the other could take over. In this case Admiral Turner, as Expeditionary Force Commander, was embarked in a command ship with General Holland Smith as Expeditionary Troops Commander, while Admiral Harry Hill, as Attack Force Commander and General Schmidt, as Landing Force Commander, were embarked in the other command ship. The VAC chief of staff was to comment on the command relationships at Iwo Jima in these terms:

> The Navy was of course in command afloat. The Landing Force Commander assumed command ashore after setting up a command post there. General Holland Smith could have assumed command ashore by setting up a headquarters ashore. He did not do so, nor to the best of my knowledge did he ever issue any command to the troops ashore. In fact, he had only a skeleton staff, and as he remarked to General Schmidt the only reason he went on the expedition was in case something happened to General Schmidt.[6]

When Admiral Nimitz coined his phrase about the uncommon valor displayed by Americans who served on Iwo Jima, he was referring not only to the Marines who did the lion's share of the fighting, but also to personnel of the U. S. Army and Navy, on the ground, at sea, and in the air, who supported them. According to one historical evaluation:

> Without supplies and medical care the assault would have ground to a halt, and without close air, naval gunfire, and artillery support, there would have been no neutralization to permit the tank-infantry demolition teams to advance.[7]

Based on sound doctrine, training, and experience, the participating services and arms developed excellent teamwork that could not have been surpassed. In view of the depth and extent of the Japanese defenses, naval gunfire had only a limited effect. Long and medium range bombardment accomplished little, and even area fire failed to do much damage to underground enemy defenses. Following the operation, Admiral Blandy was to make this comment in dealing with the preliminary bombardment:

> It was not until fire support ships, their spotting planes, and the support aircraft had worked at the objective for two days, had become familiar with the location and appearance of the defenses, and had accurately attacked them with close-range gunfire and low-altitude air strikes, that substantial results were achieved.[8]

---

[4] Morehouse, *Iwo Jima Campaign*, p. 93.
[5] *TG 53.2 AR*, p. 2.
[6] *Rogers ltr.*
[7] Iseley and Crowl, *U. S. Marines and Amphibious War*, p. 501.
[8] *TF 52 AR*, p. 10.

SUMMARY

This statement leads directly into the only deep-seated controversy to develop from the Iwo Jima operation, that of the duration of the naval gunfire support.[9] This dispute still simmers more than 25 years after the event, and it appears doubtful that it will ever be completely resolved to the satisfaction of all concerned. The issues in this case are clear:

> Previous amphibious assaults had amply demonstrated that against such defenses only deliberate, short-range destructive fire would be effective. And both Marine and Navy commanders knew that even under the most favorable conditions this method of bombardment was extremely time consuming.[10]

Then, as now, the lines in the naval gunfire controversy were clearly drawn, and little room remained for compromise. Most of the Marines who fought on Iwo Jima give credit to the high degree of precision which naval gunfire had reached since the early operations of World War II, but at the same time firmly agree with one former Marine participant who commented that "undoubtedly, longer bombardment before D-Day would have materially shortened the battle and saved many lives."[11]

It would serve no useful purpose at this time to rekindle the barely submerged passions that have occasionally popped to the surface regarding this subject. Even minute inspection of all available data does not lead to concrete and infallible conclusions that would stand up to prolonged investigation. Thus the controversy simply becomes one of the vantage point occupied by each of the participants at the time of the operation. To a Marine who went ashore on D-Day or later and saw the carnage wrought by the Japanese shore guns among his comrades, it becomes inconceivable that, regardless of time limits and restrictions on ammunition expenditure, more was not done to assure that enemy shore defenses were knocked out prior to the landings. This feeling is born of a mixture of anger and frustration, known only to those who have been exposed to superior enemy firepower for any length of time, bereft of the possibility to reply at once and in kind. Little has yet been devised to relieve the initial feeling of helplessness experienced by the rifleman who hits a hostile beach under the muzzle of still functioning enemy guns.

From the Navy's vantage point, the situation was slightly different. In the first place, the Iwo Jima operation had been tightly wedged in a time frame between the invasion of Luzon and the coming assault on Okinawa. Under such pressure, perhaps the best that could be achieved was neutralization, not destruction of the enemy artillery as

---

[9] In his version of the Iwo operation, Samuel Eliot Morison mentions an attack on Navy strategy and Marine Corps tactics launched by a segment of the American press, accusing both of being wasteful of American lives in paying an exorbitant price for the seizure of heavily defended objectives of limited usefulness. Deplorable as was the loss of lives at Iwo Jima, the American public then, as now, came to realize that the cost of victory is high. Despite expressions of public anguish at the losses sustained at Iwo Jima, the value of the objective for continued operations never was in doubt, nor did the issue, for lack of an alternate solution, ever assume the dimensions of a public controversy.

[10] Bartley, *Iwo Monograph*, p. 202.

[11] Heinl, *Soldiers of the Sea*, p. 484.

desired by the Marines. The naval viewpoint is summed up in this statement:

> There is no reason to believe that ten or even thirty days of naval and air pounding would have had much more effect on the defenses than the bombardment that was delivered. The defenses were such, by and large, that the only way they could be taken out was the way they were taken out, by Marine Corps infantry and demolitions.... Aerial bombardment and naval gunfire simply could not reach underground into the maze of caves and tunnels, yet these had to be cleared or sealed shut before the island could be secured as an air base on the Bonins' road to Tokyo.[12]

This line of reasoning carries little weight with Marines who faced the maze of virtually untouched pillboxes and covered emplacements between the Southern and Central Airfields and those to the east and west of the latter. These defenses were situated in more or less open terrain that was largely accessible to direct fire at relatively short ranges from vessels standing offshore. It required the herculean efforts of men in eight days of costly fighting to reduce these fortifications. In the words of General Harry Schmidt: "With additional time available for pre-D-Day firing naval guns might have accomplished much in this area to facilitate its capture."[13] The Navy has contended that:

> ... heavy ammunition replenishment at sea had not been service tested and the bombarding ships were far from a supply base and could not carry enough ammunition for the prolonged bombardment desired by the Marines.[14]

Neither the validity of this contention nor the flow of time itself have done much to cool the passions of Marines who underwent the trial by "fire and steel" on Iwo Jima. There simply appears to be no way to equate the feelings of men who have watched their comrades and friends torn apart by enemy weapons with the cold realities of logistics, statistics, and strategy. Thus, for the purposes of this history, the controversy must remain unsolved.

Let it be said for the record that, once the Marines had gone ashore, naval gunfire was furnished to the satisfaction of the landing force. In this connection, the positive must be accentuated. One account summed up the quality of naval gunfire support in these words:

> The cooperation of these vessels, from the largest battleship to the small, specialized gunboats, was excellent. The nature of the terrain continued to limit their effectiveness, however, and in most instances only neutralization was obtained. Supporting ships and craft were quick to observe enemy activity and take it under fire after first checking with units ashore to determine that the shelling would not endanger friendly troops.[15]

General Kuribayashi himself unwittingly paid tribute to the accuracy of American naval gunfire support when he passed word to his superiors that the power of bombardment from ships required reevaluation:

> The beach positions we made on this island by using many materials, days and great efforts, were destroyed within three days so that they were nearly unable to be used again....
> Power of the American warships and aircraft makes every landing operation possible to whatever beachhead they like,

---
[12] Morison, *Victory in the Pacific*, p. 73.
[13] *VAC NGF Rpt*, pp. 21–22.
[14] Forrestel, *Admiral Spruance*, p. 168.

[15] Bartley, *Iwo Monograph*, p. 203.

and preventing them from landing means nothing but great damages."[16]

The same factors that limited the success of naval gunfire also proved a hindrance to the effectiveness of the preinvasion air bombardment. The bombing of Iwo Jima and adjacent islands over a period of several months by high-altitude B-24 bombers based in the Marianas had prevented the Japanese from enjoying the unrestricted use of the two airfields on Iwo Jima. On the other hand, the increasingly heavy air raids did much to drive the enemy underground. In evaluating the results of this extensive bombing, Air Force historians themselves conclude that, despite "the heavy going over the island had received, weather conditions and the topography of Iwo Jima had rendered the results much less decisive than had been expected."[17]

While bombers of the Seventh Air Force had concentrated mostly on the destruction or neutralization of the operational airfields in the Bonins, Admiral Durgin's carrier pilots assaulted those defenses that would interfere with the amphibious assault and the subsequent push inland. Deficiencies in the armament of the support aircraft and the small size of the bombs they carried severely limited the effectiveness of these attacks. Even when a target had been pinpointed, the bombs proved too small to smash buried blockhouses. The use of napalm, which was badly needed to strip enemy positions on Iwo Jima of their natural cover, also proved disappointing when, in numerous instances, the liquid failed to ignite.

On D minus 1, as the weather cleared and the carrier pilots had become familiar with the terrain and the targets on the island, more was accomplished than during the two preceding days. Japanese defenses on the slopes of Mount Suribachi and emplacements above the East Boat Basin proved to be particularly attractive targets for the Navy flyers, who not only bombed these targets but also strafed them with 5-inch rockets. The latter were effective due to their accuracy but lacked the destructive power required against the formidable enemy fortifications. In evaluating the effectiveness of these air strikes, the advance commander of the air support control units only allowed that they "conceivably weakened the areas commanding the landing beaches."[18]

Greatly contrasting with the inconclusive results obtained from the above air strikes was the support furnished by the pilots of Task Force 58 on D-Day. The Marine and Navy flyers, whose heroic efforts were clearly visible to Navy personnel and Marines about to hit the Iwo Jima beaches, drew vociferous praise. As long as Vice Admiral Mitscher's carriers remained at Iwo, the carrier squadrons were able to furnish all the ground support requested, but on D plus 4, when the large carriers departed, a shortage of aircraft quickly developed. Planes needed for ground support had to be diverted to such other duties as antisubmarine patrols, strikes against other islands in the Bonins, and sea rescue operations.

As a rule, response of aviation to requests from ground units was quick,

---

[16] *Horie Rpt*, p. 13.
[17] Craven and Cate, *The Pacific*, p. 584.
[18] *TF 52 AR*, Encl D, p. 4.

though on many occasions more than an hour elapsed before the supporting aircraft appeared on the scene. Even then, the normally overcrowded Support Air Request Net proved to be the weak link in obtaining air strikes without undue loss of time. It is ironic that Iwo Jima Marines were denied the close support that was to become the trademark of Marine aviation, while Army troops in the Philippines at this time were reaping the benefits from exactly that type of support furnished by Marine dive bombers.[19] As in other campaigns, each echelon intervening between the ground unit requesting air strikes and the pilots furnishing the support resulted in loss of time and attendant confusion. Once again, the crux of the matter was control of support aircraft by the ground units, something that higher headquarters were still most reluctant to grant. At the conclusion of operations in the Marshalls and the Marianas:

> Marine commanders pressed hard for increased use of Marine air in close support. They wanted pilots, planes, and a control system oriented to ground needs and quickly responsive to strike requests. The winds of change were in the air in the summer of 1944 and refinements in close support techniques were coming. Operations later in the year saw planes bombing and strafing closer to frontline positions and evidenced a steady increase in the employment of Marine squadrons in this task as well as in air-to-air operations.[20]

In the case of Iwo Jima, it is significant that all three participating Marine divisions unanimously recommended that in future operations, the air liaison parties be given more direct control over aircraft during close support missions.[21] The start made in this direction during 1944 proved to be only the first step in an uphill and time-consuming struggle, some of which still had not been resolved at the time of the Korean War.

Throughout the Iwo operation, air observers played an important role. Fighter-type aircraft, flown by especially trained pilots of VOC–1, augmented the float planes normally used to spot naval gunfire. On an improvised basis, Marine artillery and tactical observers operated from carrier-based torpedo bombers until the small observation planes of the VMO squadrons had gone ashore. In spite of the difficulties, the latter held their own. One historical account was to sum up their performance this way:

> Like other Marines on Iwo, the VMO squadrons had to prove they could take it. The little planes and their pilots and ground crews were subjected to everything from *kamikazes* to artillery fire to faulty launching gear, and all of these took their toll.[22]

Aside from difficulties encountered with the overcrowded Support Air Request Net, communications on and around Iwo Jima functioned exceedingly well. The multiplicity of wire and radio nets complicated the situation, and there were instances of enemy jamming and interference between sets. The performance of communications personnel

---

[19] For the role played by Marine aviation during operations in the Philippines, see Part IV of this volume.

[20] Shaw, Nalty, and Turnbladh, *Central Pacific Drive*, p. 584.

[21] *3d MarDiv AR*, Anx G, App. 1, p. 3; *4th MarDiv OpRpt*, Anx C, pp. 6–7; *5th MarDiv AR*, Anx G, App. 1, p. 3.

[22] Sherrod, *Marine Corps Aviation in World War II*, p. 348.

was rated as excellent. Wire was widely used and with good effect. Radio bridged the gap where wire could not be employed. It was a far cry from the unsatisfactory radio equipment that had been employed in the early operations in the Pacific, notably at Tarawa. The short distances involved at Iwo Jima, as well as the very slow rate of advance, eased the burden of maintaining and expanding communications: there never was any serious breakdown. As in previous operations, the Navajo talkers performed an outstanding service, and their employment contributed materially to the effective and speedy transmittal of urgent classified radio traffic without danger of enemy interception.[23]

Contributing to the overall success of the Iwo Jima operation was close coordination between the supporting arms. The systems of coordination used at the headquarters of the three divisions were similar, though General Erskine's division maintained an installation known as the "supporting arms tent,'" whose organization and functions have been described in these words:

> The basic method of coordination between supporting arms was to achieve close personal liaison on all levels. Targets were freely interchanged according to the method of attack best suited, and, whenever operations were in progress or prospect, the artillery, naval gunfire, and air officers were together or readily accessible to each other by wire. Plans for scheduled fires or pre-King-Hour preparations were habitually prepared jointly, and so presented to the G-3, Chief of Staff, and the Commanding General. Much of the success achieved may be traced to the separate maintenance of a "supporting arms tent,"

so-called, adjacent to the G-3 Section. In this center, wire communications converged from the division switchboard, from the similar 5th Amphibious Corps establishment, from the division artillery fire direction center, and from the naval gunfire and air radio centrals. It was thus possible to establish any sort of communications necessary, and to plan without interruption, while being within a few steps of the G-3 Section.[24]

Throughout the operation, close liaison was maintained between the corps artillery, air, and naval gunfire officers and the Commander, Landing Force Air Support Control Unit, in the Joint Operations Rooms on board the USS *Auburn* and subsequently through facilities of the supporting arms tent at VAC headquarters ashore.[25]

The performance of the shore based artillery at Iwo Jima deserves special mention. Standard tactics, vindicated in previous operations, were employed. It quickly became evident, though, that the 75mm and the 105mm howitzers of the division artillery battalions were far from adequate for the destruction of the type of emplacements encountered on the island. In fact, the 155mm guns and howitzers of the corps artillery frequently had to score up to a dozen hits in one place before they caused major damage to some of the strongest enemy installations.[26] In performing its mission, artillery was further handicapped by limited observation, which often prevented forward observers from seeing more than 200 yards ahead. As a result, great dependence was placed on aerial spotting, particularly for counter-bat-

---

[23] *VAC Sig Bn Rpt*, p. 5.

[24] *3d MarDiv AR*, p. 53.
[25] *VAC NGF Rpt*, p. 38.
[26] *VAC Arty Rpt*, p. 29.

tery and destruction fire. Despite such limitations, officers and men of the corps and division artillery carried out their mission in an exemplary fashion.

From 23 February to 1 March, the VAC artillery fired its maximum number of missions, most of them counterbattery. During the first four days in March, normal missions were fired, but the amount of ammunition expended had to be reduced since expenditure exceeded the inflow. After a breather on 5 March, when no preparations were fired, both the corps and division artillery made a maximum effort on the following day. On 6 March, a heavy time-on-target preparation was fired in which 11 division and corps artillery battalions participated. Despite the higher expenditure of ammunition, amounting to 2,500 rounds for the corps and 20,000 rounds of 75mm and 105mm for the division artillery, this massive concentration had no decisive effect.

In discussing the performance of the artillery during the Iwo Jima operation, General Schmidt underscored another aspect:

> A feature of the employment of artillery in the Iwo Jima operation not noted in the report was that the bulk of the artillery ashore was sited around Airfield No. 1. During the greater portion of the time artillery was firing continuously (approximately 450,000 rounds fired during operation) at the same time Airfield No. 1 was being used for aircraft operation to capacity. This was also true even after Airfield No. 2 began operating. It is considered remarkable that no friendly planes were hit and that aircraft operations were not impeded by our artillery or vice versa. The method of control employed for the protection of planes taking off or landing was simply to have an individual of the firing unit placed to observe whether any aircraft were in the line of fire and to give warning if that were the case.[27]

Engineer support to VAC during Operation DETACHMENT was generally excellent. The task of constructing and maintaining roads in the VAC area was assigned to the 2d Separate Engineer Battalion, which also accomplished the preliminary work in restoring the Southern Airfield. It was the work carried out by this unit that enabled small observation aircraft to operate from this airfield by D plus 7. The further completion of additional strips on this airfield was the shared accomplishment of these Marine engineers and the 62d Naval Construction Battalion.

In addition to executing their important task of constructing roads, operating water points, and erecting various buildings and supply dumps, Marine engineers also had a combat mission to perform. The latter was the responsibility of the division engineers who cleared mines, dozed trails that enabled tanks to approach the front lines, and performed such other jobs as were designed to help the infantry advance over treacherous terrain. Much of this work was carried out under direct enemy observation and fire. Engineers, individually or in small groups, joined the infantry in demolishing the numerous enemy caves and strongpoints. For the hard-toiling engineers, there were only two bright sides to the operation: the sand-clay fill obtained from quarries on the island made excellent road

---
[27] *1st Prov Fd Arty Gp AR*, 1st Endorsement.

construction material; and "engineer operations were further facilitated in that no bridges were required."[28]

The employment of amphibious vehicles on Iwo Jima featured a greater variety than had been previously used, including armored amphibian tractors, amphibian trucks, and sea-going jeeps. First to hit the beach were the LVT(A)s of the 2d Armored Amphibian Battalion, equipped with one 75mm howitzer, one .50 caliber machine gun mounted in the turret ring, one .30 caliber machine gun mounted in front of the assistant driver, and one .30 caliber machine gun mounted in front of the howitzer loader. Once within effective range of the beaches, the LVT(A)s were to open fire with all weapons. After going ashore, these vehicles were to move about 50 yards inland and protect the following assault waves by firing on targets to their front and flanks.

Almost immediately, the steep terraces and the composition of the beaches caused the vehicles to bog down. A few made it across the first terrace only to become stalled on the second. While neither the LVT(A)s nor the following LVTs containing the assault troops drew voluminous enemy fire, progress of the LVTs upon reaching the beaches also was stymied by the loose volcanic ash and the steep terraces. Since in many instances the beach was very narrow and the surf broke very close to the steep ledge, many LVTs swamped. Some of the vehicles were thrown broadside on the beach where sand and salt water filled them.

It soon became apparent that the volcanic cinders and sand would not support wheeled vehicles. Only the LVTs, caterpillar tractors, and other tracked vehicles had a chance of making it inland across this treacherous ground. As emphasized in one report: "Supplies and equipment were hauled from ships directly to the front lines, and had it not been for LVTs the troops ashore could not have been supplied during the early stages of the landing."[29] Because of their importance to the logistics effort, it became necessary to use these vehicles around the clock during the early phase of the operation.

One of the new types of equipment to be used by all three Marine divisions during the Iwo operation was the 3½-ton Clever-Brooks trailer, employed to haul cargo and medical supplies. Major difficulty was encountered in launching these amphibious trailers in the rough seas and getting them across the steep terraces. LVTs were generally able to bring the trailers ashore, but attempts to have the DUKWs perform this service resulted in the loss of both the trailer and DUKW. While comments on both the LVT and DUKWs were generally favorable, VAC concluded: "The amphibian trailers did not prove to be of any particular or specific help during the operation."[30]

The amphibian truck, the DUKW, had the primary mission of bringing the division artillery ashore on D-Day. Personnel to operate these vehicles was furnished both by the Marine Corps and the U.S. Army. The difficulty in land-

---

[28] Morehouse, *Iwo Jima Campaign*, p. 144.
[29] *Ibid.*, p. 133.
[30] *VAC AR*, Anx B, App. 4, G–4 Rpt.

ing the artillery resulted from the high surf and the tactical situation ashore. While some of the DUKWs landed without difficulty, others were swamped after exhausting their limited fuel supply or developing mechanical problems. Others that were overloaded, sank almost immediately after disembarking from the LSTs. Many of the DUKWs ran afoul of the steep beaches and broached when the front wheels dug down into the sand or volcanic ash and could not get sufficient traction to pull the vehicles forward. Following the initial landings, DUKWs hauled supplies, especially ammunition, evacuated the wounded, and performed mail and messenger runs.

Another amphibious vehicle that proved its worth during the Iwo operation was a light cargo carrier, dubbed the "Weasel." This tracked carrier had been issued to the three Marine divisions participating in DETACHMENT in November 1944. At Iwo Jima, the Weasels hauled light supplies, evacuated the wounded, and were used to string telephone lines. Their versatility in overcoming loose sand and the steep terrain made them the ideal all-purpose vehicle, and they were soon pressed into service as messenger or command cars or for the purpose of hauling trailers and small artillery pieces over terrain that wheeled vehicles could not negotiate. In addition to their versatility, the Weasels offered a poor target for the enemy because of their speed and low silhouette. The only difficulty encountered with these vehicles was at sea, where the high swells occasionally proved more than they could handle. It is interesting to note that a total of 133 DUKWs were destroyed during the Iwo Jima operation, amounting to 53 percent of those employed; only 9 Weasels were lost in combat, accounting for 13 percent of the number that were disembarked. The remaining 61 vehicles remained in operating condition until the Marines left Iwo Jima.[31]

One of the most successfully handled, yet difficult aspects of the Iwo Jima operation pertained to the treatment and evacuation of the wounded. The bitterness of the fighting, from the first to the last day of battle, coupled with the large number of men simultaneously locked in combat, placed an extremely heavy burden on the medical units, both ashore and afloat. During the initial days of the operation, doctors and corpsmen alike occupied a precarious foothold on beaches that were exposed to enemy fire of all calibers. As often as not, the medical personnel ashore became casualties themselves, especially the corpsmen attached to the combat units or the beach evacuation stations. It was not a rare occurrence for corpsmen to be hit as they carried litters with wounded to the rear or cared for the wounded at the evacuation stations. Casualties among medical officers and corpsmen were correspondingly high: 738, among them 197 killed.[32]

In order to take care of the Iwo Jima casualties, medical plans had been drawn up well in advance of the operation. As a result, during the first nine days of the battle, once a casualty had arrived

---

[31] *VAC AR*, Anx B.

[32] U. S. Navy Bureau of Medicine, Statistics Division, World War II Casualties, dtd 1Aug-52, as cited in Bartley, *Iwo Monograph*, p. 195.

at one of the evacuation stations, he could expect prompt evacuation to one of the hospital LSTs that were lying 2,000 yards offshore. These LSTs acted as collection centers from which the casualties were forwarded to APAs and hospital ships. Initially, the transport of casualties from the beaches to the hospital LSTs was handled by landing craft, LVTs, and DUKWs. However, increasingly rough surf eventually prevented the use of small landing craft, and amphibious vehicles were employed exclusively. The DUKWs, in particular, proved useful because they handled well in the surf and alongside the big ships, and patients were more comfortable inside the DUKWs than inside the wet, bouncing LVTs.[33]

In addition to the hospital ships *Bountiful, Samaritan,* and *Solace,* and the hospital transport *Pinkney,* the LSV *Ozark* was pressed into service as an auxiliary hospital ship. Together with transports that were leaving the combat area, these ships evacuated 13,737 casualties.[34] An additional 2,449 men were airlifted to the Marianas.

Because of the small size of Iwo Jima, distances from the front lines to battalion aid stations were invariably short. Nevertheless, the difficult terrain and constant exposure to enemy fire made even such short distances extremely hazardous both for corpsmen and patients alike. At first, LVTs and Weasels were widely used in order to bring casualties to the beaches; during the latter phase of the operation when roads had been constructed that were passable for wheeled vehicles, jeeps oftentimes carried casualties to the rear.

The availability of whole blood to treat the victims of extensive loss of blood and shock undoubtedly saved many lives. Such transfusions of whole blood had not been used in any previous Central Pacific campaigns. Landing force medical facilities alone used more than 5,000 pints. By D plus 25, 12,600 pints had been used, nearly one pint for every patient evacuated.[35] Once the situation on the beaches had stabilized, hospital tents went up wherever a place for them could be found, and as electric power became available, the shore based hospitals were able to operate around the clock. In evaluating the efficiency of the medical care provided at Iwo Jima, VAC was to report:

> The medical service for the Iwo Jima operation approached nearer the ideal than during any previous operations in the Central Pacific Area, and it is firmly believed that the casualties received the maximum medical care possible commensurate with the military situation.[36]

One of the most difficult problems that had to be overcome during Operation DETACHMENT was that of supplying the landing force. Heavy surf, the deep volcanic ash, the enemy's complete coverage of the beaches with artillery, mortars, and small arms fire, and congestion at the beaches all combined to increase the complexity of logistics. Only the abandonment of carefully laid plans and timely improvisation saved the day, making possible an uninterrupted flow of supplies to the frontline units that kept the operation going.

---

[33] *TF 56 MedRpt,* pp. 8–9.
[34] *TF 53 OpRpt,* Part VI, pp. 5, 12.
[35] *VAC MedRpt,* p. 12; *TF 56 MedRpt,* p. 19.
[36] *VAC AR,* Anx B.

Iwo Jima provided a testing ground for the vehicles that shuttled back and forth through the heavy surf in an attempt to land badly needed cargo when and where required. Beyond that, it became a proving ground for men of the beach and shore parties, the frequently unpublicized and unsung heroes of the battle of logistics. Previously, little had been done to provide these parties with proper training, experience, and continuity of function. The force that went ashore on Iwo Jima included beefed-up pioneer battalions, which were further reinforced with men from the replacement drafts and division headquarters personnel, as well as U. S. Army port troops.

Taken as a whole, this conglomeration of units performed well in a situation which was considerably more complex than had been envisioned in the planning for the invasion. It had not been intended to bring any of these men, except for advance elements, ashore until the beaches were reasonably secure. Yet circumstances dictated a departure from previous plans and more than 10,000 of these service troops were landed on D-Day. Once ashore, under the most difficult circumstances, these men performed splendidly, though their presence added to the congestion and increased the number of casualties.

As it turned out, between 60 and 70 percent of the supplies unceremoniously dumped on the beaches were salvaged and either moved inland or incorporated into the hastily established beach dumps set up by forward elements of the division shore parties which went ashore with the fifth and sixth assault waves. These advance elements carried out their mission in an exemplary fashion despite the most adverse conditions imposed by the terrain and the heavy enemy fire. The casualties among these units were correspondingly heavy, some of them being reduced to half strength.

In order to keep the logistics effort from foundering in the deep volcanic ash, Marston matting and armored bulldozers had to be pressed into service. Once again, the American penchant for improvisation proved to be a decisive factor in getting troops and supplies off the crowded beaches. Marston matting was of tremendous value in serving as the only usable roadways over which vehicles could move inland during the initial phase of the assault. The armored bulldozer was employed on the beaches to level sand terraces and cut routes inland. Their steel plates protected both driver and engine from enemy fire. On northern Iwo, these machines and their drivers performed an equally important service in clearing roads into previously impassable terrain under fire.

The movement of supplies across the beaches was in no small way facilitated by the presence of Navy cranes, as well as other equipment designed to expedite the unloading of the cargo vessels. In this connection, the expertise of TF 53 and its commander proved invaluable. In line with his extensive logistical experience, Admiral Hill was keenly aware of the requirements that had to be met and had at an early time recommended that ample cargo handling equipment be available for Operation DETACHMENT.[37] Despite all preparations, the

---

[37] BGen Leland S. Swindler ltr to CMC, dtd 14May53, in *Iwo Comments*.

tactical situation prevailing on Iwo Jima on D-Day caused the beaches to become so congested that on the following day underwater demolition teams had to be employed to assist in clearing lanes through the wreckage for incoming vessels.

It needs to be emphasized that, all difficulties to the contrary, no acute supply shortages developed for the assault troops, though in the days following the landings units were living from hand to mouth. Such shortages as did develop involved 60mm mortar illumination shells, grenades, cylinders for charging flamethrowers, and ordnance spare parts. As an expedient, these items were flown to Iwo Jima from Saipan, the first extensive use of air supply by the Marines.[38]

The timing of the logistics support at Iwo Jima, an extremely important factor in an amphibious operation, proved to be well conceived and executed. Liaison teams from the 8th Field Depot, which constituted the VAC shore party, accompanied the 4th and 5th Marine Divisions ashore. As of 22 February, units of the field depot came ashore and rendered valuable service in assisting the divisional shore parties. Two days later, when VAC assumed control ashore, the field depot took over and the unloading continued without interruption. At this time, the beaches were still under enemy fire, which caused temporary work stoppages but proved unable to interfere seriously with the unloading. On D plus 6, 25 February, general unloading got under way. The opening of the western beaches to small landing craft on 2 March removed the entire unloading operation from the threat posed by variable weather conditions. Henceforth, the menace of heavy surf pounding the eastern side of the island could be overcome by switching shipping to the western beaches.

In evaluating the overall success of the logistics effort at Iwo Jima, it appears appropriate to comment:

> ... the wonder is not that things were confused but that the vast quantities of supplies actually crossed the beaches so quickly. Expertly handled ship-to-shore communications and a high degree of coordination between Navy and Marine logistical control personnel afloat and ashore did much to overcome the difficulties inherent in the situation.[39]

The official VAC report dealing with Operation DETACHMENT echoes this sentiment and, speaking of the adversities facing the Marines that went ashore on Iwo Jima, concludes:

> The fact that these factors failed to impose any limitations on the conduct of operations reflects the highest credit on all concerned. Without the tireless support through unprecedented difficulties rendered by the expeditionary force and the supply agencies of the landing force, the sustained assault of the Corps would have been impossible.[40]

Finally, a word about the tactics employed on Iwo Jima both by the assault force and the defending Japanese. The small size of the island permitted little or no maneuverability to either force, and once the first Marines had

---

[38] *VAC Logistics Rpt*, pp. 12, 16.

[39] Isely and Crowl, *U. S. Marines and Amphibious War*, pp. 519–520.

[40] *TF 56 AR*, Encl B, Comments and Recommendations, p. 4.

gone ashore, the fighting that was to typify the entire operation was dictated by General Kuribayashi, whose defensive organization "was the most intelligent and complete one yet encountered."[41] Basically, the Japanese conducted a position defense which was effective, intense, and notable for its economy of forces. There was no employment of mobile reserves, nor was there a withdrawal through a series of defensive lines. All precautions had been taken to assure that enemy troops were not exposed to the American supporting arms. General Kuribayashi's defense was simple; it was this very simplicity that made it so effective.

The enemy plan was based on the concept that a maximum number of weapons of all calibers were to fire more or less continuously from well-concealed and -protected positions until they were destroyed. Almost from the beginning of the operation the American supporting arms were handicapped by the geographical limitations of the island, the character of the terrain, and the strength of the enemy defenses. The heavier Japanese installations, in particular, often proved impervious to field artillery of light and medium calibers and required the destructive power of main battery naval gunfire. During the latter phase of the fighting, the proximity of the Marines to enemy positions frequently denied them the benefit of adequate heavy fires or bombardment.

Even though few underwater obstacles interfered with the Iwo Jima landings, the minefields ashore were the strongest yet encountered in the Pacific Theater, indicative of the progress made by the Japanese in this sphere of defensive warfare. The operation also saw the first use of antipersonnel mines by the Japanese in the Central Pacific.[42]

The Japanese made more widespread use of rockets than in earlier operations, though on Iwo Jima their effect was limited. Some of the rocket launchers were installed in locations from where they could be fired at certain areas. Movable rocket launchers were kept in caves, moved outside and fired, then pulled back into the caves. During the early phase of the Iwo Jima operation, the Japanese fired large rockets towards the northern slope of Mount Suribachi. However, due to the inaccuracy of this fire, the missiles went beyond the mountain and finally fell into the sea. If anything, these large weapons were well adapted for harassing fire, but their accuracy was doubtful.

In contrast to the relative inefficiency of the enemy rockets, the Japanese artillery performed better than had been anticipated by the invasion force. Coordination, volume, and accuracy of the enemy artillery fire, especially during the days immediately following the invasion, initially made it appear as if the Japanese were massing their fire, thus taking a page out of the book dealing with American artillery doctrine. It was subsequently determined that prior to the American landings, the enemy had

---

[41] *Ibid.*, p. 1.

[42] Detailed information on this subject can be found in Military Intelligence, War Department, *Minefield Patterns in the Defense of Iwo Jima*, Intelligence Bulletin (Washington, D.C., June 1945), pp. 15–19.

registered his artillery on critical terrain features against which he massed his fire, rather than relying on current observation.

General Kuribayashi's use of mortars was exceptionally skillful and very effective. In fact, it was this weapon, and the large number used, that inflicted more casualties on the Marines than any other support weapon. During the latter part of the campaign, the Japanese apparently suffered a shortage of mortar ammunition which restricted their choice of targets to Marine weapons, vehicles, and large groups of personnel. As with rocket launchers, the Japanese skillfully hid their mortars, either emplacing them on reverse slopes or moving them out of caves to fire, and quickly moving them back under cover.

Among the weapons Marines encountered on Iwo Jima for the first time were the 320mm spigot type mortar, new types of mobile rocket launchers and rockets, and 90mm and 120mm howitzers.

The landing force also made use of several innovations, sometimes on an experimental basis. Thus the rolling barrage, dating back to World War I, found renewed use during the operation. Generally, this type of artillery support proved successful, though the troops often did not advance as rapidly as expected. This required continuous modification of the barrage schedule resulting in repeating fires in certain blocks and delaying the lifting of fires from others.[43] With respect to the utilization of mortars, in accordance with recommendations following operations in the Marianas, an effort was made to develop a craft mounting the 4.2-inch chemical mortar. As a result, three 4.2s were mounted on an LCI and successfully employed on D-Day and thereafter.

The effectiveness of the enemy mortar fire gave rise to the recommendation that a larger mortar be adopted, and that possibly a 120mm mortar battalion be added to each division. Marines who had been on the receiving end of enemy 47mm gunfire felt that a 57mm gun should be substituted for their own 37mm piece. Similarly, a tank with thicker armor and heavier armament than the Sherman would have facilitated operations on Iwo Jima. A great majority of the Shermans were equipped with small flamethrowers that proved their worth by squirting fire through one or two of their machine gun ports, but a tank capable of shooting a flame for about 100 yards from a turret-mounted tube proved the most efficient. In order to deceive the Japanese, who tended to concentrate their fire against any type of flamethrower, these tubes outwardly were exact replicas of the 75mm gun.

In his letter to President Roosevelt, Rear Admiral Ichimaru somewhat contemptuously referred to American material superiority as opposed to Japanese fighting spirit.[44] While there can be no doubt that such material superiority did in fact exist, it is equally

---

[43] *TF 51 AR*, Pt V, Sec C, p. 3.

[44] RAdm Ichimaru ltr to President Roosevelt, n.d., as cited in Morehouse, *Iwo Jima Campaign*, App F, p. 17DD.

clear that other important factors were at work which the Japanese admiral pointedly ignored. Not least among these were the outstanding leadership and discipline of the men who came to take Iwo Jima or die in the attempt; the physical stamina and mental power of endurance of these men, both tempered in months or years of thorough training; and the intangible, indefinable something known as esprit de corps or morale, that induces men to give their last in a common cause.

Without all of the above qualities, the individual Marine could not have gone on to victory on Iwo Jima, a battle that has been linked to "throwing human flesh against reinforced concrete."[45] For the men of the landing force that assaulted and captured one of the strongest enemy bastions in the Pacific, the operation was the supreme test. Judging by the performance of these men and the results attained, the inevitable conclusion can be drawn that a heavily defended objective can be seized by such a force regardless of its size, the difficulty of its terrain, and the degree of man-made defensive perfection. An amphibious assault against such an objective will be successful if it can be isolated by surface and air superiority and prepared by naval bombardment and bombing.

---

[45] Isely and Crowl, *U. S. Marines and Amphibious War*, p. 475.

CHAPTER 13

Conclusions

The ground operations discussed in this volume, notably Peleliu and Iwo Jima, span the period of seven months from September 1944 to the end of March 1945. Within the overall context of World War II, this time span was most significant. In Europe, this period saw the advance of Soviet forces into Germany proper, the collapse of the German allies in Scandinavia and the Balkans, and the slow but steadily accelerating drive of the Western Allies into western Germany.

An ingenious offensive in the Ardennes and the introduction of new types of rockets failed to halt the steamroller that was beginning to engulf the *Reich* from the west, east, and the south. Dissent within the ranks of the Germans themselves had been all but snuffed out following the abortive attempt on Hitler's life in late July. The harsh measures that followed in the wake of the Generals' Plot all but silenced those who might have raised their voices against the continuation of a war that the overwhelming majority of the military, as well as the civilian population, already had to consider lost. The heavy Allied air raids, carried out in such force that entire cities were literally obliterated from the face of the earth only underscored the fact that time was on the side of the Allies. Despite reports of the miraculous effect of those wonder weapons already existing and those yet to come, both pessimism and fear were dominant: pessimism as to what would happen to the country and its people once the Allies had won; fear of death from the air for the civilian populace; fear of death or capture on the part of the military, particularly those facing a merciless enemy on the Eastern front; fear of the numerous foreign workers who, in many cases forcibly conscripted and not always well-treated, posed an increasing threat to internal security as the ring closed around Germany.

Finally, there was fear of the ruling police and semi-military organizations whose measures against military personnel and civilians alike became ever more menacing as the strategic situation deteriorated. During the late fall and throughout the winter of 1944-1945, the German war machine still functioned efficiently despite heavy losses in personnel and materiel, devastation from the air, increasing shortages in raw materials, and covert popular discontent. The German offensive in the Ardennes, the last of the great German offensives of World War II, represented but the final gasp of a machine that had waged almost unlimited *blitzkrieg* during the initial years of the war. When this offensive fell short of its goals and could not be sustained, the end of the war in Europe became a visible goal,

729

at the most only months away. As one history of that war was to sum it up:

> ... the roads back over the Eifel led straight to the decimation and collapse of the German armies on the banks of the Oder River, along the Danube, in the Ruhr pocket, and, at last, to the bunkers of Berlin.[1]

In comparison with operations in Europe, the war in the Pacific Theater during the latter part of 1944 and through the early months of 1945 showed certain similarities as well as marked differences. The vital gains in territory and raw materials made by the Japanese during the early months of the war had realized for them most of the tactical and strategic objectives they had embarked on. Beginning with the American landings in the Solomons, prolonged operations in New Guinea, and the American recapture of islands in the Aleutians, the Japanese situation had very gradually deteriorated, though such setbacks were in no way overly worrisome to the Japanese leaders who continued to maintain an optimistic outlook as to the eventual outcome of the war. They hoped that, in time, a negotiated peace would permit Japan to retain at least some of the vital areas from which she drew her raw materials.

The heavy American losses at Tarawa only strengthened the Japanese belief that the United States would not be willing to continue paying such a heavy price for each island that would have to be seized before the war was carried into the Home Islands. Meanwhile, despite increasingly heavy interference by American submarines with Japanese shipping, raw materials continued to flow to Japan from the conquered territories: urgently needed rubber arrived from Burma, Malaya, and Indochina; vital food products and petroleum made their way north from the Philippines and from the former Dutch East Indies; and war plants in Manchuria and Korea were producing at full capacity. The vast pool of Japanese manpower had been barely touched by combat losses, though the caliber of the aviators was diminishing.

Both the Japanese military and the civilian population stood solidly behind the government, at whose apex was the Emperor against whom no voice of dissent could be raised. The entire population was in some way involved in the war effort. There was absolute confidence in the leadership and the foreign policy pursued by the country. The borders of Japan were secure. There were still the numerous island outposts to the south and west; much of the Chinese mainland, especially the vital coastal areas, was under Japanese control and the possibility of Russia's entry into the war against Japan on the side of the Allies appeared remote. Within the Home Islands, the entire nation was functioning as a military-civilian team under quasi-military rule. There were few foreigners in the Home Islands, aside from closely guarded Allied prisoners of war and civilian internees, including missionaries, all of whom represented an infinitesimally small number that posed no threat to the Japanese war effort. Their presence

---

[1] Hugh M. Cole, *The Ardennes: Battle of the Bulge—The U. S. Army in World War II* (Washington: Office of the Chief of Military History, Department of the Army, 1955), p. 673.

in the country was not a factor in maintaining the agriculture or industry of Japan.

The spring and summer of 1944 saw a rapid acceleration of Allied operations in the Central Pacific, primarily an American effort. Based on the bitter lessons of Tarawa, U. S. Marines had perfected their planning and refined their techniques until their drive into the Marianas "saw the flowering of a vital skill, logistics planning, whose incredible complexity met the need to sustain massive assaults and at the same time provide a continuous flow of men, supplies, and equipment for a host of existing and future requirements."[2]

Noting the change in the strategic situation in the Pacific brought about by American seizure of the Gilberts and Marshalls, one postwar survey has noted that:

> The United States position was firm indeed in early March 1944. The initiative had been won, adequate forces were in sight, and it was possible to plan in orderly fashion for future operations. Japan, on the other hand, was faced with the most urgent need for devising means to counter the unpredictable but obviously intended blows at her inner perimeter, with forces so limited that opposition with the slightest chance of a favorable outcome could only be offered under ideal conditions.[3]

The stage was now set for an American advance into the inner perimeter of Japan's defense. The possibility of an American invasion of the Marianas in the spring and summer of 1944 hardly came as a surprise for the Japanese, who nearly a year earlier had already designated these islands as an "absolute strategic area within the absolute zone of national defense."[4] What did cause great surprise and consternation were the might of the American naval bombardment, notably at Saipan, the great speed of the landing operations, and the overwhelming superiority of the Americans in the air, which underscored the loss of the well-trained and seasoned aviators that Japan had possessed at the beginning of the war.

The success of the American landings on Saipan only nine days after the Normandy invasion, coupled with the subsequent operations against Tinian and Guam, struck the Japanese with the same impact that the Allied invasion of Europe had on the Germans. In either case it was less the initial success of the landings that confounded the defenders than the fact that the invasion force could not be confined to the beaches or driven back into the sea. There were several fringe benefits for the Americans inherent in the Saipan operation. First, the fact that "it lured the Japanese carriers to defeat might alone be enough to call it the decisive operation of the Central Pacific Campaign."[5] The capture of Saipan provided the Americans with a base from which giant B-29s would soon be able to launch a devastating air offensive against the Home Islands. The sea battle in the Marianas resulted in the loss of most of the carriers and air strength of the *Combined Fleet*, which gave American aircraft full control of the air while the U. S. Navy dominated the Central

---

[2] Shaw, Nalty, and Turnbladh, *Central Pacific Drive*, p. 583.

[3] USSBS, *Pacific Campaigns*, p. 204.

[4] Hayashi and Coox, *Kogun*, p. 109.

[5] Shaw, Nalty, and Turnbladh, *Central Pacific Drive*, p. 583.

Pacific. Without support from sea or air, Tinian and Guam were for all practical purposes isolated plums ripe for the picking. Since the loss of 300 naval aircraft had all but wiped out naval strength in the Marianas and the Japanese Army had only few planes with sufficient range to fly from bases on Iwo Jima to Saipan, there was no hope that Japan would regain command of the air over the Marianas. With this realization went any Japanese hopes of recapturing either Saipan, Guam, or Tinian.

Beyond this, from the Japanese point of view:

> ... there appeared a wide gap in the absolute zone of national defense in the Central Pacific region. The advance of the U. S. Navy toward Japanese waters was facilitated by this breach, which threatened the very security of the homeland. Even more painful for Japan, the American Air Force began to bomb the main islands from bases on Saipan and Guam —raids which began on September 24.[6]

Following the successful Allied invasion of Normandy, and in the weeks that followed, it is interesting to note that a group of German general officers, many of them members of the General Staff, concluded that the war could no longer be won and set about to remove Hitler before attempting to reach a negotiated peace with the Allies. In Japan, at approximately the same time, the situation was directly reversed. It was recognized that, with the loss of Saipan, the war situation had reached a critical phase. However, while the Emperor and the senior statesman "grew anxious and perturbed,"[7] the military radiated an air of optimism, which went so far as highly placed officers making profuse assurances "that our fleet had emerged victorious from the engagement (in the Philippine Sea). They even drank hilariously to the spectacular victory."[8]

In Germany the question of continuing the war or finding a way to the peace-table resulted in an ever widening chasm between the Armed Forces and the Nazi Party, with the former favoring an end to the war. In Japan, the military closed ranks in favor of fighting to the last man, woman, and child, if necessary, though major differences as to the further prosecution of the war remained between the Army and Navy. The dismissal of Tojo as Premier on 18 July preceded the assassination attempt against Hitler by two days. Whereas the abortive General's Plot resulted in a major upheaval in the German ranks with numerous courts martials and summary executions in its wake, the transition from the Tojo Government to a new cabinet took place in an orderly fashion, though it was far from routine. Never having been questioned, the stature and authority of the Emperor remained unchanged. In order to put and end to Army-Navy antagonism, both the War Minister and the Chief of Staff made efforts aimed at resolving the long-standing rivalries between the two Services, though the time was late.

While the drive across the Central Pacific was aimed directly at the Japanese Home Islands, General Douglas MacArthur was embarked on the road to Tokyo over a more circuitous south-

---

[6] Hayashi and Coox, *Kogun*, p. 109.
[7] *Ibid.*

[8] *Ibid.*, p. 208.

erly route which would take him from New Guinea to the Philippines. As compared to the European Theater, this drive might be likened to the Allied invasion of North Africa and the subsequent moves to Sicily and Italy. Where the seizure of North Africa and Italy had been intended to open a door into Europe through the supposedly "soft belly" in the south, MacArthur's strategy of isolating Japan from her sources of supply in the Philippines and freeing the inhabitants of these islands from Japanese oppression, as he had promised, was to serve as a stepping stone towards the invasion of the Home Islands. Both in southern Europe, as in the southern Pacific, the respective campaigns proved costly, arduous, and time-consuming. Neither the recapture of the Philippines nor the plodding advance up the Appenine Peninsula yielded quick results that would have brought the war to a rapid end in either theater; nor was there any clear agreement in early 1944 where MacArthur would go once the liberation of the Philippines had been accomplished.

It is in the light of this overall situation that the seizure of the southern Palaus, Operation STALEMATE, must be viewed. During the early part of 1944, the Palaus represented one of the key strongholds in Japan's second line of defense. Once New Guinea and the Marshall Islands had been seized by the Americans, the Central Carolines had been bypassed, and the Marianas had fallen, the Palaus moved into the first line of defense for Japan. They became the most powerful and strategic enemy outposts halfway between the Central Pacific drive in the northeast and Mac-Arthur's drive from the south. Since the Palaus were situated only 500 miles east of the Philippine island of Mindanao, their permanent neutralization from sea or air was impractical; as result, the southernmost of these islands became the target of invasion.

At the time Admiral Nimitz, General MacArthur, as well as the Joint Chiefs of Staff, were in general agreement as to the necessity of securing the southern Palaus, notably Peleliu and Angaur, as well as islands closest to Guam, notably Yap and Ulithi in the Northern Carolines. Possession of the smaller islands to the northeast and south of Babelthuap, the largest and most heavily-defended island in the Palaus, would permit the neutralization of that stronghold. At the same time that a joint force of Marines and Army troops assaulted Peleliu and Angaur respectively, MacArthur's forces prepared to assault Morotai, located about halfway between the western tip of New Guinea and Celebes, 480 miles southwest of Peleliu. Seizure of Peleliu and Angaur to the north (with Morotai as a stepping stone in the south) would effectively screen General MacArthur's drive into the Philippines, at the same time providing vital airstrips to the Americans from which aircraft could neutralize enemy forces and such air power as remained to the Japanese on adjacent islands.

The overall situation that had developed by mid-summer made it possible to scrap the planned operation against Yap Island in the northern Carolines. The invasions of Peleliu and Morotai took place on 15 September, followed two days later by the assault on Angaur. Fighting on Peleliu, in particular, proved long, bitter, and costly, so much so that at the conclusion of the operation doubts arose as to whether results had been worth the effort, particularly in view of the fact that last-minute changes in plans for subsequent operations, specifically the invasion of the Philippines, "made it all but impossible to fit the Palaus into the operational role originally planned for them."[9] The capture of Angaur also failed to provide immediate support to MacArthur's forces. Terrain difficulties and inadequate gasoline storage facilities prevented the operation of bombers from Angaur until 21 October, the day after American forces had landed on Leyte in the central Philippines.[10] Even then, it was not until 17 November that the first bomber mission was flown against the Philippines from a field in the Palaus. In time, Angaur became an important base for heavy bombers and an aircraft staging point, from which operations on Luzon could be supported. Aircraft based on Morotai did not fly sorties against Leyte, but flew many missions over Mindanao and other islands in the southern Philippines. After 7 October, fighters based on Morotai flew cover for Allied bombers en route to Mindanao and the Visayan Islands.

An unexpected dividend accruing to American forces from the seizure of the Palaus was the capture of Ulithi Atoll by Army troops. Seized in an unopposed operation from 22–24 September, this atoll became an extremely valuable base for the U. S. Pacific Fleet. As the war progressed, it became an important staging area for the fleet and amphibious forces taking part in the invasion of Okinawa. Generally speaking, seizure of some islands in the western Carolines, including Peleliu, gained for the Allies valuable bases, though the accelerating drive towards Japan made it necessary to convert these newly seized bases to uses other than those originally anticipated.

For the men of the 1st Marine Division who assaulted Peleliu, the seizure of the island meant a hard and bloody campaign. Of particular interest is the ratio of forces employed by both opponents. At Attu in the Aleutians, the American forces had enjoyed a numerical superiority of 5:1. The ratio was 2.5:1 in favor of the attacking force at Saipan, and at Guam it amounted to 2:1.[11] In the Palaus, the defending Japanese were considerably superior in number to the invasion force. Yet the latter was able to bring its full striking power to bear against the objective, while the main Japanese garrison on adjacent Babelthuap was effectively blocked by the U. S. Navy from giving any relief to its hard-pressed comrades in arms on Peleliu.

Completion of the operation in the Western Carolines placed the United States in a favorable position for carrying the war to the enemy at an accelerated pace. Since early summer of 1944, the Japanese situation had deteriorated alarmingly. Even while Japan attempted to bolster her sagging line of defense, the Japanese air garrison in the Philippines had suffered staggering losses, as had Japanese ship-

---

[9] Smith, *Approach to the Philippines*, p. 572.
[10] *Ibid.*, p. 573.

[11] Hayashi and Coox, *Kogun*, pp. 110–111.

CONCLUSIONS 735

ping, both through U.S. submarine action and later through carrier and shore-based air strikes.

The arrival of 1945 saw an almost complete reversal of the still fairly stable position of Japan just one year earlier. The final months of 1944 had faced the Japanese with almost unimaginable reverses that the nation could no longer compensate for. Loss of the Philippines to General MacArthur's forces was not only a very sore blow to Japanese pride, but more practically:

> The Southern Resources Area, the prize for which the war had been fought, was gone and American fleets sailed with impunity to the shores of eastern Asia. All hope of future resistance had depended upon oil and now the tankers were sunk and the oil cut off. The surface fleet was gone, and so were 7,000 aircraft, expended in four months defense of the last supply line. Suicide attack, bleeding tactics, were now the last hope of this shrunken empire, and even these economical methods of defense suffered from the blockade.[12]

From the Marine Corps point of view, the tactical development of close air support had been one of the most distinguishing features of the Peleliu operation. The remarkable performance of Marine aviators during the capture of Ngesebus Island had been but a forerunner of what Marine air was shortly to accomplish in the Philippines in support of Army troops. This development had been slow in coming, the inevitable result of the early wartime naval training of Marine pilots, which devoted little serious attention to closely coordinated air attacks in support of ground units. By late 1944 the winds of change had begun to blow at a stiffer pace, and the employment of Marine air for close support missions became a distinct possibility. In anticipation of such a development, MAG-24, then stationed at Bougainville, began the crash training of Marine pilots for close support. A radical departure from orthodox methods was the adoption of direct communications between pilots and ground-based air liaison parties. The performance of Marine aviators on Luzon Island and in the Southern Philippines was to become an outstanding chapter in a long history of excellent achievements, combining raw courage with skill and flexibility. The activities of Marine air in the Philippines constituted one of the few opportunities that Marine air groups had to show their skill in close air support. Except for a brief period of employment during the early days of the Iwo Jima operation, there would be little occasion for the Marine flyers to give any further demonstration of their close support prowess. Only later, on Okinawa, would Marine pilots have a final opportunity to perfect their close support tactics.[13]

The early days of 1945 were bleak ones for Germans and Japanese alike. In the case of the former, the Ardennes offensive had failed and only further weakened the depleted divisions of the *Reich*, which was now under aerial attack around the clock, while invading armies were striking at her interior from three directions. For the Japanese, the fortunes of war had come full

---

[12] USSBS, *Pacific Campaigns*, p. 289.

[13] For a detailed account of Marine Corps operations on Okinawa, see Frank and Shaw, *Victory and Occupation*, Pt. II.

circle. The spirit of optimism that had still filled the people of Japan with hope during the summer of 1944 had now vanished. The news from the battlefronts was all bad, and it could no longer be kept from the populace. The thought of rebellion against the Emperor was still unacceptable to the Japanese, but there were some effects, notably to morale: "At home the bad news began to be known and mutterings of negotiated conditional peace arose even in the armed forces. Japan was defeated: it remained only necessary to persuade her of the fact."[14]

As the war situation deteriorated for the Axis, the peoples of Germany and Japan realized that nothing short of a miracle could still save their situation. In Germany, the die-hard optimists looked for a reversal of imminent defeat through the V-Weapons, whose development assumed ever grander proportions, though reality lagged far behind wishful thinking. As early as 1943, the Japanese received word that Germany was working on atomic weapons, but nuclear physicists maintained that such weapons were not far enough advanced for use in World War II. Nevertheless, an attempt was made to employ science in a bid to solve the numerous military problems.

During 1944, an increasing number of scientists and technical experts were pressed into service in order to test a number of unorthodox devices that were to be employed in the decisive battle. Thus, the Japanese Army experimented with a thermal ray and bombs that would be guided to their targets by sources of heat, notably American troopships. Actual experiments had been carried out during the summer of 1944, but the onrush of events overtook the slow experimentation before a multitude of technical problems could be eliminated. In the end, the "weapons of science" could not be put to any practical use, and "weapons for decisive combat thus came to mean suicidal expedients," such as the *kamikaze*.[15] The only practical Japanese secret weapon ever to be used against the United States was a balloon bomb, which for about six months after 1 November 1944, was released daily from Japan. Purpose of the bomb was a psychological one: "Americans were to be made to feel uneasy because of surprise explosions scattered throughout the United States." While a number of these balloons actually reached the Continental United States, their effectiveness was practically nil; only a few grass fires resulted from 9,000 incendiary balloons launched.

The invasion of Iwo Jima must be viewed in the light of what the loss of the island would do to Japanese civilian morale, coupled with the benefits the use of the island's three airfields would provide to the Allied air effort against Japan. Because of the serious losses incurred in the Philippines and other campaigns, together with a breakdown in the pilot replacement program and a critical shortage of fuel, the Japanese Army and Navy Air Forces were no longer effective deterrents to American incursions at sea or in the air. On the other hand, the American potential for waging war was at its height. The Amer-

---

[14] USSBS, *Pacific Campaigns*, p. 290.

[15] Hayashi and Coox, *Kogun*, p. 118.

icans were stronger in numbers, better trained, and moving forward with an overwhelming offensive power. "United States domination of the Pacific Ocean Area was complete and the time was at hand to strike in earnest toward the heart of the Japanese Empire."[16]

The Iwo Jima operation was wedged in time into a very narrow period, barely preceded by the American landings on Luzon and shortly followed by the invasion of Okinawa. The ambitious plans for this decisive period almost exceeded the capabilities of a fully mobilized United States, particularly when the Tokyo carrier strikes were included. As a result, the landings at Iwo Jima took place under the shadow of the major invasion of Luzon in the south, the imminent assault against the Ryukyus, and a carrier-based aerial assault against the Home Islands. This accelerated schedule of events contributed to the reduction in the number of days available for the prelanding bombardment of Iwo Jima. That the island could be taken at all in view of the strength of its defenses and the casualties incurred by the attacking Marines is proof of the latters' courage, highly advanced state of training, and the soundness of amphibious doctrine that had become an integral part of Marine Corps tactics.

Control of Iwo Jima provided the Americans with airfields 600 miles closer to the Home Islands, opening the doors wide to a full-scale aerial assault on Japan. The early months of 1945 thus saw a further extension of American power towards the inner defenses of Japan. Even as bitter fighting raged on Iwo Jima, a huge American invasion armada was already en route to Okinawa, which was ultimately to turn into "the most difficult operation undertaken in the Pacific by United States forces,"[17] though from the point of view of the Marine Corps, the Iwo Jima campaign remains aptly designated as "The Supreme Test."[18] A comparison of the Iwo Jima and Okinawa operations does not fall within the purview of this volume; the latter operation has been most aptly described elsewhere in this series.[19]

The seizure of Iwo Jima eliminated a strong Japanese bastion of defense near the Home Islands; it provided the Americans with forward airfields; and the U. S. presence on Iwo Jima was decisive in neutralizing other fortified enemy islands in the Bonins. As the war in Europe thundered to its conclusion, the inevitability of defeat following the fall of Iwo Jima was impressed on all Japanese. As the shadow of American airpower and the specter of an all-out assault against the Home Islands themselves became a distinct possibility, Japanese diplomats began delicate maneuvers behind the scenes to save what could be salvaged from a misguided and misconceived war. Japanese defeats in the Pacific also were beginning to have international repercussions, notably with regard to the Soviet Union, which was beginning to waver in its neutrality towards Japan. The horror of atomic warfare was yet unheard of dur-

---

[16] USSBS, *Pacific Campaigns*, p. 320.

[17] USSBS, *Pacific Campaigns*, p. 324.

[18] Isely and Crowl, *U. S. Marines and Amphibious War*, ch 10.

[19] See Frank and Shaw, *Victory and Occupation*, Pt II.

ing these early months of 1945. But each succeeding American assault across the Central Pacific had driven the nails of defeat deeper into the coffin that bore the remains of Japanese dreams, and it was on islands such as Peleliu and Iwo Jima that these dreams were finally laid to rest.

Bibliographical Notes

This history is predominantly based on official Marine Corps records comprising the diaries, reports, plans, journals, and orders of the commands and units that participated in the operations covered by this volume. Such records of the other Services as were pertinent to the subject matter have been consulted and used. Activities on high strategic levels have been reconstructed with the help of the records of the Joint Chiefs of Staff or official publications that derived a considerable portion of their basic data from JCS records.

Since this volume deals with a number of seemingly unrelated topics, ranging from an administrative history of the Fleet Marine Force, Pacific, to major operations in the Western Pacific, not to mention aviation activities in widely separated areas, a large number of sources had to be consulted. Some of these were pertinent to only one area or period of time while others offered detailed information on a scope encompassing the entire volume. Unless otherwise noted, all of the official records cited are on file with or obtainable through the Library and Documentation Sections, Reference Branch, Historical Division, Headquarters, U. S. Marine Corps.

A number of published works of general interest have been consulted frequently during the preparation of this volume. The more important of these are listed below.

In order to bridge the inevitable gaps and inadequacies that occur in the sources consulted, extensive use was made of the knowledge of key participants in the actions described. These men, representing all Services, generously offered time and effort in replying to specific questions, making themselves available for interviews, and furnishing critical comments on draft manuscrips of this volume and preliminary monographs. The historical offices of the Army, Navy, and Air Force have conducted a detailed review of draft chapters and furnished much material of value to this history. The War History Office of the Defense Agency of Japan has read and commented on the passages dealing with Japanese operations on Peleliu, Iwo Jima, and in the Philippines, providing valuable information that has been incorporated into the narrative.

Books

Wesley Frank Craven and James Lee Cate, eds. *The Pacific: Matterhorn to Nagasaki, June 1944 to August 1945—The Army Air Forces in World War II*, v. 5. Chicago: University of Chicago Press, 1953. The Air Force official history covering the final year of World War II with particular emphasis on the development and employment of the B-29 bomber and operations in the Western and Southwestern Pacific. This well documented book is a reliable source for the operations of Army Air Forces units in the Pacific and their vital part in the defeat of Japan.

Jeter A. Isely and Philip A. Crowl. *The U. S. Marines and Amphibious War*. Princeton: Princeton University Press, 1951. An outstanding source of information dealing with the adoption, development, and perfection of amphibious warfare and application of these techniques during various phases of World War II. The authors' critical comments on each major operation and their conclusions are invaluable for a clear perspective of warfare in the Pacific Theater.

VAdm E. P. Forrestel. *Admiral Raymond A. Spruance, USN—A Study in Command*. Washington: Department of the Navy, 1966. Record of a naval leader's service to his country in war and peace. This well documented and illustrated biography not only tells the story of a man and his brilliant career in the Pacific during World War II but also outlines some of the major naval operations of World War II.

FAdm William F. Halsey and LCdr J. Bryan

III. *Admiral Halsey's Story.* New York: Whittlesey House, McGraw-Hill Publishing Company, Inc., 1947. The life and service of one of the most prominent American naval commanders in World War II. In addition to gaining a close look at the human side of this great naval leader, the reader is also presented with the background and development of some of the great naval actions in the Western Pacific during World War II.

FAdm Ernest H. King and Cdr Walter M. Whitehill. *Fleet Admiral King: A Naval Record.* New York: W. W. Norton & Company, Inc., 1952. An autobiography covering the entire span of service of this great naval leader, highlighting his part in the formulation of American strategy within the high-level command structure employed in World War II.

FAdm William D. Leahy. *I Was There.* New York: Whittlesey House, McGraw-Hill Publishing Company, 1950. The autobiography of another high-ranking naval officer who served as Chief of Staff under Presidents Roosevelt and Truman. In addition to highly relevant comments on top-level Allied conferences which the author attended, a sizable portion of the book deals with his most delicate prewar appointment as American Minister to the Vichy Government and his official and personal relations with prominent Vichy persons.

Samuel Eliot Morison. *History of United States Naval Operations in World War II,* v. XII, XIII, XIV. Boston: Little, Brown and Company, 1958, 1959, 1960. These three volumes by Rear Admiral Morison, *Leyte, June 1944-January 1945, The Liberation of the Philippines, 1944-1945,* and *Victory in the Pacific, 1945* give an excellent account of Navy operations in the Southwestern and Western Pacific. Though prepared with Navy collaboration and support, these volumes nevertheless bear the personal imprint of the author, whose masterful description of the naval operations of this period is without equal.

Robert Sherrod. *History of Marine Corps Aviation in World War II.* Washington: Combat Forces Press, 1952. An unofficial history, but prepared with substantial research support from the Marine Corps, this work contains information on Marine aviation units not to be found elsewhere. It represents the most comprehensive source in its field published to date.

Robert Ross Smith. *The Approach to the Philippines—The War in the Pacific—United States Army in World War II.* Washington: Office of the Chief of Military History, Department of the Army, 1953. An excellent account of the strategy and tactics that were employed in laying the basis for the recapture of the Philippines, specifically during amphibious and ground operations in New Guinea and the southern Palau Islands.

United States Strategic Bombing Survey (Pacific), Naval Analysis Division. *The Campaigns of the Pacific War,* 1 vol. and *Interrogations of Japanese Officials,* 2 vols. Washington: Government Printing Office, 1946. The three volumes give an interesting account of World War II as seen through Japanese eyes. Prepared shortly after the end of hostilities, this series is deficient in accuracy and perspective. Yet the information and viewpoints provide an insight into Japanese military thinking, both through translation of pertinent documents and through interviews.

The War Reports of General of the Army George C. Marshall, Chief of Staff, General of the Army H. H. Arnold, Commanding General, Army Air Forces; Fleet Admiral Ernest J. King, Commander-in-Chief, United States Fleet and Chief of Naval Operations. Philadelphia and New York: J. B. Lippincott Company, 1947. Collection of the official reports of the chiefs of the armed services, issued during World War II and the immediate postwar period. Excellent material for reviewing the big picture of World War II operations.

PART I

INTRODUCTION

Official Documents

The operational span of ground operations in this volume covers the invasion of the southern Palaus as a preliminary step in the reconquest of the Philippines and the subsequent decision to seize Iwo Jima in the Volcano-Bonins as an advanced base in the direction of the Home Islands. For the strategy and tactics employed by the United States during this crucial period of the war in the Southwestern and Western Pacific during the latter part of 1944 and early 1945, a variety of sources were required. These ranged from records of the Joint and Combined Chiefs of Staff as cited in previously published official histories to the minutes of CominCh-CinCPac Conferences conducted during the summer of 1944. In some instances, copies of reports and minutes portraying the evolution of Anglo-American strategy can be found in the files of the World War II Division, Federal Records Center, The National Archives which has recently relocated to Suitland, Maryland.

Information on the status of Marine Corps units and personnel during the period covered has been derived from such tables of organization station lists and status sheets for air and ground units as were readily available in the archives of the Historical Division. Additional sources of information were the monthly FMF air and ground status reports prepared within the Division of Plans and Policies and the Division of Aviation, HQMC, and the Annual Reports of the Commandant of the Marine Corps to the Secretary of the Navy.

Japanese Sources

In appraising the strategic and tactical situation from the Japanese side, our view is necessarily limited by the factors of time, distance, availability of enemy persons and records, and linguistics. A full exploitation of official Japanese wartime records on a scale even remotely resembling that of captured German military records by the Allies proved impossible. On the tactical level, few of the Japanese garrison commanders and their staffs survived the fighting; as a result, such information as was obtainable had to be gleaned from American intelligence surveys prepared by higher headquarters, mostly based on the interrogation of the few prisoners that were taken or such Japanese military records, mostly of a tactical nature, that fell into American hands.

Fortunately for the historian and researcher, during the immediate postwar period while the occupation of Japan was in full swing, General MacArthur's headquarters utilized its available resources to initiate a study program with the help of former Japanese officials. This program culminated in the preparation of a series of monographs detailing Japanese activities in widespread areas of the Pacific and Asia. These early studies which varied greatly in scope, quality, and accuracy underwent a further process of refinement in the mid-1950s, at which time they were published in the form of monographs under the auspices of the Office of the Chief of Military History, Department of the Army. A complete listing of these monographs is contained in *Guide to Japanese Monographs and Japanese Studies on Manchuria 1945-1960* (Washington, 1961) prepared by OCMH, which also exercises custody over this collection.

Of primary interest for the purposes of this volume were those monographs dealing with Japanese preparations for the defense of the Philippines during the summer of 1944. Monograph No. 45 comprising the *History of the Army Section, Imperial General Headquarters*, gives an insight into the prosecution of the war as seen through eyes of Japanese on the elevated level of command in an exhaustive study of 382 pages. Monograph No. 48, *Central Pacific Operations Record*, Volume I, (December 1941-August 1945) furnished considerable information on the defense of Iwo Jima, while No. 49, Volume II of the same title, was useful in providing a general outline of the Japanese situation in the Pacific for most of 1944.

Books and Periodicals

The first three volumes of this series, *Pearl Harbor to Guadalcanal, Isolation of Rabaul*, and *Central Pacific Drive*, as well as the last, *Victory and Occupation*, have served as a useful basis for the background information that had to be incorporated into the fourth, particularly with respect to the development and employment of amphibious doctrine. An appropriate setting was arrived at with the help of the following:

Ray S. Cline. *Washington Command Post: The Operations Division—The War Department—United States Army in World War II*. Washington: Office of the Chief of Military History, Department of the Army, 1951. An official Army history outlining high-level planning in the Operations Division of the War Department during World War II. An excellent source based on important primary data.

John Miller, Jr. "The Casablanca Conference and Pacific Strategy," *Military Affairs*, v. 13, no. 4 (Winter 49). A concise account of this high-level conference and its results.

Walter Millis, ed. *The Forrestal Diaries*. New York: The Viking Press, 1951. The personal files and papers of the former Secretary of the Navy and later Secretary of Defense dealing with top level planning, decisions, and conferences during the later phase of World War II. An important source for evaluating the Administration's plans in the realm of international affairs, the conclusion of the war in the Pacific, and the formulation of plans for the postwar period.

Louis Morton. "American and Allied Strategy in the Far East," *Military Review*, v. 29, no. 9 (Dec49). This article deals with planning for the eventual drive across the Pacific towards the Japanese Home Islands.

Adm Raymond A. Spruance. "The Victory in the Pacific," *Journal of the Royal United Service Institution*, v. 91, no. 564 (Nov46). A brief but well prepared look at World War II operations in the Pacific Theater stressing planning and strategy.

United States Army, War Department. *Handbook on Japanese Military Forces*. TM-E 30–480. Washington, 1Oct44. A basic source on the organization and equipment of Japanese land forces with useful detail on weapons characteristics and textbook tactics.

PART II

FLEET MARINE FORCE, PACIFIC

Official Documents

The evolution of amphibious doctrine from the mid-1930s to the end of World War II directly reflects on the size and shape of the organization employed to implement this doctrine. In tracing the origin and development of the Fleet Marine Force, pertinent information was obtained from the official files at Headquarters, Marine Corps.. The material found fruitful for this purpose included the Annual Reports of the Commandant of the Marine Corps which, for the years under consideration, faithfully mirrored the increasing size and complexity of the organization. The evolution of amphibious doctrine is further reflected in Marine Corps and Navy manuals dealing with landing operations, issued between the two world wars, again notably during the 1930s. Information on the development of landing craft and amphibious vehicles was obtained from Headquarters Marine Corps files and those of the Department of the Navy Bureau of Ships. For a look at Fleet Marine Force organization and plans shortly before the United States entered the war, the "Report of the General Board on Expansion of the U. S. Marine Corps," of 7 May 1941, in the custody of the Operational Archives Branch, Naval History Division, proved of great value.

Additional information was obtained from Volume I in this series, Part I, "Introduction to the Marine Corps," which thoroughly discusses this subject matter and the resulting Marine Corps posture on the eve of World War II.

In connection with the parallel growth of Marine aviation several sources proved important. Among these, the Marine Corps Aviation Status Sheets, prepared by the Division of Aviation; an *Administrative History of Aircraft, Fleet Marine Force, Pacific*; the *War Diary, Marine Aircraft Wings, Pacific*, and the *War Diary of Aircraft, Fleet Marine Force Pacific* made a major contribution in following the expansion of Marine Corps aviation in World War II.

Unofficial Sources

The official material enumerated above was further supplemented with letters of comment on draft manuscripts obtained mostly from retired officers connected with the Fleet Marine Force following its establishment and those who played a part in it during the succeeding phases of its evolution. Many of the men who occupied leading positions during the two decades covered are no longer among the living. Nevertheless, their views, as expressed in statements, directives, and other correspondence have trickled down to us and have been carefully considered in the development of conclusions. An unpublished draft entitled "FMFPac Administrative History—The Development of FMFPac" in the custody of the Documentation Section, Reference Branch of the Historical Division served as a valuable guide in the reconstruction of the organizational development.

Books and Periodicals

Robert D. Heinl, Jr. *Soldiers of the Sea— The United States Marine Corps, 1775-1962.* Annapolis: United States Naval Institute, 1962. An outstanding labor of love by an author who combines great writing skill with his intricate knowledge of the Marine Corps scene both in peace and war. Not always with the greatest objectivity, the narrative provides comprehensive coverage of the organization and operations of the Marine Corps including its struggles afar and at home.

Once again, Isely and Crowl, *U. S. Marines and Amphibious War* provided valuable information on early amphibious doctrine and the evolution of the Fleet Marine Force.

Clyde H. Metcalf. *A History of the United States Marine Corps.* New York: G. P. Putnam's Sons, 1939. A valuable historical work showing the triumphs and tribulations of the Marine Corps in time of war and peace. Of special interest in this context for its coverage of the lean years following World War I to the beginning buildup in the late 1930s that foreshadowed World War II.

John H. Russell, Jr., "Birth of the Fleet Marine Force," *U. S. Naval Institute Proceedings*, v. 72, no. 515 (Jan/46). An authoritative contribution by a former Assistant Commandant and later Commandan who was closely involved with the Fleet Marine Force in its early years.

General Holland M. Smith, "Development of Amphibious Tactics in the U. S. Navy," *Marine Corps Gazette*, v. 38, nos. 6, 7, 8, 9, 10 (Jun-Oct48). A five-part article written by the man who made a major contribution to implementation of amphibious doctrine and the development of the Fleet Marine Force.

Holland M. Smith and Percy Finch, *Coral and Brass.* New York: Charles Scribner's Sons, 1949. An autobiography in which the author discussses his noteworthy military career with valuable comments on the military operations of World War II and his part in the development of the FMFPac.

PART III

.THE PALAUS: GATEWAY TO THE PHILIPPINES

Official Documents

The seizure of the southern Palaus as finally executed in Operation STALEMATE II resulted in the neutralization of the entire island group. The high level planning that preceded this operation, one of the most vicious and costly to be fought in the Pacific, spanned the period of nearly six months, during which time the progress of the war in the Pacific forced several revisions in the basic operation plan. The planning and execution of STALEMATE II resulted in a wealth of documentation ranging from minutes of the CCS and JCS to detailed plans on the corps and division level. On the tactical level, considerable information was available in the form of war diaries, appendices, and annexes including reports of general and special staff officers and sections, unit journals, and after action reports. While these vary greatly in scope and content, they nevertheless provide a comprehensive basis for an operational narrative, since all fields ranging from personnel, intelligence, and operations to logistics have been covered. If anything, the sheer quantity of material available from official sources, extending from the corps down to battalion level often made the selection of pertinent data a difficult undertaking. In those instances where a conflict existed between accounts on different reporting levels, the version of the unit most closely concerned with the action described has been utilized.

Unofficial Documents

In addition to the voluminous official sources, a number of unofficial documents were available in the form of letters that passed between various high-level participants in Operation STALEMATE II, particularly in the correspondence between Generals Geiger and Rupertus, and General Vandegrift, then Commandant of the Marine Corps. These letters are part of a personal correspondence file which the Commandant maintained with general and flag officers, and which ultimately came to be placed in the custody of the Archives of the Historical Division.

During the preparation of the historical monograph, *The Assault on Peleliu*, the author, Major Frank O. Hough, prepared numerous notes in the form of a card file. These cards, though no longer complete, contain substantial information on all phases of STALEMATE II and may be examined through the Documentation Section, Reference Branch, of the Historical Division.

MajGen Oliver P. Smith. "Personal Narrative." The personal journal of the Assistant Division Commander of the 1st Marine Division covering the period from 28 January-1 November 1944, including very perceptive comments on the Peleliu campaign.

After the draft chapters of the above monograph had been completed, they were circulated among the higher ranking participants in the operation for critique and comment. The replies received brought to light much additional information of varying quality, ranging from outstanding to average, which were assembled in a folder designated as the Peleliu Comment File. To these comments, dating back to the early 1950s, must be added a similar critique of the chapters in this volume. Both comment files are in the custody of the Historical Division, which will make them available to the serious researcher.

Japanese Sources

Compared to the wealth of official records available from American sources, those from the Japanese side are at best sparse. Among a large cache of documents captured on Saipan a number dealt with Japanese defensive preparations in the Palaus. These were exploited, translated in the rough, and made available to the assault units prior to the invasion. The interrogations of the relatively few prisoners of war taken on Peleliu also provide a source of information, though intelligence obtained in this way is of a conflicting nature, since prisoners frequently made their disclosures with a view towards pleasing their captors, so that material thus obtained must be viewed with a grain of salt.

On a more professional level, the U.S. Army monograph series prepared in Japan in the postwar period offers a wide range of material not to be found elsewhere, particularly Monograph No. 48, *Central Pacific Operations Record*, v. II. A recently published official Japanese History of World War II numbering several volumes undoubtedly contains much information that could fill existing gaps in the narrative of this volume. Unfortunately, publishing deadlines and lack of resources for the translation and exploitation of this material prevented its utilization.

In the years since the end of World War II, a number of books dealing with operations in the Central and Western Pacific have been published in Japan. Some of these, of varying degrees of quality, have been translated into English and are listed below.

Books and Periodicals

Once again Craven and Cate, *Matterhorn to Nagasaki*; Isely and Crowl, *U.S. Marines and Amphibious War*; Sherrod, *History of Marine Corps Aviation*, and Smith, *Approach to the Philippines* constitute invaluable sources. Other works which shed considerable light on the Peleliu operation are:

LtCol Kimber H. Boyer. "The 3d Armored Amphibian Battalion—Palau Operation, 15 September-20 October 1944." Quantico: Marine Corps Schools, Amphibious Warfare School, Senior Course, 1948-49. A brief historical tactical study of the Peleliu operation on the battalion level.

RAdm Worrall R. Carter. *Beans, Bullets, and Black Oil*. Washington: Government Printing Office, 1953. Official history of Navy logistics in the Pacific during World War II.

Burke Davis. *Marine!—The Life of Lieutenant General Lewis B. (Chesty) Puller*. Boston: Little, Brown, and Company, 1962. The story of one of the great fighting men of the Corps and the experiences of the 1st Marines, which he commanded, in the Peleliu assault.

Saburo Hayashi and Alvin D. Coox. *Kogun*. Quantico: Marine Corps Association, 1959. Translated from the Japanese, this account of the plans and activities of the Japanese Army High Command during World War II was prepared by a former staff officer in the *Imperial General Headquarters*.

Maj Frank O. Hough. *The Assault on Peleliu*. Washington: Historical Division,

HQMC, 1950. This official monograph contains a detailed account of Operation STALEMATE including interesting appendices on Japanese cave positions and the role of Marine Corps aviation on Peleliu.

George P. Hunt. *Coral Comes High.* New York: Harper and Brothers, 1946. An account of Pacific operations including Peleliu from the company commander's point of view. More human interest than history, but nevertheless important in portraying the feelings of men in battle.

George McMillan. *The Old Breed: A History of the First Marine Division in World War II.* Washington: Infantry Journal Press, 1949. A unit history describing the performance of the units and men of the 1st Division, without which the complete story of the Peleliu operation could not be told.

MajGen Paul J. Mueller (USA), Chairman, 81st Wildcat Division Historical Committee, et al. *The 81st Infantry Wildcat Division in World War II.* Washington: Infantry Journal Press, 1948. A detailed account of the 81st Division's operation on Angaur Island and the subsequent employment of its regiments on Peleliu.

Jeremiah A. O'Leary. "Hell in the Umurbrogol," *True Magazine,* v. 17, no. 101 (Oct45). Human interest story of the ferocious fighting that took place on Peleliu.

PART IV

MARINES IN THE PHILIPPINES

Official Documents

Beyond the employment of the V Amphibious Corps Artillery on Leyte, the story of Marines in the Philippines is primarily one of Marine aviation in support of U.S. Army units. A variety of sources were consulted in order to obtain a balanced product. On the strategic level, heavy reliance was placed on minutes and records of the Combined and Joint Chiefs of Staff, reports, plans, and official correspondence on the CinCPac level. On the tactical level, records of the U. S. Sixth Army proved valuable for the Leyte and Luzon Campaigns, while Eighth Army records were consulted for a reconstruction of operations in the Southern Philippines. The bulk of this material, including war diaries and journals and after action reports of the U. S. Army corps and divisions involved are in the custody of the World War II Records Division, NARS, Suitland, Maryland.

Records of the Marine Corps consulted are predominantly those of aviation units on the aircraft group and squadron level. There is great variance in the coverage of events as to depth and scope between units, which resulted in gaps that had to be bridged through the use of both official and unofficial published works.

Unofficial Documents

Upon completion of a historical monograph on Marine Aviation in the Philippines, the draft manuscript was circulated for comment and critique to interested parties who had taken part in the operation. Many of these individuals responded and their comments have been cited throughout this section. Similarly, the draft chapters of this volume were sent to key participants and to the historical agencies of the other services, and the replies received have been used as applicable in revising the narrative. All such comments are retained in the files of the Documentation Section, Reference Branch of the Historical Division.

By no means all of the material uncovered by draft comments has been used in this book or in the historical monograph that preceded it. The files contain much unpublished information that may be of value to the future researcher or student of this phase of Marine aviation activities, particularly with regard to the doctrine of Marine close air support that evolved from childhood to adolescence during this phase of the war.

Japanese Sources

Once again, the number of official Japanese sources is quite limited when compared to the U. S. Army, Navy, and Marine Corps records available dealing with this subject matter. Nevertheless, the OCMH monograph series does provide information in its *Philippines Operations Record,* Phases II and III, that bridges the gap to some extent. Additional information is available from *35th Army Operations, 1944-45* and the interrogation of senior Japanese commanders in the postwar era. On the higher level of command, Monograph No. 45, *History of the Army Section, Imperial General Staff, 1941-45* provides valuable clues in portraying the strategy employed by the Japanese High Command during this period of the war.

Books and Periodicals

In addition to the overall sources, particularly the previously cited Morison volumes on *Leyte* and *The Liberation of the Philippines*, Craven and Cate, *The Pacific—Matterhorn to Nagasaki*, and Sherrod, *History of Marine Corps Aviation in World War II*, the following were extensively consulted:

Maj Charles W. Boggs, Jr. *Marine Aviation in the Philippines*. Washington: Historical Division, HQMC, 1951. An official monograph depicting Marine close support of Army units in the Philippines, outlining in detail the development of the Marine doctrine of close air suport. The narrative covers the entire period of liberation of the Philippines from the Leyte landings to the end of the war.

John A. DeChant. *Devilbirds: The Story of United States Marine Corps Aviation in World War II*. New York: Harper and Brothers, 1947. Relatively brief but good description of Marine dive bomber operations on Luzon.

M. Hamlin Cannon. *Leyte: The Return to the Philippines—The War in the Pacific—United States Army in World War II*. Washington: Office of the Chief of Military History, Department of the Army, 1953. Excellent account and official Army history of the recapture of Leyte, the first island to be liberated in the Philippines. Useful as a background for the movements and operations of the VAC artillery on Leyte.

General Robert L. Eichelberger and Milton Mackaye. *Our Jungle Road to Tokyo*. New York: The Viking Press, 1950. The march across the Southwest Pacific as seen through the eyes of the Commanding General of I Corps and subsequently of the Eighth Army. Based on an earlier series in the *Saturday Evening Post*, the volume furnishes interesting details on Eighth Army operations in the Philippines.

Frank O. Hough. *The Island War: The United States Marine Corps in the Pacific*. Philadelphia and New York: J. B. Lippincott Company, 1947. Relatively brief description of Marine aviation activities in the Philippines is of primary importance in this context.

General George C. Kenney. *General Kenney Reports*. New York: Duell, Sloan, and Pearce, 1949. The personal history of the Commander of the Allied Air Forces in the Southwest Pacific. A sizable portion of this book deals with the Philippines and thus serves as valuable background material for this section.

Capt Samuel H. McAloney, "Is Air Support Effective?" *Marine Corps Gazette*, v. 29, No. 11 (Nov45). One of the members of an air liaison party discusses his experiences in obtaining close air support for Army troops on Luzon.

Robert Ross Smith. *Triumph in the Philippines—The War in the Pacific—United States Army in World War II*. Washington: Office of the Chief of Military History, Department of the Army, 1963. The official Army history dealing with the liberation of the Central and Southern Philippines was of great value for providing the setting in which Marine aviation operated during the final phase of World War II.

Maj Bertram C. Wright, USA. *The First Cavalry Division In World War II*. Tokyo: Toppan Printing Company, Ltd., 1947. This division history furnishes an excellent account of the drive that culminated in the liberation of Manila and the support given to the division by Marine aviators.

PART V

MARINE AVIATION IN THE WESTERN PACIFIC

Official Documents

The discussion of Marine aviation activities in the Western Pacific is largely based on the records of the units concerned. Included in the documents are special action reports, war diaries, and informal combat reports on the wing, aircraft group, and squadron level. It should be remembered that the type of information contained in the official documents is but a reflection of the mission entrusted to Marine aviation in the Central and Western Pacific, which in 1944 and almost to the end of the war consisted primarily of neutralizing Japanese bases and involved little of the close air support envisioned by Marine planners and subsequently used in the Philippines in support of Army units. There is also a wide variance in quality and detail of coverage, depending on the skill of the personnel assigned to the task and the value placed by the command on the importance of maintaining official records. Nevertheless, despite occasional gaps, the overall coverage is adequate to permit a comprehensive view of the part played by Marine aviation in the trek of the American forces across the Pacific. All of the official records used are in the custody of the World War II Records Division, National Archives and Records Service, Suitland, Maryland and may be obtained from that agency, or through the Historical Division, HQMC.

Unofficial Documents

There is no body of letters and interviews in the Marine Corps Historical Division archives relating to air operations against the bypassed islands in the Central and Western Pacific as there is in the case of other campaigns which have been covered in historical monographs. A few pertinent letters among the papers acquired from the Sherrod aviation history project are of limited value to a history of a wide scope.

During the preparation of this volume, the two chapters comprising this section were sent out to a number of individuals who had participated in the operations covered therein. In response, numerous written comments were received to round out the strategical and tactical picture. Certain key individuals in their comments helped to clarify command problems that were encountered during this phase of the war in the area involved. Generally, as seen from the vantage point of time and experience, the comments received proved an invaluable source of information to supplement the material found in official sources.

Japanese Sources

Japanese records used in this account consisted primarily of monographs touching upon enemy air operations and defensive preparations in the Marshalls, Marianas, and Palaus. Once again, an English translation of the official Japanese Army history of World War II would have been invaluable, since official World War II records dealing with this subject matter were not available. Much of the information from the Japanese side was obtained from postwar interrogations of Japanese officials contained in the USSBS *Interrogations*, and the postwar writings of Japanese who had participated in these operations.

Books and Periodicals

Valuable background material for this section was obtained from the previously cited Isely and Crowl, *U. S. Marines and Amphibious War*; King and Whitehill, *Fleet Admiral King*; Sherrod, *Marine Corps Aviation in World War II*; Heinl, *Soldiers of the Sea*; and Morison, *Victory in the Pacific*. In addition to these, the following proved valuable in the preparation of this section:

Major Carl W. Hoffman. *Saipan—The Beginning of the End*. Washington: Historical Division, HQMC, 1950. A detailed historical monograph dealing with the Saipan operation, of value as background material for the establishment of an airfield that was to become of vital importance in the conduct of air operations in the Pacific.

Major Carl W. Hoffman. *The Seizure of Tinian*. Washington: Historical Division, HQMC, 1951. Excellent account of the Tinian operation, which furnishes valuable background material for the subsequent use of the island as a base from which the major attacks against the Home Islands were launched that brought an end to the war.

Major Orlan R. Lodge. *The Recapture of Guam*. Washington: Historical Branch, G-3 Division, HQMC, 1954. The official Marine Corps monograph concerning the Guam operation, furnishing valuable background material for an appreciation of the air situation in the Central Pacific during the final phase of World War II.

Masatake Okumiya, Jiro Horikoshi, and Martin Caidin. *Zero!* New York: E. P. Dutton & Company, Inc., 1956. The title of this well-researched and written work is misleading, in that its scope goes far beyond a discussion of the well known Mitsubishi fighter, its development, and its employment. The book dwells on Japanese air operations in the Pacific throughout the war and provides a valuable insight into Japanese internal and foreign policy during the war years.

PART VI

IWO JIMA

Official Documents

Operation DETACHMENT probably received closer study in its inception and planning, more detailed analysis by the numerous staff sections of headquarters of varying levels for historical purposes, and extensive coverage by the news and information media than any of the Pacific amphibious assaults previously executed in World War II. Since this was an all-Marine operation involving three divisions at the very threshold of Japan, in fact against a target administratively a part of the Home Islands, the importance attached to DETACHMENT is reflected both in the volume and quality of the available material. Where gaps are readily apparent in other operations, none appear in this instance; to the contrary, the data available for research on Iwo Jima tends to be overwhelming. Instead of being compelled to bridge gaps, the researcher is nearly overwhelmed with a profusion of action reports, unit diaries and journals, operation plans and orders, dispatches, letters, and preoperation studies by units that took part in the campaign. Mindful of criticism voiced as to excessive casualties after Tarawa, every precaution was taken at Iwo Jima to avoid any gap in the planning of the operation. This care is reflected in every facet of the planning phase, from the amount of intelligence collected to the evacuation of the wounded and burial of the dead.

In order to avoid repetition and to obtain a balanced account of the operation, the reports of the higher echelons were used to reconstruct the "big picture," while on the lower level the records of the unit most directly involved in the action were utilized.

In addition to the voluminous records dealing with Operation DETACHMENT, the very length and difficulty of the campaign gave rise to much soul-searching on the division and corps level, which is reflected in very detailed reports on the performance of men and equipment under the conditions peculiar to the operation, as well as on organizational problems encountered. All of the official documents pertaining to Operation DETACHMENT are in the custody of the World War II Records Division, National Archives and Records Service, Suitland, Maryland.

Unofficial Documents

The vast lode of official material is supplemented by a large quantity of information from unofficial sources. Thus, in the course of preparing the official monograph *Iwo Jima—Amphibious Epic*, its author, Lieutenant Colonel Whitman S. Bartley, requested comments from individuals who had taken part in the campaign. In response, approximately 175 participants in the operation contributed to the finished product through written comments or personal interviews. The information thus obtained was used to supplement or corroborate the hundreds of documents consulted during the preparation of the monograph. In the same way, valuable information was received that had never found its way into the official records, though time and space did not permit all of the personal recollections and anecdotes to be incorporated into the narrative.

Similarly, comments from participants in the operation were solicited upon completion of the draft chapters of this work. The passage of time had taken its toll among the survivors of the operation, but nevertheless much additional information was obtained in this fashion which otherwise might never have found its way into these pages. All of the comments, both for the historical monograph and for this volume repose in the files of the Documentation Section, Reference Branch of the Historical Division.

Japanese Sources

There is some variety in the Japanese sources available for Operation DETACHMENT. First, a number of enemy documents, diaries, and letters were seized in the course of the campaign, which were translated, for the most part on the division level, and either filed with VAC or forwarded to higher headquarters. Additional information on the defense of Iwo Jima was obtained through the interrogation of prisoners of war. For the most part, little information beyond that of a limited tactical nature could be thus obtained with the exception that one of the publishers of one of Japan's major dailies was, for reasons unknown, serving on Iwo Jima in an enlisted status. He was well versed in the realm of the big picture of the Japanese war effort and civilian morale in the Home Islands, and from this vantage point was able to contribute much to an overall appraisal of conditions in Japan during this phase of the war.

Time and resources did not permit the translation and use of the recently published official Japanese History of World War II, which, beyond doubt, would have contributed much to balancing the narrative from the enemy side of the hill. Comments by the War History Office of the Defense Agency of Japan also provided worthwhile information that was incorporated into the narrative.

Help in bringing to life the major Japanese participants in the Iwo Jima campaign arrived from a totally unexpected source, and it is in this respect that the Iwo Jima chapters differ from others in this volume. In writing an excellent book on the Iwo operation, which will be cited below, Richard F. Newcomb had numerous interviews conducted in Japan with members of the families of the long-deceased Japanese commanders, veterans of the campaign in Japan, and others who in some way were either connected with these individuals or the planning for the defense of the island. In making this voluminous file available to the Historical Division for use in this volume, Mr. Newcomb made a major contribution to removing the shadow of anonymity that cloaks these men who fought hard and gave all for their country. This material has been alternately referred to in the narrative as the *Newcomb File* or *Newcomb Notes*; a photostatic copy of it reposes in the archives of the Historical Division.

Books and Periodicals

The scope, size, and public awareness of the Iwo Jima operation have resulted in much published material on this campaign. As a result, only those sources consulted on a large scale are listed below. Valuable background material was contained in the previously cited Craven and Cate, The *Pacific—Matterhorn to Nagasaki*; Isely and Crowl, *U. S. Marines and Amphibious War*; Hayashi and Coox, *Kogun*; Heinl, *Soldiers of the Sea*; Smith and Finch, *Coral and Brass*; Mills, *The Forrestal Diaries*; and Morison, *Victory in the Pacific*.

Robert A. Aurthur and Kenneth Cohlmia. *The Third Marine Division*. Washington: Infantry Journal Press, 1948. One of the division histories published in the wake of World War II. Of primary interest in this context because of coverage of the Iwo Jima operation and the division's part in it.

Howard M. Conner. *The Spearhead—The World War II History of the 5th Marine Division*. Washington: Infantry Journal Press, 1950. An excellent account of the first major operation in which the division took part. Since this was the only campaign for the division, the author was able to devote more detail to this narrative than is the case with the histories of the other two divisions on Iwo. He has put this advantage to good use.

T. Grady Gallant. *The Friendly Dead*. New York: Doubleday and Company, Inc., 1964. A participant's account of the horrors of the battle that saw heroism, gallantry, and brutal death on an unprecedented scale.

Col Robert D. Heinl, Jr. "Target Iwo," *U. S. Naval Institute Proceedings*, v. 89, no. 7 (Jul 1963). Well written account of the factors affecting the preliminary bombardment of the objective, prepared by one who was intimately involved in this aspect of the operation.

Capt Raymond Henri. *Iwo Jima—Springboard to Final Victory*. New York: U. S. Camera Publishing Corporation, 1945. Pictorial account with brief narrative of the Iwo campaign, outstanding for its pictorial coverage.

Capt Raymond Henri et al. *The U. S. Marines on Iwo Jima*. Washington: The Infantry Journal, 1945. The operation as seen through the eyes of five official Marine combat correspondents. An interesting human drama account of one of history's large, impersonal battles. Also contains numerous interesting photographs of the action.

Clive Howard and Joe Whitley. *One Damned Island After Another.* Chapel Hill: The University of North Carolina Press, 1946. The history of the U. S. Army Seventh Air Force, written mostly from a public relations point of view. Nevertheless of value to this narrative because of its account of pre-invasion bombings of Iwo Jima.

Robert Leckie. *Strong Men Armed.* New York: Random House, 1962. Well illustrated human interest account of the Marines in World War II; its coverage of Iwo Jima added considerable flavor to the narrative.

Capt Clifford P. Morehouse. *The Iwo Jima Operation.* Washington: Historical Division, HQMC, 1946. Detailed historical monograph on the Iwo Jima operation containing some information on units and casualties not covered elsewhere.

Richard F. Newcomb. *Iwo Jima.* New York, Chicago, and San Francisco: Holt, Rinehart, and Winston, 1965. An outstanding reconstruction of the battle as seen from both sides, covering both the operational aspects and the human side. This book and the author's notes made a major contribution to the writing of this volume.

Carl W. Proehl. *The Fourth Marine Division in World War II.* Washington: Infantry Journal Press, 1946. Well written and illustrated account of the division's exploits in World War II, with good coverage of the Iwo Jima campaign. The color photography is outstanding and the map work superior.

Saburo Sakai, Martin Caidin, and Fred Saito. *Samurai!* New York: Ballantine Books, 1957. An account by one of Japan's air aces of his experiences on Iwo prior to the invasion. A much needed bit of writing that helped to balance the account of the action.

Col Donald M. Weller. "Salvo—Splash!— The Development of NGF Support in World War II." *U. S. Naval Institute Proceedings,* pt 1, v. 80, no. 8 (Aug/54). Valuable account of the experiences of a Marine officer who played a leading part in this aspect of Operation DETACHMENT.

CONCLUSIONS

Official Documents

The period covered by the ground operations in this volume extends from mid-September 1944 to the end of March 1945. The Peleliu and Iwo Jima campaigns which fall within this time frame were not isolated operations; momentous events were under way in other theaters of operations that eventually paved the way for final victory. The road to Peleliu and Iwo Jima had begun as a tortuous path that led from Guadalcanal to Tarawa. The lessons learned on each island and paid for with the blood of countless Americans paved the way for the seizure of the Marshalls and Marianas, which in turn served as springboards for the continued advance into the western Pacific.

In itself, this volume shows neither the beginning of the war nor its conclusion. The bloody battles fought in two major operations were but signposts pointing the way to the heart of the enemy's defenses. With the introduction of new defensive tactics by the Japanese and progress made in the art and science of amphibious warfare by the Marines, Peleliu was to become a struggle of endurance, Iwo Jima a contest of the will. Beyond the immediate tactical results of these operations, there were political overtones, both in Japan, the United States, and the Soviet Union. Progress of the war in the Pacific influenced Allied operations in Europe, where events, in turn, had a measurable effect on Allied resources in the Pacific.

Since the concluding part of this volume was designed to bring the two major operations described into balance with the big picture of the war, the sources, of necessity, had to be obtained from the policy-making level. These include the records of the Combined and Joint Chiefs of Staff as cited in previously published official histories, as well as the minutes of such high-level and far-reaching conferences as those held at Teheran in November 1943 and Quebec in September 1944, not to mention the important Roosevelt-Nimitz-MacArthur meeting in Hawaii in late July of the same year. The Iwo Jima campaign nearly coincided with the Yalta Conference, which set the tone for the overall strategic concept of the war, including that phase beyond the unconditional surrender of Germany to the ultimate surrender of Japan to be brought about in cooperation with other Pacific powers and the Soviet Union.

Unofficial Documents

The brevity of this part of the volume did not permit the discussion of foreign policy and the political overtones dictating strategy during the phase of the war to be covered in more than very general terms. The unofficial documents pertinent in this context are the numerous comments received on the draft chapters of this volume, as well as some of those submitted on Volume III of this series, *Central Pacific Drive* and Volume V, *Victory and Occupation*. All of these comments are filed in the archives of the Historical Division

Books and Periodicals

Among the books most widely used in the preparation of this section were the previously cited Cline, *Washington Command Post;* Craven and Cate, *The Pacific—Matterhorn to Nagasaki;* Halsey and Bryan, *Admiral Halsey's Story;* Isely and Crowl, *U. S. Marines and Amphibious War;* Hayashi and Coox, *Kogun;* Leahy, *I Was There,* and Morison, *Victory in the Pacific.* In addition, the following contributed substantially to this section.

Hugh M. Cole. *The Ardennes: The Battle of the Bulge—The U. S. Army in World War II.* Washington: Office of the Chief of the Military History, Department of the Army, 1965. An excellent account of the last major German counteroffensive of the war with resulting implications for the defeat of Germany.

Benis M. Frank and Henry I. Shaw, Jr. *Victory and Occupation—History of U. S. Marine Corps Operations in World War II*, v. V. Washington: Historical Branch, G-3 Division, HQMC, 1968. The official Marine Corps history of the Okinawa campaign and the occupation of Japan and North China.

Henry I. Shaw, Jr., Bernard C. Nalty, and Edwin T. Turnbladh. *Central Pacific Drive—History of U.S. Marine Corps Operations in World War II*, v. III. Washington: Historical Branch, G-3 Division, HQMC, 1966. The official Marine Corps history of the campaigns in the Gilberts, Marshalls, and Mariannas, which formed the basis for continued operations in the Western Pacific.

APPENDIX B

Guide to Abbreviations

A-1 (etc)	Corps Artillery Staff Officer, Personnel (See G-1)
A-20	Army twin-engine attack plane, the Douglas Havoc
AA	Antiaircraft
AAA	Antiaircraft Artillery
AAF	Army Air Forces
AAR	After Action Report
AcftCarrs	Aircraft Carriers
ACofS	Assistant Chief of Staff
ADC	Air Defense Command; Assistant Division Commander
Adm	Admiral
Admin	Administrative
Adv	Advance
AF	Air Force
AFB	Air Force Base
AFPOA	Army Forces, Pacific Ocean Areas
AirDel	Air Delivery
AirFMFPac	Aircraft, Fleet Marine Force, Pacific
AK	Cargo vessel
AKA	Cargo ship, attack
Alex	Alexandria
ALP	Air Liaison Party
Ammo	Ammunition
Amphib	Amphibian; Amphibious
Amtrac	Amphibian tractor
AN/VRC	Army-Navy Vehicle, Radio Communication
Anx	Annex
AP	Armor-piercing
APA	Attack transport
APD	High-speed transport
App	Appendix
Ar	Army
AR	Action Report
ArmdAmph	Armored Amphibian
Arty	Artillery
Asslt	Assault
Asst	Assistant
AT	Antitank
ATC	Air Transport Command (Army)
Avn	Aviation
AWS	Air Warning Squadron
B-17	Army four-engine bomber, the Boeing Flying Fortress
B-24	Army four-engine bomber, the Consolidated Liberator
B-25	Army twin-engine bomber, the North American Mitchell
B-26	Army twin-engine bomber, the Martin Marauder
B-29	Army four-engine bomber, the Boeing Super-Fortress
BAR	Browning Automatic Rifle
Btry	Battery
BB	Battleship
"Betty"	Japanese two-engine Mitsubishi bomber
BGen	Brigadier General
BLT	Battalion Landing Team
Bn	Battalion
Bomb	Bombardment
Br	Branch
Brig	Brigade
Bu	Bureau
Bul	Bulletin
BuMed	Bureau of Medicine and Surgery
BuPers	Bureau of Naval Personnel
C-1 (etc)	Corps Staff Officer, Personnel (See G-1)
C-47	Army twin-engine transport, the Douglas Skytrain
C-54	Army four-engine transport, the Douglas Skymaster
Cal	Caliber
CAP	Combat Air Patrol
Capt	Captain
CAS	Close Air Support

752

GUIDE TO ABBREVIATIONS

CASCU	Commander, Air Support Control Unit	DDT	Insecticide made of dichloro-diphenyl-trichloroethane
"Catalina"	PBY patrol bomber made by Consolidated-Vultee	DE	Destroyer Escort
		Def	Defense
Cav	Cavalry	Dep	Depot
CCS	Combined Chiefs of Staff	Det	Detachment
Cdr	Commander	DETACHMENT	Iwo Jima Operation
CEC	Civil Engineer Corps	"Devastator"	TBD, torpedo-bomber made by Douglas
CenPac	Central Pacific		
CG	Commanding General	Dir	Director
Chap	Chapter	Disp	Dispatch
CinCAFPac	Commander in Chief, Army Forces in the Pacific	Div	Division
		DOW	Died of Wounds
CinCPac	Commander in Chief, Pacific Fleet	Dtd	Dated
		DUKW	Amphibian truck
CinCPOA	Commander in Chief, Pacific Ocean Areas	Ech	Echelon
		Ed	Editor; edited
CinCUS	Commander in Chief, United States Fleet	Encl	Enclosure
		Engr	Engineer
Cm	centimeter	Enl	Enlisted
CMC	Commandant of the Marine Corps	Evac	Evacuation
		Ex	Executive
CMCS	Commandant, Marine Corps Schools	ExO	Executive Officer
		ExTrps	Expeditionary Troops
Cmt	Comment	F-1	Force staff officer, Personnel (See G-1)
CNO	Chief of Naval Operations		
CO	Commanding Officer	F2A	Marine single-engine fighter, the Brewster "Buffalo"
Co	Company		
CofS	Chief of Staff	F4F	Navy-Marine single-engine fighter, the Grumman Wildcat
Col	Colonel		
Com	Commander (Units)		
ComCenPacFor	Commander, Central Pacific Forces	F4U	Navy-Marine single-engine fighter, the Chance-Vought Corsair
Comd	Command		
CominCh	Commander in Chief, U. S. Fleet	F5A	Army photo plane version of the P-38
Conf	Confidential	F6F	Navy-Marine single-engine fighter, the Grumman Hellcat
Const	Construction		
CP	Command Post		
Cpl	Corporal	FAdm	Fleet Admiral
CT	Combat Team	FAirWest	Fleet Air, West Coast
CTF	Commander Task Force	FAirWing	Fleet Air Wing
CTG	Commander Task Group	FDC	Fire direction center
CV	Aircraft carrier	FEAF	Far East Air Forces
CVE	Escort carrier	FEC	Far East Command
CWO	Chief Warrant Officer	Fld	Field
D	Diary	FLINTLOCK	Marshall Islands Operation
D-1 (etc)	Division staff officer, Personnel (See G-1)	Flot	Flotilla
		Flt	Fleet
DA	Department of the Army	FMF	Fleet Marine Force
"Dauntless"	SBD, scout-bomber made by Douglas	FO	Field order; forward observer

FRC	Federal Records Center	Inf	Infantry
FSCC	Fire Support Coordination Center	Info	Information
		Intel	Intelligence
Fwd	Forward	Inter	Interrogation
G-1	Division (or larger unit) Personnel Office(r)	Intvw	Interview
		IsCom	Island Command
G-2	Division (or larger unit) Intelligence Office(r)	J2F	Navy-Marine Corps single-engine amphibian, the Grumman Duck
G-3	Division (or larger unit) Operations and Training Office(r)	JANAC	Joint Army-Navy Assessment Committee
G-4	Division (or larger unit) Logistics Office(r)	JANIS	Joint Army-Navy Intelligence Study
GarFor	Garrison Forces	JASCO	Joint Assault Signal Company
G.B.	General Board		
Gd	Guard	JCS	Joint Chiefs of Staff
Gen	General	JICPOA	Joint Intelligence Center, Pacific Ocean Areas
GHQ	General Headquarters		
GO	General Order	Jnl	Journal
GPO	Government Printing Office	"Judy"	Japanese single-engine Aichi bomber
Gnd	Ground		
GroPac	Group Pacific	JWPC	Joint War Plans Committee
Gru	Group	"Kate"	Japanese single-engine attack aircraft
GSA	General Services Administration		
		KIA	Killed in Action
"Hamp"	Japanese Mitsubishi fighter, identical to "Zero"	Lb.	pound
		LCC	Landing Craft, Control
Hd	Head	LCI	Landing Craft, Infantry
HE	High Explosive	LCI(G)	Landing Craft, Infantry (Gunboat)
HF	High Frequency		
H&I	Harassing and Interdiction	LCM	Landing Craft, Mechanized or Medium
Hist	History; historical		
HistDiv	Historical Division	LCS	Landing Craft, Support
HMS	His Majesty's Ship	LCT	Landing Craft, Tank
Hosp	Hospital	LCVP	Landing Craft, Vehicle and Personnel
How	Howitzer		
Hq	Headquarters	LD	Line of Departure
HQMC	Headquarters, United States Marine Corps	LFASCU	Landing Force Air Support Control Unit
HRS	Historical Reference Section	LMG	Light Machine Gun
H&S	Headquarters and Service	Loc	Located; location
IGHQ	Imperial General Headquarters	Log	Logistics; logistical
		LSD	Landing Ship, Dock
IIIAC	III Amphibious Corps	LSM	Landing Ship, Medium
IJA	Imperial Japanese Army	LST	Landing Ship, Tank
IJN	Imperial Japanese Navy	LST(H)	Landing Ship, Tank (Hospital)
IMAC	I Marine Amphibious Corps		
IMB	Independent Mixed Brigade	LSV	Landing Ship, Vehicle
IMR	Independent Mixed Regiment	Lt	Lieutenant
In	Inch(es)	LtCol	Lieutenant Colonel
Incl	Including; Inclosure (Army)	LtGen	Lieutenant General

GUIDE TO ABBREVIATIONS

Ltr	Letter	NCB	Naval Construction Battalion
LVT	Landing Vehicle, Tracked	NCO	Noncommissioned officer
LVT(A)	Landing Vehicle, Tracked (Armored)	N.d.	No date
		ND	Navy Department
M-1	Standard issue rifle, U. S., World War II	NGF	Naval Gunfire
		NHD	Naval History Division
M-4	Medium Tank, U. S.	No.	Number
M-5	Light Tank, U. S.	NorSols	Northern Solomons
MAG	Marine Aircraft Group	O	Officer; order
MAGsZam	Marine Aircraft Groups, Zamboanga	O-1	Phase line designation
		OB	Order of Battle
MAHA	Marine Aircraft, Hawaiian Area	Obj	Objective
		OCMH	Office of the Chief of Military History
Maj	Major		
MajGen	Major General	Ofc	Office
Mar	Marine(s)	OIC	Officer in Charge
MarFAirWest	Marine Fleet Air, West Coast	Op	Operation
MASG	Marine Air Support Group	OP	Observation Post
MAW	Marine Aircraft Wing	OPlan	Operation Plan
MAWG	Marine Air Warning Group	Ord	Ordnance
MAWPac	Marine Aircraft Wings, Pacific	Org	Organization(al)
		OS2U	Navy single-engine float plane, the Chance-Vought Kingfisher
MBDAG	Marine Base Defense Aircraft Group		
MBDAW	Marine Base Defense Aircraft Wing	OY	Navy-Marine single-engine observation plane, the Consolidated-Vultee Sentinel
MC	Medical Corps (Navy)		
MCAS	Marine Corps Air Station	P., pp.	Page; pages
Med	Medical	P-38	Army twin-engine fighter, the Lockheed Lightning
Memo	Memorandum		
MGCIS	Marine Ground Control Intercept Squadron	P-39	Army single-engine fighter, the Bell Aircobra
MIA	Missing in Action	P-40	Army single-engine fighter, the Curtiss Warhawk
MIAPD	Missing in Action, Presumed Dead	P-47	Army single-engine fighter, the Republic Thunderbolt
MID	Military Intelligence Division	P-51	Army single-engine fighter, the North American Mustang
MIS	Military Intelligence Section		
		P 61	Army twin-engine night fighter, the Northrop Black Widow
Misc	Miscellaneous		
MLR	Main Line of Resistance		
Mm	Millimeter	Pac	Pacific
Mov	Movement	PackHow	Pack Howitzer
MP	Military Police	PB	Patrol Boat
Mph	Miles per hour	PBJ	Navy-Marine twin-engine bomber, the North American Mitchell
MS	Manuscript		
Msg	Message		
MT	Motor Transport	PBM	Navy twin-engine seaplane, the Martin Mariner
NARS	National Archives and Records Service		
		PBO	Navy twin-engine bomber, the Lockheed Hudson
Nav	Navy; naval		

PB2Y	Navy twin-engine seaplane, the Consolidated Coronado
PB4Y	Navy-Marine four-engine bomber, the Consolidated Liberator
PBY-5A	Navy-Marine two-engine patrol bomber with amphibian boat hull, the Consolidated Catalina
Per	Personnel; Periodic
PFC	Private First Class
Phib	Amphibious; Amphibious Forces
PhibsPac	Amphibious Forces, Pacific Fleet
Pion	Pioneer
Plt	Platoon
POA	Pacific Ocean Areas
POW	Prisoner of War
Prelim	Preliminary
Prov	Provisional
Pt	Parts(s)
Pub	Public
Pvt	Private
R-1 (etc)	Regimental Staff Officer (See G-1)
R4D	Navy-Marine twin-engine transport, the Douglas Skytrain
R5D	Navy-Marine four-engine transport, the Douglas Skymaster
RAAF	Royal Australian Air Force
RB	Reference Branch
Rec	Reception
Recon	Reconnaissance
Recs	Records
Regt	Regiment
Reinf	Reinforced
Rev	Revised
RJ	Road Junction
RLT	Regimental Landing Team
RNZAF	Royal New Zealand Air Force
Rpt	Report
S-1 (etc)	Battalion (or regimental) Staff Officer, Personnel (See G-1)
SAR	Special Action Report
SBD	Navy-Marine single-engine dive bomber, the Douglas Dauntless
SB-24	Army night bombing version of the B-24
SB2C	Navy-Marine single-engine dive bomber, the Curtiss-Wright Helldiver
SB2U	Navy-Marine single engine dive bomber, the Vought-Sikorsky Vindicator
SCAP	Supreme Commander Allied Powers
SCAT	South Pacific Combat Air Transport Command
SCR	Signal Corps Radio
Sct	Scout
Sec	Section
SecNav	Secretary of the Navy
Sep	Separate
Ser	Serial
Serv	Service
Sgt	Sergeant
SgtMaj	Sergeant Major
Sig	Signal
Sit	Situation
SMS	Marine Service Squadron
SNLF	Special Naval Landing Force
SoPac	South Pacific
Spec	Special
Spt	Support
Sqd	Squad
Sqdn	Squadron
S.S.	U. S. Merchant Ship
STALEMATE..	Palaus Operation
Strat	Strategic
Subj	Subject
Sum	Summary
Sup	Support; Supply
Suppl	Supplement
Svc	Service
SWPA	Southwest Pacific Area
T/A	Table of Allowances
Tac	Tactical
TAF	Tactical Air Force
TAGO	The Adjutant General's Office
TBF	Navy-Marine single-engine torpedo bomber, the Grumman Avenger
TBM	Navy-Marine single-engine torpedo bomber, the General Motors Avenger
TBS	Talk Between Ships Radio
TBX	Medium-powered field radio

GUIDE TO ABBREVIATIONS

757

TBY	Portable low-power field radio	VAdm	Vice Admiral
TCS	Vehicle mounted, high frequency radio	VB	Navy Dive Bomber Squadron
		Veh	Vehicle
		VF	Navy Fighter Squadron
T/E	Table of Equipment	VHF	Very High Frequency
TF	Task Force	Vic	Vicinity
TG	Task Group	"Vindicator"	Scout bomber, the Vought-Sikorsky SB2U
T.H.	Territory of Hawaii		
TIO	Target Information Officer	VLR	Very Long Range
Tk	Tank	VMB	Marine Bomber Squadron
TM	Technical Manual	VMD	Marine Photographic Squadron
TNT	Trinitro-toluol, a high explosive		
		VMF	Marine Fighter Squadron
T/O	Table of Organization	VMF(N)	Marine Night Fighter Squadron
TO	Theater of Operations		
TOT	Time on Target	VMJ	Marine Utility Squadron
TQM	Transport Quartermaster	VMO	Marine Observation Squadron
Trac	Tractor	VMR	Marine Transport Squadron
Trans	Transport	VMSB	Marine Scout Bomber Squadron
TransDiv	Transport Division		
Trk	Truck	VMTB	Marine Torpedo Bomber Squadron
Trng	Training		
Trps	Troops	VP	Navy Patrol Squadron
U	Unit	VS	Navy Scouting Squadron
UDT	Underwater Demolitions Team	W-1 (etc)	Wing Staff Officer, Personnel (See G-1)
USA	United States Army	WarD	War Diary
USAF	United States Air Force	WD	War Department
USAFCP	United States Army Forces, Central Pacific Area	Wes	West
		WesLandFor	Western Landing Force
USAFPOA	United States Army Forces, Pacific Ocean Areas	WIA	Wounded in Action
		"Wildcat"	Navy-Marine single-engine fighter made by Grumman
USMC	United States Marine Corps		
USN	United States Navy	WO	Warrant Officer
USNI	United States Naval Institute	WP	White Phosphorus
USNR	United States Naval Reserve	Wpns	Weapons
USS	United States Ship	WW	World War
USSBS	United States Strategic Bombing Survey	"Zeke"	Japanese single-engine Mitsubishi fighter, also known as Zero.
USSR	Union of Soviet Socialist Republics		
		"Zero"	Same as above
V	Volume	ZofA	Zone of Action
VAC	V Amphibious Corps		

APPENDIX C

Military Map Symbols

UNIT SIZE

I	Company
II	Battalion
III	Regiment
X	Brigade
XX	Division
XXX	Corps

UNIT SYMBOLS

⬭ (LVT)	LVT
⊠ RCN	Reconnaissance
SVC	Service
◯ (in box)	Tank

UNIT SYMBOLS

☐	Basic Unit
USMC	USMC Unit (When units of other services shown)
▭	Enemy Unit
◿	Cavalry
•	Artillery
⊓	Engineer/Pioneer
⊠	Infantry
⊡	Enemy Tank

EXAMPLES

WPN ⊠ 7	Weapons Company, 7th Marines
3 ⊡ 26	3d Company, 26th Tank Regiment (Japanese)
B ⊓ 1 PION(+)	B Company, 1st Pioneer Battalion (Reinforced)
3 ⊠ 321 (III)	3d Battalion, 321st Infantry Regiment
XX ◿ 1	1st Cavalry Division
XX ⊠ 1	1st Marine Division

K.W. White

APPENDIX D

Chronology

The following listing of events is limited to those coming within the scope of this book, and those forecasting events to be treated in the volume to follow.

1935
5 Jun .... Aviation Section of the Headquarters staff is taken from the Division of Operations and Training and established as an independent section in the Office of the Commandant.

9 Jul .... Marine Corps Schools at Quantico, Virginia, publishes the Tentative Landing Operations Manual.

1 Sep .... Headquarters, Fleet Marine Force, is transferred from Quantico, Virginia, to San Diego, California.

1936
1 Apr .... Division of Aviation established at Headquarters Marine Corps.

1937
27 Jan .... The 1st and 2d Marine Brigades, the U. S. Army 1st Expeditionary Brigade, and the 1st and 2d Marine Aircraft Groups conduct Fleet Exercise No. 3 near San Diego, California.

1938
1 Jul .... Marine Corps Reserve reconstituted to consist of a Fleet Marine Corps Reserve, an Organized Marine Corps Reserve, and a Volunteer Marine Corps Reserve.

1939
1 Sep .... World War II breaks out in Europe.

8 Sep .... The President proclaims a "limited national emergency". Marine Corps strength increased to 25,000 men.

1940
Jun .... Congress authorizes the Navy to begin a 10,000-plane construction program, with 1,167 aircraft allocated for Marine aviation. Marine Corps plans to organize 4 groups of 11 squadrons each.

5 Oct .... Secretary of the Navy puts all organized Marine reserve ground units and aviation squadrons on short notice for call to active duty.

1941
15 Mar .... The Fleet Marine Force is divided, with the 1st Marine Division at Quantico, Virginia, becoming part of the Atlantic Fleet and the 2d Marine Division at San Diego, California, becoming part of the Pacific Fleet.

Jun .... First Joint Training Force (JTF-1), consisting of the 1st Marine Division, the 1st Marine Aircraft Group, and the U. S. Army 1st Infantry Division organized at Quantico, Virginia, under the command of Major General Holland M. Smith.

1 Nov .... Second Joint Training Force (JTF-2), composed of the 2d Marine Division, the U.S. Army 3d Infantry Di-

759

	vision, and the 2d Marine Aircraft Wing organized at Camp Elliott, San Diego, California, to become a part of the Pacific Fleet.
7Dec	Japanese attack Pearl Harbor.

1942

9Apr	End of American resistance on Bataan.
6May	Japanese capture Corregidor.
23May	Training Center, Fleet Marine Force, organized at Marine Barracks, New River, North Carolina, to include all Fleet Marine Force units and replacements except the 1st Marine Division.
7Aug	1st Marine Division lands on Guadalcanal.
15Aug	Marine Aircraft Wings, Pacific, established at San Diego, California, under Major General Ross E. Rowell.

1943

14-23Jan	Casablanca Conference. Agreement reached to advance toward Philippines through Central and Southwest Pacific, and to terminate hostilities only upon unconditional surrender of Japan.
21Jan	Marine Fleet Air, West Coast (MarFAirWest) organized under Colonel Lewie G. Merritt at San Diego, California.
26Jan	Headquarters of the 2d Marine Aircraft Wing established at Efate, New Hebrides.
9Feb	End of organized Japanese resistance on Guadalcanal.
12-25May	Trident Conference in Washington gives general approval to plan for a drive on Japan through the Central Pacific.
14-24Aug	Quadrant Conference at Quebec. CCS decide to attack Japan along both Central and Southwest Pacific routes.
4Sep	V Amphibious Corps organized under Maj-Gen Holland M. Smith to train and control troops for amphibious landings in the Central Pacific.
20Nov	Marines land on Betio Island, Tarawa Atoll, Gilbert Islands.
21Dec	Dive bombers of the 4th Base Defense Aircraft Wing carry out an attack against Jaluit Atoll, the first such target in the Marshall Islands.
30Dec	Advance Headquarters of the 4th Marine Base Defense Aircraft Wing established on Tarawa Atoll, Gilbert Islands.

1944

31Jan-7Feb	U. S. forces invade and capture Majuro and Kwajalein Atolls in the Marshall Islands.
4Feb	Marine aircraft carry out first photographic reconnaissance of the Japanese base at Truk in the Carolines.
17Feb	Combined Marine-Army force lands on Eniwetok Atoll in the Marshalls.
12Mar	JCS direct seizure of Southern Marianas, target date 15 Jun 1944.
28Apr	The 1st Marine Division (Rein), commanded by Major General William H. Rupertus, is relieved on New Britain and prepares to move to Pavuvu in the Russell Islands.
15Jun	The Marine V Amphibious Corps under Lieutenant General Holland M. Smith lands on Saipan in the Ma-

	riana Islands. U. S. Navy carrier task force strikes Volcano-Bonin Islands in first raid on these groups. First B-29 strikes launched from China bases against mainland of Japan. FEAF established under Lieutenant General George C. Kenney. AirNorSols formed under Major General Ralph J. Mitchell.
19-20Jun	Battle of the Philippine Sea. Carrier aircraft of TF 58 engage planes from enemy carriers and inflict crippling losses.
24Jun	U. S. Navy carrier task force again hits Volcano-Bonin Islands, including Iwo Jima.
4Jul	Renewed carrier attacks against Volcano-Bonins.
14Jul	Joint Staff Study for Operation STALEMATE (invasion of the Palaus) issued.
21Jul	III Amphibious Corps lands on Guam in the Marianas.
24Jul	4th Marine Division lands on Tinian in the Marianas.
1Aug	End of organized enemy resistance on Tinian.
10Aug	End of organized Japanese resistance on Guam.
15Aug	III Amphibious Corps, upon completing its operation in the Mariannas, is committed to invasion of the Palaus.
15Sep	The 1st Marine Division, under Major General Rupertus, lands on the southwestern shore of Peleliu Island. U. S. Army troops land on Morotai, Netherlands East Indies, and capture airfield on that island. JCS decide to invade Central rather than Southern Philippines and advance target date for invasion of Leyte from 20 December to 20 October 1944.
17Sep	81st Infantry Division, as part of III Amphibious Corps, lands on Angaur.
23Sep	U. S. Army troops seize Ulithi as advance naval base.
28Sep	The 3d Battalion, 5th Marines (Rein), under Major John H. Gustafson, lands on Ngesebus and Kongauru Islands in the Palaus, supported by VMF-114.
30Sep	Peleliu, Angaur, Ngesebus, and Kongauru declared occupied.
3Oct	JCS directive orders occupation of one or more islands in the Volcano-Bonins.
9Oct	Admiral Nimitz informs General Smith that Iwo Jima is to be the objective in the Volcano-Bonins.
12Oct	Peleliu becomes a Marine island command similar to Guam and Tinian.
14Oct	V Amphibious Corps directed to prepare plans for the Iwo Jima operation.
18Oct	Landing on Homonhon Island.
20Oct	U. S. Army troops invade Leyte. The 1st Marine Division (Rein) on Peleliu is relieved by the U. S. Army 81st Infantry Division.
21Oct	Marine Carrier Groups, Aircraft, Fleet Marine Force, Pacific, established at Santa Barbara, California, under Colonel Albert D. Cooley. Marine 5th and 11th 155mm Artillery Battalions as part of XXIV Corps Artillery in general support of the U. S. Army 7th Infantry Division on Leyte.
23-26Oct	Battle of Leyte Gulf which ends in U. S. naval victory.

4Nov	VMF-122, commanded by Major Joseph H. Reinburg, supports U. S. Army landing on Pulo Anna Island south of the Palaus.	5Jan	U. S. Navy vessels shell Iwo Jima.
5Nov	Marine Corsair fighter-bombers based in the Marshalls hit Nauru Island in the Gilberts, setting a distance record for Corsairs with full bomb loads.	9Jan	U. S. Sixth Army invades Luzon.
		24Jan	U. S. naval surface force shells Iwo Jima.
		25Jan	First Marine dive bombers arrive on Luzon.
		27Jan	Marine dive bombers fly their first mission in the Philippines.
11-12Nov	U. S. Navy surface forces rock Iwo Jima with heavy bombardment.	1Feb	Aircraft of Saipan-based Marine Bombing Squadron 612 begin nightly rocket attacks against enemy shipping and installations in the Volcano Islands.
16Nov	Marine Corsairs from Peleliu and Avengers from Ulithi launch a coordinated attack against Yap Island, west of Ulithi.	1-4Feb	Marine dive bombers of MAG-24 and MAG-32 protect the left flank of the 1st Cavalry Division during its drive to Manila.
25Nov	CinCPOA issues operation plan for invasion of Iwo Jima. Tentative date 3 February 1945.	13Feb	Final rehearsals for Iwo Jima operation concluded off coast of Tinian.
3Dec	VMF(N)-541 and VMF-115, -211, -218, and -313 of MAG-12 arrive at Tacloban, Leyte, to provide air defense.	15-16Feb	V Amphibious Corps Land-Force departs Marianas after final rehearsals for assault on Iwo Jima.
7Dec	MAG-12 aircraft, under Colonel William A. Willis, support U. S. Army landings at Ormoc, Leyte.	16Feb	TF 58 under Admiral Mitscher launches two day air strike against the Japanese mainland to divert attention from the imminent Iwo Jima operation.
8Dec	U. S. Navy surface units shell Iwo Jima.		
11Dec	Major Marine air attack on Japanese convoy, Ormoc Bay.	16-18Feb	Amphibious Support Force (TF 52) bombs and shells Iwo Jima in the course of the preparatory bombardment.
15Dec	MAG-12 aircraft support landing of U. S. Army on Mindoro in the Philippines.		
24-27Dec	U. S. Navy surface units bombard Volcano-Bonin Islands including Iwo Jima.	19Feb	The 4th and 5th Marine Division seize foothold on Iwo Jima.
25Dec	Leyte declared secured. Eighth Army relieves Sixth Army.	21Feb	21st Marines of the 3d Marine Division committed in zone of action of the 4th Division. Enemy executes *kamikaze* attack on support ships off Iwo Jima.
1945			
2-12Jan	MAG-14 with VMO-251 and VMF-212, -222, and -223 land at Guiuan, Samar.	23Feb	Combat patrol of the 28th Marines raises Old Glory

25Feb	on Mount Suribachi. Manila falls to U. S. Army troops.
25Feb	3d Marine Division committed on Iwo Jima. General unloading of cargo gets under way. Elements of MAG-32 arrive on Mindoro, Philippines, to support U. S. Army troops.
26Feb	Two Marine artillery spotter planes from the USS *Wake Island* land on Iwo Jima and become the first American planes to land on the island.

1945

27Feb	3d Marine Division captures the Central Airfield on Iwo Jima and seizes Hills Peter and Oboe.
28Feb	U. S. Army troops invade Palawan in the Philippines.
2Mar	5th Marine Division captures Hill 362A on Iwo Jima.
3Mar	Elements of MAG-12, MAG-24, and MAG-32 support U.S. Army landings on Masbate, Burias, and Ticao Islands in the Philippines.
	3d Marine Division clears Northern Airfield on Iwo Jima.
4Mar	First B-29 bomber lands on Iwo Jima after being damaged over Japan.
6Mar	U. S. Army Air Forces 15th Fighter Group arrives on Iwo Jima with P-51s and P-61s.
7Mar	Major General James E. Chaney (USA), Island Commander, assumes responsibility for Iwo Jima base development, air defense, and airfield operation.
	3d Marine Division launches predawn attack against Hill 362C and captures this objective later in the day.
8Mar	4th Marine Division repels counterattack during the night 8-9 March.
9Mar	General Holland M. Smith transfers his command post from the *Eldorado* to the *Auburn*. Admiral Turner and his staff on board *Eldorado* depart for Guam.
	Real Admiral Harry W. Hill assumes duties of Senior Officer Present Afloat, Iwo Jima.
10Mar	MAG-12 and MAG-32 aircraft support U. S. Army landings on Zamboanga in the Philippines. American troops land on Mindanao in the Philippines.
11Mar	Iwo-based Army Air Forces fighters assume responsibility for providing air defense and ground support missions when last Navy escort carriers leave.
14Mar	Official flag raising ceremony marks proclamation of U. S. Naval Military Government in the Volcano Islands. Commander, Expeditionary Troops, departs for Guam.
15Mar	Corsairs of MAG-12 arrive on Zamboanga. Close support of the U. S. Army 41st Infantry Division gets under way.
16Mar	Cushman's Pocket on Iwo Jima eliminated. End of organized resistance in zone of action of the 3d Marine Division.
	Last enemy pocket in 4th Division zone wiped out.
	Iwo Jima declared secured at 1800.
18Mar	U. S. Army troops invade Panay in the Philippines.

20Mar	U. S. Army 147th Infantry Regiment arrives on Iwo Jima for garrison duty.
23Mar	Dive bombers of MAG-32 move from Luzon to Zamboanga.
25Mar	5th Marine Division eliminates final enemy pocket of resistance on Iwo Jima.
26Mar	Japanese launch early morning attack against Marine and U. S. Army bivouac areas on Iwo Jima. Capture and occupation phase announced completed as of 0800.
	Commander, Forward Area, Central Pacific, assumes responsibility for defense and development of Iwo Jima.
	Major General Chaney assumes operational control of all units on Iwo Jima.
	V Amphibious Corps command post on Iwo Jima closed. Major General Schmidt departs Iwo Jima by air.
	U. S. Army troops invade Cebu in the Philippines, supported by aircraft of MAG-12.
1Apr	Invasion of Okinawa gets under way.
	U. S. Army troops land in the Sulu Archipelago and on Jolo Island in the Philippines.
14Apr	MAG-24 dive bombers fly last Marine aviation mission on Luzon.
17Apr	MAG-12, MAG-14, and MAG-32 support U. S. Army landings on Mindanao in the Philippines.
18Apr	Last Marines depart from Iwo Jima.
20Apr	Dive bombers of MAG-24 move from Luzon to Malabang.
22Apr	MAG-24 dive bombers begin operations from Malabang.
7May	End of war in European Theater.
25May	JCS direct invasion of Japan, scheduled for 1 November 1945.
21Jun	End of organized resistance on Okinawa.
6Aug	Atomic bomb dropped on Hiroshima.
9Aug	Atomic bomb dropped on Nagasaki.
	Russia invades Manchuria.
2Sep	Japanese sign instrument of surrender in Tokyo Bay.

APPENDIX E

Fleet Marine Force Status—31 August 1944[1]

Units and Locations	USMC Off	USMC Enl	USN Off	USN Enl
Outside U.S.A.				
Hawaiian Area				
Oahu				
Headquarters and Service Battalion, FMFPac	228	1,378	14	12
Transient Center, FMFPac	334	5,599	43	313
3d Base Headquarters Battalion, FMFPac	23	205	38	9
13th Antiaircraft Artillery Battalion, FMFPac	40	1,125	3	30
Headquarters Company, Supply Service, FMFPac	74	257	1	5
6th Base Depot, Supply Service, FMFPac	169	4,211	8	41
8th Field Depot, Supply Service, FMFPac	24	424	1	13
Headquarters and Service Battalion, VAC	82	601	8	22
Signal Battalion, VAC	42	534	9	8
Corps Transport Company, VAC	4	115	0	0
Amphibious Reconnaissance Battalion, VAC	20	288	0	12
Air Delivery Section, VAC	3	91	0	0
Headquarters, 2d Laundry Company VAC	1	24	0	0
4th Platoon, 2d Laundry Company, VAC	1	61	0	0
Headquarters Squadron, Marine Aircraft Wings, Pacific	46	110	2	0
Marine Bomber Squadron 611, 2d MAW	69	467	1	8
Marine Bomber Squadron 612, 2d MAW	68	477	1	8
Headquarters Squadron 3, 3d MAW	68	519	11	18
Marine Observation Squadron 5, 3d MAW	9	28	0	0
Air Warning Squadron 4, 3d MAW	14	233	0	5
Marine Airborne Aircraft Warning Squadron 5, 3d MAW	13	168	0	4
Service Squadron 15, 3d MAW	8	229	0	0
Marine Fighter Squadron 321, 3d MAW	48	248	1	8
Marine Scout-Bomber Squadron 343, 3d MAW	48	292	1	8
Marine Transport Squadron 953, 3d MAW	86	369	0	0
Headquarters Squadron, MAG–32	47	350	9	13
Service Squadron 32, MAG–32	11	242	0	0
Marine Scout Bomber Squadron 142, MAG–32	49	296	1	8
Marine Fighter Squadron 313, MAG–13	47	245	1	8

See footnote at end of table.

	Strength			
Units and Locations	USMC		USN	
	Off	Enl	Off	Enl
Marine Fighter Squadron 322, MAG–13	47	247	1	8
Marine Fighter Squadron 323, MAG–13	50	249	1	8
Marine Scout-Bomber Squadron 332, MAG–13	48	294	1	8
Area Sub-Total	1,821	19,976	156	577

Hawaii

2d Provisional Marine Detachment, FMFPac	13	296	1	7
1st Service and Supply Battalion, FMFPac	22	477	0	4
Headquarters Battery, VAC Artillery	27	155	3	9
2d 155mm Howitzer Battalion, VAC Artillery	34	591	1	9
5th 155mm Howitzer Battalion, VAC Artillery	35	711	1	12
10th 155mm Gun Battalion, VAC Artillery	33	724	1	12
11th 155mm Gun Battalion, VAC Artillery	54	847	4	21
12th 155mm Gun Battalion, VAC Artillery	1	150	0	0
26th Marines (Reinforced)	188	4,188	18	224
27th Marines (Reinforced)	199	4,461	19	219
Special and Service Troops, 5th Marine Division	137	1,213	8	24
Area Sub-Total	743	13,813	56	541

Kaui

1st Provisional Marine Detachment, FMFPac	18	288	2	0
8th Antiaircraft Artillery Battalion, FMFPac	51	1,029	4	27
3d Service and Supply Battalion, Supply Service, FMFPac	11	278	0	2
3d Platoon, 2d Laundry Company, VAC	1	61	0	0
2d Antiaircraft Artillery Battalion, VAC Artillery	49	1,227	4	32
5th Antiaircraft Artillery Battalion, VAC Artillery	63	1,230	3	32
7th Antiaircraft Artillery Battalion, VAC Artillery	63	1,214	4	32
16th Antiaircraft Artillery Battalion, VAC Artillery	56	1,219	4	29
Area Sub-Total	312	6,546	21	154

Maui

3d Provisional Marine Detachment, FMFPac	16	347	1	3
2d Service and Supply Battalion, Supply Service, FMFPac	6	268	0	0
Medical Battalion, VAC	1	90	28	218
1st Platoon, 2d Laundry Company, VAC	1	61	0	0

See footnote at end of table.

FLEET MARINE FORCE STATUS

Units and Locations	USMC Off	USMC Enl	USN Off	USN Enl
10th Amphibian Tractor Battalion (less Company A), VAC	20	319	1	9
11th Amphibian Tractor Battalion (plus Companies D and E, less Companies A and C), VAC	21	523	2	9
Company C, 11th Amphibian Tractor Battalion, VAC	6	133	0	0
1st Joint Assault Signal Company, VAC	32	252	14	0
4th 155mm Howitzer Battalion	28	568	1	11
4th Marine Division	757	13,133	123	969
Area Sub-Total	888	15,694	170	1,219
Midway				
6th Defense Battalion	69	1,492	5	22
Headquarters Squadron 23, MAG–23	25	337	6	16
Service Squadron 23, MAG–23	11	255	0	0
Marine Fighter Squadron 314, MAG–23	61	249	1	8
Marine Scout-Bomber Squadron 333, MAG–23	50	298	1	8
Area Sub Total	216	2,631	13	54
Southwest Pacific				
Auckland, New Zealand				
3d Field Depot, Supply Service, FMFPac	15	106	2	8
Russell Islands				
4th Base Depot, Supply Service, FMFPac	94	2,613	7	26
30th, 31st and 32d Depot Companies, Supply Service, FMFPac	12	479	0	0
2d Platoon, 1st Laundry Company, IIIAC	1	61	0	0
3d Armored Amphibian Battalion (Prov), IIIAC	32	767	1	9
1st Amphibian Tractor Battalion, IIIAC	29	473	1	10
6th Amphibian Tractor Battalion, IIIAC	24	462	1	9
4th and 5th Marine War Dog Platoons, IIIAC	3	191	0	0
5th Separate Wire Platoon, IIIAC	1	43	0	0
6th Separate Wire Platoon, IIIAC	1	44	0	0
12th Antiaircraft Artillery Battalion, IIIAC Artillery	60	1,321	4	31
1st Marine Division	897	16,822	130	968
Marine Observation Squadron 3, MAWPac	9	28	0	0
Area Sub-Total	1,163	23,304	144	1,053

See footnote at end of table.

	Strength			
Units and Locations	USMC		USN	
	Off	Enl	Off	Enl
Emirau				
Headquarters Squadron 12, MAG–12	39	311	6	27
Service Squadron 12, MAG–12	17	265	1	0
Marine Fighter Squadron 115, MAG–12	47	238	1	8
Marine Fighter Squadron 215, MAG–12	45	222	1	1
Marine Scout-Bomber Squadron 243, MAG–12	46	273	1	9
Headquarters Squadron 61, MAG–61	36	386	7	16
Service Squadron 61, MAG–61	10	249	0	0
Marine Photographic Squadron 254, MAG–61	53	470	2	8
Marine Bombing Squadron 433, MAG–61	67	411	1	8
Marine Bombing Squadron 443, MAG–61	69	410	0	0
Marine Transport Squadron 952, 2d MAW	66	375	1	8
Area Sub-Total	495	3,610	21	85
Green Island				
Headquarters Squadron 14, MAG–14	39	364	7	22
Service Squadron 14, MAG–14	14	266	1	0
Marine Fighter Squadron 218, MAG–14	45	227	1	8
Marine Scout-Bomber Squadron 235, MAG–14	57	280	2	8
Marine Scout-Bomber Squadron 341, MAG–14	46	263	0	0
Marine Bombing Squadron 423, MAG–14	62	398	1	8
Area Sub-Total	263	1,798	12	46
Guadalcanal				
16th Field Depot, Supply Service, FMFPac	43	1,204	3	16
29th Depot Company, Supply Service, FMFPac	4	148	0	0
9th Ammunition Company, Supply Service, FMFPac	7	248	0	0
1st Battalion, 29th Marines (Reinf)	34	817	2	39
Headquarters, 1st Laundry Company, IIIAC	1	24	0	0
1st Platoon, 1st Laundry Company, IIIAC	1	61	0	0
3d Platoon, 1st Laundry Company, IIIAC	1	61	0	0
4th Platoon, 1st Laundry Company, IIIAC	1	61	0	0
8th Amphibian Tractor Battalion, IIIAC	26	499	1	9
4th Joint Assault Signal Company, IIIAC	35	343	9	115
3d Separate Wire Platoon, IIIAC	1	32	0	0
3d 155mm Howitzer Battalion, Corps Artillery, IIIAC	34	678	3	9
8th 155mm Gun Battalion, Corps Artillery, IIIAC	39	730	2	12
9th 155mm Gun Battalion, Corps Artillery, IIIAC	34	642	2	12
3d Antiaircraft Artillery Battalion, Corps Artillery, IIIAC	60	1,279	5	31

See footnote at end of table.

FLEET MARINE FORCE STATUS

Units and Locations	USMC Off	USMC Enl	USN Off	USN Enl
4th Antiaircraft Artillery Battalion, Corps Artillery, IIIAC	61	1,243	5	34
11th Antiaircraft Artillery Battalion, Corps Artillery, IIIAC	57	1,283	4	30
29th Marines (Reinf)	198	3,886	18	205
54th Replacement Battalion	9	612	1	9
Marine Observation Squadron 1, MAWPac	9	28	0	0
Area Sub-Total	655	13,879	55	521
Ellice Islands				
51st Defense Battalion	54	1,326	6	32
Munda, New Georgia				
Marine Air Base Squadron 1, 1st MAW	15	380	4	10
Marine Scout-Bomber Squadron 241, 1st MAW	26	255	1	8
Marine Bombing Squadron 413, 1st MAW	57	401	2	0
Marine Scout-Bomber Squadron 244, MAG-14	29	262	1	8
Area Sub-Total	127	1,298	8	35
Torokina, Bougainville				
Headquarters Squadron 1, 1st MAW	67	531	8	11
Marine Fighter Squadron 222, 1st MAW	32	221	1	6
Headquarters Squadron 24, MAG-24	30	365	7	23
Service Squadron 24, MAG-24	13	304	0	0
Marine Scout-Bomber Squadron 133, MAG-24	47	286	1	8
Marine Fighter Squadron 212, MAG-24	14	235	1	8
Marine Fighter Squadron 223, MAG-24	44	238	1	8
Marine Scout-Bomber Squadron 236, MAG-24	31	258	1	9
Marine Observation Squadron 251, MAG-24	50	239	1	8
Marine Transport Squadron 152, MAG-25	68	385	0	0
Marine Transport Squadron 153, MAG-25	62	353	1	8
Area Sub-Total	458	3,415	22	89
Espiritu Santo, New Hebrides				
Marine Air Defense Squadron 1, 1st MAW	21	358	4	7
Headquarters Squadron 2, 2d MAW	66	422	7	28
Air Warning Squadron 3, 2d MAW	18	248	0	6
Marine Torpedo Bomber Squadron 232, 2d MAW	41	295	1	15

See footnote at end of table.

	Strength			
Units and Locations	USMC		USN	
	Off	Enl	Off	Enl
Marine Fighter Squadron 312, 2d MAW	47	249	1	8
Headquarters Squadron 11, MAG–11	23	59	8	15
Service Squadron 11, MAG–11	36	578	0	6
Marine Fighter Squadron 114, MAG–11	48	250	0	8
Marine Fighter Squadron 121, MAG–11	47	249	1	8
Marine Fighter Squadron 122, MAG–11	47	249	1	8
Marine Scout-Bomber Squadron 134, MAG–11	47	312	1	8
Marine Night Fighter Squadron 541, MAG–11	29	308	1	8
Area Sub-Total	470	3,577	25	125
Noumea and Tontouta, New Caledonia				
Transient Center, Forward Echelon, FMFPac	17	408	3	5
Headquarters (SoPac-Admin), Supply Service, FMFPac	3	10	0	0
1st Field Depot, Supply Service, FMFPac	38	664	3	13
Headquarters Squadron 25, MAG–25	33	334	9	231
Service Squadron 25, MAG–25	15	348	0	0
Area Sub-Total	106	1,764	15	249
Central Pacific				
Engebi				
Headquarters Squadron 22, MAG–22	39	365	7	22
Service Squadron 22, MAG–22	12	248	0	0
Air Warning Squadron 1, MAG–22	12	201	2	6
Marine Fighter Squadron 113, MAG–22	48	238	1	8
Marine Scout-Bomber Squadron 151, MAG–22	51	311	1	8
Marine Fighter Squadron 422, MAG–22	49	229	1	8
Area Sub-Total	211	1,592	12	52
Eniwetok				
10th Antiaircraft Artillery Battalion (Reinf), VAC Artillery	65	1,403	4	29
Marine Night Fighter Squadron 533, MAG–22	36	308	1	8
Area Sub-Total	101	1,711	5	37

See footnote at end of table.

FLEET MARINE FORCE STATUS 771

| | Strength ||||
| Units and Locations | USMC || USN ||
	Off	Enl	Off	Enl
Guam				
1st Base Headquarters Battalion, FMFPac	52	379	33	123
5th Field Depot	64	1,447	4	16
Company A, 10th Amphibian Tractor Battalion, VAC	3	138	0	0
Company A, 11th Amphibian Tractor Battalion, VAC	5	130	0	0
Headquarters and Service Battalion, IIIAC	171	1,261	17	81
Signal Battalion, IIIAC	60	1,109	2	11
Motor Transport Battalion, IIIAC	32	609	2	11
Medical Battalion, IIIAC	1	151	35	312
Air Delivery Section, IIIAC	3	164	0	2
1st Armored Amphibian Battalion, IIIAC	35	644	2	10
3d Amphibian Tractor Battalion, IIIAC	36	777	2	12
4th Amphibian Tractor Battalion, IIIAC	27	541	2	8
2d Separate Engineer Battalion, IIIAC	35	721	3	20
1st Marine War Dog Platoon, IIIAC	0	32	0	0
2d and 3d Marine War Dog Platoons, IIIAC	2	98	0	0
3d Joint Assault Signal Company, IIIAC	35	340	9	0
1st Separate Wire Platoon, IIIAC	1	41	0	0
Headquarters Battery, Corps Artillery, IIIAC	26	159	0	0
1st 155mm Howitzer Battalion, IIIAC Artillery	34	631	2	16
7th 155mm Gun Battalion, IIIAC Artillery	37	664	2	12
9th Defense Battalion, IIIAC Artillery	67	1,388	4	31
14th Defense Battalion, IIIAC Artillery	71	1,488	4	25
3d Marine Division	872	16,057	139	988
1st Provisional Marine Brigade	445	9,012	46	433
1st Replacement Draft	86	1,462	60	415
Marine Fighter Squadron 211, MAG-12	48	235	1	8
Marine Transport Squadron 253, MAG-15	67	333	0	0
Headquarters Squadron 21, MAG-21	38	322	8	19
Service Squadron 21, MAG-21	14	277	0	0
Air Warning Squadron 2, MAG-21	10	161	0	3
Marine Scout Bomber Squadron 131, MAG-21	47	328	1	8
Marine Fighter Squadron 216, MAG-21	46	234	1	8
Marine Fighter Squadron 217, MAG-21	47	229	1	7
Marine Fighter Squadron 225, MAG-21	45	239	1	8
Marine Scout-Bomber Squadron 242, MAG-21	47	328	1	8
Marine Fighter Squadron 321, MAG-21	48	230	1	7
Marine Night Fighter Squadron 534, MAG-21	37	310	1	8
Area Sub-Total	2,694	42,669	384	2,610

See footnote at end of table.

	Strength			
Units and Locations	USMC		USN	
	Off	Enl	Off	Enl
Kwajalein				
Headquarters Squadron 15, MAG–15	42	351	6	21
Marine Transport Squadron 252, MAG–15	59	322	1	10
Marine Transport Squadron 353, MAG–15	93	413	1	8
Area Sub-Total	194	1,086	8	39
Majuro				
1st Antiaircraft Artillery Battalion (Reinf), VAC Artillery	28	573	3	14
Headquarters Squadron 4, 4th MBDAW	90	635	11	20
Headquarters Squadron 13, MAG–13	31	351	7	22
Service Squadron 13, MAG–13	15	288	0	0
Marine Scout-Bomber Squadron 231, MAG–13	51	299	1	8
Marine Scout-Bomber Squadron 331, MAG–13	49	295	1	8
Marine Observation Squadron 155, MAG–31	44	248	1	8
Area Sub-Total	308	2,689	24	80
Makin				
Marine Scout-Bomber Squadron 245, MAG–13	51	285	1	8
Marine Fighter Squadron 111, MAG–31	53	347	1	8
Area Sub-Total	104	632	2	16
Roi-Namur				
15th Depot Company, Supply Service, FMFPac	5	197	0	0
15th Antiaircraft Artillery Battalion (Reinf), VAC Artillery	48	1,164	4	21
Headquarters Squadron 31, MAG–31	34	407	8	18
Service Squadron 31, MAG–31	12	308	0	0
Marine Fighter Squadron 224, MAG–31	84	283	1	8
Marine Fighter Squadron 311, MAG–31	48	258	1	8
Marine Fighter Squadron 441, MAG–31	49	309	1	8
Area Sub-Total	280	2,926	15	63
Saipan				
7th Field Depot, Supply Service, FMFPac	90	1,780	5	34
2d Platoon, 2d Laundry Company, VAC	1	61	0	0
2d Armored Amphibian Battalion, VAC	33	771	2	14

See footnote at end of table.

FLEET MARINE FORCE STATUS

Units and Locations	USMC Off	USMC Enl	USN Off	USN Enl
2d Amphibian Tractor Battalion, VAC	27	584	1	13
5th Amphibian Tractor Battalion, VAC	23	562	1	9
1st Amphibian Truck Company, VAC	6	174	0	0
2d Amphibian Truck Company, VAC	9	185	0	0
2d Joint Assault Signal Company, VAC	35	391	10	0
1st Provisional Rocket Detachment, VAC	3	54	0	0
2d Provisional Rocket Detachment, VAC	3	54	0	0
17th Antiaircraft Artillery Battalion, VAC Artillery	49	1,215	4	23
18th Antiaircraft Artillery Battalion, VAC Artillery	66	1,412	4	22
2d Marine Division	924	17,113	131	965
3d Replacement Draft	130	2,629	15	30
4th Separate Wire Platoon, IIIAC	1	43	0	0
Marine Observation Squadron 2, 3d MAW	9	28	0	0
Marine Observation Squadron 4, 3d MAW	9	29	0	0
Marine Night Fighter Squadron 532, MAG-31	33	249	1	8
Area Sub-Total	1,451	27,633	174	1,118
Tinian				
2d Base Headquarters Battalion, FMFPac	46	359	45	105
1st Separate Engineer Battalion, IIIAC	33	727	4	17
2d Separate Wire Platoon, IIIAC	1	41	0	0
Area Sub-Total	80	1,127	49	122
Miscellaneous				
Aviation personnel attached to Marine divisions, amphibious corps, and JASCOs	78	227	0	0
West Coast, U.S.A.				
San Diego				
Headquarters Company, Marine Training and Replacement Command, San Diego Area	41	145	2	5
Headquarters Squadron, Marine Fleet Air, West Coast	56	332	3	1
Area Sub-Total	97	477	5	6
Camp Elliott				
Base Depot, Fleet Marine Force, San Diego	91	760	2	20

See footnote at end of table.

| | \multicolumn{4}{c}{Strength} |
| Units and Locations | \multicolumn{2}{c}{USMC} | \multicolumn{2}{c}{USN} |
	Off	Enl	Off	Enl
Camp Gillespie				
Marine Scout-Bomber Squadron 141, MBDAG-41	48	302	1	8
Camp Pendleton				
Headquarters Battalion, Marine Training Command, SDA	172	1,847	45	256
Schools Regiment, Marine Training Command, SDA	178	2,573	9	0
Specialist Training Regiment, Marine Training Command, SDA	170	2,162	46	866
Infantry Training Regiment (10 battalions), Marine Training Command, SDA	129	9,868	1	0
9th Amphibian Tractor Battalion	26	510	0	0
5th Marine Division (less RCT 26 and RCT 27)	374	7,000	73	525
5th Joint Assault Signal Company	35	365	0	0
7th Replacement Draft	14	536	12	100
8th Replacement Draft	44	1,107	1	0
9th Replacement Draft	64	1,251	10	5
10th Replacement Draft	63	4,685	1	170
52d Defense Battalion	55	1,278	7	32
8th Field Depot (Rear Echelon)	46	770	0	0
Sound Ranging Sections (3-4-5)	3	66	0	0
Marine Fighter Squadron 471, MBDAG-43	49	277	1	8
Area Sub-Total	1,422	34,295	206	1,962
Corvallis				
Headquarters Squadron 35, MAG-35	185	857	8	30
Service Squadron 35, MAG-35	22	302	0	0
Area Sub-Total	207	1,159	8	30
Camp Kearney				
Marine Photographic Squadron 154, Marine Fleet Air, West Coast	59	427	2	8
El Centro				
Headquarters Squadron 43, MBDAG-43	64	804	7	27
Service Squadron 43, MBDAG-43	8	319	0	0
Marine Fighter Squadron 461, MBDAG-43	47	252	1	3
Marine Fighter Squadron 462, MBDAG-43	52	257	1	2
Marine Fighter Squadron 472, MBDAG-43	48	254	1	0
Area Sub-Total	219	1,886	10	32

See footnote at end of table.

FLEET MARINE FORCE STATUS

	Strength			
	USMC		USN	
	Off	Enl	Off	Enl
El Toro				
Headquarters Squadron 41, MBDAG-41	42	378	7	30
Service Squadron 41, MBDAG-41	16	277	0	0
Marine Scout-Bomber Squadron 132, MBDAG-41	47	307	1	5
Marine Scout-Bomber Squadron 144, MBDAG-41	48	313	1	2
Marine Scout-Bomber Squadron 234, MBDAG-41	46	307	1	2
Marine Scout-Bomber Squadron 454, MBDAG-41	46	324	1	3
Marine Scout-Bomber Squadron 464, MBDAG-41	31	316	1	2
Headquarters Squadron 46, MBDAG-46	72	341	6	17
Service Squadron 46, MBDAG-46	15	324	0	0
Marine Scout-Bomber Squadron 474, MBDAG-46	30	348	1	8
Marine Fighter Squadron 481, MBDAG-46	151	328	1	8
Marine Fighter Squadron 482, MBDAG-46	155	350	1	8
Marine Scout-Bomber Squadron 484, MBDAG-46	30	364	1	8
Area Sub-Total	729	4,277	22	93
Miramar				
Supply Squadron 5, Marine Fleet Air, West Coast	16	299	0	0
Headquarters and Service Squadron 2, 2d AWG	12	105	0	0
Air Warning Squadron 6, 2d AWG	14	259	0	6
Air Warning Squadron 7, 2d AWG	13	251	0	6
Air Warning Squadron 8, 2d AWG	15	258	0	6
Air Warning Squadron 9, 2d AWG	16	255	0	6
Marine Airborne Air Warning Squadron 10, 2d AWG	14	166	0	4
Air Warning Squadron 11, 2d AWG	16	255	0	6
Air Warning Squadron 12, 2d AWG	18	261	0	6
Marine Airborne Air Warning Squadron 15, 2d AWG	13	167	0	4
Marine Airborne Air Warning Squadron 20, 2d AWG	14	167	0	4
Headquarters Squadron, Personnel Group	270	215	28	0
Marine Wing Service Squadron 1, Personnel Group	12	1,124	0	0
Marine Wing Service Squadron 2, Personnel Group	5	1,167	0	160
Marine Wing Service Squadron 3, Personnel Group	6	958	0	10
Marine Wing Service Squadron 4, Personnel Group	4	1,716	0	0
Headquarters Squadron 33, MAG-33	30	362	7	16
Service Squadron 33, MAG-33	11	258	7	16
Area Sub-Total	499	8,243	42	256
Oxnard				
Marine Fighter Squadron 214, MBDAG-42	48	274	1	8

See footnote at end of table.

	Strength			
Units and Locations	USMC		USN	
	Off	Enl	Off	Enl
Mojave				
Headquarters Squadron 44, MBDAG-44...............................	32	458	8	16
Service Squadron 44, MBDAG-44..	10	396	0	0
Marine Fighter Squadron 124, MBDAG-44............................	49	246	1	8
Marine Fighter Squadron 213, MBDAG-44............................	49	252	1	7
Marine Fighter Squadron 451, MBDAG-44............................	47	243	1	8
Marine Fighter Squadron 452, MBDAG-44............................	48	252	1	8
Headquarters Squadron 51, MAG-51.....................................	38	309	9	19
Marine Observation Squadron 351, MAG-51	47	249	1	8
Marine Fighter Squadron 511, MAG-51.................................	46	242	1	8
Marine Fighter Squadron 512, MAG-51.................................	45	233	1	8
Area Sub-Total	411	2,880	24	90
Santa Barbara				
Headquarters Squadron 42, MBDAG-42...............................	44	478	5	18
Service Squadron 42, MBDAG-42..	17	338	0	0
Marine Fighter Squadron 112, MBDAG-42............................	47	241	2	8
Marine Fighter Squadron 123, MBDAG-42............................	49	249	1	8
Marine Fighter Squadron 221, MBDAG-42............................	45	242	1	8
Headquarters Squadron 45, MBDAG-45...............................	43	392	7	18
Service Squadron 45, MBDAG-45..	17	248	0	0
Marine Night Fighter Squadron 542, MBDAG-45.................	31	303	1	8
Headquarters Squadron 48, MBDAG-48 (Org 3Aug44)......	0	0	0	0
Service Squadron 48, MBDAG-48 (Org 3Aug44).................	0	0	0	0
Marine Torpedo-Bomber Squadron 143, MBDAG-48...........	46	239	1	8
Marine Torpedo-Bomber Squadron 233, MBDAG-48...........	45	303	2	8
Marine Scout-Bomber Squadron 943, MBDAG-48...............	33	223	0	0
Area Sub-Total	417	3,256	20	84
East Coast, U.S.A.				
Camp Lejeune				
Headquarters Battalion, Marine Training Command..........	28	811	0	0
Range Battalion, Marine Training Command......................	9	242	0	0
Coast Guard Detachment, Marine Training Command.......	0	0	39	1,409
Quartermaster Battalion, Marine Training Command........	57	750	0	0
Schools Regiment, Marine Training Command....................	153	1,250	0	0
Specialist Training Regiment, Marine Training Command	397	6,870	0	0
Infantry Training Regiment (7 battalions), Marine				

See footnote at end of table.

777

| Units and Locations | Strength ||||
| | USMC || USN ||
	Off	Enl	Off	Enl
Training Command	157	7,402	0	11
Corps Evacuation Hospitals (I, II, III)	0	0	79	604
10th Ammunition Company	7	279	0	0
11th Ammunition Company	3	104	0	0
7th Separate Infantry Battalion	18	677	2	21
Area Sub-Total	829	18,575	120	2,045
Norfolk				
Marine Base Depot, FMF	20	426	0	8
Quantico				
Infantry Training Battalion, MCS	36	993	2	38
Field Artillery Training Battalion, MCS	22	582	0	0
Area Sub-Total	58	1,575	2	38
Bogue				
Air Warning Squadron 16, 1st AWG	15	260	0	6
Headquarters Squadron 93, MAG-93	25	330	6	18
Service Squadron 93, MAG-93	10	190	0	0
Marine Scout-Bomber Squadron 934, MAG-93	34	188	1	8
Marine Scout-Bomber Squadron 941, MAG-93	35	188	1	7
Marine Scout-Bomber Squadron 942, MAG-93	6	81	0	0
Area Sub-Total	125	1,237	8	39
Cherry Point				
Headquarters Squadron 9, 9th MAW	63	429	7	13
Marine Wing Service Squadron 9, 9th MAW	15	183	0	0
Marine Transport Squadron 352, 9th MAW	127	434	1	8
Marine Photographic Squadron 354, 9th MAW	59	449	1	8
Marine Night Fighter Squadron 531, 9th MAW	17	166	1	4
Headquarters and Service Squadron 1, 1st AWG	91	900	3	8
Air Warning Squadron 17, 1st AWG	11	245	0	6
Air Warning Squadron 18, 1st AWG	10	164	0	6
Headquarters Squadron 53, MAG-53	45	290	5	19
Service Squadron 53, MAG-53	7	264	0	0
Marine Night Fighter Squadron 543, MAG-53	29	307	1	8
Marine Night Fighter Squadron 544, MAG-53	32	279	0	6

See footnote at end of table.

	Strength			
Units and Locations	USMC		USN	
	Off	Enl	Off	Enl
Headquarters Squadron 62, MAG-62	58	686	6	6
Service Squadron 62, MAG-62	19	424	0	0
Marine Bombing Squadron 453, MAG-62	15	157	0	0
Marine Bombing Squadron 463, MAG-62	11	73	0	0
Marine Bombing Squadron 473, MAG-62	10	45	0	0
Marine Bombing Squadron 483, MAG-62	4	3	0	0
Marine Bombing Squadron 621, MAG-62	78	402	1	8
Marine Bombing Squadron 622, MAG-62	60	325	1	8
Marine Bombing Squadron 623, MAG-62	46	314	1	8
Marine Bombing Squadron 624, MAG-62	30	236	0	8
Headquarters Squadron 92, MAG-92	18	154	1	4
Marine Fighter Squadron 921, MAG-92	40	61	0	2
Marine Fighter Squadron 922, MAG-92	38	60	0	2
Marine Fighter Squadron 924, MAG-92	106	351	1	8
Headquarters Squadron 94, MAG-94	15	107	2	15
Service Squadron 94, MAG-94	3	43	0	0
Area Sub-Total	1,057	7,551	32	155
Congaree				
Headquarters Squadron 52, MAG-52	17	45	7	19
Service Squadron 52, MAG-52	13	669	0	0
Marine Fighter Squadron 521, MAG-52	48	158	1	8
Marine Fighter Squadron 522, MAG-52	45	156	1	8
Marine Fighter Squadron 523, MAG-52	48	161	0	8
Marine Fighter Squadron 524, MAG-52	50	155	0	8
Area Sub-Total	221	1,344	9	51
Eagle Mountain Lake				
Marine Scout-Bomber Squadron 931, MAG-93	47	268	1	8
Marine Scout-Bomber Squadron 932, MAG-93	50	274	1	6
Marine Scout-Bomber Squadron 933, MAG-93	30	268	1	5
Area Sub-Total	127	810	3	19
Greenville				
Marine Fighter Squadron 913, MAG-91	42	177	1	8

	Strength			
Units and Locations	USMC		USN	
	Off	Enl	Off	Enl
Kinston				
Headquarters Squadron 91, MAG-91	16	190	5	19
Service Squadron 91, MAG-91	8	169	0	0
Marine Fighter Squadron 911, MAG-91	44	183	1	8
Marine Fighter Squadron 912, MAG-91	44	180	0	8
Marine Fighter Squadron 914, MAG-91	39	145	0	0
Area Sub-Total	151	867	6	35
Newport				
Headquarters Squadron 34, MAG-34	26	487	6	22
Service Squadron 34, MAG-34	10	265	0	0
Marine Scout-Bomber Squadron 334, MAG-34	49	279	1	8
Marine Scout-Bomber Squadron 342, MAG-34	49	295	1	8
Marine Scout-Bomber Squadron 344, MAG-34	49	295	2	8
Marine Bombing Squadron 613, MAG-62	65	418	1	8
Marine Bombing Squadron 614, MAG-62	66	423	1	8
Area Sub-Total	314	2,462	12	62
New River				
Marine Scout-Bomber Squadron 944, MAG-94	61	393	1	8
Oak Grove				
Air Warning Squadron 14, 1st AWG	16	248	0	6
Service Squadron 51, MAG-92	11	271	0	8
Marine Fighter Squadron 513, MAG-92	47	229	1	8
Marine Fighter Squadron 514, MAG-92	48	218	1	8
Area Sub-Total	122	966	2	30
Vero Beach				
Air Warning Squadron 13, 1st AWG	18	256	0	6
Total FMF (Ground) Overseas	8,810	163,333	1,191	7,855
Total FMF (Air) Overseas	4,477	31,696	208	1,070
Total FMF (Ground) in U.S.A.	2,412	55,499	331	4,070
Total FMF (Air) in U.S.A.	4,980	39,376	208	1,031
Total FMF Overseas	13,287	195,029	1,399	8,925
Total FMF in U.S.A.	7,392	94,875	539	5,101
Total FMF	20,679	289,904	1,938	14,026

[1] Strength figures and unit designations were abstracted from the FMF Status Reports, Ground and Air, for August 1944 held in the Archives of the Historical Division, Headquarters Marine Corps. Units en route or ordered to the indicated area are listed under those areas regardless of their temporary locations.

APPENDIX F

Table of Organization F—100—Marine Division
5 May 1944 [1]

Unit	USMC Off	USMC Enl	USN Off	USN Enl	Totals Off	Totals Enl
Division Headquarters	(66)	(186)	(4)	(1)	(70)	(187)
Headquarters Battalion	101	883	7	13	108	896
Headquarters Company	(73)	(394)	(7)	(9)	(80)	(403)
Signal Company	(17)	(275)			(17)	(275)
Military Police Company	(6)	(96)			(6)	(96)
Reconnaissance Company	(5)	(118)		(4)	(5)	(122)
Tank Battalion	35	585	1	9	36	594
Headquarters & Service Company	(14)	(99)	(1)	(9)	(15)	(108)
3 Tank Companies (each)	(7)	(162)			(7)	(162)
Service Troops	58	1,343	66	422	124	1,765
Service Battalion	(29)	(702)	(2)	(18)	(31)	(720)
Headquarters Company	(9)	(48)	(2)	(9)	(11)	(57)
Service & Supply Company	(13)	(483)		(9)	(13)	(492)
Ordnance Company	(7)	(171)			(7)	(171)
Motor Transport Battalion	(28)	(501)	(1)	(9)	(29)	(510)
Headquarters & Service Company	(13)	(171)	(1)	(9)	(14)	(180)
3 Transport Companies (each)	(5)	(110)			(5)	(110)
Medical Battalion	(1)	(140)	(63)	(395)	(64)	(535)
Headquarters & Service Company	(1)	(15)	(28)	(45)	(29)	(60)
5 Medical Companies (each)		(25)	(7)	(70)	(7)	(95)
Engineer Battalion	41	842	1	20	42	862
Headquarters & Service Company	(23)	(263)	(1)	(20)	(24)	(283)
3 Engineer Companies (each)	(6)	(193)			(6)	(193)
Pioneer Battalion	38	672	3	32	41	704
Headquarters & Service Company	(11)	(81)	(3)	(32)	(14)	(113)
3 Pioneer Companies (each)	(9)	(197)			(9)	(197)
Artillery Regiment	159	2,415	8	57	167	2,472
Headquarters & Service Battery	(23)	(193)	(4)	(9)	(27)	(202)
2 105mm Howitzer Battalions (each)	(33)	(556)	(1)	(12)	(34)	(568)
Headquarters & Service Battery	(15)	(133)	(1)	(12)	(16)	(145)
3 Howitzer Batteries (each)	(6)	(141)			(6)	(141)
2 75mm Pack Howitzer Battalions (each)	(35)	(555)	(1)	(12)	(36)	(567)
Headquarters & Service Battery	(14)	(132)	(1)	(12)	(15)	(144)
3 Pack Howitzer Batteries (each)	(7)	(141)			(7)	(141)
3 Infantry Regiments (each)	137	2,936	11	134	148	3,070
Headquarters & Service Company	(24)	(218)	(5)	(14)	(29)	(232)
Weapons Company	(8)	(195)			(8)	(195)
3 Infantry Battalions (each)	(35)	(841)	(2)	(40)	(37)	(881)
Headquarters Company	(14)	(157)	(2)	(40)	(16)	(197)
3 Rifle Companies (each)	(7)	(228)			(7)	(228)
Division Totals	843	15,548	119	955	962	16,503

[1] All unit strength figures enclosed in parentheses are included in strength totals of parent units.

TABLE OF ORGANIZATION F—100—MARINE DIVISION

MAJOR WEAPONS AND TRANSPORTATION—MARINE DIVISION

Weapons	Number	Transportation	Number
Carbine, .30 cal., M–1	10,953	Ambulance:	
Flamethrower, portable, M2–2	243	¼-ton, 4 x 4	52
Flamethrower, mechanized, E4–5	24	½-ton, 4 x 4	12
Gun:		Car, 5-passenger	3
37mm, M3, antitank	36	Station wagon, 4 x 4	3
75mm, motor carriage, M–3, w/armament, radio-equipped (TCS)	12	Tractor: miscellaneous	71
		Trailer:	
Gun, Machine:		¼-ton, cargo	135
.30 cal., M1919A4	302	½-ton, dump	19
.30 cal., M1917A1	162	1-ton, cargo	155
.50 cal., M2	161	1-ton, water	74
Gun, submachine, .45 cal.	49	miscellaneous	110
Howitzer:		Truck:	
75mm pack	24	¼-ton, 4 x 4	323
105mm	24	¼-ton, 4 x 4, with radio	85
Launcher, rocket, antitank, M1A1	172	1-ton, 4 x 4, cargo	224
Mortar:		1-ton, 4 x 4, reconnaissance	11
60mm	117	2½-ton, 6 x 6, cargo	150
81mm	36	2½-ton, 6 x 6, dump	53
Pistol, .45 cal.	399	miscellaneous	68
Rifle, .30 cal., M–1	5,436		
Rifle, Browning, automatic	853		
Shotgun, 12 gauge	306		
Tank, Army medium, with armament	46		
Vehicle, recovery, M32B2	3		

APPENDIX G

Marine Task Organization and Command List[1]

MARINE GROUND UNITS

A. PELELIU (6 September–14 October 1944)

Expeditionary Troops

CG	MajGen Julian C. Smith
CofS	Col Dudley S. Brown
F-1	Col Harry E. Dunkelberger
F-2	LtCol Edmund J. Buckley
F-3	Col Robert O. Bare
F-4	LtCol Jesse S. Cook, Jr.

III Amphibious Corps

(15Sep–14Oct))

CG	MajGen Roy S. Geiger
CofS	Col Merwin H. Silverthorn
C-1	LtCol Peter A. McDonald
C-2	Col William F. Coleman
C-3	Col Walter A. Wachtler
C-4	Col Francis B. Loomis, Jr.

III Amphibious Corps Headquarters and Service Battalion

(15Sept–14Oct44)

CO .... LtCol Floyd A. Stephenson

---

[1] Unless otherwise noted, names, positions held, organization titles, and periods of service were taken from the muster rolls of the units concerned, held in the Diary Unit, Files Section, Records Branch, Personnel Department, Headquarters Marine Corps. Units are listed only for those periods, indicated by the dates below parent unit designation, for which they are entitled to campaign participation credit. This information is derived from muster rolls and the U. S. Bureau of Naval Personnel, *Navy and Marine Corps Awards Manual*—NAVPERS 15,790 (Rev. 1953) with changes (Washington, 1953–1958). The muster rolls have been the final authority when there is a conflict of unit entitlement within the overall campaign period as cited by the *Awards Manual*. In the case of Marine air units, many of which participated in the campaigns as flight or advance echelons only, the unit commander who was actually in the combat area is shown where muster rolls reveal this information. In order to conserve space, only units of battalion and squadron size, or larger, and sizable separate detachments are listed for each operation, although smaller organizations may have participated also.

III Amphibious Corps Troops

(15Sep–14Oct44)

CO .... Col Max D. Smith

3d Base Headquarters Battalion

(22Sep–14Oct44)

CO .... LtCol William O. Smith

1st Amphibian Tractor Battalion

(15Sep–14Oct44)

CO .... Maj Albert F. Reutlinger (to 21-Sep44)
Capt Arthur J. Noonan (from 22Sep44 to 10Oct44)
LtCol Maynard M. Nohrden (from 11Oct44)

3d Armored Amphibian Battalion

(15Sep–14Oct44)

CO .... LtCol Kimber H. Boyer

3d 155mm Howitzer Battalion

(15Sep–14Oct44)

CO .... LtCol Richard A. Evans

6th Amphibian Tractor Battalion

(15Sep–14Oct44)

CO .... Capt John I. Fitzgerald, Jr.

7th Antiaircraft Artillery Battalion

(6Sep–14Oct44)

CO .... LtCol Henry R. Paige

8th Amphibian Tractor Battalion

(15Sep–14Oct44)

CO .... LtCol Charles B. Nerren

8th 155mm Howitzer Battalion

(15Sep–14Oct44)

CO .... Maj George V. Hanna, Jr.

12th Antiaircraft Artillery Battalion

(15Sep–14Oct44)

CO .... LtCol Merlyn D. Holmes

16th Field Depot

(15Sep–14Oct44)

CO .... LtCol Harlan C. Cooper

Headquarters, 1st Marine Division
(15Sep–14Oct44)

CG	MajGen William H. Rupertus
ADC	BGen Oliver P. Smith
CofS	Col John T. Selden
D-1	Maj William E. Benedict (to 23-Sep44)
	LtCol Harold O. Deakin (from 24Sep44)
D-2	LtCol John W. Scott, Jr.
D-3	LtCol Lewis J. Fields
D-4	LtCol Harvey C. Tschirgi

Division Headquarters and Service Battalion
(15Sep–14Oct44)

CO	Col Joseph F. Hankins (KIA 3-Oct44)
	LtCol Austin C. Shofner (from 3Oct44)

1st Engineer Battalion
(15Sep–14Oct44)

CO	LtCol Levi W. Smith, Jr.

1st Medical Battalion
(15Sep–2Oct44)

CO	Cdr Emil E. Napp, MC, USN

1st Motor Transport Battalion
(14Sep–2Oct44)

CO	Capt Robert B. McBroom

1st Pioneer Battalion
(15Sep–14Oct44)

CO	LtCol Robert G. Ballance

1st Service Battalion
(15Sep–2Oct44)

CO	Col John Kaluf

1st Tank Battalion
(15Sep–14Oct44)

CO	LtCol Arthur J. Stuart

1st Marines
(15Sep–2Oct44)

CO	Col Lewis B. Puller
ExO	LtCol Richard P. Ross, Jr.
R-3	Maj Bernard T. Kelly

1st Battalion, 1st Marines

CO	Maj Raymond G. Davis

2d Battalion, 1st Marines

CO	LtCol Russell E. Honsowetz

3d Battalion, 1st Marines

CO	LtCol Stephen V. Sabol

5th Marines
(15Sep–14Oct44)

CO	Col Harold D. Harris
ExO	LtCol Lewis W. Walt
R-3	Maj Walter S. McIlhenny (to 16-Sep44)
	Capt Donald A. Peppard (from 17Sep44)

1st Battalion, 5th Marines

CO	LtCol Robert W. Boyd

2d Battalion, 5th Marines

CO	Maj Gordon D. Gayle

3d Battalion, 5th Marines

CO	LtCol Austin C. Shofner (WIA 15Sep44)
	LtCol Lewis W. Walt (night 15-16Sep44)
	Maj John H. Gustafson (from 16-Sep44)

7th Marines
(15Sep–14Oct44)

CO	Col Herman H. Hanneken
ExO	LtCol Norman Hussa
R-3	Maj Walter Holomon

1st Battalion, 7th Marines

CO	LtCol John J. Gormley

2d Battalion, 7th Marines

CO	LtCol Spencer S. Berger

3d Battalion, 7th Marines

CO	Maj E. Hunter Hurst

11th Marines
(15Sep–14Oct44)

CO	Col William H. Harrison
ExO	LtCol Edson L. Lyman
R-3	LtCol Leonard F. Chapman, Jr.

1st Battalion, 11th Marines

CO	LtCol Richard W. Wallace

2d Battalion, 11th Marines

CO	LtCol Noah P. Wood, Jr.

3d Battalion, 11th Marines

CO	LtCol Charles M. Nees

4th Battalion, 11th Marines
CO .... LtCol Louis C. Reinberg

Island Command, Peleliu (1st Echelon)
(15Sep–14Oct44)
CO .... BGen Harold D. Campbell

B. PHILIPPINES
(20October–11December 1944)

Headquarters, V Amphibious Corps Artillery
(20Oct–29Nov44)
CG .... BGen Thomas E. Bourke
ExO .... Col Bert A. Bone
CofS .... Col Harold C. Roberts
A-1 .... Capt George K. Acker
A-2 .... Maj Leo S. Unger
A-3 .... LtCol Floyd R. Moore
A-4 .... LtCol Richard H. Crockett

5th 155mm Howitzer Battalion
(21Oct–11Dec44)
CO .... LtCol James E. Mills

11th 155mm Gun Battalion
(21Oct–11Dec44)
CO .... LtCol Thomas S. Ivey

C. IWO JIMA (19February–26March 1945)

Expeditionary Troops
(19Feb–16Mar45)
CG .... LtGen Holland M. Smith
CofS .... Col Dudley S. Brown
G-1 .... Col Russell N. Jordahl
G-2 .... Col Edmond J. Buckley
G-3 .... Col Kenneth H. Weir
G-4 .... Col George R. Rowan

Amphibious Reconnaissance Battalion, FMFPac
(19Feb–16Mar45)
CO .... Maj James L. Jones

V Amphibious Corps
(19Feb–16Mar45)
CG .... MajGen Harry Schmidt
CofS .... BGen William W. Rogers
C-1 .... Col David A. Stafford
C-2 .... Col Thomas R. Yancey, USA
C-3 .... Col Edward A. Craig
C-4 .... Col William F. Brown

V Corps Headquarters and Service Battalion
(19Feb–16Mar45)
CO .... Capt Cyril M. Milbrath

V Corps Troops
(19Feb–16Mar45)
CO .... Col Alton A. Gladden

V Corps Signal Battalion
(19Feb–16Mar45)
CO .... LtCol Alfred F. Robertshaw

V Corps Medical Battalion
(19Feb–16Mar45)
CO .... LCrd William B. Clapp, MC, USN

2d Separate Engineer Battalion
(19Feb–16Mar45)
CO .... LtCol Charles O. Clark

8th Field Depot
(19Feb–16Mar45)
CO .... Col Leland S. Swindler

1st Provisional Field Artillery Group
(19Feb–16Mar45)
CO .... Col John S. Letcher
ExO .... LtCol Marin H. Floom
G-3 .... Maj William D. Winters, Jr.

2d 155mm Howitzer Battalion
(19Feb–16Mar45)
CO .... Maj Earl J. Rowse

4th 155mm Howitzer Battalion
(19Feb–16Mar45)
CO .... LtCol Douglas E. Reeve

V Corps Provisional LVT Group
(19Feb–16Mar45)
CO .... LtCol Harry W. G. Vadnais

2d Armored Amphibian Battalion
(19Feb–16Mar45)
CO .... LtCol Reed M. Fawell, Jr.

3d Amphibian Tractor Battalion
(19Feb–16Mar45)
CO .... LtCol Sylvester L. Stephan

5th Amphibian Tractor Battalion
(19Feb–16Mar45)
CO .... Maj George L. Shead

10th Amphibian Tractor Battalion
(19Feb–16Mar45)
CO .... Maj Victor J. Croizat

MARINE TASK ORGANIZATION AND COMMAND LIST

24th Replacement Draft
(19Feb–16Mar45)
CO .... Maj Ralph E. Boulton

V Corps Evac Hosp No. 1
(19Feb–16Mar45)
CO .... Capt H. G. Young, MC, USN

11th Amtrac Battalion
(19Feb–16Mar45)
CO .... LtCol Albert J. Roose

27th Replacement Draft
(19Feb–16Mar45)
CO .... Capt Charles R. Puckett

28th Replacement Draft
(19Feb–16Mar45)
CO .... Maj Michael V. DiVita

30th Replacement Draft
(19Feb–16Mar45)
CO .... Capt Donald J. Kendall, Jr.

31st Replacement Draft
(19Feb–16Mar45)
CO .... Capt Thomas B. Tighe

34th Replacement Draft
(19Feb–16Mar45)
CO .... Capt Neil A. Weathers, Jr.

Island Commander, Iwo Jima
(19Feb–16Mar45)
CO .... MajGen James E. Chaney, USA

Headquarters, 3d Marine Division
(19Feb–16Mar45)
CG .... MajGen Graves B. Erskine
ADC .... Col John B. Wilson
CofS .... Col Robert E. Hogaboom
D-1 .... Maj Irving R. Kriendler
D-2 .... LtCol Howard J. Turton
D-3 .... Col Arthur H. Butler
D-4 .... LtCol James D. Hittle

Division Headquarters and Service Battalion
(19Feb–16Mar45)
CO .... LtCol Jack F. Warner (to 14-Mar 45)
LtCol Carey A. Randall (from 14Mar45)

3d Engineer Battalion
(19Feb–16Mar45)
CO .... LtCol Walter S. Campbell

3d Medical Battalion
(19Feb–16Mar45)
CO .... Cdr Anthony E. Reymont, MC, USN

3d Motor Transport Battalion
(19Feb–16Mar45)
CO .... LtCol Ernest W. Fry, Jr.

3d Pioneer Battalion
(19Feb–16Mar45)
CO .... LtCol Edmund M. Williams

3d Service Battalion
(19Feb–16Mar45)
CO .... LtCol Paul G. Chandler

3d Tank Battalion
(19Feb–16Mar45)
CO .... Maj Holly H. Evans

3d Marines
(19Feb–5Mar45)
CO .... Col James A. Stuart
ExO .... LtCol Newton B. Barkley
R-3 .... Capt Paul H. Groth

1st Battalion, 3d Marines
CO .... LtCol Ronald R. Van Stockum

2d Battalion, 3d Marines
CO .... LtCol Thomas R. Stokes

3d Battalion, 3d Marines
CO .... LtCol Ralph L. Houser

9th Marines
(19Feb–16Mar45)
CO .... Col Howard N. Kenyon
ExO .... LtCol Paul W. Russell
R-3 .... Maj Calvin W. Kunz

1st Battalion, 9th Marines
CO .... LtCol Carey A. Randall (to 6-Mar45)
Maj William T. Glass (from 6-14Mar45)
LtCol Jack F. Warner (from 14-Mar45)

2d Battalion, 9th Marines
CO .... LtCol Robert E. Cushman, Jr.

3d Battalion, 9th Marines
CO .... LtCol Harold C. Boehm

21st Marines
(19Feb–16Mar45)
- CO .... Col Hartnoll J. Withers
- ExO .... LtCol Eustace R. Smoak
- R-3 .... Capt Andrew Hedesh

1st Battalion, 21st Marines
- CO .... LtCol Marlowe C. Williams (WIA 22Feb45)
  - Maj Clay M. Murray (from 22-Feb45, WIA 22Feb45)
  - Maj Robert H. Houser (from 22-Feb45)

2d Battalion, 21st Marines
- CO .... LtCol Lowell E. English (WIA 2Mar45)
  - Maj George A. Percy (from 2-Mar45)

3d Battalion, 21st Marines
- CO .... LtCol Wendell H. Duplantis

12th Marines
(19Feb–16Mar45)
- CO .... LtCol Raymond F. Crist, Jr.
- ExO .... LtCol Bernard H. Kirk
- R-3 .... LtCol Thomas R. Belzer

1st Battalion, 12th Marines
- CO .... Maj George B. Thomas

2d Battalion, 12th Marines
- CO .... LtCol William T. Fairbourn

3d Battalion, 12th Marines
- CO .... LtCol Alpha L. Bowser, Jr.

4th Battalion, 12th Marines
- CO .... Maj Joe B. Wallen

Headquarters, 4th Marine Division
(19Feb–16Mar45)
- CG .... MajGen Clifton B. Cates
- ADC .... BGen Franklin A. Hart
- CofS .... Col Merton J. Batchelder
- D-1 .... Col Orin H. Wheeler
- D-2 .... LtCol Gooderham L. McCormick
- D-3 .... Col Edwin A. Pollock
- D-4 .... Col Matthew C. Horner

Division Headquarters and Service Battalion
(19Feb–16Mar45)
- CO .... Col Bertrand T. Fay

4th Engineer Battalion
(19Feb–16Mar45)
- CO .... LtCol Nelson K. Brown

4th Medical Battalion
(19Feb–16Mar45)
- CO .... Cdr Reuben L. Sharp, MC, USN

4th Motor Transport Battalion
(19Feb–16Mar45)
- CO .... LtCol Ralph L. Schiesswohl

4th Pioneer Battalion
(19Feb–16Mar45)
- CO .... LtCol Richard G. Ruby

4th Service Battalion
- CO .... LtCol John E. Fondahl

4th Tank Battalion
- CO .... LtCol Richard K. Schmidt

23d Marines
(19Feb–16Mar45)
- CO .... Col Walter W. Wensinger
- ExO .... LtCol Edward J. Dillon
- R-3 .... Maj Henry S. Campbell

1st Battalion, 23d Marines
- CO .... LtCol Ralph Haas (KIA 20Feb-45)
  - LtCol Louis B. Blissard (from 20Feb45)

2d Battalion, 23d Marines
- CO .... Maj Robert H. Davidson (WIA 7Mar45)
  - LtCol Edward J. Dillon (from 7-11Mar45)
  - Maj Robert H. Davidson (from 11Mar45)

3d Battalion, 23d Marines
- CO .... Maj James S. Scales

24th Marines
(19Feb–16Mar45)
- CO .... Col Walter I. Jordan
- ExO .... LtCol Austin R. Brunelli (to 8-Mar45)
  - None shown (8–16Mar 45)
- R-3 .... Maj Webb D. Sawyer

MARINE TASK ORGANIZATION AND COMMAND LIST

1st Battalion, 24th Marines
CO .... Maj Paul S. Treitel (to 8Mar45)
LtCol Austin R. Brunelli (from 8Mar45)

2d Battalion, 24th Marines
CO .... LtCol Richard Rothwell

3d Battalion, 24th Marines
CO .... LtCol Alexander A. Vandegrift, Jr. (WIA 23Feb45)
Maj Doyle A. Stout (from 23-Feb45)

25th Marines
(19Feb–16Mar45)
CO .... Col John R. Lanigan
ExO .... LtCol Clarence J. O'Donnell
R-3 .... Maj John H. Jones

1st Battalion, 25th Marines
CO .... LtCol Hollis U. Mustain (KIA 21Feb45)
Maj Fenton J. Mee (from 21Feb45)

2d Battalion, 25th Marines
CO .... LtCol Lewis C. Hudson, Jr. (WIA 20Feb45)
LtCol James Taul (from 20Feb45)

3d Battalion, 25th Marines
CO .... LtCol Justice M. Chambers (WIA 22Feb45)
Capt James C. Headley (from 22-Feb45)

14th Marines
(19Feb–16Mar45)
CO .... Col Louis G. DeHaven
ExO .... LtCol Randall M. Victory
R-3 .... Maj Frederick J. Karch

1st Battalion, 14th Marines
CO .... Maj John B. Edgar, Jr.

2d Battalion, 14th Marines
CO .... Maj Clifford B. Drake

3d Battalion, 14th Marines
CO .... LtCol Robert E. MacFarlane (WIA 19Feb45)
Maj Harvey A. Feehan (from 19–23Feb45)
LtCol Carl A. Youngdale (from 23Feb–10Mar 45)
Maj Harvey A. Feehan (from 10-Mar45)

4th Battalion, 14th Marines
CO .... LtCol Carl A. Youngdale (to 23-Feb45)
Maj Roland J. Spritzen (from 23-Feb–10Mar45)
LtCol Carl A. Youngdale (from 10Mar45)

Headquarters, 5th Marine Division
(19Feb–16Mar45)
CG .... MajGen Keller E. Rockey
ADC .... BGen Leo D. Hermle
CofS .... Col Ray A. Robinson
D-1 .... Col John W. Beckett
D-2 .... LtCol George A. Roll
D-3 .... Col James F. Shaw, Jr.
D-4 .... Col Earl S. Piper

Headquarters Battalion, 5th Marine Division
(19Feb–16Mar45)
CO .... Maj John Ayrault, Jr.

5th Engineer Battalion
(19Feb–16Mar45)
CO .... LtCol Clifford H. Shuey

5th Medical Battalion
(19Feb–16Mar45)
CO .... LCdr William W. Ayres, MC, USN

5th Motor Transport Battalion
(19Feb–16Mar45)
CO .... Maj Arthur F. Torgler, Jr.

5th Pioneer Battalion
(19Feb–16Mar45)
CO .... Maj Robert S. Riddell

5th Service Battalion
(19Feb–16Mar45)
CO .... Maj Francis P. Daly (KIA 22-Feb45
None shown (from 22–27Feb45)
Maj Gardelle Lewis (from 27Feb-45)

5th Tank Battalion
(19Feb–16Mar45)
CO .... LtCol William R. Collins

26th Marines
(19Feb–16Mar45)
CO .... Col Chester B. Graham
ExO .... Col Lester S. Hamel
R–3 .... LtCol William K. Davenport, Jr.

1st Battalion, 26th Marines
CO .... LtCol Daniel C. Pollock (WIA 19Mar45)
Maj Albert V. K. Gary (from 19-Mar45)

2d Battalion, 26th Marines
CO .... LtCol Joseph P. Sayers (WIA 23Feb45)
Maj Amedeo Rea (from 23Feb45)

3d Battalion, 26th Marines
CO .... LtCol Tom M. Trotti (KIA 22-Feb45)
Capt Richard M. Cook (22Feb45 only)
Maj Richard Fagan (from 23-Feb45)

27th Marines
(19Feb–16Mar45)
CO .... Col Thomas A. Wornham
ExO .... Col Louis C. Plain (WIA 19Feb-45)
LtCol James P. Berkeley (from 15Mar45)
R–3 .... LtCol Justin G. Duryea (to 5Mar-45)
Capt Franklin L. Smith (from 5Mar45)

1st Battalion, 27th Marines
CO .... LtCol John A. Butler (KIA 5-Mar45)
LtCol Justin G. Duryea (from 5-Mar45, WIA 9Mar45)
Maj William H. Tumbelston (from 9Mar45, WIA 14Mar45)
Maj William H. Kennedy, Jr. (from 14Mar45)

2d Battalion, 27th Marines
CO .... Maj John W. Antonelli (WIA 9-Mar45)
Maj Gerald F. Russell (from 9-Mar45)

3d Battalion, 27th Marines
CO .... LtCol Donn J. Robertson

28th Marines
(19Feb–16Mar45)
CO .... Col Harry B. Liversedge
ExO .... LtCol Robert H. Williams
R–3 .... Maj Oscar F. Peatross (to 14-Mar45)
LtCol Charles E. Shepard, Jr. (from 15Mar45)

1st Battalion, 28th Marines
CO .... LtCol Jackson B. Butterfield

2d Battalion, 28th Marines
CO .... LtCol Chandler W. Johnson (KIA 2Mar45)
Maj Thomas B. Pearce, Jr. (from 2Mar45)

3d Battalion, 28th Marines
CO .... LtCol Charles E. Shepard, Jr. (to 14Mar45)
Maj Tolson A. Smoak (from 14-Mar 45)

13th Marines
(19Feb–16Mar45)
CO .... Col James D. Waller
ExO .... LtCol Kenyth A. Damke
R–3 .... LtCol Jack Tabor

1st Battalion, 13th Marines
CO .... LtCol John S. Oldfield

2d Battalion, 13th Marines
CO .... Maj Carl W. Hjerpe

3d Battalion, 13th Marines
CO .... LtCol Henry T. Waller

4th Battalion, 13th Marines
CO .... Maj James F. Coady

MARINE AIR UNITS

*Headquarters Squadron Detachment,
1st Marine Aircraft Wing[2]..
(C—10Mar–4Jul45)[3]*

CO, HQ
  Sqn-1 .... Capt Robert W. Baile

*Advance Echelon, 2d Marine Aircraft Wing
(B—24Sep–14Oct44)*

CG .... MajGen James T. Moore
AWC .... BGen Harold D. Campbell
CofS .... Col John Wehle
W-1 .... Maj William K. Lations
W-2 .... (None shown)
W-3 .... Col Ronald D. Salmon
W-4 .... LtCol Walter T. Brownell
CO, Hq
  Sqn-2 .... Maj Charles C. Campbell

4th Marine Base Defense Aircraft Wing
(Redesignated 4th Marine Aircraft Wing
effective 10Nov44)
(A—25Dec43–26Mar45)

CG .... BGen Lewie G. Merritt (to 15-May44)
              BGen Thomas J. Cushman (from 15May–20Aug44)
              MajGen Louis E. Woods (from 21Aug44)
AWC .... (None shown to 20Aug44)
              BGen Thomas J. Cushman (from 21Aug–31Oct44)
              (None shown from 1Nov44)
CofS .... Col Frank H. Lamson-Scribner
W-1 .... Maj Maurice L. McDermond (to 15Mar44)
              Maj Lloyd E. Pike (from 16 Mar–5Sep44)
              Col Lawrence T. Burke (from 6-Sep–17Nov44)
              LtCol Corey C. Brayton (from 18-Nov44)

W-2 .... Capt Charles J. Greene, Jr. (to 10Oct44)
              Capt Thomas C. Andrews (from 11Oct44)
W-3 .... Col Lawrence T. Burke (to 2 Feb-44)
              Col Carson A. Roberts (from 3-Feb–12Apr44)
              Col Lawrence T. Burke (from 13-Apr–16Jun44)
              LtCol Lee C. Merrell, Jr. (from 16Jun–15Sep44)
              Col Calvin R. Freeman (from 16-Sep44–1Feb45)
              Maj Elmer G. Glidden, Jr. (from 2Feb–14Mar45)
              LtCol Martin A. Severson (from 15Mar45)
W-4 .... Maj Melville M. Nenefee (to 30-Sep44)
              Maj Granville Mitchell (from 1-Oct44)
CO, Hq-
  Sqn-4 .... Maj Melchior B. Trelfall (to 15-Oct44)
              Maj Charles C. Boyer (from 16-Oct–14Dec44)
              LtCol Alfred C. Cramp (from 15-Dec44–24Jan45)
              2dLt Robert J. Brown, Jr. (from 25Jan–3Feb45)
              Maj George F. Webster (from 4-Feb45)

Marine Aircraft Group 11
Advance Echelon (B—15Sep–14Oct44)
Rear Echelon (B—25Sep–14Oct44)
CO .... Col Caleb T. Bailey
ExO .... Col John S. Holmberg
GruOpsO .... LtCol Jeslyn R. Bailey
CO, Hq
  Sqn-11 .. Capt Cornelius Cole II
CO,
  SMS-11 .. Maj Leslie T. Bryan, Jr.

Marine Aircraft Group 12
Advance Echelon (C –3Dec44–4July45)
Rear Echelon (C—17Mar–4Jul45)
CO .... Col William A. Willis (to 26Feb-45)
              Col Verne J. McCaul (from 27-Feb45)

---

[3] Under each unit listed below there will appear a letter designation for each major area in which the unit operated, and dates of major involvement. Following are the campaigns and dates of entitlements, though individual units may have continued operations beyond the cutoff dates, particularly during the final months of the war.
A. Marshalls-Marianas-Bypassed Islands 25Dec43–26Mar45
B. Peleliu 6Sep–14Oct44
C. Philippines 10Oct44–20Jul45
D. Iwo Jima 15Feb–16Mar45

[2] Headquarters, 1st Marine Aircraft Wing did not move to the Philippines until August 1945, shortly before the end of World War II.

ExO .... LtCol John L. Winston
GruOpsO.... LtCol Frederick E. Leek
CO, Hq-
 Sqn–12 .. Capt Francis L. O'Melia
CO,
 SMS–12 .. Capt William B. Freeman

Marine Aircraft Group 13
(A—31Jan44–26Mar45)
CO .... Col Lawrence Norman (to 16Dec-44)
  LtCol Chauncey V. Burnett (from 17Dec44)
ExO .... Col Athur F. Binney (to 15Jul-44)
  LtCol Avery R. Kier (from 16-Jul–4Sep44)
  LtCol Zane Thompson, Jr. from 5Sep–8Oct44)
  LtCol Chauncey V. Burnett (from 9Oct–16Dec44)
  LtCol Zane Thompson, Jr. (from 17Dec44–3Feb45)
  LtCol Edward J. Moore (from 4-Feb–11Mar45)
  LtCol John V. Kipp (from 12-Mar45)
GruOpsO.... LtCol Zane Thompson, Jr. (to 9-May44)
  LtCol Avery R. Kier (from 10 May–15Jul44)
  LtCol Zane Thompson, Jr. (from 16Jul–4Sep44)
  LtCol Paul R. Byrum, Jr. (from 5Sep–8Oct44)
  LtCol Zane Thompson, Jr. (from 9Oct–16Dec44)
  Maj James C. Otis (from 17Dec-44–10Mar45)
  LtCol Edward J. Moore (from 11-Mar45)
CO, Hq-
 Sqn–13 .. Maj Harlan Rogers (to 22Apr44)
  Maj Stanley W. Burke (from 23-Apr–3Dec44)
  Capt Clement F. Hahn, Jr. (from 4Dec44)
CO,
 SMS-13 .. Maj David Ahee (to 9Jun44)
  LtCol Corey C. Brayton, Jr. (from 10Jun–7Nov44)
  Maj Joseph A. Gray (from 8 Nov-44)

Marine Aircraft Group 14
Advance Echelon (C—11Jan–15May45)
Rear Echelon (C—23Feb–28May45)
CO .... Col Zebulon C. Hopkins (to 17-May-45)
  Col Edward A. Montgomery (from 18May45)
ExO .... LtCol Curtis W. Smith, Jr.
GruOpsO.... Maj William C. Humberd
CO, Hq-
 Sqn–14 .. Capt Robert M. Crooks
CO,
 SMS–14 .. Capt Droel H. Looney

Marine Aircraft Group 15
(A—1Apr44–25Mar45)
CO .... LtCol Ben Z. Redfield (to 31May-44)
  Col Thomas J. McQuade (from 1-Jun–30Sep44)
  LtCol Ben Z. Redfield (from 10-Oct44)
ExO .... Maj Neil R. MacIntyre (to 31May-44)
  LtCol Ben Z. Redfield (from 1Jun–30Sep44)
  LtCol George D. Omer (from 1–31Oct44)
  LtCol Stanley W. Trachta (from 1Nov44–28Feb45)
  LtCol Edward F. Knight (from 1Mar45)
GruOpsO .... Maj Ridgway Baker (to 1Oct44)
  Maj Clifford R. Banks, Jr. (from 1–31Oct44)
  LtCol Edward F. Knight (from 1-Nov44–21Jan45)
  Maj Charles W. Sommers, Jr. (from 22Jan–5Mar45)
  LtCol Desmond E. Canavan (from 6Mar45)
CO,Hq-
 Sqn–15 .. Capt Louis F. Ferguson (to 15-Oct44)
  Maj Melchior B. Trelfall (from 16-Oct44–6Mar45)
  Maj Peter Ficker (from 7Mar45)
CO,
 SMS–15 .. Maj Thomas H. Ray (to 8Sep44)
  1st Lt Thomas F. Wade, Acting (from 9Sep–5Nov44)
  Maj Thomas H. Ray (from 6Nov-44)

Marine Aircraft Group 21
(A—27Jul44–26Mar45)

CO	Col Peter P. Schrider (to 6Sep44)
	Col Edward B. Carney (from 7-Sep44)
ExO	LtCol James A. Booth, Jr. (to 2-Oct44)
	(None shown 3Oct–28Nov44)
	LtCol George D. Omer (from 29-Nov44–7Jan45)
	LtCol Wilfred J. Huffman (from 8Jan45)
GruOpsO	LtCol Robert W. Clark (to 3Sep44)
	LtCol James A. Embrey, Jr. (from 4Sep44–6Mar45)
	LtCol John S. Carter (from 7Mar-45)
CO, Hq-Sqn-21	Maj Robert F. Higley
CO, SMS-21	Maj Charlton B. Ivey (to 22Aug44)
	Capt Albert I. Haas (from 23Aug44–30Jan45)
	LtCol George E. Congdon (from 31Jan45)

Marine Aircraft Group 22
(A—19Feb44–26Mar45)

CO	Col James M. Daly (to 9Oct44)
	Col Daniel W. Torrey, Jr. (from 10Oct44)
ExO	LtCol Richard D. Hughes (to 14-Aug44)
	(None shown from 15–19Aug44)
	Col Edward B. Carney (from 20-Aug–17Sep44)
	LtCol Harrison Brent, Jr. (from 18Sep44–7Jan45)
	LtCol Elmer A. Wrenn (from 8-Jan45)
GruOpsO	LtCol Julian F. Walters (to 24Jul44)
	LtCol Charles R. Luers (from 25-Jul–3Aug44)
	LtCol Harrison Brent, Jr. (from 4Aug–17Sep44)
	LtCol Charles R. Luers (from 18-Sep–9Nov44)
	Maj Thomas C. Colt, Jr. (from 10Nov44)

CO, Hq-Sqn-22	1stLt John W. Hackner, Jr. (to 20-Nov44)
	Maj Alfred C. Cramp (from 21-Nov–18Dec44)
	Capt Lindsay K. Dickey (from 19-Dec44)
CO, SMS-22	Capt John A. Hood (to 15Aug44)
	Capt Arthur Blakeney (from 16-Aug44–25Jan45)
	Maj Bruce Prosser (from 26Jan-45)

Marine Aircraft Group 24
Advance Echelon (C—11Jan–8Apr45)
Rear Echelon (C—22Jan–8Apr45)

(C—22Jan–4Jul45)

CO	LtCol Lyle H. Meyer (to 31May-45)
	Col Warren E. Sweetser, Jr. (from 1Jun45)
ExO	LtCol John H. Earle, Jr.
GruOpsO	LtCol Keith B. McCutcheon
CO, Hq-Sqn-24	Capt J. Devereaux Wrather, Jr.
CO, SMS-24	Capt Horace C. Baum, Jr. (to 21-Jan45)
	Maj William K. Snyder (from 22-Jan45)

Marine Aircraft Group 25
(C—30Oct44–1Apr45)

CO	Col Allen C. Koonce (to 13Feb45)
	Col Harold C. Major (from 14Feb-45)
ExO	LtCol John P. Coursey (to 13Nov-44)
	LtCol William H. Klenke, Jr. (from 25Nov44–8Feb45)
	Col Warren E. Sweetser, Jr. (from 9Feb45)
GruOpsO	LtCol Theodore W. Sanford, Jr. (to 4Mar45)
	LtCol William H. Klenke, Jr. (from 5Mar45)

CO, Hq-
Sqn-25 .. Capt LeRoy M. James (to 21Oct-44)
Maj Theodore E. Beal (from 22-Oct-9Nov44)
Maj Charles J. Prall (from 10-Nov44)
CO,
SMS-25 .. LtCol Hillard T. Shepard (to 14-Nov44)
LtCol Albert S. Munsch (from 15-Nov44)

Marine Aircraft Group 31
(A—7Feb44–26Mar45)
CO .... Col Calvin R. Freeman (to 12Sep44)
LtCol Ralph K. Rottet (from 13-Sep–13Dec44)
LtCol Martin A. Severson (from 13Dec44–5Mar45)
Col John C. Munn (from 6Mar45)
ExO .... Col Edward B. Carney (to 16Aug-44)
LtCol Ralph K. Rottet (from 17-Aug–13Dec44)
LtCol Richard D. Hughes (from 13Dec44–15Jan45)
LtCol Gordon E. Hendricks (from 16Jan45)
GruOpsO .... LtCol Ralph K. Rottet (to 16 Aug-44)
LtCol Richard D. Hughes (from 17Aug–12Sep44)
LtCol Kenneth D. Kerby (from 13–30Sep44)
LtCol Lee C. Merrell, Jr. (from 1Oct–21Dec44)
LtCol Kirk Armistead (from 22-Dec44)
CO, Hq-
Sqn-31 .. Capt Warren S. Adams II (to 9-Apr44)
Capt James C. Woodhull, Jr. (from 10Apr–31Dec44)
Capt William L. Thompson (from 1Jan–4Feb45)
Maj Leon A. Danco (from 5Feb45)
CO,
SMS-31 .. Capt Neil A. Vestal (to 14Mar44)
Capt John Zouck (from 15Mar44–18Feb45)
Maj Archibald M. Smith, Jr. (from 19Feb45)

Marine Aircraft Group 32
Group Echelon (C—27Jan–22Feb45)
Flight Echelon (C—31Jan–22Feb45)
Advance Echelon (C—10Mar–4Jul45)
Rear Echelon (C—17Mar–4Jul45)
CO .... Col Clayton C. Jerome
ExO .... LtCol John L. Smith
GruOpsO .... LtCol Wallace T. Scott
CO, Hq-
Sqn-32 .. Capt Harold L. Maryott (to 17-Mar45)
1stLt Robert W. Mazur (from 18-Mar45)
CO,
SMS-32 .. Maj Jack D. Kane

Air Warning Squadron 1
(A—20Feb44–26Mar45)
CO .... Capt William D. Felder (to 20-Dec44)
Capt Edward R. Stainback (from 21Dec44)

Advance Echelon, Marine Observation Squadron 1
(D—19Feb–8Mar45)
CO .... Lt Anthony E. Barrett, Jr.

Air Warning Squadron 3
(C—17Apr–4Jul45)
CO .... Capt Harold W. Swope (to 1Jul45)
Capt Freeman R. Cass (from 2-Jul45)

Advance Echelon, Marine Observation Squadron 3
(B—15Sep–14Oct44)
CO .... Capt Wallace J. Slappey, Jr.

Air Warning Squadron 4
(C—10Mar–4Jul45)
CO .... Capt Charles T. Porter

Marine Observation Squadron 4
(D—19Feb–16Mar45)
CO .... 1stLt Thomas Rozga

Marine Observation Squadron 5
(D—19Feb–16Mar45)
CO .... 1stLt Roy G. Miller

MARINE TASK ORGANIZATION AND COMMAND LIST

Marine Fighter Squadron 111
(A—7Mar44–26Mar45)
CO .... Maj J. Frank Cole (to 6Apr44)
Maj William E. Clasen (7Apr–27Oct44)
Maj William T. Herring (28Oct44–1Mar45)
Maj Robert D. Kelly (from 2Mar-45)

Marine Fighter Squadron 112
(USS *Bennington*)
(D—15Feb–4Mar45)
CO .... Maj Herman Hansen, Jr.

Marine Fighter Squadron 113
(A—15Jan44–26Mar45)
CO .... Capt Loren D. Everton (to 7Sep-44)
Maj Charles Kimak (from 8Sep–18Dec44)
Maj Philip R. White (from 19Dec-44–20Feb45)
Maj Hensley Williams (from 21-Feb45)

Marine Fighter Squadron 114
Ground Echelon (B—15Sep–14Oct44)
Flight Echelon (B—26Sep–14Oct44)
CO .... Capt Robert F. Stout

Marine Fighter Squadron 115
(C—17Dec44–4Jul45)
CO .... Maj John H. King, Jr. (to 29May-45)
Maj John S. Payne (from 30May-45)

Marine Fighter Squadron 121
Ground Echelon (B—15Sep–14Oct44)
CO .... Maj Walter J. Meyer

Marine Fighter Squadron 122
Ground Echelon (B—15Sep–14Oct44)
Flight Echelon (B—1–14Oct44)
CO .... Maj Joseph H. Reinburg

Advance Echelon Marine Fighter Squadron 123
(USS *Bennington*)
(D—15Feb–4Mar45)
CO .... Maj Everett V. Alward (to 25-Feb45)
Maj Thomas E. Mobley (from 25-Feb45)

Marine Fighter Squadron 124
(USS *Essex*)
(C—3–22Jan45)
(D—15Feb–4Mar45)
CO .... Maj William A. Millington

Marine Scout-Bomber Squadron 133
(C—22Jan–4Jul45)
CO .... Maj Lee A. Christoffersen (to 8-Mar45)
Maj Floyd Cummings (from 9-Mar45)

Marine Torpedo-Bomber Squadron 134
Ground Echelon (B—30Sep–14Oct44)
Flight Echelon (B—6–14Oct44)
CO .... Maj Russell R. Riley

Marine Scout-Bomber Squadron 142
Ground Echelon (C—22Jan–4Jul45)
Flight Echelon (C—27Jan–4Jul45)
CO .... Capt Hoyle R. Barr (to 8Jun45)
Maj James L. Fritsche (from 9-Jun45)

Marine Scout-Bomber Squadron 151
(A—29Feb44–26Mar45)
CO .... LtCol Gordon H. Knott (to 30Oct-44)
Maj Randolph C. Berkeley, Jr. (from 31Oct–4Dec44)
Maj Bruce Prosser (from 5Dec44–25Jan45)
Maj Robert J. Shelley, Jr. (from 25Jan45)

Marine Observation Squadron 155
(redesignated Marine Fighter Squadron 155, effective 31Jan45)
(A—1Nov44–26Mar45)
CO .... Capt John P. Haines, Jr. (to 13-Jan45)
Maj John E. Reynolds (from 14-Jan–14Feb45)
Maj Wayne M. Cargill (from 15-Feb45)

Marine Fighter Squadron 211
(C—5Dec44–4Jul45)

CO .... Maj Stanislaus J. Witomski (to 30Jan45)
Maj Philip B. May (from 31Jan–20Mar45)
Maj Angus F. Davis (from 21Mar-45)

Marine Fighter Squadron 212
(C—19Jan–14May45)
CO .... Maj Quinton R. Johns (to 27Apr45)
Maj John P. McMahon (from 28-Apr45)

Marine Fighter Squadron 213
(USS *Essex*)
(C—3–22Jan45)
(D—15Feb–4Mar45)
CO .... Maj Donald P. Frame (to 28Jan45)
Maj Louis R. Smunk (from 29Jan–4Feb45)
Maj David E. Marshall (from 5-Feb45)

Advance Echelon, Marine Fighter Squadron 216
(USS *Wasp*)
(D—15Feb–4Mar45)
CO .... Maj George E. Dooley

Advance Echelon, Marine Fighter Squadron 217
(USS *Wasp*)
(D—15Feb–4Mar45)
CO .... Maj Jack R. Amende, Jr. (to 16-Feb45)
Maj George E. Buck (from 17Feb-45)

Marine Fighter Squadron 218
(C—10Mar–4Jul45)
CO .... Maj John M. Massey

Advance Echelon, Marine Fighter Squadron 221
(USS *Bunker Hill*)
(D—15Feb–4Mar45)
CO .... Maj Edwin S. Roberts, Jr.

Marine Fighter Squadron 222
(C—11Jan–14May45)
CO .... Maj Roy T. Spurlock (to 27Apr45)
Maj Harold A. Harwood (from 28Apr45)

Flight Echelon, Marine Fighter Squadron 223
(C—19Jan–15May45)
CO .... Maj Robert F. Flaherty (to 24Mar45)
Maj Robert W. Teller (from 25-Mar–16Apr45)
Maj Howard E. King (from 17-Apr45)

Marine Fighter Squadron 224
(A—1Jan44–26Mar45)
CO .... Maj Darrell D. Irwin (to 24Aug44)
Maj Howard A. York (from 24-Aug–31Dec44)
Maj James W. Poindexter (from 31Dec44)

Marine Scout-Bomber Squadron 231
(A—4Feb44–1Aug45)
CO .... Maj Elmer G. Glidden, Jr. (to 4-Sep44)
Maj William E. Abblitt (from 5-Sep44–3Feb45)
Maj Joseph W. White, Jr. (from 3Feb45)

Marine Scout-Bomber Squadron 233
(C—26Jun–6Jul45)
CO .... Capt Edmund W. Berry

Marine Scout-Bomber Squadron 236
Advance Echelon (C—11Jan–4Jul45)
Rear Echelon (C—28Jan–4Jul45)
CO .... Maj Fred J. Frazer

Marine Scout-Bomber Squadron 241
Advance Echelon (C—22Jan–4Jul45)
Rear Echelon (C—25Jan–4Jul45)
CO .... Maj Benjamin B. Manchester, III (to 19Feb45)
Maj Jack L. Brushert (from 20-Feb45)

Advance Echelon, Marine Torpedo-Bomber Squadron 242
(C—8–16Mar45)
CO .... Maj William W. Dean

Marine Scout-Bomber Squadron 243
Ground Echelon (C—22Jan–4Jul45)
Flight Echelon (C—31Jan–4Jul45)
CO .... Maj Joseph W. Kean, Jr.

MARINE TASK ORGANIZATION AND COMMAND LIST 795

Marine Scout-Bomber Squadron 244
Ground Echelon (C—22Jan–4Jul45)
Flight Echelon (C—31Jan–4Jul45)
CO .... Maj Vance H. Hudgins

Marine Scout-Bomber Squadron 245
(A—1Jun44–15Aug45)
CO .... Maj Julian F. Acers (to 23Sep44)
Maj Robert F. Halladay (from 24-Sep44–30Jun45)
Maj John E. Bell (from 1Jul45)

Marine Fighter Squadron 251
(C—2Jan–12May45)
CO .... Maj William C. Humberd (to 9-Feb45)
Maj William L. Bacheler (from 10Feb–14Apr45)
Maj Thomas W. Furlow (from 15-Apr45)

Marine Transport Squadron 252
(D—3–9Mar45)
CO .... LtCol Russell A. Bowen

Marine Transport Squadron 253
(D—3–16Mar45)
CO .... LtCol John V. Kipp (to 9Mar45)
Maj Jack F. McCollum (from 10-Mar45)

Marine Fighter Squadron 311
(A—15May44–20Jan45)
CO .... Maj Harry B. Hooper, Jr. (to 23-Oct44)
Maj Charles M. Kunz (from 24-Oct44)

Marine Fighter Squadron 313
Ground Echelon (C—3Dec44–1Jun45)
Flight Echelon (C—18Dec44–1Jun45)
CO .... Maj Joe J. McGlothin, Jr. (to 26-Apr45)
Capt Jay E. McDonald (from 27–29Apr45)
1stLt John M. Lomac (from 30-Apr45)

Marine Scout-Bomber Squadron 331
Flight Echelon (A—25Feb44–1Aug45)
Ground Echelon (A—2Mar44–1Aug45)

CO .... Maj Paul R. Byrum, Jr. to 9May-44)
Maj James C. Otis (from 10May–15Dec44)
Maj John H. McEniry (16Dec44–2Feb45)
Maj Winston E. Jewson (from 3-Feb45)

Marine Scout-Bomber Squadron 341
Ground Echelon (C—22Jan–4Jul45)
Flight Echelon (C—28Jan–4Jul45)
CO .... Maj Christopher F. Irwin (to 3-May45)
Maj Robert J. Bear (from 4May-45)

Marine Transport Squadron 353
(B—6–14Oct44)
(D—8–16Mar45)
CO .... Maj John R. Walcott

Marine Fighter Squadron 441
(A—1Jan44–6Apr45)
CO .... Maj James B. Moore (to 4Apr44)
Maj Grant W. Metzger (from 5-Apr44–20Jan45)
Maj Robert O. White (from 21-Jan45)

Marine Fighter Squadron 422
(A—24Jan44–25Apr45)
CO .... Maj John S. MacLaughlin, Jr. MIA 24Jan44)
Maj Edwin C. Fry (from 25Jan–1Feb44)
Maj Elmer A. Wrenn (from 2Feb–31Dec44)
Maj Elkin S. Dew (from 1Jan45)

Advance Echelon, Marine Fighter Squadron 451
(USS *Bunker Hill*)
(D—15Feb–4Mar45)
CO .... Maj Henry A. Ellis, Jr.

Marine Fighter Squadron 511
(USS *Block Island*)
(C—26Jun–6Jul45)
CO .... Capt James L. Secrest

Marine Fighter Squadron 512
(USS *Gilbert Islands*)
(C—26Jun–6Jul45)
CO .... Maj Blaine H. Baesler

Marine Night Fighter Squadron 532
(A—27Feb–23Oct44)
CO .... Maj Everett H. Vaughan (to 23-Sep44)
Capt Warren S. Adams II (from 24Sep44)

Marine Night Fighter Squadron 534
(A—4Aug44–15Aug45)
CO .... Maj Ross S. Mickey (to 23May45)
Maj James B. Maguire, Jr. (from 24May–15Jun45)
Maj Clair C. Chamberlain (from 21Jun45)

Marine Night Fighter Squadron 541
Ground Echelon (A—15Sep44–28Aug45)
Flight Echelon (A—24Sep–3Dec44)
Flight Echelon (C—4Dec44–10Jan45)
Flight Echelon (A—11Jan–28Aug45)
CO .... LtCol Peter D. Lambrecht (to 20-Jun45)
Maj Norman L. Mitchell (from 21Jun–7Jul45)
Maj Reynolds A. Moody (from 8Jul45)

Marine Bombing Squadron 611
Ground Echelon (C—17Mar–4Jul45)
Flight Echelon (C—30Mar–4Jul45)
CO .... LtCol George A. Sarles (KIA 30-May45)
Maj Robert R. Davis (from 1–19-Jun45)
Maj David Horne (from 20Jun45)

Marine Bombing Squadron 612
(D—15Feb–16Mar45)
CO .... Maj Lawrence F. Fox

Marine Bombing Squadron 613
(A—23Dec44–26Mar45)
CO .... Maj George W. Nevils

Marine Transport Squadron 952
(B—1–14Oct44)
(D—1–16Mar45)
CO .... Maj Malcolm S. Mackay

APPENDIX H

Marine Casualties[1]

Location and Date	KIA Officer	KIA Enlisted	DOW Officer	DOW Enlisted	WIA Officer	WIA Enlisted	MIAPD Officer	MIAPD Enlisted	TOTAL Officer	TOTAL Enlisted
Marines										
Peleliu[2] (6Sep–14Oct44)	66	984	18	232	301	5,149	0	36	385	6,401
Iwo Jima (19Feb–26Mar45)	215	4,339	60	1,271	826	16,446	3	43	1,104	22,099
Aviation[3]	66	49	3	6	91	212	44	32	204	299
Sea-duty	4	61	0	9	8	142	0	63	12	275
Total Marines	351	5,433	81	1,518	1,226	21,949	47	174	1,705	29,074
Naval Medical Personnel Organic to Marine Units[4]										
Peleliu	1	49	0	11	11	238	0	0	12	298
Iwo Jima	4	183	0	22	19	622	0	0	23	827
Marine Aviation[5]	0	2	0	0	2	10	0	0	4	10
Total Navy	5	234	0	33	32	870	0	0	39	1,135
Grand Total	356	667	0	1,551	1,258	22,817	47	174	1,744	30,209

[1] These final Marine casualty figures were compiled from records furnished by Statistics Unit, Personnel Accounting Section, Records Branch, Personnel Department, HQMC. Figures for the Peleliu Operation were certified and released on 1 June 1950; those for Iwo Jima in August 1952. Naval casualties were taken from NavMed P-5021, *The History of the Medical Department of the Navy in World War II* (Washington: Government Printing Office, 1953). The key to the abbreviations used at the head of columns in the table follows: KIA, Killed in Action; DOW, Died of Wounds; WIA, Wounded in Action; MIAPD, Missing in Action, Presumed Dead. Because of the casualty reporting method used during World War II, a substantial number of DOW figures are also included in the WIA column.

[2] Includes Ngesebus.

[3] Includes bypassed Marshalls, Carolines, Palau, Philippines, and Volcano Bonin Islands, overall period covering February 1944 - June 1945.

[4] See Footnote (1) above.

[5] Time frame identical to (3) above.

APPENDIX I

Unit Commendations

THE SECRETARY OF THE NAVY
Washington

The President of the United States takes pleasure in presenting the PRESIDENTIAL UNIT CITATION to the

FIRST MARINE DIVISION (REINFORCED)

consisting of

FIRST Marine Division; First Amphibian Tractor Battalion, FMF; U.S. Navy Flame Thrower Unit Attached; Sixth Amphibian Tractor Battalion (Provisional), FMF; Third Armored Amphibian Battalion (Provisional), FMF; Detachment Eighth Amphibian Tractor Battalion, FMF; 454th Amphibian Truck Company, U.S. Army; 456th Amphibian Truck Company, U.S. Army; Fourth Joint Assault Signal Company, FMF; Fifth Separate Wire Platoon, FMF; Sixth Separate Wire Platoon, FMF,

for service as set forth in the following

CITATION:

"For extraordinary heroism in action against enemy Japanese forces at Peleliu and Ngesebus from September 15 to 29, 1944. Landing over a treacherous coral reef against hostile mortar and artillery fire, the FIRST Marine Division, Reinforced, seized a narrow, heavily mined beachhead and advanced foot by foot in the face of relentless enfilade fire through rain-forests and mangrove swamps toward the air strip, the key to the enemy defenses of the southern Palaus. Opposed all the way by thoroughly disciplined, veteran Japanese troops heavily entrenched in caves and in reinforced concrete pillboxes which honeycombed the high ground throughout the island, the officers and men of the Division fought with undiminished spirit and courage despite heavy losses, exhausting heat and difficult terrain, seizing and holding a highly strategic air and land base for future operations in the Western Pacific. By their individual acts of heroism, their aggressiveness and their fortitude, the men of the FIRST Marine Division, Reinforced, upheld the highest traditions of the United States Naval Service."

For the President,

JOHN L. SULLIVAN,
Secretary of the Navy

UNIT COMMENDATIONS

EXTRACT

GENERAL ORDERS) 　　　　　　　　　　　　　　　 WAR DEPARTMENT
No. 22　　　　　)　　　　　　　　　　　Washington, D. C., 14 February 1947
　　　　　　　　　　　　　　　　　　　　　　　　　　　　　　　　　Section
BATTLE HONORS — Citation of Unit　　　　　　　　　　　　　　　　XV
XV — BATTLE HONORS.

The Marine Night Fighter Squadron 541 is cited for extraordinary performance of duty in action against the enemy at Leyte, Philippine Islands, from 3 to 15 December 1944. During a critical period in the fight for the control of the Philippine Islands, the pilots and ground crews of this unit signally distinguished themselves by the intrepidity and unyielding determination with which they overcame exceptionally adverse weather conditions and operational difficulties engendered by lack of ground facilities and incomplete radar directional coverage. Their superb airmanship and daring resourcefulness displayed in outstanding night patrol and interception work, which forestalled destruction of airfield facilities, and in the completeness of cover provided for numerous vital convoys and Patrol Torpedo boat patrols, effectively thwarted enemy attempts to prevent consolidation and further expansion of the foothold gained by United States forces in the Philippines. Achieving a record unparalleled at that time, the unit, composed of but 15 aircraft and 22 pilots, flew 136 sorties totaling 298.6 combat hours, destroyed 18 enemy aircraft in aerial combat without unit loss or damage, and on numerous occasions pitted consummate skill and accuracy against overwhelming numerically superior enemy strength. The extraordinary performance of the air and ground personnel of the Marine Fighter Squadron 541 in overcoming the greatest of aerial hazards and maintenance difficulties reflects the highest credit on themselves and the military service of the United States.

BY ORDER OF THE SECRETARY OF WAR:

OFFICIAL:　　　　　　　　　　　　　　　　　　　　　　DWIGHT D. EISENHOWER,
　　　　　　　　　　　　　　　　　　　　　　　　　　　　　　　Chief of Staff
　　EDWARD F. WITSELL
　　Major General
　　The Adjutant General

THE SECRETARY OF THE NAVY
Washington

The President of the Unites States takes pleasure in presenting the PRESIDENTIAL UNIT CITATION to

MARINE AIRCRAFT GROUP TWELVE

for service as set forth in the following

CITATION:
"For extraordinary heroism in action against enemy Japanese forces in the Philippine Islands from December 3, 1944, to March 9, 1945. Operating from the captured airfield at Tacloban, Marine Aircraft Group TWELVE employed Corsairs as bombing planes to strike destructive blows at escorted enemy convoys and to prevent the Japanese from reinforcing their beleagured garrisons by landing troops and supplies on western Leyte. Undeterred by intense aerial opposition and accurate antiaircraft fire, these pilots provided effective cover for ground troops, shore installations and Fleet units and, on several occasions, when ground troops were held up by heavy enemy fire, bombed and strafed Japanese positions, thereby enabling our land forces to advance unopposed. As hostile resistance lessened on Leyte, Marine Aircraft Group TWELVE expanded its sphere of operations to strike at enemy garrisons on the Visayan Islands and southern Luzon and to support the Lingayen beachheads, neutralizing the enemy's lines of communication, his harbors, airfields and escape routes, and ranging far from base to provide aerial cover for ships of the SEVENTH Fleet and merchant-ship convoys operating in the area. During February and the early part of March, this courageous Group gave direct support to Guerrilla units fighting on Cebu Island and aided in their rapid advance and the ultimate neutralization of the island. Well supported by skilled and dependable ground personnel, the gallant pilots of Marine Aircraft Group TWELVE caused the Japanese severe losses in airplanes, installations and surface craft, contributing to the achievement of air superiority so essential to the success of the campaign and thereby upholding the highest traditions of the United States Naval Service."

For the President,

FRANCIS P. MATTHEWS,
Secretary of the Navy

UNIT COMMENDATIONS

The Secretary of the Navy
Washington

The President of the United States takes pleasure in presenting the PRESIDENTIAL UNIT CITATION to

ASSAULT TROOPS OF THE FIFTH AMPHIBIOUS CORPS, REINFORCED
UNITED STATES FLEET MARINE FORCE

for service as set forth in the following

CITATION:
"For extraordinary heroism in action during the seizure of enemy Japanese-held Iwo Jima, Volcano Islands, February 19 to 28, 1945. Landing against resistance which rapidly increased in fury as the Japanese pounded the beaches with artillery, rocket and mortar fire, the Assault Troops of the FIFTH Amphibious Corps inched ahead through shifting black volcanic sands, over heavily mined terrain, toward a garrison of jagged cliffs barricaded by an interlocking system of caves, pillboxes and blockhouses commanding all approaches. Often driven back with terrific losses in fierce hand-to-hand combat, the Assault Troops repeatedly hurled back the enemy's counterattacks to regain and hold lost positions, and continued the unrelenting drive to high ground and Motoyama Airfield No. 1, captured by the end of the second day. By their individual acts of heroism and their unfailing teamwork, these gallant officers and men fought against their own battle-fatigue and shock to advance in the face of the enemy's fanatical resistance; they charged each strongpoint, one by one, blasting out the hidden Japanese troops or sealing them in; within four days they had occupied the southern part of Motoyama Airfield No. 2; simultaneously they stormed the steep slopes of Mount Suribachi to raise the United States Flag; and they seized the strongly defended hills to silence guns commanding the beaches and insure the conquest of Iwo Jima, a vital inner defense of the Japanese Empire."

The following Assault Troops of the FIFTH Amphibious Corps, United States Fleet Marine Force, participated in the Iwo Jima Operation from February 19 to 28, 1945:

9th Marines; 21st Marines; 3rd Engineer Battalion (less detachment); 3rd Tank Battalion; 3rd Joint Assault Signal Company (less detachment); Reconnaissance Company, Headquarters Battalion, THIRD Marine Division; Liaison and Forward Observer Parties, 12th Marines; Pilots and Air Observers, Marine Observation Squadron 1; 23rd Marines; 24th Marines; 25th Marines; Companies A, B, and C, 4th Tank Battalion; Companies A, B, and C, 4th Engineer Battalion; 1st Joint Assault Signal Company; 1st, 2nd, and 3rd Platoons, Military Police Company, Headquarters Battalion, FOURTH Marine Division; Companies A, B, and C, 4th Pioneer Battalion; 10th Amphibian Tractor Battalion; 5th Amphibian Tractor Battalion; Reconnaissance Company, Headquarters Battalion, FOURTH Marine Division; Companies A and B and Detachment,

Headquarters Company, 2nd Armored Amphibian Battalion; 7th Marine War Dog Platoon; Pilots and Air Observers, Marine Observation Squadron 4; Liaison and Forward Observer Parties, 14th Marines; 1st Provisional Rocket Detachment; 26th Marines; 27th Marines; 28th Marines; 5th Engineer Battalion; 5th Tank Battalion; 6th War Dog Platoon; 5th Joint Assault Signal Company; 3rd Amphibian Tractor Battalion; 11th Amphibian Tractor Battalion; Companies A, B, and C, 5th Pioneer Battalion; Reconnaissance Company, Headquarters Battalion, FIFTH Marine Division; 1st, 2nd, and 3rd Platoons, Military Police Company, Headquarters Battalion, FIFTH Marine Division; 3rd Provisional Rocket Detachment; Pilots and Air Observers, Marine Observation Squadron 5; Liaison and Forward Observer Parties, 13th Marines; Companies C, D, and Detachment, Headquarters Company, 2nd Armored Amphibian Battalion.

For the President,

JOHN L. SULLIVAN
Secretary of the Navy

UNIT COMMENDATIONS

The Secretary of the Navy
Washington

The Secretary of the Navy takes pleasure in commending the

III AMPHIBIOUS CORPS SIGNAL BATTALION

for service as set forth in the following

CITATION:
"For extremely meritorious service in support of military operations, while attached to the I Marine Amphibious Corps during the amphibious assault on Bougainville, and attached to the III Amphibious Corps during operations at Guam, Palau and Okinawa, during the period from November 1, 1943 to June 21, 1945. The first American Signal Battalion to engage in amphibious landings in the Pacific Ocean Areas; the III Amphibious Corps Signal Battalion pioneered and developed techniques and procedures without benefit of established precedent, operating with limited and inadequate equipment, particularly in the earlier phase of these offensive actions, and providing its own security while participating in jungle fighting, atoll invasions and occupation of large island masses. Becoming rapidly experienced in guerrilla warfare and the handling of swiftly changing situations, this valiant group of men successfully surmounted the most difficult conditions of terrain and weather as well as unfamiliar technical problems and, working tirelessly without consideration for safety, comfort or convenience, provided the Corps with uninterrupted ship-shore and bivouac communication service continuously throughout this period. This splendid record of achievement, made possible only by the combined efforts, loyalty and courageous devotion to duty of each individual, was a decisive factor in the success of the hazardous Bougainville, Guam, Palau and Okinawa Campaigns and reflects the highest credit upon the III Amphibious Corps Signal Battalion and the United States Naval Service."

All personnel attached to the III Amphibious Corps Signal Battalion who actually participated in one or more of the Bougainville, Guam, Palau and Okinawa operations are hereby authorized to wear the NAVY UNIT COMMENDATION Ribbon.

JAMES FORRESTAL
Secretary of the Navy

The Secretary of the Navy
Washington

The Secretary of the Navy takes pleasure in commending the

THIRD 155-mm. HOWITZER BATTALION

for service as set forth in the following

CITATION:
"For outstanding heroism in support of military operations against enemy Japanese forces on Peleliu, Palau Islands, from 15 to 29 September 1944. Landing on an unestablished beachhead between 300 and 400 yards deep despite rugged terrain and fanatic opposition, the Third 155-mm. Howitzer Battalion established a position across a 200-yard front and emplaced its weapons precariously on top of solid rock within 300 yards of heavily entrenched, well concealed Japanese fortifications on commanding ground. The Battalion effectively utilized its 155-mm. howitzers in the same method of operation as demolitions to pound hostile pillboxes, machine-gun positions and troop concentrations with heavy fire and succeeded in annihilating the enemy, breaking down the hillsides and closing the caves in the sheer coral cliffs with rubble. Ordered later to hold a defensive sector on the front lines, the men and officers of the Battalion functioned effectively as an infantry unit despite the lack of specific training, and resolutely held the line until relieved. Resourceful and daring in the unorthodox employment of howitzers, the Third 155-mm. Howitzer Battalion provided unfailing support vital to the conquest of this strategic enemy stronghold, thereby upholding the highest traditions of the United States Naval Service."

All personnel attached to and serving with the Third 155-mm. Howitzer Battalion during this period are hereby authorized to wear the NAVY UNIT COMMENDATION Ribbon.

FRANCIS P. MATTHEWS
Secretary of the Navy

UNIT COMMENDATIONS

The Secretary of the Navy takes pleasure in commending the

MARINE AIRCRAFT GROUP ELEVEN

for service as follows:

"For outstanding heroism in support of military operations against enemy Japanese forces during the Peleliu Campaign and the consolidation of the Western Carolines from September 15, 1944, to January 31, 1945. Performing valuable service during the early stages of the Peleliu Campaign by coordinating with ground units in unloading, establishing the air base and furnishing riflemen and stretcher bearers, Marine Aircraft Group ELEVEN commenced air operations on September 24 while the airfield was still under direct enemy fire. Assigned the mission of providing close support for ground troops which necessitated utmost precision because of close in-fighting between the opposing forces, the officers and men evolved new and unique tactics as exemplified in the development of steep-angle glide-bombing with varied fuse settings for diversified targets; low-level precision skip-bombing of almost impregnable caves in precipitous cliffs; and the employment of napalm bombs without fuses to be fired simultaneously by phosphorus shells from infantry weapons. By their resourcefulness, courage and skill, the flight personnel and ground crewmen of Marine Aircraft Group ELEVEN achieved an illustrious combat record in keeping with the highest traditions of the United States Naval Service."

All personnel attached to and serving with Marine Aircraft Group ELEVEN, consisting of Headquarters and Headquarters Squadron, Marine Aircraft Group ELEVEN; Marine Service Squadron, Marine Aircraft Group ELEVEN; Marine Fighting Squadron ONE HUNDRED FOURTEEN; Marine Fighting Squadron ONE HUNDRED TWENTY ONE; Marine Fighting Squadron ONE HUNDRED TWENTY TWO; Marine Night Fighting Squadron FIVE HUNDRED FORTY ONE; and Marine Torpedo Bombing Squadron ONE HUNDRED THIRTY FOUR, from September 15, 1944, to January 31, 1945, are authorized to wear the NAVY UNIT COMMENDATION Ribbon.

JOHN L. SULLIVAN
Secretary of the Navy

THE SECRETARY OF THE NAVY
Washington

The Secretary of the Navy takes pleasure in commending the

EIGHTH 155-mm. GUN BATTALION

for service as set forth in the following

CITATION:
"For outstanding heroism in action against enemy Japanese forces on Peleliu, Palau Islands, from 17 to 29 September 1944. Landing heavy material over treacherous coral reefs in the face of fanatic opposition, the Eighth 155-mm. Gun Battalion pushed forward to the southern edge of the airfield where the enemy was concentrating the fire of heavy mortars and anti-boat and anti-tank guns. Undeterred by infiltrating Japanese troops and intense mortar barrages, this Battalion went into firing position and rendered effective support to the Eighty-First Army Division. Moving around the outlying islands in LVT'S equipped with radar, this gallant Battalion prevented the reinforcement of hostile defenses on Peleliu and, in the later stages, denied routes of escape to the remnants of the defending garrison. When the infantry was confronted by an almost impenetrable barrier of man-made and natural defenses which withstood the onslaughts of tank and demolition squads and the fire of mortars, machine guns and small arms, elements of the Battalion moved forward and boldly emplaced a 155-mm. gun in an unprotected position close to the enemy. Braving intense hostile fire which caused several casualties, this indomitable group courageously fired its weapon at point-blank range and succeeded in exploding concealed ammunition dumps, annihilating the enemy and completely eliminating the strong point, thus permitting the infantry to clear the area. By their valor, determination and fighting spirit, the officers and men of the Eighth 155-mm. Gun Battalion rendered invaluable service in breaking down the enemy's resistance and in hastening the conquest of this strategic Japanese stronghold, achieving a gallant combat record in keeping with the highest traditions of the United States Naval Service."

All personnel attached to and serving with the Eighth 155-mm. Gun Battalion during this period are hereby authorized to wear the NAVY UNIT COMMENDATION Ribbon.

FRANCIS P. MATTHEWS
Secretary of the Navy

UNIT COMMENDATIONS 807

THE SECRETARY OF THE NAVY
Washington

The Secretary of the Navy takes pleasure in commending the

MARINE BOMBING SQUADRON SIX HUNDRED TWELVE

for service as follows:

"For outstanding heroism in action against enemy Japanese forces during numerous offensive missions in the Central Pacific Area from November 1, 1944, to May 31, 1945. Aggressive and courageous in the execution of their manifold assignments, the pilots and aircrewmen of Marine Bombing Squadron SIX HUNDRED TWELVE served heroically despite severe weather and relentless opposition in a series of air-sea rescues, special experimental operations and highly successful night, low-level rocket attacks against strongly defended shipping and shore installations. By their expert airmanship and superb skill, they saved the lives of several B-29 crews, developed and tested valuable new technical equipment and destroyed or extensively damaged 29 Japanese ships. This outstanding record of service and combat achievement, made possible only by the teamwork and steadfast devotion to duty of the pilots, flight crews and maintenance men of Marine Bombing Squadron SIX HUNDRED TWELVE, is in keeping with the highest traditions of the United States Naval Service."

The pilots, aircrewmen and ground crews attached to Marine Bombing Squadron SIX HUNDRED TWELVE during the above mentioned period are hereby authorized to wear the NAVY UNIT COMMENDATION Ribbon.

JAMES FORRESTAL
Secretary of the Navy

The Secretary of the Navy
Washington

The Secretary of the Navy takes pleasure in commending the

MARINE AIRCRAFT GROUP THIRTY-TWO

for service as follows:

"For exceptionally meritorious service in support of the United States SIXTH Army in the Lingayen Gulf and Manila, Philippine Islands, Areas, from January 23 to March 15, 1945. After landing at Lingayen with the assault forces on D-day, Marine Aircraft Group THIRTY-TWO operated continuously against Japanese forces, flying a series of more than 8,000 daring and brilliantly executed sorties despite relentless air and ground force opposition. Dauntless and determined, these units penetrated numerous hostile defenses ahead of our advancing troops and, destroying vital ammunition and fuel dumps, bridges, gun bastions and troop concentrations, effectively reduced the enemy's power to resist and contributed materially to our ground forces' sweeping victory in this area. The heroic achievements of Marine Aircraft Group THIRTY-TWO reflect the skill, personal valor and steadfast devotion to duty of these courageous officers and men, and are in keeping with the highest traditions of the United States Naval Service."

All personnel of the United States Armed forces serving with Marine Aircraft Group THIRTY-TWO during the above period are hereby authorized to wear the NAVY UNIT COMMENDATION Ribbon.

JAMES FORRESTAL
Secretary of the Navy

UNIT COMMENDATIONS

THE SECRETARY OF THE NAVY
Washington

The Secretary of the Navy takes pleasure in commending the

MARINE AIRCRAFT GROUP TWENTY-FOUR

for service as follows:

"For exceptionally meritorious service in support of the United States SIXTH Army in the Lingayen Gulf and Manila, Philippine Islands Area, from January 23 to April 10, 1945. After landing at Lingayen with the assault forces on D-day, Marine Aircraft Group TWENTY-FOUR operated continuously against Japaneses forces, flying a series of more tha n 8,000 daring and brilliantly executed sorties despite relentless air and ground force opposition. Dauntless and determined, these units penetrated numerous hostile defenses ahead of our advancing troops and, destroying vital ammunition and fuel dumps, bridges, gun bastions and troop concentrations, effectively reduced the enemy's power to resist and contributed materially to the sweeping victory of our ground forces in this area. The heroic achievements of Marine Aircraft Group TWENTY-FOUR reflect the skill, personal valor and steadfast devotion to duty of these courageous officers and men, and are in keeping with the highest traditions of the United States Naval Service."

All personnel of the United States Armed Forces serving with Aircraft Group TWENTY-FOUR during the above period are hereby authorized to wear the NAVY UNIT COMMENDATION Ribbon.

JAMES FORRESTAL
Secretary of the Navy

THE SECRETARY OF THE NAVY
Washington

The Secretary of the Navy takes pleasure in commending the

SUPPORT UNITS OF THE FIFTH AMPHIBIOUS CORPS
UNITED STATES FLEET MARINE FORCE

for service as follows:

"For outstanding heroism in support of Military Operations during the seizure of enemy Japanese-held Iwo Jima, Volcano Islands, February 19 to 28, 1945. Landing against resistance which rapidly increased in fury as the Japanese pounded the beaches with artillery, rocket and mortar fire, the Support Units of the FIFTH Amphibious Corps surmounted the obstacles of chaotic disorganization, loss of equipment, supplies and key personnel to develop and maintain a continuous link between thousands of assault troops and supply ships. Resourceful and daring whether fighting in the front line of combat, or serving in rear areas or on the wreck-obstructed beaches, they were responsible for the administration of operations and personnel; they rendered effective fire support where Japanes pressure was greatest; they constructed roads and facilities and maintained communications under the most difficult and discouraging conditions of weather and rugged terrain; they salvaged vital supplies from craft lying crippled in the surf or broached on the beaches; and they ministered to the wounded under fire and provided prompt evacuation to hospital ships. By their individual initiative and heroism and their ingenious teamwork, they provided the unfailing support vital to the conquest of Iwo Jima, a powerful defense of the Japanese Empire."

All personnel attached to and serving with the following Support Units of the FIFTH Amphibiius Corps, United States Fleet Marine Force, during the Iwo Jima Operation from February 19 to 28, 1945, are authorized to wear the NAVY UNIT COMMENDATION Ribbon.

Headquarters & Service Battalion; Medical Battalion; Signal Battalion; Motor Transport Company; Detachment, 1st Separate Radio Intelligence Platoon; Detachment, Signal, Headquarters, Air Warning Squadron 7 - Army Fighter Command; Detachment, 568th Signal Air Warning Battalion - Army; Detachment, 726th Signal Air Warning Company - Army; Detachment, 49th Signal Construction Battalion - Army; Detachment 44 - 70th Army Airways Communications Service - Army; Detachment, Communication Unit 434 (Group Pacific 11); Landing Force Air Support Control Unit No. 1; 2nd Separate Engineer Battalion; 62nd Naval Construction Battalion; 2nd Separate Topographical Company; Detachment, 23rd Naval Construction Battalion (Special); 8th Field Depot (plus Headquarters Shore Party); 33rd Marine Depot Company; 34th Marine Depot Company; 36th Marine Depot Company; 8th Marine Ammunition Company; Detachment, 8th Naval Construction Regiment; Corps Evacuation Hospital No. 1; 2nd Bomb Disposal Company; 156th Bomb Disposal Squad - Army; Company B, Amphibious Reconnaissance Battalion, Fleet Marine Force; A and C Platoons, 38th Field Hospital - Army; Joint Intelligence Corps, Pacific Ocean Area, Intelligence Teams No. 22, 23, 24, and 25; **Detachment,**

Joint Intelligence Corps, Pacific Ocean Area, Enemy Materiel and Salvage Platoon; Detachment, 1st Platoon, 239th Quartermaster Salvage and Collection Company - Army; Detachment, Headquarters, Army Garrison Forces, APO 86; Detachment Headquarters, 147th Infantry - Army; Detachment, Headquarters, 7th Fighter Command - Army; Detachment, 47th Fighter Squadron - Army; Detachment, 548th Night Fighter Squadron - Army; Detachment, 386th Air Service Group (Special) - Army; Detachment, Group Pacific 11; Detachment, Port Director; Detachment, Garrison Beach Party; Headquarters & Service Battery, 1st Provisional Artillery Group; 2nd 155-mm. Howitzer Battalion; 4th 155-mm. Howitzer Battalion; 473rd Amphibian Truck Company - Army; Detachment, Headquarters & Headquarters Battery, 138th Antiaircraft Artillery Group - Army; Detachment, 506th Antiaircraft Gun Battalion - Army; Detachment, 483rd Antiaircraft Air Warning Battalion - Army; 28th and 34th Replacement Drafts (less Advance Groups and those assigned assault units); Headquarters Battalion, THIRD Marine Division, (less Reconnaissance Company); 3rd Marine War Dog Platoon; 3rd Service Battalion (less detachment); 3rd Pioneer Battalion (less 2nd Platoon, Company C), 3rd Medical Battalion (less Company C); 3rd Motor Transport Battalion (less Company C); 12th Marines (less detachment); Marine Observation Squadron 1 (less detachment); Headquarters Battalion, FOURTH Marine Division, (less Reconnaissance Company and 1st, 2nd, and 3rd Platoons, Military Police Company); 4th Motor Transport Battalion; 4th Medical Battalion; 133rd Naval Construction Battalion; 4th Tank Battalion (less Companies A, B, and C); 4th Engineer Battalion (less Companies A, B, and C); 4th Service Battalion; 4th Pioneer Battalion (less Companies A, B, and C); 442nd Port Company - Army; 14th Marines (less detachment); 4th Marine Amphibian Truck Company; 476th Amphibian Truck Company - Army; Marine Observation Squadron 4 (less detachment); Detachment, 726th Signal Air Warning Company - Army (FOURTH Marine Division- Reinf.); 24th and 30th Replacement Drafts (less Advance Groups and those assigned assault units); Headquarters Battalion, FIFTH Marine Division, (less Reconnaissance Company and 1st, 2nd, and 3rd Platoons, Military Police Company); 5th Medical Battalion; 13th Marines (less detachment); 5th Marine Amphibian Truck Company; 471st Amphibian Truck Company - Army; Marine Observation Squadron 5 (less detachment); Detachment, 726th Signal Air Warning Company - Army (FIFTH Marine Division-Reinf.); 5th Pioneer Battalion (less Companies A, B, and C); 31st Naval Construction Battalion; 592nd Port Company - Army; 5th Motor Transport Battalion; 5th Service Battalion; 27th and 31st Replacement Drafts (less Advance Groups and those assigned assault units).

JOHN L. SULLIVAN
Secretary of the Navy

The Secretary of the Navy
Washington

The Secretary of the Navy takes pleasure in commending

MARINE AIRCRAFT GROUPS, ZAMBOANGA

consisting of the following Marine Aircraft Groups:

Marine Aircraft Group TWELVE	March 10 - June 30, 1945
Marine Aircraft Group THIRTY TWO	March 16 - June 30, 1945
Marine Aircraft Group TWENTY FOUR	April 11 - June 30, 1945

for service as set forth in the following

CITATION:
"For exceptionally meritorious service and outstanding heroism in support of elements of the EIGHTH Army during operations against enemy Japanese forces on Mindanao, Philippine Islands, and in the Sulu Archipelago. After landing with the assault forces, Marine Air Groups, ZAMBOANGA, effected wide coverage of battle areas in flights made extremely hazardous by dense jungles, precipitous cloud-obscured mountains and adverse weather conditions. The gallant officers and men of these Groups penetrated hostile defenses to press relentless attacks and reduce vital enemy targets, disrupt communications and troop concentrations, and destroy ammunition and fuel dumps despite intense antiaircraft fire over Japanese objectives. The vital service rendered during these campaigns in providing convoy cover, fighter defense and close aerial support of ground forces is evidence of the courage, skill and devotion to duty of the pilots, aircrewmen and ground personnel operating as a well coordinated team, and reflects the highest credit upon Marine Aircraft Groups, ZAMBOANGA, and the United States Naval Service."

All personnel attached to and serving with Marine Aircraft Group 12, 32 or 24 during their respective periods of service as designated are authorized to wear the NAVY UNIT COMMENDATION Ribbon.

FRANCIS P. MATTHEWS
Secretary of the Navy

Index

Abuyog, 310, 321-322
ACETYLENE Island, 181n, 183-184
Acker, Capt George K., 314
Adams, Maj Hank, 248
Admiralty Islands, 67, 83, 292, 315, 363, 407
Advance Base Force, 14, 16
Advance base warfare, 14
AGGRAVATE, 181n, 183
  Aineman Island, 414
Ainsworth, RAdm Walden L., 278
Air activities
  American, 43, 95, 99, 227, 236, 340, 363, 368, 373, 381, 388, 718, 735
    air alerts, 624
    air attacks, 172, 450, 455-456, 735
    air combat, 278, 378, 385, 434, 561
    air coordination, 305-306, 354, 377, 385
    air cover, 328
    air defense, 319, 326, 598, 708
    air drops, 597
    air escort, 601
    air freight, 604
    air gunfire, 280, 605, 719
    air liaison officers, 171, 352-353, 390
    air liaison parties, 106n, 277, 283, 306-308, 342-344, 349, 351, 353, 356, 368, 370, 378, 718, 735
    airlift, 723
    air neutralization, 184
    air preparation, 210
    air observation, 281, 317, 320, 373, 600, 668, 671, 686, 719
    air observers, 660, 707, 718
    air offensive, 492
    air photography, 163, 368, 472, 474, 486
    air raids, 717, 729
    air reconnaissance, 382, 486
    air-sea rescue, 103, 717
    air strikes, 135-137, 141-142, 157, 172, 177, 224, 226, 241-242, 249, 260, 282-283, 306, 314, 327, 332, 335, 342, 346, 350-354, 366-367, 370, 372, 381, 383, 386, 399, 412, 415, 423, 430, 435, 453, 472-473, 485-486, 490, 500, 504, 534, 551, 558, 562-563, 586, 591-592, 601, 611, 638, 643-644, 648, 665, 668, 672, 676, 698, 714-715, 717-718, 735
    air superiority, 670, 728
    air supply, 725
    air support, 63, 97, 101, 153, 180, 211, 256, 283-284, 303, 306, 309, 350, 354, 356, 373, 384, 531, 538, 547, 555, 558, 611, 636, 643, 684, 686, 691, 699, 717
      bombing support, 190, 221, 728
      carrier-based support, 76-77, 106n, 283, 292, 306, 340, 424, 436, 489, 491, 737
      close air support, 17, 83, 99, 216, 283-284, 291, 304-307, 328, 332, 339-340, 343, 347, 349, 352-353, 368, 370, 378, 384-385, 387-388, 390, 393, 397, 423, 435, 440, 495, 512, 598, 640, 655, 699, 714, 718, 735
    dive bombing, 305, 374, 388
    emergency landings, 325, 438, 464, 597-598, 601
    fighter missions, 291
    ground controllers, 328, 385
    rocket strikes, 141, 506
    strafing, 190, 211, 221, 283
  Japanese
    air attacks, 71, 190, 318-319, 325, 328, 330, 335, 400, 413, 451, 570
    air defense, 298
    air efforts, 337, 375, 396
    air garrisons, 340, 734
    air neutralization, 309
    air power, 309, 331, 405, 432, 597
    air strength, 298, 331, 336, 379, 393, 405, 450, 466, 530, 601, 731
    air support, 70, 670
Aircraft
  American, 81, 184, 199, 210-211, 224, 262, 264, 329, 350, 361-362, 376, 381, 393, 412, 417, 422-423, 493n, 548, 554, 644, 716, 720
    Types
      B-24s (Liberators), 101-102, 193, 218, 399, 459, 473, 485 485n, 487, 495-496, 499, 504, 717
      B-25s (Mitchells), 353, 412
      B-29s (Super Fortresses), 429, 429n, 438, 462-464, 476, 479, 487, 597-598, 600-601, 679, 683, 731
      bombers, 43, 59, 325, 400, 407, 413, 430,

813

462, 487, 500, 503–504, 598, 717, 734
C–46s (Commandos), 199, 604
C–47s (Skytrains), 199, 326, 604
C–54s (Skymasters), 427
carrier-based, 5, 40, 64, 77, 82, 102–103, 108, 141–142, 152–153, 165, 232, 298, 301, 422, 436, 495–496, 500, 530, 574, 587, 595, 610, 621, 623, 633, 638-640, 718
dive bombers, 43, 143, 340, 342–344, 346–347, 350, 352, 359, 370, 378–379, 382–383, 385, 393, 407, 412, 422, 718
escort fighters 439, 600–601
F4Us (Corsairs), 99, 143, 211, 228, 256, 284, 326–332, 335, 339, 365, 368, 371–372, 375, 378, 383, 399, 401–402, 404, 408, 412–414, 416, 428–429, 432–433, 436, 503
F6Fs (Hellcats), 100, 199, 326–327, 333, 371, 399, 412, 427, 429, 436, 451–452
F6F–Ns, 429, 432
FMs, 371
fighter-bombers, 108, 386, 412, 416, 429
fighters, 58, 172, 328, 350, 362, 379, 382–383, 399, 404, 407, 413, 422, 429, 435, 452, 495, 499, 503, 576, 597, 600, 691, 718
floatplanes, 101
flying boats, 367, 439
J2F–6s, 429
L–4s, 317, 370
L–5s, 212
medium bombers, 43, 325, 382–383, 429
night fighters, 193, 199, 326–328, 330, 333, 371, 400, 411, 413, 422, 425, 429, 526, 560
OS2Us, 495
OYs, 429, 432, 595
observation planes, 101, 426, 429, 436–437, 495, 595, 617, 658, 718, 720
P–40s, 329
P–47s, 423
P–51s, 436, 464, 598, 643, 643n
P–61s, 326, 328, 371, 526, 598
PBJs (Mitchells), 371, 373–374, 380, 387, 429, 436, 485
PBYs, 199, 371
R4Ds (Skytrains), 371, 408, 437–438, 597
R5Cs (Commandos), 437, 597
reconnaissance planes, 415, 417
SB2Cs (Helldivers), 371, 389, 418

SBDs (Dauntlesses), 339, 342–344, 346, 353–354, 356–357, 370–371, 378, 383–386, 388, 399, 414
spotting planes, 317–318, 386, 436, 714
TBFs (Avengers), 193, 318, 371, 426, 429,, 433–434
TBMs (Avengers), 429
torpedo bombers, 43, 422, 424, 426–427, 429, 432, 576, 595
transports, 325, 356, 632-363, 401, 412, 422, 438, 480, 597, 604
utility planes, 429
Japanese, 71, 259, 276, 278, 300, 312, 324, 328, 366–367, 382, 429, 450, 484, 732
Types
Bettys (medium bombers), 276, 356
bombers, 407, 411, 413, 452
carrier-based, 300
dive bombers, 330
fighters, 101, 327–330, 375, 400, 412, 451–452
float planes, 71, 228, 259
heavy bombers, 300
Lilys (light bombers), 374
medium bombers, 276
night bombers, 326
night fighters, 326, 330
torpedo bombers, 330, 451-452
transports, 321–322
Zeros (fighters), 399, 404, 412, 451–452, 495
Airfield No. 1 (Iwo Jima), 449n, 459, 471, 479, 495, 504, 514–516, 518–519, 525, 528, 547, 549, 551, 557, 560, 563–565, 571, 595, 597–598, 600, 603–604, 633, 651, 716, 720
Airfield No. 2 (Iwo Jima), 447, 449n, 459, 471, 479, 509, 525, 548, 555–558, 561–563, 565–567, 569, 574–576, 586, 595, 597, 600, 616, 644–647, 649, 701, 716, 720
Airfield No. 3 (Iwo Jima), 459, 574, 578, 581–586, 600, 684, 708
Airfields
American, 58, 118, 152–153, 162, 173, 177, 179, 181, 187, 189, 192–193, 199, 204, 212, 214, 217, 222–224, 227–228, 237, 241, 259, 268, 273–274, 277–281, 287, 298, 314–315, 319, 323, 325, 339, 361, 363, 365, 463, 485n, 600–601, 608
Japanese, 58, 117, 120–124, 126, 131, 134, 139, 141, 144, 156, 161, 180, 324, 336, 393, 395–396, 405
AK–*98*, 316

INDEX   815

Akalokul, 58
Akarakoro Point, 190
Aleutian Islands, 6, 21, 23, 467, 730, 734
Allender, LCdr Byron E., 151*n*
Allied
  air effort, 736
  invasion fleet, 340
  invasion, North Africa, 733
  news service, 612
  planners, 614
  powers, 613
  prisoners of war, 730
  ships, 336
Allied Forces, 5, 54, 179, 301, 382, 440, 448, 729, 730, 732, 734
Allies, Western, 729
AMAZEMENT Island, 181, 181*n*, 183
AMELIORATE, 181*n*, 183–184. *See also* Falalop Island.
Amiangai, 208
Ammunition
  American, 87–88, 128, 152, 240, 269, 279, 318, 476–477, 492, 523, 553, 601, 611, 678, 689, 720, 722
    artillery, 88, 127, 603, 610
    bombs, 108, 227, 408, 530, 534, 548, 551, 565, 613, 644, 691
    8-inch, 363, 587, 610
    81mm mortar, 152, 209, 523, 526, 563, 597
    15-inch, 587
    .50 caliber, 414, 551
    5-inch, 610
    14-inch, 145, 563, 565, 610
    40mm, 261, 315, 497, 505
    gas shells, 613
    high-explosive shells, 145, 156
    machine gun, 87, 127, 173
    mortar shells, 597, 611
    napalm bombs, 224–225, 249, 254, 256, 271, 283–284, 370, 378–379, 385–386, 416, 432, 436, 487, 499, 503, 506, 523, 530, 536, 611, 638, 658, 677, 717
    155mm howitzer, 587
    105mm, 152, 587, 672
    pyrotechnics, 258
    rockets, 241, 387, 418, 436, 481, 495, 497, 503, 505, 530, 534, 551, 565, 590, 611, 623, 631, 638, 649, 674, 685, 707, 727, 729
    75mm, 155, 587, 615, 644, 650, 672, 705
    16-inch, 610
    smoke, 154, 160, 206, 209, 230, 262, 352, 497, 501, 568, 589, 635
    star shells, 152, 270, 281, 526, 589, 610, 678–679, 725
    .30 caliber, 173
    tracer, 408
    12-inch, 610
    20mm, 261, 315, 578
  Japanese, 226, 249, 530, 654, 695
    aerial bombs, 72, 193, 258, 375, 636*n*
    aerial torpedos, 565–566
    antipersonnel bombs, 424
    armor-piercing shells, 123, 513
    artillery, 231, 367, 527, 545
    .50 caliber, 415, 420
    gas shells, 624
    illuminating, 258
    mortar, 526, 662, 673, 675, 727
Amoy, 293, 465
Amphibious assault operations, 10, 13–17, 33–34, 43, 71, 84, 168, 211, 278–279, 281, 286, 304, 359, 448, 463, 478, 487, 505, 715
Amphibious doctrine, tactics, 10, 268, 737
Amphibious exercises, 14, 162, 483
Amphibious Training Command, 304
Amphitheater, 568, 572, 595, 616, 646–648, 650, 656–657, 661, 663–665, 667, 671–672, 681–682
Anderson, Capt Carl E., 602; RAdm, 602 *n*
Angat River, 346
Angaur, 52, 55, 57, 59, 62–63, 68–69, 79–80, 88, 134, 161–163, 165–166, 168–169, 171–175, 177–179, 181, 183–184, 187, 223, 279, 284–287, 430–431, 433, 733–734
  operation, 166, 173, 177–178, 180
Annapolis, Maryland, 14
Anso, Maj Kenro, 659
Antonelli, Maj. John W. A., 508, 514, 618, 642–643
Apamama Island, 398–399, 413
Apennine Peninsula, 733
Apra Harbor, 426
Arakabesan, 57
Ardennes, 729
  offensive, 735
Arkansas, 493, 503
Armor. *See also* Army Units; Marine Units; Weapons.
  American, 153–154, 158, 172, 212, 235, 272–273, 512, 514–515, 517, 519, 534, 549, 554, 565–567, 584, 592, 618, 621, 623, 628, 631–632, 637, 639, 647–649, 662, 672–673, 676, 687, 691, 727
  Japanese, 123

Armstrong, PFC P. E., 344n
Army Air Forces, 102, 307, 309, 325, 332, 359, 361, 366, 377, 386, 393, 396, 407, 436, 462, 464, 486–487, 496, 500, 640, 699, 712
  Units
    Far East Air Forces, 301, 303, 324–325, 359, 365, 388
    Strategic Air Forces, 417
    Fifth Air Force, 78, 101, 301, 307, 312, 326, 328, 332–334, 339, 353, 382, 389
    Seventh Air Force, 396, 412, 473, 485, 717
    Thirteenth Air Force, 301, 309, 334, 359, 362, 366, 368, 377, 382, 384, 390
    Fourteenth Air Force, 334
    Twentieth Air Force, 334
    VII Bomber Command, 485, 485n
    XX Bomber Command, 463–464
    V Fighter Command, 333
    VII Fighter Command, 603, 710
    XIII Fighter Command, 388
    308th Bombardment Wing, 339, 342–344, 346, 349, 354
    310th Bombardment Wing, 331
    313th Bombardment Wing, 487
    15th Fighter Group, 598, 598n
    21st Fighter Group, 708
    48th Bombardment Squadron, 412
    419th Night Fighter Squadron, 368
    28th Photographic Reconnaissance Squadron, 473
    9th Troop Carrier Squadron, 438, 597, 604
    973d Aviation Engineer Battalion, 367
    465th Aviation Squadron, 708
    76th Fighter Control Center, 368
    77th Fighter Control Center, 371, 383
Army-Navy joint communications procedure, 35
Army Units
  Chemical Warfare Service, 477, 613
  Field Service Command, 30
  Pacific Ocean Areas, 476
  Southwest Pacific Area, 291, 293, 293n
  Garrison Force Zero, 603
  Sixth Army, 309–310, 315–316, 320–321, 325, 334, 337, 339–340, 342, 348–349, 357–359
  Eighth Army, 332, 358–359, 365, 367, 374, 382
  Tenth Army, 38, 465
  I Corps, 20, 352
  X Corps, 310, 315, 319, 321, 337, 359, 381–384, 386–387
  XIV Corps, 303, 337, 342, 352

  XXIV Corps, 63, 65, 301, 314–321, 323
  XXIV Corps Artillery, 314, 319, 323
  Americal Division, 375–377
  1st Cavalry Division, 301, 310, 334, 342–344, 346–348, 351–352, 354
  1st Infantry Division, 20, 34, 353
  3d Infantry Division, 34
  6th Infantry Division, 352–354
  7th Infantry Division, 34, 310, 315–318, 321, 400
  9th Infantry Division, 34, 36, 315
  11th Airborne Division, 322, 354
  24th Infantry Division, 310, 365, 384, 387, 390
  25th Infantry Division, 354
  31st Infantry Division, 381, 384–386, 390
  32d Infantry Division, 310
  37th Infantry Division, 307, 346, 354
  38th Infantry Division, 354
  40th Infantry Division, 354, 375–376
  41st Infantry Division, 359, 362, 366–368, 370–371, 373–374, 378–379, 390
  43d Infantry Division, 354
  77th Infantry Division, 63, 181, 310, 328, 332, 427
  81st Infantry Division, 63, 79, 96, 153, 162–163, 165, 170, 175, 177–180, 186–187, 250, 252, 254, 258, 260, 262, 264, 274, 282, 284–286. *See also* Wildcats.
  96th Infantry Division, 180–181, 310, 315–316, 318, 321
  1st Cavalry Brigade, 354
  Infantry Regiments
    20th, 315
    33d, 315
    124th, 385
    147th, 608, 708, 711
    162d, 374
    163d, 374
    321st, 166, 168–171, 173–176, 178, 180, 186–187, 190, 192–193, 197, 201–202, 204, 209, 217–218, 221–224, 237, 242, 246, 249, 251, 254, 261
    322d, 166, 168–173, 176, 178–180
    323d, 163, 168, 180–181, 183–184, 251, 257–259, 264
  726th Amphibian Tractor Batallion, 254
  287th Artillery Observation Battalion, 314, 316–318, 322
  506th Antiaircraft Artillery Battalion, 603, 708
  154th Engineer Battalion, 254

INDEX

Field Artillery Battalions
  198th, 314, 316–317, 319
  226th, 314, 316–320
Infantry Battalions
  1/162, 371
  1/321, 170–171, 173–176, 189, 192, 210, 254, 256–257
  1/322, 171–174
  1/323, 250, 254, 256–257, 262
  2/15, 190, 226
  2/162, 371
  2/321, 173–174, 176, 178, 189, 192, 195, 197, 199, 201, 206–207, 214, 223, 250, 254, 256–257
  2/322, 171–174, 176, 187, 193
  2/323, 257, 260–262
  3/124, 385
  3/321, 173–176, 187, 189, 192, 195, 198, 200, 206–207, 250, 254, 257
  3/322, 171–174, 197, 199
  6th Ranger Battalion, 310
  710th Tank Battalion, 174, 187, 224, 228–229, 240, 254
  471st Amphibian Truck Company, 475, 516
  295th Joint Assault Signal Company, 384
  442d Port Company, 602
  592d Port Company, 602
  38th Field Hospital, 603, 710
Arnold, MajGen William H., 377, 463–464
Artillery
  American, 80–81, 84, 103, 129, 132, 135, 137, 142, 151–153, 157, 161, 173, 175, 187, 190, 195, 205, 208, 210, 224, 242, 244, 246, 254, 269, 272, 274, 281, 291, 300–301, 314, 316–320, 322–323, 379–380, 416, 423, 484, 504, 508, 516, 521, 530–531, 534, 538, 549–550, 552, 554–556, 560, 563, 565–567, 573, 576–585, 587, 589, 591, 605, 611, 617, 623–624, 626–627, 632–635, 638–639, 648–652, 654, 658, 661–663, 666–669, 671–674, 676, 679, 681, 684, 686, 691, 697 699, 704, 708, 714, 717, 719–722, 726–727
  Filipino, 348
  Japanese, 109, 115, 122, 127–128, 134, 141–142, 156, 177, 278, 350, 407, 453–454, 454n, 456–457, 474, 493n, 497–498, 519–520, 525–526, 531, 533–534, 538, 545, 549 551, 553–554, 557–558, 561, 564, 566, 568, 570, 575, 582, 584, 586–587, 595, 597, 603, 617, 624, 626, 629, 647, 651, 653, 655–656, 658, 662, 666, 669,
  671, 674, 677, 718, 723, 726
Asbill, Maj Edward L., 671
Asia, 294
  Eastern, 735
  Southeast, 51, 294, 463
Asias (village), 58–59, 148
Aslito Airfield, 423–424
Atlantic Ocean, 21, 444
Atomic warfare, 737. *See also* Weapons.
Atsuchi, Capt Kanehiko, 533n; Col, 533, 533n, 536, 537n, 538, 542
Attu, 467, 734
Auburn, 605, 607, 619
Auckland, New Zealand, 431
Aur Atoll, 418
Auriga, 314, 316
Australia, 291, 444
Aviators. *See* Pilots.
Axis, 736
Aycrigg, Lt William A., 403
Azores, 43

Babelthuap Island, 57, 60–62, 68–69, 79, 162–163, 166, 175, 190, 193, 222, 225, 232, 241–242, 262, 264–265, 281, 432–433, 733–734
Baker, Maj Harry F., 437
Baker, Col R. M., 15
Baldy Ridge, 224, 226, 228, 234, 237–238, 241–242, 244–245
Balete Pass, 357
Baliuag, 346
Balkans, 443, 729
Ballance, LtCol Robert G., 84, 86
Baltic Sea, 443
Bangkal, 379
Bangkok, 463
Banika Island, 89–90, 95, 393, 400
Bard, Capt Elliott E., 42
Basilan Island, 374
Basilan Strait, 363, 366, 374
Basilone, GySgt John, 514
Bataan Peninsula, 348, 690
Batangas Peninsula, 342
Bates, Lt Wesley C., 512
Battle for Leyte Gulf, 312, 321, 323, 443
Battle of Midway, 430
Battle of the Philippine Sea, 443
Baybay, 310, 321
Bayfield, 648
Bayug Airfield, 325
Beach, Capt C. C., 415n
Beaches, 58, 72, 77, 79, 86–87, 94, 118, 121, 128,

131, 259–260, 274, 472, 482, 527, 603, 617, 623, 717, 722, 724
Blue, 163, 165–166, 168–169, 508, 519, 525, 557
Blue 1, 316, 471, 471n, 508, 519–521, 548
Blue 2, 471, 471n, 519–521, 525
Brown, 602
Green, 165, 169, 471, 513, 516, 526
Green 1, 471, 508, 510
Green 2, 173
Orange, 79, 81–82, 106, 108, 119n, 137, 187, 232, 268, 602
Orange 1, 80, 115
Orange 2, 80, 115–117, 121, 129
Orange 3, 80, 116, 119, 119n, 120, 131, 152, 233
Purple, 187, 201, 228, 236, 251, 258, 268, 274, 602–603
Purple 2, 603
Red, 163, 165–166, 168, 176, 472, 508, 514
Red 1, 471, 508, 512–513, 515, 552
Red 2, 471, 508, 513, 515
Scarlet, 193
White, 79–82, 106, 108, 110, 144, 264, 268, 274, 602
White 1, 108–110, 112
White 2, 110
Yellow, 424, 508–509, 517, 525, 555
Yellow 1, 471, 508, 517–518, 522, 526, 548, 552, 560
Yellow 2, 471, 508, 516–517, 519
Beachheads, 73, 85, 430. *See also* Beaches.
Beachmasters, 85, 87
Beach parties, 282, 601. *See also* Shore party activities.
Belgium, 6
Bell, BGen Marcus B., 187, 211, 264n
Benedict, LtCol William E., 97n, 109n,
Berger, LtCol Spencer S., 92n, 147, 229, 253, 275
Berlin, 730
Betio Island, 396–397, 401
Biak, 71, 457
Bismarck Archipelago, 438
Bismarck Sea, 537
Bivouac areas, 151
Blackburn, Capt Donald D., 348
Blaha, Capt Nathan D. 424
Blanchard, Capt Rolfe T., 329n, 372
Blandy, RAdm William H. P., 63, 165–166, 181, 278, 483, 492–493, 493n, 495–496, 498–502, 714

Blessman, 500
Blissard, LtCol Louis B., 649, 652
Block Island, 435
Bloody Gorge, 616
Bloody Nose Ridge, 157, 223–225, 228, 279
Blow, Maj Rex, 382
Boats. *See* Landing Craft; Ships.
Boehm, Col Harold C., 575, 575n, 582n, 588–590, 591n, 686
Bohemia, 9
Bohol Island, 327, 359, 361, 375, 377
Bollman, Capt Howard W., 413
Bombardments, 71, 102–104, 108, 112, 132, 145, 153, 165, 211, 221, 227, 278–281, 335, 386, 409, 452–453, 455, 486–487, 489, 491–493, 493n, 495–496, 498, 501–506, 509, 517, 526, 531, 533, 547, 565, 574, 576, 610, 646, 714, 726, 728, 731, 737. *See also* Naval gunfire.
Bongao Island, 378
Bonins, 64, 68, 102, 436, 444–445, 448, 450–451, 459, 461–462, 462n, 463-464, 466, 472, 475, 484–485, 505, 537, 597, 654, 716–717, 737
Borneo, 6, 294, 309, 358, 366, 374, 378
Bougainville, 284, 305–307, 335, 342, 346, 362–363, 388–389, 393, 467, 735
Bountiful, 723
Bourke, BGen Thomas E., 291, 300–301, 314, 316–318, 323; LtGen, 319n
Bowdoin, Maj George E., 248n
Boyd Ridge, 221, 229, 231–237, 241–242, 250, 254, 257, 260
Boyd, LtCol Robert W., 115, 123
Boyer, LtCol Kimber H., 93
Bozarth, Capt Clyde L., 276n
Brant, Capt Robert E., 123
Brayton, LtCol Corey C., 415n
Brisbane, 291–292, 301
British whaling captains, 445
Brodie gear, 436–437
Brown, Col Dudley S., 61
Brunelli, LtCol Austin R., 680
Buckley, Col Edmond J., 474
Buckley, LtCol Joseph E., 93n
Buckner, LtGen Simon B., Jr., 465
Burauen, 310, 316–317, 319–320, 322
Buri Airfield, 322–323, 325
Burma, 730
Burnette, Maj Robert W., 91
Burrfish, 78
Bushido, 69
Butler, LtCol John A., 305, 508, 634

INDEX 819

Butterfield, LtGen Jackson B., 508, 513, 625, 627
Byers, SSgt A. A., 344n
Bypassed islands, 412, 415, 418
Byrum, Maj Paul R., Jr., 399

Cabanatuan, 343, 346
Cagayan, 381
Caldera Point, 366
California, 17, 437, 468, 500
Campbell, LtCol Harold D., 42; BGen, 46, 98, 265, 398, 430, 595
Camp Dunlap, 23
Camp Elliott, 20–21
Camp Holcomb, 20
Camp Kearney Field, 437
Camp Lejeune, 20, 39
Camp Pendleton, 23, 468
Camp Tarawa, 482
Cape Esperance, 94, 165
Cape Gallatin, 169
Cape Gloucester, 89, 94, 268, 275
Cape Isabel, 409
Cape Ngaramudel, 173
Cape Ngatpokul, 168
Cape Pkulangelul, 172
Capisan, 370
Carey, Maj Roland, 662
Cargill, Maj Wayne M., 417
Caribbean, 15–17, 21, 36
Carleson, Maj Roger T., 42
Carney, Col Edward B., 429
Caroline Islands, 3, 6, 16, 54, 67–68, 101, 395, 412, 733–734. *See also* Western Caroline Islands.
Castle, Capt Donald E., 636
Catskill, 314
Casualties
 American, 113–114, 120, 124, 128, 130–132, 136, 138, 141, 144, 147–148, 150, 154, 161, 166, 179, 185, 189, 198–199, 208–209, 212, 216, 218, 225, 227, 231, 236, 242–243, 253, 257, 273–274, 281–282, 284–285, 322, 336, 356, 375, 386, 390, 408, 412, 438, 451, 471, 479, 504, 513, 517, 520–521, 525, 525n, 531, 536–537, 545, 551, 560, 574–575, 597, 602, 604–605, 608, 612, 614–615, 617, 624, 630–631, 633–636, 636n, 644, 648, 659–660, 665, 689, 695, 699, 701, 703, 705, 710–711, 715n, 722–723
 Japanese, 109, 113, 121, 126, 136, 138, 177, 177n, 179, 185, 208–209, 218, 226–227, 232, 253, 261, 265, 276, 300, 333, 350, 352, 376, 385, 396, 409, 415, 426, 453, 531, 533, 536, 538, 545, 562, 605, 626, 629, 639, 665, 679, 689
Catabato, 381–382
Cates, MajGen Clifton B., 467, 505, 517, 519, 521, 554, 557, 563, 579, 610, 645, 647, 652, 661, 665, 669–670, 672, 677, 681–682, 694, 700, 708
Catmon Hill, 319n
Caves. *See* Terrain.
Cebu, 294, 358–359, 361, 363, 374–376, 388
Cebu City, 375
Celebes, 102, 294, 733
Celebes Sea, 309
Cemeteries, 712
Central America, 8, 15
Central Intelligence Agency, 612
Central Pacific, 3, 23–24, 51–52, 54, 266, 293, 309, 318, 393, 395–398, 400–401, 405, 407, 414, 416, 432, 437–438, 440, 462–463, 466, 478, 491, 723, 726, 731–733, 738
Chamberlain, Sgt Reid, 690
Chambers, LtCol Justice M., 519–520, 559
Chaney, MajGen James E., 603, 708
Chapman, LtCol Leonard F., Jr., 92n
Chappell, Maj C. J., Jr., 42
Charan Kanoa, 424–425
Charlie Dog Ridge, 568, 645, 648, 682
Chase, BGen William C., 343–344, 347
Chateau-Thierry, 468
Centaurus, 101
Chemical officers, 613
Chemical warfare, 91, 612–614
Chenango, 426
Chesapeake Bay, 36, 304
Chester, 493, 500
Chichi Jima, 64, 445, 448–449, 451, 455, 462n, 496, 543, 561, 598, 700, 702, 705–707
Chidori Airfield, 449n, 453, 457
Chilton, Cdr W. P., 499
China, 3, 6, 9, 16, 51, 62, 69, 293–294, 298, 309, 334, 458, 463–464, 467
China-Burma-India Theater, 334
China Wall, 221, 241, 248, 250, 256, 260–264
Chinese, 54, 276, 730
Christianity, 294
Christmas Day, 438
Clark Field, 342, 357
Clark, RAdm Joseph J., 451–453, 595
Clausewitz, 330

Coady, Maj James F., 515
Cobia, 455
Cole, Col J. Frank, 395n, 400
Coleman, Col William F., 186n, 210n, 211n; BGen, 221n
Colhoun, 624
Collins, LtCol William R., 564–565
Colorado, 409
Columbia Victory, 602–603
Columbus, Ohio, 610
Combat efficiency, 185, 227, 592, 608, 661, 694
Combat information center, 497
Combat loading, 17, 83n
Commandant of the Marine Corps, 15, 24, 27, 29, 36, 46, 253 n, 428
Commander, Air, Iwo Jima, 597–598
Commander, Aircraft, Northern Solomons, 362
Commander, Aircraft, Solomons, 46
Commander, Air Forces, Pacific Fleet, 29, 38, 47, 99, 477
Commander, Amphibious Forces, Pacific Fleet, 48, 466, 473, 490, 490n, 491n, 492n
Commander, Beach Party Group, 602
Commander, Fifth Fleet, 491, 492n
Commander, Forward Area, Central Pacific, 64, 710
Commander, Forward Areas, Western Pacific, 184
Commander, Garrison Air Force, Western Carolines, 99
Commander in Chief, Pacific Fleet, 26, 28–30, 36, 293, 421
Commander in Chief, Pacific Ocean Areas, 26, 38–39, 60–61, 77–78, 83, 98, 101, 134, 301, 417, 421, 464, 469
Commander in Chief, United States Fleet, 24
Commander, Joint Expeditionary Force, 486, 608
Commander, Landing Force Air Support Control Unit, 503
Commander, Marianas Area, 36
Commander, Marshall-Gilberts Area, 36
Commander, Service Forces, Pacific Fleet, 477–478
Commander, South Pacific, 99, 301
Commander, Support Aircraft, 103, 108, 283
Commander, Ulithi Fire Support Group, 183
Commander, Western Pacific Task Forces, 62
Commanding General, Aircraft, Fleet Marine Force, Pacific, 47
Commanding General, Army Forces, Western Pacific, 39
Commanding General, Expeditionary Troops, Third Fleet, 64
Commanding General, Fleet Marine Force, Pacific, 28–29, 31, 47, 477, 482, 491n, 492, 492n
Commanding General, V Amphibious Corps, 24, 490n, 491n
Commanding General, Marine Garrison Forces, 14th Naval District, 38
Commanding General, Pacific Ocean Areas, 477–478
Commanding General, Samoan Force, 46
Communications
 American, 14, 17, 35, 151, 178, 204, 222, 241, 274, 277, 350, 368, 370, 377, 383–384, 402n, 411, 612, 615, 620n, 693, 703, 722–723, 725
 Equipment, 94, 130, 139, 368
 Radios, 207, 259, 277, 384, 390, 402, 404, 486n, 589, 612, 620n, 626, 719
 SCR–193, 308
 SCR–300, 277
 SCR–542, 308
 SCR–610, 277
 tank, 154
 Japanese, 278, 455, 586, 612, 646, 656–657,
 Radios, 120, 202, 377, 449, 451, 456, 461, 487, 702
Communism, 8–9
Congress, 445
Connolly, RAdm Richard L., 25
Cook, Capt Richard M., 558
Cooley, Maj Albert D., 42; Col, 47, 423
Coolidge, President Calvin, 6–7
Corregidor, 291, 296, 354, 690
Court of International Justice, 4
Craig, LtGen Edward A., 608n, 624n
Cram, LtCol Jack R., 436
Crist, LtCol Raymond F., Jr., 573
Crowl, Philip A., 52, 279n
Crown, Maj John A., 119, 204
Cuba, 14, 19
Culebra, 19
Cunningham, Maj Alfred A., 41
Cushman's Pocket, 686–687, 689, 691–692
Cushman, LtCol Robert E., 414, 416, 574, 577, 584, 591

D-Day, 86, 273, 280–284
Dagami, 316–317, 319–321
Dagupan, 337, 339, 372
Daly, LtCol James M., 401, 411
Danube River, 730

INDEX 821

Dardanelles, 33
Dardanelles-Gallipoli operation, 14
Dark, Col Robert F., 187, 192, 199, 250–251, 257
Dato, 379
Davao, 366, 381, 384–385
Davis, Maj Raymond G., 145
Davidson, Maj Robert, 508, 517, 654, 674
Day, Maj William R., 558
Dead Man's Curve, 232–233
Deakin, Col Harold O., 95n, 150n, 274n
Dean, Maj William W., 598
Death Valley, 160, 221, 226, 232, 254, 261–263, 707
DeBell, Maj George J., 233n
Deep Passage, 409
Defenses
  American, 549
    antiaircraft, 101, 328, 330, 486n, 499, 708
    barbed wire, 675
    emplacements, 666
    fire, 661
    field fortifications, 14
    land mines, 14
    sandbags, 246, 248, 256–257, 260, 508
  Japanese, 66, 71–73, 101–103, 112, 134, 137, 144, 152, 161, 168, 177, 185, 189, 192, 199, 207, 217, 221, 227, 234, 237–238, 240, 242, 244–246, 249, 256–257, 262–264, 268, 276, 279, 284, 316, 346, 352, 366, 379–381, 385–386, 407, 436, 453–454, 457, 474, 484, 491, 496, 499, 528, 531–538, 546, 549, 564, 570, 573, 627, 645, 684–686, 695, 697–698, 700–701, 714, 717, 766, 731
    antiaircraft, 102, 329, 400, 412, 415–417, 424, 428–429, 433–434, 495, 499, 506, 568
    antiboat, 110, 116, 119, 121, 474–475, 497–498, 506
    antiinvasion mines, 72
    antitank, 72–73, 116, 120, 139, 141, 156, 171, 176, 205, 208, 268, 273, 346, 376, 459, 474, 513–514, 566, 572, 584, 625, 627–629, 655
    barbed wire, 72, 120, 163, 454
    beach, 71–72, 81, 108, 176, 267
    blockhouses, 104, 120, 134–135, 208, 211, 456, 459, 473–474, 485n, 486, 493n, 500, 508, 510, 513, 517, 528, 530, 539, 545, 548, 550, 562, 572, 620, 636n, 644, 649, 698, 717

booby traps, 156, 178, 199, 257, 407, 426, 562, 600, 697
bunkers, 135, 156, 171, 173, 273, 459, 528, 536, 545, 548, 558, 562, 572, 580, 590, 635, 647–649, 654, 665
buried aerial torpedoes, 565
camouflage, 548, 550
coastal, 321, 407, 493n, 496, 624–625
concrete fortifications, 73, 120, 135, 145, 376, 454–455, 629, 646, 666
dugouts, 171, 192, 201, 212, 242, 379, 550, 555, 642, 685–686
emplacements, 75, 156, 160, 200, 280, 473, 486, 495, 523, 542, 550, 554, 567, 584, 591, 618, 621, 635, 639–640, 665–666, 672, 675, 694, 698, 716
fortifications, 75, 134–135, 138, 145, 154–156, 165, 169, 171, 173, 185, 208, 216, 274, 278, 448, 454–455, 458–459, 487, 531, 545, 627, 639, 673, 717
foxholes, 651
machine gun positions, 119, 127, 134, 136, 172, 242, 261, 636, 647
mine fields, 251, 276, 375–376, 407, 479, 498, 513, 517, 520, 550, 554–555, 572, 600, 627, 640, 649, 676, 726
observation posts, 75, 550
obstacles, 72, 268, 271
pillboxes, 73, 75, 79, 92, 112, 116, 118, 120–121, 134, 136, 138, 145, 152, 154–157, 163, 169, 171, 173, 176, 198, 200, 208, 212, 268, 271, 273, 350–351, 371, 379, 407, 453, 455, 458–459, 473–474, 482, 485n, 486, 493n, 500, 508, 510, 513–514, 517–518, 520, 528, 530–531, 536, 538–539, 545, 548, 550, 554–555, 558, 560, 562, 566–567, 572, 577, 590–591, 605, 610, 614n, 618, 621, 627, 631–632, 635, 639, 643, 647–651, 654, 663, 665–666, 668, 672, 685, 687, 693, 698, 716
pockets, 693–694, 706
rifle pits, 73, 136, 160, 171
rocket positions, 655
spider foxholes, 698
spider-traps, 517, 528, 691, 701
tetrahedrons, 72, 79, 138, 163
trenches, 117, 120, 171, 370, 379, 566, 651, 687
trip wires, 473
tunnels, 75, 205, 221, 453, 456, 530, 538, 540, 566, 572, 586, 613, 622, 637, 639, 645, 663–664, 689–690, 692

underground fortifications, 75, 154, 279, 453, 455–456
DeHaven, Col Louis G., 472, 521–522
Deho, 379
del alle, BGen Pedro A., 428
Demolitions. *See* Weapons.
Denmark, 19
Deputy Commander, Aircraft, Landing Force, 503
Deputy Commanding General, Fleet Marine Force, Pacific, 30–31
DETACHMENT Operation, 435, 465, 467–469, 482, 487, 489–491, 714, 720, 722–725
de Villalobos, Ruy Lopez, 54
Digos, 395
Dillon, LtCol Edward J., 674, 678
Dipolog, 365–367, 371–372
Director of Marine Corps Aviation, 41
Disarmament conferences, 5–6
Disarmament treaty, 6
Doe, MajGen Jens A., 366, 373, 378
Doherty, Capt. Albert J., 204
Dominican Republic, 467
Donlan, Capt Pat, 662–663
Doswell, Maj Menard, III, 433
Downs, 1stLt Willis A., 374n
Drake, Maj Clifford B., 521–522
Drydocks, 83, 184
Dulag, 310, 312, 314–317, 320, 325
Dunn, Col Ray A., 179
DuPage, 108, 278n
Duplantis, LtCol Wendell H., 558
Durgin, RAdm Calvin T., 492, 495, 500, 560, 717
Duryea, LtCol Justin G., 634, 642
Dutch East Indies, 358, 730

East Boat Basin, 220, 353, 459, 469, 471, 474, 500, 509, 547, 553, 555, 569, 646, 650, 711
East Indies, 287, 294
East Prussia, 143
East Road, 145–146, 157–159, 189, 198–202, 206, 221, 224, 226, 228–233, 236–238, 240, 251
Eberhardt, Capt Fred C., 526
Edgar, Maj John B., Jr., 521
Edmondson, Maj Robert W., 424
Efate Island, 98, 430–431, 730
Eichelberger, LtGen Robert L., 332, 359; Gen, 377, 386, 390
El Centro, California, 45
Eldorado, 484

Eleventh Naval District, 21
Eli Malk, 57
Eller, RAdm Ernest M., 80n, 283, 437n
Ellice Islands, 396, 398–401, 404
Ellis, Maj Donald K., 548
Ellis, Maj Earl H., 16; LtCol, 66n
Elmore, 278n
Emirau Island, 363, 373, 416, 432, 435, 438
Emperor Meiji, 459
Engebi Island, 408–413
England, 6
English, 54
English, LtCol Lowell E., 558, 582
Engineers. *See also* Army units; Marine units.
    American, 135–136, 156, 193, 204, 209, 224, 226, 231, 234, 258, 263, 271, 282, 325, 337, 376, 383, 398, 484, 514, 520, 531, 554, 595, 600, 602, 610, 627, 640–641, 652, 765, 681, 705, 720–721
    Japanese, 453, 647
Eniwetok Atoll, 64, 83, 278, 314–315, 405, 408–409, 412–413, 420, 438, 526
Enterprise, 560
Equipment. *See* Supplies and equipment.
Ermilio, LCdr Dominick J., 594
Erskine, MajGen Graves B., 467, 565, 573–574, 577–581, 583–585, 588–590, 592–593, 602, 607, 610, 616–617, 627, 635, 647, 652, 659, 686, 691–692, 700–701, 703–704, 708, 711, 719
Espiritu Santo Island, 98–101, 430–431, 433, 438
Essex, 335, 435, 503
Estes, 493, 499
Ethiopia, 9
Europe, 5, 440, 729–731, 733, 737
Europeans, 444–445
European Theater, 714, 733
Evans, Lt E. Graham, 635
Evans, Maj Holly H., 574
Everglades, 35
Everton, Maj Loren D., 400, 412, 416
Ewa, 21, 41–42, 45–47

Fagan, Maj Richard, 558, 618
Fais, 434
Falalop Island, 433–434
Fanshaw Bay, 424
Far East, 6
Farrell, BGen Walter G., 46
Fascism, 8
Fascist dictatorships, 4
Fawell, LtCol Reed M., Jr., 505, 618

INDEX   823

Feehan, Maj Harvey A., 522
Ferguson, Capt, 197
Fertig, Col Wendell W., 359, 381–382
Fields, Capt Thomas M., 620
Filipinos, 296, 347, 350, 381, 387
   Forces, 348, 381, 407
   Guerrillas, 348–352, 359, 361, 363, 365, 370–371, 375–377, 379–384, 386, 690
Fire direction centers, 153, 319, 611. *See also* Artillery.
Fitzgerald, Captain John I., Jr., 93
Five Brothers Ridge, 221, 224–226, 229–231, 233, 240, 244, 246, 254, 256–257, 260–261, 441
Five Sisters Hill, 157–158, 160, 221, 231, 237, 248, 250, 256–257
Flag raising (Iwo Jima), 542–543, 543n, 545, 593
Fleet Anchorage, 181
Fleet War Plans Division, 465
FLINTLOCK Operation, 401
Flock, Lt Charles F., 370
Florida, 35
Flyers. *See* Pilots.
FORAGER Operation, 61, 301, 422
Formosa, 6, 51, 62, 276, 293, 297–299, 321, 324, 335–337, 435, 450, 464–465, 476
Forrestal, Mr. James V., 442, 484, 564
Fort Bragg, N. C., 35–36
Fort, RAdm George H., 63, 83, 95, 104n, 165, 186, 211, 278–280, 286; VAdm, 78n
Fort Stotsenburg, 342
Forward observers, 153, 597, 628, 719. *See also* Artillery.
Fourteen Points, 7
Frame, Maj Donald P., 435
France, 4–7, 19, 443, 467
Frank, Mr. Benis M., 90n
Freeman, Col Calvin B., 398, 401, 407–408
Fremont, 165, 278
French Samoa, 398
Frogmen, 495, 497–498, 500
Fukudome, VAdm Shigeru, 298
Funafuti, 396, 398, 401–404
Futrell, Dr. Robert F., 486n

Gabbert, LtCol John T. L. D., 389
Gambier Bay, 405
Garakayo Islands, 242, 250
Garangaoi Cove, 173–174
Garapan Plain, 670
Garekoru, 59, 160, 190, 192–193, 195, 197–201

Gayle, Maj Gordon D., 208, 242
Geiger, BGen Roy S., 42, 45–46; MajGen, 25, 61, 63–64, 79, 89, 104, 131, 165, 175, 185–187, 211, 246, 252, 278–279, 286, 428, 433; LtGen, 31–32
Gela, 281
Geneva, Switzerland, 6
Geneva Conference, 7
Geneva Conventions, 377, 420
German colonies, 3, 6, 55
German General's Plot, 729, 732
Germans, 395, 458, 675, 729–732, 735–736
German Siegfried Line, 443
German Sixth Army, 430
Germany, 4, 8–9, 67, 408, 430, 443, 729, 732 736
Gilbert Islands, 6, 23, 288, 395–396, 399–401, 404, 407, 415, 422, 443, 462, 731
Gilberts-Marshalls Operations, 407
Gilberts operation, 395–396, 399
Glidden, Maj Elmer G., Jr., 405
Godolphin, Capt Francis B., 343n, 344n
Gormley, LtCol John J., 119n, 121, 137
Gorokottan Island, 262
Goto, Major Ushio, 69, 163, 168–171, 176–177, 177n, 179–180,
Graham, Col Chester B., 471, 515, 557–558, 567, 569, 617, 627, 639
Great Britain, 4–6, 19
Great Depression, 9
Green Island, 363
Green, Maj Thomas C., 42
Griffin, Maj David R., 202n
Grinlinton Pond, 257–258, 261
Griswold, MajGen Oscar W., 352
Guadalcanal, 44–45, 52, 61, 77, 89–90, 94–97, 99, 101, 165, 237, 253, 266, 268, 284, 291–293, 305, 327, 389, 393, 410, 422, 428, 430–431, 438–439, 457, 466, 514, 678
Guam, 6, 25, 30–32, 36, 60–61, 63–64, 79, 184, 277, 279–280, 282, 310, 323, 388, 425–429, 429n, 438, 444, 466–469, 473, 477, 480, 483–484, 489, 505, 538, 564, 578, 597, 598n, 604, 612, 711, 731–734
Guimba, 342, 347
Guiuan, 335
Guiuan strip, 339
Gustafson, Maj John H., 141, 212

H. L. *Edwards*, 190
Haas, LtCol Ralph, 508, 517, 526
Hague Conventions, 377

Haha Jima, 496, 598
Haiti, 467
Hale, MajGen Willis H., 414
Halsey, Adm William F., 62–63, 65, 66n, 82, 102, 181, 245, 278, 286, 291, 293, 293n, 301, 303, 309, 325–326, 335, 420, 430, 435, 465
Hanneken, Col Herman H., 119, 130, 135, 137
Hankins, Col Joseph F., 233
Hanlon, Capt B. Hall, 492
Hansen, Lt John E., 402, 404, 536
Harding, President Warren G., 5, 7
Harmon, LtGen Millard F., 417, 464, 483
Harris, SSgt Charles E., 536
Harris, Col Harold D., 115, 122, 139, 141–143, 208, 237–238, 240, 240n, 241, 245, 254, 303; BGen, 115n
Harrison, Col William H., 104–105
Hart, BGen Franklin A., 505, 556
Hawaiian Islands, 6, 16–17, 23–24, 30–32, 45, 96, 162, 301, 314, 363, 400–401, 408–409, 436, 438, 445, 462, 468, 477–478, 482–483, 604–605, 612, 708, 713
Hawkins Field, 401, 404
Headley, Capt James C., 559, 650, 664
Headquarters, Marine Corps, 23, 27, 38, 221
Heinl, Maj Robert D., Jr., 589n
Hellzapoppin Ridge, 305, 346, 389
Henderson, Col Frederick P., 426n
Henderson Field, 45, 393, 428
Heritage, Maj Gordon W., 426–427
Hermle, BGen Leo D., 505, 516, 706
Higashi, 445, 673, 680
Higashi Rock, 495
Higashiyama, 159, 260. *See also* Walt's Ridge.
Hill, RAdm Harry W., 466, 502, 524, 700, 714
Hill B, 222
Hill Oboe, 576–577, 616
Hill Peter, 574, 576–577, 616
Hill Row, 205
Hill 3, 214
Hill 80, 202, 204
Hill 100, 157, 199, 206–207
Hill 120, 234, 244
Hill 140, 244–246, 249, 254
Hill 165, 640
Hill 200, 146–147, 157
Hill 205, 147
Hill 210, 146–147
Hill 215, 637
Hill 260, 157
Hill 300, 224, 260. *See also* Kansokuyama.
Hill 331, 589–590

Hill 357, 583–584
Hill 362, 590, 687
Hill 362A, 220, 581n, 616, 618, 621–623, 625–630
Hill 362B, 581, 582n, 583–584, 616, 629–632, 635, 691
Hill 362C, 445, 582n, 583, 585–586, 588, 591, 616, 684–685
Hill 382, 447, 455, 568, 572, 646–647, 649–663, 665, 668–669, 682
Hilo, Hawaii, 477, 482
Hiraiwa Bay, 474, 633
Hirohito, Emperor, 732, 736
Hitler, Adolph, 9, 729, 732
Hjerpe, Maj Carl W., 515
Hobby, 402, 404
Hodge, MajGen John R., 63, 318
Hoeck, 1stLt G. A., 638n
Hoffman, BGen Hugh, 344n
Holcomb, Gen Thomas, 19, 44
Holland, TSgt R. B., 344n
Hollandia, 292, 310, 327
Home Islands, 39–40, 57, 428, 443–445, 448–450, 463, 466, 484, 493, 496, 597, 611, 618, 730–732. *See also* Japan.
Hong Kong, 6, 294, 435, 451
Honolulu, Hawaii, 476
Honolulu, 132
Honshu, 490
Honsowetz, LtCol Russell E., 147, 157
Hoover, President Herbert, 7, 246, 401, 414, 613, 710
Hoover, VAdm John H., 184; Adm, 64
Hope, Bob, 90n
Hopkins, Col Zebulon C., 304n, 334
Hori, Col Shizuichi, 457–458, 533n, 539n, 706, 706n, 707, 717n
Hough, Maj Frank O., 52, 150n
Houser, Maj Robert H., 559n, 562, 588
Hudson, LtCol Lewis C., 520, 548
Hungary, 8
Hunt, Capt George P., 110, 112–113, 144
Hurst, Maj E. Hunter, 119–120, 137, 226, 229, 234; LtCol, 197n

ICEBERG Operation, 465, 572
Ichimaru, RAdm Toshinosuka, 454, 461, 499, 499n, 564, 586, 669–670, 680, 702, 706, 706n
Idaho, 493, 496, 498, 500, 563, 565
IDENTICAL Island, 181n, 183–184
Ikeda, Col Masuo, 453, 562, 566, 643, 701–705, 710

INDEX

Iloilo River, 375
Inaoka, Maj Masauru, 711
Independence, 396
Indianapolis, 281, 560
Indochina, 453, 730
Indonesia, 294, 358
Infantry
  American, 87, 211, 240, 251, 273, 305, 307, 317, 352, 366–368, 371, 374–375, 379, 385–386, 423, 521, 531, 565, 567, 574, 576, 581–582, 584, 592, 608, 618, 621, 628, 633, 639, 647, 649–650, 657, 681, 686, 716, 720. *See also* Army units and Marine units.
Inoue, LtGen Sadae, 68–72, 76, 156, 159, 163, 169–170, 179, 180n, 190, 222, 232, 259, 263, 265, 285–286
Inouye, Capt Samaji, 457, 543, 586, 675, 677–680, 702, 706
Intelligence
  American, 163, 173, 177, 183, 209, 271, 280, 284, 335–336, 340, 343, 349, 352, 359, 366, 368, 469, 472, 475–476, 489, 499, 523, 570, 638–639, 646, 651, 693, 698
Irwin, Maj Darrell D., 400
Islamic religion, 294
Island Mail, 409
Isolationism, 5, 8, 15
Italy, 4–9, 530, 733
Ivey, LtCol Thomas S., 314
Iwahig, 362
Iwo Jima Operation, 397, 465, 468, 472, 476, 435–438, 444–445, 447–449, 449n, 450–454, 454n, 455–459, 461, 462n, 463–469, 471–485, 485n, 486–487, 490–497, 500–504, 506, 510, 512, 514–519, 521–523, 525–528, 530–533, 535–543, 545–548, 550, 552–556, 559–565, 568–573, 577, 579–581, 586, 588, 592–593, 597–598, 598n, 600–605, 607–608, 610–614, 614n, 615–618, 620, 620n, 622–626, 628–631, 633–634, 636, 640–644, 646–647, 657, 669, 688, 691, 693–695, 697–715, 715n, 716–719, 721–729, 732, 736–738
  Operation, 397, 465, 468, 472, 476, 482, 482, 564, 579, 597, 601, 604, 617, 645, 710–711, 713, 715, 715n, 720, 722–723, 726, 735, 737
Izu Shoto, **444**

Jack, Maj Samuel S., 42
Jaluit Airfield, 396
Jaluit Atoll, 412–414, 416, 420
Jaluit Island, 399, 405, 412, 415
Jaluit lagoon, 399
Japan 4–6, 8–10, 16, 23, 30, 32, 51, 54–55, 62, 67, 76, 241, 265, 276, 293–294, 296–297, 300, 326, 377, 405, 421, 430, 435–436, 348, 444–445, 448, 451, 453–454, 462–465, 476, 484, 489–491, 495, 598, 600–601, 614–615, 669, 683, 706, 711, 730–737.
  invasion of, 387–388
  Japanese, 57–58, 66, 117, 119, 121, 136, 138, 144–145, 147, 158, 160, 177, 190, 201–202, 207, 209, 212, 214, 216–219, 221–223, 225, 227–228, 230–232, 234–235, 237–238, 240–242, 246, 249–251, 253, 256–258, 261–264, 267–268, 270, 276–277, 279, 285, 287, 296–297, 300, 306, 310, 312, 314–315, 317–318, 320–325, 328–329, 332, 335–336, 340, 346, 348–352, 356–357, 359, 361, 366–367, 370, 372, 374, 376–377, 379, 382, 386–387, 389, 393, 395, 399–400, 407, 409–11, 413, 415–418, 420, 426, 430, 436, 445, 449n, 451, 474, 484, 490, 526, 543, 558, 602, 613, 624, 670, 688, 697–698, 700, 710–711, 735–737
  Army-Navy relations, 732
  bases, 52, 400, 417
  civilians, 55, 265, 381, 445, 450, 453
  diplomats, 737
  Emperor, 8, 485, 730
  Empire, 451, 700, 737
  food, 530, 695
  Imperial Government, 706
  installations, 101, 108, 143, 279, 383, 414, 417, 490, 498–500, 514, 550, 719, 726
  leaders, 443, 449, 730
  mandated territory, 57
  Military Academy, 457
  military doctrine, 457
  Minister of War, 324, 451, 732
  morale, 332, 414, 682, 736
  policy, 445, 614
  phosphate plant, 172–174, 208, 216
  Prime Minister, 707
  repatriation, 265
  Samurai family, 450
  secret weapon, 736
  strength, 163, 175, 180, 189, 258, 276, 285, 336, 340, 381, 458n, 472 473
  surrender, 178, 222, 265, 421, 693, 704–705
  thermal ray, 736
  Tokyo Prefecture, 445
  transportation system, 335
  war effort, 730

war production, 450
weather station, 449, 456
Japanese Units
  Imperial General Headquarters, 67–68, 70–71, 76, 297–298, 706
  Army, 208, 221, 276, 297, 332, 361, 371, 383, 407, 448, 457, 614n, 620, 726, 732, 736
    Kwantung Army, 67
    Southern Area Army, 76
    First Combined Air Force, 298. *See also* First Air Fleet, Fourth Air Army
    Fourth Air Army, 298, 337
    Fourteenth Area Army, 298, 300, 340, 348, 358
    Twenty-Third Army, 451
    Thirty-First Army, 68, 76, 78, 449, 453
    Thirty-Fifth Army, 298, 361
    1st Infantry Division, 321
    14th Infantry Division, 68
    16th Infantry Division, 315
    30th Infantry Division, 359
    35th Infantry Division, 67–68
    100th Infantry Division, 359
    102d Infantry Division, 361
    109th Infantry Division, 433, 455, 475, 533n
    1st Amphibious Brigade, 68
    2nd Independent Mixed Brigade, 453, 457–458, 569, 572, 647, 647n, 654, 693, 711
    53d Independent Mixed Brigade, 68–69
    54th Independent Mixed Brigade, 359, 361
    Infantry Regiments
      2nd, 264
      15th, 68–69
      26th, 698
      41st, 321
      59th, 68–69
      145th, 453, 562, 643, 701, 703, 705
    26th Tank Regiment, 454–455, 590, 692
    10th Independent Antitank Battalion, 553n
    Independent Infantry Battalions
      309th, 569, 647n, 651
      310th, 572, 647
      311th, 572, 647n
      312th, 647n
      314th, 572, 647n
      346th, 69
    Infantry Battalions
      1/59, 163, 175
      2/15, 69, 193, 195
      3/15, 69, 135
      3/17, 643
      3/145, 659
    Antiaircraft units
      126th, 69
      144th, 69
    Miscellaneous
      45th Guard Force Detachment, 69
  Navy, 178, 208, 265, 276, 298, 300, 312, 319, 329, 439–440, 443, 449–450, 454n, 670, 677, 680, 732
    Air Fleets
      First, 298
      Second, 298
    Combined Fleet, 67, 76, 297–298, 407, 499, 701
    Imperial Fleet, 64, 68, 297, 312, 319, 325, 407, 461, 493
    First Mobile Fleet, 298
    Second Fleet, 298
    Third Fleet, 298
    Fifth Fleet, 298
    Sixth Fleet, 298
    Chichi Jima Naval Base, 449
    204th Naval Construction Battalion, 454
    214th Naval Construction Battalion, 75, 208
    Naval Guard Force, 457, 475, 677
    Special Naval Landing Force, 379
    Striking Force, 298
    Special Attack Unit, 537. *See also* Kamikazes.
    Miscellaneous
      Angaur Sector Unit, 69, 166, 169
      Antitank Battalion, 454
      Cavalry, 451
      Chichi Jima Branch, Army Fortification Department, 448
      Demolition detachment, 592
      Field Hospital, 647
      Garrison units, 138, 163, 169–170, 178, 222, 237, 278, 358–359, 361–362, 377, 381, 387, 415, 448, 453, 493, 704
        Anguar, 163, 165, 175, 179–180, 184
        Chichi Jima, 449, 705
        Iwo Jima, 458n, 537, 670, 700, 702
        Leyte, 329
        Peleliu, 76, 134, 189–190, 214, 232, 265
      Imperial Guards, 451
      Korean labor force, 69
      Naval engineers, 221
      Palau Sector Group, 68–71, 76
      Parachute units, 450
      Peleliu Area Unit, 222

INDEX 827

Shimbu Group, 352
Special Counterattack units, 267
Special Counterlanding Force, 134
Stragglers, 376, 426, 664, 675, 692
Suicide Squads, 156
Suicide Swimmers, 561
Suribachi Sector Unit, 533
Volcano-Bonin Defense Sector, 475
Java, 297
Jeans, Capt Cloyd R., 402–403
Jerome, Col Clayton C., 219, 304, 336–337, 339, 352, 356, 363, 366–368, 372–373, 382, 390; BGen, 280n
Jeru, Capt George E., 85n
Johnson, LtCol Chandler W., 508, 539–540, 629
Johnson, Capt Robert C., 560
Johnson, Col Robert F., 711
Johnston Island, 21, 438
Joint Army-Navy Board, 16
Joint Chiefs of Staff, 24, 38, 51, 60, 62, 65, 151, 286, 292–293, 303, 462, 465, 733
Joint Expeditionary Forces, 62
Joint Intelligence Center (Pacific Ocean Areas), 30, 60
Joint Marine-Army training, 21
Joint Navy-Marine planning, 83
Joint Planning, 468
Joint Staff Planners, 464
Joint Staff Study, 50
Joint Training Forces
  1st, 20
  2d, 21
Joint War Plans Committee, 462, 464
Jolo Island, 361, 378–380
Jordan, Col Walter I., 471, 519, 563, 567, 569, 659, 663, 665, 667, 672
June, Col Frank M., 433
Jungle Warfare. *See* Tactics.

Kabacan, 381
Kaempfer, Maj William P., 548
Kaido, Col Chosaku, 456
Kalinin Bay, 401, 407
Kaluf, Col John, 80n, 282n
Kama Rock, 603, 698
Kamikazes, 323–325, 328, 331, 336, 340, 459, 537, 718, 736
Kamilianlul Mountain, 210
Kamilianlul ridges, 202
Kaneohe, Hawaii, 398
Kangoku Rock, 472, 603, 698
Kansokuyama, 159, 235, 260. *See also* Hill 300.

Kauffman, Cdr D. L., 498n
Kavieng, 303, 444
Kazan Retto, 444
KEENSET, 181n, 183–184
Kellum, Maj William C., 433
Kenney, LtGen George C., 291–292, 301, 303, 326, 334, 362; Gen, 65n
Kenyon, Col Howard N., 564, 573, 582, 584, 687
Keokuk, 537
Kessing, Como Oliver O., 434
Kibawe Trail, 387
Kibbe, Cdr R. L., 102n
Kimes, Maj Ira L., 42
KING II Operation, 310, 315
King, Adm Ernest J., 35, 293, 395, 397, 462–463, 465
King, Maj John H., 329
Kingman, RAdm Howard F., 278
Kingsbury, Maj Robert T., III, 326n
Kinkaid, VAdm Thomas C., 303, 309, 326, 334
Kiska Operation, 467
Kita village, 445, 455–456, 633, 639, 695
Kitano Point, 447, 455, 459, 577, 593, 624, 640, 642–643, 684, 698, 691, 695, 698, 700
Knott, Maj Gordon H., 411
Koiso, Premier Kuniaki, 707n
Kojima, Cpl Kyutaro, 711
Kolombangara Island, 393
Kongauru Island, 211–212, 223, 250
Korea, 730
Korean civilians and laborers, 206, 209, 216, 222, 265, 276, 418, 420, 639, 711
Korean War, 718
Koror Island, 57, 62, 68, 71, 134, 166, 190, 232, 281, 433
Koror Town, 101
Kossol Passage, 57, 103, 232
Kossol Roads, 152, 287
Koyatau, Riichi, 543n
Krueger, LtGen Walter, 309, 321, 339, 348, 351, 357
Krulewitch, LtCol Melvin L., 681
Kumamoto, 659
Kuribayashi, Capt Tadamichi, 451; LtCol, 451; Col, 451; BGen, 451; MajGen, 451; LtGen, 450–451, 451n, 453–459, 475, 484, 493, 523, 525–528, 533, 537, 539, 546–547, 551, 556, 561, 568, 572, 584–586, 593, 615, 623, 628, 630, 633, 641–644, 669–670, 679, 682–683, 685, 695
Kuribayashi, Yoshii, 451n
Kurihama, 484

Kurihara, SgtMaj Masao, 237*n*
Kurile Islands, 415, 443
Kuroda, LtGen Shigenori, 298, 300
Kurpoat, Sgt Henry S., 516
Kwajalein, 400, 405, 407, 409, 411, 417, 438, 467
Kyushu, 39, 659

Lae, 451
Lake Aztec, 176
Lake Pinalay, 385
Lake Salome, 174
Lambrecht, LtCol Peter D., 326
Lanboyan Point, 365
Landing barges, 195
Landing craft. *See also* Ships.
  American, 19, 35, 181, 184, 195, 241, 267, 503, 508, 522, 548, 601, 607, 634, 725
    Types
      LCIs (Landing Craft, Infantry), 108, 135, 166, 171, 497–498, 503, 554, 727
      LCI(G)s Landing Craft, Infantry (Gunboat), 132, 166, 496–497, 503, 626, 708
      LCI(M)s (Landing Craft, Infantry, (Mortar), 166, 504, 523, 555
      LCI(R)s (Landing Craft, Infantry, (Rocket), 315, 504, 530
      LCMs (Landing Craft, Mechanized), 88, 166, 516
      LCPs (Landing Craft, Personnel), 85
      LCTs (Landing Craft, Tank), 35, 84, 272, 459, 602
      LCVP (Landing Craft, Vehicle, Personnel), 19, 34–35, 85, 88, 127, 166, 516, 518, 522, 542
  Japanese, 195, 258, 278
Landing exercises and techniques, 17, 19
Landing forces, 269, 731
Lang, Lt Frank C., 413
Lanigan, Col John R., 471, 509, 519–520, 549–551, 555, 649–650, 660, 663, 671, 692, 694
Larkin, LtCol Claude A., 42; Col, 45; BGen, 46; MajGen, 303, 388
Larsen, MajGen Henry L., 428
Lauesen, Lt Christian F., 402
    LCI-*392*, 418, 420
    LCI-*394*, 420
    LCI-*438*, 497
    LCI-*449*, 497
    LCI-*450*, 498
    LCI-*457*, 498
    LCI-*466*, 498

LCI-*469*, 498
LCI-*474*, 497
LCI-*479*, 420
LCI-*484*, 420
LCI-*491*, 420
League of Nations, 4–5, 7, 9, 55, 66
Leek, LtCol Frederick E., 372–373, 373*n*
Lehnert, Lt Robert E., 402
Lejeune, MajGen John A., 16
Letcher, Col John S., 652; BGen, 480*n*, 605*n*, 614*n*, 624*n*
Lethbridge Report, 612*n*
Leutze, 497
Lexington, 40–42
Leyte, 54, 181, 287, 291, 294, 301, 303, 309–310, 312, 315–327, 330–335, 339, 342, 358–359, 361, 363, 366–367, 377–378, 381, 443, 443, 461, 734
Leyte Gulf, 300, 310, 312, 318, 330, 335–337, 366
Leyte Operation, 314, 318, 320, 323, 328, 332–334, 345, 358
Lighthouse Hill. *See* Palomas Hill.
Line of departure, 84, 505–506, 517, 522, 615, 649
Lingayen, 337, 339, 342, 348
Lingayen Airfield, 339
Lingayen Gulf, 334–335, 337, 342
Liscome Bay, 396
LITHARGE, 181*n*, 183–184
Little Slot, 221
Liversedge, Col Harry B., 471, 509, 512, 528, 530, 539, 545, 625
Logistics, 82, 476, 716, 725
London Naval Treaty, 7
Los Angeles, Calif., 454
Los Negros, 363
LOSSAU, 183
Loud, Cdr Wayne R., 63
Louisville, 106, 190, 278, 281
Lovell, Stanley P., 612*n*
Low Countries, 19
Lowery, Sgt Louis R., 542
LSM *216*, 517–518
LST *776*, 436–437
LST *477*, 537
LST *779*, 543, 552
LST *807*, 560
LST *929*, 479
LST *930*, 479
LST *931*, 479
LST *1032*, 552
LST *1033*, 479

INDEX

Lummus, 1stLt Jack, 640–641
Lunga Point, 537
Luzon, 21, 62, 287, 291, 293–294, 296–298, 303, 312, 324, 327, 331–332, 334–337, 339–343, 348–349, 351–352, 356–358, 361, 366, 368, 370, 377, 382–383, 433, 435, 443, 457, 465, 734–735, 737
Luzon Operation, 332, 334, 348, 353, 357, 715
Lyman, Col E. L., 248*n*

MacArthur, Gen Douglas, 9, 24, 51–52, 54, 62, 65, 181, 286, 296, 301, 303, 309, 326, 333, 336–337, 342–343, 358, 386, 390, 465, 732–735
MacFarlane, LtCol Robert E., 521
Mackay, Maj Malcolm S., 437; LtCol, 438, 597
Magai Channel, 183
Main Valley, 221
Major, Col Harold C., 388
Majuro Atoll, 400, 400*n*, 405, 407, 438
Makin Island, 396, 398–399, 400*n*, 408, 412
Malabang Field, 383
Malabang landing, 373*n*
Malacanan Palace, 343
Malakal, 57, 281
Malanaphy, Cdr Michael J., 492
Malaya, 730
Malayan, 55, 294
Malaybaley, 385
Maloelap Airfield, 396, 405
Maloelap Atoll, 412–413, 415
Manchuria, 9, 67–68, 454, 458, 463, 730
Mangaldan, 337, 339–340, 342, 352, 356–357, 370, 373, 381–383
Mangaldan Field, 339, 354
Manila, 294, 296, 303, 334, 342–344, 346–347, 349, 351–354
  Liberation of, 348
Manila Bay, 296, 354
Manila Bay, 423
Manila, John, 514. *See also* Basilone, GySgt John.
Manus Island, 83, 315
Maps and charts, Japanese, 472
Marakina Watershed, 354
Marcus Island, 283*n*, 444
Marianas, 3, 6, 25–26, 30, 51, 54, 60, 67–68, 70, 292–293, 301, 395, 397, 416, 422, 428, 429, 436, 443–444, 449, 453, 462–464, 466–468, 477–478, 483, 485, 495, 500, 504, 527, 559, 592, 598, 600, 604, 614, 713, 717–718, 723, 731–733

Marianas Operation, 26, 60, 62, 64, 84, 86, 153, 424, 465
Marianas Turkey Shoot, 423
Marine units
 Air
  Aircraft, Fleet Marine Force, Pacific, 27–30, 40, 47, 433
  Marine Aircraft, Hawaiian Area, 46
  Marine Aircraft, Northern Solomons, 301, 303, 387, 388
  Marine Aircraft, South Pacific, 46
  Marine Aircraft, Defense Force, Samoan Area, 46
  Marine Fleet Air, West Coast, 27, 30, 45–46
  Marine Garrison Air Force, Western Carolines, 431
  Marine Air Support Control Units, Amphibious Forces, Pacific, 48
  Marine Aircraft Wings, Pacific, 28, 44–47, 99
  1st Marine Aircraft Wing, 27, 41–47, 301, 303–304, 312, 347, 362, 387–389
  2d Marine Aircraft Wing, 27, 41–42, 44–47, 98, 98*n*, 99, 212, 377, 388, 425, 430–431
  3d Marine Aircraft Wing, 27, 46–47
  4th Marine Aircraft Wing, 27, 44–47, 398–399, 401, 404*n*, 412, 414, 416, 420, 422, 425
  Marine Aircraft Wings, Pacific, Service Group, 44–45
  Marine Carrier Groups, Aircraft, Fleet Marine Force, Pacific, 47, 423, 434–435
  Marine Aircraft Groups, 340, 342
  Marine Aircraft Group 11, 42, 98, 100–101, 127, 282, 430
  Marine Aircraft Group 12, 326–333, 335, 339, 342, 359, 362–363, 365–368, 372–373, 378, 390
  Marine Aircraft Group 13, 398, 400, 407
  Marine Aircraft Group 14, 334–335, 339, 359, 362–363, 375–376, 390
  Marine Aircraft Group 15, 413, 437
  Marine Aircraft Group 21, 42, 393, 426–429
  Marine Aircraft Group 22, 401, 411
  Marine Aircraft Group 23, 45
  Marine Aircraft Group 24, 303–304, 306–308, 335, 337, 339, 342–344, 347–349, 354, 356–357, 362–363, 368, 373, 382, 384, 387–389, 735

829

Marine Aircraft Group 25, 98, 430
Marine Aircraft Group 31, 398, 400, 407–408
Marine Aircraft Group 32, 303–304, 335, 339, 342–344, 347–349, 352, 354, 356–357, 359, 362–363, 366–368, 371, 373, 378, 388, 390
Marine Aircraft Group 41, 45
Marine Aircraft Group 42, 45
Marine Aircraft Group 43, 45
Marine Aircraft Group 44, 45
Marine Aircraft Group 45, 433–434
Marine Aircraft Group 51, 47, 423
Marine Aircraft Group 61, 327, 363, 388
Second Marine Aircraft Group (Oahu), 20
Marine Aircraft Group (Dagupan), 339, 350, 354, 356, 368
Marine Aircraft Groups (Mindanao), 363
Marine Aircraft Groups (Zamboanga), 370–374, 382, 384, 388
Marine Aircraft Service Group 48, 435
Marine Aircraft Support Groups, 47
Provisional Air Support Command, 47
Landing Force Air Support Control Unit, 503, 605, 611, 719
Marine Base Defense Aircraft Group 45, 98n, 433
Marine Base Defense Aircraft Group 48, 47, 423
Base Air Detachment 3, 42
AWS–1, 411
AWS–2, 429
AWS–3, 363, 383
AWS–4, 363, 366, 368
AWS–5, 425
Headquarters Squadron, Marine Aircraft Wings, Pacific, 44–46
HqSqn–11, 101
HqSqn–12, 45
VMB–413, 363, 388
VMB–423, 388
VMB–433, 363, 388
VMB–611, 363, 373–374, 380, 386
VMB–612, 429, 436, 485
VMF–111, 42, 398, 400, 400n, 412
VMF–113, 400, 411–412, 416
VMF–114, 99, 101, 210–211, 226, 232, 241–242, 256, 259, 283–284, 430, 432–433
VMF–115, 326, 329, 363, 368, 378
VMF–121, 42, 99, 101, 430
VMF–122, 99, 101, 228, 430
VMF–124, 335, 435–436, 503

VMF–151, 398
VMF–155, 417
VMF–211, 42, 326, 328–329, 363, 368, 378, 383
VMF–212, 334, 340, 363
VMF–213, 335, 435
VMF–216, 427, 429
VMF–217, 427, 429
VMF–218, 326, 328–329, 363, 368, 383
VMF–221, 42
VMF–222, 334, 340, 363, 375–376
VMF–223, 334, 363, 375–376
VMF–224, 398, 400, 408, 416
VMF–225, 427, 429
VMF–241, 398
VMF–251, 363, 375–376
VMF–252, 42
VMF–311, 398
VMF–312, 433
VMF–313, 326, 328–330, 363, 368, 378
VMF–321, 429
VMF–422, 398, 401, 403–404, 409–411
VMF–441, 398, 400, 416
VMF(N)–531, 400
VMF(N)–532, 400, 408, 411, 413, 425
VMF(N)–534, 427, 429
VMF(N)–541, 99, 259, 326–328, 330, 333, 430, 432
VMF(N)–542, 433–434
VMJ–152, 42
VMJ–252, 413
VMJ–353, 397–398, 413
VMO squadrons, 718
VMO–1, 426–427, 429
VMO–2, 424–425, 429
VMO–3, 153, 432
VMO–4, 424–425, 436–437, 595, 646, 650, 665, 671
VMO–5, 436–437, 595
VMO–151, 42
VMO–251, 42, 334–335
VMR–253, 429, 438–439, 604
VMR–353, 438, 604
VMR–952, 437–438, 597, 604
VMS–3, 42
VMSB–131, 42
VMSB–132, 42
VMSB–133, 339, 346, 383, 385, 388
VMSB–142, 339, 346, 353, 370, 380, 383
VMSB–151, 398, 411
VMSB–231, 42, 405, 412
VMSB–232, 42

INDEX 831

VMSB-236, 339, 370, 378, 380, 388
VMSB-241, 339, 346, 353, 383-385, 388
VMSB-243, 339, 353, 363, 380
VMSB-244, 339, 353, 383, 388
VMSB-331, 398-399, 407, 412n, 418
VMSB-341, 339, 353, 380, 383
VMSB-354, 420
VMTB-131, 367, 429
VMTB-134, 100-101
VMTB-232, 433-434
VMTB-242, 429, 598
Ground
  Fleet Marine Force, 10, 17, 19, 21, 23-29, 32-33, 36, 38-40, 44, 47-48, 464, 466-467, 476, 489
  Headquarters, Fleet Marine Force, 17, 26-27, 30-31, 36, 38-39, 46
  Amphibious Corps, Atlantic Fleet, 20, 467
  Department of the Pacific, 38
  Administrative Command, Fleet Marine Force, Pacific, 26-27, 30
  Marine Garrison Force, 246, 475
  Amphibious Training Staff, FMFPac, 21
  Headquarters and Service Battalion, FMFPac, 27
  Marine Supply Service, FMFPac, 477
  Service Command, FMFPac, 30
  Supply Service, FMFPac, 27-28, 30, 477
  Transient Center (Marianas Area), FMFPac, 31
  Marine Corps Expeditionary Force, 16-17
  Marine Service of Supply, Amphibious Troops, Pacific, 24
  Expeditionary Troops, 83, 162, 181, 469, 471, 474, 484, 607, 714
  Force Amphibian Tractor Group, 27
  Force Antiaircraft Artillery, 27
  Force Artillery, 27
  Force Reserve, 27
  Force Service Troops, 27
  Fleet Base Defense Force, 17
  FMF Transient Center, 27
  I Marine Amphibious Corps, 3, 21, 23-25
  II Marine Amphibious Corps, 24
  X-Ray Provisional Amphibious Corps, 61, 64, 78-79
    Redesignated III Amphibious Corps, 66
  III Amphibious Corps, 25-27, 30, 61, 63, 64, 79, 88, 96, 162-163, 165, 168, 177, 181, 186-187, 246, 252, 278n, 430
  V Amphibious Corps, 23-27, 30, 38-39, 61, 102, 300-301, 425, 436, 466-469, 471, 471n, 472-473, 476-480, 482-483, 489, 491-492, 504, 522, 522n, 523, 525-526, 528, 547-549, 554-557, 560-561, 563-565, 565n, 567-569, 571-573, 577-579, 579n, 580, 583, 585-588, 593, 597-598, 603, 605, 608, 608n, 610, 624, 629, 633, 635, 638, 643n, 644, 647, 670-672, 685, 700n, 711-712, 714, 719-721, 723, 725
    Administrative Command, 24-25
    Supply Service, 25
  V Corps Artillery, 301, 314, 316-319, 323, 565, 574, 580, 605, 708, 720
  I Corps Supply Service, 25
  III Corps Headquarters and Troops, 27
  V Corps Headquarters and Troops, 27
  1st Marine Division, 19-20, 27, 34, 36, 63, 77-79, 83, 86, 89, 94, 96, 100, 106, 127, 130, 138, 158-159, 161-162, 165, 185, 187, 200, 209, 216, 218, 223, 225, 227, 232, 236, 240, 245, 249-251, 253-254, 266, 269, 271, 274-275, 277, 281-283, 283n, 284, 286, 430, 433, 734
  2d Marine Division, 19, 27, 34, 97, 266, 395-396, 425, 464
  3d Marine Division, 27, 389, 437, 464, 467-469, 471, 473, 478n, 483-484, 515, 525, 537, 553-555, 558, 563-565, 565n, 572-579, 579n, 580-582, 582n, 583-587, 589-593, 616-617, 623, 626-627, 630, 634, 638, 644n, 645, 647, 649, 652, 655, 659, 672-673, 676, 680, 684, 686, 688-689, 691, 701-702, 704, 708, 711, 711n, 712
  4th Marine Division, 27, 400, 407-408, 423, 425, 437, 466-469, 471, 471n, 472-473, 478n, 479n, 482-483, 498, 502, 505-506, 508-509, 517-518, 521, 523, 525-526, 528, 549, 551-552, 554-558, 560-561, 563-564, 565n, 569-571, 595, 602-603, 605, 616, 636n, 642, 644n, 645-647, 649-652, 654, 657-661, 665, 668-677, 680-683, 692-693, 695, 702, 708, 711n, 712, 714, 725
  5th Marine Division, 25, 27, 34, 437, 467-469, 471-473, 478n, 479n, 480, 482-484, 498, 502, 505-506, 508-509, 512, 516-517, 521, 525, 528, 549, 551-552, 554-558, 560-561, 563-565, 565n, 567, 569, 571, 573, 575-579, 579n, 580-581, 581n, 582n, 583-587, 591-592, 602-603, 605, 616-618, 620, 622, 624, 626-627, 629-636, 636n, 637 638, 640-641, 643-644, 644n, 645, 658, 676, 686, 688, 691, 695,

697–698, 700–705, 707, 711n, 712, 714, 725
6th Marine Division, 27
1st Marine Brigade, 17, 19, 344n
2d Marine Brigade, 17, 19, 344n
1st Marines, 80–86, 91, 110, 116, 122, 126, 130, 134, 141, 143–146, 148, 155–159, 161, 186–187, 189, 192, 201, 223–224, 228, 237, 280, 467
3d Marines, 564, 565n, 573, 607–608, 608n
5th Marines, 80, 91, 96, 115–116, 118, 122, 126, 128–129, 134, 139, 141–143, 146, 148, 152, 155, 185, 201, 204–205, 207, 210, 214, 218, 223, 236–238, 240, 242, 249–250, 252, 254, 593
6th Marines, 467
7th Marines, 19, 80–81, 96, 118, 121, 126–127, 129–130, 134, 138, 146, 148, 153, 155, 185, 192, 200, 207, 216, 222–228, 233–234, 236–238, 252, 269, 276
9th Marines, 564, 573–578, 581–585, 587–588, 590–592, 617–618, 648, 665, 667, 672, 686–687, 690, 711
11th Marines, 80, 91, 94, 105, 129, 153, 202, 207, 233, 250
12th Marines, 573, 579, 579n, 580, 587, 589, 697
13th Marines, 472, 482, 515–516, 521, 548, 554, 579n, 617, 621, 624–625, 627–628, 636, 643, 697, 701
14th Marines, 472, 545, 552, 560, 568, 579n, 587, 655, 671, 675–676, 697
20th Marines, 408
21st Marines, 305–306, 484, 515, 551, 554–559, 561–563, 565–567, 573–575, 578, 580–588, 590–591, 593, 623, 636, 647, 655–656, 690–691, 701, 711
22d Marines, 408
23d Marines, 471, 509, 517–519, 521, 549–551, 554–558, 647, 649–652, 654–656, 658–659, 661–662, 665, 667–670, 672, 674–678, 680–681, 692, 694
24th Marines, 471–472, 519, 521, 557, 563, 565, 567–569, 647–648, 659–661, 663, 666–668, 671, 673, 675–681
25th Marines, 471, 471n, 509, 519–521, 548–551, 554–557, 560, 647, 649–651, 656, 658, 660–661, 664–665, 669–670, 673, 675–676, 678, 680–682, 692, 694
26th Marines, 469–471, 484, 515, 549, 557–558, 561, 565–567, 569, 575, 616–618, 620–621, 627, 629–636, 639, 643, 699–703, 706–707
27th Marines, 471–472, 509, 513–515, 548–550, 554–557, 621–623, 625, 633–636, 638, 642–643, 686, 697–702, 707
28th Marines, 471, 482, 509–510, 512–513, 516, 528, 530–531, 533–534, 536, 538–539, 542, 545, 547, 553, 624–628, 630, 632–633, 635, 637, 640, 642–643, 697, 699–701, 703, 707
29th Marines, 39
Field Depots
  1st, 28
  3d, 28
  5th, 28, 477
  7th, 28
  8th, 28, 478, 602, 708, 725
  16th, 28, 86, 99, 150, 225, 246, 282
Base Depots
  4th, 28
  6th, 28, 477
1st Provisional Field Artillery Group, 652
Amphibian Tractor Battalions
  1st, 28, 92, 229, 252, 271
  2d, 28
  3d, 28
  4th, 28
  5th, 28
  6th, 28, 93
  8th, 28
  10th, 28
  11th, 28, 643
Amphibious Reconnaissance Battalion, 698
Antiaircraft Artillery Battalions
  1st, 27
  2d, 27
  3d, 27
  4th, 27
  5th, 27
  7th, 27, 175, 179
  8th, 27
  9th, 27
  10th, 27
  11th, 27
  12th, 27, 265
  14th, 27
  15th, 28
  16th, 28
  17th, 28
  18th, 28
Armored Amphibian Battalions
  1st, 28
  2d, 28, 472, 505, 618, 648, 671, 698, 721

INDEX 833

    3d, 28, 93, 242, 252
Artillery Battalions
    1/11, 80
    1/12, 575, 686
    1/13, 515, 639
    1/14, 521–522, 555, 573, 575, 661, 668
    2/11, 80, 116, 123, 195, 228
    2/13, 515
    2/14, 521–522, 652, 668
    3/11, 80, 129, 153, 269
    3/13, 515–516, 531
    3/14, 521–522, 552, 668
    4/11, 86, 248, 252, 254
    4/12, 708
    4/13, 515, 574, 578
    4/14, 472, 522, 552, 668
Base Headquarters Battalions
    1st, 28
    3d, 28
Defense Battalions, 19, 21, 43
    52d, 28
Engineer Battalions
    1st Separate, 28, 114, 204
    2d Separate, 28, 595, 720
    1st, 152, 156, 204, 240
    3d, 573
    4th, 647
    5th, 545, 628
Infantry Battalions
    1/1, 114, 144–147, 157–159, 161, 189
    1/5, 115–117, 122–124, 126, 139, 141, 143, 201–202, 204–205, 209, 214, 216–217, 236–237, 240, 250
    1/7, 119, 119n, 121, 129n, 135–138, 159–160, 190, 200, 210, 212, 223–229, 231, 236, 250–252
    1/9, 574–577, 581–582, 586, 590–591, 685–688
    1/21, 306, 558–559, 559n, 562, 578, 580, 582–586, 588–589, 591–592, 626, 686, 691
    1/23, 508, 517–519, 526, 548, 550, 554, 558, 647, 649, 652, 654–656, 658, 660, 665, 667, 671–672, 674, 680, 687, 692, 779
    1/24, 519–521, 547–548, 550–551, 555, 557, 559–560, 568–569, 647–648, 658, 660–662, 666–667, 672, 674–676, 680–681
    1/25, 508, 519–520, 526, 547, 550–551, 554–555, 559, 650–651, 654, 656–657, 660, 664–665, 667, 671, 673–675, 681–682, 694
    1/26, 515, 547, 549, 554, 557, 567, 617, 621, 623, 633–635, 638–641, 697, 703, 706–707
    1/27, 508, 513–514, 549, 554–555, 621–623, 633–634, 636, 642
    1/28, 508–510, 512–514, 525n, 526, 530, 534, 536, 538, 543, 545, 625–626, 629–630, 637, 640, 643, 707
    2/1, 110, 113–115, 123, 126, 134, 144–147, 157–159, 229
    2/5, 117–118, 123, 126, 139, 141–143, 201, 205–206, 208–209, 216–217, 232–233, 237–238, 241–242, 244–246
    2/7, 80, 119, 130–131, 138, 144, 146–147, 157, 159–160, 190, 207, 224–231, 234, 236, 251–252
    2/9, 574–575, 575n, 576–577, 581–582, 585–586, 590–592, 684, 686, 688
    2/21, 558–559, 562, 566–567, 578, 580, 582–587, 591, 686, 691
    2/23, 508, 517–519, 550, 554, 558, 647, 654–655, 658, 667, 672–674, 676–681, 692
    2/24, 519, 547, 549, 554, 557, 567–568, 636n, 647–648, 658–663, 665–668, 672, 675–676, 680–682, 693–694
    2/25, 520, 547–548, 550–551, 555, 559, 561, 567, 647–650, 654, 656–658, 664–665, 667, 669–670, 673, 681–682, 693–694
    2/26, 561, 567, 617–618, 620, 624, 626–627, 629–631, 635, 699–700
    2/27, 508, 513–515, 549, 557, 561, 617–618, 621, 623, 636–637, 639–642
    2/28, 508–510, 512–514, 530–531, 535–536, 538–540, 543, 625–630, 633, 637, 640–641, 707
    3/1, 110, 113, 144–145, 147, 156–157, 159–160, 187, 189, 192, 197
    3/4, 522
    3/5, 116–117, 119–120, 126, 128, 139, 141–143, 148, 201–202, 205, 210–212, 214, 228–229, 231–232, 237, 240, 246, 249–251, 433
    3/7, 116–119, 119n, 120–121, 134–138, 141, 159–160, 192–193, 195, 197–200, 224–225, 227–229, 231, 234, 236–238, 252, 697
    3/9, 575, 575n, 576, 578, 580–583, 585–593, 626, 629–631, 685–687
    3/21, 566–567, 576, 578, 580–581, 585–

587, 591–592, 685–687
  3/23, 518–519, 547, 556, 558, 647, 649, 651–655, 658, 660, 664, 667, 671–672
  3/24, 520–521, 567–568, 647–650, 656, 659–661, 665–667, 672, 676–677, 681
  3/25, 508, 519–521, 547–548, 550, 555, 559, 561, 650–651, 654, 657–658, 664, 667, 669–671, 673, 680–682, 693
  3/26, 558, 567, 617–618, 626–627, 630–631, 635–636, 639, 643, 699–700, 703, 707
  3/27, 515, 547, 549, 554, 621, 623, 625, 633, 637, 643, 691, 703, 706–707
  3/28, 512–513, 530–531, 534–536, 538–540, 625–626, 629–630, 633, 637, 643, 701, 703, 706–707
1st Medical Battalion, 148, 251
Motor Transport Battalions
  1st, 88, 252
  5th, 643
155m Howitzer Battalions
  1st, 27
  2d, 27, 552
  3d, 27, 80, 153, 254
  4th, 27
  5th, 27, 314–319, 320n, 322
155mm Gun Battalions
  7th, 27
  8th, 27, 80, 153, 254
  9th, 27
  10th, 27
  11th, 27, 314, 316–317, 319n
  12th, 27
Pioneer Battalions
  1st, 84, 86, 147, 152, 225, 282
  3d, 573, 602
  5th, 703, 708, 710, 724
1st Seacoast Artillery Battalion, 28
1st Service Battalion, 86, 282
Service and Supply Battalions
  1st, 28
  2d, 28
  3d, 28
  4th, 28
Tank Battalions
  1st, 88, 115, 124, 155, 228, 272
  3d, 484, 573–574, 578, 581, 591, 685, 687–688
  4th, 472, 509, 517, 519, 548–550, 555, 560, 647–648, 650, 666–668, 676
  5th, 472, 512–515, 531, 538, 549, 554, 560, 565, 618, 625–628, 631, 639, 641

Provisional Battalion, 675, 681
4th Provisional Battalion, 681
Amphibian Truck Companies
  4th, 521
  5th, 516
2d Bomb Disposal Company, 600
Joint Assault Signal Company (JASCO), 103, 282, 332, 384
4th Joint Assault Signal Company, 277
War Dog Platoons,
  4th, 158
  6th, 624
1st Provisional Rocket Detachment, 662, 655
3d Rocket Detachment, 621
Demolition teams, 135–137, 156, 169, 209, 214, 216, 226, 262, 271, 531, 621, 633, 636, 649, 667, 685, 689, 697, 706
Marine Detachment (Provisional), U. S. Army Forces, Western Pacific, 39
Marine Detachment, Sixth Army, 39
Marine Detachment, Tenth Army, 38
Marine Detachment (Provisional), Marianas Area, 31
1st Division Military Police Company, 233
7th Marines Weapons Company, 224, 227
Marine Corps Air Station, Cherry Point, N.C., 20, 100
Marine Corps Air Station, Mojave, Calif., 45, 47, 423
Marine Corps Base, San Diego, Calif. 17
Marine Corps Equipment Board, 17, 35
Marine Corps Schools, Quantico, Va., 17, 60
Marshall, General of the Army George C., 614
Marshalls, 3, 16, 48, 54, 60, 67, 85n, 110, 279, 288, 292, 315, 392, 395–396, 399–400, 400n, 401, 405, 407–409, 411–414, 416–417, 420–422, 428, 449, 462, 466–467, 478, 713, 718, 731, 733
Masilay, 371
Mason, Col Arthur T., 172n
Matsunaga, RAdm Teiichi, 451
Matsushita, Maj Nagahiko, 533n
Maui, 468, 482–483
McAloney, Capt Samuel H., 344n, 351n, 368, 378–379
McBroom, Maj Robert B., 89
McCarthy, LCdr Daniel J., 538
McCaul, Maj Vernon J., 42; Col, 304, 363, 388; LtGen, 304n
McConaughy, Capt James L., Jr., 351–352, 379
McCutcheon, LtCol Keith B., 304, 306–307, 337,

INDEX
835

343, 372, 382, 389; MajGen, 343n, 373n
McGlothlin, Maj Joe H., 329, 401-402
McQuade, Maj Thomas J., 42
Mears, Capt Dwayne E., 510
Meat Grinder, 616, 645, 647-648, 651, 661, 682
Medical Activities, 55, 83, 139, 142-143, 148, 150-151, 185, 225, 227, 234-235, 238, 266, 274-275, 398-399, 427, 431, 438, 477, 517, 525, 536, 545, 551, 557, 567, 569, 597, 602-604, 610, 613, 629, 635, 642, 648, 668, 677-678, 682, 689, 699, 721-723, 761
Mee, Maj Fenton, 5; LtCol, 525n, 555, 650, 653, 656, 660, 674
Megee, Col Vernon E., 47-48, 503-504, 504n, 597; Gen, 598n
Melanesian, 55
Merritt, Col Lewie G., 45; BGen, 388, 398, 401, 414, 416
Meyer, Col Lyle H., 303, 307, 339, 356, 387
Micronesia, 16, 54-55
Middle Village, 174
Midway, 17, 21, 342, 401, 438-439
Mille Airstrip, 396
Mille Atoll, 400n, 405, 412-413, 415, 418, 421
Miller, Sgt P. J., 344n, 479
Miller, Lt Roy G., 320, 436
Millington, LtCol William A., 435-436, 503-504, 506
Mills, LtCol James E., 314; Col, 319n
Minami village, 445, 447, 459, 568, 642, 646, 648, 650, 660, 666, 673, 676, 682
Mindanao, 52, 64-65, 291-293, 303, 309, 321, 332, 356-359, 361-363, 365-366, 374, 380-388, 390, 733-734
Mindoro Island, 331, 334, 336, 358, 363, 381
Mississinewa, 434
Missoula, 540
Mitchell, Maj Norman L., 259
Mitchell, MajGen Ralph J., 46, 301, 303n, 312, 314, 326, 334-335, 362-363, 387
Mitscher, RAdm Marc A., 405, 493, 495-496, 717; VAdm, 64, 102
Moluccas, 52
Monte Cassino, 530
Monitor, 314
Montgomery, Field Marshal Sir Bernard L., 307-308
Moore, BGen Ernest, 598, 708
Moore, Maj James B., 400
Moore, MajGen James T., 47, 98-99, 430-431, 433, 598n
Moran, Lt Robert P., 402-403

Moret Field, 367-368, 370-374, 379-384, 388
Moret, Capt Paul, 42; LtCol, 367
Morison, Samuel Eliot, 715n
Mormacport, 101
Moro guerrillas, 379
Morotai Island, 52, 62, 65, 293, 309-310, 381, 733-734
Mortimer Valley, 260
Moses, Col Martain, 318
Motoyama Plateau, 471, 571-574, 577, 579, 632
Motoyama tableland, 580, 593
Motoyama village, 445, 447, 449n, 459, 539, 574, 577-578, 581, 584-586, 634, 684, 686
Mt. Bangkal, 379
Mt. Daho, 379-380
Mt. Dato, 379
Mt. Mataba, 353-354
Mt. McKinley, 106, 187
Mt. Olympus, 106, 108, 278, 314
Mt. Oyama, 262
Mt. Patikul, 379
Mt. Suribachi, 453, 455-459, 469, 471, 473, 483, 487, 495-498, 500, 502-503, 508-510, 512-513, 516, 525-526, 528, 530-531, 533, 533n, 534-540, 542-543, 545, 547, 553, 564-565, 593, 604, 611, 618, 624-626, 634, 646, 677-679, 700, 726
Mudge, MajGen Verne D., 343n, 344n, 347, 352
Mueller, MajGen Paul J., 63, 165, 168-169, 171-173, 175, 177, 179, 181, 186, 211, 232n, 237n, 252, 254, 259n, 260-262, 263n, 264, 278
Mugai Channel, 181
Mulcahy, Col Francis P., 46; MajGen, 47, 388
Munda Airstrip, 428
Munday, Maj Jack R., 123n, 129n
Munich Settlement, 9
Murahori, 1stLt, 190
Murai, MajGen Kenjiro, 70, 259, 263; LtGen, 264
Murphy, LCdr Raymond P., 595
Murray, Maj Clay, 559n, 562
Murray, 420
Mussolini, Benito, 9
Mustain, LtCol Hollis U., 508, 519, 550, 555

Nakagawa, Col Kunio, 68-70, 72, 146-148, 156-157, 159, 161, 169, 179, 217, 219, 222, 225, 229-230, 233, 235, 245, 248-249, 258, 260-264; LtGen, 267
Nakayama, 146. *See also* Hill 200.
Namur Island, 407. *See also* Roi-Namur.
Nanomea, 396, 401-402, 404

Nanpo Shoto, 444–445, 464
Nansei Shoto, 465
Napalm, 92, 92n, 136, 153, 169
Napp, Cdr Emil E., 90n
Nashville, 311
Natives, 265, 317, 365, 398, 402, 404, 418, 420
Natoma Bay, 423
Nauru, 396, 399, 415
Navajo Marine Code Talkers, 620, 620n, 621, 719
Naval gunfire, 17, 34, 36, 63, 78, 83, 94, 103–105, 108, 112, 119n, 135, 137, 146, 153, 162, 166, 168–169, 177, 190, 208, 210, 221, 278–279, 280–282, 288, 314, 368, 404, 475, 483, 486–487, 489–493, 495, 501, 504–505, 512, 534, 536, 547–550, 555–556, 558, 562–563, 567, 573, 576, 579n, 582, 584, 587, 589, 605, 611, 617, 620–621, 623, 633, 638, 640, 643, 646, 648, 654, 658, 661–662, 668, 671–672, 674, 684, 714–719, 726
Naval liaison officers, 282
Naval liaison parties, 308
Naval losses, 312
Naval Treaty of 1922, 4, 6
Naval War College, 15
Navy, 13, 24, 41, 63–64, 278, 307, 325, 334, 342, 388, 430, 436, 452, 670, 714, 732, 734
  Bureau of Aeronautics, 41
  Bureau of Naval Personnel, 279
  General Board of the Navy, 14, 20, 40, 43
Navy Units. *See also* Task Organizations.
  U. S. Fleet, 17, 395, 735
  Atlantic Fleet, 19–20
  Pacific Fleet, 19, 23, 184, 734
    Third Fleet, 63–64, 102, 245, 278, 293, 300, 303, 309, 334–336, 430, 435
    Fifth Fleet, 23, 68, 70, 77, 101, 422, 435, 466, 491, 502
  Seventh Fleet, 300–301, 307, 309, 326, 335
  Amphibious Force, Atlantic Fleet, 20
  Amphibious Force, Pacific Fleet, 21, 23, 467
  Amphibious Support Force, 483, 492, 502
  Attack Forces
    Eastern, 63
    Luzon, 336
    Northern, 25, 502
    Southern, 25
    Ulithi, 183
    Western, 63, 83, 102, 165, 186, 283
  Covering Force, 63–64, 483, 492, 498, 500, 503
  Fast Carrier Forces, 64, 101, 435, 495
  Fleet Naval Landing Forces, 25, 63–64, 425

  Joint Expeditionary Force, 483
  Joint Expeditionary Force, 466, 483
  Pacific Forces
    Central, 23
    Southwest, 62
  Service Force, Pacific, 477
  Fleet Air Wing 2, 398
  Transport Division, 28, 316
  Transport Division 32, 484
  Amphibious Group 2, 476
  Attack Groups
    Angaur, 63, 165
    Peleliu, 63
    Ulithi, 181
  Defense Group, 634
  Escort Carrier Group, 96
  Fast Carrier Groups, 102
  Fire Support Group, 64, 102–103, 278
  Mine Group, 492
  Submarine Offensive Reconnaissance Group, 102
  Support Carrier Group, 492, 495, 500, 598
  Transport Groups, 95
  Transport Group 3, 83
  Underwater Demolition Group, 492
  Air Evacuation Squadron 2, 597
  Destroyer Squadron, 54
  Interpretation Squadron 2, 473
  Naval Construction Battalions (Seabees), 89, 204, 274, 335, 398, 408, 484, 517, 526, 564, 595, 600, 701, 710, 712
    9th, 560
    15th, 89
    31st, 479, 479n, 564, 594, 602
    33d, 152, 204, 272
    51st, 433
    62d, 479, 595, 720
    73d, 152, 204
    93d, 335
    98th, 708
    133d, 479, 479n. 594–595, 602, 634
    1054th, 152
  Photographic Squadrons
    4th, 472
    5th, 472
  Service Squadron 10, 478
  Transport Squadrons
    11, 484
    15, 584
    16, 484
  Underwater Demolition teams (UDT), 78–79, 83, 103, 110, 165, 183, 207, 268, 490,

INDEX 837

493n, 496–499, 725
UDT 13, 495
UDT 15, 500
VC–21, 283n
VOC–1, 718
Air Support Unit, 492
Fire Support Unit One, 498
Fire Support Unit Two, 498
Gunboat Support Unit One, 492
Gunboat Support Unit Two, 492
Peleliu Fire Support Unit, 96
Kossol Passage Detachment, 63, 103
Shore-Based Aircraft, Forward Area, 414
Navy Yard, 270
Nazi Party, 732
Negro Marines, 150, 516, 602
Negros Island, 294, 331, 358–359, 361, 374–378
Nemoto, Captain, 264
Netherlands, 6
Netherlands Indies, 51, 55
Nevada, 493, 496, 498, 500, 503, 624
New Bern, N. C., 41
New Britain, 77, 89, 237, 266, 303, 363, 444
New Caledonia, 367, 438
Newcomb, Richard F., 458n, 533n, 543n, 677n, 678n
New Georgia, 305, 389, 393, 428, 430
New Guinea, 51–52, 67–68, 97, 287, 291–292, 309, 432, 439, 444, 730, 733
New Hebrides, 95, 98, 100, 430, 433
New Ireland, 303, 363
New London, Conn., 14
New Mexico, 336
Newport, R.I., 14–15
New River Base, N.C., 20
Newton, VAdm John H., 293
New York, 493, 500, 503
Ngardololok, 59, 142–143, 201, 217
Ngarekeukl, 189–190
Ngarmoked Island, 57, 135–138
Ngercheu Island, 265
Ngeregong, 261–262
Ngesebus Airfield, 73, 211
Ngesebus Island, 58, 61, 73, 80, 148, 189, 202, 205–212, 214, 219, 222–223, 242, 250, 276, 281, 84, 306, 735
Nicaragua, 16–17, 305, 467
Nichols Field, 354
Nimitz, Adm Chester W., 24, 26, 29–30, 38, 44–47, 51–52, 52n, 60–62, 65, 98, 278, 286, 292–293, 326, 388, 395–396, 420, 427, 430, 462–466, 491n, 612, 712, 714, 733

Nine-Power Treaty, 6
Nishi, LtCol Baron Takeichi, 454–455, 459, 590–591, 628, 646, 652, 655, 684, 692; Col, 706
Nishi Ridge, 616, 625, 628–630
Nishi Village, 618, 630, 632, 635, 637
Nisshu Maru, 455
Noble, RAdm Albert G., 381
Noguchi, Capt Iwao, 711
Norfolk, Va., 35
Norman, Col Lawrence, 398
Normandy, 731–732
North Africa, 733
North Carolina, 20
North Carolina, 493, 503
Northern Solomons, 303
Northrop Aviation, 326
Norway, 19
Noumea, 431
Novaliches, 346
Nui Island, 402–403
Nukufetau, 399
Nutting, Capt Lewis, 605

Oahu, 21, 183, 417, 477, 483
Obata, Gen Hideyoshi, 449, 453
Observers, Japanese, 128, 141
Ocean Island, 415
OCTAGON Conference, 65
Oder River, 730
Office of Strategic Services (OSS), 612
Ofstie, RAdm Ralph, 278, 281
Ogasawara Gunto, 444
Okinawa, 30, 32, 39, 47, 184, 266, 277, 309, 377, 387–388, 465, 490, 572, 614, 715, 734–735, 737
Old Baldy, 260
Oldendorf, RAdm Jesse B., 103–104, 106, 287n, 279–280
Oldfield, LtCol John S., 515
Old Glory, 445
O'Leary, TSgt Jeremiah A., Jr., 235n
Ommaney Bay, 336
O'Neill, Capt Donald D., 425
Ormoc, 321, 325, 327–328, 330
Orote Field, 426–428
Orote Peninsula, 425–426
Osaka Yama, 628. *See also* Hill 362A.
Osborne, 1stLt Stanley, 662–663
Osuka, MajGen Kotau, 453, 457–458, 475
Ota, Lt Hideo, 711
Owi Island, 335, 432

Oyama, 260
Oyanagi, Leading Private Yutaka, 683n
Ozark, 723

Pacific Islands, 55
Pacific Ocean, 54, 439–440, 444, 713–714, 731, 737, 764
Pacific Ocean Areas, 24, 29, 38, 41, 54, 60
Pacific Theater, 21, 292, 504, 522, 588, 612–613, 620n, 726, 730
Pacific War, 54
Pagan Island, 429
Palampon, 332
Palaus, 16, 47, 52, 54–55, 57–62, 64–68, 71, 76–78, 82, 96–98, 101–102, 105, 134, 162, 165, 180, 183, 189, 193, 223, 227, 232, 245, 253, 259, 265, 279, 286–287, 293, 326, 407, 430, 433, 457, 733–734
Palawan Island, 358–359, 361–362, 365
Palmyra Island, 21, 438
Palo, 310
Palomas Hill, 174, 176. *See also* Lighthouse Hill.
Palompon, 331
Panaon Straits, 310
Panay, 294, 358–359, 361, 363, 370, 374–376, 378
Panay Islands, 328, 331
Parang, 381–383
Parangon, 381
Parker, Capt Elton C., 492
Parris Island, S.C., 35–36
Parry Islands, 408–409
Password CHEVROLET, 620
Patikul, 379
Patrick, MajGen Edwin D., 352–354
Patrols, 269, 611, 637, 692
  antisubmarine, 100, 278, 433, 561, 598, 611, 717
Pearce, Maj Thomas B., Jr., 629
Pearl Harbor, 20, 26, 30, 32, 41, 44–45, 60–61, 67, 94, 98–99, 220, 303, 315, 409, 423, 429, 431, 449, 451, 465, 467–468, 476–477, 501, 537, 677
  Japanese attack, 29, 40, 42, 44
Peatross, LtCol Oscar F., 513n
Peleliu, 3, 36, 57–59, 62–63, 66, 70–73, 75–81, 83–84, 86, 88–89, 92–94, 97, 100–106, 116, 118, 120, 122n, 124, 127–129, 131, 135–136, 138–139, 141–143, 150–51, 153, 155–156, 162, 165, 169, 175, 177, 179–181, 184–197, 189–190, 192–193, 195, 198–202, 204–205, 207, 209–211, 214, 216–219, 221–223, 225, 227–228, 232–233, 236–237, 241–242, 244–246, 249–250, 253–254, 258–263, 265, 267–269, 271–273, 275–286, 288, 300, 306, 309, 326–327, 333, 335, 430–431, 431n, 432, 438, 443, 445, 489, 505, 729, 733–734, 738
Peleliu Airfield, 66, 95, 98–99, 115, 152, 165, 185, 236, 263, 276, 430, 432, 438
Peleliu Island Command, 86, 89, 98, 134, 152, 156, 264–265, 282
Peleliu Operation, 94, 96, 100, 153–154, 161, 185, 190, 207, 214, 266, 270–271, 273–274, 278, 280–281, 284, 285n, 287, 324, 433, 735
Pennsylvania, 145
Pensacola, 493, 495–497, 563, 565, 624
Peppard, Maj Donald A., 237n
Peralta, Col, 375
Percy, Maj George A., 562, 582
Perry, Commo Matthew, 445, 484
Philadelphia, Pa., 14
Philippines, 3, 6, 14, 51–52, 54, 65, 67, 70–71, 76, 102, 179, 181, 184, 279, 287, 291–294, 296–298, 303–304, 306–307, 309, 312, 324, 327, 332–333, 335–337, 340, 342, 348, 354, 356, 358–359, 361–363, 366, 375–377, 380–382, 384, 387–390, 423, 433, 440, 443–444, 447, 457, 461, 463, 465, 469, 718, 718n, 730, 732–736
Philippines Operation, 286, 291, 300, 307, 334, 351, 358, 374, 377, 387, 389–390, 416
Photographs, 221, 275, 318, 382
Pilots
  American, 40–42, 48, 153, 225, 241, 274, 283, 291, 301, 312, 314, 327–328, 330–335, 342, 346, 348–349, 351–352, 354, 356, 359, 362, 365, 367, 370, 374–376, 380, 383–390, 393, 396–397, 400–401, 407, 411–413, 415–417, 420, 422–424, 427–428, 433–437, 440, 472, 485, 490, 493, 499–500, 523, 597, 717–718, 718n, 735
  Japanese, 399–400, 439, 452, 454
Pinckney, 479, 723
Pipes, Sgt Joe L., 516
Plain, Col Louis C., 514
Planning
  American, 51–52, 57–58, 60, 98, 346, 483, 485, 590, 542, 559n, 590, 593, 612, 721
  Japanese, 300, 340, 450
Plaridel, 346
Poland, 8–9, 19
Pollock, LtCol Daniel C., 515, 549
Polynesian, 55

INDEX 839

Ponape Island, 407, 412, 415–416
Pontoon causeways, 152
Pope, Capt Everett P., 157–158, 234
Portland, 281
Portugal, 6, 8
Pratt & Whitney radial engine, 399
President Monroe, 409–410, 710
Price, RAdm John D., 398
Prisoners of War
    Japanese, 134, 138, 175, 195, 199, 207–209, 218, 222, 225, 236, 253, 258, 276–277, 285, 361–362, 370, 418, 522, 551, 626, 644, 690, 692–694, 703–704, 710–711
    Korean, 209, 216, 276, 644
Psychological warfare, 276, 417, 693, 704
Puerta Princesa, 362
Puller, Col Lewis B., 110, 112, 114, 129–130, 134, 144, 147–148, 157, 187
Pusan, Korea, 454
Putnam, Maj Paul A., 42

Quantico, Va., 14, 16–17, 19, 21, 35–36, 39, 41–42, 304, 388
Quarry, Iwo Jima, 525
Quebec, Canada, 65
Quebec (QUADRANT) Conference, 60
Quezon City, 354
Quezon, Manuel L., 296

Rabaul, 303, 393
Radar, 100, 259, 323–324, 326, 328, 330, 373, 404, 408, 411, 425, 486n, 487, 572, 611, 646, 653, 662
Radar Hill, 205, 214, 216–217
Radio Tokyo, 499, 707
Railroads, 171, 171n, 172, 176
Ramsey, LtCol Frederick A., Jr., 130n
Randall, LtCol Carey A., 574
Rea, Maj Amedeo, 561, 618
Reconnaissance activities, 318, 474
Redfield, LtCol Ben Z., 413
Rees, Col James E., 353
Reeves, RAdm John W., Jr., 151
Reich, 2dLt Richard, 662–663
Reinberg, LtCol Louis, 248
Reinforcements
    American, 155
    Japanese, 190, 201, 281, 321–322, 324–325, 328, 382, 453, 664, 670
RENO V Operation, 293n
Rentz, Maj John N., 445n
Replacements, 86, 139, 147–148, 480, 483, 546, 586, 592–593, 602, 608, 633, 688–689, 699, 702, 724
Rescue Activities, 401, 440
Research and Development, OSS. *See* Office of Strategic Services.
Reservoir Hill, 350–351
Reutlinger, Maj Albert F., 93
Reynolds, Maj John E., 417
Rhineland, 9
Richardson, LtGen Robert K., Jr., 464
Ridderhof, Col Stanley E., 388
Ridge 3, 242, 245
Ridge 120, 244
Ridlon, Capt Walter, 663
Roach, Capt Phil E., 510
Roads, 202, 210, 325, 479, 634
Roane, Capt Eugene S., Jr., 322
Robertson, Capt Armand, 95–96
Robertson, LtCol Donn J., 515, 549, 702
Robinson, Col Ralph R., 60
Rockey, MajGen Keller E., 468, 512, 549, 554–555, 557, 579, 581, 598, 610, 617, 626–627, 630, 633, 635, 638, 642–644, 691, 695, 699–702, 706
Rocky Point, 168–169, 171
Rodgers, RAdm Bertram J., 483, 492, 498, 500, 502
Rogers, BGen Ford O., 265
Rogers, Capt John F., 402
Rogers, Col William W., 466; MajGen, 466n, 522n, 565n, 579n, 608n, 700n, 714n,
Roi-Namur, 400, 400n, 401, 405, 407–408, 411, 466–467, 477, 636n
Roll, LtCol George A., 638
Roosevelt, President Franklin D., 9, 19, 65, 613, 614n, 673, 706, 706n, 727
Rosenthal, Joe, 543
Ross, Col Richard P., Jr., 150n
Rota Island, 428–429
Rothwell, LtCol Richard, 519, 558, 562
Rowell, Col Ross E., 41; BGen, 42; MajGen 44, 44n, 45, 45n, 46
Rowse, Maj Earl J., 552
Royal Air Force, 408
Royal Australian Air Force Command, 301, 309, 382
Royal, RAdm Forrest B., 366
Royal Netherlands Marine Corps, 39–40
Royal New Zealand Air Forces, 301, 362
Rozga, Lt Thomas, 425, 436
Rue, Lt Charles C., 370
Ruhl, PFC Donald J., 535

Ruhr Pocket, 730
Rupertus, MajGen William H., 63, 77, 79, 83, 94, 97, 129–132, 151, 165, 185–186, 189–190, 193, 199, 200–201, 204, 206, 210–211, 223–224, 228, 236, 242, 251, 253n, 266, 278, 278n, 279, 284, 286, 433
Russell, Maj Gerald F., 642
Russell Islands, 77, 88, 100, 115, 186, 393, 400
Russell, MajGen John H., 17
Russia. *See* Union of Soviet Socialist Republics.
Ryukyus, 297, 335, 444, 464, 737

Sabol, LtCol Stephen V., 110, 113, 145
Saipan, 25, 32, 51, 59–61, 71, 76, 78, 105, 168, 173–174, 176, 184, 263, 267, 275–277, 323, 421, 423–425, 428–430, 438, 443–444, 450, 453, 457, 461, 464, 467–468, 472, 474, 476, 478, 480, 484, 487, 489, 491, 498, 504, 573, 597, 725, 731–732, 734
Saipan Operation, 26, 225, 423–424, 462, 466
Saito, Fred, 533n, 543n, 677n, 678n
Salt Lake City, 493, 498
Samar, 65, 294, 310, 312, 317, 330, 334–335, 339, 358–359, 365, 377–378
Samaritan, 479, 537, 723
Samoa, American, 21, 46, 398
Sample, RAdm William D., 278
Samurai, 677
San Bernardino Straits, 312
Sanderson, BGen Lawson H. M., 420
San Diego, Calif., 17, 21, 23, 41–42, 44–45, 328, 431
San Diego Union (newspaper), 400
San Fabian, 339, 356
San Fernando, 342, 350
San Francisco, Calif., 286, 465
Sangamon, 426
Sanga Sanga, 378
San Ildefonso, 346
San Isidro, 331
San Jose, Calif., 316–317, 353
San Jose del Monte, 346
San Pablo, 325
San Roque Airfield, 367
Santa Barbara, Calif., 45, 47, 423
Santa Cruz, 439
Santa Maria, 346, 367
Santee, 427
Santo Tomas, 343
Santo Tomas University, 347
Sarangani Bay, 382, 384, 387
Saratoga, 40–42, 537

Sarles, LtCol George H., 373, 386
Saufley, 378
Savory, Nathaniel, 445
Sayers, LtCol Joseph C., 561
Sayre Highway, 385–386
Scales, Maj James S., 518, 649, 652–653
Scandinavia, 729
Schmidt, MajGen Harry, 466–468, 476, 482, 490–491, 491n, 492, 505, 515, 517, 547, 551–553, 563–564, 569, 576–577, 593, 603, 607, 608n, 610, 627, 633, 635, 638, 670–671, 676, 700, 710, 714, 716, 720
Schmidt, LtCol Richard K., 509, 648
Schrider, Maj Peter P., 304, 425, 429
Schrier, 1st Lt Harold G., 540, 542
Scott, LtCol Wallace T., 356, 373
Sea Runner, 253
Sea Sturgeon, 251, 253
Seawolf, 78
Secretary of the Navy, 484, 542, 713
Selden, Col John T., 131; BGen, 131n
Senda, MajGen Sadasue, 458, 569, 572, 586, 647, 654, 680, 693, 693n, 694–695, 702
Sengebau, Kulas, 265n
Service and Supply Activities. *See* Army units; Logistics; Marine Units; Supply and equipment.
Sevik, Lt Edward A., 413
Shanghai, 321
Shanley, Capt James V., 235, 244
Sharp, RAdm Alexander, 492
Sharpe, 1stLt Winfield S., 372
Shepard, LtCol Charles E., Jr., 513
Sherman, Capt Forrest P., 465
Shimbu Line, 351, 353. *See also* Japanese Defenses.
Ships. *See also* Landing craft.
  American, 86, 169, 323, 445, 493n, 499, 548, 603, 714, 716
    amphibious command ships, 475, 523, 714
    battleships, 82, 103, 165–166, 210, 278, 475, 493, 498–499, 574, 587, 625, 634, 644, 665
    barges, 87, 127, 184, 232, 269, 314, 367, 375
    cargo vessels, 82, 87, 478, 573, 603, 722
    carriers, 97, 102, 278, 281, 283, 293, 312, 317, 323–325, 336, 395, 397, 405, 407, 423–424, 426, 429, 435, 437, 451–452, 459, 475, 523, 537, 560, 565, 717
    cruisers, 82, 103, 160, 165–166, 181, 210, 278–279, 336–337, 400, 407, 459, 475, 484, 489, 498, 504, 551, 554–555, 574, 587, 625, 634–644, 665

INDEX 841

destroyer escorts, 312–313, 420, 607
destroyer minesweepers, 607
destroyers, 103, 108, 132, 162, 165–166, 181, 190, 195, 210, 261, 278–279, 312, 329–330, 336, 378, 383, 400, 402, 404, 407, 420, 475, 484, 493, 496–498, 504, 530, 554–555, 591–592, 607, 634, 637, 644, 658, 665, 668, 691, 699
  escort carriers, 424, 432
  gunfire support ships, 81, 211, 493, 495–498, 501, 503–504, 523, 554, 649, 658, 671–672, 679, 714
  liberty ships, 431
  LSDs (Landing Ships, Dock), 84, 88, 96, 607
  LSMs (Landing Ships, Medium), 379, 475, 482, 509, 517, 520, 601
  LSTs (Landing Ships, Tank), 84, 95–97, 103, 129, 153, 162, 166, 187, 232–233, 270, 329, 356, 366, 436, 475, 477, 479–480, 480n, 482, 484, 503, 522–523, 560–561, 601, 607, 722
  LST(H)s (Landing Ships, Hospital), 83, 479, 480n, 517, 522–523, 560, 604, 723
  LSVs (Landing Ships, Vehicle), 314, 732
  minelayers, 400, 530, 607
  minesweepers, 103, 165, 183, 335, 420, 491, 495–496, 607
  motor torpedo boats, 327, 361
  patrol craft, 84, 181, 261, 315, 497, 505, 607, 665, 716
  repair ships, 607
  submarines, 381, 444, 453–455, 473
  supply and support ships, 233, 253, 502, 531, 597, 648, 651,
  tankers, 82
  tenders, 607
  transports, 19, 85, 87, 96–97, 162, 168, 181, 212, 251, 274, 328–329, 335, 367, 429, 475, 498, 502–503, 522–523, 525, 540, 552, 573, 597, 604, 607, 610, 714, 723, 736
  tugs, 601, 607
Japanese, 278, 281, 324, 327 330, 333, 399, 730
  barges, 166, 190, 259, 278, 420, 432, 526
  battleships, 312
  cargo vessels, 328–329, 399
  carriers, 300, 312, 731
  coast defense vessels, 321
  cruisers, 312
  destroyers, 312, 321, 328

  escorts, 329
  submarines, 259, 312, 366, 396, 415, 417, 434, 450, 484
  tankers, 447, 735
  tenders, 399
  torpedo boats, 366, 407
  transports, 321, 328, 453
hip-to-shore movement, 119n, 239
Shofner, LtCol Austin C., 116–118
Sho-Go Operations, 297, 312, 321
Shore fire control parties, 35, 277. *See also* Air activities; Naval gunfire.
Shore party activiites, 17, 34, 84, 86, 88, 94, 127, 143, 148, 152, 204, 282, 478, 480, 483, 523, 553, 592–593, 601–602, 708, 710, 724–725
Siari, 365
Siberia, 67
Sibert, MajGen Franklin C., 381, 383
Sicily, 281, 733
Silverthorn, LtGen Merwin H., 32n, 27n
Sindangan, 365
Singapore, 294, 337, 382
Siskin, Chaplain Edgar E., 109n
Slappey, Capt Wallace J., 432
Smith, Sgt E. Payson, Jr., 373n
Smith, LtCol John, 379
Smith, Maj Holland M., 15, 19; Maj Gen, 20–21, 23, 434n; LtGen, 24–26, 29–31, 33–36, 304, 423, 428, 433, 464, 466, 487, 489–492, 492n, 501, 523, 542, 603, 608, 608n, 610–613, 700, 714
Smith, MajGen Julian C., 61, 63–64, 76, 79, 186, 211, 278; LtGen 80, 80n, 89, 162–163, 181, 181n
Smith, BGen Oliver P., 77, 129–131, 211, 253; MajGen, 60n
Smith, Maj Perry K., 142; Col, 363
Smoak, Col Eustace, 588
Smoke screen
  American, 135, 231, 279, 322, 357, 385, 497–498, 637, 650, 652, 660, 666
  Japanese, 227, 592, 698
Smyth, PFC George, 562
Solace, 479, 542, 723
Solomons, 6, 67, 83, 87, 97, 291–293, 301, 326–327, 334, 342–343, 362–363, 393, 428, 466–467, 730
Song of Iwo Jima, 700
Sorol, 434
South America, 8
South China Sea, 334, 435
South Pacific, 21, 23, 45–46, 398, 431, 733

Southwest Pacific Area, 24, 51–52, 101–102, 291–292, 301, 303, 334–335, 358, 416, 438, 457
Spain, 8, 9, 54, 294
Spanish American War, 14, 54
Spatz, Lt Donald, 413
Spearfish, 473
Spritzen, LtCol Roland J., 553*n*
Spruance, VAdm Raymond A., 23, 422, 435, 465–466, 469, 489–491, 492*n*, 501, 560, 713; Adm, 465*n*
Spurlock, Maj Roy T., 327
STALEMATE Operation, 52, 59–62, 162, 266, 278, 430, 733
STALEMATE II Operation, 59, 62–65, 82, 84, 89, 97–98, 100–101, 180, 287, 315
Stalingrad, 430
Stark, Adm H. R., 40, 42–43
Stars and Stripes, 207, 542, 564, 626, 678. See also Flag raising and Old Glory.
Steele, 413
Stein, Cpl Tony, 625
Stephenson, Capt Edward V., 578
Stiles, Maj Wilfrid H., 431
St. Matthias Group, 373
Stout, Maj Doyle A., 568, 648, 661
Stout, Maj Robert F., 225, 432–433
Strategy, 395, 715*n*, 716
Streit, Maj Victor H., 226
Stuart, LtCol Arthur J., 88*n*, 122*n*, 124*n*, 154*n*, 210*n*, 272*n*
Stuart, Col James A., 607
Subic Bay, 21, 342
Sudentenland, 9
Suifuzan Hill, 235, 260
Sulphur, 444, 455–456, 572, 579, 600, 638
Sulphur Island, 444
Sulu Archipelago, 358–359, 361, 363, 371, 374, 378, 389, 385
Sulu Sea, 335, 368
Sumatra, 297
Supplies and equipment. See also Ammunition; Logistics.
    American, 85, 87, 128, 152, 273, 478, 478*n*, 522, 551, 553, 597, 601–602, 610, 612–613, 627, 722–725
        aviation, 477–478
        cargo, 721, 724
        clothing, 610
        communications, 308, 368, 370, 379, 383, 389, 413, 515, 597, 719
        dumps and storage, 86–87, 122, 126–128, 151–152, 264, 269, 282, 318, 526, 551, 553, 600, 608, 658, 701, 720, 724
        equipment, 92, 152, 184, 208, 266, 269, 272, 277, 325, 523, 611, 651
        explosives, 514, 531, 669, 711, 716
        food and rations, 83, 87, 128, 282, 398, 410, 477, 523, 553, 557
        fuel and lubricants, 87–88, 241, 476–477, 526, 536, 607, 610, 612–614, 641, 664, 712, 722
        gas masks, 638
        matting, 333, 478, 601–602, 724
        smoke pots, 256
        spare parts, 155, 266, 277
        water, 87–88, 128, 129*n*, 135–136, 150, 190, 241, 257, 271, 275, 352, 398, 447, 477, 480, 523, 553, 557, 602, 607, 634
    Japanese, 382, 415, 457, 473, 654, 659
        dumps and storage, 150, 200, 275, 278, 281, 331, 353, 383, 493*n*, 562, 617, 638, 641
        gas munitions, 614
        signal, 259
        smokeless powder, 177, 584
        water, 258, 262, 530, 611, 620, 695
Support Air Request Net, 718
Surigao City, 382
Surigao Straits, 312, 327, 330
Sutherland, LtGen R. K., 293*n*
Suwanee, 426
Suzuki, LtGen Sosaku, 361
Sweetser, Col Warren E., Jr., 387–388
Swift, MajGen Innis P., 352
Swindler, Col Leland S., 478; BGen, 724*n*

Tachiiwa Point, 447, 459, 578, 642, 675–677, 681
Tacloban, 310, 312, 314, 316, 325–328, 330–331
Tacloban Airfield, 310, 330, 333
Tactics
    American, 715*n*, 725, 737
        amphibious patrols, 260
        armored support, 209, 518, 550, 564, 566, 635
        counterbattery fire, 202, 320, 554–555, 639, 656, 660, 666, 669, 673, 719–720
        gas warfare, 612–614
        harassing and interdiction fire, 153, 281, 414, 651, 654, 661, 671
        infiltration, 705
        jungle warfare, 305
        night attacks, 91, 588, 590
        sabotage, 349
        search and kill missions, 318, 401

INDEX   843

supporting arms coordination, 134, 282, 308, 320, 331, 333, 482, 555, 657–658, 666, 684, 716, 719

tank-infantry assault, 110, 174, 177, 234, 281, 514, 519, 536, 567, 580, 592, 623, 627, 687, 714
Japanese, 278, 315, 322
  Banzai attacks, 71, 122, 156, 169–170, 175, 261, 263, 457–458, 522*n*, 525–527, 533, 538, 556, 641–642; 678–679, 705, 708
  chemical warfare, 614
  counterattacks, 72, 115, 121, 126, 132, 147, 158, 170–171, 176, 198, 202, 205, 245, 257, 267, 350, 556, 559, 679, 682
  counterbattery fire, 279, 655, 661
  counterlandings, 242, 261
  guerrillas, 461
  harassing and interdiction fire, 73, 320, 726
  incendiary balloons, 736
  infiltration, 170, 174, 207, 220, 225, 249, 261, 319–320, 322, 525–526, 539, 545, 556, 558, 585–586, 630, 632, 638, 661, 665, 677, 686, 697
  rocket barrages, 660–664
  sniping, 135, 141, 168, 172, 187, 201, 208, 232–233, 246, 248, 251, 263, 320*n*, 351, 426, 543, 560, 564, 578, 595, 623, 625, 635, 637, 639, 641, 646, 649–651, 656, 667, 669
  suicide attacks, 156, 323, 330–331, 335–336, 435, 735
  tank attacks, 123
  withdrawal, 180
Tada, Col Tokechi, 232*n*, 263, 458, 508, 548, 550, 559, 650, 657
Takasago Maru, 420
Talevera, 342
Tanauan, 315, 320
Tanauan Airfield, 325, 331, 333, 339
Tarawa, 32, 52, 78, 105, 287–288, 395–401, 408, 438, 466–467, 487, 489, 505, 719, 730–731
Taroa, 400
Taroa Airfield, 405. *See also* Maloelap Airfield.
Task Organizations
  Central Pacific, 160
  TF 18, 20
  TF 30, 63–64
  TF 31, 63
  TF 32, 60, 83, 102, 165, 186, 283

TF 33, 63
TF 38, 64–65
TF 50, 466
TF 51, 466
TF 52, 523
TF 53, 25, 502, 724
TF 54, 483, 493, 498, 500, 503, 654, 668, 671,
TF 55, 25
TF 56, 466
TF 57, 399
TF 58, 405, 408, 435–436, 475–476, 489, 493, 495–496, 501, 503, 523, 560, 564, 717
TF 59, 11, 46
TG 32.1, 63
TG 32.2, 63, 165, 181
TG 32.9, 63, 103
TG 51.5, 634
TG 52.2, 492, 495
TG 52.3, 492
TG 52.4, 492
TG 56.1, 466
TG 58.1, 451
TG 58.4, 451
TG 58.5, 560
TG 59.6, 431
TG 78.1, 366
TG 78.2, 381
TU 52.2.2, 492
Tawi Tawi Group, 378
Tennessee, 409, 493, 496, 498, 500
Tentative Landing Operations Manual, 17
Tenzan, 260, 644
Terrain, 77, 723, 726
  caves, 57, 70, 73, 75, 92, 104, 112, 134, 138, 145–146, 154, 156, 160–161, 177, 192, 198, 201–202, 205, 208–209, 212, 214, 216–271, 221–223, 225–226, 230, 234, 236, 240–242, 245–246, 248, 251, 256, 258, 261–265, 270–271, 276, 279, 351, 426, 432, 453, 455, 459, 473, 493*n*, 508, 528, 530–531, 539–540, 542–543, 545, 548, 554, 560, 569, 572, 577, 580, 586, 589–592, 611, 613, 614*n*, 618, 620–621, 626, 628 629, 631–633, 635, 639, 642–643, 645–646, 468–650, 652, 663, 668, 672, 684–687, 689, 691–692, 695, 697–701, 704, 706–707, 716, 720, 726–727
  escarpments, 721–722
  hydrographic conditions, 165
  jungles, 192
  promontories, 73, 119, 134–136, 136*n*, 137 138, 146, 153

ravines, 693
reefs, 58–59, 78–79, 81, 84–88, 94, 103, 108–110, 113, 119, 127, 129, 131, 148, 152, 163, 183, 216–217, 241, 266, 268–270, 272, 41, 478, 496
ridges, 134, 141–142, 146–147, 153, 185, 189–190, 193, 195, 198, 200–201, 204–205, 214, 216–217, 219
sand, 721–722, 724
swamps, 141–142
terraces, 721, 724
tunnels, 695, 716
volcanic ash and rock, 452, 455, 478, 483, 506, 509, 516–517, 519, 538, 557, 600–601, 686, 690–691, 721–724
Terrar, Lt Edward F., 426
Terry, 624
Texas, 493, 503
Thompson, Lt Earl C., 402
Thurnau, Lt Theodore, 403–404
Timor, 297
Tinian, 25, 32, 36, 60, 184, 424, 429, 429n, 467–468, 484, 598, 731–732
Titcomb Field, 383–384, 388
Titcomb, Capt Jack, 344n, 351, 383
Tobiishi Point, 539, 545
Tojo, Gen Hideki, 430, 450; Premier, 732
Tokyo, 67, 288, 294, 296, 377, 428, 435, 451, 458–459, 463–464, 487, 491, 493, 495, 537, 560, 669–670, 683, 700, 716, 732, 737
Tokyo Bay, 421, 444
Torokina, 301
Totsuke, LtCol Ryoichi, 375
Toyoda, Adm Soemu, 297–298, 300, 499, 499n, 564, 670, 680
Treitel, Maj Paul S., 550, 560, 569, 680
Trotti, LtCol Tom M., 558
Truk, 60, 67, 101, 292, 407–408, 449
Tryon, 101
Tulagi, 95
Tulagi-Purvis Bay, 83
Tumatangas, 379
Tumbelston, Maj William H., 642
Turkey Hill, 572
Turkey Knob, 353, 568, 595, 616, 646–647, 650–651, 654, 656–658, 660–661, 663–665, 667, 669, 672–673, 675, 680–682
Turner, RAdm Richmond K., 23; VAdm, 25, 466, 475–476, 484, 489–491, 501, 608, 608n, 612, 700, 714
Tuscaloosa, 493

Twining, MajGen Nathan, 46
Tutuila, 398

Ujelang Atoll, 416
Ulithi Atoll, 52, 59, 62, 66, 162–163, 180–181, 184, 250, 254, 257, 286–287, 430–435, 443, 478, 733–734
Umayam River Valley, 386
Umurbrogol, 58, 73, 75, 108, 147–148, 156, 161, 190, 192, 200, 210, 219, 228, 237, 240, 248, 258
Umurbrogol Mountain, 57, 145, 177
Umurbrogol Pocket, 192, 206, 216, 218, 221, 224, 227, 231, 236, 240–242, 244–246, 249–251, 254, 257, 259–262, 270, 284
Umurbrogol Ridges, 58, 146, 189, 199, 219, 222–223, 236–237, 265
Union of Soviet Socialist Republics, 4–5, 8, 443, 675, 729–730, 737
United Press, 400
United States, 4–8, 171n, 294, 296, 400, 429, 444, 451, 467, 480, 483, 604, 612–614, 700, 734, 736–737
 aid programs, 274
 Armed Forces, 9, 348, 351, 462, 644
 Army, 17, 23, 161, 187, 200, 248, 291, 303, 307, 332, 342–343, 361, 384, 393, 409, 484, 708, 710–711, 714, 718, 721, 724
 Marine Corps, 9–10, 13, 15, 19, 39, 52, 397, 620n, 712, 721, 735
  doctine, 333, 714
  history, 396
  morale, 664
  replacements, 688
  strength, 15, 19–20, 39, 44, 688
  training, 688, 714
  shipping losses, 324, 556
  units of fire, 83n
Urukthapel, 57

Valencia, 385
Vandegrift, LtGen Alexander A., 186n, 252n, 247; Gen, 24–25, 29, 253, 288n, 423
Vandegrift, LtCol Alexander A., Jr., 521, 568
Vandegrift Letters, 158n
Vaughan, Maj Everette H., 400; Col, 401n
Vegetation, 192
Vehicles
 American, 722
  Alligators, Roebling, 35
  ambulances, 274

INDEX 845

amphibians, 87–88, 94, 127–128, 130–131, 139, 148, 156, 269, 273, 312, 721–723
amphibian tractors, 13, 17, 35, 78, 84, 92–94, 106, 108–109, 148, 187, 224, 266–267, 274, 282, 315, 321, 432, 473, 483, 503, 505, 508, 516, 548, 553, 573
amphibian trailers, 88, 127–128, 269, 477–478, 482, 721
amphibian trucks, 85, 87–88, 92–94, 103, 109, 115, 127, 129, 131–132, 148, 228, 269–270, 274, 277, 282, 344, 477, 479, 482–483, 515–516, 521–522, 552–553, 573, 601–602, 657, 721–723
armored tankdozers, 699
bulldozers, 127, 138, 152, 168, 238, 242, 262, 480, 516, 521, 523, 459, 601–602, 605, 610–611, 615, 628, 647, 685–688, 701, 705, 707, 712, 724
cargo carriers (Weasels), 478, 482, 523, 530, 601, 722–723
cranes, 724
jeeps, 308, 344, 350, 368, 378–379, 384, 701
LVTs (Landing Vehicle, tracked), 35, 85, 87, 92, 94, 104, 106, 108–110, 115–117, 127–128, 130–132, 136, 139, 144, 148, 151, 155, 166, 206, 210–211, 216–217, 233, 240, 257, 262, 269, 271–273, 280, 375, 447, 472–473, 478, 503, 506, 508, 516, 518–519, 523, 551, 601, 721–723
LVT(A)s (Landing Vehicle, Tracked (Armored)), 35, 84–85, 92–93, 106, 108–109, 114, 116, 129, 137, 146, 158, 195, 209–210, 212, 242, 266, 277, 472, 505, 508, 569, 618, 620, 648, 650, 721
LVT(F)s (Landing Vehicle, Tracked (Flamethrower)), 155, 157, 201, 206, 208, 226, 229–230, 241, 263–264
tank retriever, 156, 273, 518
tractors, 109, 127, 506, 552–553, 721
trailers, 722
trucks, 151, 274, 350, 379, 513, 517, 522, 534, 655,
wheeled vehicles, 447, 473, 478, 516–517, 721–723
Japanese
armor, supporting, 177
bulldozers, 459
motor vehicles, 641
prime movers, 617
tanks, 687
trailers, 641

Vella Lavella Island, 393
Venable, Col Benjamin W., 176
Versailles Peace Conference, 7
Versailles, Treaty of, 16
Vicksburg, 493, 498
VICTOR Operations, 358, 362
　VICTOR I, 358, 375, 377
　VICTOR II, 358, 375, 377
　VICTOR III, 359
　VICTOR IV, 359, 365, 378
　VICTOR V, 359, 380–382
Virgin Islands, 42
Visayan Islands, 309, 734
Visayan Sea, 327, 332, 358, 374
Visayas, 65, 294, 298, 309–310, 321, 374, 377–378
Vogel, MajGen Clayton B., 21
Vogelkop Peninsula, 292
Volcano Islands, 436, 443–444, 484, 462n
Volckmann, Maj Russell W., 348; Col, 349, 351; BGen, 348n

Wachi, Capt Tsunezo, 458n
Wachtler, BGen Walter A., 82n, 240n
Wake Island, 6, 21, 42, 415, 420–421, 444
Wake Island, 437, 493, 595
Walker, Maj Thomas J., Jr., 42
Waller, Col James D., 472, 515
Wallis Island, 398–399, 411
Walsh, Senator Joseph, 288n
Walsh, GySgt William G., 622
Walt, LtCol Lewis W., 118, 123, 141, 210
Walt's Ridge, 157–158, 160, 221, 224, 229–234, 237, 240, 244, 246, 248, 250, 254, 256–257, 260
Walter Colton, 431
War Dogs, 91, 143. *See also* Marine units.
Washington, 493, 503
Washington Conference, 6, 15
Washington, D. C., 5, 279, 462, 613
Washington, President George, 5, 445
Wasp, 436
Watson, Col Arthur P., 257, 264
Watson, Sgt Sherman B., 539
Wattie Ridge, 224, 233, 246
Wattie, Lt. Robert T., 238
Weapons
　American, 195, 655, 689
　　antiaircraft guns, 356, 477, 501
　　antitank guns, 91, 116, 687

atomic weapons, 204
automatic weapons, 91–92, 126, 132, 144, 589
bayonets, 223, 566
bazookas, 91–92, 115, 124, 135, 152, 214, 216, 266, 271, 566, 578, 633, 652, 659, 666, 693, 708
BARs, 266, 708
demolitions, 91–92, 114, 134, 138, 216, 266, 590, 629, 631, 650, 666, 681, 687, 689, 699, 705
8-inch howitzers, 500, 504
81mm mortars, 230, 270, 518, 568, 575, 582, 640, 648, 697
.50 caliber machine guns, 272, 463, 628, 721
5-inch guns, 500, 504
5-inch rockets, 503, 717
flamethrowers, 91–92, 134–36, 138, 152, 155, 169, 176, 200, 204, 209, 216, 223, 256–257, 262, 264, 266, 270–271, 273, 514, 531, 536, 567, 569, 576, 578, 589–590, 614, 621, 631, 633, 666, 681, 687, 689–690, 695, 699, 707, 725, 727
flamethrower tanks, 238, 273, 512, 531, 621, 626, 628, 641, 666–668, 673, 675, 687–688, 694, 699, 707, 710
4.2-inch mortars, 108, 270, 503, 554, 610, 727
4.5-inch rockets, 108, 503, 621, 655
14-inch guns, 500
40mm guns, 166, 503, 654
.45 caliber pistols, 708
grenade launchers, 115, 124
grenades, 144, 262, 514, 531, 569, 611, 614, 620, 636, 652, 659, 666, 678, 686, 689, 693–694, 713, 725
guns, 156, 477
half-tracks, 136–138, 200, 230–231, 531, 534, 548, 630, 632, 657, 673, 684
howitzers, 94, 116, 124, 246, 248, 482, 521–522, 552, 554–555, 565, 721
M-1 rifles, 697, 707–708
machine guns, 91, 108–109, 123, 272, 472, 566, 635, 698, 701
medium tanks, 208, 233, 649–650, 673
mines, 109, 134, 632, 656, 675, 691, 720
mortars, 87, 92, 109, 121, 142, 144, 157, 166, 171, 173, 187, 230, 270, 272, 477, 508, 523, 566, 575, 629, 635, 637, 698, 727
naval guns, 209, 376, 423, 540, 716

90mm guns, 603
155mm guns (Long Toms), 154, 209, 228, 230, 248, 301, 719
155mm howitzers, 301, 477, 625, 638, 652, 719
105mm guns, 240, 242, 516, 634, 691
105mm howitzers, 83–84, 129, 129n, 269–270, 472, 515, 521, 552, 568, 719–720
120mm mortars, 727
rifles, 91, 109, 566, 613–614, 659, 689, 698
rocket launchers, 627, 631, 639, 655, 662, 666, 676, 685
rockets, 108, 166, 534, 637
satchel charges, 652, 659
7.2-inch rockets, 685
75mm guns, 108, 209, 214, 217, 269, 516, 520, 534, 621, 634, 640–641, 727
75 mm guns (self-propelled), 135, 176
75mm howitzers (pack), 84, 93, 116, 129n, 246, 261, 272, 521, 639, 657, 719–721
16-inch guns, 504
60mm mortars, 92, 126, 241, 270, 510, 568, 582, 666, 693
tank dozers, 156, 273, 512, 520, 652, 706–707
tanks, 81, 85, 88, 91, 110, 115–117, 120, 123–124, 134–139, 141, 143, 145–146, 153–161, 166, 168, 171, 173–74, 200–201, 205–206, 209–212, 214, 217, 226, 229–232, 235–236, 238, 241, 251, 256–257, 262–264, 272–274, 277, 281, 353, 472–473, 483, 509, 512–515, 517–520, 531, 534, 536, 538, 550, 553, 555, 558, 560, 563–567, 569, 574, 576–578, 582, 584, 590–591, 618, 621, 626–628, 630, 633–634, 639, 641, 644, 646–647, 649–653, 655–657, 659, 662, 664, 666–668, 672, 676–677, 681, 684–690, 693, 698–699, 706–707, 727
.30 caliber machine guns, 272, 771
37mm guns, 108, 115, 123–124, 136–137, 158, 251, 269, 531, 534, 568, 575, 621, 629–630, 632, 636, 640, 667, 684, 727
toxic gases, 613–614
20mm guns, 166, 463, 654
white phosphorus grenades, 235, 567
Filipino, 348
Japanese, 73, 109, 137, 156, 193, 221, 231, 240, 256, 267, 449, 454, 498, 518, 531, 538, 553, 585, 587, 604, 617, 639, 655, 666, 668, 675, 681, 689, 723, 726
antiaircraft guns, 135, 415, 449, 493n, 549

INDEX   847

antipersonnel land mines, 667, 690, 726
antitank guns, 177, 209, 249, 316, 353, 474, 493n, 513, 519–520, 536, 565–568, 572, 574, 582, 587, 591, 634, 646–647, 684
automatic weapons, 75, 117, 136, 205–206, 209, 240, 256, 273, 320, 453, 456, 458, 575, 618, 625, 648, 655
bamboo spears, 678
bangalore torpedoes, 154
chemicals, 142, 614, 614n, 620, 638
coastal guns, 458, 474–475, 498, 500, 531
demolitions, 154, 200, 320, 367, 526, 592, 691
dual-purpose guns, 146, 474, 572
80mm (naval) guns, 454
81mm mortars, 267, 454
5-inch guns, 135, 500
57mm guns, 83, 646, 649, 727
flares, 533
4.7-inch gun, 610
40mm guns, 144, 415
47mm antitank guns, 73, 109, 112, 454, 562, 591, 628, 646, 649, 665, 684, 727
grenades, 134, 249, 259, 320, 514, 526, 535, 542, 545, 614n, 622, 630–631, 637–639, 656, 659, 678, 688, 691, 708
guns, 473
knee mortars, 637–638, 676
knives, 630
light tanks, 684
machine guns, 73, 112, 142, 160, 168, 177, 226, 249, 449, 474, 493n, 518–519, 535, 539, 549–550, 554, 563, 568, 574, 584, 589, 617, 621–622, 650, 656, 660, 662, 664–665, 675, 678, 689, 697, 703
medium tanks, 316, 684
mines, 72, 79, 115, 119, 135–136, 152, 156, 160, 163, 193, 199, 249, 258, 267, 269, 320, 426, 473–474, 482, 486, 508–509, 512, 519–520, 528, 536, 545, 548–549, 564–566, 584, 641, 647, 726
Molotov cocktails, 592
mortars, 118–119, 122, 127–128, 134, 141, 154, 156, 160, 168, 177, 205–206, 231, 353, 367, 453, 459, 513–514, 519–520, 523, 525, 527, 531, 533–535, 538, 549–550, 553–554, 557–561, 566–568, 573–575, 585, 587, 595, 603–604, 617–618, 621, 624–629, 634, 639, 648–651, 653–656, 685, 660–662, 664, 668–669, 671–672, 674–677, 681–682, 692, 723, 727
mountain guns, 146

naval mines, 367
90mm howitzers, 727
150mm guns, 497
150mm mortar, 221, 267, 454
140mm guns, 533
120mm howitzers, 449, 727
pistols, 630
rifles, 142, 177, 249, 449, 535, 568, 575, 662, 697, 703
rocket launchers, 407, 454, 459, 726–727
rockets, 142, 267, 453–454, 519, 527, 550, 592, 649–651, 655, 677, 692, 726
sabers, 630
satchel charges, 628
70mm guns, 202, 249
75mm guns, 73, 205, 268, 316, 454
6-inch guns, 530
60mm mortars, 510, 675
small arms, 206, 209, 617, 623, 625, 692
tanks, 122–124, 126, 267, 281, 316, 454–455, 523, 586, 591, 652, 655
37mm antitank guns, 73, 202, 205, 209, 268, 454, 591, 675
320mm mortars, 454, 727
torpedoes, 396, 452, 624–625, 636n
20mm rockets, 267
20mm cannon, 139, 249, 379, 415, 454
25mm antiaircraft guns, 268, 449, 454
200mm (naval) guns, 267
Weather, 233
humidity, 55
rain, 55
temperature, 141
Weller, LtCol Donald M., 489, 493, 499; Col, 279n
Welles, 403
Wells, 1stLt George G., 540
Wensinger, Col Walter W., 471, 509, 517–519, 549–550, 647–649, 656, 670, 680–681
West Coast, 400, 411
Western Caroline Islands, 52, 55, 62, 97, 99, 151, 184, 429, 431–434, 455, 734. *See also* Caroline Islands.
Western Pacific, 3, 59, 397, 465, 614
West Field, 429n
West Indies, 19
West Road, 189, 192, 195, 198, 200–202, 204, 206, 209, 222, 224, 226, 228, 232–233, 236–238, 240, 242, 246, 249, 254,
White, Maj Philip R., 326n
Whitehead, MajGen Ennis C., 382
White Plains, 424–425

Wickel, 2dLt James J., 232n, 259n, 263n
Wildcat Bowl, 221, 256, 260–263
Wildcats, 263–264, 399. *See also* 81st Infantry Division under Army units.
Wildcat Trail, 210
Wilkinson, VAdm Theodore S., 63–64, 103–104, 181, 278
Williams, LtCol Marlowe C., 558–559; Col, 559n
Williams, BGen Robert H., 543n
Willis, 2dLt William A., 112
Willis, Col William A., 326, 363
Wills, Maj Donald H., 372
Wilson, Lt Walter A., 402, 404
Wilson, President Woodrow, 3–5, 7
Wintle, 420
Withers, Col Hartnoll J., 551, 555, 558
Witomski, Maj Stanislaus J., 326n
Woleai, 101
Woods, MajGen Louis E., 388, 416, 420; LtGen, 404n
Worden, LtCol Waite W., 66n, 70n, 129n, 132n, 153n, 180n, 190n, 248n, 285n
World Disarmament Conference, 7
World War I, 3–5, 7–8, 14, 54, 448, 467, 504, 613, 727

World War II, 3, 55, 448, 467–468, 522, 543, 588, 612, 620n, 713, 715, 729, 736
Wornham, Col Thomas A., 471, 509, 513, 549, 556, 621, 639, 643
Wotje Atoll, 400, 405, 412–415, 417–418
Wright engines, 463
Wright, Lt Frank J., 512
Wurtsmith, BGen Paul D., 333n

Yamashita, Gen Tomoyuki, 300, 377
Yap, 54, 59, 62, 64, 68–69, 101–102, 180–181, 184, 286, 430, 432–434, 444, 783
Yap Air Base, 52
Yap Operation, 63, 65, 181, 301
Yokohama, 484
Yokosuka, 449
Yorktown, 399
Youngdale, LtCol Carl A., 552

Zambales Mountains, 342
Zamboanga, 356, 359, 362–363, 365–368, 371–373, 378–379, 382, 388, 390
Zamboanga Peninsula, 361, 363, 365–366, 370–371, 374, 381
Zeros. *See* Aircraft, Japanese.
Zonne, Maj Edmund L., 397

MAP I

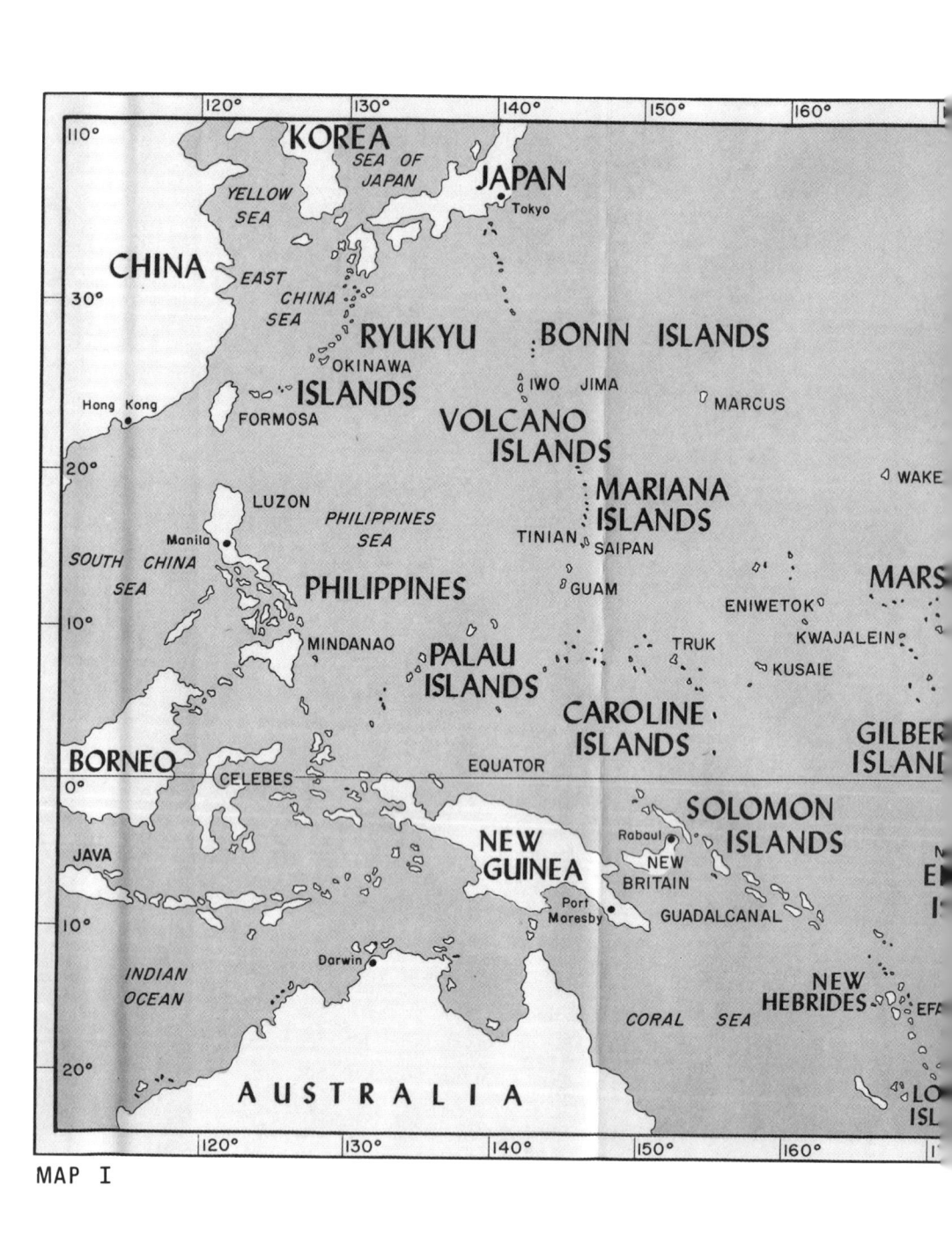

| 180° | 170° | 160° | 150° | 140° | 130° |

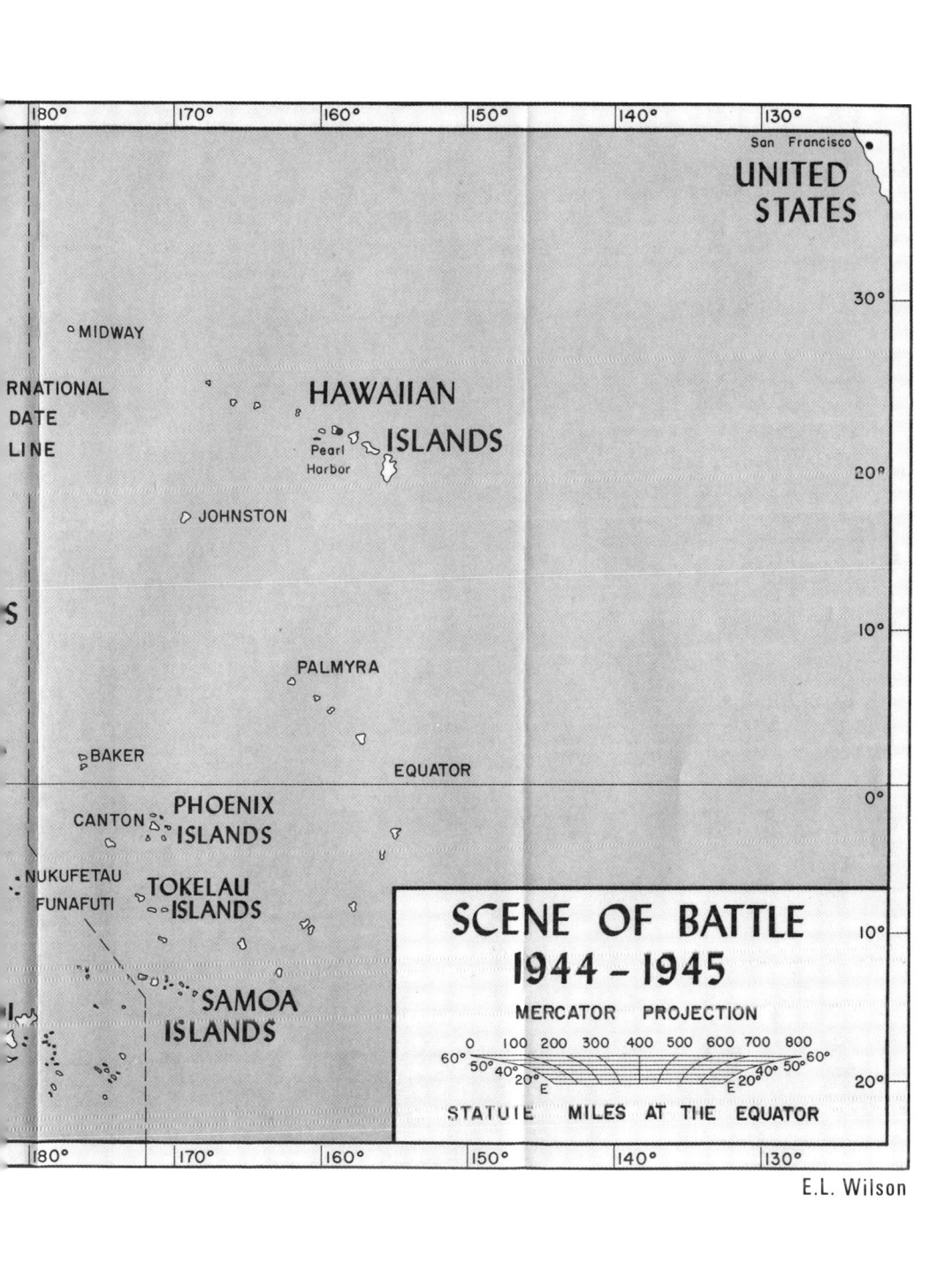

San Francisco
UNITED STATES

30°

○ MIDWAY

HAWAIIAN ISLANDS
Pearl Harbor

20°

○ JOHNSTON

10°

PALMYRA

○ BAKER
EQUATOR

0°

CANTON **PHOENIX ISLANDS**

NUKUFETAU
FUNAFUTI **TOKELAU ISLANDS**

SCENE OF BATTLE
1944 – 1945

10°

SAMOA ISLANDS

MERCATOR PROJECTION

0 100 200 300 400 500 600 700 800
60° 50° 40° 20° E   E 20° 40° 50° 60°

STATUTE MILES AT THE EQUATOR

20°

| 180° | 170° | 160° | 150° | 140° | 130° |

E.L. Wilson

Map II

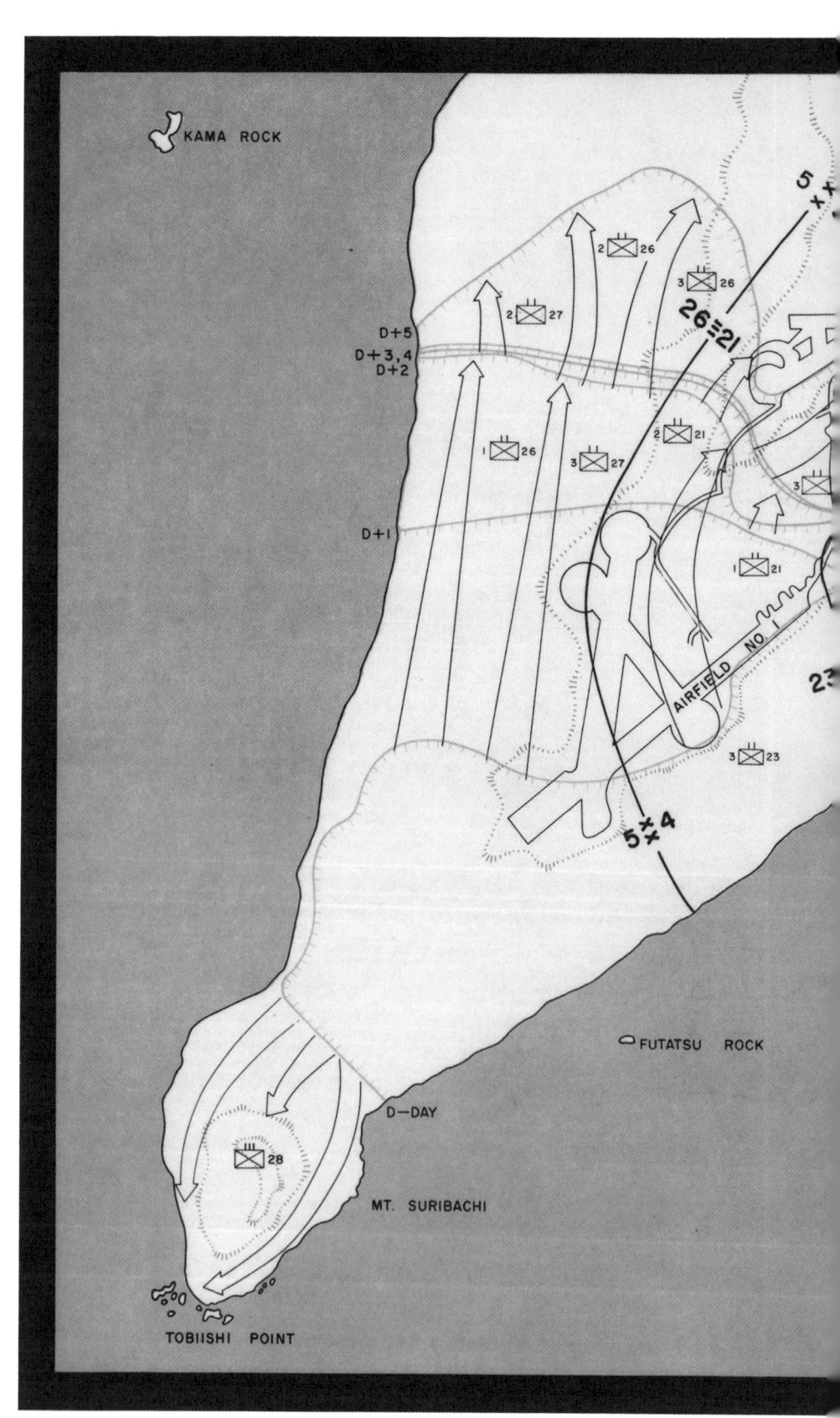

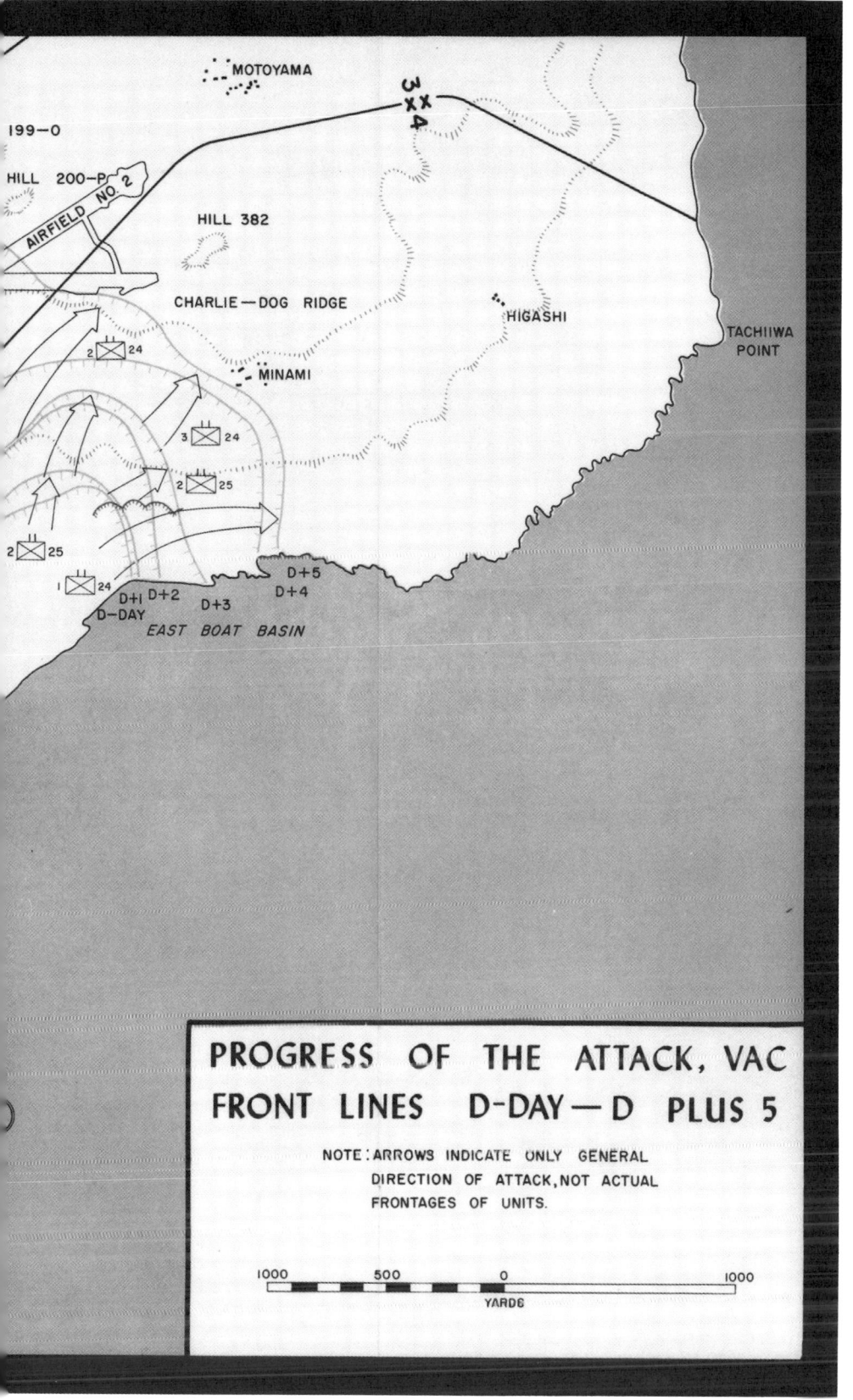

PROGRESS OF THE ATTACK, VAC FRONT LINES D-DAY — D PLUS 5

NOTE: ARROWS INDICATE ONLY GENERAL DIRECTION OF ATTACK, NOT ACTUAL FRONTAGES OF UNITS.

E.L. Wilson

Map III

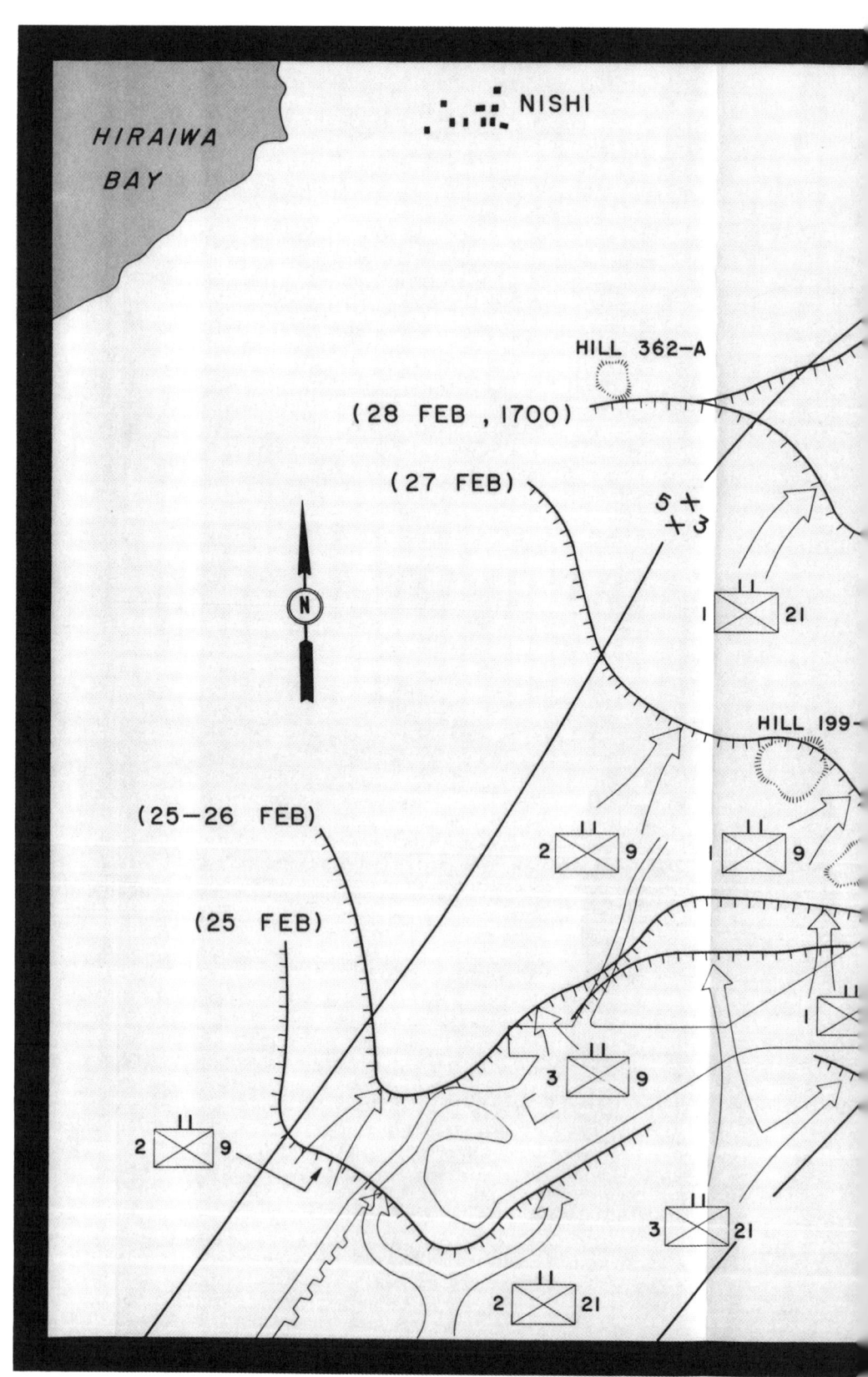

AIRFIELD NO. 3
(UNDER CONSTRUCTION)

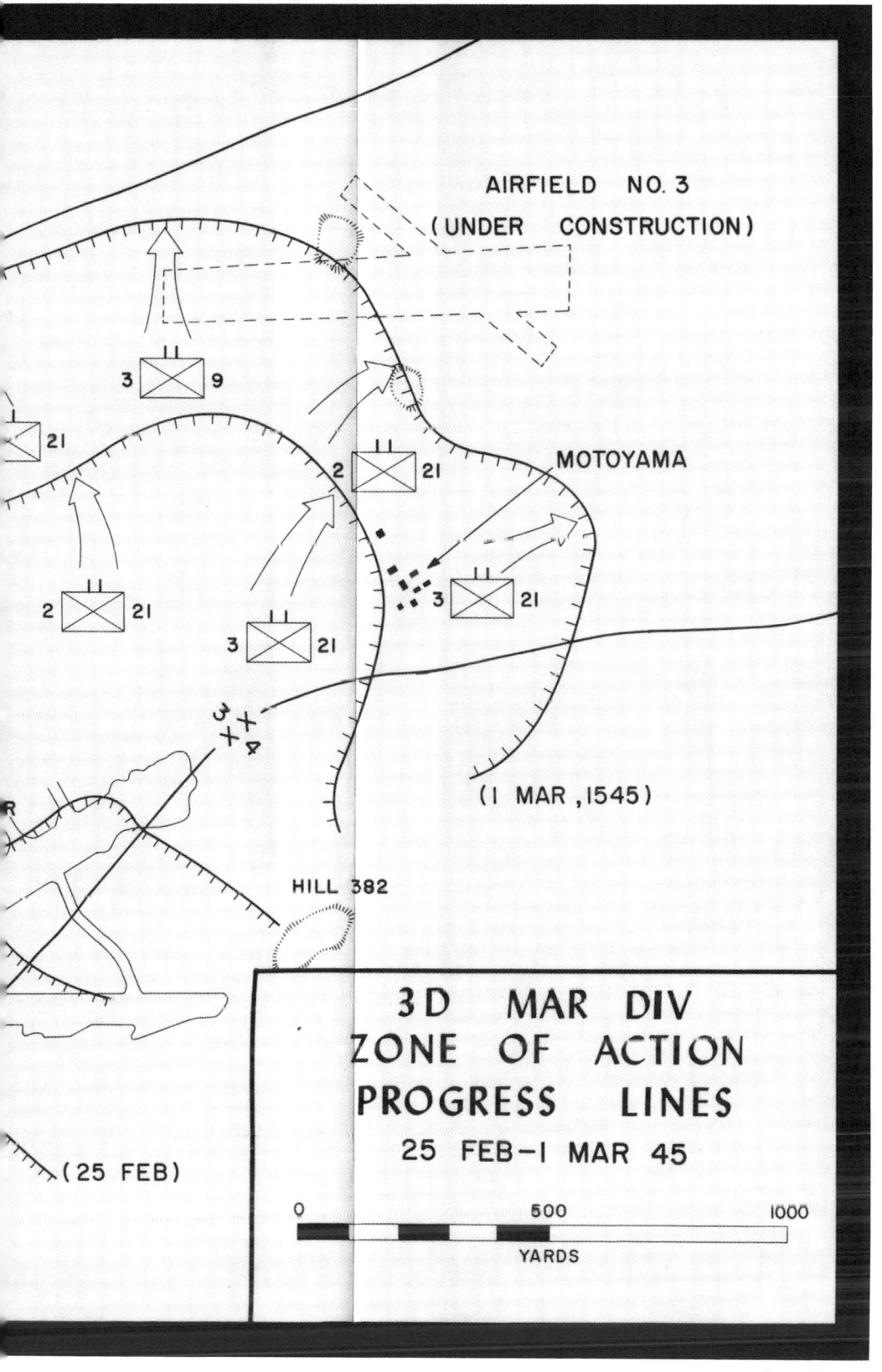

MOTOYAMA

(1 MAR, 1545)

HILL 382

(25 FEB)

**3D MAR DIV
ZONE OF ACTION
PROGRESS LINES
25 FEB-1 MAR 45**

0   500   1000
YARDS

E.L. Wilson

Map IV

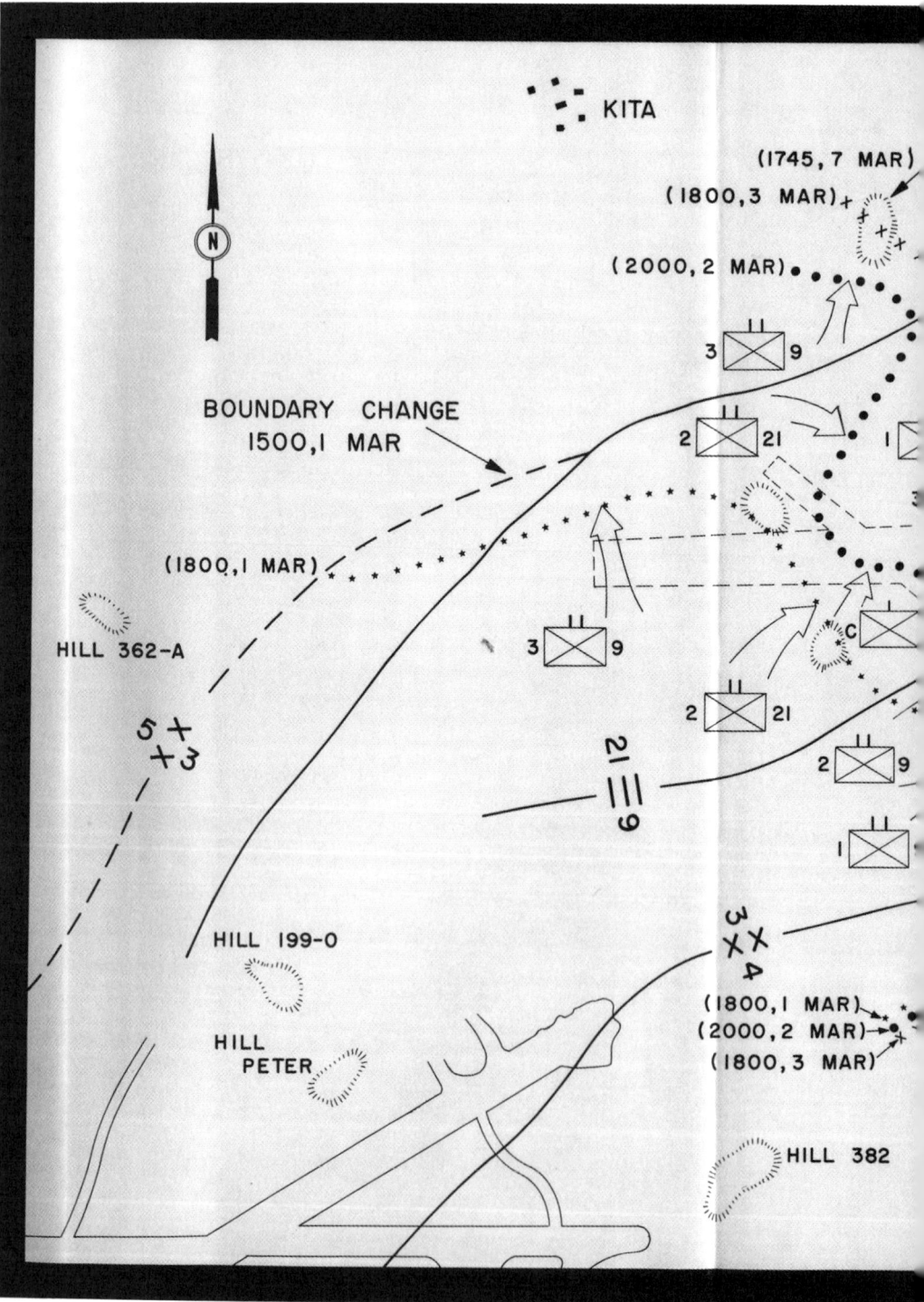

362-B

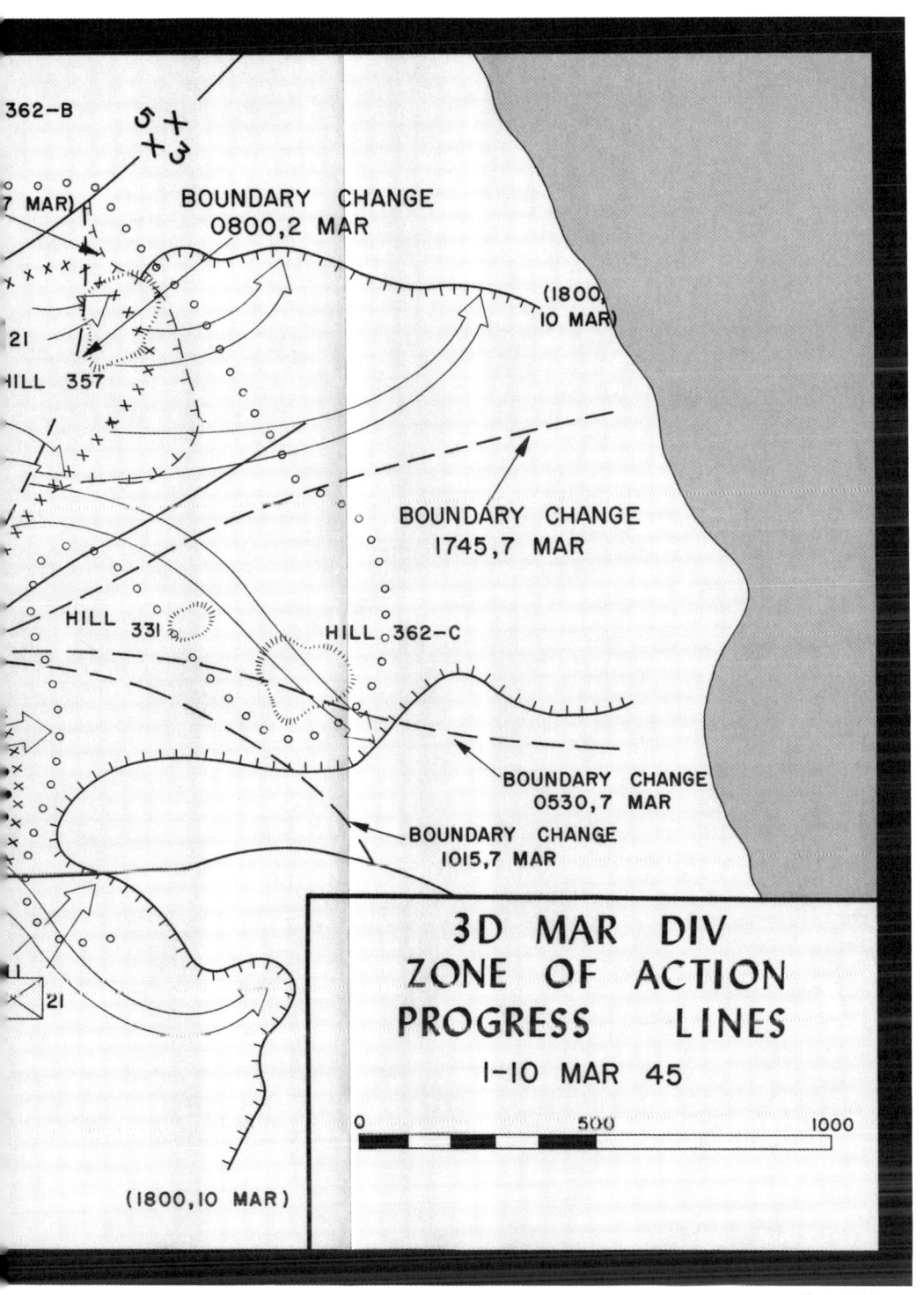

BOUNDARY CHANGE
0800, 2 MAR

(1800, 10 MAR)

HILL 357

BOUNDARY CHANGE
1745, 7 MAR

HILL 331

HILL 362-C

BOUNDARY CHANGE
0530, 7 MAR

BOUNDARY CHANGE
1015, 7 MAR

**3D MAR DIV
ZONE OF ACTION
PROGRESS LINES
1-10 MAR 45**

0   500   1000

(1800, 10 MAR)

E. L. Wilson

Map V

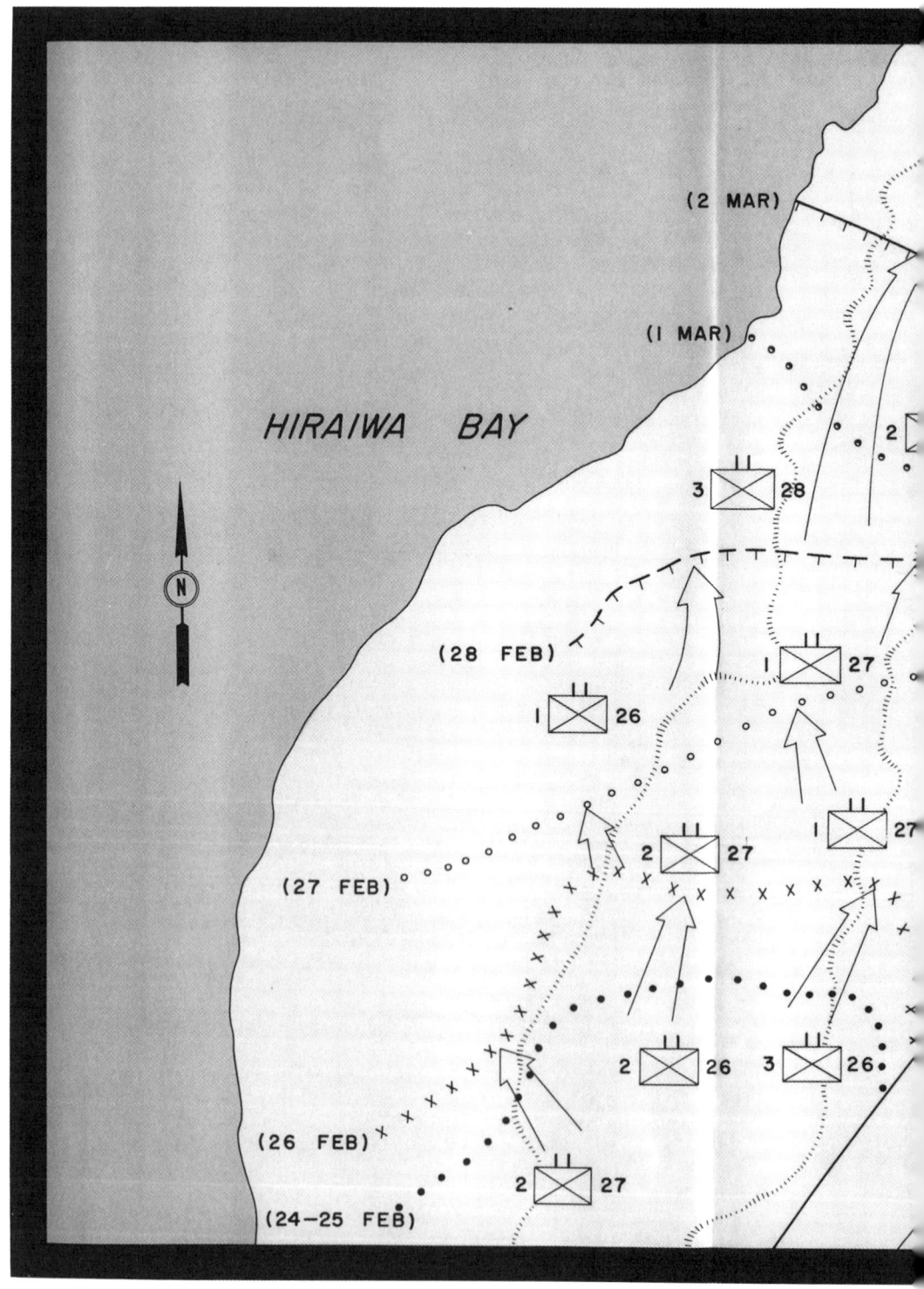

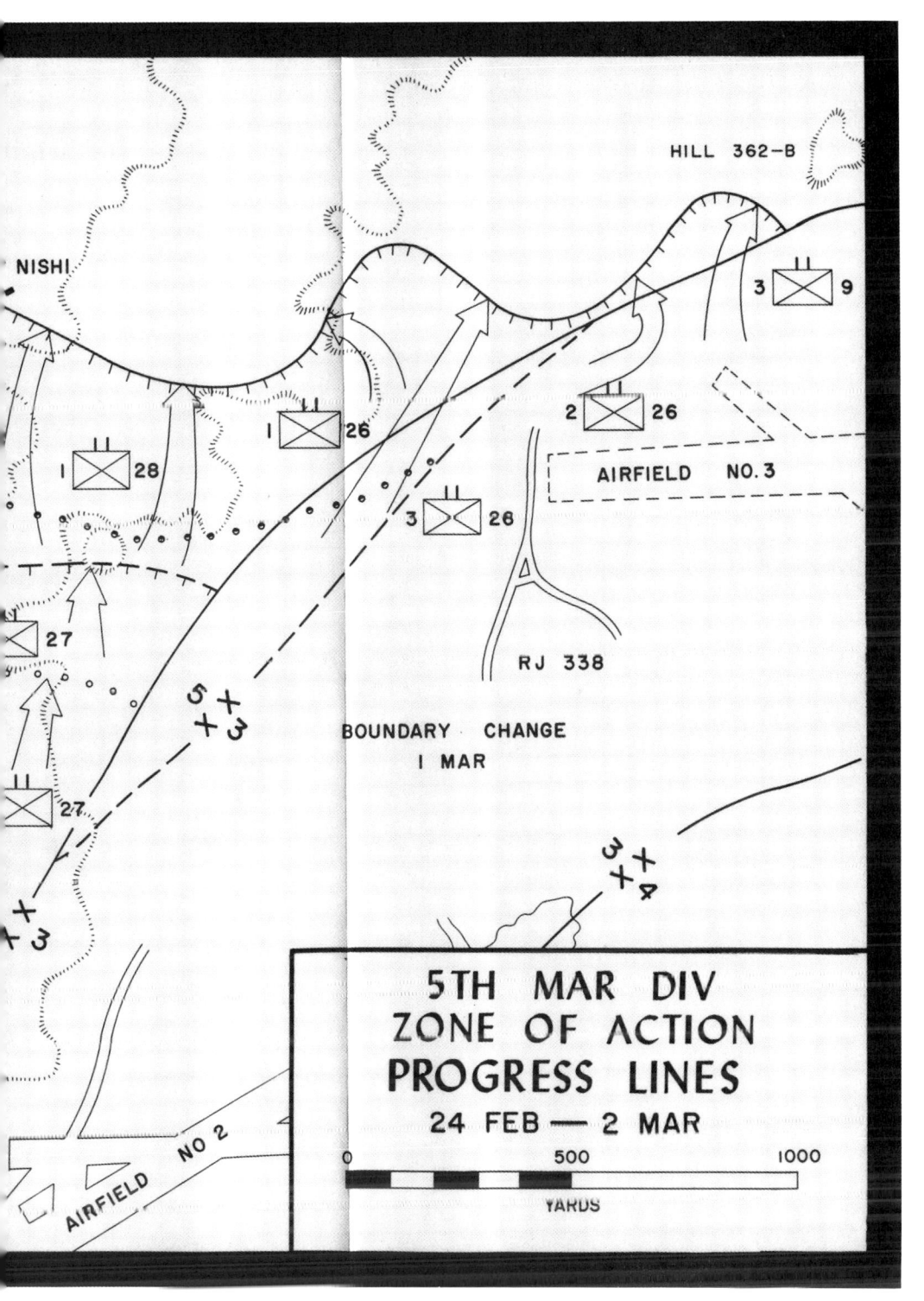

5TH MAR DIV
ZONE OF ACTION
PROGRESS LINES
24 FEB — 2 MAR

Map VI

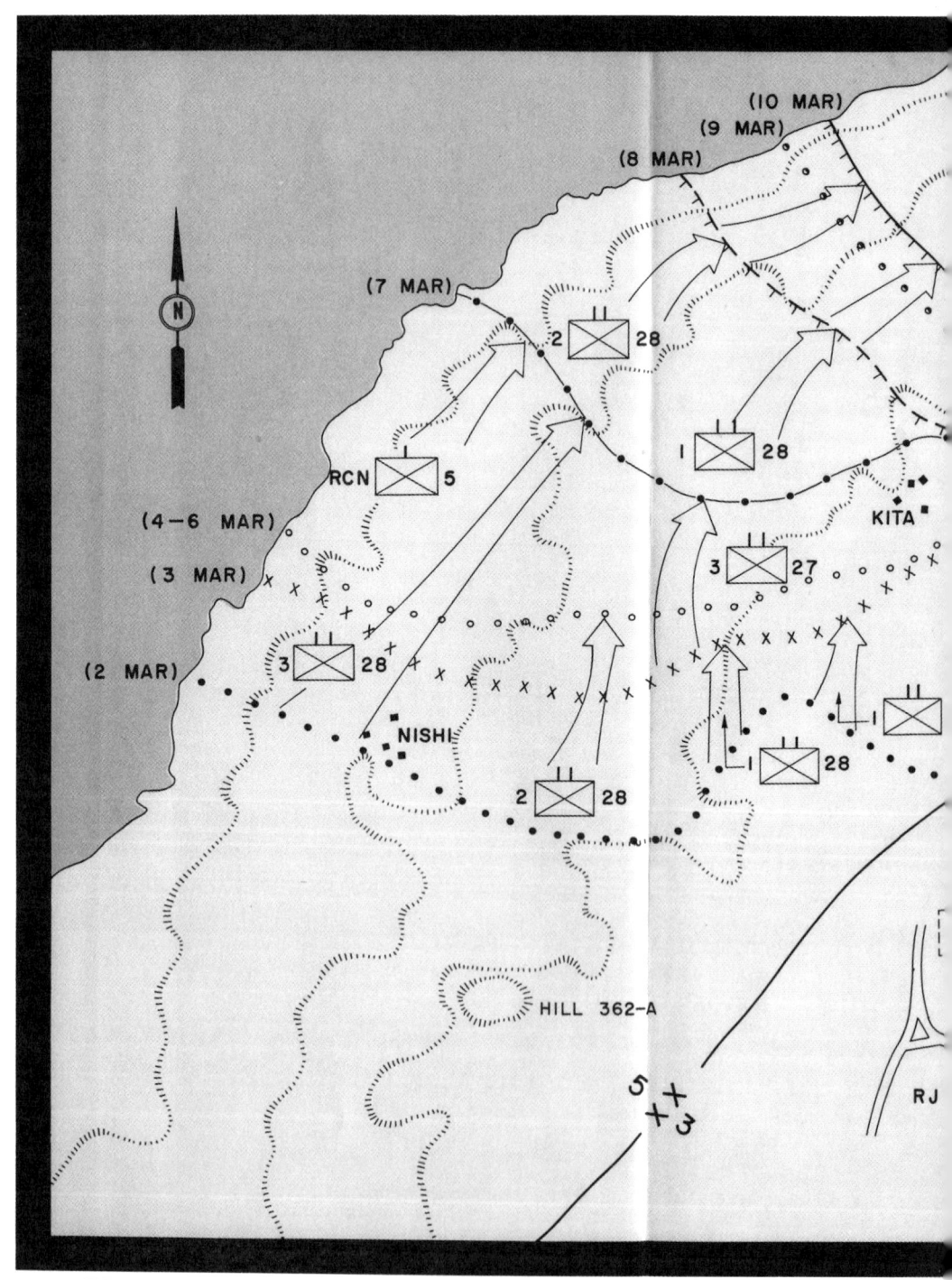

HILL 362-B

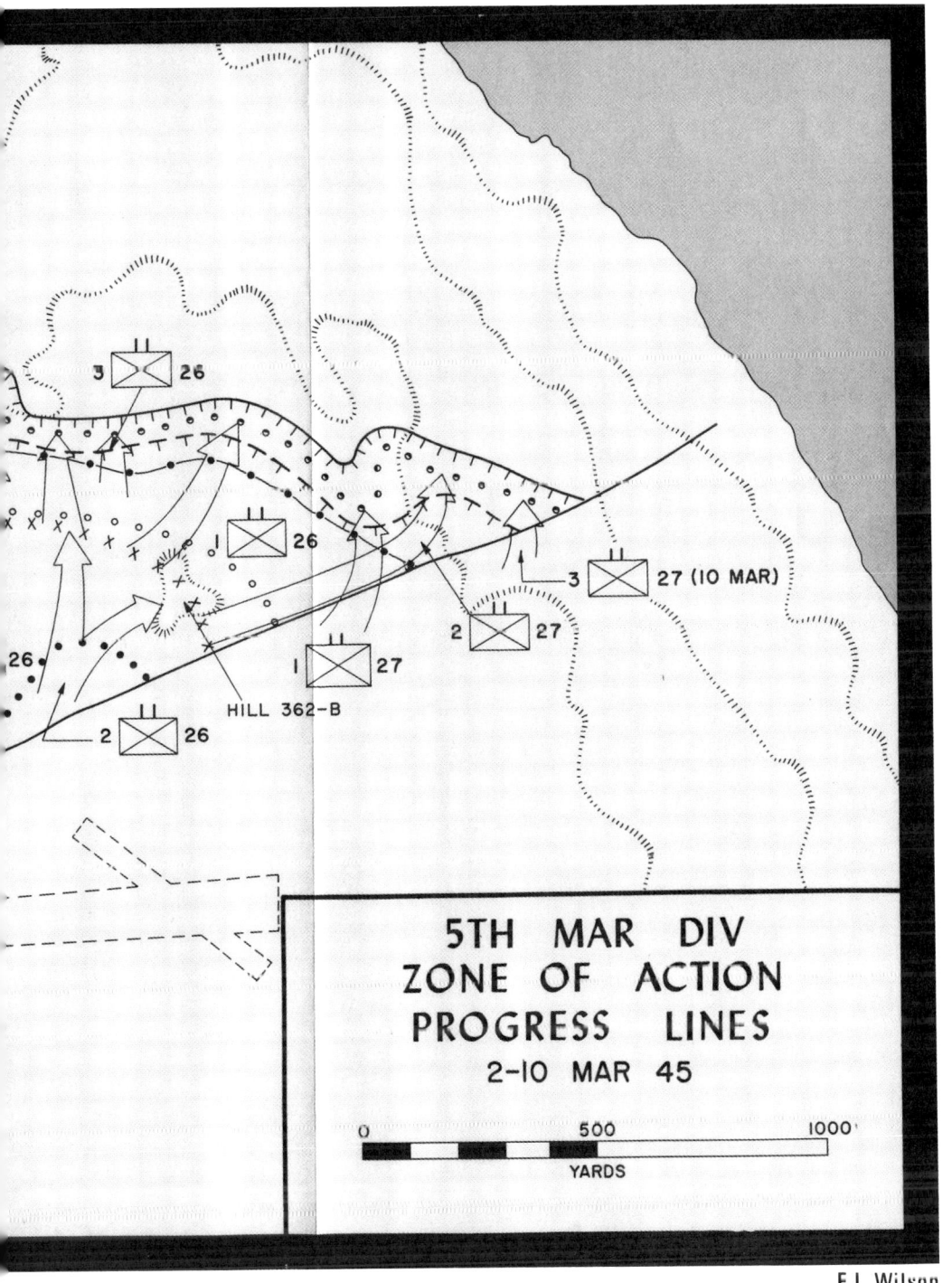

**5TH MAR DIV
ZONE OF ACTION
PROGRESS LINES
2-10 MAR 45**

0   500   1000
YARDS

E.L. Wilson

Map VII

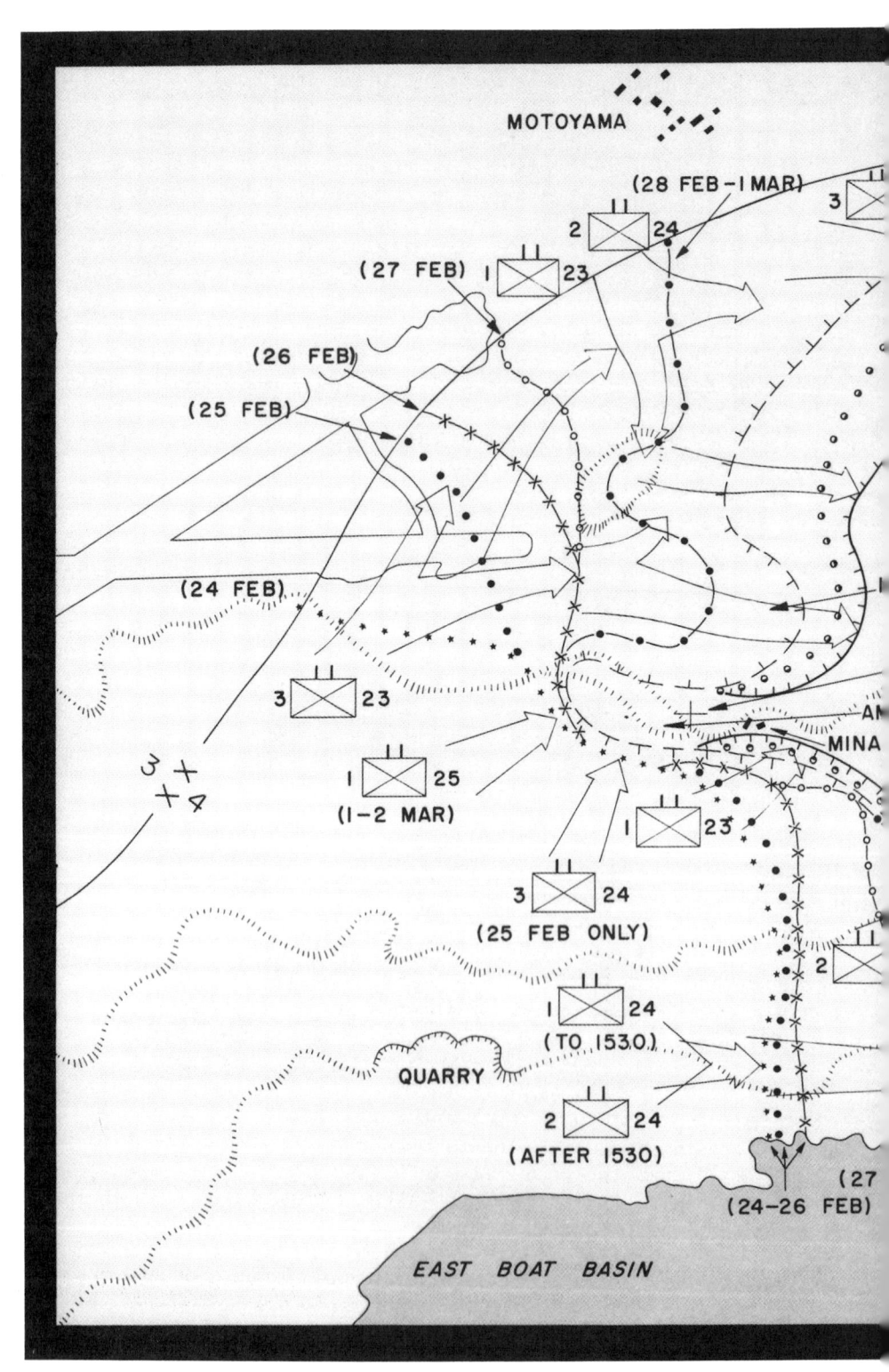

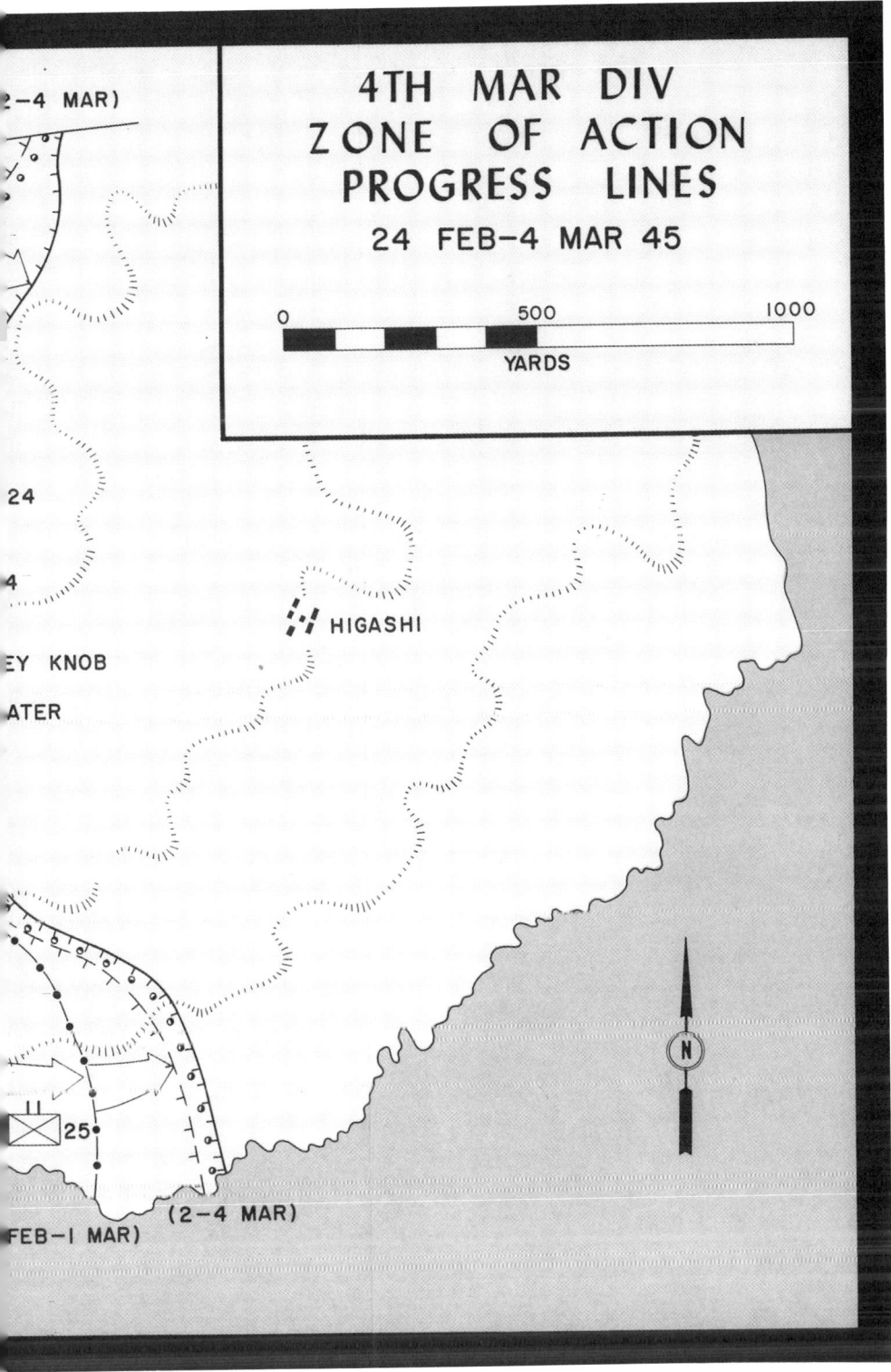

4TH MAR DIV ZONE OF ACTION PROGRESS LINES
24 FEB-4 MAR 45

HIGASHI

E.L. Wilson

MOTOYAMA

TURKEY KNOB

**4TH MAR DIV
ZONE OF ACTION
PROGRESS LINES
5-10 MAR 45**

0   500   1000
YARDS

Map VIII

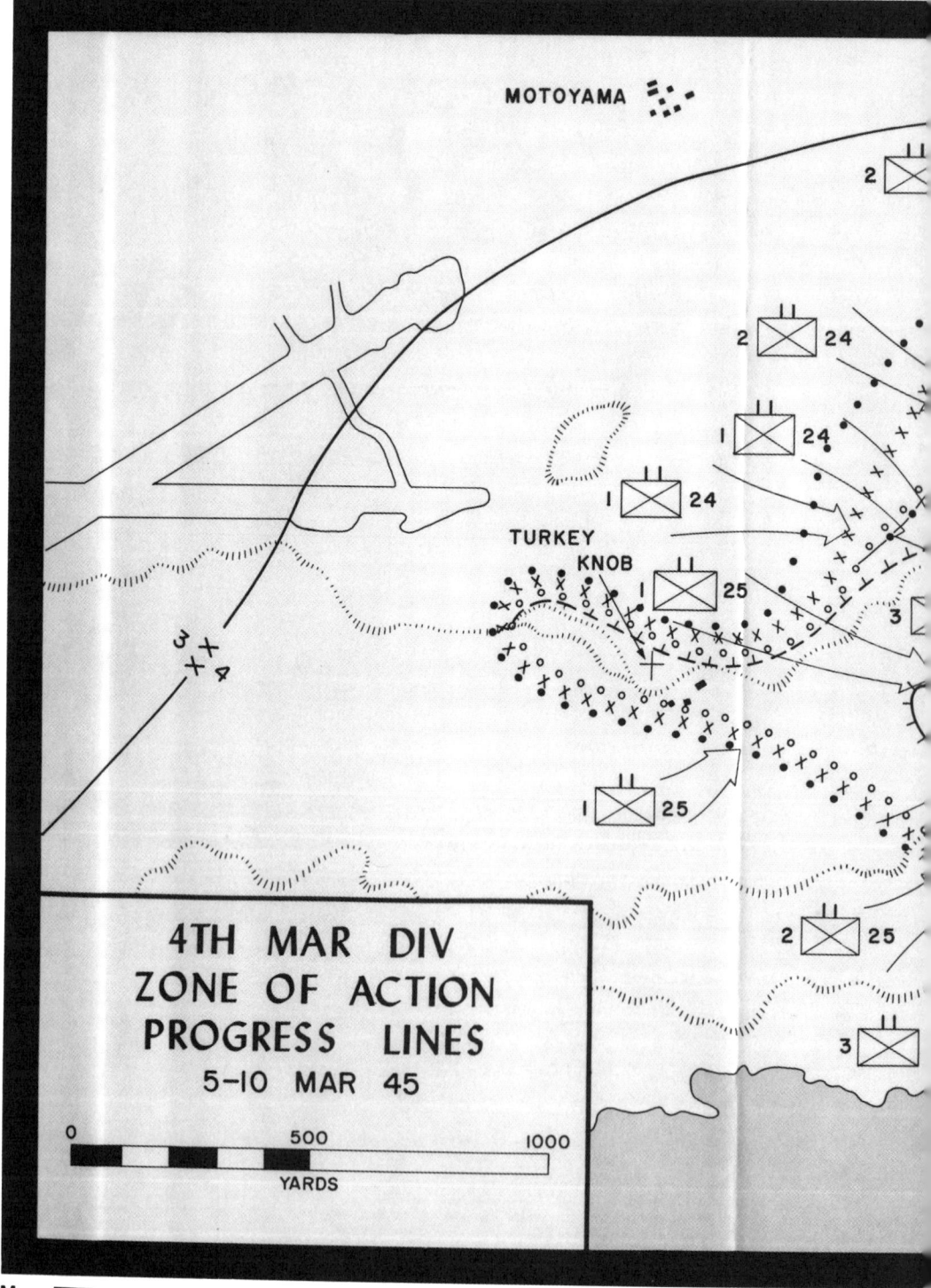

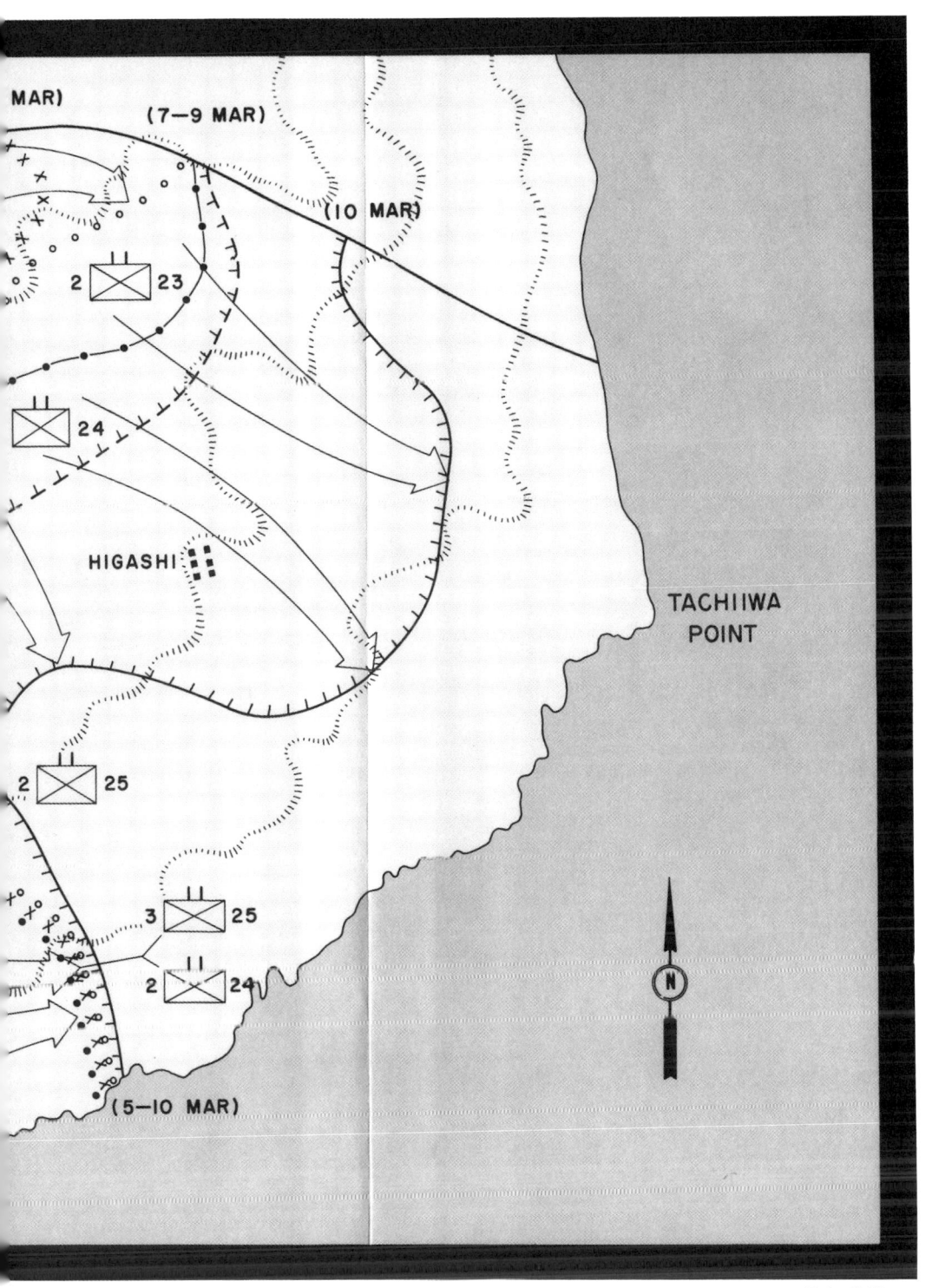

(MAR) (7-9 MAR)

(10 MAR)

2 ⊠ 23

⊠ 24

HIGASHI

TACHIIWA POINT

2 ⊠ 25

3 ⊠ 25

2 ⊠ 24

(5-10 MAR)

N

E.L. Wilson

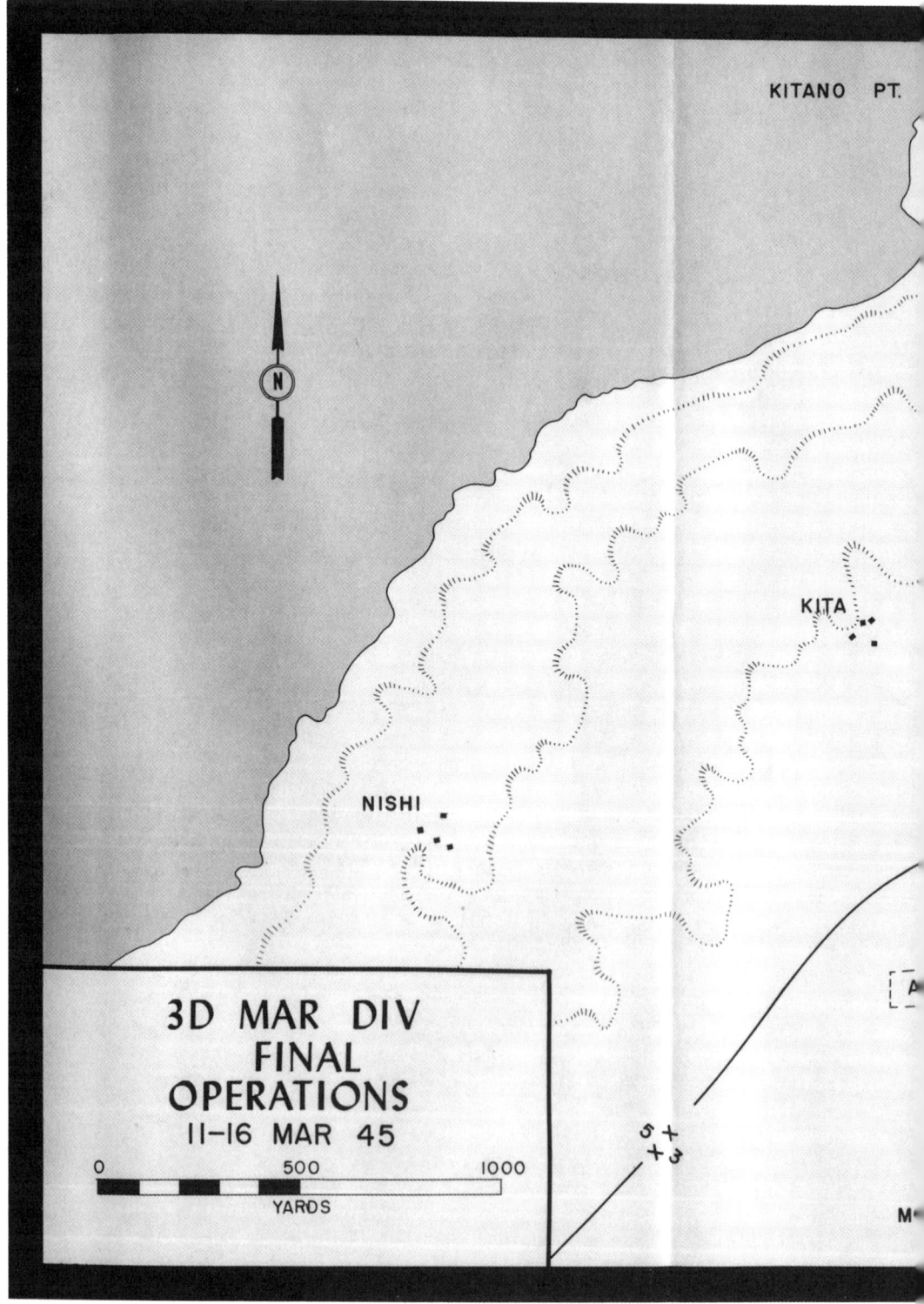

Map IX

(16 MAR)

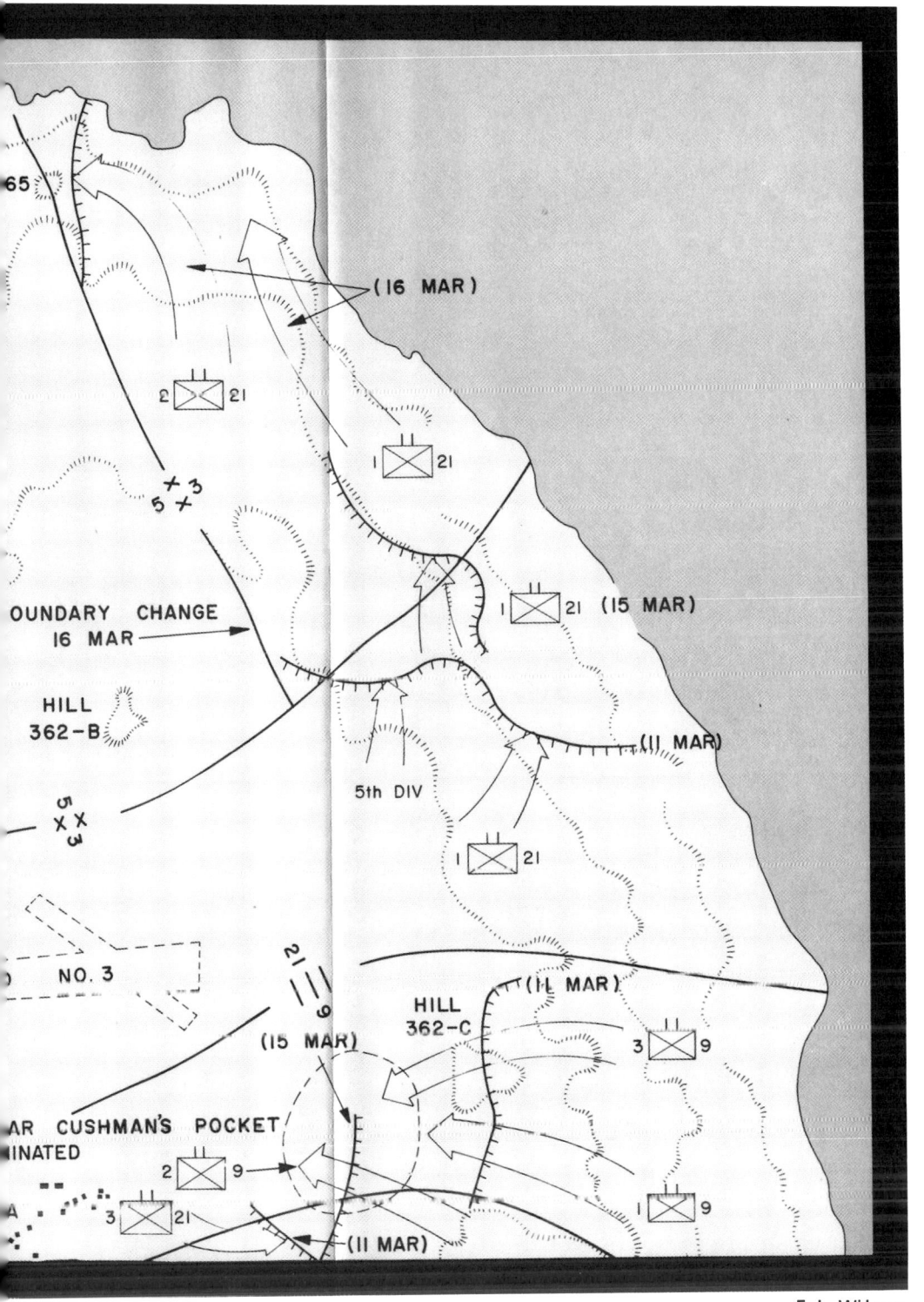

2 ☒ 21

1 ☒ 21

BOUNDARY CHANGE
16 MAR

1 ☒ 21 (15 MAR)

HILL
362-B

(11 MAR)

5th DIV

1 ☒ 21

NO. 3

(15 MAR)

HILL
362-C

(11 MAR)

3 ☒ 9

CUSHMAN'S POCKET
INATED

2 ☒ 9

3 ☒ 21

(11 MAR)

1 ☒ 9

E.L. Wilson

Map X

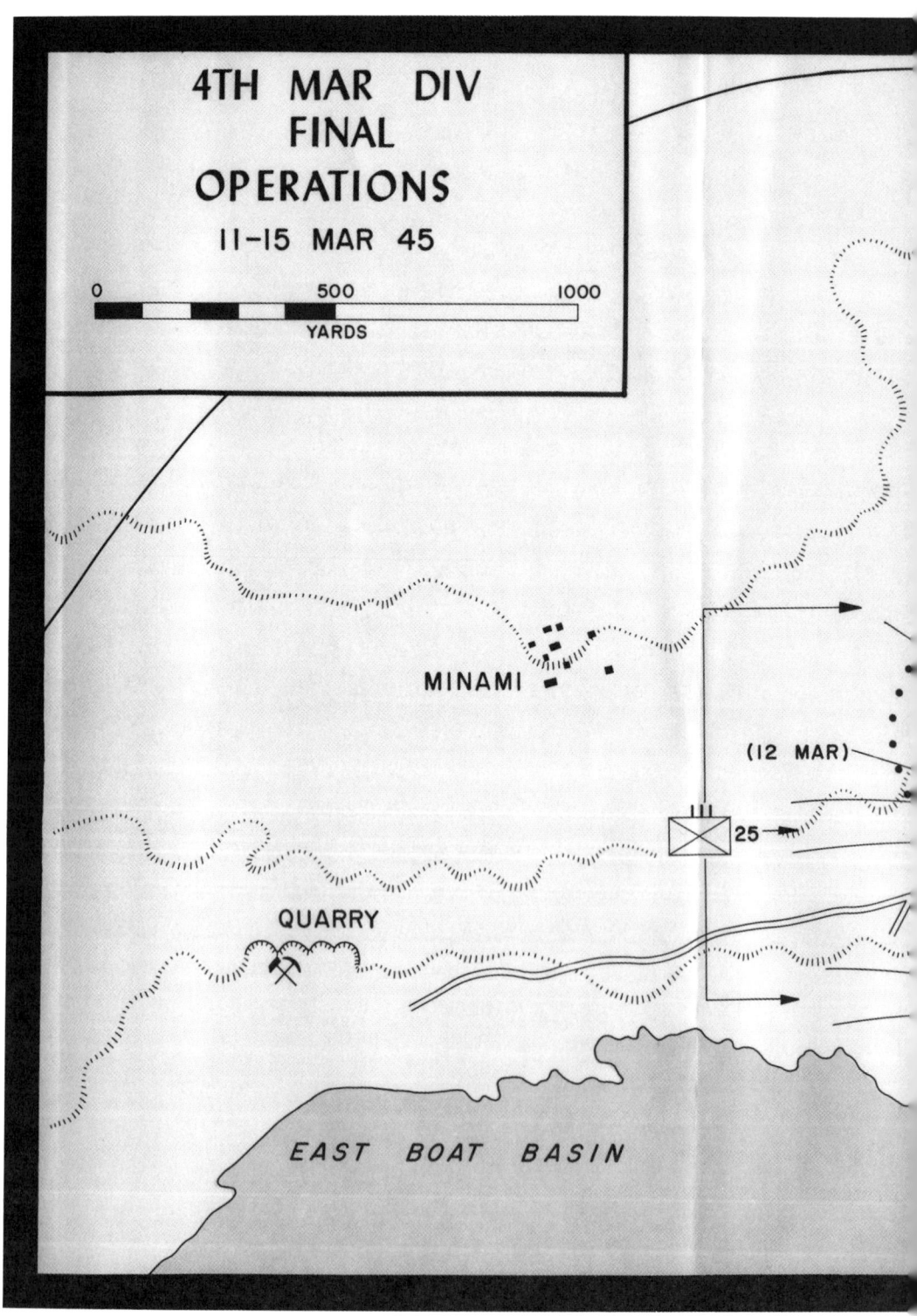

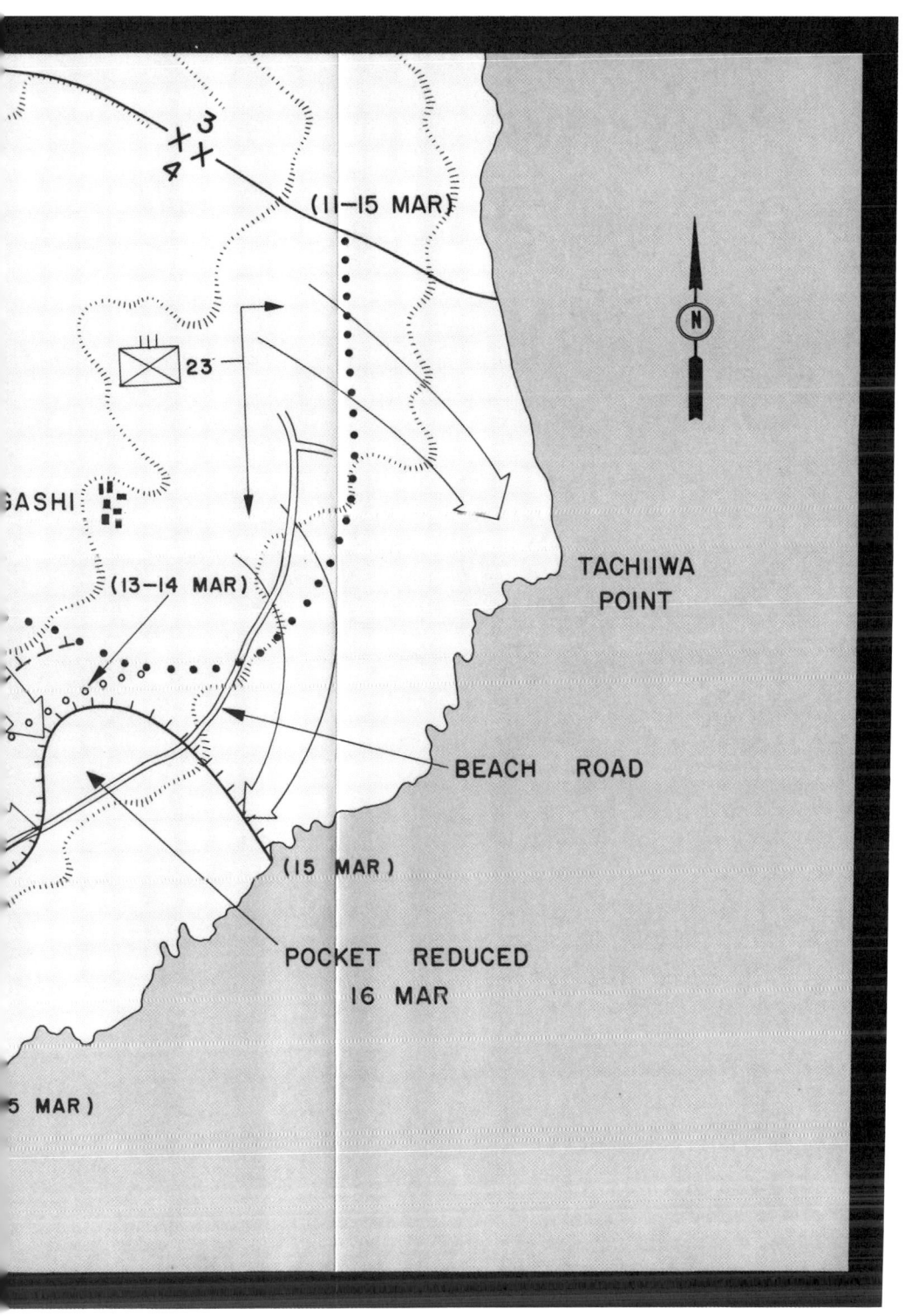

(11-15 MAR)

23

GASHI

(13-14 MAR)

TACHIIWA
POINT

BEACH ROAD

(15 MAR)

POCKET REDUCED
16 MAR

5 MAR)

E. L. Wilson

KITANO POINT

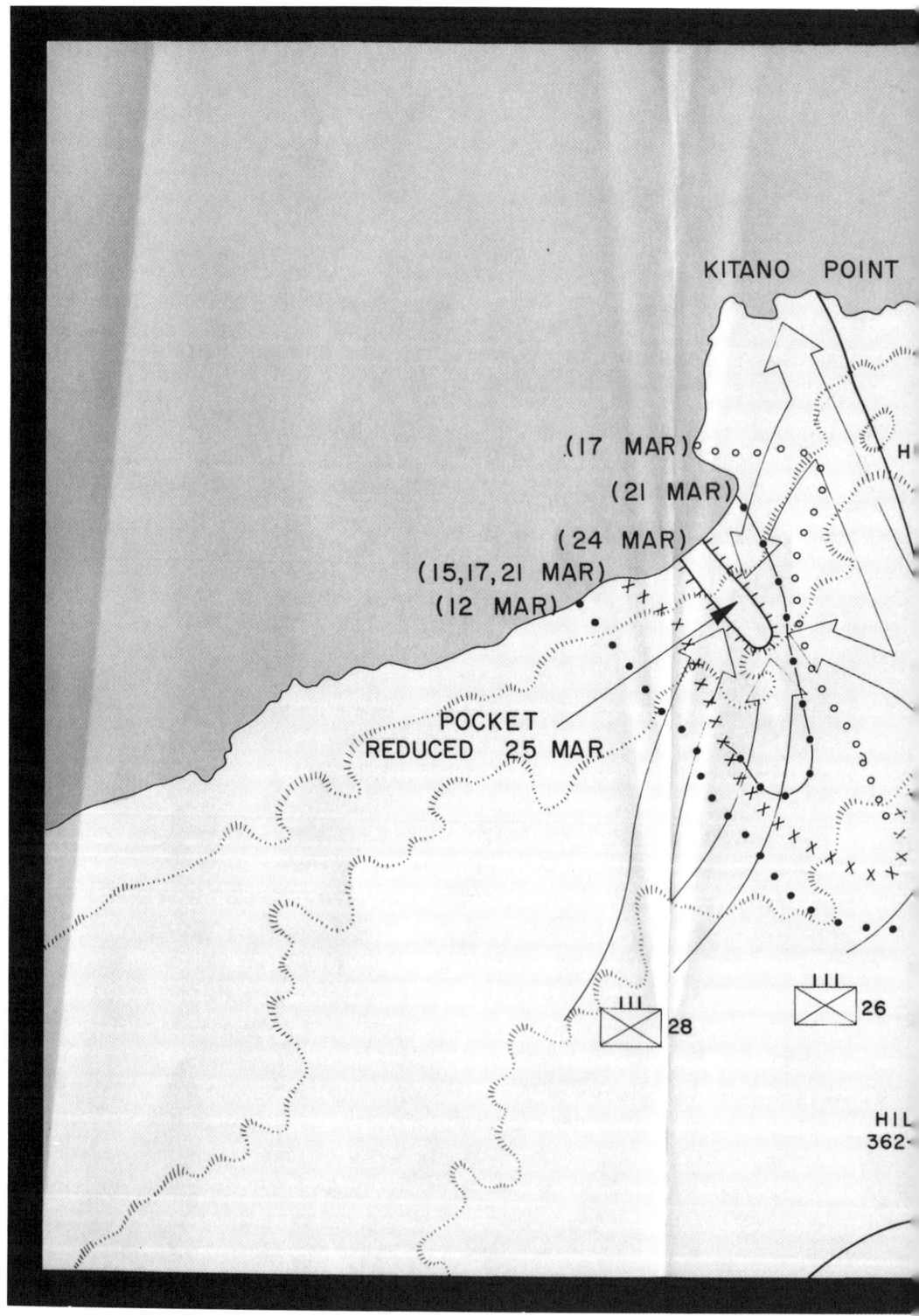

(17 MAR)
(21 MAR)
(24 MAR)
(15,17,21 MAR)
(12 MAR)

POCKET
REDUCED 25 MAR

28   26

HIL
362-

Map XI

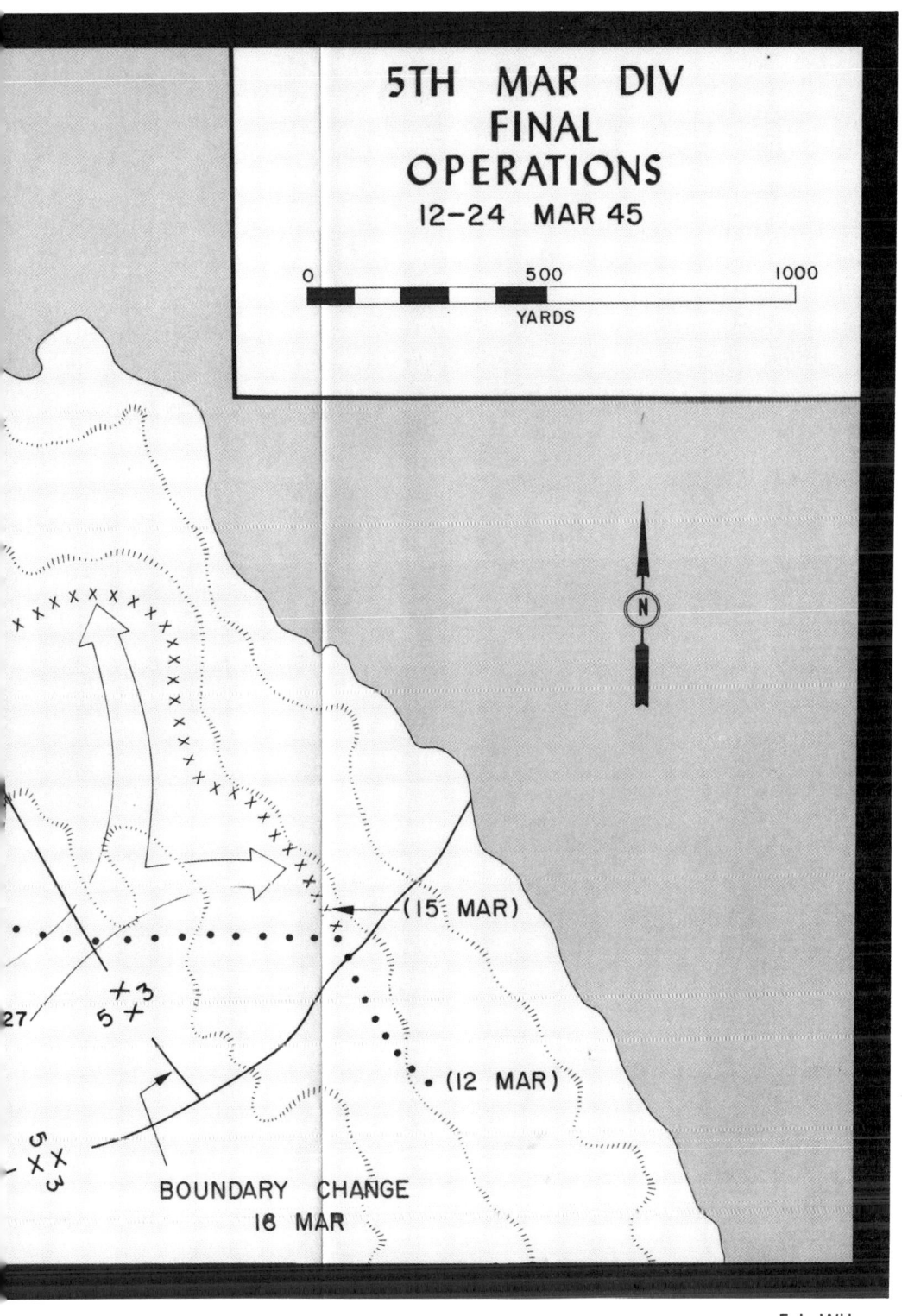

5TH MAR DIV
FINAL
OPERATIONS
12-24 MAR 45

0 — 500 — 1000
YARDS

N

(15 MAR)

(12 MAR)

BOUNDARY CHANGE
16 MAR

E.L. Wilson